Supply Chain Management

Colorado State University

Robert M. Monczka | David Alan Collier | John J. Coyle

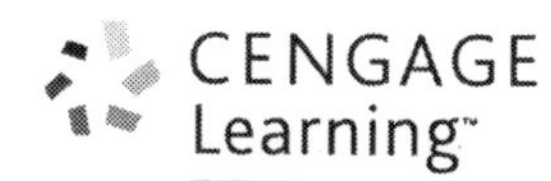

Australia • Brazil • Japan • Korea • Mexico • Singapore • Spain • United Kingdom • United States

Supply Chain Management: Colorado State University

Robert M. Monczka | David Alan Collier | John J. Coyle

Executive Editors:
Michele Baird
Maureen Staudt
Michael Stranz

Project Development Manager:
Linda deStefano

Senior Marketing Coordinators:
Sara Mercurio
Lindsay Shapiro

Production/Manufacturing Manager:
Donna M. Brown

PreMedia Services Supervisor:
Rebecca A. Walker

Rights & Permissions Specialist:
Kalina Hintz

Cover Image:
Getty Images*

ISBN-13: 978-1-4240-5562-3

ISBN-10: 1-4240-5562-8

Cengage Learning
5191 Natorp Boulevard
Mason, Ohio 45040
USA

Cengage Learning is a leading provider of customized learning solutions with office locations around the globe, including Singapore, the United Kingdom, Australia, Mexico, Brazil, and Japan. Locate your local office at:
international.cengage.com/region

Cengage Learning products are represented in Canada by Nelson Education, Ltd.

For your lifelong learning solutions, visit **custom.cengage.com**

Visit our corporate website at **cengage.com**

Printed in the United States of America

CONTENTS

PART ONE OPERATION

PART TWO PURCHASING AND SUPPLY

PART THREE LOGISTICS.

OPERATION

Taken from OPERATIONS MANAGEMENT GOOD SERVICE & VALUE CHAINS by David Alan Collier | James R. Evans, 2007

Chapter Outline

CHAPTER 4

Operations Strategy

Learning Objectives

1. To understand how customer wants and needs drive strategic thinking in a firm and their consequences for designing and managing operations within the value chain.

2. To learn the five major competitive priorities important to business success and what they mean for operations.
3. To understand the process of strategic planning at the organizational level and its relationship to operations strategy.
4. To understand how operations strategy can support and drive the achievement of organizational objectives, and to learn the key elements of an operations strategy.
5. To understand the operations design choices and infrastructure decisions from the perspective of defining an operations strategy and trade-offs that need to be made in developing a viable operations strategy.
6. To be able to identify and understand the seven decision areas in Hill's operations strategy framework.
7. To be able to analyze a real organization's operations strategy and apply the strategy development framework.

Getty Images

- Rival golf club equipment manufacturers TaylorMade and Callaway are both based in Carlsbad, California. That's about where the similarity ends. Callaway made clubs for average golfers, while TaylorMade took the clubs pro golfers were using and adjusted them to suit amateurs. Callaway focused on management and production efficiency while sticking to core product designs, much the way Ford built cars around a basic chassis. TaylorMade, however, was constantly reinventing its product lines, and in an industry that expected product cycles to last 18 months or longer, began releasing new drivers and irons in rapid-fire succession. Even new product launches show the difference between these companies: Callaway typically launched products with lengthy PowerPoint presentations, while TaylorMade turned them into huge pep rallies. TaylorMade's strategy seems to have paid off; late in 2003 it overtook Callaway in market share for metalwoods.[1]

- George Huber addressed his management team at New Mexico National Bank and Trust, "The results of our first customer survey are in, and there are a few surprises. We knew they wanted competitive rates on savings and checking accounts, but more importantly, the survey indicates that friendly service and convenience are actually *more* important. We've been devoting all our resources to keeping costs low, but this throws a new twist into the mix." "What this means for us," interjected Paul Westel,

VP of operations, "is that we need to take a hard look at our current strategy. We've been focusing on the wrong priorities. This also means that we need to better analyze where we locate our ATMs and branch operations, and whether we should partner with a grocery store or maybe even a fast-food chain to establish a presence in their stores." "And," noted Deb Hamilton, VP of human resources, "we need to revamp our hiring and training programs; we've been getting a lot of complaints lately about 'uncaring' tellers." CFO Sarah Reimer observed, "This can affect nearly everything we do!" "That's right," said George. "I want each of you to think about what these results mean for your area of the business and report back to me next week. I'll suggest a new statement of our mission and vision. We need to start at the top."

Getty Images/PhotoDisc

- "Dad, don't you have a big account at Global Financial Services?" Jessie Parker asked. "Sure," her father replied. "They provide excellent service; whenever I call to talk to a broker, I get routed to a 'preferred client' advisor. They get me off the phone quickly with all my questions answered." "That's what I thought," said Jessie. "I opened an account with them when I started my job after graduating last year, but I've noticed that I have to wait quite a long time for an advisor to answer. While I'm waiting, a recording is urging me to visit their web site for frequently asked questions or to use their automated phone system. I'm much more comfortable speaking to a live person. I wonder how big an account I need to be a 'preferred client'?"

Discussion Questions: What differences would the different strategies chosen by Callaway and TaylorMade—sticking to core product designs versus continual innovation—have for key operations management decisions (consider the decision areas discussed in Chapter 2 for designing value chains)? Should organizations create strategies in response to customer wants and needs, or should they create strategies and then try to influence customer behavior to meet the strategic goals?

Every organization has a myriad of choices in deciding where to focus its efforts—for example, on low cost, high quality, quick response, or flexibility and customization—and in designing their operations to support their chosen strategy. The differences between Callaway and TaylorMade clearly show the significantly different strategies that competitors in the same industry can choose. As the second episode suggests, these choices should be driven by the most important customer requirements and expectations. In particular, what happens in operations—on the front lines and on the factory floor—must support the strategic direction the firm has chosen. In recent years, to respond to a significant financial crisis since the 9/11 terrorist attacks, several major U.S. airlines have closed or plan to close hubs in the long-standing hub-and-spoke system, adding instead more direct city-to-city flights.

In a strategy to become more efficient and cut costs, airlines are making major changes in their operating and value chain structure, which will undoubtedly have implications for customers. However, an industry consultant noted that "hubs are essential . . . but the hub model is changing in how it is operated." One change by Delta in its Atlanta hub is abandoning the concept of having groups of flights scheduled closely together to allow passengers to connect easily. This decision was made to obtain cost savings and efficiencies that are expected to outweigh any revenue effects.[2]

Any change in a firm's customer benefit package or strategic direction typically has significant consequences for the entire value chain and for operations. Although it may be difficult to change the *structure* of the value chain, operations managers have considerable freedom in determining what components of the value chain to emphasize, selecting technology and processes, making human resource policy choices, and in making other relevant decisions to support the firm's strategic emphasis. Fidelity Investments (the basis for the third episode), for instance, discovered that when a customer does limited business and calls a service representative too frequently, costs can outweigh profits.[3] So when such customers called, Fidelity's reps began teaching them how to use its automated phone lines and web site, which were designed to be friendlier and easier to use. These customers could talk to a service representative, but the phone system routed them into longer queues so the most profitable customers could be served more quickly. If these lower-account-balance customers switched to lower-cost channels such as the web site, Fidelity became more profitable. If they did not like the experience and left, the company became more profitable without them. However, 96 percent of them stayed and most switched to lower-cost channels, and customer satisfaction actually increased as these customers learned to get faster service. This operations strategy helped the firm to lower costs and focus on the most profitable customers. In essence, Fidelity influences customer behavior within its value chain to create better operational efficiency.

Competitive advantage *denotes a firm's ability to achieve market and financial superiority over its competitors.*

Competitive advantage *denotes a firm's ability to achieve market and financial superiority over its competitors.* In the long run, a sustainable competitive advantage provides above-average performance and is essential to survival of the business. Creating a competitive advantage requires a fundamental understanding of two things. First, management must understand customer wants and needs—and how the value chain can best meet these needs through the design and delivery of customer benefit packages that are attractive to customers. Second, management must build and leverage operational capabilities to support desired competitive priorities. **Competitive priorities** *represent the strategic emphasis that a firm places on certain performance measures and operational capabilities within a value chain.* In other words, operations must be aligned strategically with customer needs to create value. Understanding competitive priorities and their relationships to customer benefit packages provides a basis for designing the processes that create and deliver goods and services. These issues will be addressed in detail in Chapters 6 and 7. For now, we will focus on understanding how managers think about customer wants and needs and competitive priorities, and then discuss how managers develop an operations strategy, build capability, and achieve competitive advantage.

Competitive priorities *represent the strategic emphasis that a firm places on certain performance measures and operational capabilities within a value chain.*

Learning Objective
To understand how customer wants and needs drive strategic thinking in a firm and their consequences for designing and managing operations within the value chain.

UNDERSTANDING CUSTOMER WANTS AND NEEDS

Because the fundamental purpose of an organization is to provide goods and services of value to customers, it is important to first understand customer needs and requirements and also to understand how customers evaluate goods and services. However, a company usually cannot satisfy all customers with the same goods and services. Often, customers must be segmented into several natural groups, each with unique wants and needs. These segments might be based on buying behavior, geography, demographics, sales volume, profitability, or expected levels of service. By understanding differences among such segments, a company can design the most appropriate customer benefit packages, competitive strategies, and processes to create the goods and services to meet the unique needs of each segment.

To correctly identify what customers expect requires being "close to the customer." There are many ways to do this, such as having employees visit and talk to customers, having managers talk to customers, and doing formal marketing research. Marriott Corporation, for example, requires their top managers to annually work a full day or more in the hotels as bellhops, waiters, bartenders, front-desk service providers, and so on to gain a true understanding of customers' wants and needs and the types of issues that their hotel service providers must face in serving the customer. Good marketing research includes such techniques as focus groups, salesperson and employee feedback, complaint analysis, on-the-spot interviews with customers, videotaped service encounters, mystery shoppers, telephone hotlines, Internet monitoring, and customer surveys.

Identifying and defining the true wants and needs of customers are not easy, as customers may not always know what they want. Traditional market research may not always provide accurate information on latent needs and may even backfire. For example, Ford listened to a sample of customers and asked if they wanted a fourth door on the Windstar minivan. Only about a third thought it was a great idea, so Ford scrapped the idea. Chrysler, on the other hand, spent a lot more time living with owners of vans and observing their behavior, watching them wrestle to get things in and out, noting all the occasions where a fourth door would really be convenient, and was very successful after introducing a fourth door.[4] Thus, a company must make special effort to identify these goods and service features.

Sony and Seiko, for instance, go beyond traditional market research and produce dozens, even hundreds, of audio products and wristwatches with a variety of features to help them understand what excites and delights the customer. Those models that do not sell are simply dropped from the product lines. Of course, the cost per unit of these items is relatively low. To practice this strategy effectively, marketing efforts must be supported by highly flexible manufacturing systems that permit rapid setup and quick response to changing volumes and product features.

Creating breakthrough goods or services sometimes requires that companies ignore customer feedback and take risks. As Steve Jobs of Apple Computer noted about the iMac, "That doesn't mean we don't listen to customers, but it's hard for them to tell you what they want when they've never seen anything remotely like it. Take desktop video editing. I never got one request from someone who wanted to edit movies on his computer. Yet now that people see it, they say, 'Oh my God, that's great!' "[5]

Dissatisfiers, Satisfiers, and Exciters/Delighters

Japanese professor Noriaki Kano suggested three classes of customer requirements:

1. **Dissatisfiers:** *requirements that are expected in a good or service.* In an automobile, a radio and driver-side air bag are expected by the customer, who generally do not state so but assume them as given. For a hotel, the customer assumes the hotel room is safe and clean. If these features are not present, the customer is dissatisfied, sometimes very dissatisfied.

Dissatisfiers: *requirements that are expected in a good or service.*

2. **Satisfiers:** *requirements that customers say they want.* Many car buyers want a sunroof, power windows, or antilock brakes. Likewise, a hotel guest may want an

Satisfiers: *requirements that customers say they want.*

exercise room, hot tub, or a restaurant in the hotel. Providing these goods and service features creates customer satisfaction by fulfilling customer's wants and needs.

Exciters/delighters: *new or innovative good or service features that customers do not expect.*

3. **Exciters/delighters:** *new or innovative good or service features that customers do not expect.* The presence of unexpected features leads to surprise and excitement and enhances the customer's perceptions of value. Collision avoidance systems or an automobile navigation system, for example, can surprise and delight the customer and enhance the customer's feeling of safety. Adding exciting music and laser lights can entertain and delight customers as they shop for clothes in retail stores. Within the framework of the customer benefit package introduced in Chapter 1, these features are usually peripheral goods or services.

In the Kano classification system, dissatisfiers and satisfiers are relatively easy to determine through routine marketing research. For example, the hot-selling Ford F-150 pickup truck relied on extensive consumer research at the beginning of the redesign process. Perhaps one of the best examples of understanding customer needs and using this information to improve competitiveness is Frank Perdue's chicken business.[6] Perdue learned what customers' key purchase criteria were. These included a yellow bird, high meat-to-bone ratio, no pinfeathers, freshness, availability, and brand image. He also determined the relative importance of each criterion and how well the company and its competitors were meeting each one. By systematically improving his ability to exceed customers' expectations relative to the competition—that is, provide the exciters/delighters—Perdue gained market share even though his chickens were premium-priced. Among Perdue's innovations was using a jet engine to dry the chickens after plucking, allowing the pinfeathers to be singed off.

As customers become familiar with new goods and service features that delight them, these same features become part of the standard customer benefit package over time. Eventually, exciters/delighters become satisfiers. For instance, antilock brakes and air bags certainly were exciters/delighters when they were first introduced. Now, most car buyers expect them as a standard part of the customer benefit package associated with automobiles. Likewise, wireless computer access in hotel rooms once differentiated one hotel from another with business customers but now are an ordinary part of most hotel's customer benefit package. In fact, the absence of hotel room online computer capability is a dissatisfier today. Camera phones were a customer delighter and quickly became a satisfier in the highly competitive cell phone market. As goods and service features evolve, customer expectations continually increase, reaching new performance plateaus for that industry.

Basic customer expectations—dissatisfiers and satisfiers—are generally considered the minimum performance level required to stay in business and are often called **order qualifiers.**

Order winners *are goods and service features and performance characteristics that differentiate one customer benefit package from another and win the customer's business.*

Basic customer expectations—dissatisfiers and satisfiers—are generally considered the minimum performance level required to stay in business and are often called **order qualifiers**. The unexpected features that surprise, entertain, and delight customers by going beyond the expected often make the difference in closing a sale. **Order winners** *are goods and service features and performance characteristics that differentiate one customer benefit package from another and win the customer's business.* For example, decades ago financing the sale of an automobile was not nearly as important as financing and leasing options today. If three automobiles are roughly equal in terms of goods quality, manufacturer and dealer service quality, and price (that is, price and quality parity), then an attractive leasing package bundled with the other goods and services may very well be the order winner.

Search, Experience, and Credence Attributes

Consumers want quality in the goods and services they purchase. The concept of quality can mean several different things, from a vague notion of "excellence" to the ability of a production process to conform to engineering specifications. One of the more popular definitions is *fitness for intended use*. This characterizes how well a good or service performs its function and meets a customer's needs. For example, does an automobile have advanced safety features? Is the car fun to drive? Will it start every day in all weather conditions? Are the brakes working and safe? Is it free from rattles and squeaks? Is the cost of maintenance low? Are the controls easy to read and use? Consumers, therefore, evaluate various goods and service attributes in forming perceptions about the quality of goods and services.

Research suggests that customers use three types of attributes in evaluating the quality of goods and services: search, experience, and credence.[7] **Search attributes** *are those that a customer can determine prior to purchasing the goods and/or services.* These attributes include things like color, price, freshness, style, fit, feel, hardness, and smell. Goods such as supermarket food, furniture, clothing, automobiles, and houses are high in search attributes. **Experience attributes** *are those that can only be discerned after purchase or during consumption or use.* Examples of these attributes are friendliness, taste, wearability, safety, fun, and customer satisfaction. **Credence attributes** *are any aspects of a good or service that the customer must believe in but cannot personally evaluate even after purchase and consumption.* Examples would include the expertise of a surgeon or mechanic, the knowledge of a tax advisor, or the accuracy of tax preparation software. In these situations, the customer does not have the opportunity, expertise, or experience to evaluate the quality of the good or service, but can only have faith and trust that the good performs as it should or the service provider has done the job right. This classification has several important implications for operations. For example, the most important search and experience attributes should be evaluated during design, measured during manufacturing, and drive key operational controls to ensure that they are built into the good with high quality. Credence attributes stem from the nature of services (see Chapter 1), the design of the service system, and the training and expertise of the service providers.

Search attributes *are those that a customer can determine prior to purchasing the goods and/or services.*

Experience attributes *are those that can only be discerned after purchase or during consumption or use.*

Credence attributes *are any aspects of a good or service that the customer must believe in but cannot personally evaluate even after purchase and consumption.*

These three evaluation criteria form an evaluation continuum from easy to difficult, as shown in Exhibit 4.1. This model suggests that goods are easier to evaluate than services, and that goods are high in search qualities whereas services are high in experience and credence attributes. Of course, goods and services are usually combined and configured in unique ways, making for an even more complex customer evaluation process.

In this new millennium, customers are placing more emphasis on intangible attributes than on tangible attributes. Customers purchase things that add value to how they feel (the ambience of a restaurant), how much fun they have (climbing a rock wall in a retail store while shopping), how well they are informed (knowing their exact location while driving via a global positioning system), how they are treated (the empathy the doctor and staff exhibit when a serious injury victim arrives in the hospital), and how they can share experiences (e-mailing a picture from a camera phone). Avis discovered, for example, that customers were typically anxious when returning rental cars. They were worried about making their flights and communicating with their offices. In response, Avis installed monitors showing flight departure times and status and built a communications center for people who needed to make phone calls, send faxes, or plug in laptops.[8] Thus, understanding experience and credence attributes is important for businesses to succeed.

Customers evaluate services in ways that are often different from the ways they evaluate goods. These are summarized here along with significant issues that affect operations.

- Customers seek and rely more on information from personal sources than from nonpersonal sources when evaluating services prior to purchase. Operations must ensure that accurate information is available and that experiences with prior services and service providers results in positive experiences and customer satisfaction.

Exhibit 4.1
How Customers Evaluate Goods and Services

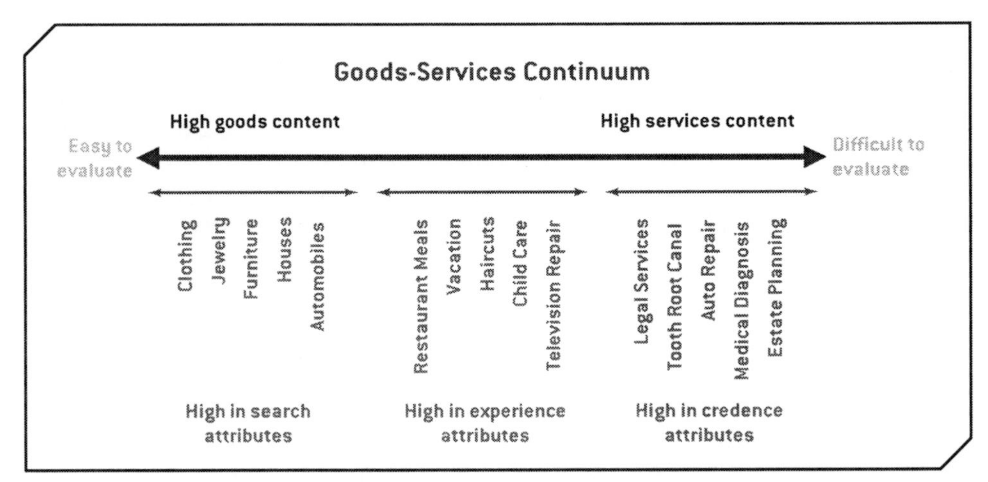

Source: Adapted from V. A. Zeithamel, "How Consumer Evaluation Processes Differ Between Goods and Services," in J. H. Donnelly and W. R. George, eds., *Marketing in Services*, published by the American Marketing Association, Chicago, 1981, pp. 186–199. Reprinted with permission from the American Marketing Association.

- Customers use a variety of perceptual features in evaluating services. The design and daily operations of service facilities must create a positive image and meet or exceed their expectations. Safety, friendliness, professionalism, and speed of service are examples that can enhance or damage the customer's perception of the value of the service.
- Customers normally adopt innovations in services more slowly than they adopt innovations in goods. Examples include new medical treatments, different curricula in secondary schools, and different banking technology such as off-site tellers accessed through video screens. Service processes must be flexible to accommodate rapid innovation.
- Customers perceive greater risks when buying services than when buying goods. Because services are intangible, customers cannot look at or touch them prior to the purchase decision. They only experience the service when they actually go through the process. This is why many are hesitant to use online banking or bill paying.
- Dissatisfaction with services is often the result of customers' inability to properly perform or coproduce their part of the service. A wrong order placed on the Internet can be the result of customer error despite all efforts on the part of the company to provide clear instructions. The design of services must be sensitive to the needs to educate customers on their role in the service process.

These insights help to explain why it is more difficult to design services and service processes than goods and manufacturing operations.

COMPETITIVE PRIORITIES

Learning Objective
To learn the five major competitive priorities important to business success and what they mean for operations.

Every organization is concerned with building and sustaining a competitive advantage in its markets. A strong competitive advantage is driven by customer needs and aligns the organization's resources with its business opportunities. A strong competitive advantage is difficult to copy, often because of a firm's culture, habits, or sunk costs. For example, why doesn't every company copy Dell's superior direct personal computer business model? Dell's approaches are hardly a secret; Michael Dell has even written a book about it. Competitors have copied its web site with stunning precision, but they face far greater difficulty copying other processes—order entry, billing, customer contact centers, purchasing, scheduling, assembly, and logistics—that Dell has built around its direct model over several decades. Competitors are burdened by longstanding relationships with suppliers and distributors and by a different culture.[9]

Competitive advantage can be achieved in different ways, such as outperforming competitors on price or quality, responding quickly to changing customer needs in designing goods and services, or providing rapid design or delivery (see the OM Spotlight on BMW). In general, organizations can compete on five key competitive priorities:

1. cost,
2. quality,
3. time,
4. flexibility, and
5. innovation.

In Chapter 3 we discussed how these can be measured to evaluate operations performance. How operations are designed and managed can have a significant impact on these performance measures. Here we want to investigate their role in defining an operations strategy.

All of these competitive priorities are vital to success. For example, no firm today can sacrifice quality simply to reduce costs or emphasize flexibility to the extent that it would make its goods and services unaffordable. However, organizations generally make trade-offs among these competitive priorities and focus their efforts along one or two key dimensions. For example, Dell Computer (1) manufactures PCs with high goods quality, (2) configures them to customer specifications, and

OM SPOTLIGHT

BMW[10]

The banner "Customers Drive our Future" greets visitors to BMW's Spartanburg, South Carolina, plant, which produces roadsters and sport utility vehicles. BMW operates one of the cleanest and quietest assembly plants in the industry, with three distinctive competencies: speed, flexibility, and quality. BMW's approach to meeting its cost challenges is to speed things up. The idea here is as you speed things up, costs decrease. The plant was launched in 23 months. The X5 SUV was developed in 35 months, and the company has an aggressive 30% reduction target for new product development cycles. The way to customize every car to meet individual customer's needs is to have "efficient flexibility." With 22 color options when the Z3 roadster was introduced, 123 center consoles, and 26 wheel options, BMW has become a master at information technology and logistics. Its demand flexibility extends to management and people; it is introducing two 10-hour shifts to accommodate the growth of the X5. Finally, its commitment to quality, as exemplified by consistent fit and finish tolerances and elimination of tolerance "stack-up" with a new door-hanging technology, is imperative to meet the needs of its demanding customer base. These attributes are a stark contrast to the traditional German style of operations, which is essentially to engineer until it can't be engineered any more.

BLOOMBERG NEWS\Landov

(3) tries to deliver them quickly to customers. However, they are not always the least-expensive machines available, and customers must wait longer to get them as opposed to picking one off the shelf at a retail store. Hence, high goods quality and flexibility are top competitive priorities at Dell whereas cost and delivery time are of somewhat lesser importance.

Cost

Many firms gain competitive advantage by establishing themselves as the low-cost leader in an industry. These firms handle high volumes of goods and services and achieve their competitive advantage through low prices. Examples of firms that practice a low-cost strategy are Honda Motor Co., Marriott's Fairfield Inns, Merck-Medco On-line Pharmacy, Southwest Airlines (see the OM Spotlight), and Wal-Mart's Sam's Club.

Almost every industry has a low-price market segment. Although prices are generally set outside the realm of operations, low prices cannot be achieved without strict attention to cost and the design and management of operations (see the OM Spotlight on IBM). Costs accumulate through the value chain and include the costs of raw materials and purchased parts, direct manufacturing cost, distribution, post-sale services, and all supporting processes. Design significantly affects the costs of manufacturing, warranty and field repair, and such non-value-added costs as redesign and rework. General Electric, for example, discovered that 75 percent of its manufacturing costs are determined by design. Through good design and by chipping away at costs, operations managers help to support a firm's strategy to be a low-price leader. They emphasize achieving economies of scale and finding cost advantages from all sources in the value chain.

Low cost can result from high productivity and high capacity utilization. More importantly, improvements in quality lead to improvements in productivity, which in turn lead to lower costs. Thus, a strategy of continuous improvement is essential to achieving a low-cost competitive advantage. Lower costs also result from

OM SPOTLIGHT

Southwest Airlines[11]

The only major airline that has been profitable during 2001 and 2002 is Southwest Airlines. Other major U.S. airlines have had to collectively reduce costs by $18.6 billion or 29 percent of their total operating expenses to operate at the same level (cost per mile) as Southwest. The high-cost airlines such as United and American face enormous pressure from low-fare carriers such as Southwest Airlines. Mr. Roach, a long-time industry consultant says, "The industry really is at a point where survival is in question." For example, the cost to fly one seat one mile on US Airways is 69 percent higher than on Southwest. US Airways filed for bankruptcy in August, 2002. Northwest and Continental Airlines all have costs at least 40 percent higher than Southwest, and Northwest and Delta have recently filed for bankruptcy.

Historically, large network carriers such as United and American Airlines did not have to match Southwest's cost per seat-mile because they could command higher prices due to premium service, first-class cabins, frequent flyer loyalty, and greater network breadth and amenities. But while everyone else's passenger volume is down, Southwest's has increased. Now all carriers are forced to cut service, eliminate flights to smaller cities, use smaller, more fuel-efficient planes, and reduce the frequency of flights. American, by one study's estimate, needs to cut costs by $3.6 billion per year and so far has only been able to reduce costs by $1.1 billion. A low-cost strategy can reshape industry structure and allow the firm to survive in an economic downturn.

OM SPOTLIGHT

IBM[13]

In IBM's manufacturing strategy for a high-volume, low-cost product (summarized next), notice the planned involvement of manufacturing in the design, development of production processes, and quality-assurance systems. Note also how all the components of the business strategy relate to the ultimate objectives of high volume and low cost. For instance, automated production helps to achieve a high volume of production; customizing in distribution centers eliminates the need for great product variety in the manufacturing function itself and reduces the cost of maintaining large manufacturing inventories. The key elements of its strategy are:

- *Early manufacturing involvement* in the design of the product both for make-versus-buy decisions and for assurance that the production processes can achieve required tolerances.
- *Design for automation* by minimizing the number of parts, eliminating fasteners, providing for self-alignment with no adjustments, making parts symmetrical where possible, avoiding parts that interfere with automation, making parts rigid and stiff, providing close tolerances, and making assembly one-sided.
- *Limited models and features* to ensure stable product design, group engineering changes for the "model year," and customization of the product in distribution centers.
- *Building to plan* for finished goods owned by sales, continuous-flow manufacturing, supplier integration, zero defects, reduction of work-in-process inventory, and a multiskilled, focused team.
- *Defect-free* at shipment.

innovations in product design and process technology that reduce the costs of production and from efficiencies gained through meticulous attention to operations. Many Japanese firms have exploited this approach. Japanese companies adopted many product innovations and process technologies that were developed in the United States. They refined the designs and manufacturing processes to produce high-quality products at low costs, resulting in higher market shares.

A cost leader can achieve above-average performance if it can command prices at or near the industry average. However, it cannot do so with an inferior product. For example, the problems with focusing on costs at the expense of quality are illustrated by the case of the Schlitz Brewing Company.[12] In the early 1970s, Schlitz, the second-largest brewer in the United States, began a cost-cutting campaign. It included reducing the quality of ingredients in its beers by switching to corn syrup and hop pellets and shortening the brewing cycle by 50 percent. In the short term, it achieved higher returns on sales and assets than Anheuser-Busch (and the acclaim of Wall Street analysts). *Forbes* magazine stated, "Does it pay to build quality into a product if most customers don't notice? Schlitz seems to have a more successful answer." But customers do recognize inferior products. Soon after, market share and profits fell rapidly. By 1980, Schlitz's sales had declined 40 percent, the stock price fell from \$69 to \$5, and the company was eventually sold. The product must be perceived as comparable with competitors' or the firm will be forced to discount prices well below competitors' prices to gain sales. This can cancel any benefits that result from cost advantage.

Quality

The role of quality in achieving competitive advantage was demonstrated by several research studies. PIMS Associates, Inc., a subsidiary of the Strategic Planning Institute, for example, maintains a database of 1,200 manufacturing companies and studies the impact of goods quality on corporate performance.[14] PIMS researchers have found the following:

- Businesses offering premium quality goods usually have large market shares and were early entrants into their markets.
- Quality is positively and significantly related to a higher return on investment for almost all kinds of market situations. PIMS studies have shown that firms with superior goods quality can more than triple return on sales over goods perceived as having inferior quality.
- A strategy of quality improvement usually leads to increased market share but at a cost in terms of reduced short-run profitability.
- High goods quality producers can usually charge premium prices.

Exhibit 4.2 summarizes the impact of quality on profitability. The value of a good or service in the marketplace is influenced by the quality of its design. Improvements in performance, features, and reliability will differentiate the good or service from its competitors, improve a firm's quality reputation, and improve the perceived value of the customer benefit package. This allows the company to command higher prices and achieve an increased market share. This, in turn, leads to increased revenues that offset the added costs of improved design. Improved conformance in production leads to lower manufacturing and service costs through savings in rework, scrap, and warranty expenses. The net effect of improved quality of design and conformance is increased profits. In addition, the four models of organizational performance described in Chapter 3—Malcolm Baldrige National Quality Award Criteria, balanced scorecard, value chain model, and the service-profit chain—highlight many of these same performance relationships.

In many industries, strategies often led to trade-offs between quality and cost; some company strategies are willing to sacrifice quality in order to develop a low-cost advantage. Such was the case with new automobile start-ups, especially with Hyundai Motor Co. However, goods quality has evolved over the years and now is generally considered to be an order qualifier (see the OM Spotlight on Hyundai). Operations managers deal with quality issues on a daily basis; these include ensuring that goods are produced defect-free or that service is delivered flawlessly. In the long run, it is the design of goods and service processes that ultimately define the quality of outputs and outcomes.

Time

In today's society, time is perhaps the most important source of competitive advantage. Customers demand quick response, short waiting times, and consistency

Exhibit 4.2
Interlinking Quality and Profitability Performance

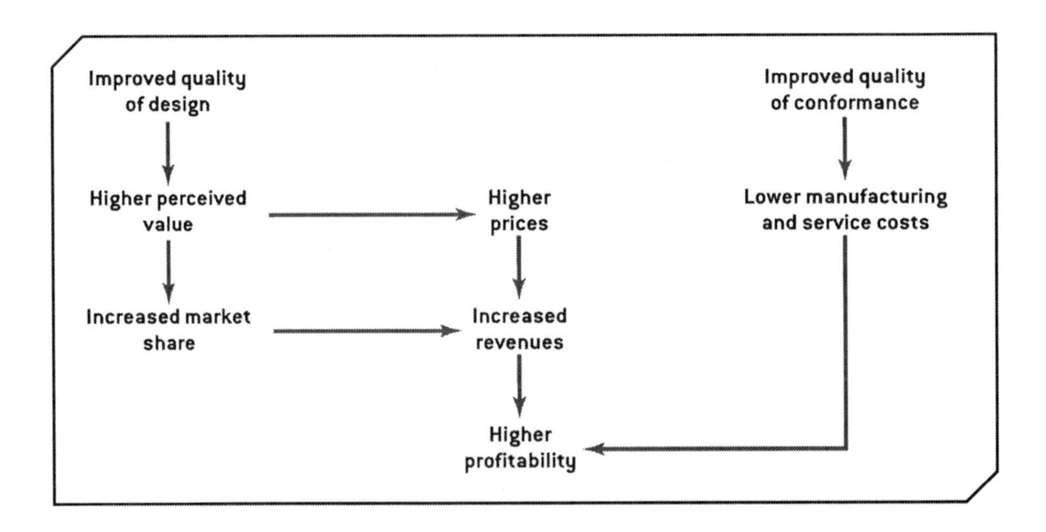

OM SPOTLIGHT

Hyundai Motor Company[15]

Hyundai Motor Company automobiles had been viewed as low-cost knockoffs of Japanese cars. When Hyundai's new CEO, Chung Mong Koo, took over in 1999, he walked on the factory floor and demanded a peek under the hood of a Sonata sedan. He didn't like what he saw: loose wires, tangled hoses, bolts painted four different colors. On the spot, he demanded that the bolts be painted black and ordered workers not to release any car unless all was orderly under the hood. The plant chief recalls Chung fuming: "The only way we can survive is to raise our quality to Toyota's level." Within months, he established quality-control units, promoted a pair of U.S. designers, and sold 10 percent of the company to Daimler-Chrysler with the aim of building a strategic alliance. He poured money into research and development to build cars that not only compete on price but also on quality. Hyundai bought several new Toyota and Honda SUVs and tore them apart to analyze them and devise features that would set their product apart. Hyundai innovations ranged from a cup holder large enough to hold a liter soft drink bottle to extra power ports for cell phones. Their strategy is to be the low-cost producer (the order winner) and maintain competitive goods quality (the order qualifier). Not long after, Hyundai rose near the top of the J.D. Powers' Initial Quality ranking.

in performance. Many firms such as Charles Schwab, Clarke American Checks, CNN, Dell, FedEx, and Wal-Mart know how to use time as a competitive weapon to create and deliver superior goods and services.

Reductions in flow time serve two purposes. First, they speed up work processes so that customer response is improved. Deliveries can be made faster and more often on time. Second, reductions in flow time can only be accomplished by streamlining and simplifying processes and value chains to eliminate non-value-added steps such as rework and waiting time. This forces improvements in quality by reducing the opportunity for mistakes and errors. By reducing non-value-added steps, costs are reduced as well. Thus, flow-time reductions often drive simultaneous improvements in quality, cost, and productivity (see the OM Spotlight on Procter & Gamble). Developing processes and using technology efficiently to improve speed and time reliability are some of the most important activities for operations managers.

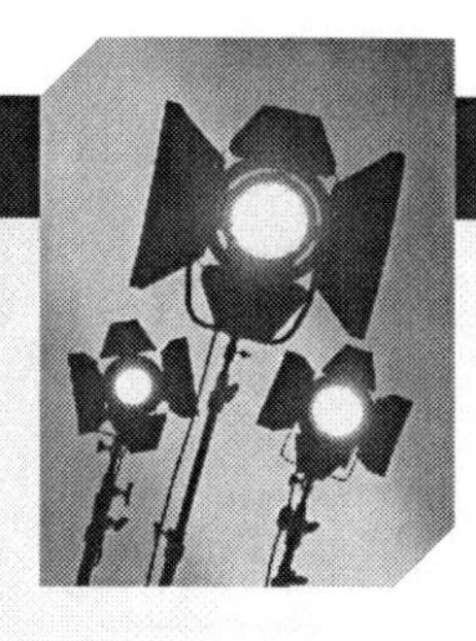

OM SPOTLIGHT

Procter & Gamble

One example of flow-time reduction is Procter & Gamble's over-the-counter (OTC) clinical division, which conducts clinical studies that involve testing drugs, health care products, or treatments in humans.[16] Such testing follows rigorous design, conduct, analysis, and summary of the data collected. P&G had at least four different ways to perform a clinical study and needed to find the best way to meet its research and development needs. To do this, it focused on flow-time reduction. Its approach built on fundamental high-performance management principles: focusing on the customer, fact-based decisions, continual improvement, empowerment, the right leadership structure, and an understanding of work processes. An example is shown in Exhibit 4.3. The team found that final reports took months to prepare. Only by mapping the existing process did they fully understand the causes of long flow times and the amount of rework and recycling during review and sign-off. By restructuring the activities from sequential to parallel work and identifying critical measurements to monitor the process, they were able to reduce the time from several months to less than 4 weeks.

Exhibit 4.3 Final Report "Is" and "Should" Process Example

How a Final Report Is Actually Prepared

Treatments complete
Complete statistics
Draft statistical and medical summaries
Integrate summaries, make consistent with basic protocol into draft report
Sequential review, negotiate changes one-on-one
Perform quality control corrections
Circulate for final sign-off
Changes required?
Yes
No
Investigator signs final report

How a Final Report Should Be Prepared

Treatments complete
Initial draft report prepared from basic protocol information during treatment phase
Complete statistics
Draft statistical and medical summaries
Integrate summaries in draft report
Perform quality control corrections
Board review of draft product
Care teams meet to integrate comments, final sign-off
Investigator signs final report

Source: David A. McCarney, Robert W. Bogs, and Linda M. Bayuk, "More, Better, Faster From Total Quality Effort," *Quality Progress*, August 1999, pp. 43–50. © 1999. American Society for Quality. Reprinted with permission.

Significant reductions in flow time cannot be achieved simply by focusing on individual subprocesses; cross-functional processes must be examined all across the organization. This forces the company to take a system's view of operations and to engage in cooperative behaviors.

Flexibility

Success in globally competitive markets requires a capacity for both design and demand flexibility. The automobile industry, for example, is constantly developing new models. Companies that can exploit flexibility by building several different vehicles on the same assembly line at one time, enabling them to switch output as demand shifts, will be able to sell profitably at lower volumes. This is one key advantage that Japanese manufacturers have over U.S. automakers. Honda's two plants that produce Acura's MDX crossover sport utility vehicle and the less-expensive Honda Pilot can produce any combination of 300,000 MDX, Pilot, and Odyssey minivans. This allows Honda to concentrate on whatever model happens to be in greatest demand.[17] In contrast, competitors like Ford, GM, and DaimlerChrysler have as many as three factories dedicated to a single vehicle.

Enablers of design flexibility include close relationships with customers to understand their emerging wants and needs, outsourcing and make-versus-buy trade-offs, empowering employees as decision makers, effective manufacturing and information technology, and close supplier and customer relationships. For example, Harley-Davidson's annual output is relatively small (around 52,000 bikes per year). However, it offers numerous models, accessories, and customized features that make almost every bike unique. It can do so because its manufacturing operations are built around programmable robots and other forms of flexible automation.[18]

Flexibility is manifest in mass customization strategies that are becoming increasingly prevalent today. **Mass customization** *is being able to make whatever goods and services the customer wants, at any volume, at any time for anybody, and for a global organization, from any place in the world.*[19] Some examples include Sign-tic company signs that are uniquely designed for each customer from a standard base sign structure; business consulting; Levi's jeans that are cut to exact measurements; personal web pages; estate planning; Motorola pagers customized in different colors, sizes, and shapes; personal weight-training programs; and modular furniture that customers can configure to their unique needs and tastes. Customer involvement might occur at the design (as in the case of Sign-tic signs), fabrication (Levi's jeans), assembly (Motorola pagers), or postproduction (modular furniture) stages of the value chain. Mass customization requires companies to align their activities around differentiated customer segments and to design goods, services, and operations around flexibility. High levels of flexibility might require special strategies such as modular designs, interchangeable components, and postponement strategies. These allow companies to build standard components and configure them at the last possible moment to meet customers' unique needs. Flexible operations require sharing manufacturing lines and specialized training for employees. They also require attention to outsourcing decisions, agreements with key suppliers, and innovative partnering arrangements, because delayed shipments and a complex supply chain can hinder flexibility.

Mass customization *is being able to make whatever goods and services the customer wants, at any volume, at any time for anybody, and for a global organization, from any place in the world.*

Innovation

Innovation *is the discovery and practical application or commercialization of a device, method, or idea that differs from existing norms.* Innovations in all forms encapsulate human knowledge. Over the years, innovations in goods (such as telephones, automobiles, refrigerators, computers, optical fiber, satellites, and cell phones) and services (self-service, all-suite hotels, health maintenance organizations, and Internet banking) have improved the overall quality of life. Within business organizations, innovations in manufacturing equipment (computer-aided design, robotic automation, and smart tags) and management practices (customer satisfaction surveys, quantitative decision models, and the Malcolm Baldrige criteria) have allowed organizations to be more efficient and better meet customers' needs.

Innovation *is the discovery and practical application or commercialization of a device, method, or idea that differs from existing norms.*

Many firms focus on research and development for innovation as a core component of their strategy. Such firms are on the leading edge of product technology, and their ability to innovate and introduce new products is a critical success factor. Product performance, not price, is the major selling feature. When competition enters the market and profit margins fall, these companies often drop out of the market while continuing to introduce innovative new products. These companies focus on outstanding product research, design, and development; high product quality; and the ability to modify production facilities to produce new products frequently.

As global competition increases, the ability to innovate has become almost essential for remaining competitive. National Cash Register, for example, clung to outdated mechanical technologies for years while competitors developed innovative new electronic systems. The lack of innovation nearly destroyed the company. Today, leading companies do not wait for customers to change; they use innovation to create new customer needs and desires. At 3M, for example, every division is expected to derive 25 percent of its sales each year from products that did not exist 5 years earlier. This forces managers to think seriously about innovation. Such a spirit of continuous improvement not only will result in new products, but also will help operations managers to create better processes.

Learning Objective
To understand the process of strategic planning at the organizational level and its relationship to operations strategy.

STRATEGIC PLANNING

The direction an organization takes and the competitive priorities it chooses are driven by its strategy. The concept of strategy has different meanings for different people. **Strategy** *is a pattern or plan that integrates an organization's major goals, policies, and action sequences into a cohesive whole.*[20] Basically, a strategy is the approach by which an organization seeks to develop the capabilities required for achieving its competitive advantage. Effective strategies develop around a few key competitive priorities—such as low cost or fast service time—which provide a focus for the entire organization and exploit an organization's **core competencies**—*the strengths unique to that organization.* Such strengths might be a particularly skilled or creative work force, good customer relationship management, clever bundling of goods and services, strong supply chain networks, extraordinary service, marketing expertise, or the ability to rapidly develop new products or change production-output rates.

Strategy *is a pattern or plan that integrates an organization's major goals, policies, and action sequences into a cohesive whole.*

Core Competencies—*the strengths unique to that organization.*

Strategic planning *is the process of determining long-term goals, policies, and plans for an organization.*

Strategic planning *is the process of determining long-term goals, policies, and plans for an organization.* The objective of strategic planning is to build a position that is so strong in selected ways that the organization can achieve its goals despite unforeseeable external forces that may arise. Strategy is the result of a series of hierarchical decisions about goals, directions, and resources; thus, most large organizations have three levels of strategy: corporate, business, and functional. At the top level, *corporate strategy* is necessary to define the businesses in which the corporation will participate and develop plans for the acquisition and allocation of resources among those businesses. *The businesses in which the firm will participate are often called* **strategic business units (SBUs)** *and are usually defined as families of goods or services having similar characteristics or methods of creation.* For small organizations, the corporate and business strategies frequently are the same.

The businesses in which the firm will participate are often called **strategic business units (SBUs)** *and are usually defined as families of goods or services having similar characteristics or methods of creation.*

SBUs might be organized by process or customer benefit packages such as home, life, automobile, and medical insurance, or Medicare versus private insurance customer benefit packages, or by physical goods such as the steel, glass, and plastics divisions. Or in some organizations by target market segments such as food for babies, adults, and the elderly or computer chips for the personal computer, server, cell phone, and handheld digital assistant target market segments.

For example, at one point during Jack Welch's tenure as CEO of General Electric, he formulated a strategy in which each business was to be either number 1 or number 2 in its market. Those that could not meet this corporate objective were sold. A corporate strategy requires consideration of such factors as current market share, internal strengths and weaknesses, and competitors' strengths and weaknesses. Corporate strategic planning addresses such questions as: What are our objectives? What are our greatest challenges? What must we do particularly well? How will we measure success?

The second level of strategy is generally called *business strategy*, and defines the focus for SBUs. The major decisions involve which markets to pursue and how best to compete in those markets, that is, what competitive priorities the firm should pursue. Strategic plans generally differ among SBUs but must be consistent with the overall corporate strategy. For example, an appliance division of a large goods-producing firm might decide to produce standard dishwashers and compete on low costs, while an electronics division might focus on customized products and compete on innovation and design flexibility.

Finally, the third level of strategy is *functional strategies*, the means by which business strategies are accomplished. *A* **functional strategy** *is the set of decisions that each functional area—marketing, finance, operations, research and development, engineering, and so on—develops to support its particular business strategy.*

A **functional strategy** *is the set of decisions that each functional area—marketing, finance, operations, research and development, engineering, and so on—develops to support its particular business strategy.*

Our particular focus will be on **operations strategy**—*how an organization's processes are designed and organized to produce the type of goods and services to support the corporate and business strategies.* Business strategy has historically emphasized marketing and financial considerations, and operations strategy has received the least amount of high-level management attention. In some organizations, operations is not considered a factor of the corporate strategy. Consequently, operations managers have often been placed in the position of having to react to strategic plans that were developed from primarily financial and marketing perspectives, often with disastrous results. For example, a marketing-driven strategy might require a wide line of goods with required short delivery times; these would necessitate short production runs and fast changeover that a firm's facilities might not be designed for.

Operations strategy—*how an organization's processes are designed and organized to produce the type of goods and services to support the corporate and business strategies.*

Today, managers have recognized that the value chain can be leveraged to provide a distinct competitive advantage and that operations is a core competency for the organization. Whoever has superior operational capability over the long term is the odds-on favorite to win the industry shakeout. Before we address operations strategy in detail, we discuss the typical strategic planning process that most organizations use.

The Strategic Planning Process

The strategic planning process consists of two main parts: *development* and *implementation*. **Strategy development** *refers to a company's approach, formal or informal, for making key long-term business decisions.* The process typically takes into account customer and market requirements, the competitive environment, industry structure and nonindustry competitors, financial and societal risks, human resource capabilities and needs, technological capabilities, and supplier capabilities. This strategy development process might include environmental scanning, global and local business intelligence, market or sales forecasts, target market characteristics and analysis, quantitative models or simulations, evaluating alternative "what-if" scenarios, and other tools to develop strategies to bridge the gap between where the organization is now and where it wants to be in 2, 4, or 10 years. Strategies might involve developing new goods or services, expanding existing or entering new markets, growing revenue, adding new peripheral services, reducing cost, controlling the value chain, providing great service, or establishing global alliances. Strategies

Strategy development *refers to a company's approach, formal or informal, for making key long-term business decisions.*

might also be directed toward making the company a preferred supplier, a low-cost producer, a technology leader, or a market innovator.

Strategy implementation *refers to the development of specific action plans derived from strategy that clearly describe the things that need to be done, human resource plans and support, performance measures and indicators, and resource deployment to ensure that plans and strategies are successfully executed.*

The **strategic mission** *of a firm defines its reason for existence.*

Strategy implementation *refers to the development of specific action plans derived from strategy that clearly describe the things that need to be done, human resource plans and support, performance measures and indicators, and resource deployment to ensure that plans and strategies are successfully executed.* The alignment of corporate strategy with functional strategies is a key task of senior management. Usually, both of these steps are integrated into one strategic planning process, especially in smaller organizations.

In most organizations, the organization's mission and values drive strategy. *The* **strategic mission** *of a firm defines its reason for existence.* For example, the strategic mission of Pal's Sudden Service (see Chapter 1 for an introduction to this company) is "To deliver excellence in food service while providing a menu focused on exceptional quality." *The* **strategic vision** *describes where the organization is headed and what it intends to be.* Pal's strategic vision is shown at the left.

Values *are attitudes and policies for all employees to follow that direct the journey to achieving the organization's vision.* Values are reinforced through conscious and subconscious behavior at all levels of the organization. Over time, customers recognize a strong organizational value system through repetitive service encounters, and this interaction and experience builds customer loyalty, and eventually profits. The service-profit chain introduced in Chapter 3 is one way strong organizational values and clear corporate objectives lead to increasing market share, customer satisfaction, and profits. Pal's Values and Code of Ethics statement is shown on the left.

Pal's Vision Statement

To be the preferred quick service restaurant in our market achieving the largest market share by providing:

- The quickest, friendliest, most accurate service available
- A focused menu that delights customers
- Daily excellence in our product, service, and systems execution
- Clean, organized, sanitary facilities
- Exceptional value
- A fun, positive and profitable experience for all stakeholders

Source: Pal's Sudden Service

Pal's Values and Code of Ethics

Positive Energy
We will always nurture a positive, enthusiastic atmosphere, which will foster mutual trust and respect among employees, customers, and suppliers. Further, we will always operate with open agendas, positive interactions and genuine motives.

Honesty and Truthfulness
We will always be honest and truthful in all relationships, respecting and relying on each other.

Employee Well Being
We will always provide a safe, healthy, and desirable workplace.

Citizenship
We will always provide community involvement through personal and company contributions of time, efort, and resources. Through our best effort and consideration, we will always protect public health, safety, and the environment.

Golden Rule
We will always do unto others as we would have them do unto us.

Source: Pal's Sudden Service

A firm's strategic mission and values guides the development of strategies by establishing the context within which daily operating decisions are made and how resources are allocated and setting limits on available strategic options. In addition, they help to make trade-offs among the various performance measures and between short- and long-term goals. The approaches that Pal's listed in its Vision Statement essentially define the basic strategy needed to achieve its vision of being the preferred quick-service restaurant. However, the business environment can easily change, and strategies need to respond dynamically to such changes. For instance, a small company like Pal's might find itself in a tight labor market and would need to develop strategies to address this threat. This is done through some type of a systematic "what-if" strategic planning process.

The Pal's strategic planning process, which is performed annually, focuses on a 2-year planning horizon. The major steps are as follows:

Step 1—Gather and Analyze Strategic Performance Data (strengths, weaknesses, opportunities, and threats): In addition to collecting data from all levels of the organization, Pal's gathers data from our primary stakeholders (i.e., customers/market, employees, community, competitors, banks, regulatory, suppliers/partners, and food industry). The leadership team analyzes all data using a SWOT (Strengths, Weaknesses, Opportunities, and Threats) analysis and risk review.

Step 2—Review/Analyze Existing Strategic Directions/Documents: Analyzed data from step 1 are used to evaluate the appropriateness of the existing strategic documents/outputs (Mission, Values/Code of Ethics, and Key Business Drivers).

Step 3—Revise/Develop Strategy: Results of the SWOT analysis and risk data from step 1 are used to perform various functions (e.g., visioning, forecasting, projections, options development, brainstorming, scenarios). Strategic documents and outputs from step 2 are used as references to ensure consistency is maintained during the establishment of short-term and longer-term strategic objectives and action plans. Strategic data analyses and interpretations are carefully evaluated against their own operational requirements, capabilities, and available capital before strategic objectives and plans are chosen.

Step 4—Deploy Objectives and Action Plans: Deploying objectives and action plans to all levels of the Pal's organization and to all stakeholders involves developing item-specific action (implementation) plans, which are analyzed and integrated into a single, coordinated, large-scale action plan designed to accomplish the overall objective.

Step 5—Review Progress and Results: The Leadership Team reviews progress and results using Pal's Management Review Process.

Step 6—Continually Evaluate and Improve Strategic Planning Process: The Leadership Team devotes part of its annual planning agenda to evaluating and improving strategic objective selection, action planning, deployment, our capabilities for tracking and achieving performance relative to plans, improvement planning, benchmarking, innovation, problem solving, and performance.

The **strategic vision** *describes where the organization is headed and what it intends to be.*

Values *are attitudes and policies for all employees to follow that direct the journey to achieving the organization's vision.*

Pal's strategic planning process demonstrates how one company approaches the challenges of strategic planning. Each organization has its own unique ways of doing strategy development and implementation. The next step is to translate business strategy into operations.

OPERATIONS STRATEGY

Learning Objective
To understand how operations strategy can support and drive the achievement of organizational objectives, and to learn the key elements of an operations strategy.

An **operations strategy** *defines how an organization will execute its chosen business strategies.* Developing an operations strategy involves translating competitive priorities into operational capabilities by making a variety of choices and trade-offs for design and operating decisions. That is, operating decisions must be aligned with achieving the desired competitive priorities. For example, if corporate objectives are to be the low-cost and mass-market producer of a good, then adopting an assembly line type of process is how operations can help achieve this corporate objective.

An **operations strategy** *defines how an organization will execute its chosen business strategies.*

What kind of an operations strategy might a company like Pal's Sudden Service have? Consider the implications for operations management of the basic strategy stated in its vision:

1. *The quickest, friendliest, most accurate service available.* To achieve quick and accurate service, Pal's needs highly standardized processes. The staff at each Pal's facility is organized into process teams along the order-taking, processing, packaging, and order-completion line. The process layout is designed so that raw materials enter through a delivery door and are worked forward through the store with one process serving the next. Employees must have clearly defined roles and responsibilities, understanding of all operating and service procedures

and quality standards, and job flexibility through cross-training to be able to respond to volume cycles and unplanned reassignments of work activities. To ensure friendly service, Pal's uses specific performance criteria to evaluate and select employees who demonstrate the aptitude, talents, and characteristics to meet performance standards, invests heavily in training, and pays close attention to employee satisfaction.

2. *A focused menu that delights customers.* They must understand their customers' likes and dislikes of their products and services as well as their competitors'. Although this would fall within the realm of marketing, such a marketing strategy must be coordinated with operations to ensure that planned response times can be achieved and that any menu changes can be quickly adapted to its operations. Such questions as these are addressed during the design stage: Are our customer needs data and market trend data objective, valid, and credible? What new capabilities will we need? What similar or related things are our competitors doing? Do our suppliers have the capacity to support this new offering? Is the appropriate technology available? Does Pal's have the capability to fully support this new offering? Pal's new product design process begins with customer-defined quality, focuses on maintaining or improving critical cycle times for speed, tests new technologies, and assesses overall feasibility and capability of new designs.
3. *Daily excellence in product, service, and systems execution.* Successful day-to-day operations requires employees to effectively apply Pal's On-Line Quality Control process, consisting of four simple steps: standardize the method or process, use the method, study the results, and take control. With Pal's high-speed work, processes are running so rapidly that visual operational standards must be mentally ingrained to achieve compliance to standards. Visual standardization is a critical element of training and development. Each employee is thoroughly trained and coached on precise work procedures and process standards, focusing on developing a visual reference to verify product quality. Performance is also maintained through various process automation and measurement components to minimize variation and ensure accuracy. Employees are also trained to analyze results against process standards and measures and are given the authority to recognize problems and take appropriate action.
4. *Clean, organized, sanitary facilities.* Pal's focuses on prevention—eliminating all possible causes of accidents—first, then finding and eliminating causes of actual incidents. In-house health and safety inspections are conducted monthly using the FDA Food Service Sanitation Ordinance. Results are compiled and distributed to all stores within 24 hours with any identified improvements applied in each store.
5. *Exceptional value.* Value is created by continually improving the goods and services that customers receive while maintaining low costs. Through methods of listening and learning from customers and studies of industry standards and best practices, Pal's has designed the following into its operations: convenient locations with easy ingress and egress, long hours of operation (6:00 A.M. to 10:00 P.M.), easy-to-read 3-D menus, direct fact-to-face access to order taker and cashier/order deliverer, fresh food (cooked hot dogs are discarded after 10 minutes if not purchased), a 20-second delivery target, and a web site for contacting the corporate office and stores. Pal's selects suppliers carefully to ensure not only product quality and on-time delivery but also the best price for the volume level purchased. Overall supply chain costs are minimized by maintaining only a few, long-term core suppliers.

From this discussion of Pal's Sudden Service, it is clear that how operations are designed and implemented can have a dramatic effect on business performance and achievement of the strategy. Therefore, operations require close coordination with functional strategies in other areas of the firm, such as marketing and finance. For example, decisions to discount goods to increase demand might put such a strain on operations that it would be impossible to satisfy the resulting volume of demand and, hence, dissatisfy many customers. Financial decisions to reduce costs might adversely impact quality by reducing technology or training investments. Similarly, operations decisions such as updating facilities or technology might temporarily reduce production and impact marketing efforts. It is important that managers understand the relationships between operations and other areas of the firm and take a systems view when making key decisions.

In some companies, the operations strategy *is* their business strategy. Wal-Mart, for example, focuses its competitive strategy on controlling the entire value chain to create a competitive advantage that few competitors can copy easily (see the OM Spotlight). Wal-Mart places huge order quantities with its suppliers and demands substantial price discounts, frequent delivery of the best-selling goods, and supplier management of the inventory in the 2,600 U.S. Wal-Mart stores. The company established optical laboratories next to airport cargo hubs to supply their 1,500 optical operations within Wal-Mart stores. Information system capability allows Wal-Mart to make and execute these order requirements better than other retailers. The dominant player within the value chain is not suppliers, wholesalers, manufacturers, distributors, or transportation firms, but the retail store toward the end of the value chain—Wal-Mart!

OM SPOTLIGHT

Wal-Mart[21]

Wal-Mart has more than 3,000 stores across the United States and about 1,000 stores internationally. The Retail Divisions include Wal-Mart Stores, Sam's Club, Supercenters, Neighborhood Markets, International, and Walmart.com. Specialty Divisions include Tire & Lube Express, Pharmacy, Vacations, Used Fixture Auctions, and Optical. Wal-Mart employees more than 962,000 associates in the United States and 282,000 internationally. Sam Walton's strategy was simple: "Give people high value, low prices, and a warm welcome."

Sam Walton built Wal-Mart on the revolutionary philosophies of excellence in the workplace, customer service, and always having the lowest prices. The company was founded on the Three Basic Beliefs Mr. Sam established in 1962 and which are continually stressed by senior executives:

1. *Respect for the Individual*—"We are a group of dedicated, hardworking, ordinary people who have teamed together to accomplish extraordinary things. We have very different backgrounds, different colors and different beliefs, but we do believe that every individual deserves to be treated with respect and dignity." Don Soderquist, senior vice chairman of Wal-Mart Stores, Inc. (retired).
2. *Service to Our Customers*—"Wal-Mart's culture has always stressed the importance of Customer Service. Our Associate base across the country is as diverse as the communities in which we have Wal-Mart stores. This allows us to provide the Customer Service expected from each individual customer that walks into our stores." Tom Coughlin, president and chief executive officer, Wal-Mart Stores division.
3. *Strive for Excellence*—"Sam was never satisfied that prices were as low as they needed to be or that our products' quality was as high as they deserved—he believed in the concept of striving for excellence before it became a fashionable concept." Lee Scott, president and chief executive officer of Wal-Mart Stores, Inc.

John Zich/Bloomberg News/Landov

This approach leads to low cost, fast and reliable delivery, a broad selection of goods, and volume and product flexibility—all the things that create value for its customers. Wal-Mart also uses service to enhance the shopping and buying experience by having greeters to direct and help customers as they enter the huge stores, which often include banking, optical, shoe and leather, pharmacy, gasoline, and automobile repair services. In an annual survey by WSL Strategic Retail, a consulting firm, 25 percent of Americans say Wal-Mart is their favorite store, and 58 percent of children age 8 to 18 declared Wal-Mart their favorite place to shop. Wal-Mart is also credited with a substantial impact on productivity in the U.S. economy in the 1990s. As Bradford C. Johnson wrote in an article in the *McKinsey Quarterly*, "More than half of the U.S. productivity acceleration in the retailing of general merchandise can be explained by only two syllables: Wal-Mart."[22]

A Framework for Operations Strategy

Operations design choices *are the decisions management must make as to what type of process structure is best suited to produce goods or create services.*

Infrastructure *focuses on the nonprocess features and capabilities of the organization and includes the work force, operating plans and control systems, quality control, organizational structure, compensation systems, learning and innovation systems, and support services.*

A useful framework for strategy development that ties corporate and marketing strategy to operations strategy was proposed by Professor Terry Hill at Templeton College, Oxford University and is shown in Exhibit 4.4.[23] It was originally designed for goods-producing organizations, but it can also be applied to service-providing firms. This framework defines the essential elements of an effective operations strategy in the last two columns—*operations design choices* and *building the right infrastructure.*

Operations design choices *are the decisions management must make as to what type of process structure is best suited to produce goods or create services.* It typically addresses six key areas—types of processes, value chain integration and outsourcing, technology, capacity and facilities, inventory and service capacity, and trade-offs among these decisions. **Infrastructure** *focuses on the nonprocess features and capabilities of the organization and includes the work force, operating plans and control systems, quality control, organizational structure, compensation systems, learning and innovation systems, and support services.* The infrastructure must support process choice and provide managers with accurate and timely information to make

Exhibit 4.4 Hill's Strategy Development Framework

Corporate Objectives	Marketing Strategy	How Do Goods and Services Qualify and Win Orders in the Marketplace? (Competitive Priorities)	Operations Strategy	
			Operations Design Choices	Infrastructure
• Growth • Survival • Profit • Return on investment • Other market and financial measures • Social welfare	• Goods and services markets and segments • Range • Mix • Volumes • Standardization versus customization • Level of innovation • Leader versus follower alternatives	• Safety • Price (cost) • Range • Flexibility • Demand • Goods and service design • Quality • Service • Goods • Environment • Brand image • Delivery • Speed • Variability • Technical support • Pre- and postservice support	• Type of processes and alternative designs • Supply chain integration and outsourcing • Technology • Capacity and facilities (size, timing, location) • Inventory • Trade-off analysis	• Work force • Operating plans and control system(s) • Quality control • Organizational structure • Compensation system • Learning and innovation systems • Support services

Source: T. Hill, *Manufacturing Strategy: Text and Cases*, 3rd ed., Burr Ridge, IL: McGraw-Hill, 2000, p. 32 and T. Hill, "Operations Management: Strategic Context and Managerial Analysis," 2nd ed. Prigrame MacMillan, 2005, p. 50. Reprinted with permission from McGraw-Hill Companies.

good decisions. These decisions lie at the core of organizational effectiveness and suggest that the integrative nature of operations management is one of the most important aspects of success.

A key feature of this framework is the link between operations and corporate and marketing strategies. Clearly, it is counterproductive to design a customer benefit package and an operations system to produce and deliver it, and then discover that these plans will not achieve corporate and marketing objectives. This linkage is described by the four major decision loops illustrated in Exhibit 4.5. Decision loop #1 ties together corporate strategy—which establishes the organization's direction and boundaries—and marketing strategy—which evaluates customer wants and needs and target market segments. By focusing on the desired set of competitive priorities and target markets, the organization can develop a set of relative priorities for each target market segment.

The output of loop #1 is the input for loop #2. Decision loop #2 describes how operations evaluates the implications of competitive priorities in terms of process choice and infrastructure. The key decisions are: Do we have the process capability to achieve the corporate and marketing objectives per target market segment? Are our processes capable of consistently achieving order winner performance in each market segment? What drives loop #2 is a rank ordering of competitive priorities for each market segment as determined by the corporate and marketing managers. For example, if a 2-day financial loan approval flow time (processing time) is desired by the corporate and marketing strategies (loop #1) but the current process is not capable of doing this work in less than 10 days (loop #2), then the corporate, marketing, and operations areas need to revise their strategies and plans. By using the latest information technology at a cost of $10 million the loan approval process can be upgraded to achieve the 2-day target flow time.

Decision loop #3 lies within the operations function of the organization and involves determining if process choice decisions and capabilities are consistent with infrastructure decisions and capabilities. Much of this book is devoted to these issues. The fourth decision loop (loop #4) represents operations' input into the corporate and marketing strategy. Corporate decision makers ultimately decide how to allocate resources to achieve corporate objectives.

The management decisions represented by these four loops are iterative and highly integrated. The more integration and communication about "what is desired" and "what is possible," the better the organization is at achieving its objectives. We will now examine the specific elements of operations strategy in this strategy development framework.

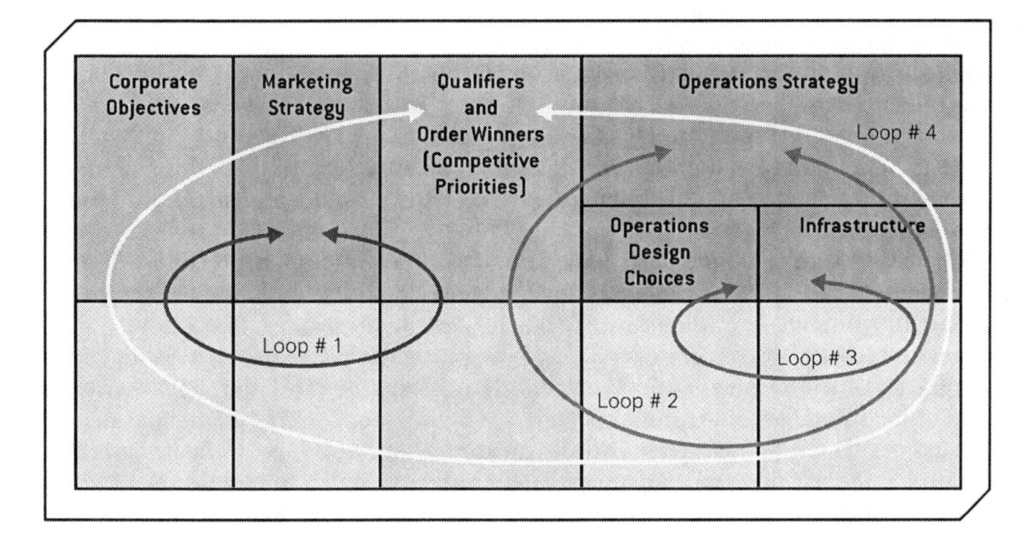

Exhibit 4.5
Four Key Decision Loops in Terry Hill's Generic Strategy Framework

Learning Objective
To understand the operations design choices and infrastructure decisions from the perspective of defining an operations strategy and trade-offs that need to be made in developing a viable operations strategy.

OPERATIONS DESIGN CHOICE AND INFRASTRUCTURE DECISIONS

A key aspect of configuring an operations strategy is selecting and designing the key value creation processes for manufacturing and service delivery systems. Although we will examine advantages and disadvantages of process decisions and their impact on competitive priorities in Chapter 7, our focus here is on how process choice is related to strategy from a "big-picture," strategic-level perspective.

Types of Processes

In Chapter 1, we classified processes by their *purpose*:

1. *value creation processes* that focus on primary goods and service creation and delivery,
2. *support processes* that provide the infrastructure for value creation processes, and
3. *general management processes* that coordinate the value creation and support processes.

In each of these categories, operations managers have choices in selecting technology and designing processes. For example, the process of providing information to prospective students in a campus visit could be designed in several ways. Students and their parents might be herded in large groups from one function, such as admissions, financial aid, and college departments, to another in a fixed sequence. An alternative is to take smaller groups through the different functions in different sequences so that college representatives can provide more personalized attention. Virtual campus tours could also be used to reinforce actual student visits. Similar choices exist in manufacturing and other types of service processes. One of the key issues in selecting processes is to appropriately match the process to the type of good or service being produced to support competitive priorities. Other process choice issues and ways to think about processes are the subjects of Chapters 7 and 8.

Supply Chain Integration and Outsourcing

The second element of operations design choices noted in Exhibit 4.4 addresses the role of suppliers in the value chain. We introduced many of these issues in Chapter 2. Key strategic questions to consider are: Should we make components in our facilities or purchase them from external suppliers? Should we outsource support functions such as software integration or benefits administration? Should we acquire suppliers or distributors or merge with them? Should we use one or several suppliers? Should we enter into alliances with suppliers, intermediaries, or customers? Should we enter new global or local markets and does our supply chain have the capability to support this decision? What are the implications of these decisions on the information systems we need to successfully implement our strategies and plans?

Issues of cost, quality, time, and flexibility enter into such decisions. Supply chain integration might include strategic partnerships that enhance collaboration among firms that have different core competencies, joint ventures, or licensing agreements. Increased integration of suppliers, or partnership strategies, requires more complex control by operations managers. For instance, both Palm and Microsoft license their handheld operating system to many manufacturers of personal digital assistants (PDAs), and electronics firms outsource assembly operations to contract manufacturers. Many firms outsource support services like human resources or call center operations. Hewlett-Packard, for example, successfully bid on Procter &

Gamble's outsourcing of its entire information technology operation. These issues will be explored further in Chapter 9.

Technology

The technology choices impact cost, flexibility, quality, time, and innovativeness. In a fast-food restaurant, for example, should sandwiches be made to customers' orders or made to one or more specifications and stored? (See the OM Spotlight on McDonald's.) Likewise, a grocery store must decide whether or not to use scanners as opposed to manual keying in of prices. A custom product strategy requires on-time delivery, quality, and the capability to design and manufacture different products. On the other hand, companies that manufacture high-volume types of products usually benefit most from standardization in design, low manufacturing cost, and high availability of the product through inventories and distribution channels.

Technology decisions directly influence cost, flexibility, quality, and speed. A process-oriented system employing general-purpose equipment allows for flexibility in manufacturing different products. A product-oriented system, with special-purpose equipment dedicated to the production of one or a few products, provides high volume and low unit costs. In designing service delivery, questions often focus on what level of technology, mechanization, and automation should be used. Many service processes are moving toward increased levels of self-service, often computer-based, to replace traditional human interaction. For example, a bank customer has the choice of using automatic tellers or human tellers or the Internet. Issues of technology will be addressed further in Chapter 5.

Capacity and Facilities

Capacity *measures the amount of output that can be produced over a period of time.*

Capacity *measures the amount of output that can be produced over a period of time.* A firm must make many strategic decisions about capacity, such as the amount of

OM SPOTLIGHT

McDonald's[24]

McDonald's used to make food to stock, storing sandwiches in a large tray used to fulfill customer orders. Although the company has about 25,000 restaurants, it had lost some of its competitive edge. Sales went flat in the mid-1990s and independent market testing showed a widening gap with competition in food quality. Worse, the customers of fast food like variety, and when they switch foods they switch restaurants. The make-to-stock system was not meeting these new demands. After 5 years of lab and market testing, McDonald's rolled out the new "Just for You" system, which began in March 1998, to create a make-to-order environment. This required a massive change in computer technology with computers coordinating orders; food production equipment using "rapid toasters" and temperature-controlled "launching zones" to replace the old heat lamps and holding bins; new food preparation tables; and retraining efforts for the entire domestic food production organization of over 600,000 crew members.

However, this system has apparently backfired. Sales did not improve as expected and customers complained about slow service. The new system increased the average service time from 2 to 3 minutes per order, and 15-minute waits were not uncommon. McDonald's stock price decreased, and rivals such as Wendy's captured additional market share.

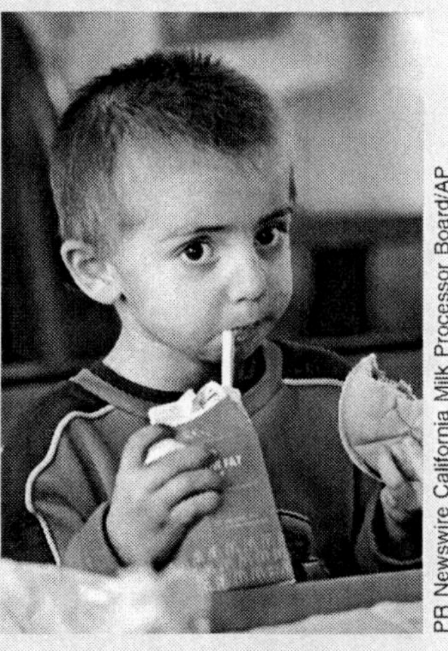

PR Newswire California Milk Processor Board/AP

capacity to have, the timing of capacity changes, and the type of capacity. Consequences of capacity decisions normally influence cost, flexibility, time, and quality. For example, what is the economic effect of expanding a facility versus building a new one, or of having one large facility versus several small ones? An airline might consider changing from large jets (which provide economies of scale) to smaller jets and more frequent flights (which provide a greater degree of customer service). Too high a capacity or too many facilities requires a high fixed-cost structure, while too low a capacity or not enough facilities close to the customers can result in inadequate service quality, resulting in the loss of (dissatisfied) customers. Capacity will be discussed more in Chapters 10 and 11.

Facilities decisions can have significant influence on costs and customer service. For instance, oil companies often locate processing plants near supplies of crude oil to achieve economies of scale. Individual distribution outlets are located much closer to customers. Decisions on how to structure product groups within plants, what types of processes to develop, and what volume to produce and when are important, especially in rapidly changing industries. For instance, in the semiconductor industry, small, low-volume plants are built for new products with considerable risk, whereas high-volume plants are used for stable and mature products. Facility location and capacity decisions in services require many service facilities located close to customers. A manufacturer may have five factories and ten distribution warehouses; many service firms have thousands of stores and locations and hundreds of warehouses. McDonald's and Wal-Mart, for example, have, respectively, over 30,000 and 4,000 stores worldwide. This dramatically complicates the management of facilities and is called "multisite management," which is explained in more detail in Chapter 8.

Inventory

In goods-producing firms, the role of inventory—goods stored for future use—is an important operations management decision because it provides capacity to meet demand and respond to demand variation at various stages within the supply chain. Operations managers need to consider where to position inventory within the supply chain and how much inventory to have at each stage. Managing inventories is the subject of Chapters 12 and 13.

In service organizations, as discussed in Chapter 1, physical inventory does not exist; however, adequate service capacity must be designed into the system to buffer against peak demand and variations in demand. In a service organization, service capacity substitutes for physical inventory. Key service capacity decisions include the amount of staff to schedule by day of the week and by department, the amount of additional safety needed, such as nurses and trucks, and the pricing of perishable service capacity (for instance, airline seats and hotel rooms). Inventory and service capacity decisions have a major impact on process structure, choice, efficiency, and effectiveness. Chapters 10 and 11 address service capacity in more detail.

Trade-Off Analysis

The sixth decision area for process choice in Exhibit 4.4 is trade-off analysis. The trade-offs between process choice decisions are many and often complex. Operations managers must make trade-offs between capacity and service; manual and automated equipment; alternative process designs; inventory, cost, and service; quality and costs; and the number and location of service facilities. Such decisions may be based on economics or other performance measures such as quality, time, and volume. Chapters 1 and 3 provided some basic methods for examining trade-offs, such as computing break-even quantities for make-or-buy decisions, the value of a loyal customer, and the productivity of employees.

BUILDING THE RIGHT INFRASTRUCTURE

Learning Objective
To be able to identify and understand the seven decisions areas in Hill's operations strategy framework.

The second component of Hill's operations strategy approach depicted in Exhibit 4.4 is infrastructure. Infrastructure represents the "behind-the-scenes" processes in a value chain, that is, the key supporting and general management processes. How these are designed and executed can easily mean the difference between success and failure in achieving organizational objectives.

Work Force

The management of the work force has important long-term implications for operations strategy. How work and jobs are designed to promote empowerment, innovation, and problem solving; the amount of training provided to employees; recognition and rewards; incentive and compensation systems; and sustaining a positive and motivating work environment are key operations management challenges. Because of varying levels in demand, many service organizations like Pal's Sudden Service are forced to use part-time employees and staff that are cross-trained in a variety of skills. Employees with more customer contact must understand customer interactions and have better "people skills" than task-oriented personnel who work behind the scenes. The focus on human resources was highlighted in Chapter 3 by Category 5 (Human Resource Focus) of the Baldrige criteria, two of the four performance areas (Innovation and Learning, Internal Performance) in the balanced scorecard, and the focus on the employee and internal performance in the service-profit chain. Some aspects of work design are addressed in Chapter 8.

Operating Plans and Control Systems

How operations are planned and controlled affects cost, quality, and dependability. Actual decisions are more of a tactical and operational nature, but the policies used for making such decisions have long-term effects. Scheduling, material control, capacity allocation, waiting lines, and day-to-day quality control are just some of the issues we will address throughout this book. Operating decisions such as short-term staffing and scheduling have profound effects on costs, customer satisfaction, and efficiency. For instance, many managers of grocery and discount department stores are able to shift employees from such ancillary activities as stocking shelves to staffing checkout lines as demand increases, and therefore reallocate staff capacity to improve customer service. These issues are addressed further in Chapter 14.

Quality Control

All goods and services are not designed or produced in the same fashion; for example, Cadillac automobiles, although part of General Motors, use more sophisticated technology and manufacturing processes that provide a higher level of quality (along with associated higher prices) than other GM brands. To illustrate this point, David Garvin describes the differences between Steinway & Sons and Yamaha, two of the leading manufacturers of pianos.[25] Steinway & Sons has been the industry leader because of the even voicing, sweetness of register, duration of tone, long lives, and fine cabinetwork of its pianos, each of which is handcrafted and unique in sound and style. Yamaha, in contrast, has developed a reputation for manufacturing quality pianos in a very short time. Yamaha did that by emphasizing reliability and conformance (low on Steinway's list of priorities), rather than artistry and uniqueness. Unlike Steinway & Sons, Yamaha produces its more standardized pianos on an assembly line. Whatever dimensions of quality a company chooses to emphasize should reflect customer needs and expectations. Yamaha and Steinway have successfully fulfilled two different sets of such needs and expectations, both valid.

Management has many decisions to make regarding quality control. These include what quality characteristics to monitor and measure, where in the manufacturing or service delivery process to measure them, how often to take measures and analyze the data, and what actions to take when quality problems are discovered. Quality management and control issues are discussed further in Chapters 15 and 16.

Organization Structure

Organizational structure greatly influences the ability of a firm to satisfy its customers. Traditionally, the functional structure, as represented by the typical organization chart, divides the organization into such functions as marketing, finance, operations, and so on, providing a clear chain of command and allowing specialization in work. However, it separates employees from customers, both external and internal, can inhibit agility and process improvement, and requires many handoffs between functions. A pure process-based organization, on the other hand, is designed around teams dedicated to specific processes or projects, which are often self-managed, and promotes speed, flexibility, and internal cooperation (see Exhibit 1.7 in Chapter 1).

The Baldrige criteria, described in Chapter 3, support the notion of "organizing by process." Each process should be driven by the customer—from identifying customer wants and needs to ending with postsale services and follow-up. By assigning each process to a "process owner" or manager, responsibility and authority are clearly defined. A matrix organization blends elements of both of these organizational structures by configuring process or project teams from different functions, while maintaining functional control over individuals and technologies.

Compensation Systems

Building the human infrastructure is probably the most difficult of all management tasks. Work-force management involves many complex decisions, such as recognition and reward, advancement opportunities, training and continued education, benefits, team building and communication, empowerment, negotiation, work environment, and job shift and displacement policies. For example, compensation systems can focus on individual or team performance or some combination of them. A team-based compensation system requires a supporting organizational culture and training on team communication and brainstorming skills. An individual-based compensation system encourages independence, empowerment, and rewards the higher-performing employees. Each approach has advantages and disadvantages; however, the approach that is selected becomes a part of the operations strategy and therefore should support the achievement of a company's strategic goals and objectives.

Learning and Innovation Systems

Learning is the basis for continuous improvement and technological change. How do we record and disseminate job, process, market, and organizational knowledge accurately and quickly throughout the organization? How can we leverage past experiences in the future? What training and information support does each job need? How do we manage legacy knowledge systems while new knowledge is acquired? How do we ensure we do not have to reinvent internal and external knowledge over and over again? How can we institutionalize learning within the organization? These are the kinds of questions operations managers must help answer if the organization is to survive. Mass customization is very much dependent on learning systems. Information technology provides the capability to store organizational knowledge and use it at key points in the process to increase quality, productivity, and speed while lowering costs.

Innovation within the organization is coupled with good learning systems. The successful introduction of new goods and services and the processes that create them continuingly adds value to the firm's customer benefit packages. Rapid introduction of goods and services, a high percent of total sales from new goods and services, and research and development expense as a percent of total sales dollars are just a few of the metrics that help managers evaluate innovation.

Support Services

Support services often represent 30 to 70 percent of the cost of being in business. Each support service has at least one process. Support service processes provide services to internal (employee benefit packages) or external (customer benefit packages) customers and in doing so, create the infrastructure for an organization's primary processes. Exhibit 4.6 shows a typical list of support services to help you appreciate the amount of resources committed to support processes and why they are vital to a company's success.

Support service processes cost money, influence customer satisfaction, and consume time. Despite their importance, they often are not documented, measured, evaluated, well managed, or continuously improved. Such lack of management attention occurs both in goods-producing and service-providing organizations. In most cases, support services offer a significant opportunity for improvement in organizational effectiveness that translates to bottom-line savings.

Exhibit 4.6
Examples of Support Process

Union grievance procedures	Financial systems	Regulatory procedures
Travel services	Benefits administration	Customer-contact procedures
Training programs	Strategic planning	Health systems and procedures
Computer software services	Customer complaint processes	Research and development
CBP warranty processes	Waste management	Recognition and reward programs
Advertising programs	Company communication systems	Refund and recall procedures
Sales programs	Employee counseling	Legal and tax procedures
Supplier programs	Security and safety systems	Conference/meeting administration
Claims processing	Marketing research	
Environmental programs	Accounting systems	
Franchise systems		
Repair services		

APPLYING THE STRATEGY DEVELOPMENT FRAMEWORK: A CASE STUDY OF MCDONALD'S

Learning Objective
To be able to analyze the operations strategy and apply the strategy development framework to a real organization.

McDonald's Corporation is the world's leading food-service retailer with more than 30,000 restaurants in 121 countries serving 46 million customers each day. Because almost everyone on the planet is familiar with McDonald's goods and service delivery system, we will use it to illustrate Hill's strategy development framework.[26] Despite the operational problems that the company has encountered in recent years (as discussed in an earlier OM Spotlight), the company's vision provides the basis for its strategy:

McDonald's vision is to be the world's best quick service restaurant experience. Being the best means providing outstanding quality, service, cleanliness and value, so that we make every customer in every restaurant smile. To achieve our vision, we focus on three worldwide strategies:

(1) ***Be The Best Employer***
Be the best employer for our people in each community around the world.

(2) ***Deliver Operational Excellence***
Deliver operational excellence to our customers in each of our restaurants.

(3) ***Achieve Enduring Profitable Growth***
Achieve enduring profitable growth by expanding the brand and leveraging the strengths of the McDonald's system through innovation and technology.

Exhibit 4.7
McDonald's Customer Benefit Package

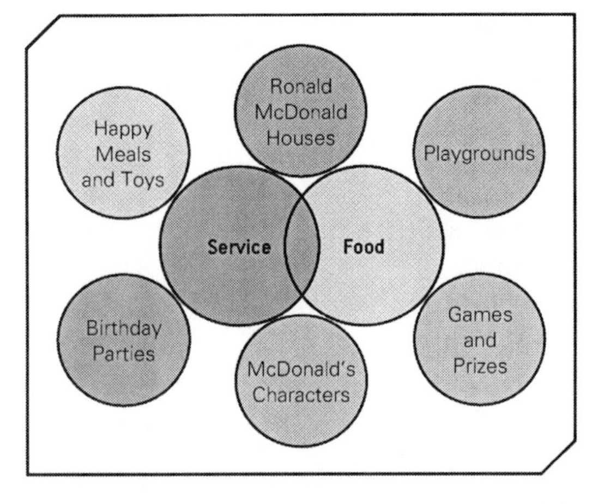

PR Newswire McDonald's; Lego; Limited Too/AP

What is the customer benefit package (CBP) that McDonald's offers? Exhibit 4.7 shows the CBP, in which goods and service content (food and fast service) are equally important and the primary mission and are supported by peripheral goods and services. To support this CBP, operations must design facilities, processes, equipment, and jobs that can create and deliver the primary and peripheral goods and services to meet corporate and competitive priority goals.

Exhibit 4.8 illustrates how Hill's strategy framework can be applied to McDonald's. One corporate objective is profitable growth. Global research suggests that time pressures are causing people to eat out more than ever. The more people eat out, the more variety they want. That is why McDonald's bought such restaurant chains as Boston Market, and Chipotle (Mexican). Not only did McDonald's gain thousands of prime locations with these acquisitions, but it also broadened its food variety and portfolio. The long-term strategy is that "one brand can't be all things to all people," and these acquisitions allow it to follow the strategy of variety. This provides McDonald's with many attractive strategies, such as combo restaurants with several of these brands under one roof or a mix of these restaurants in a high traffic area. Designing the value chain to support such clusters of restaurants would represent a challenge to operations yet provide McDonald's with economies of scale and even lower costs.

The marketing strategy to support profitable growth consists of adding both company-owned and franchised McDonald's and Partner Brand restaurants. McDonald's is committed to franchising as a key strategy to grow and leverage value chain capabilities. Approximately 70 percent of McDonald's restaurants worldwide are owned and operated by independent business people—the franchisee.

The core competency to profitable growth is maintaining low cost and fast service. To support this strategy, McDonald's has many operational decisions to make such as: Adopt an assembly line approach to process design? Standardize store design to make process flow, training, and performance evaluation consistent among stores? Standardize equipment and job design work activities? The french fryer equipment and procedure is a good example of standardizing equipment design. There is "only one way to make french fries" in 30,000 stores worldwide and this contributes to the consistent quality of goods, fast service, and a standardized training program. Likewise, ordering by the numbers and digital printouts of customer orders in the drivethrough improves order accuracy and speed of service. Of course,

Exhibit 4.8 Applying the Hill's Strategy Development Framework to McDonald's

Corporate Objective Examples	Marketing Strategy Examples	How Do Goods and Services Qualify and Win Orders in the Marketplace? (Competitive Priorities)	Operations Strategy	
			Operating Design Choice Examples	**Infrastructure Examples**
Profitable Growth	Add worldwide 1,300 McDonald's restaurants and 150 new Partner Brand restaurants using company-owned and franchised stores	Competitive priorities tie the corporate and marketing strategies to the operational strategy ⟷	• Flow shop process design • Standardized store design • Equipment design • Job design • Order-taking process • Capacity and facility size, location, and clusters	• Hiring process and criteria • First job training • Recognition and rewards • Training for the unexpected • Keeping it simple • Manager trainee program • Coaching and counseling • Teamwork • e-mail capabilities
Operational Excellence	Ideal store location, best training and employee well-being programs	• #1 Low prices • #2 Quick service (delivery speed) • #3 High service quality	• Global value chain coordination • Suppliers • Resource scheduling • Inventory placement and control • Distribution centers • Standardized operational and job procedures	• Operating plans and control system(s) • Shift management • Supplier relations and negotiation • Equipment maintenance • Online network capability • Distribution centers
Leverage Strengths Through Innovation and Technology	Develop new food items, store and food mix Tie demand analysis to promotions	⟷ • #4 High goods quality	• Store equipment technology • Value chain information systems to tie stores, distribution centers, and suppliers together • New food products	• Quality control • Laboratory testing • Organizational structure • Compensation systems
Diversity	Long-standing commitment to a diverse work force	• #5 Demand flexibility	• Training and franchising • Process performance • Career paths	• Learning and innovation systems • Hamburger University
Social Responsibility	Being a good neighbor and partner with the local community	• #6 Brand image ⟷	• Trade-off analysis • Recycling processes • Package redesign, shipping, warehousing	• Support services • Ronald McDonald House • Mobile health centers • Youth camps

the entire human resource function is built around the needs of McDonald's value chain and operating systems. Examples of supportive infrastructure include good hiring criteria, recognition and reward programs, training, and promotion criteria.

A second corporate objective is *operational excellence*. The ultimate objective of operational excellence is satisfied customers. Operational excellence includes value chain, process, equipment, and job efficiencies, as well as superior people-related performance, all focused to support the service encounter. McDonald's strategy is to deliver exceptional customer experiences through a combination of great-tasting food, outstanding service, a good place to work, profitable growth, and consistent value. To put sparkle in McDonald's service, initiatives include training for the unexpected and keeping it simple.

To accomplish operational excellence requires answers to some of the previous questions plus answers to questions such as: How do we measure operational performance? How do we train front- and back-office employees to achieve corporate objectives? What are alternative career progression paths? What equipment and technology reduce the opportunities for errors and service upsets? What supply chain structure best services our global network of stores? Where should we locate our distribution centers? What should be the capacity of each distribution center? How many employees should work in the store on each day of the week (that is, What is the staff schedule?)?

A third corporate objective is leveraging innovation and technology capabilities. In the United States, 40 distribution centers support more than 12,000 restaurants and about 350 suppliers. Information technology is used to coordinate the activities of McDonald's value chain. In Russia, McDonald's also operates a $45-million state-of-the-art food processing and distribution center. It employees 450 people and supplies all McDonald's restaurants in Russia and 17 other countries. Every hour, the distribution center (called McComplex) produces about 15,500 buns, 13,500 pies, 15,000 kilograms of beef patties, and 2,900 liters of milk. McComplex has eight flow shop assembly lines that include meat, pie, dairy, fry, liquid, cheese, and garnish lines. All food items from over 100 suppliers are monitored through laboratory testing for conformance to quality standards. Video training, online ordering, automated french fry machines, debt cards, and daily performance reporting by store, district, region, and country are just a few of the uses of technology that support corporate strategy and objectives.

Another corporate objective is developing and maintaining a diverse work force. Diversity at McDonald's is understanding, recognizing, and valuing the differences that make each person unique. It has won many awards over the years for its diversity practices, including *Fortune* magazine's Top Places for Minorities to Work, Best Employer for Asians, and Top 50 Places for Hispanic Women to Work. In the United States, minorities and women currently represent over 34 percent of McDonald's franchisees. Hamburger University, located in Oak Brook, Illinois, has trained over 65,000 mangers in 22 different languages and also manages ten international training centers in places like Australia, England, Japan, and Germany. McDonald's takes pride in the fact that it is the "first job" for many young people throughout the world. These first-job employees learn about McDonald's values, behavior and dress standards, customer relationships, schedules, efficient operation of the delivery system, performance systems, and so on. Many of these ideas and practices are carried throughout life for thousands of people worldwide.

McDonald's supports its social responsibility objective with over 200 Ronald McDonald House charities. Social responsibility activities also include funding immunization programs for 1 million African children, Olympic youth camps, disaster relief, and sponsored mobile health centers in underserved areas.

PR Newswire McDonald's

Other corporate objectives not shown in Exhibit 4.7 include a high return on investment, exploring nontraditional locations for stores, and commitment to the environment. To support a high return on investment and exploring nontraditional store locations, McDonald's is partnering with other firms such as Amoco, Chevron, airports, and hospitals. In support of its environment-friendly corporate objective, it has purchased over $4 billion of recycled goods and redesigned its packaging to reduce total annual weight by over 400 million pounds. The success of each of these corporate initiatives requires good operations skills such as project management, inventory management, logistics, capacity analysis, scheduling, quality control, and facility location analysis. For each of these corporate initiatives to be successful requires someone in McDonald's to excel in process design and management.

Competitive priorities are derived from McDonald's vision statement and strategy. The ranking in Exhibit 4.8 reflects their importance. The competitive priorities tie the corporate and marketing strategies to the operations strategy. The competitive priorities provide direction on key operations strategy issues listed in the last two columns of Exhibit 4.8. One job of senior McDonald's managers is to check all four decision loops in Exhibit 4.5 for inconsistencies or conflicts in their logic. Operations managers spend the majority of their time evaluating loops #2 and #3, but they must also communicate any potential conflicts or inconsistencies back to corporate and marketing managers through loop #4. The development of a world-class strategy for an organization is an immense challenge with many opportunities for strategic mismatches, failures, and inconsistencies.

SOLVED PROBLEMS

SOLVED PROBLEM #1

Define the customer benefit package for a health club or recreation center or gymnasium you frequent (check out the web site of your favorite club, center, or gym for more information), and use this to describe the organization's strategic mission, strategy, competitive priorities, and how it wins customers. What are the order qualifiers and winners for this organization? Second, make a list of example processes that create and deliver each good or service in the CBP you selected, and briefly describe process procedures and issues.

Solution:

One example is depicted here. Of course, health clubs and recreation centers often have unique features to differentiate them from their competition.

Mission: The mission of our health club is to offer many pathways to a healthy living style and body.

Strategy: We strive to provide our customers with superior:

- customer convenience (location, food, communication, schedules, etc.);
- clean facilities, equipment, uniforms, parking lot, and the like;
- friendly professional staff that care about you;
- ways to improve and maintain your body and mind's health and well-being.

Competitive Priorities: #1 Priority—many pathways to healthy living and a healthy body (design flexibility), #2—friendly professional staff and service encounters (service quality), #3—everything is super clean (goods and environmental quality), #4—customer convenience in all respects (time), #5—price (cost).

How to win customers? Providing a full-service health club with superior service, staff, and facilities. (Although you would not see this in company literature, this health club provides premium service at premium prices.)

Key Processes

- The food ordering and supply, preparation, delivery, and cleanup processes define the *food-service value chain.* Key procedures and issues include how the food service in the health club ensures accurate and timely ordering of all raw materials necessary to make the food served to customers; how they make the chicken salad or the six kinds of pasta served daily; whether they throw away all food at the end of the day to ensure fresh food the next day; the type of goods and service quality standards used; how the club trains all kitchen staff; and how it manages kitchen, silver and dinnerware, food, and uniform inventories.
- The *childcare process* includes rigorous procedures for checking children in and out of the childcare area. Issues include whether the childcare staff is mature, trained, and CPR certified;

what offerings are available, such as fitness classes for kids, a library and study area, educational videos, and a computer lab; the check-in and check-out process to ensure children's security; whether medicines may be administered; activities planned throughout the day; and the qualifications of the caregivers.
- The *swimming lesson process* includes a sign-up phase, potential participant medical examination phase, and a series of classes taught by certified swimming instructors who are trained in emergency services such as CPR. Issues include how the swimming class age groups (target markets) should be segmented; whether a swimming aerobics class is offered to senior citizens; how the health club keeps people safe yet teaches them to swim and have fun; lesson plans for each day; and how to schedule the 20 different swimming classes going on in May.
- The *personal trainer process* requires high design flexibility since each exercise and training program is customized to the individual. Key issues include how customers and professional trainers are assigned and scheduled; what procedures are in place when customers want to change personal trainers; how customized training programs are developed for all ages and sizes of people; what training is required of all personal trainers; whether enough personal trainer staff capacity is available; and whether the trainer keeps records of workouts and medical histories.

SOLVED PROBLEM #2

California Aggregates, a supplier of construction materials such as ready-mix concrete, sand, gravel, and other products, conducted a survey of its customers to understand their most important wants and needs. The survey revealed the following:

- Responsive to special needs
- Easy to place orders
- Consistent product quality
- On-time delivery
- Accurate invoices
- Lowest prices
- Attractive credit terms
- Salespeople's skills
- Helpful dispatchers
- Courteous drivers
- Fair and quick problem resolution

a. Draw an example customer benefit package, and define the company's strategic mission.

b. What elements of operations design choices and infrastructure in Hill's strategy framework would an operations strategy have to address to meet these customer requirements?

Solution:

Strategic mission: California Aggregates provides aggregate materials to meet or exceed customer requirements at the right price at the right time and in a friendly and helpful manner.

- Responsive to special needs—organizational structure, learning and innovation systems, skilled work force
- Easy to place orders—type of process, technology, supply chain integration
- Consistent product quality—type of process, supply chain integration and outsourcing, operating plans and control systems, quality control
- On-time delivery—type of process, technology, capacity and facilities, inventory, operating plans and control systems
- Accurate invoices—technology, support services
- Lowest prices—type of process, supply chain integration and outsourcing, trade-off analysis, inventory
- Attractive credit terms—supply chain integration and outsourcing, support services
- Salespeople's skills—work force, compensation systems, learning systems
- Helpful dispatchers—work force, compensation systems, learning systems
- Courteous drivers—work force, compensation systems, learning systems
- Fair and quick problem resolution—work force, organizational structure, learning systems, operating plans and control systems

KEY TERMS AND CONCEPTS

Capacity
Competitive advantage
Competitive priorities
Core competencies
Corporate, business, and functional levels of strategy
Cost
Customer wants and needs analysis
Dissatisfiers, satisfiers, and exciters/delighters
Flexibility
Functional strategy
Infrastructure
Innovation
Mass customization
Operations design choices
Operations strategy
Order qualifiers and winners
Quality
Search, experience, and credence attributes
Strategic business units (SBUs)
Strategic mission and vision
Strategic planning
Strategic values
Strategy
Strategy development
Strategy development framework
Strategy implementation
Time

QUESTIONS FOR REVIEW AND DISCUSSION

1. Discuss the role of operations management in overall business strategy. Why is OM critical to a successful strategy?
2. What do we mean by the term *competitive advantage*? What might the competitive advantage be for each of the following companies:
   a. Home Depot
   b. Southwest Airlines
   c. Dell Computer
   d. Toyota
   e. Avis
3. Describe some approaches that companies use to understand their customers' wants and needs. What are the advantages and disadvantages of these approaches?
4. Contrast dissatisfiers, satisfiers, and exciters/delighters. Why is this classification important for companies to understand, particularly from a strategic point of view?
5. Select a business you are familiar with and identify and explain example dissatisfiers, satisfiers, and exciters/delighters. You might look up the business on the Internet or visit the library.
6. Explain the difference between an order qualifier and an order winner. Provide some examples.
7. Give some examples of search, experience, and credence attributes for an automobile, an automobile repair service center, and cable television.
8. Select businesses you are familiar with and identify and provide examples of customers using search, experience, and credence quality to evaluate the good or service. You might also look up the businesses on the Internet or visit the library.
9. Explain the interlinking model of quality and profitability (Exhibit 4.2). How does it connect to business and operations strategy?
10. What are competitive priorities? Provide some examples of how OM influences the five major types of competitive priorities.
11. Is it possible for a world-class organization to achieve superiority in all five major competitive priorities—price (cost), quality, time, flexibility, and innovation? Explain. Justify. Provide examples pro or con.
12. Select a business you are familiar with and identify and rank order its competitive priorities as best you can, then identify the order qualifiers and winners. Justify your reasoning.
13. Explain the concept of mass customization and the role of customer participation in the process.
14. What is the difference between corporate, business, and functional strategy?
15. Select a business you are familiar with and identify its three levels of strategy—corporate, business, and functional.
16. What do we mean by *core competencies*?

17. Describe the components of the strategic planning process. What makes a good strategic planning process?
18. Why is it important to understand and communicate a firm's mission, vision, and values? How do these help direct strategy?
19. How is strategy development and implementation alike and unalike in huge conglomerate organizations such as General Electric versus small organizations such as Pal's Sudden Service? Explain.
20. What is *operations strategy*? How does it relate to corporate strategy?
21. Explain Hill's strategy development framework. What are the key elements of operations strategy within this framework?
22. Based on firsthand knowledge or research, what is the length of the useful life cycle for a good or service and its implications for any three of the following: automobiles, a cruise ship, a cruise vacation, PC operating system software, refrigerator, electric coffee maker, space shuttle, college textbooks, a night's stay in a hotel room, downloading music online, online auctions, and a beer. How does the good or service life cycle affect strategy?

PROBLEMS AND ACTIVITIES

1. Define the customer benefit package in (a) the "old days" when the automobile (that is, the physical good) itself was enough to make the sale, and (b) then do the same thing with services that complement the sale today. Define the automobile manufacturer or dealer's strategic vision, strategy, competitive priorities, and ways of winning customer orders in both situations. What are the order qualifiers and winners? What would operations have to be good at to make this a successful business or organization? Make a list of the processes you will need to implement this strategy. You can check out the web site of your favorite organization for more information.
2. A hotel has determined that its customers' most important wants and needs are
   - having correct reservation information,
   - honoring the reservation (ensuring that a room is available for a confirmed reservation),
   - fulfilling any special room type or location requests,
   - check-in speed,
   - cleanliness and servicing of the room,
   - check-out speed,
   - staff efficiency in responding to requests,
   - staff attitude and behavior,
   - having all items in the room in working order.

a. Draw the CBP for this hotel as best you can.

b. What elements of operations design choices and infrastructure in Hill's strategy framework would an operations strategy have to address to meet these customer requirements?

3. Define and draw the customer benefit package (see Chapter 1 for additional discussion) for any organization you are familiar with, such as
   - sporting goods store,
   - haircut salon,
   - a personal computer manufacturer,
   - college bar or restaurant,
   - the university, college, or technical school you attend,
   - pizza business,
   - a sports team,
   - library,
   - wireless telephone service,
   - an Internet business,
   - used-book exchange or bookstore.

   You can check out the web site of your favorite organization for more information. Usually you can find the organization's mission and value statements on the web.

a. Define the firm's strategic vision, strategy, and competitive priorities. What are the order qualifiers and winners? What would operations have to be good at to make this a successful business or organization?

b. Make a list of the key processes you will need to implement this customer benefit package and strategy. How important is operations in the success of this organization? Explain/justify. (See Solved Problem #1 for an example format.)

c. Apply Professor Hill's framework to the organization you select.

4. Find a customer survey or satisfaction questionnaire from a local restaurant.
   a. Does each of the customer attributes surveyed address dissatisfiers, satisfiers, or exciters/delighters?
   b. What elements of process choice and infrastructure in Hill's strategy framework would an operations strategy have to address to meet these customer requirements?
5. Using the information about Pal's Sudden Service provided in this chapter, apply Hill's generic strategy framework in a fashion similar to the McDonald's example. How do the strategies of Pal's and McDonald's appear to differ? What differences exist in their operations strategies and decisions?
6. Apply Hill's generic strategy framework to one of the organizations in Questions 1, 2, 3, or 4. This will require some research to identify corporate objectives and competitive priorities. See the McDonald's example in the chapter for guidance.
7. Explore the web sites for several companies on the Fortune 500 list. Based on the information you find, on which competitive priorities do these firms appear to focus? What can you say about their operations strategy (either explicit or implied)?

CASES

THE LAWN CARE COMPANY

"Chris, we make the highest quality grass seed and fertilizer in the world. Our brands are known everywhere!" stated Caroline Ebelhar, the vice president of manufacturing for The Lawn Care Company. "Yah! But the customer doesn't have a Ph.D. in organic chemistry to know the difference between our grass seed and fertilizer compared to our competitors'! We need to be in the lawn care application service business, not just be the manufacturer of super perfect products," responded Chris Kilbourne, the vice president of marketing, as he walked out of Ebelhar's office. This on-going debate among Lawn Care's senior management team had not been resolved but the chief executive officer, Steven Marion, had been listening very closely. A major strategic decision would soon have to be made.

The Lawn Care Company, a fertilizer and grass seed manufacturer, with sales of almost $1 billion, sold some of its products directly to parks and golf courses. Customer service in this goods-producing company was historically very narrowly defined as providing "the right product to the right customer at the right time." Once these goods were delivered to the customer's premises and the customer signed the shipping documents, Lawn Care's job was done. For many park and golf course customers, a local subcontractor or the customers themselves applied the fertilizer and seed. These application personnel often did the job incorrectly using inappropriate equipment and methods. The relationship between these non-Lawn Care application service personnel, The Lawn Care Company, and the customer was also not always ideal. When the customer made claims because of damaged lawns, the question then became one of who was at fault? Did the quality of the physical product or the way it was applied cause the damage? Either way, the customers' lawns were in poor shape, and in some cases, the golf courses lost substantial revenue if a green or hole was severely damaged or not playable.

One of Lawn Care's competitors began an application service for parks and golf courses that routinely applied the fertilizer and grass seed for its primary customers. This competitor bundled the application service to the primary goods, fertilizer and grass seed, and charged a higher price for this service. The competitor learned the application business in the parks and golf course target market segment and was beginning to explore expanding into the residential lawn care application service target market. The Lawn Care Company sold the "highest quality physical products" in the industry. Its competitor sold the customer "a beautiful lawn with a promise of no hassles." To the competitor, this included an application service bundled to grass seed and fertilizer.

Questions

a. Define and draw the current customer benefit package for the firm and its competitors.
b. Define the organization's strategic mission, strategy, competitive priorities, and how it wins customers. What are the order qualifiers and winners?

c. Make a list of example processes that create and deliver each good or service in the CBP you selected, and briefly describe process procedures and issues.
d. What pre- and postservices could Lawn Care possibly offer its customers to complement the sale of the grass seed and fertilizer?
e. What problems, if any, do you see with its current strategy, vision, customer benefit package design, and pre- and postservices?
f. Should the company offer lawn care application services to the professional market? If not, why? If so, justify. What do you have to be good at to offer outstanding lawn care application services at multiple sites?
g. What are your final recommendations regarding a revised business strategy, vision, customer benefit package, the role of pre- and postservices, and so on?

THE GREATER CINCINNATI CHAMBER OF COMMERCE

Founded in 1839 to facilitate the growth and ease of commerce, the Greater Cincinnati Chamber of Commerce is a membership organization of approximately 6,700 businesses and organizations in the region that surrounds Cincinnati, Ohio. The chamber's stated purpose is to serve its members, and its mission is simple: to present Cincinnati as one of the world's favorite American business centers. The chamber delivers a diverse range of products and services, including

- new business attraction,
- business retention,
- government advocacy,
- education and training services,
- networking events,
- festivals and events,
- "Business Connections" membership directory,
- ChamberVision newsletter.

Although technically a not-for-profit organization, many chamber services are expected to generate an excess of revenues over expenses, which is required to support a variety of non-revenue-producing chamber programs. The chamber serves the region from its headquarters office located in downtown Cincinnati.

In 1996, the management group, with active involvement of a number of key board members, established the vision to guide the chamber's efforts supporting the region into the future. The vision was to "run with the gazelles," focusing on becoming as effective as other chamber benchmark cities (the "gazelles") in terms of business development and job creation. The chamber detailed its mission to guide that service as follows:

To strengthen the economic vitality and quality of life in the Greater Cincinnati region by

- generating job growth through local, national, and international economic development,
- influencing government regulations and legislation that affect business, and
- providing services that help local businesses prosper and grow.

In early 2000, the management group recognized that the vision, "run with the gazelles," while providing the region with its overall goal, did not adequately support the other key aspect of the chamber's role, helping each individual member meet the challenges of growth and success. The management group defined a new vision for the organization itself:

Be the first place that businesses in the region go for solutions to the competitive challenges of growth

Packaged with the still valid and important regional vision of running with the gazelles and the existing mission, the management group created "Beyond 2000," the chamber's revised strategic plan, combining the two complementary visions with the day-to-day foundation of the mission to fully focus the chamber for the future.

The chamber is organized in a series of product-focused departments, as shown in the table. These five departments interact directly with customer segments to develop and deliver chamber products and services.

Department	Key Services
Business Development	Educational services, networking events and activities
Downtown Council	Downtown street festivals and events
Economic Development	Business attraction—national and international, retention and expansion assistance
Government Affairs	Information, advocacy activities
Member Benefits	Benefits products to improve members' bottom line

Support groups assist these line departments in product and service delivery functions that include information services, administration, human resources, marketing/communications, and finance. In addition, the Chamber's Membership/Member Relations department serves chamber staff and members in providing information and access to chamber products and services, including membership.

The chamber has ongoing relationships with affiliate organizations housed within the chamber's downtown Cincinnati office. Those affiliates include the Cincinnati Minority Supplier Development Council, the Cincinnati Minority Enterprise Business Mentoring Program, and The Japan-America Society. The chamber participates in the Tri-State Chamber Collaborative, an organization of ten chamber senior executives, eight representing geographic segments of the region and two that represent the local Hispanic and African-American chambers. The Chamber Collaborative focuses on projects of regional importance where common goals exist and cooperation is critical to regional success. The chamber supports the Metropolitan Growth Alliance (MGA), an organization of local business leaders focused on generating regional economic growth. In 1998, the MGA sponsored a study to identify areas for action to ensure long-term regional health and vitality. The chamber had a lead role in facilitating the process of that study toward its release of results in May 1999.

In 1998, the chamber began the process of forming the Partnership for Greater Cincinnati, a broad-based initiative to unify the region's marketing efforts and economic development efforts and infrastructure. The Regional Marketing Partners (RMP) lead this marketing effort. Membership in the RMP includes five economic development leaders representing seven counties and the City of Cincinnati in the three-state area, as well as key leaders representing local chambers, industry, and the Greater Cincinnati-Northern Kentucky International Airport. More than 180 business and government entities are aligned with this effort designed to bring the vision to "run with the gazelles" to reality. More than 1,500 chamber members invested in the Partnership in 2000 through a voluntary option presented on their annual chamber dues invoice. The chamber maintains an active role in addressing issues of regional and community development and redevelopment. The chamber's reputation and credibility positions it as the organization that brings others to the table and facilitates solutions to community challenges.

In 1996, the chamber initiated efforts internally to create a team-based environment. The management group attended training in basics of team development and facilitation skills. Through this leadership initiative, the chamber has fostered the development of a culture of employee involvement. In 1998, the management group participated in a chamber-sponsored organizational development process, the Center for Excellence. This process trained the management group in the basics of Total Quality and Continuous Improvement and resulted in an implementation plan to improve performance throughout the organization. In 1999, the chamber expanded this plan through the development of the "Measurement Report Card," emphasizing measurement as the tool to drive effectiveness. This Measurement Report Card links the Strategic Plan, Program of Work, and departmental and work group measures into one unified system and incorporates a broadened set of measures, coupling financial goals with penetration and satisfaction data through the quarterly operations report.

Discussion Questions

1. Characterize the customer benefit package that the chamber offers. What other peripheral goods might the chamber provide to complement its services? How might this affect its strategy?
2. What sources of competitive advantage do you feel the chamber has? Who does it compete with?
3. Critique its mission and strategy. At what operational processes must it excel to accomplish its mission and vision?
4. In many areas, a chamber of commerce is primarily in the travel and tourism business. How does the Greater Cincinnati Chamber of Commerce appear to differentiate itself from these types of organizations?
5. Visit the chamber's web site at www.gccc.com. Has its focus changed since the time on which this case is based?

ENDNOTES

[1] Rynecki, Davie, "One Town, Two Rivals," *Fortune*, July 26, 2004, pp. 110–119.
[2] Pilcher, James, "Airlines Changing Hub Plans," *Cincinnati Enquirer*, September 12, 2004, pp. F1, F4.
[3] Selden, Larry, and Colvin, Geoffrey, "Will this Customer Sink Your Stock?" *Fortune*, September 30, 2002, pp. 127–132.
[4] "Getting an Edge," *Across the Board*, February 2000, pp. 43–48.
[5] "Apple's One-Dollar-a-Year Man," *Fortune*, January 24, 2000, pp. 71–76.
[6] Buzzell, Robert D., and Gale, Bradley T., *The PIMS Principles: Linking Strategy to Performance*, New York: The Free Press, 1987.

[7] Zeithaml, V. A., "How Consumer Evaluation Processes Differ Between Goods and Services," in J. H. Donnelly and W. R. George, eds., *Marketing in Services*, Chicago: American Marketing Association, 1981, pp. 186–199.
[8] Caudron, Shari, "All Shopped Out," *Across the Board*, September/October 2002, pp. 31–34.
[9] Selden, Larry, and Colvin, Geoffrey, "Will Your E-Business Leave You Quick or Dead?", *Fortune*, May 28, 2001, pp. 112–124.
[10] Ettlie, John E., "BMW: Believing the Banner," *Automotive Manufacturing and Production*, April 2001, p. 38.
[11] "Southwest Sets Standards on Costs," *Wall Street Journal*, October 9, 2002, p. A2. Reprinted by permission of Dow Jones, Inc. via Copyright Clearance Center.
[12] Gale, Bradley T., "Quality Comes First When Hatching Power Brands," *Planning Review*, July/August 1992, pp. 4–9, 48.
[13] Hales, H. Lee, "Time Has Come for Long-Range Planning of Facilities Strategies in Electronic Industries," *Industrial Engineering*, April 1985.
[14] *The PIMS Letter on Business Strategy*, Cambridge, MA: The Strategic Planning Institute, no. 4, 1986.
[15] *Business Week*, December 17, 2001, p. 84.
[16] McCamey, David A., Bogs, Robert W., and Bayuk, Linda M., "More, Better, Faster from Total Quality Effort," *Quality Progress*, August 1999, pp. 43–50.
[17] "Attack of the Killer Crossovers," *Business Week*, January 28, 2002, pp. 98–100.
[18] Grant, Robert M., Krishnan, R., Shani, Abraham B., and Baer, Ron, "Appropriate Manufacturing Technology: A Strategic Approach," *Sloan Management Review* 33, no. 1 (Fall 1991), pp. 43–54.
[19] Lafamore, G. Berton, "The Burden of Choice," *APICS—The Performance Advantage*, January 2001, pp. 40–43.
[20] Quinn, James Brian, *Strategies for Change: Logical Incrementalism*, Homewood, IL: Richard D. Irwin, 1980.
[21] Portions adapted from www.walmartstores.com, July 27, 2002.
[22] "Credit Wal-Mart for 1990's Productivity Boom," *The Columbus Dispatch*, Columbus, Ohio, March 3, 2002, p. C2.
[23] Hill, T., *Manufacturing Strategy: Text and Cases*, 3rd ed., Burr Ridge, IL: McGraw-Hill, 2000.
[24] Ettlie, John E., "What the Auto Industry Can Learn from McDonald's," *Automotive Manufacturing & Production*, October 1999, p. 42; Stires, David, "Fallen Arches," *Fortune*, April 29, 2002, pp. 74–76.
[25] Garvin, David A., *Managing Quality: The Strategic and Competitive Edge*, New York: The Free Press, 1988.
[26] www.mcdonalds.com/corporate/info/vision/index.html. This example is the book author's interpretation of McDonald's public information with the objective of illustrating Professor Terry Hill's generic strategy development framework. It may or may not be perfectly accurate and it is only partially complete due to space limitations.

Chapter Outline

CHAPTER 11

Forecasting and Demand Planning

Learning Objectives

1. To understand the need for forecasts and the implications of information technology for forecasting in the value chain.
2. To understand the basic elements of forecasting, namely, the choice of planning horizon, different types of data patterns, and how to calculate forecasting errors.
3. To be aware of different forecasting approaches and methods.
4. To understand basic time-series forecasting methods, be aware of more advanced methods, and use spreadsheet models to make forecasts.

5. To learn the basic ideas and method of regression analysis.
6. To understand the role of human judgment in forecasting and when judgmental forecasting is most appropriate.
7. To know that judgment and quantitative forecast methodologies can complement one another, and therefore improve overall forecast accuracy.

- Russ Newton recently joined Health Products, Inc., a company that designs and manufactures hospital equipment, such as beds and other specialized furniture. Russ had worked for the firm as a co-op while he was in business school, and his ability to develop Microsoft Excel applications impressed his supervisors. Russ's new manager had just the job for him. The company's top managers had expressed the need for better data to support their strategic planning. Their forecasts of the market potential for key products had not been very accurate in recent years. Most forecasting was done simply by gathering sales managers' opinions, and very little had been driven by data or an understanding of the key factors, such as governmental policies, population demographics, and hospital occupancy rates and capital spending, that influence demand. Russ was assigned to develop a forecasting model to predict the market growth for each of the firm's five product categories. In talking to various managers in the company, Russ was overwhelmed with the many factors that the managers thought would influence demand and the huge amount of economic and industry data that was available. He was a bit apprehensive and wondered how he could approach this important assignment.

- Mandy Alan, the national sales forecasting manager at Galaxy Communications, surveyed the managers gathered in the conference room. Galaxy Communications is a regional telecom, offering traditional residential and commercial telephone service as well as wireless plans. "We're getting a lot of customer complaints," she said. "We always seem to be running out of stock of key equipment for installation and repair, and customers complain about long waits for customer service. It seems to me that we simply can't do a good job of forecasting the demand for each type of telecommunication service so that we can accurately determine our equipment and staffing needs. We need help and we need it quickly. Any ideas?"

- The demand for rental cars in Florida and other warm climates peaks during college spring break season. Call centers and rental offices are flooded with customers wanting to rent a vehicle. National Car Rental took a unique approach by developing a customer-identification forecasting model, by which it identifies all customers who are young and rent cars only once or twice a year. These demand analysis models allow National to call this target market segment in February, when call volumes are lower, to sign them up again. The proactive strategy is designed to both boost repeat rentals and smooth out the peaks and valleys in call center volumes.[1]

PRNewsFoto/Volkswagen of America, Inc. and Scholastic Corporation

Discussion Questions: Think of a pizza delivery franchise located near a college campus. What factors that influence demand do you think should be included in trying to forecast demand for pizzas? How might these factors differ for a franchise located in a suburban residential area?

Forecasting *is the process of projecting the values of one or more variables into the future.* Good forecasts are needed in all organizations to drive analyses and decisions related to operations. Forecasting is a key component in many types of integrated operating systems that we described in Chapter 5, such as supply chain management, customer relationship management, and revenue management systems.

Forecasting *is the process of projecting the values of one or more variables into the future.*

The first episode highlights both the complexity of modern forecasting and the importance of using good analytical approaches instead of simply "going with the gut" and using salespersons' opinions. In the health care industry, for example, the demand for hospital beds and related products is driven in part by population demographics, hospital admissions and surgical procedures rates, hospital construction, interest rates, and many other factors. Identifying these factors, collecting historical data to understand trends, and building a useful forecasting model is a very challenging task. Good models can provide the type of information that top managers need to plan product development, long-term capacity decisions, and other key strategic decisions.

Forecasting is also vital for daily operations, as the second episode illustrates. Poor forecasting can result in poor inventory and staffing decisions, resulting in part shortages, inadequate customer service, and many customer complaints. In the telecommunications industry, competition is fierce; and goods and services have very short life cycles. Changing technology, frequent price wars, and incentives for customers to switch services increase the difficulty of providing accurate forecasts.

Many firms integrate forecasting with value chain and capacity management systems to make better operational decisions. National Car Rental, for example, is using data analysis and forecasting methods in its value chain to improve service and reduce costs. Instead of accepting customer demand as it is and trying to plan resources to meet the peaks and valleys, its models help to shift demand to low demand periods and better use its capacity. The proactive approach to spring break peak demand helps plan and coordinate rental office and call center staffing levels and schedules, vehicle availability, advertising campaigns, and vehicle maintenance and repair schedules. Many commercial software packages also tie forecasting modules into supply chain and operational planning systems.

Good forecasting and demand planning systems result in higher capacity utilization, reduced inventories and costs, more efficient process performance, more flexibility, improved customer service, and increased profit margins. In this chapter, we discuss the role of forecasting in OM. We begin by describing the role of forecasting in the broader context of demand planning. Then we introduce a variety of quantitative and qualitative forecasting methods and approaches.

Learning Objective
To understand the need for forecasts and the implications of information technology for forecasting in the value chain.

FORECASTING AND DEMAND PLANNING

Organizations make many different types of forecasts. Consider a consumer products company, such as Procter & Gamble, that makes many different goods in various sizes. Top managers need long-range forecasts expressed in total sales dollars for use in financial planning and for sizing and locating new facilities. At lower organizational levels, however, managers of the various product groups need aggregate forecasts of sales volume for their products in units that are more meaningful to them—for example, pounds of a certain type of soap—to establish production plans. Finally, managers of individual manufacturing facilities need forecasts by brand and size—for instance, the number of 64-ounce boxes of Tide detergent—to plan material usage and production schedules. For such a company, forecasts also need to be tied to different global markets and must be consistent across organizational levels to be effective planning aids. In addition, special forecasts—such as forecasts of material and production costs, prices, and so on—may be required for new products and promotional items. Clearly, forecasts are of many different types and in different units of measurement, depending on their purpose. Similarly, airlines need long-range forecasts of demand for air travel to plan their purchases of airplanes and short-term forecasts to develop seasonal routes and schedules; university administrators require enrollment forecasts; city planners need forecasts of population trends to plan highways and mass transit systems; and restaurants need forecasts to be able to plan for food purchases.

In many organizations, such as the airline, hospitality, and retail industries, demand is highly seasonal over a year or may vary significantly with the day of the week or the time of day. Grocery stores, banks, and similar organizations need very short-term forecasts to plan work-shift scheduling and vehicle routing and make other operating decisions to accommodate such variations in demand. Many firms that provide customized services find it easy to forecast the number of customers that will demand service in a particular time period but quite difficult to forecast the mix of services that will be required or the time it will take to provide those services. Hence, such firms need special forecasts of service mix. Operations managers would find it quite difficult to do their jobs without good forecasts.

Accurate forecasts are needed throughout the value chain, as illustrated in Exhibit 11.1, and are used by all functional areas of an organization, such as accounting, finance, marketing, operations, and distribution. One of the biggest problems with forecasting systems is they are driven by different departmental needs and incentive systems, and therefore, multiple sets of data exist for similar customers, work orders, and process performance. This leads to conflicting forecasts and organizational inefficiencies. One way to avoid these problems is by having only one integrative database that helps synchronize the value chain.

Forecasting is typically included in comprehensive value chain and demand-planning software systems. These systems integrate marketing, inventory, sales, operations planning, and financial data. For example, the SAP Demand Planning module enables companies to integrate planning information from different de-

Exhibit 11.1 The Need for Forecasts in a Value Chain

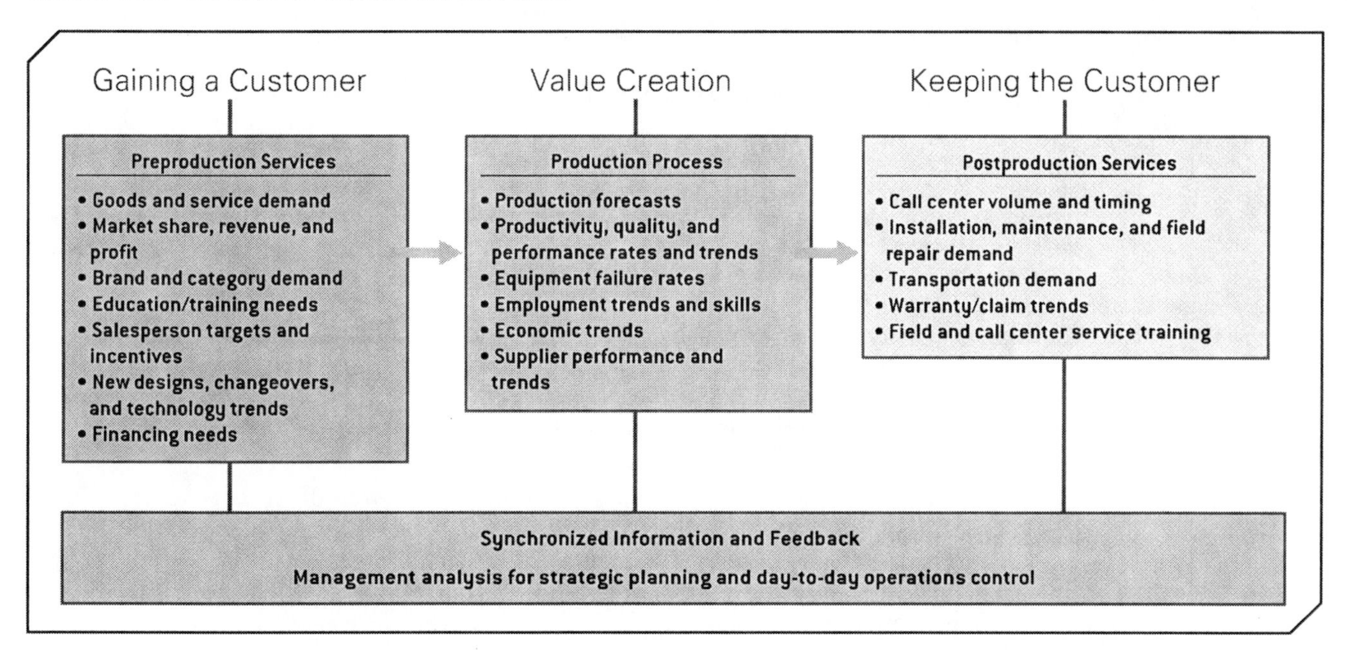

partments or organizations into a single demand plan. Some software vendors are beginning to use the words *demand planning* or *demand chain* instead of *supply chain*. This name change highlights the fact that customer's wants and needs define the customer benefit package and that customer demand pulls goods and services through the supply chain. We discuss the ideas and methods of pulling goods and services through the value chain in Chapter 9.

SAP Demand Planning offers these key capabilities:[2]

- *Multilevel planning*—SAP Demand Planning enables a firm to view, forecast, and plan products on any level and in any dimension. Planning can be based on product, geography, or time and can be initiated from the top down or from the bottom up.
- *Data analysis*—Managers can easily analyze planning data in tables and as graphics, and intuitive navigation features enable them to move through various levels of data.
- *Statistical forecasting*—SAP Demand Planning supports a full range of forecasting methods that use past sales to identify level, trend, or seasonal patterns and regression tools to predict consumer behavior by determining the impact of causal factors such as price, number of displays, number of stores, weather, and demographics.
- *Trade promotion support*—SAP Demand Planning generates promotion-driven forecasts on top of a baseline forecast. Firms can model promotional demand based on profitability goals or historical patterns. Using historical sales estimates, SAP Demand Planning can automatically detect a promotion pattern that occurred in the past.
- *Collaborative demand planning*—This capability enables planners to share demand plans among key players in the value chain. Users can pilot collaborative planning processes and deploy them widely and access graphics that enable them to view large amounts of data. Firms can also collect, forecast, and plan demand from multiple input sources. Finally, users can view planning books over the Internet, allowing easy access for suppliers and customers with limited IT capabilities.

OM SPOTLIGHT

Collaborative Demand Planning at Colgate-Palmolive[3]

Colgate-Palmolive is a global consumer products company with such products as toothpaste, laundry detergents, pet foods, and soap and operates in over 200 countries. About 80 percent of its employees are located outside the United States. The company uses an integrated operating system to give its customers and suppliers complete access to business-critical data such as order status, forecasts, production plans and schedules, and worldwide inventory status. The system provides the platform for collaboration on many supply chain decisions such as demand planning.

To reduce supply chain costs, Colgate-Palmolive implemented three supply chain strategies simultaneously. First, it established a vendor-managed inventory program (see Chapter 9) with key customers to reduce channel inventory and cycle times. Colgate also wanted to move from regional to global sourcing of raw materials, component parts, and packaging. Finally, Colgate implemented a collaborative supply chain planning process with its suppliers and customers to manage promotional demand, improve forecasts, and synchronize activities along the supply chain. These initiatives have improved on-time order performance from 70 to 98 percent for vendor-managed inventories, reduced total inventories by 10 percent, and improved customer order fulfillment rates to 95 percent.

Victor Fisher/Bloomberg News/Landov

Information technology provides the capability to share time-sensitive information all along the value chain. This information sharing is reducing the need for forecasting in the traditional sense (see the OM Spotlight on Colgate-Palmolive). In the past, companies conducted planning based on known customer orders or forecasts of future customer orders. By sharing information across the value chain about customer order status, customer and supplier delivery schedules, backorders, and inventory status, companies in the value chain reduce their need for forecasts and also improve the accuracy of the forecasts they have to make. SAP calls this *collaborative demand planning* (see Exhibit 11.2).

Exhibit 11.2
Impact of Collaborative Demand Planning

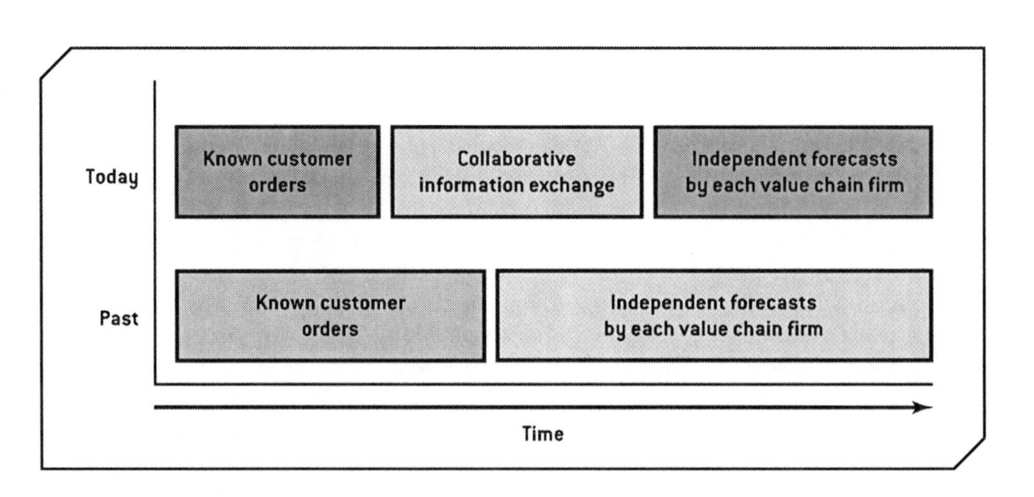

BASIC CONCEPTS IN FORECASTING

Learning Objective
To understand the basic elements of forecasting, namely, the choice of planning horizon, different types of data patterns, and how to calculate forecasting errors.

Before diving into the process of developing forecasting models, it is important to understand some basic concepts that are used in model development. These concepts are independent of the type of model and provide a foundation for users to make better use of the models in operations decisions.

Forecast Planning Horizon

Forecasts of future demand are needed at all levels of organizational decision-making. *The* **planning horizon** *is the length of time on which a forecast is based.* Long-range forecasts cover a planning horizon of 1 to 10 years and are necessary to plan for the expansion of facilities and to determine future needs for land, labor, and equipment. When and where to build new retail stores, factories, schools, libraries, distribution centers, hospitals and clinics, and emergency service facilities for the police and fire departments are dependent on long-range forecasts. Mistakes in long-term forecasts can result in firms overbuilding their infrastructure, and therefore, creating huge cost disadvantages. Likewise, long-term forecast mistakes also result in underbuilding, and therefore, missed opportunities to gain market share and generate revenue.

The **planning horizon** *is the length of time on which a forecast is based.*

Intermediate-range forecasts over a 3- to 12-month period are needed to plan work-force levels, allocate budgets among divisions, schedule jobs and resources, and establish purchasing plans. For example, a purchasing department may negotiate a substantial discount by contracting to order a large amount of a particular good or service over the next year. Intermediate-range forecasts also help human resources departments plan for future hiring, employee training, and so on.

Short-range forecasts focus on the planning horizon of up to 3 months and are used by operations managers to plan production schedules and assign workers to jobs, to determine short-term capacity requirements, and to aid shipping departments in planning transportation needs and establishing delivery schedules.

The **time bucket** *is the unit of measure for the time period used in a forecast.* A time bucket might be a year, quarter, month, week, day, hour, or even a minute. For a long-term planning horizon, a firm might forecast in yearly time buckets; for a short-range planning horizon, the time bucket might be an hour or less. Customer call centers, for example, forecast customer demand in 5-, 6-, or 10-minute intervals. Selecting the right planning horizon length and time bucket size for the right situation is an important part of forecasting.

The **time bucket** *is the unit of measure for the time period used in a forecast.*

Data Patterns in Times Series

Statistical methods of forecasting are based on the analysis of historical data, called a time series. *A* **time series** *is a set of observations measured at successive points in time or over successive periods of time.* A time series provides the data for understanding how the variable that we wish to forecast has changed historically. For example, the daily ending Dow Jones stock index is one example of a time series; another is the monthly volume of sales for a product. To explain the pattern of data in a time series, it is often helpful to think in terms of five characteristics: *trend, seasonal, cyclical, random variation, and irregular (one-time) variation.* Different time series may exhibit one or more of these characteristics. Understanding these characteristics is vital to selecting the appropriate forecasting model or approach.

A **time series** *is a set of observations measured at successive points in time or over successive periods of time.*

TRENDS

*A **trend** is the underlying pattern of growth or decline in a time series.*

*A **trend** is the underlying pattern of growth or decline in a time series.* Although data generally exhibit random fluctuations, a trend shows gradual shifts or movements to relatively higher or lower values over a longer period of time. This gradual shifting over time is usually due to such long-term factors as changes in performance, technology, productivity, population, demographic characteristics, and customer preferences.

For example, a manufacturer of industrial photographic equipment may see substantial month-to-month variability in the number of cameras sold. Reviewing the sales over the past 10 years, however, this manufacturer may find a steady increase in the annual sales volume. Exhibit 11.3 shows a straight-line, or linear, trend, that explains the steady increase in the sales data over time.

Trends can be increasing or decreasing and can be linear or nonlinear. Exhibit 11.4 shows various trend patterns. Linear increasing and decreasing trends are shown in Exhibit 11.4(a) and (b), and nonlinear trends are shown in Exhibit 11.4(c) and (d).

SEASONAL PATTERNS

***Seasonal patterns** are characterized by repeatable periods of ups and downs over short periods of time.*

***Seasonal patterns** are characterized by repeatable periods of ups and downs over short periods of time.* Seasonal patterns may occur over a year; for example, the demand for cold beverages is low during the winter, begins to rise during the spring, peaks during the summer months, and then begins to decline in the autumn. Manufacturers of coats and jackets, however, expect the opposite yearly pattern. Exhibit 11.5 shows an example of natural gas usage in a single-family home over a two-year period, which clearly exhibits a seasonal pattern.

We generally think of seasonal patterns occurring within 1 year, but similar repeatable patterns might occur over the weeks during a month, over days during a week, or hours during a day. For instance, pizza delivery peaks on the weekends, and grocery store traffic is higher during the evening hours. Likewise, customer call center volume might peak in the morning and taper off throughout the day. Different days of the week might have different seasonal patterns.

Exhibit 11.3
Linear Trend of Industrial Photographic Equipment

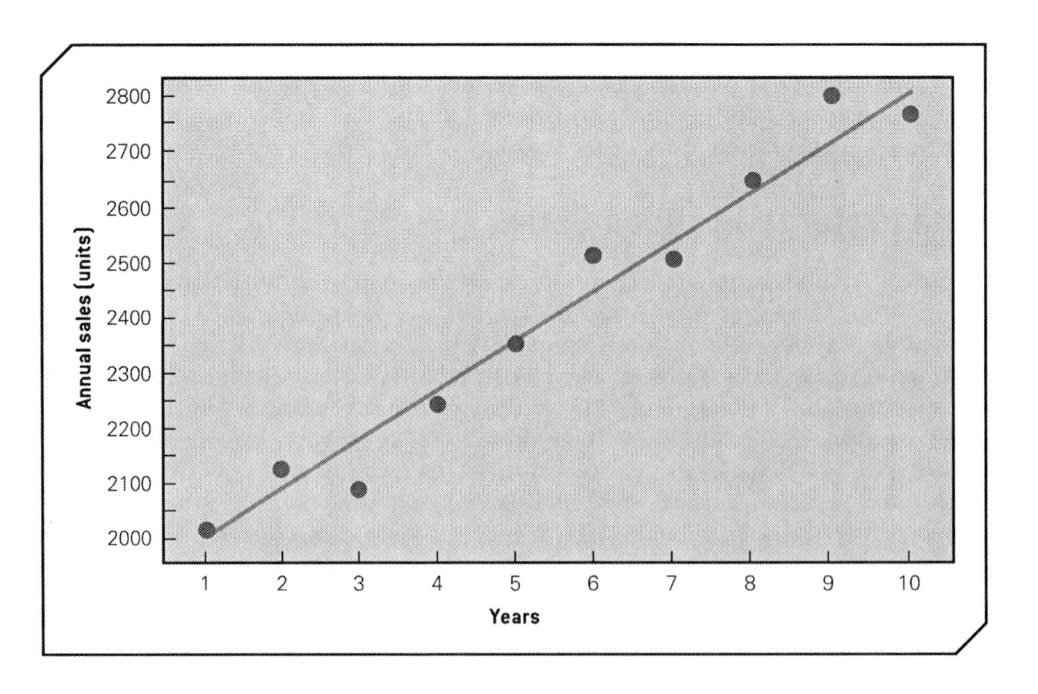

Exhibit 11.4 Example Linear and Nonlinear Trend Patterns

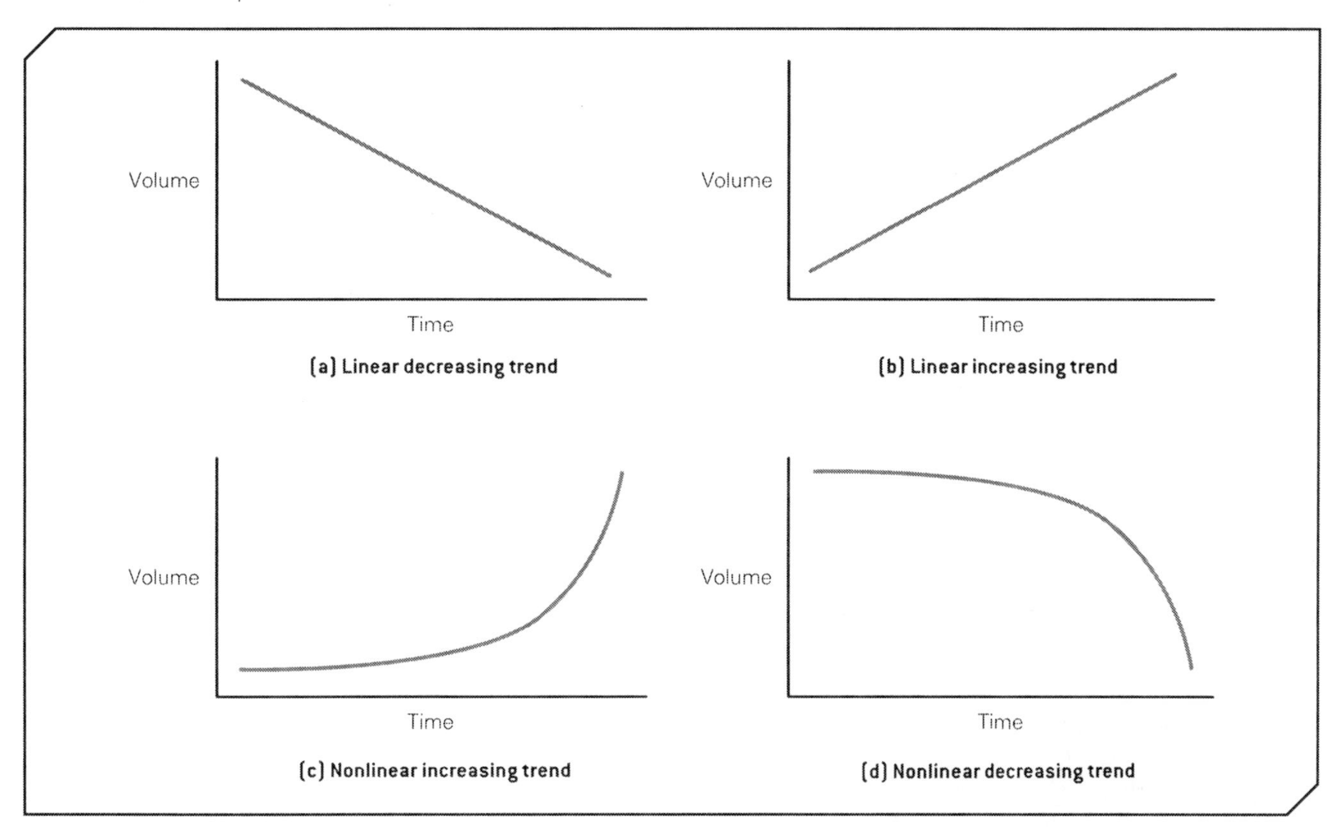

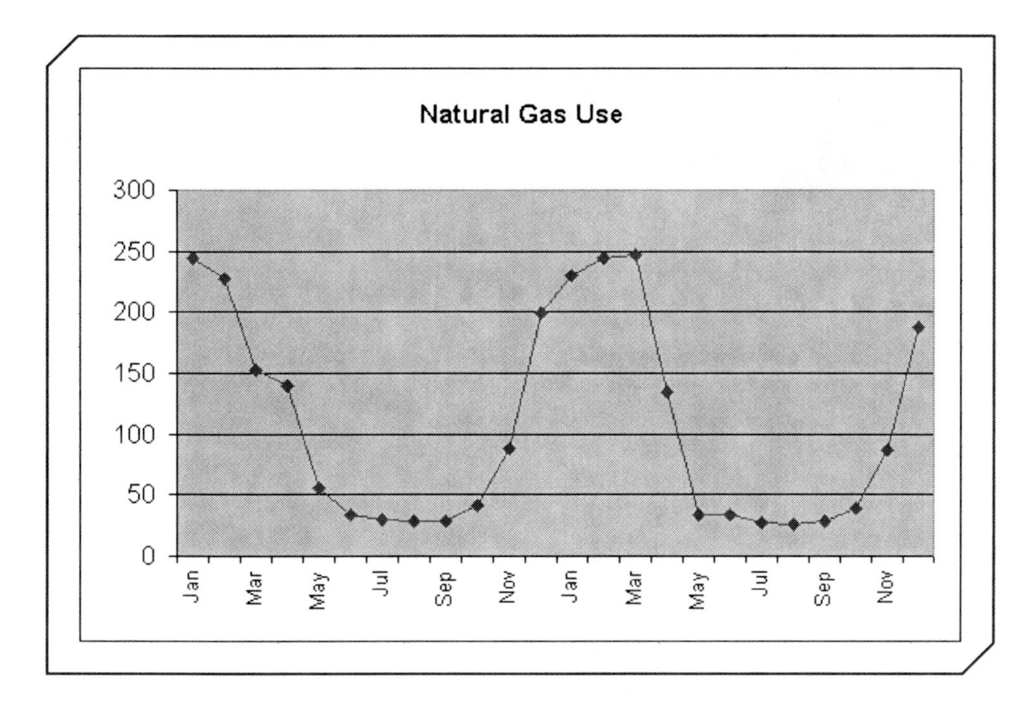

Exhibit 11.5
Seasonal Pattern of Home Natural Gas Usage

CYCLICAL PATTERNS

Cyclical patterns *are regular patterns in a data series that take place over long periods of time.*

Cyclical patterns *are regular patterns in a data series that take place over long periods of time.* Exhibit 11.6 shows an example of multiyear cyclical movements occurring along with an increasing trend. A common example of a cyclical pattern is the movement of stock market values during "bull" and "bear" market cycles.

RANDOM VARIATION

Random variation *(sometimes called* **noise***) is the unexplained deviation of a time series from a predictable pattern, such as a trend, seasonal, or cyclical pattern.*

Random variation *(sometimes called* **noise***) is the unexplained deviation of a time series from a predictable pattern, such as a trend, seasonal, or cyclical pattern.* Random variation is caused by short-term, unanticipated, and nonrecurring factors and is unpredictable. Because of random variation, forecasts are never 100 percent accurate. In the ideal situation, random variation should be normally distributed about the average. That is crucial for operations managers to remember when using forecasts in decision-making. The best that can be hoped for is to identify the trend, seasonal, and/or cyclical patterns that a time series might exhibit in order to develop a useful forecast.

IRREGULAR (ONE-TIME) VARIATION

Irregular variation *is one-time variation that is explainable.*

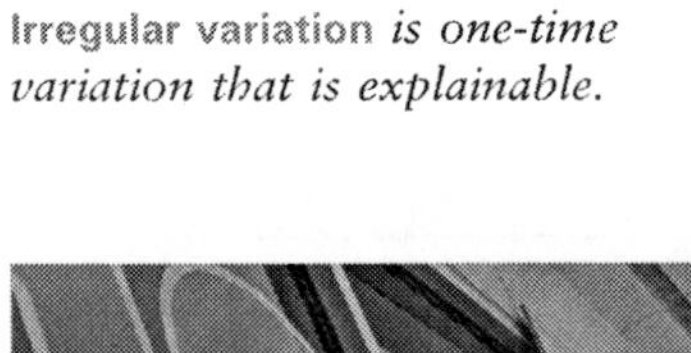

Irregular variation *is one-time variation that is explainable.* For example, a hurricane can cause a surge in demand for building materials, food, and water. Likewise, a major snowstorm can reduce retail sales significantly. After the 9/11 terrorist attacks on the United States, many forecasts that predicted U.S. financial trends and airline passenger volumes had to be discarded due to the effects of this one-time event. One-time events result in data outliers that can normally be discarded. In some cases, such as 9/11, the irregular variation has a longer-term effect on data patterns.

Matt Stroshane/Bloomberg News/Landov

An example of a time series is given in the spreadsheet in Exhibit 11.7. These data represent the call volumes over 24 quarters from a call center at a major financial institution. The data are plotted on a chart in Exhibit 11.8. We can see both an increasing trend over the entire 6 years along with seasonal patterns within each of the years. For example, during the first three quarters of each year, call volumes increase,

Exhibit 11.6
Trend and Business Cycle Characteristics (each data point is 1 year apart)

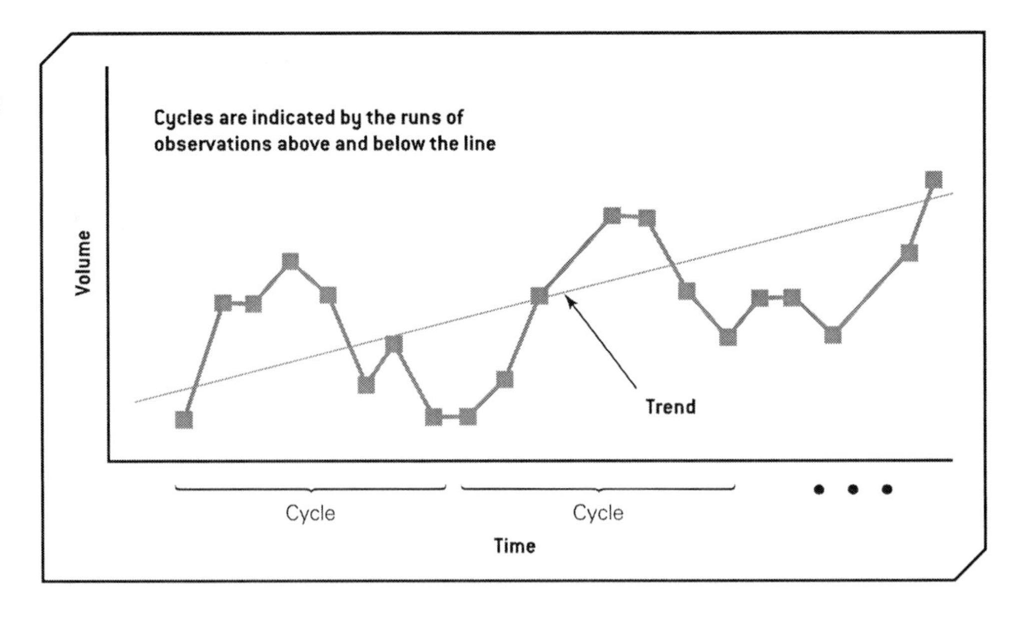

	A	B	C	D
1	Period	Year	Quarter	Call Volume
2	1	1	1	362
3	2	1	2	385
4	3	1	3	432
5	4	1	4	341
6	5	2	1	382
7	6	2	2	409
8	7	2	3	498
9	8	2	4	387
10	9	3	1	473
11	10	3	2	513
12	11	3	3	582
13	12	3	4	474
14	13	4	1	544
15	14	4	2	582
16	15	4	3	681
17	16	4	4	557
18	17	5	1	628
19	18	5	2	707
20	19	5	3	773
21	20	5	4	592
22	21	6	1	627
23	22	6	2	725
24	23	6	3	854
25	24	6	4	661

Exhibit 11.7
Call Center Volume

followed by a rapid decrease in the fourth quarter as customers presumably turn their attention to the holiday season. To develop a reliable forecast for the future, we would need to take into account both the long-term trend and the annual seasonal pattern. Operations managers can use this information to better plan staffing levels and schedules, vacations, and project and technology changeovers.

Forecast Errors and Accuracy

All forecasts are subject to error, and understanding the nature and size of errors is important to making good decisions. For example, the top managers of the health care products company in one of the opening episodes who need to predict the size of the hospital bed market for the next year will want to know if their forecast has a 5 percent, 10 percent, or 50 percent error.

We denote the historical values of a time series by $A_1, A_2, \ldots, A_T$. In general, A_t represents the value of the time series for period t. We will let F_t represent the forecast value for period t. When we make this forecast, we will not know the actual value of the time series in period t, A_t. However, once A_t becomes known, we can assess how well our forecast was able to predict the actual value of the time series. **Forecast error** *is the difference between the observed value of the time series and the forecast, or* $A_t - F_t$. Because of the inherent inability of any model to forecast accurately, we use quantitative measures of forecast accuracy to evaluate how well the forecasting model performs. Clearly, we want to use models that have small forecast errors.

Forecast error *is the difference between the observed value of the time series and the forecast, or* $A_t - F_t$.

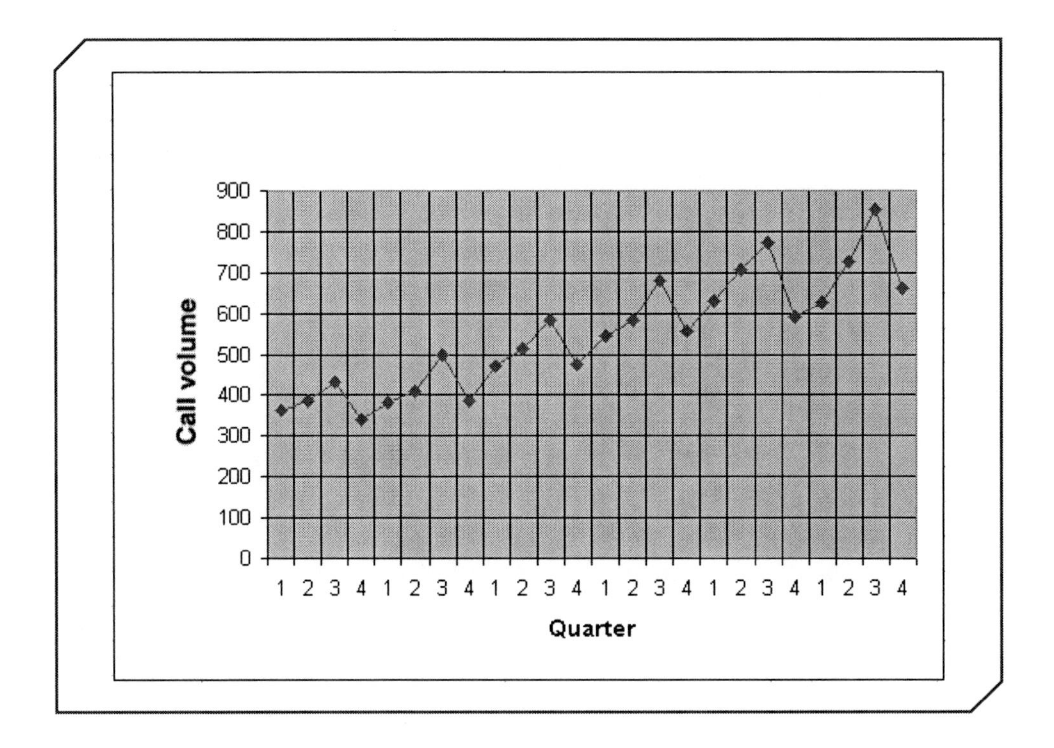

Exhibit 11.8
Chart of Call Volume

Suppose that a forecasting method provided the forecasts in column E of Exhibit 11.9 for the call volume time series we discussed earlier. The forecast errors are computed in column F. As a means of measuring forecast accuracy, we might simply add up the forecast errors. However, if the errors are random (as they should be if the forecasting method is appropriate), some errors will be positive and some will be negative, resulting in a sum near zero regardless of the size of the individual errors.

One way to avoid this problem is by squaring the individual forecast errors and then averaging the results over all T periods of data in the time series. This measure is called the mean square error, or MSE, and is calculated as

$$\text{MSE} = \frac{\sum(A_t - F_t)^2}{T} \tag{11.1}$$

For the call center data, this is computed in column H of Exhibit 11.9. The sum of the squared errors is 87910.6, and therefore MSE is 87,910.6/24 = 3,662.94. MSE is probably the most commonly used measure of forecast accuracy. (Sometimes the square root of MSE is computed; this is called the *root mean square error, RMSE.*)

Another common measure of forecast accuracy is the mean absolute deviation (MAD), computed as

$$\text{MAD} = \frac{\sum|(A_t - F_t)|}{T} \tag{11.2}$$

This measure is simply the average of the sum of the absolute deviations for all the forecast errors. Using the information in column J of Exhibit 11.9, we compute MAD as 1,197/24 = 49.88.

Exhibit 11.9 Forecast Error of Example Time Series Data

	A	B	C	D	E	F	G	H	I	J	K	L
1	Period	Year	Quarter	Call At Volume	Forecast Ft	Error (At - Ft)		Squared Error		Absolute Deviation		Percentage Error
2	1	1	1	362	343.8	18.20		331.24		18.2		5.03%
3	2	1	2	385	361.6	23.40		547.56		23.4		6.08%
4	3	1	3	432	379.4	52.60		2766.76		52.6		12.18%
5	4	1	4	341	397.2	-56.20		3158.44		56.2		16.48%
6	5	2	1	382	415	-33.00		1089.00		33		8.64%
7	6	2	2	409	432.8	-23.80		566.44		23.8		5.82%
8	7	2	3	498	450.6	47.40		2246.76		47.4		9.52%
9	8	2	4	387	468.4	-81.40		6625.96		81.4		21.03%
10	9	3	1	473	486.2	-13.20		174.24		13.2		2.79%
11	10	3	2	513	504	9.00		81.00		9		1.75%
12	11	3	3	582	521.8	60.20		3624.04		60.2		10.34%
13	12	3	4	474	539.6	-65.60		4303.36		65.6		13.84%
14	13	4	1	544	557.4	-13.40		179.56		13.4		2.46%
15	14	4	2	582	575.2	6.80		46.24		6.8		1.17%
16	15	4	3	681	593	88.00		7744.00		88		12.92%
17	16	4	4	557	610.8	-53.80		2894.44		53.8		9.66%
18	17	5	1	628	628.6	-0.60		0.36		0.6		0.10%
19	18	5	2	707	646.4	60.60		3672.36		60.6		8.57%
20	19	5	3	773	664.2	108.80		11837.44		108.8		14.08%
21	20	5	4	592	682	-90.00		8100.00		90		15.20%
22	21	6	1	627	699.8	-72.80		5299.84		72.8		11.61%
23	22	6	2	725	717.6	7.40		54.76		7.4		1.02%
24	23	6	3	854	735.4	118.60		14065.96		118.6		13.89%
25	24	6	4	661	753.2	-92.20		8500.84		92.2		13.95%
26						Sum		87910.60	Sum	1197	Sum	218.13%
27						**MSE**		**3662.94**	**MAD**	**49.88**	**MAPE**	**9.09%**

A third measure of forecast error is the mean absolute percentage error (MAPE):

$$\text{MAPE} = \frac{\sum|(A_t - F_t)/A_t| \times 100}{T} \tag{11.3}$$

This is simply the average of the percentage error for each forecast value in the time series. These calculations are shown in column L of Exhibit 11.9, resulting in MAPE = 218.13%/24 = 9.09 percent. Using MAPE, the forecast differs from actual call volume on average by plus or minus 9.09 percent.

A major difference between MSE and MAD is that MSE is influenced much more by large forecast errors than by small errors (because the errors are squared). The values of MAD and MSE depend on the measurement scale of the time-series data. For example, forecasting profit in the range of millions of dollars would result in very large values, even for accurate forecasting models. On the other hand, a variable like market share, which is measured as a fraction, will always have small values of MAD and MSE. Thus, the measures have no meaning except in comparison with other models used to forecast the same data. MAPE is different in that the measurement scale factor is eliminated by dividing the absolute error by the time-series data value. This makes the measure easier to interpret. The selection of the best measure of forecasting accuracy is not a simple matter; indeed, forecasting experts often disagree on which measure should be used.

Learning Objective
To be aware of different forecasting approaches and methods.

Statistical forecasting *is based on the assumption that the future will be an extrapolation of the past.*

Judgmental forecasting *relies upon opinions and expertise of people in developing forecasts.*

TYPES OF FORECASTING APPROACHES

Forecasting methods can be classified as either statistical or judgmental. **Statistical forecasting** *is based on the assumption that the future will be an extrapolation of the past.* Statistical forecasting methods use historical data to predict future values. Many different techniques exist; which technique should be used depends on the variable being forecast and the time horizon. Statistical methods can generally be categorized as *time-series methods*, which extrapolate historical time-series data, and *regression methods*, which also extrapolate historical time-series data but can also include other potentially causal factors that influence the behavior of the time series. **Judgmental forecasting** *relies upon opinions and expertise of people in developing forecasts.* For example, suppose that we are asked to forecast the length of time before a current technology becomes obsolete. Certainly past data are no help here. The forecast can only be developed in a qualitative fashion by experts who are knowledgeable about changing technology. As we will discuss later, many organizations use a combination of both types of approaches. Exhibit 11.10 summarizes some of the basic forecasting approaches that are used in business; however, many other methods exist that are not listed here. See the OM Spotlight for an interesting contrast of statistical versus judgmental forecasts.

Forecasting Software

Microsoft Excel provides a convenient platform to implement many of the forecasting techniques shown in Exhibit 11.10. It is relatively easy to design spreadsheets for simple forecasting approaches that we will discuss in this chapter. Excel also has some built-in tools for some of these techniques. In addition to Excel, many

Exhibit 11.10 Classification of Basic Forecasting Methods

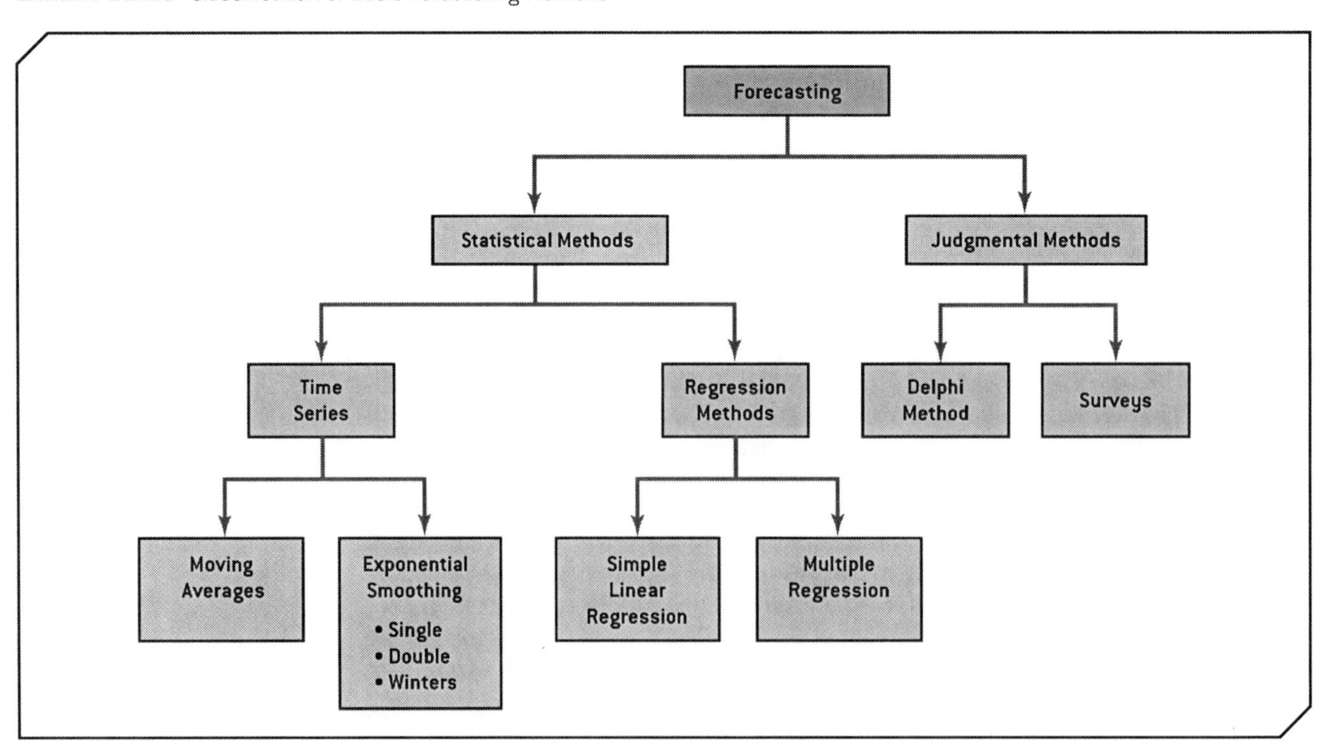

OM SPOTLIGHT

Statistical Versus Judgmental Forecasting[4]

A $2 billion consumer packaged goods company gained significant benefits from implementing a better forecasting system. At the time, the company was selling roughly 1,000 make-to-stock finished goods at 10,000 customer shipment locations, which were served through ten regional distribution centers. The company needed good weekly forecasts for each of the 1,000 finished goods by distribution center. The forecasting approach depended heavily on numbers generated by sales representatives. However, this approach had failed to work. First, the sales representatives had no particular interest in forecasting. They had no training or skill in forecasting and their judgment forecasts on an item and weekly basis were not very good. Second, forecast errors for individual items cancelled each other out when they were aggregated to the assigned distribution center.

Today, standard statistical forecasting approaches are integrated into all company forecasts. Sales representatives have more time to build customer relationships and generate revenue. The company also established a weekly consensus process to review and override the statistical forecasts at the product group level only. Modest changes in the statistical forecasts are made about half the time. However, of these override decisions, only 40 percent improved the original forecasts—60 percent of the time management overrides made the forecasts worse!

commercial software packages and general statistical analysis programs, such as SPSS, Minitab, and SAS, have forecasting features or modules. With these software packages, users must choose the forecasting model and may also have to specify the model parameters. This requires a solid understanding of the assumptions and capabilities of the various models, some in-depth knowledge of the mathematics behind the procedures, and often numerous experimental trials to identify the best forecasting model. Various other stand-alone software packages exist that automate some of these tasks. Some will find the optimal model parameters that will minimize some measure of forecast accuracy. Others will even attempt to determine the best forecasting method to use automatically.

CBPredictor is an Excel add-in that was developed by Decisioneering, Inc., and is included in *Crystal Ball* on the text CD-ROM. *CBPredictor* includes many different time-series forecasting approaches that we will discuss in this chapter. We will illustrate how *CBPredictor* works after we present these approaches. Surveys of forecasting software packages are routinely published in *ORMS Today*, a publication of the Institute for Operations Research and the Management Sciences (INFORMS).[5] See www.orms-today.com for further information.

STATISTICAL FORECASTING MODELS

Learning Objective
To understand basic time-series forecasting methods, be aware of more advanced methods, and use spreadsheet models to make forecasts.

A wide variety of statistical forecasting models have been developed, and we cannot discuss all of them. However, we present some of the basic and more popular approaches used in OM applications.

Single Moving Average

A moving average (MA) forecast is an average of the most recent "k" observations in a time series.

The single moving average concept is based on the idea of averaging random fluctuations in a time series to identify the underlying direction in which the time series is changing. *A moving average (MA) forecast is an average of the most recent "k" observations in a time series.* Thus, the forecast for the next period ($t + 1$), which we denote as F_{t+1}, for a time series with t observations is

$$\begin{aligned} F_{t+1} &= \sum(\text{most recent "}k\text{" observations})/k \\ &= (A_t + A_{t-1} + A_{t-2} + \cdots + A_{t-k+1})/k \end{aligned} \qquad \textbf{(11.4)}$$

MA methods work best for short planning horizons when there is no major trend, seasonal, or business cycle patterns, that is, when demand is relatively stable and consistent. As the value of k increases, the forecast reacts slowly to recent changes in the time series because more older data are included in the computation. As the value of k decreases, the forecast reacts more quickly. If a significant trend exists in the time-series data, moving-average-based forecasts will lag actual demand, resulting in a bias in the forecast.

To illustrate the moving-averages method, consider the data presented in Exhibit 11.11. These data and chart show the number of gallons of milk sold each month at Gas-Mart, a local convenience store. To use moving averages to forecast the milk sales, we must first select the number of data values to be included in the moving average. As an example, let us compute forecasts based on a 3-month moving average ($k = 3$). The moving-average calculation for the first 3 months of the milk-sales time series, and thus the forecast for month 4, is

$$F_4 = \frac{172 + 217 + 190}{3} = 193.00$$

Since the actual value observed in month 4 is 233, we see that the forecast error in month 4 is $233 - 193 = 40$. The calculation for the second 3-month moving average (F_5) is

$$F_5 = \frac{217 + 190 + 233}{3} = 213.33$$

This provides a forecast for month 5. The error associated with this forecast is $179 - 213.33 = -34.33$. A complete summary of these moving-average calculations is shown in Exhibit 11.12. The mean square error for these forecasts is 1,457.33.

The number of data values to be included in the moving average is often based on managerial insight and judgment. Thus, it should not be surprising that for a particular time series, different values of k lead to different measures of forecast accuracy. One way to find the best number is to use trial and error to identify the value of k that minimizes MSE for the historical data. Then, if we were willing to assume that the number that is best for the past will also be best for the future, we would forecast the next value in the time series using the number of data values that minimized the MSE for the historical time series. Exhibit 11.13 shows an analysis of 2-, 3-, and 4-month moving averages for the milk-sales data. We see that among these options, a 3-month moving average forecast provides the smallest value of MSE.

MICROSOFT EXCEL DATA ANALYSIS MOVING AVERAGE TOOL

Excel provides a simple tool for computing moving-average forecasts. From the *Tools* menu, select *Data Analysis*, and then *Moving Average*. (The *Data Analysis* tools are a standard Excel feature. If they do not appear under the *Tools* menu,

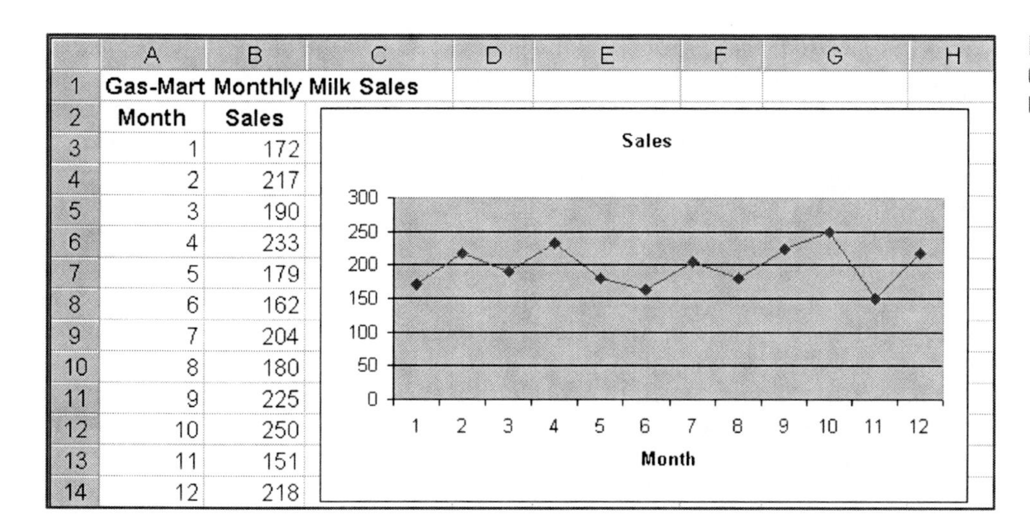

Gas-Mart Monthly Milk Sales	
Month	Sales
1	172
2	217
3	190
4	233
5	179
6	162
7	204
8	180
9	225
10	250
11	151
12	218

Exhibit 11.11 Gas-Mart Milk Sales Time-Series Data

Exhibit 11.12 Summary of 3-Month Moving-Average Forecasts

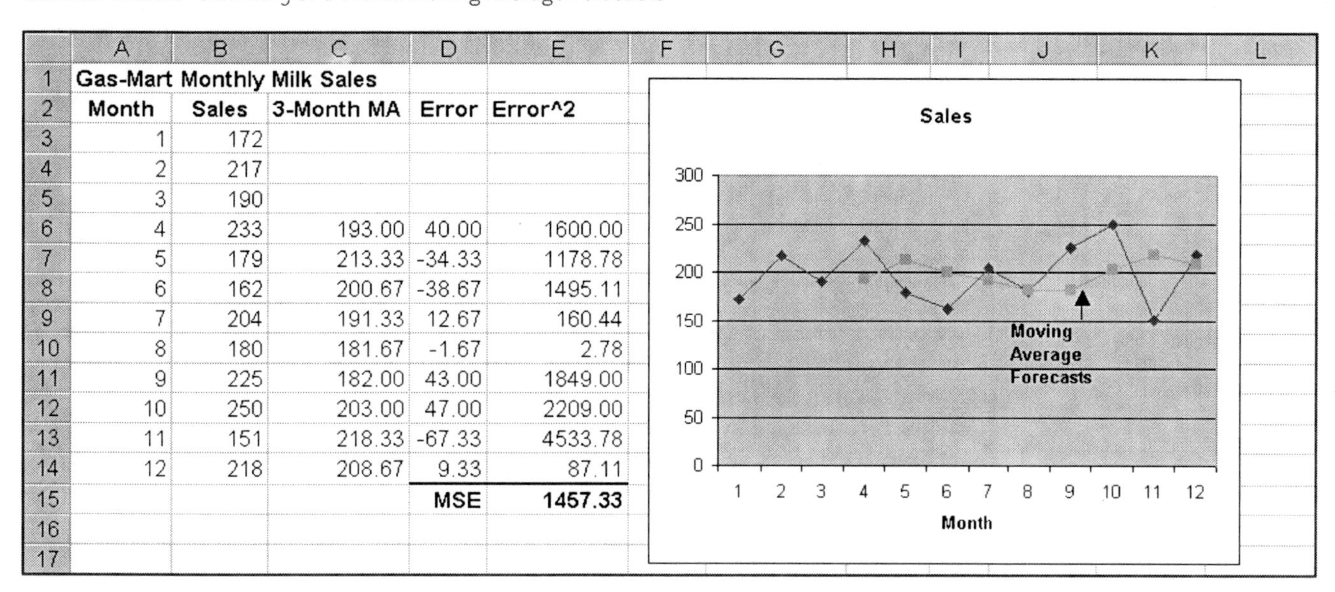

Gas-Mart Monthly Milk Sales				
Month	Sales	3-Month MA	Error	Error^2
1	172			
2	217			
3	190			
4	233	193.00	40.00	1600.00
5	179	213.33	-34.33	1178.78
6	162	200.67	-38.67	1495.11
7	204	191.33	12.67	160.44
8	180	181.67	-1.67	2.78
9	225	182.00	43.00	1849.00
10	250	203.00	47.00	2209.00
11	151	218.33	-67.33	4533.78
12	218	208.67	9.33	87.11
			MSE	**1457.33**

Exhibit 11.13 Milk-Sales Forecast Error Analysis

Gas-Mart Monthly Milk Sales									Squared Errors		
Month	Sales	2-Month MA	Error	3-Month MA	Error	4-Month MA	Error		2-Month MA	3-Month MA	4-Month MA
1	172										
2	217										
3	190	194.50	-4.50						20.25		
4	233	203.50	29.50	193.00	40.00				870.25	1600.00	
5	179	211.50	-32.50	213.33	-34.33	203.00	-24.00		1056.25	1178.78	576.00
6	162	206.00	-44.00	200.67	-38.67	204.75	-42.75		1936.00	1495.11	1827.56
7	204	170.50	33.50	191.33	12.67	191.00	13.00		1122.25	160.44	169.00
8	180	183.00	-3.00	181.67	-1.67	194.50	-14.50		9.00	2.78	210.25
9	225	192.00	33.00	182.00	43.00	181.25	43.75		1089.00	1849.00	1914.06
10	250	202.50	47.50	203.00	47.00	192.75	57.25		2256.25	2209.00	3277.56
11	151	237.50	-86.50	218.33	-67.33	214.75	-63.75		7482.25	4533.78	4064.06
12	218	200.50	17.50	208.67	9.33	201.50	16.50		306.25	87.11	272.25
									16147.75	13116.00	12310.75
								MSE	**1614.78**	**1457.33**	**1538.84**

select *Add-Ins* from the *Tools* menu and select them.) In the dialog box that Excel displays, you need to enter the *Input Range* of the data, the *Interval* (the value of k), and the first cell of the *Output Range*. To align the actual data with the forecasted values in the worksheet, select the first cell of the *Output Range* to be one row below and to the right of the first time-series value. You may also obtain a chart of the data and the moving averages as well as a column of standard errors by checking the appropriate boxes. However, we do *not* recommend using the chart or error options because the forecasts are not properly aligned with the data (the forecast value aligned with a particular data point represents the forecast for the *next* month) and thus can be misleading. Rather, we recommend that you generate your own chart as we did in Exhibit 11.12. Exhibit 11.14 shows the results produced by the *Moving Average* tool (with some customization of the chart to show the months on the x axis). Note that the forecast for month 4 is aligned with the actual value for month 3 on the chart. Compare this to Exhibit 11.12 and you can see the difference.

Weighted Moving Average

In the simple moving average approach, the data are weighted equally. This may not be desirable, as we might wish to put more weight on recent observations than on older observations, particularly if the time series is changing rapidly. For example, you might assign a 60 percent weight to the most recent observation, 30 percent to the observation two periods prior, and the remaining 10 percent of the weight to the observation three periods prior. A general formula for a weighted moving-average forecast obtained by weighting the most recent k observations is

$$F_{t+1} = w_t A_t + w_{t-1} A_{t-1} + w_{t-2} A_{t-2} + \cdots + w_{t-k+1} A_{t-k+1} \quad \textbf{(11.5)}$$

where w_t represents the weight assigned to time period t. Note that all the weights must add to 1.0. Exhibit 11.15 shows a comparison of a 60-30-10 percent weighted moving average with the original 3-month moving-average model. We see that the weighted forecasts provide a smaller MSE. An interesting problem is to determine the best set of weights. We leave this to you as a problem at the end of the chapter.

Exhibit 11.14 Results of Excel Moving Average Tool (note misalignment of forecasts with the time series)

	A	B	C
1	**Gas-Mart Monthly Milk Sales**		
2	**Month**	**Sales**	**Forecast**
3	1	172	
4	2	217	#N/A
5	3	190	#N/A
6	4	233	193
7	5	179	213.333333
8	6	162	200.666667
9	7	204	191.333333
10	8	180	181.666667
11	9	225	182
12	10	250	203
13	11	151	218.333333
14	12	218	208.666667
15			206.333333

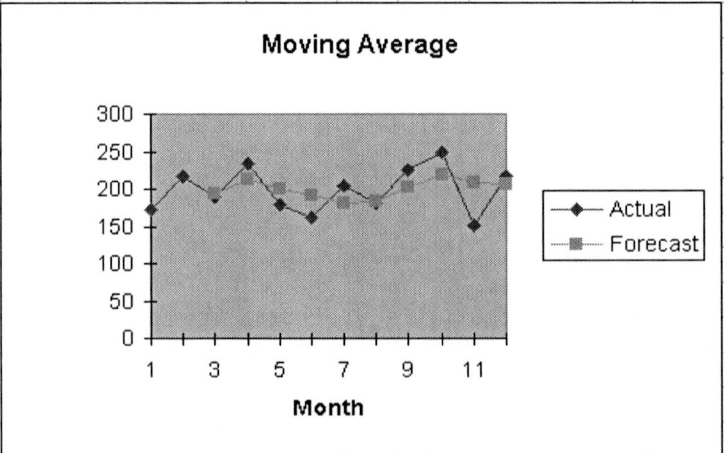

Exhibit 11.15 Comparison of 3-Month Moving Average and Weighted Moving Average Models

	A	B	C	D	E	F	G	H	I
1	Gas-Mart Monthly Milk Sales							Error Analysis	
2	Month	Sales	3-Month MA	Error	3-Month Weighted	Error		3-Month MA	3-Month Weighted
3	1	172							
4	2	217							
5	3	190							
6	4	233	193.00	40.00	187.30	45.70		1600.00	2088.49
7	5	179	213.33	-34.33	210.50	-31.50		1178.78	992.25
8	6	162	200.67	-38.67	201.80	-39.80		1495.11	1584.04
9	7	204	191.33	12.67	209.70	-5.70		160.44	32.49
10	8	180	181.67	-1.67	176.40	3.60		2.78	12.96
11	9	225	182.00	43.00	176.40	48.60		1849.00	2361.96
12	10	250	203.00	47.00	198.90	51.10		2209.00	2611.21
13	11	151	218.33	-67.33	200.50	-49.50		4533.78	2450.25
14	12	218	208.67	9.33	225.10	-7.10		87.11	50.41
15								13116.00	12184.06
16							MSE	**1457.33**	**1353.78**

Single Exponential Smoothing

Single Exponential smoothing (SES) *is a forecasting technique that uses a weighted average of past time-series values to forecast the value of the time series in the next period.* SES forecasts are based on averages using and weighting the most recent actual demand more than older demand data. SES methods do not try to include trend or seasonal effects. The basic exponential-smoothing model is

$$F_{t+1} = \alpha A_t + (1 - \alpha)F_t = F_t + \alpha(A_t - F_t) \qquad \textbf{(11.6)}$$

where α is called the **smoothing constant** ($0 \leq \alpha \leq 1$). To use this model, set the forecast for period 1, F_1, equal to the actual observation for period 1, A_1. Note that F_2 will also have the same value.

Using the two preceding forms of the forecast equation, we can interpret the simple exponential smoothing model in two ways. In the first model shown in Equation 11.6, the forecast for the next period, F_{t+1}, is a weighted average of the forecast made for period t, F_t, and the actual observation in period t, A_t. The second form of the model in Equation 11.6, obtained by simply rearranging terms, states that the forecast for the next period, F_{t+1}, equals the forecast for the last period, F_t, plus a fraction, α, of the forecast error made in period t, $A_t - F_t$. Thus, to make a forecast once we have selected the smoothing constant, we need only know the previous forecast and the actual value.

To illustrate the exponential-smoothing approach to forecasting, consider the milk-sales time series presented in Exhibit 11.16 using $\alpha = 0.2$. As we have said, the exponential-smoothing forecast for period 2 is equal to the actual value of the time series in period 1. Thus, with $A_1 = 172$, we will set $F_1 = 172$ to get the computations started. Using Equation (11.6) for $t = 1$, we have

$$F_2 = 0.2A_1 + 0.8F_1 = 0.2(172) + 0.8(172) = 172.00$$

For period 3 we obtain

$$F_3 = 0.2A_2 + 0.8F_2 = 0.2(217) + 0.8(172) = 181.00$$

Single Exponential smoothing (SES) *is a forecasting technique that uses a weighted average of past time-series values to forecast the value of the time series in the next period.*

By continuing these calculations, we are able to determine the monthly forecast values and the corresponding forecast errors shown in Exhibit 11.16. The mean squared error is MSE = 1285.28. Note that we have not shown an exponential-smoothing forecast or the forecast error for period 1, because F_1 was set equal to A_1 to begin the smoothing computations. You could use this information to generate a forecast for month 13 as

$$F_{13} = 0.2A_{12} + 0.8F_{12} = 0.2(218) + 0.8(194.59) = 199.27$$

Exhibit 11.17 is the plot of the actual and the forecast time-series values. Note in particular how the forecasts "smooth out" the random fluctuations in the time series.

Exhibit 11.16
Summary of Single Exponential Smoothing Milk-Sales Forecasts with $\alpha = 0.2$

	A	B	C	D	E
1	Gas-Mart Monthly Milk Sales				
2		Alpha	0.2		
3	Month	Sales	Exponential Smoothing Forecast	Error	Error^2
4	1	172	172.00		
5	2	217	172.00	45.00	2025.00
6	3	190	181.00	9.00	81.00
7	4	233	182.80	50.20	2520.04
8	5	179	192.84	-13.84	191.55
9	6	162	190.07	-28.07	788.04
10	7	204	184.46	19.54	381.91
11	8	180	188.37	-8.37	69.99
12	9	225	186.69	38.31	1467.44
13	10	250	194.35	55.65	3096.44
14	11	151	205.48	-54.48	2968.44
15	12	218	194.59	23.41	548.18
16				MSE	1285.28

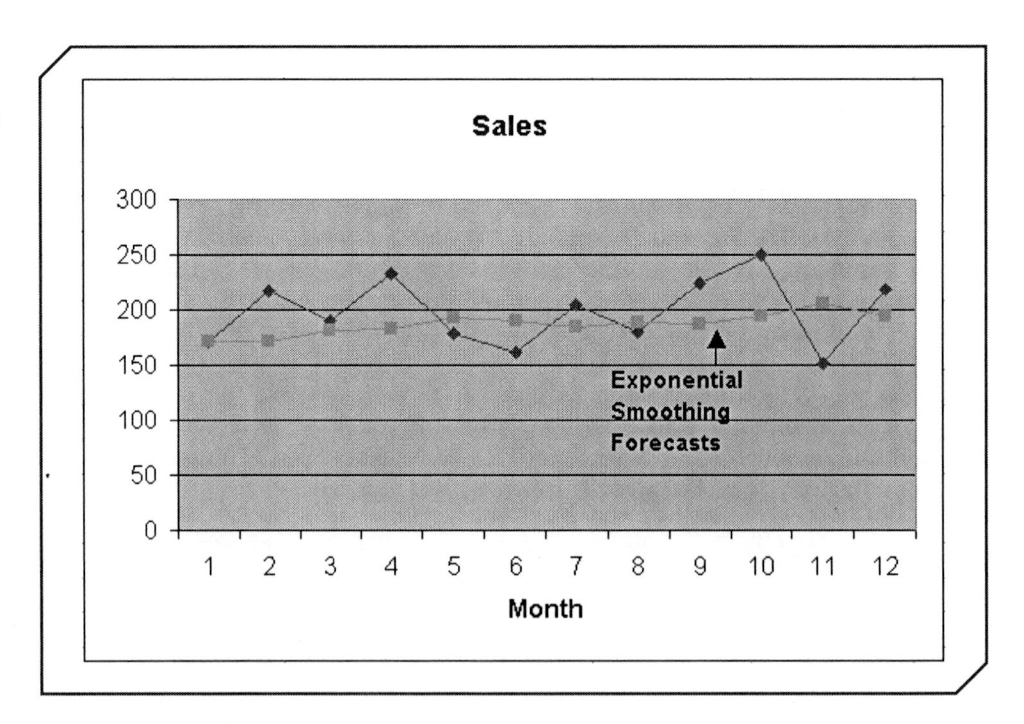

Exhibit 11.17
Graph of Single Exponential Smoothing Milk-Sales Forecasts with $\alpha = 0.2$

By repeated substitution for F_t in the equation, it is easy to demonstrate that F_{t+1} is a decreasingly weighted average of all past time-series data. To see this, suppose we have a time series with three observations: A_1, A_2, and A_3. Initially, $F_1 = A_1$. Thus, the forecast for period 2 is

$$F_2 = \alpha A_1 + (1 - \alpha)F_1$$
$$F_2 = \alpha A_1 + A_1 - \alpha A_1$$
$$F_2 = A_1$$

To obtain the forecast for period 3 (F_3), we substitute $F_2 = A_1$ in the expression for F_3. The result is

$$F_3 = \alpha A_2 + (1 - \alpha)F_2$$
$$F_3 = \alpha A_2 + (1 - \alpha)A_1$$

To go one step further, substituting this expression for F_3 in the expression for F_4, we obtain

$$\begin{aligned} F_4 &= \alpha A_3 + (1 - \alpha)F_3 \\ &= \alpha A_3 + (1 - \alpha)[\alpha A_2 + (1 - \alpha)A_1] \\ &= \alpha A_3 + \alpha(1 - \alpha)A_2 + (1 - \alpha)^2 A_1 \end{aligned}$$

We see that F_4 is a weighted average of the first three time-series values and that the sum of the weights is equal to 1. For instance, if $\alpha = 0.2$, then

$$F_3 = 0.2A_2 + 0.8A_1$$
$$F_4 = 0.2A_3 + (0.2)(0.8)A_2 + (1 - 0.2)^2 A_1 = 0.2A_3 + 0.16A_2 + 0.64A_1$$

As the number of data points increases, the weights associated with older data get progressively smaller. For example, we see that the weight on A_2 dropped from 0.2 to 0.16, and the weight on A_1 dropped from 0.8 to 0.64 as we added a new data point.

A similar argument can be made to show that any forecast F_{t+1} is a weighted average of *all* the previous time-series values. Thus, exponential smoothing models "never forget" past data as long as the smoothing constant is strictly between 0 and 1. In contrast, MA methods "completely forget" all the data older than k periods in the past. Typical values for α are in the range of 0.1 to 0.5. When $\alpha = 0.1$, exponential smoothing assigns about 90 percent of the weight to the last 22 periods. With $\alpha = 0.5$, exponential smoothing assigns about 90 percent of the weight to the last 4 periods. Thus, larger values of α place more emphasis on recent data. If the time series is very volatile and contains substantial random variability, a small value of the smoothing constant is preferred. The reason for this choice is that since much of the forecast error is due to random variability, we do not want to overreact and adjust the forecasts too quickly. For a fairly stable time series with relatively little random variability, larger values of the smoothing constant have the advantage of quickly adjusting the forecasts when forecasting errors occur and therefore allowing the forecast to react faster to changing conditions.

The smoothing constant is approximately related to the value of k in the moving-average model by the following relationship:

$$\alpha = 2/(k + 1) \qquad \textbf{(11.7)}$$

Therefore, an exponential smoothing model with $\alpha = 0.5$ is roughly equivalent to a moving-average model with $k = 3$. Equation (11.7) allows one to switch between a k-period simple moving average and exponential smoothing with a smoothing constant α, with similar results. Similar to the MA model, we can experiment to find the best value for the smoothing constant to minimize the mean square error or one of the other measures of forecast accuracy. Using a spreadsheet, we could easily evaluate a range of smoothing constants to try to find the best values.

One disadvantage of exponential smoothing is that if the time series exhibits a positive trend, the forecast will lag the actual values and, similarly, will overshoot the actual values if a negative trend exists. It is good practice to analyze new data to see whether the smoothing constant should be revised to provide better forecasts. If values of α greater than 0.5 are needed to develop a good forecast, then other types of forecasting methods might be more appropriate.

CBPredictor

CBPredictor is an Excel add-in that is included with certain versions of *Crystal Ball.* The student version of *Crystal Ball* that accompanies this text includes *CBPredictor.* After *CBPredictor* has been installed, it may be accessed in Excel from the *CB Run* menu; if the menu is not present in Excel, make sure that the *Crystal Ball* box is checked in the *Tools...Add-Ins* window. When *CBPredictor* is started, the dialog box shown in Exhibit 11.18 appears. The dialog box contains four tabs that query you for information one step at a time. *Input Data* allows you to specify the data range on which to base your forecast; *Data Attributes* allows you to specify the type of data and whether or not seasonality is present; *Method Gallery* (see Exhibit 11.19) allows you to select any or all of eight time-series methods, including single moving average, single exponential smoothing, and other methods we briefly describe in the next section. *CBPredictor* will run each method you select and will recommend the one that best forecasts your data, along with the best model parameters (such as the number of periods in the moving average or the value of α in exponential smoothing). The final tab, *Results,* allows you to specify a variety of reporting options.

We will illustrate the use of *CBPredictor* for the single moving-average and single exponential methods as selected in the Methods Gallery dialog in Exhibit 11.19. After running *CBPredictor,* several new worksheets are created in the Excel workbook: *Report, Chart, Results Table,* and *Methods Table.* The *Report* worksheet contains the calculated forecasts for the best model along with forecast error analysis. Exhibit 11.20 shows a portion of the results. *CBPredictor* found that single exponential smoothing provided the best model with α = 0.178. The forecast for month 13 is 198.21, with a 90 percent confidence interval of (136.67, 259.74).

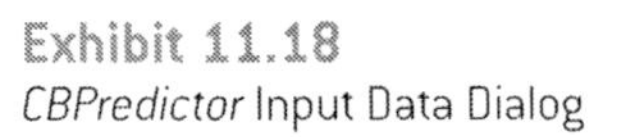
Exhibit 11.18
CBPredictor Input Data Dialog

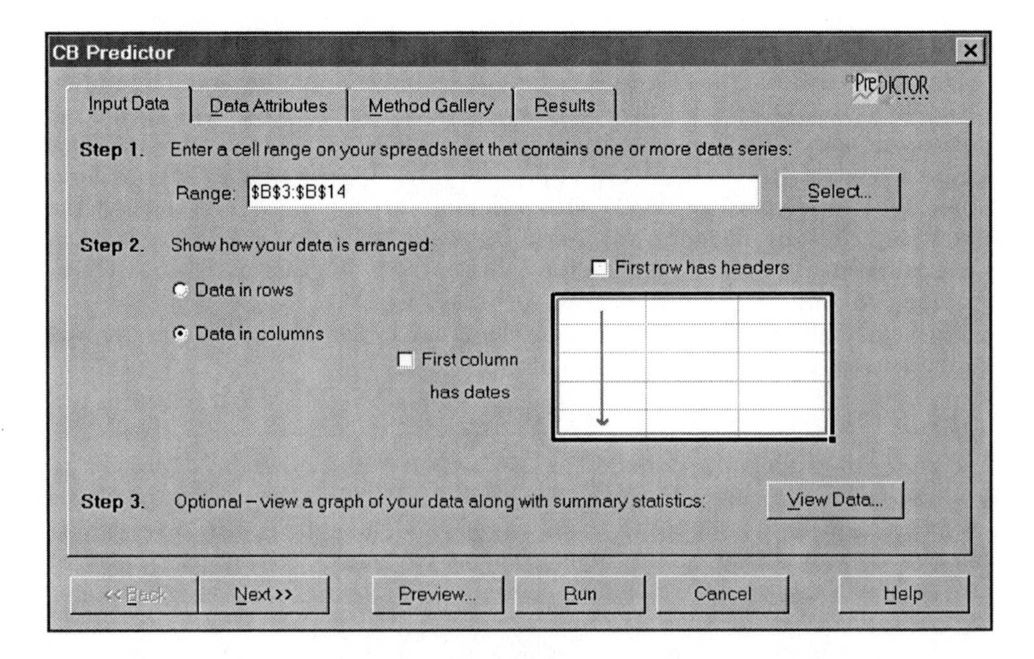

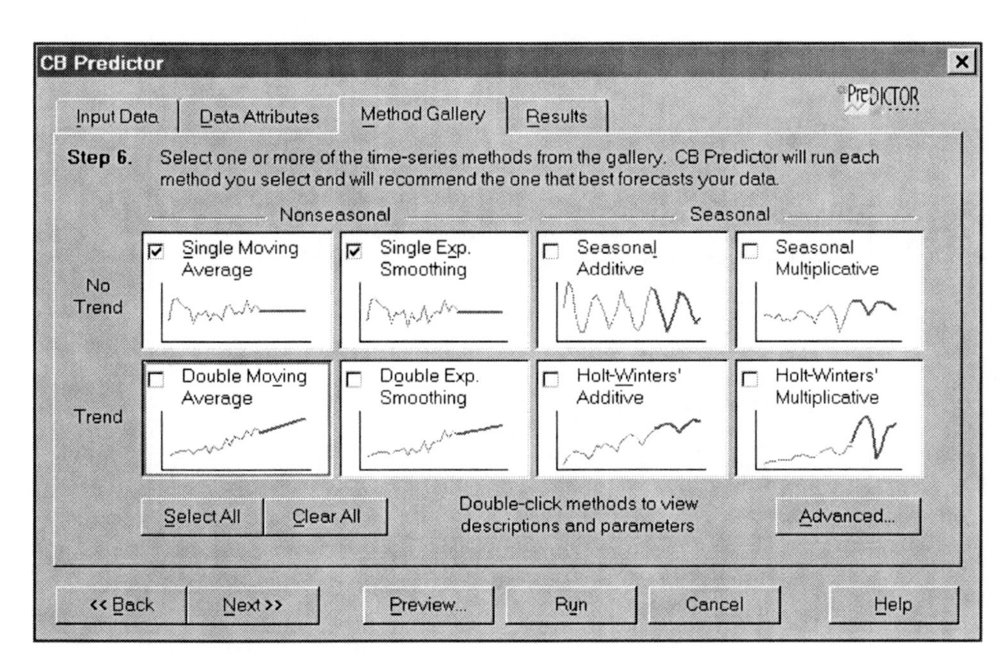

Exhibit 11.19
CBPredictor Methods Gallery Dialog

Because this confidence interval has a large range—123.07 gallons of milk—there is a significant potential for error in using the point estimate forecast of 198.21. The *Report* worksheet also shows the RMSE, MAD, and MAPE error metrics along with some advanced statistical measures. The Durbin–Watson statistic checks for autocorrelation, which measures how strongly successive values of the data may be correlated with each other, with values of 2 indicating no autocorrelation. The Ljung–Box statistic measures whether a set of autocorrelations are significantly different from a set of autocorrelations that are all zero. Large values suggest that the model used is poor. Theil's U statistic is a relative error measure that compares the results with a naïve forecast. A value less than 1 means that the forecasting technique is better than guessing; a value equal to 1 means that the technique is about as good as guessing; and a value greater than 1 means that the forecasting technique is worse than guessing. In this example, we see that the forecasting techniques provide managers with a useful decision aid. The other worksheets provide the information used in the *Report* in a bit more detail. These features make *CBPredictor* a simple yet very powerful tool for forecasting.

Advanced Forecasting Models

As we noted, MA and SES models work best for time series that do not exhibit trend or seasonality. Several other methods are often used when trend or seasonal factors exist. These are

- *Double moving average*—used for time series with a linear trend
- *Double exponential smoothing*—used for time series with a linear trend
- *Seasonal additive*—used for time series with seasonality that is relatively stable over time
- *Seasonal multiplicative*—used for time series with seasonality that is increasing or decreasing in magnitude over time
- *Holt–Winters additive*—used for time series with both a linear trend and seasonality that is relatively stable over time
- *Holt–Winters multiplicative*—used for time series with both a linear trend and seasonality that is increasing or decreasing in magnitude over time

Exhibit 11.20
Portions of *CBPredictor Report* Worksheet

Summary:
Number of series: 1
Periods to forecast: 1
Seasonality: none
Error Measure: RMSE

Series: ColumnB

Method: Single Exponential Smoothing
Parameters:
Alpha: 0.178
Error: 34.290

Series Statistics:
Mean: 198.4166667
Std. Dev.: 30.72298025
Minimum: 151
Maximum: 250
Ljung-Box: 2.3033

Forecast:

Date	Lower: 5%	Forecast	Upper: 95%
Period 13	136.6726327	198.207667	259.7427014

Method Errors:

	Method	RMSE	MAD	MAPE
Best:	Single Exponential Smoothing	34.29	28.697	14.23%
2nd:	Single Moving Average	36.563	31.457	16.45%

Method Statistics:

	Method	Durbin-Watson	Theil's U
Best:	Single Exponential Smoothing	2.289	0.717
2nd:	Single Moving Average	2.449	0.576

Method Parameters:

	Method	Parameter	Value
Best:	Single Exponential Smoothing	Alpha	0.178
2nd:	Single Moving Average	Periods	5

The theory and formulas for these models are quite a bit more complicated than for single moving average or single exponential smoothing, so we shall not cover them here. Instead, we will demonstrate the use of *CBPredictor* for applying some of these methods. Note that the graphs shown in the *Method Gallery* in Exhibit 11.19 suggest visually the method that is best suited for the data. Therefore, to select the proper method, you should always chart a time series first to scope out its characteristics or simply let *CBPredictor* run all models and identify the best.

To illustrate this, let us use the call center time series in Exhibit 11.7. This time series shows both a linear trend as well as seasonality. The seasonal pattern also appears to be increasing in magnitude over time, suggesting that the Holt–Winters multiplicative method is most appropriate. However, we will run all models in *CBPredictor* and see if this is true.

In the Data Attributes tab of the *CBPredictor* dialog, note that we specify that the data are in quarters with a seasonality of 4 quarters (see Exhibit 11.21). This ensures that the seasonal models will be tested. In the *Results* tab, we also specify that *CBPredictor* forecast the next four quarters. As expected, the Holt–Winters multiplicative model has the best error measures, as shown in Exhibit 11.22. You can see from the chart that the model provides a very good fit to the time series. The chart shows how well the model has forecasted the historical data along with forecasts for the next four quarters. The confidence intervals show that the fore-

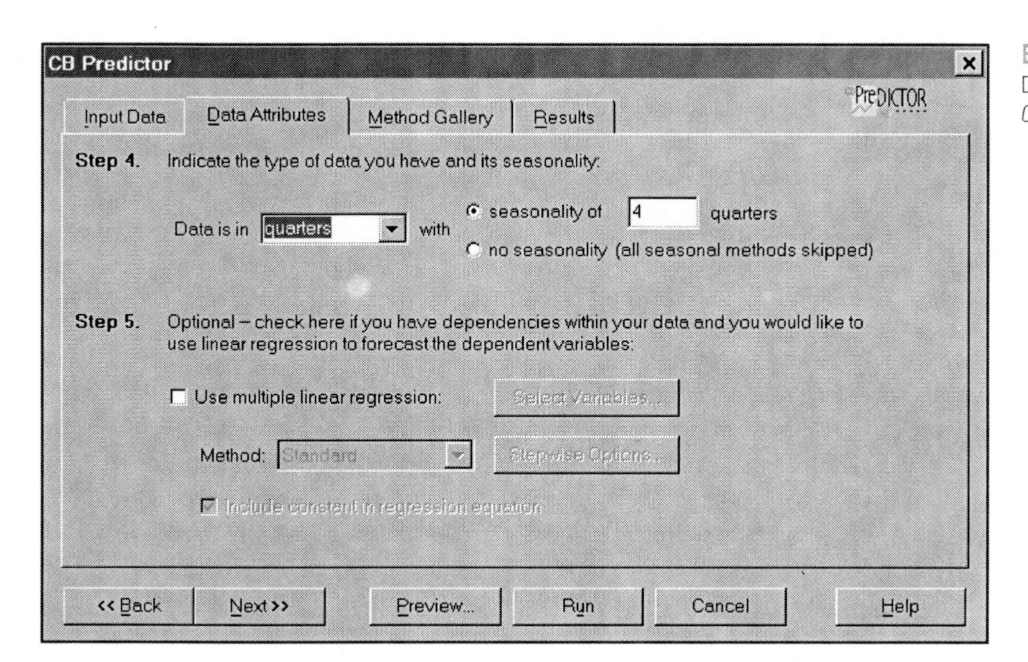

Exhibit 11.21
Data Attributes Tab of *CBPredictor* Dialog

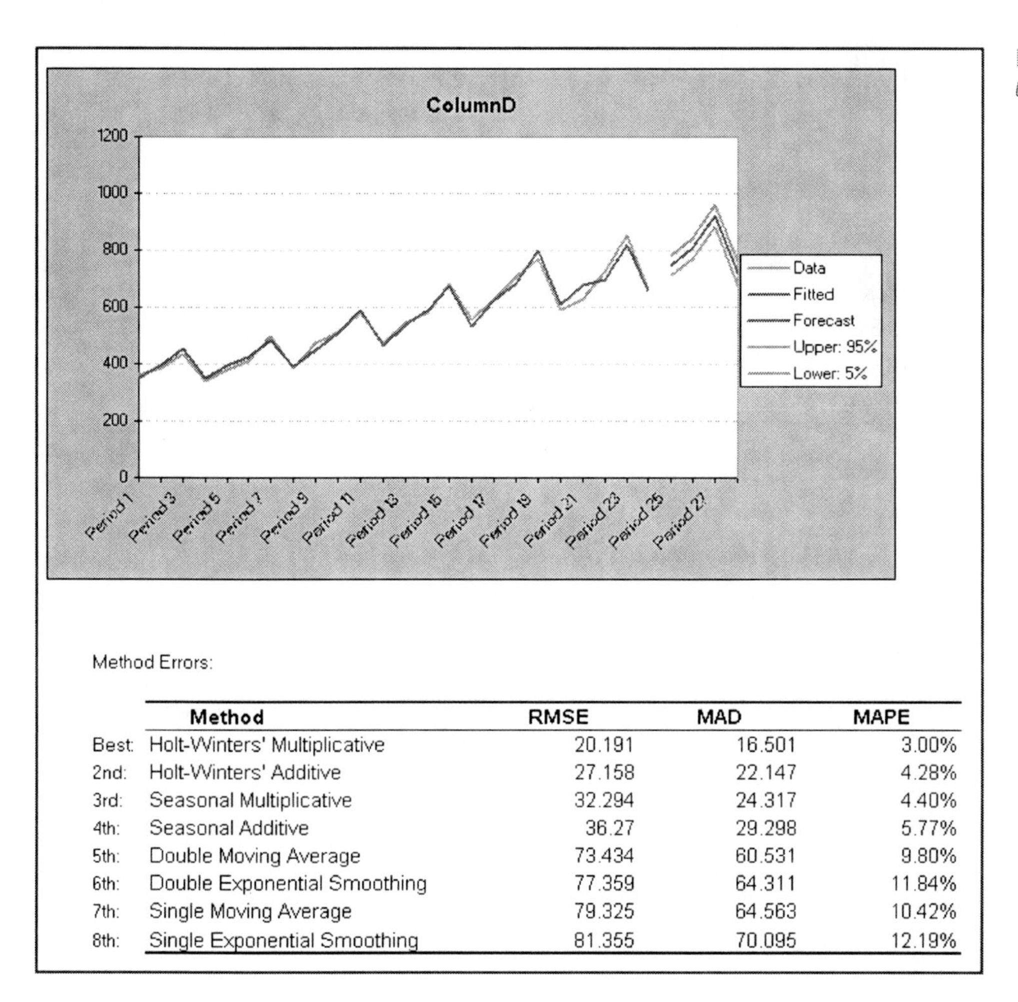

	Method	RMSE	MAD	MAPE
Best:	Holt-Winters' Multiplicative	20.191	16.501	3.00%
2nd:	Holt-Winters' Additive	27.158	22.147	4.28%
3rd:	Seasonal Multiplicative	32.294	24.317	4.40%
4th:	Seasonal Additive	36.27	29.298	5.77%
5th:	Double Moving Average	73.434	60.531	9.80%
6th:	Double Exponential Smoothing	77.359	64.311	11.84%
7th:	Single Moving Average	79.325	64.563	10.42%
8th:	Single Exponential Smoothing	81.355	70.095	12.19%

Exhibit 11.22
CBPredictor Results

casts should be quite accurate. *CBPredictor* pastes the forecasts in the data worksheet as specified in the *Results* tab. These are shown in Exhibit 11.23.

Exhibit 11.23
Call Center Volume Forecasts for Year 7

	A	B	C	D	E
1	Period	Year	Quarter	Call Volume	
2	1	1	1	362	
3	2	1	2	385	
4	3	1	3	432	
5	4	1	4	341	
6	5	2	1	382	
7	6	2	2	409	
8	7	2	3	498	
9	8	2	4	387	
10	9	3	1	473	
11	10	3	2	513	
12	11	3	3	582	
13	12	3	4	474	
14	13	4	1	544	
15	14	4	2	582	
16	15	4	3	681	
17	16	4	4	557	
18	17	5	1	628	
19	18	5	2	707	
20	19	5	3	773	
21	20	5	4	592	
22	21	6	1	627	
23	22	6	2	725	
24	23	6	3	854	
25	24	6	4	661	Forecasts
26	25	7	1		748.1127808
27	26	7	2		808.7917057
28	27	7	3		921.1043844
29	28	7	4		719.5947499

Learning Objective
To learn the basic ideas and method of regression analysis.

Regression analysis *is a method for building a statistical model that defines a relationship between a single dependent variable and one or more independent variables, all of which are numerical.*

REGRESSION AS A FORECASTING APPROACH

Regression analysis *is a method for building a statistical model that defines a relationship between a single dependent variable and one or more independent variables, all of which are numerical.* Regression analysis has wide applications in business; however, we will restrict our discussion to simple applications in forecasting. We will first consider only simple regression models in which the value of a time series (the dependent variable) is a function of a single independent variable, time.

Exhibit 11.24 shows total energy costs over the past 15 years at a manufacturing plant. The plant manager needs to forecast costs for the next year to prepare a budget for the VP of finance. The chart suggests that energy costs appear to be increasing in a fairly predictable linear fashion and that energy costs are related to time by a linear function

$$Y_t = a + bt \qquad \textbf{(11.8)}$$

where Y_t represents the estimate of the energy cost in year t. If we can identify the best values for a and b, which represent the intercept and slope of the straight line

Exhibit 11.24 Factory Energy Costs

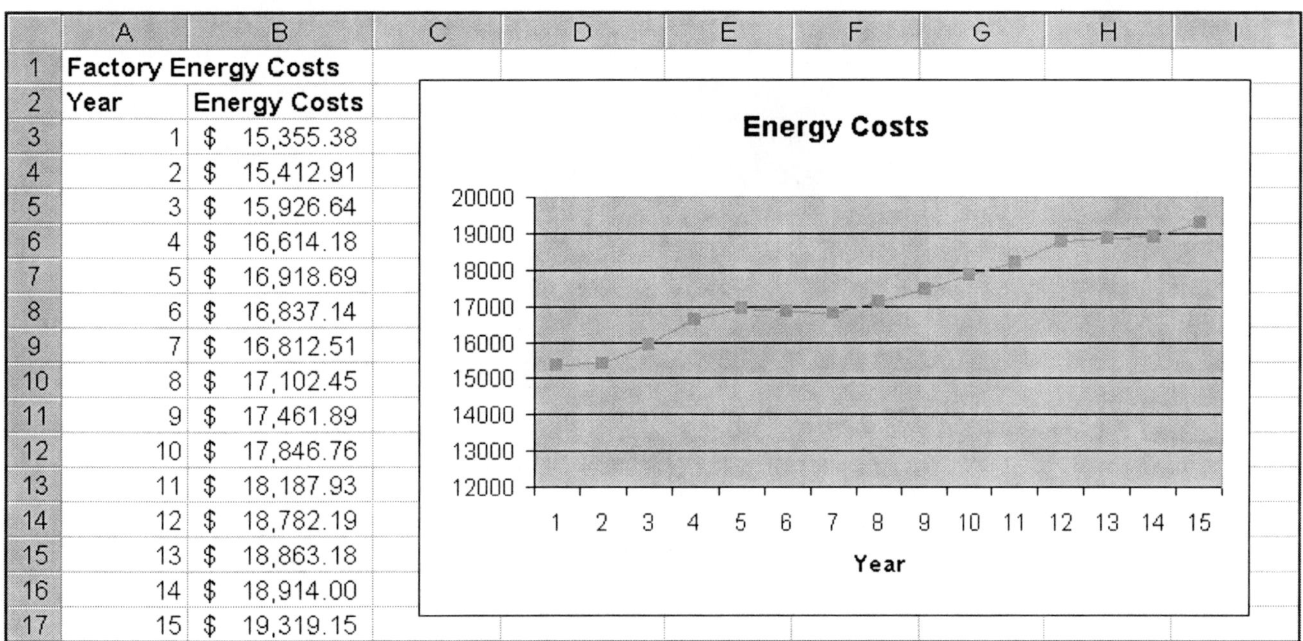

Factory Energy Costs	
Year	Energy Costs
1	$ 15,355.38
2	$ 15,412.91
3	$ 15,926.64
4	$ 16,614.18
5	$ 16,918.69
6	$ 16,837.14
7	$ 16,812.51
8	$ 17,102.45
9	$ 17,461.89
10	$ 17,846.76
11	$ 18,187.93
12	$ 18,782.19
13	$ 18,863.18
14	$ 18,914.00
15	$ 19,319.15

that best fits the time series, we can forecast cost for the next year by computing $Y_{16} = a + b(16)$.

Simple linear regression finds the best values of a and b using the *method of least squares*. The method of least squares minimizes the sum of the squared deviations between the actual time-series values (A_t) and the estimated values of the dependent variable (Y_t).

EXCEL'S ADD TRENDLINE OPTION

Excel provides a very simple tool to find the best-fitting regression model for a time series. First, select the chart in the worksheet. Then select the *Add Trendline* option from the *Chart* menu. The dialog box in Exhibit 11.25 is displayed, and you may choose among a linear and a variety of nonlinear functional forms to fit the data. Selecting an appropriate nonlinear form requires some advanced knowledge of functions and mathematics, so we will restrict our discussion to the linear case. From the *Options* tab (see Exhibit 11.26), you may customize the name of the trendline, forecast forward or backward, set the intercept at a fixed value, and display the regression equation and R-squared value on the chart by checking the appropriate boxes. Once Excel displays these results, you may move the equation and R-squared value for better readability by dragging them with a mouse. For the linear trendline option only, you may simply click on the data series in the chart to select the series, and then add a trend line by clicking on the right mouse button (try it!). Exhibit 11.27 shows the result. The model is

$$\text{Energy cost} = \$15{,}112 + 280.66(\text{Time})$$

Thus, to forecast the cost for the next year, we compute

$$\text{Energy cost} = \$15{,}112 + 280.66(16) = \$19{,}602.56$$

We could forecast further out into the future if we wish, but realize that the uncertainty of the accuracy of the forecast will be higher. The R^2 value is a measure of how much variation in the dependent variable (energy cost) is explained by the independent variable (time). The maximum value for R^2 is 1.0; therefore, the high

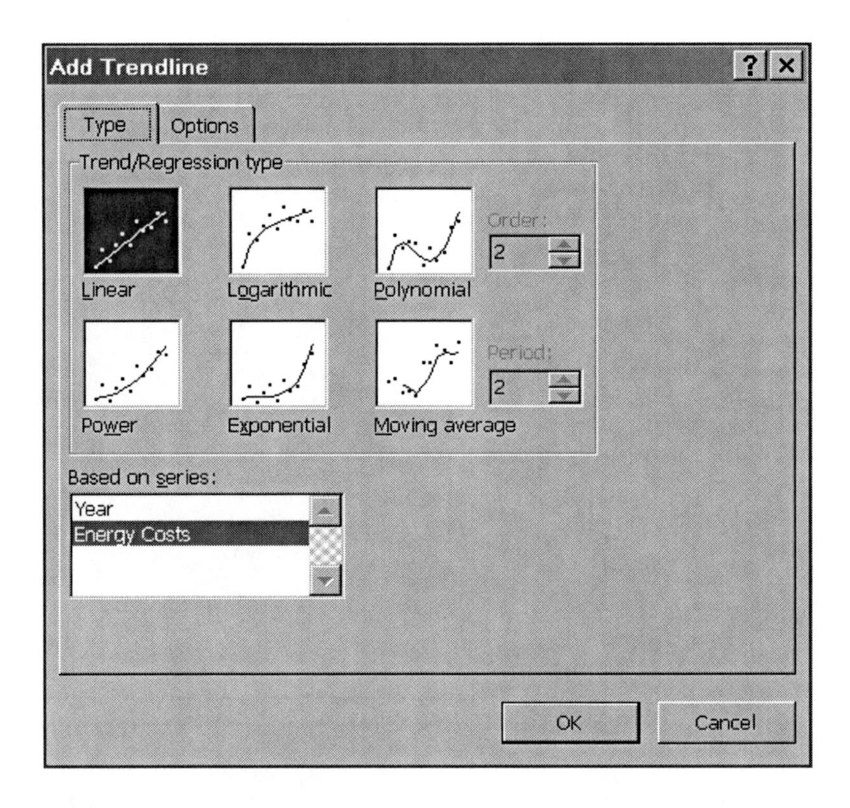

Exhibit 11.25
Add Trendline Dialog

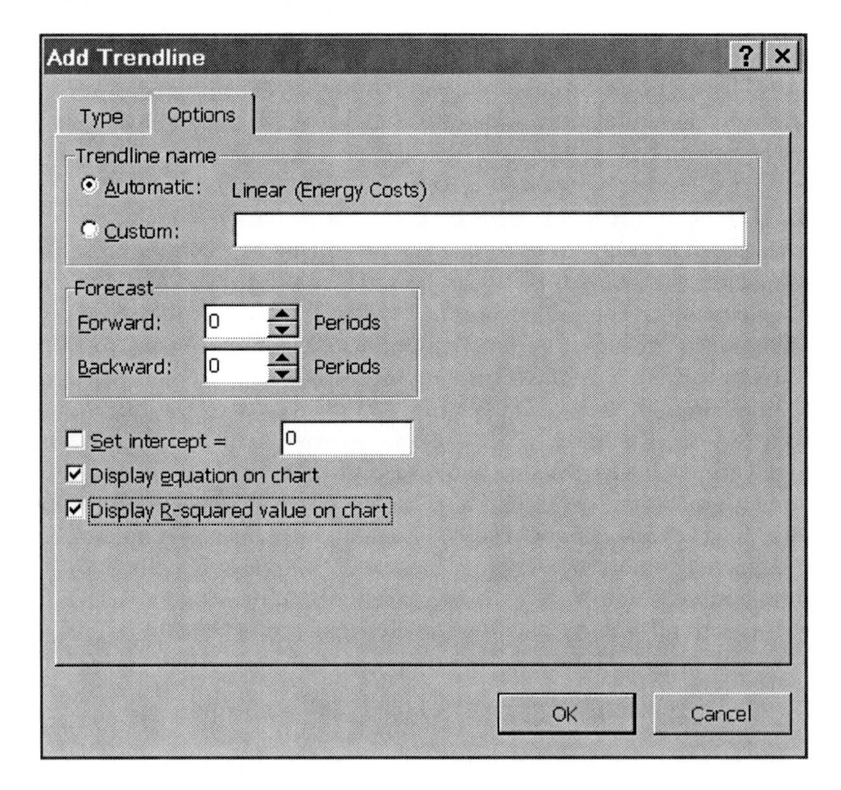

Exhibit 11.26
Add Trendline Options Tab

value of 0.97 suggests that the model will be a good predictor of cost. *CBPredictor* also has a regression option that can be selected in the *Data Attributes* tab. This option is useful for multiple linear regression models that involve several independent variables, which we illustrate next.

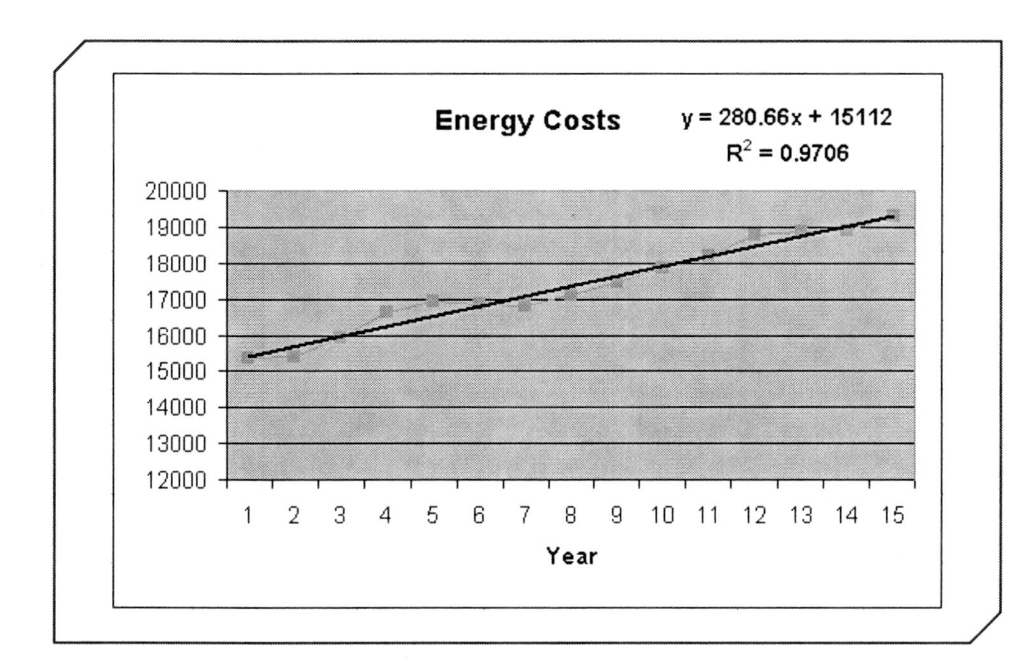

Exhibit 11.27
Least-Squares Regression Model for Energy Cost Forecasting

Causal Forecasting Models with Multiple Regression

In more advanced forecasting applications, other independent variables such as economic indexes or demographic factors that may influence the time series can be incorporated into a regression model (see OM Spotlight: California Electric Power Plant Closings). *A linear regression model with more than one independent variable is called a* **multiple linear regression model.**

A linear regression model with more than one independent variable is called a **multiple linear regression model.**

To illustrate the use of multiple linear regression for forecasting with causal variables, suppose that we wish to forecast gasoline sales. Exhibit 11.28 shows the sales over 10 weeks during June through August along with the average price per gallon. Exhibit 11.29 shows a chart of the gasoline-sales time series with a fitted

OM SPOTLIGHT

California Electric Power Plant Closings[6]

The California Independent System Operator's Board of Governors unanimously approved to close two electric power-generating plants in San Francisco by 2007. Both fossil-fuel power plants are well documented for polluting the environment. Community leaders are asking for a guaranteed date to close the two power plants down but PG&E Corporation and the board of governors cannot specify a date. Former Mayor Willie Brown promised to shut down these two plants in 1998. A PG&E spokesperson said, "If the electrical load grows unexpectedly fast, we are going to have to redo our action plan." Whether the plants can be closed is based on a demand forecast that is subject to much controversy. Area demographics, weather patterns, and economic growth patterns are all part of a demand forecast based on regression analysis.

Getty Images/PhotoDisc

Exhibit 11.28
Gasoline Sales Data

	A	B	C
1			
2	Gasoline Sales	Week	Price Per Gallon
3	10420	1	$ 1.95
4	7388	2	$ 2.20
5	7529	3	$ 2.12
6	11932	4	$ 1.98
7	10125	5	$ 2.01
8	15240	6	$ 1.92
9	12246	7	$ 2.03
10	11852	8	$ 1.98
11	16967	9	$ 1.82
12	19782	10	$ 1.90
13		11	$ 1.80

regression line. During the summer months, it is not unusual to see an increase in sales as more people go on vacations. The chart shows that the sales appear to increase over time with a linear trend, making linear regression an appropriate forecasting technique.

The fitted regression line is

$$\text{Sales} = 6{,}382 + 1{,}084.7 \times \text{Week}$$

The R^2 value of 0.6842 means that that about 68 percent of the variation in the data is explained by time. Using the model, we would predict sales for week 11 as

$$\text{Sales} = 6{,}382 + 1{,}084.7 \times 11 = 18{,}313.7$$

However, we also see that the average price per gallon changes each week, and this may influence consumer sales. Therefore, the sales trend might not simply be a factor of steadily increasing demand, but might also be influenced by the average price. Multiple regression provides a technique for building forecasting models that not only incorporate time, in this case, but other potential causal variables.

Exhibit 11.29
Chart of Sales Versus Time

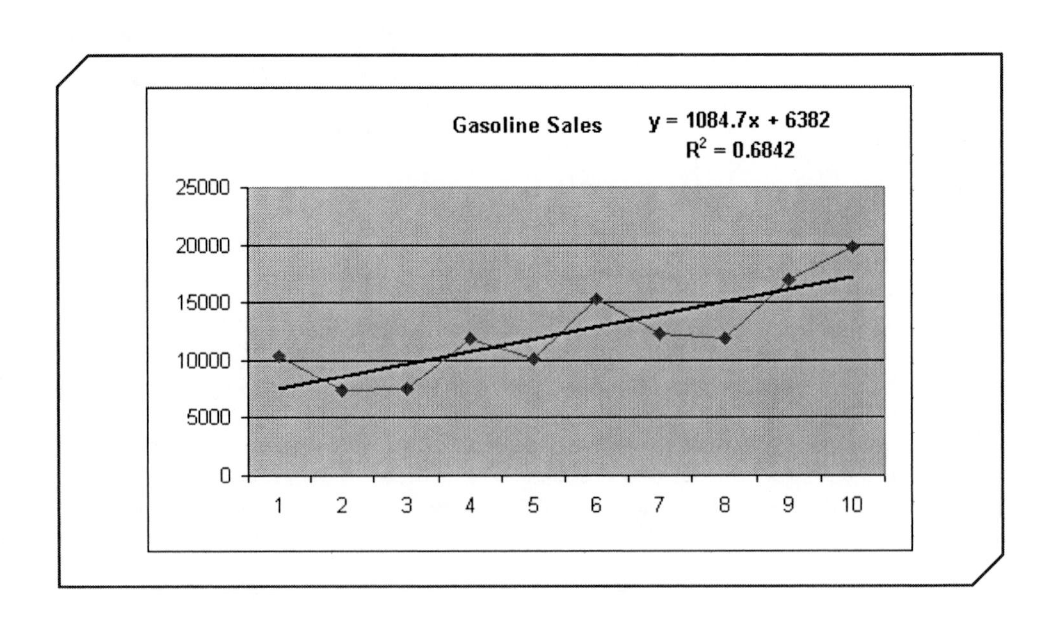

Thus, to forecast gasoline sales (that is, the dependent variable) we propose a model using two independent variables (weeks and price):

$$\text{Sales} = \beta_0 + \beta_1 \times \text{Week} + \beta_2 \times \text{Price}$$

Using the Excel Data Analysis tool for Regression, we obtain the results shown in Exhibit 11.30. The regression model is

$$\text{Sales} = 47{,}747.81 + 640.71 \times \text{Week} - 19{,}550.6 \times \text{Price}$$

This makes sense because as price increases, sales should decrease. Notice that the R^2 value is higher when both variables are included, explaining almost 86 percent of the variation in the data. The p-values for both variables are small, indicating that they are statistically significant variables in predicting sales.

Based on trends in crude oil prices, the company estimates that the average price for the next week will drop to \$1.80. Then, using this model we would forecast the sales for week 11 as

$$\text{Sales} = 47{,}747.81 + 640.71 \times 11 - 19{,}550.6 \times \$1.80 = \$19{,}604.54$$

Notice that this is higher than the pure time-series forecast because the price per gallon is estimated to fall in week 11 and result in a somewhat higher level of sales. The multiple regression model provides a more realistic and accurate forecast than simply extrapolating the historical time series. The theory of regression analysis is much more complex than presented here, so we caution you to consult more advanced books on the subject for a more complete treatment.

JUDGMENTAL FORECASTING

Learning Objective
To understand the role of human judgment in forecasting and when judgmental forecasting is most appropriate.

When no historical data are available, only judgmental forecasting is possible. But even when historical data are available and appropriate, they cannot be the sole basis for prediction. The demand for goods and services is affected by a variety of factors, such as global markets and cultures, interest rates, disposable income,

Exhibit 11.30 Multiple Regression Results

	A	B	C	D	E	F	G
1	SUMMARY OUTPUT						
2							
3	*Regression Statistics*						
4	Multiple R	0.92577504					
5	R Square	0.857059425					
6	Adjusted R Square	0.81621926					
7	Standard Error	1702.092291					
8	Observations	10					
9							
10	ANOVA						
11		*df*	*SS*	*MS*	*F*	*Significance F*	
12	Regression	2	121596103.7	60798051.87	20.98569971	0.001104191	
13	Residual	7	20279827.17	2897118.167			
14	Total	9	141875930.9				
15							
16		*Coefficients*	*Standard Error*	*t Stat*	*P-value*	*Lower 95%*	*Upper 95%*
17	Intercept	47747.81095	14266.13592	3.346933691	0.012302289	14013.78411	81481.8378
18	Week	640.7098599	241.6857585	2.651003782	0.032893732	69.21426278	1212.205457
19	Price Per Gallon	-19550.5999	6720.128757	-2.909259719	0.022684465	-35441.16797	-3660.031835

inflation, and technology. Competitors' actions and government regulations also have an impact. Thus, some element of judgmental forecasting is always necessary. One interesting example of the role of judgmental forecasting occurred during a national recession. All economic indicators pointed toward a future period of low demand for manufacturers of machine tools. However, the forecasters of one such company recognized that recent government regulations for automobile pollution control would require the auto industry to update its current technology by purchasing new tools. As a result, this machine tool company was prepared for the new business.

The **Delphi method** *consists of forecasting by expert opinion by gathering judgments and opinions of key personnel based on their experience and knowledge of the situation.*

One approach that is commonly used in judgmental forecasts is the Delphi method. *The* **Delphi method** *consists of forecasting by expert opinion by gathering judgments and opinions of key personnel based on their experience and knowledge of the situation.* In the Delphi method, a group of experts, possibly from both inside and outside the organization, are asked to make a prediction, such as industry sales for the next year. The experts are not consulted as a group so as not to bias their predictions—for example, because of dominant personalities in the group—but make their predictions and justifications independently. The responses and supporting arguments of each individual are summarized by an outside party and returned to the experts along with further questions. Experts whose opinions fall in the midrange of estimates as well as those whose predictions are extremely high or low (that is, outliers) might be asked to explain their predictions. The process iterates until a consensus is reached by the group, which usually takes only a few rounds.

The Delphi method can be used to predict qualitative as well as numerical outcomes. For instance, a company might be interested in predicting when a new law or regulation might pass the legislature. In a Delphi exercise, experts would be asked to select a date and justify it or select responses along some continuum, such as "highly certain" to "highly uncertain," or "strongly agree" to "strongly disagree."

Delphi results based on a few individuals are more risky than for larger groups and can be very inaccurate. However, some interesting research has observed that although any one individual might not develop accurate predictions, group consensus is often quite good.

Another common approach to gathering data for judgmental forecasts is a survey using a questionnaire, telephone contact, or personal interview. For example, telecommunication executives might be surveyed and ask to predict the cost of specific telephone services during the next 5 years. These data can be summarized and analyzed using basic statistical tools to help develop a reliable forecast. Sample sizes are usually much larger than with the Delphi method and expert opinion; however, the cost of such surveys can be high because of the labor involved, postage, low response rates, and postsurvey processing. Electronic surveys using the Internet have reduced these costs and increased the speed of obtaining results. Companies most often rely on managers' opinions for short-range forecasts and on group opinions for longer-range forecasts.

The major reasons given for using judgmental methods rather than quantitative methods are (1) greater accuracy, (2) ability to incorporate unusual or one-time events, and (3) the difficulty of obtaining the data necessary for quantitative techniques. Also, judgmental methods seem to create a feeling of "ownership" and add a commonsense dimension.

Learning Objective
To know that judgment and quantitative forecast methodologies can complement one another, and therefore improve overall forecast accuracy.

FORECASTING IN PRACTICE

In practice, managers use a variety of judgmental and quantitative forecasting techniques. Statistical methods alone cannot account for such factors as sales promotions, competitive strategies, unusual economic or environmental disturbances, new product introductions, large one-time orders, labor union strikes, and so on. Many managers begin with a statistical forecast and adjust it to account for such factors. Others may develop independent judgmental and statistical forecasts and then combine them, either objectively by averaging or in a subjective manner. It is impossible to provide universal guidance as to which approaches are best, for they depend on a variety of factors, including the presence or absence of trends and seasonality, the number of data points available, length of the forecast time horizon, and the experience and knowledge of the forecaster. Often, quantitative approaches will miss significant changes in the data, such as reversal of trends, while qualitative forecasts may catch them, particularly when using indicators as discussed earlier in this chapter. The events of 9/11, for example, made it difficult to use trends based on historical data. Quantitative forecasts often are adjusted judgmentally as managers incorporate environmental knowledge that is not captured in quantitative models.

The first step in developing a practical forecast is to understand the purpose of the forecast. For instance, if financial personnel need a sales forecast to determine capital investment strategies, a long (2- to 5-year) time horizon is necessary. For such forecasts, using aggregate groups of items is usually more accurate than using individual-item forecasts added together. These forecasts would probably be measured in dollars. In contrast, production personnel may need short-term forecasts for individual items as a basis for procurement of materials and scheduling. In this case, dollar values would not be appropriate; rather, forecasts should be made in terms of units of production. The level of aggregation often dictates the appropriate method. Forecasting the total amount of soap to produce over the next planning period is certainly different from forecasting the amount of each individual product to produce. Aggregate forecasts are generally much easier to develop, whereas detailed forecasts require more time and resources.

The choice of a forecasting method depends on other criteria as well. Among them are the time span for which the forecast is being made, the needed frequency of forecast updating, data requirements, the level of accuracy desired (see the OM Spotlight on Holland Hitch), and the quantitative skills needed. The time span is one of the most critical criteria. Different techniques are applicable for long-range,

OM SPOTLIGHT

Holland Hitch Company—Forecast Cost Versus Accuracy[7]

Courtesy of The Holland Group, Inc.

The Holland Hitch Company, part of the Holland Group, manufactures the coupling device used to hitch the tractor to the trailers. In the midst of a business process reengineering initiative, executives at Holland Hitch Company realized that they needed better forecast accuracy. To evaluate different forecasting software vendors, Holland Hitch had each vendor develop a forecast for this year based on the actual sales data from last year. Many other criteria were used in evaluating each vendor such as the ease of integrating with other demand planning and supply chain modules, scalability, reasonable software and training costs, and forecast accuracy. The software vendor who was hired developed forecasts across Holland's major product lines with an average of 98 percent accuracy. Other benefits of the new forecasting system were much better customer service and an increase in inventory turnover rates from the 2–3 range to the 9–10 range. These operational benefits far exceeded the cost to implement and maintain the forecasting system.

intermediate-range, and short-range forecasts. Also important is the frequency of updating that will be necessary. For example, the Delphi method takes considerable time to implement and thus would not be appropriate for forecasts that must be updated frequently.

Bias is the tendency of forecasts to consistently be larger or smaller than the actual values of the time series.

Forecasters should also monitor a forecast to determine when it might be advantageous to change or update the model. A *tracking signal* provides a method for doing this by quantifying **bias** – *the tendency of forecasts to consistently be larger or smaller than the actual values of the time series.* The tracking method used most often is to compute the cumulative forecast error divided by the value of MAD at that point in time; that is,

$$\text{Tracking signal} = \Sigma(A_t - F_t)/\text{MAD} \quad \textbf{(11.9)}$$

Typically, tracking signals between plus or minus 4 indicate that the forecast is performing adequately. Values outside this range indicate that you should reevaluate the model used.

SOLVED PROBLEMS

SOLVED PROBLEM #1

A retail store records customer demand during each sales period. Use the following demand data to develop three-period and four-period moving-average forecasts and single exponential smoothing forecasts with α = 0.5. Compute the MAD, MAPE, and MSE for each. Which method provides the better forecast?

Period	Demand	Period	Demand
1	86	7	91
2	93	8	93
3	88	9	96
4	89	10	97
5	92	11	93
6	94	12	95

Solution:

	A	B	C	D	E
1	Solved Problem 1				Exponential
2	Period	Demand	3-Month MA	4-Month MA	Smoothing
3	1	86			86
4	2	93			86
5	3	88			89.5
6	4	89	89.00		88.75
7	5	92	90.00	89.00	88.88
8	6	94	89.67	90.50	90.44
9	7	91	91.67	90.75	92.22
10	8	93	92.33	91.50	91.61
11	9	96	92.67	92.50	92.30
12	10	97	93.33	93.50	94.15
13	11	93	95.33	94.25	95.58
14	12	95	95.33	94.75	94.29
15		MAD	1.93	2.09	2.53
16		MSE	5.96	6.21	9.65
17		MAPE	2.04%	2.22%	2.71%

Based on these error metrics, the 3-month moving average is the best method among these three. The chart showing these forecasts is shown next.

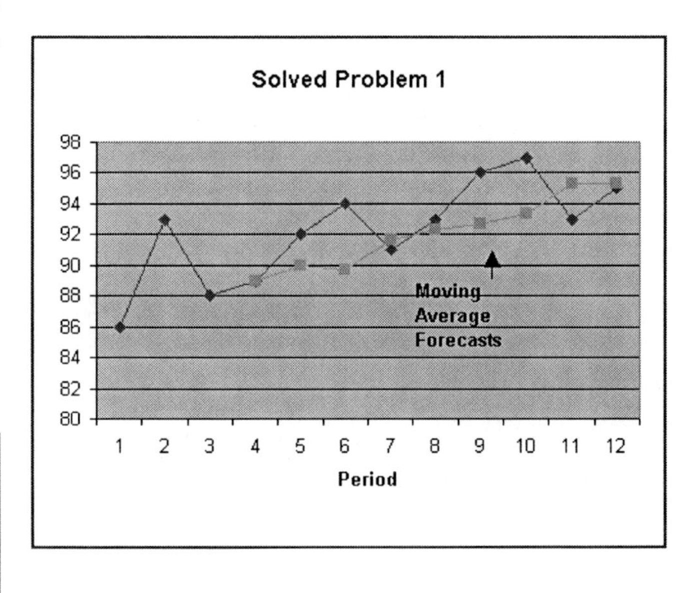

SOLVED PROBLEM #2

Average attendance figures at a major university's home football games have generally been increasing as the team's performance and popularity has been improving:

Year	Attendance
1	26,000
2	30,000
3	31,500
4	40,000
5	33,000
6	32,200
7	35,000

Solution:

A chart of these data and a fitted trend line are shown next. The forecast for the next year (Year 8) would be

$$\text{Attendance} = 1{,}175(8) + 27{,}829 = 37{,}229$$

However, Year 4 appears to be an unusual value, or "outlier." Outliers can significantly change the results. If we delete this value, we obtain the model $Y = 1{,}175x + 26{,}583$ with $R^2 = 0.82$. The forecast would be $1{,}175(8) + 26{,}583 = 35{,}983$. Checking for outliers is an important preliminary step before doing regression. However, you should only delete outliers for logical reasons. Here, if the large attendance was because of a cross-state rivalry that was a one-time event, then it should not be included in the model.

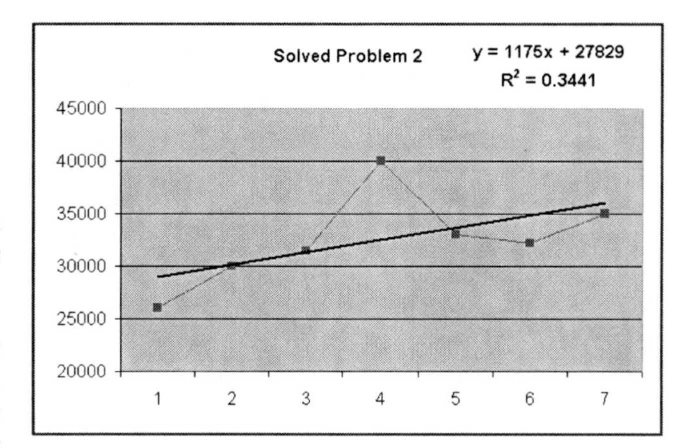

SOLVED PROBLEM #3

The data shown in Exhibit 11.31 represent the number of orders received by a supplier for a particular item from business customers. What is the best forecasting model that the firm should use? Before reading on, what method do you think *CBPredictor* will choose based on the form of the time series in Exhibit 11.31?

Solution:

Using *CBPredictor*, be sure to note that the data are in days with no seasonality in the *Data Attributes* tab. All methods were selected, and the Double Moving Average method with 8 periods was found to be the best, as shown in the following figure.

Methods	Rank	RMSE	MAD	MAPE	Durbin-Watson	Theil's U	Periods	Alpha	Beta
Double Exponential Smoothing	4	21.039	16.658	15.063	1.937	1.171		0.612	0.446
Double Moving Average	**1**	**13.292**	**10.474**	**8.277**	**1.663**	**0.885**	**8**		
Single Exponential Smoothing	3	16.783	12.33	11.834	1.888	0.763		0.357	
Single Moving Average	2	13.725	10.694	8.464	1.127	1.009	10		

If you examine the *CBPredictor Method Gallery*, you should have guessed that either a double exponential smoothing or double moving-average model would be the best because the time series show random fluctuation around a linear trend.

The chart at the right shows the fitted model against the time series. Because double exponential smoothing "smooths out" single exponential smoothing forecasts, it requires twice the number of periods before actually generating a forecast. Thus, the fitted line does not begin until period 16.

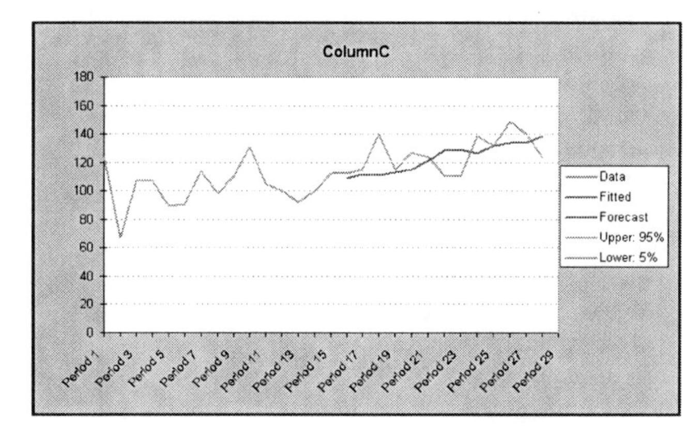

Exhibit 11.31 Data for Solved Problem #3

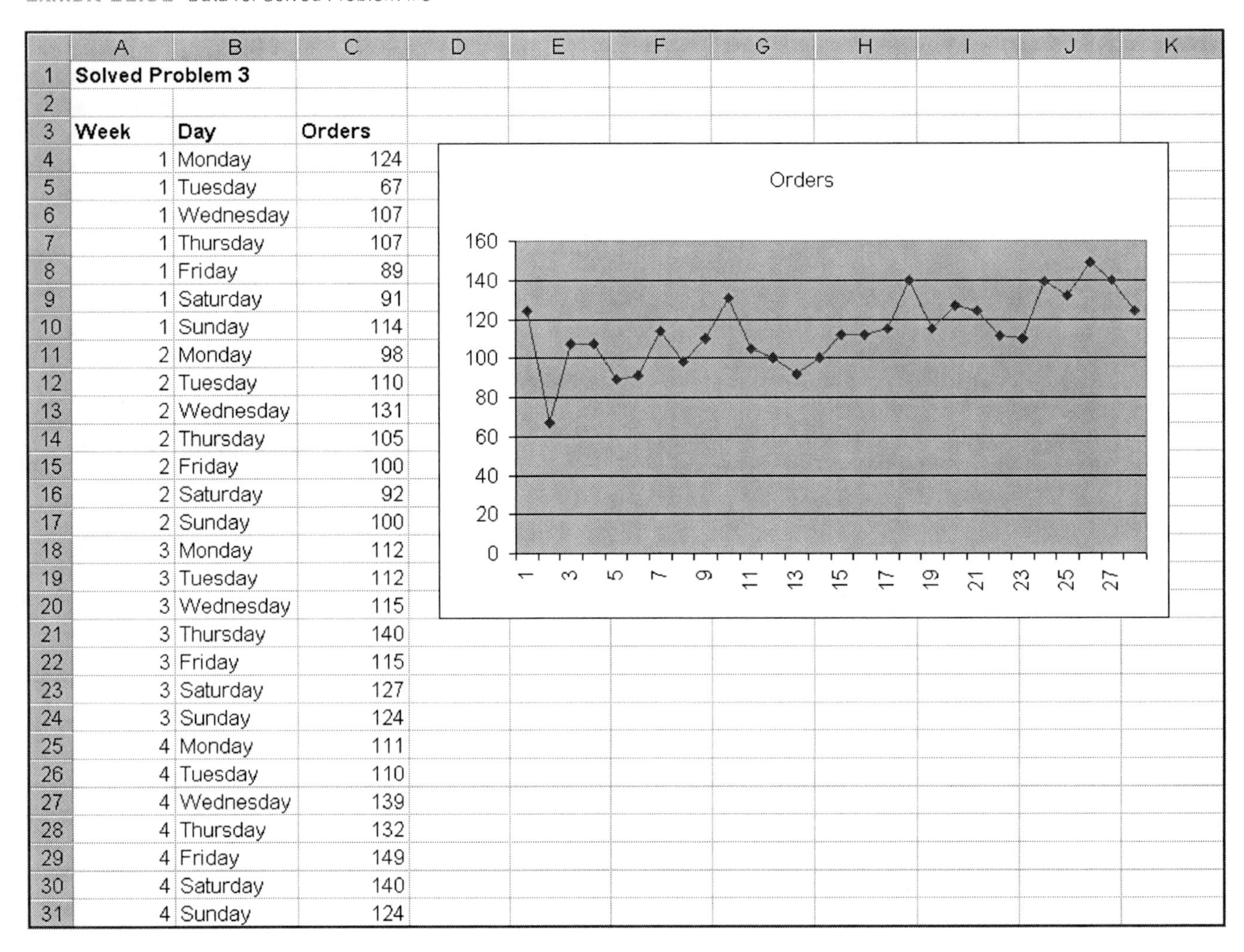

	A	B	C
1	**Solved Problem 3**		
2			
3	**Week**	**Day**	**Orders**
4	1	Monday	124
5	1	Tuesday	67
6	1	Wednesday	107
7	1	Thursday	107
8	1	Friday	89
9	1	Saturday	91
10	1	Sunday	114
11	2	Monday	98
12	2	Tuesday	110
13	2	Wednesday	131
14	2	Thursday	105
15	2	Friday	100
16	2	Saturday	92
17	2	Sunday	100
18	3	Monday	112
19	3	Tuesday	112
20	3	Wednesday	115
21	3	Thursday	140
22	3	Friday	115
23	3	Saturday	127
24	3	Sunday	124
25	4	Monday	111
26	4	Tuesday	110
27	4	Wednesday	139
28	4	Thursday	132
29	4	Friday	149
30	4	Saturday	140
31	4	Sunday	124

KEY TERMS AND CONCEPTS

Bias
CBPredictor
Data patterns
- Business cycle
- Irregular variation
- Random variation (noise)
- Seasonal
- Time series
- Trend—linear and nonlinear

Forecast errors and accuracy
- Mean absolute deviation (MAD)
- Mean absolute percentage error (MAPE)
- Mean squared deviation (MSD)

Forecasting
Judgmental forecasting methods
- Delphi
- Market surveys

Moving averages
Multiple linear regression model
Planning horizon
- Intermediate-range
- Long-range
- Short-range

Regression analysis
Simple regression as a forecasting tool
Single exponential smoothing (SES)
Smoothing constant
Statistical forecasting methods
Time bucket size
Tracking signal
Weighted averages

QUESTIONS FOR REVIEW AND DISCUSSION

1. What is forecasting? Why is it important at all levels of an organization and in operations in particular?
2. Discuss some forecasting issues that you encounter in your daily life. How do you make your forecasts?
3. How are forecasts used throughout the value chain?
4. What is the role of forecasting in demand planning processes?
5. Explain the importance of selecting the proper planning horizon in forecasting.
6. What is a time series, and what characteristics might it have?
7. Explain why time series might exhibit trend, cyclical, and seasonal patterns.
8. Summarize the different types of forecasting methods that are used in business.
9. What is the difference between statistical and judgmental forecasting methods?
10. Define *forecast error*. Explain how to calculate the three common measures of forecast accuracy.
11. What capabilities does *CBPredictor* have that make it superior to simply using Excel and the Data Analysis tools?
12. Explain how to compute single moving-average forecasts.
13. What is the difference between single moving average and weighted moving average? When might you choose one over the other?
14. Explain the process of single exponential smoothing.
15. How does exponential smoothing incorporate all historical data into a forecast?
16. Summarize the advanced types of forecasting models available in *CBPredictor*. To what types of time series are they most applicable?
17. How does regression differ from time-series methods?
18. What is the value of using judgmental forecasting techniques? How might one choose between statistical and judgmental methods?
19. Explain how judgmental forecasting might be used to predict the timing of market saturation of a new high-tech product.
20. Discuss some practical ways to design a forecasting system for an organization.
21. Interview a previous employer about how it makes forecasts. Document in one page what you discovered, and describe it using the ideas discussed in this chapter.
22. What is bias in forecasting? Explain the importance of using tracking signals to monitor forecasts.

PROBLEMS AND ACTIVITIES

1. Forecasts and actual sales of MP3 players at *Just Say Music* are as follows:

Month	Forecast	Actual Sales
March	150	170
April	220	229
May	205	192
June	256	271
July	250	238
August	260	255
September	270	290
October	280	279
November	296	301

   a. Plot the data and provide insights about the time series.
   b. What is the forecast for December, using a three-period moving average?
   c. What is the forecast for December, using a four-period moving average?
   d. Compute the MAD, MAPE, and MSE for parts b and c and compare your results.
   e. Might double exponential smoothing work better? Why or why not? Use *CBPredictor* to answer this question.

2. For the data in Problem 1, find the best single exponential smoothing model by evaluating the MSE for α from 0.1 to 0.9, in increments of 0.1.

3. The monthly sales of a new business software package at a local discount software store were as follows:

Week	1	2	3	4	5	6
Sales	360	415	432	460	488	512

a. Plot the data and provide insights about the time series.
b. Find the best number of weeks to use in a moving-average forecast based on MSE.
c. Find the best single exponential smoothing model to forecast these data.

4. The president of a small manufacturing firm is concerned about the continual growth in manufacturing costs in the past several years. The data series of the cost per unit for the firm's leading product over the past 8 years are given as follows:

Year	Cost/Unit ($)	Year	Cost/Unit ($)
1	20.00	5	26.60
2	24.50	6	30.00
3	28.20	7	31.00
4	27.50	8	36.00

a. Construct a chart for this time series. Does a linear trend appear to exist?
b. Develop a simple linear regression model for these data. What average cost increase has the firm been realizing per year?

5. Canton Supplies, Inc. is a service firm that employs approximately 100 people. Because of the necessity of meeting monthly cash obligations, the chief financial officer wants to develop a forecast of monthly cash requirements. Because of a recent change in equipment and operating policy, only the past 7 months of data are considered relevant

Month	Cash Required ($1,000)	Month	Cash Required ($1,000)
1	205	5	230
2	212	6	240
3	218	7	246
4	224		

a. Plot the data.
b. What forecasting method do you recommend and why?
c. Use your recommendation to obtain a forecast for Month 8.

6. The Costello Music Company has been in business 5 years. During that time its sales of electric organs have grown from 12 units to 76 units per year. Fred Costello, the firm's owner, wants to forecast next year's organ sales. The historical data follow:

Year	1	2	3	4	5
Sales	12	28	34	50	76

a. Construct a chart for this time series.
b. What forecasting method do you recommend and why?
c. Use your recommendation to obtain a forecast for Years 6 and 7.

7. Consider the quarterly sales data for Kilbourne Health Club shown here:

	Quarter				
Year	1	2	3	4	Total Sales
1	4	2	1	5	12
2	6	4	4	14	28
3	10	3	5	16	34
4	12	9	7	22	50
5	18	10	13	35	76

a. Develop a 4-period moving average model and compute MAD, MAPE, and MSE for your forecasts.
b. Find a good value of α for a single exponential smoothing model and compare your results to part (a).
c. Apply *CBPredictor* to find the best model to forecast sales for the next four quarters.

8. The number of component parts used in a production process each of the last 10 weeks is as follows:

Week	Parts	Week	Parts
1	200	6	210
2	350	7	280
3	250	8	350
4	360	9	290
5	250	10	320

a. Developing moving average models with 2, 3, and 4 periods. Compare them using MAD, MAPE, and MSE to determine which is best.
b. Use *CBPredictor* to find the best forecast for the next week.

9. The manufacturer of gas outdoor grills provides sales data for the last 3 years as follows:

	Quarter Number			
Year	1	2	3	4
1	20,000	40,000	50,000	20,000
2	30,000	60,000	60,000	50,000
3	40,000	50,000	70,000	50,000

a. Develop single exponential smoothing models with $\alpha = 0.2$, 0.4, and 0.6. Compare these models using MAD, MAPE, and MSE metrics to identify the best one.
b. Use *CBPredictor* to find the best forecasting model. What are your forecasts for the next four quarters?

10. The historical demand for the Panasonic Model 304 Pencil Sharpener is: January, 80; February, 100; March, 60; April, 80; and May, 90 units.
a. Using a 4-month moving average, what is the forecast for June? If June experienced a demand of 100, what is the forecast for July?
b. Using single exponential smoothing with $\alpha = 0.2$, if the forecast for January had been 70, compute what the exponential forecast would have been for the remaining months through June.

c. Develop a linear regression model, and compute a forecast for June, July, and August.
d. Using a weighted moving average with weights of 0.30, 0.25, 0.20, 0.15, and 0.10, what is June's forecast?

11. Two experienced managers are resisting the introduction of a computerized exponential smoothing system, claiming that their judgmental forecasts are much better than any computer could do. Their past record of predictions is as follows:

Week	Actual Demand	Manager's Forecast
1	4,000	4,500
2	4,200	5,000
3	4,200	4,000
4	3,000	3,800
5	3,800	3,600
6	5,000	4,000
7	5,600	5,000
8	4,400	4,800
9	5,000	4,000
10	4,800	5,000

Based on whatever calculations you think appropriate, are the manager's judgmental forecasts performing satisfactorily?

12. A chain of grocery stores had the following weekly demand (cases) for a particular brand of laundry soap:

Week	1	2	3	4	5	6	7	8	9	10
Demand	31	22	33	26	21	29	25	22	20	26

a. Develop three- and four-period moving average forecasts, and compute MSE for each. Which provides the better forecast? What would be your forecast for week 11?
b. Develop an exponential smoothing forecast with smoothing constants of $\alpha = 0.1$ and 0.3. What would be your forecast for week 11?
c. Compute the tracking signal for each of your forecasts in parts (a) and (b). Is there any evidence of bias?
d. Might a different model provide better results?

13. Sales of surfboards for the last 5 years are shown here in millions of dollars.

Year, Quarter	Time (X)	Sales (Y)
1, Q1	1	2
1, Q2	2	4
1, Q3	3	5
1, Q4	4	4
2, Q1	5	3
2, Q2	6	5
2, Q3	7	7
2, Q4	8	5
3, Q1	9	4
3, Q2	10	8
3, Q3	11	9
3, Q4	12	6
4, Q1	13	5
4, Q2	14	8
4, Q3	15	10
4, Q4	16	6
5, Q1	17	6
5, Q2	18	7
5, Q3	19	9
5, Q4	20	7

a. Forecast the four quarters of Year 6 using *CBPredictor*.
b. If annual sales in Year 6 were forecast to be $40 million, what is the forecast of sales by quarter?

CASES

BANKUSA: FORECASTING HELP DESK DEMAND BY DAY (A)

"Hello, is this the Investment Management Help Desk?" said a tired voice on the other end of the telephone line at 7:42 A.M. "Yes you have the right place, how can I help you?" said Thomas Bourbon, the customer service representative (CSR) who received this inquiry. "Well, I've got a problem. My best customer, with assets of over $10 million in our bank, received his monthly trust account statement. He says we inaccurately computed the market value of one of his stocks by using an inaccurate share price. He says this error makes his statement $42,000 too low. I assured him we would research the problem and get back to him by the end of the day. Also, do you realize that I waited over 4 minutes before you answered my telephone call!" said the trust administrator, Chris Eddins. "Mr. Eddins, give me the customers' account number and the stock in question, and I'll get back to you within the hour. Let's solve the customer's problem first. I apologize for the long wait," said Bourbon in a positive and reassuring voice.

The Help Desk supports fiduciary operations activities worldwide by answering questions and inquiries from company employees, such as portfolio managers, stock traders, backroom company process managers, branch bank managers, accountants, and trust account administrators. These internal customers originate over

98 percent of the volume of Help Desk inquiries. Over 50 different internal processes and organizational units call the Help Desk. Some external customers such as large estate and trust administrators are directly tied via the Internet to their accounts and occasionally call the Help Desk directly.

The Help Desk is a unit of the bank's fiduciary operations group. The Help Desk services internal and external customers through the identification, resolution, and reduction of future investment services inquiries. Fiduciary Operations is an area of the bank that supports many of the products and services of the BankUSA Investment Management Division. The Investment Management Division manages over $300 billion in assets for individual and institutional portfolios and mutual funds. Fiduciary Operations employs over 1,000 people with a wide range of skills, such as information and financial officers, process managers, and human resource management employees.

The Help Desk is the primary customer contact unit within Fiduciary Operations. The Help Desk employs 14 full time customer service representative (CSRs), 3 CSR support employees, and 3 managers, for a total of 20 people. The 3 CSR support employees do research on a full-time basis in support of the CSRs answering the telephone.

The skill of the Help Desk's customer service representative is critical in providing good, friendly, and competent service to both internal and external customers. The bank and its geographically dispersed businesses call the Help Desk but seldom if ever visit the call (contact) center. Although Fiduciary Operations supports many activities of the bank, such as executing billions of dollars of financial transactions daily, the interaction with the Help Desk is where company employees and managers form their impression of Fiduciary Operations. Most often these inquiries are because someone is having a problem or needs a correct and quick answer to an external customer's question.

The Help Desk handles about 2,000 calls a week. Although the Help Desk was the primary gateway and contact center for Fiduciary Operations, the pressure to reduce unit cost was ongoing. Forecast accuracy was a key input to better staffing decisions that minimize costs and maximize service. The data in Exhibit 11.32 is the number of calls per week (Call Volume), day of the week (DOW), and day of week ID (DOW ID). The data set of 16 daily observations is contained on the textbook's CD.

The senior manager of the Help Desk, Dot Gifford, established a team to try to evaluate short-term forecasting at the Help Desk. The "Help Desk Staffing Team" consisted of Gifford, Bourbon, Chris Paris, and a new employee of the bank, David Hamlet, with an undergraduate major in operations management at a leading business school. This four-person team was charged with developing a long-term forecasting procedure for the Help Desk. Gifford asked the team to make an informal presentation of their analysis in 10 days. The primary job of analysis fell on Samantha Jenkins, the newly hired operations analyst. It would be her chance to make a good first impression on her boss and colleagues.

Question for Part A of the Case: Using the information in Exhibit 11.32, what should Jenkins do to determine the best method or methods to forecast these data?

Exhibit 11.32

Example Call Volume Data by Day for BankUSA [see the file BankUSA Forecasting Case Data.xls on the student CD-ROM]

Day	CALL VOLUME	DOW	DOW ID
1	413	Fri	5
2	536	Mon	1
3	495	Tue	2
4	451	Wed	3
5	480	Thu	4
6	400	Fri	5
7	525	Mon	1
8	490	Tues	2
9	492	Wed	3
10	519	Thu	4
11	402	Fri	5
12	616	Mon	1
13	485	Tues	2
14	527	Wed	3
15	461	Thu	4
16	370	Fri	5

BANKUSA: FORECASTING HELP DESK DEMAND BY HOUR OF THE DAY (B)

Review the background on BankUSA in part A of the preceding case.

Question for Part B of the Case: The team's objectives are stated as: (1) What forecasting methods should we adopt? (2) What is the forecast for each day of next week (that is, days 11 to 15)? (3) How might these forecasts be used to drive staff planning and scheduling? Using the data in Exhibit 11.33, help Jenkins meet these objectives.

Exhibit 11.33 Help Desk Inquiry Volumes by Hour of Day (B)

Time of Day	Monday Day 1	Tuesday Day 2	Wednesday Day 3	Thursday Day 4	Friday Day 5	Weekly Total	Monday Day 6	Tuesday Day 7	Wednesday Day 8	Thursday Day 9	Friday Day 10	Weekly Total
7:00–7:30 A.M.	2	0	0	0	0	**2**	0	0	1	1	1	**3**
7:30–8:00 A.M.	2	2	4	0	3	**11**	3	4	3	0	2	**12**
8:00–8:30 A.M.	6	4	5	5	7	**27**	15	4	5	3	7	**34**
8:30–9:00 A.M.	16	26	10	7	16	**75**	12	11	5	9	9	**46**
9:00–9:30 A.M.	17	20	18	14	23	**92**	22	11	21	18	16	**88**
9:30–10:00 A.M.	22	19	29	23	23	**116**	25	18	25	29	20	**117**
10:00–10:30 A.M.	31	24	24	33	18	**130**	31	30	31	35	15	**142**
10:30–11:00 A.M.	29	40	29	31	21	**150**	26	30	24	33	27	**140**
11:00–11:30 A.M.	21	37	28	28	23	**137**	18	24	25	34	28	**129**
11:30–12:00 P.M.	19	24	28	23	22	**116**	32	32	27	23	22	**136**
12:00–12:30 P.M.	33	28	18	17	20	**116**	24	18	26	27	19	**114**
12:30–1:00 P.M.	18	18	16	15	18	**85**	17	32	20	23	18	**110**
1:00–1:30 P.M.	18	15	20	16	15	**84**	23	16	25	16	22	**102**
1:30–2:00 P.M.	23	24	15	25	15	**102**	15	18	16	19	13	**81**
2:00–2:30 P.M.	28	13	15	26	18	**100**	17	22	20	26	26	**111**
2:30–3:00 P.M.	20	23	23	26	25	**117**	26	27	16	20	18	**107**
3:00–3:30 P.M.	17	28	16	21	21	**103**	23	20	25	28	22	**118**
3:30–4:00 P.M.	30	22	31	18	23	**124**	21	22	19	32	18	**112**
4:00–4:30 P.M.	25	27	22	17	24	**115**	25	22	12	30	13	**102**
4:30–5:00 P.M.	14	16	17	8	20	**75**	26	20	18	18	12	**94**
5:00–5:30 P.M.	17	14	7	5	8	**51**	13	15	13	13	9	**63**
5:30–6:00 P.M.	5	12	5	2	10	**34**	5	5	6	6	5	**27**
6:00–6:30 P.M.	4	5	3	1	0	**13**	4	3	1	1	3	**12**
6:30–7:00 P.M.	1	3	1	0	0	**5**	1	0	0	1		**2**
Total	**418**	**444**	**384**	**361**	**373**	**1,980**	**424**	**404**	**384**	**445**	**345**	**2,002**

ENDNOTES

[1] "Holding Patterns," *CIO Magazine*, www.cio.com/archive May 15, 1999.
[2] http://www.sap.com/solutions/scm/demand/.
[3] "Colgate Supports Its Worldwide Brands with mySAP Supply Chain Management," http://www.sap.com/solutions/business-suite/scm/customersuccess/index.aspx, December 6, 2004.
[4] Gilliland, M., "Is Forecasting a Waste of Time?" *Supply Chain Management Review*, www.manufacturing.net/scm, July/August 2002.
[5] See, for example, Yurkiewicz, Jack, "Forecasting Software Survey," *ORMS Today* 30, no. 1, February 2003, pp. 44–51.
[6] "Cal ISO Okays Plan to Shut 2 San Francisco Power Plants," The Wall Street Journal Online, November 10, 2004, http://online.wsj.com/article.
[7] http://www.i2.com/web505/media/F8875AFA-990B-484B-A91F87436BB8B8AB.pdf.

Chapter Outline

CHAPTER 15 Quality Management

Learning Objectives

1. To learn how quality management has evolved and changed focus over the years and why organizations need to continue to place a significant amount of emphasis on quality.

2. To understand what quality means in manufacturing and service operations, how organizations should address customer expectations and perceptions, and how quality is integrated into operations through customer focus, continuous improvement, and employee involvement.

3. To understand the quality philosophies and principles of Deming, Juran, and Crosby and how these individuals influenced the quality management practices of today's organizations.

4. To become acquainted with the International Organization for Standardization's ISO 9000:2000 requirements, documentation, and certification for meeting a family of quality standards used in many international markets.

5. To understand the principal activities that organizations must incorporate into an effective quality management system to support operations.

6. To understand the basic philosophy and methods of Six Sigma and how it is applied in organizations to improve quality and operations performance.

7. To learn about the features of elementary quality analysis and improvement tools and be able to apply them to practical business problems.

• "Wow!" exclaimed Lauren when she saw the ski runs at Deer Valley Resort in Park City, Utah. "Thanks for taking me! This sure beats the little ski hill we have in the Midwest." "You bet. Too bad Mom doesn't ski; look at what she's missing. Just take it slow and make sure I can keep up with you!" replied her dad. He knew that Deer Valley has been called "The Ritz-Carlton" of ski resorts, and this was his first trip to Utah also. He was expecting exceptional services and a superior ski vacation experience after all he had read in ski magazines.

He wasn't disappointed. When he drove up to the slopes, a curbside ski valet took their equipment from his car, parking lot attendants directed him to the closest available parking, and a shuttle transported them from the lot to Snow Park Lodge. From the shuttle, he and his daughter walked to the slopes on heated pavers that prevent freezing and assist in snow removal. At the end of the day, they were able to store their skis without charge at the lodge and easily retrieve them the next morning. "I really can't believe how short the lift lines are!" Lauren observed. "Neither can I," replied

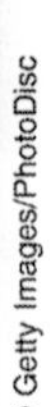

© Getty Images/PhotoDisc

her dad, "I especially like the complimentary mountain tours so we can get to know this place a little better." In one ski magazine, he had read about how the resort offers tours for both expert and intermediate skiers and limits the number of skiers on the mountain to reduce lines and congestion. Everyone is committed to ensuring that each guest has a wonderful experience, from "mountain hosts" stationed at the top of the lifts who answer questions and provide directions, to the friendly workers at the cafeterias and restaurants, whose food is consistently rated number one by ski-enthusiast magazines. "Lauren, what do you say we take a break for lunch? I heard the turkey chili is fantastic!"

- Haller Breweries' CEO Ray White gathered his management team. "Ladies and gentlemen, we are facing a crisis. Sales have fallen 40 percent over the past year, and just in case you hadn't noticed, our stock price slipped from $70 a few years ago to less than $10." George Green, the company's chief financial officer, replied, "I can't understand it. After our cost reduction program a few years ago, we dramatically increased the return on sales and asset utilization." Operations Manager Stephanie Scarlet jumped in, "Yes, we switched to corn syrup and hop pellets in our brewing formula and shortened the brewing time by 50 percent. *Business News* magazine even confirmed our strategy in that article—what was it? Oh, yeah. 'Does it Pay to Build Quality if Customers Don't Notice?' " "Well," replied Mr. White, "maybe they did."

- Although Hyundai Motor Co. dominated the Korean car market, it had a poor reputation for quality overseas, with doors that didn't fit properly, frames that rattled, and engines that delivered poor acceleration. In addition, the company was losing money. When Chung Mong Koo became CEO in 1999, he visited Hyundai's plant at Ulsan. To the shock of his employees, who hardly ever see a CEO, Chung walked onto the factory floor and looked under the hood of a Sonata sedan. He didn't like what he saw: loose wires, tangled hoses, bolts painted four different colors—the kind of sloppiness that would never be seen in a Japanese car. On the spot, he instructed the plant chief to paint all bolts and screws black and ordered workers not to release a car unless all was orderly under the hood. "You've got to get back to basics. The only way we can survive is to raise our quality to Toyota's level" he fumed.[2] The next year, U.S. sales rose by 42 percent, and in 2004, Hyundai tied with Honda as the second-best carmaker on the J.D. Powers Initial Quality ranking.

DOUG KANTER/BLOOMBERG NEWS/Landov

Discussion Questions: What satisfying service experiences similar to the Deer Valley episode have you personally encountered? Can you cite some examples of poor quality that you have received in a good or service? How have these experiences shaped your perceptions of the quality of the organization you were dealing with and your subsequent purchase decisions?

The concept of quality is fundamental to business operations. In 1887, William Cooper Procter, grandson of the founder of Procter & Gamble, told his employees, "The first job we have is to turn out quality merchandise that consumers will buy and keep on buying. If we produce it efficiently and economically, we will earn a profit, in which you will share." Procter's statement addresses three issues that are critical to operations managers: *productivity*, *cost*, and *quality*. Of these, the most significant factor in determining the long-run success or failure of any organization is quality. High quality of goods and services can provide an organization with a competitive edge; reduces costs due to returns, rework, scrap, and service upsets; increases productivity, profits, and other measures of success; and most importantly, generates satisfied customers, who reward the organization with continued patronage and favorable word-of-mouth advertising. The Deer Valley episode is a good example of this.

However, as the second example—which was based on the actual experience of Schlitz Brewing Co., once the second-largest brewer in the United States that eventually met its demise[3]—suggests, quality cannot be sacrificed simply for cost reduction or the hope of increased profits. The long-term sustainability of any organization depends on meeting customers' quality expectations.

The third example shows the importance of leadership, persistence, and an almost fanatical obsession with quality. One of the keys to Hyundai's success, in addition to investing heavily in research and development and employee training, was creating a quality control czar, who studied quality manuals of U.S. and Japanese automakers and developed their own, making it clear who is responsible for each manufacturing step, what outcome is required, and who checks and confirms performance levels. When customers reported faulty warning lights and hard-to-start engines, Chung set up a $30 million computer center where 71 engineers simulate harsh conditions to test electronics, reducing problems in these areas from 23.4 to 9.6 per 100 vehicles.[4]

Today, the high quality of goods and services is simply expected by consumers and business customers and is essential to survival and competitive success. To understand this better, just consider Ford Motor Company. During the 1980s, Ford fought its way from the bottom of Detroit's Big Three automakers to the top of the pack by a concerted effort to improve quality and better meet customer needs and expectations. It quickly became a highly profitable business. However, on January 12, 2002, a newspaper headline read "Ford to cut 35,000 jobs, close 5 plants." CEO William Ford is cited as stating, "We strayed from what got us to the top of the mountain, and it cost us greatly. . . . We may have underestimated the growing strength of our competitors. There were some strategies that were poorly conceived, and we just didn't execute on the basics of our business." The article goes on to observe that Ford "has been dogged by quality problems that forced the recall of several new models, including the Explorer, one of the top money-makers."[5] One of the key elements of Ford's 2002 Revitalization Plan was to "Continue Quality Improvements." In fact, the *top two* "vital few priorities" set by Ford's president for North America were "Improve quality."

Quality must be addressed throughout the value chain, beginning with suppliers and extending through operations and postsale services. **Quality management** *refers to systematic policies, methods, and procedures used to ensure that goods and services are produced with appropriate levels of quality to meet the needs of customers.* From the perspective of operations, quality management deals with key issues relating to how goods and services are designed, created, and delivered to meet customer expectations. We discussed the strategic role of quality and important design issues for goods and services earlier in this book. Our focus in this chapter is how operations should be managed to ensure that outputs meet the requirements established in design activities; that is, what must managers do on a daily basis to ensure quality? This chapter and the next focus on the philosophy and tools of modern quality management.

Quality management *refers to systematic policies, methods, and procedures used to ensure that goods and services are produced with appropriate levels of quality to meet the needs of customers.*

A BRIEF HISTORY OF QUALITY MANAGEMENT

Learning Objective
To learn how quality management has evolved and changed focus over the years and why organizations need to continue to place a significant amount of emphasis on quality.

Why so much emphasis on quality today? It helps to review a bit of history. Quality assurance, usually associated with some form of measurement and inspection activity—two important aspects of quality management—has been an important aspect of production operations throughout history.[6] Egyptian wall paintings from around 1450 B.C. show evidence of measurement and inspection. Stones for the pyramids were cut so precisely that even today it is impossible to put a knife blade between the blocks. The Egyptians' success was due to the consistent use of well-developed methods and procedures and precise measuring devices.

During the Industrial Revolution, the use of interchangeable parts and the separation of work into small tasks necessitated careful control of quality, leading to the dependence on inspection to identify and remove defects. Eventually, production organizations created separate quality departments. This artificial separation of production workers from responsibility for quality assurance led to indifference to quality among both workers and their managers. During World War II, many quality specialists were trained to use statistical tools, and statistical quality control became widely known and gradually adopted throughout manufacturing industries. However, because upper managers had delegated so much responsibility for quality to others, they gained little knowledge about quality, and when the quality crisis hit years later, they were ill-prepared to deal with it. Concluding that quality was the responsibility of the quality department, many upper managers turned their attention to output quantity and efficiency because of the shortage of civilian goods.

During this time, two U.S. consultants, Dr. Joseph Juran and Dr. W. Edwards Deming, introduced statistical quality control techniques to the Japanese to aid them in their rebuilding efforts. A significant part of their educational activity was focused on upper management, rather than quality specialists alone. With the support of top managers, the Japanese integrated quality throughout their organizations and developed a culture of continuous improvement.

Improvements in Japanese quality were slow and steady; some 20 years passed before the quality of Japanese products exceeded that of Western manufacturers. By the 1970s, primarily due to the higher quality levels of their products, Japanese companies had made significant penetration into Western markets. Most major U.S. companies answered the wake-up call by instituting extensive quality improvement campaigns, focused not only on conformance but also on improving design quality. A Westinghouse (now CBS) vice president of corporate productivity and quality summed up the situation by quoting Dr. Samuel Johnson's remark: "Nothing concentrates a man's mind so wonderfully as the prospect of being hanged in the morning."

One of the most influential individuals in the quality revolution was W. Edwards Deming. In 1980, NBC televised a special program entitled *If Japan Can . . . Why Can't We?* The widely viewed program revealed Deming's key role in the development of Japanese quality, and his name was soon a household word among corporate executives. Although Deming had helped to transform Japanese industry three decades earlier, it was only then that U.S. companies asked for his help. From 1980 until his death in 1993, his leadership and expertise helped many U.S. companies to revolutionize their approach to quality.

As organizations began to integrate quality principles into their management systems, the notion of total quality management, or TQM, became popular. TQM represented a focus on quality throughout the value chain, rather than simply during production operations, and the involvement of every individual and function in the organization. Quality took on a new meaning of organization-wide performance excellence rather than an engineering-based technical discipline. Unfortunately, with all the hype and rhetoric (and the unfortunate three-letter acronym, TQM, that turns some individuals off), many companies that scrambled to institute quality programs failed in their haste. As a result, TQM met some harsh criticism. However, those organizations that succeeded in building and sustaining quality have reaped the rewards associated with higher customer loyalty, employee satisfaction, and business performance. Despite the demise of TQM as a quality "program," its basic principles took root in many organizations and have remained important management practices. Today, most people simply use the term *total quality* to refer to the original notion of TQM.

In recent years, a new interest in quality has emerged in corporate boardrooms under the concept of *Six Sigma*, a customer-focused and results-oriented approach to business improvement. Six Sigma integrates many quality tools and techniques that have been tested and validated over the years, with a bottom-line orientation that has high appeal to senior managers. We discuss Six Sigma in more detail later in this chapter. Health care is one industry that is adopting fundamental quality principles and methods, including Six Sigma initiatives (see the OM Spotlight below).

OM SPOTLIGHT

Poor Quality Costs in U.S. Health Care[7]

"Poor quality in health care costs the typical employer an estimated $1,700 to $2,000 for each covered employee each year," said Jim Mortimer, president of the Midwest Business Group on Health. That is about a third of the $4,900 spent on each employee on health care last year. IBM, General Motors, and Xerox are among the firms that offer lower monthly premiums to employees who choose health plans with the best quality results. Diane Bechel, a health care expert at Ford Motor Company, estimated that the company saved more than $5,000 on care for each of 500 employees, retirees, and family members who used hospitals that met certain quality standards, including a lot of experience with certain surgical procedures and good communication with patients. Verizon, IBM, Xerox, and Empire Blue Cross recently started to pay a 4 percent bonus for employee care to a handful of hospitals that met quality and patient safety goals for prescription drug orders and intensive care units. Eight hospitals so far have received the bonuses. Incentives like these from Fortune 500 companies are driving Six Sigma and other quality management initiatives in U.S. health care.

One U.S. government study for Medicare and Medicaid Services projects national spending on health care to soar to $2.82 trillion in 2011, almost double 2001's $1.42 trillion. If current trends continue, "the cost of poor-quality care will likely exceed $1 trillion by 2011," the study said.

UNDERSTANDING QUALITY

Learning Objective
To understand what quality means in manufacturing and service operations, how organizations should address customer expectations and perceptions, and how quality is integrated into operations through customer focus, continuous improvement, and employee involvement.

In Chapter 3, we discussed performance measurement. Recall that quality (of goods and services, as well as environmental quality) was one of the major types of performance measures that drive operations. Quality can be a confusing concept, partly because people view quality in relation to differing criteria based on their individual roles in the value chain. In addition, the meaning of quality has evolved as the quality profession has grown and matured. Neither consultants nor business professionals agree on a universal definition. A study that asked managers of 86 firms in the eastern United States to define quality produced several dozen different responses, including

1. perfection
2. consistency
3. eliminating waste
4. speed of delivery
5. compliance with policies and procedures
6. providing a good, usable product
7. doing it right the first time
8. delighting or pleasing customers
9. total customer service and satisfaction[8]

Many of these perspectives relate to a good or service's **fitness for use**—*the ability of a good or service to meet customer needs.* Understanding fitness-for-use criteria is important in the design process, as we discussed in Chapter 6. It is also important to understand that "fit for use" can mean different things to different people and that customer perceptions of quality are as important to understand as any measurable characteristics that a firm can quantify. Many people view quality by comparing features and characteristics of goods and services to a set of expectations, which may be promulgated by marketing efforts aimed at developing quality as an image variable in their minds. A framework for evaluating quality of both goods and services and identifying where to focus design and improvement efforts is the GAP model, which we discuss next.

Fitness for Use *is the ability of a good or service to meet customer needs.*

The GAP Model[9]

The GAP model recognizes that there are several ways to misspecify and mismanage the creation and delivery of high levels of quality. These "gaps" are shown in the model in Exhibit 15.1 and explained in the following list. The model clearly shows the complexity and interdisciplinary nature of service management and that there are many opportunities to make mistakes.

- **Gap 1** *is the discrepancy between customer expectations and management perceptions of those expectations.* Managers may think they understand why customers buy a good or service, but if their perception is wrong, then all subsequent design and delivery activities may be misdirected.
- **Gap 2** *is the discrepancy between management perceptions of what features constitute a target level of quality and the task of translating these perceptions into executable specifications.* This represents a mismatch between requirements and design activities that we discussed in Chapter 6.
- **Gap 3** *is the discrepancy between quality specifications documented in operating and training manuals and plans and their implementation.* Gap 3 recognizes that the manufacturing and service delivery systems must execute quality specifications well.

Exhibit 15.1 Gap Model of Quality

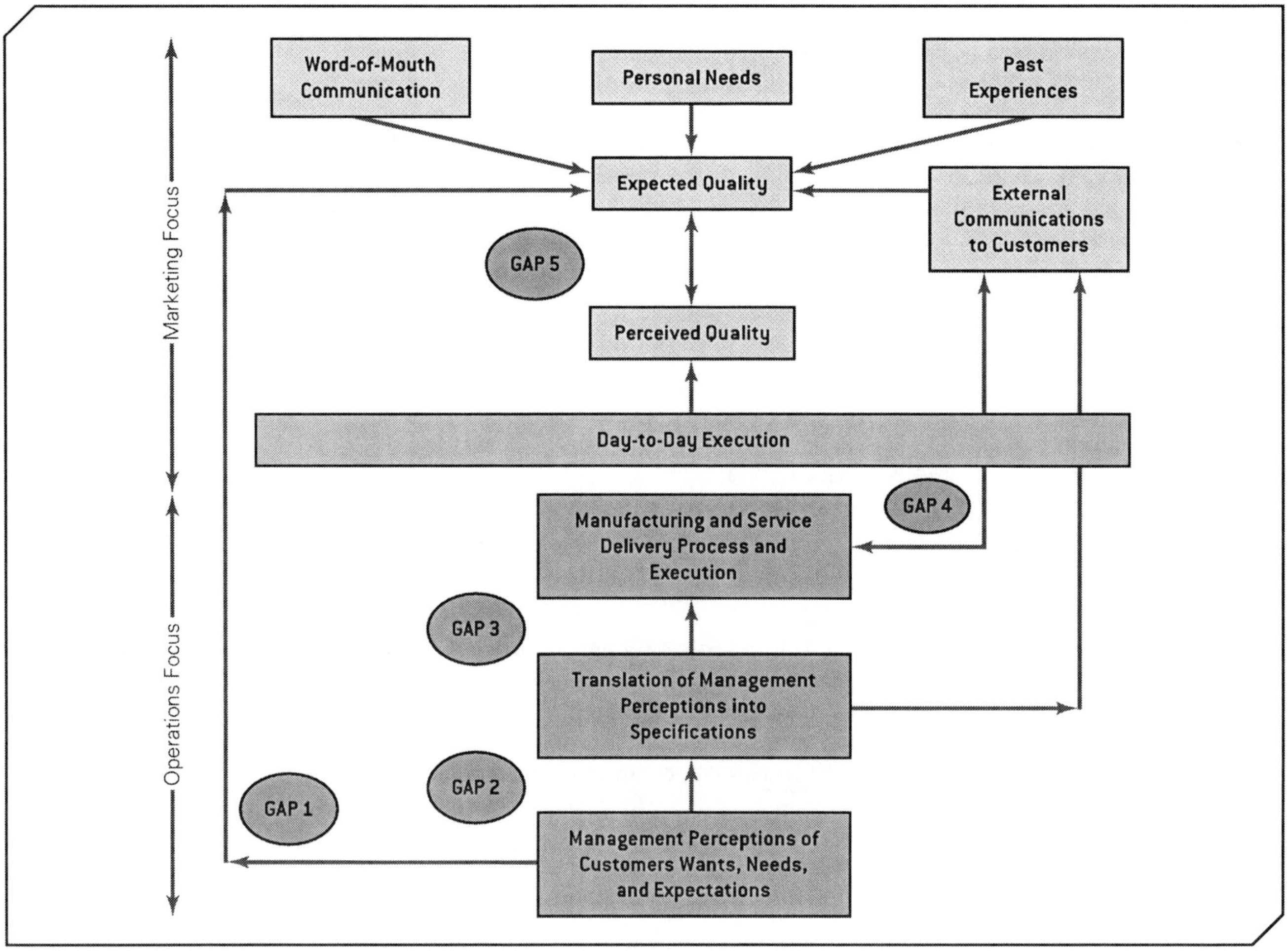

Source: Parasuraman, A., Zeithaml, V. A., and Berry, L. L., "A Conceptual Model of Service Quality and Its Implications for Future Research," *Journal of Marketing*, Fall 1985, Vol. 49, pp. 41–50. Reprinted with permission from the American Marketing Association.

- Gap 4 *is the discrepancy between actual manufacturing and service delivery system performance and external communications to the customers.* The customer should not be promised a certain type and level of quality unless the delivery system can achieve or exceed that level.
- Gap 5 *is the difference between the customer's expectations and perceptions.* The fifth gap depends on the other four. This is where the customer judges quality and makes future purchase decisions.

Managers can use this model to analyze goods and services and the processes that make and deliver them to identify and close the largest gaps and improve performance. Failure to understand and minimize these gaps can seriously degrade the quality of a service and risk losing customer loyalty.

Quality in Operations

From an operations perspective, however, the most useful definition is how well the output of a manufacturing or service process conforms to the design specifications.

Quality of conformance *is the extent to which a process is able to deliver output that conforms to the design specifications.* **Specifications** *are targets and tolerances determined by designers of goods and services.* Targets are the ideal values for which production is to strive; tolerances are the permissible variation. We briefly discussed design specifications in Chapter 5 in the context of goods and service design. If a part is produced within the defined tolerance, for example, 0.236 ± 0.003 cm, then it conforms to the specifications. Specifications are meaningless, however, if they do not reflect attributes that are deemed important to the consumer. Ensuring quality of conformance is a major responsibility of operations managers. This is accomplished through **quality control**—*the means of ensuring consistency in processes to achieve conformance.* The next chapter addresses this topic in more depth.

Quality of conformance *is the extent to which a process is able to deliver output that conforms to the design specifications.*

Specifications *are targets and tolerances determined by designers of goods and services.*

Quality Control *is the means of ensuring consistency in processes to achieve conformance.*

Service quality *is consistently meeting or exceeding customer expectations (external focus) and service delivery system performance criteria (internal focus) during all service encounters.* Excellent service quality is achieved by the consistent delivery to the customer of a clearly defined customer benefit package, and associated process and service encounters, defined by many internal and external standards of performance. Performance standards are analogous to manufacturing specifications. For example, "on-time arrival" for an airplane might be specified as within 15 minutes of the scheduled arrival time. The target is the scheduled time, and the tolerance is specified to be 15 minutes.

Service quality *is consistently meeting or exceeding customer expectations (external focus) and service delivery system performance criteria (internal focus) during all service encounters.*

Quality is more than simply ensuring that goods and services consistently conform to specifications. Achieving high-quality goods and services depends on the commitment and involvement of everyone in the entire value chain. The principles of total quality are simple:

1. a focus on customers and stakeholders,
2. a process focus supported by continuous improvement and learning, and
3. participation and teamwork by everyone in the organization.

First, the customer is the principal judge of quality. Thus, a quality-focused company's efforts need to extend well beyond merely meeting specifications, reducing defects and errors, or resolving complaints. They must include knowing what the customer wants, how the customer uses its goods or services, and anticipating needs that the customer may not even be able to express; designing new goods and services that truly delight the customer; responding rapidly to changing consumer and market demands; and continually developing new ways of enhancing customer relationships.

The importance of a process, as well as a customer, focus can be described by what W. Edwards Deming told Japanese managers in 1950. While presenting to a group of Japanese industrialists (collectively representing about 80 percent of the nation's capital), he drew the diagram shown in Exhibit 15.2. This diagram depicts not only the relationships among inputs, processes, and outputs but also the roles of consumers and suppliers, the interdependency of organizational processes, the usefulness of consumer research, and the importance of continuous improvement of all elements of the production system. Deming told the Japanese that understanding customers and suppliers was crucial to planning for quality. He advised them that continuous improvement of both products and production processes through better understanding of customer requirements is the key to capturing world markets. Deming predicted that within 5 years Japanese manufacturers would be making products of the highest quality in the world and would have gained a large share of the world market. He was wrong. By applying these ideas, the Japanese penetrated several global markets in less than 4 years!

The third principle is perhaps the most important. When managers give employees the tools to make good decisions and the freedom and encouragement to make contributions, they virtually guarantee that better-quality goods and services will result. Employees who are allowed to participate—both individually and in

Exhibit 15.2
Deming's View of a Production System

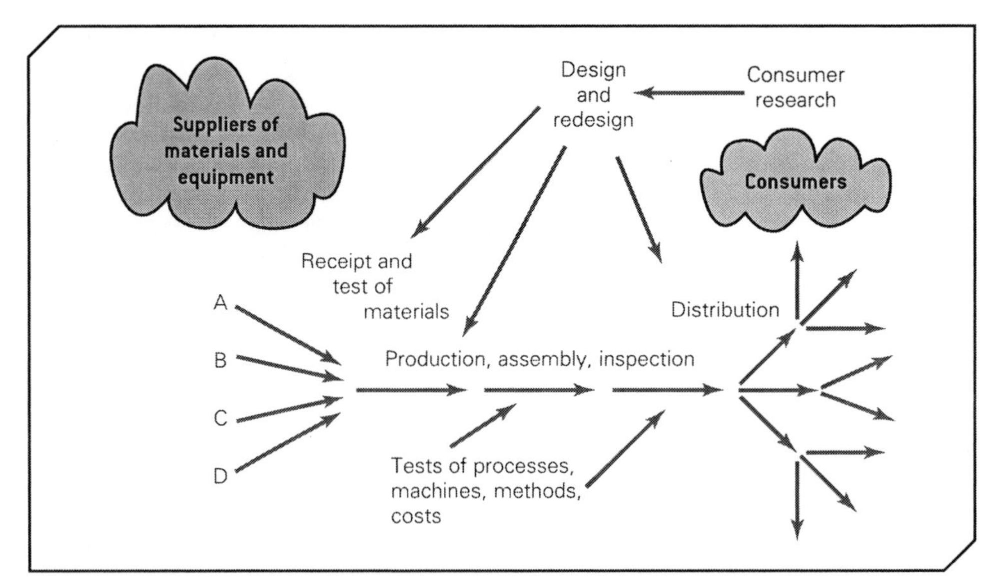

Source: Reprinted from *Out of the Crisis*, p. 5, by W. Edwards Deming, by permission of MIT and the W. Edwards Deming Institute. Published by MIT Center for Advanced Educational Services, Cambridge, MA 02139. © 1986 by The W. Edwards Deming Institute.

teams—in decisions that affect their jobs and the customer can make substantial contributions to quality. Empowering employees to make decisions that satisfy customers without constraining them with bureaucratic rules shows the highest level of trust. Another important element of total quality is teamwork, which focuses attention on both internal and external customer-supplier relationships and encourages the involvement of everyone in attacking systemic problems, particularly those that cross functional boundaries.

Every business function plays an important role in achieving quality. For example,

- Marketing and sales personnel are responsible for determining the needs and expectations of consumers.
- Product design and engineering functions develop technical specifications for products and production processes to meet the requirements determined by the marketing function.
- The purchasing department must select quality-conscious suppliers and ensure that purchase orders clearly define the quality requirements specified by product design and engineering.
- Production control must ensure that the correct materials, tools, and equipment are available at the proper time and in the proper places in order to maintain a smooth flow of production.
- Finance must authorize sufficient budgeting for equipment, training, and other means of assuring quality.
- A firm's legal department ensures that the firm complies with laws and regulations regarding such things as product labeling, packaging, safety, and transportation and has proper procedures and documentation in place in the event of liability claims against it.

Quality and Business Results

There is considerable evidence that investment in quality—not only in goods, services, and processes but in the quality of management itself—yields numerous benefits. A survey of almost 1,000 executives conducted by Zenger-Miller Achieve noted significant benefits from quality initiatives, including increased employee participation, improved product and service quality, improved customer satisfaction, improved productivity, and improved employee skills.[10] The Malcolm Baldrige National Quality Award (MBNQA) criteria and the model depicted in Exhibit 3.3 champion this notion. Baldrige Award recipients provide compelling evidence that a focus on quality leads to exceptional business results.

One of the most celebrated studies was published by Kevin Hendricks and Vinod Singhal in 1997.[11] Based on objective data and rigorous statistical analysis, the study showed that when implemented effectively, total quality management approaches improve financial performance dramatically. Using a sample of about 600 publicly traded companies that have won quality awards either from their customers (such as automotive manufacturers) or through Baldrige and state and local quality award programs, Hendricks and Singhal examined performance results from 6 years before to 4 years after winning the first quality award. The primary performance measure tracked was the percent change in operating income and a variety of measures that might affect operating income: percent change in sales, total assets, number of employees, return on sales, and return on assets. These results were compared to a set of control firms that were similar in size to the award winners and in the same industry. The analysis revealed significant differences between the sample and the control group. Specifically, the growth in operating income of winners averaged 91 percent versus 43 percent for the control group. Winners also experienced a 69 percent jump in sales (compared to 32 percent for the control group), a 79 percent increase in total assets (compared to 37 percent), a 23 percent increase in the number of employees (compared to 7 percent), an 8 percent improvement on return on sales (compared to 0 percent), and a 9 percent improvement on return on assets (compared to 6 percent). Small companies actually outperformed large companies, and over a 5-year period, the portfolio of winners beat the S&P 500 index by 34 percent.

A sample of specific operational and financial results that companies taking a total quality path have achieved include

- Among associates at Clarke American, overall satisfaction has improved from 72 percent to 84 percent over a 5-year period. Rising associate satisfaction correlated with an 84 percent increase in revenue earned per associate. Annual growth in company revenues also increased from a rate of 4.2 percent to 16 percent, compared to the industry's average annual growth rate of less than 1 percent over a 5-year period.
- Dana Corporation–Spicer Driveshaft Division lowered internal defect rates by more than 75 percent. Employee turnover is below 1 percent, and economic value added increased from $15 million to $35 million in 2 years.
- Texas Nameplate Company increased its national market share from less than 3 percent to 5 per cent over 3 years, reduced its defects from 3.65 percent to about 1 percent of billings, and increased on-time delivery from 95 to 98 percent.
- Pal's Sudden Service, a privately owned quick-service restaurant chain in eastern Tennessee, had customer quality scores averaging 95.8 percent, compared with 84.1 percent for its best competition, and improved order delivery speed by over 30 percent.
- KARLEE, a contract manufacturer of precision sheet metal and machined components, reduced waste from 1.5 percent of sales to less than 0.5 percent of sales while nearly doubling productivity over a 5-year period.
- SSM Health Care's share of the St. Louis market has increased substantially while three of its five competitors have lost market share. It has achieved a AA credit rating from Standard and Poor's for 4 consecutive years, a rating attained by fewer than 1 percent of U.S. hospitals.

Learning Objective
To understand the quality philosophies and principles of Deming, Juran, and Crosby and how these individuals influenced the quality management practices of today's organizations.

INFLUENTIAL LEADERS IN MODERN QUALITY MANAGEMENT

Many individuals have made substantial contributions to quality management thought and applications. However, three people—W. Edwards Deming, Joseph M. Juran, and Philip B. Crosby—are regarded as "management gurus" in the quality revolution. Their insights on measuring, managing, and improving quality have had profound impacts on countless managers and entire corporations around the world and laid the foundation for today's quality management practices.

W. Edwards Deming

© Catherine Karnow/CORBIS

Dr. W. Edwards Deming worked for Western Electric during its pioneering era of statistical quality control in the 1920s and 1930s. Deming recognized the importance of viewing management processes statistically. During World War II, he taught quality control courses as part of the U.S. national defense effort, but he realized that teaching statistics only to engineers and factory workers would never solve the fundamental quality problems that manufacturing needed to address. Despite numerous efforts, his attempts to convey the message of quality to upper-level managers in the United States were ignored.

Unlike other management gurus and consultants, Deming never defined or described quality precisely. In his last book, he stated, "A product or a service possesses quality if it helps somebody and enjoys a good and sustainable market."[12] The Deming philosophy focuses on bringing about improvements in product and service quality by reducing variability in goods and services design and associated processes. Deming professed that higher quality leads to higher productivity and lower costs, which in turn leads to improved market share and long-term competitive strength. The Deming "Chain Reaction" theory (see Exhibit 15.3) summarizes this view. Deming stressed that top management has the overriding responsibility for quality improvement.

In his early work in the United States, Deming preached his 14 Points. Although management practices today are vastly different than when Deming first began to preach his philosophy, the 14 Points still convey important insights for operations managers as well as every other manager in an organization. We briefly summarize the key issues.

Point 1: *Create a Vision and Demonstrate Commitment* An organization's basic purpose is to serve its customers and employees. It must define its values, mission, and vision of the future to provide long-term direction for its management and employees. This responsibility lies with top management, who must show commitment to quality and long-term success.

Point 2: *Learn the Philosophy* Companies cannot survive if goods and services of poor quality leave their customers dissatisfied. Thus, companies must take a customer-driven approach with a never-ending cycle of improvement, and engage all employees—from the boardroom to the stockroom—in learning the principles of quality and performance excellence. Although many of these principles are indeed ingrained in managers and front-line employees through training and reinforcement of organizational values, managers need to continually renew themselves to learn new approaches and relearn many older ones.

Point 3: *Understand Inspection* Traditionally, inspection had been the principal means for quality control—let the "quality control" department find and remove

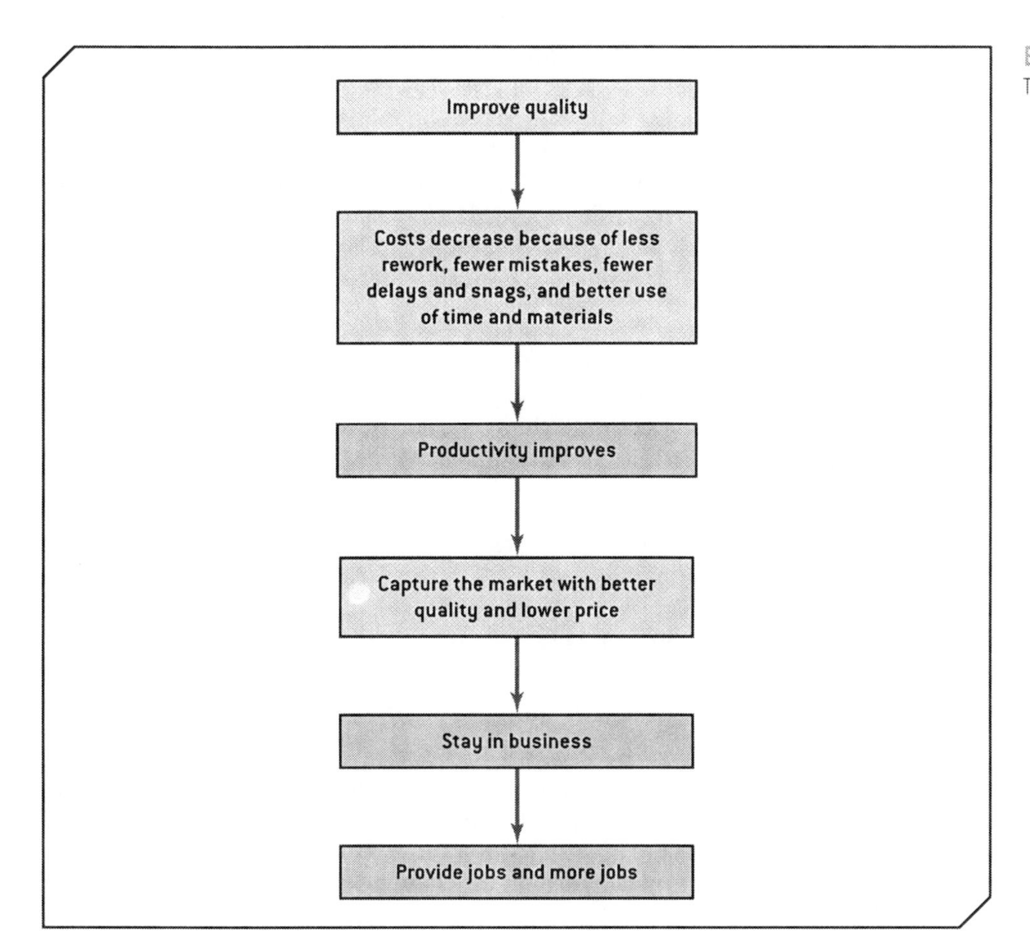

Exhibit 15.3
The Deming Chain Reaction

defective goods. This adds little value to the product, decreases productivity, and increases costs, and as we discussed earlier in this book, cannot even be done in service industries. Deming encouraged organizations to use inspection as an information-gathering tool for improvement and give this responsibility to the workers who do the work. Through better understanding of variation and statistical principles, managers can eliminate many sources of unnecessary inspection, thus reducing non-value-added costs associated with operations.

Point 4: *Stop Making Decisions Purely on the Basis of Cost* In 1931, Walter Shewhart noted that price has no meaning without quality.[13] Nevertheless, many managers will sacrifice quality for cost. Deming recognized that the direct costs associated with inferior materials that arise from scrap and rework during production or customer returns, as well as the loss of customer goodwill, can far exceed the cost "savings" achieved by using them. Today's emphasis on the value chain takes a system's view with the objective of minimizing total costs and developing stronger partnerships with customers and suppliers.

Point 5: *Improve Constantly and Forever* When quality improves, productivity improves and costs decrease, as the Deming Chain Reaction suggests. Traditionally, continuous improvement was not a common business practice; today, it is recognized as a necessary means for survival in a highly competitive and global business environment. The tools for improvement are constantly evolving, and organizations need to ensure that their employees understand and apply them effectively. This requires training, the focus of the next point.

Point 6: *Institute Training* Effective training results in improvements in quality and productivity, and also adds to worker morale. Training must transcend basic job skills like running a machine or following the script when talking to customers. For example, at Honda of America in Marysville, Ohio, all employees start out on the production floor, regardless of their job classification. Today, many companies have excellent training programs for technology related to direct production but still fail to enrich the ancillary skills of their work force. This is where some of the most lucrative opportunities exist to impact key business results.

Point 7: *Institute Leadership* Leadership goes far beyond the executive suite. For operations managers, it involves providing guidance to help employees do their jobs better with less effort, eliminating fear, encouraging innovation and risk taking, and facilitating teamwork. Leadership was, is, and will continue to be a challenging issue in every organization, particularly as new generations of managers replace those who have learned to lead.

Point 8: *Drive Out Fear* No system can work without the mutual respect of managers and workers. Fear is manifested in many ways: fear of reprisal, fear of failure, fear of the unknown, fear of relinquishing control, and fear of change. Creating a culture without fear is a slow process that can be destroyed in an instant with a transition of leadership and a change in corporate policies. Therefore, today's managers need to continue to be sensitive to the impact that fear can have on their organizations.

Point 9: *Optimize the Efforts of Teams* Teamwork helps to break down barriers between departments and individuals and helps them see how elements of the value chain are interrelated. The lack of cooperation often leads to poor quality because other departments cannot understand what their internal customers want and do not get what they need from their internal suppliers.

Point 10: *Eliminate Exhortations* Many early attempts to improve quality focused solely on behavioral change and involved posters, slogans, and motivational programs. However, the major source of many problems is the system itself. Improvement occurs by understanding the nature of processes and making decisions based on data and information.

Point 11: *Eliminate Numerical Quotas* Many organizations manage front-line workers by numbers and often compensate and reward individuals based on quantity not quality, for example, setting standards on the number of calls that a call center operator must process each hour, rather than focusing on the quality of the customer interaction. Workers may shortcut quality to reach the goal. Once a standard is reached, little incentive remains for workers to continue production or to improve quality.

Point 12: *Remove Barriers to Pride in Work* Front-line workers are often treated as, in Deming's words, "a commodity." They are given monotonous tasks, provided with inferior machines, tools, or materials, told to run defective items to meet sales pressures, and report to supervisors who know nothing about the job. Organizations must develop a work environment that is enriching, motivating, and enjoyable.

Point 13: *Encourage Education and Self-Improvement* The difference between this point and Point 6 is subtle. Point 6 refers to training in specific job skills; Point 13 refers to continuing, broad education for self-development. Organizations must invest in their people at all levels to ensure success in the long term. Today, many companies understand that elevating the general knowledge base of their work force—outside of specific job skills—has many benefits. However, others still view this as a cost that can be easily cut when financial trade-offs must be made.

Point 14: *Take Action* Any cultural change begins with top management and includes everyone. Changing an organizational culture generally meets with skepticism and resistance that many firms find difficult to deal with, particularly when many of the traditional management practices Deming felt must be eliminated are deeply ingrained in the organization's culture.

The 14 Points have become the basis for many organization's quality approaches (see the OM Spotlight on Hillerich & Bradsby Co.).

Joseph Juran

Joseph Juran also worked at Western Electric in the 1920s as it pioneered in the development of statistical methods for quality. He spent much of his time as a corporate industrial engineer and published the *Quality Control Handbook* in 1951, one of the most comprehensive quality manuals ever written. Like Deming, Juran taught quality principles to the Japanese in the 1950s and was a principal force in their quality reorganization. Juran proposed a simple definition of quality: "fitness for use."

Unlike Deming, however, Juran did not propose a major cultural change in the organization, but rather sought to improve quality by working within the system familiar to managers. He argued that employees at different levels of an organization

OM SPOTLIGHT

Hillerich & Bradsby[14]

Hillerich & Bradsby Co. (H&B) has been making the Louisville Slugger brand of baseball bat for more than 115 years. In the mid-1980s, the company faced significant challenges from market changes and competition. CEO Jack Hillerich attended a 4-day Deming seminar, which provided the basis for the company's current quality efforts. Returning from the seminar, Hillerich decided to see what changes that Deming advocated were possible in an old company with an old union and a history of labor-management problems. Hillerich persuaded union officials to attend another Deming seminar with five senior managers. Following the seminar, a core group of union and management people developed a strategy to change the company. They talked about building trust and changing the system "to make it something you want to work in."

Employees were interested, but skeptical. To demonstrate their commitment, managers examined Deming's 14 Points and picked several they believed they could make progress on through actions that would demonstrate a serious intention to change. One of the first changes was the elimination of work quotas that were tied to hourly salaries and a schedule of warnings and penalties for failures to meet quotas. Instead, a team-based approach was initiated. While a few workers took advantage of the change, overall productivity actually improved as rework decreased because workers were taking pride in their work to produce things the right way first. H&B also eliminated performance appraisals and commission-based pay in sales. The company has also focused its efforts on training and education, resulting in an openness for change and capacity for teamwork. Today, the Deming philosophy is still the core of H&B's guiding principles.

JOHN SOMMERS/Reuters/Landov

speak in their own "languages." (Deming, on the other hand, believed statistics should be the common language.) Juran stated that top management speaks in the language of dollars; workers speak in the language of things; and middle management must be able to speak both languages and translate between dollars and things. Thus, to get top management's attention, quality issues must be cast in the language they understand—dollars. Hence, Juran advocated the use of quality cost measurement, discussed later in this chapter, to focus attention on quality problems. At the operational level, Juran focused on increasing conformance to specifications through elimination of defects, supported extensively by statistical tools for analysis. Thus, his philosophy fit well into existing management systems.

Like Deming, Juran advocated a never-ending spiral of activities that includes market research, product development, design, planning for manufacture, purchasing, production process control, inspection and testing, and sales, followed by customer feedback. Juran's prescriptions focus on three major quality processes, called the Quality Trilogy: (1) quality planning—the process of preparing to meet quality goals; (2) quality control—the process of meeting quality goals during operations; and (3) quality improvement—the process of breaking through to unprecedented levels of performance. At the time he proposed this structure, few companies were engaging in any significant planning or improvement activities. Thus, Juran was promoting a major cultural shift in management thinking.

Unlike Deming, however, Juran specified a detailed program for quality improvement. Such a program involves proving the need for improvement, identifying specific projects for improvement, organizing support for the projects, diagnosing the causes, providing remedies for the causes, proving that the remedies are effective under operating conditions, and providing control to maintain improvements. Juran's approach is reflected in the practices of a wide variety of organizations today.

Philip B. Crosby

Philip B. Crosby was corporate vice president for quality at International Telephone and Telegraph (ITT) for 14 years after working his way up from line inspector. After leaving ITT, he established Philip Crosby Associates in 1979 to develop and offer training programs. He also authored several popular books. His first book, *Quality Is Free*, sold about 1 million copies and was greatly responsible for bringing quality to the attention of top corporate managers in the United States. The essence of Crosby's quality philosophy is embodied in what he calls the Absolutes of Quality Management and the Basic Elements of Improvement. Crosby's Absolutes of Quality Management include the following points:

- *Quality means conformance to requirements, not elegance.* Requirements must be clearly stated so that they cannot be misunderstood. Requirements act as communication devices and allow workers to take measurements to determine conformance to those requirements. Any nonconformance is the absence of quality.
- *There is no such thing as a quality problem.* Problems are functional in nature. Thus, a firm may experience accounting problems, manufacturing problems, design problems, front-desk problems, and so on, and the burden of responsibility for such problems falls on these functional departments. The quality department should measure conformance, report results, and lead the drive to develop a positive attitude toward quality improvement. This Absolute is similar to Deming's third point.
- *There is no such thing as the economics of quality; doing the job right the first time is always cheaper.* Crosby supports the premise that "economics of quality" has no meaning. Quality is free. What costs money are all actions that involve not doing jobs right the first time. The Deming chain reaction sends a similar message.

- *The only performance measurement is the cost of quality, which is the expense of nonconformance.* Crosby calls for measuring and publicizing the cost of poor quality. Quality cost data are useful to call problems to management's attention, to select opportunities for corrective action, and to track quality improvement over time. Such data provide visible proof of improvement and recognition of achievement. Juran supported this approach.
- *The only performance standard is "Zero Defects (ZD)."* This simply represents the philosophy of preventing defects in goods and services rather than finding them after the fact and fixing them.

Crosby's Basic Elements of Improvement are *determination*, *education*, and *implementation*. Determination means that top management must take quality improvement seriously. Education provides the means by which everyone in an organization learns quality principles. Finally, every member of the management team must understand the implementation process.

Comparisons of Quality Philosophies

In spite of the fact that they have significantly different approaches to implementing organizational change, the philosophies of Deming, Juran, and Crosby are more alike than different. Each views quality as imperative for future competitiveness in global markets, makes top management commitment an absolute necessity; demonstrates that quality management practices will save, not cost, money; places responsibility for quality on management, not the workers; stresses the need for continuous, never-ending improvement; acknowledges the importance of the customer and strong management–worker partnerships; and recognizes the need for and difficulties associated with changing the organizational culture.

The individual nature of business firms complicates the strict application of any one specific philosophy. Although each of these philosophies can be highly effective, a firm must first understand the nature and differences of the philosophies and then develop a quality management approach that is tailored to its individual organization. Any approach should include goals and objectives, allocation of responsibilities, a measurement system and description of tools to be employed, an outline of the management style that will be used, and a strategy for implementation. After taking these steps, the management team is responsible for leading the organization through successful execution.

ISO 9000:2000

Learning Objective
To become acquainted with the International Organization for Standardization's ISO 9000:2000 requirements, documentation, and certification for meeting a family of quality standards used in many international markets.

As quality became a major focus of businesses throughout the world, various organizations developed standards and guidelines. As the European Community moved toward the European free trade agreement, which went into effect at the end of 1992, quality management became a key strategic objective. To standardize quality requirements for European countries within the Common Market and those wishing to do business with those countries, a specialized agency for standardization, the International Organization for Standardization (IOS), founded in 1946 and composed of representatives from the national standards bodies of 91 nations, adopted a series of written quality standards in 1987. They were revised in 1994, and again (significantly) in 2000. The most recent version is called the ISO 9000:2000 family of standards. The standards have been adopted in the United States by the American National Standards Institute (ANSI) with the endorsement and cooperation of the American Society for Quality (ASQ) and are recognized by about 100 countries.

ISO 9000 defines *quality system standards*, based on the premise that certain generic characteristics of management practices can be standardized and that a well-designed, well-implemented, and carefully managed quality system provides confidence that the outputs will meet customer expectations and requirements. The standards were created to meet five objectives:

1. Achieve, maintain, and seek to continuously improve product quality (including services) in relationship to requirements.
2. Improve the quality of operations to continually meet customers' and stakeholders' stated and implied needs.
3. Provide confidence to internal management and other employees that quality requirements are being fulfilled and that improvement is taking place.
4. Provide confidence to customers and other stakeholders that quality requirements are being achieved in the delivered product.
5. Provide confidence that quality system requirements are fulfilled.

The standards prescribe documentation for all processes affecting quality and suggest that compliance through auditing leads to continuous improvement. The standards are intended to apply to all types of businesses, including electronics and chemicals, and to services such as health care, banking, and transportation. In some foreign markets, companies will not buy from suppliers who are not certified to the standards. For example, many products sold in Europe, such as telecommunication terminal equipment, medical devices, gas appliances, toys, and construction products, require product certifications to assure safety. Often, ISO certification is necessary to obtain product certification. Thus, meeting these standards is becoming a requirement for international competitiveness (see OM Spotlight: Rehtek Machine Co.).

The ISO 9000:2000 standards consist of three documents:

- ISO 9000—Fundamentals and vocabulary
- ISO 9001—Requirements
- ISO 9004—Guidance for performance improvement

OM SPOTLIGHT

Rehtek Machine Co.[15]

Many small companies do not have the resources to redo their processes, documentation, and quality control systems. Stephen Reh, president of Rehtek Machine Co., spent $30,000 to upgrade equipment and computerize operations at his 12-employee contract-manufacturing firm. Reh hired a consulting firm to help him become ISO certified. Rehtek Machine Co. received a U.S. federal grant designed to help small firms improve their manufacturing operations. The consultants helped train internal ISO auditors, draw process flow diagrams, and document every work activity and manufacturing step to meet ISO standards. Many operational improvements were made as this ISO documentation was developed. Reh said, "Everything is traceable from when it comes in the door to when it leaves. There is no more confusion on the shop floor. With set procedures in place, I can sleep at night, knowing everyone is making parts according to written quality specifications. One of the first things our customers ask is are we ISO certified."

Courtesy of Rehtek Machine Company

ISO 9000 provides definitions of key terms. ISO 9001 provides a set of minimum requirements for a quality management system and is intended to demonstrate compliance with recognized quality principles to customers and for third-party certification. ISO 9004 focuses on improving the quality management system beyond these minimum requirements. The ISO 9000:2000 standards structure these into four major sections: Management Responsibility; Resource Management; Product Realization; and Measurement, Analysis, and Improvement[16] and are supported by the following eight principles:

Principle 1—Customer-Focused Organization Organizations depend on their customers and therefore should understand current and future customer needs, meet customer requirements, and strive to exceed customer expectations.

Principle 2—Leadership Leaders establish unity of purpose and direction of the organization. They should create and maintain the internal environment in which people can become fully involved in achieving the organization's objectives.

Principle 3—Involvement of People People at all levels are the essence of an organization and their full involvement enables their abilities to be used for the organization's benefit.

Principle 4—Process Approach A desired result is achieved more efficiently when related resources and activities are managed as a process.

Principle 5—System Approach to Management Identifying, understanding, and managing a system of interrelated processes for a given objective improves the organization's effectiveness and efficiency.

Principle 6—Continual Improvement Continual improvement should be a permanent objective of the organization.

Principle 7—Factual Approach to Decision Making Effective decisions are based on the analysis of data and information.

Principle 8—Mutually Beneficial Supplier Relationships An organization and its suppliers are interdependent, and a mutually beneficial relationship enhances the ability of both to create value.

ISO 9000 provides a set of good basic practices for initiating a basic quality management system and is an excellent starting point for companies with no formal quality assurance program. For companies in the early stages of developing a quality program, the standards enforce the discipline of control that is necessary before they can seriously pursue continuous improvement. The requirements of periodic audits reinforce the stated quality system until it becomes ingrained in the company.

Many organizations have realized significant benefits from ISO 9000. At DuPont, for example, ISO 9000 has been credited with increasing on-time delivery from 70 to 90 percent, decreasing cycle time from 15 days to 1.5 days, increasing first-pass yields from 72 to 92 percent, and reducing the number of test procedures by one-third. Sun Microsystems' Milpitas plant was certified in 1992, and managers believe that it has helped deliver improved quality and service to customers.[17] In Canada, Toronto Plastics, Ltd. reduced defects from 150,000 per million to 15,000 per million after 1 year of ISO implementation.[18] The first home builder to achieve registration, Michigan-based Delcor Homes, reduced its rate of correctable defects from 27.4 to 1.7 percent in 2 years and improved its building experience approval rating from the mid-60s to the mid-90s on a 100-point scale.[19]

Learning Objective
To understand the principal activities that organizations must incorporate into an effective quality management system to support operations.

DESIGNING QUALITY MANAGEMENT AND CONTROL SYSTEMS

First and foremost, any effective quality management system must extend throughout the value chain, and all managers in the value chain need to incorporate quality management principles into their activities. The Baldrige Criteria for Performance Excellence, described in Chapter 3, provide a framework and focus on quality management at the organizational level. At the operations level, the ISO 9000 standards define the basic elements of an effective quality management system. The following sections describe the key elements of a good quality management and control system that operations managers should apply. Additional tools for control will be introduced in the next chapter.

Contract Management, Design Control, and Purchasing

Because the ultimate objective of quality assurance is to provide goods and services that meet customer needs and requirements, the quality system should provide for contract review to ensure that customer requirements are adequately defined and documented and that the company has the capability to meet these requirements. For companies that design products, the quality system should clearly delineate responsibilities for design and development activities, the organizational and technical interfaces between groups, product requirements, and any legal or regulatory requirements. For example, if the sales and marketing or engineering departments work directly with customers in establishing designs, then the process of how this is done and communicated should be defined. In addition, processes for design review and for verifying design outputs against input requirements should be defined. In some service organizations, such as retail sales, health care, or insurance, establishing a contract and providing the service occur simultaneously. This would require appropriate training to ensure that requirements are met.

The purchasing function is critical because designs often require components or materials supplied by other firms. The purchasing function should include processes for evaluating and selecting suppliers on the basis of their ability to meet requirements, appropriate methods for controlling supplier quality, and means of verifying that purchased product conforms to requirements.

Process Control

Process control is ensuring that a process performs as it should and taking corrective action when it does not. A good process control system should include documented procedures for all key processes; a clear understanding of the appropriate equipment and working environment; methods for monitoring and controlling critical quality characteristics; approval processes for equipment; criteria for workmanship, such as written standards, samples, or illustrations; and maintenance activities. For example, Cincinnati Fiberglass, a small manufacturer of fiberglass parts for trucks, has a control plan for each production process that includes the process name, tool used, standard operating procedure, tolerance, inspection frequency, sample size, person responsible, reporting document, and reaction plan. Of particular importance is the ability to trace all components of a product back to key process equipment and operators and to the original material from which it was made. Process control also includes monitoring the accuracy and variability of equipment, operator knowledge and skills, the accuracy of measurement results and data used, and environmental factors such as time and temperature. Process control should be the responsibility of every employee who "owns" a process.

Many organizations fall into the trap of trying to control every possible quality characteristic. Time and resources preclude this goal. Process control indicators should be closely related to cost or performance, be economical to measure, and should provide information for improvement. Good places to take control measurements are before relatively high-cost operations or where significant value is added to the product; before processing operations that may make detection of defectives difficult or costly, such as operations that may mask or obscure faulty attributes, as, for example, painting; and after operations that are likely to generate a high proportion of defectives.

From a strict economic standpoint, one need only inspect everything or nothing. To illustrate this, let us consider the decision between having 100 percent inspection and no inspection after an intermediate assembly operation for an electronic calculator. To make this decision, we must compare the inspection cost to the penalty cost incurred if a nonconforming item is missed. Suppose it costs an average of 25¢ per unit for the inspector's time, equipment, and overhead. If a nonconforming part is assembled at this stage of production, the calculator will not work properly during final inspection. Rejected calculators must be disassembled and repaired; the work involved averages $8 per unit. The problem is thus to establish a break-even point for the quality level. For a lot size of 100 items, for example, 100 percent inspection costs 100(0.25), or $25. The cost of no inspection depends on the quality level—that is, the proportion nonconforming. If the proportion nonconforming is p, then an average of $100p$ units require rework at a cost of $8 each. Thus, the average cost of no inspection is $800p$. The break-even proportion of defective items is found by setting $25 = 800p$. Thus, $p = .03125$. Hence, if the proportion nonconforming is greater than .03125, it is more economical to inspect each assembly.

One should also consider the result of allowing a nonconforming item to continue through production or on to the consumer. If the result might be a safety hazard, costly repairs or correction, or some other intolerable condition, the conclusion would probably be to use 100 percent inspection.

Corrective Action and Continual Improvement

Errors in production and service will occur, for example, because of confusing instructions or drawings, unclear verbal directions, inadequate training, poor designs, confusing customer specifications, or incapable equipment. As soon as nonconforming items or errors are identified, they should be brought to the attention of someone who is authorized to take action and prevent further expense. The quality system should clearly state what actions should be taken and what should be done with any nonconforming items, for example, repair, rework, or scrap. Using techniques for quality improvement such as Six Sigma to identify the root cause and develop a solution, corrective action should be taken to eliminate or minimize the recurrence of the problem. Permanent changes resulting from corrective actions should be recorded in work instructions, product specifications, or other quality-system documentation.

Controlling Inspection, Measuring, and Test Equipment

Measuring quality characteristics generally requires the use of the human senses—seeing, hearing, feeling, tasting, and smelling—and the use of some type of instrument or gauge to measure the magnitude of the characteristic. Gauges and instruments used to measure quality characteristics must provide correct information; this is done through metrology. **Metrology** *is the collection of people, equipment, facilities, methods, and procedures used to assure the correctness or adequacy of measurements.*

Metrology *is the collection of people, equipment, facilities, methods, and procedures used to assure the correctness or adequacy of measurements.*

Metrology is vital to quality control because of the emphasis on quality by government agencies, the implications of measurement error on safety and product liability, and the reliance on improved quality control methods such as statistical process control. The need for metrology stems from the fact that every measurement is subject to error. Whenever variation is observed in measurements, some portion is due to measurement system error. Some errors are systematic; others are random. The size of the errors relative to the measurement value can significantly affect the quality of the data and resulting decisions. The evaluation of data obtained from inspection and measurement is not meaningful unless the measurement instruments are accurate and precise. To understand this, consider the fact that the total observed variation in operating systems output is the sum of the true process variation (which is what we actually want to measure) plus variation due to measurement:

$$\sigma^2_{\text{total}} = \sigma^2_{\text{process}} + \sigma^2_{\text{measurement}}$$

If the measurement variation is high, the observed results will be biased, leading to inaccurate assessment of process capabilities.

Repeatability, *or* **equipment variation,** *is the variation in multiple measurements by an individual using the same instrument.*

Reproducibility, *or* **operator variation,** *is the variation in the same measuring instrument when it is used by different individuals to measure the same parts.*

Repeatability, *or* **equipment variation,** *is the variation in multiple measurements by an individual using the same instrument.* This is a measure of how precise and accurate the equipment is. **Reproducibility,** *or* **operator variation,** *is the variation in the same measuring instrument when it is used by different individuals to measure the same parts.* This indicates how robust the measuring process is to the operator and environmental conditions. Most manufacturers conduct gage repeatability and reproducibility studies to quantify these types of variation.

Records, Documentation, and Audits

All the elements required for a quality system, such as control processes, measuring and test equipment, and other resources needed to achieve the required quality of conformance, should be documented in a quality manual, which serves as a permanent reference for implementing and maintaining the system. A quality manual need not be very complex; a small company might need only a dozen pages, whereas a large organization might need manuals for all key functions. Sufficient records should be maintained to demonstrate conformance to requirements and verify that the quality system is operating effectively. Typical records that might be maintained are inspection reports, test data, audit reports, and calibration data. They should be readily retrievable for analysis to identify trends and monitor the effectiveness of corrective actions. Other documents, such as drawings, specifications, inspection procedures and instructions, work instructions, and operation sheets are vital to achieving quality and should likewise be controlled.

Because many documents and data are generated during a product's life cycle, the quality system should include a means of controlling them. This includes such things as keeping documents and data up-to-date and removing obsolete documents, unless they are needed for legal purposes. In many situations, it is appropriate to have procedures for identifying and tracing products during all stages of production, delivery, and installation, even down to individual parts or batches. This is critical, for instance, in the food or drug industries in the event of any product recalls.

Internal audits *focus on identifying whether documented procedures are being followed and are effective and report the issues to management for corrective action.*

Keeping the quality control system up-to-date is not always easy. This can be facilitated through **internal audits,** *which focus on identifying whether documented procedures are being followed and are effective and report the issues to management for corrective action.* Internal audits generally include a review of process records, training records, complaints, corrective actions, and previous audit reports. Managers must use audit findings as a tool for continuous improvement, not as means of placing blame on individuals.

A typical internal audit begins by asking those who perform a process regularly to explain how it works.[20] Their statements are compared to written procedures, and compliance and deviations are noted. Next, the trail of paperwork or other data is examined to determine whether the process is consistent with the intent of the written procedure and the worker's explanation. Internal auditors also need to analyze whether the process is meeting its intent and objectives, thus focusing on continuous improvement.

Challenges Facing Global Companies

Multinational corporations face special challenges in implementing quality management systems.[21] Six key factors have been identified:

1. Cultural limitations
2. Insufficient management preparation
3. Insufficient employee preparation
4. Employee attitudes
5. Specific legal regulations
6. Technological limitations

Cultural differences are fairly obvious. One of the reasons that many Western nations had difficulty implementing many of the approaches developed in Japan, such as problem-solving teams, was largely due to such differences. Because quality depends so heavily on management leadership, the lack of quality-consciousness in senior management makes it difficult to introduce and implement new concepts and ideas. Many companies find the greatest challenges in Africa, China, and Central and Eastern Europe. However, as many managers have attended top business schools in the United States and in Europe, this is becoming less of a factor. Companies find employees better prepared and with better attitudes in Australia and Oceania, as well as in many parts of Asia (excluding China), while the greatest challenges again lie in Africa, China, and Central and Eastern Europe. In these regions also, companies face legal challenges because of differences in regulations. However, with the exception of Africa, technological limitations do not appear to inhibit the implementation of quality management systems.

Changing attitudes and mind-sets is a difficult process that require significant investment in education and genuine understanding by managers who run operations outside of their native land.

SIX SIGMA

Learning Objective
To understand the basic philosophy and methods of Six Sigma and how it is applied in organizations to improve quality and operations performance.

Six Sigma *is a business improvement approach that seeks to find and eliminate causes of defects and errors in manufacturing and service processes by focusing on outputs that are critical to customers and results in a clear financial return for the organization.* The term *Six Sigma* is based on a statistical measure that equates to at most 3.4 errors or defects per million opportunities. An ultimate "stretch" goal of all organizations that adopt a Six Sigma philosophy is to have all critical processes, regardless of functional area, at a six-sigma level of capability—a level of near zero defects. Six Sigma has garnered a significant amount of credibility over the last decade because of its acceptance at such major firms as Motorola, Allied Signal (now part of Honeywell), Texas Instruments, and General Electric. It is facilitated through use of basic and advanced quality improvement and control tools by individuals and teams whose members are trained to provide fact-based decision-making information.

Six Sigma *is a business improvement approach that seeks to find and eliminate causes of defects and errors in manufacturing and service processes by focusing on outputs that are critical to customers and results in a clear financial return for the organization.*

Measuring Quality in Six Sigma

A **defect** *is any mistake or error that is passed on to the customer.*

A **unit of work** *is the output of a process or an individual process step.*

In Six Sigma terminology, *a* **defect** *is any mistake or error that is passed on to the customer* (many people also use the term *nonconformance*). *A* **unit of work** *is the output of a process or an individual process step.* We can measure output quality by defects per unit (DPU), a popular quality measure that we introduced in Chapter 3:

Defects per unit = Number of defects discovered/Number of units produced

However, an output measure such as this tends to focus on the final product, not the process that produces the product. In addition, it is difficult to use for processes of varying complexity, particularly service activities. Two different processes might have significantly different numbers of opportunities for error, making appropriate comparisons difficult. The Six Sigma concept characterizes quality performance by *defects per million opportunities (dpmo)*, computed as DPU × 1,000,000/opportunities for error (or, as is often used in services, *errors per million opportunities—epmo*). For example, suppose that an airline wishes to measure the effectiveness of its baggage handling system. A DPU measure might be lost bags per customer. However, customers may have different numbers of bags; thus the number of opportunities for error is the average number of bags per customer. If the average number of bags per customer is 1.6, and the airline recorded 3 lost bags for 8,000 passengers in one month, then

$$\text{epmo} = (3/8{,}000) \times 1{,}000{,}000/1.6 = 234.375$$

The use of dpmo and epmo allows us to define quality broadly. In the airline case, this might mean every opportunity for a failure to meet customer expectations from initial ticketing until bags are retrieved.

Six Sigma represents a quality level of at most 3.4 defects per million opportunities. The theoretical basis for Six Sigma is explained by Exhibit 15.4 in the context of manufacturing specifications. A six-sigma quality level corresponds to a process variation equal to half of the design tolerance while allowing the mean to shift as much as 1.5 standard deviations from the target. This figure was chosen by Motorola because field failure data suggested that Motorola's processes drifted by this amount on average. The allowance of a shift in the distribution is important, since no process can be maintained in perfect control. Under this assumption, the area in either tail of the shifted curves *beyond* the six-sigma range (the tolerance limit) is only 0.0000034, or 3.4 parts per million. If the process mean is held exactly on target (the shaded distribution in Exhibit 15.4), only 1 defect per billion would be expected (the area under each tail)!

In a similar fashion, we could define three-sigma quality, five-sigma quality, and so on. A 5-sigma level corresponds to 233 dpmo, 4-sigma to 6,200 dpmo, and 3-sigma to 66,803 dpmo. What may be quite surprising to realize is that a change from 3 to 4-sigma represents a 10-fold improvement; from 4 to 5 sigma, a 30-fold improvement; and from 5- to 6-sigma, a 70-fold improvement—difficult challenges for any organization. Many companies have adopted this standard to challenge their own improvement efforts.

The sigma level can easily be calculated on an Excel spreadsheet using the formula

=NORMSINV(1 − Number of Defects/Number of Opportunities) + 1.5

or equivalently,

=NORMSINV(1 − dpmo/1,000,000) + 1.5

Using the airline example discussed earlier, if we had 3 lost bags for 8,000(1.6) = 12,800 opportunities, we would find =NORMSINV(1 − 3/12800) + 1.5 = 4.99828, or about a 5-sigma level. The truth is less impressive. It was reported that 3.67 mishandled baggage reports per 1,000 passengers were filed in May 2003, which was up from 3.31 per 1,000 a year earlier.[22] This result yields a sigma level of only 4.33, assuming 1.6 bags per passenger.

Although originally developed for manufacturing in the context of tolerance-based specifications, the Six Sigma concept has been adopted to any process and has come to signify a generic quality level of at most 3.4 defects per million opportunities. It has been applied in product development, new business acquisition, customer service, accounting, and many other business functions. For example, suppose that a bank tracks the number of errors reported in customers' checking account statements. If it finds 12 errors in 1,000 statements, this is equivalent to an error rate of 12,000 per million, (somewhere between 3.5 and 4 sigma levels).

Implementing Six Sigma

Six Sigma has developed from simply a way of measuring quality to an overall strategy to accelerate improvements and achieve unprecedented performance levels within an organization by finding and eliminating causes of errors or defects in processes by focusing on characteristics that are critical to customers.[23] The core philosophy of Six Sigma is based on some key concepts:[24]

1. emphasizing dpmo as a standard metric that can be applied to all parts of an organization: manufacturing, engineering, administrative, software, and so on
2. providing extensive training followed by project team deployment to improve profitability, reduce non-value-added activities, and achieve cycle time reduction
3. focusing on corporate sponsors responsible for supporting team activities, helping to overcome resistance to change, obtain resources, and focus the teams on overall strategic objectives
4. creating highly qualified process improvement experts ("green belts," "black belts," and "master black belts") who can apply improvement tools and lead teams
5. ensuring that appropriate metrics are identified early in the process and that they focus on business results
6. setting stretch objectives for improvement

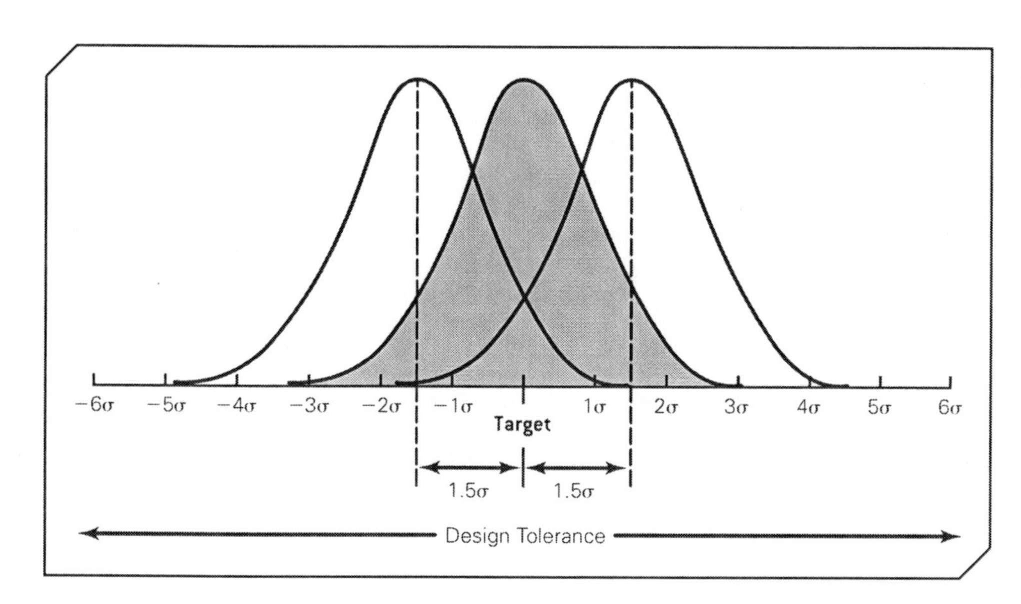

Exhibit 15.4
Six-Sigma Quality

The recognized benchmark for Six Sigma implementation is General Electric (see the OM Spotlight). GE's Six Sigma problem-solving approach (DMAIC) employs five phases:

1. *Define (D)*
   - Identify customers and their priorities.
   - Identify a project suitable for Six Sigma efforts based on business objectives as well as customer needs and feedback.
   - Identify CTQs (*critical to quality characteristics*) that the customer considers to have the most impact on quality.
2. *Measure (M)*
   - Determine how to measure the process and how is it performing.
   - Identify the key internal processes that influence CTQs and measure the defects currently generated relative to those processes.
3. *Analyze (A)*
   - Determine the most likely causes of defects.
   - Understand why defects are generated by identifying the key variables that are most likely to create process variation.
4. *Improve (I)*
   - Identify means to remove the causes of the defects.
   - Confirm the key variables and quantify their effects on the CTQs.
   - Identify the maximum acceptable ranges of the key variables and a system for measuring deviations of the variables.
   - Modify the process to stay within the acceptable range.

OM SPOTLIGHT

General Electric

The efforts by General Electric in particular, driven by former CEO Jack Welch, have brought significant media attention to the concept and have made Six Sigma a very popular approach to quality improvement. In the mid-1990s, quality emerged as a concern of many employees at GE. Jack Welch invited Larry Bossidy, then CEO of AlliedSignal, who had phenomenal success with Six Sigma, to talk about it at a corporate executive council meeting. The meeting caught the attention of GE managers and as Welch stated, "I went nuts about Six Sigma and launched it," calling it the most ambitious undertaking the company had ever taken on.[25] To ensure success, GE changed its incentive compensation plan so that 60 percent of the bonus was based on financials and 40 percent on Six Sigma and provided stock option grants to employees in Six Sigma training. In their first year, GE trained 30,000 employees at a cost of $200 million and got back about $150 million in savings. From 1996 to 1997, GE increased the number of Six Sigma projects from 3,000 to 6,000 and achieved $320 million in productivity gains and profits. By 1998, the company had generated $750 million in Six Sigma savings over and above its investment and would receive $1.5 billion in savings the next year.

GE had many early success stories. GE Capital, for example, fielded about 300,000 calls each year from mortgage customers who had to use voice mail or call back 24 percent of the time because employees were busy or unavailable. A Six Sigma team analyzed one branch that had a near perfect percentage of answered calls and applied their knowledge of their best practices to the other 41 branches, resulting in a 99.9 percent chance of customers' getting a representative on the first try. A team at GE Plastics improved the quality of a product used in CD-ROMs and audio CDs from a 3.8 sigma level to a 5.7 level and captured a significant amount of new business from Sony.[26] GE credits Six Sigma with a 10-fold increase in the life of CT scanner X-ray tubes, a 400% improvement in return on investment in its industrial diamond business, a 62 percent reduction in turnaround time at railcar repair shops, and $400 million in savings in its plastics business.[27]

5. *Control (C)*
    - Determine how to maintain the improvements.
    - Put tools in place to ensure that the key variables remain within the maximum acceptable ranges under the modified process.

Project teams are fundamental to Six Sigma. Six Sigma projects require a diversity of skills that range from technical analysis, creative solution development, and implementation (see the OM Spotlight on Ford Motor Company). Thus, Six Sigma teams not only address immediate problems but also provide an environment for individual learning, management development, and career advancement. Six Sigma teams are comprised of several types of individuals:

- *Champions*—senior-level managers who promote and lead the deployment of Six Sigma in a significant area of the business. Champions understand the philosophy and tools of Six Sigma, select projects, set objectives, allocate resources, and mentor teams. Champions own Six Sigma projects and are responsible for their completion and results; typically they also own the process that the project is focused on improving. They select teams, set strategic direction, create measurable objectives, provide resources, monitor performance, make key implementation decisions, and report results to top management. More importantly, champions work toward removing barriers—organizational, financial, personal—that might inhibit the successful implementation of a Six Sigma project.
- *Master Black Belts*—full-time Six Sigma experts who are responsible for Six Sigma strategy, training, mentoring, deployment, and results. Master Black Belts are highly trained in how to use Six Sigma tools and methods and provide advanced technical expertise. They work across the organization to develop and coach teams, conduct training, and lead change, but are typically not members of Six Sigma project teams.
- *Black Belts*—fully trained Six Sigma experts with up to 160 hours of training who perform much of the technical analyses required of Six Sigma projects, usually on a full-time basis. They have advanced knowledge of tools and DMAIC methods and can apply them either individually or as team leaders. They also mentor and develop Green Belts. Black Belts need good leadership and communication skills in addition to technical skills and process knowledge. They should be highly motivated, eager to gain new knowledge, and well respected among their peers. As such, Black Belts are often targeted by the organization as future business leaders.
- *Green Belts*—functional employees who are trained in introductory Six Sigma tools and methodology and work on projects on a part-time basis, assisting Black Belts while developing their own knowledge and expertise. Typically, one of the requirements for receiving a Green Belt designation is to successfully complete a Six Sigma project. Successful Green Belts are often promoted to Black Belts.
- *Team Members*—individuals from various functional areas who support specific projects.

Six Sigma has many benefits. For example, from 1996 to 1998, GE increased the number of Six Sigma projects from 200 to 6,000. From all these efforts, GE expected to save $7 to $10 billion over a decade. Other companies also report significant results. Between 1995 and the first quarter of 1997, Allied Signal reported cost savings exceeding $800 million from its Six Sigma initiative. Citibank groups have reduced internal callbacks by 80 percent, credit process time by 50 percent, and cycle times of processing statements from 28 days to 15 days.[28]

OM SPOTLIGHT

Ford Motor Company[29]

Ford Motor Company began developing its Six Sigma quality approach, called Consumer Driven Six Sigma, in 1999. However, the company didn't really get serious about reclaiming its motto of the 1980s, "Quality is Job 1," until 2001. That was when JD Power and Associates' Initial Quality Study ranked Ford last among the Big-Seven automakers. By 2003, the same survey ranked Ford number four and found that it was the most improved automaker of the group.

The company now has more than 200 Master Black Belts, 2,200 Black Belts, nearly 40,000 Green Belts, and 3,000 Project Champions. Ford's training of Green, Black, Master Black Belts, and Project Champions generally follows the conventional Six Sigma training process. Black Belt training is "hands-on" and "just in time." Each trainee gets 1 week of full-time training per month for 4 months. The other 3 weeks of the month require that the trainee apply the training to a live project. Ford's Six Sigma teams typically have a member of management, a Master Black Belt (MBB), a Black Belt (BB), and several Green Belts (GB) assigned to take on various roles in a project.

BBs are expected to handle two to three projects at a time. They can choose their own projects but are asked to choose them carefully to ensure that they contribute to waste elimination and/or customer satisfaction improvement. The goal is that at least half of the reduction of "Things Gone Wrong," (in "Ford-speak") will be improved through successful Six Sigma projects. Ford has implemented a unique project tracking system that has helped to promote organizational learning. The system allows member of project teams to observe what other teams are working on via an internal database.

Leaders are also expected to have hands-on involvement as Project Champions. Senior leaders are required to partner with MBBs to run performance cells. These cells are managed similarly to a manufacturing cell and benefit from the technical expertise of the MBB and the administrative experience of the manager. The process keeps new projects coming in and ensures that projects that are underway stay on track.

Overall, Ford's Six Sigma approach has contributed impressively to the bottom line. More than 6,000 projects have been completed in just 3 years, and Six Sigma has saved over $1 billion since its inception.

JEFF KOWALSKY/EPA/Landov

Six Sigma in Services and Small Organizations

Because Six Sigma was developed in the manufacturing sector, and most publicity has revolved around such companies as Motorola and GE, many people in the service sector think that Six Sigma applies only to large manufacturing companies. Nothing can be further from the truth.[30] All Six Sigma projects have three key characteristics: a problem to be solved, a process in which the problem exists, and one or more measures that quantify the gap to be closed and can be used to monitor progress. These characteristics are present in all business processes; thus, Six Sigma can easily be applied to a wide variety of transactional, administrative, and service areas in both large and small firms. Many financial services firms, like J.P. Morgan Chase & Co. and GE Capital, have used it extensively.

It is generally agreed that 50 percent or more of the total savings opportunity in an organization lies outside of manufacturing. Both manufacturing and service processes have "hidden factories," those places where the defective "product" is sent to be reworked or scrapped (revised, corrected, or discarded, in nonmanufacturing terms). Find the hidden factory and you have found one good place to look for opportunities to improve the process. Performing manual account reconciliation in accounting, revising budgets repeatedly until management will accept them, and making repeat sales calls to customers because all the information requested by the customer was not available are all examples of the hidden factory.

Because service processes are largely people-driven, measurements are often nonexistent or ill-defined, as many believe that there are no defects to measure. Therefore, one must often create good measurement systems before collecting any data. In applying Six Sigma to services, there are four key measures of the performance: *accuracy*, as measured by correct financial figures, completeness of information, or freedom from data errors; *cycle time*, which is a measure of how long it takes to do something, such as pay an invoice; *cost*, that is, the internal cost of process activities (in many cases, cost is largely determined by the accuracy and/or cycle time of the process; the longer it takes, and the more mistakes that have to be fixed, the higher the cost); and *customer satisfaction*, which is typically the primary measure of success.

Consider how a janitorial service company might use DMAIC. In the Define stage, a key question would be to define what a defect represents. One might first create a flowchart of the cleaning process, specifying what activities are performed. One example of a defect might be leaving streaks on windows, because it is a source of customer dissatisfaction—a CTQ. In the Measure stage, the firm not only would want to collect data on the frequency of defects but also information about what products and tools employees use. The Analyze stage might include evaluating differences among employees to determine why some appear better at cleaning than others. Developing a standard operating procedure might be the focus of the Improve stage. Finally, Control might entail teaching employees the correct technique and measuring improvement over time. The following OM Spotlight describes some real applications of Six Sigma in service organizations.

OM SPOTLIGHT

Six Sigma Applications in Services[31]

In one application at CNH Capital, Six Sigma tools were applied to decrease asset management cycle time in posting repossessions to a bid list and remarketing web site. Cycle time was reduced 75 percent, from 40 days to 10 days, resulting in significant ongoing dollar savings. A facility management company had a high level of "days sales outstanding." Initially, it tried to fix this by reducing the term of days in its billing cycle, which, however, upset customers. Using Six Sigma, it found that a large percentage of accounts with high days sales outstanding received invoices from the company having numerous errors. After understanding the source of the errors and making process changes, the invoice process improved and days sales outstanding was reduced. At DuPont, a Six Sigma project was applied to improve cycle time for an employee's application for long-term disability benefits.[32] Some examples of financial applications of Six Sigma include[33]

- reducing the average and variation of days outstanding of accounts receivable
- closing the books faster
- improving the accuracy and speed of the audit process
- reducing variation in cash flow
- improving the accuracy of journal entry (most businesses have a 3–4 percent error rate)
- improving the accuracy and cycle time of standard financial reports

Six Sigma faces some challenges in small organizations. First, the culture in small organizations is usually less scientific and employees typically do not think in terms of processes, measurements, and data. Second, the processes are often invisible, complex, and not well defined or well documented. Small organizations are often confused and intimidated by the size, costs, and extensive technical training they see in large organizations that implement "formal" Six Sigma processes. Because of this, they often don't even try to adopt these approaches. Small organizations are usually lean by necessity, but not always effectively so. Their processes often operate at quality levels of 2 to 3 sigma, and they are not even aware of it. Small companies often need to bring in consultants for training or improvement initiatives in the early stages of learning. This can help to develop in-house expertise and put them on the right track.

Learning Objective
To learn about the features of elementary quality analysis and improvement tools and be able to apply them to practical business problems.

TOOLS FOR QUALITY ANALYSIS AND IMPROVEMENT

The tools used in Six Sigma efforts have been around for a long time and may be categorized into seven general groups:

- *elementary statistical tools* (basic statistics, statistical thinking, hypothesis testing, correlation, simple regression)
- *advanced statistical tools* (design of experiments, analysis of variance, multiple regression)
- *product design and reliability* (quality function deployment, reliability analysis, failure mode and effects analysis)
- *measurement* (cost of quality, process capability, measurement systems analysis)
- *process control* (control plans, statistical process control, reducing variation)
- *process improvement* (process improvement planning, process mapping, mistake-proofing)
- *implementation and teamwork* (organizational effectiveness, team assessment, facilitation tools, team development)

You may have covered some of these tools, such as statistics and teamwork, in other courses, and some, such as quality function deployment and statistical process control, are discussed in other chapters of this book. In this section, we present some of the more important tools for quality analysis and improvement.

Cost of Quality Measurement

Quality problems expressed as the number of errors or defects—the principal metrics at the operations level—have little impact on top managers, who are generally concerned with financial and market performance, until they are translated and aggregated into financial measures. An effective way for operations managers to understand quality and how it affects what they do is to consider the costs associated with goods, services, or environmental quality. *The* **cost of quality** *refers specifically to the costs associated with avoiding poor quality or those incurred as a result of poor quality.* Cost of quality analysis can help operations managers communicate with senior-level managers, identify and justify major opportunities for process improvements, and evaluate the importance of quality and improvement in operations.

The **cost of quality** *refers specifically to the costs associated with avoiding poor quality or those incurred as a result of poor quality.*

Prevention costs *are those expended to keep nonconforming goods and services from being made and reaching the customer.*

QUALITY COST CLASSIFICATION

Quality costs can be organized into four major categories: prevention costs, appraisal costs, internal-failure costs, and external-failure costs. **Prevention costs** *are* *those expended to keep nonconforming goods and services from being made and reaching the customer.* They include

- *quality planning costs*—such as salaries of individuals associated with quality planning and problem-solving teams, the development of new procedures, new equipment design, and reliability studies
- *process-control costs*—which include costs spent on analyzing processes and implementing process control plans
- *information-systems costs*—which are expended to develop data requirements and measurements
- *training and general management costs*—which include internal and external training programs, clerical staff expenses, and miscellaneous supplies

Appraisal costs *are those expended on ascertaining quality levels through measurement and analysis of data to detect and correct problems.* They include

- *test and inspection costs*—those associated with incoming materials, work-in-process, and finished goods, including equipment costs and salaries
- *instrument maintenance costs*—those associated with the calibration and repair of measuring instruments
- *process-measurement and process-control costs*—which involve the time spent by workers to gather and analyze quality measurements

Appraisal costs *are those expended on ascertaining quality levels through measurement and analysis of data to detect and correct problems.*

Internal-failure costs *are costs incurred as a result of unsatisfactory quality that is found before the delivery of a good or service to the customer.* Examples include

- *scrap and rework costs*—including material, labor, and overhead
- *costs of corrective action*—arising from time spent determining the causes of failure and correcting problems
- *downgrading costs*—such as revenue lost by selling a good or service at a lower price because it does not meet specifications
- *process failures*—such as unplanned equipment downtime or service upsets or unplanned equipment repair

Internal-failure costs *are costs incurred as a result of unsatisfactory quality that is found before the delivery of a good or service to the customer.*

External-failure costs *are incurred after poor-quality goods or services reach the customer.* They include

- *costs due to customer complaints and returns*—including rework on returned items, cancelled orders, discount coupons, and freight premiums
- *goods and services recall costs and warranty and service guarantee claims*—including the cost of repair or replacement as well as associated administrative costs
- *product-liability costs*—resulting from legal actions and settlements

External-failure costs *are incurred after poor-quality goods or services reach the customer.*

An example of a prevention cost in a pizza business would be processing customer-satisfaction survey results as a basis for improved training programs. Appraisal costs might be measuring the weight of the cheese used in a pizza before pizza assembly to ensure the correct amount or the time associated with inspecting each pizza before delivery to the customer. A burned pizza that is discarded would be an internal-failure cost. Given the short shelf life of a pizza, inaccurate order taking could also cause one to throw away the finished pizza (good). The cost of pizzas sent back by customers or discounts offered because of late delivery would be examples of external-failure costs. These data can be broken down by customer benefit package, process, department, work center, time, job, service encounter type, or cost category to make data analysis more convenient and useful to managers.

Standard accounting systems are generally able to provide quality-cost data for direct labor, overhead, scrap, warranty expenses, product-liability costs, and maintenance, repair, and calibration efforts on test equipment. However, they are not structured to capture many types of important cost-of-quality information. Costs related to service upsets, poor goods or service design, remedial engineering effort, rework, in-process inspection, and engineering-change losses must usually be estimated or collected through special efforts. Although prevention costs are the most important, it is usually easiest to determine appraisal, internal-failure, external-failure, and prevention costs, in that order.

Like productivity measures, quality costs are often reported as an index—that is, the ratio of the current value to a base-period value. Some common quality-cost indexes are quality cost per direct labor hour, quality cost per manufacturing cost dollar, quality cost per sales dollar, and quality costs per unit of production. All of those ratios and indexes, although extensively used in practice, have a fundamental problem. A change in the denominator can appear to be a change in the level of quality or productivity alone. For instance, if direct labor is decreased through managerial improvements, the direct-labor-based index will increase even if there is no change in quality. Also, the common inclusion of overhead in manufacturing cost is certain to distort results. And in services, how to allocate overhead to specific services is an ongoing problem. Nevertheless, such indexes can help in comparing quality costs over time. Generally, sales bases are the most popular, followed by cost, labor, and unit bases.[34]

Consider a printing company that produces a variety of books, brochures, reports, and other printed material for business customers. The printing manager has tracked quality-related costs over the past year. Sales were $16.2 million last year. What do the following data suggest?

Cost Element	Amount ($)
Proofreading	$ 710,000
Quality planning	10,000
Press downtime	405,000
Bindery waste paper	75,000
Checking and inspection	60,000
Customer complaints and job redo	40,000
Printing plate revisions	40,000
Quality-improvement projects	20,000
Other waste	55,000
Correction of typographic errors	300,000
Total quality-related costs	$1,715,000

The first step in the cost-of-quality analysis is to assign each quality-cost element to the appropriate category—prevention, appraisal, internal failure, or external failure:

Prevention	
Quality planning	$ 10,000
Quality-improvement projects	20,000
Total	30,000
Appraisal	
Proofreading	$710,000
Checking and inspection	60,000
Total	770,000
Internal failure	
Press downtime	$405,000
Bindery waste paper	75,000
Printing plate revisions	40,000
Other waste	55,000
Correction of typographical errors	300,000
Total	875,000
External failure	
Customer complaints and rework	$ 40,000

Internal-failure costs account for 51 percent ($875,000/$1,715,000) of the total quality-related costs, external failure 2.3 percent, prevention 1.8 percent, and appraisal costs account for 44.9 percent. Hence, although the company is spending a lot of money in appraisal (detection) activities, it still has a significant amount of internal failure. Apparently, much more effort needs to be expended on quality-improvement initiatives, particularly to reduce press downtime and typographical errors, and better practices and training for proofreading. The company is in the very early stages of continuous improvement with 95.9 percent of its quality costs in appraisal and internal-failure costs. Interestingly, external-failure costs are relatively low, meaning that it catches and corrects most errors prior to delivering the goods to customers or it doesn't do a good job of measuring customer retention and repeat business rates. Moreover, quality costs are 10.6 percent of sales, a dismal performance statistic! It is not unusual for quality costs to represent 20 percent or more of sales in manufacturing companies and over 30 percent of operating costs in service companies. Top-performing companies have quality cost as a percent of sales in the 1 percent to 5 percent range.

COMPUTING QUALITY-COST INDEXES

A company collects quality costs by cost category and product for each time period, say 1 month, as shown in the upper portion of Exhibit 15.5. It might compute a total quality-cost index as

$$\text{Quality-cost index} = \text{Total quality costs/Direct labor costs}$$

Alternatively, it might compute individual indexes by category, product, and time period, as summarized in the lower portion of Exhibit 15.5.

Such information can be used to identify areas that require improvement. Of course, it is up to managers and engineers to discover the precise nature of the improvement needed. For example, a steady rise in internal-failure costs and decline in appraisal costs might indicate a problem in assembly, maintenance of testing equipment, or control of purchased parts.

Quality costs in service organizations differ from those in manufacturing organizations. In manufacturing, they are primarily product-oriented; in services, they are process- and service-provider-dependent and usually more difficult to identify and quantify. Since quality in service organizations depends on service-provider and customer interaction, appraisal costs tend to account for a higher percentage of

Exhibit 15.5
Computing Quality-Cost Indexes

	January		February	
Cost Category	**Product A**	**Product B**	**Product A**	**Product B**
Prevention	$2,000	$4,000	$2,000	$4,000
Appraisal	$10,000	$20,000	$13,000	$21,000
Internal failure	$19,000	$106,000	$16,000	$107,000
External failure	$54,000	$146,000	$52,000	$156,000
Total	$85,000	$276,000	$83,000	$288,000
Standard direct labor costs	$35,000	$90,000	$28,000	$86,000
Quality-Cost Index				
Prevention	0.057	0.044	0.071	0.047
Appraisal	0.286	0.222	0.464	0.244
Internal failure	0.543	1.178	0.571	1.244
External failure	1.543	1.622	1.857	1.814
Total	2.429	3.067	2.964	3.349

total quality costs than they do in manufacturing. In addition, internal-failure costs tend to be lower for high-contact service organizations, because there is little opportunity to correct an error before it reaches the customer—at which point it represents an external failure. Such "service upsets" should be resolved on-the-spot by empowered and well-trained service providers. In fact, research has shown that good service recovery generally improves customer satisfaction and loyalty.

External-failure costs can become an extremely significant out-of-pocket expense to consumers of services. Consider the costs of interrupted service, such as telephone, electricity, or other utilities; delays in waiting to obtain service or excessive time in performing the service; errors made in billing, delivery, or installation; or unnecessary service. For example, a family moving from one city to another may have to pay additional costs for lodging and meals if the moving van does not arrive on the day promised; if a doctor's prescription needs to be changed because of faulty diagnosis, the patient pays for unnecessary drugs; if a computer makes a billing error, several phone calls, letters, and copies of cancelled checks may be needed to correct the mistake.

The "Seven QC Tools"

Seven simple tools—flowcharts, checksheets, histograms, Pareto diagrams, cause-and-effect diagrams, scatter diagrams, and control charts—termed the *Seven QC* (quality control) *Tools* by the Japanese, support quality improvement problem-solving efforts.[35] The Seven QC Tools are designed to be simple and visual so that workers at all levels can use them easily and provide a means of communication that is particularly well suited in group problem-solving efforts. We will briefly review each of these to explain their role in quality improvement.

FLOWCHARTS

To understand a process, one must first determine how it works and what it is supposed to do. Flowcharting, or process mapping, identifies the sequence of activities or the flow of materials and information in a process. Flowcharts help the people who are involved in the process understand it much better and more objectively. Understanding how a process works enables a team to pinpoint obvious problems, error-proof the process, streamline it by eliminating non-value-added steps, and reduce variation. Many types of flowcharts are used to communicate "how work gets done," and we have seen examples in previous chapters, for instance, Exhibit 1.7 for Pal's Sudden Service, Exhibit 3.3 on the time required to process reports.

Once a flowchart is constructed, it can be used to identify quality problems as well as areas for productivity improvement. Questions such as "How does this work activity or workstation affect the customer?", or "Can we improve or even eliminate this work activity?" or "Should we control a critical quality characteristic at this point?" trigger the identification of process design and improvement opportunities.

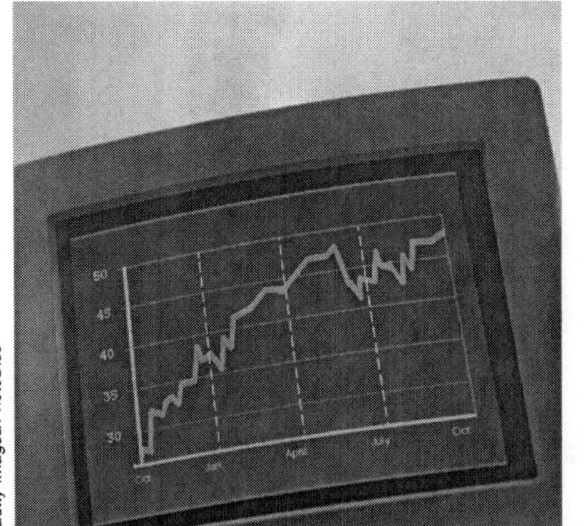

RUN CHARTS AND CONTROL CHARTS

A **run chart** is a line graph in which data are plotted over time. The vertical axis represents a measurement; the horizontal axis is the time scale. The daily newspaper usually has several examples of run charts, such as the Dow Jones Industrial Average. Run charts show the performance and the variation of a process or some quality or productivity indicator over time. They can be used to track such things as production volume, costs, and customer satisfaction indexes. Run charts summarize data in a graphical fashion that is easy to understand and interpret, identify process changes and trends over time, and show the effects of corrective actions.

The first step in constructing a run chart is to identify the measurement or indicator to be monitored. In some situations, one might measure the quality characteristics for each individual unit of process output. For low-volume processes, such as chemical production or surgeries, this would be appropriate. However, for high-volume production processes or services with large numbers of customers or transactions, it would be impractical. Instead, samples taken on a periodic basis provide the data for computing basic statistical measures such as the mean, range or standard deviation, proportion of items that do not conform to specifications, or number of nonconformances per unit.

Constructing the chart consists of the following steps:

Step 1. *Collect the data.* If samples are chosen, compute the relevant statistic for each sample, such as the average or proportion.

Step 2. *Examine the range of the data.* Scale the chart so that all data can be plotted on the vertical axis. Provide some additional room for new data as they are collected.

Step 3. *Plot the points on the chart and connect them.* Use graph paper if the chart is constructed by hand; a spreadsheet program is preferable.

Step 4. *Compute the average of all plotted points and draw it as a horizontal line through the data.* This line denoting the average is called the center line (CL) of the chart.

If the plotted points fluctuate in a stable pattern around the center line, with no large spikes, trends, or shifts, they indicate that the process is apparently under control. If unusual patterns exist, then the cause for lack of stability should be investigated and corrective action should be taken. Thus, run charts can identify messes caused by lack of control.

A **control chart** is simply a run chart to which two horizontal lines, called *control limits*, are added: the *upper control limit (UCL)* and *lower control limit (LCL)*, as illustrated in Exhibit 15.6. Control limits are chosen statistically so that there is a high probability (generally greater than .99) that points will fall between these limits if the process is in control. Control limits make it easier to interpret patterns in a run chart and draw conclusions about the state of control. The next chapter addresses this topic in much more detail.

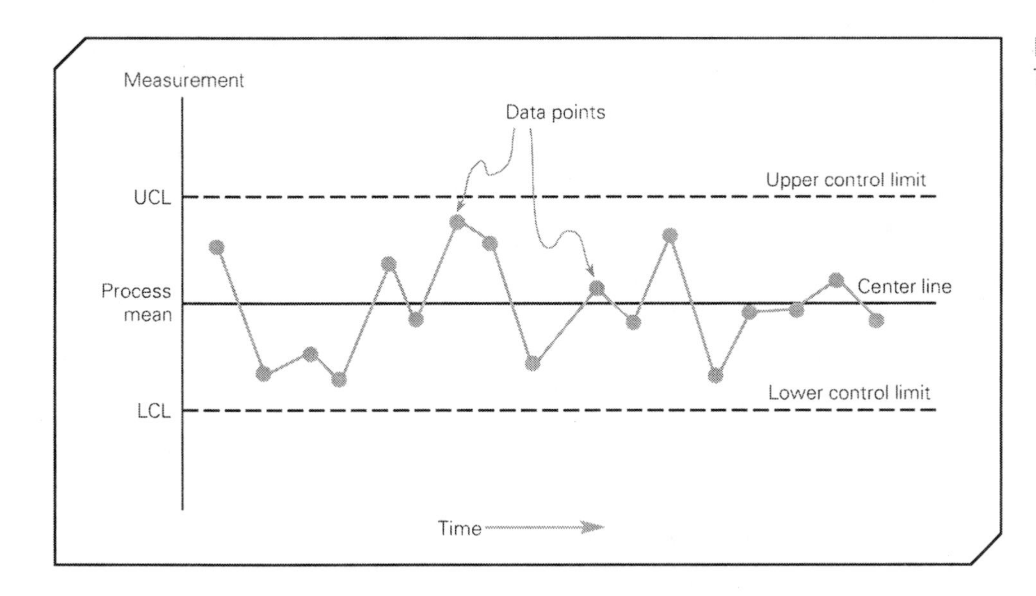

Exhibit 15.6
The Structure of a Control Chart

CHECKSHEETS

Checksheets are simple tools for data collection. Nearly any kind of form may be used to collect data. **Data sheets** are simple columnar or tabular forms used to record data. However, to generate useful information from raw data, further processing generally is necessary. Checksheets are special types of data collection forms in which the results may be interpreted on the form directly without additional processing. For example, in the checksheet in Exhibit 15.7, one can easily identify the most frequent causes of defects.

HISTOGRAMS

A histogram is a basic statistical tool that graphically shows the frequency or number of observations of a particular value or within a specified group. Histograms provide clues about the characteristics of the parent population from which a sample is taken. Patterns that would be difficult to see in an ordinary table of numbers become apparent. You are probably quite familiar with histograms from your statistics classes.

PARETO ANALYSIS

The *Pareto principle* was observed by Joseph Juran in 1950. Juran found that most effects resulted from only a few causes. For instance, in an analysis of 200 types of field failures of automotive engines, only 5 accounted for one-third of all failures; the top 25 accounted for two-thirds of the failures. He named this technique after Vilfredo Pareto (1848–1923), an Italian economist who determined that 85 percent of the wealth in Milan was owned by only 15 percent of the people. Pareto analysis separates the vital few from the trivial many and provides direction for selecting projects for improvement. For example, the checksheet in Exhibit 15.7 provides the data for a Pareto analysis. We see that the most frequent defect is Incomplete,

Exhibit 15.7
Defective Item Checksheet

Check Sheet

Product:

Manufacturing stage: final insp.

Type of defect: scar, incomplete, misshapen

Total no. inspected: 2530

Remarks: all items inspected

Date:

Factory:

Section:

Inspector's name:

Lot no.

Order no.

Type	Check	Subtotal
Surface scars	////// ////// ////// ////// ////// ////// //	32
Cracks	////// ////// ////// ////// ///	23
Incomplete	////// ////// ////// ////// ////// ////// ////// ////// ////// ///	48
Misshapen	////	4
Others	////// ///	8
	Grand total	115
Total rejects	////// ////// ////// ////// ////// ////// ////// ////// ////// ////// ////// ////// ////// ////// ////// ////// ////// /	86

Source: Ishikawa, Kaoru, "Defective Item Checksheet," p. 33 from *Guide to Quality Control*, 1982. Asian Productivity Organization. Reprinted with permission.

followed by Surface scars and Cracks. These should be the issues that management attacks first.

Pareto diagrams can also progressively help focus in on specific problems. Exhibit 15.8 shows one example. At each step, the Pareto diagram stratifies the data to more detailed levels (or it may require additional data collection), eventually isolating the most significant issues.

Exhibit 15.8
Use of Pareto Diagrams for Progressive Analysis

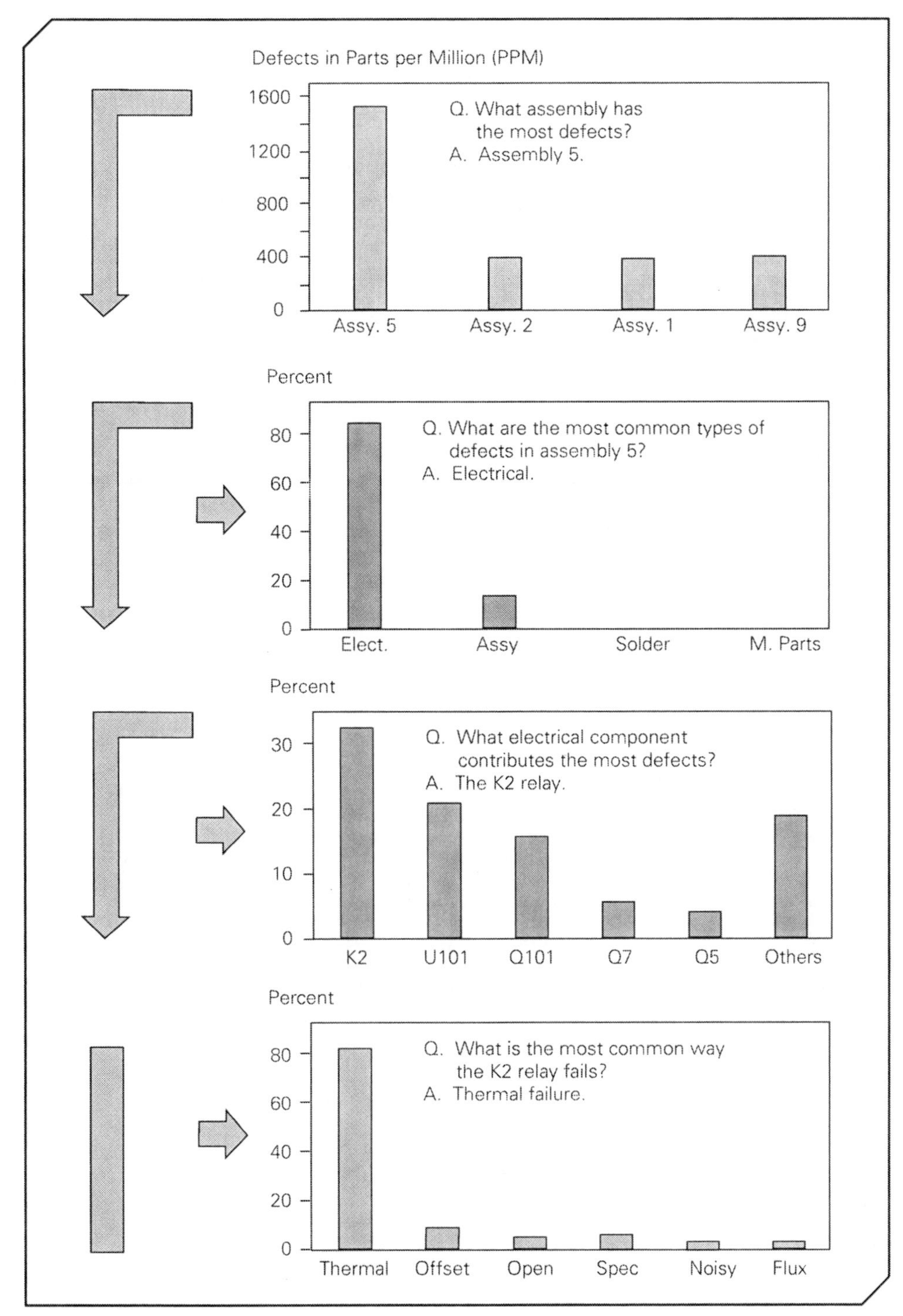

Source: *Small Business Guidebook to Quality Management*, Office of the Secretary of Defense, Quality Management Office, Washington, DC (1988).

CAUSE-AND-EFFECT DIAGRAMS

The cause-and-effect diagram is a simple, graphical method for presenting a chain of causes and effects and for sorting out causes and organizing relationships between variables. Because of its structure, it is often called a *fishbone diagram*. An example of a cause-and-effect diagram is shown in Exhibit 15.9. At the end of the horizontal line, a problem is listed. Each branch pointing into the main stem represents a possible cause. Branches pointing to the causes are contributors to those causes. The diagram identifies the most likely causes of a problem so that further data collection and analysis can be carried out.

SCATTER DIAGRAMS

Scatter diagrams are the graphical component of regression analysis. Although they do not provide rigorous statistical analysis, they often point to important relationships between variables, such as the percentage of an ingredient in an alloy and the hardness of the alloy. Typically, the variables in question represent possible causes and effects obtained from cause-and-effect diagrams. For example, if a manufacturer suspects that the percentage of an ingredient in an alloy is causing quality problems in meeting hardness specifications, an employee group might collect data from samples on the amount of ingredient and hardness and plot the data on a scatter diagram, which might indicate that lower quantities of the ingredient in the alloy are associated with increased quality problems.

Exhibit 15.9 Cause-and-Effect Diagram for Hospital Emergency Admission

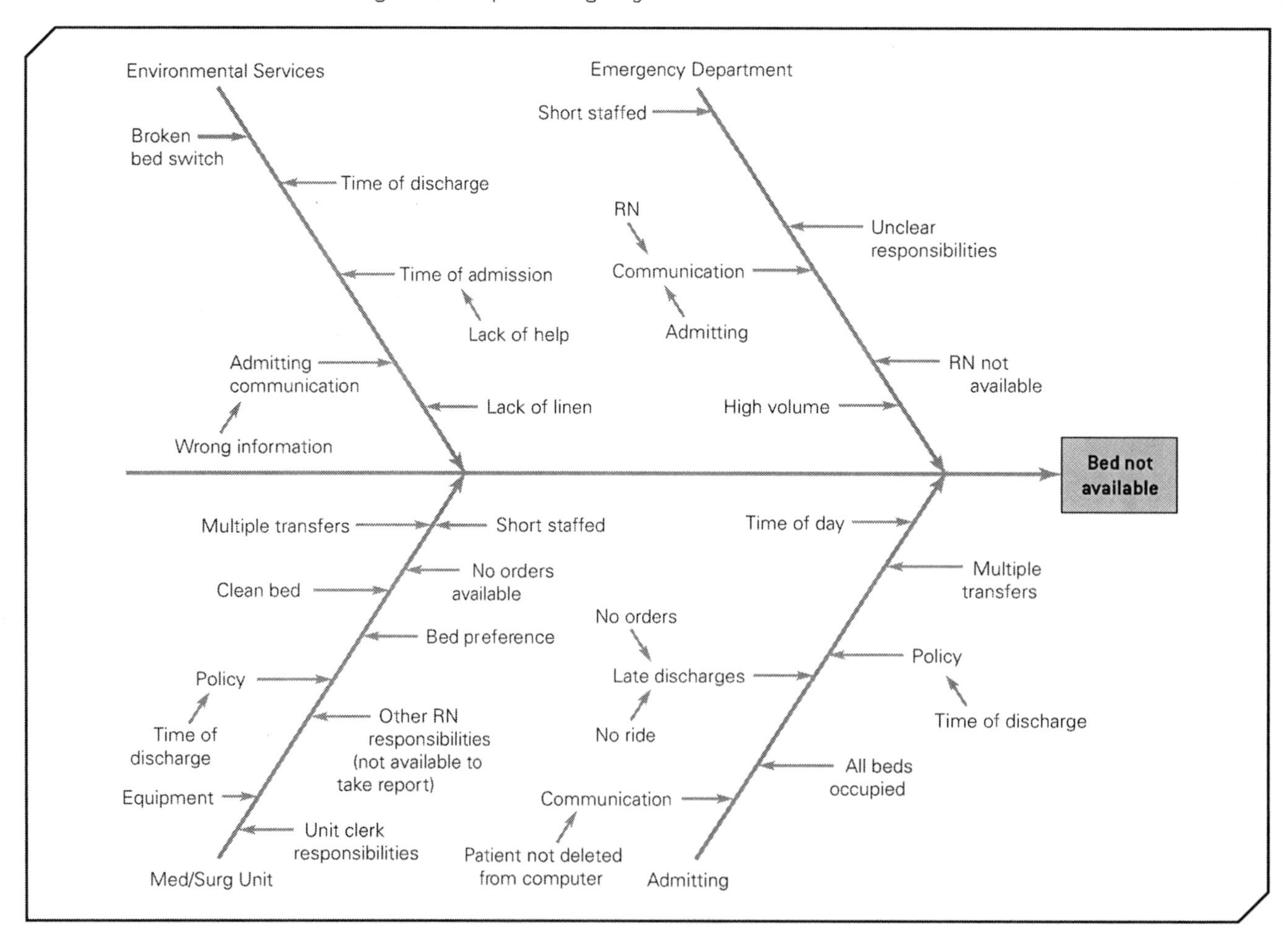

Using the Seven QC Tools for Improvement

The QC tools can be applied to the different steps of the Six Sigma DMAIC process to support the overall problem-solving and improvement effort, as shown in Exhibit 15.10.

Exhibit 15.10
Application of the Seven QC Tools in Six Sigma

Tool	DMAIC Application
Flowcharts	Define, Control
Checksheets	Measure, Analyze
Histograms	Measure, Analyze
Cause-and-effect diagrams	Analyze
Pareto diagrams	Analyze
Scatter diagrams	Analyze, Improve
Control charts	Control

Deming advocated a process similar to DMAIC to guide and motivate improvement activities, which has become known as the *Deming cycle*. The Deming cycle is composed of four stages: *plan*, *do*, *study*, and *act* (PDSA), as illustrated in Exhibit 15.11. (The third stage—study—was formerly called *check*, and the Deming cycle was known as the *PDCA cycle*.)

The Plan stage consists of studying the current situation and describing the process: its inputs, outputs, customers, and suppliers; understanding customer expectations; gathering data; identifying problems; testing theories of causes; and developing solutions and action plans. In the Do stage, the plan is implemented on a trial basis—for example, in a laboratory, pilot production process, or with a small group of customers—to evaluate a proposed solution and provide objective data. Data from the experiment are collected and documented. The Study stage determines whether the trial plan is working correctly by evaluating the results, recording the learning, and determining if any further issues or opportunities need be addressed. Often, the first solution must be modified or scrapped. New solutions are proposed and evaluated by returning to the Do stage. In the last stage, Act, the improvements become standardized and the final plan is implemented as a "current best practice" and communicated throughout the organization. This process

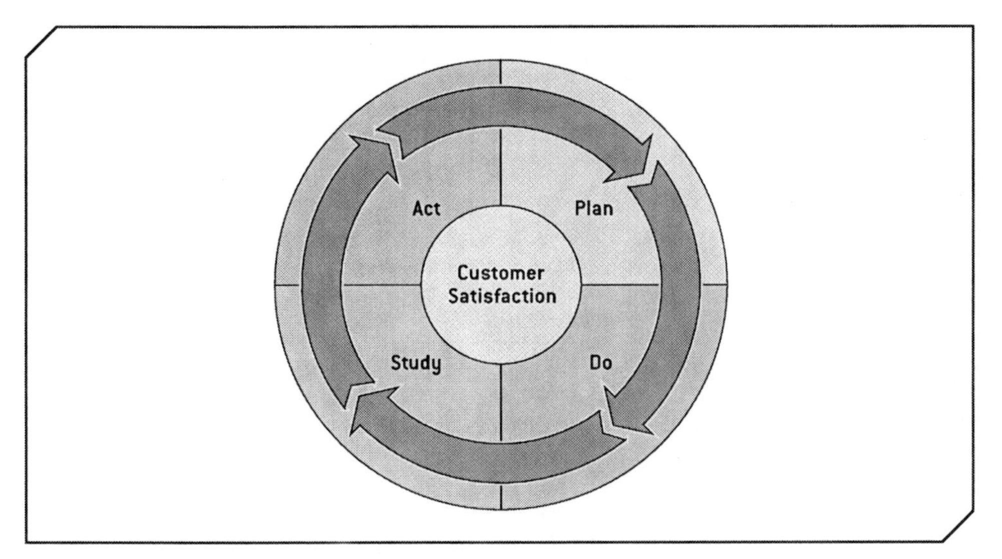

Exhibit 15.11
The Deming Cycle

then leads back to the Plan stage for identification of other improvement opportunities. Exhibit 15.12 summarizes the steps in the Deming cycle in more detail. The Seven QC tools can be used to facilitate the steps in the Deming cycle in a fashion similar to the DMAIC process as described in Exhibit 15.10.

Kaizen[36]

Kaizen *focuses on small, gradual, and frequent improvements over the long term with minimum financial investment and with participation by everyone in the organization.*

The concept of continuous improvement advocated by Deming was embraced by Japanese organizations, leading to an approach known as *kaizen.* **Kaizen** *focuses on small, gradual, and frequent improvements over the long term with minimum financial investment and with participation by everyone in the organization.* In the kaizen philosophy, improvement in all areas of business—cost, meeting delivery schedules, employee safety and skill development, supplier relations, new product development, or productivity—serve to enhance the quality of the firm. Thus, any activity directed toward improvement falls under the kaizen umbrella. At Nissan Motor Co., Ltd., for instance, management seriously considers any suggestion that saves at least 0.6 seconds in a production process. Activities to establish traditional quality control systems, install robotics and advanced technology, institute employee suggestion systems, maintain equipment, and implement just-in-time production systems all lead to improvement.

Three things are required for a successful kaizen program: operating practices, total involvement, and training.[37] First, operating practices expose new improvement opportunities. Practices such as just-in-time reveal waste and inefficiency as well as poor quality. Second, in kaizen, every employee strives for improvement. Top management, for example, views improvement as an inherent component of corporate strategy and provides support to improvement activities by allocating resources effectively and providing reward structures that are conducive to improvement. Middle management can implement top management's improvement goals by establishing, upgrading, and maintaining operating standards that reflect those

Exhibit 15.12 Detailed Steps in the Deming Cycle*

Plan
1. Define the process—its start, end, and what it does.
2. Describe the process—list the key tasks performed and the sequence of steps, people involved, equipment used, environmental conditions, work methods, and materials used.
3. Describe the players—external and internal customers and suppliers and process operators.
4. Define customer expectations—what the customer wants, when, and where, for both external and internal customers.
5. Determine what historical data are available on process performance, or what data needs to be collected to better understand the process.
6. Describe the perceived problems associated with the process, for instance, failure to meet customer expectations, excessive variation, long cycle times, and so on.
7. Identify the primary causes of the problems and their impacts on process performance.
8. Develop potential changes or solutions to the process, and evaluate how these changes or solutions will address the primary causes.
9. Select the most promising solution(s).

Do
1. Conduct a pilot study or experiment to test the impact of the potential solution(s).
2. Identify measures to understand how any changes or solutions are successful in addressing the perceived problems.

Study
1. Examine the results of the pilot study or experiment.
2. Determine whether process performance has improved.
3. Identify further experimentation that may be necessary.

Act
1. Select the best change or solution.
2. Develop an implementation plan—what needs to be done, who should be involved, and when the plan should be accomplished.
3. Standardize the solution, for example, by writing new standard operating procedures.
4. Establish a process to monitor and control process performance.

*Adapted from *Small Business Guidebook to Quality Management,* Office of the Secretary of Defense, Quality Management Office, Washington DC (1998).

goals; by improving cooperation between departments; and by making employees conscious of their responsibility for improvement and developing their problem-solving skills through training. Supervisors can direct more of their attention to improvement rather than "supervision," which, in turn, facilitates communication and offers better guidance to workers. Finally, workers can engage in improvement through suggestion systems and small group activities, self-development programs that teach practical problem-solving techniques, and enhanced job performance skills. All this requires significant training, both in the philosophy and in tools and techniques.

The kaizen philosophy has been widely adopted and is used by many firms in the United States and around the world. For example, at ENBI Corporation, a New York manufacturer of precision metal shafts and roller assemblies for the printer, copier, and fax machine markets, kaizen projects have resulted in a 48 percent increase in productivity, a 30 percent reduction in cycle time, and a 73 percent reduction in inventory.[38] Kaizen has been successfully applied in the Mercedes-Benz truck factory in Brazil, resulting in reductions of 30 percent in manufacturing space, 45 percent in inventory, 70 percent in lead time, and 70 percent in setup time over a 3-year period. Sixteen employees have full-time responsibility for kaizen activities.[39]

A **kaizen blitz** *is an intense and rapid improvement process in which a team or a department throws all its resources into an improvement project over a short time period, as opposed to traditional kaizen applications, which are performed on a part-time basis.* Blitz teams are generally comprised of employees from all areas involved in the process who understand it and can implement changes on the spot. Improvement is immediate, exciting, and satisfying for all those involved in the process (see the OM Spotlight on Magnivision).

A **kaizen blitz** *is an intense and rapid improvement process in which a team or a department throws all its resources into an improvement project over a short time period, as opposed to traditional kaizen applications, which are performed on a part-time basis.*

Poka-Yoke (Mistake-Proofing)

Human beings tend to make mistakes inadvertently. Typical process-related mistakes include omitted processing steps, processing errors, setup or changeover errors, missing information or parts, not handling service upsets properly, wrong information or parts, and adjustment errors. Errors can arise from

- forgetfulness due to lack of concentration,
- misunderstanding because of the lack of familiarity with a process or procedures,
- poor identification associated with lack of proper attention,
- lack of experience,
- absentmindedness,
- delays in judgment when a process is automated, or
- equipment malfunctions.

Poka-yoke *(POH-kah YOH-kay) is an approach for mistake-proofing processes using automatic devices or methods to avoid simple human error.* The poka-yoke concept was developed and refined in the early 1960s by the late Shigeo Shingo, a Japanese manufacturing engineer who developed the Toyota production system.[40]

Poka-yoke *(POH-kah YOH-kay) is an approach for mistake-proofing processes using automatic devices or methods to avoid simple human error.*

Poka-yoke is focused on two aspects: prediction, or recognizing that a defect is about to occur and providing a warning, and detection, or recognizing that a defect has occurred and stopping the process. Many applications of poka-yoke are deceptively simple, yet creative, and usually, they are inexpensive to implement. One of Shingo's first poka-yoke devices involved a process at the Yamada Electric plant in which workers assemble a switch having two push buttons supported by two springs.[42] Occasionally, the worker would forget to insert a spring under each button, which led to a costly and embarrassing repair at the customer's facility. In the old method, the worker would take two springs out of a large parts box and then assemble the switch. To prevent this mistake, the worker was instructed first to place two springs in a small dish in front of the parts box, and then assemble

OM SPOTLIGHT

Kaizen Blitz at Magnivision[41]

Many companies use kaizen blitz to drive improvements. Some examples of using it at Magnivision include the following:

- The molded lens department ran two shifts per day, using 13 employees, and after 40 percent rework yielded 1,300 pieces per day. The production line was unbalanced and work piled up between stations. This added to quality problems as the work-in-process was often damaged. After a 3-day blitz, the team reduced the production to one shift of 6 employees and a balanced line, reducing rework to 10 and increasing yield to 3,500 per day, saving over $179,000.
- In retail services, a blitz team investigated problems that continually plagued employees and discovered that many were related to the software system. Some of the same customer information had to be entered in multiple screens, sometimes the system took a long time to process information, and sometimes it was difficult to find specific information quickly. Neither the programmers nor the engineers were aware of these problems. By getting everyone together, some solutions were easily determined. Estimated savings were $125,000.

the switch. If a spring remains in the dish, the operator knows immediately that an error has occurred. The solution was simple, cheap, and provided immediate feedback to the employee.

Many other examples can be cited:

- Machines have limit switches connected to warning lights that tell the operator when parts are positioned improperly on the machine.
- Fast-food restaurants used automated french-frying machines that can only be operated one way and the french fries are prepackaged and the equipment automated to reduce the chance of human error.
- A device on a drill counts the number of holes drilled in a workpiece; a buzzer sounds if the workpiece is removed before the correct number of holes has been drilled.
- One production step at Motorola involves putting alphabetic characters on a keyboard, then checking to make sure each key is placed correctly. A group of workers designed a clear template with the letters positioned slightly off center. By holding the template over the keyboard, assemblers can quickly spot mistakes.
- A proxy ballot for an investment fund will not fit into the return envelope unless a small strip is detached. The strip asks the respondent to check if the ballot is signed and dated, a major source of error in returning proxy votes.
- Computer programs display a warning message if a file that has not been saved is to be closed.
- A 3.5-inch diskette is designed so that it cannot be inserted unless the disk is oriented correctly (try it!). These disks are not perfectly square, and the beveled right corner of the disk allows a stop in the disk drive to be pushed away if it is inserted correctly.

Process simulation *is an approach for building a logical model of a real process, and experimenting with the model to obtain insight about the behavior of the process or to evaluate the impact of changes in assumptions or potential improvements to it.*

Process Simulation

Process simulation *is an approach for building a logical model of a real process, and experimenting with the model to obtain insight about the behavior of the process* *or to evaluate the impact of changes in assumptions or potential improvements to it.* Process simulation has been used routinely in business to address complex operational problems, so it is no wonder that it is a useful tool for Six Sigma applications, especially those involving customer service improvement, cycle time reduction, and reducing variability. Process simulation should be used when the process is very complex and difficult to visualize, involves many decision points, or when the goal is to optimize the use of resources for a process.[43]

Building a process simulation model involves first describing how the process operates, normally using a process map. The process map includes all process steps, including logical decisions that route materials or information to different locations. Second, all key inputs such as how long it takes to perform each step of the process and resources needed must be identified. Typically, the activity times in a process are uncertain and described by probability distributions; this is what normally makes it difficult to evaluate process performance and identify bottlenecks without simulation. The intent is for the model to duplicate the real process so that "what-if?" questions can easily be evaluated without having to make time-consuming or costly changes to the real process. Once the model is developed, the simulation process repeatedly samples from the probability distributions of the input variables to create a distribution of potential outputs.

As an example, a common customer support process is the help desk or call center process responsible for answering and addressing customers' questions and complaints.[44] Typically, customer satisfaction ratings of the help desk are generally very low. Although this process is common, it is difficult to analyze with conventional Six Sigma tools. The measure phase usually identifies "time to resolve an issue" and "quality of the issue resolution" as the two CTQs. When these are measured, performance is generally less than a 1-sigma level, so significant improvement potential exists.

Help desks are much too complex to analyze using basic Six Sigma tools. Most help desks have two or three levels of support. When a call comes in, it often waits in a queue. When a level 1 person is available, he or she takes the call. If this person cannot resolve the issue, the call is forwarded to level 2. If the level 2 rep cannot resolve the call, it is forwarded to engineering or a similar support group. Between each of these levels, the call may end up waiting in several more queues, or the customer may be asked to wait for a callback.

By developing a process simulation model, a Black Belt can validate the model against the real process by collecting whatever data are available for model inputs, running the model, and statistically matching the results with data collected during the measure phase. Once the model is validated, analysis can begin. Most simulation packages provide operational output data for all the process steps, resource utilization data, and any additional variables tracked throughout the process. When the data are collected, it becomes a fairly straightforward task to analyze it statistically, identify bottlenecks, develop proposed solutions, and rerun the simulation to confirm the results.

To provide a simple illustration, suppose that in a phone support center, incoming calls arrive on a random basis with an average time between calls of about 5 minutes and a support representative evaluates the nature of each problem.[45] Each call takes anywhere between 30 seconds and 4 minutes, although most can be handled in about 2 minutes. The representative is able to resolve 75 percent of the calls immediately. However, 25 percent of the calls require that other support representatives do research and make a return call to the customer. The research itself combined with the return call requires an average of 20 minutes, although this time may vary quite a bit, from as little as 5 minutes to over 35 minutes. Exhibit 15.13 shows the process map for this situation, including the support representative resources.

Exhibit 15.13
Process Map for Help Desk Simulation Model

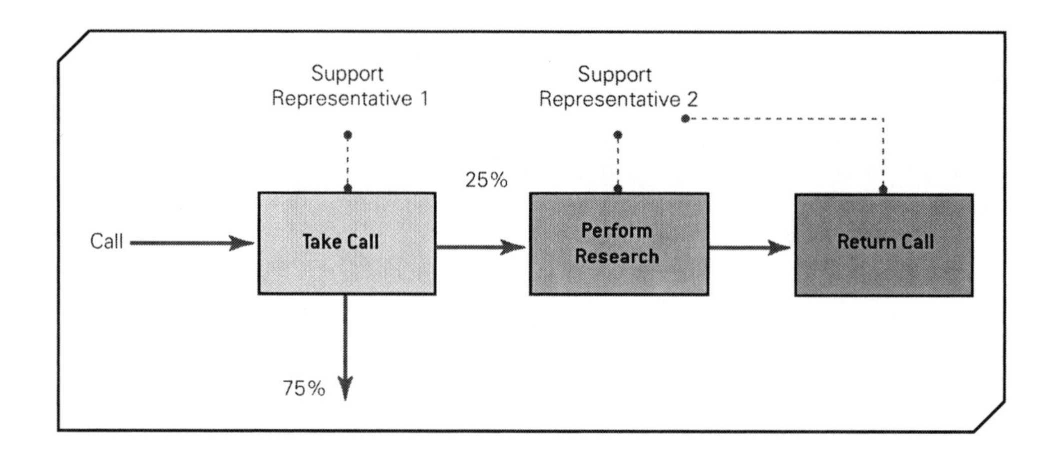

It is difficult to perform a process simulation, even for as simple a process as this, without some type of commercial simulation software. For this example, we used a package called ProcessModel,* which facilitates the simulation process by allowing you to build the model by simply "dragging and dropping" the process map symbols on the computer screen, entering the appropriate data input descriptions, and running the model. As the model runs, ProcessModel provides a visual animation of the process, allowing you to see the buildup of calls at each support stage to gain insight into the system performance.

Standard output reports, such as the one shown in Exhibit 15.14, are generated automatically. By examining these results (see the circled entries in the figure), we see that support problems waited in the *Return Call inQ* activity on average over 496 minutes and as many as 51 calls were waiting at any one time. Thus, this activity should be identified as a problem area suitable for process improvement efforts. In the RESOURCES section, we see that Support 1 was busy about half the time, while Support 2 was busy nearly 100 percent of the time. Any time human resource utilization is above 80 percent for extended periods, the system will most likely result in long waiting times and queue lengths, requiring more resources or changes in the assignment of resources. This suggests that better allocation of resources should improve performance. To reduce the customer waiting time, we

Exhibit 15.14 ProcessModel Simulation Results

Scenario = Normal Run
Replication = 1 of 1
Simulation Time = 40 hr

ACTIVITIES

Activity Name	Scheduled Hours	Capacity	Total Entries	Average Minutes Per Entry	Average Contents	Maximum Contents	Current Contents	% Util
Take Call inQ	40	999	504	1.01	0.21	5	0	0.02
Take Call	40	1	504	2.17	0.45	1	0	45.62
Perform Research inQ	40	999	114	112.50	5.34	11	4	0.53
Perform Research	40	10	110	19.92	0.91	1	1	9.13
Return Call inQ	40	999	109	496.78	22.56	51	51	2.26
Return Call	40	1	58	3.00	0.07	1	0	7.25

Source: ProcessModel Simulation Results from ProcessModel, Inc. Reprinted with permission.

Exhibit 15.14 (Continued)

ACTIVITY STATES BY PERCENTAGE (Multiple Capacity)

Activity Name	Scheduled Hours	% Empty	% Partially Occupied	% Full
Take Call inQ	40	84.85	15.15	0.00
Perform Research inQ	40	10.50	89.50	0.00
Perform Research	40	8.67	91.33	0.00
Return Call inQ	40	2.06	97.94	0.00

ACTIVITY STATES BY PERCENTAGE (Single Capacity)

Activity Name	Scheduled Hours	% Operation	% Idle	% Waiting	% Blocked
Take Call	40	45.62	54.38	0.00	0.00
Return Call	40	7.25	92.75	0.00	0.00

RESOURCES

Resource Name	Units	Scheduled Hours	Number of Times Used	Average Minutes Per Usage	% Util
Support 1	1	40	504	2.17	45.62
Support 2	1	40	168	14.08	98.58

RESOURCE STATES BY PERCENTAGE

Resource Name	Scheduled Hours	% In Use	% Idle	% Down
Support 1	40	45.62	54.38	0.00
Support 2	40	98.58	1.42	0.00

ENTITY SUMMARY (Times in Scoreboard time units)

Entity Name	Qty Processed	Average Cycle Time (Minutes)	Average VA Time (Minutes)	Average Cost
Call	390	4.19	2.18	0.43
HardCall	58	596.99	24.99	8.04

VARIABLES

Variable Name	Total Changes	Average Minutes Per Change	Minimum Value	Maximum Value	Current Value	Average Value
Avg BVA Time Entity	1	0.00	0	0	0	0
Avg BVA Time Call	391	6.10	0	0	0	0
Avg BVA Time HardCall	59	39.04	0	0	0	0

might add additional support representatives or cross-train and share the existing representatives. The simulation model can easily be modified to incorporate these changes, and the impacts on the results can be evaluated. Clearly, trying to do this in the real process would be costly and disruptive, with no guarantee that it would work.

Simulation is a rich and complex topic. Many good books exist about process simulation and we encourage you to find and explore some of them.

SOLVED PROBLEMS

1. The following cost-of-quality data were collected at the installment loan department of the Hamilton Bank. Classify these data into the appropriate cost-of-quality categories and analyze the results. What suggestions would you make to management?

Loan Processing

1.	Run credit check:	$26.13
2.	Review documents:	$3,021.62
3.	Make document corrections; gather additional information:	$1,013.65
4.	Prepare tickler file; review and follow up on titles, insurance, second meetings:	$156.75
5.	Review all output:	$2,244.14
6.	Correct rejects and incorrect output:	$425.84
7.	Reconcile incomplete collateral report:	$78.34
8.	Respond to dealer calls; address associate problems; research and communicate information:	$2,418.88
9.	Compensate for system downtime:	$519.38
10.	Conduct training:	$1,366.94

Loan Payment

1.	Receive and process payments:	$1,045.00
2.	Respond to inquiries when no coupon is presented with payments:	$783.64

Loan Payoff

1.	Receive and process payoff and release documents:	$13.92
2.	Research payoff problems:	$14.34

Solution:

Cost Elements	Costs	Quality Cost Categories Subtotal	Proportion
APPRAISAL			
Run credit checks	$26.13		
Loan Payment and Loan Payoffs			
Receive and process (2 items)	$1,058.92		
Inspection			
Review documents	$3,021.63		
Prepare tickler file, etc.	$156.75		
Review all output	$2,244.14		
		$6,507.57	.496
PREVENTION			
Conduct training	$1,366.94		
		$1,366.94	.104
INTERNAL FAILURE COSTS			
Scrap and Rework			
Make document corrections	$1,013.65		
Correct rejects	$425.84		
Reconcile incomplete collateral reports	$78.34		
Compensate for system downtime	$519.38		
Loan Payment or Payoff			
Respond to inquiries—no coupon	$783.64		
Research payoff problems	$14.34		
		$2,820.85	.215
EXTERNAL FAILURE COSTS			
Respond to dealer calls, etc.	$2,418.88		
		$2,418.88	.185
Total costs		$13,114.24	

The external failure costs for the bank are not extremely high. However, they do represent 18.5 percent of the total quality costs. The process of working with dealers should be investigated to determine if it can be simplified, better communications established, and problems avoided in the future. The highest cost category is in appraisal costs at $6,507.57 and 49.6 percent of total quality costs. If the categories of "document review" and "review all output" can be reduced without compromising the quality of the lending procedure, these costs could be greatly improved.

2. A watch manufacturer has the option of inspecting each crystal. If a bad crystal is assembled, the cost of disassembly and replacement after the final test and inspection is $1.40. Each crystal can be tested for 8 cents. Perform a break-even analysis to determine the percent nonconforming for which 100 percent inspection is better than no inspection at all.

Solution:

$C_1 = \$0.08$
$C_2 = \$1.40$
$C_1/C_2 = 0.057$

Therefore, if the actual error rate is greater than 0.057, 100 percent inspection is best; otherwise, no inspection is warranted.

3. A hotel estimates that each business guest encounters 20 "moments of truth" during service encounters on a typical overnight stay. On average, the hotel has 1,000 business customers on Monday through Friday and has an average of six complaints per week. What is the epmo measure, and how close is the hotel operating to a Six Sigma level?

Solution:
The weekly number of opportunities for error is (1,000 customers/day)(20 moments of truth per customer) (5 days/week) = 100,000. Six complaints per 100,000 opportunities is equivalent to 60 complaints per million. Using the Excel formula NORMSINV(1 − 6/100000) + 1.5, this is equivalent to a sigma level of 5.35, approaching a 6-sigma level.

4. An analysis of customer complaints at a large mail-order house revealed the following data:

Billing errors	867
Shipping errors	1,960
Unclear charges	9,650
Long delays	6,672
Delivery errors	452

Construct a Pareto diagram for these data. What conclusions can you draw?

Solution:
Total errors are 19,601. The data for each complaint category are as follows (percentages rounded to whole numbers):

Complaint	Number	Percent	Cumulative Percent
Unclear charges	9,650	49	49
Long delays	6,672	34	83
Shipping errors	1,960	10	93
Billing errors	867	4	97
Delivery errors	452	2	100

Almost half the errors are due to unclear charges, and over 80 percent are attributable to the first two categories. These are the ones to which managers should direct their attention.

KEY TERMS AND CONCEPTS

Acceptance sampling
Appraisal costs
Attribute
Black Belt
Cause-and-effect diagram
Champion
Checksheet
Common causes of variation
Control chart
Cost of quality
Critical to quality (CTQ)
Defect
Defects per unit (DPU)
Defects per million opportunities (dpmo)
Deming cycle
Deming's 14 Points
DMAIC—Define, Measure, Analyze, Improve, Control
Equipment variation
Errors per million opportunities (epmo)
External-failure costs
Fitness for use
Flowchart
GAP Model
Green Belt
Histogram
Internal audit
Internal-failure costs
ISO 9000:2000
Kaizen
Kaizen blitz
Lot
Master Black Belt
Metrology
Nonconformance

Operator variation
Pareto analysis
Pareto diagram
Poka-yoke
Prevention costs
Process simulation
Quality control
Quality management
Quality manual
Quality of conformance
Quality system standards
Repeatability
Reproducibility
Run chart
Scatter diagram
Service quality
Seven QC Tools
Six Sigma
Special causes of variation
Specifications
Stable system
Total quality
Total quality management
Unit of work
Variable data

QUESTIONS FOR REVIEW AND DISCUSSION

1. Define *quality management*. Why is it important for every manager to understand?
2. What does the history of quality management suggest to today's managers?
3. Explain the five gaps in the GAP Model. What can operations do to reduce these gaps?
4. What is the most useful definition of quality from an operations perspective? How might an operations manager use this definition in making daily decisions?
5. How do you define *service quality*? How is it similar and different from the manufacturing definition?
6. Explain the three principles of total quality.
7. Are the basic elements of total quality really any different from the practices that every manager should perform? Why do some managers find them difficult to accept?
8. How does Deming's view of a production system in Exhibit 15.2 correspond to the notion of a value chain introduced in Chapter 2?
9. Summarize the impact of quality on business results. Can you state that quality is a key "driver" of business results?
10. Summarize Deming's philosophy as expressed in the 14 Points. Explain how it differs from traditional management practices and why.
11. How might Deming's 14 Points be applied in running a college or university? How about an individual classroom?
12. Explain the Deming chain reaction.
13. What is the Deming cycle, and how does it support continuous improvement activities?
14. Explain the purpose and structure of ISO 9000:2000. How do the principles of ISO 9000 compare with the Malcolm Baldrige criteria discussed in Chapter 3?
15. Summarize the basic elements of an effective quality management system at the operations level.
16. Explain how service quality is measured. How does it differ from manufacturing, and how can such measurements be used for controlling quality in services?
17. What is Six Sigma? How is it measured?
18. Explain the key concepts used in implementing a Six Sigma quality initiative.
19. Summarize the DMAIC process for problem solving.
20. What types of individuals participate in Six Sigma projects? How do their skills differ?
21. Explain issues that service and small organizations face in implementing Six Sigma.
22. What does "cost of quality" mean? Why is it important?
23. Explain the classification of quality costs. Provide some specific examples in a fast-food operation and in the operation of your college or university.
24. How is Pareto analysis beneficial in analyzing quality costs?
25. Summarize the Seven QC Tools used for quality improvement, and provide an example of each.
26. Explain the concept of kaizen. What must an organization do to successfully operate a kaizen initiative?
27. What is a kaizen blitz? How does it differ from the original notion of kaizen?

28. What is poka-yoke? Provide some examples in your daily life.

29. How can process simulation be used in quality management activities?

PROBLEMS AND ACTIVITIES

1. Analyze the following cost data. What implications do these data suggest to managers?

	Product		
	A	B	C
Total sales	$537,280	$233,600	$397,120
External failure	42%	20%	20%
Internal failure	45%	25%	45%
Appraisal	12%	52%	30%
Prevention	1%	3%	5%

Note: Figures represent percentages of quality costs by product.

2. Compute a sales-dollar index base to analyze the quality-cost information in the following table, and prepare a memo to management.

	Quarter			
	1	2	3	4
Total sales	$4,120	$4,206	$4,454	$4,106
External failure	$40.80	$42.20	$42.80	$28.60
Internal failure	$168.20	$172.40	$184.40	$66.40
Appraisal	$64.20	$67.00	$74.40	$166.20
Prevention	$28.40	$29.20	$30.20	$40.20

3. Given the cost elements in the following table, determine the total percentage in each of the four major quality-cost categories.

Cost Element	Amount ($)
Incoming test and inspection	7,500
Scrap	35,000
Quality training	0
Inspection	25,000
Test	5,000
Adjustment cost of complaints	21,250
Quality audits	2,500
Maintenance of tools and dies	9,200
Quality control administration	5,000
Laboratory testing	1,250
Design of quality assurance equipment	1,250
Material testing and inspection	1,250
Rework	70,000
Quality problem solving by product engineers	11,250
Inspection equipment calibration	2,500
Writing procedures and instructions	2,500
Laboratory services	2,500
Rework due to vendor faults	17,500
Correcting imperfections	6,250
Setup for test and inspection	10,750
Formal complaints to vendors	10,000

4. Use Pareto analysis to investigate the quality losses in a paper mill given the following data. What conclusions do you reach?

Category	Annual Loss ($)
Downtime	38,000
Testing costs	20,000
Rejected paper	560,000
Odd lot	79,000
Excess inspection	28,000
Customer complaints	125,000
High material costs	67,000

5. A manufacturer estimates that the proportion of nonconforming items in one process is 3.5 percent. The estimated cost of inspecting each item is $0.50, and the cost of replacing a nonconforming item after it leaves the production area is $25. What is the best economic inspection decision?

6. The cost to inspect a credit card statement in a bank is $0.75, and correction of a mistake later amounts to $500. What is the break-even point in errors per thousand transactions for which 100 percent inspection is no more economical than no inspection?

7. A bank has set a standard that mortgage applications be processed within 8 days of filing. If, out of a sample of 1,000 applications, 75 fail to meet this requirement, what is the epmo metric, and how does it compare with a six-sigma level?

8. Over the last year, 965 injections were administered at a clinic. Quality is measured by the proper amount of dosage as well as the correct drug. In two instances, the incorrect amount was given, and in one case, the wrong drug was given. What is the epmo metric and how does it compare with a 6-sigma level?

9. The *Wall Street Journal* reported on February 15, 2000 that about 750,000 airplane components are manufactured, machined, or assembled for Boeing Co. by workers from the Seattle Lighthouse for the Blind. A Boeing spokeswoman noted that the parts have an "exceptionally low" rejection rate of one per thousand. What is the dpmo metric, and how does it compare with a 6-sigma level?

10. A flowchart for a fast-food drive-through window is shown in Exhibit 15.15. Determine the important quality characteristics inherent in this process, and suggest possible improvements.

11. The following list gives the number of seconds customers have waited for a telephone service representative today. Construct a histogram, and discuss any conclusions you might reach.

5	7	7	15	3
21	15	22	10	8
10	6	8	18	4
14	5	7	8	10

12. The manager at a pizza franchise has logged customer complaints over the past 3 months. From the data given, construct a Pareto diagram. What should the manager do?

Type of complaint	Frequency
Wrong order	3
Late delivery	17
Not enough toppings	1
Not hot enough	8
Excessive wait in dining room	12

13. Fourteen batches of a raw material were tested for the percentage of a particular chemical (x). It is believed that the amount of this chemical influences an important quality characteristic of the final product (y). The test data follow. Construct a scatter diagram of the data, and discuss any conclusions you might reach.

x	y
3.5	7.0
3.2	8.0
4.5	8.4
1.0	7.6
3.8	10.5
5.4	9.2
5.3	11.7
6.1	10.1
6.1	11.0
6.9	10.7
7.4	9.6
7.5	8.2
8.5	9.1
8.2	11.1

14. The following list gives the number of defects found in 30 samples of 100 electronic assemblies taken on

Exhibit 15.15

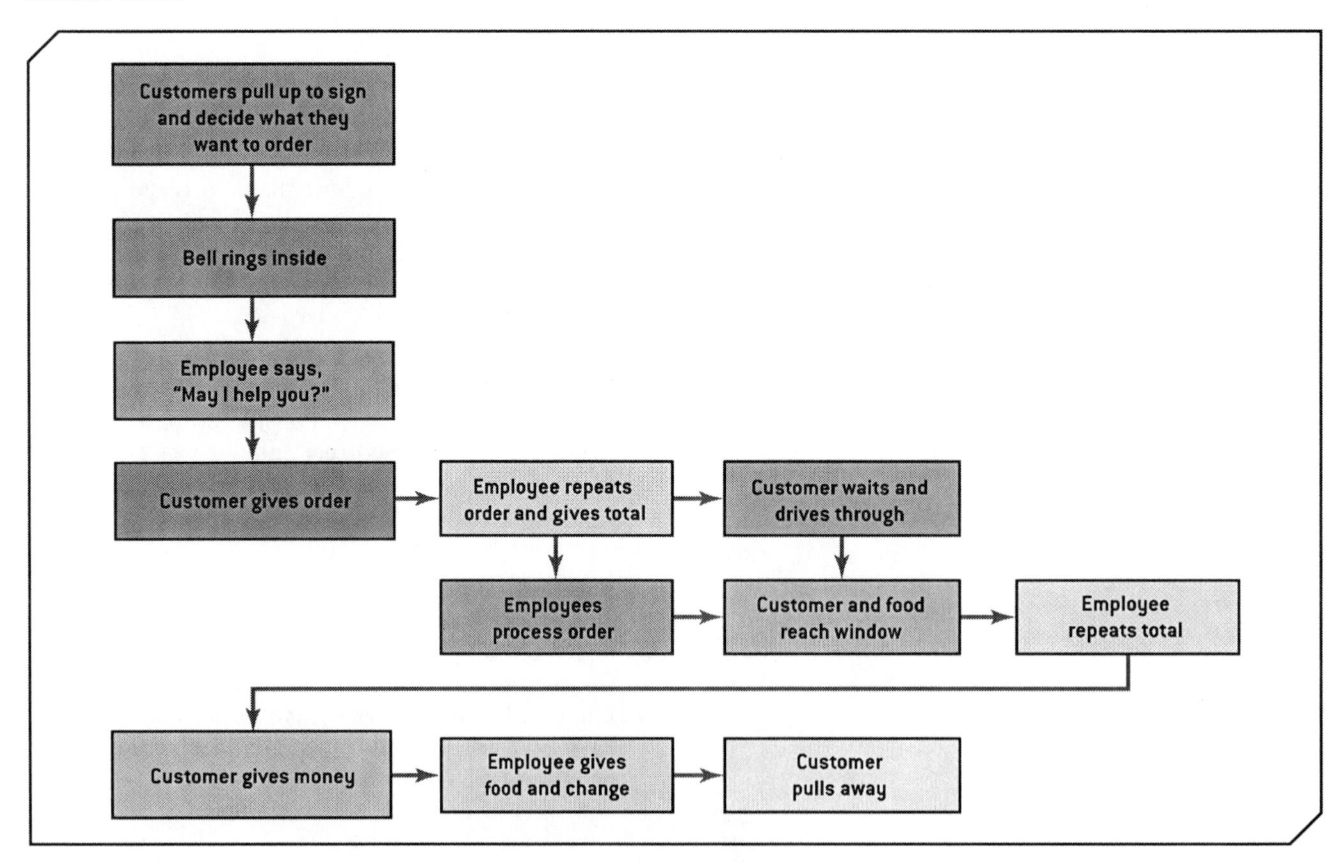

a daily basis over 1 month. Plot these data on a run chart, computing the average value (center line). How do you interpret the chart?

1	6	5	5	4	3	2	2	4	6
2	1	3	1	4	5	4	1	6	15
12	6	3	4	3	3	2	5	7	4

15. A catalog order-filling process for personalized printed products can be described as follows. Telephone orders are taken over a 12-hour period each day. Orders are collected from each order clerk at the end of the day and checked for errors by the supervisor, usually the next morning. Because of the supervisor's heavy work load, this 1-day batch of orders usually does not get to the data-processing department until after 1:00 P.M. Orders are invoiced by the data-processing department in 1-day batches and then printed and "matched back" with the original orders. (At this point, if the order is for a new customer, it is returned to the person who did the new-customer verification and set up the new account for that customer, both of which must be done before an order from a new customer can be invoiced.) The next step is order verification and proofreading. The orders, with invoices attached, are given to a person who verifies that all required information is present and correct. If there is a question, it is checked by computer or by calling the customer. Finally, the completed orders are sent to the typesetting department of the printshop.
    a. Develop a flowchart for this process.
    b. Discuss opportunities for improving the quality of service in this situation.
16. An independent outplacement service helps unemployed executives find jobs. One of the major activities of the service is preparing resumes. Three word processors work at the service and type resumes and cover letters. They are assigned to individual clients, currently about 120. Turnaround time for typing is expected to be 24 hours. The word-processing operation begins with clients placing work in the assigned word processor's bin. When the word processor picks up the work (in batches), it is logged in by use of a clock time stamp, and the work is typed and printed. After the batch is completed, the word processor puts the documents in the clients' bins, logs in the time delivered, and picks up new work. A supervisor tries to balance the workload for the three word processors. Lately, many of the clients have been complaining about errors in their documents—misspellings, missing lines, wrong formatting, and so on. The supervisor has told the word processors to be more careful, but the errors persist.
    a. Develop a cause-and-effect diagram that might help to identify the source of errors.
    b. How might the supervisor study ways to reduce the amount of errors? What tools might the supervisor use to do so, and how might they be applied?
17. Interview managers of a local company that has achieved or is pursuing ISO 9000 registration. What problems does it face or did it encounter in achieving registration?
18. List some of the common processes you perform as a student. How might you go about controlling and improving them?
19. Develop cause-and-effect diagrams for the following problems:
    a. poor exam grade
    b. no job offers
    c. too many speeding tickets
    d. late for work or school
20. Search the Internet for examples and applications of Six Sigma. Write a report on current industry practice and the benefits cited.
21. Select some process in your work or personal life (for example, something to do with a fraternity, car maintenance, or home activities), and discuss how you would apply the Six Sigma DMAIC approach to improve this process. Be specific, addressing such things as how you would collect the data, what tools you might use for analysis, and so on.

CASES

WELZ BUSINESS MACHINES

Welz Business Machines sells and services a variety of copiers, computers, and other office equipment. The company receives many calls daily for service, sales, accounting, and other departments. All calls are handled centrally through customer service representatives and routed to other individuals as appropriate. A number of customers have complained about long waits when calling for service. A market research study found that customers become irritated if the call is not answered within five rings. Scott Welz, the company president, authorized the customer service department manager, Tim, to study this problem and find a method to shorten the call-waiting time for its customers.

Tim met with the service representatives to attempt to determine the reasons for long waiting times. The following conversation ensued:

Tim: "This is a serious problem; how a customer phone inquiry is answered is the first impression the customer receives from us. As you know, this company was founded on efficient and friendly service to all our customers. It's obvious why customers have to wait: you're on the phone with another customer. Can you think of any reasons that might keep you on the phone for an unnecessarily long time?"

Robin: "I've noticed that quite often the party I need to route the call to is not present. It takes time to transfer the call and then wait to see if it is answered. If the party is not there, I end up apologizing and have to transfer the call to another extension."

Tim: "You're right, Robin. Sales personnel often are out of the office for sales calls, absent on trips to preview new products, or not at their desks for a variety of reasons. What else might cause this problem?"

Ravi: "I get irritated at some customers who spend a great deal of time complaining about a problem that I cannot do anything about except refer to someone else. Of course, I listen and sympathize with them, but this eats up a lot of time."

LaMarr: "Some customers call so often, they think we're long-lost friends and strike up a personal conversation."

Tim: "That's not always a bad thing, you realize."

LaMarr: "Sure, but it delays my answering other calls."

Nancy: "It's not always the customer's fault. During lunch times, we're not all available to answer the phone."

Ravi: "Right after we open at 9:00 A.M., we get a rush of calls. I think that many of the delays are caused by these peak periods."

Robin: "I've noticed the same thing between 4 and 5 P.M."

Tim: "I've had a few comments from department managers that they received routed calls that didn't fall in their areas of responsibility and had to be transferred again."

Mark: "But that doesn't cause delays at our end."

Nancy: "That's right, Mark, but I just realized that sometimes I simply don't understand what the customer's problem really is. I spend a lot of time trying to get him or her to explain it better. Often, I have to route it to someone because other calls are waiting."

Ravi: "Perhaps we need to have more knowledge of our products."

Tim: "Well, I think we've covered most of the major reasons as to why many customers have to wait. It seems to me that we have four major reasons: the phones are short-staffed, the receiving party is not present, the customer dominates the conversation, and you may not understand the customer's problem. We need to collect some information next about these possible causes. I will set up a data-collection sheet that you can use to track some of these things. Mark, would you help me on this?"

Over the next 2 weeks, the staff collected data on the frequency of reasons why some callers had to wait:

Reason	Total Number
A. Operators short-staffed	172
B. Receiving party not present	73
C. Customer dominates conversation	19
D. Lack of operator understanding	61
E. Other reasons	10

Discussion Questions

a. From the conversation between Tim and his staff, draw a cause-and-effect diagram.

b. Perform a Pareto analysis of the data collected.

c. What actions might the company take to improve the situation?

NATIONAL FURNITURE

National Furniture is a large retail design and furniture store. The store often orders special merchandise at the request of its customers. However, the store has recently experienced problems with the on-time delivery of these special orders. Sometimes the orders are never received, resulting in very irate customers!

The process of fulfilling a special order begins with the sales associate who records the customer information and obtains approval from a manager to process the order. The sales associate puts the form in a bin for the office manager to fax the order form to the special-order department at the regional office. When the office manager faxes the special-order forms from the bin, she files them in a notebook. If there is a problem with the order, the manager receives notification and contacts the sales associate who took the order to decide what needs to be done next. Typical problems that are often observed include sales associates not filling out the order form completely or entering a request date that is impossible to fulfill. Sometimes the sales associate does not put the form in the proper bin, so the form never gets faxed. Other times, sales associates are asked to obtain more information from the customer but fail to call the customer back or do not inform the office associate to re-fax the form after getting additional information from the customer.

At the regional office, the special-order department receives the fax from the store, reviews it, and informs the store if additional information is needed. When all the information is complete, it processes the order. Sometimes it loses or misplaces the form after it arrives on the fax machine, orders the wrong merchandise, or fails to notify the store when additional information is needed or when the merchandise should be expected to arrive.

Discussion Questions

1. Develop a flowchart for administering special orders. What steps might you suggest to improve this process?
2. Construct a cause-and-effect diagram for identifying reasons why special orders are not received on time.
3. Discuss the relationship between the process map and the cause-and-effect diagram. How can they be used together to attack this problem?
4. How can you mistake-proof this process?

RENEWAL AUTO SERVICE

Renewal Auto Service (RAS) is a quick-service vehicle oil and lubricant change service somewhat similar to Jiffy Lube, FasLube, and Speedy Lube. The primary customer benefit package consists of providing oil, oil filters, air filters, and lubricants by polite and friendly employees who regularly interact with customers. However, RAS seeks to differentiate itself from the competition by focusing on peripheral goods and services and a customer-friendly servicescape. These include two blends of fresh coffee, tea, sodas, current magazines, and a television in the customer waiting room. Customers receive vehicle maintenance brochures and discount coupons for their next visit. RAS also offers services that competitors do not, including cleaning the vehicle's windows outside and inside; vacuuming carpets; reviewing service history with the customer; checking tire pressure, belts, hoses, windshield wipers, coolant levels, and filters; and explaining the technical aspects of vehicle service if the customer asks or if a potential safety or mechanical problem is discovered.

The facility layout consists of three service bays with a pit below each bay for draining and changing oil and lubricants. Aboveground are all necessary tools and equipment. The customer waiting area is carpeted and

Exhibit 15.16 RAS Customer Quarterly Example Survey Results ($n = 2.6$)

Survey Question	Average Score on 1 (worst) to 5 (best) Scale
1. The total time you spent in RAS was as expected.	4.59
2. My service experience during each repeat visit is of consistent high quality.	3.94
3. Store managers monitor my vehicles maintenance and repair very well.	4.36
4. Store managers understand my individual wants and needs.	3.77
5. Standards of performance at RAS are clearly visible inside the store.	4.54
6. Standards of performance at RAS are clearly advertised in the media and help me understand what to expect during vehicle service.	4.68
7. The facility is clean and well maintained.	4.64
8. The customer waiting area is really nice and why I come here.	4.79
9. Service personnel are polite, friendly, and clearly explain technical details if I ask.	3.85
10. Store managers always go over the vehicle checksheet with me prior to paying the bill.	4.40
11. Cleaning the vehicle windows and vacuuming are extra services that I like.	4.66
12. Knowing the vehicle history makes me feel secure that I am doing the right thing in terms of vehicle maintenance and repair.	4.43
13. RAS employees are really good at what they do.	4.10
14. RAS is clearly better than competitors.	4.35

larger than competitors', with comfortable sofas and chairs. A large glass window in the waiting area allows customers to see their vehicle being serviced in any of the three bays. Employees are professionally dressed in clean blue uniforms with their first name embroidered on them. To maintain a professional appearance, employees are required to wash their arms and hands after each service job.

A comprehensive vehicle checklist is used to ensure completeness of the work and as a means of quality control. The standard time to complete a job is 16 minutes in the bay area, plus 9 minutes for customer check-in and checkout. Store managers and assistant managers are trained and empowered to approve free service if the customer is dissatisfied for any reason.

RAS surveys customers regularly as a way of understanding their perceptions of service quality. Results from 206 customer surveys over the past 3 months for nine RAS area stores are summarized in Exhibit 15.16. Samples of good and bad written customer comments are also shown in Exhibit 15.17. The vice presidents of marketing, human resource management, and operations were asked to analyze these data to determine what actions might be necessary to reward or improve performance. The V.P. of Operations, Thomas Margate, thought he would try to apply the GAP model to analyze this information. A final report to the CEO was due in 2 weeks. What recommendations would you make? (Hint: See if you can assign each survey question to a gap.)

Exhibit 15.17
Five Good and Five Bad Sample RAS Customer Written Comments

1. I come to RAS because of their outstanding vehicle technical knowledge and skills.
2. Believe it or not, I really like their coffee and enjoy reading their magazines.
3. The mechanics are very careful and conscientious when working on my car.
4. When I complained there were streaks on my windows, they redid my windows and gave me a discount coupon for my next visit—real nice people.
5. Very fast and convenient service—I'll be back.
6. Store managers are super but the employees don't like to talk to us customers.
7. I won't come back; a mechanic keeps staring at me!
8. I felt pressured to buy the air and fuel filter and I don't even know what these parts do.
9. All the mechanics seem hurried while I was there.
10. The mechanic got grease on my fender and when I asked him to please clean it off he shrugged and wiped it off with a cleaner.

ENDNOTES

[1] Harrington, H. James, "Looking for a Little Service," *Quality Digest*, May 2000; www.qualitydigest.com

[2] "Hyundai Gets Hot," *Business Week*, December 17, 2001, pp. 84–85.

[3] Gale, Bradley T., "Quality Comes First When Hatching Power Brands," *Planning Review*, July–August 1992, pp. 4–9, 48.

[4] "Hyundai: Kissing Clunkers Goodbye," *BusinessWeek*, May 17, 2004, p. 45.

[5] *The Cincinnati Enquirer*, January 12, 2002, pp. A1, A9.

[6] Early history is reported in Dague, Delmer C., "Quality—Historical Perspective," *Quality Control in Manufacturing*, Warrendale, PA: Society of Automotive Engineers, February 1981; and Provost, L. P., and Norman, C. L., "Variation through the Ages," *Quality Progress* 23, no. 12, December 1990, pp. 39–44. Modern events are discussed in Karabatsos, Nancy, "Quality in Transition, Part One: Account of the '80s," *Quality Progress* 22, no. 12, December 1989, pp. 22–26; and Juran, Joseph M., "The Upcoming Century of Quality," address to the ASQC Annual Quality Congress, Las Vegas, May 24, 1994. A comprehensive historical account may be found in Juran, J. M., *A History of Managing for Quality*, Milwaukee, WI: ASQC Quality Press, 1995.

[7] Freudenheim, M., "Study Finds Inefficiency in Health Care," *The New York Times*, 2002, http://www.nytimes.com/2002/06/11/business/11CARE.html.

[8] Tamimi, Nabil, and Sebastianelli, Rose, "How Firms Define and Measure Quality," *Production and Inventory Management Journal* 37, no. 3, Third Quarter, 1996, pp. 34–39.

[9] Parasuraman, A., Zeithaml, V. A., and Berry, L. L., "A Conceptual Model of Service Quality and Its Implications for Future research," *Journal of Marketing* 49, Fall 1985, pp. 41–50.

[10] "Progress on the Quality Road," *Incentive*, April 1995, p. 7.

[11] Hendricks, Kevin B., and Singhal, Vinod R., "Does Implementing an Effective TQM Program Actually Improve Operating Performance? Empirical Evidence from Firms That Have Won Quality Awards," *Management Science* 43, no. 9, September 1997, pp. 1258–1274. The results of this study have appeared in extensive business and trade publications such as *Business Week*, *Fortune*, and others.

[12] Deming, W. Edwards, *The New Economics for Industry, Government, Education*, Cambridge, MA: MIT Center for Advanced Engineering Study, 1993.
[13] Shewhart, Walter A., *Economic Control of Quality of a Manufactured Product*, New York: Van Nostrand, 1931.
[14] Adapted from Jacques, March Laree, "Big League Quality," *Quality Progress*, August 2001, pp. 27–34.
[15] "ISO 9000 Certification Can Be Boost for Small Companies," *The Columbus Dispatch*, Columbus, Ohio, January 22, 2002, p. C6.
[16] Source: http://www.bsi.org.uk/iso-tc176-sc2/—Document: "Transition Planning Guidance for ISO/DIS 9001:2000," ISO/TC 176/SC 2/N 474, December, 1999.
[17] "ISO 9000 Update," *Fortune*, September 30, 1996, p. 134[J].
[18] Eckstein, Astrid L. H., and Balakrishnan, Jaydeep, "The ISO 9000 Series: Quality Management Systems for the Global Economy," *Production and Inventory Management Journal* 34, no. 4, Fourth Quarter 1993, pp. 66–71.
[19] "Home Builder Constructs Quality with ISO 9000," *Quality Digest*, February 2000, p. 13.
[20] Taormina, Tom, "Conducting Successful Internal Audits," *Quality Digest*, June 1998, pp. 44–47.
[21] Karaszewski, Robert, "Quality Challenges in Global Companies," *Quality Progress*, October 2004, pp. 59–65.
[22] "Up, Up, and Away?" *Fortune*, July 21, 2003, p. 149.
[23] Snee, Ronald D., "Why Should Statisticians Pay Attention to Six Sigma?" *Quality Progress*, September 1999, pp. 100–103.
[24] Marash, Stanley A., "Six Sigma: Business Results Through Innovation," ASQ's 54th Annual Quality Congress Proceedings, pp. 627–630.
[25] Welch, Jack, *Jack: Straight from the Gut*, New York: Warner Books, 2001, pp. 329–330.
[26] Ibid., pp. 333–334.
[27] "GE Reports Record Earnings With Six Sigma," *Quality Digest*, December 1999, p. 14.
[28] Rucker, Rochelle, "Six Sigma at Citibank," *Quality Digest*, December 1999, pp. 28–32.
[29] Smith, Kennedy, "Six Sigma at Ford Revisited," *Quality Digest,* 23, no. 6, June 2003, pp. 28–32.
[30] This discussion of the applicability of Six Sigma to services is adapted from Bisgaard, Soren, Hoerl, Roger W., and Snee, Ronald D., "Improving Business Processes with Six Sigma," *Proceedings of ASQ's 56th Annual Quality Congress*, 2002, CD-ROM, and Smith, Kennedy, "Six Sigma for the Service Sector," *Quality Digest*, May 2003, pp. 23–28.
[31] Adapted from Keim, Elizabeth, Fox, LouAnn, and Mazza, Julie S., "Service Quality Six Sigma Case Studies," *Proceedings of the 54th Annual Quality Congress of the American Society for Quality*, 2000, CD-ROM.
[32] Palser, Lisa, "Cycle Time Improvement for a Human Resources Process," *ASQ's 54th Annual Quality Congress Proceedings*, 2000, CD-ROM.
[33] Hoerl, Roger, "An Inside Look at Six Sigma at GE," *Six Sigma Forum Magazine*, 1, no. 3, May 2002, pp. 35–44.
[34] Sullivan, Edward, and Owens, Debra A., "Catching A Glimpse of Quality Costs Today," *Quality Progress*, 16, no. 12, December 1983, pp. 21–24.
[35] *Reports of Statistical Application Research, Japanese Union of Scientists and Engineers*, 33, no. 2, June 1986.
[36] Imai, Masaaki, *KAIZEN—The Key to Japan's Competitive Success*, New York: McGraw-Hill, 1986.
[37] Robinson, Alan, ed., *Continuous Improvement in Operations*, Cambridge, MA: Productivity Press, 1991.
[38] Tonkin, Lea A. P., "Kaizen Blitz℠ 5: Bottleneck-Bashing comes to Rochester, NY," *Target* 12, no. 4, September/October 1996, pp. 41–43.
[39] Oakeson, Mark, "Makes Dollars & Sense for Mercedes-Benz in Brazil," *IIE Solutions*, April 1997, pp. 32–35.
[40] From *Poka-yoke: Improving Product Quality by Preventing Defects*. Edited by NKS/Factory Magazine, English translation copyright © 1988 by Productivity Press, Inc., P.O. Box 3007, Cambridge, MA 02140, 800-394-6868. Reprinted by permission.
[41] Chilson, Eleanor, "Kaizen Blitzes at Magnivision: $809,270 Cost Savings," *Quality Management Forum*, 29, no. 1, Winter 2003.
[42] Robinson, Harry, "Using Poka Yoke Techniques for Early Defect Detection," Paper presented at the Sixth International Conference on Software Testing and Analysis and Review (STAR '97).
[43] Fleming, Steve, and Manson, E. Lowry, "Six Sigma and Process Simulation," *Quality Digest*, March 2002.
[44] Ibid.
[45] This example is adapted from a tutorial for ProcessModel, a commercial simulation package. ProcessModel, Inc., 32 West Center, Suite 209, Provo, Utah 84601.

Chapter Outline

CHAPTER 16

Quality Control and SPC

Learning Objectives

1. To understand the elements of good control systems, variation in processes, the difference between common and special causes of variation, quality control metrics, and the design of quality control systems.

2. To understand variation in manufacturing and service processes, metrics for quantifying variation, and the role of control charts and

statistical process control methods in helping managers control variation.

3. To be able to construct and interpret simple control charts for both continuous and discrete data, to understand how to select the proper chart, and to understand the role of SPC in processes approaching Six Sigma capability.

4. To understand the concept of process capability and be able to analyze process capability data, compute process capability indexes, and interpret the results.

- In early June 1999, almost 100 Belgian children fell ill after drinking Coca-Cola. This incident caused the Belgian Health Ministry to require Coke to recall millions of cans of product in Belgium and to cease product distribution. Later, France and the Netherlands also halted distribution of Coke products as the contamination scare spread. It was quickly determined that contaminated carbon dioxide had been used during the carbonation process at the Antwerp bottling facility. According to the official statement from Coca-Cola, "Independent laboratory testing showed that the cause of the off-taste in the bottled products was carbon dioxide. That carbon dioxide was replaced and all bottles with off-taste have been removed from the market. The issue affects the taste of the soft drinks only. . . ."

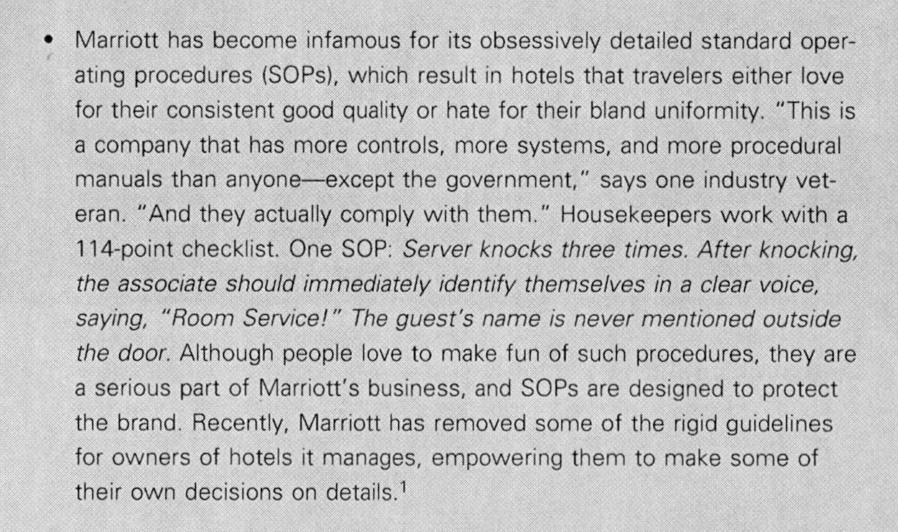

- Marriott has become infamous for its obsessively detailed standard operating procedures (SOPs), which result in hotels that travelers either love for their consistent good quality or hate for their bland uniformity. "This is a company that has more controls, more systems, and more procedural manuals than anyone—except the government," says one industry veteran. "And they actually comply with them." Housekeepers work with a 114-point checklist. One SOP: *Server knocks three times. After knocking, the associate should immediately identify themselves in a clear voice, saying, "Room Service!" The guest's name is never mentioned outside the door.* Although people love to make fun of such procedures, they are a serious part of Marriott's business, and SOPs are designed to protect the brand. Recently, Marriott has removed some of the rigid guidelines for owners of hotels it manages, empowering them to make some of their own decisions on details.[1]

- Frank Roy, the new plant manager at a large pharmaceutical company that manufactures syringes with a self-contained, single dose of an

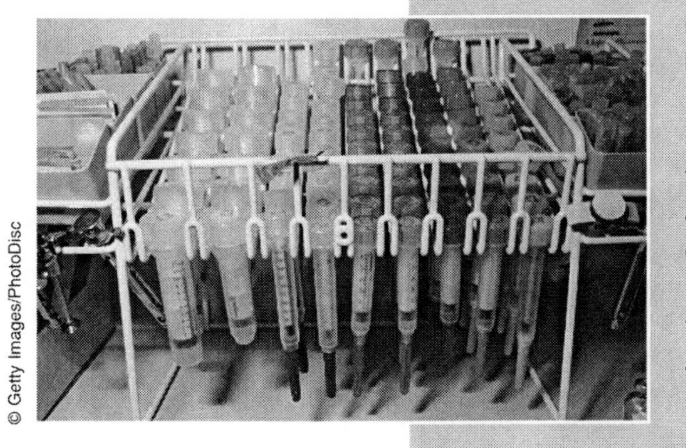
© Getty Images/PhotoDisc

injectable drug is concerned about the increased scrap that his process seems to be making. His engineering manager, Edith Berger, explained how the process works. "In the first stage, we fill sterile liquid drug into glass syringes and seal them with rubber stoppers. Next, we insert the cartridge into a plastic syringe and 'tack' the containment cap at a precisely determined length of the syringe (4.920 inches). If the tacking process results in a shorter than desired length, it leads to pressure on the cartridge stopper and a partial or complete activation of the syringe. We have to scrap these. This step seems to be producing more and more scrap and reworked syringes over the last several weeks." "What happens if the length is too long?" asked Frank. Edith replied, "If the process results in a longer than desired length, the syringe will likely be damaged in shipment and handling. However, we can rework these manually to attach the cap at a lower position. This process requires a 100 percent inspection of the tacked syringes and increases our cost." "We can't remain competitive and incur these unnecessary costs," stated Frank emphatically. "We need to get this situation under control—quickly!"

Discussion Questions: What role do you think quality control plays in creating satisfying customer experiences? What opportunities for improved quality control or use of SOPs can you think of at your college or university (e.g. bookstore, cafeteria)?

The task of **quality control** *is to ensure that a good or service conforms to specifications and meets customer requirements by monitoring and measuring processes and making any necessary adjustments to maintain a specified level of performance.*

Value chains are complex networks of internal and external processes and customer-supplier relationships. The ability to satisfy the ultimate customer—the consumer or external business customer—depends on the ability to satisfy the needs and requirements of all internal customers within the value chain. This requires a significant amount of attention to quality control at key process steps throughout the value chain. *The task of* **quality control** *is to ensure that a good or service conforms to specifications and meets customer requirements by monitoring and measuring processes and making any necessary adjustments to maintain a specified level of performance.* The consequences of a lack of good quality control systems and procedures can be serious and potentially cause large financial losses or affect a company's reputation, as the first episode illustrates. Health care is one industry that has been highly criticized for its lack of effective quality control systems. For instance, a hospital in Philadelphia promised to evaluate and redesign its laboratory procedures after state investigators confirmed that faulty lab tests led to dozens of patients receiving overdoses of a blood-thinning medication, resulting in the deaths of two patients. Retests found that 932 lab tests were improperly performed without being caught. Lawsuits on behalf of the dead patients were pending.[2]

The second episode shows the importance of quality control in ensuring consistent service experiences and creating customer satisfaction. Simple control mechanisms such as checklists and standard operating procedures provide cost-effective means of doing this. Contacting customers after a poor service experience only uncovers the damage that has already occurred, requires extraordinary measures for service recovery, and often results in lost customers. In the third episode, the pharmaceutical company has recognized the need to reduce both scrap and unnecessary inspection by instituting better controls and improving the process. Control should be performed by those who know the process best—the people who do the work. Focusing on the process, rather than the output, in a prevention-oriented strategy of control is preferable to inspecting the results and trying to deal with them.

In this chapter we focus on

- understanding quality control systems in manufacturing and service organizations;
- the foundations of statistical process control—understanding variation, selecting metrics to control, and building control charts;
- developing and using different types of control charts for manufacturing and service applications; and
- understanding the concept of process capability and how to measure it.

QUALITY CONTROL SYSTEMS

Learning Objective
To understand the elements of good control systems, variation in processes, the difference between common and special causes of variation, quality control metrics, and the design of quality control systems.

Any control system has three components:

1. a performance standard or goal,
2. a means of measuring actual performance, and
3. comparison of actual performance with the standard to form the basis for corrective action.

As one practical example, golf balls must meet five standards to conform to the Rules of Golf: minimum size, maximum weight, spherical symmetry, maximum initial velocity, and overall distance.[3] Methods for measuring such quality characteristics may be automated or performed manually. For instance, golf balls are measured for size by trying to drop them through a metal ring—a conforming ball sticks to the ring while a nonconforming ball falls through; digital scales measure weight to one-thousandth of a gram; and initial velocity is measured in a special machine by finding the time it takes a ball struck at 98 mph to break a ballistic screen at the end of a tube exactly 6.28 feet away. By comparing the measurements to the standard, golf ball manufacturers can determine whether their goods conform to the Rules of Golf. If they find some nonconformances, then some corrective action must be taken to either redesign the goods or correct the process that makes them. As another example, DaimlerChrysler manufactures the PT Cruiser at the company's Toluca Assembly Plant in Mexico. To ensure quality, the Toluca plant verifies parts, processes, fit, and finish every step of the way—from stamping and body to paint and final assembly. The quality control practices include visual management through quality alert systems, which are designed to call immediate attention to abnormal conditions. The system provides visual and audible signals for each station for tooling, production, maintenance, and material flow.[4]

Similar control measures are taken in services (we introduced service quality metrics in the previous chapter). Fast-food restaurants, for example, have carefully designed their processes for a high degree of accuracy and fast response time, using hands-free intercom systems, microphones that reduce ambient kitchen noise, and screens that display a customer's order. Timers at Wendy's count every segment of the order completion process to help managers control performance and identify problem areas.

Good control systems make economic sense. The importance of control is often explained by the *1:10:100 Rule* (see Exhibit 16.1):

If a defect or service error is identified and corrected at the design stage, it might cost $1 to fix. If it is first detected during the production process, it might cost $10 to fix. However, if the defect is not discovered until it reaches the customer, it might cost $100 to correct.

Exhibit 16.1
Economic Implications of the 1:10:100 Rule

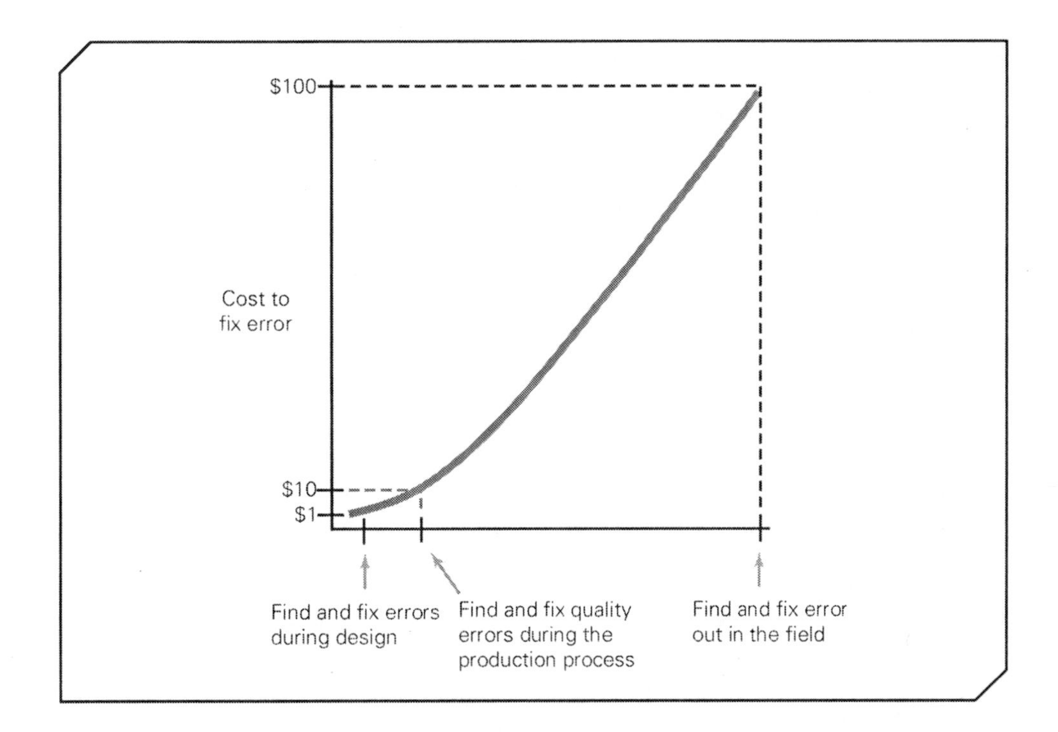

This rule is often cited in software development. Errors in software are easy to fix early in the design and development phase. However, if a "programming bug" is not detected until the software reaches system testing, it is much more costly to fix and often results in delays in the launch date of the software. If the bugs are not found until the software is released, the cost can be very high, especially if repairs must be done at the customer's site, as is often the case with software that is embedded in industrial equipment. For commercial software, the damage to customer relationships and the long-term potential loss of future business can be staggering. It is not unusual for the ratio to be more like 1:100:1,000 or 1:1,000:10,000 in these situations.

The actual numbers are irrelevant, and the exact ratios differ among firms and industries. However, the fact is that the cost of repair or service recovery grows dramatically the further that defects and errors move along the value chain. This rule clearly supports the need for control and a focus on prevention by building quality "at the source." **Quality at the source** *means the people responsible for the work control the quality of their processes by identifying and correcting any defects or errors when they first are recognized or occur.* This requires that employees have good data collection, observation, and analysis skills, as well as the proper tools, training, and support of management.

Quality at the source *means the people responsible for the work control the quality of their processes by identifying and correcting any defects or errors when they first are recognized or occur.*

Quality Control Practices in Manufacturing

In manufacturing, control is generally applied at three key points in the supply chain: at the receiving stage from suppliers, during various production processes, and at the finished goods stage.

Incoming Control and Acceptance Sampling If incoming materials are of poor quality, then the final manufactured good will certainly be no better. The purpose of receiving control is to ensure conformance to requirements before value-adding operations begin. Historically, the quality of incoming materials has been evaluated by the receiving function through reliance on a technique known as acceptance sampling. **Acceptance sampling** *is the process of making decisions on whether to accept or reject a group of items (formally called a* **lot***) purchased from some external supplier based on specified quality characteristics.* Typically, a sample is inspected and the results are compared with acceptance criteria. The acceptance criteria are determined statistically by defining a sampling plan. For example, a sampling plan might be to inspect n items from a production lot and count the number of nonconforming items in the sample. If this number is less than or equal to a statistically determined value c, the lot is accepted; otherwise, it is rejected. Acceptance sampling is relatively inexpensive and particularly well suited to destructive testing situations. It takes less time than complete inspection. It also requires less handling, which decreases the chance of damage. As with any sampling procedure, however, there is the risk of making an incorrect decision. That is, based on a sample of the items in a lot, a lot of poor quality might be accepted or a lot of good quality might be rejected. *The probability of rejecting a lot of good quality is commonly referred to as the* **producer's risk**. *The probability of accepting a lot of poor quality is called the* **consumer's risk**.

Acceptance sampling *is the process of making decisions on whether to accept or reject a group of items (formally called a* **lot***) purchased from some external supplier based on specified quality characteristics.*

The probability of rejecting a lot of good quality is commonly referred to as the **producer's risk**.

The probability of accepting a lot of poor quality is called the **consumer's risk**.

Although many companies still practice it, acceptance sampling has lost favor as an inspection practice because it is based on detection and not prevention. The burden of supplying high-quality product should rest with the suppliers themselves. Occasional inspection might be used to audit compliance, but suppliers should be expected to provide documentation and statistical evidence that they are meeting required specifications. If supplier documentation is done properly, incoming inspection can be completely eliminated. Acceptance sampling is also flawed from a statistical point of view. If a supplier maintains effective control over the process to keep variation stable over time, then the conclusion that a particular lot is unacceptable results only from statistical sampling error, not because the quality is any different from that of the other lots.

In-Process Control In-process quality control systems are needed to ensure that defective outputs do not leave the process and, more importantly, to prevent them in the first place. In designing in-process quality control systems, three key issues should be considered: *what to control, where to control,* and *how much data to gather*. Many organizations fall into the trap of trying to control every possible product or process characteristic. This can be a wasteful practice. Instead, experts suggest that the characteristics measured and controlled should be closely related to cost or key customer requirements, be easy to gather, and provide useful information to help the organization improve. The decision of where to control is fundamentally an economic one. An organization must consider trade-offs between the explicit costs of detection, repair, or replacement and the implicit costs of allowing a nonconformity to continue through the production process. These costs are sometimes difficult or even impossible to quantify. As a result, the decision is often made judgmentally. For example, a firm might choose to inspect work before relatively high-cost operations or where significant value is added to the product; before processing operations that may make detection of defectives difficult or costly, such as operations that may mask or obscure faulty attributes—for example, painting; or after operations that are likely to generate a high proportion of defectives.

The final question is whether to inspect nothing, everything, or just a sample. Unless a manufactured good requires destructive testing (in which case, sampling is necessary) or faces critical safety concerns (in which case, complete inspection is warranted or regulated by law), the best choice can be addressed economically. In fact, on a strict economic basis, the choice is to have either no inspection or complete inspection; a model for this was presented in Chapter 15.

Finished Goods Control Finished goods control is often focused on verifying that the product meets customer requirements. For many consumer products, this consists of functional testing. For instance, a manufacturer of televisions might do a simple test on every unit to make sure it operates properly. However, the company might not test every aspect of the television, such as picture sharpness or other characteristics. These aspects might already have been evaluated through in-process controls. Modern technology now allows for such tests to be conducted rapidly and cost-effectively. For example, imaging scanners along food packaging lines easily check for foreign particles.

Quality Control Practices in Services

Many of the same practices described in the previous section can be applied to quality control for back-office service operations such as check or medical insurance claim processing. However, one of the key differences between goods and services cited in Chapter 1 was "customers participate in many service processes, activities, and transactions." Customers introduce more uncertainty into service processes than in goods-producing processes. Therefore, front-office services that involve substantial customer contact must be controlled differently (see the OM Spotlight on The Ritz-Carlton). The day-to-day execution of thousands of service encounters is a challenge for any service-providing organization.

One way to control quality in services is to prevent sources of errors and mistakes in the first place by using the poka-yoke approaches described in Chapter 15. Another way is to hire and train service providers in service management skills as part of a prevention-based approach to quality control. The GAP model, also introduced in the previous chapter, can provide a framework for quality control by focusing on the key areas—the gaps—that service organizations must constantly strive to reduce.

Customer satisfaction measurement can provide the basis for effective control systems in services. Customer satisfaction instruments often focus on service attributes such as attitude, lead time, on-time delivery, exception handling, accountability, and technical support; image attributes such as reliability and price; and overall satisfaction measures. At FedEx, customers are asked to rate everything from billing to the performance of couriers, package condition, tracking and tracing capabilities, complaint handling, and helpfulness of employees. Xerox sends specific surveys to buyers, managers, and users. Buyers provide feedback on their perceptions of the sales processes, managers provide input on billing and other administrative processes, and users provide feedback on product performance and technical support. Customer satisfaction measurement should not be confined to external customers. Information from internal customers also contributes to the assessment of the organization's strengths and weaknesses. Often, the problems that cause employee dissatisfaction are the same issues that cause dissatisfaction in external customers. By controlling the appropriate things inside the organization, positive results can be achieved outside the organization. As J. W. Marriott once said, "Happy employees make happy customers."

Actionable *means that responses are tied directly to key business processes, so that what needs to be corrected or improved is clear and information can be translated into cost/revenue implications to support good management decisions.*

The types of questions to ask in a satisfaction survey must be properly worded to achieve **actionable** results. **Actionable** *means that responses are tied directly to key business processes, so that what needs to be corrected or improved is clear and information can be translated into cost/revenue implications to support good management decisions.* One example of a simple satisfaction survey for Hilton Hotels is shown in Exhibit 16.2. The survey asks direct and detailed questions about the guest bathroom, including such potential dissatisfiers as shower water pressure and temperature and bathtub/sink drainage, and likelihood of future recommendation and also has space for open-ended comments.

Satisfaction surveys create a lot of data. Most service firms simply track trends and usually have standards for determining when low scores, such as those below 4.0 on a 5.0 ordinal scale, should be investigated and corrective action taken. In-

Exhibit 16.2
Hilton Hotel Guest Survey

Completely fill in your response ● Correct **GUEST**Scope

Hilton

Please rate your satisfaction with the comfort level of your accommodations.

	Level of Satisfaction							
	Low			Avg.			High	N/A
	1	2	3	4	5	6	7	
Accommodations look and smell clean and fresh:	☐	☐	☐	☐	☐	☐	☐	☐
Clean and comfortable linens:	☐	☐	☐	☐	☐	☐	☐	☐
Comfort level of pillow:	☐	☐	☐	☐	☐	☐	☐	☐
Comfort level of mattress:	☐	☐	☐	☐	☐	☐	☐	☐
Easily regulated room temperature:	☐	☐	☐	☐	☐	☐	☐	☐
Housekeeping during stay:	☐	☐	☐	☐	☐	☐	☐	☐
Overall satisfaction with this Hilton:	☐	☐	☐	☐	☐	☐	☐	
Likelihood you would recommend Hilton:	☐	☐	☐	☐	☐	☐	☐	
Likelihood, **if returning to the area**, you would return to this Hilton:	☐	☐	☐	☐	☐	☐	☐	
Value of accommodations for price paid:	☐	☐	☐	☐	☐	☐	☐	

Primary purpose of visit? ☐ Individual business ☐ Convention/Meeting ☐ Pleasure
How many times have you been a guest at this Hilton? ☐ 1 ☐ 2 ☐ 3 ☐ 4 ☐ 5+
Did you have a hotel product or service problem during your stay? ☐ Yes ☐ No
If yes—did you report it to the staff? ☐ Yes ☐ No
If yes—was it resolved to your satisfaction? ☐ Yes ☐ No
If yes—what was the nature of the problem? ____________

Please share any thoughts on any other aspects of your visit, including the names of any staff members who made your stay more enjoyable: ____________

Name: Daytime Phone:
Date of Stay: Room:
PLEASE DO NOT WRITE BELOW THIS LINE FD2

Source: Reprinted with permission of UniFocus, LP. © 2000 UniFocus.

dividual comments are often reviewed by customer service representatives or by general management. Survey results are often used in performance reviews, so managers have incentives to ensure that customers are satisfied.

Many companies have integrated customer feedback into their continuous improvement activities and in redesigning goods and services. For example, Skilled Care Pharmacy, located in Mason, Ohio, is a $25-million, privately held, regional provider of pharmaceutical products delivered within the long-term care, assisted-living, hospice, and group home environments. Skilled Care developed a Customer Grade Card, benchmarked from Baldrige winner Wainwright Industries, to measure customer satisfaction and provide a simple control mechanism. The Grade Card uses the school-like A-B-C-D scoring system shown in Exhibit 16.3. The scores from the four questions covering Quality, Responsiveness, Delivery, and Communication are converted from letters to numbers and averaged. Any questions that were graded C or below generate an immediate phone call and/or personal visit to the facility by the Customer Care Team to investigate and resolve the issue. An example of how the feedback was used for improvement revolved around low scores received for "Delivery." Management determined there was potential risk for losing valuable customers. Upon investigation, it became evident that the issue was not timely

Exhibit 16.3
Skilled Care's Customer Grade Card Scoring System

A = Customer Totally Satisfied	100 points
B = Customer Generally Satisfied	90 points
C = Customer Generally Dissatisfied	50 points
D = Customer Totally Dissatisfied	0 points

delivery, but the system of cutoff times for ordering medications for same-day delivery. If the customer missed the cutoff time, it did not receive the order until the next day; therefore, Skilled Care was considered to be "late." The response to this customer need was to extend pharmacy ordering hours and aggressively modify staff schedules for the order processing and pharmacy departments. In turn, it was able to offer an additional 5 hours for customers to phone or fax medication orders for receipt the same day. As a result, satisfaction scores for "Delivery" rose dramatically.

OM SPOTLIGHT

The Ritz-Carlton Hotel Company

The approach used by the Ritz-Carlton Hotel Company to control quality is proactive because of its intensive personalized service environment.[5] Systems for collecting and using quality-related measures are widely deployed and used extensively throughout the organization. For example, each hotel tracks a set of Service Quality Indicators on a daily basis. The Ritz-Carlton recognizes that many customer requirements are sensory (see the idea of a servicescape in Chapter 5) and, thus, difficult to measure. However, by selecting, training, and certifying employees in their knowledge of the Ritz-Carlton Gold Standards of service, they are able to assess their work through appropriate sensory measurements—taste, sight, smell, sound, and touch—and take appropriate actions.

The company uses three types of control processes to deliver quality:

1. Self-control of the individual employee based on their spontaneous and learned behavior.
2. Basic control mechanism, which is carried out by every member of the work force. The first person who detects a problem is empowered to break away from routine duties, investigate and correct the problem immediately, document the incident, and then return to their routine.
3. Critical success factor control for critical processes. Process teams use customer and organizational requirement measurements to determine quality, speed, and cost performance. These measurements are compared against benchmarks and customer satisfaction data to determine corrective action and resource allocation.

In addition, the Ritz-Carlton conducts both self- and outside audits. Self-audits are carried out internally at all levels, from one individual or function to an entire hotel. Process walk-throughs occur daily in hotels; senior leaders assess field operations during formal reviews at various intervals. Outside audits are performed by independent travel and hospitality rating organizations. All audits must be documented, and any findings must be submitted to the senior leader of the unit being audited. They are responsible for action and for assessing the implementation and effectiveness of recommended corrective actions.

KJELD DUITS/EPA/Landov

FOUNDATIONS OF STATISTICAL PROCESS CONTROL

Learning Objective
To understand variation in manufacturing and service processes, metrics for quantifying variation, and the role of control charts and statistical process control methods in helping managers control variation.

Statistical process control (SPC) *is a methodology for monitoring quality of manufacturing and service delivery processes to help identify and eliminate unwanted causes of variation.* The outputs of any goods- or service-producing process have some variation. Variation occurs for many reasons, such as inconsistencies in material inputs; changes in environmental conditions (temperature, humidity); machine maintenance cycles; tool wear; and human fatigue. Some variation is obvious, such as inconsistencies in meal delivery times or food quantity at a restaurant; other variation—such as minute differences in physical dimensions of machined parts—is barely perceptible, but can be determined through some type of measurement process. Understanding variation and choosing the right metrics to monitor a process are vital prerequisites for implementing statistical process control systems.

Statistical process control (SPC) *is a methodology for monitoring quality of manufacturing and service delivery processes to help identify and eliminate unwanted causes of variation.*

Understanding Variation

Walter Shewhart is credited with recognizing the distinction between two principal types of variation at Bell Laboratories in the 1920s. **Common cause variation** *is the result of complex interactions of variations in materials, tools, machines, information, workers, and the environment.* Such variation is a natural part of the technology and process design and cannot be controlled; that is, we cannot influence each individual output of the process. It appears at random, and individual sources or causes cannot be identified or explained. However, their combined effect is usually stable and can be described statistically. For example, if you would measure and record the times it takes to cook and deliver a customer's meal at a restaurant on a typical Saturday night, you would observe some statistical variation, which would be due to the random mix and sequence of orders in the kitchen, variations in the preparation and cooking times, and variation in waiting for servers to pick the meals up.

Common cause variation *is the result of complex interactions of variations in materials, tools, machines, information, workers, and the environment.*

Common causes of variation generally account for about 80 to 95 percent of the observed variation in a process. It can be reduced only if better technology, process design, or training is provided. This clearly is the responsibility of management. One of the goals of the Six Sigma approaches that we discussed in the previous chapter is to try to identify significant sources of common cause variation and reduce it through improvements in the design of processes and application of technology. Statistical analysis techniques, such as Design of Experiments that you might have encountered in other courses, help to isolate individual sources of variation so they can be improved.

Special (or assignable) cause variation *arises from external sources that are not inherent in the process, appear sporadically, and disrupt the random pattern of common causes.* Special cause variation occurs sporadically and can be prevented or at least explained and understood. For example, a tool might break during a process step, a worker might be distracted by a colleague, or a bus load of tourists stops at a restaurant (resulting in unusual wait times). Special cause variation tends to be easily detectable using statistical methods because they disrupt the normal pattern of measurements. When special causes are identified, short-term corrective action generally should be taken by those who own the process and are responsible for doing the work, such as machine operators, order-fulfillment workers, and so on.

Special (or assignable) cause variation *arises from external sources that are not inherent in the process, appear sporadically, and disrupt the random pattern of common causes.*

A system governed only by common causes is called a **stable system**. Understanding a stable system and the differences between special and common causes of variation is essential for managing any system. If we don't understand the variation in a system, we cannot predict its future performance. For example, suppose that under normal circumstances, the lead time to produce and deliver a customer's

A system governed only by common causes is called a **stable system**.

order is between 20 and 25 days. If the system is stable, salespeople can promise delivery to customers within this time frame. However, if special causes that are not controlled cause the range of the lead times to sometimes increase from 15 to 30 days, or jump to an average of 30–35 days with no predictability, salespeople will not be able to provide any assurance to their customers about delivery. This might result in disruptions of normal work schedules, unnecessary outsourcing costs, or customer complaints.

Keeping special cause variation from occurring is the essence of quality control. *If no special causes affect the output of a process, we say that the process is* **in control***; when special causes are present, the process is said to be* **out of control**. A process that is in control does not need any changes or adjustments; an out-of-control process needs correction. However, employees often make two basic mistakes when attempting to control a process:

If no special causes affect the output of a process, we say that the process is **in control***; when special causes are present, the process is said to be* **out of control**.

1. adjusting a process that is already in control, or
2. failing to correct a process that is out of control.

While it is clear that a truly out-of-control process must be corrected, many workers mistakenly believe that whenever process output is off-target, some adjustment must be made. Actually, overadjusting a process that is in control will *increase* the variation in the output. Thus, employees must know when to leave a process alone to keep variation at a minimum.

In Chapter 2 we introduced many of the basic metrics that are used to measure and evaluate quality, including nonconformities per unit, defects per million opportunities (dpmo), and service errors per million opportunities (epmo). Operations managers use such metrics as a basis for quality control. Methods for measuring such quality characteristics may be automated or performed manually by the work force. One of the most popular approaches to quality control is the use of statistical process control, which we describe later in this chapter.

Quality Control Metrics and Measurement

Controlling a process begins with understanding how a process works: what materials, equipment, information, people, and other resources are needed; what steps and activities occur during the process; who makes decisions at various stages in the process and what information is needed to make those decisions; and if things go wrong, what needs to be done to correct them.

Data for process control generally come from some type of measurement or inspection process. The true purpose of inspection is to provide information to control and improve the process effectively. Thus, inspection activities must be integrated throughout the production process, usually at the receipt of incoming materials, during the manufacturing process, and upon completion of production, to provide useful information for daily control as well as for long-term improvement.

Quality control metrics and indicators can be either discrete or continuous. *A* **discrete metric** *is one that is calculated from data that are counted.* In quality control, discrete measurements are often called *attributes data.* Visual inspection and observation is often used to gather such data. For example, we might observe whether a quality characteristic is either present or absent in the product or service under consideration. A dimension on a machined part is either within tolerance or out of tolerance, an order is either complete or incomplete, or a service experience is either good or bad. We can count the number of parts within tolerance, the number of complete orders, or the number of good service experiences. The number of acceptable outcomes is an example of a discrete metric. Usually, we divide this by the total number to obtain the fraction or percentage of parts, orders, or service experiences that are acceptable. This is a more common discrete metric used in quality control. In other cases, the entity that we are analyzing can have multiple

A **discrete metric** *is one that is calculated from data that are counted.*

defects or errors. For instance, an order might be missing one or more items. If we only look at whether the order is good or bad, we have no information on whether a bad order has only one missing item or many. If we count the number of defects or errors for each order and compute the average number of errors per order, we have a more relevant metric. Another common example of a discrete metric that many organizations use is the number of complaints per customer or per time period (see OM Spotlight: Bad Service Is Remembered). An obvious approach to address this is to count the frequency and type of complaints, identify those that occur the most, and take action.

A **continuous metric** *is one that is calculated from data that are measured as the degree of conformance to a specification on some continuous scale of measurement.* In quality control, continuous measurements are often called *variables data.* Examples are length, weight, and time. Thus, rather than determining whether the diameter of a shaft is just in or out of tolerance, we might measure the actual value of the diameter. Customer waiting time, order lead time, and the weight of cereal in a box are other examples. Continuous metrics are generally summarized with such statistics as averages and standard deviations.

A **continuous metric** *is one that is calculated from data that are measured as the degree of conformance to a specification on some continuous scale of measurement.*

It is important to understand that collecting discrete data is usually easier than collecting continuous data since the assessment can usually be done more quickly by a simple inspection and count, whereas continuous metrics require the use of some type of measuring instrument. In a statistical sense, however, discrete data provide less information than continuous data and require a larger sample size to obtain the same amount of statistical information about the quality of what is measured. This difference can become significant when inspection of each item is time-consuming or expensive.

Service Quality Metrics and Measurement

One of the challenges of developing effective quality management systems for services is measurement. Most quality metrics in "back office" service environments revolve around goods and information. These are well defined and relatively easy to measure. Examples in services include time (waiting time, service time, delivery time) and number of nonconformances. Insurance companies, for example, measure the time to complete different transactions such as new issues, claim payments, and cash surrenders. Hospitals measure the percentage of nosocomial infections and

OM SPOTLIGHT

Bad Service Is Remembered[6]

The American Customer Satisfaction Index rated automobile service the highest followed by gas stations, supermarkets, retail stores, hotels, motion pictures, computer stores, banking, restaurants, telecommunications, utilities, hospitals, newspapers, and airlines. As we drop down this list, we find organizations for which many customers have had bad experiences. For example, the Public Utilities Commission of Ohio found that "rude customer-service representatives" and "automated answering systems" that block callers from getting through to a real person are two of the top ten customer complaints. High prices, billing errors, missed installation and repair appointments, service outages, broken promises by service providers, waiting for service, and weather-related service upsets are the other top ten customer complaint categories. Gas, electric, telephone, and water utilities were the focus of the study. "Customers don't forgive and forget; bad service is remembered," said one Ohio consultant on customer service.

the percentage of unplanned readmissions to the emergency room, intensive care, or operating room within, say, 48 hours. Other quality characteristics are observable. These include the types of errors (wrong kind, wrong quantity, wrong delivery date, and so on). Hospitals might monitor the completeness of medical charts and the quality of radiology readings, measured by a double-reading process.

In services with high customer contact, many key quality measures are perceptual; that is, they measure customer perceptions of the quality of service. Employee courtesy, promptness, competency, behavior, treatment of the customer, ability to solve a customer's problem, and so on are some common examples. Even though human behavior can be observed, the task of describing and classifying the observations is far more difficult. Individual customers may perceive actual performance differently and be influenced by many factors unrelated to the actual performance of the service. Thus, the major obstacle is developing operational definitions of service provider and customer behavioral characteristics. The focus of this interaction is the service encounter. For example, how does one define courteous versus discourteous, empathy versus anger toward the customer or understanding versus indifferent? Defining such distinctions is best done by comparing behavior against understandable standards. For instance, a standard for "courtesy" might be to address the customer as "Mr." or "Ms." Failure to do so is an instance of an error. "Promptness" might be defined as greeting a customer within 5 seconds of entering the store or answering letters within 2 days of receipt. These behaviors can easily be recorded and counted. As described in Chapter 5 on service guarantees, "script dialogues" help to standardize service provider responses to certain service encounter situations.

Another issue with service quality metrics is whether to use customer perception-based or internal process-based measures. It is not uncommon to find that customer perceptions do not agree with actual operational measures. For example, customers might perceive their waiting time to be 4 or 5 minutes (and state their dissatisfaction) when the true waiting time might only be a minute and a half. This might result from prior expectations. The GAP model described in Chapter 15 can help uncover such discrepancies between customer expectations and perceptions after service. Nevertheless, perceived wait time is the "real" wait time, and management must identify ways to change perceptions, for example, by using advertising to set proper expectations, engaging customers in other activities to distract perceptions of long waits, and designing the facility so the entire waiting line is not apparent.

An established instrument for measuring the external customer perceptions of service quality is SERVQUAL.[7] The initial instrument identified ten dimensions of service quality performance: (1) reliability, (2) responsiveness, (3) competence, (4) access, (5) courtesy, (6) communication, (7) credibility, (8) security, (9) understanding/knowing the customer, and (10) tangibles. These were reduced to five dimensions based on further research: tangibles, reliability, responsiveness, assurance, and empathy. Assurance consolidated competence, courtesy, credibility, and security attributes, and is defined as the "knowledge and courtesy of service providers and their ability to convey trust and confidence." Empathy is defined as "caring, individual attention the firm provides its customers" and incorporates the attributes of access, communication, and understanding the customer. SERVQUAL is designed to apply to all service industries; however, measures specific to a certain industry or business or process may provide more accurate measures.

Internal measurements of service quality are commonly collected using some type of data sheet or checklist. Time is easily measured by taking two observations: starting time and finishing time. Many observed data assume only "yes" or "no" values. For example, a survey of pharmaceutical operations in a hospital might include the following questions:

- Are drug storage and preparation areas within the pharmacy under the supervision of a pharmacist?
- Are drugs requiring special storage conditions properly stored?

- Is patient, staff, and doctor interaction handled in a professional and friendly manner?
- Are drug emergency boxes inspected on a monthly basis?
- Is the drug emergency box record book filled out completely?

Simple checksheets can be designed to record the types of errors that occur.

Exhibit 16.4 shows some examples of many types of quality metrics used in service organizations.

Control Charts

SPC uses control charts—graphical tools that indicate when a process is in control or out of control—to measure quality. *A* **control chart** *is simply a run chart to which two horizontal lines, called* **control limits**, *are added: the upper control limit (UCL) and lower control limit (LCL).* The general structure is illustrated in Exhibit 16.5. Control limits are chosen statistically to provide a high probability (generally greater than .99) that points will fall between these limits if the process is in control. Control limits make it easier to interpret patterns in a run chart and draw conclusions about the state of control. If sample values fall outside the control limits or if nonrandom patterns occur in the chart, then special causes may be affecting the process; the process is not stable. Thus, a control chart provides a statistical basis for concluding when special causes occur in a process.

A **control chart** *is simply a run chart to which two horizontal lines, called* **control limits**, *are added: the upper control limit (UCL) and lower control limit (LCL).*

If evaluation and correction are done in real time, then the chance of producing nonconforming output is minimized. Thus, as a problem-solving tool, control charts allow employees to identify quality problems as they occur. Of course, control charts alone cannot determine the source of the problem. This requires knowledge and creativity on the part of the workers to diagnose the process and identify the root cause (see OM Spotlight: Dow Chemical Company).

Exhibit 16.4
Examples of Service Quality Metrics

Organization	Quality Measure
Hospital	Lab test accuracy Insurance claim accuracy On-time delivery of meals and medication Patient satisfaction
Bank	Check-processing accuracy Time to process loan requests
Insurance company	Claims-processing response time Billing accuracy
Post Office	Sorting accuracy Time of delivery Percentage of express mail delivered on time
Ambulance	Response time
Police Department	Incidence of crime in a precinct Number of traffic citations Empathy and respect toward crime victims
Hotel	Proportion of rooms satisfactorily cleaned Checkout time Number of complaints received
Transportation	Proportion of freight cars correctly routed Dollar amount of damage per claim
Auto service	Percentage of time work completed as promised Number of parts out of stock Politeness of service advisor

Exhibit 16.5
Structure of a Control Chart

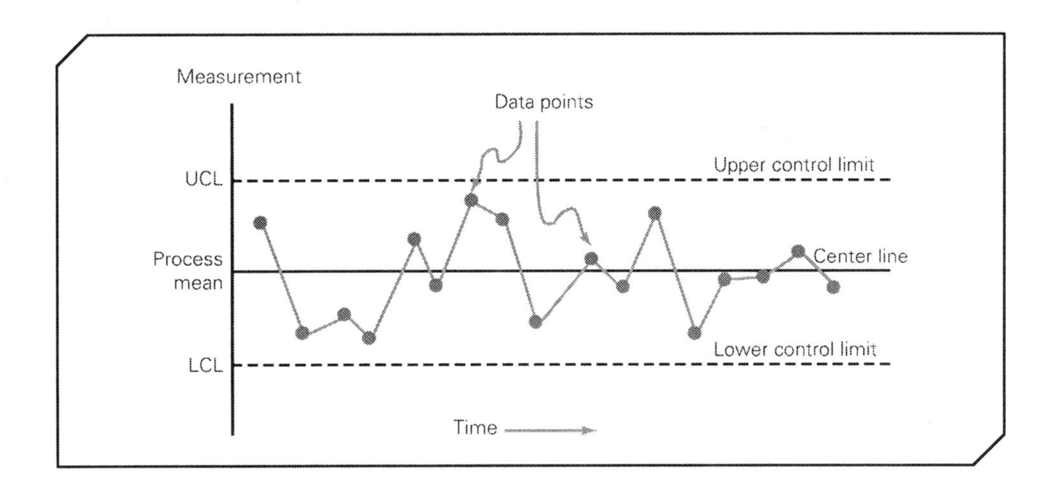

OM SPOTLIGHT

Dow Chemical Company[8]

The magnesium department of the Dow Chemical Company plant in Freeport, Texas, has produced magnesium, a silvery light metal, for nearly a century. It was the first major group in Texas Operations to train all of its technical people and managers in the use of statistical quality control (SQC) techniques, following the example set by the automobile industry.

Some of the earliest successful applications of SQC were in chemical-process areas. Exhibit 16.6 shows the improvement in the dryer analysis after SQC and retraining were implemented. In addition to the fact that the process control required significant improvement, differences between operators existed. The dark circles in Exhibit 16.6 represent one operator in question; the open circles represent the other operators. On examination, it was found that the operator had not been properly trained in the use of SQC, even though the operator had been performing the analysis for 2 years. There was immediate improvement in the consistency of the operators' analyses after retraining.

The use of control charts in the control room made the operators realize that their attempts to fine-tune the process introduced a great deal of unwanted variation. The before-and-after range charts (*R*-charts) show the improvement; see Exhibit 16.7.

As with many chemical and manufacturing operations, when the variability of the feedstock to one operation is reduced, it is possible to reduce the variability of the basic operation. With tighter control over the concentration of magnesium hydroxide from the filter plant, Dow was able to exert much tighter control on the subsequent neutralization operation. As seen in Exhibit 16.8, the differences are substantial. The upper control limit (UCL) on the second range chart is about where the center line is on the first. A similar situation exists on the $\bar{x}$-charts. These improvements resulted without any additional instrumentation or operators.

Another application involved the casting operation. On primary magnesium, for example, Dow calculated a process-capability index—the ratio of the specified tolerance to the six-sigma natural variation—of meeting minimum magnesium content of 99.8 percent purity and found it to be over 10, based on more than 10,000 samples. Thus, there had been little incentive to use control charts in this operation because of the comfortable level of compliance. However, ingots are also graded according to their surface quality. Using control charts, Dow found that although the process was in control, the number of rejects was much higher than desired. After several months of analysis and modifications, the process was improved.

Dow has had success everywhere it has used SQC in the magnesium process. Savings of several hundred thousand dollars per year have been realized, and new applications are continually being discovered.

PR Newswire DOW CHEMICAL USA

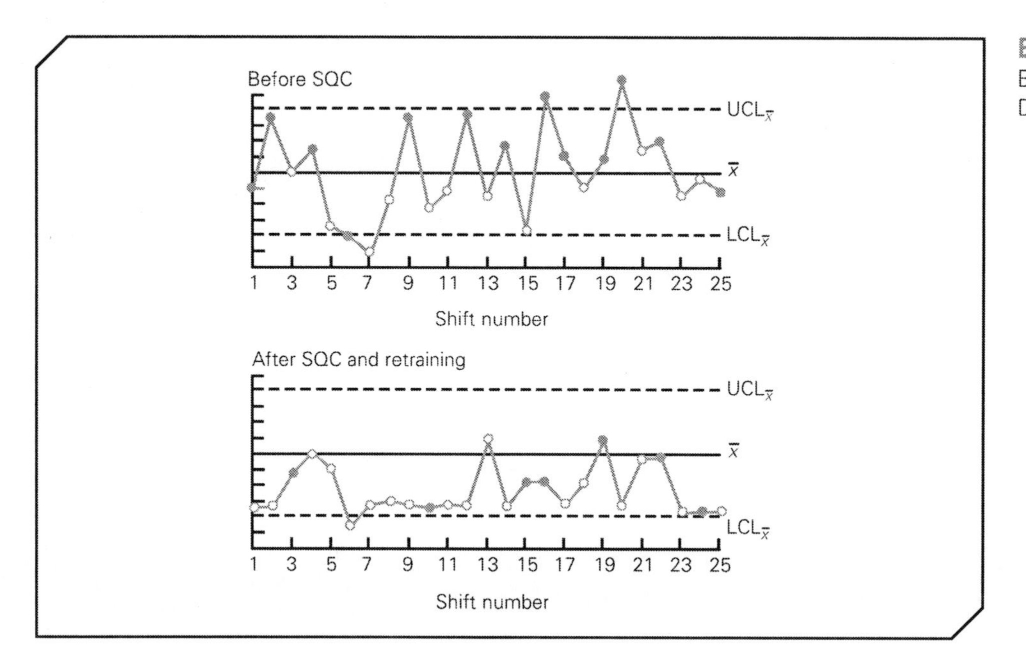

Exhibit 16.6
Before-and-After $\bar{x}$-Charts on Dryer Analysis

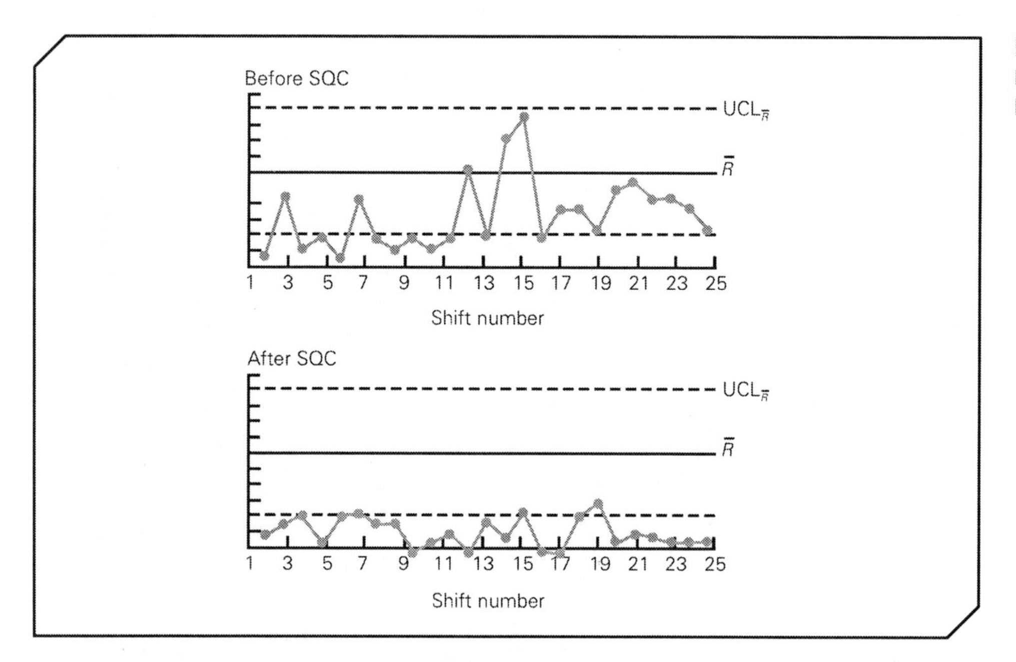

Exhibit 16.7
Before-and-After R-Charts on Dryer Analysis

The benefits of using control charts can be summarized as follows:

- Control charts are simple, effective tools for achieving statistical control. They can be maintained at the workstation by the employee who runs a machine or process, thus giving the people closest to the operation reliable information on when action should be taken and when it should not.
- When a process is in statistical control, its performance to specification is predictable. Both producer and customer can rely on consistent quality levels, and both can rely on stable costs for achieving that quality level.
- After a process is in statistical control, management can attack the systemic causes of variation in an effort to reduce it, by, for instance, improving technology or employee training.
- Control charts provide a common language for communication between the people on different shifts operating a process; between line production (operator,

Exhibit 16.8 $\bar{x}$- and R-Charts on Neutralizer Excess Alkalinity Before and After SQC

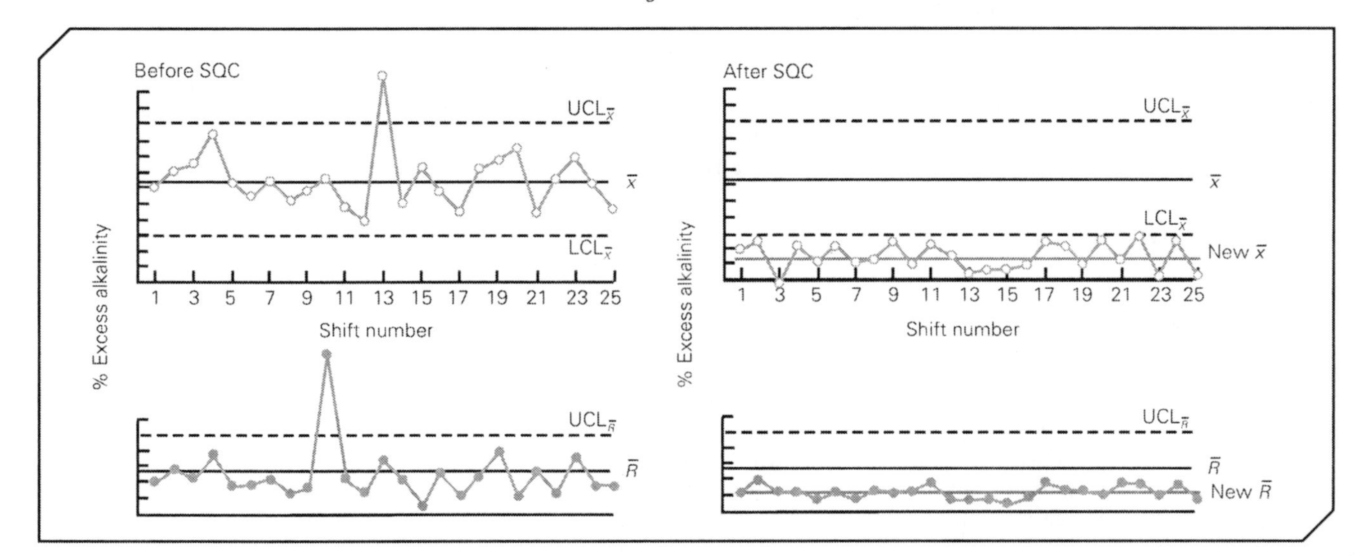

supervisor) and support activities (maintenance, material control, process engineering, quality control); between different stations in the process; between supplier and user; and between the manufacturing/assembly plant and the design-engineering activity.

By distinguishing special from common causes of variation, control charts give a good indication of whether problems are correctable locally or require management action. This minimizes the confusion, frustration, and cost of misdirected problem-solving efforts.

SPC Methodology

Control charts are relatively simple to use. The following is a summary of the steps required to develop and use control charts. Steps 1 through 4 focus on setting up an initial chart; in step 5, the charts are used for ongoing monitoring; and finally, in step 6, the data are used for process capability analysis.

1. Preparation
   a. Choose the metric to be monitored.
   b. Determine the basis, size, and frequency of sampling.
   c. Set up the control chart.
2. Data collection
   a. Record the data.
   b. Calculate relevant statistics: averages, ranges, proportions, and so on.
   c. Plot the statistics on the chart.
3. Determination of trial control limits
   a. Draw the center line (process average) on the chart.
   b. Compute the upper and lower control limits.
4. Analysis and interpretation
   a. Investigate the chart for lack of control.
   b. Eliminate out-of-control points.
   c. Recompute control limits if necessary.
5. Use as a problem-solving tool
   a. Continue data collection and plotting.
   b. Identify out-of-control situations and take corrective action.
6. Determination of process capability using the control chart data

CONSTRUCTING CONTROL CHARTS

Learning Objective
To be able to construct and interpret simple control charts for both continuous and discrete data, to understand how to select the proper chart, and to understand the role of SPC in processes approaching Six Sigma capability.

Many different types of control charts exist. All are similar in structure, but the specific formulas used to compute control limits for them differ. Moreover, different types of charts are used for different types of metrics. Continuous data usually require $\bar{x}$-("x-bar") and R-charts. Discrete data usually require p-, c-, or u-charts.

Constructing $\bar{x}$- and R-Charts

The first step in developing $\bar{x}$- and R-charts is to gather data. Usually, about 25 to 30 samples are collected. Samples between size 3 and 10 are generally used, with 5 being the most common. The number of samples is indicated by k, and n denotes the sample size. For each sample i, the mean (denoted $\bar{x}_i$) and the range (R_i) are computed. These values are then plotted on their respective control charts. Next, the *overall mean* and *average range* calculations are made. These values specify the center lines for the $\bar{x}$- and R-charts, respectively. The overall mean (denoted $\bar{\bar{x}}$) is the average of the sample means $\bar{x}_i$:

$$\bar{\bar{x}} = \frac{\sum_{i=1}^{k} \bar{x}_i}{k} \quad (16.1)$$

The average range ($\bar{R}$) is similarly computed, using the formula

$$\bar{R} = \frac{\sum_{i=1}^{k} R_i}{k} \quad (16.2)$$

The average range and average mean are used to compute upper and lower control limits (UCL and LCL) for the R- and $\bar{x}$-charts. Control limits are easily calculated using the following formulas:

$$\begin{aligned} UCL_R &= D_4\bar{R} \qquad & UCL_{\bar{x}} &= \bar{\bar{x}} + A_2\bar{R} \\ LCL_R &= D_3\bar{R} \qquad & LCL_{\bar{x}} &= \bar{\bar{x}} - A_2\bar{R} \end{aligned} \quad (16.3)$$

where the constants D_3, D_4, and A_2 depend on the sample size (see Appendix B).

The control limits represent the range between which all points are expected to fall if the process is in statistical control. If any points fall outside the control limits or if any unusual patterns are observed, then some special cause has probably affected the process. The process should be studied to determine the cause. If special causes are present, then they are *not* representative of the true state of statistical control, and the calculations of the center line and control limits will be biased. The corresponding data points should be eliminated, and new values for $\bar{\bar{x}}$, $\bar{R}$, and the control limits should be computed.

In determining whether a process is in statistical control, the R-chart is always analyzed first. Because the control limits in the $\bar{x}$-chart depend on the average range, special causes in the R-chart may produce unusual patterns in the $\bar{x}$-chart, even when the centering of the process is in control. (An example of such distorted patterns is given later in this chapter.) Once statistical control is established for the R-chart, attention may turn to the $\bar{x}$-chart.

An Example of an $\bar{x}$-Chart and R-Chart

The Goodman Tire and Rubber Company periodically tests its tires for tread wear under simulated road conditions. To study and control its manufacturing processes, the company uses $\bar{x}$- and R-charts. Twenty samples, each containing three radial tires, were chosen from different shifts over several days of operation. Exhibit 16.9 is a spreadsheet that provides the data, sample averages and ranges, and control limits. Since $n = 3$, the control limit factors for the R-chart are $D_3 = 0$ and $D_4 = 2.57$. The control limits as computed in the spreadsheet are

$$UCL = D_4\overline{R} = 2.57(10.8) = 27.8$$

$$LCL = D_3\overline{R} = 0$$

For the $\overline{x}$-chart, $A_2 = 1.02$; thus the control limits are

$$UCL = 31.88 + 1.02(10.8) = 42.9$$

$$LCL = 31.88 - 1.02(10.8) = 20.8$$

The R- and $\overline{x}$-charts for the sample data, charted with Microsoft Excel (the Excel templates are included on the Student CD-ROM), are shown in Exhibits 16.10 and 16.11, respectively.

Interpreting Patterns in Control Charts

The location of points and the patterns of points in a control chart enable one to determine, with only a small chance of error, whether or not a process is in statistical control. A process is in control when the control chart has the following characteristics:

1. No points are outside control limits.
2. The number of points above and below the center line is about the same.
3. The points seem to fall randomly above and below the center line.
4. Most points, but not all, are near the center line, and only a few are close to the control limits.

You can see that these characteristics are evident in the R-chart in Exhibit 16.10. Therefore we would conclude that the R-chart is in control.

These characteristics stem from the assumption that the distribution of sample means, which we plot on the chart, is normal (see Exhibit 16.12). You may recall from statistics that the sampling distribution of the mean is approximately normal regardless of the original distribution. The formulas used for the upper and lower

Exhibit 16.9 Excel Template for $\overline{x}$- and R-Charts

X-bar and R-Chart

This spreadsheet is designed for up to 50 samples, each of a constant sample size from 2 to 10. Enter data ONLY in yellow-shaded cells.

Enter the number of samples in cell E6 and the sample size in cell E7. Then enter your data in the grid below.

Click on sheet tabs for a display of the control charts. Specification limits may be entered in cells N7 and N8 for process capability.

Number of samples (<= 50)	30				
Sample size (2 - 10)	3				
Grand Average	31.877778	A2	D3	D4	d2
Average Range	10.8	1.02	0	2.57	1.69

Process Capability Calculations		Six sigma	38.28
Upper specification	50	Cp	1.306
Lower specification	0	Cpu	0.947
		Cpl	1.666
		Cpk	0.947

DATA	1	2	3	4	5	6	7	8	9	10	11	12	13	14	15
1	31	26	25	17	38	41	21	32	41	29	26	23	17	37	18
2	42	18	30	25	29	42	17	26	34	17	31	19	24	35	25
3	28	35	34	21	35	36	29	28	33	30	40	25	32	17	29
Average	33.67	26.33	29.67	21	34	39.67	22.33	28.67	36	25.33	32.33	22.33	24.33	29.67	24
LCLx-bar	20.83	20.83	20.83	20.83	20.83	20.83	20.83	20.83	20.83	20.83	20.83	20.83	20.83	20.83	20.83
Center	31.88	31.88	31.88	31.88	31.88	31.88	31.88	31.88	31.88	31.88	31.88	31.88	31.88	31.88	31.88
UCLx-bar	42.93	42.93	42.93	42.93	42.93	42.93	42.93	42.93	42.93	42.93	42.93	42.93	42.93	42.93	42.93
Range	14	17	9	8	9	6	12	6	8	13	14	6	15	20	11
LCLrange	0	0	0	0	0	0	0	0	0	0	0	0	0	0	0
Center	10.8	10.8	10.8	10.8	10.8	10.8	10.8	10.8	10.8	10.8	10.8	10.8	10.8	10.8	10.8
UCLrange	27.8	27.8	27.8	27.8	27.8	27.8	27.8	27.8	27.8	27.8	27.8	27.8	27.8	27.8	27.8

DATA	16	17	18	19	20	21	22	23	24	25	26	27	28	29	30
1	30	28	40	18	22	36	29	40	34	31	41	36	35	38	42
2	42	36	29	29	34	22	37	35	44	37	45	41	49	45	44
3	31	32	31	28	26	26	31	46	42	39	34	34	40	40	32
Average	34.33	32	33.33	25	27.33	28	32.33	40.33	40	35.67	40	37	41.33	41	39.33
LCLx-bar	20.83	20.83	20.83	20.83	20.83	20.83	20.83	20.83	20.83	20.83	20.83	20.83	20.83	20.83	20.83
Center	31.88	31.88	31.88	31.88	31.88	31.88	31.88	31.88	31.88	31.88	31.88	31.88	31.88	31.88	31.88
UCLx-bar	42.93	42.93	42.93	42.93	42.93	42.93	42.93	42.93	42.93	42.93	42.93	42.93	42.93	42.93	42.93
Range	12	8	11	11	12	14	8	11	10	8	11	7	14	7	12
LCLrange	0	0	0	0	0	0	0	0	0	0	0	0	0	0	0
Center	10.8	10.8	10.8	10.8	10.8	10.8	10.8	10.8	10.8	10.8	10.8	10.8	10.8	10.8	10.8
UCLrange	27.8	27.8	27.8	27.8	27.8	27.8	27.8	27.8	27.8	27.8	27.8	27.8	27.8	27.8	27.8

Exhibit 16.10 *R*-Chart for Goodman Tire Example

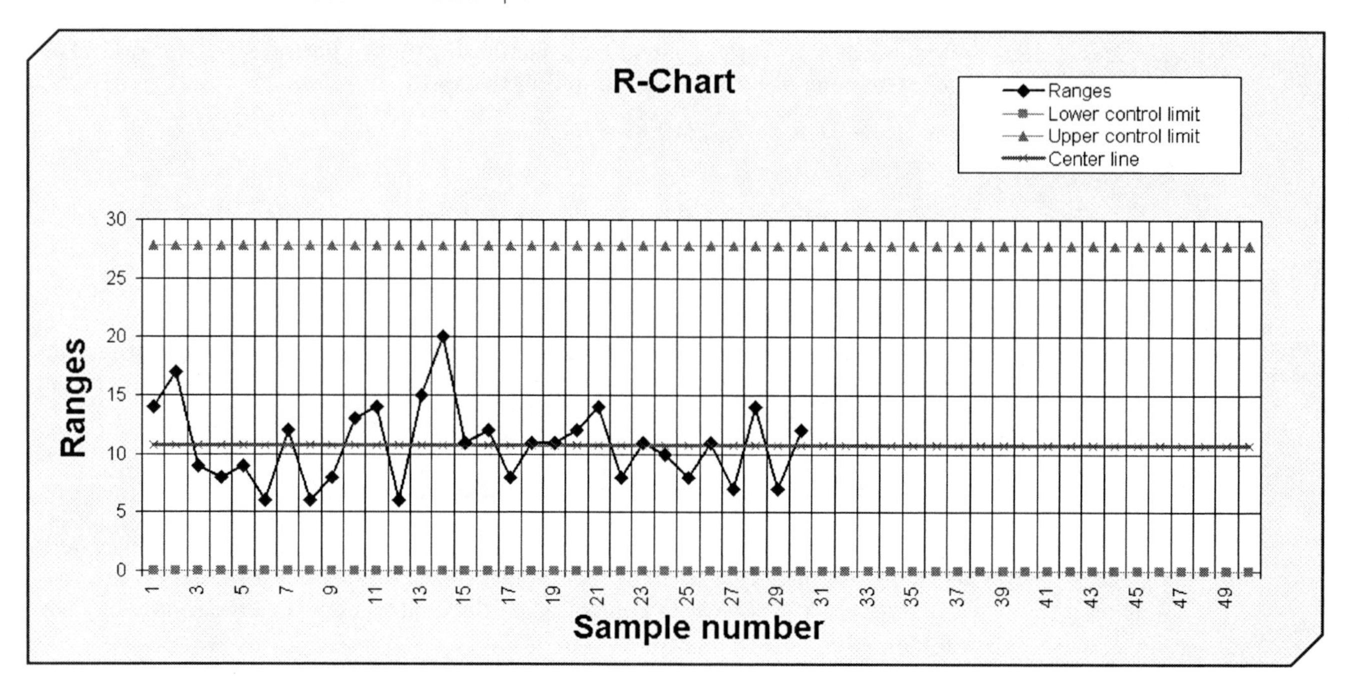

Exhibit 16.11 $\bar{x}$-Chart for Goodman Tire Example

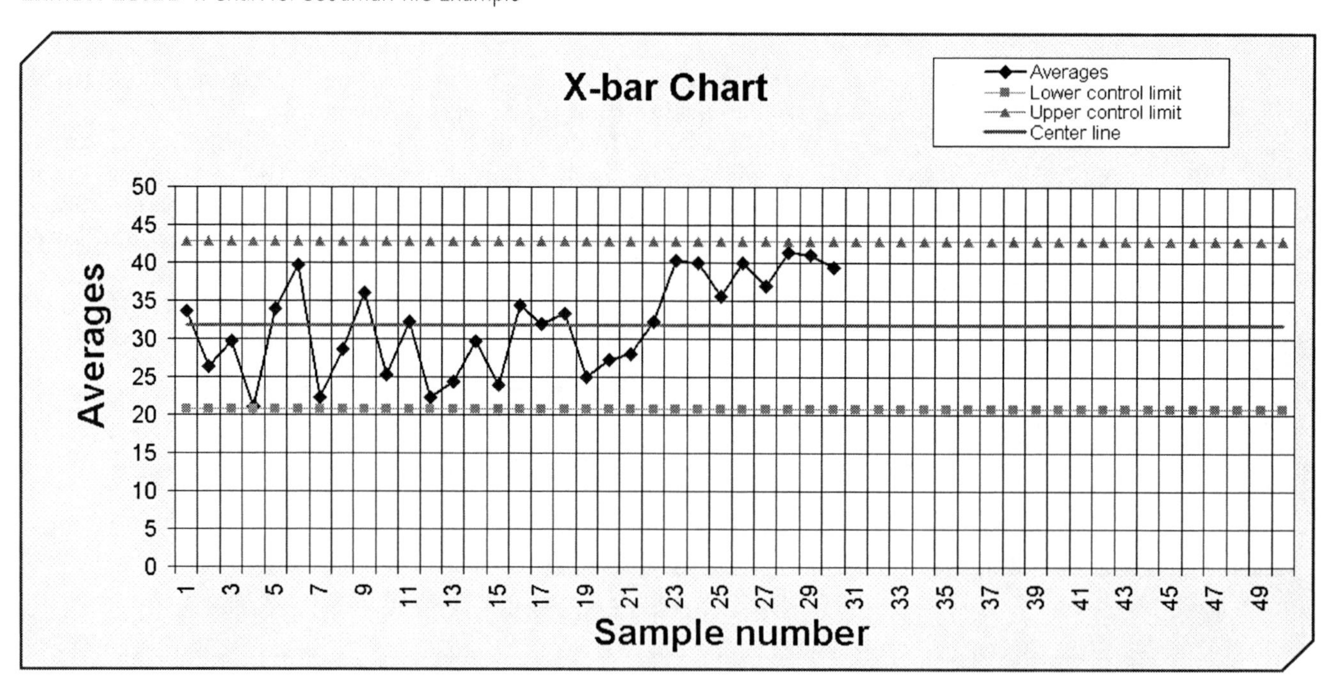

control limits set them to be 3 standard deviations from the overall mean. Thus, it will be highly unlikely that any sample mean will fall outside the control limits. Because the normal distribution is symmetric, about the same number of points should fall above as below the center line. Finally, about 68 percent of a normal distribution falls within 1 standard deviation of the mean; thus, most—but not all—points

Exhibit 16.12 Samples in a Controlled Process from a Normal Distribution

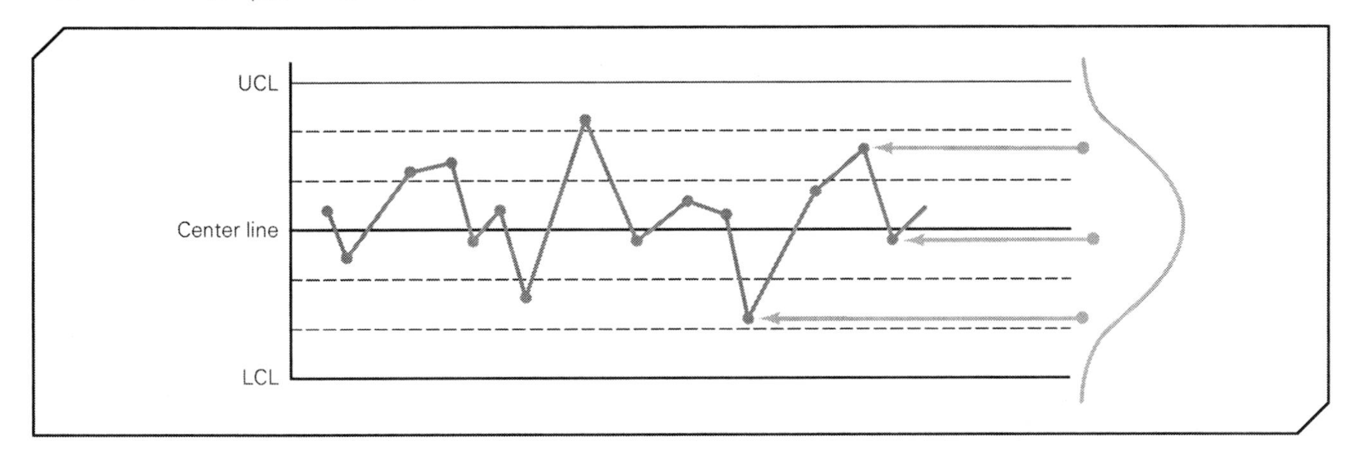

should be close to the center line. These characteristics will hold provided that the mean and variance of the original data have not changed during the time the data were collected; that is, the process is stable.

When a process is out of control, we typically see some unusual characteristics. An obvious indication that a process may be out of control is a point that falls outside the control limits. If such a point is found, you should first check for the possibility that the control limits were miscalculated or that the point was plotted incorrectly. If neither is the case, this can indicate that the process average has changed.

Another indication of an out-of-control situation is a sudden shift in the average. For example, in Exhibit 16.11, we see that the last eight points are all above the center line, suggesting that the process mean has increased. This might suggest that something is causing excessive tread wear in recent samples, perhaps a different batch of raw material or improper mixing of the chemical composition of the tires. Some typical rules that are used to identify a shift include

- 8 points in a row above or below the center line
- 10 of 11 consecutive points above or below the center line
- 12 of 14 consecutive points above or below the center line
- 2 of 3 consecutive points in the outer one-third region between the center line and one of the control limits
- 4 of 5 consecutive points in the outer two-thirds region between the center line and one of the control limits.

Some of these rules are illustrated in Exhibit 16.13. Note that if the average in the range chart shifts *down*, it indicates that the variation has decreased. This is good, and every effort should be made to understand why this occurred and to maintain the improvement.

A third thing to look for in a control chart is an increasing or decreasing trend. As tools wear down, for example, the diameter of a machined part will gradually become larger. Changes in temperature or humidity, general equipment deterioration, dirt buildup on fixtures, or operator fatigue may cause such a trend. About six or seven consecutive points that increase or decrease in value usually signify a gradual change. A wave or cycle pattern is also unusual and should be suspect. It might be a result of seasonal effects of material deliveries, temperature swings, maintenance cycles, or periodic rotation of operators. Whenever an unusual pattern in a control chart is identified, the process should be stopped until the problem has been identified and corrected.

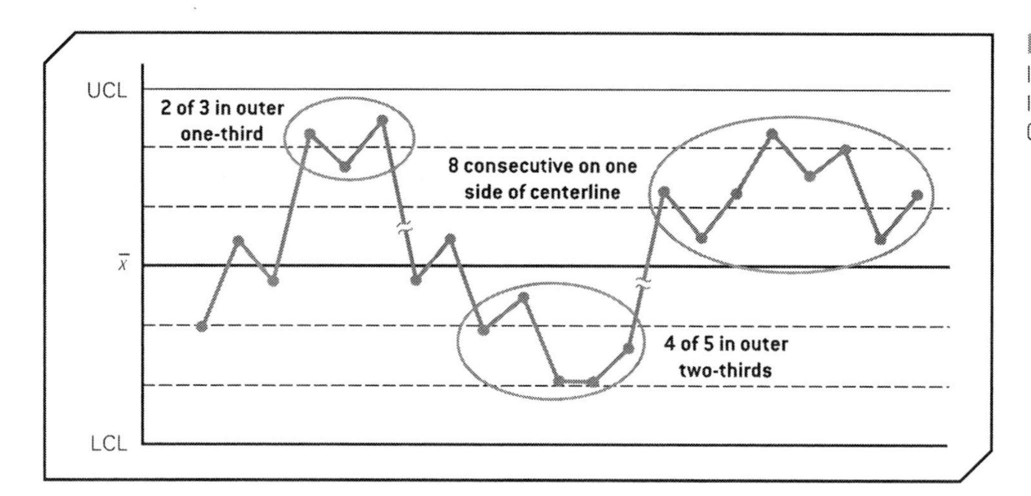

Exhibit 16.13
Illustration of Some Rules for Identifying Out-of-Control Conditions

All of these guidelines, which are used extensively in practice, stem from basic statistical principles and probability calculations. Analysts can also conduct formal statistical hypothesis tests, such as a number-of-runs test, to draw inferences about the state of control. More advanced books on SPC provide details of these approaches.

Constructing *p*-Charts

Recall that many quality characteristics assume only two values, such as good or bad, pass or fail, and so on. The proportion of nonconforming items can be monitored using a control chart called a *p-chart*, where p is the proportion of nonconforming items found in a sample. Often, it is also called a *fraction nonconforming* or *fraction defective* chart.

As with continuous data, a p-chart is constructed by first gathering 25 to 30 samples of the attribute being measured. The size of each sample should be large enough to have several nonconforming items. If the probability of finding a nonconforming item is small, a sample size of 100 or more items is usually necessary. Samples are chosen over time periods so that any special causes that are identified can be investigated.

Let us suppose that k samples, each of size n, are selected. If y represents the number nonconforming in a particular sample, the proportion nonconforming is y/n.

Let p_i be the fraction nonconforming in the ith sample; the average fraction nonconforming for the group of k samples, then, is

$$\bar{p} = \frac{p_1 + p_2 + \cdots + p_k}{k} \tag{16.4}$$

(Note that this formula applies only when all sample sizes are the same!) This statistic reflects the average performance of the process. One would expect a high percentage of samples to have a fraction nonconforming within 3 standard deviations of $\bar{p}$. An estimate of the standard deviation is given by

$$s_{\bar{p}} = \sqrt{\frac{\bar{p}(1 - \bar{p})}{n}} \tag{16.5}$$

Therefore, upper and lower control limits are given by

$$\begin{aligned} \text{UCL}_p &= \bar{p} + 3s_{\bar{p}} \\ \text{LCL}_p &= \bar{p} - 3s_{\bar{p}} \end{aligned} \tag{16.6}$$

If LCL_p is less than zero, a value of zero is used.

Analysis of a *p*-chart is similar to that of an $\bar{x}$- or *R*-chart. Points outside the control limits signify an out-of-control situation. Patterns and trends should also be sought to identify special causes. However, a point on a *p*-chart below the lower control limit or the development of a trend below the center line indicates that the process might have improved, based on an ideal of zero defectives. Caution is advised before such conclusions are drawn, because errors may have been made in computation.

In other words, errors in calculating control limits can lead to conclusions that the process has improved when in fact it has not.

An Example of a *p*-Chart

The operators of automated sorting machines in a post office must read the ZIP code on letters and divert the letters to the proper carrier routes. Over a month's time, 25 samples of 100 letters were chosen, and the number of errors was recorded. Exhibit 16.14 is a spreadsheet summarizing the data and control chart calculations (available on the Student CD-ROM). The proportion of errors in each sample is simply the number of errors divided by 100. Adding the proportions defective and dividing by 25 yields

$$\bar{p} = \frac{.03 + .01 + \cdots + .01}{25} = .022$$

The standard deviation is computed as

$$s_{\bar{p}} = \sqrt{\frac{0.022(1 - 0.022)}{100}} = .01467$$

Thus UCL = .022 + 3(.01467) = .066, and LCL = .022 − 3(.01467) = −.022. Since the LCL is negative and the actual proportion nonconforming cannot be less than zero, the LCL is set equal to zero. Exhibit 16.15 shows the control chart. Although no values above the UCL or below the LCL were observed in this example, the occurrence of such values might indicate operator fatigue or the need for more experience or training.

Variable Sample Size

Often, 100 percent inspection is performed on process output during fixed sampling periods; however, the number of units produced in each sampling period may vary. In this case, the *p*-chart would have a variable sample size, and $\bar{p}$ must be computed differently. One way of handling this variation is to compute a standard deviation for each individual sample. Thus, if the number of observations in the *i*th sample is n_i, control limits are given by

$$\bar{p} \pm 3\sqrt{\frac{\bar{p}(1 - \bar{p})}{n_i}} \qquad \textbf{(16.7)}$$

$$\text{where } \bar{p} = \frac{\sum \text{number nonconforming}}{\sum n_i}$$

The data given in Exhibit 16.16 represent 20 samples with varying sample sizes. The value of $\bar{p}$ is computed as

$$\bar{p} = \frac{18 + 20 + 14 + \cdots + 18}{137 + 158 + 92 + \cdots + 160} = \frac{271}{2{,}980} = .0909$$

Exhibit 16.14 Data and Calculations for p-Chart Example

	A	B	C	D	E	F	G	H	I	J	K	L	M
1	**Fraction Nonconforming (p) Chart**												
2	This spreadsheet is designed for up to 50 samples. Enter data ONLY in yellow-shaded cells.												
3	Click on the sheet tab to display the control chart (some rescaling may be needed).												
4													
5	**Average (p-bar)**		**0.022**										
6	**Avg. sample size**		**100**										
7										**Approximate Control Limits Using**			
8			**Sample**	**Fraction**	**Standard**					**Average Sample Size Calculations**			
9	**Sample**	**Value**	**Size**	**Nonconforming**	**Deviation**	**LCLp**	**CL**	**UCLp**		**LCLp**	**CL**	**UCLp**	
10	1	3	100	0.0300	0.0146683	0	0.022	0.066		0	0.022	0.066005	
11	2	1	100	0.0100	0.0146683	0	0.022	0.066		0	0.022	0.066005	
12	3	0	100	0.0000	0.0146683	0	0.022	0.066		0	0.022	0.066005	
13	4	0	100	0.0000	0.0146683	0	0.022	0.066		0	0.022	0.066005	
14	5	2	100	0.0200	0.0146683	0	0.022	0.066		0	0.022	0.066005	
15	6	5	100	0.0500	0.0146683	0	0.022	0.066		0	0.022	0.066005	
16	7	3	100	0.0300	0.0146683	0	0.022	0.066		0	0.022	0.066005	
17	8	6	100	0.0600	0.0146683	0	0.022	0.066		0	0.022	0.066005	
18	9	1	100	0.0100	0.0146683	0	0.022	0.066		0	0.022	0.066005	
19	10	4	100	0.0400	0.0146683	0	0.022	0.066		0	0.022	0.066005	
20	11	0	100	0.0000	0.0146683	0	0.022	0.066		0	0.022	0.066005	
21	12	2	100	0.0200	0.0146683	0	0.022	0.066		0	0.022	0.066005	
22	13	1	100	0.0100	0.0146683	0	0.022	0.066		0	0.022	0.066005	
23	14	3	100	0.0300	0.0146683	0	0.022	0.066		0	0.022	0.066005	
24	15	4	100	0.0400	0.0146683	0	0.022	0.066		0	0.022	0.066005	
25	16	1	100	0.0100	0.0146683	0	0.022	0.066		0	0.022	0.066005	
26	17	1	100	0.0100	0.0146683	0	0.022	0.066		0	0.022	0.066005	
27	18	2	100	0.0200	0.0146683	0	0.022	0.066		0	0.022	0.066005	
28	19	5	100	0.0500	0.0146683	0	0.022	0.066		0	0.022	0.066005	
29	20	2	100	0.0200	0.0146683	0	0.022	0.066		0	0.022	0.066005	
30	21	3	100	0.0300	0.0146683	0	0.022	0.066		0	0.022	0.066005	
31	22	4	100	0.0400	0.0146683	0	0.022	0.066		0	0.022	0.066005	
32	23	1	100	0.0100	0.0146683	0	0.022	0.066		0	0.022	0.066005	
33	24	0	100	0.0000	0.0146683	0	0.022	0.066		0	0.022	0.066005	
34	25	1	100	0.0100	0.0146683	0	0.022	0.066		0	0.022	0.066005	

The control limits for sample 1 are

$$\text{LCL}_p = .0909 - 3\sqrt{\frac{.0909\ (1 - .0909)}{137}} = .017$$

$$\text{UCL}_p = .0909 + 3\sqrt{\frac{.0909\ (1 - .0909)}{137}} = .165$$

Because the sample sizes vary, the control limits are different for each sample. The p-chart is shown in Exhibit 16.17. Note that points 13 and 15 are outside the control limits.

An alternative approach is to use the average sample size, $\overline{n}$, to compute approximate control limits. Using the average sample size, the control limits are computed as

$$\text{UCL}_p = \overline{p} + 3\sqrt{\frac{\overline{p}(1 - \overline{p})}{\overline{n}}}$$
$$\text{LCL}_p = \overline{p} - 3\sqrt{\frac{\overline{p}(1 - \overline{p})}{\overline{n}}} \qquad \textbf{(16.8)}$$

Exhibit 16.15 *p*-Chart for ZIP Code Reader Example

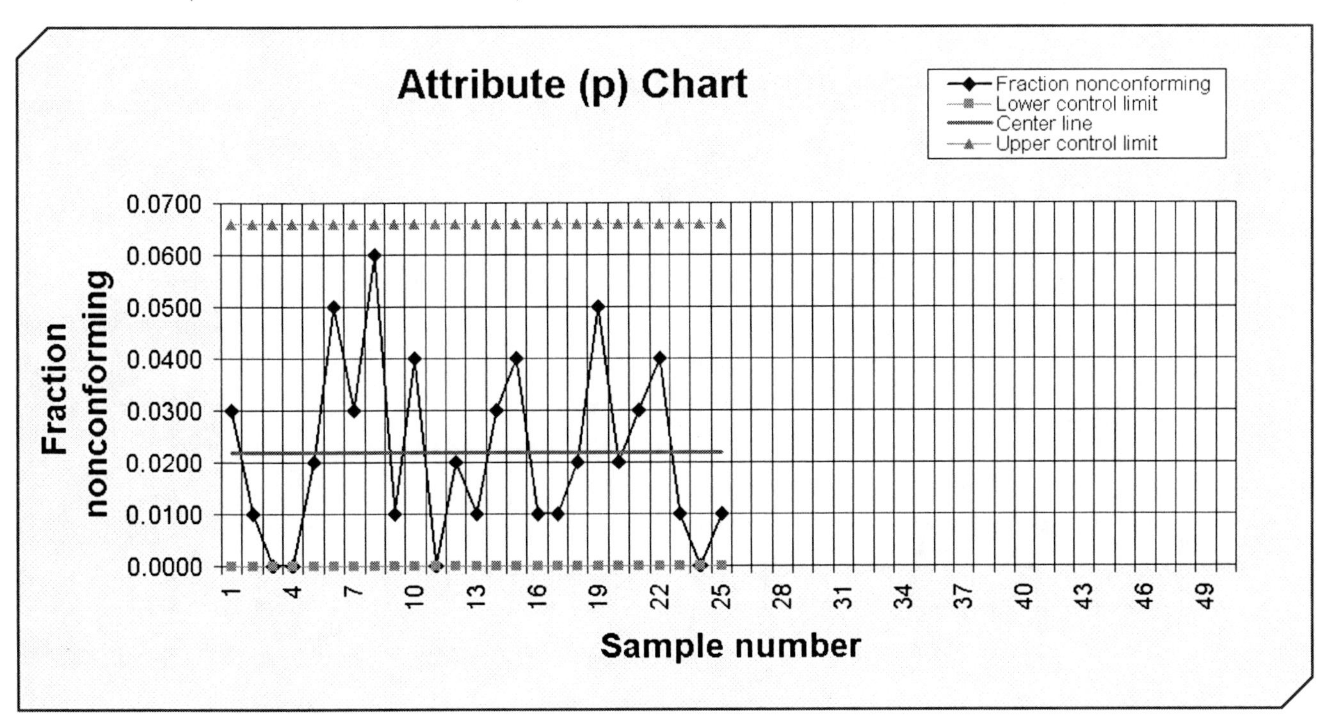

Exhibit 16.16 Data and Calculations for Variable Sample Size Example

	A	B	C	D	E	F	G	H	I	J	K	L	M
1	**Fraction Nonconforming (p) Chart**												
2	This spreadsheet is designed for up to 50 samples. Enter data ONLY in yellow-shaded cells.												
3	Click on the sheet tab to display the control chart (some rescaling may be needed).												
4													
5	**Average (p-bar)**		**0.09103124**										
6	**Avg. sample size**		**148.85**										
7										**Approximate Control Limits Using**			
8			**Sample**	**Fraction**	**Standard**					**Average Sample Size Calculations**			
9	**Sample**	**Value**	**Size**	**Nonconforming**	**Deviation**	**LCLp**	**CL**	**UCLp**		**LCLp**	**CL**	**UCLp**	
10	1	18	137	0.1314	0.0245759	0.0173	0.091	0.1648		0.020299	0.091031	0.161763	
11	2	20	158	0.1266	0.0228845	0.0224	0.091	0.1597		0.020299	0.091031	0.161763	
12	3	14	92	0.1522	0.02999	0.0011	0.091	0.181		0.020299	0.091031	0.161763	
13	4	6	122	0.0492	0.0260429	0.0129	0.091	0.1692		0.020299	0.091031	0.161763	
14	5	11	85	0.1294	0.0312004	0	0.091	0.1846		0.020299	0.091031	0.161763	
15	6	22	187	0.1176	0.0210353	0.0279	0.091	0.1541		0.020299	0.091031	0.161763	
16	7	6	156	0.0385	0.0230307	0.0219	0.091	0.1601		0.020299	0.091031	0.161763	
17	8	9	117	0.0769	0.0265936	0.0113	0.091	0.1708		0.020299	0.091031	0.161763	
18	9	14	110	0.1273	0.0274267	0.0088	0.091	0.1733		0.020299	0.091031	0.161763	
19	10	12	142	0.0845	0.0241393	0.0186	0.091	0.1634		0.020299	0.091031	0.161763	
20	11	8	140	0.0571	0.0243112	0.0181	0.091	0.164		0.020299	0.091031	0.161763	
21	12	13	179	0.0726	0.0215002	0.0265	0.091	0.1555		0.020299	0.091031	0.161763	
22	13	5	195	0.0256	0.0205993	0.0292	0.091	0.1528		0.020299	0.091031	0.161763	
23	14	15	162	0.0926	0.0226002	0.0232	0.091	0.1588		0.020299	0.091031	0.161763	
24	15	25	140	0.1786	0.0243112	0.0181	0.091	0.164		0.020299	0.091031	0.161763	
25	16	12	135	0.0889	0.0247573	0.0168	0.091	0.1653		0.020299	0.091031	0.161763	
26	17	16	186	0.0860	0.0210918	0.0278	0.091	0.1543		0.020299	0.091031	0.161763	
27	18	12	193	0.0622	0.0207058	0.0289	0.091	0.1531		0.020299	0.091031	0.161763	
28	19	15	181	0.0829	0.0213811	0.0269	0.091	0.1552		0.020299	0.091031	0.161763	
29	20	18	160	0.1125	0.022741	0.0228	0.091	0.1593		0.020299	0.091031	0.161763	

Exhibit 16.17 *p*-Chart for Variable Sample Size Example

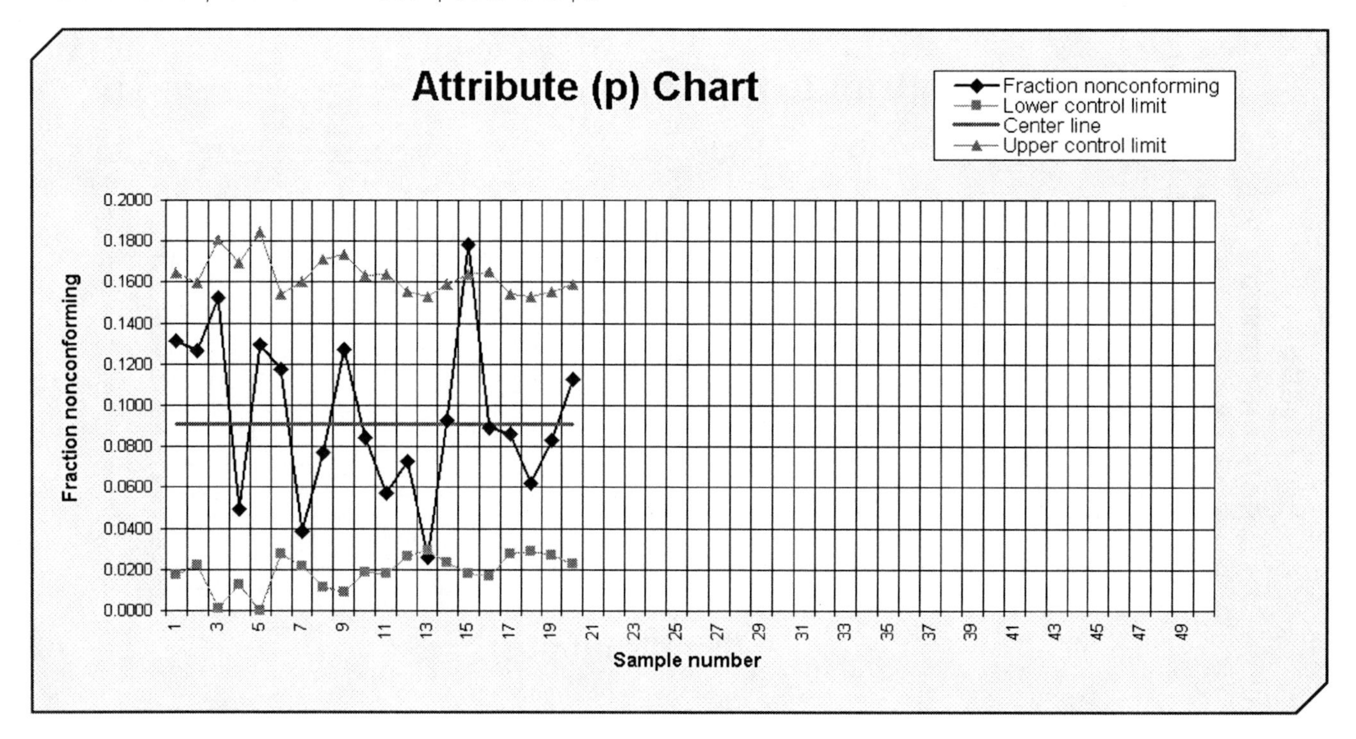

These result in an approximation to the true control limits. For the data in Exhibit 16.16, the average sample size is computed as 148.85, found by dividing the sum of the nonconformances in column B by the sum of the sample sizes used in column C. Using this value, the upper control limit is calculated to be .1618, and the lower control limit is .0203. However, this approach has several disadvantages. Because the control limits are only approximate, points that are actually out of control may not appear to be so on this chart. Second, runs or nonrandom patterns are difficult to interpret because the standard deviation differs between samples as a result of the variable sample sizes. Hence, this approach should be used with caution. Exhibit 16.18 shows the control chart for this example with approximate control limits using the average sample size. Note the difference in sample 13; this chart shows that it is in control, whereas the true control limits show that this point is out of control.

As a general guideline, use the average sample size method when the sample sizes fall within 25 percent of the average. For this example, 25 percent of 149 is 37.21. Thus, the average could be used for sample sizes between 112 and 186. This guideline would exclude samples 3, 6, 9, 11, 13, and 18, whose control limits should be computed exactly. If the calculations are performed on a computer, sample size is not an issue. However, for situations where workers need to do this manually, then using approximate limits is easier.

Constructing *c*- and *u*-Charts

A *p*-chart monitors the proportion of nonconforming items, but a nonconforming item may have more than one nonconformance. For instance, a customer's order may have several errors, such as wrong item, wrong quantity, wrong price, and so on. To monitor the number of nonconformances per unit, we use a *c*-chart or a *u*-chart. These charts are used extensively in service applications because most

Exhibit 16.18 *p*-Chart Using Average Sample Size

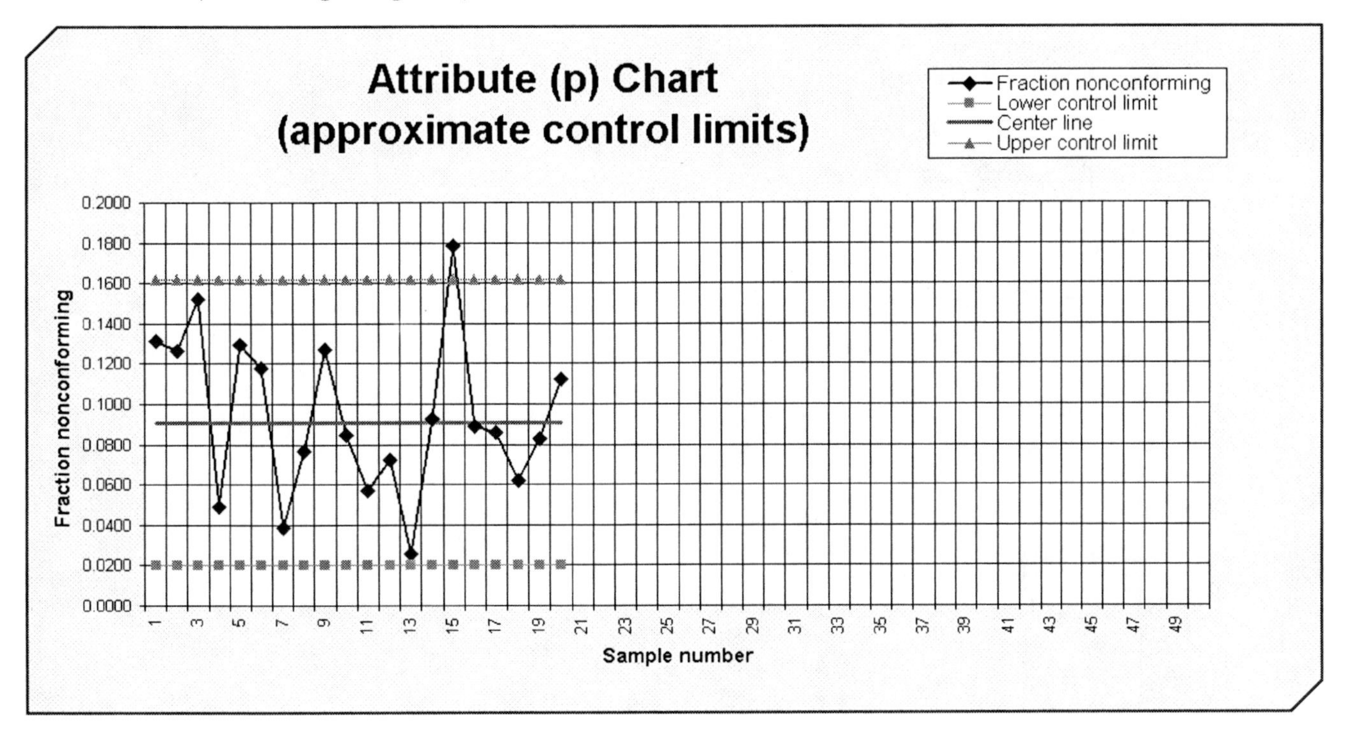

managers of service processes are interested in the number of errors or problems that occur per customer (or patient, student, order), and not just the proportion of customers that experienced problems. The *c*-chart is used to control the *total number* of nonconformances per unit when the size of the sampling unit or number of opportunities for errors is constant. If sampling unit sizes or number of opportunities for errors vary for each unit or customer, a *u*-chart is used to monitor the *average number* of nonconformances per unit.

The *c*-chart is based on the Poisson probability distribution. To construct a *c*-chart, we must first estimate the average number of nonconformances per unit, $\bar{c}$. This is done by taking at least 25 samples of equal size, counting the number of nonconformances per sample, and finding the average. Since the standard deviation of the Poisson distribution is the square root of the mean, we have

$$s_c = \sqrt{\bar{c}} \qquad \textbf{(16.9)}$$

Thus, control limits are given by

$$UCL_c = \bar{c} + 3\sqrt{\bar{c}}$$
$$LCL_c = \bar{c} - 3\sqrt{\bar{c}} \qquad \textbf{(16.10)}$$

An Example of a *c*-Chart

Exhibit 16.19 shows the number of machine failures over a 25-day period. The total number of failures is 45; therefore, the average number of failures per day is

$$\bar{c} = \frac{45}{25} = 1.8$$

Exhibit 16.19
Machine Failure Data for c-Chart

	A	B	C	D	E	F	G	H	I
1	**Average Number of Defects (c) Chart**								
2	This spreadsheet is designed for up to 50 samples. Enter data ONLY in yellow-shaded cells.								
3	Click on the sheet tab to display the control chart (some rescaling may be needed).								
4									
5	**Average (c-bar)**		1.8						
6	**Standard deviation**		1.341640786						
7									
8		**Number**							
9	**Sample**	**of Defects**	**LCLc**	**CL**	**UCLc**				
10	1	2	0	1.8	5.8249224				
11	2	3	0	1.8	5.8249224				
12	3	0	0	1.8	5.8249224				
13	4	1	0	1.8	5.8249224				
14	5	3	0	1.8	5.8249224				
15	6	5	0	1.8	5.8249224				
16	7	3	0	1.8	5.8249224				
17	8	1	0	1.8	5.8249224				
18	9	2	0	1.8	5.8249224				
19	10	2	0	1.8	5.8249224				
20	11	0	0	1.8	5.8249224				
21	12	1	0	1.8	5.8249224				
22	13	0	0	1.8	5.8249224				
23	14	2	0	1.8	5.8249224				
24	15	4	0	1.8	5.8249224				
25	16	1	0	1.8	5.8249224				
26	17	2	0	1.8	5.8249224				
27	18	0	0	1.8	5.8249224				
28	19	3	0	1.8	5.8249224				
29	20	2	0	1.8	5.8249224				
30	21	1	0	1.8	5.8249224				
31	22	4	0	1.8	5.8249224				
32	23	0	0	1.8	5.8249224				
33	24	0	0	1.8	5.8249224				
34	25	3	0	1.8	5.8249224				

Hence, control limits for a c-chart are given by

$$UCL_c = 1.8 + 3\sqrt{1.8} = 5.82$$

$$LCL_c = 1.8 - 3\sqrt{1.8} = -2.22, \text{ or zero}$$

The chart shown is in Exhibit 16.20 and appears to be in control. Such a chart can be used for continued control or for monitoring the effectiveness of a quality improvement program.

As long as the subgroup size is constant, a c-chart is appropriate. In many cases, however, the subgroup size is not constant or the process does not yield discrete, measurable units. For example, in the production of textiles, photographic film, or paper, there is no convenient set of items to measure. In such cases, a standard unit of measurement is used, such as nonconformances per square foot or defects per square inch. The control chart used in these situations is called a u-chart.

The variable u represents the average number of nonconformances per unit of measurement, that is, $u = \frac{c}{n}$, where n is the size of the subgroup (such as square feet). We compute the center line, $\overline{u}$, for k samples each of size n_i as follows:

© Getty Images/PhotoDisc

$$\bar{u} = \frac{c_1 + c_2 + \cdots + c_k}{n_1 + n_2 + \cdots + n_k} \quad (16.11)$$

The standard deviation of the *i*th sample is estimated by

$$s_u = \sqrt{\frac{\bar{u}}{n_i}} \quad (16.12)$$

The control limits, based on 3 standard deviations for the *i*th sample, are then

$$UCL_u = \bar{u} + 3\sqrt{\frac{\bar{u}}{n_i}}$$
$$LCL_u = \bar{u} - 3\sqrt{\frac{\bar{u}}{n_i}} \quad (16.13)$$

Note that if the size of the subgroups varies, so will the control limits.

An Example of a *u*-Chart

A catalog distributor ships a variety of orders each day. The packing slips often contain errors such as wrong purchase order numbers, wrong quantities, or incorrect sizes. Exhibit 16.21 shows the data collected during August. Since the sample size varies each day, a *u*-chart is appropriate. To construct the chart, we first compute the average number of errors per slip, *u*, as shown in column C of Exhibit 16.21, by dividing the total number of errors (209) by the total number of packing slips (2,785):

$$\bar{u} = \frac{209}{2{,}785} = 0.075$$

Exhibit 16.20 *c*-Chart for Machine Failures

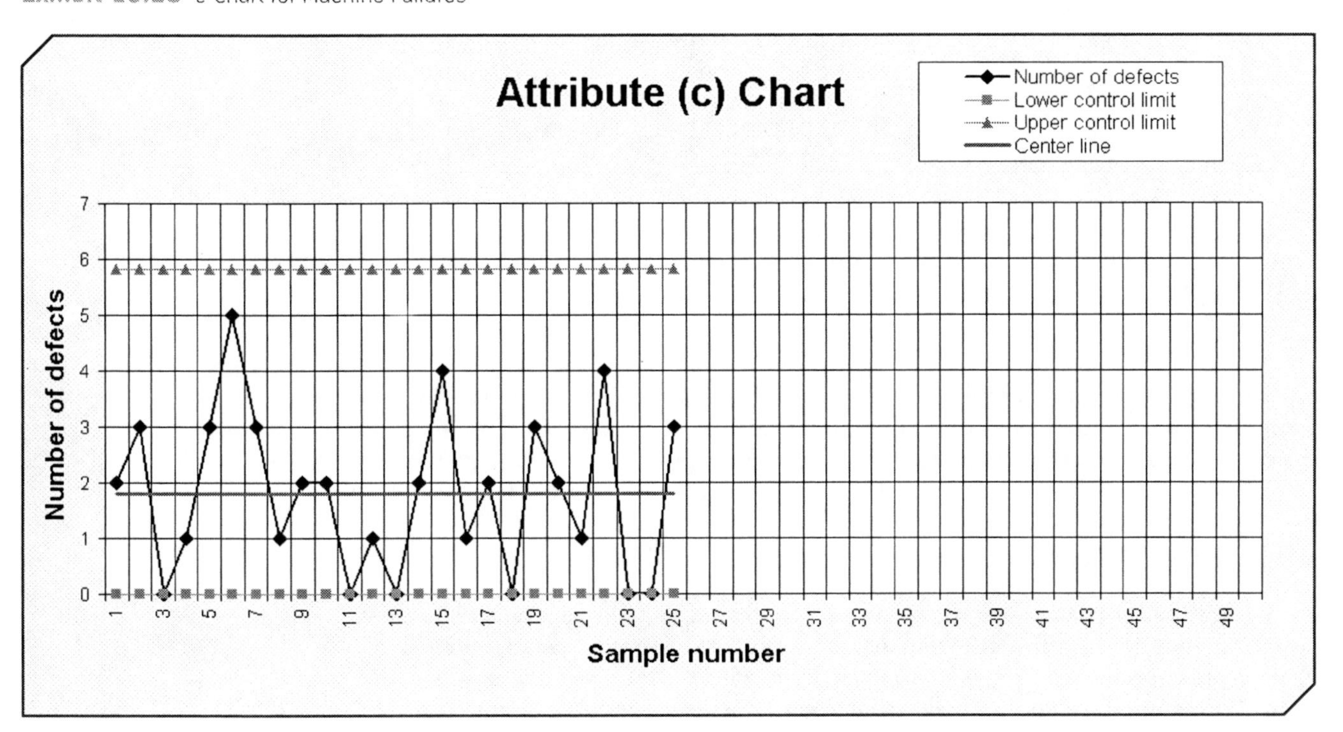

Exhibit 16.21
Data and Calculations for *u*-Chart Example

	A	B	C	D	E	F	G	H
1	**Average Number of Defects Per Unit (u) Chart**							
2	This spreadsheet is designed for up to 75 samples. Enter data ONLY in yellow-shaded cells.							
3	Click on the sheet tab to display the control chart (some rescaling may be needed).							
4								
5	**Average (u-bar)**		**0.075044883**					
6								
7			**Sample**					
8		**Number**	**Unit**	**Defects**	**Standard**			
9	**Sample**	**of Defects**	**Size**	**per unit**	**Deviation**	**LCLu**	**CL**	**UCLu**
10	1	8	92	0.0870	0.028561	0	0.075	0.161
11	2	15	69	0.2174	0.032979	0	0.075	0.174
12	3	6	86	0.0698	0.02954	0	0.075	0.164
13	4	13	85	0.1529	0.029713	0	0.075	0.164
14	5	5	123	0.0407	0.024701	9E-04	0.075	0.149
15	6	5	87	0.0575	0.02937	0	0.075	0.163
16	7	3	74	0.0405	0.031845	0	0.075	0.171
17	8	8	83	0.0964	0.030069	0	0.075	0.165
18	9	4	103	0.0388	0.026992	0	0.075	0.156
19	10	6	60	0.1000	0.035366	0	0.075	0.181
20	11	7	136	0.0515	0.02349	0.005	0.075	0.146
21	12	4	80	0.0500	0.030628	0	0.075	0.167
22	13	2	70	0.0286	0.032742	0	0.075	0.173
23	14	11	73	0.1507	0.032063	0	0.075	0.171
24	15	13	89	0.1461	0.029038	0	0.075	0.162
25	16	6	129	0.0155	0.024119	0.003	0.075	0.147
26	17	6	78	0.1410	0.031018	0	0.075	0.168
27	18	3	88	0.1477	0.029202	0	0.075	0.163
28	19	8	76	0.0789	0.031423	0	0.075	0.169
29	20	9	101	0.0594	0.027258	0	0.075	0.157
30	21	8	92	0.0326	0.028561	0	0.075	0.161
31	22	2	70	0.1143	0.032742	0	0.075	0.173
32	23	9	54	0.1667	0.037279	0	0.075	0.187
33	24	5	83	0.0964	0.030069	0	0.075	0.165
34	25	13	185	0.0108	0.020141	0.015	0.075	0.135
35	26	5	137	0.0657	0.023405	0.005	0.075	0.145
36	27	8	79	0.0633	0.030821	0	0.075	0.168
37	28	6	76	0.1711	0.031423	0	0.075	0.169
38	29	7	147	0.0340	0.022594	0.007	0.075	0.143
39	30	4	80	0.1000	0.030628	0	0.075	0.167

The standard deviation for a particular sample size, n_i, is therefore

$$s_u = \sqrt{\frac{0.075}{n_i}}$$

As with a *p*-chart with variable sample sizes, we substitute the sample size in the formula for the standard deviation to find individual control limits. Exhibit 16.22 is the control chart generated from the spreadsheet. One point (number 2) appears to be out of control. Note that the control limits vary because of different sample sizes.

Choosing between *c*- and *u*-Charts

Since the *c*- and *u*-charts apply to situations in which the quality characteristics inspected do not necessarily come from discrete units, confusion may arise as to which chart is appropriate. The key issue to consider is whether the sampling unit is constant. For example, suppose an electronics manufacturer produces circuit boards.

Exhibit 16.22 Example of u-Chart

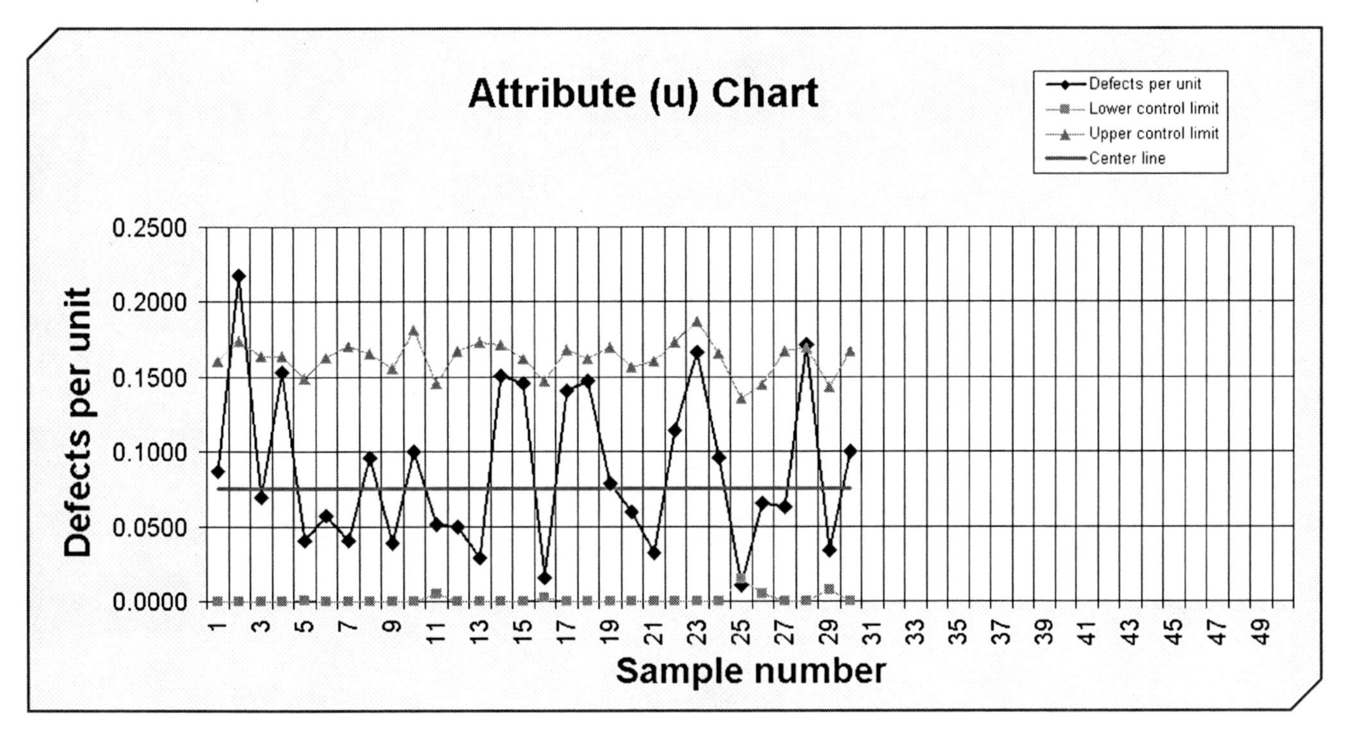

The boards may contain various defects, such as faulty components, missing connections, and so on. The sampling unit is the circuit board. If it is constant (all boards are the same), a c-chart is appropriate. If the process produces boards of varying sizes with different numbers of components and connections, a u-chart would apply.

Summary of Control Charts

Exhibit 16.23 summarizes the formulas needed for the various types of control charts we discussed in this chapter. Exhibit 16.24 provides a simple set of guidelines for choosing the proper chart. Both manufacturing and service organizations have numerous opportunities to apply all these charts throughout their value chains. The OM Spotlight on IBM shows one example of how control charts were used successfully to improve preemployment physical examinations and purchase-order processing systems.

Exhibit 16.23
Summary of Control Chart Formulas

Type of Chart	LCL	CL	UCL
$\bar{x}$ (with $\bar{R}$)	$\bar{\bar{x}} - A_2\bar{R}$	$\bar{\bar{x}}$	$\bar{\bar{x}} + A_2\bar{R}$
R	$D_3\bar{R}$	$\bar{R}$	$D_4\bar{R}$
p	$\bar{p} - 3\sqrt{\frac{\bar{p}(1-\bar{p})}{n}}$	$\bar{p}$	$\bar{p} + 3\sqrt{\frac{\bar{p}(1-\bar{p})}{n}}$
c	$\bar{c} - 3\sqrt{\bar{c}}$	$\bar{c}$	$\bar{c} + 3\sqrt{\bar{c}}$
u	$\bar{u} - 3\sqrt{\frac{\bar{u}}{n}}$	$\bar{u}$	$\bar{u} + 3\sqrt{\frac{\bar{u}}{n}}$

Exhibit 16.24 Choosing the Right Control Chart

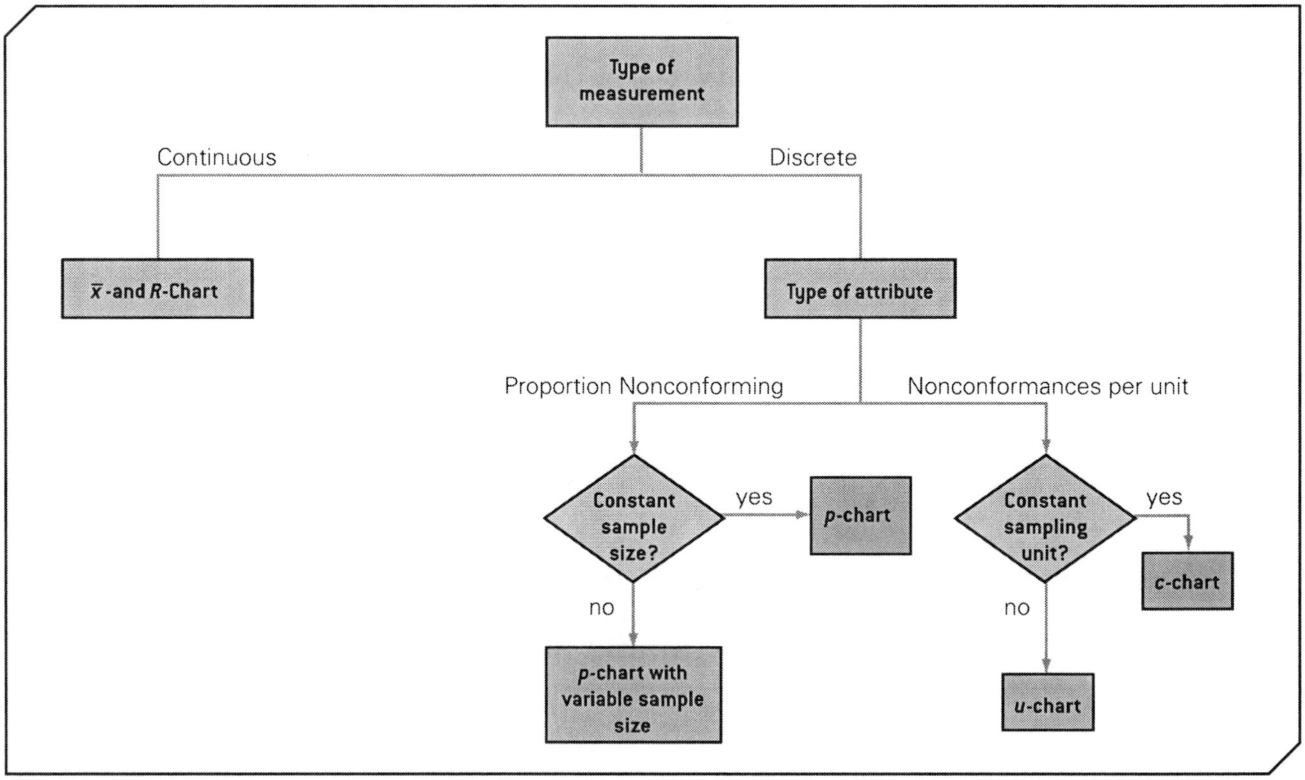

PRACTICAL ISSUES IN SPC IMPLEMENTATION

Although SPC has been around a long time, there are still many organizations that do not use it despite its value. Companies considering using it must address the same fundamental issues in organizational change as they would in implementing an ERP or CRM system. Management must be dedicated to its success. This means that training and other resources such as instrument calibration and maintenance must be committed. Management commitment will be evident at times when control charts dictate that corrective action must delay a shipment, for example. If management ignores what SPC suggests, then workers will quickly see that they are wasting their time and stop using the technique. In addition, users must understand the economics associated with SPC in designing appropriate control charts. This is discussed next.

Control Chart Design

Designing control charts involves three key issues:

1. sample size,
2. sampling frequency, and
3. tightness of control limits.

A small sample size is desirable to keep the cost associated with sampling low. The time a worker spends taking the sample measurements and plotting a control chart represents nonproductive time (in a strict accounting sense only!). On the other hand, large sample sizes provide greater degrees of statistical accuracy in

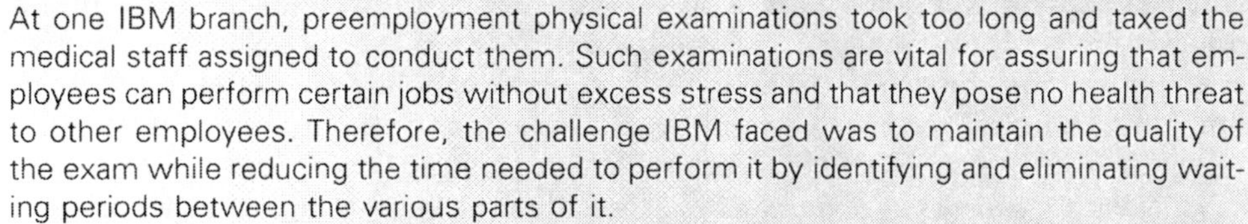

IBM[9]

At one IBM branch, preemployment physical examinations took too long and taxed the medical staff assigned to conduct them. Such examinations are vital for assuring that employees can perform certain jobs without excess stress and that they pose no health threat to other employees. Therefore, the challenge IBM faced was to maintain the quality of the exam while reducing the time needed to perform it by identifying and eliminating waiting periods between the various parts of it.

Preliminary control charts revealed that the average time required for the examination was 74 minutes, but the range varied greatly. New equipment and additional training of the medical staff were suggested as means of shortening the average time. Initial charts indicated that the process was out of control, but continued monitoring and process improvements lowered the average time to 40 minutes, and both the average and range were brought into statistical control with the help of $\bar{x}$- and *R*-charts.

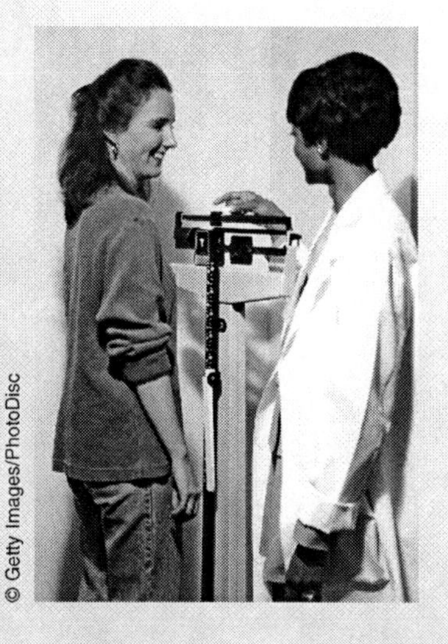
© Getty Images/PhotoDisc

Another problem involved purchase orders. The steps in processing purchase orders are fairly routine. The person requesting an item or service fills out a requisition and forwards it to a buyer who translates it into an order. The buyer selects a vendor, usually after a number of bids. But at this IBM branch, time and money were being lost by human error in the purchase-order processing system, and both requesters and buyers were contributing to the problem. Of great concern were nonconforming documents originated by the purchasing department itself. The department started to count them. Data on weekly purchase orders and orders in error were monitored, and a *p*-chart was constructed that showed an average error rate of 5.9 percent. After the buyers reviewed the data, they found that the process had actually changed during the data collection period, resulting in a shift in the mean to 3.7 percent. The use of the chart also showed out-of-control conditions resulting from vacations. Substitute buyers created a high percentage of rework because of the workload and their unfamiliarity with particular aspects of the process. Preventive measures were created for peak vacation periods to provide sufficient coverage and ensure that backup personnel understood the process better.

estimating the true state of control. Large samples also allow smaller changes in process characteristics to be detected with higher probability. In practice, samples of about 5 have been found to work well in detecting process shifts of 2 standard deviations or larger. To detect smaller shifts in the process mean, larger sample sizes of 15 to 25 must be used.

For attributes data, too small a sample size can make a *p*-chart meaningless. Even though many guidelines such as "use at least 100 observations" have been suggested, the proper sample size should be determined statistically, particularly when the true portion of nonconformances is small. If p is small, n should be large enough to have a high probability of detecting at least one nonconformance. For example, statistical calculations can show that if $p = .01$, then the sample size must be at least 300 to have at least a 95 percent chance of finding at least one nonconformance. This has significant implications for processes approaching Six Sigma quality levels, which we discuss in the next section.

Managers must also consider the sampling frequency. Taking large samples on a frequent basis is desirable but clearly not economical. No hard-and-fast rules exist for the frequency of sampling. Samples should be close enough to provide an opportunity to detect changes in process characteristics as soon as possible and reduce the chances of producing a large amount of nonconforming output. However, they should not be so close that the cost of sampling outweighs the benefits that can be realized. This decision depends on the individual application and volume of output.

These decisions depend on the risk of drawing the wrong conclusions similar to those in statistical hypothesis testing. For example, we could say that a Type I error occurs when an incorrect conclusion is reached that a special cause is present when in fact one does not exist. This error results in the cost of trying to find a nonexistent problem. Similarly, a Type II error occurs when special causes are present but are not signaled in the control chart because points fall within the control limits by chance. Type I errors result in an unnecessary search for a special cause of variation and may be costly in terms of lost production time and testing effort. Type II errors can be more damaging, especially if an out-of-control process is not recognized and defectives are not caught.

Standard control limits, such as those in Exhibit 16.23, are based on 3 standard deviation ranges about the mean value. These essentially provide low risk of making Type I errors. However, the wider the control limits, the greater the risk of a Type II error. Thus, in some situations, for example, when the costs associated with a Type II error is large, it may be advantageous to tighten these limits so that any nonconformances can be more easily detected even though more false alarms might occur.

Exhibit 16.25 shows how costs associated with these errors and sampling and testing should influence sample size and sample frequency decisions.

Controlling Six Sigma Processes

SPC is a useful methodology for processes that operate at a low sigma level, for example 3-sigma or less. However, when the rate of defects is extremely low, standard control charts are not effective. For example, in using a p-chart for a process with a high sigma level, few defectives will be discovered even with large sample sizes. For instance, if $p = .001$, a sample size of 500 will only have an expected number of $500(.001) = 0.5$ defects. Hence, most samples will have only zero or one defect, and the chart will provide little useful information for control. Using much larger sample sizes would only delay the timeliness of information and increase the chances that the process may have changed during the sampling interval. Small sample sizes will typically result in a conclusion that any observed defect indicates an out-of-control condition, thus implying that a controlled process will have zero defects, which may be impractical. In addition, conventional SPC charts will have higher frequencies of false alarms and make it difficult to evaluate process improvements. These issues are important for Six Sigma practitioners to understand, in order not to blindly apply tools that may not be appropriate.

PROCESS CAPABILITY

Learning Objective
To understand the concept of process capability and be able to analyze process capability data, compute process capability indexes, and interpret the results.

Process capability *refers to the natural variation in a process that results from common causes.* Knowing process capability allows one to predict, quantitatively, how well a process will meet specifications and to specify equipment requirements and

Exhibit 16.25
Economic-Based Decisions in Designing SPC Procedures

Source of Cost	Sample Size	Sampling Frequency	Control Limits
Type I error	large	high	wide
Type II error	large	high	narrow
Sampling and testing	small	low	—

Process capability ***refers to the natural variation in a process that results from common causes.***

A ***process capability study*** *is a carefully planned study designed to yield specific information about the performance of a process under specified operating conditions.*

the level of control necessary. *A* **process capability study** *is a carefully planned study designed to yield specific information about the performance of a process under specified operating conditions.* Typical questions that are asked in a process capability study are

- Where is the process centered?
- How much variability exists in the process?
- Is the performance relative to specifications acceptable?
- What proportion of output will be expected to meet specifications?

One of the properties of a normal distribution is that 99.73 percent of the observations will fall within 3 standard deviations from the mean. Thus, a process that is in control can be expected to produce a very large percentage of output between $\mu - 3\sigma$ and $\mu + 3\sigma$, where μ is the process average. Therefore, the natural variation of the process can be estimated by $\mu \pm 3\sigma$ and characterizes the capability of the process. One way of computing the standard deviation in this formula is to take a sample of data, compute the sample standard deviation, s, and use it as an estimate of σ. A second approach, often used in conjunction with an $\bar{x}$- and R-chart, is to estimate σ by dividing the average range by a constant, d_2, which can be found in Appendix B. That is,

$$\sigma = \frac{\bar{R}}{d_2} \tag{16.14}$$

Capability Versus Control

Process capability has no meaning if the process is not in statistical control because special causes will bias the mean or the standard deviation. Control and capability are two different concepts. As shown in Exhibit 16.26, a process may be capable or not capable, or in control or out of control, independently of each other. Clearly, we would like every process to be both capable and in control. If a process is neither capable nor in control, we must first get it in a state of control by removing special causes of variation and then attack the common causes to improve its capability. If a process is capable but not in control, we should work to get it back in control. Therefore, we should use control charts to first eliminate any special causes before computing the process capability.

Exhibit 16.26
Capability Versus Control (arrows indicate the direction of appropriate management action)

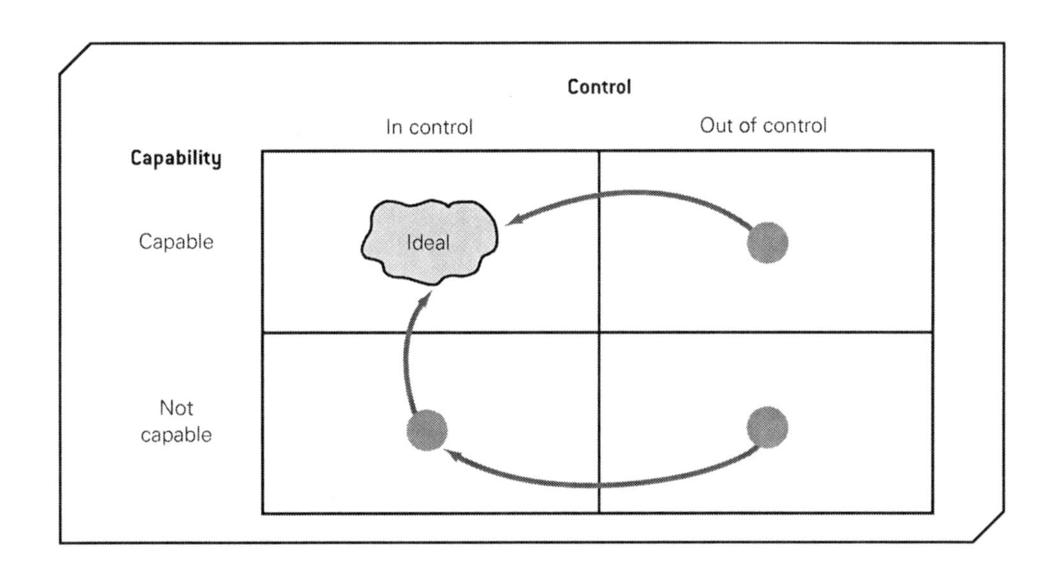

The process capability is usually compared to the design specifications to indicate the ability of the process to meet the specifications. Exhibit 16.27 illustrates four possible situations that can arise when the observed variability of a process is compared to design specifications. In part a, the range of process variation is larger than the design specification; thus it will be impossible for the process to meet specifications a large percentage of the time. Managers can either scrap or rework nonconforming parts (100 percent inspection is necessary), invest in a better process with less variation, or change the design specifications. In part b, the process is able to produce according to specification, although it will require close monitoring to ensure that it remains in that position. In part c, the observed variation is tighter than the specifications; this is the ideal situation from a quality control viewpoint, since little inspection or control is necessary. Finally, in part d, the observed variation is the same as the design specification, but the process is off-center; thus some nonconforming product can be expected.

Process Capability Index

The relationship between the natural variation and specifications is often quantified by a measure known as the **process capability index.** The process capability index, C_p, is defined as the ratio of the specification width to the natural tolerance of the process. C_p relates the natural variation of the process with the design specifications in a single, quantitative measure. In numerical terms, the formula is

$$C_p = \frac{\text{UTL} - \text{LTL}}{6\sigma} \tag{16.15}$$

where

UTL = upper tolerance limit
LTL = lower tolerance limit
σ = standard deviation of the process (or an estimate based on the sample standard deviation, s)

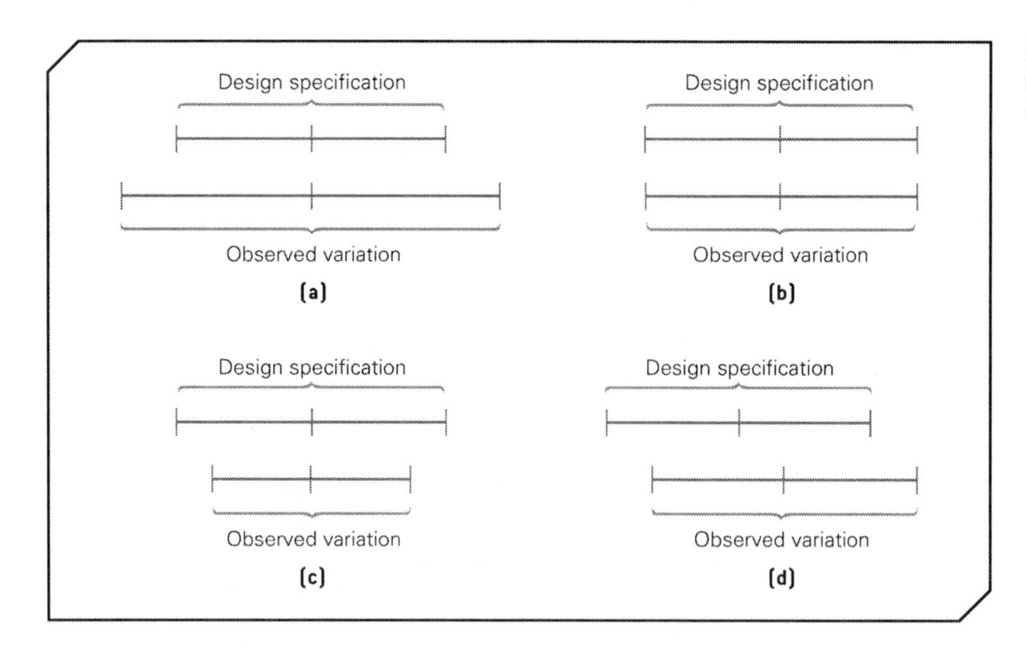

Exhibit 16.27
Process Capability Versus Design Specifications

Note that when $C_p = 1$, the natural variation is the same as the design tolerance (as in Exhibit 16.27(b)). Values less than 1 mean that a significant percentage of output will not conform to the specifications. Values of C_p exceeding 1 indicate good capability; in fact, many firms require C_p values of 1.66 or greater from their suppliers, which equates to a tolerance range of about 10 standard deviations. Because 6 standard deviations generally cover the normal variation of output, a 10-standard deviation range provides adequate comfort so that even if the process shifts a moderate amount and is undetected, nearly all of the output will still be conforming.

The value of C_p does not depend on the mean of the process; thus, a process may be off-center such as in Exhibit 16.27(d) and still show an acceptable value of C_p. To account for the process centering, one-sided capability indexes are often used:

$$C_{pu} = \frac{\text{UTL} - \mu}{3\sigma} \text{ (upper one-sided index)} \quad \textbf{(16.16)}$$

$$C_{pl} = \frac{\mu - \text{LTL}}{3\sigma} \text{ (lower one-sided index)} \quad \textbf{(16.17)}$$

$$C_{pk} = \min(C_{pl}, C_{pu}) \quad \textbf{(16.18)}$$

For example, a high value of C_{pu} indicates that the process is very capable of meeting the upper specification. C_{pk} is the "worst case" and provides an indication of whether both the lower and upper specifications can be met regardless of where the process is centered. This is the value that most managers pay attention to.

The Excel template for the $\bar{x}$- and R-chart calculates process capability information. Suppose that the specifications for tread wear for the Goodman Tire example used earlier require a maximum tread wear loss of 50 hundredths of an inch (the upper specification), with a lower specification of zero, and a target tread wear of 25. As we noted earlier, we must remove special cause variation before calculating process capability indexes. In the Goodman Tire example, we saw that the last eight samples appeared to have an unusual pattern in the control chart. These should be eliminated (in the Excel template, simply highlight the data for these samples and press the Delete key, and be sure to change the number of samples in cell E6). The result is shown in Exhibit 16.28.

The "Six Sigma" spread of 39.31 in cell R6 represents the range of plus or minus 3 standard deviations on either side of the mean (the denominator in the formula for C_p). Because the specification range is 50 (the numerator in the formula for C_p), we find that C_p is greater than 1.0 and represents good capability. Because the average tread wear is 29.16, the process is not centered on the target, and therefore the upper capability index is just barely greater than 1 while the lower capa-

Exhibit 16.28 Process Capability Calculations for Goodman Tire

	A	B	C	D	E	F	G	H	I	J	K	L	M	N	O	P	Q	R
5																		
6	Number of samples (<= 50)				22					Process Capability Calculations						Six sigma		39.31
7	Sample size (2 - 10)				3					Upper specification				50		Cp		1.272
8										Lower specification				0		Cpu		1.06
9	Grand Average		29.1666667		A2	D3	D4	d2								Cpl		1.484
10	Average Range		11.0909091		1.023	0	2.574	1.693								Cpk		1.06

bility index is much higher. In general, process capability is determined to be 29.16 ± 19.655, or 9.505 to 48.818. This means that as long as the process remains in control, the tread wear for individual tires can be expected to vary between about 19 and 49 hundredths of an inch when evaluated under the same simulated road conditions.

Process capability is important both to product designers and to process owners. If product specifications are too tight, the product will be difficult to manufacture. Employees who run the processes will be under pressure and will have to spend a lot of time adjusting the process and inspecting output. Control charts and process capability information are often integrated in unique ways within companies, as the OM Spotlight on Corning illustrates.

OM SPOTLIGHT

Corning Incorporated[10]

Corning Incorporated has adapted statistical quality control in a unique fashion at several of its electronic plants in the United States and in Europe. In its approach, called process control management (PCM), the burden of continuous checking is placed on the operators, and processes that continually produce excellent-quality products are seldom checked by personnel. Data obtained from several operations are fed into the system and tabulated to produce a picture of current operations. These data are available to production, quality control, and engineering for analysis and evaluation. Quality control may then increase its monitoring of processes that are questionable, while reducing involvement with those running with consistent excellence. Annual savings have been estimated at more than $200,000 in direct labor and $300,000 in yield improvement.

Analysis is based on past experience, historical data, process-capability studies, and other statistical methods. Each machine in a process is categorized as one of four quality levels identified by color codes. Level I denotes a problem-free, excellent machine or process and is identified by the color blue. Most of the machines of a process should enter this category. The manufacturing costs are low, and requirements for the next operation or for final release to the customer are satisfied. Under level 1, it is necessary only to verify that changes have not occurred. Full trust is given to production personnel at this level, and it is assumed that the process will continue in full control and produce excellent-quality parts under constant operator verification. Quality control personnel make only occasional random checks on these processes.

In level 2, the machine or process is classified as workable and is identified by the color green. This level requires that the process inspector be directed to the same machine more often than required by level 1. The machine chosen and the frequency of visits by quality control (QC) personnel is higher. Production personnel still exercise full control, but QC monitors the processes more closely to detect any deterioration and trend toward a level-3 classification.

Level 3 denotes borderline operations, and the identifying color is yellow. The inspectors are directed to step up the monitoring of these machines. Very tight control is required, and every effort is expended to bring the offending machines back into the relative safety of level 2.

In level 4, machines designated out of control (color red) are immediately shut down and repaired. Parts produced for evaluation after the machine is repaired are segregated into lots for special consideration by QC. Maximum support is provided by QC whenever machines reach this level.

Conventional control charts and process-capability studies are used to designate the levels. They enable operators to immediately detect changes in the process and alert QC personnel. QC support is directed from the process-control monitor console, which may be operated manually or be computer-supported or fully computerized. This support provides continuously adjusted levels of machines and processes and directs QC personnel to the next machine to be checked.

Corning has found that the system maintains and improves quality by motivating production department personnel and by charging them with the responsibility for making acceptable products without sacrificing yield. It also has improved interdepartmental communications by developing a feeling of teamwork. Each plant has its own adaptation of PCM to fit its specific needs.

SOLVED PROBLEMS

1. A production process, sampled 30 times with a sample size of 8, yielded an overall mean of 28.5 and an average range of 1.6.
   a. Construct R- and $\bar{x}$-charts for this process.
   b. At a later stage, 6 samples produced these sample means: 28.001, 28.25, 29.13, 28.72, 28.9, 28.3. Is the process in control?
   c. Does the following sequence of sample means indicate that the process is out of control: 28.3, 28.7, 28.1, 28.9, 28.01, 29.01? Why or why not?

Solution:

From Appendix B with $n = 8$, we have $A_2 = 0.37$, $D_3 = 0.14$, and $D_4 = 1.86$.

a. For the $\bar{x}$-chart:

$$\text{UCL} = 28.5 + 0.37(1.6) = 29.092$$
$$\text{LCL} = 28.5 - 0.37(1.6) = 27.908$$

For the R-chart:

$$\text{UCL} = 1.86(1.6) = 2.976$$
$$\text{LCL} = 0.14(1.6) = 0.224$$

b. The sample mean of 29.13 is above the UCL, signifying an out-of-control condition.
c. All points are within the control limits, and there do not appear to be any shifts or trends evident in the new data.

2. Over several weeks, 20 samples of 50 packages of synthetic-gut tennis strings were tested for breaking strength; 38 packages failed to conform to the manufacturer's specifications. Compute control limits for a p-chart.

Solution

$\bar{p} = 38/1{,}000 = 0.038$ and the standard deviation is $\sqrt{(0.038)(0.962)/50} = .027$

Control limits:

$$\text{UCL} = 0.038 + 3(0.027) = 0.119$$
$$\text{LCL} = 0.038 - 3(0.027) = -0.043,$$
so set LCL = 0

3. A controlled process shows an overall mean of 2.50 and an average range of 0.42. Samples of size 4 were used to construct the control charts. What is the process capability? If specifications are 2.60 ± 0.25, how well can this process meet them?

Solution:

From Appendix B, $d_2 = 2.059$ and $s = \bar{R}/d_2 = 0.42/2.059 = 0.20$. Thus, the process capability is $2.50 \pm 3(0.020)$, or 1.90 to 3.10. Because the specification range is 2.35 to 2.85 with a target of 2.60, we may conclude that the observed natural variation exceeds the specifications by a large amount. In addition, the process is off-center (see Exhibit 16.29).

Exhibit 16.29
Comparison of Observed Variation and Design Specifications for Solved Problem 3.

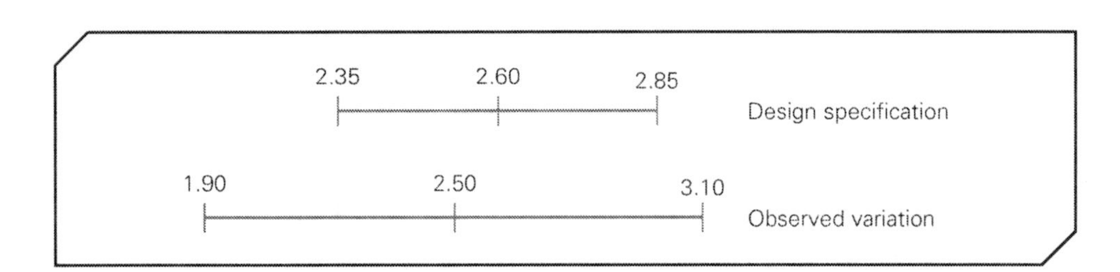

KEY TERMS AND CONCEPTS

Acceptance sampling
c- and u-charts
C_p, C_{pu}, C_{pl}, C_{pk} indexes
Common cause variation
Consumer's risk
Continuous metric
Control chart
Control chart patterns
Control limits
Discrete metric
In control
1:10:100 rule

Out of control
p-charts
Process capability
Process capability index
Process capability study
Producer's risk
Quality control
Quality at the source
Special cause variation
Stable system
Statistical process control (SPC)
$\bar{x}$- and R-charts

QUESTIONS FOR REVIEW AND DISCUSSION

1. What is quality control? Why is it necessary in any organization?
2. Explain the three components of any control system, and provide an example different from the one in the text.
3. What is the 1:10:100 rule? Why is it important for managers to understand?
4. What is "quality at the source"?
5. Describe the basic quality control practices used in manufacturing. In what service contexts can they be applied?
6. How does quality control in services involving customer contact differ from typical manufacturing practices?
7. How can customer satisfaction measurement provide useful information for control in services?
8. What is statistical process control?
9. What is the difference between common and special causes of variation?
10. What do we mean when we say that a process is "in control" or "out of control"?
11. Provide some examples in business or daily life in which a controlled process is erroneously adjusted and an out-of-control process is ignored.
12. Explain the difference between a discrete and a continuous metric. Provide some examples different from those in the text.
13. Explain the characteristics of service quality metrics for high-contact services. How do they differ from "back-office" services?
14. What is a control chart and what benefits can control charts provide?
15. Summarize the process used to apply SPC.
16. Describe the various types of control charts and their applications.
17. Discuss how to interpret control charts. What types of patterns indicate a lack of control?
18. What is the purpose of a process-capability study?
19. List some applications of control charts in service organizations.
20. Describe how to choose the correct control chart for a business application.
21. Develop a "personal-quality checklist" on which you tally nonconformances in your personal life (such as being late for work or school, not completing homework on time, not getting enough exercise, and so on). What type of chart would you use to monitor your performance?
22. What is the difference between capability and control?
23. What is a process capability index? Explain how process capability indexes are computed and how to interpret the results.

PROBLEMS AND ACTIVITIES

1. Thirty samples of size 3 resulted in an overall mean of 16.51 and average range of 1.30. Compute control limits for $\bar{x}$- and R-charts.
2. Twenty-five samples of size 5 resulted in an overall mean of 5.42 and an average range of 20. Compute control limits for $\bar{x}$- and R-charts, and estimate the standard deviation of the process.

3. Use the sample data in Exhibit 16.30 to construct $\bar{x}$- and R-charts. Assume that the sample size is 5.
4. Develop x- and R-charts for the data in Exhibit 16.31.
5. Thirty samples of size 3, listed in Exhibit 16.32, were taken from a machining process over a 15-hour period.
   a. Compute the mean and standard deviation of the data, and plot a histogram.
   b. Compute the mean and range of each sample, and plot them on control charts. Does the process appear to be in statistical control? Why or why not?
6. In testing the resistance of a component used in a microcomputer, the data in Exhibit 16.33 were obtained.

   Construct $\bar{x}$- and R-charts for these data. Determine if the process is in control. If it is not, eliminate any assignable causes, and compute revised limits.
7. Twenty-five samples of 100 items each were inspected, and 68 were found to be defective. Compute control limits for a p-chart.
8. At a pizza restaurant, a 20-week study of 30 pizzas per week found a total of 18 pizzas made improperly. Construct a p-chart to monitor this process.
9. The proportions nonconforming for an automotive piston are given in Exhibit 16.34 for 20 samples. Two hundred units are inspected each day. Construct a p-chart and interpret the results.
10. One hundred insurance claim forms are inspected daily for 25 working days, and the number of forms with errors are recorded as in Exhibit 16.35. Construct a p-chart. If any points are outside the control limits, assume that assignable (special) causes have been determined. Then construct a revised chart.
11. Find control limits for a c-chart with $\bar{c} = 9$.
12. Consider the following data showing the number of errors per thousand lines of code for a software development project. Construct a c-chart and interpret the results.

Sample	1	2	3	4	5	6	7	8	9	10
Number of Errors	4	15	13	20	17	22	26	17	20	22

Exhibit 16.30 Data for Problem 3

Sample	$\bar{x}$	R	Sample	$\bar{x}$	R
1	95.72	1.0	11	95.80	.6
2	95.24	.9	12	95.22	.2
3	95.18	.8	13	95.56	1.3
4	95.44	.4	14	95.22	.5
5	95.46	.5	15	95.04	.8
6	95.32	1.1	16	95.72	1.1
7	95.40	.9	17	94.82	.6
8	95.44	.3	18	95.46	.5
9	95.08	.2	19	95.60	.4
10	95.50	.6	20	95.74	.6

Exhibit 16.31 Data for Problem 4

	Observations				
Sample	1	2	3	4	5
1	3.05	3.08	3.07	3.11	3.11
2	3.13	3.07	3.05	3.10	3.10
3	3.06	3.04	3.12	3.11	3.10
4	3.09	3.08	3.09	3.09	3.07
5	3.10	3.06	3.06	3.07	3.08
6	3.08	3.10	3.13	3.03	3.06
7	3.06	3.06	3.08	3.10	3.08
8	3.11	3.08	3.07	3.07	3.07
9	3.09	3.09	3.08	3.07	3.09
10	3.06	3.11	3.07	3.09	3.07

Exhibit 16.32 Data for Problem 5

Sample	Observations		
1	3.55	3.64	4.37
2	3.61	3.42	4.07
3	3.61	3.36	4.34
4	4.13	3.50	3.61
5	4.06	3.28	3.07
6	4.48	4.32	3.71
7	3.25	3.58	3.51
8	4.25	3.38	3.00
9	4.35	3.64	3.20
10	3.62	3.61	3.43
11	3.09	3.28	3.12
12	3.38	3.15	3.09
13	2.85	3.44	4.06
14	3.59	3.61	3.34
15	3.60	2.83	2.84
16	2.69	3.57	3.28
17	3.07	3.18	3.11
18	2.86	3.69	3.05
19	3.68	3.59	3.93
20	2.90	3.41	3.37
21	3.57	3.63	2.72
22	2.82	3.55	3.56
23	3.82	2.91	3.80
24	3.14	3.83	3.80
25	3.97	3.34	3.65
26	3.77	3.60	3.81
27	4.12	3.38	3.37
28	3.92	3.60	3.54
29	3.50	4.08	4.09
30	4.23	3.62	3.00

Exhibit 16.33 Data for Problem 6

Sample	Observations		
1	414	388	402
2	408	382	406
3	396	402	392
4	390	398	362
5	398	442	436
6	400	400	414
7	444	390	410
8	430	372	362
9	376	398	382
10	342	400	402
11	400	402	384
12	408	414	388
13	382	430	400
14	402	409	400
15	399	424	413
16	460	375	445
17	404	420	437
18	375	380	410
19	391	392	414
20	394	399	380
21	396	416	400
22	370	411	403
23	418	450	451
24	398	398	415
25	428	406	390

Exhibit 16.34 Data for Problem 9

Sample	Proportion Nonconforming	Sample	Proportion Nonconforming
1	.04	11	.07
2	.05	12	.09
3	.03	13	.05
4	.02	14	.04
5	.02	15	.03
6	.04	16	.04
7	.04	17	.03
8	.06	18	.05
9	.04	19	.02
10	.08	20	.04

13. Find control limits for a u-chart with 9 total errors and $n = 4$; also with $n = 5$ and $n = 6$.

14. A trucking company is studying its billing process. Over a 15-day period, it obtained the results in Exhibit 16.36.

    Construct a u-chart for errors per bill. Is the process in control? Is the process satisfactory?

15. Discuss the interpretation of each of the control charts presented in Exhibit 16.37.

16. For Problem 4, estimate the natural variation in the process by first computing the sample standard deviation and then computing $\overline{R}/d_2$. Why is there a difference?

Exhibit 16.35 Data for Problem 10

Day	Number Nonconforming	Day	Number Nonconforming
1	2	14	2
2	1	15	1
3	2	16	3
4	3	17	4
5	0	18	0
6	2	19	0
7	0	20	1
8	2	21	0
9	7	22	2
10	1	23	8
11	3	24	2
12	0	25	1
13	0		

Exhibit 16.36 Data for Problem 14

Day	No. of Bills	No. of Errors
1	54	6
2	76	8
3	67	8
4	89	20
5	76	13
6	84	11
7	61	11
8	73	10
9	90	14
10	98	10
11	82	13
12	64	13
13	72	10
14	88	11
15	86	12

17. Suppose that a specification calls for LTL = 2.0, and UTL = 6.0. A sample of 100 parts found $\mu = 4.5$ and $\sigma = 0.5$. Compute C_p, C_{pl}, C_{pu}, and C_{pk}. Should the manager consider any action based on these results?

18. Determine the process capability for the data in Problem 6. Suppose the specifications for the resistance are 400 ± 40. Compute the capibility indexes. What would you conclude?

19. General Hydraulics, Inc., manufactures hydraulic machine tools. It has had a history of leakage trouble resulting from a certain critical fitting. Twenty-five samples of machined parts were selected, one per

Exhibit 16.37
Control Charts for Problem 15

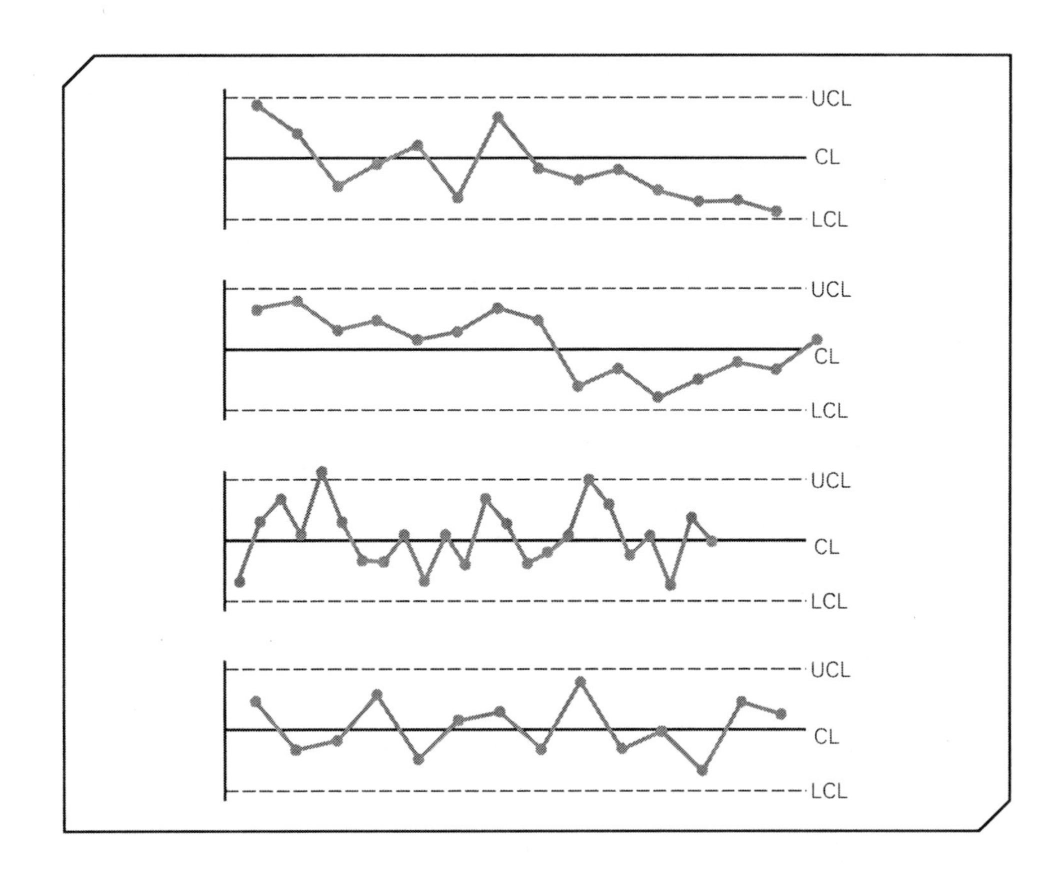

Exhibit 16.38 Data for Problem 19, Part a

Sample	Diameter Measurement (cm) Observation 1	2	3	4
1	10.94	10.64	10.88	10.70
2	10.66	10.66	10.68	10.68
3	10.68	10.68	10.62	10.68
4	10.03	10.42	10.48	11.06
5	10.70	10.46	10.76	10.80
6	10.38	10.74	10.62	10.54
7	10.46	10.90	10.52	10.74
8	10.66	10.04	10.58	11.04
9	10.50	10.44	10.74	10.66
10	10.58	10.64	10.60	10.26
11	10.80	10.36	10.60	10.22
12	10.42	10.36	10.72	10.68
13	10.52	10.70	10.62	10.58
14	11.04	10.58	10.42	10.36
15	10.52	10.40	10.60	10.40
16	10.38	10.02	10.60	10.60
17	10.56	10.68	10.78	10.34
18	10.58	10.50	10.48	10.60
19	10.42	10.74	10.64	10.50
20	10.48	10.44	10.32	10.70
21	10.56	10.78	10.46	10.42
22	10.82	10.64	11.00	10.01
23	10.28	10.46	10.82	10.84
24	10.64	10.56	10.92	10.54
25	10.84	10.68	10.44	10.68

shift, and the diameter of the fitting was measured. The results are given in Exhibit 16.38.

a. Construct control charts for the data in the table.
b. It was discovered that the regular machine operator was absent when samples 4, 8, 14, and 22 were taken. How will this affect the results in part a?
c. Exhibit 16.39 presents measurements taken during the next ten shifts. What information does this provide to the quality control manager?

Exhibit 16.39 Data for Problem 19, Part c

Sample	Additional Observation 1	2	3	4
1	10.40	10.76	10.54	10.64
2	10.60	10.28	10.74	10.86
3	10.56	10.58	10.64	10.70
4	10.70	10.60	10.74	10.52
5	11.02	10.36	10.90	11.02
6	10.68	10.38	10.22	10.32
7	10.64	10.56	10.82	10.80
8	10.28	10.62	10.40	10.70
9	10.50	10.88	10.58	10.54
10	10.36	10.44	10.40	10.66

CASES

BANKUSA: SECURITIES CONTROL

"Beverly, it takes Securities Control (SC) 15 to 30 days to identify errors originating from other groups, and then a few days more for these groups to fix the errors. During this time period, BankUSA is exposed to considerable market risk that can and *has* cost the bank a lot of money," said Craig Anderson, director of security operations, during the meeting. "Craig, our process designs and systems are not responsive enough to avoid this type of market risk," responded Beverly Thompson, the manager of SC. "Yes, that is correct," said Lori Andrew, supervisor of securities processing. "Well," said Anderson, "what are you two doing to help fix this problem? A $1 million mistake and we are all fired!"

"Craig, we are collecting data to help the process managers identify the source of errors by type. If we can send these process managers these 'error type' data along with the outage reports, they should be able to make improvements in process design and eliminate these errors (outages) and the risk associated with them," said Andrew. Also, Thompson stated, "Craig, we are trying to get the U.S. Federal Reserve to provide us with daily reconciliation reports that would allow us to identify the errors in a much more timely fashion than our current weekly reports. But to do this we also have to overcome some system changes in our internal accounting systems. Also, the national securities settlement systems are not integrated and are the source of many errors."

As Thompson and Andrew left the meeting, they discussed another problem facing Beverly and other process managers at Fiduciary Operations. "Lori, we also need to address the problem of outages that are sometimes not quickly resolved because several processes must work together to fix the cause of the outage," Thompson said. "Yes," Andrew said as someone handed her a piece of paper as they walked down the hallway, "Relogs can add 2 to 10 days to the 15- to 35-day outage research time, and therefore, expose us to more market risk and possible economic consequences. We must address this issue too!" (A "relog" occurs when an SC associate identifies the error as belonging to one department, and when that department receives the documentation and researches it, it concludes the error belongs to another department. A relog form is then filled out and SC inputs this information into the SC tracking system, and the outage is reassigned to the appropriate department.)

After Thompson returned to her office, she thought that if she did a perfect job and helped the other departments and processes "mistake-proof" their processes, her SC department would be eliminated. SC was a third-party internal control function that audits other internal processes to help ensure that no errors hurt customer service or BankUSA's economic performance.

Although not a pleasant thought, Thompson's long-term goal was to eliminate her department. The costs of failure could range from an annoyed customer whose account statement was not accurate to several hundred thousand dollars due to the bank having to buy shares at higher market prices then if the trade was done on-time and accurately. Of course, SC was one operations process in a complex value chain of other non-BankUSA institutions, such as the U.S. Federal Reserve, that could cause an error. Types of errors included:

1. incorrect number of shares or trade price per share for an account,
2. incorrect account numbers and/or credit or debit in the wrong account,
3. a transaction recorded in other non-BankUSA systems that does not show up in BankUSA's systems,
4. a failed trade where Security Settlement, a process within BankUSA, booked the trade to BankUSA's system but the trade was not executed,
5. receiving or sending shares to the wrong institution.

Once these are identified, SC generates reports that go back to the process or department primarily responsible for correcting these outages. These reports go to the following six internal BankUSA processes: (1) Account Processing, (2) Security Settlement, (3) Trade Support, (4) Asset Collection, (5) Conversions, and (6) Corporate Reorganization. Any one of these internal processes, a combination of several processes, or an outside non-BankUSA institution could be the root cause of the outage.

Discussion Questions

1. Develop a statistical process control chart for the data in Exhibit 16.40. What insights, if any, are gained? How might this information be used in a continuous improvement initiative?
2. What type of information should SC be collecting? What types of reports should SC be generating to help these six processes reduce or eliminate errors and identify non-BankUSA root causes?
3. Given that SC is currently a "detection-based quality management system," develop a step-by-step action plan to move toward a "prevention-based quality management system."
4. What are your final recommendations?

Exhibit 16.40 Weekly Errors Reported by Securities Control

Month	Week No.	Total Errors	Total No. Security Assets Processed	Month	Week No.	Total Errors	Total No. Security Assets Processed
January	1	68	6,597	June	24	442	5,796
January	2	618	6,613	June	25	523	5,778
January	3	340	6,640	June	26	476	5,757
January	4	326	6,607	June	27	818	5,721
January	5	220	6,592	June	28	245	5,702
February	6	261	6,627	July	29	82	5,639
February	7	414	6,605	July	30	977	6,344
February	8	535	6,638	July	31	647	6,329
February	9	257	6,671	July	32	937	6,315
March	10	214	6,669	July	33	401	6,295
March	11	265	6,684	August	34	604	6,280
March	12	367	6,677	August	35	1054	6,322
March	13	622	6,600	August	36	977	6,342
March	14	220	6,605	August	37	324	6,300
April	15	105	6,675	August	38	68	6,354
April	16	554	6,555	September	39	261	6,325
April	17	707	6,633	September	40	602	6,305
April	18	401	6,671	September	41	923	6,293
May	19	228	6,668	September	42	672	6,281
May	20	664	6,683	September	43	109	6,248
May	21	282	6,713				
May	22	137	6,745				
May	23	249	5,807				

DEAN DOOR CORPORATION

The Dean Door Company (DDC) manufactures steel and aluminum exterior doors for commercial and residential applications. DDC landed a major contract as a supplier to Walker Homes, a builder of residential communities in several major cities throughout the southwestern United States. Because of the large volume of demand, DDC expanded its manufacturing operations to three shifts and hired additional workers.

Not long after DDC began shipping windows to Walker Homes, it received some complaints about excessive gaps between the door and frame. This was somewhat alarming to DDC, because its reputation as a high-quality manufacturer was the principal reason that it was selected as a supplier to Walker Homes. DDC placed a great deal of confidence in its manufacturing capability because of its well-trained and dedicated employees, and it never felt the need to consider formal process control approaches. In view of the recent complaints, however, Jim Dean, the company president, suspected that the expansion to a three-shift operation, the pressures to produce higher volumes, and the push to meet just-in-time delivery requests were causing a breakdown in quality.

On the recommendation of the plant manager, Dean hired a quality consultant to train the shift supervisors and selected line workers in statistical process control methods. As a trial project, the plant manager wants to evaluate the capability of a critical cutting operation that he suspects might be the source of the gap problem. The target specification for this cutting operation is 30.000 inches with a tolerance of 0.125 inch. Thus, the upper and lower specifications are LSL = 29.875 inches and USL = 30.125 inches. The consultant suggested inspecting five consecutive door panels in the middle of each shift over a 10-day period and recording the dimension of the cut. Exhibit 16.41 shows 10 days' data collected for each shift, by operator.

Discussion Questions

1. Interpret the data in Exhibit 16.41, establish a state of statistical control, and evaluate the capability of the process to meet specifications. Consider the following questions: What do the initial control charts tell you? Do any out-of-control conditions exist? If the process is not in control, what might be the likely causes, based on the information that is available?

Exhibit 16.41
DDC Production Data

			Observation				
Shift	**Operator**	**Sample**	**1**	**2**	**3**	**4**	**5**
1	Terry	1	30.046	29.978	30.026	29.986	29.961
2	Jordan	2	29.972	29.966	29.964	29.942	30.025
3	Dana	3	30.046	30.004	30.028	29.986	30.027
1	Terry	4	29.997	29.997	29.980	30.000	30.034
2	Jordan	5	30.018	29.922	29.992	30.008	30.053
3	Dana	6	29.973	29.990	29.985	29.991	30.004
1	Terry	7	29.989	29.952	29.941	30.012	29.984
2	Jordan	8	29.969	30.000	29.968	29.976	29.973
3	Cameron	9	29.852	29.978	29.964	29.896	29.876
1	Terry	10	30.042	29.976	30.021	29.996	30.042
2	Jordan	11	30.028	29.999	30.022	29.942	29.998
3	Dana	12	29.955	29.984	29.977	30.008	30.033
1	Terry	13	30.040	29.965	30.001	29.975	29.970
2	Jordan	14	30.007	30.024	29.987	29.951	29.994
3	Dana	15	29.979	30.007	30.000	30.042	30.000
1	Terry	16	30.073	29.998	30.027	29.986	30.011
2	Jordan	17	29.995	29.966	29.996	30.039	29.976
3	Dana	18	29.994	29.982	29.998	30.040	30.017
1	Terry	19	29.977	30.013	30.042	30.001	29.962
2	Jordan	20	30.021	30.048	30.037	29.985	30.005
3	Cameron	21	29.879	29.882	29.990	29.971	29.953
1	Terry	22	30.043	30.021	29.963	29.993	30.006
2	Jordan	23	30.065	30.012	30.021	30.024	30.037
3	Cameron	24	29.899	29.875	29.980	29.878	29.877
1	Terry	25	30.029	30.011	30.017	30.000	30.000
2	Jordan	26	30.046	30.006	30.039	29.991	29.970
3	Dana	27	29.993	29.991	29.984	30.022	30.010
1	Terry	28	30.057	30.032	29.979	30.027	30.033
2	Jordan	29	30.004	30.049	29.980	30.000	29.986
3	Dana	30	29.995	30.000	29.922	29.984	29.968

What is the process capability? What do the process capability indexes tell the company? Is DDC facing a serious problem that it needs to address? How might the company eliminate the problems found by Walker Homes?

2. The plant manager implemented the recommendations that resulted from the initial study. Because of the success in using control charts, DDC made a decision to continue using them on the cutting operation. After establishing control, additional samples were taken over the next 20 shifts, shown in the second part of the table, in Exhibit 16.42. Evaluate whether the process remains in control, and suggest any actions that should be taken. Consider the following issues: Does any evidence suggest that the process has changed relative to the established control limits? If any out-of-control patterns are suspected, what might be the cause? What should the company investigate?

Exhibit 16.42
Additional Production Data

Shift	Operator	Sample	Observation				
			1	2	3	4	5
1	Terry	31	29.970	30.017	29.898	29.937	29.992
2	Jordan	32	29.947	30.013	29.993	29.997	30.079
3	Dana	33	30.050	30.031	29.999	29.963	30.045
1	Terry	34	30.064	30.061	30.016	30.041	30.006
2	Jordan	35	29.948	30.009	29.962	29.990	29.979
3	Dana	36	30.016	29.989	29.939	29.981	30.017
1	Terry	37	29.946	30.057	29.992	29.973	29.955
2	Jordan	38	29.981	30.023	29.992	29.992	29.941
3	Dana	39	30.043	29.985	30.014	29.986	30.000
1	Terry	40	30.013	30.046	30.096	29.975	30.019
2	Jordan	41	30.043	30.003	30.062	30.025	30.023
3	Dana	42	29.994	30.056	30.033	30.011	29.948
1	Terry	43	29.995	30.014	30.018	29.966	30.000
2	Jordan	44	30.018	29.982	30.028	30.029	30.044
3	Dana	45	30.018	29.994	29.995	30.029	30.034
1	Terry	46	30.025	29.951	30.038	30.009	30.003
2	Jordan	47	30.048	30.046	29.995	30.053	30.043
3	Dana	48	30.030	30.054	29.997	29.993	30.010
1	Terry	49	29.991	30.001	30.041	30.036	29.992
2	Jordan	50	30.022	30.021	30.022	30.008	30.019

ENDNOTES

[1] Brown, Eryn, "Heartbreak Hotel?" *Fortune*, November 26, 2001, pp. 161–165.
[2] "Hospital to Revise Lab Procedures After Faulty Tests Kill 2," *The Columbus Dispatch*, Columbus, Ohio, August 16, 2001, p. A2.
[3] "Testing for Conformity: An Inside Job," *Golf Journal*, May 1998, pp. 20–25.
[4] "DaimlerChrysler's Quality Practices Pay Off for PT Cruiser," *News and Analysis*, Metrologyworld.com, 3/23/2000.
[5] Adapted from the Ritz-Carlton Hotel Company 1992 and 1999 Application Summaries for the Malcolm Baldrige National Quality Award.
[6] "Waiting Game," *The Columbus Dispatch*, Columbus, Ohio, January 13, 2002, pp. E1–E2.
[7] Parasuraman, A., Zeithaml, V. A., and Berry, L. L., "A Conceptual Model of Service Quality and Its Implications for Future Research," *Journal of Marketing* 49, Fall 1985, pp. 41–50.
[8] Wilson, Clifford B., "SQC + Mg: A Positive Reaction," *Quality Progress*, April 1988, pp. 475–479.
[9] McCabe, W. J., "Improving Quality and Cutting Costs in a Service Organization," *Quality Progress*, June 1985, pp. 85–89.
[10] Adapted from Basile A. Denissoff, "Process Control Management," *Quality Progress* 13, 6, June 1980, pp. 14–16.

Chapter Outline

CHAPTER 17

Lean Operating Systems

Learning Objectives

1. To learn the basic principles of lean operating systems—elimination of waste, increased speed and response, improved quality, and reduced cost—and the benefits they provide to organizations.

2. To understand the basic tools and approaches that organizations use to create a lean organization and to recognize how to apply these tools appropriately.

3. To understand how manufacturing firms apply lean tools and concepts.

4. To understand how lean tools and concepts are applied to service organizations.

5. To understand the concepts and philosophy of just-in-time operating systems and the challenges that managers face in managing JIT systems.

- "Where's our pizza?" Rachel asked. "I don't know," said her dad, "but I think I have an idea. . . ." Peering back across the next table into the kitchen, Steve saw mass confusion. The kitchen is crammed with workers running in all directions. Some workers are rushing about madly while others stand by idly, unsure of what to do. Other workers are cleaning up discarded pieces of dough and excess toppings from the floor. Several assistant managers are directing every step of the pizza-making process. Next to each workstation are piles of unfinished pizzas waiting for the addition of sauce, toppings, or cheese. Between the oven and the packaging table are piles of pizzas that have been set aside because they were made incorrectly. In one corner of the kitchen are stacked boxes of dough, meats, and cheeses from suppliers, none of which has been checked or properly stored. "Be patient, Rachel," Steve sighed, "we'll get it eventually. . . ."

© Getty Images/PhotoDisc

- Porsche, the maker of high-end German sports cars, found sales falling to 25 percent of their 1986 peak by 1992.[1] When Wendelin Wiedeking took over as head of the company, he pushed his workers to adopt Japanese-style lean production methods. He hired two Japanese efficiency experts and personally chopped the top half off a row of shelves with a circular saw to reduce inventories. Along with more flexible, negotiated work rules, Porsche revamped its assembly process so that production of 1997 911 models would take only 60 hours, compared to 120 hours for its predecessor. The time to develop a new model was cut from 7 years to 3.

JOCHEN ECKEL/BLOOMBERG NEWS/Landov

Porsche uses 300 parts suppliers, down from nearly 1,000, and a quality-control program has helped reduce the number of defective parts by a factor of 10.

- A medical laboratory had been improving the time it took from the receipt of a test sample to completion and had achieved a 30 percent reduction, primarily by using new technology. However, doctors were still asking for faster responses. The lab quality coordinator did some research and found some examples of manufacturing plants that had reduced cycle time by as much as 90 percent with little capital investment. The coordinator discovered that these improvements were not achieved simply by making each step work faster but also by identifying and reducing waste that existed between the process steps, such as movement, waiting, and inventory. By learning how these manufacturers accomplish these improvements, he was able to apply similar ideas to his laboratory service and reduce the processing time by another 20 percent.[2]

Discussion Questions: Explain the operational implications that Steve's observations of the pizza kitchen would have in creating value for customers. Can you cite any personal experiences in your work or around your school where you have observed similar inefficiencies? Why would less inventory, as suggested in the Porsche example, lead to greater efficiencies in production? Don't you think the opposite would occur?

The first scenario may be a bit difficult to imagine for a pizza business. However, it describes the classic mass-production environment typical of U.S. automobile plants a couple of decades ago: workers doing different tasks with no clear sense of teamwork and cooperation; messy factories, piles of excess inventory and raw materials awaiting inspection, and defective parts waiting disposition. The impacts on the customer were often long delivery lead times and cars having significant defects or wrong options.

Now picture a much different situation in the pizza kitchen, which is analogous to how a typical Japanese automobile plant operated several decades ago: Indirect workers, who add no value to the product, are nowhere to be seen; all workers are adding value to the pizzas. The space between production operations is small, allowing little room to store excess inventory and fostering close communication among workers. Pizzas flow smoothly from one preparation step to the next. When an incorrect order is discovered, all work stops and the team works together to uncover the reason and prevent it from occurring again. Every pizza coming out of the oven is correct and immediately boxed for delivery to the customer. There are no large supplies of dough and other ingredients; the restaurant's suppliers deliver them fresh daily. Such an organization, focused on its core capabilities and devoid of any waste, is called *lean*.

Lean enterprise *refers to approaches that focus on the elimination of waste in all forms, and smooth, efficient flow of materials and information throughout the value chain to obtain faster customer response, higher quality, and lower costs.* Manufacturing and service operations that apply the principles of lean enterprise are often called **lean operating systems**. Lean concepts were initially developed and implemented by the Toyota Motor Corporation, and lean operating systems are often

Lean enterprise *refers to approaches that focus on the elimination of waste in all forms, and smooth, efficient flow of materials and information throughout the value chain to obtain faster customer response, higher quality, and lower costs.*

benchmarked with "the Toyota production system." As one article about Toyota observed, to see the Toyota production system in action is to "behold a thing of beauty":

A Toyota assembly plant fairly hums: Every movement has a purpose, and there is no slack. Tour a typical auto plant, and you see stacks of half-finished parts, assembly lines halted for adjustment, workers standing idle. At Toyota the workers look like dancers in a choreographed production: retrieving parts, installing them, checking the quality, and doing it all in immaculate surroundings.[3]

Lean enterprise has been adopted by many companies around the world, such as Porsche, highlighted in the second episode, and has led to substantial improvements and results. More importantly, lean thinking is not just for manufacturing; the principles are simple and can easily be adapted to service organizations such as banks, hospitals, and restaurants, as the third episode illustrates. For example, banks require quick response and efficiency to operate on low margins, making many of their backroom processes, such as check sorting and mortgage processing, natural candidates for lean enterprise solutions.[4] The handling of paper checks and credit card slips, for instance, involves a physical process like an assembly line. The faster a bank moves checks and mortgages (that is, information) through its system, the sooner it can collect its funds and the better its returns on invested capital.

Why is being a lean organization important? One answer stems from the concept of value, which customers clearly expect from an organization's goods and services. As we noted earlier in this book, value is enhanced by improving the customer benefit package while simultaneously reducing the costs associated with providing it. Eliminating waste, becoming more efficient, and providing faster customer response all increase value. Secondly, cost pressures in every industry are driving companies to become more efficient, and therefore, lean operating systems are necessary for survival. Many airlines, for instance, continue to struggle to survive in the aftermath of 9/11, yet Southwest Airlines has continued to be successful because of applying lean thinking to its operations. Recent start-ups such as JetBlue, which managed to be ranked #1 in customer service and quality in 2003 while maintaining a low cost structure, are driving the major U.S. airlines to become leaner.

Lean thinking is more than a set of tools and approaches; it is a mindset that must be understood and adopted by managers and workers at all levels of the organization. Every step in the value chain affects the creation of value in some way; thus, lean principles and thinking must be applied broadly to the entire value chain. The power of information technology is helping entire industries to rethink, redefine, and restructure their value chains. Dell Computer, for example, is a recognized leader in applying lean thinking and radically changing the value chain for purchasing personal computers. Today, RFID tags are facilitating more lean thinking in organizations; we have discussed applications of RFID in Chapters 5 and 7. Six Sigma quality improvement tools are also being integrated with lean principles to simultaneously attack issues affecting quality, speed, and cost.

In this chapter we discuss the principles of lean operating systems and how they are applied in both manufacturing and service.

PRINCIPLES OF LEAN OPERATING SYSTEMS

Learning Objective
To understand the basic objectives of lean operating systems—elimination of waste, increased speed and response, improved quality, and reduced cost—and the benefits they provide to organizations.

Lean operating systems have four basic principles:

1. elimination of waste
2. increased speed and response
3. improved quality
4. reduced cost

As simple as these may seem, organizations required disciplined thinking and application of good operations management tools and approaches to achieve them.

Eliminate Waste

Lean, by the very nature of the term, implies doing only what is necessary to get the job done. Any activity, material or operation that does not add value in an organization is considered waste. Exhibit 17.1 shows a variety of specific examples. The Toyota Motor Company classified waste into seven major categories:

1. *Overproduction:* for example, making a batch of 100 when there are orders only for 50 in order to avoid an expensive setup, or making a batch of 52 instead of 50 in case there were rejects. Overproduction ties up production facilities, and the resulting excess inventory simply sits idle.
2. *Waiting time:* for instance, allowing queues to build up between operations, resulting in longer lead times and higher work-in-progress.
3. *Transportation:* the time and effort spent in moving products around the factory as a result of poor layout.
4. *Processing:* the traditional notion of waste, as exemplified by scrap that often results from poor product or process design.
5. *Inventory:* waste associated with the expense of idle stock and extra storage and handling requirements needed to maintain it.
6. *Motion:* as a result of inefficient workplace design and location of tools and materials.
7. *Production defects:* the result of not performing work correctly the first time.

Eliminating waste requires an attitude of continuous improvement and sensitivity to finding potential sources of waste and taking appropriate action. This requires the involvement and cooperation of everyone in the value chain. It also requires training and constant reinforcement by managers and supervisors. Improvement initiatives must also be implemented without disrupting current process efficiency and customer service.

Increase Speed and Response

Lean operating systems focus on quick and efficient response in designing and getting goods and services to market, producing to customer demand and delivery requirements, responding to competitor's actions, collecting payments, and addressing customer inquiries or problems. Better process design, exploiting information technology, and improved management practices, such as short cash-to-cash conversion cycles as described in Chapter 9, and Just-in-Time as described later in this chapter are some ways to meet this goal.

Exhibit 17.1 Common Examples of Waste in Organizations

Excess capacity	Overproduction	Waiting time
Inaccurate information	Produce too early	Accidents
Excess inventory	Long distance traveled	Too much space
Long changeover and setup times	Retraining and relearning time and expense	Unnecessary movement of materials, people and information
Spoilage	Scrap	Equipment breakdowns
Clutter	Rework and repair	Knowledge bottlenecks
Planned product obsolescence	Long unproductive meetings	Non-valued-added process steps
Excessive material handling	Poor communication	Misrouting jobs

Perhaps the most effective way of increasing speed and response is to *synchronize the entire value chain*. By this we mean that not only are all elements of the value chain focused on a common goal but that the transfer of all physical materials and information are coordinated to achieve a high level of efficiency. This coordination might be driven by the master production schedule in an automobile assembly plant, for example, or daily sales information from all the stores in a large retail chain. Information technology has vastly improved the ability to synchronize value chains, as we have discussed in several chapters throughout this book. In addition, partnerships with suppliers and customers ensure high quality and responsive delivery.

Improve Quality

Lean operating systems cannot function if raw materials are bad, processing operations are not consistent, or machines break down. Poor quality disrupts work schedules and reduces yields, requiring extra inventory, processing time, and space for scrap and parts waiting for rework. All these are forms of waste and increase costs to the customer.

Eliminating the sources of defects and errors in all processes in the value chain greatly improves speed and agility and supports the notion of continuous flow. Using mistake-proofing approaches discussed in Chapter 15 in designing processes, improving training, or even eliminating certain work activities can help to achieve this objective. In addition, reducing process variability improves customer service, quality, and speed, while reducing costs and required capacity. This is one of the primary goals of Six Sigma quality initiatives described in Chapter 15. Many firms are now adopting the idea of "*Lean Six Sigma*," and combining lean and Six Sigma tools, concepts, and approaches.

Reduce Cost

Certainly, reducing cost is an important objective of lean enterprise. Anything that is done to reduce waste and improve quality often reduces cost at the same time. More efficient equipment, better preventive maintenance, and smaller inventories reduce costs in manufacturing firms. Simplifying processes, such as using customer labor via self-service in a fast-food restaurant, depositing a check using an automatic teller machine, and completing medical forms online before medical service are ways for service businesses to become leaner and reduce costs. Outsourcing processes for which an organization does not have sufficient expertise is another way.

Benefits of Lean Operating Systems

Proponents of lean operating systems cite many benefits, including reductions in cycle (processing) times, improvements in space utilization, increases in process throughput, smooth workloads, reductions in work-in-process and finished goods inventories, improvements in communication and information sharing in the value chain, improvements in quality and customer service, and reductions in cash flow and working capital required to run the business (see the OM Spotlight on TI Automotive).

Becoming lean requires a focus on details, discipline, persistence, and hard work to achieve results. Surveys have noted that mid-sized and large companies are likely to be familiar with lean principles and have systems in place; however, small firms have much less familiarity with the principles. Thus, considerable opportunity exists for adopting lean practices in small businesses.

OM SPOTLIGHT

TI Automotive[5]

TI Automotive (www.tiautomotive.com) is a global supplier of fully integrated vehicle fuel storage, braking, power train, and air-conditioning systems. Company sales were $2.3 billion with 130 facilities in 29 countries, 20,000 employees, and 31 manufacturing plants located in North America. In 2004, it was awarded new supply contracts worth more than $100 million from three auto manufacturers—PSA Peugeot Citröen, Toyota, and Volkswagen.

TI Automotive has implemented lean practices throughout its value chain, improving purchasing, engineering change order processing, and shipment to customers. For example, it switched from a "push-batch-queue processing" to a "pull and extended enterprise" system, achieving many of the benefits cited in the text. For example, inventory turns steadily improved from 12.7 to 22. This improvement resulted in $41 million in additional free cash flow and contributed significantly to the company's bottom line. Product quality improved from over 500 defects per million to less than 50 defects per million. Almost all TI facilities are ISO 9000 certified.

TI Automotive calls its lean practices "Common Sense Manufacturing." Much effort is spent trying to diffuse these practices to all facilities and employees as quickly as possible. According to TI Automotive, some of the keys to quickly diffusing lean practices include: (1) properly characterize and identify target innovators and early adopter groups, (2) support and invest in early innovators, (3) recognize the importance of communication channels and use them, (4) create slack resources to support successful change, (5) make early innovators' activity visible throughout the organization, and (6) require managers to lead by example, that is, "if the leader doesn't eat sauerkraut, don't expect others to do so."

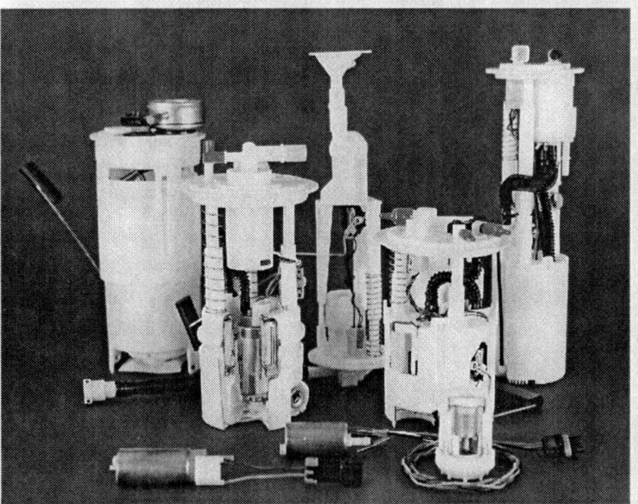
TI Automotive

LEAN TOOLS AND APPROACHES

Learning Objective
To understand the basic tools and approaches that organizations use to create a lean organization and to recognize how to apply these tools appropriately.

Meeting the objectives of lean enterprise requires disciplined approaches for designing and improving processes. Many of the tools that we have discussed in previous chapters, such as quality function deployment, value stream mapping, and the seven basic quality management tools, are important in lean thinking. In addition to these, organizations use several other tools and approaches to create a lean organization. These are summarized in this section.

Value Stream Mapping

Value stream mapping was introduced in Chapter 7. Recall that a value stream map shows the process flows in a manner similar to an ordinary process map. However, the difference is that value stream maps highlight value-added versus non-value-added activities and include times that activities take. This makes them well suited for lean enterprise analyses. They allow one to measure the impact of value-added and non-value-added activities on the total lead time of the process and compare this to the **takt time**—*the ratio of the available work time to the required production volume necessary to meet customer demand.* If the value stream is faster than

Takt time *is the ratio of the available work time to the required production volume necessary to meet customer demand.*

the takt time, it generally means that waste in the form of overproduction is occurring; when it is less, the firm cannot meet customer demand. Value stream maps might also include other information such as machine uptime and reliability, process capacity, and size of batches moving through the process. Developing value stream maps is usually one of the first steps in applying lean principles.

Small Batch and Single-Piece Flow

Batching—*the process of producing large quantities of items as a group before being transferred to the next operation.*

One of the practices that inhibits increasing speed and response in manufacturing or service processing of discrete parts such as a manufactured part, invoices, medical claims, or home loan mortgage approvals is **batching**—*the process of producing large quantities of items as a group before being transferred to the next operation.* Batching results in buildup of inventories and often leads to delays in delivery as customers wait for their order to be scheduled. The alternative to batching is continuous flow (which we introduced in Chapter 7), which is typically used to produce goods such as chemicals and gasoline. Continuous flow processes, by their very nature, are highly efficient because materials move through operations without stopping. Lean operating systems seek to apply the principles of continuous flow to the production of discrete parts by reducing batch sizes, ideally to a size of one—that is, using *single-piece flow*. Many companies justify batching on the basis that pallet loads or other full containers can be moved more easily between operations. However, simple changes in plant layout and material handling systems often can support one-piece flow. Single-piece flow allows companies to better match production to customer demand (particularly if processing times are large), avoid large and expensive inventory buildups, and ensure uninterrupted movement of work-in-process through the production system.

To understand this, consider the following comparison of batch processing versus single-piece flow in Exhibit 17.2. Assume that the batch size is 100 items and that each item must be processed sequentially on three workstations. Remember, in a batch process the entire lot size is produced at workstation A before it is moved to workstation B, and so on. Therefore, it takes 3,500 seconds to process a batch of 100 items through the three workstations, as depicted in Exhibit 17.3a.

Now consider single-piece flow, as shown in Exhibit 17.3b, where the first item is processed in 5 seconds then immediately moves on to the second workstation (we assume zero delay time in moving from one workstation to another). The first item completes processing at workstation B in a total of 25 seconds, and then moves on to workstation C, finishing in a total of 35 seconds. Note that B is the bottleneck workstation; items arrive for processing at B faster than B is capable of processing them, and therefore cannot be completed faster than 20 seconds apart. So, items 2 through 100 will all be completed by workstation B in 99(20 seconds) = 1,980 seconds after item #1. Thus, the last item leaves B at time 25 + 1,980 = 2,005 seconds from the start of production. Because workstation C is not the bottleneck,

Exhibit 17.2
Batch versus Single-Piece Flow Processing

Workstation	Batch Size (Q)	Processing Time per Item	Total Time per Batch (seconds)
A	100	5 seconds	500
B*	100	20 seconds	2,000
C	100	10 seconds	1,000
		Total	3,500

*Bottleneck workstation
Source: Adapted from Jeffrey K. Pinto and Om P. Kharbanda, "How to Fail in Project Management (Without Really Trying)" Business Horizons, July/August 1996, pp. 45–53. © 1996, with permission from Elsevier.

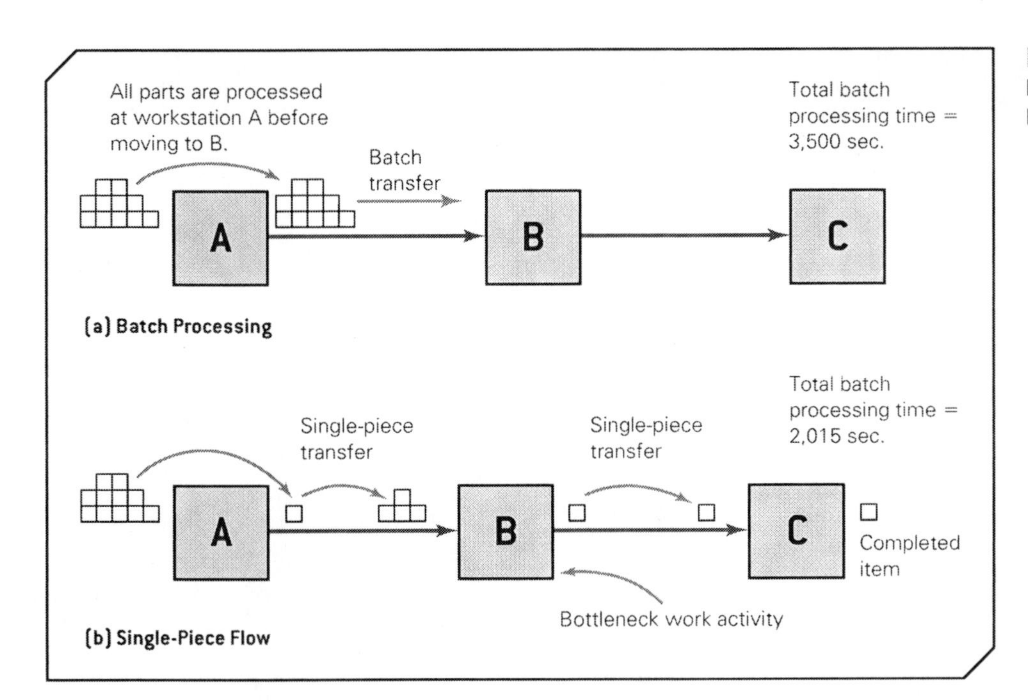

Exhibit 17.3
Batch versus Single Piece Flow Processing

every item that arrives from B can immediately be processed, so the 100th item is completed by time 2,005 + 10 = 2,015 seconds. This reduces the time from the batch process by (3,500 − 2,015)/3,500, or about 42 percent.

Batching is often necessary when producing a broad goods or service mix with diverse requirements on common equipment. When making different goods, manufacturers often need to change dies, tools, and fixtures on equipment, resulting in expensive and time-consuming setups and teardowns. For services, preprinted forms or software may have to be changed or modified. By running large batches, setups and teardowns are reduced, providing economies of scale. However, this often builds up inventory that might not match market demand, particularly in highly dynamic markets. A better strategy would be to use small batches or single-piece flow. However, to do this economically requires the ability to change between products quickly and inexpensively. Many companies have made remarkable improvements in reducing product setup times, making small-batch or single-piece flow a reality in job shop environments (see the OM Spotlight on Harley-Davidson). For example, Yammar Diesel reduced a machining-line tool setting from 9.3 hours to 9 minutes; a U.S. chain-saw manufacturer reduced setup time on a punch press from more than 2 hours to 3 minutes; and a midwestern manufacturer was able to cut equipment setup time on a 60-ton press from 45 minutes to 1 minute. This was accomplished through process improvements such as storing the required tools next to the machine, using conveyors to move the tools in and out of the machine, and improving the labeling and identification. Previously, the setup tools were poorly identified, poorly organized, and stored far from the machine, requiring a forklift to transport them. The machine operator can perform the new changeovers or setups with no indirect assistance.

Another way to improve performance when batching is necessary is to move a *portion* of a completed batch before the entire batch is finished. This is called a transfer batch. *A* **transfer batch** *is part of the original batch (lot) size that is completed at one workstation and moved to the next downstream workstation.* For example, in Exhibit 17.3a if the batch size is 100 items, a transfer batch of 20 items would allow downstream workstations to get the original batch out sooner.

A **transfer batch** *is part of the original batch (lot) size that is completed at one workstation and moved to the next downstream workstation.*

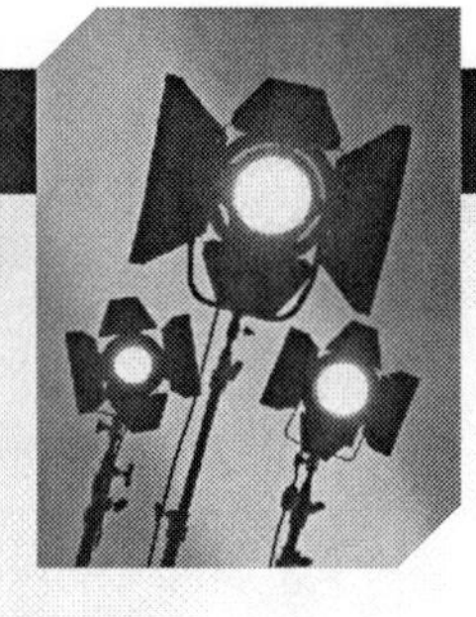

OM SPOTLIGHT

Harley-Davidson[6]

Feature Photo Service HARLEY-DAVIDSON CO.

After Harley-Davidson's market share fell from a near monopoly to less than 30 percent in the early 1980s, the company embarked on an aggressive strategy for improving quality and manufacturing efficiency. Lean production was an important part of that effort. Simple design changes, in both products and processes, helped it achieve dramatic reductions in setup time. For example, using "C"-shaped spacing washers instead of "O" types enabled operators to loosen nuts and slide in the "C" washers from the side to reposition a machine instead of taking the nuts off and lifting the machine to replace the "O" washers. Another change involved two crankpins that were similar except for a hole drilled at a 45-degree angle in one and at a 48-degree angle in the other. It took 2 hours to reposition the machine for the new operation. Engineers designed a common hole angle in the two parts, and changeovers could be made by simply inserting or removing a set of spacers on the fixture that held the crankpin for drilling. Setup time was reduced to 3 minutes.

The 5Ss

Workers cannot be efficient if their workplaces are messy and disorganized. Much time can be wasted looking for the right tool or moving around piles of materials that may be scattered about. Efficient manufacturing plants are clean and well organized. Firms use the "5S" principles to create this work environment. *The* 5Ss *are derived from Japanese terms: seiri (sort), seiton (set in order), seiso (shine), seiketsu (standardize), and shitsuke (sustain).*

The **5S Principles** *are* **seiri** *(sort),* **seiton** *(set in order),* **seiso** *(shine),* **seiketsu** *(standardize), and* **shitsuke** *(sustain).*

- *Sort* refers to ensuring that each item in a workplace is in its proper place or identified as unnecessary and removed.
- *Set in order* means to arrange materials and equipment so that they are easy to find and use.
- *Shine* refers to a clean work area. Not only is this important for safety, but as a work area is cleaned, maintenance problems such as oil leaks can be identified before they cause problems.
- *Standardize* means to formalize procedures and practices to create consistency and ensure that all steps are performed correctly.
- Finally, *sustain* means to keep the process going through training, communication, and organizational structures.

These principles define a system for workplace organization and standardization. By applying these, workers develop a mindset for lean thinking that carries over into all aspects of their work.

Visual Controls

Visual controls *are indicators for operating activities that are placed in plain sight of all employees so that everyone can quickly and easily understand the status and performance of the work system.* Visual signaling systems are known as *andon*, drawing from the Japanese term where the concept first originated. For example, if a machine fails or a part is defective or manufactured incorrectly, a light might turn on or a buzzer might sound, indicating that immediate action should be taken. Many firms have cords that operators can pull that tell supervisors and other workers that a problem has occurred. Some firms, such as Honda (on the manufacturing floor) and J.P. Morgan Chase (at its call centers), use electronic "scoreboards" to keep track of daily performance. These scoreboards are located where everyone can see them and report key metrics such as volume, quality levels, speed of service, and so on.

Visual controls *are indicators for operating activities that are placed in plain sight of all employees so that everyone can quickly and easily understand the status and performance of the work system.*

Efficient Layout and Standardized Operations

The layout of offices, equipment, and processes is designed according to the best operational sequence, by physically linking and arranging work activities and process steps most efficiently, often in a linear or cellular arrangement (see Chapters 7 and 8 and the OM Spotlight: Omark). Standardizing the individual tasks by clearly specifying the proper methods and procedures to do the work reduces wasted human movement and energy.

Technology

Although most of the tools and approaches for lean enterprise that we describe are quite simple, technology is becoming increasingly important in creating lean operating systems. Chapter 5 provides many examples on how technology improves performance, so we will not repeat them here. Here, we provide some additional examples to help you understand how organizations use technology to become leaner.

New forms of automated reasoning, learning, and control are now being used in selected factory operating systems.[8] These include *expert systems* that use a set of "intelligent rules" to make logical decisions to solve a specific problem or control an operation or machine, advanced search algorithms to solve complex optimization problems, and "intelligent agents" that perform tasks such as machine scheduling,

OM SPOTLIGHT

Omark[7]

The benefits of improved layout can be seen at Omark's Guelph, Ontario, factory, which makes chain saws. Originally, the distance the product had to travel within the plant was 2,620 feet and flow time was 21 days. Within 2 years, the distance was reduced to 173 feet and the time to 3 days by moving metal-forming machines together and eliminating much of the work-in-process (WIP) inventory. Omark's ultimate strategy is to fill orders from the factory and eliminate finished-goods warehouses altogether.

material transfer, and web auction bidding. For example, Sandia National Laboratories developed an expert system that monitors and controls a factory's brazing oven, which is used to solder ceramic parts to metal parts at high temperatures. Expert systems are being developed to continually analyze a production line to improve flexibility and trim changeover times. Advanced search algorithms are being applied to operating the shop floor in new-generation ERP packages sold by Oracle, SAP, i2 Technologies, Peoplesoft, and other vendors. Intelligent agents have been used to predict when injection-molding machines are about to turn out defective products by sifting through reams of data in real time, looking for patterns that are good predictors of defective parts. When problems are identified, the operator is notified and the machine is recalibrated. If the problem threatens delivery to a key customer, the sales and plant manager might get an automatic pager alert. These technologies can eliminate the limitations and errors associated with human judgment and clearly support the four objectives of lean enterprise.

Despite the fact that most customers do not like automated telephone answering systems, such systems streamline operations and lead to dramatic reductions in costs. For example, it costs a call center about $7 on average to handle a telephone call using a real person, $2.25 per call to handle an Internet transaction with human intervention at some point in the encounter, and only 20 to 50 cents for handling a telephone call using automated technology with no human intervention. In medical practices, technology enables a reduction of the office staff to physician ratio by one-half while speeding up the examination, order fulfillment, and payment processes.

Supplier Relationship Management

Lean operating systems will not work with suppliers who miss delivery dates or provide poor-quality goods or services. The fulfillment process requires collaborative partnerships between suppliers and their customers where communication is often on a real-time basis. This includes suppliers of information, energy, transportation, warehousing, packaging, and manufactured goods (see OM Spotlight: Saturn Corporation).

In a lean environment, shipments are received in reusable, standardized containers, each containing fixed quantities, so that there is no reason to unpack and count all incoming goods. In fact, shipping containers usually are designed to go directly to the assembly line and are designed to fit in a predesigned space. This practice also eliminates the potential for damage through handling and saves space.

OM SPOTLIGHT

Saturn Corporation[9]

Saturn's automobile plant in Spring Hill, Tennessee, manages its suppliers so well that in 4 years it had to stop its production line just once and for only 18 minutes because the right part was not delivered at the right time. Saturn maintains virtually no inventory. A central computer directs trucks to deliver preinspected and presorted parts at precise times to the factory's 56 receiving docks, 21 hours a day, 6 days a week. Of Saturn's more than 300 suppliers, most are not even located near the plant, but are in 39 states and an average of 550 miles away from Spring Hill. Ryder System, the Miami transportation services company, manages the Saturn network. Tractors pulling trailers that are 90 percent full on average arrive daily at a site 2 miles from Saturn's factory. The drivers uncouple the trailers, which contain bar-coded, reusable plastic containers full of parts, and shuttle tractors deliver them to the plant. Saturn is linked electronically with all its suppliers and reorders parts each time a car comes off the assembly line, an example of a pull production system in action.

Single Minute Exchange of Dies (SMED)

Long setup times waste manufacturing resources. Short setup times, on the other hand, enable a manufacturer to have frequent changeovers and move toward single-piece flow, thus achieving high flexibility and product variety. Reducing setup time also frees up capacity for other productive uses. **Single Minute Exchange of Dies (SMED)** *refers to quick setup or changeover of tooling and fixtures in processes so that multiple products in smaller batches can be run on the same equipment.* SMED was pioneered by Toyota and other Japanese manufacturers and has been adopted by companies around the world. Some remarkable examples are Yammar Diesel's reduction of a machining-line tool setup from 9.3 hours to 9 minutes, a U.S. chain-saw manufacturer's reduction of setup time on a punch press from more than 2 hours to 3 minutes, and a midwestern manufacturer's reduction of setup time on a 60-ton press from 45 minutes to 1 minute. This was accomplished through simple process improvements such as storing the required tools next to the machine, using conveyors to move the tools in and out of the machine, and improving the labeling and identification. Although SMED originated in a factory setting, the same principles of reducing non-value-added setup and changeover time apply for any good-producing or service-providing process (see OM Spotlight: Sunset Manufacturing).

Single Minute Exchange of Dies (SMED) *refers to quick setup or changeover of tooling and fixtures in processes so that multiple products in smaller batches can be run on the same equipment.*

Stable Production Schedules

Lean operating systems require uniform and stable production plans and schedules. This is accomplished by using small lot sizes, freezing the production schedule, and using a pull operating system. Such stabilizing practices level out the workloads at workstations. The ideas and methods of Chapter 11 on forecasting and Chapter 13 on aggregate planning, master production scheduling, and resource planning are used to develop stable and repetitive schedules.

OM SPOTLIGHT

Sunset Manufacturing[10]

An example of how even a small business can adopt lean production principles in order to realize significant improvements is found at Sunset Manufacturing, Inc. of Tualatin, OR, a 35-person, family-owned machine shop. Because of competitive pressures and a business downturn, Sunset began to look for ways to simplify operations and cut costs. At a Kaizen event, it determined that SMED and the 5S approach could yield benefits. Several actions were taken, including: (1) standardizing parts across milling machines, (2) reorganizing the tool room, (3) incorporating the SMED approach in machine setups, and (4) implementing what was termed "dance cards" that gave operators the specific steps required for SMED of various machines and products. The results were impressive and gratifying. Tool preparation time dropped from an average of 30 minutes to less than 10 minutes, isolation and identification of worn tools was improved, safety and appearance in the tool room due to 5S application was apparent, machine setup time was reduced from an average of 216 minutes to 36 minutes (an 86 percent improvement), and the entire Kaizen event resulted in an estimated savings of $33,000 per year, with a cost to implement of less than half of that amount. The net impact was to allow smaller lots to be run, a 75 percent reduction in setup scrap, a more competitive organization to emerge, and a morale boost for team members.

Quality at the Source

Quality at the source requires doing it right the first time, and therefore, eliminates the opportunities for waste. It reduces cost as implied by the 1:10:100 Rule we discussed in Chapter 16. Employees inspect, analyze, and control their own work to guarantee that the good or service passed on to the next process stage conforms to specifications. Of course, this requires a flexible and well-educated work force to learn the concepts and methods of lean operating systems and quality management. By inspecting your own work, inspection stations and jobs along the process can be eliminated, resulting in a leaner operating system.

Continuous Improvement and Six Sigma

In order to make lean principles work, one must get to the root cause of problems and permanently remove them. Continuous improvement initiatives that we discussed in Chapter 15 are vital in lean environments, as is teamwork among all managers and employees.

Six Sigma, in particular, has emerged to be a useful and complementary approach to lean production and has led to a new concept know as *Lean Six Sigma*. For example, lean systems assume high-quality output so as to maintain an uninterrupted process flow, so a processing time reduction project might involve aspects of both lean concepts and Six Sigma. A firm might apply lean tools to streamline an order entry process and discover that significant rework is occurring because of incorrect addresses, customer numbers, or shipping charges that results in high variation of processing time. Six Sigma tools might then be used to drill down to the root cause of the problems and identify a solution.

However, major differences exist between lean enterprise and Six Sigma, such as:

- Lean enterprise addresses more visible problems in processes, for example, inventory, material flow, and safety, while Six Sigma is more concerned with less visible problems, for example, process variation.
- Lean tools are more intuitive, simpler, and easier to apply in the workplace, while some Six Sigma tools are more advanced, such as statistical analysis of variance, design of experiments, and simulations.
- Lean tools generally require less training, whereas Six Sigma tools require advanced training and expertise in statistics, control charts, and Black Belt or Master Black Belt specialists. For example, the lean tool of the 5Ss is easier to grasp than statistical methods used with control charts.

Despite these differences, they both aim to eliminate waste from the value chain and improve the design and operation of goods, services, and processes. Both are driven by customer requirements and market strategies, focus on real dollar savings, and have the ability to make significant financial impacts on the organization, and both can be used in nonmanufacturing environments, require senior leadership commitment, and use a systematic methodology for implementation. Because of these similarities, many industry training programs and consultants have begun to focus on Lean Six Sigma, drawing upon the best practices of both approaches.

Total Productive Maintenance

Lean operating systems require that all equipment and processes operate reliably. Unplanned downtime is far worse than planned downtime and scheduled maintenance. For example, a $38 roller bearing on a manufacturer's plastics extruder machine failed, resulting in misalignment of the shaft and destroying the gears, the pinion shaft, three other bearings, and an oil seal. The actual cost of materials loss and equipment repair was $13,000 plus 3 days of lost production, which was valued at over $25,000. A routine inspection by an experienced maintenance mechanic or machine operator could have prevented almost all of this loss.[11]

Therefore, maintenance should be addressed proactively, rather than reactively by fixing failures and breakdowns. **Total productive maintenance (TPM)** *is focused on ensuring that operating systems will perform their intended function reliably.* The goal of TPM is to prevent equipment failures and downtime; ideally, to have "zero accidents, zero defects, and zero failures" in the entire life cycle of the operating system.[12] TPM has been described as the health care system for the operating system. TPM seeks to

Total productive maintenance (TPM) *is focused on ensuring that operating systems will perform their intended function reliably.*

- maximize overall equipment effectiveness and eliminate unplanned downtime
- create worker "ownership" of the equipment by involving them in maintenance activities
- foster continuous efforts to improve equipment operation through employee involvement activities

Better equipment maintenance can increase production yields, productivity, and capacity and reduce energy losses, rework and defects, and production line shutdowns. Maintenance is the responsibility of all employees. TPM promotes practices by which employees preserve and protect their own equipment and are responsible for routine maintenance such as cleaning or tightening (see the OM Spotlight on Eastman Chemical). Equipment maintenance staff and engineers are responsible for diagnosis of problems, major repair, and inspections.

In services, reliability of computers, software, and information networks is of paramount importance. Many banks, for example, go so far as to set up a second almost duplicate operations center in case the primary operations center is out of service for some reason.

Equipment performance deteriorates over time. When equipment performance reaches a point of failure, it can idle part or all of a process or factory, which is very expensive. Thus, TPM tries to predict equipment failure rates and perform maintenance before a problem arises, as illustrated in Exhibit 17.4. With TPM, the time before deterioration in equipment performance is increased substantially. Two key TPM questions to answer are (1) How can the start of deterioration in performance be detected? (2) When should action be taken? Statistical process control charts (Chapter 15) can help in answering these questions.

OM SPOTLIGHT

Eastman Chemical Company[13]

Within 5 years of starting TPM at Eastman Chemical Company, more than 120 teams were functioning, comprising over 85 percent of the facility. In its implementation, maintenance personnel work with operators in work zones within the plant with a focus on continuous improvement of processes through improved equipment reliability and maintainability. More than 3,000 tasks have been identified as TPM tasks, 80 percent of which are being performed by the equipment operators themselves. These include repairing equipment, changing filters, lubricating, and adjusting.

Prior to TPM, a mixer stoppage would last approximately 1 hour while maintenance personnel came and reset a tripped motor starter. Subsequently, an operator can restore production in 15 minutes or less. In one instance, after a power plant failure, a team restored production approximately 3 days sooner than would have been possible under the traditional maintenance organization, saving the company several million dollars.

Exhibit 17.4 TPM Equipment Issues and Benefits

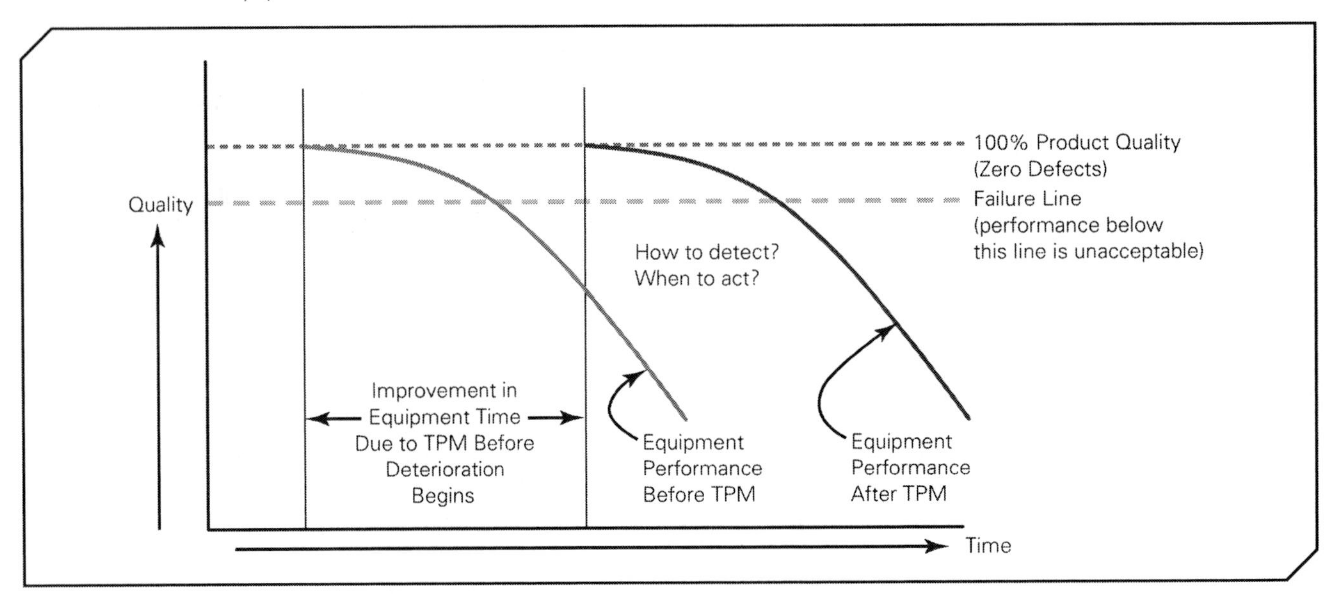

Because of its importance in lean thinking, TPM has recently been called "lean maintenance." Lean maintenance is more than preventing failures of equipment and processes; it now includes maintenance and backup systems for software and electronic network systems such as the Internet or wireless networks.

Manufactured Good Recovery

In an effort to reduce costs and essentially "do more with less," which is the essence of lean thinking, many companies are actively recovering and recycling parts (sometimes called *green manufacturing*). This can occur at various points of the supply chain, as shown in Exhibit 17.5. Once a manufactured good is discarded, one option is to resell the good or its various component parts. Other options include

- *Repairing* a manufactured good by replacing broken parts so it operates as required.
- *Refurbishing* the good by updating its looks and/or components; for example, cleaning, painting, or perhaps replacing parts that are near failure.
- *Remanufacturing* the good by returning it to close to its original specifications. This is usually done by disassembling it, cleaning or replacing many of the parts, and testing it to ensure it meets certain performance and quality standards. Certified remanufactured parts typically result in higher gross profit margins than the original, as high as 20 percent to 60 percent (see OM Spotlight: Remanufacturing Printer Ink Cartridges).
- *Cannibalizing* parts for use as replacement parts in other goods.
- *Recycling* goods by disassembling them and selling the parts or scrap materials to other suppliers. If the residual value of the manufactured good has been extracted or it is not economical to do so, the part ends up being incinerated or dumped in a landfill.

For example, a major automobile manufacturer became interested in remanufacturing transmissions to reduce the need to purchase a 10- to 20-year supply of transmission parts to service future customer needs. Each certified remanufactured transmission meets the original transmission performance and quality specifications.

Exhibit 17.5 Integrated Manufactured Good Recovery Value Chain[15]

Service Parts

Raw Materials → Parts Fabrication → Module Assembly → Manufactured Good Assembly → Distribution → Customers/Users →

2

6 5 4 3 1

7 and 8

Waste Management
7 — Incineration
8 — Landfill

Manufactured Good
2 — Repair
3 — Refurbishing
4 — Remanufacturing
5 — Cannibalization
6 — Recycling

Direct Reuse
1— Direct reuse/resale

A remanufactured transmission sells for 50 percent to 75 percent of a new one. The customer wins by lowering the total cost of replacement, and the company wins by reducing its inventory carrying costs.

The next two sections take you on tours of two goods-producing and two service-providing companies. The objective is to expose you to lean thinking in a wide variety of companies using the four basic principles of lean operating systems.

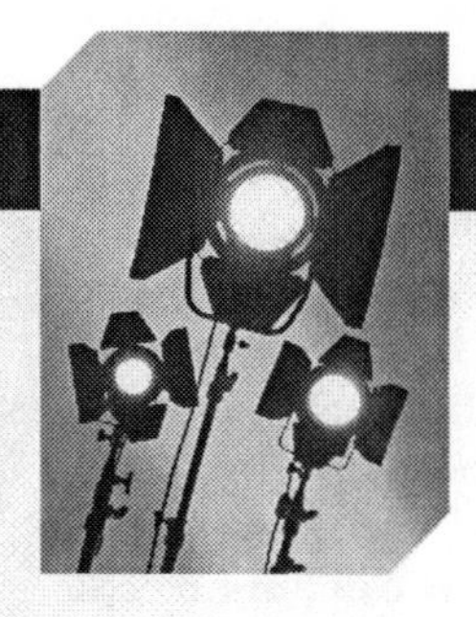

OM SPOTLIGHT

Remanufacturing Printer Ink Cartridges[14]

"I paid $90 for the printer, and one ink cartridge is $36," Brian Evans said, pausing on his way out of a New York office-supply store. Companies such as Lexmark, Hewlett-Packard, Canon, and Epson have coupled low-priced inkjet and laser printers with high-priced disposable ink cartridges. But the business model has sprung a leak—remanufacturing ink cartridges.

One objective of lean operating systems is zero waste. Buying a new replacement ink cartridge reminds us that printer manufacturers create obsolete ink cartridges by design. New ink cartridges cost one-third to one-half the cost of some printers. The strategy is to almost give away the printer and make profits from the perishable items such as ink and toner cartridges. Entrepreneurs have started selling refilling kits and remanufacturing ink cartridges for less than one-half the price of a new cartridge. Printer manufacturers are resisting this infringement on their profits.

Learning Objective
To understand how manufacturing firms apply lean tools and concepts.

LEAN MANFACTURING TOURS

Lean manufacturing plants look significantly different from traditional plants. They are clean and organized, devoid of long and complex production lines and high levels of work-in-process, have efficient layouts and work area designs, use multiskilled workers that perform both direct and indirect work such as maintenance, and have no incoming or final inspection stations. In this section, we "tour" two manufacturing firms to examine how they focus on the four major lean objectives. In the next section, we will tour some service organizations that apply similar principles.

Gorton's of Gloucester[16]

Perhaps you have seen advertisements with the trademark "Gorton's Fisherman" highlighting the great-tasting and high-quality seafood produced by Gorton factories. Gorton, headquartered in Gloucester, Massachusetts, has been processing seafood for over 150 years. In 1998, the company embarked on a lean operating system initiative because one of its senior managers walked through the factory and noticed that raw material was brought in through the second floor freight entrance and then stored on multiple floors. The seafood was processed on the second and third floors and then shuttled back to cold storage on the first floor. Conveyers connected the processes on each floor but this senior manager challenged factory management to address the "lack of visual flow." Some of the ways in which Gorton's is applying lean principles are summarized next.

Eliminate Waste The old operating system led to many forms of waste. Miscommunication among operations on different floors created excessive handling and movement of seafood, boxes, and pallets, and the entire process often stopped or slowed down due to bottlenecks. Before lean practices were implemented, cold storage included 40,000 square feet of expensive warehouse space to keep all the raw material, work-in-process, and finished goods inventory. Today, the factory has less than 10,000 square feet of cold storage warehouse space and 50 percent less inventory, increasing working capital and reducing operating expense. The new system also freed up an entire floor of the factory for other uses, which was eventually used to produce seven new retail brand seafood lines.

Increase Speed and Response One lean systems objective was to simplify the factory by putting all seafood production on one floor. Process and value stream maps drawn for the current processes found them to be incredibly complex, with much wasted movement and lack of communication between floors. Each section of the process was isolated physically and communicating operations information was difficult. The company embarked on a two-year effort to organize the production process on one floor as a pull system. By eliminating most of the old conveyer system, all production was organized on one floor. Process flow became more continuous and stable, and the production area was much easier to clean. Employees could also see the process from beginning to end, and communication improved, resulting in fewer slowdowns and stoppages. Raw materials are now replenished only when needed. The physical changes also led to cultural changes. Employee morale increased and they could see when they needed to speed up or help out other workstations.

The new layout and improved equipment enhanced the speed and efficiency of the production process. They also reduced setup and changeover times to different products and supported continuous flow production, improving the flexibility to adapt to different production order sizes needed to meet demand. Gorton's has also applied lean practices to its new product development processes, focusing on bringing new and innovative products to market quickly and effectively.

Improve Quality Gorton's production engineers began working with their equipment suppliers to redesign the batter, breader, tempering, and cutting machines. Many of these machines were invented by Gorton's decades ago and were designed to operate in a batch production environment. The new machines were designed to reduce the variability in their output, had fewer moving parts to minimize breakdowns, simplified maintenance designs that were easy to access, and were much easier to clean.

Reduce Cost Gorton's worked with suppliers who deliver the fish, flour, batter, boxes, and so on, so that they had the information necessary to deliver goods only when necessary. What they make they sell, and consequently, food is fresher. Gorton's hosts an annual Operations Conference that includes its suppliers, large retail customers, and truckers, so everyone in the value chain can communicate with each other. At each annual conference, performance results are reported, and Gorton's gives an award called the "Gorton's Lean Corporate Challenge" to the supplier who best contributed to Gorton's lean journey.

Gorton's is also studying the use of lean practices and tools in administrative areas such as purchasing, office services, distribution, quality control, accounts receivable, and accounts payable. Its goal is to become the "Toyota of Food Processing."

Timken Company[17]

The Timken Company (www.timken.com) is a leading global manufacturer of highly engineered bearings and alloy steels and related products and services. NASA's Mars rovers use Timken precision bearings in wheel transmissions, gearboxes, rotating cameras, camera masts, and solar array panel drives. Timken employs about 18,000 employees in over 50 factories and more than 100 sales, design, and distribution centers located throughout the world.

PR Newswire THE TIMKEN COMPANY

Timken divides its business into three major groups—industrial, automotive, and steel. The industrial group accounts for about 40 percent of total sales and manufactures bearings for the aerospace, mining, agriculture, rail, heavy industry, and distribution industries. The automotive group also accounts for another 40 percent of sales and manufactures bearings and power train products, often in bundled subassemblies and modules. For both of these groups, Timken places increasing emphasis on pre- and postproduction services, such as integrated engineering solutions to customer requirements. The steel group accounts for the remaining sales and produces specialty alloy steel bars and tubes used in the other two groups.

Like most manufacturers, Timken faced intense, survival-threatening, global competition, and like many others, it placed itself on the leading edge of U.S. industrial revival. In 1989, the company launched "Vision 2000," a program of lean production initiatives that developed throughout the 1990s. A key element was increased productivity through lean-manufacturing operating principles and technologies, some of which we highlight next.

Eliminate Waste Timken's automotive business uses a "Boot Camp" in which a certain factory identifies several improvement opportunities and Timken employees and managers from other sites then try to solve these specific problems at the host factory. This is similar to a *kaizen blitz* (see Chapter 15). The problems often focus on removing non-value-added steps from processes, reducing process and equipment variation, and eliminating waste. The boot camp approach allows "fresh eyes" to evaluate improvement opportunities and present solutions to host plant management. Timken has also worked with the U.S. Department of Energy to improve the manufacture and performance of seamless tube and pipe so as to help steel producers eliminate unnecessary processing steps.

Increase Speed and Response Timken has focused on improving its product development process—a nonmanufacturing, information-intensive process—with the objective to radically reduce the total cycle time for new product development with fewer errors and to be more responsive to customer requests, competitor capabilities, and marketplace changes. Timken's objective of an integrated supply chain also focuses on agility to better meet customer wants and needs.

Timken exploited many of the technologies we described in Chapter 6, such as computer-aided design and computer-aided manufacturing (CAD/CAM), to better meet customer needs and improve design for manufacturability. It developed flexible manufacturing systems to facilitate rapid, cost-effective changeover from one product to another, combining the advantages of batch and mass production. Lean manufacturing's most distinguishing characteristic at Timken, however, was the authority and responsibility it gave to people on the shop floor. Initiatives aimed at empowering shop floor employees included more open communication, enhanced training, widespread adoption of a team approach to problem solving and decision-making, and changes in measures of performance and rewards. Teams helped to redesign machinery and reorganize equipment into flexible manufacturing cells. Timken's customers, themselves under tremendous pressure to bring new products to market, needed quicker response times. Timken research facilities led pilot production programs that enabled machine operators to have early input into the design process and resulted in significant cost savings.

Improve Quality Quality standards are determined for all manufacturing processes, and worldwide quality audits make sure that these standards are being met. Each plant is certified to ISO 9000 or other quality certifications. Timken has applied Six Sigma tools to minimize process variation. One initiative was to improve machine operator efficiency and reduce variability. Workstation processes were standardized and machine operator walking and movement time was eliminated or reduced. The result was improved quality and reduced scrap.

Total quality and continuous improvement has long been a focus for Timken. Through programs like Breakthrough and Accelerated Continuous Improvement, thousands of improvement ideas have been implemented, saving millions of dollars. In some cases, the stretch targets of 40 percent improvement in costs, quality, and service were exceeded. All manufacturing machinery must meet the company's Capability Policy for quality and consistency. Even new equipment is tested and modified to meet specifications. Sometimes these tests are conducted on the plant floor; at other times, equipment is brought to one of its research facilities for more extensive modification. As a natural evolution from traditional total quality approaches, Timken embraced Six Sigma.

Reduce Cost Timken redefined its mission statement in 1993 to be "the best-performing manufacturing company in the world as seen through the eyes of our customers and shareholders." Management made structural changes aimed at pushing its engineering culture to become more business oriented. Markets were segmented, with associates from marketing, sales, application engineering, and manufacturing forming teams, each focusing on a single market. Today, Timken factories, suppliers, and customers share information using the Internet. Purchasing, order fulfillment, manufacturing strategy implementation, Lean Six Sigma, and logistics have been brought together to create an "integrated supply chain model." The purpose of this focus is to reduce asset intensity, improve customer service and systems support, respond faster to customer needs, and better manage inventory levels.

Exhibit 17.6 Timken's DMAIC Toolkit for Lean Six Sigma

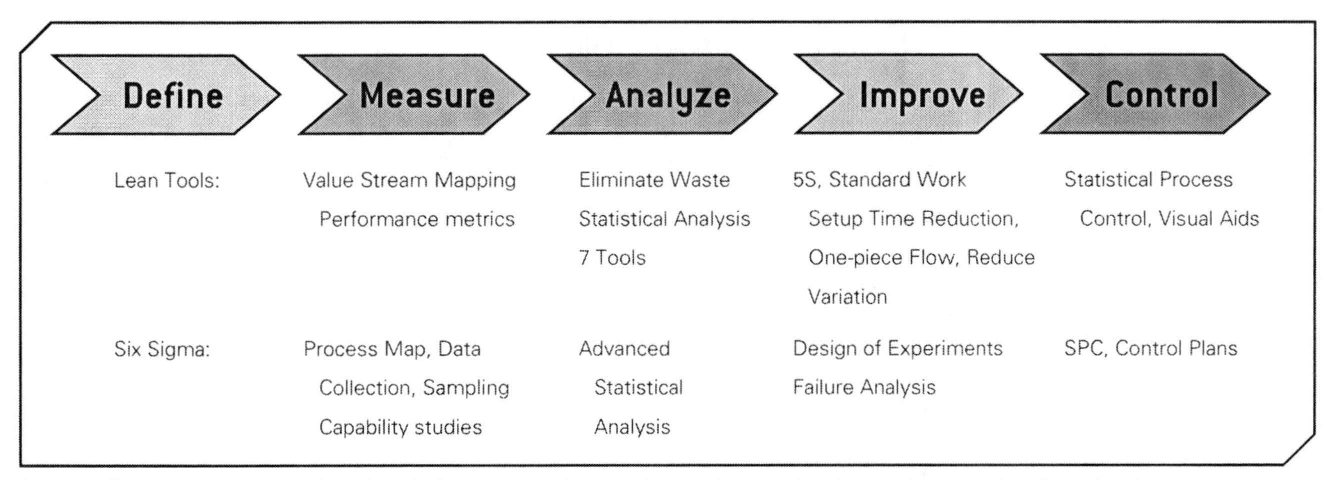

Source: Ellis, R., and Hankins, K., "The Timken Journey for Excellence," Presentation for the Center of Excellence in Manufacturing Management, Fisher College of Business, Ohio State University, Columbus, Ohio, August 22, 2003.

In the late 1990s, Timken decided to integrate its lean manufacturing practices and Six Sigma initiatives into one unified program, Lean Six Sigma. The objective of Timken's Lean Six Sigma program is "to identify and deliver value to our customers and shareholders by improving the flow of product and information through waste elimination and variation reduction." All manufacturing processes are flowcharted and the DMAIC problem-solving framework is used to generate process improvements. Exhibit 17.6 shows the wide variety of lean and Six Sigma analysis tools used throughout the company. The automotive business achieved a net documented savings of $7 million from Lean Six Sigma projects in 1 year alone.

LEAN SERVICE TOURS

Learning Objective
To understand how lean tools and concepts are applied to service organizations.

Service organizations can benefit significantly from applying lean principles. Value chains identify many preproduction services, such as financing and good/service design, and postproduction processes, such as installation/repair and consulting and technical support services (refer back to Exhibits 2.1 to 2.3). Synchronized information and feedback flows tie these different processes together.

Lean principles are not always transferable to "front-office" services that involve high customer contact and service encounters. In these situations, the service provider and firm do not have complete control over creating the service. Different customers, service encounter situations, and customer and employee behaviors cause the creation and delivery of the service to be much more variable and uncertain than producing a manufactured good in the confines of a factory. However, "back-office" service processes, such as hospital laboratory testing, check processing, and college application processing, are nearly identical to many manufacturing processes. Time, accuracy, and cost are all important to their performance, and therefore they can clearly benefit from the application of lean principles.

The following discussion shows how lean concepts have been used at SBC Communications and Southwest Airlines.

SBC Communications

SBC Communications is a major telecommunications company that provides local, long-distance, digital satellite television, and wireless and Internet access products to residential and commercial customers. One of its services is telephone installation and repair. When customers contact a call center and request telephones to be installed, removed, or repaired, the call center creates a trouble report.[18]

Eliminate Waste Excess capacity, a form of waste, is reflected in too many technicians and trucks, both of which are very expensive. By increasing technician/truck utilization by applying lean principles, excess capacity can be reduced. Unnecessary movement of technicians/trucks from job site to job site is also very wasteful and expensive. The objective of the dispatching function is to minimize the distance traveled per technician/truck. Other forms of waste in this value chain include rework, inaccurate information, missed customer appointment times, customers not being home when they said they would be, long waiting times, unnecessary rescheduling, doing non-value-added tasks, and retraining and relearning time and expense due to technician job turnover rates.

One example of how SBC addressed waste revolves around order processing. The old process batched work orders and trouble reports and processed them the evening before the next day's work. When service technicians arrived the next day, they received a printout of their work schedule and the order they should visit customer sites. This approach did not consider the changes that often occurred throughout the workday, such as customers not being home or calling to change their request. Hence, the service technicians were constantly calling in to update and revise their job assignments throughout the day. Applying lean principles to this situation, the company decided to process one trouble report at a time to each service repair technician. This is analogous to the single-piece flow idea in a lean manufacturing system. All changes to the status of trouble reports were handled in the main dispatching office. After technicians finished each job, they called the dispatcher to get their next job assignment. The dispatcher could better coordinate job assignments, taking into account technicians' locations and skills.

Increase Speed and Response Speed of service is clearly very important when a customer's telephone does not work. To respond quickly and effectively, representatives must promptly and courteously answer the customers' telephone call and quickly process the trouble report, the technician must show up when promised and perform the work professionally, and the next telephone bill must accurately reflect what was promised and done. Improving the accuracy of the standard times to perform different types of installation and repair jobs is very important to the objective of speed and response. Training also plays a role in how fast technicians can do this work. Convenience supports speed and response in a service business. For example, the appointment time must be convenient for the customer.

Improve Quality Regardless of whether the service provider is a technician or telephone customer service representative, the quality of service encounters is critical to long-term customer satisfaction. The telephone call center, a front-office, high-customer-contact function, must get accurate information as to exactly what the customer wants done. If the information at the beginning of the process is inaccurate, then rework, rescheduling, and return visits may result. Because the customer service representative is in direct contact with customers, human behavior and service management skills must be considered in meeting quality requirements. SBC identified the top ten types of service inquiries and developed standard responses (called script dialogues) to standardize service provider responses to frequently asked questions. Similar issues arise when the technician interacts with the customer and enters the home or facility. However, in such high-contact situations, lean methods and practices do not transfer as well from manufacturing.

Missed appointments, even if they arise because the customer might have forgotten, are damaging service upsets. One way of reducing this type of quality error is for the dispatching function to call customers the morning of the appointment to ensure they will be home and that the technician will have access to the facility. SBC was able to reduce the standard deviation of missed appointment times by 50 percent.

Reduce Cost Today's information and cell phone technology allows all repair technicians and job assignments in a geographical area to be coordinated more efficiently and faster than in the past. The central information processing center—the dispatching function—has more timely information than any single technician and truck. The dispatching function sets the pace of this value chain. For this service, the dispatching function is similar to a factory's master production schedule or gateway workstation. The dispatching function's objectives are to maximize customer service and technician/truck utilization and minimize costs. Therefore, smart and timely information means more can be done with fewer resources.

Southwest Airlines

BARRY SWEET/Landov

Since its inception, Southwest Airlines has shown lean performance when compared to other major airlines. For example, in fiscal year 2001, the average cost to fly one available passenger seat 1 mile was 7.6¢. The next best was American West at 8.8¢, followed by TWA at 9.3¢, and all others were higher—up to 71 percent higher. One study suggested that for all other U.S. major airline carriers to get down to Southwest's cost per average seat mile, $18 billion in costs needed to be taken out of their budgets![19] What is even more significant is that Southwest has historically operated small planes and short-distance flights and therefore cannot capitalize on economies of scale available to larger airlines.

Exhibit 17.7 shows the total operating costs of the average major domestic U.S. airline. The vast majority of total airline cost focuses on operations management activities: traffic servicing (13 percent), aircraft servicing (7 percent), flight operations (47 percent), reservations and sales (10 percent), and passenger in-flight service (7 percent). Note that the first three are low-contact (back-office) operations, whereas passenger in-flight service and reservations and sales are high-contact service management functions. Therefore, taking a lean approach to all operations is vital to airline performance. Southwest is clearly a lean airline—it does more with less than any other airline competitor. Let us examine some of the reasons.

Eliminate Waste In the airline industry, idle time is the largest form of waste. Southwest locates its planes at noncongested airports to help it minimize airplane turnaround time. Fewer ancillary services reduce the opportunity for waste and inefficiencies. Southwest also enjoys a much lower employee turnover rate than its competitors, resulting in lower training costs. Its frequent-flyer program is simple: Customers receive a free flight after eight paid flights. Other major airline programs are much more complex, requiring substantial overhead to track and report frequent-flyer points earned.

All the resources at Southwest work to keep the airplanes in the air earning revenue—the primary focus of its strategy. The more time spent on the ground, the less revenue. It relies on motivated employees, a culture focused on the customer, and teamwork to accomplish this strategy. Southwest employees are cross-trained and organized into teams to accomplish all key operational activities. For example, all employees cooperate to ensure timely takeoffs and landings; it is not unusual to see pilots helping load baggage if this will get the plane off on time. This maintains smooth system schedules and reduces the need for reschedules and reticketing, both of which are a form of rework. As one example—in as fast as 15 minutes—Southwest can change the flight crew; deplane and board 137 passengers; unload

Exhibit 17.7 Total Operating Costs for Average U.S. Major Airline Carriers[20]

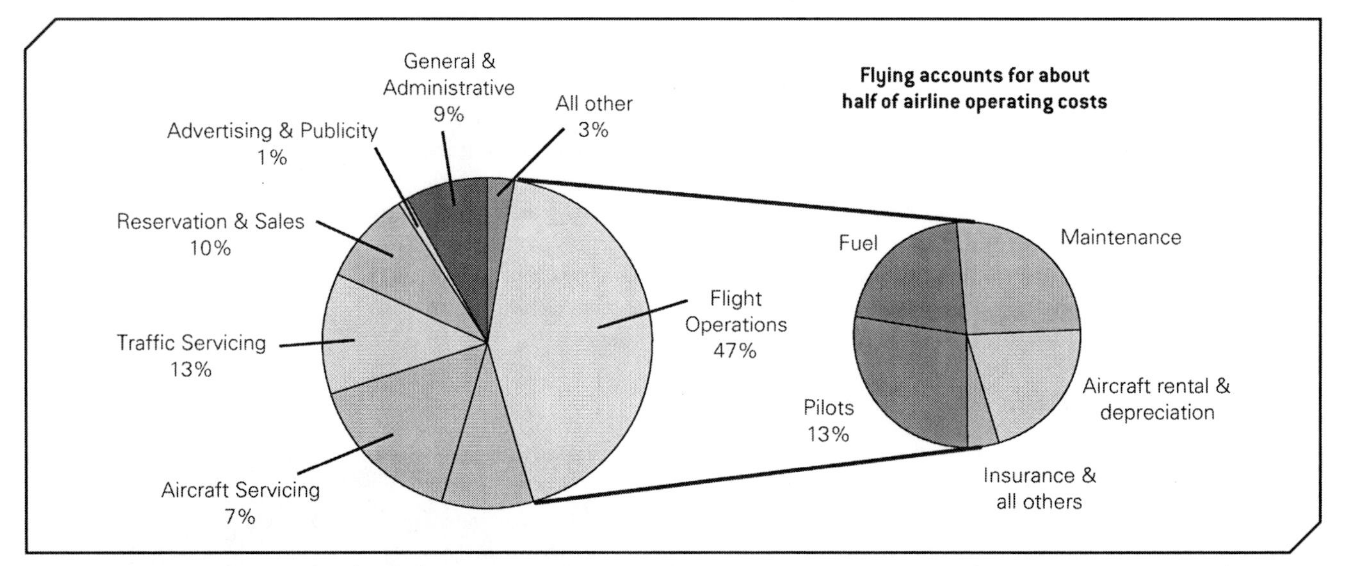

Source: "Unisys R2A Scorecard-Airline Industry Cost Management," figure 1, Unisys Corporation, Vol. 1, Issue 2, Nov. 2002. This report may be copied, in whole or in part, provided all legends, copyright, proprietary and other notices which appear herein are reproduced. © 2002 Unisys Corporation. Reprinted with permission of Unisys Corporation.

97 bags, 1,000 pounds of mail, and 25 pieces of freight; load another 123 bags and 600 pounds of mail; and pump 4,500 pounds of jet fuel into the aircraft.[21]

Increase Speed and Response Southwest uses a much simpler structure and operating system than competitors. It uses only one type of aircraft—the Boeing 737—making it easier to schedule crews, perform maintenance, and standardize such activities as boarding, baggage storage and retrieval, and cabin operations. It books direct flights from point A to B and does not rely on the hub-and-spoke system used by competitors. This makes it easier for many customers to get to their destinations, instead of, for instance, flying from Orlando to Cincinnati or Detroit and then connecting back to Nashville. A simple operating structure reduces the time it takes to make decisions and allows employees to focus on the key drivers of airline performance such as turnaround time. For example, if Southwest can turn its planes around on average in at most 1/2 hour while competitors take 1 hour, then, assuming a 90-minute flight, approximately one to two more flights per day per plane can be made. This can be a significant economic and strategic advantage.

Southwest was the first airline to introduce ticketless travel. Customers simply get a confirmation number and show up on time. A significant proportion of customers book their flights directly on Southwest.com. No in-flight full-service meals are provided either, simplifying cabin operations and eliminating the need to stock meals, which increases the time to clean up from the previous flight and prepare for the next flight. Instead, Southwest was the first airline to offer continental breakfast in the gate area, and flight attendants serve drinks and peanuts using specially designed trays. If a customer misses a flight, he or she can use the ticket for a future flight with no penalty; this reduces paperwork and processing, contributing to a leaner operation.

Improve Quality Simplified processes reduce variability in flight schedules, a major source of customer complaints, and therefore improve customers' perceptions of quality and satisfaction. Southwest encourages carry-on baggage; hence, there is less opportunity for losing, misrouting, or damaging baggage. People-oriented employees are carefully chosen and empowered to both serve and entertain passengers.

Reduce Cost Short setup and turnaround time translates into higher asset utilization and reduces the need for costly inventories of aircraft. Southwest does not have assigned seating; customers wait on a first-come, first-served basis and board in zones. This lowers costs, and only a few employees are needed to coordinate passenger boarding. In addition, rather than carry the high overhead costs of airplane maintenance and repair, Southwest outsources these tasks to third parties.

JUST-IN-TIME SYSTEMS

Learning Objective
To understand the concepts and philosophy of just-in-time operating systems and the challenges that managers face in managing JIT systems.

Just-in-Time (JIT) was introduced at Toyota during the 1950s and 1960s to address the challenge of coordinating successive production activities. An automobile, for instance, consists of thousands of parts. It is extremely difficult to coordinate the transfer of materials and components between production operations. Traditional factories use a **push system**, *which produces finished goods inventory in advance of customer demand using a forecast of sales.* Parts and subassemblies are "pushed" through the operating system based on a predefined schedule that is independent of actual customer demand. In a push system, a model that might not be selling well is still produced at the same predetermined production rate and held in finished goods inventory for future sale, whereas enough units of a model in high demand might not get produced.

A **push system** *produces finished goods inventory in advance of customer demand using a forecast of sales.*

Another problem was that traditional automobile production systems relied on massive and expensive stamping press lines to produce car panels. The dies in the presses weighed many tons and specialists needed up to a full day to switch them for a new part. To compensate for long setup times, large batch sizes were produced so that machines could be kept busy while others were being set up. This resulted in high work-in-process inventories and high levels of indirect labor and overhead.

Toyota created a system based on a simple idea: Produce the needed quantity of required parts each day. This concept characterizes a **pull system**, *in which employees at a given operation go to the source of required parts, such as machining or subassembly, and withdraw the units as they need them.* Then just enough new parts are manufactured or procured to replace those withdrawn. As the process from which parts were withdrawn replenishes the items it transferred out, it draws on the output of its preceding process, and so on. Finished goods are made to coincide with the actual rate of demand, resulting in minimal inventories and maximum responsiveness.

A **pull system** *is one in which employees at a given operation go to the source of required parts, such as machining or subassembly, and withdraw the units as they need them.*

JIT systems are based on the concept of pull rather than push. In a JIT system, a key gateway workstation (such as final assembly) withdraws parts to meet demand and therefore provides real-time information to preceding workstations about how much to produce and when to produce to match the sales rate. By pulling parts from each preceding workstation, the entire manufacturing process is synchronized to the final-assembly schedule. JIT operating systems prohibit all process workstations from pushing inventory forward only to wait idle if it is not needed.

The name "just-in-time" arose from this concept of making parts from upstream processes only when needed by downstream processes. In this fashion, a JIT system can produce a steady rate of output to meet the sales rate in small, consistent batch sizes to level loads and stabilize the operating system. This dramatically reduces the inventory required between stages of the production process, thus greatly reducing costs and physical capacity requirements. Thus, JIT represents a very efficient inventory control process. An ideal JIT system would have single-piece flow if possible. Of course, to make this happen, a JIT system could not tolerate defects or long setup times; hence, continuous improvement is vital to improve quality and speed.

Operation of a JIT System

As noted, JIT systems produce according to the rate of sales. Takt time is the production rate for one good or service based on the rate of sales. Takt time is a term used in lean operating systems and is equivalent to cycle time for assembly-line balancing as described in Chapter 8, and is computed using Equation (17.1).

$$\text{Takt time} = \frac{\text{Available time per time period}}{\text{Market demand rate per time period}} \quad \textbf{(17.1)}$$

For example, an 8-hour workday that includes 1 hour for lunch and breaks effectively has 25,200 seconds per workday (7 hours/day × 3,600 seconds/hour). If the rate of sales is 400 units per day, then the takt time is (25,200 seconds/day)/(400 units/day) = 63 seconds/unit. If the production process pulls units through the system at the rate of 63 seconds/unit, the pace of production will match the pace of sales.

A simple generic JIT system with two process cycles—one for the customer and a second for the supply process—is shown in Exhibit 17.8. Conceptually, the customer can be an internal or external customer, and the customer-supply configuration in Exhibit 17.8 can be chained together to model a more complex sequence of production or assembly operations. In this process, the customer cycle withdraws what is needed at the time it is needed according to sales. The supply cycle creates the good to replenish only what has been withdrawn by the customer. The storage area is the interface and control point between the customer and supply cycles.

A ***Kanban*** *is a flag or a piece of paper that contains all relevant information for an order: part number, description, process area used, time of delivery, quantity available, quantity delivered, production quantity, and so on.*

Slips, called Kanban cards (*Kanban* is a Japanese word that means "visual record" or "card"), are circulated within the system to initiate withdrawal and production items through the production process. *A* ***Kanban*** *is a flag or a piece of paper that contains all relevant information for an order: part number, description,*

Exhibit 17.8 A Two-Card Kanban JIT Operating System

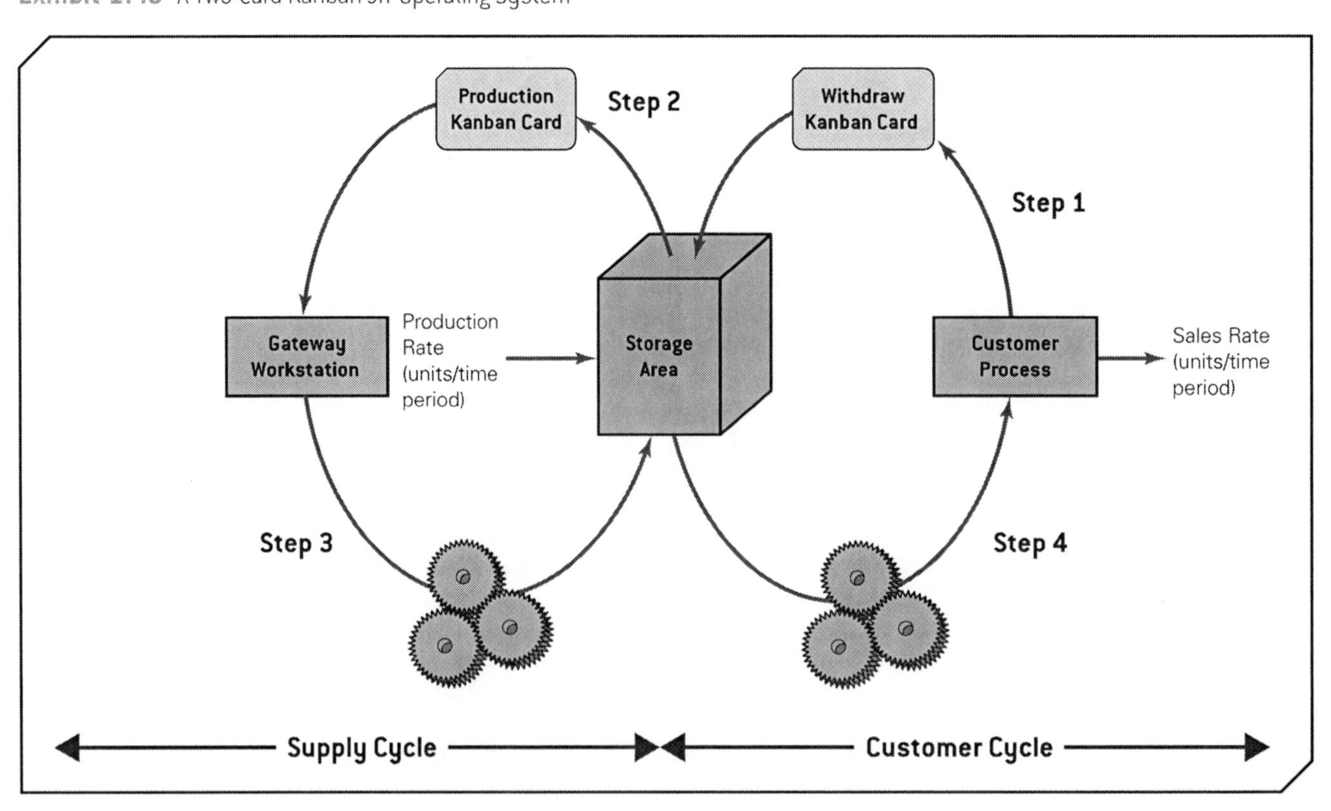

process area used, time of delivery, quantity available, quantity delivered, production quantity, and so on. Because of this, a JIT system is sometimes called a Kanban system.

The Kanban system begins when the customer buys or uses the good and an empty container is created. The withdraw Kanban (step 1) authorizes the material handler to transfer empty containers to the storage area. Withdraw Kanbans trigger the movement of parts. The material handler detaches the withdraw-ordering Kanban that was attached to the empty container and places the Kanban card in the storage area or on the Kanban receiving post, leaving the empty container(s) (step 1). A material handler for the supply cycle places a production Kanban on the empty container and this authorizes the gateway workstation to produce parts (step 2). Production Kanbans trigger the production of parts. The container holds a small lot size of parts. Without the authorization of the production Kanban, the gateway workstation and all other workstations may be idle. The gateway workstation must be scheduled to meet the sales rate and it pulls parts from all other workstations. The other workstations in the process do not need to be scheduled because they get their production orders from the production Kanban that pulls parts through the supply process. The supply process returns a full container of parts to the storage area with the production Kanban attached (step 3). The Kanban process is complete when the material handler for the customer process picks up a full container of parts and takes the production Kanban card off the container. Normally, the material handler drops off a withdrawal Kanban and empty container when picking up a full container of parts.

Note that the Kanban cards and containers are simple visual controls. Some JIT systems use the containers themselves as the signaling device and do not use Kanban cards. An empty or full container automatically tells everyone what to do and when to do it. Other types of visual controls used to pull parts through the production process include using cabinet drawers or marked-off spaces on the floor in the storage area. When the drawers or marked-off floor spaces are empty, that is the visual signal to produce another container of parts and fill the empty drawer or space.

To illustrate some examples of using Kanbans, truck drivers from component plants for a General Electric lamp division collect Kanban cards and empty containers when they unload. The card signals which components are to be delivered on the next trip. At a Hewlett-Packard plant, the signal for a subassembly shop that makes computer-system modules to send another plastic tub of parts forward is removal of the present plastic tub of parts from a sensing platform. At another Hewlett-Packard facility, an empty "Kanban square" outlined in yellow tape is the visual signal for the preceding workstation to forward another disk-drive unit.

JIT practice is to set the lot size or container size equal to about 5 percent to 20 percent of a day's demand or between 20 to 90 minutes worth of demand. The number of containers in the system determines the average inventory levels. The following equation is used to calculate the number of Kanban cards (K) required:

$$K = \frac{\text{Average daily demand during the lead time plus a safety stock}}{\text{Number of units per container}}$$

$$= \frac{d(p + w)(1 + \alpha)}{C} \qquad \textbf{(17.2)}$$

where K = the number of Kanban cards in the operating system.

d = the average daily production rate as determined from the master production schedule.

w = the waiting time of Kanban cards in decimal fractions of a day (that is, the waiting time of a part).

p = the processing time per part, in decimal fractions of a day.
C = the capacity of a standard container in the proper units of measure (parts, items, etc.).
α = a policy variable determined by the efficiency of the process and its workstations and the uncertainty of the workplace, and therefore, a form of safety stock usually ranging from 0 to 1. However, technically, there is no upper limit on the value of α.

For example, suppose that d = 50 parts/day, w = 0.20 day, p = 0.15 day, C = 5 parts, and α = 0.5. Then the number of Kanban cards is calculated, using Equation (17.2), as

$$K = \frac{50(0.2 + 0.15)(1 + 0.5)}{5} = 5.25 \text{ containers} \cong 6 \text{ (rounded up to 6)}$$

The number of Kanban cards is directly proportional to the amount of work-in-process inventory. Managers and employees strive to reduce the number of cards in the system through reduced lead time (p or w), lower α values, or through other improvements. The maximum authorized inventory in the operating system is $K \times C$. In the previous example, $K \times C$ = 6 Kanban sets × 5 parts per container = 30 parts.

Note that the numerator of Equation (17.2) is similar to the reorder point (r) in a FQS inventory system (see Chapter 11). Rewriting this as $d(p + w) + \alpha d(p + w)$, the first term is analogous to the demand during the lead time and the second to safety stock to buffer against inefficiencies and uncertainty. Once the system is running, supervisors can delete or add Kanban cards from or to the system as they observe that certain workstations need less or more work-in-process inventory.

WIP inventory is often viewed as an analogy to the water level in a lake, as shown in Exhibit 17.9. High levels hide critical inefficiencies such as equipment breakdowns, high scrap rates, and unreliable suppliers. By reducing inventory (and the number of Kanbans) these inefficiencies are exposed and must be solved to operate an effective JIT system.

JIT in Service Organizations

Although JIT has had its biggest impact in manufacturing, many service organizations are increasingly applying it. At the Nashua Corporation, for example, a JIT-oriented study of administrative operations reduced order-cycle time from 3 days to 1 hour, office space requirements by 40 percent, and errors by 95 percent and

Exhibit 17.9 A Water-Level Analogy of Waste

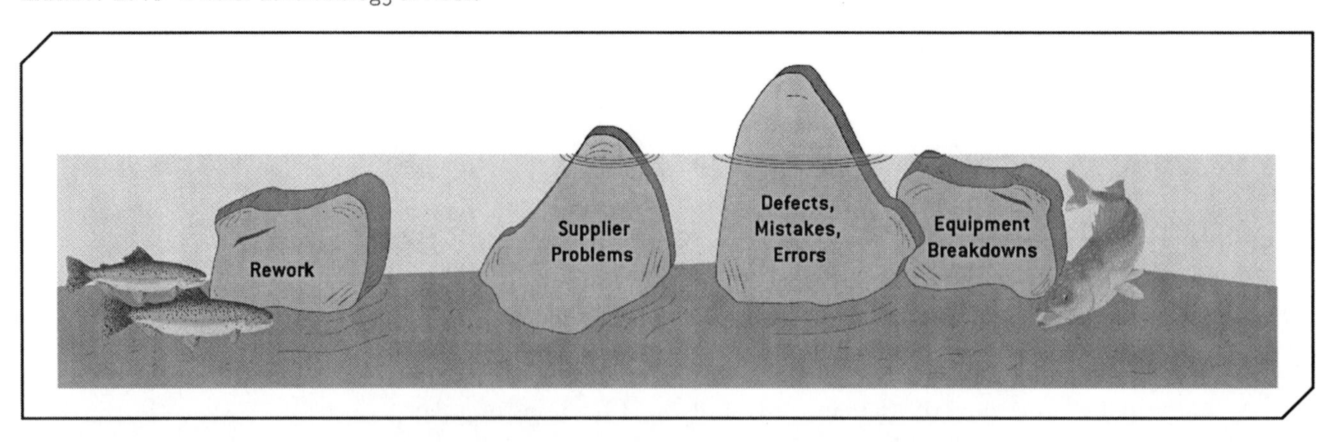

OM SPOTLIGHT

Baxter International[24]

St. Luke's Episcopal Hospital in Houston has applied JIT to its dispensing of hospital supply products. Most hospitals maintain a large inventory of supplies in a central storeroom and replenish the supplies needed in the various areas of the hospital on a regular basis. St. Luke's adopted a radical strategy; it closed its warehouse and sold its inventory to Baxter International Inc., a major hospital supplier. Baxter has become a partner with the hospital in managing, ordering, and delivering supplies. Baxter fills orders in exact, sometimes small, quantities and delivers them directly to the hospital departments, including operating rooms and nursing floors. The hospital is now saving $350,000 annually due to staff reductions and $162,500 by eliminating its inventory. Its storeroom has been converted to patient care and other productive uses.

increased productivity by 20 percent.[22] One overnight package-delivery service saw its inventory investment climb from $16 million to $34 million with conventional inventory-management techniques.[23] Implementing JIT reduced its inventory investment, but the company's major objective was to increase profits by providing a 99.9 percent level of service to its customers. Before JIT implementation, its service level—computed by dividing the number of items filled weekly by the number of items requested—was 79 percent. After JIT, the level was 99 percent, and the firm looked forward to meeting its goal. Baxter International is another service company that has experienced the benefits of a JIT system (see the OM Spotlight).

Designing Effective JIT Systems

Designing and implementing a well-run JIT system may seem simple but it is not (see OM Spotlight: The Hazards of One-Piece Flow). The entire value chain must synchronize its activities. Some of the challenging characteristics of a well-designed JIT system are summarized in Exhibit 17.10. These characteristics require knowledge and expertise in almost every topic previously covered in this book. Hence, JIT is an integrative operating system that demands the best ideas, methods, and management practices.

Exhibit 17.10 Example JIT Characteristics and Best Practices

- Setup/changeover time minimized
- Excellent preventive maintenance
- Mistake-proof job and process design
- Stable, level, repetitive master production schedule
- Phantom bill of materials with zero lead time
- Fast processing times
- Clean and uncluttered workspaces
- Very little inventory to hide problems and inefficiencies
- Use production cells with no wasted motion
- May freeze the master production schedule
- Use reusable containers
- Outstanding communication and information sharing
- Keep it simple and use visual controls
- High quality approaching zero defects
- Small repetitive order/lot sizes
- Minimize the number of parts/items
- Minimize the number of bill-of-material levels
- Facility layout that supports continuous or single-piece flow
- Minimize distance traveled and handling
- Clearly defined performance metrics
- Minimize the number of production, inventory, and accounting transactions
- Good calibration of all gauges and testing equipment
- Employees trained in quality management concepts and tools
- Excellent employee recognition and reward systems
- Employee cross-training and multiple skills
- Empowered and disciplined employees

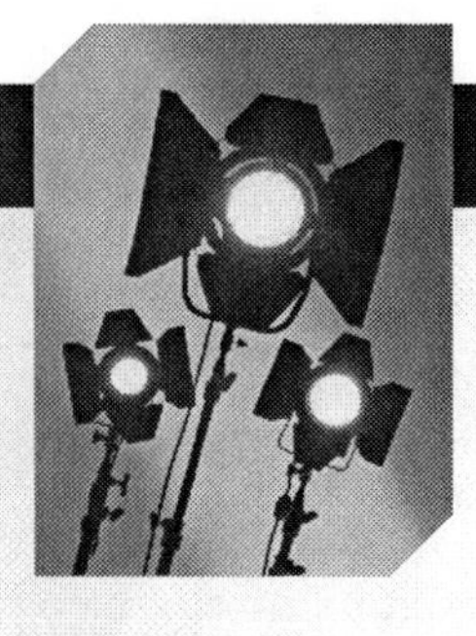

OM SPOTLIGHT

The Hazards of One-Piece Flow[25]

An investment foundry manufactures small parts for aircraft and stationary turbine engines. The company has about 4,000 active part numbers, and they have wide variations in routings and work content. The technology is difficult, making yields and scrap rates unpredictable. Much of the equipment is large and expensive. The company had tried to apply JIT principles, but the complex product and process mix had baffled all attempts to put them into practice. For example, the product and process did not lend itself to one-piece flow. Operation times were very short, about 15–20 seconds. The parts were very small (about 1-1/2 inches). One process step, shot-blasting, required a large batch (number) of parts in order to function properly. Compounding this was the excessive distance between machines. Only after 3 years of trial and error did the firm understand the real principles of JIT and understand how to adapt it to its environment. One partial solution was to redefine the word *piece* as a JIT container of 20 castings. Small carriers were built to carry 20 castings, and queues were set up to allow accumulation of a reasonable batch quantity for shot blasting.

SOLVED PROBLEMS

SOLVED PROBLEM #1

Bracket Manufacturing uses a Kanban system for a component part. The daily demand is 800 brackets. Each container has a combined waiting and processing time of 0.34 days. The container size is 50 brackets and the safety factor (α) is 9 percent.

a. How many Kanban card sets should be authorized?

b. What is the maximum inventory of brackets in the system of brackets?

c. What are the answers to (a) and (b) if waiting and processing time is reduced by 25 percent?

d. If we assume one-half the containers are empty and one-half full at any given time, what is the average inventory in the system for the original problem?

Solution:

a. Using Equation (17.2):

$$K = \frac{d(p + w)(1 + \alpha)}{C}$$

$$= \frac{(800 \text{ units})(0.34)(1 + 0.09)}{50} = 5.93$$

$\cong$ 6 (rounded up to 6)

Thus, 6 containers and 6 Kanban card sets are necessary to fulfill daily demand.

b. The maximum authorized inventory is $K \times C = 6 \times 50 = 300$ brackets.

c. $$K = \frac{d(p + w)(1 + \alpha)}{C}$$

$$= \frac{(800 \text{ units})(0.255)(1 + 0.09)}{50} = 4.45$$

$\cong$ 5 (rounded up to 5)

Thus, 5 containers and 5 Kanban card sets are necessary to fulfill daily demand. The maximum authorized inventory is now $K \times C = 5 \times 50 = 250$ brackets.

d. The average inventory under this assumption is 300/2 = 150 brackets. Many variables in the JIT system determine whether this assumption is valid or not. For example, for a given combination of daily demand, processing and waiting times, and other process inefficiencies and uncertainties, it is possible for more or less containers to be empty (full).

SOLVED PROBLEM #2

TAC Manufacturing is implementing lean ideas and methods in its factory. It wants to compute the takt time based on its gateway assembly workstation that pulls parts from preceding workstations. The assembly workstation is available 9 hours a day; with 1 hour for lunch and breaks, it's available 8 hours per day. Daily demand is 1,000 units per day.

a. What is the takt time?

b. Show that cycle time used in balancing an assembly line is the same as takt time used by lean practitioners.

Solution:

a. Using Equation (17.1), Assembly workstation takt

$$\text{time} = \frac{(8 \times 60 \times 60)}{1{,}000} = \frac{28{,}800 \text{ seconds/day}}{1{,}000 \text{ parts/day}}$$
$$= 28.8 \text{ seconds/part}$$

b. From Chapter 8, cycle time is related to the output rate (R) by the following equation:

$$C = A/R \qquad \textbf{(Equation 8.2)}$$

where A = available time to produce the output and R = output rate. By definition they are the same, so cycle time = takt time = 28.8 seconds/part.

KEY TERMS AND CONCEPTS

Batching
Continuous improvement
Efficient layout and standardized work
5Ss (sort, set in order, shine, standardize, and sustain)
JIT characteristics and best practices
Just-in-time (Kanban) system
Lean enterprise
Lean operating systems
Lean Six Sigma
Manufactured Good Recovery Options
- Cannibalize
- Recycle
- Refurbish
- Remanufacture
- Repair
- Resell

Number of Kanban cards (K)
Pull operating system
Push operating system
Quality at the source
Seven types of waste
Single minute exchange of dies (SMED)
Single-piece flow
Supplier relationships
Synchronous value chain operation
Takt time
Total productive maintenance (TPM)
Transfer batch
Value stream mapping
Visual controls (andon)
Zero waste

QUESTIONS FOR REVIEW AND DISCUSSION

1. What is lean enterprise?
2. Explain the four fundamental objectives of lean operating systems.
3. What are the categories of waste as defined by Toyota? Can you cite some examples from your work experience or around your college or university?
4. Provide some examples of different types of waste in an organization with which you are familiar, such as an automobile repair shop or a fast-food restaurant.
5. What do we mean by "synchronize the entire value chain"? Why is this important to becoming lean?
6. How does quality improvement support lean enterprise?

7. What are the benefits of adopting lean operating systems?
8. Describe three lean tools and how they contribute to lean objectives.
9. What is takt time, and how does it help to assess performance of the value chain?
10. Explain the limitations of batching and how single-piece flow overcomes these limitations. Under what conditions is batching useful?
11. What are the "5Ss"? Why are they important to becoming lean?
12. What benefits do visual controls have for lean operating systems?
13. Explain the importance of short setup times in a lean environment. What approach is used to reduce setup times?
14. What types of "setups" do you perform in your work or school activities? How might you reduce the setup times?
15. What is Lean Six Sigma? Why are lean and Six Sigma concepts highly complementary?
16. Explain the role of total productive maintenance in lean operating systems.
17. Summarize the options for manufactured good recovery. How does this approach support lean objectives?
18. Would you buy a certified remanufactured automobile transmission for 60 percent of the price of a newly manufactured transmission? Why or why not?
19. Explain the role of technology in lean operating systems. Can you think of other types of technology that can support lean enterprise?
20. Explain the difference between push and pull systems. What advantages do pull systems have over push systems?
21. What is a Kanban? Explain how a Kanban system operates.
22. Explain the water-level analogy with WIP inventory.
23. Describe some of the key features of good JIT systems.
24. What is the role of suppliers in JIT systems?
25. Does a high alpha value (say $\alpha = 2$ or 3) in Equation (17.2) negate the benefits of a Kanban/JIT operating system? Explain.
26. Explain how the JIT concept can be adapted to service organizations.
27. Interview a manager at a local company that uses JIT. Report on how it is implemented and the benefits the company has realized.
28. Identify and explain one key lesson or best practice from each of the following lean operating system tours: (a) Gortons, (b) Timken, (c) SBC Communications, and (d) Southwest Airlines.
29. Compare the lean-service system of Southwest Airlines to a full-service airline such as United or British Airways on the following: (a) airplane boarding process, (b) cabin service, (c) ticket transfer to other Southwest flights, (d) frequent-flyer program, (e) baggage handling, (f) seat assignment system, and (g) service encounters.
30. Search the Internet for some manufacturing or service tours similar to the ones in this chapter. Classify their practices according to lean principles in a manner similar to the examples.

PROBLEMS AND ACTIVITIES

1. Bracket Manufacturing uses a Kanban system for a component. Daily demand is 1,000 units. Each container has a combined waiting and processing time of 0.85 days. If the container size is 70 and the alpha value (α) is 13 percent, how many Kanban card sets should be authorized? What is the maximum authorized inventory?
2. Lou's Bakery has established that JIT should be used for chocolate chips due to the high probability of the kitchen heat melting the chips. The average demand is 180 cups of chocolate chips per week. The average setup and processing time is 1/2 day. Each container holds exactly 2 cups. The current safety stock factor is 5 percent. The baker operates 6 days per week.
   a. How many Kanbans are required for the bakery?
   b. What is the maximum authorized inventory?
   c. If the average setup and processing time is reduced to 3/8ths of a day due to better training and retention of experienced employees, what are the answers to (a) and (b)?

3. An automobile transmission manufacturer is considering using a JIT approach to replenishing its stock of transmissions. Daily demand for transmission #230 is 25 transmissions per day and they are built in groups of six transmissions. Total assembly and waiting time is 3 days. The supervisor wants to use an alpha value (α) of 3, or 300%.
   a. How many Kanbans are required?
   b. What is the maximum authorized inventory?
   c. What are the pros and cons of using such a high alpha (α) value?
4. CDC Discrete Fabricators wants to produce parts in batches of 300. Each part must be processed sequentially from workstation A to B to C to D. The following information is also provided:

Workstation	Batch Size (Q)	Processing Time per Part
A	300	20 seconds
B	300	15 seconds
C	300	10 seconds
D*	300	25 seconds

*Bottleneck workstation

   a. How many seconds are required to produce the batch under the assumptions of batch processing?
   b. How many seconds are required to produce the batch under the assumptions of single-piece flow processing?
   c. Compare the two solutions in terms of time saved and any other issue(s) you think important.

CASES

COMMUNITY MEDICAL ASSOCIATES

Community Medical Associates (CMA) is a large health care system with two hospitals, 25 satellite health centers, and 56 outpatient clinics. CMA had 1.5 million outpatient visits and 60,000 inpatient admissions the previous year. Just a few years ago, CMA's health care delivery system was having significant problems with quality of care. Long patient waiting times, uncoordinated clinical and patient information, and medical errors plagued the system. Doctors, nurses, lab technicians, managers, and medical students in training were very aggravated with the labyrinth of forms, databases, and communication links. Accounting and billing were in a situation of constant confusion and correcting medical bills and insurance payments. The complexity of the CMA information and communication system overwhelmed its people.

Prior to redesigning its systems, physicians were faced with a complex array of appointments and schedules in order to see patients in the hospital, centers, and clinics. For example, an elderly patient with shoulder pain would get an X-ray at the clinic but have to set up an appointment for a CAT scan in the hospital. Furthermore, the patient's blood was sent to an off-site lab while physician notes were transcribed from tape recorders. Radiology would read and interpret the X-rays and body scans in a consultant report. Past and present medication records were kept in the hospital and off-site pharmacies. Physicians would write out on paper prescriptions for each patient. Billing and patient insurance information was maintained in a separate database. The patient's medical chart was part paper-based and part electronic. The paper medical file could be stored at the hospital, center, or clinic. Nurses handwrote their notes on each patient, but their notes were seldom input into the patient's medical records or chart.

"We must access one database for lab results, then log off and access another system for radiology, then log off and access the CMA pharmacy system to gain anintegrated view of the patient's health. If I can't find the patient's records within 5 minutes or so, I have to abandon my search, and tell the patient to wait or make another appointment," said one doctor. The doctor continued, "You have to abandon the patient because you have to move on to patients you truly can diagnose and help. If you don't abandon the patient, you might make clinical decisions about the patient's health without having a complete set of information. Not having all the medical information fast has a direct impact on quality of care and patient satisfaction."

Today, CMA uses an integrated operating system that consolidates over 50 CMA databases into one. Health care providers in the CMA system now have access to these records through 7,000 computer terminals. Using many levels of security and some restricted databases, all patient information is accessible in less than 2 minutes. For example, sensitive categories of patient records, such as psychiatric and AIDS problems, were kept in super-restricted databases. It had cost CMA

$4.46 to retrieve and transport a single patient's paper-based medical chart to the proper location whereas the more complete and quickly updated electronic medical record costs $0.82 to electronically retrieve and transport once. A patient's medical records are retrieved on average 1.4 times for outpatient services and 6.8 times for inpatient admissions. In addition, CMA has spent more money on database security, although it has not been able to place a dollar value on this. Electronic security audit trails show who logs on, when, how long they view a specific file, and what information they viewed.

The same doctor who made the previous comments 2 years ago now said, "The speed of the system is what I like. I can now make informed clinical decisions for my patients. Where it used to take several days and sometimes weeks to transcribe my patient medical notes, it now takes no more than 48 hours to see them pop up on the CMA system. Often my notes are up on the system the same day. I'd say we use about one-half the paper we used with the old system. I also find myself editing and correcting transcription errors in the database—so it is more accurate now."

The next phase in the development of CMA's integrated system was to connect it to suppliers, outside labs and pharmacies, other hospitals, and to doctor's home computers.

Case Assignment Questions

1. Explain how CMA used the four principles of lean operating systems to improve performance.
2. Draw a current and future state of the value chain for CMA's situation as best you can from case information. Give two examples of how the value chain could be synchronized to improve value chain performance.
3. Do you think applying operations management concepts and methods such as Six Sigma and lean principles can reduce U.S. health care costs? Explain. Provide examples that show how OM can help the U.S. health care industry.

BENCHMARKING JIT AT TOYOTA[26]

Richard Keever is the plant manager for a supplier of axles and other components for SUVs produced by one of the domestic automobile manufacturers. His company had been using traditional batch production methods, but as the industry has become more competitive, and customers have been demanding just-in-time deliveries, Keever realized that he must make the transition to a JIT operating environment to improve speed and response, as well as reduce cost, to help sustain the company's current competitive advantage.

Keever is well aware of Toyota's reputation for lean enterprise and decided to make a benchmarking trip to the Toyota Motor Manufacturing (TMM) plant in Long Beach, California, to learn about its JIT processes. TMM fabricates, assembles, and paints four models of truck beds for Toyota light trucks. In touring the plant and talking with the plant's managers, many of whom were there when JIT was initially implemented back in the 1970s, Keever learned much about their approaches and implementation challenges.

Kanban is used at the Toyota Long Beach plant to control the flow of material and production operations. The Kanbans in this plant are traveling paper tickets containing detailed information that provides control requirements and even satisfies accounting and Internal Revenue Service needs. This is in contrast to many Japanese plants, where Kanbans are simple (usually triangular) pieces of metal with limited information. However, the managers were quick to point out that Kanban, by itself, is only a small piece of the total JIT planning and control system. The environment created by the Kanban attention and JIT philosophy is mostly responsible for continuous improvements in manufacturing and for reducing the WIP inventory.

Kanbans are often combined with bar coding to obtain rapid access to inventory-level information and to facilitate WIP cycle counting. Many types of Kanbans are used to trigger different operations or to order raw material. The Kanbans are placed on hooks on a board beside the entrance to each area. The hook board is the staging area for the Kanbans, which circulate between the suppliers and the warehouse, the warehouse and the press department, and so on.

TMM cycles 4,000 to 5,000 Kanbans per day, which requires an immense amount of manual sorting and placing on the proper hooks each day. The company uses a single-Kanban method of recirculation, whereby the Kanban represents both the authority to produce and also the move and identification ticket. The hook board is color-coded, as are the Kanbans, to indicate raw material or other stages of manufacturing. The motto, of course, is "no Kanban—no production."

An attempt is made to decrease the number of Kanbans each month to constantly drive down the in-process inventory and increase the inventory cycles. The objective is to reduce the lot sizes to one and the WIP inventory to zero. However, the schedule is not as rigid as in many other plants. A small safety stock is considered acceptable to allow for some flexibility in shifting the sequence of the operations or the mixture of the products. It also enables the plant to meet the schedule without exhausting the supply and interrupting the line. In the paint and stamping operations, the nature of manufacturing calls for a certain quantity per production run. In this case, a number of Kanbans accumulate before they trigger the production of the preceding operation.

The master schedule is used to calculate the number of Kanbans. The calculations are simple and mostly manual. The products are made to order, which is anticipatory due to the difficulty of coordination with Japan in terms of the precise timing and destination of the orders. Additional flexibility is built in to allow for changing priorities. Ideally, the truck should arrive in time for the bed to be assembled and then shipped to the dealers and delivered to the customers. Study teams are constantly working to coincide the orders without sacrificing the flexibility and the ability to deliver the trucks to the customers.

Visual controls are used wherever possible, using color, light boards, hook boards, charts, and graphs. The visual controls facilitate immediate identification of problems, such as shortage or excess of parts as well as any other unusual occurrence. Visual controls are also extended to testing and shipping areas. They are easy to understand and inexpensive and they allow for immediate detection. There is a control chart for each critical operation, graphing the performance of that operation versus the acceptable level. A buzzer is used to indicate a problem or a failure in a function. An unusually long buzz notifies the supervisor that the machine is out of sequence and additional help should be dispatched.

A computerized board in the assembly area contains many colored lights indicating the status of machines and orders. Another board provides information on the scheduled versus the actual production as well as the reason for the variance. It provides workers with immediate feedback and general awareness to assist them in taking corrective action when needed.

At TMM, many workers voluntarily belong to quality improvement teams, which meet weekly in paid overtime. The company initially established a team in the press area and then in the paint and the maintenance areas. The overall trend has been a rapid growth in the number of quality teams, the number of suggestions made, and the quality and complexity of suggestions. These teams were a great source of problem solving in preparation for JIT implementation.

The quality teams are particularly useful in implementing changes that workers tend to oppose. A JIT system requires many drastic changes in manufacturing. Quality teams may be used to educate workers as to the benefits of JIT and convince them that making the necessary changes is worthwhile. Quality teams may also be used to implement and support the required changes very quickly. They usually solve a number of smaller problems while they are working on the main problem. Employee suggestions are well recognized by TMM managers and rewarded, though not necessarily financially. The company has firmly maintained the policy of retaining any worker whose job is eliminated in the productivity-improvement process by transferring his or her employment to another area.

Prior to using the JIT system at the Long Beach plant, the amount of raw material and WIP inventories and also of finished goods in the shipping area was of great concern to managers. Another concern was hidden problems in quality and material-handling procedures. A worker could produce several hours' worth of defective units before they were discovered. When JIT was first implemented, the immediate improvement was the reduction of inventories, which resulted in a major reduction in carrying and handling costs. The average WIP inventory was lowered by about 45 percent and the raw-material inventory by approximately 24 percent in 1 year. The warehousing cost of material was reduced by about 30 percent; the carrying and control costs were lowered accordingly.

As the inventory was drained, the overloaded buildings were emptied, and many hidden problems in handling and moving the material surfaced. The warehouse was reorganized, and the additional space was utilized for other productive purposes. Improvements in handling procedures resulted in shorter movement distances and fewer needs for equipment.

The material was delivered directly to the point of use. About 30 percent of the forklifts were eliminated as the average movement time and distance were reduced. In the production area, the number of presses was reduced by 30 percent. The same operations were performed with an approximately 20 percent reduction in labor, and the production volume per shift was increased by 40 percent in less than 2 years. Some of these improvements were direct results of JIT production, but many were simply due to changes made by the workers, inspired by the JIT atmosphere. The outgoing product quality was improved and warranty costs and replacement parts were reduced substantially.

The most noticeable improvements were in worker attitudes and awareness. The JIT environment offers continuous challenge in the sense that there is no reserved inventory to comfort production. As a problem arises in the sequence, the line comes to a halt immediately. Thus, the workers are constantly stimulated to discover problems and fix them. As a side benefit, absentee rates and labor turnover were substantially reduced.

During his flight back, Richard began thinking of what he needed to do to plan for implementing JIT in his plant.

Case Assignment Questions

1. What lessons did Keever learn from his benchmarking trip to Toyota?
2. What significant challenges or barriers might he face in his plant if he implemented JIT?
3. What should he tell his managers and workers tomorrow?
4. Develop a plan to implement JIT with an emphasis on what to do early in the JIT initiative.

JIT IN MAIL-ORDER PROCESSING[27]

Semantodontics is a direct marketing company that sells nationally by catalog to dentists. One of its major product lines is "personalized brochures, business cards, and patient medical handouts for dental practices." This product line was creating a larger-than-normal number of customer complaints, resulting in an increasing number of calls to the customer service department. A study of the reasons for customer service calls indicated that 64 percent of them involved two questions: What is this charge on my statement? and Where is my order?

After some investigation, both of these questions were found to be related to the long lead times required to produce personalized printed products. Customers often waited 3 or more weeks, and some statements mailed at the end of the month showed charges for orders invoiced but not yet printed. Therefore, the company began to study the process involved in meeting customer orders.

Exhibit 17.11 is a flowchart of the order-filling process. In the first step, telephone orders were taken over a 12-hour period each day. They were collected at the end of the day and checked for errors by the supervisor of the call center, usually the following morning. Depending on how busy the supervisor was, the 1-day batch of print orders would often not get to the data-processing department until after 1:00 P.M.

In the data-processing step, the telephone orders were invoiced, still in 1-day batches. Then the invoices were printed and matched back to the original orders. This step usually took most of the next day to complete. At this point in the process, if the order was for a new customer, it was sent to the person who did customer verification and set up new customer accounts on the computer. Setting up a new account would often delay an order by a day or more.

The next step was order verification and proofreading. Once invoicing was completed, the orders with invoices attached were given to a person who verified that all the required information was present and correct to permit typesetting. If there was a question at this time, the order was checked by computer or by calling the customer. It was common for this step to have a 2-day backlog of orders waiting for verification.

Finally, the completed orders were sent to the typesetting department of the print shop. Using current methods, an order for an existing customer took at least 4 days to flow from the order taker to typesetting. Often, a new customer's order took a day or two longer. In addition, there was often more than a 1-day backlog of orders at each step in the process.

Case Assignment Questions

1. Evaluate the current process from the perspective of lean operating systems and as a value stream. Outline some improvements to make this operation leaner and explain why you think your ideas will lead to improved performance.
2. It was determined that the new-customer setup procedure was the bottleneck for about 20 percent of the orders. Customer verification required looking up the customer in various directories or checking with the customer by telephone. This often took a day or more to complete. Can you think of ways to improve this?
3. Should Semantodontics set up a web site for online ordering by customers with or without human intervention? What problems do you anticipate with ordering personalized printed material online for a dental practice? Explain.
4. Define a possible future state map for this process, and explain why it should be adopted.

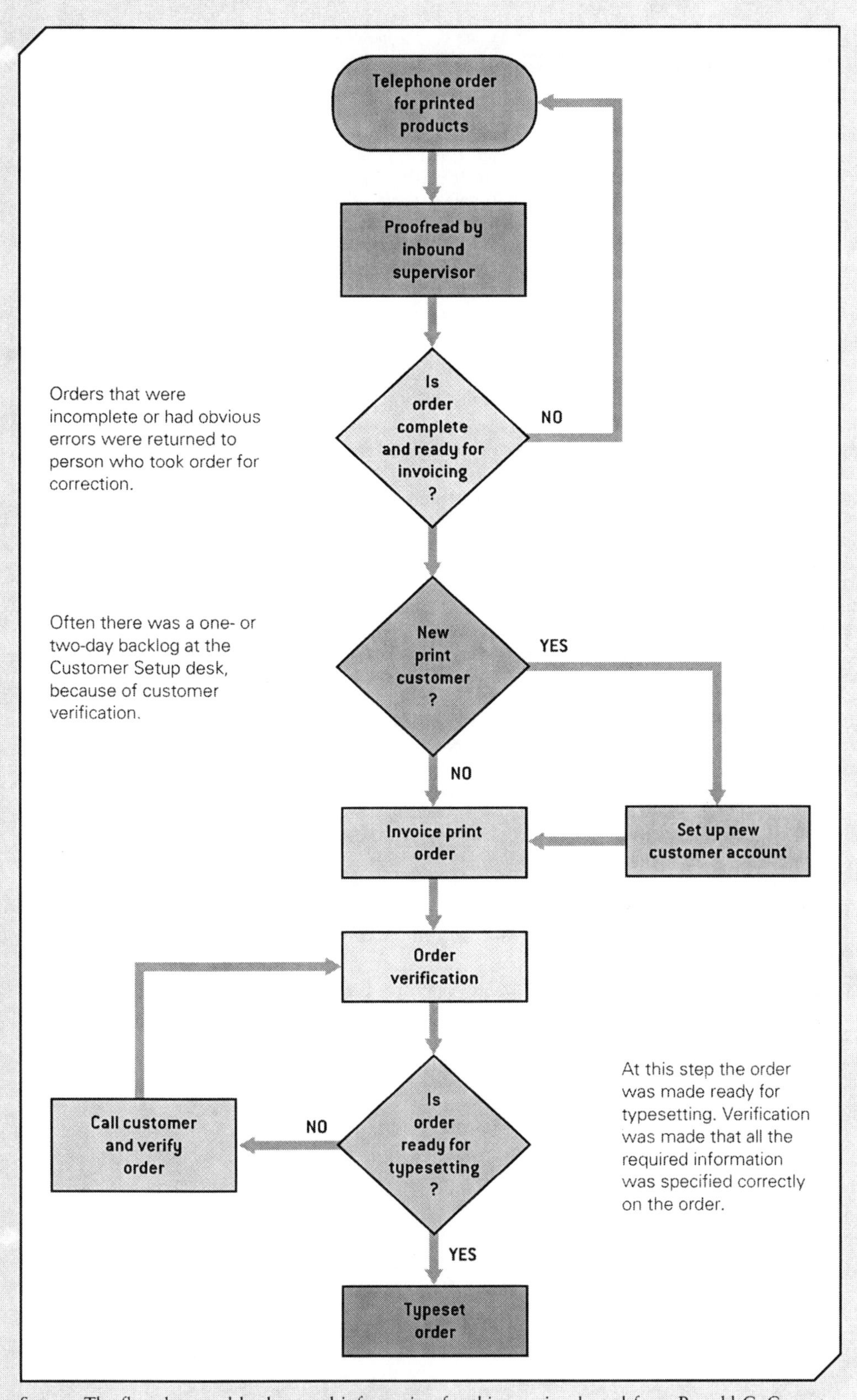

Exhibit 17.11
Flowchart of Semantodontics Order-Filling Process

Source: The flowchart and background information for this case is adapted from Ronald G. Conant, "JIT in Mail-Order Operation Reduces Processing Time from Four Days to Four Hours," *Industrial Engineering* 20, no. 9 (1988), pp. 34–37. Reprinted with permission from Industrial Engineering.

ENDNOTES

[1] Woodruff, David, "Porsche is Back—and Then Some," *Business Week*, September 15, 1997, p. 57.
[2] Okes, Duke, "Organize Your Quality Toolbelt," *Quality Progress*, July 2002, pp. 25–29.
[3] Taylor, Alex, III, "How Toyota Defies Gravity," *Fortune*, December 8, 1997, pp. 100–108.
[4] Goland, Anthony R., Hall, John, and Clifford, Devereaux A., "First National Toyota," *The McKinsey Quarterly*, no. 4, 1998, pp. 58–66.
[5] Sources include the web site (http://www.tiautomotive.com) and a presentation by Eva Stewart, Lean Manufacturing Manager, TI Automotive, Center for Excellence in Manufacturing Management (CEMM), Fisher College of Business, Ohio State University, April 12, 2004.
[6] Van, Jon, "Leaks No Longer Stain Harley-Davidson Name," *Chicago Tribune*, November 4, 1991, p. 16.
[7] Schonberger, Richard J., "Just-in-Time Production Systems: Replacing Complexity with Simplicity in Manufacturing Management," *Industrial Engineering* 16, no. 10, October 1984, pp. 52–63.
[8] "Thinking Machines," *Business Week Online*, August 7, 2000. http://www.businessweek.com/archives/2000/b3693096.arc.htm.
[9] Henkoff, Ronald, "Delivering the Goods," *Fortune*, November 28, 1994, pp. 64–78.
[10] Conner, Gary, "Benefiting from Six Sigma," *Manufacturing Engineering*, February 2003, pp. 53–59.
[11] http://www.strategosinc.com/mnt.htm.
[12] Nakajima, Seiichi, "Explanation of New TPM Definition," *Plant Engineer* 16, no. 1, pp. 33–40.
[13] Maggard, Bill N., and Rhyne, David M., "Total Productive Maintenance: A Timely Integration of Production and Maintenance," *Production and Inventory Management Journal* 33, no. 4, Fourth Quarter 1992, pp. 6–10.
[14] "Ink Fight Stains Printer Companies," *The Columbus Dispatch*, Columbus, Ohio, May 6, 2002, p. E4.
[15] Thierry, M., Salomon, M., Nunen, J., and Wassenhove, L., "Strategic Issues in Product Recovery Management," *California Management Review* 37, no. 2, Winter 1995, p. 118.
[16] Whiteacre, J., "Lean Success in the Plant, the Supply Chain, and the Office," http://www.leanadvisors.com/lean/articles/gortons2004.cfm.
[17] Ellis, R., and Hankins, K., "The Timken Journey for Excellence," Presentation for the Center of Excellence in Manufacturing Management, Fisher College of Business, Ohio State University, Columbus, Ohio, August 22, 2003. Also see Timken's 2003 Annual Report and "From Missouri to Mars—A Century of Leadership in Manufacturing," http://www.timken.com.
[18] Collier, D. A., and Wilson, D. D., "The Role of Automation and Labor in Determining Customer Satisfaction in a Telephone Repair Service," *Decision Sciences* 28, no. 3, 1997, pp. 689–708; and Collier, D. A., and Wilson, D. D., "A Structural Equation Model of a Telephone Repair Service Process," *Proceedings of the Western Decision Sciences Institute*, Hawaii, March 25–29, 1997, pp. 584–586.
[19] "Unisys R2A Scorecard—Airline Industry Cost Measurement," Figure 1, *Unisys Corporation* 1, no. 2, November 2002, pp. 1–2.
[20] "Unisys R2A Scorecard—Airline Industry Cost Measurement," Figure 8, *Unisys Corporation* 1, no. 2, November 2002, p. 5.
[21] Freiberg, Kevin, and Freiberg, Jackie, *Nuts!*, Austin, TX: Bard Press, 1996, p. 59.
[22] Dickinson, Paul E., Dodge, Earl C., and Marshall, Charles S., "Administrative Functions in a Just-in-Time Setting," *Target*, Fall 1988, pp. 12–17.
[23] Inman, R., and Mehra, S., "JIT Implementation within a Service Industry: A Case Study," *International Journal of Service Industry Management* 1, no. 3, 1990, pp. 53–61.
[24] Freudenheim, Milt, "Removing the Warehouse from Cost-Conscious Hospitals," *The New York Times*, Sunday, March 3, 1991, p. F5.
[25] http://www.strategosinc.com/onepieceflow_1.htm.
[26] The information about Toyota is adapted from Sepehri, Mehran, "How Kanban System Is Used in an American Toyota Motor Facility," *Industrial Engineering* 17, no. 2, 1985.
[27] The flowchart and background information for this case is adapted from Conant, Ronald G., "JIT in a Mail-Order Operation Reduces Processing Time from Four Days to Four Hours," *Industrial Engineering* 20, no. 9, 1988, pp. 34–37.

PURCHASING
and
SUPPLY

Taken from PURCHASING AND SUPPLY CHAIN MANAGEMENT by Robert M. Monczka | Robert B. Handfield | Larry C. Giunipero | James L. Patterson, 2009

Chapter 6

SUPPLY MANAGEMENT AND COMMODITY STRATEGY DEVELOPMENT

Learning Objectives

After completing this chapter, you should be able to

- Align the supply management and enterprise objectives
- Recognize a category strategy
- Understand category strategy development
- Identify the types of supply management strategies
- Understand e-reverse auctions
- Develop sourcing strategies

Chapter Outline

Building the 787 Dreamliner: The Critical Role of Supply Management

Boeing Co. recently announced that its new wide-body jet, the 787 Dreamliner, will be delayed by at least six months, a blow for the company's ambitious plan to revamp how it builds airplanes by having suppliers take on a greater role. Jim McNerney, their CEO, noted that "notwithstanding the challenges that we are experiencing in bringing forward this game-changing product, we remain confident in the design of the 787, and in the fundamental innovation and technologies that underpin it." This strategy indeed represents an entirely new approach to building airplanes that relies much more on sourcing strategy. In planning for the 787, Boeing remade its production process to rely heavily on major suppliers as risk-sharing partners. In return for investing more up front and taking on a share of the development costs, suppliers have been given major sections of the airplane to build. The wing sections are made in Japan, whereas factories in Italy, South Carolina, and Wichita, Kansas, assemble the bulk of the fuselage. The parts are flown aboard modified 757 cargo planes to Everett, Washington, for final assembly.

Boeing says that when the system is up and running, it will eventually be able to snap together Dreamliners in as little as three days, not unlike how plastic model airplanes are assembled. Further, Boeing officials say the system has reduced the company's upfront development costs by billions of dollars. The downside? Boeing has less control over the day-to-day progress of the Dreamliner program than it has had for any new airliner in its history.

However, unlike the delays that have plagued Airbus, which has delayed its A380 jetliner by two years, Boeing says the problems don't point to a fundamental flaw in its design, but rather involve difficulties in the supply chain. For example, since the summer of 2007, the industry has been beset by a shortage in titanium and aluminum fasteners used to hold airplanes together. Boeing's problems were exacerbated because suppliers are working with composite materials instead of the more familiar aluminum. After a major ceremony on July 8 when the first Dreamliner was unveiled before a crowd of more than 15,000 guests, the plane actually had to be largely disassembled by unfastening the thousands of fasteners on the body. Suppliers hadn't preinstalled wiring or other major components needed to make the system work smoothly. Once engineers got inside, it became evident that it would take more time to put the plane back together than anticipated.

Outsourcing design to suppliers has definitely proven to increase the risk associated with developing new products. For more than a year, teams of Boeing experts have lived on the road, troubleshooting problems at factories all over the globe, and making sure they have enough raw materials to do their work. In some cases, such as with a factory that was erected in Charleston, South Carolina, by Italy's Alenia Aeronautica SpA and Bought Aircraft Industries Inc. of Dallas, relatively inexperienced workers were hired from the local area to begin building an airplane that is technically more advanced than any commercial airplane in history! "If there's a lesson learned, you'd start earlier and do a little more training with our people there," said Scott Carson, chief executive of Boeing's Commercial Airplanes unit. Carson noted that unlike the previous schedule, the new delivery schedule has a margin built in for unexpected problems that might arise during flight testing, which gives Boeing "much more confidence in our ability to deliver this plane on time."

Source: J. L. Lunsford, "Boeing Delays 787 by Six Months as Suppliers in New Role Fall Behind," *Wall Street Journal,* October 11, 2007, p. A1.

Remaining competitive means that supply management must contribute to profitability by focusing on not only cost savings, but contributions to top-line growth and innovation. World-class supply management requires that leaders align with business unit stakeholders, understand their direct and indirect requirements for success, develop a deep insight into the global supply market's ability to meet these requirements, and negotiate contracts and manage supplier relationships that create a competitive advantage. This is a dynamic and difficult task, given the complexity and challenges that exist under current market conditions.

This chapter focuses on the contribution that supply management can make to a firm's competitive position and how this contribution should filter down to category management teams. A **category** refers to a specific family of products or services that are used in delivering value to the end customer. We begin by discussing how supply management executives can contribute to the strategic plan at the companywide level. In order to contribute to corporate strategy, supply management must be able to translate corporate objectives into specific supply management goals. Supply management goals serve as the driver for both strategic supply management processes and detailed commodity strategies—specific action plans that detail how goals are achieved through relationships with suppliers. To illustrate this, we provide a step-by-step process employed by category teams that is used to define business requirements, research the supply market, and develop a plan to source the product or services. We conclude with some specific examples of category strategies that best-in-class firms are deploying to cope with an increasingly challenging set of circumstances in today's supply market.

Aligning Supply Management and Enterprise Objectives

A company's leadership team, in defining how the firm will compete and succeed in the global environment, must clearly and succinctly communicate the following to their executive team:

- What markets will the firm compete in, and on what basis?
- What are the long-term and short-term business goals the company seeks to achieve?
- What are the budgetary and economic resource constraints, and how will these be allocated to functional groups and business units?

When faced with these challenges, business unit functions must then work together to define their functional strategies, which are a set of short-term and long-term plans that will support the enterprise strategy.

The first part of this process requires that the leadership team understand its key markets and economic forecasts, and provide a clear vision of how the enterprise will differentiate itself from its competitors, achieve growth objectives, manage costs, achieve customer satisfaction, and maintain continued profitability in order to meet or exceed the expectations of stakeholders.

Although it is beyond the scope of this chapter to go into detail regarding corporate strategies, the economics associated with corporate strategy are fairly straightforward. An organization must take in more revenues than it spends on operating costs

Exhibit 6.1 How Companies Create Shareholder Value

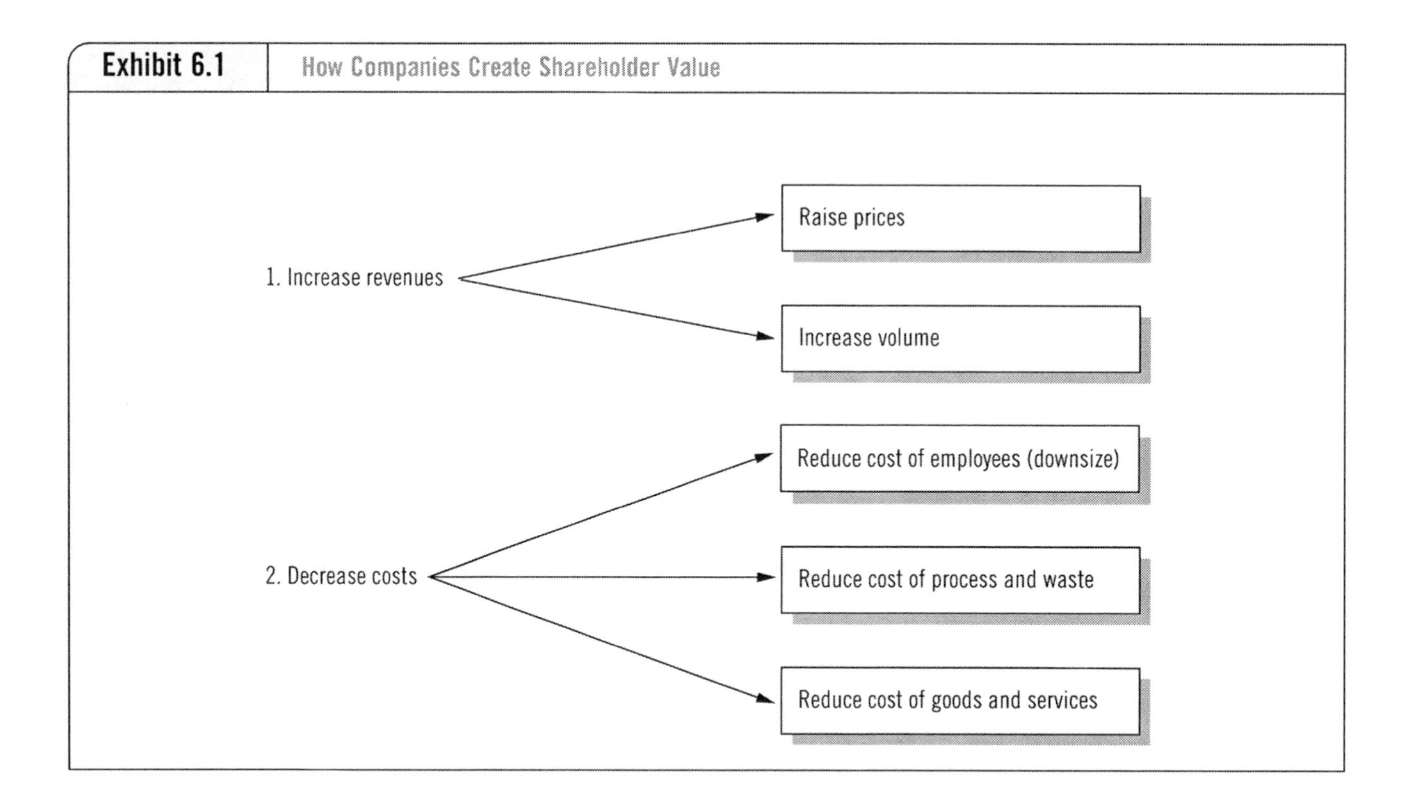

in the long term to grow and increase profits. As shown in Exhibit 6.1, there are two fundamental ways of balancing this equation: increase revenues or decrease costs.

Increasing revenues involves either raising prices or keeping prices stable and increasing volume. Simultaneously, costs must be held steady or must increase at a rate smaller than the rate of increasing revenues. However, this option has become increasingly more difficult to realize over the last several years. Since 2004, prices for commodities such as nickel, steel, oil and gas, coal, resin feedstocks, and copper have doubled or tripled. To combat these trends, many firms have sought new suppliers in China, India, and Asia, to counteract these higher costs with lower labor costs. As a result, inflation has been largely kept at bay, and the number of competitively priced, higher-quality products has increased. Today, there are only a few markets in which a seller can increase or even hold prices steady. For example, the price of automobiles has remained largely stable, even as the cost of materials going into these cars has increased dramatically.

Reducing costs has become an area of intense interest. Faced with global competition, companies are constantly searching for ways to reduce costs and pass the savings on to customers while preserving their profit margins and maintaining a return to shareholders.

Reducing the cost of materials and services has remained an important enterprise objective. Another is innovation. Firms are constantly seeking to find the next new technology that will create new markets and capture a share of consumers' wallets. Consider the iPod and the massive market for online music that followed this innovation.

Integrative Strategy Development

The process of aligning supply management goals with corporate objectives is especially important for supply management and supply chain managers. These managers often face some very broad directives from corporate management—for example, to reduce costs or to improve quality. The strategy development process takes place on four levels:

- Corporate Strategies: These strategies are concerned with (1) the definition of businesses in which the corporation wishes to participate and (2) the acquisition and allocation of resources to these business units.
- Business Unit Strategies: These strategies are concerned with (1) the scope or boundaries of each business and the links with corporate strategy and (2) the basis on which the business unit will achieve and maintain a competitive advantage within an industry.
- Supply Management Strategies: These strategies, which are part of a level of strategy development called functional strategies, specify how supply management will (1) support the desired competitive business-level strategy and (2) complement other functional strategies (such as marketing and operations).
- Commodity Strategies: These strategies specify how a group tasked with developing the strategy for the specific commodity being purchased will achieve goals that in turn will support the supply management–, business unit–, and ultimately corporate-level strategies.

Companies that are successful in deploying supply chain strategies do so because the strategy development process is **integrative**. This means that the strategy is drafted by (or has significant input from) those people responsible for implementation.

Exhibit 6.2 Components of Integrative Strategy Development

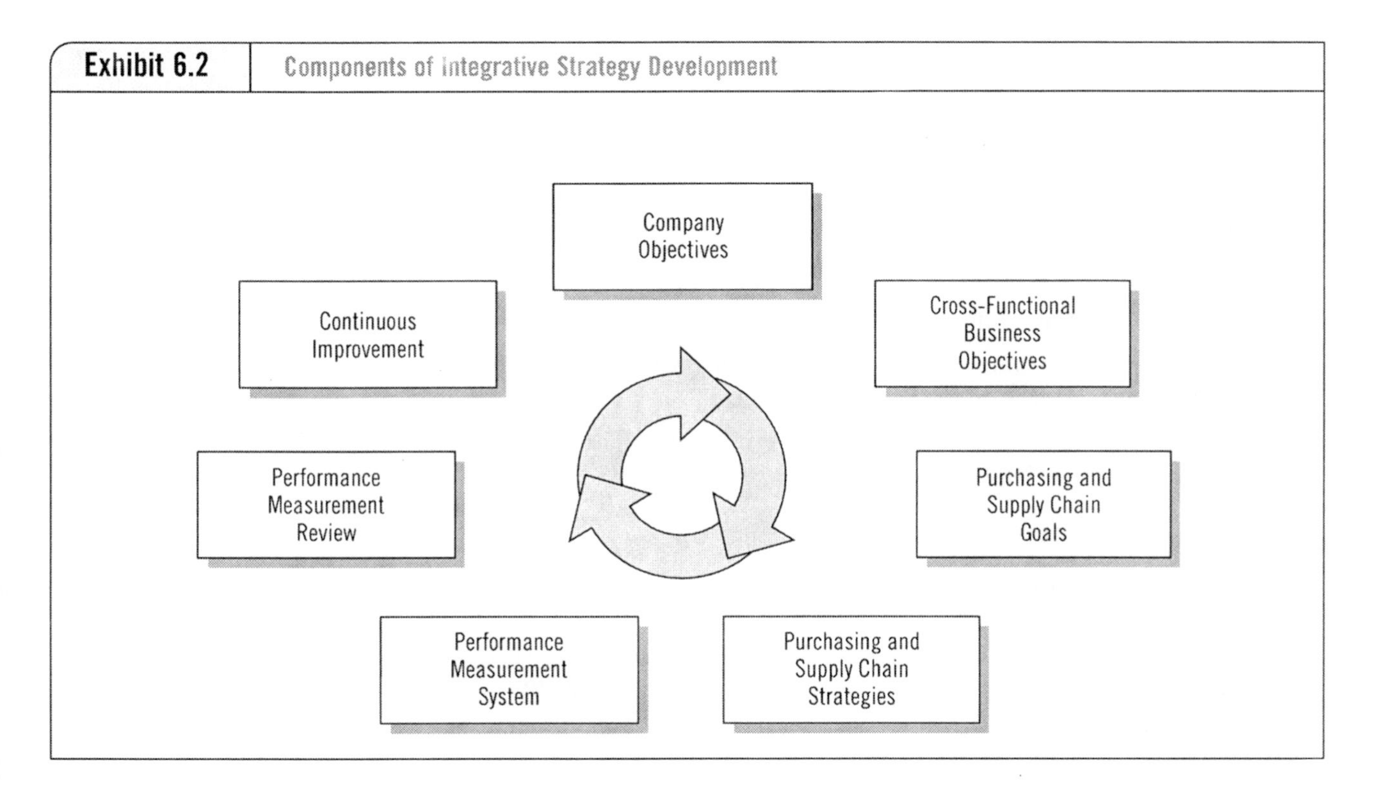

Integrative supply chain strategies occur when corporate strategic plans are effectively "cascaded" into specific supply management and commodity goals, through a series of iterative planning stages (shown in Exhibit 6.2). Corporate strategy evolves from corporate objectives, which effectively evolve from a corporate mission statement drafted by the chief executive officer (CEO), functional executives, and the board of directors. Corporate strategies are crafted by the CEO, taking into consideration the organization's competitive strengths, business unit and functional capabilities, market objectives, competitive pressures and customer requirements, and macroeconomic trends. What distinguishes an integrative strategy development process is that business unit executives, as well as corporate supply management executives, provide direct input during the development of corporate strategy.

Translating Supply Management Objectives into Supply Management Goals

A major output of the strategy development process is a set of functional strategic objectives, including supply management strategic objectives. As supply management managers interact with other members within their business, as well as with corporate executives, a major set of strategic directives should begin to emerge. These strategic objectives may or may not provide details concerning how they are to be achieved. However, the process is not yet complete. Unless supply management executives can effectively translate broad-level objectives into specific supply management goals, these strategies will never be realized.

Supply management must couple each objective with a specific goal that it can measure and act upon. These specific goals become the initial step for a detailed commodity strategy formulation process. Remember—objectives drive goals, whether at the highest levels of an organization or at the functional or department level. The following are examples of corporatewide supply management goals associated with various supply management objectives.

Cost-Reduction Objective

- Be the low-cost producer within our industry. (Goal: Reduce material costs by 15% in one year.)
- Reduce the levels of inventory required to supply internal customers. (Goal: Reduce raw material inventory to 20 days' supply or less.)

Technology/New-Product Development Objective

- Outsource non-core-competency activities. (Goal: Qualify two new suppliers for all major services by end of the fiscal year.)
- Reduce product development time. (Goal: Develop a formal supplier integration process manual by the end of the fiscal year.)

Supply Base Reduction Objective

- Reduce the number of suppliers used. (Goal: Reduce the total supply base by 30% over the next six months.)
- Joint problem-solve with remaining suppliers. (Goal: Identify $300,000 in potential cost savings opportunities with two suppliers by the end of the fiscal year.)

Sourcing Snapshot

Ford Rebuilds Its Supply Base

In the latest sign of how U.S. automakers are rethinking their business, Ford Motor Co. plans to overhaul its $90-billion-a-year global purchasing process to offer larger, long-term contracts to a smaller group of suppliers on future models, a switch that could save billions of dollars a year. In particular, Ford will tap seven major suppliers in its initial effort to streamline parts purchasing (see table below as compiled from company sources).

COMPANY (LOCATION)	SOME KEY PRODUCTS
Autoliv (Stockholm)	Safety systems such as seat belts and airbags
Delphi (Troy, Michigan)	Steering systems; remote keyless entry systems
Johnson Controls (Milwaukee)	Seats; instrument panels; batteries
Lear (Southfield, Michigan)	Seats; instrument panels; acoustics
Magna International (Aurora, Ontario)	Center consoles; interior mirrors; transmission parts
Visteon (Van Buren Township, Michigan)	Heating and cooling systems; lighting
Yazaki (Tokyo)	Wire harnesses; advanced electronics

The initial phase of the plan covers more than $35 billion in Ford purchasing for 20 key parts such as seats, tires, and bumpers. Ford will cut by more than half the number of suppliers from whom it buys these parts, starting with vehicles that will be built in 2008–2009 and beyond, Ford officials said.

That effort in turn promises a shake-up in the beleaguered auto-parts industry, a key part of the nation's manufacturing base. In recent months, several auto suppliers have filed for Chapter 11 bankruptcy protection amid broader pressure on the industry from the rising price of oil, steel, and other commodities and their inability to raise prices as car companies maintain steep consumer discounts.

Globally, there are an estimated 5,000 direct suppliers of parts to the auto industry, with combined sales in excess of $500 billion, according to CSM, a Farmington Hills, Michigan–based auto research and production firm.

Ford's move to revamp how it buys everything from paint to health care is the latest stage in the efforts of Chairman and Chief Executive Officer William Clay Ford Jr. to turn around the nation's No. 2 automaker, whose automotive business reported a $1.1 billion operating loss in the second quarter and whose debt recently was downgraded to junk-bond status. It comes at a time when the big U.S. automakers are facing profit-margin squeezes from steep discounting, rising gasoline prices, and fierce competition from Asian rivals.

Source: J. McCracken, "Ford Seeks Big Savings by Overhauling Supply System: No. 2 Automaker Will Offer Larger and Longer Contracts but Use Fewer Companies," *Wall Street Journal*, September 29, 2005, p. A1.

Supply Assurance Objective

- Assure uninterrupted supply from those suppliers best suited to filling specific needs. (Goal: Reduce cycle time on key parts to one week or less within six months.)

Quality Objective

- Increase quality of services and products. (Goal: Reduce average defects by 200 ppm on all material receipts within one year.)

The next level of detail requires translating companywide supply management goals into specific commodity-level goals.

What Is a Category Strategy?

Although not always the case, companies often use commodity teams to develop supply management strategies. Supply management strategies often apply to categories—general families of purchased products or services. Examples of major commodity classifications across different industries include body side moldings (automotive), microprocessors (computer), steel (metalworking), cotton (apparel), wood (pulp and paper), petroleum products (chemicals), outsourced business processes (IT programming, call centers), and office supplies (all industries). A category team is often composed of personnel from the operational group, product design, process engineering, marketing, finance, and supply management. The personnel involved should be familiar with the commodity being evaluated.

For instance, if the team is tasked with supply management computers, then users from information systems should be included. If the team purchases vehicles and vehicle parts, then it would be a good idea to include maintenance managers who are familiar with the characteristics of these commodities. In general, the more important the commodity, the more likely that cross-functional members and user groups will be involved. Together, the commodity team will develop a commodity strategy that provides the specific details and outlines the actions to follow in managing the commodity.

As noted in previous sections and shown in Exhibit 6.2, supply management derives its strategic direction from corporate objectives and the business unit strategy development process.

The business unit functional strategy acts as the driver for the cross-organizational supply management strategies that emerge for the major products and services purchased by the business unit. These in turn translate into supply management goals. Once supply management has identified a set of broad-level goals that it must achieve, another set of more detailed strategies should emerge at the commodity/service/product family level. The process of supply management strategy deployment effectively begins at the commodity/product family level.

Before initiating any category strategy, there must be buy-in from the key stakeholders, especially at the senior leadership level. Without executive commitment, strategic sourcing results are unlikely to be successful. To ensure buy-in of the corporate team, supply management must clearly define the "prize" or carrot at the end of the stick, to obtain the go-ahead to pursue the strategy. To enable an effective category strategy, the team must:

1. Spend money on resources initially, including assessment of current spend, data collection, market research, training, and people.
2. Validate the savings or contribution to other company objectives achieved by supply management and drive them to the bottom line.

3. Sustain the initiative through presentations to senior executives who support the move toward an integrated supply management function with other functional groups in the supply chain, including marketing, research and development, and accounting.

The individual who will ensure that this can happen will often report to the chief financial officer (CFO)—so making a solid business case is an important element in building support for category strategies in most firms.

A study[1] conducted by Accenture, Stanford, and INSEAD found that 89% of senior executives at leading companies view supply chains as critical or very important to their company and industry, and 89% also agreed investments in supply chain capabilities have increased in the last three years. Chief financial officers are especially interested. Driven by cost-cutting needs and general dissatisfaction with supply chain performance, CFOs are adding supply chain management to the financial levers they already control.[2] They see this activity as integral to meeting their strategic goals and view the supply chain as having a large or very important effect on their ability to achieve corporate objectives. Above all else, CFOs consider reducing operating costs as a key goal of their supply chain, with improving customer service coming in a close second. This suggests that CFOs are not just obsessed with financial rigor but also appreciate the importance of customer-relationship management to the future of their organizations.

According to the survey, 34% of CFOs have taken more of a leadership role in supply chain management, and 49% believe that they will be playing such a role in two years. And CFOs see themselves as suited to the task; they wield significant corporate power, yet have no ax to grind in a supply chain sense because they are not bound by the traditional political and organizational ties that anchor this discipline within companies. CFOs can bring "a certain degree of coherence to what may be a fragmented reporting structure," said Gene Long, president of UPS Consulting. Because they are already charged with managing cash and capital allocations, in a supply chain sense they "probably are in a critical position to be able to manage the tradeoffs that should be made," Long said. Also, he said CFOs are adept at quantifying value, something that supply management can benefit from. In many cases this is already happening; 20% of respondents said that senior supply chain professionals already report to the CFO, but the survey indicates that this will become more widespread, enabling financial executives to take a more proactive role.

The most common approach for building a business case is through an annual process review of where the company is spending its money: the "spend analysis."

Conducting a Spend Analysis

As we discussed in Chapter 2, a robust procure to pay process is critical, in order to facilitate an accurate spend analysis. Why is it important to capture the transaction-level data associated with all purchasing processes? Because from time to time the firm must identify opportunities for savings through a process known as a spend analysis. A spend analysis becomes a critical input into building category strategies.

A **spend analysis** is an annual review of a firm's entire set of purchases. This review provides answers to the following questions:

- What did the business spend its money on over the past year? (This value is an important component in calculating the cost of goods sold in the financial statement. Purchased goods and materials are often more than 50% of the total cost of goods sold.)

- Did the business receive the right amount of products and services given what it paid for them? (This is an important requirement to meet the legal requirements of the Sarbanes Oxley Act, which requires accountability and correct reporting of financial statements to the SEC.)
- What suppliers received the majority of the business, and did they charge an accurate price across all the divisions in comparison to the requirements in the POs, contracts, and statements of work? (This is an important component to ensure contract compliance.)
- Which divisions of the business spent their money on products and services that were correctly budgeted for? (This is an important component for planning annual budgets for spending in the coming year.)
- Are there opportunities to combine volumes of spending from different businesses, and standardize product requirements, reduce the number of suppliers providing these products, or exploit market conditions to receive better pricing? (This is an important input into strategic sourcing planning, the topic of the next chapter in the book.)

Moreover, a spend analysis provides insights and clarity into these questions and becomes an important planning document for senior executives in finance, operations,

Exhibit 6.3 Best Practices in Spend Analysis

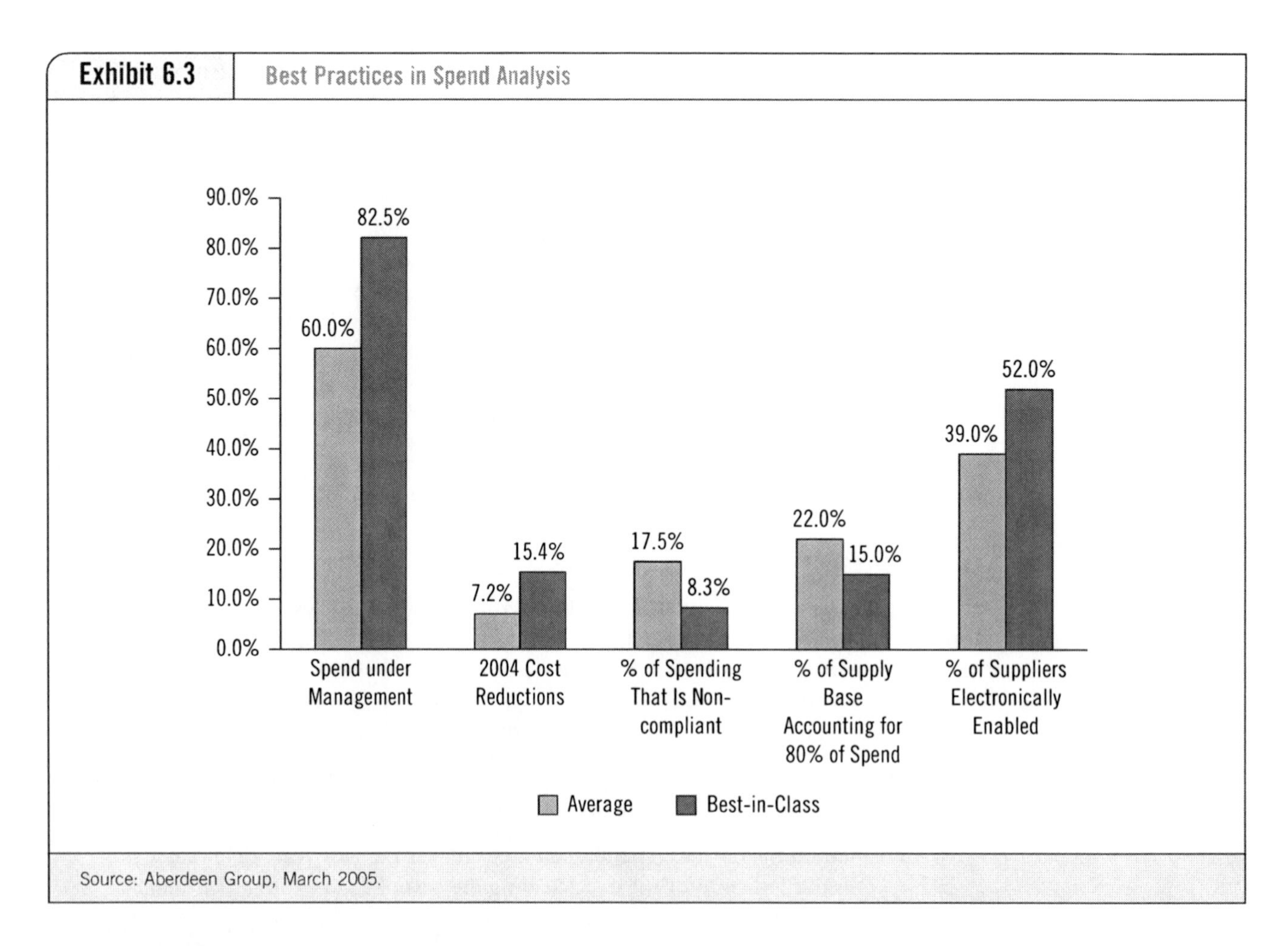

Source: Aberdeen Group, March 2005.

marketing, purchasing, and accounting. Despite the importance of this element, many firms struggle to develop a comprehensive and accurate spend analysis report. This is because purchasing was for many years a paper-based system, and figures were not entered correctly into accounting systems. Even with the evolution of sophisticated enterprise systems such as SAP and Oracle, purchasing transactions are often entered incorrectly, which elicits the old phrase "garbage in, garbage out." Another problem is that many enterprises have grown through mergers and acquisitions. When a new division is acquired, they may be using a different system from the acquiring company, and so the data is not easily translatable. For this reason, many firms are undergoing major initiatives to streamline procurement through electronic procurement systems that will revamp the purchase to pay process and automate different portions to capture transactions more effectively. Indeed, the research shown by Aberdeen Research in Exhibit 6.3 on p. 197 suggests that "best in class" firms are more likely to have a higher proportion of their spend under management, which has led to important improvements such as cost reductions, reduction of noncompliant purchases, supply base reduction, and electronically enabled suppliers.

Spend Analysis Spreadsheet

Assuming that a spend database is available and is reasonably accurate, how do firms produce a spend analysis? The best way to illustrate is to go through a specific example of a spend analysis and identify the requirements at each stage.

Exhibit 6.4 Example of Spend Analysis

SUPPLIER	COMMODITY	ANNUAL SPEND
REBATE CO	Rebate Fulfillment & Call Center	$329,873,663
INVEST CO	Investments	$130,328,512
ADVERT CO	Advertising	$ 56,134,490
REPAIR CO	Service Repairs	$ 49,339,218
BENEFITS CO	Benefits	$ 48,969,149
HARDWARE CO	Hardware	$ 40,572,450
PARTCO	Service Parts	$ 39,910,372
TELECOM	Telecommunications	$ 31,055,599
DISPLAY CO	Store Displays	$ 30,020,969
PENPAPER CO	Paper	$ 29,175,843
LABOR CO	Contract Labor	$ 27,880,363
SUPPLY CO	Paper	$ 23,844,707
CONTRACT CO	General Contracting	$ 22,579,113
OFFICE CO	Paper	$ 22,257,690
GRAPHICS CO	Graphic Design	$ 21,966,989
PAYMENT CO	Business & Management Services	$ 20,380,275
FREIGHT CO	Surface Freight	$ 19,369,010
PAPER CO	Paper	$ 15,603,682
SERVICE PLAN CO	Service Plan	$ 15,478,827
SERVICE CO	Service Parts	$ 14,868,023
CONSUMER CO	Consumer Financing	$ 14,833,333
ENERGY CO	Energy	$ 14,087,177

Exhibit 6.4 shows spend data sorted by descending dollar. Note that the dataset contains information on the general classification or "commodity," the primary supplier for that category, and the dollar amount spent with that supplier in that commodity. It is important to note that there may be multiple suppliers that supply a single commodity, and vice versa (multiple commodity classifications supplied by a single supplier). The entire spreadsheet is NOT shown in this case; in fact, the spreadsheet has over 2,500 lines in it, and this would be considered a simple spend analysis. Many datasets have literally millions of transactions in them. With this information in hand, you can proceed as follows:

1. The first step is to take this information and sort the data by commodity. In this case, a commodity is a "category" of spending.
2. From the commodity sort, find the total spend by commodity. (Hint: The subtotal or pivot table functions in Excel can help.) Calculate the total spend by commodity.
3. Make a chart of the top 10 commodities by descending $ spend. A Pareto chart is used to show the total value of spend that occurs within each category. As shown in Exhibit 6.5, the top 10 categories of spending are rebate fulfillment and call center spending, advertising, general contracting, hardware, investments, paper, service parts, business and management services, contract labor, and telecommunications. These areas represent the highest level of spend and, therefore, the biggest opportunity for sourcing analysis and opportunities for cost savings and price reductions. But we aren't done yet!
4. From the commodity sort, find the number of suppliers by commodity. (Hint: The pivot table function in Excel can help.) Perform a descending sort of number of suppliers by commodity.

Exhibit 6.5 Pareto Chart of Spend by Commodity Category

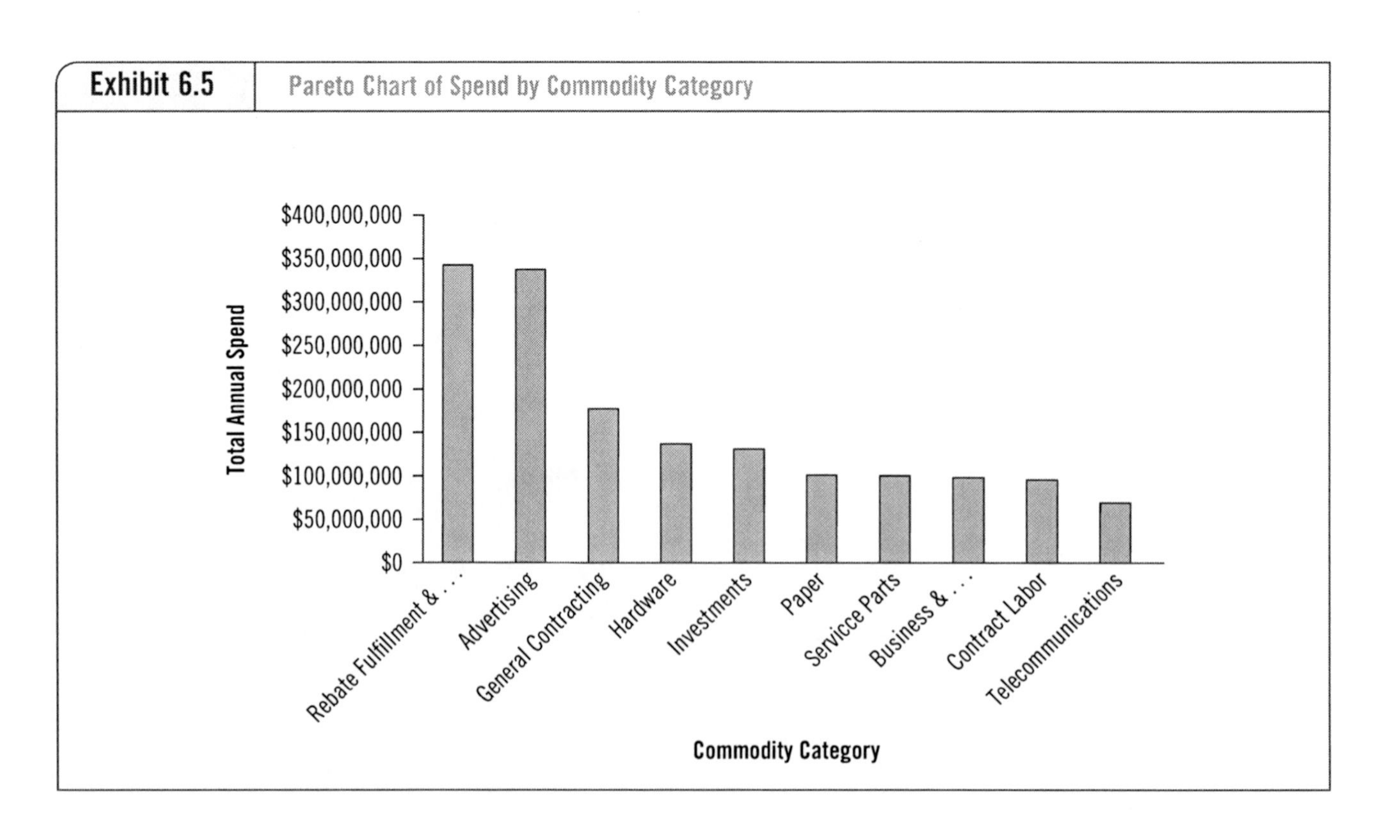

5. Make a chart of the top ten commodities by descending number of suppliers. As shown in Exhibit 6.6, the advertising category has the highest number of suppliers within it, followed by other miscellaneous small dollar suppliers (who might be supplying office products or other noncritical items), energy, security, general contracting, and business and management services. It is amazing that this firm is using almost 2,500 different suppliers of advertising! However, this is not uncommon, as business units will often use their own local preferred supplier, because they are nearby and they know them. Although this is appropriate in some cases, it may also be an opportunity for supply base reduction and further cost savings.
6. From the commodity sort, find the average spend per supplier by commodity. Perform an ascending sort of average spend per supplier. Exhibit 6.7 shows the categories that have the lowest volume of spending by supplier. A low spend per supplier figure is indicative that there are too many suppliers in that category, as the volume per supplier should be increased. It is interesting that none of these parameters show up in the other two charts, suggesting that there may or may not be an opportunity worth pursuing in the categories shown in these charts.
7. Applying the concept of Pareto analysis to the chart of top 10 commodities by descending $ spend, what are the recommendations for savings opportunities?

From Exhibit 6.5, the areas of Rebate Fulfillment and Advertising are clear areas for savings opportunities. As shown in Exhibit 6.8, total spend for this company is $2,449,428,985, of which 14% ($342M) and 13.8% ($336M) are in these two areas alone. Note that overall, these 10 categories constitute 65% of the company's total spend. Further analysis shows that rebate fulfillment only has eight suppliers, although

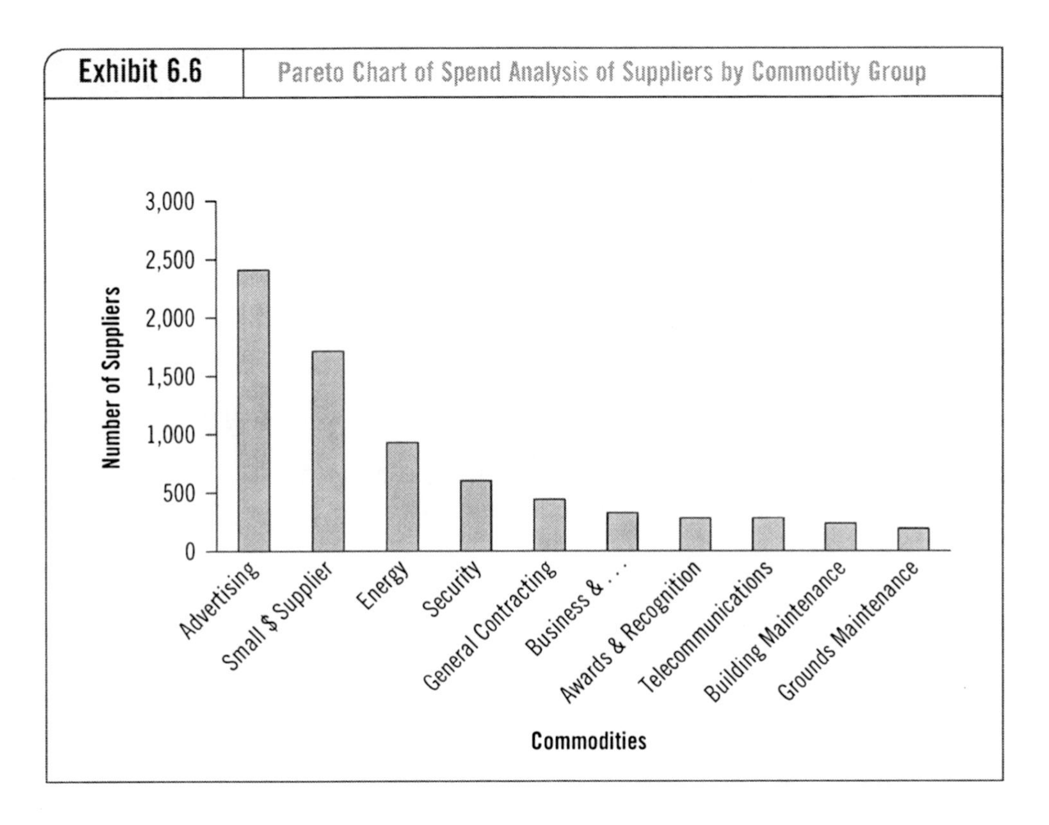

Exhibit 6.7 Pareto Chart of Spend per Supplier by Commodity

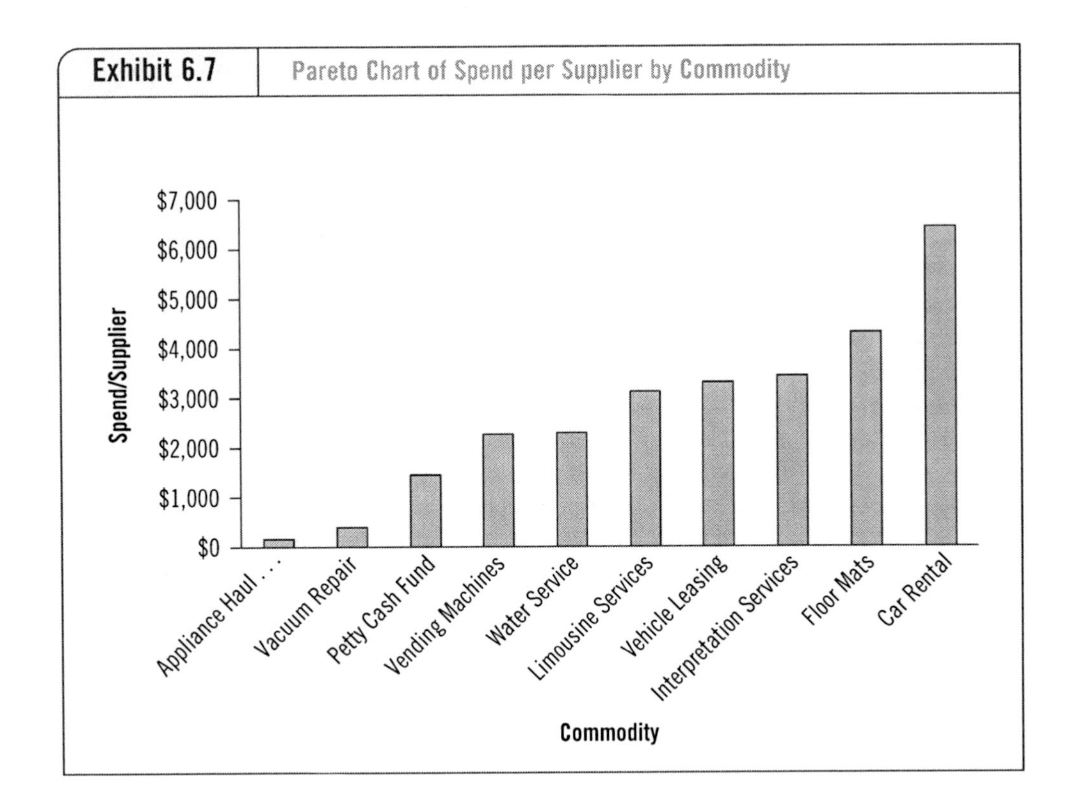

Exhibit 6.8 Pareto Chart by Percentage of Total Spend by Category

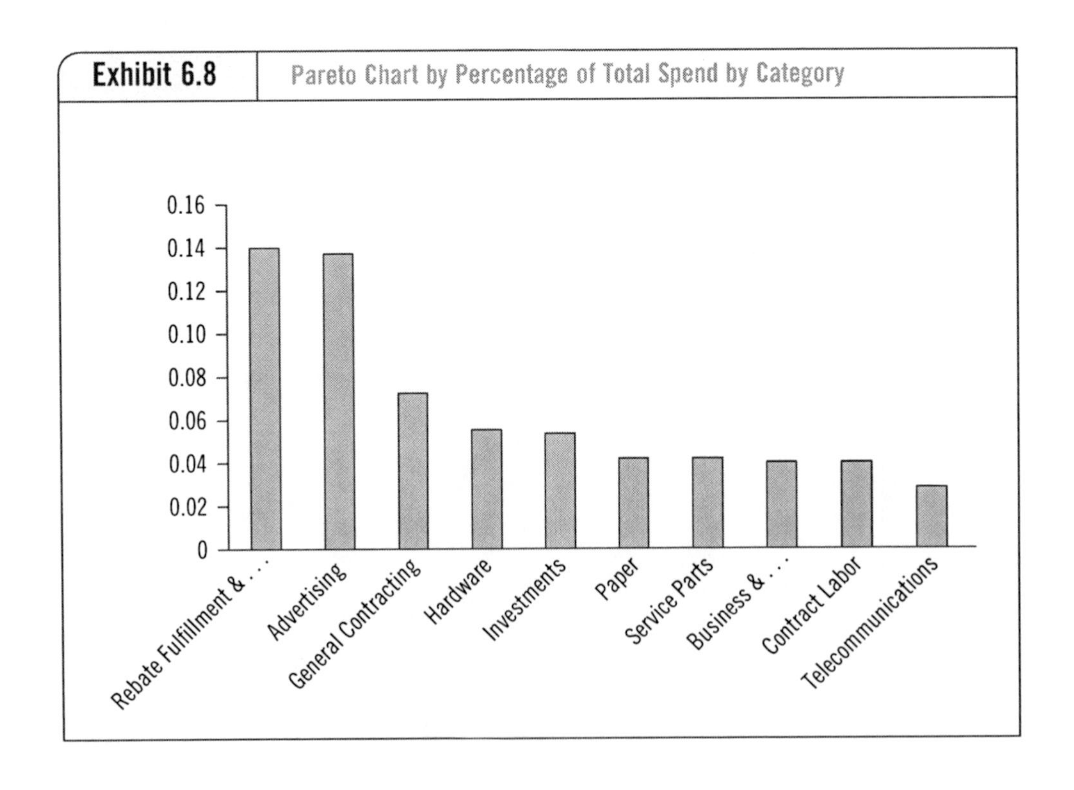

advertising has close to 2,400! Clearly, by reducing the number of suppliers in the advertising sector, spend volumes can be leveraged and more favorable pricing can be achieved, leading to a significant cost savings (perhaps on the order of 5–10%), which could lead to a net bottom line contribution of between $17M and $33M!

The same logic applies to general contracting, although the size of this opportunity is not as great. With close to 500 suppliers of this service, and the third highest spend ($175M), further negotiation and supply base reduction could lead to additional savings of $8–$17M. Combined, these two initiatives alone could contribute up to $50M of net savings to this enterprise, which could either be utilized in other investments, or passed on to shareholders in the form of increased profitability and shareholder value.

Not bad for a day's work!

From this analysis, the supply management team might approach the senior leadership team and ask for resources to deploy two category management teams: one in the rebate fulfillment services area, and another in the advertising sector. If approved, the deliverables might be, say, a 5% savings on current spend in these two areas.

Sourcing Snapshot

Shipping Shortages Drive Raw Material Costs

Category strategies do not just focus on commodities and goods, but also on services such as transportation. For many commodities, raw material costs are increasingly being driven by the cost of shipping. The cost of shipping raw materials across the world's oceans has reached an all-time high in October 2007, pushing up prices of grain, iron ore, coal, and other commodities. The average price of renting a ship to carry raw materials from Brazil to China has nearly tripled to $180,000 from $65,000 a year ago. In some cases, ocean shipping can be more expensive than the cargo itself. Iron ore, for example, costs about $60 a ton, but ship owners are charging about $88 a ton to carry it from Brazil to Asia. The trend is forcing many manufacturers to pay more for basic ingredients, which will probably be passed on to consumers, affecting everything from automobiles to washing machines and bread. The main reason for these shipping rates escalating is that there are not enough bulk ships. The shortage is related to the fact that explosive growth in China, India, and other developing nations is driving a need for importing of raw materials, such as iron ore from Brazil. Experts believe that shipping rates are not through escalating, either. New batches of bulk freighters are not expected to come online until 2010. "All of the ship owners are making a lot of money because these are numbers the market has never seen," said John P. Dragnis, commercial director of Goldenport Inc., one of the largest providers of ships to commodity sellers. And even when ships are available, bottlenecks at port facilities can cause delays, driving up the costs of shipments. At many ports in Brazil, Australia, and elsewhere, wait times have increased by 35%. The Baltic Exchange Dry Index, which reflects rates to transport bulk commodities such as coal, iron ore, and grains in vessels of typical sizes, is up from 4000 in October of 2006 to 11,000 in October 2007. Don't expect it to go away soon, as Chinese and Indian manufacturers tie up more ships in their hunger for more raw materials to drive their economies.

Source: R. G. Matthews, "Ship Shortage Pushes Up Prices of Raw Materials," *Wall Street Journal,* November 12, 2007, p. A1.

Category Strategy Development (Strategic Sourcing)

Once the decision has been made to outsource a product or service, firms will typically use a process known as strategic sourcing to decide to whom to outsource the product or service, as well as the structure and type of relationship that should be established. A sourcing strategy is typically focused on a category of products or services, and for that reason, the strategy is sometimes called a category strategy. A category strategy is a decision process used to identify which suppliers should provide a group of products or services, the form of the contract, the performance measures used to measure supplier performance, and the appropriate level of price, quality, and delivery arrangements that should be negotiated. A typical category may include many smaller subcategories. For example, a category around information technology may include subcategories such as laptops, desktops, servers, and keyboards. If a firm outsources accounting services, the category strategy may include tax accountants and managerial accountants. The strategic sourcing decision is typically made by a cross-functional team, composed of sourcing professionals, operations managers, finance, or other stakeholders for the product or service. A stakeholder is someone who is impacted by the sourcing decision. They have a stake in the game, so to speak, so their input in the sourcing decision is critical to reaching a successful sourcing decision. The sourcing process is described below and is shown in Exhibit 6.9.

Exhibit 6.9 Strategic Sourcing Process

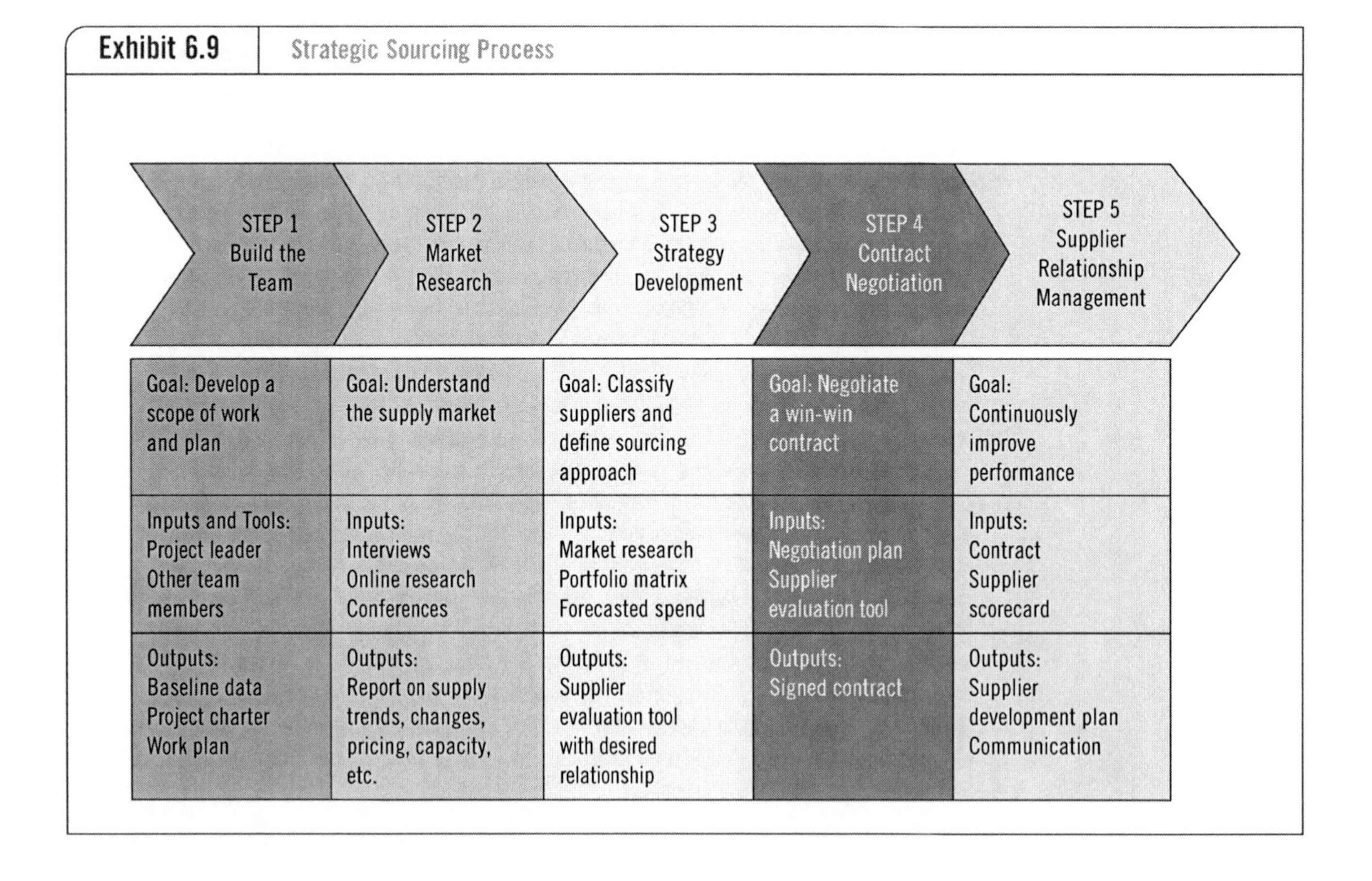

Step 1: Build the Team and the Project Charter

Companies are increasingly using a team approach to sourcing decision making by bringing together personnel from multiple functions who are familiar with the product to be purchased. Part of the first phase of the category management process is to identify the people who should be involved, as well as the key subject matter experts who may be part of the extended team. Once developed, the team should then define the scope of the category strategy, publish a project charter, and develop a work plan and communication plan. These steps help to define the purpose, boundaries, and goals of the process; identify the tasks involved; and provide a plan for communicating the results to the primary stakeholders.

A category team can be composed of personnel from operations, product design, process engineering, marketing, finance, and purchasing. The personnel involved should be familiar with the commodity being evaluated. For instance, if the team is tasked with purchasing computers, then users from information systems should be included. If the team purchases vehicles and vehicle parts, then it would be a good idea to include maintenance managers who are familiar with the characteristics of these commodities. In general, the more important the commodity, the more likely that cross-functional members and user groups will be involved. Together, the commodity team will develop a commodity strategy that provides the specific details and outlines the actions to follow in managing the commodity. Strong skills in team building and leadership, decision making, influencing internal users and suppliers, and compromising in reaching a team consensus are therefore critical skills found in individuals who will succeed in these roles.

Every sourcing team should begin by assigning a project lead, who will coordinate meetings, project deliverables, and requirements. The project lead will assemble a group of subject matter experts from various stakeholder groups in the team to provide feedback and assist with delivering the project charter. The project charter is a clear statement of the goals and objectives of the sourcing project, which is officially announced shortly after the team's first few meetings. The project charter can be issued before or after the cross-functional sourcing team has been formed, and in fact, it can be used to garner interest from potential participants in the process. The purpose of a project charter is to demonstrate management support for the project and its manager.

Step 2: Conduct Market Research on Suppliers

The second step when developing a sourcing strategy is to fully understand the purchase requirement relative to the business unit objectives. Also involved in this step is a thorough supplier spend analysis to determine past expenditures for each commodity and supplier, as well as the total expenditures for the commodity as a percentage of the total. Note that the spend analysis identified in the prior section looked at spending for the entire company. A category spend analysis will drill down to a more granular level and identify the specific business units that are purchasing the products or services, and which suppliers they are currently using. Generally, this produces a Pareto chart as shown before; often one or a handful of suppliers are the primary sources of the majority of spending in a particular category. After understanding the spend, the category team should also educate themselves as to what is happening in the marketplace, as well as what their internal customer requirements are. Just as you would perform research before buying a car (e.g., going online, reading reviews of vehicles, looking into gas mileage, and looking at warranty history reports at

Consumer Reports), teams perform the same type of market research on the supply base. This is critical in building and understanding the key suppliers, their capabilities, and their capacity to perform and meet the stakeholders' requirements.

To make an informed decision about sourcing, several pieces of information are needed. These include the following:

- Information on total annual purchase volumes. This is often an important element from the spend analysis. This analysis should show how much was spent on the category of goods or services by supplier, by business unit, and by subgroups.
- Interviews with stakeholders to determine their forecasted requirements. For example, if the annual purchase volume last year was $10 million, is this figure expected to go up or down next year based on the predicted amount of work? Stakeholders should also be interviewed to determine any new sourcing elements that may not have been included in last year's figure.
- External market research identifying information on key suppliers, available capacity, technology trends, price and cost data and trends, technical requirements, environmental and regulatory issues, and any other data that is available. In effect the team must educate themselves through a detailed analysis of the marketplace and identify how best to meet the forecasted demand (generated by the spend analysis and interviews with stakeholders) given the market conditions that will occur in the next year.

The data can be collected in a number of ways. For example, the team might elect to meet with a supplier that is an expert on the marketplace, or an external consultant who specializes in studying certain markets (e.g., chemicals, resins, IT providers). These interviews are often the best source of information and are not published. Secondary data sources are published available databases, reports, websites, and so on. Examples might be a "state of the industry" report purchased from a consulting company or a publicly available database such as the Census of U.S. Manufacturers or the U.S. Department of Labor Statistics. The problem with secondary data such as these is that they are often outdated and may not provide the specific information the team is looking for.

When conducting market research, the team may use an outsourced provider such as Beroe (www.beroe-inc.com), ICE, or Global Outlook. However the data are collected, the team must also process and integrate the data to ensure that they are relevant and can be effectively communicated to stakeholders. The whole point of conducting market research is to understand the prevailing market conditions and the ability of current or potential new suppliers to effectively deliver the product or service. In that respect, supply market intelligence becomes one of the most important and critical stepping stones for an effective category strategy. As one manager noted, "Supply market intelligence may be the only competitive advantage of the future!"

Where do most firms go to find good market intelligence? There are multiple sources of market and supplier information available. The key here is to **triangulate**, which means that you need to explore, compare, and contrast data from multiple sources before you can validate it. Triangulation is part of the scientific method and requires that you establish corroborating data to validate a given hypothesis. The more data points you have supporting the hypothesis, the greater the likelihood that the hypothesis is correct. Your job is to go through these sources and identify key elements that support your hypothesis.

- Trade journals are a great place to start. These journals provide good leads and recent updates to what is happening in the industry.
- Start also with annual reports for supplier companies, as well as other customers, and make sure you read the notes to investors.
- The Internet is great and provides a ton of leads.
- Don't forget the power of books. Many people just start by using Google, which leads you to a massive set of links that may or may not be useful. A visit to a university library can lead you to some great reference books and trade journals, with multiple leads for further information.
- The power of snowball sampling is important. This means finding experts in a particular category, who can refer you to other experts whom you can also talk to.
- There are trade consultants who can provide information, but they are very often costly.
- Category managers will also visit trade association conferences and trade websites. These conferences offer a great opportunity to network and learn more from other people who know a lot about what is going on in the industry.
- You've got to be scanning the headlines.
- Suppliers are about the best sources. Don't just talk to salespeople. Talk to the line and their purchasing people.
- Investment analyst reports, as well as interviews, can provide very good information on what is happening in certain industries where they are investing.

Collecting the data is just the first part of the job. To effectively represent and communicate the market conditions, category teams may employ a number of different data representation tools to portray and explain the current situation. Three tools we will discuss here are Porter Five Forces analysis, SWOT analysis, and supplier analysis.

Porter Five Forces

Porter Five Forces was created to describe competitive forces in a market economy. Porter Five Forces is a heavy-hitting strategy development tool that is used widely for business strategy development and sales and marketing strategies. The five forces are the forces that shape an industry (see Exhibit 6.10).

Michael Porter's industry analysis methodology was introduced in his book *Competitive Strategy,* first published in 1980 and now in its 60th printing. The powerful tool provides understanding of an industry with a simple framework.

Data for creation of a Five Forces analysis requires a review of all of the different data sources described to date in this section. It may also involve deep market intelligence through focused discussions with key stakeholders and subject matter experts. The tool helps to predict supplier and buyer behavior in the marketplace and is a critical element in shaping supply strategy. Five Forces analysis is close to a crystal ball and can be used to predict the future. It is also a helpful educational tool to lead stakeholders to understand current supply market conditions. When you understand your supplier's needs, you can figure out how you can help them help you.

Exhibit 6.10 Porter's Five Forces Analysis

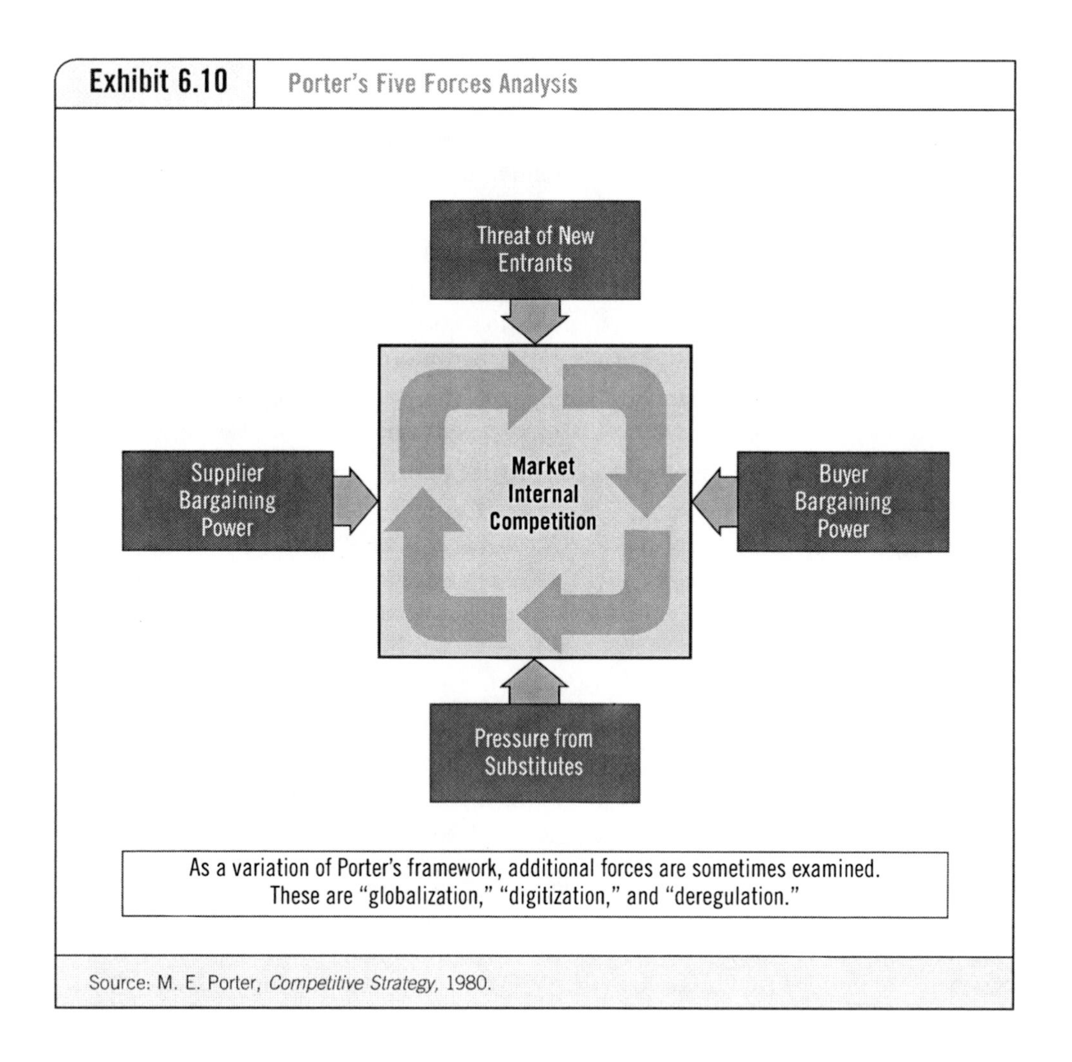

Source: M. E. Porter, *Competitive Strategy*, 1980.

The following are the five forces:

1. Higher levels of competition create more options for buyers and suppliers. Factors include the following:
   - Speed of industry growth
   - Capacity utilization
   - Exit barriers
   - Product differences
   - Switching costs
   - Diversity of competitors
2. The threat of new entrants. Examples here might be the new set of Chinese and other low-cost-country manufacturers that are entering many of the traditional U.S. manufacturing strongholds such as electronics and automobiles. Factors include the following:
   - Capital markets
   - Availability of skilled workers
   - Access to critical technologies, inputs, or distribution
   - Product life cycles

- Brand equity/customer loyalty
- Government deregulation
- Risk of switching
- Economies of scale

3. The threat of substitute products and services. For example, there are a new set of growing composites, thermosets, and carbon fibers that are replacing traditional elements such as steel. Factors influencing this include the following:
   - Relative performance of substitutes
   - Relative price of substitutes
   - Switching costs
   - Buyer propensity to substitute
4. The power of buyers. For example, as buyers begin to consolidate specifications and develop industry standards, increasing power is created over suppliers in the marketplace. Factors include the following:
   - Buyer concentration
   - Buyer volume
   - Buyer switching costs
   - Price sensitivity
   - Product differences
   - Brand identity
   - Impact on quality or performance
   - Buyer profits
   - Availability of substitutes
5. The power of suppliers. As many supply markets begin to consolidate, fewer suppliers means that a greater amount of supplier power exists in markets. Factors include the following:
   - Prices of major inputs
   - Ability to pass on price increases
   - Availability of key technologies or other resources
   - Threat of forward or backward integration
   - Industry capacity utilization
   - Supplier concentration
   - Importance of volume to supplier

Generally speaking, summarizing these elements requires that participants take a high-level view of the marketplace and begin to brainstorm and review the implications of these changes in the marketplace.

SWOT Analysis

An analysis that examines strengths, weaknesses, opportunities, and threats (SWOT) can provide insight even with limited data. (It is often a good way to figure out what data you have and where there are gaps.) As a strategic planning tool, the goal is to minimize weakness and threats, and exploit strengths and opportunities (see Exhibit 6.11).

Exhibit 6.11 SWOT Analysis

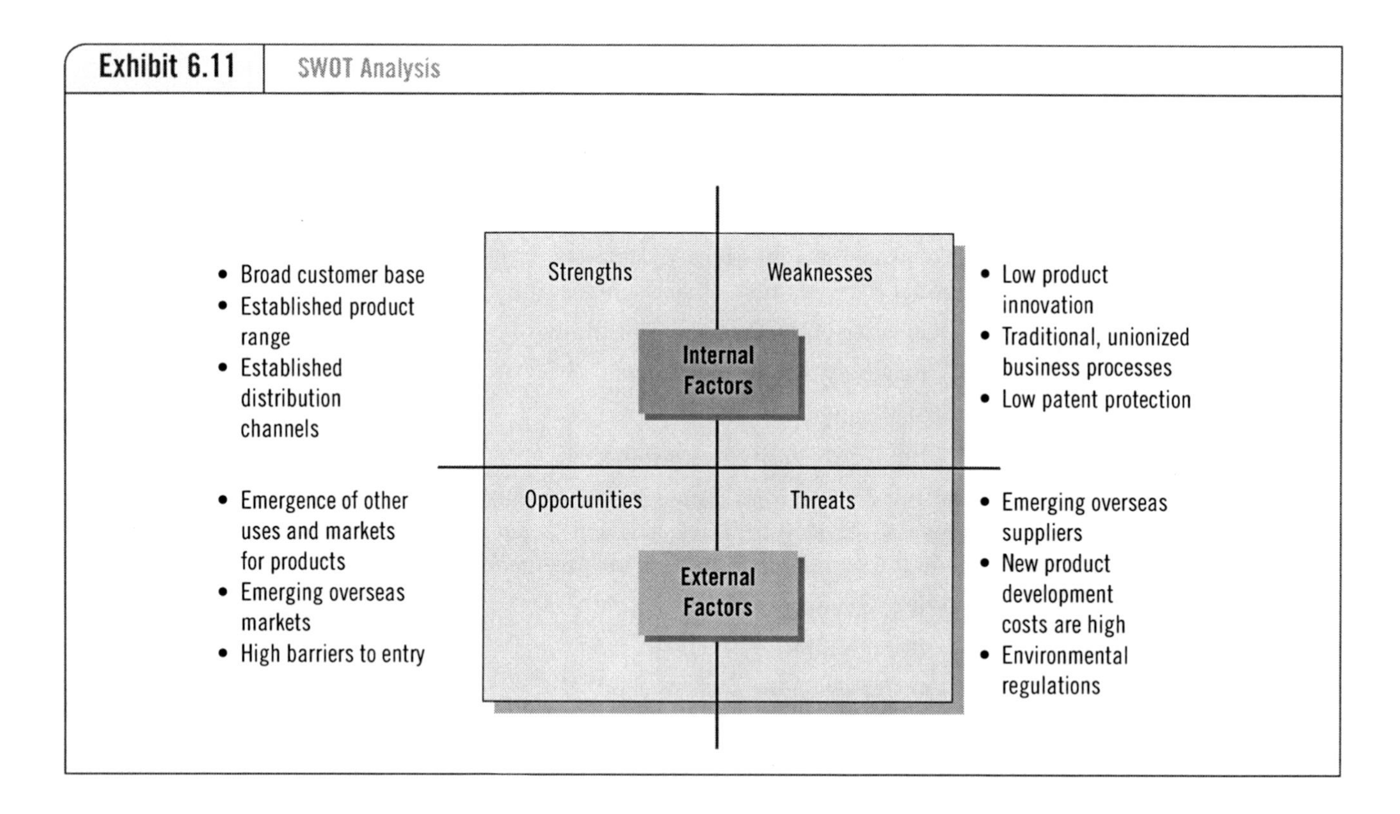

Supplier Analysis

Establish Benchmarks through Industry Databases

Benchmarking is an important element in building competitive strategy. Benchmarking requires identifying the critical performance criteria that are being benchmarked and identifying relative competitive performance. Industry benchmarks involve comparisons of performance with firms in the same industry, whereas external benchmarks involve best practices and performance levels achieved by firms that are not within the same industry.

The Center for Advanced Supply Management Studies has a number of supply management benchmark reports that can provide comparative insights into supply management performance. A number of reports on various components of supply strategy can also be found through consulting organizations, such as Aberdeen Group, Gartner, Procurement Strategy Council, Hackett Group, and other firms.

Requests for Information

A request for information (RFI) is generally used before a specific requisition of an item is issued. Most organizations will issue an RFI if they have determined that there are several potential suppliers. The RFI is a solicitation document that is used by organizations to obtain general information about services, products, or suppliers. This document does not constitute a binding agreement by either the supplier or the purchaser. The information gathered from an RFI can be disseminated throughout the organization or to specific departments.

This procedure is generally used when a large or complicated purchase is being considered and the potential pool of suppliers must be prequalified. In this case an

RFI is a questionnaire or inquiry into the supplier's background. This is used to determine if the supplier meets the minimum standards needed to successfully bid on the project and, if awarded, successfully complete the project

Value Chain Analysis

Value chain analysis is used to help identify the cost savings opportunities that exist within the supply chain. The goal is to be able to understand, identify, and exploit cost savings opportunities that may have been overlooked by business unit managers or even by suppliers in bringing the products and services to the appropriate location.

Some of the best data for value chain analysis comes from books, industry journals, and discussions with suppliers. The tool provides insights into where products originate (from dirt) and where they end up (cradle to grave). A good value chain analysis can provide insights into where in the market you need to be buying. Examples of value chain analysis are discussed in Chapter 12.

Supplier Research

Supplier research is required to identify the specific capabilities and financial health of key suppliers that are in the supply base or that may not currently be in the supply base. Some of the key elements that should be documented and included in a comprehensive supplier analysis study include the following:

- Cost structure
- Financial status
- Customer satisfaction levels
- Support capabilities
- Relative strengths and weakness
- How the buying company fits in their business
- How the company is viewed
- Core capabilities
- Strategy/future direction
- Culture

Identifying the major suppliers in a market is an important first step of any supplier analysis, especially when you are talking about global market share. This tells you who the world prefers, who the world is buying from! It is also critical to understand global capacity versus global demand and trends.

Step 3: Strategy Development

Once the team have educated themselves to the point that they feel they know enough about the supply market conditions, the forecasted spend, and the user stakeholder requirements, they are faced with a different challenge. The team must convert all of this data into meaningful knowledge and apply some meaningful tools to structure the information so that it will render an effective decision. Two tools are most often used in this process: a portfolio analysis matrix (sometimes called the strategic sourcing matrix), and the supplier evaluation scorecard.

Exhibit 6.12 Strategy Portfolio Matrix for Category Management

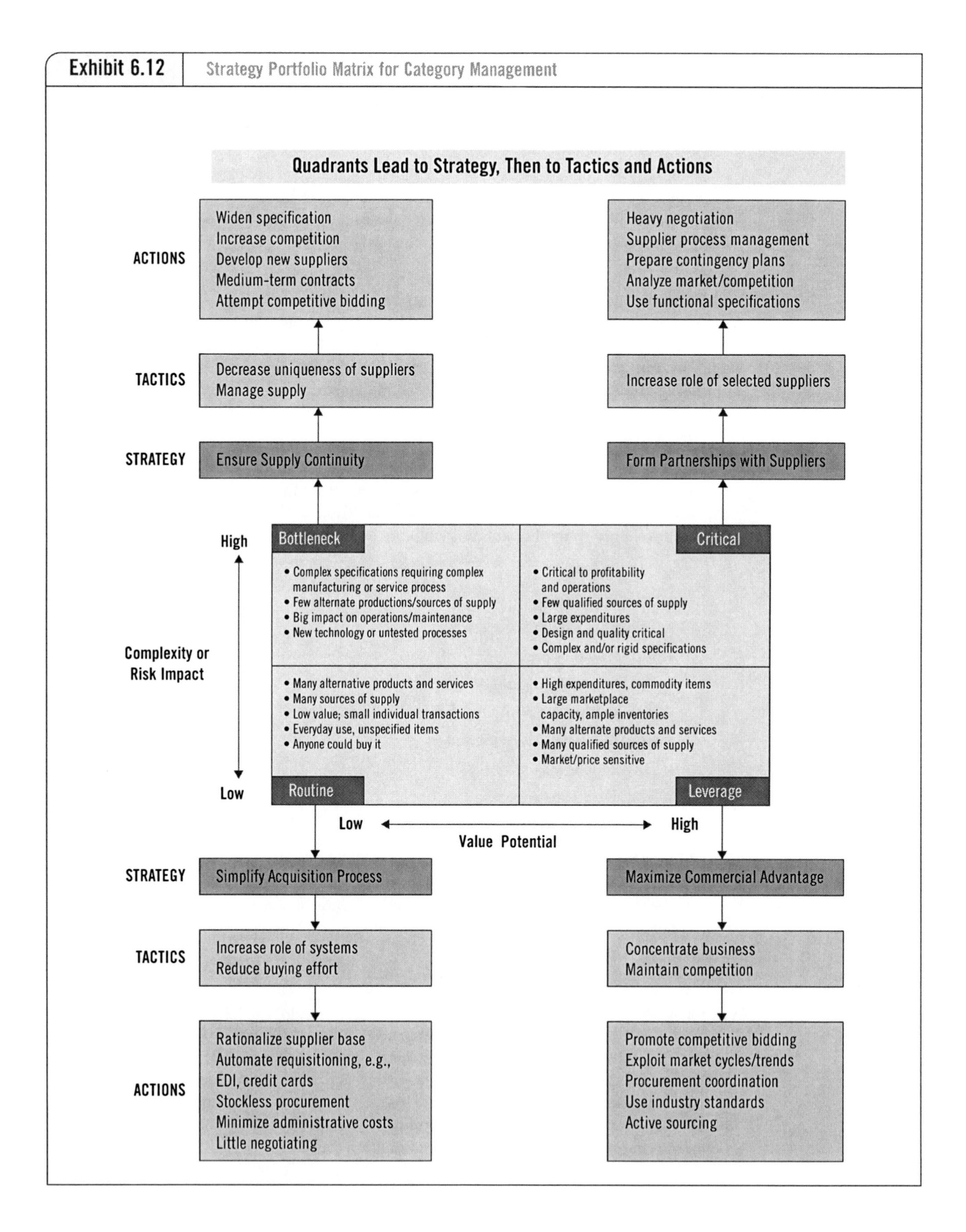

Portfolio Analysis

Portfolio analysis is a tool to structure and segment the supply base, and is used as a means of classifying suppliers into one of four types. The objective is to categorize every purchase or family of purchases into one of four categories. The premise of portfolio analysis is that every purchase or family of purchases can be classified into one of four categories or quadrants: (1) Critical, (2) Routine, (3) Leverage, and (4) Bottleneck.[3] By effectively classifying the goods and services being purchased into one of these categories, those responsible for proposing a strategy are able to comprehend the strategic importance of the item to the business. The results of this analysis can then be compared to the current sourcing strategy for the category group, and tactics and actions defined for moving forward. Exhibit 6.12 on p. 211 summarizes the essential elements of strategy, tactics, and actions associated with managing categories that fall into each of the different quadrants in the matrix, and these are described in greater detail below.

Critical Commodity—Strategic Supplier

Generally speaking, the goals for a strategic commodity are to develop a competitive advantage, support and leverage the supplier's core competencies, develop best-in-class suppliers, support the company's overall strategy, and improve value-added services beyond a simple purchasing agreement. If the annual spend on the item is high, then it also makes sense for the company to establish a strategic preferred supplier. A preferred supplier designation indicates that the selected supplier should receive the business under most conditions. Formally designating a supplier as strategic builds a foundation for achieving higher levels of information sharing and improvement. In the words of Dave Nelson, a guru in supply management who has worked at Honda, John Deere, and Delphi, "If you develop the right relationship with your supply base, you can have 10,000 additional brains thinking about ways to improve your product and generate cost savings. And that is very powerful!"[4]

Routine Commodity

Products and services in this category are readily available and often are low in cost. Examples include janitorial services, facilities management, and office suppliers. The goal for the team is to reduce the number of items in this category through substitution, elimination of small-volume spend, elimination of duplicate SKUs, rationalization of the number of units to control costs, and simplification of the procurement process using electronic tools (e.g., electronic data interchange, auto-order systems, online vendor catalogs, and purchasing cards). For example, at GlaxoSmithKline, a pharmaceutical company, the chief procurement officer discovered that the R&D group was using 50 different types of Bunsen burners and beakers simply because scientists have particular preferences that they acquired in graduate school.

The team will also try to find suppliers that can automate the purchasing process to the greatest extent possible. For example, companies such as Staples and Office-Depot will consolidate a company's purchases of paper and office supplies, and enable users to order supplies directly from their online catalog. A supplier catalog allows users to order directly through the Internet using a company procurement card (just like a credit card), with the delivery made directly to the site the next day.

Leverage Commodity—Preferred Supplier

As in the case of a common commodity, a leverage commodity also provides the opportunity for savings. These items or services have a high volume of internal consumption, are readily available, are important to the business, and represent a significant portion of spend. Because of their importance to the business, the need to maintain a high level of quality and compliance with corporate objectives is paramount. Preferred suppliers are awarded the business under these conditions with the understanding that they will be expected to significantly reduce the cost of supplying these items or services over time, in return for a significant volume of business and possible multiyear agreements. A high level of service is also expected, which may include supplier capabilities such as management of on-site inventory, e-purchasing capabilities, and ability to quickly respond to customer requirements. In so doing, the supplier will also be expected to maintain a high level of quality and to reduce the total cost to the business of managing this commodity.

One of the tools often used for this category of spend is an e-reverse auction (e-RA), an online auction that awards the business to the lowest bidder (as opposed to the highest bidder, as in a traditional auction, hence the terminology "reverse auction").

Bottleneck Commodity—Transactional Supplier

The final combination often found in developing sourcing strategy is for bottleneck commodities, which have unique requirements or niche suppliers yet are significant to the business. Such items tend to be expensive, due to the exclusive market position maintained by the supplier. The goal of the team is to not run out and to ensure continuity of supply. In such cases, an optimal strategy might be to scan the marketplace and develop an agreement with a supplier to enable a streamlined accounts payable and receiving process. If the supplier is relatively small, this may involve sending an IT team to establish this capability at the supplier's location, with some minimal technology investment required. After a competitive bid, a detailed negotiation should take place that establishes high levels of service as critical to the business, with specific service level agreements detailed. The supplier must be validated to ensure that it can deliver in a responsive manner, is capable of handling orders from multiple locations, and is responsible for managing inventory of the item. In service agreements, the supplier must be led to understand the specific requirements around providing the service.

Supplier Evaluation

Once the portfolio analysis is completed, the team must then dive into the category and evaluate individual suppliers as to their suitability, narrowing the list down to a critical few. The ultimate result of this step is to make supplier recommendations, so the team must first identify current and potential suppliers, determine any information technology requirements, and identify opportunities to leverage the commodity expenditures with similar commodities.

Some of the criteria used to evaluate suppliers, as well as the tools that can be used to do so, are discussed in the next chapter, which describes weighted point supplier evaluation systems. Here we limit ourselves to a brief description of the different criteria that a company may use to assess potential suppliers, which include the following capabilities:

- Process and design capabilities
- Management capability
- Financial condition and cost structure
- Planning and control systems
- Environmental regulation compliance
- Longer-term relationship potential
- Supplier selection scorecards

These criteria are worth talking about in more detail. Although it may not be possible to obtain all the relevant information, data that can be obtained will help the buying firm assess the potential for a successful match.

Process and Design Capabilities

Because different manufacturing and service processes have various strengths and weaknesses, the buying firm must be aware of these characteristics upfront. When the buying firm expects suppliers to perform component design and production, it should also assess the supplier's design capability. One way to reduce the time required to develop new products is to use qualified suppliers that are able to perform product design activities.

Management Capability

Assessing a potential supplier's management capability is a complicated, but important, step. Different aspects of management capability include management's commitment to continuous process and quality improvement, its overall professional ability and experience, its ability to maintain positive relationships with its workforce, and its willingness to develop a closer working relationship with the buyer.

Financial Condition and Cost Structure

An assessment of a potential partner's financial condition usually occurs during the evaluation process. Evaluation teams will typically evaluate the different financial ratios that determine whether a supplier can invest in resources, pay its suppliers and its workforce, and continue to meet its debt and financial obligations. These elements are important in determining whether the supplier will continue to be a reliable source of supply, and that supply will not be disrupted.

Planning and Control Systems

Planning and control systems include those systems that release, schedule, and control the flow of work in an organization. As we shall see in later chapters, the sophistication of such systems can have a major impact on supply chain performance.

Environmental Regulation Compliance

The 1990s brought about a renewed awareness of the impact that industry has on the environment. The Clean Air Act of 1990 imposes large fines on producers of ozone-depleting substances and foul-smelling gases, and governments have introduced laws regarding recycling content in industrial materials. As a result, a supplier's ability to comply with environmental regulations is becoming an important criterion for supply chain alliances. This includes, but is not limited to, the proper disposal of hazardous waste. (This is discussed in a later chapter.)

Longer-Term Relationship Potential

In some cases, a firm may be looking to develop a long-term relationship with a potential supplier. This is particularly true if the supplier is in the "Critical" quadrant, and the category of spend is high volume and critical to the company's business. This approach requires that the parties share their mutual goals, establish metrics to guide the relationship, and develop a series of ongoing discussions on how issues and conflicts can be resolved in a mutually beneficial manner. These relationships may also involve joint cost-savings projects and new-product development efforts, which are also described in a later chapter on integration.

This is not a complete list of criteria that can be applied when evaluating the possibility of a closer, longer-term relationship. This list does provide, however, a framework concerning the types of issues that are important in this area.

Supplier Selection Scorecards

During the selection stage, oftentimes companies need a structured way to evaluate alternative suppliers. This can be particularly hard when the criteria include not just quantitative measures (such as costs and on-time delivery rates), but other, more qualitative factors, such as management stability or trustworthiness. A supplier selection scorecard may be used as a decision support tool. The team will assign a weight to the different categories and develop a numerical score for each supplier in each category, thereby developing a final performance score.

The need for assessment does not end with the selection decision, however. After the buyer-supplier relationship has been established, buyers also must track supplier performance over time. The ability to rank suppliers across multiple criteria can be especially helpful in identifying which suppliers are providing superior performance, and which are in need of some work.

After making the selection using some of the different supplier evaluation tools, the team must reach consensus on the strategy. The team may even take the suppliers short list and hold meetings with the selected suppliers to enable an effective decision. Finally, the suppliers are chosen that best fit the commodity strategy to be employed, based on their performance in the supplier analysis.

Step 4: Contract Negotiation

After the sourcing strategy has been determined and suppliers have been recommended, it is time to implement the strategy and negotiate the contract. Effective implementation of the strategy includes establishing tasks and time lines, assigning accountabilities and process ownership, and ensuring adequate resources are made available to the process owners. The strategy should also be communicated to all stakeholders, including suppliers and internal customers, in order to obtain buy-in and participation.

Before entering into contract negotiations, the commodity team should perform an analysis of market and pricing issues so that a fair price for both parties can be agreed upon. This analysis attempts to define the marketplace, including best price, average price, and the business unit's price, and determines expected trends in pricing. In preparation for negotiations, the buyer should develop a negotiation plan and an ideal contract. There should also be a contingency plan in case negotiations with the recommended suppliers do not go as expected. Finally, the negotiation is conducted, and a contract is signed.

For some items, firms may maintain a list of preferred suppliers that receive the first opportunity for new business. A **preferred supplier** has demonstrated its performance capabilities through previous purchase contracts and, therefore, receives preference during the supplier selection process. By maintaining a preferred supplier list, purchasing personnel can quickly identify suppliers with proven performance capabilities. Competitive bidding and negotiation are two methods commonly used for final supplier selection when there is not a preferred supplier.

Competitive Bidding

Competitive bidding in private industry entails a request for bids from suppliers with whom the buyer is willing to do business. This process is typically initiated when the purchasing manager sends a request for quotation (RFQ) to qualified suppliers. The RFQ is a formal request for the suppliers to prepare bids, based on the terms and conditions set by the buyer. Purchasers often evaluate the resulting bids based on price. If the lowest bidder does not receive the purchase contract, the buyer has an obligation to inform that supplier why it did not receive the contract. Competitive bidding is most effective when the following conditions apply:[5]

- The buying firm can provide qualified suppliers with clear descriptions of the items or services to be purchased.
- Volume is high enough to justify the cost and effort.
- The firm does not have a preferred supplier.

Buying firms use competitive bidding when price is a dominant criterion and the required items or services have straightforward specifications. In addition, government agencies often require competitive bidding. If there are major nonprice variables, then the buyer and seller usually enter into direct negotiation. Competitive bidding can also be used to identify a short list of suppliers with whom the firm will begin detailed purchase contract negotiation.

More advanced online tools are becoming available that feature the ability to negotiate issues beyond price with multiple suppliers. With these tools, e-procurement managers no longer have to spend hours in face-to-face meetings arguing over details with suppliers. A buyer simply fills out an RFQ template and forwards the document electronically to suppliers.[6] Suppliers can respond electronically with online proposals detailing price, payment terms, shipping methods, or any other issue relevant to the buyer. These tools enable a buyer to negotiate the process simultaneously with more than one supplier, which leads to efficiencies and lower prices due to increased competition (similar to reverse auctions).

Negotiation

Negotiation is a more costly, interactive approach to final supplier selection. Face-to-face negotiation is best when the following conditions apply:

- The item is a new or technically complex item with only vague specifications.
- The purchase requires agreement about a wide range of performance factors.
- The buyer requires the supplier to participate in the development effort.
- The supplier cannot determine risks and costs without additional input from the buyer.

Negotiations with a supplier should occur only when a purchaser feels confident about the level of planning and preparation put forth. However, planning is not an open-ended process; buyers must usually meet deadlines that satisfy the needs of internal customers within the purchaser's firm. Thus, the buyer faces pressure to conduct the negotiation within a reasonable amount of time.

Step 5: Supplier Relationship Management

The strategic sourcing process does not end when a contract is signed with a supplier. Although the sourcing team may disband and go their separate ways once the contract is signed, typically one member of the team will continue to work with the supplier in the role of supplier relationship manager. This individual must continuously monitor the performance of the sourcing strategy, as well as the supplier. The buying firm should revisit the sourcing strategy at predetermined intervals, to ensure that it is achieving its stated objectives, and may need to make modifications to the strategy if it is not working as planned or if there are changes in the market. The buying firm should also continuously monitor the performance of suppliers based on predetermined and agreed-upon criteria such as quality, delivery performance, and continuous cost improvement. And there should be a plan in place to manage any conflicts that occur with suppliers.

One of the most important tools used to monitor supplier performance is the supplier scorecard. Just like the supplier evaluation matrix, the scorecard often reflects the same set of categories used during the evaluation process, but the scores are updated typically once a quarter, and reviewed with the supplier. Over time, the nature of the classifications used in the scorecard may also change, as the stakeholders' requirements and their requests may change. Scorecards typically include the categories of price, quality, and delivery reliability used in the evaluation process, but the team may also choose to add categories such as "Responsiveness" (how quickly does the supplier return a call when there is a problem?). These scorecards are used in regularly scheduled review meetings with suppliers, so that deficiencies in performance can be noted, discussed, and acted upon.

Regular reviews must be held to determine if the strategy is successful or whether it requires modification. The review may include feedback and input from key suppliers. In any case, all suppliers should be advised of results along with future expectations. Supply management personnel play a key role in this review because they are often the primary contact for the supplier with responsibility for supplier performance measurement. Earlier decisions may have to be revisited and re-evaluated if suppliers do not perform as expected.

The key goals defined in Step 2 must be revisited periodically to identify modifications to the original strategy. Key elements of the results-monitoring process include the following:

- Conduct regular review meetings (at least annually) to determine if the strategy is well aligned with an organization's objectives.
- Share results with top management to provide additional momentum to the strategy; be sure to report the performance improvements achieved through the strategy.

- Assess internal customers' and suppliers' perceptions. Are they satisfied with what has happened? If not, why not, and can the strategy be altered to improve the situation?
- Determine whether key goals are being achieved. If they are not being achieved, what is the contingency plan? If the goals are being achieved, are there any lessons to be learned?
- Provide feedback to those involved.

These strategy development steps are relatively general—they describe the steps to follow only when proposing and executing a strategy. However, the actual outcomes of the commodity strategy development process may vary considerably, depending on the specific commodity and the supply market.

Types of Supply Management Strategies

Organizations can employ a variety of different strategies that may be unique to each commodity. Although we cannot cover all of the possible variations of strategies that may emerge, we will briefly review some of the most common and important supply management strategies. As we will see later, certain strategies are used more often than others, depending on how advanced an organization is at the supply management strategy development process. Each of these strategies or supply management approaches is covered in greater detail in other chapters throughout the book.

Supply Base Optimization

Supply base optimization is the process of determining the appropriate number and mix of suppliers to maintain. Although this has also been referred to as **rightsizing**, it usually refers to reducing the number of suppliers used. Moreover, suppliers that are not capable of achieving world-class performance, either currently or in the near future, may be eliminated from the supply base. This process is continuous because the needs of the business unit are always changing. Optimization requires an analysis of the number of suppliers required currently and in the future for each purchased item. For example, General Motors was ready to eliminate 160 suppliers worldwide that it considered poor performers in 2003 and 2004. Chapter 9 discusses supply base optimization in detail.

Supply Risk Management

Events in 2005 such as Hurricane Katrina and corresponding escalating commodity prices have highlighted more than ever the impact of disruptions on supply chain operations and global competition. Although many events are not easily predicted, there are many other sources of supply chain disruption that have the potential to be better managed, thereby reducing the impact on firm agility and profitability.

As firms outsource a greater proportion of products and services from China, India, and other low-cost countries, the hidden perils of these approaches are often not considered, especially within the context of enterprise risk management (ERM). Global outsourcing affords many benefits in the form of lower prices and expanded market access, but only recently have senior executives begun to recognize the increased risk attributed to the higher probability of product and service flow disruptions in global sourcing networks. A major disruption in the offshore supply chain can shut down a company and have dire consequences for profitability. This was felt most drastically in the last few years, when such events as 9/11, the war in Iraq, the West Coast port workers' strike, and increased regulatory and customs delays brought supply chain operations to a standstill. Recently, the impact of Hurricane Katrina was felt by companies relying on supplies of critical commodities produced on the Gulf Coast such as fuel, natural gas, chemicals, and resins. Other, less serious events that can also impact customer service include fire and theft, poor communication of customer requirements, part shortages, and quality problems.

The impact of supply chain disruptions, although difficult to quantify, can be costly. A study investigated stock market reactions when firms publicly announced that they were experiencing supply chain glitches or disruptions causing production or shipping delays.[7] Results of the study of 519 supply chain problem announcements showed that stock market reactions decrease shareholder value by 10.28%. A follow-up study assessed the effect 827 publicly announced disruptions had on long-run stock price (one year before the disruption and two years after) and found a mean abnormal return of nearly −40% along with significant increases in equity risk.[8] Their results also showed that the majority of supply chain disruptions involved parts shortages, lack of response to customer-requested changes, production problems, ramp-up problems, and quality problems.

Many recent events illustrate this phenomenon. For example, Boeing experienced supplier delivery failure of two critical parts with an estimated loss to the company of $2.6 billion. In 2002, less than 100 workers in the longshoremen's union strike disrupted West Coast port operations. As a result, it took six months for some containers to be delivered and schedules to return to normal. Finally, Hurricane Katrina resulted in billions of dollars of lost revenue to major retailers such as British Petroleum, Shell, Conoco Phillips, and Lyondell, as well as causing gasoline shortages in many parts of the United States, resulting in lost economic activity. Given these and other events, it is not surprising that supply chain disruptions have caught the attention of executives.

In a survey of *BusinessWeek* Global 1000 companies, supply chain disruptions were perceived to be the single biggest threat to their companies' revenue streams. Although senior executives now recognize that supply chain disruptions can be devastating to an enterprise's bottom line, strategies to mitigate supply chain disruptions are typically not well developed or even initiated. A troubling statistic is that only between 5 and 25% of Fortune 500 companies are estimated to be prepared to handle a major supply chain crisis or disruption.

One factor that is increasing the risk exposure to supply chain disruption is the increasing propensity of companies to outsource processes to global suppliers. The complexity associated with multiple hand-offs in global supply chains increases the probability of disruptions. As the number of hand-offs required to ship products through multiple carriers, multiple ports, and multiple government checkpoints increases, so does the probability of poor communication, human error, and missed shipments. One executive we interviewed from a major electronics company noted: "We have successfully outsourced production of our products to China. Unfortunately, we now recognize that we do not have the processes in place to manage risk associated with this supply chain effectively!"[9] In this environment, questions arise such as, What steps can an organization take to design its supply chains to ensure uninterrupted material availability? Is it possible to respond in an agile manner to customer requirements in a global sourcing environment? These are issues that supply chain managers must think through in the future, to build effective contingency plans before these disruptions occur, so that there is a plan when they do occur.

Global Sourcing

Global sourcing is an approach that requires supply management to view the entire world as a potential source for components, services, and finished goods. It can be used to access new markets or to gain access to the same suppliers that are helping global companies become more competitive. Although true global sourcing is somewhat limited in most industries, more and more companies are beginning to view the world as both a market and a source of supply.

The major objective of global sourcing is to provide immediate and dramatic improvements in cost and quality as determined through the commodity research process. Global sourcing is also an opportunity to gain exposure to product and process technology, increase the number of available sources, satisfy countertrade requirements, and establish a presence in foreign markets. This strategy is not contradictory to supply base optimization because it involves locating the worldwide best-in-class suppliers for a given commodity. Some buyers also source globally to introduce competition to domestic suppliers.

There are several major barriers to global sourcing that must be overcome. Some serious issues are that some firms are inexperienced with global business processes and practices, and there are few personnel qualified to develop and negotiate with global suppliers or manage long material pipelines. In addition, more complex logistics and currency fluctuations require measuring all relevant costs before committing to a worldwide source.

Finally, organizations may not be prepared to deal with the different negotiating styles practiced by different cultures, and they may have to work through a foreign host national in order to establish contacts and an agreement. Chapter 10 addresses global sourcing in detail.

Longer-Term Supplier Relationships

Longer-term supplier relationships involve the selection of and continuous involvement with suppliers viewed as critical over an extended period of time (e.g., three years and beyond). In general, the use of longer-term supplier relationships is growing in importance, and there will probably be greater pursuit of these relationships through longer-term contracts. Some purchasers are familiar with the practice, whereas for others it represents a radical departure from traditional short-term approaches to supply base management.

Longer-term relationships are sought with suppliers that have exceptional performance or unique technological expertise. Within the portfolio matrix described earlier, this would involve the few suppliers that provide items and services that are critical or of higher value. A longer-term relationship may include a joint product development relationship with shared development costs and intellectual property. In other cases, it may simply be an informal process of identifying suppliers that receive preferential treatment. Chapter 14 discusses longer-term relationships and contracts.

Early Supplier Design Involvement

Early supplier design involvement and selection requires key suppliers to participate at the concept or predesign stage of new-product development. Supplier involvement may be informal, although the supplier may already have a purchase contract for the production of an existing item. Early involvement will increasingly take place through participation on cross-functional product development teams. This strategy recognizes that qualified suppliers have more to offer than simply the basic production of items that meet engineering specifications. Early supplier design involvement is a simultaneous engineering approach that occurs between buyer and seller, and seeks to maximize the benefits received by taking advantage of the supplier's design capabilities. This strategy is discussed in detail in Chapter 4; the Good Practice Example at the end of this chapter also highlights how one company has successfully employed early involvement.

Supplier Development

In some cases, purchasers may find that suppliers' capabilities are not high enough to meet current or future expectations, yet they do not want to eliminate the supplier from the supply base. (Switching costs may be high or the supplier has performance potential.) A solution in such cases is to work directly with a supplier to facilitate improvement in a designated functional or activity area. Buyer-seller consulting teams working jointly may accelerate overall supplier improvement at a faster rate than will actions taken independently by the supplier. The basic motivation behind this strategy is that supplier improvement and success lead to longer-term benefits to both buyer and seller. This approach supports the development of world-class suppliers in new areas of product and process technology. Chapter 9 discusses supplier development in detail.

Total Cost of Ownership

Total cost of ownership (TCO) is the process of identifying cost considerations beyond unit price, transport, and tooling. It requires the business unit to define and measure the various cost components associated with a purchased item. In many cases, this includes costs associated with late delivery, poor quality, or other forms of supplier nonperformance. Total cost of ownership can lead to better decision making because it identifies all costs associated with a supply management decision and the costs associated with supplier nonperformance. Cost variances from planned results can be analyzed to determine the cause of the variance. Corrective action can then prevent further problems. TCO is discussed in detail in Chapters 10 and 11.

E-Reverse Auctions

An e-RA is an online, real-time dynamic auction between a buying organization and a group of pre-qualified suppliers who compete against each other to win the business to supply goods or services that have clearly defined specifications for design, quantity, quality, delivery, and related terms and conditions. These suppliers compete by bidding against each other online over the Internet using specialized software by submitting successively lower-priced bids during a scheduled time period. This time period is

Sourcing Snapshot *Reverse Auctions*

Reverse auctions can be used for one specific product/service in a spot buy or for contracts to provide the products or services over the course of a year. The goal of reverse auctions is to bring buyers and sellers together to expose prices on a dynamic and real-time basis. A reverse auction involves suppliers bidding on a clearly specified buyer requirement. All activity takes place online. The majority of reverse auctions are completed in 30 minutes or less (although some have been stretched out over 12 hours). A recent auction carried out by a large engineering project construction firm for a large commodity group included multiple suppliers from Japan, Korea, and the United States. The pricing behaviors that were evidenced in the auction stunned the buying company executives who witnessed them. The price paid for the commodity was well below the group's expectation of market price. One executive who participated said, "It showed us just how little we really knew about what the market was doing." Reverse auctions can provide some deep insights into true market pricing, especially in situations when there is available capacity in a supply marketplace.

Source: Interview with executive, Supply Chain Resource Cooperative executive meeting, North Carolina State University, Raleigh, April 2004.

usually only about an hour, but multiple, brief extensions are usually allowed if bidders are still active at the end of the initial time period.

The use of e-RAs has been facilitated by a number of company internal and external developments including the following:

- Buyers' and suppliers' ability to communicate in real time, worldwide, via the Internet.
- Development of robust, user-friendly Internet-based software systems to support worldwide e-RAs hosted by a third party or conducted by the buying company with little or no outside assistance.
- Significant improvements in goods and service quality and cycle-time reductions have resulted in buying companies requiring superior quality and service. Therefore, buyers have emphasized low price as a major sourcing-decision variable.

E-RAs are discussed in Chapter 13.

Evolving Sourcing Strategies

If we compare the level of supply management strategy evolution to the strategies available, there is clearly an implementation sequence that emerges. Exhibit 6.13 presents the sequence of supply management strategy execution based on research from multiple studies and interviews with many executives. Organizations tend to evolve through four phases as they become mature and sophisticated in their supply management strategy development.

Exhibit 6.13 Stages of Supply Management Strategy Evolution

1. BASIC BEGINNINGS	2. MODERATE DEVELOPMENT	3. LIMITED INTEGRATION	4. FULLY INTEGRATED SUPPLY CHAINS
• Quality/cost teams • Longer-term contracts • Volume leveraging • Supply-base consolidation • Supplier quality focus	• E-RAs • Ad hoc supplier alliances • Cross-functional sourcing teams • Supply-base optimization • International sourcing • Cross-location sourcing teams	• Global sourcing • Strategic supplier alliances • Supplier TQM development • Total cost of ownership • Nontraditional purchase focus • Parts/service standardization • Early supplier involvement • Dock to stock pull systems	• Global supply chains with external customer focus • Cross-enterprise decision making • Full-service suppliers • Early sourcing • Insourcing/outsourcing to maximize core competencies of firms throughout the supply chain • E-systems

Phase 1: Basic Beginnings

In the initial stages of supply management strategy development, supply management is often characterized as a lower-level support function. Supply management adopts essentially a short-term approach and reacts to complaints from its internal customers when deliveries are late, quality is poor, or costs are too high. The only impetus for change here is the demand for change by management. The primary role of supply management managers is to ensure that enough supply capacity exists, which usually means that suppliers are viewed in an adversarial manner. However, the amount of resources for improvement is limited, usually because the highest-ranking supply management manager likely reports to manufacturing or materials management. Performance measures focus on efficiency-related measures and price reduction. Information systems are location or facility focused and primarily transaction based.

In Phase 1, supply management often focuses on supply base optimization, and more attention is paid to total quality management than to other progressive supply management strategies. In a sense, these two strategies represent the building blocks from which to pursue increasingly sophisticated strategies. A reduced supply base is necessary because of the increased two-way communication and interaction necessary for successful execution of more complicated strategies. TQM also provides the fundamental focus on process that is required to implement supply management strategies.

Phase 2: Moderate Development

The second phase of the strategy progression usually occurs as an organization begins to centrally coordinate or control some part of the supply management function across regional or even worldwide locations. Supply management councils or lead buyers may be responsible for entire classes of commodities, and companywide databases by region may be developed to facilitate this coordination. The primary purpose of this coordination is to establish companywide agreements in order to leverage volumes to obtain lower costs from volume discounts. Single sourcing with long-term agreements may eventually emerge as a policy for leveraged or consolidated purchase families. At this stage, limited cross-functional integration is occurring. In addition, e-RAs have recently been selectively used to leverage purchases and improve goods and service pricing by between 15 and 30%.

The approaches in Phases 1 and 2—supply base optimization, TQM, and long-term contracting—have the potential, over time, to effect a steady increase in supplier contributions and improvements, but the performance change rate may not be dramatic.

Purchasers must now begin to pursue strategic supplier relationships that focus on customer needs and the organization's competitive strategy. In Phase 2, buyers may begin to establish better relationships with critical suppliers while continuing to optimize the supply base. The supply management department may now be evaluated on the achievement of competitive objectives, and suppliers are viewed as a resource. As such, there may be some informal channels of functional integration developing between supply management, engineering, manufacturing, marketing, and accounting. Some of this may occur through infrequent cross-functional team decision making. The execution of supply management strategy still takes place primarily at the business unit or local level.

Phase 3: Limited Integration

A number of supply management initiatives discussed in this book, including concurrent engineering, supplier development, lead-time reduction, and early supplier involvement, characterize this phase. In this environment, supply management strategies are established and integrated early into the product and process design stage, and first- and second-tier suppliers are becoming actively involved in these decisions. Supply management is evaluated on the basis of strategic contribution, and resources are made available according to strategic requirements. Extensive functional integration occurs through design and sourcing teams that focus on product development, building a competitive advantage, and total cost analysis for new and existing products and services. Supply management is viewed as a key part of the organizational structure with a strong external customer focus. As such, multiple customer-oriented measurements are used to identify performance improvements. Information systems include global databases, historical price and cost information, joint strategy development efforts with other functional groups, and the beginning of total cost modeling.

Phase 4: Fully Integrated Supply Chains

In the final and most advanced phase, supply management has assumed a strategic orientation, with reporting directly to executive management and a strong external, rather than simply internal, customer focus. Non-value-added activities such as purchase order follow-up and expediting have been automated, allowing purchasers to focus their attention on strategic objectives and activities. Organizations demand a higher performance standard from suppliers. Executives take aggressive actions that will directly improve supplier capability and accelerate supplier performance contributions.

Examples of aggressive actions include developing global supplier capabilities, developing full-service suppliers, and adopting a systems thinking perspective that encompasses the entire supply chain. In such a mode, insourcing core activities add the greatest value, whereas components of the value chain are often outsourced to upstream or downstream parties that are more capable.

Such a system can directly affect the ability of the supply base to meet world-class expectations and often involves direct intervention in the supplier's operating systems and processes.

Relatively few organizations have evolved to this phase. However, for those that succeed, a number of tangible and intangible benefits accrue from the progression of supply management from a supportive role to an integrated activity. These include price reductions across all product lines ranging from 5 to 25%; improved quality, cost, and delivery performance in the range of 75 to 98% in six to eight months; and a supply base that is better than the competition's. Supply management is now in a position to influence rather than react to the supply base, and it can actually develop key suppliers in cases where a weak link exists. Moreover, all of these processes help establish the critical capabilities required of a global leader.

Observations on Supply Management Strategy Evolution

It is important that the supply management student recognize an important point about the sequence shown in Exhibit 6.13 and the phases just discussed: Few organizations have fully executed the more complex strategies found in Phases 3 and 4. This is due to a variety of factors including the relative complexity of higher-level strategies, the resources and commitment necessary to execute the strategy, a lack of a supply base optimization effort, and personnel who lack the skills and capabilities necessary for developing advanced sourcing strategies. However, those that successfully execute more sophisticated and comprehensive sourcing strategies should realize greater performance improvement over time. The following Good Practice Example illustrates how one company developed a higher-level commodity strategy. This strategy may be considered to be within the Phase 3–4 category of maturity.

Good Practice Example

Commodities Forecasting: It's All in Your Head

Strong global growth has pushed industrial commodity prices to new heights in 2006 and 2007. This has wreaked havoc with procurement budgets and created a quandary for buyers trying to forecast pricing trends in the second half of 2007 and into 2008. In a nutshell, forecasting has been muddled by supplier consolidations, pricing volatility, economic uncertainties, monetary unpredictability, and geopolitical concerns.

But forecasts are critical in business. Estimated prices are the core of product-development budgets. Those estimates are also the basis for evaluating buying strategies, planning quarterly cash flows, making forward pricing decisions, and implementing such risk-management plans as hedges.

So what's a buyer to do in the face of all the economic uncertainty? Use his or her head.

Of the three types of commodity price forecasts—those based on personal judgment, those relying exclusively on historical price data, and those incorporating commodity futures prices at the time of the forecast together with historical price data—the judgmental forecasts have the best record of accuracy.

According to Aasim Husain, of the International Monetary Fund's research department in Washington, analysis indicates that "judgmental forecasts tend to outperform the model-based forecasts over short horizons of one quarter for several commodities." They're also the most popular, he says.

Purchasing surveys show that many buying groups tend to use homegrown projections or forecasts developed for them by various research organizations. Academicians explain that's because statistical models can be short-circuited by the volatility of energy, metals, chemicals, plastic resins, wood products, and other production materials.

But if you're going to use personal judgment in commodities forecasting, you have to base it on the right factors. Analysts and buyers alike agree that the most critical data to review are the following:

- Market intelligence
- Global economic trends
- Supplier safeguards against volatility
- Your own company's selling strategies

Even in calm economic times, those tools are critical. With the current volatility in commodities, they're essential. "The commodity markets are crazy these days," says Peter Connelly, CPO at diversified manufacturer Leggett & Platt in Carthage, Missouri, which buys $3.7 billion annually in production and packaging materials. "Prices are affected by local and world demand and supply trends, global currency movements, the economic policies of such developing economies as Brazil, Russia, India, and China—and even today's instant communications."

The latest demand boom for base metals is in its third year and has elevated nonferrous metals pricing to record highs. Steel prices are reflecting iron ore, scrap, ferroalloy, and energy costs—rather than demand trends—probably for the first time.

"Pricing cycles for commodities are shrinking," says the global procurement manager at a Detroit-area auto parts company. "The steel cycle used to be 7 to 10 years in length from peak to valley in prices. Nowadays, it's more like 18 months due to the rapid change in delivery of information."

Atop all that, says Leggett & Platt's Connelly, "supplier consolidation and pricing volatility is making forecasting difficult and, actually, past a 90-day window very inaccurate." Rather than a sign of the top for commodity prices, analysts worry that the deal making could help put a lid on supply and put even more pressure on a host of commodity prices.

This view is supported by research director Anirvan Banerji at the Economic Cycle Research Institute in New York. Most forecasters have a dismal record of predicting the timing of cyclical turns in economic growth, jobs, and inflation, Banerji writes, "because most people and forecasting models expect recent patterns to persist in the near future." This is "a sure recipe for being surprised on prices by the next turn in the global industrial cycle."

And then, there is nature. The late-summer hurricanes of 2005 taught energy and petrochemical buyers just how fast supply can be disrupted and prices can explode.

"It's all about energy and raw materials these days," says Dan DiMicco, CEO of Nucor Corp., the Charlotte, North Carolina–based steelmaker. "With the volatility in and high level of materials pricing nowadays, nobody wants to carry inventory—whether it's in the raw materials at my mills or the finished products we ship to our customers."

INTELLIGENCE IS KING

Stating that "in a commodity market today, intelligence is king," DiMicco tells a recent steel industry conference that "to run as efficiently as we can, mills and service centers will have to start at the customer—and talk to buyers about what they really need and what they expect they will be paying. Only then can we take some volatility out of the metals market—and come to some equitable long-term arrangements on price and supply."

So, the foundation for any successful commodity forecasting program must be based on detailed market knowledge that can smooth out current volatility and help ensure against disrupted flow of raw materials, says Mike Burns, global business director for polyethylene at supply chain consultancy Resin Technology Inc. in Fort Worth, Texas.

Burns insists that buyers "emerge from their comfortable silos" and get knowledgeable about global economics, supply, demand, and sourcing alternatives—"whatever they need to know to become expert about their company, their industry, and their regional and global supply chain." Solid market facts are needed to develop effective buying plans, and that includes accurate price forecasting, says Burns in an interview.

IT'S A SMALL WORLD

A key piece of advice from this purchasing coach and several top-level buyers interviewed: Whatever the commodity, watch the international marketplace to determine supply, demand, pricing, and trading trends. That's because economic conditions that affect supply and prices are changeable—and usually global. "Buyers have got to know demand, as best as they can, but not just demand in North America—demand globally," says Burns.

Today's lean and highly outsourced supply chains leave procurement teams with little visibility to anticipate and react to global risks, complain some analysts. That's why they suggest that buyers learn as much as possible about global supply chains and determine what safeguards their world supplier organizations are putting in place to maintain continuous supply and honor agreed-upon future pricing.

"The days of going out with an RFQ and a spreadsheet of needed materials are over," agrees the commodities buyer for a Chicago-based multinational corporation. "Past-paid price averages are just the start of what we'll expect to pay in the future. We have to work closely with materials engineering and quality folks on the materials specifications and then we

	2005		2006		2007	
	FORECAST	ACTUAL	FORECAST	ACTUAL	FORECAST	ACTUAL*
Aluminum	80	85	104	116	91	127
Copper	156	167	279	305	237	269
Nickel	625	666	945	1102	870	1878
Lead	41	44	51	60	44	81
Tin	314	335	345	397	278	577
Zinc	59	64	130	148	119	164

*First quarter 2007

Forecast: World Bank; Actual: London Metal Exchange

have to find out what's available. Remember, you can't buy all over the world for the same price—ever."

Yet another essential weapon in the commodities-forecasting wars is knowledge of your own company's strategies. "The key to future pricing is to remember that the company's sourcing strategy is there to support the company's business," says Dan Ronchetto, vice president of global direct materials for Greif in Delaware, Ohio. "So, the purchasing organization has to know how the company sells into the market—what the competitive dynamics are and how competitors are competing."

In an interview, Ronchetto says the sourcing strategy has to be in line with the company's sales strategy. If a company's sales are on an annual fixed basis, then purchasing arrangements should be on an annual fixed-prices basis. "The bottom line is the key issue! Wall Street doesn't like surprises or volatility," he says. And it's not just for public companies. Sourcing strategy has to be aligned with overall business strategy and how end customers are served. "If you sell monthly, buy monthly," Ronchetto advises. Fixed two-year or three-year contracts are disappearing into indexing to adjust quarterly market changes, he says.

Some analysts suggest that futures prices on commodity exchanges in London and New York may be the best measure of imminent sales price trends. The various commodity futures exchange markets do provide a mechanism for price discovery on an aggregate level through arbitrage between multiple buyers and sellers.

To many buyers, though, futures trading is just one of several possible tools to guesstimate future pricing—and only for certain raw materials. Although nonferrous metals are traded globally, other materials—such as resins and lumber products—have limited regional exchange liquidity, and other materials, such as steel, have yet to find a trading floor. Also, price discovery at any given location—whether that is New York, Chicago, Winnipeg, London, Tokyo, or Shanghai—is not necessarily definitive because supply and demand relationships are murky.

Nevertheless, buyers are the ones expected to navigate the terrain. Says Greif's Ronchetto, "My CFO and other chief financial officers also are putting more and more pressure on manufacturing and purchasing colleagues to reduce corporate costs." And forecasts, however unscientific, are an important tool in that effort.

TEN FORECASTING TIPS FOR BUYERS

1. Determine corporate price goals; if necessary, adjust them to economic realities.
2. Reduce purchasing pricing strategies to 30, 60, or 90 days.

3. Adjust actual timing of buys to weekly, monthly, or quarterly events.
4. Analyze and, if necessary, adjust the structure of supply-contract agreements.
5. Pay attention to inventory levels to determine comfort of spot versus contract buys.
6. Ensure true supply tie-in with buying company's operational action plans.
7. Study global pricing and sourcing trends of commodities—and their feedstocks.
8. Survey primary suppliers' operating rates, inventory, and costs.
9. Analyze the secondary sourcing market for alternative suppliers.
10. Determine potential alternatives of supply and prices of commodity products.

Source: T. Stundza, "Resin Technology Inc.," *Purchasing* online, www.purchasing.com, May 14, 2007.

CONCLUSION

Category management is perhaps one of the most important ways that supply managers create value for their stakeholders. Category teams must effectively scan the market environment, conduct research on suppliers and cost drivers, analyze internal spend characteristics, and establish appropriate strategies for managing these relationships. In doing so, supply managers depict and create insights for stakeholders on key elements of their supply environment that shape their operational, financial, and market planning decisions. Effective category strategies also create the foundation for cost management, contract frameworks, and ongoing supplier performance management metrics and relationships. These elements will be discussed in greater detail in later chapters, but it is important for students to understand how to conduct research and analysis leading to these actions.

KEY TERMS

category, 190

integrative, 192

preferred supplier, 216

rightsizing, 218

spend analysis, 196

supply base optimization, 218

triangulate, 205

DISCUSSION QUESTIONS

1. Select a commodity that you believe might be chosen for a strategic commodity analysis in the industries listed below. Describe the factors impacting each commodity, using a Porter Five Forces analysis. Justify why you believe the commodity is strategic to that industry, and the approach to be used in developing a commodity strategy.
   - Oil (West Texas intermediate) versus gasoline (discuss differential)
   - Metals
   - Chemicals
   - Plastic resins
   - Shipping
   - Wood products and other production materials
   - Aeronautical equipment
   - Machine tools
   - Telecommunications
   - Paper
2. Why has supply management traditionally not been involved in the corporate strategic planning function?
3. Describe a set of supply management goals that might be aligned with the following corporate objective made by an automotive manufacturer: "To be the number one in customer satisfaction."
4. Describe where you think the following commodities—paper clips, machine tools, castings, personal computers, fuel, computer chips, printers, styrofoam cups, paper, custom-designed networks—might fall within the portfolio matrix. Under what circumstances might one of these items fall into more than one quadrant of the matrix, or evolve from one quadrant to another?

5. Under what conditions might you consider single-sourcing an item in the leveraging category of the portfolio matrix?
6. When conducting research, what are some advantages and disadvantages of the different types of information you might obtain from the Internet? Which types of Internet sites are likely to be more reliable as compared with personal interviews?
7. Why is it important to establish a document explaining the commodity strategy and share it with others? What are the possible consequences of not doing so?
8. Why must organizations develop suppliers? Is supplier development a long-term trend or just a fad? Explain.
9. Supply base optimization must occur before long-term agreements can be put into place. What are the implications of this statement?
10. How long do you believe it takes a company to move from a Stage 1 phase to a Stage 4 phase of supply management strategy development? In providing your response, consider all of the changes that must take place.
11. Provide a list of companies that, based on your reading of recent articles in the popular press, fit into the category of Stage 1 companies. What companies can you think of that might fall into the category of Stage 3 or 4? Provide some justification for your lists.
12. What do you think are the reasons why there are so few companies classified as Stage 4 companies? Do you think this is likely to change?

ADDITIONAL READINGS

Craighead, C. W., Blackhurst, J., Rungtusanatham, M. J., and Handfield, R. B. (2007), "The Severity of Supply Chain Disruptions: Design Characteristics and Mitigation Capabilities," *Decision Sciences,* 38(1), 131–156.

D'Avanzo, R., et al. (2003), "The Link between Supply Chain and Financial Performance," *Supply Chain Management Review,* 27(6), 40–47.

Handfield, R. (2006), *Supplier Market Intelligence,* Boca Raton, FL: Auerbach Publications.

Handfield, R., Elkins, D., Blackhurst, J., and Craighead, C. (2005), "18 Ways to Guard against Disruption," *Supply Chain Management Review,* 9(1), 46–53.

Handfield, R., and Krause, D. (1999), "Think Globally, Source Locally," *Supply Chain Management Review,* Winter, 36–49.

Handfield, R., and McCormack, K. (2005), "What You Need to Know about Sourcing in China," *Supply Chain Management Review,* 9(5), 56–62.

Monczka, R., and Trent, R. J. (1991), "Evolving Sourcing Strategies for the 1990s," *International Journal of Physical Distribution and Logistics Management,* 21(5), 4–12.

Monczka, R., and Trent, R. J. (1995), *Supply Management and Sourcing Strategy: Trends and Implications,* Tempe, AZ: Center for Advanced Supply Management Studies.

Porter, M. E. (1985), *Competitive Advantage: Creating and Sustaining Superior Performance,* New York: Free Press.

ENDNOTES

1. "A Global Study of Supply Chain Leadership and Its Impact on Business Performance," Accenture and INSEAD, white paper, 2003.

2. Developed jointly with Atlanta-based UPS Consulting, the survey titled "CFOs and the Supply Chain" was carried out by CFO Research Services. Reported in "Paying Attention: Chief Financial Officers Get Involved in Managing More Supply Chains," *Traffic World,* September 2, 2003.

3. Monczka, R., Trent, R., and Handfield, R. (2002), *Purchasing and Supply Chain Management* (2nd ed.), Cincinnati: South-Western.

4. Interview with Dave Nelson, North Carolina State University research study on design for order fulfillment, March 2007.

5. Dobler, D., Lee, L., and Burt, D. (1990), *Purchasing and Materials Management,* Homewood, IL: Irwin.

6. Waxer, C. (2001), "E-Negotiations Are In, Price-Only e-Auctions Are Out," *iSource,* June, pp. 73–76.

7. Hendricks, K., and Singhal, V. (2003), "The Effect of Supply Chain Glitches on Shareholder Wealth," *Journal of Operations Management,* 21(5), 501–522.

8. Hendricks, K., and Singhal, V. (2005), "An Empirical Analysis of the Effect of Supply Chain Disruptions on Long Run Stock Price Performance and Equity Risk of the Firm," *Production and Operations Management,* 14(1), 35–52.

9. Interview with senior executive, North Carolina State research study on global supply chain risk, October 2004.

Chapter 7

SUPPLIER EVALUATION AND SELECTION

Learning Objectives

After completing this chapter, you should be able to

- Recognize the seven-step supplier selection process as an enabler to world-class supplier selection
- Appreciate the many areas that supply professionals consider when evaluating potential suppliers
- Understand the importance of supplier visits
- Identify key criteria to narrow the supplier pool
- Learn about the resources available to identify suppliers
- Understand the importance of supplier financial analysis
- Comprehend the various factors that constitute a supplier performance evaluation
- Identify ways to reduce the time associated with supplier evaluation and selection

Chapter Outline

Selecting U.S.-Based Suppliers at Toyota Industrial Equipment Manufacturing

The need to evaluate and select suppliers comes about in many ways. During the development of purchasing strategies, selecting the right supplier is central to success. The following example shows that Toyota's supplier selection philosophy and its commitment to using U.S.-based suppliers is a central part of its supplier selection strategy.

Toyota Industrial Equipment Manufacturing (TIEM) is committed to building lift trucks in the United States and to purchasing materials and components from domestic suppliers. TIEM is the largest manufacturer of material-handling equipment in the world. Most of the products it builds for the U.S. market are made in Columbus, IN, a facility that opened in 1990 and underwent an $11 million expansion in 2005. In May, the plant celebrated the production of its 250,000th forklift truck.

These American-made lift trucks are manufactured of steel, plastic parts, and other components produced mainly by suppliers located in the United States. Roughly 60% of the Columbus plant's supply base now is domestic. TIEM's parent company in Japan, Toyota Industries Corporation (TICO), still provides some critical components such as engines, which it makes in large volumes for plants in Asia, Europe, and the United States. Sixteen years ago when the Columbus facility opened, the ratio was reversed: Local suppliers provided TIEM with 40% of the materials that went into the lift trucks made in the United States.

According to Bruce Nolting, vice president of purchasing, production control, and logistics, purchasing manages about 65 key suppliers in the United States, which provide 75% of the materials and components that go into the lift trucks built in Columbus. These key suppliers provide TIEM with critical parts, make daily deliveries or "milk runs" to the plant, and are on the kanban system, which is key to meeting the just-in-time (JIT) requirements of the Toyota production system in place at the facility.

This transition to increased purchasing through U.S. suppliers is part of TICO's overall procurement policy to buy from domestic suppliers as a way to help keep local economies healthy. In Columbus, TIEM puts these words into action; purchasing and quality assurance work closely together to qualify and develop key suppliers.

Working together, purchasing and quality assurance look for suppliers that can provide materials and components at a lower price to TIEM with as good or better quality, and the capability to provide deliveries to the plant daily or multiple times per day. They use a formula that takes into account such criteria as piece price, inventory carrying costs, and freight.

SUPPLIER QUALIFICATION AND DEVELOPMENT

Nolting's purchasing team consists of six purchasing specialists who manage categories of related materials or components, such as steel and steel products. These specialists are responsible for supplier selection, evaluation and development, and working with quality assurance, as well as cost reduction activities. Steve Pride, TIEM's purchasing manager, oversees their efforts.

Pride serves on a Toyota Material Handling Group global purchasing committee that consists of representatives of facilities in Europe and Asia. He and his team also are in daily contact with colleagues in Japan via videoconferencing and e-mail during model changes.

Looking to keep the supply base a manageable size, TIEM's purchasing and quality assurance department approach a domestic supplier that manufactures similar parts to determine whether it has the capacity to provide the plant with additional components.

"We are looking at a small supply base that supports us in 100% of our needs on a particular part," says Nolting. "Very rarely do we purchase one part number from dual sources. Our idea is to keep the number of suppliers small, but support them and make sure we feed them accurate forecast information to ensure they have ample capacity to meet our requirements." If the supplier needs assistance with equipment or tooling to take on the additional requirements, TIEM provides the resources.

To qualify a domestic supplier, purchasing and quality assurance visit the supplier's plant and conduct a thorough audit that includes a survey consisting of 130 questions, such as: How do you manage your process? How do you evaluate internal quality? Do you have standardized work in your process? The audit team also queries the supplier on its financial health.

Once a supplier is selected, the team works with suppliers on continuous improvement activities. Purchasing and quality assurance evaluate the supplier's performance using quality, cost, and delivery metrics. They issue a report card monthly and recognize top performers with an annual supplier award. Purchasing specialists work with suppliers to resolve any issues that may arise.

"I feel very committed to the suppliers we select," says Nolting. "Once we make a commitment, we do everything possible to get the supplier to the level of our expectation. We don't make many changes in our supply base."

Twice each year, purchasing and quality assurance work with a small group of suppliers on process improvements that ensure they are providing the plant with good-quality parts. The group consists of suppliers that may have had a number of rejects during a specific time period, or another quality issue.

Recently, a group of five suppliers met with purchasing and quality assurance in Columbus to resolve some recurring problems. Three of the suppliers were providing components that were causing issues in the field. The other two were providing parts that the company was rejecting at the plant.

"We ask the supplier to identify the issue and by using a format we provide, let us know how they plan to resolve it," says Nolting. "We do this in an open forum with representatives of all five suppliers meeting with our management in one room. It's proven very effective."

Key domestic suppliers provide laser- and gas-cut plate steel used to make frames and masts, tubing components that go into lift cylinders, chrome-plated rods, plastic parts, metal stampings, tires, and wheels. (MRO tool crib items bring the total number of domestic suppliers to a little more than 200.) Nolting declined to disclose the plant's annual spend.

Even so, the move to domestic suppliers hasn't been 100% successful, Nolting says. In a few cases, the company has had to move purchasing of certain components back to Japan because of quality or delivery issues.

TIEM's success with supplier development—and manufacturing in the United States—goes back to the selection process, a joint effort between purchasing and quality assurance. "We know what questions to ask," says Nolting. "We know what to look for in a supplier. We don't make many changes to our supply base. We are willing to make a commitment. I think our record really proves that we are here for the long run. A supplier hooks its wagon to this group and it can be a long, prosperous ride down the trail, so to speak."

Source: Adapted from S. Avery, "Toyota Commits to Suppliers in the U.S.," *Purchasing*, November 16, 2006.

One of the most important processes that organizations perform is the evaluation, selection, and continuous measurement of suppliers. Traditionally, competitive bidding was the primary method for awarding purchase contracts. In the past, it was sufficient to obtain three bids and award the contract to the supplier offering the lowest price. Enlightened purchasers now commit major resources to evaluating a supplier's performance and capability across many different areas. The supplier selection process has become so important that teams of cross-functional personnel are often responsible for visiting and evaluating suppliers. A sound selection decision can reduce or prevent a host of problems.

Supplier evaluation and selection decisions are taking on increased importance today. If a firm has reduced its supply base to a much smaller level, and if remaining suppliers usually receive longer-term agreements, the willingness or ability to switch suppliers is diminished. This makes selecting the right suppliers an important business decision.

This chapter focuses on different topics and issues pertaining to the evaluation and selection of suppliers. The first section provides an overview of the evaluation and selection process. The next sections present the various performance categories that a purchaser can include within the evaluation and selection process. The third section focuses on an approach for developing a tool or instrument for use during supplier evaluations. We next highlight the critical issues that confront a purchaser during the selection process. The chapter concludes with ways to reduce the time required for selection decisions.

The Supplier Evaluation and Selection Process

Most purchasing experts will agree that there is no one best way to evaluate and select suppliers, and organizations use a variety of different approaches. Regardless of the approach employed, the overall objective of the evaluation process should be to reduce purchase risk and maximize overall value to the purchaser.

An organization must select suppliers it can do business with over an extended period. The degree of effort associated with the selection relates to the importance of the required good or service. Depending on the supplier evaluation approach used, the process can be an intensive effort requiring a major commitment of resources (such as time and travel). This section addresses the many issues and decisions involved in effectively and efficiently evaluating and selecting suppliers to be part of the purchaser's supply base. Exhibit 7.1 highlights the critical steps involved in the supplier evaluation and selection process.

Recognize the Need for Supplier Selection

The first step of the evaluation and selection process usually involves recognizing that there is a requirement to evaluate and select a supplier for an item or service. A purchasing manager might begin the supplier evaluation process in anticipation of a future purchase requirement. Purchasing may have early insight into new-product development plans through participation on a product development team. In this case, engineering personnel may provide some preliminary specifications on the type of materials, service, or processes required, but will not yet have specific details. This

Exhibit 7.1 Supplier Evaluation and Selection Process

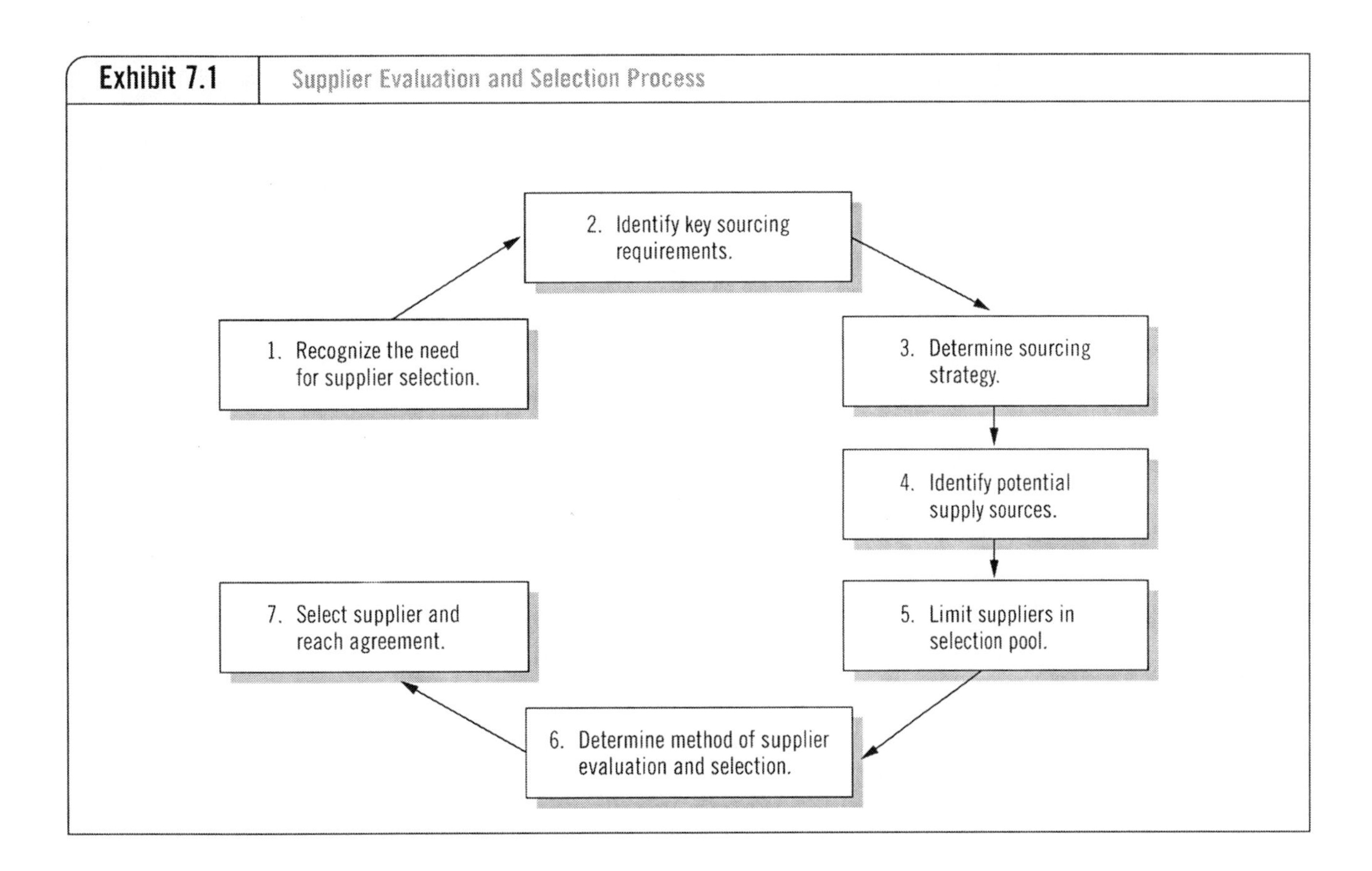

preliminary information may be enough to justify beginning an initial evaluation of potential sources of supply.

The recognition that a need exists to evaluate suppliers can come about in many different ways. Exhibit 7.2 on p. 238 identifies the most common ways that result in a need to evaluate sources of supply. Progressive purchasing groups increasingly anticipate rather than react to supplier selection needs. The complexity and value of a required purchase will influence the extent to which a buyer evaluates potential supply sources.

Identify Key Sourcing Requirements

Throughout the supplier evaluation and selection process, it is important to understand the requirements that are important to that purchase. These requirements, often determined by internal and external customers within the value chain, can differ widely from item to item. A later section discusses the various supplier performance areas where a purchaser should determine its critical sourcing requirements. Although different requirements may exist for each evaluation, certain categories—supplier quality, cost, and delivery performance—are usually included in the evaluation.

Determine Sourcing Strategy

No single sourcing strategy approach will satisfy the requirements of all purchases. Because of this, the purchasing strategy adopted for a particular item or service will influence the approach taken during the supplier evaluation and selection process. In this chapter, we will not go into detail on the processes used to develop a commodity

Exhibit 7.2	When Do Supplier Evaluation and Selection Decisions Arise?
	During new product development
	Due to poor internal or external supplier performance
	At the end of a contract
	When buying new equipment
	When expanding into new markets or product lines
	When internal users submit requisitions for goods or services
	When performing market tests
	When faced with countertrade requirements
	During outsourcing analyses
	When consolidating volumes across a business
	When conducting a reverse auction
	When current suppliers have insufficient capacity
	When reducing the size of the supply base

strategy. Chapter 6 covers this subject in detail. There are many decisions that a purchaser initially makes when developing a sourcing strategy. However, these often change as a result of market conditions, user preferences, and corporate objectives. The considerations developed during the strategy phase need to be re-evaluated during the selection process. The strategy options selected will greatly influence the supplier selection and evaluation process.

These key decisions include the following:

- Single versus multiple supply sources
- Short-term versus long-term purchase contracts
- Selecting suppliers that provide design support versus those that lack design capability
- Full-service versus non-full-service suppliers
- Domestic versus foreign suppliers
- Expectation of a close working relationship versus arm's-length purchasing

Identify Potential Supply Sources

Purchasers rely on various sources of information when identifying potential sources of supply. The degree to which a buyer must search for information or the effort put forth toward the search is a function of several variables, including how well existing suppliers can satisfy cost, quality, or other performance variables. The strategic importance or technical complexity of the purchase requirement also influences the intensity of the search. The following offers some guidelines regarding the effort and intensity of search required during supplier evaluation:

- High capability of current suppliers + High strategic importance of requirement = **Minor to moderate information search**

- High capability of current suppliers + Low strategic importance of requirement = **Minor information search**
- Low capability of current suppliers + High strategic importance of requirement = **Major information search**
- Low capability of current suppliers + Low strategic importance of requirement = **Minor to moderate information search**

The following sections discuss various resources that may be good sources of information when seeking to identify potential supply sources.

Current Suppliers

A major source of information is current or existing suppliers. Buyers often look to existing suppliers to satisfy a new purchase requirement. The advantage of this approach is that the purchaser does not have to add and maintain an additional supplier. Also, the buyer can do business with an already familiar supplier, which may limit the time and resources required to evaluate a new supplier's capabilities.

On the negative side, using existing suppliers, although perhaps easier and quicker, may not always be the best long-term approach. A purchasing manager may never know if better suppliers are available without information on other sources. For this reason, most organizations are continuously seeking new sources of supply and are expanding this search to include suppliers from around the world.

Selecting an existing supplier for a new purchase requirement may be an attractive option if a list of preferred suppliers is maintained. Designation as a **preferred supplier** means that a supplier consistently satisfies the performance and service standards defined by the buyer. A preferred supplier status conveys immediate information about the supplier's overall performance and competency. However, the buyer must still determine if a preferred supplier is capable of providing a particular purchase requirement.

Sales Representatives

All purchasers receive sales and marketing information from sales representatives. These contacts can prove to be a valuable source of information about potential sources. Even if an immediate need does not exist for a supplier's services, the buyer can file the information for future reference. A visit to a purchasing manager's office would probably reveal a set of cabinets or drawers that contain sales and marketing information.

Information Databases

Some companies maintain databases of suppliers that are capable of supporting an industry or product line. NCR, for example, maintains data on about 30,000 companies serving the computer industry. The company searches trade journals and financial newspapers for information about potential suppliers. The use of an automated database or data warehouse can quickly identify suppliers potentially qualified to support a requirement.

Maintaining a supplier database is particularly important in industries where technology changes rapidly. The database may contain information on current products, the supplier's future technology roadmap, process capability ratios, and past performance.

Databases of potential supply sources are also available for purchase from external parties. These can be especially valuable when searching for foreign sources of supply.

Experience

Experienced purchasing personnel usually have strong knowledge about potential suppliers. A buyer may have worked within an industry over many years and may be familiar with the suppliers, perhaps including international suppliers. One argument against rotating buyers too frequently between product lines or types of purchases is that a buyer may lose the expertise built up over the years. Experience and knowledge become valuable because few purchasing organizations have developed an intelligence database about suppliers.

Trade Journals

Most industries have a group or council that publishes a trade journal or magazine that routinely presents articles about different companies. These articles often focus on a company's technical or innovative development of a material, component, product, process, or service. Suppliers also use trade journals to advertise their products or services. Most buyers follow (or should follow) trade journals closely.

Trade Directories

Almost all industries publish directories of companies that produce items or provide services within an industry. Such directories can be a valuable source of initial information for a buyer who is not familiar with an industry or its suppliers. Chapter 10 provides some examples of international supplier directories. A very popular directory for domestic buyers is the *Thomas Register of American Manufacturers.* This directory can be located at www.thomasnet.com.

Trade Shows

Trade shows may be an effective way to gain exposure to a large number of suppliers at one time. Groups such as the Chemical Manufacturers Association and the American Society of Automotive Suppliers often sponsor trade shows. The National Machine Tool Builders Show in Chicago is one of the largest trade shows held in the United States. Buyers attending trade shows can gather information about potential suppliers while also evaluating the latest technological developments. Many contacts are initiated between industrial buyers and sellers at trade shows.

Second-Party or Indirect Information

This source of information includes a wide range of contacts not directly part of the purchaser's organization. A buyer can gather information from other suppliers, such as knowledge about a noncompetitor that might be valuable. Other buyers are another second-party information source. Attendees at meetings of the Institute for Supply Management can develop informal networks that provide information about potential supply sources. Other professional groups include the American Production and Inventory Control Society, the Council for Supply Chain Management Professionals, the American Manufacturing Engineering Association, and the American Society for Quality Control.

Some purchasers publicly recognize their best suppliers. Recognition may come in the form of a newspaper advertisement that highlights the achievement of superior suppliers. Ford Motor Corporation, for example, periodically purchases a full-page advertisement in the *Wall Street Journal* expressing appreciation and recognition of its best suppliers. In the advertisement, Ford lists each supplier by name and why it is being recognized. Because of Ford's approach to recognizing its best suppliers, a buyer gains visibility to a group of blue-chip suppliers.

Internal Sources

Many larger companies divide the organization into units, each with a separate purchasing operation. Sharing information across units can occur through informal meetings, strategy development sessions, purchasing newsletters, or the development of a comprehensive database containing information about potential supply sources. Internal sources, even those from diverse business units, can provide a great deal of information about potential supply sources.

Internet Searches

Buyers are increasingly using the Internet to help locate potential sources that might qualify for further evaluation. Sellers are increasingly using the Internet as an important part of their direct marketing efforts.

After collecting information about potential supply sources, the purchasing manager must begin to sift through and consolidate the information. This can be a huge task, depending on the number of suppliers and the information obtained. During its search for global suppliers for an item, Mack Trucks (part of Volvo) may collect or request information from 500 suppliers. It categorizes this information and puts it into a worldwide database for current and future reference. At some point, companies must eliminate suppliers that do not have a good fit with the buyer.

Sourcing Snapshot

Chemical Distributors Select Global Suppliers with a Customer Focus

Chemical distributors are expanding their global sourcing. International sourcing must be a win-win; their customers need to ensure that what they buy—and where they buy it from—is on their customers' wish list. Buyers at chemical distributors emphasize thorough supplier evaluation and product testing in their global supplier selection process.

Tom Corcoran is vice president of sales and sourcing at Brenntag North America, a Reading, PA–based subsidiary of the German chemical distributor that sources from and sells into a variety of overseas markets. "We don't simply look at global sourcing as leverage for better pricing, but rather we look at it as a way to expand the sourcing options for our customers," he says. That philosophy is embodied in Corcoran's unique title, which includes both sales and sourcing. As a distributor, Brenntag is, in effect, selling its suppliers to its customers, and therefore, its buyers are more closely tied to the customer side than in a typical manufacturing environment.

"Our customers clearly have an impact on where and who we source from and influence which suppliers we use in various global markets," Corcoran says. "And without the suppliers' commitment we'd have nothing to sell. Our suppliers are as important as our customers."

Corcoran says he has an advantage in global sourcing because his company is a subsidiary of the global distributor. Corcoran has counterparts in various other global regions, including Latin America and Europe, which provide leads and assistance in uncovering new suppliers on a case-by-case basis.

Also, Brenntag North America inherited a sourcing office in China when it acquired Los Angeles Chemical, which it has found it to be an extremely useful asset in its efforts to source more from China. The four sourcing employees there work to ensure that the suppliers Brenntag recruits from that market meet its needs in terms of quality and reliability. Brenntag has an office in Shanghai, and his manager there spends time interacting with suppliers and customers looking for information on how to go to market in China and extract the value out of those markets.

Beyond those regions, Corcoran says he is investigating India very closely as a potential source for new suppliers. "We have some suppliers in India now," he says, "but more and more that is becoming a strategic marketplace for us."

Shondra Garrigus is vice president of purchasing at Seattle-based TRInternational (TRI) and says the company's experience in exporting products to various global markets (most notably Europe) has helped the purchasing organization streamline its global sourcing efforts. "For a company our size—we're on the small side—to survive in the chemical industry, we have to be a little bit more innovative about how we source," Garrigus says. In the past, the company has sourced up to 75% of its products from outside the United States, but today that amount has been pared back to about 60%, due mostly to recent currency fluctuations in Europe.

Like many purchasing executives, Garrigus is focused on China. "We've gotten some materials like citric acid from China for a while, but we're rapidly expanding the list of chemicals we source from China," Garrigus says. "In the past year, we've been expanding the breadth of products coming out of China." The biggest challenge in global sourcing, she says, is educating suppliers in new regions about how to export efficiently to the U.S. market. For example, in China there are fewer regulations on the types of packaging or drums that chemicals can be shipped in.

SUPPLIER EVALUATION

As important as supplier evaluation is for manufacturers in global sourcing, it's even more important for distributors. If a manufacturer finds it has been working with a less-than-reputable supplier, it's a problem, but often the problem can be rectified before the end customer is impacted. However, poor supplier selection in distribution can have a direct impact on customer satisfaction in the distribution business.

"The same parameters we'd hold for our domestic suppliers, we hold for all of our foreign suppliers as well," says Corcoran. "That's because the customers' requirements don't change based on the supplier's location." But when it comes to global sourcing, learning by mistake is sometimes the only way.

"Anyone who has been doing this a long time has been burned on more than one occasion," says Garrigus. "It comes with the territory. But we can learn from those experiences. Beyond cost, it's most important to us to make sure we have a secure supply line for our customers.

We have to make sure the suppliers we're working with are reputable and will be around for a long time."

Both Brenntag and TRI receive requests from customers specifying that nothing they buy can be sourced from outside the United States, especially for application-specific and specialty products. Other customers prefer products from certain regions or countries.

"Sometimes customers have a valid reason, but we can sometimes break their biases by providing the right materials," says Garrigus. "We can show them that while this might not be the same supplier they are used to, this is a quality product and can save them money."

Source: Adapted from D. Hanson, "Distributors Take On Global Sourcing with a Customer Focus," *Purchasing*, March 1, 2007.

Sourcing Alternatives

Once the list of potential and current suppliers is put into a database, it is further refined considering the type of supplier a firm may wish to deal with based on the initial sourcing strategy. Major sourcing alternatives include whether to purchase from a (1) manufacturer or distributor; (2) local or national or international source; (3) small or large supplier; and (4) multiple or single supplier for the item, commodity, or service.

Manufacturer vs. Distributor

The choice of buying directly versus from a distributor is usually based on four criteria: (1) the size of the purchase; (2) the manufacturer's policies regarding direct sales; (3) the storage space available at the purchaser's facility; and (4) the extent of services required.

Economically speaking, if all else is equal, the lowest unit price will be available from the OEM. The distributor buys from the OEM and resells, therefore incurring a transaction cost, and it must make a profit. Despite the exchange cost, recent trends have increased the role of distributors in providing the purchaser a low-cost solution. First, many OEMs can't handle or choose not to handle the large volume of transactions required to sell directly. Second, buyers are requiring more services from their suppliers and distributors have stepped in to fill this need. **Vendor Managed Inventory** is a program that distributors market to manage their customer's inventory for them. Several organizations are using **integrated supply**, where a distributor is awarded a longer-term contract. Integrated suppliers are given access to the purchaser's demand data and are expected to maintain certain levels of inventory and customer service on the contracted items.

Local or National or International Suppliers

International and national suppliers may be able to offer the best price and superior technical service. Alternatively, local suppliers are more responsive to the buying firm's changing needs and can economically make frequent smaller deliveries. The popularity of JIT and quick-replenishment systems favor using more local suppliers. Local suppliers also allow the buying firm to build a degree of community goodwill through enhancing local economic activity (see the Toyota case at the beginning of this chapter). International suppliers provide opportunities to attain dramatic price savings. These savings must be evaluated against the additional inventory, communication, and logistics costs (see Chapter 10 for a complete discussion).

Large or Small Suppliers

All suppliers were at one time small suppliers. Growth over time is due to providing superior price, quality, and service compared to their competitors. Many purchasers prefer to focus on "capability to do the job" regardless of size. Size does become a factor when one firm decides to leverage its purchases from one or a few suppliers. This leveraging means that the supplier must have wide variety in its product or service offerings as well as the ability to service multiple geographic locations (in some cases worldwide locations).

Often the buying firm does not want the seller to become dependent on its business. Thus the purchaser would make sure that its purchases do not represent more than a certain percentage (e.g., 35–45%) of the supplier's total business. Finally, supply departments that are building diversity into the supply base will often deal with an increased number of small suppliers.

Multiple or Single Sourcing

Once the number of suppliers is reduced to those qualified, a decision on the optimal number of suppliers in the supply base needs to be made. Certainly there is a trend to reduce the number of suppliers. Although single sourcing provides optimum leverage and power over the supplier, multiple sourcing provides improved assurance of supply.

Limit Suppliers in Selection Pool

The result of this information gathering is that, depending upon the item under consideration, a purchaser may have many potential sources from which to choose. Unfortunately, the performance capabilities of suppliers vary widely. Limited resources also preclude an in-depth evaluation of all potential supply sources. Purchasers often perform a first cut or preliminary evaluation of potential suppliers to narrow the list before conducting an in-depth formal evaluation. Several criteria may support the narrowing of the supplier list.

Financial Risk Analysis

Most purchasers perform at least a cursory financial analysis of prospective suppliers. Although financial condition is not the only criterion upon which to evaluate a supplier, poor financial condition can indicate serious problems. A financial analysis performed during this phase of the process is much less comprehensive than the one performed during final supplier evaluation. During this phase, a purchaser is trying to get a feel for the overall financial health of the supplier. Buyers often consult external sources of information such as Dun & Bradstreet (D&B) reports to support the evaluation.

Evaluation of Supplier Performance

A prospective supplier may have an established performance record with a purchaser. A purchaser may have used a supplier for a previous purchase requirement, or a supplier may currently provide material to another part of the organization. A supplier may also have provided other types of commodities or services to the purchaser than those under consideration. Based on prior experience, a purchasing manager may consider that supplier for a different type of commodity or service.

Evaluation of Supplier-Provided Information

Buyers often request specific information directly from potential suppliers. Requests for information involve sending a preliminary survey to suppliers. The buyer uses this information to screen each supplier and to determine if the buyer's requirements appear to match the supplier's capabilities. Buyers can request information on a supplier's cost structure, process technology, market share data, quality performance, or any other area important to the purchase decision.

A major U.S. chemical producer mandates that suppliers complete requests for information (which it calls presurvey questionnaires) before conducting more detailed supplier surveys. Besides ownership, financial information, and type of business, this company attempts to determine how sophisticated the supplier's current practices are and how far along it is toward achieving total quality.

Before committing time to evaluate a supplier further, suppliers should satisfy certain entry qualifiers. **Entry qualifiers** are the basic components that suppliers must possess before they proceed to the next phase of the evaluation and selection process. One researcher identifies five qualifiers that suppliers must satisfy: financial strength, appropriate business strategy, strong supportive management, proven manufacturing capability, and design capability.[1] The time and cost associated with evaluating suppliers makes it necessary to limit suppliers in the selection pool that meet these qualifiers.

Determine the Method of Supplier Evaluation and Selection

Once an initial cut has eliminated suppliers that are not capable, the buyer or commodity team must decide how to evaluate the remaining suppliers, which may appear to be equally qualified. This requires a finer level of evaluation detail than that used in the initial process. There are a number of ways to evaluate and select suppliers from the remaining companies in the pool. These include evaluating supplier-provided information, conducting supplier visits, and using preferred supplier lists.

Evaluation from Supplier-Provided Information

Buyers often receive and evaluate detailed information directly from potential suppliers for the purpose of awarding a purchase contract. This information may come from requests for quotes or requests for proposals. Not too long ago buyers made almost all purchase decisions using this method. In recent years, however, many organizations have adopted a more direct and in-depth approach to evaluating potential suppliers. Increasingly, companies are also requesting that suppliers provide a detailed cost breakdown of their quoted price in the response to a request for quote, including details on labor, materials, overhead, and profit.

Supplier Visits

A team of cross-functional experts may visit potential suppliers. The next section discusses the criteria often used by cross-functional teams during supplier visits. Although many sources exist to discover information about a potential supplier, visiting the actual facility provides the most complete way to ensure an accurate assessment

Exhibit 7.3 Key Evaluation Criteria to Be Noted During a Supplier Visit

- ✓ Management capability
- ✓ Total quality management
- ✓ Technical capability
- ✓ Operations and scheduling capability
- ✓ Financial strength
- ✓ Personnel relations
- ✓ E-systems capabilities
- ✓ Technological sophistication and efficiency of the equipment
- ✓ ISO certifications
- ✓ Caliber of the supervision and inspection personnel
- ✓ Evidence of good management and housekeeping practices
- ✓ Types of inventory systems
- ✓ Nature of the receiving, storeroom, and shipping areas
- ✓ Quality control philosophy
- ✓ Environmental practices
- ✓ Representation of white and blue collar staffs
- ✓ Employee contract expiration dates
- ✓ Names and contact information of key decision makers

of the supplier. Site visits are expensive and require buyer time in travel and information collection. The purchaser needs to be alert and gather all necessary information while being sensitive to the supplier's limitations on restricted information. Exhibit 7.3 provides a checklist of the key evaluation criteria that should be noted during the site visit. Key personal contacts in management, operations, and marketing may be useful resources in the later stages of the selection process.

Regardless of whether the supplier is a potential or existing supplier, the purchaser should compile this data into a report that is maintained in a data warehouse or on file for easy retrieval by members of the cross-functional team. Evaluation criteria are covered in detail in the next section.

The use of teams for supplier evaluation and selection is increasing, particularly among larger organizations that have the resources to commit to this approach. The advantage to the team approach is that each team member contributes unique insight into the overall supplier evaluation. Members may have expertise in quality, engineering capabilities, or manufacturing techniques, and they may be qualified to assess suppliers in these areas.

Use of Preferred Suppliers

Increasingly, purchasers are rewarding their best suppliers by creating preferred supplier lists, which can simplify the supplier evaluation and selection process. A preferred supplier is one that consistently meets stringent performance criteria. A buyer can refer to the purchasing database to determine if there is a current supplier that can satisfy the purchase requirement. This eliminates the need to perform a time-consuming evaluation. Buyers can also use a preferred supplier list as an incentive to improve the performance of existing suppliers. Only the best suppliers should receive placement on a preferred supplier list.

Sourcing Snapshot

D&B Makes Supplier Evaluation Data Available through the Web

Imagine this scenario: You work for a small organization that simply does not have the financial or human resources to qualify suppliers. Or perhaps you have a minor purchase requirement that does not justify a major search. Do you simply hope for the best when making your selection? Will you be reluctant to try new suppliers for fear that the risk of the unknown is simply too great? For many organizations and purchase situations, supplier evaluation is a luxury when it should be a necessity.

What can you do when faced with these situations? One option is to use an external party to collect and disseminate supplier performance data. Dun & Bradstreet (D&B), a supplier of business information and receivables management services, offers its Supplier Qualifier Report over the Internet. Users around the world can now purchase with a credit card the supplier evaluation report for any of the 80 million businesses worldwide contained in D&B's database.

Designed for purchasing professionals, qualifier reports provide an objective, third-party view of suppliers. These reports provide a wide range of information about suppliers, including a business overview, history and operations, payment information, risk assessment, financial information, and public filings. The reports also indicate if a supplier is ISO 9000 registered or a minority- or women-owned business. D&B maintains that the report is a tremendous resource for companies that want to confidently do business with suppliers.

Source: From www.dnb.com, 2003.

External or Third-Party Information

Mattel Corporation's recent problem with lead paint in toys has resulted in other firms asking for third-party quality audits during the evaluation phase.[2] Sourcing Snapshot: D&B Makes Supplier Evaluation Data Available through the Web highlights another approach for securing reliable third-party information. Using third-party information can be a timely and effective way to gain insight into potential suppliers.

Select Supplier and Reach Agreement

The final step of the evaluation and selection process is to select the supplier(s) and reach a contract agreement. The activities associated with this step can vary widely depending on the purchase item under consideration. For routine items, this may simply require notifying and awarding a basic purchase contract to a supplier. For a major purchase, the process can become more complex. The buyer and seller may have to conduct detailed negotiations to agree upon the specific details of a purchase agreement.

Sourcing Snapshot — *Good Ideas When Evaluating IT Suppliers*

Buyers of information technology (IT) know that choosing the wrong supplier can create problems that last for many years. The rate of technological change can make the perfect supplier obsolete within months. Unfortunately, it is usually next to impossible to switch to a new IT supplier quickly. For this reason, the selection process takes on added importance. IT experts offer some sound suggestions when making supplier selection decisions:

- Do not rely on only one supplier. Too many companies try to complete all of their computer technology buying using one or two big suppliers. Try to build a supply network that includes some smaller suppliers that have promising emerging technologies.
- Make sure you and the supplier are moving down the same road. Evaluate each supplier's technology and product roadmaps. Are both organizations working toward platforms, capabilities, features, and functions that are compatible?
- Build your portfolio with the best. Choose suppliers that add strength to your ability to add value to your end customer. Do not select suppliers simply because they offer a good purchase price.
- Be a big fish in a little pond. Sourcing from the biggest supplier might bring a good purchase price but limits your ability to leverage. A smaller supplier may be more motivated to innovate in your direction.
- Know the supplier's Internet strategy. Understand how your suppliers are using the Internet to add value to what they develop, manufacture, service, or distribute.

Because information technology has become increasingly important to supply chain management, making the right IT supplier selection decision can mean the difference between success and failure.

Source: Adapted from "Tips on Supplier Evaluation," *InfoWorld*, October 26, 1998, p. 72.

Key Supplier Evaluation Criteria

Purchasers usually evaluate potential suppliers across multiple categories using their own selection criteria with assigned weights. Purchasers that need consistent delivery performance with short lead times to support a just-in-time production system might emphasize a supplier's scheduling and production systems. A high-technology buyer might emphasize a supplier's process and technological capabilities or commitment to research and development. The selection process for a distributor or service provider will emphasize a different set of criteria.

Most evaluations rate suppliers on three primary criteria: (1) cost or price, (2) quality, and (3) delivery. These three elements of performance are generally the most obvious and most critical areas that affect the purchaser. For critical items needing an in-depth analysis of the supplier's capabilities, a more detailed supplier evaluation study is required. The following presents the wide range of criteria that a purchaser might consider during supplier evaluation and selection.

Management Capability

It is important for a buyer to evaluate a supplier's management capability. After all, management runs the business and makes the decisions that affect the competitiveness of the supplier. A buyer should ask many questions when evaluating a supplier's management capability:

- Does management practice long-range planning?
- Has management committed the supplier to total quality management (TQM) and continuous improvement?
- Is turnover high among managers?
- What are the professional experience and educational backgrounds of the key managers?
- Is there a vision about the future direction of the company?
- Is management customer focused?
- What is the history of labor/management relations?
- Is management making the investments that are necessary to sustain and grow the business?
- Has management prepared the company to face future competitive challenges, including providing employee training and development?
- Does management understand the importance of strategic sourcing?

It may be a challenge to identify the true state of affairs during a brief visit or using a questionnaire. Nevertheless, asking these questions can help the purchasing manager to develop a feeling for the professional capabilities of the managers in the supplying organization. When interviewing managers, it is important to attempt to meet with as many people as possible in order to paint a true picture.

Employee Capabilities

This part of the evaluation process requires an assessment of non-management personnel. Do not underestimate the benefit that a highly trained, stable, and motivated workforce provides, particularly during periods of labor shortages. A purchaser should consider these points:

- The degree to which employees are committed to quality and continuous improvement
- The overall skills and abilities of the workforce
- Employee-management relations
- Worker flexibility
- Employee morale
- Workforce turnover
- Willingness of employees to contribute to improved operations

A buyer should also gather information about the history of strikes and labor disputes. This can result in a general idea of how dedicated the supplier's employees are to producing products or services that will meet or exceed the buyer's expectations.

Sourcing Snapshot

H.B. Fuller Uses Supplier Visits to Narrow the Supply Base

H.B. Fuller Corporation illustrates how first-hand information gained through supplier visits plays a large part in narrowing the supply base.

Latin America sourcing manager Roy Calderón of H.B. Fuller narrows down his list of suppliers by obtaining first-hand information. Whenever possible, that means touring supplier plants and interacting with the supplier's staff.

"I have a technical and manufacturing background, so I first try to understand the logistical and manufacturing capabilities of a supplier, as well as their quality assurance process and systems," says Calderón. What he sees at a supplier's plant helps him determine how much H.B. Fuller, headquartered in St. Paul, MN, can expect from that supplier in the way of consistent quality.

Calderón scrutinizes the plant's infrastructure as well as its production staff. "Morale and work environment is hard to put into hard numbers or dollars, but it needs to be part of a supplier's intelligence profile," he says. Though he can't visit every single one of his suppliers, he makes a point to visit at least the top 10 suppliers in his region.

When visiting a supplier, Calderón looks for any signs in the facilities that might signal future supply problems. For example, if a machine looks like it might wear out or if the plant seems like it's falling apart, he takes notice. He also inspects production line pacing as another indicator of a supplier's health. If a supplier is too busy and overloaded, it might not be responsive enough to any order changes. If it is too relaxed, it might not be economically viable for much longer. Neither extreme is encouraging, Calderón says.

Another crucial component of supplier health is the attitude of employees on the plant floor. Calderón wants to see if they seem motivated or happy. He'll speak with employees about nontechnical topics, even just to ask them how they're doing, and gauge their reaction. If the workers seem to be proud of their work, it's more likely that supplier will provide a consistently high-quality product.

Although some suppliers might want to keep Calderón in the board room offices, he insists on the broader picture. "If all I see are fancy offices and the suppliers aren't willing to show me their manufacturing process and let me talk to their employees, that's a big question mark," he says.

Source: Adapted from M. Varmazis, "How to Narrow Your Supply List," *Purchasing*, July 17, 2007.

Cost Structure

Evaluating a supplier's cost structure requires an in-depth understanding of a supplier's total costs, including direct labor costs, indirect labor costs, material costs, manufacturing or process operating costs, and general overhead costs. Understanding a supplier's cost structure helps a buyer determine how efficiently a supplier can produce an item. A cost analysis also helps identify potential areas of cost improvement.

Collecting this information can be a challenge. A supplier may not have a detailed understanding of its costs. Many suppliers do not have a sophisticated cost accounting system and are unable to assign overhead costs to products or processes. Furthermore, some suppliers view cost data as highly proprietary. They may fear that the release of cost information will undermine its pricing strategy or that competitors will gain access to its cost data, which could provide insight into a supplier's competitive advantage. Because of these concerns, buyers will often develop reverse pricing models that provide estimates of the supplier's cost structure during the initial supplier evaluation.

Total Quality Performance, Systems, and Philosophy

A major part of the evaluation process addresses a supplier's quality management processes, systems, and philosophy. Buyers evaluate not only the obvious topics associated with supplier quality (management commitment, statistical process control, defects) but also safety, training, and facilities and equipment maintenance. Alcoa defines its supplier quality requirements in four broad areas: management, quality measurement, safety and training, and facilities. Many purchasers are expecting potential suppliers to have adopted quality systems based on the Malcolm Baldrige National Quality Award (MBNQA) or International Organization for Standardization (ISO) 9000 criteria. The wide distribution of these guidelines has exposed many suppliers to the Baldrige and ISO definitions of quality.

Process and Technological Capability

Supplier evaluation teams often include a member from the engineering or technical staff to evaluate a supplier's process and technological capability. Process consists of the technology, design, methods, and equipment used to manufacture a product or deliver a service. A supplier's selection of a production process helps define its required technology, human resource skills, and capital equipment requirements.

The evaluation should include both the supplier's current and future process and technological capabilities. Assessing a supplier's future process and technological capability involves reviewing capital equipment plans and strategy. In addition, a purchaser should evaluate the resources that a supplier is committing to research and development.

A purchaser may also assess a supplier's design capability. One way to reduce the time required to develop new products involves using qualified suppliers that are able to support product design activities. The trend toward the increased use of supplier design capabilities makes this area an integral part of the supplier evaluation and selection process.

Environmental Regulation Compliance

The 1990s brought about a renewed awareness of the impact that industry has on the environment. The Clean Air Act of 1990, for example, imposes large fines on producers of ozone-depleting substances and foul-smelling gases. Recycling of industrial materials is also an issue. Purchasers certainly do not want to be associated with known environmental polluters from a public relations or potential liability standpoint.

The most common environmental performance criteria used when evaluating a supplier's performance include the following:

- Disclosure of environmental infractions
- Hazardous and toxic waste management

- Recycling management
- ISO 14000 certification
- Control of ozone-depleting substances

Herman Miller, a manufacturer of office furniture, makes environmental concerns part of the supplier evaluation and selection process. For instance, Herman Miller includes supplier packaging as an evaluation criterion. Standardized, reusable shipping containers are favored over disposable ones. Such containers also support just-in-time deliveries. Herman Miller also requires its suppliers to label the chemical composition of its plastic procured items so that recyclers will know the exact content of the plastic found in the parts.[3] DuPont's environmental program began with cutting greenhouse gas emissions at its factories by 72% since 1990, an initiative that saved $3 billion in energy costs. Now DuPont views the environmental movement as a key to increasing revenue.[4]

Financial Stability

An assessment of a potential supplier's financial condition should occur during the initial evaluation process. Some purchasers view the financial assessment as a screening process or preliminary condition that the supplier must pass before a detailed evaluation can begin. An organization may use a financial rating service to help analyze a supplier's financial condition.

Selecting a supplier in poor financial condition presents a number of risks. First, there is the risk that the supplier will go out of business. Second, suppliers that are in poor financial condition may not have the resources to invest in plant, equipment, or research that is necessary for longer-term technological or other performance improvements. Third, the supplier may become too financially dependent on the purchaser. A final risk is that financial weakness is usually an indication of underlying problems. Is the weakness a result of poor quality or delivery performance? Is it a result of wasteful spending by management? Has the supplier assumed too much debt?

There may be circumstances that support selecting a supplier in a weaker financial condition. A supplier may be developing but has not yet marketed a leading-edge technology that can provide an advantage to the purchaser. A supplier may also be in a weaker financial condition because of uncontrollable or nonrepeating circumstances.

If the supplier is publicly traded, specific financial ratios can be obtained from a variety of websites providing detailed financial ratios and industry averages to compare these ratios against. Some common ratios used to assess supplier financial health appear in Exhibit 7.4.

Some websites available to obtain such information include the following:

- Yahoo! Financial section (http://www.biz.yahoo.com)
- Morningstar (http://www.morningstar.net)
- Marketwatch (http://www.marketwatch.com)
- 411Stocks (http://www.411stocks.com)
- The Street (http://www.thestreet.com)
- Dun & Bradstreet (http://www.dnb.com)

Procurement specialists should become familiar with financial ratios because they can provide quick and valuable insights into a supplier's financial health. Moreover,

Exhibit 7.4 Interpreting Key Financial Ratios

RATIOS	INTERPRETATION
LIQUIDITY	
Current ratio = Current assets/Current liabilities	Should be over 1.0, but look at industry average; high—may mean poor asset management.
Quick ratio = (Cash + Receivables)/Current liabilities	At least 0.8 if supplier sells on credit; low—may mean cash flow problems; high—may mean poor asset management.
Note: Calculation includes marketable securities	
ACTIVITY	
Inventory turnover = Costs of goods sold/Inventory	Compare industry average; low—problems with slow inventory, which may hurt cash flow.
Fixed asset turnover = Sales/Fixed assets	Compare industry average; too low may mean supplier is not using fixed assets efficiently or effectively.
Total asset turnover = Sales/Total assets	Compare industry average; too low may mean supplier is not using its total assets efficiently or effectively.
Days sales outstanding = (Receivables × 365)/Sales	Compare industry average, or a value of 45–50 if company sells on net 30; too high hurts cash flow; too low may mean credit policies to customers are too restrictive.
PROFITABILITY	
Net profit margin = Profit after taxes/Sales	Represents after-tax return; compare industry average.
Return on assets = Profit after taxes/Total assets	Compare industry average; represents the return the company earns on everything it owns.
Return on equity = Profit after taxes/Equity	The higher the better; the return on the shareholders' investment in the business.
DEBT	
Debt to equity = Total liabilities/Equity	Compare industry average; over 3 means highly leveraged.
Current debt to equity = Current liabilities/Equity	Over 1 is risky unless industry average is over 1; when ratio is high, supplier may be unable to pay lenders.
Interest coverage = (Pretax Inc. + Int. Exp.)/Int. Exp.	Should be over 3; higher is better; low may mean supplier is having difficulty paying creditors.

purchasing managers should track such ratios for possible red flags that may signify potential financial difficulty.

Production Scheduling and Control Systems

Production scheduling includes those systems that release, schedule, and control a supplier's production process. Does the supplier use material requirements planning (MRP) to ensure the availability of required components? Does the supplier track material and production cycle time and compare this against a performance objective or standard? Does the supplier's production scheduling system support a purchaser's just-in-time requirements? What lead time does the supplier's production scheduling and control system require? What is the supplier's on-time delivery performance history? The purpose behind evaluating the production scheduling and control system is to identify the degree of control the supplier has over its scheduling and production process.

Suppliers can formally claim to have a Class A production system once they have undergone a formal review of their system by a professional external reviewer who has verified that the requisite criteria are satisfied. Companies that are considering sourcing high volumes of product with a supplier will also want to consider whether the supplier has adequate capacity.

E-Commerce Capability

The ability to communicate electronically between a buyer and seller is fast becoming a requirement during supplier selection. In the past, many considered electronic data interchange (EDI) a primary condition for doing business. However, more and more companies are moving to web-based business to business (B2B) platforms for their transactions. In early 2000, relatively few companies had implemented B2B electronic commerce platforms, but the rate of technology change in this area has now escalated rapidly.

IBM now states that the majority of its purchases (by dollar spent) occur via the Internet. However, such statements entail that suppliers have the required ability to adopt an e-commerce approach. In contrast to EDI, electronic commerce requires a relatively low investment on the part of suppliers. Besides the efficiencies that B2B e-commerce provides, these systems support closer relationships and the exchange of all kinds of information.

Purchasing managers should also evaluate other dimensions of the supplier's information technology (IT). Does the supplier have computer-aided design (CAD) capability? Does the supplier have bar coding capability or the ability to use radio frequency identification tags? Can the supplier send advance-shipping notices or accept payment by electronic funds transfer? Is the supplier able to communicate via e-mail? Evidence that the supplier is using these technologies can provide reasonable assurance that the supplier is current with e-commerce technologies.

Supplier's Sourcing Strategies, Policies, and Techniques

The concept of understanding a supplier's suppliers is part of integrated supply chain management. Unfortunately, organizations do not have the resources or personnel to investigate all of the suppliers within their supply chain. However, there are ways to obtain information on the performance capabilities of Tier 2 and even Tier 3 suppliers.

It is possible for a purchaser to develop an understanding of the purchasing approaches and techniques of suppliers that are three tiers or levels from the primary buyer. Assume that during the supplier selection process, a purchaser evaluates the sourcing strategies, approaches, and techniques of its first-tier supplier. Through discussions with the purchasing department of the first-tier supplier, the purchaser can gain insight about its second-tier suppliers. If the first-tier supplier also evaluates the sourcing strategies, approaches, and techniques of its first-tier suppliers (second-tier suppliers to the purchaser), then this can provide information about third-tier suppliers. Evaluating a potential supplier's sourcing strategies, approaches, and techniques is one way to gain greater insight and understanding of the supply chain. Because few purchasers understand their second- and third-tier suppliers, those that do can gain an important advantage over competitors.

Longer-Term Relationship Potential

A supplier's willingness to move beyond a traditional purchasing relationship should be part of the evaluation process for items and services where a longer-term relationship might be beneficial. Robert Spekman presented a number of questions that a buyer should ask when evaluating the potential of a longer-term relationship.[5] He argued that approaches emphasizing supplier efficiency, quality, price, and delivery are sometimes incomplete. Although these areas are important, they do not necessarily cover the issues upon which to base a longer-term relationship. Consider the following questions when evaluating the longer-term relationship potential of a prospective supplier:

- Has the supplier indicated a willingness or commitment to a longer-term relationship?
- Is the supplier willing to commit resources specific to this relationship?
- How early in the product design stage is the supplier willing or able to participate?
- What does the supplier bring that is unique?
- Does the supplier have an interest in joint problem solving and improvement efforts?
- Will there be free and open exchange of information across the two companies?
- How much future planning is the supplier willing to share?
- Is the need for confidential treatment of information taken seriously?
- What is the general level of comfort between the two parties?
- How well does the supplier know our industry and business?
- Will the supplier share cost data?
- Is the supplier willing to come to us first with innovations?
- Is the supplier willing to commit capacity exclusively to our needs?
- What will be the supplier's commitment to understanding our problems and concerns?

Although this is not a complete list of questions when evaluating the possibility of a longer-term relationship, it does provide a framework regarding the types of issues that are important. It is relatively straightforward to create a numerical scale to assess these questions as part of the supplier evaluation and selection process.

Developing a Supplier Evaluation and Selection Survey

Supplier evaluation often follows a rigorous, structured approach using formal surveys. An effective supplier survey should have certain characteristics. First, the survey should be comprehensive and include the performance categories considered important to the evaluation and selection process. Second, the survey process should be as objective as possible. This requires the use of a scoring system that defines the meaning of each value on a measurement scale.

A third characteristic is that the items and the measurement scales are reliable. This refers to the degree to which different individuals or groups reviewing the same items and measurement scales will arrive at the same conclusion. Reliable evaluations require well-defined measures and well-understood items.

A fourth characteristic of a sound supplier survey is flexibility. Although an organization should maintain a structure to its supplier survey, the format of the evaluation should provide some flexibility across different types of purchase requirements. The easiest way to make the process flexible is to adjust the performance categories and weights assigned to each category. The most important categories will receive a higher weight within the total evaluation score.

A final characteristic of an effective survey is that it is mathematically straightforward. The use of weights and points should be simple enough that each individual involved in the evaluation understands the mechanics of the scoring and selection process. To ensure that a supplier survey has the right characteristics, we recommend the use of a step-by-step process when creating this tool. Exhibit 7.5 presents the steps to follow when developing such a system. The following section discusses this framework and develops a sample evaluation survey.

Step 1: Identify Supplier Evaluation Categories

Perhaps the first step when developing a supplier survey is deciding the categories to include. As discussed earlier, there are many evaluation categories. For illustrative purposes, assume that a purchaser selects quality, management capability, financial condition, supplier cost structure, expected delivery performance, technological capability, systems capability, and a general category of miscellaneous performance factors as the categories to include in the evaluation. These categories would reveal the performance areas that the purchaser considers most important.

Exhibit 7.5 Supplier Evaluation and Selection Survey Development

Step	Action	Phase
Step 1	Identify supplier evaluation categories.	Develop the Survey
Step 2	Assign a weight to each evaluation category.	Develop the Survey
Step 3	Identify and weigh subcategories.	Develop the Survey
Step 4	Define scoring system for categories and subcategories.	Develop the Survey
Step 5	Evaluate supplier directly.	Assess and Select Supplier
Step 6	Review evaluation results and make selection decision.	Assess and Select Supplier
Step 7	Review and improve supplier performance continuously.	Review Performance

Step 2: Assign a Weight to Each Evaluation Category

The performance categories usually receive a weight that reflects the relative importance of that category. The assigned weights reflect the relative importance of each category. The total of the combined weights must equal 1.0.

Exhibit 7.6 shows the weight assigned to each selected performance category in our sample survey. Notice that the quality systems category receives 20% of the total evaluation, whereas systems capability receives 5%; this simply reflects the difference in relative importance to the purchaser between the two performance categories. Recall that an important characteristic of an effective evaluation system is flexibility. One way that management achieves this flexibility is by assigning different weights or adding or deleting performance categories as required.

Exhibit 7.6 Initial Supplier Evaluation

CATEGORY	WEIGHT	SUBWEIGHT	SCORE (5 PT. SCALE)	WEIGHTED SCORE	
Supplier: Advanced Micro Systems					
1. Quality Systems	20				
Process control systems		5	4	4.0	
Total quality commitment		8	4	6.4	
Parts-per-million defect performance		7	5	7.0	
					17.4
2. Management Capability	10				
Management/labor relations		5	4	4.0	
Management capability		5	4	4.0	
					8.0
3. Financial Condition	10				
Debt structure		5	3	3.0	
Turnover ratios		5	4	4.0	
					7.0
4. Cost Structure	15				
Costs relative to industry		5	5	5.0	
Understanding of costs		5	4	4.0	
Cost control/reduction efforts		5	5	5.0	
					14.0
5. Delivery Performance	15				
Performance to promise		5	3	3.0	
Lead-time requirements		5	3	3.0	
Responsiveness		5	3	3.0	
					9.0
6. Technical/Process Capability	15				
Product innovation		5	4	4.0	
Process innovation		5	5	5.0	
Research and development		5	5	5.0	
					14.0
7. Information Systems Capability	5				
EDI capability		3	5	3.0	
CAD/CAM		2	0	0	
					3.0
8. General	10				
Support of minority suppliers		2	3	1.2	
Environmental compliance		3	5	3.0	
Supplier's supply base management		5	4	4.0	
					8.2
			Total Weighted Score		80.6

Step 3: Identify and Weigh Subcategories

Step 2 specified broad performance categories included within our sample evaluation. Step 3 of this process requires identifying any performance subcategories, if they exist, within each broader performance category. For example, the quality systems category may require the identification of separate subcategories (such as those described in the Malcolm Baldrige Award criteria). If this is the case, the supplier evaluation should include any subcategories or items that make up the quality systems category.

Equally important, the purchaser must decide how to weigh each subcategory within the broader performance evaluation category. In Exhibit 7.6, the quality category includes an evaluation of a supplier's process control systems, total quality commitment, and parts per million (ppm) defects performance. The sum of the subcategory weights must equal the total weight of the performance category. Furthermore, the purchaser must clearly define the scoring system used within each category. This becomes the focus of Step 4.

Step 4: Define a Scoring System for Categories and Subcategories

Step 4 defines each score within a performance category. If an evaluation uses a 5-point scale to assess a performance category, then a purchaser must clearly define the difference between a score of 5, 4, 3, and so on. One important point is to develop a scale that clearly defines what a specific score means. For example, it is better to use a 4-point scale that is easier to interpret and is based on the language and principles of total quality management than a 10-point scale where 1–2 = poor, 3–4 = weak, 5–6 = marginal, 7–8 = qualified, and 9–10 = outstanding. The scoring values on the 10-point scale do not have descriptive definitions detailing the difference between a 1 and a 2 or a 3 and a 4, for example. A more specific way is shown in the 4-point scale below:

- Major nonconformity (0 points earned): The absence or total breakdown of a system to meet a requirement, or any noncompliance that would result in the probable shipment of a nonconforming product.
- Minor nonconformity (1 point earned): A noncompliance (though not major) that judgment and experience indicate is likely to result in the failure of the quality system or reduce its ability to ensure controlled processes or products.
- Conformity (2 points earned): No major or minor nonconformities were noted during the evaluation.
- Adequacy (3 points earned): Specific supplier performance or documentation meets or exceeds requirements given the scope of the supplier's operations.

A well-defined scoring system takes criteria that may be highly subjective and develops a quantitative scale for measurement. Effective metrics allow different individuals to interpret and score similarly the same performance categories under review. A scoring system that is too broad, ambiguous, or poorly defined increases the probability of arriving at widely different assessments or conclusions.

Step 5: Evaluate Supplier Directly

This step requires that the reviewer visit a supplier's facilities to perform the evaluation. Site visits require at least a day and often several days to complete. When factoring in travel time and postvisit reviews, we begin to realize that an organization must carefully select those suppliers it plans on evaluating. In many cases, a cross-functional team will perform the evaluation, which allows team members with different knowledge to ask different questions.

Purchasers often notify suppliers beforehand of any documentation required during the initial evaluation. For example, if a purchaser has no previous experience with a supplier, the reviewer might require a supplier to provide documentation of performance capability. The supplier will have to present evidence of process capability studies, process control systems, or delivery performance.

The following explains the calculation for the quality category in Exhibit 7.6: Quality Systems Performance Category (Weight = 20% of total evaluation).

Subcategories are the following:

- *Process control systems* (4 points out of 5 possible points equals 80%) or 0.8 × 5 sub-weight = 4.0 points
- *Total quality commitment* (4 points out of 5 possible points) = 0.8 × 8 sub-weight = 6.4 points
- *PPM defect performance* (5 points out of 5 possible points) = 1.0 × 7 sub-weight = 7.0 points
- Total for category = 17.4 points or 87% of total possible points (17.4/20)

As shown in Exhibit 7.6, Advanced Micro Systems received a total overall evaluation of 80.6%. A purchaser can objectively compare the scores of different suppliers competing for the same purchase contract or select one supplier over another based on the evaluation score. It is also possible that a supplier does not qualify at this time for further purchase consideration. Purchasers should have minimum acceptable performance requirements that suppliers must satisfy before they can become part of the supply base. In this example, the supplier performs acceptably in most major categories except delivery performance (9 out of 15 possible points). The reviewer must decide if the shortcomings in this category are correctable or if the supplier simply lacks the ability to perform.

Step 6: Review Evaluation Results and Make Selection Decision

At some point, a reviewer must decide whether to recommend or reject a supplier as a source. A purchaser may review a supplier for consideration for expected future business and not a specific contract. Evaluating suppliers before there is an actual purchase requirement can provide a great deal of flexibility to a purchaser. Once an actual need materializes, the purchaser is in a position to move quickly because it has prequalified the supplier.

It is important to determine the seriousness of any supplier shortcomings noted during the evaluation and assess the degree to which these shortcomings might affect performance. Evaluation scales should differentiate between various degrees of supplier shortcomings. Alcoa, for example, explicitly defines the difference between a performance problem and a deficiency. A **performance problem** is "a discrepancy, nonconformance, or missing requirement that will have a significant negative impact on an important area of concern in an audit statement." A **deficiency** is "a minor departure from an intended level of performance, or a nonconformance that is easily resolved and does not materially affect the required output."[6]

The primary output from this step is a recommendation about whether to accept a supplier for a purchase contract. Exhibit 7.7 illustrates a simple recommendation form issued after a supplier evaluation visit conducted by a commodity team. An important outcome from any evaluation is the identification of improvement opportunities on the part of the supplier.

Exhibit 7.7 Sample Recommendation Form

Type of Supplier: Mfg.

Qualification Survey Summary

Company Name	Foster Industries	Surveyed By:	Manufacturing Commodity Team
Address	PO Box 1256	Accompanied By:	Quality
City, State, Zip	Stroudsburg, PA 18370	Initial Survey (circled)	Resurvey
Phone	570-619-5411	Survey Date:	9/14/2004
Supplier Code	Foster	Contact:	Robert Jones
Supplier Score	80.8	**Minimum Required Score: 65**	

Recommendations

Supplier has potential to become a critical partner. However, limited design/development capability prevents continued growth. Foster will embark on implementing and upgrading design/development function for our business.

ACTION PLAN IS DUE BY: 1/1/2005

Supplier Acknowledgment:

John Weaver

9/15/2004
Date

Source: Adapted from J. Przirembel, *How to Conduct Supplier Surveys and Audits,* West Palm Beach, FL: PT Publications, 1997, p. 76.

A purchaser may evaluate several suppliers that might be competing for the same contract. The initial evaluation provides an objective way to compare suppliers side-by-side before making a final selection decision. A purchaser may decide to use more than one supplier based on the results of the supplier survey.

The authority to decide the final selection varies from organization to organization. The reviewer or team who evaluated the supplier may have the authority to make the supplier selection decision. In other cases, the buyer or team may present or justify the supplier selection decision or findings to a committee or a manager who has final authority.

Step 7: Review and Improve Supplier Performance Continuously

The supplier survey or visit is only the first step of the evaluation process. If a purchaser decides to select a supplier, the supplier must then perform according to the purchaser's requirements. The emphasis shifts from the initial evaluation and selection of suppliers to evidence of continuous performance improvement by suppliers. Chapter 9 addresses the management of a world-class supply base.

Supplier Selection

Some important issues arise during the supplier evaluation and selection process. Each has the potential to affect the final decision.

Critical Issues

Size Relationship

A purchaser may decide to select suppliers over which it has a relative size advantage. A buyer may simply have greater influence when it has a relative size advantage over the supplier or represents a larger share of the supplier's total business. For example, Allen-Edmonds Shoe Corporation, a 71-year-old maker of premium shoes, tried unsuccessfully to implement just-in-time methods to speed production, boost customer satisfaction, and save money. Unfortunately, Allen-Edmonds had difficulty getting suppliers to agree to the just-in-time requirement of matching delivery to production needs. Although domestic suppliers of leather soles agreed to make weekly instead of monthly deliveries, European tanneries supplying calfskin hides refused to cooperate. The reason? Allen-Edmonds was not a large enough customer to wield any leverage with those suppliers.

Use of International Suppliers

The decision to select a foreign supplier can have important implications during the supplier evaluation and selection process. For one, international sourcing is generally more complex than domestic buying. As a result, the evaluation and selection process can take on added complexity. It may be difficult to implement JIT with international suppliers, as lead times are frequently twice or even three times as long as lead times for domestic suppliers.

Competitors as Suppliers

Another important issue is the degree to which a buyer is willing to purchase directly from a competitor. Purchasing from competitors may limit information sharing between the parties. The purchase transaction is usually straightforward and the buyer and seller may not develop a working relationship characterized by mutual commitment and confidential information sharing.

Countertrade Requirements

The need to satisfy countertrade requirements can also affect the supplier selection decision. **Countertrade** is a broad term that refers to all trade where buyer and seller have at least a partial exchange of goods for goods. (See Chapter 10 for additional discussion.)

Boeing, a producer of commercial aircraft, purchases a portion of its production requirements in markets where it hopes to do business. An organization involved in extensive worldwide marketing may have to contend with countertrade requirements before it can sell to international customers, which can have a direct impact on the supplier evaluation and selection process. Chapter 10 addresses international purchasing and countertrade.

Social Objectives

Most purchasers are attempting to increase their business with traditionally disadvantaged suppliers, including suppliers with female, minority, or handicapped owners. Buyers may also want to conduct business with suppliers that commit to the highest environmental standards. The influence of social objectives on purchasing will continue to remain strong.

Reducing Supplier Evaluation and Selection Cycle Time

Across almost all business applications, competitive and customer pressures are forcing reductions in the time it takes to perform a task or carry out a process. These pressures are also affecting the time available to evaluate and select suppliers. Purchasing must increasingly be proactive and anticipate supplier selection requirements rather than react when a need arises.

Although supplier selection decisions come about for different reasons, many important selection decisions come about as part of the product development process. Consider the cycle time changes that the U.S. automotive industry continues to experience. In the middle of the 1980s, GM, Ford, and Chrysler required 60 months to design and bring a new car or truck to market. During the early 1990s, the benchmark for development time (sometimes referred to as concept-to-customer, or CTC, cycle time) became 48 months. By the mid-1990s world-class producers were aiming for development times of 36 months.

From the 1980s to 2003, product development cycle times changed from 60 months to a new target of 18 months, or a reduction of 70%! In many industries, development times are shortening by 30–50% every five years. Processes that support new-product development, such as supplier evaluation and selection, must also shorten accordingly.

Tools and Approaches

Most managers do not even challenge the need to reduce the time it takes to evaluate and select suppliers. The challenge is one of shortening the process while still arriving at effective decisions. Fortunately, supply managers have many tools and approaches available to help them shorten the selection cycle time. Although dozens of activities can help shorten selection time, the following presents a set of powerful ways to reduce selection time.

Map the Current Supplier Evaluation and Selection Process

Process mapping involves the identification of the steps, activities, time, and costs involved in a process. Once we understand the current evaluation and selection process, opportunities for improvement should become evident. Supply managers should measure process cycle times to identify rates of improvement against pre-established performance targets. Process mapping should be the first step in the improvement process.

Integrate with Internal Customers

The need to anticipate rather than react to supplier evaluation and selection decisions requires closer involvement with internal customers, which can be achieved in a variety of ways. Purchasing can co-locate physically with marketing, engineering, and operations to gain early insight into expected supply requirements. Involvement on new-product development teams is also an ideal way to integrate with internal customers. Allowing internal customers to forward their requirements to purchasing, perhaps through an online requisition system, can also be an effective way to integrate with internal customers, particularly for routine purchase requirements.

Data Warehouse with Supplier Information

A data warehouse consists of easy-to-access supplier data and information. The data warehouse can include information about potential suppliers, performance history of current suppliers, details of current contracts, expiration dates of supply contracts, expected forecasts for purchased items, and any other information that supports a faster selection process.

Third-Party Support

The Good Practice Example following this section highlights the use of a third or external party to provide supplier data, which can significantly reduce time and effort. Another third-party source is Dun & Bradstreet, which provides financial ratio data, the business background of supplier management, payment trends, and an overall supplier risk score. The Internet is also a source of third-party supplier information, including online directories of potential suppliers.

New Organizational Design Features

Commodity teams have become a popular way to manage important purchase requirements. These teams are responsible for understanding in depth entire families or groups of purchased goods and services. The teams are usually responsible for achieving improvements within their commodity, which may involve site visits to evaluate suppliers. Some companies also use a lead buyer model as part of their organizational design. An individual at a site or location is responsible for owning and managing a purchased item. The lead buyer usually manages items that are not critical enough for a commodity team to manage.

Preferred Supplier List

Many firms create a list of their highest-performing suppliers. These suppliers earn their place on a preferred supplier list by consistently providing the best services and products to the buyer. A preferred supplier list can provide dramatic reductions in selection time because a buyer already knows the best suppliers to consider.

Electronic Tools

IT providers have developed a host of electronic tools to improve the evaluation and selection process:[7]

- E-Learning Scorecard is a tool to use during first-time visits with suppliers to make a quick "yes or no" decision about the possibility of using the supplier. The tool requires the user to rank various criteria among suppliers.[8]
- Special Edition is a microsite developed by Northern Light Technology. This tool provides current news and information, as well as Internet links to leading supplier information.[9]
- RFP Version 2.0, developed by eBreviate, is a web-based software package that enables companies to develop customized online supplier surveys and proposal requests. A buyer can establish simultaneous communication with multiple potential suppliers, which allows users to evaluate and quantify discussions with potential suppliers in an online auction format.[10]
- Decision Analysis, developed by Kepner-Tregoe of Princeton, NJ, is a widely used supplier evaluation and selection process that uses a weighted-point system. This tool is part of Kepner-Tregoe's "Problem Solving and Decision Making" series.[11]
- SPEX evaluation kits use a four-step process that consists of industry analysis and project formalization, definition of projects, examining responses to key requirements, and evaluation and selection of suppliers.[12]

Predefined Contract Language and Shorter Contracts

Most contracts address areas that are similar. Progressive supply managers work with their legal group to develop pre-established contract language that can be cut and pasted during a supplier negotiation. The role of the legal department is to review and initial any changes from the pre-established language or approve areas the standard language does not cover. Progressive firms are also working to shorten the length of their contracts.

Good Practice Example

Eaton Corporation Wins Purchasing Medal of Excellence through Supplier Management

When Eaton CEO Alexander (Sandy) Cutler thanked the supply chain management staff for winning the Purchasing Medal of Excellence, he emphasized that the goal didn't include price reductions. Instead, he talked about values. "We want to be the most admired company in our markets through supply chain performance," he told the attendees. "Have the right ethics and the right business practices and you'll attract the best people and suppliers who'll produce the best results," Cutler said.

With that ethos as their foundation, Eaton's vice president for supply chain management Rick Jacobs and the 3,500-strong supply chain team examine suppliers' ethics and business practices as closely as they look at their product quality, core competencies, and potential for value creation. The company has an ombudsman for ethics whom employees or anyone else can confer with. And Eaton doesn't hesitate to stop doing business with suppliers whose business practices aren't up to its own high standards, regardless of their quality or prices. Eaton believes in working collaboratively with the key suppliers that make the cut and are selected for business. Eaton's supply chain team has given birth to a variety of strategic initiatives that support its supply selection and management process. Among the initiatives are the following:

- A supply chain data warehouse that integrates data from the company's myriad ERP systems to create a single repository of critical data for decision making. Its genesis was a shared service center that the supply chain organization initiated with the company's finance group. "But it only contained financial data, and we knew we needed much more, such as information on quality, logistics, non-purchase-order data, and other items so we could more effectively manage spend and monitor suppliers," Jacobs said.
- Significant progress toward the corporate goal of reducing the supply base by 50% by 2010.
- A 50% reduction in the number of incoming parts defects over the last three years, in part by eliminating poor-performing suppliers.
- Major savings and improved cross-functional communication from the work of special hub-and-spoke commodity teams composed of supply chain representatives from each of Eaton's business groups. Each team develops commodity strategies that integrate supply chain and business strategies. On each team, the hub is the business group with the highest dollar purchases in the commodity. The spokes are the remaining businesses. The electronics team, for one, reduced its supplier base from 127 to just 5 key distributors and has achieved 12% annualized savings so far.
- A 10% per-year savings in North American small-package logistics from moving 95% of shipments through a single provider. Partnering with five lead logistics suppliers across the globe for raw materials and finished goods shipments has led to 6% savings per year since 2005.
- Globalization of the indirect buy, including MRO, capital equipment, energy, information technology, telecom, and fleet services.
- Development of special software tools for improving communication with suppliers and other Eaton functional business groups. One, Worldwide Interactive Supplier Performance Evaluation Resource (WISPER), helps the supply chain team manage and evaluate suppliers. Another, Supplier Visualization, gives suppliers visibility into purchase orders, forecasts, and inventory so they can appropriately manage Eaton's inventory.
- Development and implementation of a state-of-the-art training initiative—called the Supply Chain Functional Excellence Program—that helps supply chain staff improve their knowledge and skills and prepare for advancement within the company.

EXHAUSTIVE SUPPLIER QUALIFICATION AND COORDINATION

All those and other successes begin with Eaton's rigorous process to find suppliers whose business practices match their own. For an idea of how rigorously Eaton analyzes the quality, fitness, and potential of prospective suppliers, talk to Jon Barfield, CEO and president of the Bartech Group. The Livonia, MI–based minority supplier finds and manages all of the company's temporary help. "We had discussions and did testing for the better part of a year before they decided to go with us," says Barfield, who calls his company's relationship with Eaton one of the best of all his customers.

Or talk to Gregg Hammer, national accounts manager for Pratt Industries in Conyers, GA, a supplier of corrugated containers. "They are very meticulous about analyzing suppliers' business practices, more so than most others," says Hammer. "Environmentalism is one of their big pushes, and they talked with us about that and our own views on ethics." In fact, Hammer believes Pratt's "green" practices—the fact that their products are 100% recyclable—was a big reason that Eaton increased its business with them.

Sourcing teams develop a single commodity strategy that integrates supply chain and business strategy. Among other things, the teams act as clearinghouses for information and communication, and for resolving supplier problems. For example, two business units located in the United Kingdom and the Netherlands were using the same supplier for custom electronics and electrical assemblies. The supplier was producing these assemblies at several of its plants in Hungary and Bulgaria.

Because of timing differences at the two Eaton business units, the production ramp-up started at an earlier date for the U.K. sites than for those in the Netherlands. As a result, the individual business units signed separate supplier agreements that included differing performance parameters for the relationship. That, of course, inevitably led to different performance expectations and communication issues. Because both business units were part of the electronics hub-and-spoke team, they eventually found a way to jointly set performance parameters by completing a single supply agreement with the supplier and standardizing on communication and performance. Supplier performance improved and the team agreed to consider giving more business to the supplier.

Eaton's hub-and-spoke commodities teams integrate commodity and business strategies. Here are some of the savings the teams have realized:

- Electronics team: Consolidated 127 suppliers into 5 key distributor partners. Annualized cost savings of 12%.
- Plastics team: Consolidated the resin-distribution base from 10 suppliers to 1 supplier. Savings of 5%.
- Packaging team: Consolidated 175 suppliers to 1 supplier. Savings of 12%.
- Raw materials team: Leveraged low spend ($5 million) in one group and $100 million in another group. For a similar product, saved more than 10% on the low-spend portion.

COLLABORATION IS KEY

Besides ethics, quality, and environmentally sound practices, the willingness to collaborate is critical in Eaton's evaluation of suppliers. Within the company's own walls, Jacobs and his team collaborate with virtually every function in the company, including finance, information technology, human resources, legal, and ethics, boosting the supply chain organization's image and influence internally, as well as its value. For example, representatives from product engineering, accounting, and other functions brainstorm strategies with supply chain personnel on the hub-and-spoke commodity teams. Additionally, supply chain staff are working closely with finance and information technology to develop a system to completely digitize invoicing.

Externally, the supply chain team facilitates collaboration between Eaton's engineering staff and its customers to solve design problems. Case in point: the Eaton Automotive Division's work on a supercharger for the Cadillac Northstar. Superchargers are positive-displacement devices that add power and efficiency to car engines. But they have to fit within a very tight space, and the design envelope often changes. Despite the changes, Eaton's task was to hold to its quote.

"We could only get our costs down so much through negotiations," says Jeff Place, director of supply chain management for the Automotive Group. So, Place and his team sat Eaton engineers down with the customer's engineers and the suppliers of the various components of the supercharger. Together, they identified the individual cost drivers for each component, considered the possibility of unnecessary tolerances, and identified opportunities to cut costs. "We took a product-centric view," Place says, "and collaborated with the suppliers to find the lowest cost."

In another case, the supply chain worked with suppliers of a DC motor to get the cost down. Again, the supply chain formed a team with members from engineering, staff from manufacturing, and representatives of the suppliers to identify the key cost drivers. Result: They achieved double-digit cost reductions.

THE SEARCH FOR INNOVATION

And you can't be successful without innovation. Like most progressive manufacturers, Eaton encourages—indeed, expects—its suppliers to be innovative. "That often requires bringing them in at the earliest stages of the design process so they'll understand the product better," says Mike Bungo, vice president of supply chain and operational excellence. And the supply chain team will help suppliers succeed, he says, even if it requires bringing in a master scheduler to adjust delivery dates, or posting Eaton quality engineers and technicians to strategic-supplier sites for extended periods to guide the suppliers' quality efforts.

Source: Adapted from P. E. Teague, "Eaton Wins Purchasing's Medal of Professional Excellence," *Purchasing*, September 13, 2007.

CONCLUSION

This chapter discussed one of the most important functions of business—the evaluation and selection of suppliers. When a purchaser performs these activities well, it establishes the foundation upon which to further develop and improve supplier performance. In his book *Purchasing in the 21st Century,* John Schorr maintains that a buyer should look for certain characteristics when evaluating and selecting suppliers. A good supplier does the following:

- Builds quality into the product, aiming for zero-defect production.
- Makes delivery performance a priority, including a willingness to make short and frequent deliveries to point-of-use areas at a purchaser's facility.
- Demonstrates responsiveness to a purchaser's needs by ensuring that qualified and accessible people are in charge of servicing the purchaser's account.
- Works with a purchaser to reduce lead times as much as possible. Long lead times make it difficult to plan and drive up supply chain costs.
- Provides a purchaser with information regarding capability and workload.
- Creates the future rather than fears the future.
- Reinvests part of its profits in R&D, takes a long-term view, and is willing to spend for tomorrow.
- Meets the stringent financial stability criteria used when evaluating potential new customers for credit.

A focus on selecting only the best suppliers possible will make a major contribution to the competitiveness of the entire organization. The ability to make this contribution requires careful evaluation and selection of the suppliers that provide the goods and services that help satisfy the needs of an organization's final customers.

KEY TERMS

countertrade, 262
deficiency, 260
entry qualifiers, 245
integrated supply, 243
performance problem, 259
preferred supplier, 239
Vendor Managed Inventory, 243

DISCUSSION QUESTIONS

1. Why do organizations commit the resources and time to evaluate suppliers before making a supplier selection decision?
2. Discuss the possible ways that purchasing becomes aware of the need to evaluate and select a supplier.
3. Discuss the sources of information available to a buyer when seeking information about potential sources of supply. When do you think it is appropriate to use different sources?
4. What are various methods for evaluating and selecting suppliers?
5. What are some possible indicators on a supplier visit that might cause you to question whether the managers in the company are forward-looking or whether the company is capable of becoming a best-in-class supplier?

6. Discuss the reasons why suppliers are sometimes reluctant to share cost information with buyers, particularly during the early part of a buyer-seller relationship.
7. Discuss the logic behind a purchaser trying to understand its total supply chain (i.e., the need to understand its supplier's suppliers).
8. What are the issues or questions purchasing needs to address when evaluating whether a supplier is a candidate for a longer-term relationship?
9. Define and discuss the characteristics included in an effective supplier survey.
10. How can a purchaser build flexibility into a supplier survey?
11. What are the advantages of assigning numerical scores to the categories and subcategories included in a supplier survey?
12. Why is it important to discuss promptly the results of a supplier visit or survey with the supplier? If a supplier has a weak area, under what conditions would supplier development be appropriate?
13. Discuss a situation in which a purchaser might select a supplier that is having financial difficulties.
14. Discuss the following statement: If a purchaser decides to select a supplier based on the results of the initial evaluation, the supplier must then meet the purchaser's continuous performance requirements.
15. Why must the time it takes to evaluate and select suppliers decrease? What three ways would you select to have the largest impact on reducing supplier selection time?

ADDITIONAL READINGS

Carbone, J. (1999), "Evaluation Programs Determine Top Suppliers," *Purchasing,* 127(8), 31–35.

Carter, R. (1995), "The Seven C's of Effective Supplier Evaluation," *Purchasing and Supply Management,* 44–46.

Choi, T. Y., and Hartley, J. L. (1996), "An Exploration of Supplier Selection Practices across the Supply Chain," *Journal of Operations Management,* 14, 333–343.

Dwyer, R. F., Schurr, P. H., and Oh, S. (1987), "Developing Buyer-Seller Relationships," *Journal of Marketing,* 51, 11–25.

Ellram, L. M. (1991), "A Managerial Guideline for the Development and Implementation of Purchasing Partnerships," *International Journal of Purchasing and Materials Management,* 27(3), 2–9.

Gottfredson, M., Puryear, R., and Phillips, S. (2005), "Strategic Sourcing: From Periphery to the Core," *Harvard Business Review,* 83(2), 132–139.

Gustin, C. M., Daugherty, P. J., and Ellinger, A. E. (1997), "Supplier Selection Decisions in Systems/Software Purchases," *Journal of Supply Chain Management,* 33(4), 41–46.

Przirembel, J. L. (1997), *How to Conduct Supplier Surveys and Audits,* West Palm Beach, FL: PT Publications.

Schorr, J. (1998), *Purchasing in the 21st Century,* New York: John Wiley & Sons.

Woods, J. A. (Ed.) (2000), *The Purchasing and Supply Yearbook: 2000 Edition,* New York: McGraw-Hill.

ENDNOTES

1. Howard, A. (1998), "Valued Judgments," *Supply Management,* 17, 37–38.

2. Casey, N., Zamiska, N., and Pasztor, A. (2007), "Mattel Seeks to Placate China with Apology on Toys," *Wall Street Journal,* September 22, 23, pp. A1, A7.

3. Seegers, L., Handfield, R., and Melynk, S. (1995), "Environmental Best Practices in the Office Furniture Industry," *Proceedings of the National Decision Science Institute Conference.*

4. Seegers, L., Handfield, R., and Melynk, S. (2007), "Green Movement Turns Mainstream for Corporate America," *Environmental Leader,* environmentalleader.com.

5. Spekman, R. E. (1988), "Strategic Supplier Selection: Understanding Long-Term Buyer Relationships," *Business Horizons,* pp. 80–81.

6. From Alcoa's Supplier Certification Guidelines.

7. From an in-depth literature search and summary of "Supplier Evaluation and Selection" performed by Tara Lewis and Vincent Sedlmyer, Lehigh University, 2001.

8. D. Hartley, (2000), "Looking for a Supplier? Use the E-Learning Scorecard," *Training and Development,* 54, 26.

9. "Northern Lights Simplifies the Supplier Selection Process" (2001), *Business Wire,* p. 2.

10. "eBreviate Unveils Web-Based RFP Version 2.0" (2001), *PR Newswire,* September, p. 2.

11. O'Donnell, D. (1998), "The Evaluation Effect," *Software Magazine,* June, pp. 72–78.

12. O'Donnell, pp. 72–78.

Chapter 9

SUPPLIER MANAGEMENT AND DEVELOPMENT: CREATING A WORLD-CLASS SUPPLY BASE

Learning Objectives

After completing this chapter, you should be able to

- Recognize that supplier management and development includes a variety of activities intended to improve supplier performance
- Appreciate the relationship between supplier measurement and supplier management
- Understand how to develop different types of supplier measurement tools
- Understand the importance of a manageable supply base in terms of size and quality
- Know when and how to apply supplier development tools, techniques, and approaches

Chapter Outline

Managing Suppliers Is a Priority at Honda of America Manufacturing

Honda of America Manufacturing (HAM), with several production and assembly locations in Ohio, strongly commits to longer-term relationships and supplier development with its suppliers. Long-term supplier viability is critical to Honda's profitability. First, the company fully commits to its suppliers for life. When Honda signs a sourcing contract with a supplier, it expects to maintain that relationship for 25 to 50 years. Second, the company buys 80% of the cost of every car from outside suppliers—the most of any automotive producer. Honda, therefore, commits a significant amount of its resources toward managing and developing local suppliers to ensure Honda has access to capable suppliers that can continuously meet the company's stringent performance standards.

Supplier development and improvement has one primary objective at Honda—to create and maintain a dedicated supply base that supports Honda's U.S. requirements. Pursuit of this objective requires a substantial commitment of resources to support and develop its suppliers:

- Two full-time employees help suppliers develop their employee involvement programs.
- Forty full-time engineers in the supply management department work with suppliers to improve productivity and quality.
- Over 100 engineers in the quality control department deal with incoming parts and supplier quality issues.
- Honda provides technical support to suppliers in a number of technical areas, including plastics technology, welding, stamping, and aluminum die casting.
- Honda forms special teams to help suppliers on an ad hoc basis. One supplier, for example, experienced problems resulting from rapid growth. Honda formed a four-person team that moved to the supplier's town for nine months to help correct the problems.
- A "Quality-Up" program targets suppliers with lower quality. Honda works directly with the supplier's top management team to ensure that the supplier produces a 100% quality product.
- Honda has a loaned-executive program where it sends various executives to work at the supplier's location. This supports greater understanding and communication between Honda and its suppliers, as well as creating long-term commitment and loyalty.

However, most companies are not willing to provide this level of attention and dedication to supplier management and development. A company that maintains either a laissez-faire or a reactive approach to supply base management is probably not willing to provide the necessary resources to support ongoing supplier development. Furthermore, some suppliers are not willing to expose themselves to the level of scrutiny required by Honda. Honda, for example, conducts minimal price negotiation. Instead, the company identifies a target cost and then works with a supplier to jointly meet that cost. Such detailed cost sharing can be difficult or traumatic for many independent suppliers.

This example outlines several key points about supplier management and development. First, suppliers play a critical role in the success of most organizations. Therefore, it makes sense to pay attention to a supplier's performance improvement needs. Second, a supply base that is too large and complex usually prohibits providing adequate supplier development support. There simply are not enough resources available to support and develop a large supply base. Finally, supplier development requires more than slogans and demands for better performance. It means actually committing the joint resources to make the process successful.

Although the Honda approach may seem extreme to some, few can argue with the company's demonstrated success. Automobiles produced at its Ohio assembly plants have consistently been among the highest-quality and best-selling in the United States. The success of Honda's supplier development and improvement effort is one reason the company enjoys such loyal customers.

Source: Adapted from Krause, D., and Handfield, R. (1999), *Developing a World-Class Supply Base*, Tempe, AZ: Center for Advanced Purchasing Studies, p. 102; Harrington, L. H. (1997), "Buying Better," *Industry Week*, July 21, p. 75; Fitzgerald, K. R. (1995), "For Superb Supplier Development, Honda Wins!" *Purchasing*, 21, 32; and Nelson, D., Moody, P. E., and Stegner, J. (2001), *The Purchasing Machine*, New York: Free Press. Also adapted from interviews with various company managers and other public sources.

As the opening vignette illustrates, progressive firms take the need to improve supplier performance quite seriously. Gone are the days when vertically integrated companies mass-produced products with long product life cycles. With increased global competition, companies increasingly rely on an ever-expanding network of dedicated suppliers to meet their business objectives. Businesses across every industry are beginning to realize that success requires them to organize and manage resources and processes across a network of supply chain partners put together on purpose, not haphazardly.[1]

Effective supplier management and development includes a broad array of actions taken to manage and improve a worldwide network of carefully screened and selected supply chain partners or suppliers. The primary objective of these future-oriented management and development processes is the continuous improvement of supplier capabilities. Supplier performance that is good enough today will not suffice in the marketplace of tomorrow. History shows that, unless companies are able to bring supply base performance to world-class levels, they will be at the mercy of competitors that have taken supplier performance improvement more seriously.

This chapter focuses on various ways organizations manage their supply chains. Although a number of supplier management approaches exist, most fall into the broad activities described in this chapter. The first section discusses the important relationship between supplier measurement and effective supplier management. The next section discusses supply base rationalization and optimization, the process of identifying the proper mix and number of suppliers. The third section discusses supplier development as a strategy for improvement. In the final section, we present some of the barriers faced by organizations as they attempt to improve supplier performance through supplier development. Finally, we conclude with a Good Practice Example of supplier measurement at FedEx.

Supplier Performance Measurement

An important part of supplier management involves the continuous measurement, evaluation, and analysis of supplier performance. An organization must have the tools to measure, manage, and develop the performance of its supply base. Without an effective measurement system to record and evaluate supply base performance, how do buyers really know how well their suppliers are satisfying their contractual obligations? Supplier performance measurement includes the methods and systems to collect and provide information to measure, rate, or rank supplier performance on a continuous basis. The supplier measurement system is a critical part of the sourcing process—essentially serving as a supplier's report card. Note that supplier performance measurement differs from the process used to initially evaluate and select a supplier. It is a continuous process as opposed to a unique, one-time event.

Supplier Measurement Decisions

Organizations face several key decisions when developing a supplier measurement system that are critical to the final design, implementation, and effectiveness of the system.

What to Measure

Central to the design of all supplier measurement systems is the decision about what to measure and how to weigh various performance categories. An organization must decide which performance criteria are objective (quantitative) and which are subjective (qualitative), as the metrics will be different between the two. Most of the objective, quantitative variables lie within the following three categories:

- *Delivery performance:* Purchase orders or material releases sent to a supplier have a quantity and a materials due date. A buyer can assess how well a supplier satisfies its quantity and due-date commitments. Quantity, lead time requirements, and due-date compliance also define a supplier's overall delivery performance.
- *Quality performance:* Almost all supplier measurement systems include quality performance as a critical component. Review Chapter 8 for a more in-depth discussion of supplier quality management. A buyer can evaluate a supplier's quality performance against previously specified objectives, track trends and improvement rates, and compare similar suppliers. A well-designed measurement system also helps define a buyer's quality requirements and effectively communicates them to its suppliers.
- *Cost reduction:* Buyers frequently rely on suppliers for cost-reduction assistance, which can be measured in a number of ways. One common method is to track a supplier's real cost after adjustment for inflation. Other accepted techniques involve comparing a supplier's cost against other suppliers within the same industry or against a baseline or target price. Some leading companies use the last price paid in a year as the baseline price for comparisons during the next year.

Buyers can also use a number of qualitative factors to assess supplier performance. Exhibit 9.1 on p. 310 details some of the qualitative service factors available to buyers. Although these factors are largely subjective, a buyer can still assign a score or rating to each factor. A buyer might evaluate five different qualitative factors (assume equal weighting for simplicity) along a five-point scale. The system adds the five scores and divides by the total possible points to arrive at a percentage of total points, so that a buyer can rank suppliers by the percentage of total possible points earned.

Measurement and Reporting Frequency

Two important issues relate to the regularity of measurement: reporting frequency to the buyer and reporting frequency to the supplier. A buyer (or someone responsible for the day-to-day management of suppliers) should receive a daily report sum-

Exhibit 9.1 Qualitative Service Factors

FACTOR	DESCRIPTION
Problem resolution ability	Supplier's attentiveness to problem resolution
Technical ability	Supplier's manufacturing ability compared with other industry suppliers
Ongoing progress reporting	Supplier's ongoing reporting of existing problems or recognizing and communicating a potential problem
Corrective action response	Supplier's solutions and timely response to requests for corrective actions, including a supplier's response to engineering change requests
Supplier cost-reduction ideas	Supplier's willingness to help find ways to reduce purchase cost
Supplier new-product support	Supplier's ability to help reduce new-product development cycle time or to help with product design
Buyer/seller compatibility	Subjective rating concerning how well a buying firm and a supplier work together

marizing the previous day's activities. This report allows the buyer to scan incoming receipt activity and should highlight past-due supplier receipts. A buyer should receive additional reports summarizing supplier performance on a weekly, monthly, quarterly, and annual basis.

Routine reporting of supplier performance relative to goal should happen monthly or quarterly. Buyers should also meet with suppliers on at least an annual basis to review actual performance results and identify improvement opportunities. However, a buyer should never delay reporting a supplier's poor performance, particularly when it adversely affects day-to-day operations. Poor performance must be addressed as soon as it is recognized to avoid financial or operational repercussions.

Uses of Measurement Data

A buyer can use the data gathered from its measurement system in a number of ways. The data can help identify those suppliers that are incapable of performing at expected levels so that remedial action will be taken to get performance back to acceptable levels or to find a new supplier. A measurement system also helps identify those highly capable suppliers that may qualify for longer-term partnerships or designation as preferred suppliers because of exemplary performance.

Measurement data also support supply base rationalization and optimization efforts. If suppliers do not improve performance to minimum acceptable levels, they are not likely to remain part of the supply base over the long term. Another use of supplier performance data includes determining a supplier's future purchase volume based on its past performance rating. Some companies adjust their purchase volumes periodically and reward better-performing suppliers with a higher share of purchase requirements. Adjusting volumes between suppliers provides a financial incentive for a supplier to meet or exceed the buyer's performance expectations.

A major benefit from supplier measurement is that performance data allow the buying organization to identify those areas requiring improvement. Buyers can also use the data when making sourcing decisions. These become clearer when a buyer has a reliable measurement system that rates and ranks a supplier's performance against other suppliers or other established performance standards.

Types of Supplier Measurement Techniques

All supplier measurement systems have some element of subjectivity. Even the implementation of a computerized measurement system will require subjective judgment. What data to analyze, what metrics to use, what performance categories to include, how to weight different categories, how often to generate performance reports, and how to use the performance data are all subjective to some degree. Moreover, there are no hard rules regarding the specific categories to include in supplier measurement systems; the choice will depend on what is strategically important to the buyer.

Organizations typically use one of three common measurement techniques or systems when evaluating supplier performance. Each system differs in its ease of use, level of decision subjectivity, required system resources, and implementation cost. Exhibit 9.2 compares the advantages and disadvantages of these three systems.

Categorical System

A categorical system is the easiest and most basic measurement system to put in place, but it is also the most subjective as far as measuring supplier performance. This system requires the assignment of a rating evaluation for each selected performance category. Examples of ratings typically include: excellent, good, fair, and poor. These subjective evaluations can be completed by the buyer, other internal users, or some combination of both.

The categorical approach is commonly used by smaller organizations because it is both easy and relatively inexpensive to implement. Although the categorical approach provides some structure to the measurement process, it does not provide sufficiently detailed insight into a supplier's true performance. Furthermore, because categorical systems often rely on manually collected data, an organization generates supplier

Exhibit 9.2 Comparison of Supplier Measurement and Evaluation Systems

SYSTEM	ADVANTAGES	DISADVANTAGES	USERS
Categorical	Easy to implement Requires minimal data Different personnel contribute Good for firms with limited resources Low-cost system	Least reliable Less frequent generation of evaluations Most subjective Usually manual	Smaller firms Firms in the process of developing an evaluation system
Weighted-Point	Flexible system Supplier ranking allowed Moderate implementation costs Quantitative and qualitative factors combined into a single system	Tends to focus on unit price Requires some computer support	Most firms can use this approach
Cost-Based	Total cost approach Specific areas of supplier nonperformance identified Objective supplier ranking Greatest potential for long-range improvement	Cost accounting system required Most complex so implementation costs high Computer resources required	Larger firms Firms with a large supply base

performance reports less frequently than if an automated system existed. The reliability of the categorical method is the lowest of the three measurement systems discussed here, which limits the value of this approach when assessing supplier performance. There is often significant variance in the subjective ratings.

Weighted-Point System

This approach overcomes some of the subjectivity of the categorical system. A weighted-point system weighs and quantifies scores across different performance categories. This approach usually features higher reliability and moderate implementation costs.

Weighted-point systems are also flexible—users can change the weights assigned to each performance category or the performance categories themselves, depending on what is most important to the buying organization. For example, the performance categories and weights for an MRO distributor will likely differ from those for a supplier furnishing production components.

Several important issues must be understood regarding the use of weighted-point systems. First, users must carefully select the key performance categories to measure. Second, an organization must decide how to weight each performance category. Although assigning weights is subjective, an organization can reach consensus about how to weigh the performance categories through careful planning and involvement from different functions. Third, a set of decision rules must be in place to compare a

Exhibit 9.3 Weighted-Point Supplier Measurement and Evaluation of Davis Industries for Third Quarter 2004

PERFORMANCE CATEGORY	WEIGHT	SCORE	WEIGHTED SCORE
Delivery			
On time	.10	4	.4
Quantity	.10	3	.3
Quality			
Inbound shipment quality	.25	4	1.0
Quality improvement	.10	4	.4
Cost Competitiveness			
Comparison with other suppliers	.15	2	.3
Cost-reduction ideas submitted	.10	3	.3
Service Factors			
Problem resolution ability	.05	4	.2
Technical ability	.05	5	.25
Corrective action response	.05	3	.15
New-product development support	.05	5	.25
Total Rating			**3.55**

1 = Poor, 3 = Average, 5 = Excellent

supplier's performance against a predetermined objective to provide a score for each category.

Exhibit 9.3 illustrates a sample weighted-point system based on a five-point scale, where five is the highest possible score. The weighted-point plan should provide a higher level of objectivity for most performance categories and evaluate supplier performance in more detail compared with the categorical approach. Note that actual rating scales will be much more detailed than the one presented in this exhibit.

Cost-Based System

The most thorough and least subjective of the three measurement systems is the cost-based system. This approach seeks to quantify the total cost of doing business with a supplier, as the lowest purchase price is not always the lowest total cost for an item or service.

Most companies with information system capability can readily implement a cost-based supplier measurement system. The major challenge involves identifying and recording appropriate costs that result whenever a supplier fails to perform as expected. To use such a system, an organization must estimate or calculate the additional costs that result whenever a supplier underperforms. The basic logic of the system is the calculation of a supplier performance index (SPI). This index, with a base value of 1.0 that represents satisfactory performance, is a total cost index calculated for each item or commodity provided by a supplier:

$$\text{SPI} = (\text{Total Purchases} + \text{Nonperformance Costs})/\text{Total Purchases}$$

Exhibit 9.4 illustrates a total cost–based approach for supplier measurement. The cost-based approach can also include an assessment of qualitative service factors to provide a more complete picture of supplier performance. This exhibit compares the

Exhibit 9.4 Supplier Performance Comparison through First Quarter 2005

COMMODITY: INTEGRATED CIRCUIT

PART NUMBER	SUPPLIER	UNIT PRICE	SPI	TOTAL COST
04279884	Advanced Systems	$3.12	1.20	$3.74*
	BC Techtronics	$3.01	1.45	$4.36
	Micro Circuit	$3.10	1.30	$4.03
04341998	Advanced Systems	$5.75	1.20	$6.90*
	BC Techtronics	$5.40	1.45	$7.83
	Micro Circuit	$5.55	1.30	$7.21

Service Factor Ratings:

Advanced Systems	78%
BC Techtronics	76%
Micro Circuit	87%

*Lowest-total-cost supplier for item (Unit price × SPI = Total cost).
Source: R. M. Monczka and S. J. Trecha, "Cost-Based Supplier Performance Evaluation," *Journal of Purchasing and Materials Management*, Spring 1988, 1–4.

Exhibit 9.5 Supplier Performance Report for First Quarter 2005

Supplier: Advanced Systems
Commodity: Integrated circuit
Total part numbers in commodity: 2

A. Total purchase dollars this quarter: $5,231.67

NONPERFORMANCE COSTS

EVENT	NUMBER OF OCCURRENCES	AVERAGE COST PER OCCURRENCE	EXTENDED COST
Late delivery	5	$150	$750
Return to supplier	2	$ 45	$ 90
Scrap labor costs	3	$ 30	$ 90
Material rework cost	1	$100	$100
B. Total nonperformance costs			$1,030
C. Purchase + nonperformance cost	(Line A + B)		$6,261.67
D. Supplier performance index	(Line C/A)		1.20
E. Service factor rating			78%

total cost of ownership (TCO) for each supplier for the two items in the integrated circuit category. It also compares suppliers on the basis of their service factor ratings. Note that the lowest-price supplier, BC Techtronics, is not the lowest-total-cost supplier when the costs of nonperformance are included. BC Techtronics also has a lower service rating score as compared with the other two suppliers.

Exhibit 9.5 summarizes supplier performance for a group of items comprising a single commodity. It details the total number of nonperformance occurrences, the cost of each event as identified by the buyer, and the total nonperformance cost for the quarter. Lines C and D include the figures required for the SPI calculation. Line E is the ratio of points earned to the total possible points for the qualitative or service factors.

In many cases, the actual cost per nonperformance event may be difficult to estimate or calculate, as the traditional cost accounting system is not designed to identify and capture such data. For instance, the average cost of a late delivery may vary widely, depending on its impact to the customer, potential lost sales, line shutdown costs, and so on. Therefore, many organizations get around this limitation by assigning a standard charge each time a nonperformance event occurs.

The SPI sometimes provides an incomplete or misleading assessment of supplier performance. For example, consider a supplier that delivers $100,000 of material, with one late delivery charged at $5,000. That supplier will have an SPI of ($100,000 + $5,000)/$100,000, or 1.05. This SPI appears more favorable than that of a supplier that delivers only $30,000 of material and has one late delivery, and that also charged at $5,000. The second supplier has an SPI of ($30,000 + $5,000)/$30,000, or 1.17. Although both suppliers committed the same infraction, the smaller supplier received a

Exhibit 9.6 Supplier Performance Index Calculation with Q Adjustment Factor

Q is a normalization factor that eliminates high-dollar lot biases.

Q = (Average cost of a lot of material for an individual supplier)/(Average cost of a lot of material for all suppliers)

Consider the following information for Suppliers A, B, and C, each with a single late delivery nonconformance calculated at $4,000.

Assume the average cost of all lots for suppliers of this commodity is $2,500.

	SUPPLIER A	SUPPLIER B	SUPPLIER C
3rd quarter shipments	20 lots @ $500 each	20 lots @ 1,000 each	20 lots @ $10,000
Total value of shipments	$10,000	$20,000	$200,000
Average lot cost	$500	$1,000	$10,000
Nonconformance charges	Late delivery $4,000	Late delivery $4,000	Late delivery $4,000
3rd Quarter SPI	**($10,000 + $4,000)/ $10,000 = 1.40**	**($20,000 + $4,000)/ $20,000 = 1.20**	**($200,000 + $4,000)/ $200,000 = 1.02**
Average cost of a lot from all suppliers	$2,500	$2,500	$2,500
Q calculation	$500/$2,500 = .2	$1,000/$2,500 = .4	$10,000/$2,500 = 4

Notice how different the SPI values are for the three suppliers, even though they each committed the same nonconformance. Supplier C, due to the high lot bias, has the lowest SPI.

SPI calculation with Q adjustment = Cost of material + (Nonconformance costs × Q factor)/Cost of material

Supplier A: $10,000 + ($4,000 × .2)/$10,000 = 1.08

Supplier B: $20,000 + ($4,000 × .4)/$20,000 = 1.08

Supplier C: $200,000 + ($4,000 × 4)/$200,000 = 1.08

The Q adjustment now allows a fair comparison.

comparatively more severe penalty relative to purchase volume. A normalization adjustment (Q) is required to eliminate a bias that favors higher-dollar-volume suppliers. Exhibit 9.6 illustrates how to calculate an SPI with the Q adjustment factor, which allows an "apples-to-apples" comparison between suppliers.

Management has many uses for the data derived from a comprehensive cost-based supplier measurement system. Such a system provides necessary information that a buyer may need to justify buying from a preferred supplier despite a higher unit price. The system also allows a buyer to communicate the cost of specific nonperformance occurrences to a supplier, which then helps identify improvement opportunities. Quantifying nonperformance costs can also result in a chargeback to the offending supplier for unplanned costs. Finally, a buyer can use this data to identify longer-term sources of supply based on a supplier's total cost performance history.

Each of the three types of measurement approaches featured in this chapter, although differing in their complexity and scope of use, raises a buyer's awareness about supply base performance. Supplier measurement is a powerful tool for managing and increasing the capabilities of the supply base.

Sourcing Snapshot

McDonald's Takes Supplier Measurement Seriously

To measure supplier performance, McDonald's (Oak Brook, IL) recently employed a supplier relationship management (SRM) process to its global technology buy. According to Joseph Youssef, McDonald's SRM strategy "requires dedicated supply managers, effective processes to create standardized best practices, and tools to track and evaluate the results." Youssef also indicates that an organization must manage its supply base through effective performance measurement and then make supplier-related decisions using the outputs of those measurements. He outlines four prime measurements that organizations should consider in their supplier performance management systems. The first area includes day-to-day tactical measurements such as quality, service, responsiveness, and delivery performance. The second measurement focuses on contract management: making sure that previously agreed-to contractual arrangements are followed. The third area measured is financial management. Measurements in this area track to see that accurate invoices are submitted in a timely manner and for the agreed-upon products and services. Lastly, the fourth measurement centers on the buyer-supplier relationship and the level of two-way communication between the parties.

Source: Adapted from W. Forrest, "McDonald's Applies SRM Strategy to Global Technology Buy," *Purchasing*, September 7, 2006, p. 16.

Rationalization and Optimization: Creating a Manageable Supply Base

Effective supplier management and development begins by determining an optimal number of suppliers that an organization should maintain. Supply base rationalization is the process of identifying how many and which suppliers a buyer will maintain. Supply base optimization involves an analysis of the supply base to ensure that only the most capable suppliers are kept in the supply base as it is rationalized. It often involves eliminating those suppliers that are unwilling or incapable of achieving supply management performance objectives, either currently or expected in the near future.

Supply base rationalization and optimization should be a continuous process. The elimination of both marginal and small-purchase-volume suppliers is usually the first phase of the rationalization process. Subsequent optimization requires the replacement of good suppliers with better-performing suppliers or initiating supplier development projects with existing suppliers to improve performance. Organizations must develop supplier evaluation and measurement systems to identify the best-performing suppliers and then develop stronger business relationships with those suppliers. Oftentimes, companies must search worldwide for the best suppliers.

During the early phases of supply base rationalization and optimization, the process usually results in an absolute reduction in the total number of suppliers. Reduction, however, may not always be the result for every family or group of purchased items. The key is to determine the right number of suppliers, not just arbitrarily cut down on the number. For example, a truck assembly plant in Michigan received tires and wheels from separate suppliers. OEM employees mounted and balanced the tires on the wheels inside the assembly plant in a labor- and space-intensive operation. The buyer established a new supplier near the assembly plant that then received both the tires and wheels, and assembled, balanced, and stored the wheel assemblies until shipping them to the assembly plant on a just-in-time basis. Although the company added an additional supplier to its supply base, overall system efficiency increased, and total cost declined. In this example, the optimization process resulted in the net addition of a supplier.

Advantages of a Rationalized and Optimized Supply Base

Supply base rationalization and optimization should result in real improvements in cost, quality, delivery, and information sharing between buyer and supplier. Because the process identifies the best suppliers in terms of number and quality, the remaining suppliers are often capable of performing additional tasks that improve performance or add value to the buyer-supplier relationship. Suppliers in an optimized supply base often develop longer-term relationships with buyers, which can lead to further joint improvement efforts.

Buying from World-Class Suppliers

Because of the correlation between supplier performance and supply chain success, it is not difficult to see why choosing and maintaining only the best suppliers supports higher performance throughout the supply chain. Instead of being responsible for literally hundreds or thousands of suppliers, supply management can concentrate on developing closer relationships with a smaller core group of qualified suppliers. The benefits of doing business with world-class suppliers include fewer quality and delivery problems, access to leading-edge technology, opportunities to develop collaborative relationships, and a lower product cost as supply management and engineering gain key supplier input during new-product development.

Use of Full-Service Suppliers

The remaining suppliers in a rationalized and optimized supply base are often larger on average and highly capable of offering a broad range of value-adding services. When a buyer uses full-service suppliers, it expects to reap substantial benefits in the form of access to the supplier's engineering, research and development, design, testing, production, service, and tooling capabilities. The full-service supplier approach places a greater burden on a supplier to manage an entire system of components, activities, and services, as well as to effectively manage its own supply base. The full-service supplier can also perform complete design and build work instead of the buyer performing the work internally or using several different suppliers in an uncoordinated effort.

The automobile industry provides many examples of how full-service suppliers can provide these benefits. For example, all vehicles have extensive electrical wiring systems. Traditionally, automobile manufacturers designed each individual wiring harness internally and sent the design specifications to suppliers through a competitive bidding process. It was not uncommon to have 10 different suppliers working on wiring systems for final assembly into a vehicle. Now, a single supplier, or only a few suppliers, might design and produce the entire wiring system for a new vehicle throughout the entire model life cycle. The result is lower cost, improved quality, and reduced product development time. Because of its expertise, a supplier can design the wiring systems concurrently with the overall design of the car, reducing concept-to-customer cycle time.

Reduction of Supply Base Risk

At first glance, it seems illogical that using fewer suppliers can result in reduced supply base risk. **Risk** can be defined as the magnitude of exposure to financial loss or operational disruption and stems from uncertainty. What if the single or sole source for a critical item goes on strike or has a fire at its production facility, disrupting its production process and ability to maintain an uninterrupted flow of materials? Historically, the risk of supply disruption has been the primary argument against supply base reduction or single-sourcing of purchased items.

Many buyers have now concluded that, if they select suppliers carefully and develop close and collaborative working relationships with fewer suppliers, supply risk can actually decrease. Risk does not only include supply disruption. Other supply risks include poor supplier quality, poor delivery performance, or overpaying for items due to a noncompetitive sourcing situation. However, maintaining multiple suppliers for each item can actually increase the probability and level of risk. Having more suppliers for individual items creates the opportunity for increased product variability or inconsistent quality across the supply chain.

Lower Supply Base Administrative Costs

Buyers interact with their suppliers in many ways. Examples include contacting suppliers about design and material specifications, communicating quality and other performance requirements, negotiating purchase contracts, visiting and evaluating supplier facilities and processes, providing feedback about supplier performance, collaborating with suppliers when problems occur, requesting supplier input about product design, contacting suppliers regarding engineering change orders, and transmitting material releases. These activities all have associated costs in terms of time, effort, and potential for miscommunication. For example, the administrative cost of maintaining 5,000 suppliers will be dramatically higher than the cost of maintaining a core group of 500 highly qualified suppliers. Furthermore, highly qualified suppliers require fewer problem-related interactions with the buyer. The best contacts between a buyer and seller are those that add value to the relationship rather than merely resolve problems.

Lower Total Product Cost

During the 1980s, buyers recognized the real cost of maintaining multiple suppliers for each sourced item. Acquisition and operating costs increased as a result of greater variability in product quality and delivery and smaller production volumes offered to each supplier, which did nothing to spread out the supplier's fixed costs over higher output levels. Short-term purchase contracts that award small volumes of business to multiple suppliers only increase production costs and provide no incentive for investments in process improvement. It became evident that, if fewer suppliers received larger-volume contracts, the resulting economies of scale would lower production and distribution costs. Supply base rationalization and optimization provides the opportunity to achieve lower total product costs by awarding larger volumes to fewer suppliers.

Ability to Pursue Complex Supply Management Strategies

Implementing complex supply management strategies requires a rationalized and optimized supply base. The need for more complicated activities with suppliers requires a reduced supply base due to higher levels of two-way interactions between a buyer and seller. Examples of complex supply management strategies include supplier development, early supplier design involvement, just-in-time sourcing, and the development of cost-based pricing agreements with suppliers.

Possible Risks of Maintaining Fewer Suppliers

Few supply management executives would argue in favor of maintaining multiple suppliers for every purchased item. Currently, the debate centers on maintaining a limited number of qualified suppliers for major items versus using a single source. Some organizations believe using several suppliers for a purchased item promotes and maintains a healthy level of competition between suppliers. Others, however, believe that a single source can still deliver cost and quality improvements over the life of a contract if a buyer manages that supplier appropriately. Although most buyers recognize the benefits of supply base rationalization and optimization, there are still potential risks from relying on a smaller supply base.

Supplier Dependency

Some buyers fear that a supplier can become too dependent on the buyer for its economic survival. This situation can easily occur if a buyer combines its total purchase volumes for an item with a single supplier. A smaller supplier with limited capacity may need to eliminate some existing customers in order to meet the increased requirements of its larger customer. As a result, the supplier may become too dependent on a buyer for its financial well-being. If, for some reason, the buyer no longer requires a particular item, the overly dependent supplier may no longer be financially viable. Although supply base optimization can lead to a beneficial mutual commitment between buyer and seller, it can also result in an unhealthy dependence of one party on the other.

Absence of Competition

By relying on only one or a limited number of suppliers, some buyers fear losing the advantages of a competitive marketplace. A supplier may hold the buyer hostage by unduly raising its prices or becoming too complacent. The more difficult and expensive it is to change suppliers (e.g., higher switching costs), the more likely this scenario becomes. However, organizations with substantial supply base optimization experience argue that careful supplier selection and the development of equitable contracts that address continuous improvement requirements should prevent an over-reliance on suppliers that try to take advantage of a single-source situation.

Supply Disruption

Supply disruption is a potential risk when sourcing from a single-location supplier. In 1999, a major earthquake in Taiwan disrupted the supply of computer chips in the global semiconductor industry. Chip fabrication plants were shut down for several days, and the normal level of output was curtailed for several weeks. Customers reacted by hoarding chip inventories and reducing their production of finished goods. Suppliers not affected by the quake increased their prices, resulting in a ripple effect throughout the electronics industry.[2] Likewise, labor strikes, fires, acts of nature, production or quality problems, or disruption within the supplier's own supply base can disrupt the smooth flow of materials through a supply chain. Buyers can minimize this risk by sourcing from a single supplier with multiple production facilities. For example, Dell Computer utilizes multiple sourcing for many of the key components that go into its notebook computers manufactured in Asia. If a disruption or lack of capacity occurs at one supplier's facility, Dell can quickly shift its sourcing to another facility from the same supplier or to a different supplier.[3]

Another method for minimizing supply disruption risk is to select suppliers with multiple capabilities—the practice of cross-sourcing. Here, a buyer selects or develops suppliers with multiple or redundant capabilities. If problems occur with a primary source of supply for an item, the secondary supplier, which is the supplier for another purchased item, then assumes ownership of the sourcing process. This approach requires identifying suppliers capable of producing different items or performing multiple functions throughout the production process.

Overaggressive Supply Reduction

However, buyers can move too aggressively when reducing the supply base. If this occurs, the remaining suppliers may not have adequate capacity to meet purchase requirements if demand increases substantially. This happened when a major producer of hand tools developed a wide array of products that used rechargeable nickel-cadmium batteries. The supplier found that it did not have adequate manufacturing capacity to support new-product requirements for these batteries. In this case, supply base optimization required the company to qualify new sources rather quickly. As part of the supply base optimization process, the buyer must ensure that it carefully evaluates the remaining suppliers' capacity to produce larger volumes or develop other suppliers to cover the increased volumes.

Formal Approaches to Supply Base Rationalization

In his discussion of strategic supply management, Keki Bhote offers several possible supply base reduction methods.[4] Bhote's framework contains three primary elements: (1) phasing out current suppliers, (2) selection of finalist suppliers, and (3) selection of partnership suppliers. This section focuses on several methods commonly used to rationalize the supply base.

Twenty/Eighty Rule

This approach identifies those 20% of suppliers receiving the bulk of purchase spend or that minority of suppliers that cause the most quality problems. Purchase spend and supplier quality are two possible decision criteria used to identify suppliers for elimination. Organizations often use this approach when they require a rapid reduction in the number of suppliers. A disadvantage to the 20/80 approach is the possible elimination of otherwise capable suppliers simply because they received fewer purchase dollars. This approach assumes the best suppliers receive the majority of the purchase dollars, which may not necessarily be true. In addition, the buyer may exclude suppliers with needed capabilities that are not currently utilized.

Exhibit 9.7 Supply Base Optimization and Development

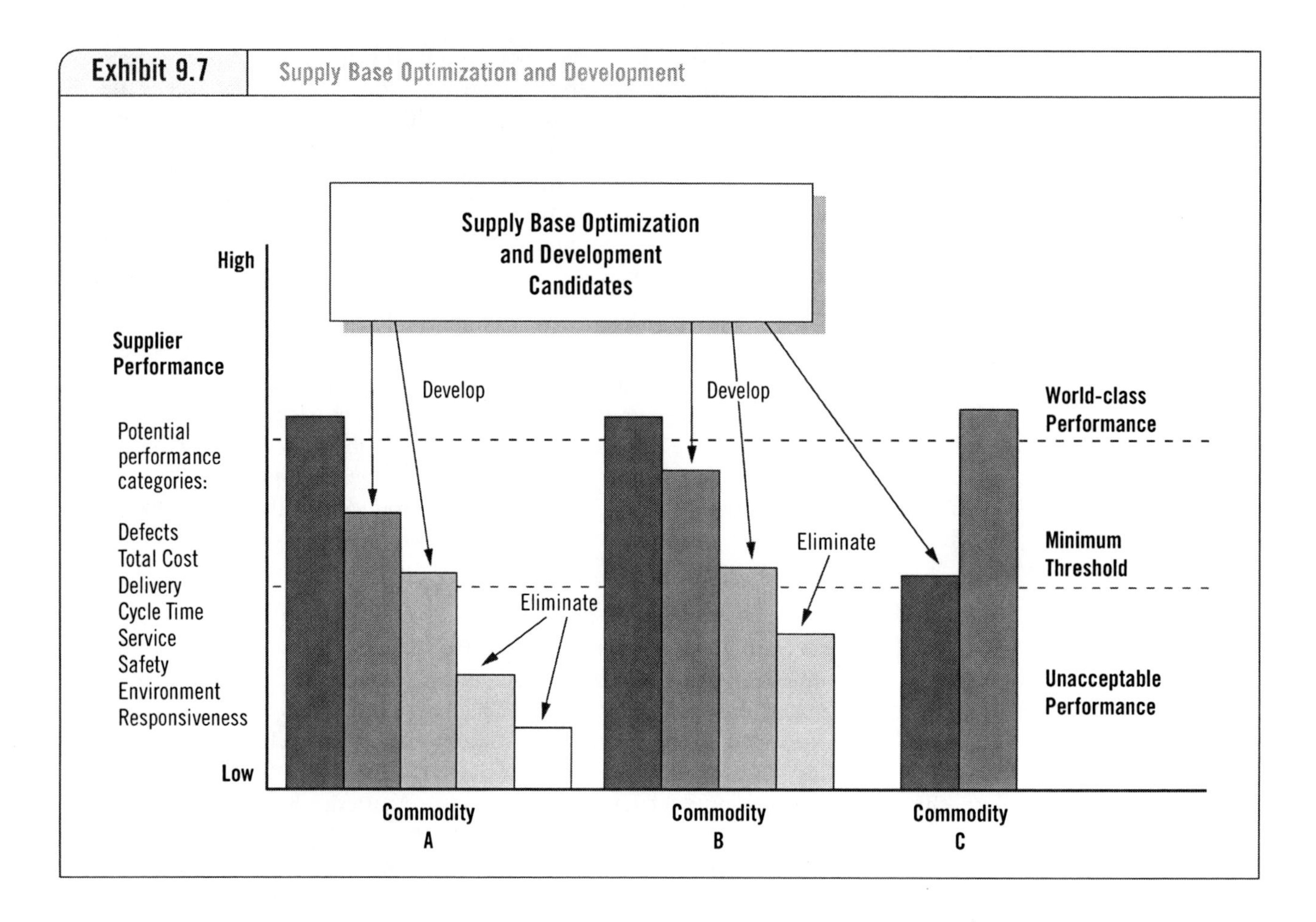

"Improve or Else" Approach

This approach provides all suppliers, regardless of their performance history, a chance to remain in the supply base. It involves notifying suppliers that they have a specified period of time in which to meet new performance requirements—from improved quality levels and delivery performance to lead time and cost reductions, or any other key performance indicator. Suppliers that fall short of expectations may soon become ex-suppliers. Although this approach has the potential for driving rapid performance improvement in the supply base, it can also be a heavy-handed way of dealing with suppliers. For example, this was the approach that General Motors' chief purchasing officer, J. Ignacio Lopez de Arriortua, used in 1992 by demanding that GM's suppliers reduce their prices by 3 to 22% or risk losing their existing supply contracts.[5]

Triage Approach

This approach requires the systematic evaluation of the performance of individual suppliers and placement into one of three categories. The first category, and most likely the largest, includes those suppliers that are marginal performers or otherwise incapable of meeting purchase performance requirements, now or in the future. The buyer targets these suppliers for immediate removal from the supply base. The second category includes those suppliers that do not consistently meet purchase requirements in all areas but demonstrate sufficient improvement potential. The most promising of these suppliers are often targets for supplier assistance and development. The third category includes those high-quality, capable suppliers requiring no improvement assistance. These suppliers are candidates for more collaborative buyer-seller relationships, which may include offering longer-term contracts in exchange for continuous improvement, as well as being considered for an alliance. The distribution of suppliers across these categories may vary across industries.

Exhibit 9.7 on p. 321 illustrates one company's triage approach to supplier reduction. This company compares suppliers against various performance criteria and segments the supply base into three groups: unacceptable performers, suppliers that meet minimum requirements but are not world class, and world-class performers worthy of closer relationships.

Competency Staircase Approach

This method requires suppliers to successfully navigate a succession of performance milestones or hurdles in order to remain in the supply base. First, all suppliers must meet a buyer's basic quality standards for consideration as potential suppliers. Suppliers must then pass a series of hurdles analogous to climbing a staircase. Each hurdle brings the supplier one step closer to its ultimate goal of remaining in the buyer's supply base.

The next hurdle may be a supplier's ability to meet a buyer's technical specifications and product performance requirements. Subsequent hurdles can include demonstrating sustained production competency, delivery capability (such as just-in-time requirements), willingness to share information, supplier size, and physical proximity to the buyer. Note that different purchase requirements will present varying sets of hurdles. Each hurdle results in fewer and fewer suppliers remaining in the supply base. The result is a strong and flexible supply base comprised of highly capable and motivated suppliers.

Summary of Supplier Rationalization and Optimization

Several conclusions about supplier rationalization and optimization can now be made. First, there are a variety of approaches to supply base rationalization and optimization. This chapter provides only a select sample of those approaches. Furthermore, an organization can combine more than one approach to meet its supply base reduction goals. Second, we do not have to limit our evaluation only to suppliers currently in the supply base. A buyer should always be open to the possibility of adding new suppliers if their use makes good business sense. Third, the benefits of supply base rationalization and optimization are real, whereas the potential drawbacks are manageable.

Supply base rationalization and optimization constitutes a critical first step toward the effective management and development of the supply base. It is difficult to manage many suppliers as efficiently as a small core group of suppliers, just as it is challenging to pursue progressive supply management strategies with too many suppliers. A large supply base also means the duplication of a wide range of supply management activities, adding to acquisition cost without a corresponding increase in value added. Finally, supplier rationalization and optimization is a continuing activity. Almost half of the companies participating in a 2000 survey reduced their supply base by 20%, and almost 15% reduced their supply base between 20 and 60% over the last

Sourcing Snapshot

Raytheon Relies on Supplier Development as a Strategic Initiative

Assuming responsibility for supply chain management at Raytheon, one of the country's largest industrial companies, Shelley Stewart Jr. brought to the job a wealth of experience in strategic sourcing, electronic commerce, and supplier diversity activities. The initiatives that he introduced or expanded at Raytheon include the following:

- Introduction of a single process for strategic sourcing for use across all Raytheon businesses
- Companywide deployment of a process for sourcing indirect materials using teams and consortiums
- Application of Raytheon's Six Sigma quality initiative to the company's supplier development effort
- Companywide adoption of the aerospace and defense industries' e-procurement exchange, Exostar, as well as FreeMarkets' reverse auction process
- Creation of a leadership development program
- Enhancement of the company's supplier diversity programs

In keeping with Raytheon's corporate goals, Stewart's organization is applying Six Sigma quality approaches to the company's supplier development activities. He has also assembled a network of Raytheon Six Sigma champions to work directly with suppliers. The Raytheon process for supplier development has six steps:

1. Identify supplier candidates for projects.
2. Define objectives and resources.
3. Baseline the opportunities and rank.
4. Analyze selected opportunities.
5. Implement projects.
6. Document and realize improvements.

When identifying suppliers, Stewart says he does not want his organization to select only suppliers "that are broken. We think we can work Six Sigma with suppliers at the higher end as well as the low end. On the other hand, I don't want suppliers to think we are using it just to attack the small and mid-size suppliers. We are going to use it across the supplier base. Six Sigma is a continuous-improvement or problem-solving tool, and all relationships have problems." Stewart says he is looking to identify not only the right suppliers for the process but also the right projects within those suppliers.

Another area where Raytheon is committed to improvement is its use of disadvantaged suppliers, some of whom are ideal candidates for supplier development. As a company, Raytheon has a series of comprehensive goals for small, women- and minority-owned supplier businesses.

For women owners of small businesses, the company held a Women's Business Forum that linked women business owners with female executives within Raytheon. Through the initiative, "we developed corporate relationships through which our executives mentored the women small business leaders. As we rationalize our supplier base, we don't want to leave some of these businesses behind," says Stewart. "So, we are bringing them along with us." To this end, his supply chain organization has a good record of creating opportunity for small businesses.

Source: Adapted from S. Avery, "Linking Supply Chains Saves Raytheon $400 Million," *Purchasing*, August 23, 2001, p. 27.

several years. Furthermore, three quarters of firms indicate they now commit 80% of their total purchase dollars with fewer than 100 suppliers.[6]

Supplier Development: A Strategy for Improvement

The first documented applications of supplier development came from Toyota, Nissan, and Honda, some as early as 1939. Toyota's *1939 Purchasing Rules* discussed the need to treat its suppliers as an integral part of Toyota and to work together to improve their collective performance. Nissan implemented its first supplier development efforts in 1963, with Honda joining the club as a result of the first Arab oil embargo in 1973.[7] However, the rest of the world has been slow to take up the supplier development banner.[8] Even the United Nations has recognized the need for supplier development; its *Guide to Supplier Development* is designed to improve the skills, capacities, and competitiveness of global industrial subcontracting and partnership exchanges.[9]

Although the concept was mentioned in several early purchasing books, early North American writings on supplier development began in earnest with researcher Michiel Leenders.[10] As broadly defined by a number of authors, supplier development is any activity undertaken by a buyer to improve a supplier's performance or capabilities to meet the buyer's short- and long-term supply needs. Organizations rely on a variety of activities to improve supplier performance, including sharing technology, providing incentives to suppliers for improved performance, promoting

Exhibit 9.8 Process for Implementation of Supplier Development Strategy

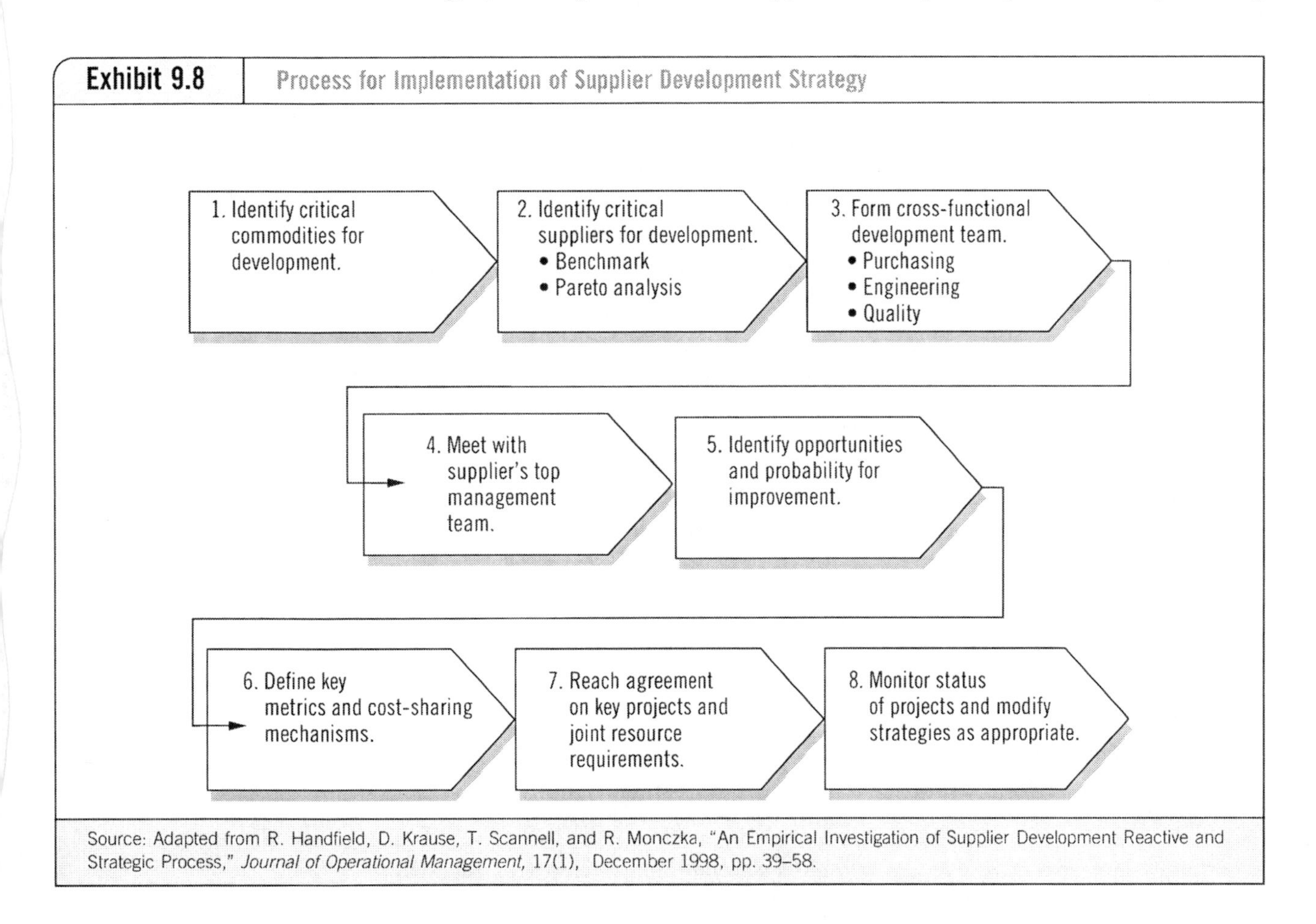

Source: Adapted from R. Handfield, D. Krause, T. Scannell, and R. Monczka, "An Empirical Investigation of Supplier Development Reactive and Strategic Process," *Journal of Operational Management*, 17(1), December 1998, pp. 39–58.

competition among suppliers, providing necessary capital, and directly involving its personnel with suppliers through activities such as training and process improvement.[11]

Direct involvement in a supplier's operations by buyer personnel is undoubtedly the most challenging part of any supplier development process. Not only must internal management and employees be convinced that investing scarce company resources in an outside supplier's operation is a worthwhile risk, but the supplier must be convinced it is in its own best interest to accept direction and assistance. Too often, the supplier is convinced that the only reason a buyer wants to engage in supplier development is to pressure the supplier to pass along all of the savings generated by reducing its price. Even if a mutual understanding of the importance of supplier development is reached, there is still the matter of implementation and allocation of needed resources by both parties, as well as ensuring that the implementation is maintained over time. Effective supplier development requires the commitment of financial capital and human resources, skilled personnel, timely and accurate information sharing, and performance measurement.

A Process Map for Supplier Development

After reviewing the strategies for more than 60 organizations, we have developed a generic process map for deploying a supplier development initiative, as shown in Exhibit 9.8.[12] Although many organizations have successfully deployed the first four stages of the process, some have been less successful in implementing the latter four stages.

Step 1—Identify Critical Commodities for Development

Not all organizations must pursue supplier development. An organization may already be sourcing from world-class suppliers due to its existing strategic supplier selection processes, or it may buy external inputs only in a very small proportion to total costs or sales. Therefore, supply managers must analyze their own individual sourcing situations to determine if a particular supplier's level of performance warrants development, and if so, which specific commodities and services will require attention.

Senior supply managers should thoroughly consider the following questions to determine if a given supplier warrants development effort.[13] A "yes" response to a majority of these questions suggests a need for supplier development.

- Do externally purchased products and services account for more than 50% of product or service value?
- Is the supplier an existing or potential source of competitive advantage?
- Do you currently purchase or plan to purchase on the basis of total cost versus initial purchase price?
- Can existing suppliers meet your competitive needs five years from now?
- Do you need suppliers to be more responsive to your needs?
- Are you willing and able to become more responsive to your suppliers' needs?
- Do you plan to treat suppliers as partners in your business?
- Do you plan to develop and maintain open and trusting relations with your suppliers?

A corporate-level executive steering committee should then develop an assessment of the relative importance of all purchased goods and services to identify where to focus any supplier development efforts. The result of this assessment is a portfolio analysis of those critical products or services that are essential for marketplace success. This discussion is an extension of the company's overall corporate-level strategic planning process and must include participants from other critical functions affected by sourcing decisions, including finance, sales and marketing, information technology, accounting, engineering, production, and design.

Step 2—Identify Critical Suppliers for Development

The supply base performance assessment system helps identify those suppliers within a commodity group that would be targeted for development. A common approach involves a routine analysis of current supplier performance. As shown in Exhibit 9.7, leading companies regularly monitor supplier performance on a facility-by-facility basis and rank suppliers from best to worst. Suppliers failing to meet predetermined minimum performance standards in quality, delivery, cycle time, late deliveries, total cost, service, safety, or environmental compliance are potential candidates for elimination from the supply base. If the supplier's product or service is essential, it should be considered for supplier development. Those suppliers that meet minimum requirements but do not provide world-class performance are the most likely candidates for development efforts. Benchmarking and Pareto analysis are two sourcing tools that can assist in the identification of possible supplier development targets.

Step 3—Form Cross-Functional Development Team

Before approaching suppliers and asking for improved performance, it is critical to develop cross-functional consensus and support from within for the initiative. Supply management executives continually emphasize that supply base improvement begins from within through buyer-focused activities—that is, the buying company must have its own house in order before expecting commitment and cooperation from suppliers. Development teams typically include members from engineering, operations, quality, and supply management.

Step 4—Meet with Supplier's Top Management Team

Once the development team's charter is established and an appropriate supplier has been identified for improvement, the team should approach the supplier's top management team and establish three relational building blocks for seeking supplier improvement: strategic alignment, measurement, and professionalism. Strategic alignment requires a business and technology alignment between the companies. It also requires alignment about key customer needs throughout the supply chain. Measurement requires an objective means of accurately assessing development results and progress in a timely manner. By approaching the supplier's top management with a solid and mutually beneficial business case for improvement, the demonstrated professionalism of all parties helps to establish a positive tone, reinforce collaboration, foster two-way communication, and develop mutual trust.

Step 5—Identify Opportunities and Probability for Improvement

At these meetings with the supplier's senior management, supply management executives should identify areas earmarked for improvement. Companies adopting a strategic approach to supply base development can usually agree upon the areas for improvement. In some cases, such areas are driven by final customer requirements and expectations.

Step 6—Define Key Metrics and Cost-Sharing Mechanisms

Development opportunities, although not necessarily specific improvement projects, are evaluated next in terms of project feasibility and potential return on investment. The parties jointly determine if the opportunities for improvement are realistic and achievable and, if so, then establish measures and improvement goals. The buyer and seller must also agree on how to divide or share the costs and benefits from the development project. A common sharing arrangement is 50/50, but the actual cost/benefit sharing must take each party's level of investment into consideration.

Step 7—Reach Agreement on Key Projects and Joint Resource Requirements

After identifying specific improvement projects to pursue, the parties must identify the resources necessary to carry out the project or development effort and make the commitment to employ them. The parties also need to reach agreement regarding the specific measures and metrics that will demonstrate success. These measures may include a defined percentage improvement in cost savings, quality, delivery or cycle time, or any other area relevant to supply chain performance. The most critical component of supplier development is that it must contain realistic and visible milestones and time horizons for improvement. What gets measured is usually what gets accomplished. The agreement should also specify the role of each party, who is responsible for the outcomes of the project, and the manner and timing for deploying already agreed-upon resources.

Step 8—Monitor Status of Projects and Modify Strategies as Appropriate

Progress must be monitored routinely after initiating a development project. Moreover, an ongoing, two-way exchange of information is needed to maintain project momentum. This can be achieved by creating visible milestones for objectives, posting progress, and creating new or revised objectives based on actual progress. Ongoing project management may require modifying the original plan, applying additional resources, developing new information, or refocusing priorities depending on events.

Supplier Development Efforts That Sometimes Don't Work

Evidence indicates that supplier development projects work—at least some of the time. Exhibit 9.9 on p. 328 presents the results of a comprehensive study of supplier development efforts and clearly indicates that, although there is no guarantee that comparable supplier development efforts will be equally successful, on average the development process produces substantial results. This does not mean that there are no barriers and challenges to successful supplier development. In fact, other studies have found these barriers to be very real. The next section describes some of the proven techniques and tools used by leading-edge companies to address the problems or barriers that may contribute to less-than-desired supplier development effectiveness.

Exhibit 9.9 Supplier Development Results

CRITERIA	BEFORE SUPPLIER DEVELOPMENT	AFTER SUPPLIER DEVELOPMENT
Incoming defects	11.65%	5.45%
% on-time delivery	79.85%	91.02%
Cycle time (from order placement to receipt, inclusively)	35.74 days	23.44 days
% orders received complete	85.47%	93.33%

Source: Krause, 1997, Survey of 527 firms.
Respondents: ISM members.

Overcoming the Barriers to Supplier Development

Barriers to supplier development fall into three classifications: (1) buyer-specific barriers, (2) buyer-supplier interface barriers, and (3) supplier-specific barriers. Companies can use a variety of approaches to overcome barriers to supplier development. In general, these approaches fall into one of three categories:

- Direct-involvement activities (hands-on): Companies often send their own personnel in to assist suppliers. These efforts are characterized as hands-on activities, where the buyer's representatives are directly involved in correcting supplier problems and increasing capabilities. An example would be the buyer assigning one of its process engineers to the supplier's facility to assist in physically rearranging its equipment to be more efficient.
- Incentives and rewards (the "carrot"): Companies also use incentives to encourage suppliers to improve, largely by means of their own efforts. For example, a buyer might agree to increase future order volumes if the desired performance improvement takes place within a specific time, or it could hold an annual award ceremony to recognize the best suppliers.
- Warnings and penalties (the "stick"): In some cases, companies may withhold potential future business if a supplier's performance is deemed unacceptable or if a lack of improvement is evident. Buyers may also use a competitive marketplace to provide a viable threat or incentive to a poorly performing supplier.

In many cases, organizations employ a combination of these three strategies to drive supplier improvement as quickly as possible, applying them judiciously in response to a particular supplier's capabilities and needs. The following sections address barriers to supplier development that are internal, external, or interface based, and provide examples of how leading companies overcome these barriers.

Buyer-Specific Barriers

A buying company will not engage in supplier development unless senior management recognizes the need for or the benefits to be gained from an investment in supplier development. Moreover, if supply management personnel have not already rationalized and optimized its supply base as discussed above, the volume of purchases with any particular supplier will likely not justify the joint investment. In addition, there may be a lack of top-level support for financing supplier development efforts in terms of both dollars and time.

Sourcing Snapshot

Guess Who's Getting into Supplier Development? The U.S. Air Force!

In the late 1990s, the Manufacturing Technology Division (ManTech) of the U.S. Air Force convened a meeting of 30 high-level supply management officials from various aerospace and defense organizations to discuss plans for supply base development. The meeting was an early step in a major ManTech initiative (dubbed the SME Initiative) that set a goal for prime and subprime Air Force contractors to foster improvements among the small- or medium-sized enterprises (SMEs) within their supply base. Underpinning the SME Initiative has been research by a ManTech team indicating that up to 80% of production for most weapons systems is now performed by suppliers, many of which are small- or medium-sized companies.

A study by the ManTech team identified a set of practices that better companies employed with their suppliers (listed in order of popularity):

1. Supplier training
2. Supplier rating, certification, and awards
3. Making customer technical expertise available to suppliers
4. Integrated customer/supplier teams to reduce supplier process waste and solve supplier problems
5. Supplier symposia and suggestion programs
6. Supplier continuous improvement programs
7. Supplier access to customer's volume discount rates
8. Structured methodology for problem solving
9. Integrated customer/supplier technology roadmaps
10. Customer development of a supplier's capability prior to outsourcing.

Under the SME Initiative, ManTech identifies critical small suppliers for direct development by either themselves or third-party consultants and incentives for prime contractors and subsystem producers to pursue supplier development policies. The U.S. Air Force knows that supplier development is essential to the success of future weapons programs.

Source: Adapted from "Air Force Pushes Its Supplier Development Program Forward," *Purchasing,* May 6, 1999, pp. 34–37.

Barrier: The Buying Company's Purchase Volume from the Supplier Does Not Justify Development Investment

Solution: Standardization and single-sourcing. Parts standardization across several product lines is a way to increase total order volumes with suppliers, which may justify a development investment. For example, IBM's Networking Hardware Division, which produces customized networking solutions for customers, is constantly striving to increase its parts commonality. Currently, over 50% of purchased components for major hardware projects contain unique items. If IBM personnel believe that using customized components will provide a market advantage, they will continue to use them. However, standardization remains an important way to leverage worldwide purchase volume and shorten new-product development cycles.

Concurrent with component standardization, many supply managers also plan to reduce their supply base, wherever possible, to achieve economies of scope and scale. Daewoo Corporation, for example, uses single-sourcing wherever possible, relying on two or more suppliers only in situations with high potential for labor disputes. Similarly, NCR, Doosan Corporation of Korea, Honda of America Manufacturing, and Rover currently use single-sourcing or are planning to move in that direction.

Barrier: No Immediate Benefit to Supplier Development Is Evident to the Buying Organization

Solution: Pursue small wins. Varity Perkins, a producer of diesel engines used in automotive and construction vehicles, found its initial supplier development efforts to be relatively unsuccessful. This resulted in lowered internal expectations and dampened enthusiasm for future development efforts. However, Varity personnel realized that part of the problem was that they were trying to accomplish too much. Thus, the company focused on a smaller group of suppliers for kaizen (or continuous improvement) efforts to gain a series of small wins and build momentum. Varity's kaizen approach achieved incremental improvements that ultimately gained renewed internal commitment for the supplier development process.

Barrier: Importance of Purchased Item Does Not Justify Development Efforts

Solution: Take a longer-term focus. Solectron, a contract manufacturer in the computer industry, has a competitive strategy that relies heavily on its supply chain management competencies. The company looks beyond the price of purchased inputs and examines how its most important suppliers affect the quality and technology of its products. Solectron expects its suppliers to provide designs offering integrated solutions that Solectron engineers can use in future product designs. Total cost and long-term strategic impact help justify ongoing investment in suppliers.

Barrier: Lack of Executive Support within the Buying Organization for Supplier Development

Solution: Prove the benefits. Support for supplier development is gained when management becomes convinced that the company can improve if supplier performance improves. For companies spending nearly 80% of their cost of goods sold on purchased inputs, such an argument is easy to make. For companies with lower percentages of purchased content, the argument may be more difficult. Proving a direct relationship between supplier improvement and increased profits can be difficult to achieve; someone within the supply management organization must document that outcome. Managers also note that efforts to optimize their companies' supply bases, combined with part standardization, can help free up scarce resources over the long term, making supplier development more palatable to internal skeptics. In addition, the total cost approach to supplier performance measurement should also prove to be an effective communication tool for demonstrating the deleterious effects of poor supplier performance. However, many companies still view supplier development resources simply as additional overhead costs rather than needed investment in supply chain performance.

Buyer-Supplier Interface Barriers

Barriers to supplier development may also originate in the interface between the buyer and supplier in areas such as open communication, alignment of organizational cultures, and trust. A reluctance to share sensitive information about costs and processes on the part of either buyer or supplier is one of the more significant interface barriers.

Barrier: Supplier Is Reluctant to Share Information on Costs or Processes

Solution: Create a supplier ombudsman. Honda of America has supplier ombudsmen who deal with the "soft side" of the business—primarily human resource issues not usually associated with cost, quality, or delivery. Because the supplier ombudsman is not directly involved in sourcing contract negotiations, suppliers are often much more willing to talk openly and honestly with the ombudsman, who can then act as a liaison between the two companies. One ombudsman emphasized that it takes time to build trust with suppliers, and trust building varies with different suppliers. If a supplier approaches the ombudsman with a problem that is the result of poor communication or misunderstanding between Honda and its supplier, the ombudsman communicates the supplier's perspective to Honda while maintaining as much confidentiality as possible. Over time, suppliers come to trust the ombudsman and appear to be more willing to share proprietary information with the company.

Barrier: Confidentiality Inhibits Information Sharing

Solution: Establish confidentiality agreements. Perhaps one of the biggest challenges in developing suppliers is sharing confidential information, especially when dealing with high-tech suppliers. Thus, many companies require nondisclosure or exclusivity agreements (i.e., the supplier provides a specific product to only one buyer) in development efforts, especially when dealing with technologically advanced products that contribute significantly to the buyer's competitiveness. However, nondisclosure agreements can benefit both parties. Ethical behavior on the part of the buyer will also support more open sharing of information with suppliers.

Barrier: Supplier Does Not Trust the Buying Organization

Solution: Spell it out. The driving forces behind kaizen events at Varity Perkins indicate that the company will not run an event without a properly executed written agreement between the parties. Although some supply management personnel at Varity Perkins prefer a "gentlemen's agreement," kaizen leaders believe the only way to gain a supplier's trust is to have the terms specifically written out and signed, especially when conducting the first supplier development event at a supplier. In one instance, it took Varity Perkins eight months to convince a supplier to consider a kaizen workshop because the supplier felt that a similar event with a different company previously failed to yield any improvements. The trust problem was compounded further because of Varity Perkins' previous reputation for arm's-length relationships with suppliers, manifested by frequent switching of suppliers based solely on price. The company has moved aggressively to reverse this perception by implementing and publicizing a new supply management philosophy emphasizing collaborative relationships with its suppliers.

Barrier: Organizational Cultures Are Poorly Aligned

Solution: Adapt a new approach to local conditions. When setting up its U.S. auto assembly plant in South Carolina, BMW quickly realized it would have to change its supplier development approach to conform to the North American supply market. BMW uses a process consulting approach to supplier development in Germany, which involves analyzing suppliers' processes and telling them what is wrong. This approach works well in a mature supplier relationship, where the supplier intuitively understands what the customer wants because the parties have worked together over time. In the United States, however, it became obvious that a very different approach was required because those long-term relationships did not exist.

When BMW started production, its U.S. suppliers frequently had difficulty understanding what was required in terms of quality and continuous improvement, resulting in strained relationships. Consequently, BMW spent a great deal of time explaining and communicating its expectations to suppliers. Eventually, BMW published a *Supplier Partnership Manual* that clearly delineated supplier responsibilities and its own expectations. The company also held supplier seminars to present its "Roadmap to Quality." These efforts have helped align buyer-supplier expectations and create a shared culture toward improvement.

Barrier: Not Enough Inducements to Participate Are Provided to the Supplier

Solution: Designed-in motivation. Although Solectron is now generally able to offer large order volumes to suppliers, that was not always the case. To gain supplier cooperation in the low-volume years, Solectron emphasized that a supplier could become designed into its products and thus have a greater potential for future business.

Solution: Financial incentives. Hyundai Motor Company uses financial incentives as one motivational tool for supplier improvement. The company rates supplier performance from 1 (highest) to 4 (lowest). Class 1 suppliers receive cash immediately on their invoices; Class 2 suppliers receive payment in 30 days; Class 3 suppliers receive payment in 60 days; and Class 4 suppliers receive no new business. Because all suppliers know how Hyundai evaluates their performance, they can take the steps necessary to ensure higher levels of performance.

Supplier-Specific Barriers

Just as buyers sometimes fail to recognize the potential benefits accruing from supplier development, a lack of recognition by the supplier may also keep its top management from fully committing to the joint effort. This lack of commitment may result in a failure to implement improvement ideas or to provide the technical and human resources necessary to support the development process. In addition, appropriate supplier follow-up may not take place once the development project has been completed, and the supplier's performance may revert back to its previous level.

Barrier: Lack of Commitment on the Part of Supplier's Management

Solution: Implement after commitment. Deere and Company's supplier development managers state that they will not engage in a supplier development project with a supplier unless the supplier's management demonstrates full commitment to the process. This involves a joint examination of the proposed improvement project and determination of the potential costs and benefits. To do so, a supply manager from

Deere arranges an initial contact meeting with the supplier's top local management to obtain its commitment and involvement. To secure this, Deere's supplier development engineers educate the supplier's management about the scope and impact of the desired improvement efforts. Once the supplier's senior management agrees to participate in principle, the supplier development engineer conducts process mapping, establishes the base case, and delineates the expected benefits hand in hand with corresponding supplier personnel. Once Deere and the supplier agree to the goals and objectives of the intended project, the next step is to determine how to share the costs and benefits. Deere typically allows the supplier to recover up front any capital-related costs required to implement the project and then splits the resulting savings 50/50 with the supplier, generally through a price decrease on future volume. By equitably sharing the resulting savings with the supplier, the supplier is more willing to engage in future development projects. In addition, success stories are shared with other possible supplier development targets to demonstrate the viability of the development process.

Barrier: Supplier's Management Agrees to Improvements but Fails to Implement the Proposals

Solution: Supplier champions. JCI Corporation, a first-tier supplier to the automotive industry, has instituted a Supplier Champions Program (SCP) designed to ensure suppliers are proficient in areas that are important to JCI's customers. The program was initiated because many of the suppliers that had attended JCI's training sessions failed to implement the tools and techniques that JCI provided. The SCP identifies what supplier personnel need to implement after they return from training. The program designates a Supplier Champion, a key supplier employee who understands JCI's expectations and demonstrates a high level of competence. The certification process requires that the Supplier Champion submit those actions to JCI that the supplier has identified for improvement. Such actions might include process mapping, failure mode effects analysis, quality control planning, best-practices benchmarking, and process auditing.

Barrier: Supplier Lacks Engineering Resources to Implement Solutions

Solution: Direct support. Honda of America Manufacturing has invested a significant amount of resources in its supplier support infrastructure, which was highlighted in the chapter opening. Of the more than 300 people then in HAM's supply management department, 50 were supplier development engineers who worked exclusively with suppliers. In one case, a small supplier did not have the capacity to keep up with requested volume, resulting in quality deterioration. HAM stationed four of its personnel at the supplier for 10 months at no charge, with additional services offered on an as-needed basis. As a result, the supplier improved its performance and now is a well-established Honda supplier.

Barrier: Supplier Lacks Required Information Systems

Solution: Direct electronic data interchange (EDI) support. At NCR Corporation, a manufacturer of ATMs, managers note that access to timely and accurate information is critical to decision making and ultimately to improved performance. An important focus of NCR's supplier development program has been to get its suppliers to invest in EDI. NCR also provides direct assistance to those suppliers producing lower-level components that do not have sufficient resources to get online. In addition, NCR provides training for suppliers and recommendations on hardware and software purchases.

Barrier: Suppliers Are Not Convinced Development Will Provide Benefits to Them

Solution: Let suppliers know where they stand. Varity Perkins revamped its supplier evaluation system to show suppliers areas of potential improvement. Previously, the company sent a quarterly report to suppliers assessing quality, delivery, and price competitiveness performance. Perkins did not use the data in any manner, and as a result, suppliers did not take the assessments seriously. When revamping the system, the measures were changed to capture the impact of supplier performance on daily operations.

Varity Perkins measured supplier delivery performance using a weekly time bucket, and on-time performance averaged 90 to 95%. With a daily time bucket, on-time performance dropped to 26% on time. Since the new measure has been in place, daily on-time delivery has improved to 90%. The supplier's history, its performance relative to Varity's other suppliers, and deviation from the mean in each evaluated area also appear on the modified report. The report also uses more graphics to make the data more meaningful.

This measurement system has become the foundation for the company's supplier development program. By allowing suppliers to view their performance relative to competitors, the company expects that suppliers will see the potential benefits of participating in supplier development activities as discussed earlier in the chapter.

Barrier: Supplier Lacks Employee Skill Base to Implement Solutions

Solution: Establish training centers. JCI Corporation realized that some suppliers, particularly smaller ones, lacked the internal skills required to implement improvement ideas. With this in mind, JCI built a facility dedicated to providing training to internal stakeholders, suppliers, and customers. Hyundai also established a domestic training center to provide supplier personnel with training in key performance areas, such as specialized welding. The suppliers and Hyundai share this cost. The South Korean government also supports this training center by providing tax benefits for building costs and making the joint training costs tax-deductible.

Solution: Provide human resource support. Hyundai Corporation recognizes that smaller suppliers with limited resources cannot consistently recruit and retain highly skilled engineers and other critical employees. Therefore, the majority of Hyundai's improvement efforts focus on smaller suppliers. Hyundai selects engineers from its own shops to spend time at supplier facilities. The engineers are co-located with their supplier counterparts, performing time/motion studies, teaching layout design, and improving productivity. Suppliers are consistently encouraged to learn, apply, and eventually teach the transferred knowledge to themselves and second-tier suppliers, a train-the-trainer approach.

Lessons Learned from Supplier Development

An underlying theme from these examples is that many of the barriers to supplier development are interrelated. It appears that, as companies work toward solving one barrier, they make concurrent progress toward solving others. Therefore, we can discern several lessons from studying supplier development successes and failures.

1. Managerial attitudes are a common and difficult barrier to overcome. A supply management executive at Honda of America noted that, although quality problems always have a solution, the attitudes of supplier management must be right before a problem can be truly resolved. Suppliers are sometimes not willing to accept outside help in the form of supplier development, either because they are too proud to accept help or because they do not see the value in improving quality or delivery performance. Management attitudes significantly affect the success of supplier development efforts. Oftentimes, suppliers feel that the resources required for improvement come at the expense of other needs. The savings must be real and readily achievable in order to get the supplier to sign on.
2. Realizing a competitive advantage from the supply chain requires a strategic orientation toward supply chain management and the alignment of supply management objectives with business unit goals. Supplier development plays a major role in helping create sustainable competitive advantage while aligning supply management and business goals. A strong supply management mission statement helps promote this strategic emphasis and alignment. Consider the following supply management mission statement from an auto parts manufacturer in the U.K.:

   > *We are committed to procure goods and services in a way that delivers our aims and objectives of becoming the most successful auto parts business in the world.*

   The company pursues this mission through (1) development of a world-class supplier base; (2) obtaining the highest-quality, most cost-effective goods and services in a timely manner; and (3) establishing long-term relationships with suppliers that strive for continuous improvement in all areas.
3. Relationship management is critical to supplier development success. Buyers can strengthen relationships with suppliers through focused supplier development activities. Besides developing mutual trust, the participants within a supply chain can begin to truly understand each other's needs and requirements, thereby making the entire supply chain stronger and more competitive. Ideally, supplier development will lead to the recognition that there is a strong co-destiny between buyer and supplier. Successful supplier development requires a strong, collaborative relationship and mutual commitment between the parties.

Pursuing supplier development activities directly with suppliers is neither quick nor easy. It requires vision, commitment, open communication, and equitable sharing of costs and benefits to work effectively. The long-term objective, of course, is to transform suppliers in such a way that continuous improvement becomes an integral part of each supplier's culture and DNA. Such joint accomplishments are achieved longitudinally and only by those companies that are patient and tenacious enough to make supplier development an important part of their supplier management processes.

Good Practice Example

Supplier Measurement Helps FedEx Manage a Worldwide Supply Base

FedEx, a worldwide leader in package delivery and logistics services, has built a solid reputation for reliable, on-time service. Throughout its history (founded in 1971), FedEx has focused on operational excellence and the ability to consistently pick up, sort, and deliver packages on time to their final destination.

Over the last 10 years, the package delivery industry has become highly competitive. Besides FedEx, customers can select UPS, DHL, or the U.S. Postal Service to deliver their packages. Even electronic mail is a source of new competition—senders simply attach large files with their electronic messages instead of sending paper copies via the overnight letter pack. FedEx must provide new services to customers, expand into new markets worldwide, and control costs if it expects to meet its growth targets.

FedEx purchases billions of dollars of goods and services annually, making supply management a major value-adding activity at the company. Furthermore, FedEx realizes that its suppliers greatly affect total costs and the ability of FedEx to serve its shippers. For example, if a supplier of aircraft replacement parts misses a delivery or ships defective parts, this affects FedEx's ability to keep its planes flying safely and on time. To help in its supply chain management efforts, the company has created a detailed supplier scorecard to evaluate supplier performance for goods, services, and fuel.

The FedEx supplier scorecard, available internally and to suppliers through the company intranet, establishes a level of uniformity among the many diverse supply management groups at FedEx. Buyers or supply chain specialists maintain scorecards for the suppliers for which they have responsibility. Completed scorecards are forwarded to a central database so they can be reviewed for procedural compliance and maintenance. The database allows supply chain specialists to perform a variety of analyses. For example, a supply manager can quickly identify those suppliers failing to meet minimum delivery requirements. The ability to perform this analysis greatly supports FedEx's supplier development and improvement efforts.

Exhibit 9.10 on p. 338 is an example of the supplier scorecard template that FedEx uses for products. The original scorecard system also featured templates with separate scoring guidelines for service and fuel suppliers. These three categories are now combined into a single robust template. The scorecard system allows the individual responsible for managing the supplier to adjust weights within the performance categories to meet the unique needs of a purchase requirement. Besides adjusting the weights, users can also determine which categories and subitems within a category to include.

Although the system offers the user substantial flexibility in selecting categories and weights, several scorecard rules apply. First, the performance category titled Diverse Supplier Development must be included in each evaluation per corporate requirements. Second, the selected performance category weights must sum to 100. Third, all subitems within a category must be scored on a 0–5 scale, which are added together and divided by the number of subitems for an average category score. This average score is then multiplied by the category weight to yield the total score for that category. When all selected categories are scored, the category totals are added to arrive at a performance level ranging from 0 to 500 points, resulting in one of the following designations:

500–450	Platinum
449–400	Gold
399–350	Silver
349–300	Bronze
<300	Requires special attention

A detailed user's manual provides guidance for subitem scoring. For example, the first performance category listed in Exhibit 9.10 is on-time delivery performance. The score is based on the number of deliveries that arrived on time divided by the total number of deliveries. The following scale determines the delivery performance score:

ON-TIME DELIVERY %	SCORE
100–95	5
94–90	4
89–80	3
79–70	2
69–60	1
<60	0

Buyers or supply chain specialists must communicate with internal customers to get additional insight into each supplier's performance history. Ideally, feedback from internal customers is incorporated into the scorecard so results can be shared with suppliers on a regular basis. Because most supplier scorecards include some qualitative assessments or judgments, suppliers may question or even disagree with parts of their score. This is not a major drawback to the system. In fact, disagreements can be positive because they open channels of communication between FedEx and its suppliers.

Users now have the ability to weight the subitems within a category rather than providing a single weight for the entire category. FedEx also expects to expand scorecard use to include a greater number of suppliers. Supply chain managers at FedEx realize that something as important as supplier management requires a rigorous measurement system that supports the attainment of supply objectives.

Exhibit 9.10 FedEx Strategic Sourcing Supplier Scorecard

Supplier Number ______ Eval. Period: From ______
FSC Code ______ To ______

Supplier Name ______ Date: ______
Address ______ FedEx Rep: ______
______ Manager: ______
Representative ______ Department: ______

CATEGORY	6 mths	3 mths	1 mth	Weight	Score	Total
1. On-Time Delivery Performance				25		
No. of on-time deliveries						
Total deliveries						
Pct. On-Time						
(100–95% = 5 // 94–90 = 4 // 89–80 = 3 // 79–70 = 2 // 69–60 = 1 // less than 60 = 0)						
2. Cycle Time Improvement (Yes / No)				5		
3. Quality				10		
A. Discrepancy rate	6 mths	3 mths	1 mth			
No. of problem receipts						
Total receipts						
Discrepancy rate (rec.)						
No. of problem invoices						
Total invoices						
Discrepancy rate (inv.)						
Total discrepancy rate						
(0–1% = 5 //2–3 = 4 // 4–6 = 3 // 7–9 = 2 // 10–12 = 1 // greater than 12 = 0)						
B. MTBF						
C. Bad from stock						
D. No. of customer / quality complaints						
E. No. of warranty claims						
F. Turn time on warranty claims						
G. Certification (yes / no)						
(Average score for quality)						
4. Service				15		
A. Flexibility						
B. Customer service responsiveness						
C. Operational compatibility / coverage / accessibility						
D. Sales person product knowledge						
E. Sales person knowledge of FedEx						
F. Post sales support						
G. Technology upgrades / enhancements						
(Average score for service)						
5. Financial Stability (measured by D&B)				5		
6. Cost				20		
A. Price competitiveness						
B. Cost trends						
C. Add-ons						
D. Frequency / value of cost-reduction ideas						
E. Supplier savings sharing						
F. Gratis service (no incremental costs)						
G. FedEx cost of quality (or benefit)						
(Average score for cost)						
7. Diverse Supplier Development (DSD) — contact DSD for scoring				10		
A. Direct reporting						
B. Indirect tier reporting (completed by DSD & Prime)						
C. Use of local suppliers						
(Average score for DSD)						
8. Optional or Supplier / Product specific				10		
A.						
B.						
C.						
(Average score for optional)						
9. TOTAL SCORE				100		

Scoring Scale: 5 = Excellent // 4 = Above average // 3 = Average // 2 = Below average // 1 = Poor // 0 = Unacceptable
Performance Level: 500–450 = Platinum // 449–400 = Gold // 399–350 = Silver // 349–300 = Bronze // <300

CONCLUSION

Effectively managing and improving supplier performance is a primary supply management and business function. Supplier management and development constitute the new model of supply management. No longer does a buyer simply purchase parts from the lowest-priced source. The activities that best describe today's enlightened buyer include planning, coordinating, managing, developing, and improving performance capabilities throughout the supply base. For many items, buyers no longer just buy parts from suppliers; they manage supplier relationships and capabilities.

Therefore, supply management must carefully select and manage a proper mix of suppliers. To accomplish this, the buying organization must invest the requisite resources for effective supplier management, including a broad-based supplier performance measurement system, contracts with preferred or certified suppliers, and a wide range of supplier development tools and techniques. An effective supplier management program helps maximize the contribution received from suppliers, lowering costs, increasing quality, and developing future capabilities.

KEY TERMS

risk, 318

DISCUSSION QUESTIONS

1. Provide reasons why most firms do not have an adequate supplier measurement system.
2. Your manager at the medium-sized company where you work has just called you in and asked you to explain why the company should spend its scarce financial resources to develop a supplier measurement system. What do you tell her?
3. Why is it critical to have a smaller supply base before committing to a supplier management and development program?
4. Discuss the advantages and disadvantages of an optimized supply base. How can a buyer overcome the disadvantages?
5. Discuss the logic behind maintaining multiple suppliers for each purchased item.
6. Discuss the logic behind maintaining a reduced number of suppliers for each item.
7. What is a full-service supplier? What are the benefits of using full-service suppliers?
8. Why is the Honda approach to supplier development and improvement not widespread among U.S. firms?
9. Many companies are now using the World Wide Web to share performance information with suppliers, thereby allowing suppliers to compare their performance to other suppliers within the buying company's supply base. Discuss the benefits of this strategy to both buyers and suppliers.
10. Discuss the different types of supplier development and support that a firm can offer. Which are the most common? Why?

11. Research has revealed that no single approach to supplier development is effective in achieving performance goals. Rather, a mix of the carrot, stick, and hands-on approaches seems to work best. Explain why you think this is the case.
12. A common statement made in some supply management organizations is, "We can't be spending money on supplier development—we're not in business to train suppliers and do their job for them!" What type of barrier does this statement represent? How would you respond to such a statement?
13. Of the barriers to supplier development mentioned in this chapter, which ones, in your opinion, are the most difficult to overcome?
14. A Chrysler executive once made the following statement: "Only about one in five supplier development efforts are truly 100% successful." Why do you think this is the case? What makes supplier development such a challenging effort?
15. Discuss the reasons why top-management commitment is essential to the success of supplier management and development.
16. What are the advantages of calculating a Supplier Performance Index? What are the challenges associated with developing a measurement system that uses SPI?
17. What is the role of the Q adjustment factor in the SPI calculation?

ADDITIONAL READINGS

Bolstorff, P., and Rosenbaum, R. (2007), *Supply Chain Excellence: A Handbook for Dramatic Improvement Using the SCOR Model* (2nd ed.), New York: AMACOM.

Butterfield, B. (2000), "Mentoring for Advantage," *Purchasing Today,* 11(3), 14.

Davenport, T. H., and Harris, J. G. (2007), *Competing on Analytics: The New Science of Winning,* Boston: Harvard Business School Press.

de Crombrugghe, A., and Le Coq, G. (2003), *Guide to Supplier Development: For Programmes to Be Implemented by Industrial Subcontracting and Partnership Exchanges (SPXs),* Vienna: United Nations Industrial Development Organization.

Desai, M. P. (1996), "Implementing a Supplier Scorecard Program," *Quality Progress,* 29(2), 73–76.

Dunn, S. C., and Young, R. R. (2004), "Supplier Assistance within Supplier Development Initiatives," *Journal of Supply Chain Management,* 40(3), 19–29.

Fitzgerald, K. R. (1995), "For Superb Supplier Development, Honda Wins!" *Purchasing,* 21, 32.

Forker, L. B., Ruch, W. A., and Hershauer, J. C. (1999), "Examining Supplier Improvement Efforts from Both Sides," *Journal of Supply Chain Management,* 35(3), 40–50.

Forrest, W. (2006), "McDonald's Applies SRM Strategy to Global Technology Buy," *Purchasing,* 135(12), 16–17.

Galt, Major J. D. A., and Dale, B. G. (1991), "Supplier Development: A British Case Study," *International Journal of Purchasing and Materials Management,* 27, 16–22.

Giunipero, L. C. (1990), "Motivating and Monitoring JIT Supplier Performance," *Journal of Purchasing and Materials Management,* 26, 19–24.

Hahn, C. K., Watts, C. A., and Kim, K. Y. (1990), "The Supplier Development Program: A Conceptual Model," *International Journal of Purchasing and Materials Management,* 26, 2–7.

Handfield, R., and Krause, D. (1999), "Think Globally, Source Locally," *Supply Chain Management Review,* Winter, 36–49.

Handfield, R. B., Krause, D. R., Scannell, T. V., and Monczka, R. M. (2000), "Avoid the Pitfalls in Supplier Development," *Sloan Management Review,* 41(2), 37–49.

Hartley, J., and Choi, T. (1996), "Supplier Development: Customers as a Catalyst of Process Change," *Business Horizons,* July–August, pp. 37–44.

Hartley, J., and Jones, G. (1997), "Process Oriented Supplier Development: Building the Capability for Change," *International Journal of Purchasing and Materials Management,* 33(3), 24–29.

Hines, P. (1994), *Creating World-Class Suppliers: Unlocking Mutual Competitive Advantage,* London: Pitman.

Humphreys, P. K., Li, W. L., and Chan, L. Y. (2004), "The Impact of Supplier Development on Buyer-Supplier Performance," *Omega: The International Journal of Management Science,* 32(2), 131–143.

Kerr, J. (2006), "The Changing Complexion of Supplier Diversity," *Supply Chain Management Review,* 10(2), 38–45.

Krause, D. R. (1997), "Supplier Development: Current Practices and Outcomes," *International Journal of Purchasing and Materials Management,* 33(2), 12–19.

Krause, D. R., and Ellram, L. M. (1997), "Critical Elements of Supplier Development: The Buying Firm Perspective," *European Journal of Purchasing and Supply Management,* 3(1), 21–31.

Krause, D. R., and Ellram, L. M. (1997), "Success Factors in Supplier Development," *International Journal of Physical Distribution and Logistics Management,* 27(1), 39–52.

Krause, D. R., Handfield, R. B., and Tyler, B. B. (2007), "The Relationship between Supplier Development, Commitment, Social Capital Accumulation and Performance Improvement," *Journal of Operations Management,* 25(2), 528–545.

Krause, D. R., and Scannell, T. V. (2002), "Supplier Development Practices: Product and Service Based Industry Comparisons," *Journal of Supply Chain Management,* 38(2), 13–22.

Lamming, R. (1993), *Beyond Partnership: Strategies for Innovation and Lean Supply,* Hertfordshire, U.K.: Prentice Hall International.

Leenders, M. R. (1965), *Improving Purchasing Effectiveness through Supplier Development,* Boston: Harvard University Press.

Li, W.-L., Humphreys, P., Chan, L. Y., and Kumaraswamy, M. (2003), "Predicting Purchasing Performance: The Role of Supplier Development Programs," *Journal of Materials Processing Technology,* 138(1–3), 243–249.

Liker, J. K., and Choi, T. Y. (2004), "Building Deep Supplier Relationships," *Harvard Business Review,* 83(1), 104–113.

Nelson, D., Moody, P. E., and Stegner, J. R. (2005), *The Incredible Payback: Innovative Solutions That Deliver Extraordinary Results,* New York: AMACOM.

Nix, N. W., Lusch, R. F., Zacharia, Z. G., and Bridges, W. (2007), "The Hand That Feeds You: What Makes Some Collaborations with Suppliers Succeed, When So Many Fail?" *Wall Street Journal,* October 27–28, p. R8.

Patterson, J. L., and Nelson, J. D. (1999), "OEM Cycle Time Reduction through Supplier Development," *Practix: Best Practices in Purchasing and Supply Chain Management,* 2(3), 1–5.

"Performance Measurement: Why It's Important to Measure Suppliers Well" (2000), *Purchasing,* 128(7), 36–39.

Prokopets, L., and Tabibzadeh, R. (2006), *Supplier Relationship Management: Maximizing the Value of Your Supply Base,* Stamford, CT: Archstone Consulting.

Robitaille, D. (2007), *Managing Supplier-Related Processes,* Chico, CA: Paton Professional.

Rogers, P. A. (2005), "Optimising Supplier Management and Why Co-Dependency Equals Mutual Success," *Journal of Facilities Management,* 4(1), 40–50.

Sako, M. (2004), "Supplier Development at Honda, Nissan and Toyota: Comparative Case Studies of Organizational Capability Enhancement," *Industrial and Corporate Change,* 13(2), 281–308.

Sánchez-Rodríguez, C., Hemsworth, D., and Martínez-Lorente, A. R. (2005), "The Effect of Supplier Development Initiatives on Purchasing Performance: A Structural Model," *Supply Chain Management,* 10(3–4), 289–301.

Teague, P. E. (2007), "How to Improve Supplier Performance," *Purchasing,* 136(4), 31–32.

Theodorakioglou, Y., Gotzamani, K., and Tsiolvas, G. (2006), "Supplier Management and Its Relationship to Buyers' Quality Management," *Supply Chain Management,* 11(2), 148–159.

Wagner, S. M. (2006), "Supplier Development Practices: An Exploratory Study," *European Journal of Marketing,* 40(5–6), 554–571.

Watts, C. A., and Hahn, C. K. (1993), "Supplier Development Programs: An Empirical Analysis," *International Journal of Purchasing and Materials Management,* 29(2), 11–17.

ENDNOTES

1. Minahan, T., and Vigoroso, M. (2002), "The Supplier Performance Measurement Benchmarking Report," http://www.aberdeen.com; accessed January 2, 2008.

2. Robinson, S. (1999), "Taiwan's Chip Plants Left Idle by Earthquake," *New York Times,* September 22.

3. Friedman, T. L. (2006), *The World Is Flat, Release 2.0,* New York: Farrar, Straus, and Giroux, p. 517.

4. Bhote, K. R. (1989), *Strategic Supply Management: A Blueprint for Revitalizing the Manufacturer-Supplier Partnership,* New York: AMACOM, pp. 75–78.

5. Greenwald, J. (1992), "What Went Wrong? Everything at Once," *Time,* http://www.time.com/time/magazine/article/0,9171,976990-6,00.html; accessed April 16, 2008.

6. Reese, A. (2000), "E-Procurement Takes On the Untamed Supply Chain," *iSource,* November, p. 108.

7. Sako, M. (2004), "Supplier Development at Honda, Nissan and Toyota: Comparative Case Studies of Organizational Capability Enhancement," *Industrial and Corporate Change,* 13(2), 281–308.

8. Lamming, R. (1993), *Beyond Partnership: Strategies for Innovation and Lean Supply,* Hertfordshire, U.K.: Prentice Hall International, pp. 215–216.

9. de Crombrugghe, A., and Le Coq, G. (2003), *Guide to Supplier Development,* Vienna: United Nations Industrial Development Organization.

10. See Leenders, M. R. (1965), *Improving Purchasing Effectiveness through Supplier Development,* Boston: Harvard University Press; and Leenders, M. R., and Blenkhorn, D. L. (1988), *Reverse Marketing: The New Buyer-Supplier Relationship,* New York: Free Press.

11. Krause and Handfield, p. 7.

12. Handfield, R., Krause, D., Scannell, T., and Monczka, R. (1998), "An Empirical Investigation of Supplier Development: Reactive and Strategic Processes," *Journal of Operations Management,* 17(1), 39–58.

13. Hahn, C. K., Watts, C. A., and Kim, K. Y. (1990), "The Supplier Development Program: A Conceptual Model," *International Journal of Purchasing and Materials Management,* 26(2), 2–7.

Chapter 10

WORLDWIDE SOURCING

Learning Objectives

After completing this chapter, you should be able to

- Identify the differences between international purchasing and global sourcing
- Understand the reasons why firms pursue international purchasing
- Identify the total costs associated with international purchasing
- Become familiar with the problems and obstacles hindering global sourcing efforts
- Understand the key factors needed for successful global sourcing efforts

Chapter Outline

Worldwide Sourcing at Selex

Selex, a U.S.-based electronics company with $2 billion in annual sales, is a company in transition. The early 1990s, which began the longest period of industrial expansion in U.S. history, were not rewarding for the company. Selex experienced eroding profit margins due to intense global competition and mature product lines (with some of its products being 20 to 25 years old), making it vulnerable to cost-reduction pressure and lower profit margins.

The company suffered through several costly product failures during the 1990s and lost market share as new competitors and technologies encroached on core markets. And, with some difficulty, the company was forced to change its culture to respond to the demands of a new marketplace. Selex has had to change from being a technology-driven company to a flexible, market-focused company.

Selex organizes supply management into three distinct groups: indirect purchasing, raw materials purchasing (any material that is required for production), and contract or finished goods purchasing (outsourced finished goods). Each group has pursued innovative approaches to worldwide sourcing.

INDIRECT PURCHASING

Previous efforts at managing indirect purchases were U.S. focused, even though Selex has a manufacturing presence in the United Kingdom, Mexico, the United States, Japan, and China. A major corporate initiative at Selex has involved the development of a global sourcing process called Sourcing Vision. Using this process, project teams systematically review Selex's worldwide indirect spend with the goal of achieving cost savings of 7 to 15% annually.

An executive steering committee oversees the Sourcing Vision process. This committee consists of the vice president of research, the vice president of supply chain management, the vice president of marketing and sales, the vice president of information technology, and the corporate controller. Each member resides at the executive vice president level, and each champions a specific global project.

Cross-functional project teams are an integral part of Sourcing Vision. Project teams engage in the following activities:

- Analyzing the industry and identifying buyer and seller strengths and weaknesses
- Defining improvement goals
- Identifying potential suppliers
- Forwarding and analyzing supplier proposals
- Determining the criteria for supplier selection
- Developing a sourcing strategy
- Making supplier selection decisions

RAW MATERIALS PURCHASING

The second major procurement group is raw materials purchasing (which most companies call direct materials). As part of its global procurement strategy, the raw materials group has focused on (1) identifying and qualifying sources worldwide and (2) aggregating volumes with leveraged agreements. This group also has responsibility for finished goods planning (which includes aggregate product planning).

A major change in raw materials procurement involved technical personnel, operations, and procurement working together worldwide to refine component materials. This cross-functional approach, which is coordinated at the corporate level, examines systems tradeoffs to arrive at an expected lowest total component cost. A second major change emphasized a commodity approach to global strategy development, with leadership roles assumed by personnel from different sites. Selex has also established lead buyers at sites for items that are not part of the coordinated commodity approach. One individual at each plant is responsible for a procurement area and becomes Selex's resident expert.

CONTRACT PURCHASING

The global outsourcing of finished products at Selex is a result of the realization that vertical integration could not support 20 to 40 new-product launches a year. Most Selex products use self-contained electronic components, which the company refers to as media. The physical housing of the product is the hardware. Selex insources media and outsources hardware because most of the innovation that customers value occurs within media rather than hardware.

Approximately seven years ago, Selex formed a contract manufacturing organization with primary responsibility for hardware outsourcing. This group now has responsibility for identifying and qualifying outsource partners, assessing product quality, and working with contract manufacturers during new-product development. As part of the contract manufacturing organization, the outsourcing director also has responsibility for two international purchasing offices (IPOs). The IPOs identify potential contract manufacturers or identify available suppliers for a specific application. The IPOs also support the indirect and raw materials purchasing groups discussed earlier.

Selex illustrates how a major corporation, faced with new competitive threats and declining markets, transformed itself from a slow, functionally driven organization into a responsive, market-driven, cross-functional enterprise. It also illustrates how three procurement groups, each taking very different approaches, have endorsed worldwide sourcing as a way to help achieve corporate objectives.

Source: Interviews with company managers. The company name was changed at the request of the company.

Globalization is dramatically changing interactions among the world's economies through increasing interdependencies. Included in several definitions of **globalization** are the terms "interdependence," "connectivity," and "integration of economies" in social, technical, and political spheres. This trend toward seamless boundaries is explored in depth by Thomas Friedman in his best seller *The World Is Flat.*[1] Information now circles the globe with such ease that 245,000 Indians housed in call centers are scheduling airline flights, soliciting credit card customers, and answering questions about mortgages and insurance policies.[2] When asked to indicate what business drivers were likely to have the most influence on their company's purchasing strategies in the next 10 years, 49% of 359 responding executives stated it would be globalization.[3]

Globalization in developing economies such as China and India represents opportunities for cost savings on the buying side and new markets on the selling side. On the selling side more affluent consumers are desiring higher-level brands. The well-known French cosmetics firm L'Oréal failed to make a profit competing in India's low-priced shampoo market. However, when it shifted its focus and advertising to the emerging middle class, with products selling for 3 to 20 times the price of those of its rivals, profits followed. The 200-million-person Indian middle class desires many foreign brands, from Tommy Hilfiger jeans to Absolut vodka.[4]

On the supply side, the cost/price benefits associated with sourcing in developing countries are a significant motivation for remaining competitive in an increasingly global environment. Several studies have indicated that cost/price savings are the number one reason for global sourcing. Other important benefits realized are availability, quality, and (to a lesser extent) innovation. Once a firm establishes sourcing roots in these countries, it facilitates entry to marketing and selling opportunities. Many larger multinationals take a more global perspective by seeking to supply their worldwide operations with common sources of supply at the lowest worldwide cost, and they are developing centralized and globally coordinated supply organizations to support these efforts.

One indicator of this increased international sourcing is the large U.S. merchandise trade deficit, which in 2006 was more than $700 billion. Much of the focus on the increasing deficit is directed toward China. The U.S. government has stepped up pressure on China to both open its markets and allow its currency to float freely. This pressure is justified; looking at the top U.S. trading partners reveals that Canada leads with China second, followed by Mexico, Japan, Germany, U.K., South Korea, France, Taiwan, and Malaysia. As is shown in Exhibit 10.1, the first four partners account for 75% of total trade. Second, two of the four largest trading partners are part of the North American Free Trade Agreement. Finally, because services such as call centers are not captured by the data, India is not listed as a top 10 trading partner. Outsourcing and offshoring of services are a large part of global sourcing strategies for the 21st-century supply manager.

Globalization is also changing the structure of many marketplaces as global companies extend their reach into all markets. Often the acquiring firm is not a U.S.-based firm. In the aluminum industry, Rio Tinto of Australia acquired Canada's Alcan Aluminum. In obtaining Alcan, Rio Tinto bested U.S.-based Alcoa's bid.[5] In the global steel industry, Germany's Thyssen Krupp is building a $2.7 billion mill outside of Mobile, AL. Scheduled for opening in 2010, the mill is the largest to be built in the United States in over 40 years. Indian steel maker Essar Global announced plans to build an integrated mill outside of Duluth, MN.[6]

Exhibit 10.1 U.S. Trading Partners, 2006

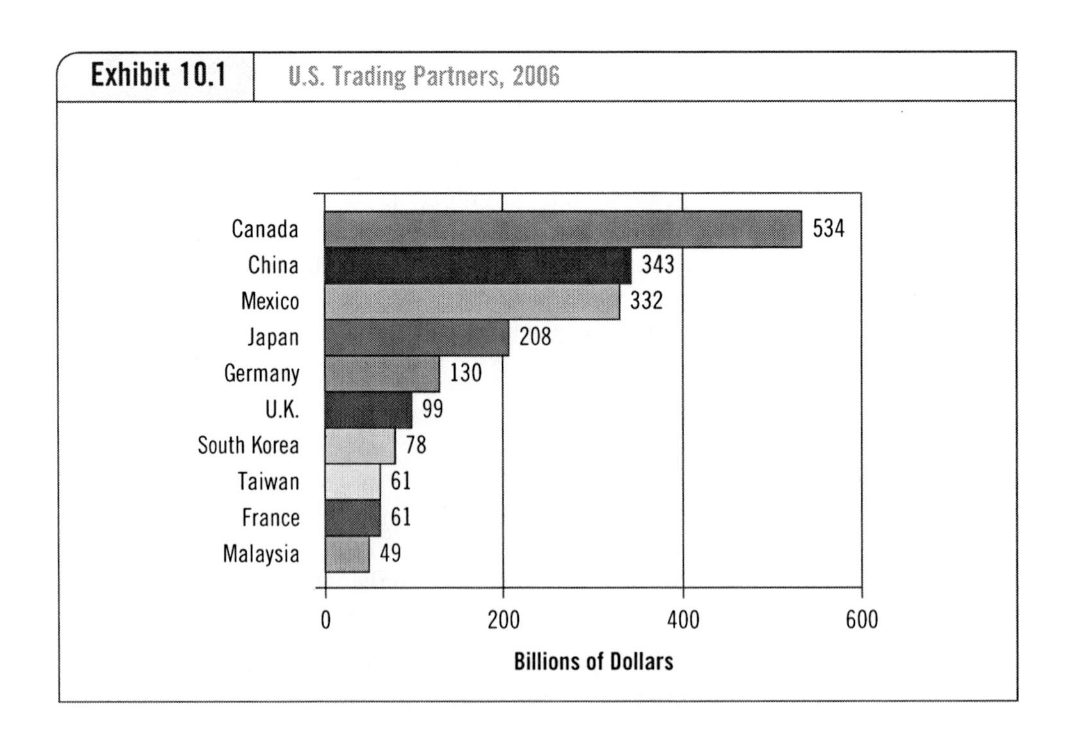

This chapter focuses on how supply managers can capture the benefits of globalization through international purchasing and global sourcing. **International purchasing** relates to a commercial purchase transaction between a buyer and a supplier located in different countries. This type of purchase is typically more complex than a domestic purchase. Organizations must contend with lengthened lead times, increased rules and regulations, currency fluctuations, customs requirements, and a host of other variables such as language and time differences.

Global sourcing, which differs from international purchasing in scope and complexity, involves proactively integrating and coordinating common items and materials, processes, designs, technologies, and suppliers across worldwide purchasing, engineering, and operating locations. Because of the differences between international buying and global sourcing, we will use the term **worldwide sourcing** for general discussions of the process of purchasing from other countries.

This chapter contains three major sections. The first section presents an overview of worldwide sourcing, including the most common reasons why companies source worldwide. The second section identifies the areas that make international purchasing more complex than domestic sourcing. The final section presents those factors that separate successful from less-successful global sourcing efforts.

Worldwide Sourcing Overview

The number of U.S. companies that practice worldwide sourcing has increased dramatically over the past three decades.[7] Between 1973 and 1975, the percentage of companies purchasing internationally more than doubled, from 21 to 45%. The oil embargo of the 1970s, coupled with shortages of other basic materials, forced purchasing to search overseas for suppliers. Many foreign producers were also becoming quality and cost leaders across a number of industries. The foreign items most sought after by U.S. companies in 1975, for example, were production machinery and equipment, followed by chemicals and mechanical and electrical components.

The percentage of U.S. companies engaged in worldwide sourcing increased from 45 to 56% from 1975 to 1982. This increase reflected the continuing inability of domestic suppliers and manufacturers to compete in terms of price, quality, and even delivery. Foreign suppliers could often provide higher-quality parts at a lower total cost. For some, survival against foreign competitors required sourcing from the same suppliers that supported the competition.

The period from 1982 through 1987 saw a sharp rise in the number of companies looking internationally for their purchase requirements—from 56 to 71%. During this time the value of the U.S. dollar increased dramatically against other currencies. U.S. imports became less expensive while U.S. firms found it difficult to export and compete in world markets. The huge trade imbalances of the 1980s reflected the strength of the U.S. dollar in world currency markets along with a continued lack of competitiveness of many U.S. companies.

Since 1987 the level of international purchasing and trade has accelerated rapidly. The end of the Cold War led to the opening of trade with emerging markets in Russia, Eastern Europe, and China, which in turn has led to the development of new markets and new sources of supply. Furthermore, import and export restrictions are lessening, partly as a function of the GATT agreement on free trade signed in

Sourcing Snapshot — *Thinking Globally and Buying Locally at Sony*

Countless organizations today face a similar scenario. They are expanding production facilities or distribution networks in a new country, and they must often develop local sources of supply to meet domestic content regulations or to minimize transportation costs. At Sony, its global procurement strategy has been to procure local parts whenever possible and to produce in those countries where the company's products are sold. In Europe, Sony sources approximately 90% of the company's product value locally; in Asia, Sony obtains 30 to 50% of product content locally. When production shifts to a new area, local suppliers are developed whenever possible. As a backup, Sony often negotiates with Japanese suppliers to ship parts to the new production facilities. If no suitable local supplier exists, purchasing may negotiate with a Japanese supplier to set up local production in the new country of operation. Although Sony does not contribute capital to suppliers to set up production facilities, it will help with training of personnel at new locations. Thus, Sony's policy is to produce as many parts as possible locally at each location.

Source: Adapted from R. Handfield and D. Krause, "Think Globally, Source Locally," *Supply Chain Management Review*, Winter 1999, pp. 36–49.

Uruguay. The North American Free Trade Agreement, passed in 1993, has also resulted in a dramatic increase in trade between the United States, Canada, and Mexico. Trade talks between the United States and other countries, such as Japan and China, also reduced trade restrictions.

The average amount of total purchases from non-U.S. sources by larger firms has increased from 9% of total purchases in 1993 to over 25% in 2000. One study indicated that 38% of the firms surveyed forecasted they would source at least 60% of their purchases on a global basis by 2010. This was up from 18% in 2000.[8] The trend toward increased international purchasing activity is clear. The growth in worldwide sourcing is likely to continue rather than decrease. As indicated earlier, business drivers most likely to have an influence on the company purchasing strategies in the next 10 years are globalization and cost leadership.[9] Besides lowest cost, there are many possible reasons why firms will continue to purchase internationally.

Why Source Worldwide?

Although the previous discussion provided some reasons for purchasing internationally, let's discuss formally the more important reasons why companies pursue worldwide sourcing.

Cost/Price Benefits

After considering all the costs associated with international purchasing, savings of 20 to 30% may be available. Cost differentials between countries arise because of

- Lower labor rates
- Different productivity levels
- Possible willingness to accept a lower profit margin

- Exchange rate differences
- Lower-cost inputs for materials
- Government subsidies

Purchasing should consider only suppliers that are capable of meeting rigid quality and delivery standards, although far too often price differentials become the primary criterion behind a foreign sourcing decision. It is important to note that in assessing the cost benefits of sourcing internationally, purchasers should include all of the relevant costs associated with sourcing items beyond piece price, which a later section discusses.

Access to Product and Process Technology

The United States is no longer the undisputed product and process technology leader in the world. Other countries have developed leading-edge technologies in a number of areas, such as electronic components. Purchasers that require these components know that Asian suppliers are technology leaders. Gaining access to the most current technology leaves many companies with little choice except to pursue worldwide sourcing.

Quality

Some countries, such as Japan and Germany, are obsessed with product quality. Producers in these countries have been able to capture an increasing share of world markets across a range of industries. U.S. purchasers stuck with domestic suppliers that produce poor quality often begin to source foreign components with the hope of improving end-product quality. The combination of consistently high quality and lower overall price has been a major contributor to the growth of U.S. companies buying internationally.

Access to the Only Source Available

Economic recessions, mergers, and government environmental regulations often result in suppliers exiting certain lines of business due to higher costs, loss of business volume, or both. This capacity reduction makes it increasingly difficult for U.S. buyers to source domestically. Although copper producers today are enjoying the benefits of high prices and tight capacity, this was not always the case. During the early and mid-1980s, U.S. copper producers closed many mines because of low copper prices and inefficient process technology. Some copper buyers turned to overseas producers to meet their requirements. A loss of supplier capability and availability in the automotive, machine tool, and electronics industries often left domestic buyers with no viable supply alternative except international sources.

Introduce Competition to Domestic Suppliers

Companies that rely on competitive forces to maintain price and service levels within their industry sometimes use worldwide sourcing to introduce competition to the domestic supply base. In industries characterized by limited domestic competition, this can diminish a supplier's power and break certain practices unfavorable to purchasers. Selex, featured at the beginning of this chapter, historically sourced many chemical products with a single large U.S. supplier. However, Selex is now qualifying suppliers in emerging countries as a way to counteract the domestic supplier's pricing power. A more competitive supply market will shift power away from U.S. suppliers as well as shift power from sellers to buyers.

React to Buying Patterns of Competitors

This is probably the least-mentioned reason for worldwide sourcing, because most firms do not want to admit that they are reacting to the practices of competitors. Imitating the action of competitors is the "fashion and fear" motive. A purchaser may try to duplicate the factors that provide an advantage to a competitor, which may mean sourcing from the same suppliers or regions of the world that a competitor uses. There may be a belief that not sourcing in the same region(s) may create a competitive disadvantage. This is especially true today with many firms believing they must source in China or risk being at a cost disadvantage.

Establish a Presence in a Foreign Market

Virtually the whole world is a potential market for goods and services from the United States, so it makes good economic and political sense to buy in those markets when planning to sell there. One way to develop goodwill in the country to assist in gaining product or service acceptance is through business relationships that will help support an expanded marketing presence.

In order to gain access to the lowest costs, cutting-edge technology, and best capabilities, organizations must scan the global landscape in search of the best suppliers. By aligning technology roadmaps with leading-edge suppliers, designers can ensure that their products and services will truly be world class, not just the best in the region. Although the exact reasons each company sources internationally will vary, they surely include some of those discussed here. Without access to worldwide sources of supply, companies may not remain competitive. A domestic company that purchases a portion of its material requirements worldwide is better than a domestic company that is no longer in business as a result of its inability to meet global competition.

Barriers to Worldwide Sourcing

Companies with little or no international experience often face obstacles or barriers when beginning worldwide sourcing. These barriers include (1) lack of knowledge and skills concerning global sourcing; (2) resistance to change; (3) longer lead times; (4) different business customs, language, and culture; and (5) currency fluctuations.

The lack of knowledge and skills pertaining to the intricacies of global sourcing inhibits a company from considering global sources. These shortcomings include a basic lack of knowledge about potential sources of supply or a lack of familiarity with the additional documentation required for international purchasing. International documentation requirements include

- Letters of credit
- Multiple bills of lading
- Dock receipts
- Import licenses
- Certificates of origin
- Inspection certificates

- Certificates of insurance coverage
- Packing lists
- Commercial invoices

Resistance to change from an established, routine procedure or shifting from a long-standing supplier are also major barriers. It is natural to resist changes that represent a radical departure from existing ways of doing business. Domestic market nationalism has also sometimes presented itself as a barrier. Buyers are sometimes reluctant to shift business from domestic sources to unknown foreign sources. Home market nationalism, although not the obstacle it was years ago, can still be an issue.

Another barrier involves managing longer lead times and extended material pipelines. With longer lead times, accurate materials forecasts over extended periods become critical. Buyers must manage delivery dates closely because of the possibility of transit or customs delays. International sourcing also introduces an additional degree of logistical, political, and financial risk.

Other barriers relate to a lack of knowledge about foreign business practices, language, and culture. Negotiations with foreign suppliers can be more difficult, and simple engineering or delivery change requests can become frustrating experiences. Meetings and negotiations with international suppliers require knowledge of the customs and culture associated with the particular country. Lack of understanding of customs can lead to serious problems in making significant progress in negotiations and in building relationships with the supplier.

Currency fluctuations can have a significant impact on the price paid for the item. Major currencies fluctuate daily, and therefore it is important for the buyer to understand the options to minimize this significant risk. Specific currency fluctuation strategies are discussed later in this chapter.

The most common method for overcoming these barriers involves education and training, which can generate support for the process as well as help overcome the anxiety associated with change. Publicizing success stories can also show the performance benefits that worldwide purchasing provides. Globally linked computer-aided design systems, electronic mail, and bar code systems that help track material through international pipelines have helped reduce the communication barriers surrounding worldwide sourcing. Some companies also insist on only working with those foreign suppliers that have U.S.-based support personnel.

Measurement and reward systems can encourage sourcing from the best suppliers worldwide. These firms measure and reward buyers on the basis of their ability to realize performance benefits from the selected use of international sources. The use of third-party or external agents can also help overcome barriers to international purchasing, particularly when first starting out. The use of brokers can be an efficient way to get your feet wet in worldwide sourcing.

Regardless of the technique used to overcome worldwide sourcing barriers, the effort will fail unless top management demonstrates its support for worldwide sourcing. Management must send the message that going international is a means to remain competitive by using the most competitive suppliers and does not represent an effort to force domestic suppliers out of business.

Sourcing Snapshot

The Balancing Act: Low Price versus Safety in Chinese Sourcing

Recent events in the food and toy industries have shown that although cost and price advantages are major factors driving global sourcing, they need to be balanced against the total cost. Mattel recalled more than 1 million lead-contaminated toys that were made in China. The recall involved 83 types of toys from the firm's Fisher-Price unit. The toys contained excessive levels of lead paint despite lead-paint regulations in both China and the United States. Experts estimate that 80% of the toys imported into the United States come from China, so the lead-paint problem is extensive. Supply managers have contract provisions limiting lead paint; however, enforcement is a problem. Using lead additives in paint is inexpensive and allows paint to dry more quickly; it also prevents corrosion of painted parts. These advantages help suppliers meet relentless cost pressures from customers.

Mattel had a 15-year trusted relationship with the supplier, so it allowed the supplier to do the product testing. Mattel's periodic quality audits also didn't catch the problem. Lack of proper testing has heightened the call for independent third-party testing. Tragically, weeks after the Mattel recall, Cheung Shu-Hung, the owner of the Chinese toy factory, reportedly committed suicide. A combination of pressure from the customer to ensure that such events would not happen again and the loss of face in government-business circles created a huge sense of shame for the owner. Mattel now must deal with the cost of recalled toys and multiple lawsuits from parents of children exposed to the lead paint. One of the classes of these suits involves medical monitoring, which allows families to sue toy makers and others before their children show any kind of injury. Should these types of lawsuits be allowed, a significant amount of Mattel's resources would be tied up for the immediate future.

Another toy company, Toys "R" Us, voluntarily recalled 128,700 military toys sold under the Elite Operations brand. According to the company the toys originally passed two tests, the first before they were put into production and the second after first shipment. Subsequent periodic tests conducted by a third party discovered the lead. As a result of the recall, the firm set up a cross-functional team that meets monthly to discuss safety issues.

McDonald's Corporation, another of the world's largest toy buyers, has found the Chinese lead-paint problem to be so pervasive that it has started managing deep into the supply chain. The firm monitors its Chinese toy manufacturers' paint sources back to the paint manufacturers. It requires its Chinese toy makers to use only these approved sources.

Supply managers must take a proactive and hands-on approach to any potential safety risks and factor the costs into the sourcing process. Wal-Mart Corporation worked with its shrimp supplier Rubicon, LLC, to upgrade its 150 Thai shrimp farms. By the end of 2007 these farms must meet a set of environmental and social standards backed by Wal-Mart, Darden Restaurants, and other large shrimp buyers. Wal-Mart is the largest U.S. buyer of shrimp, importing 20,000 tons annually or 3.4% of U.S. total shrimp imports. The Global Aquaculture Alliance will develop similar standards for farming of tilapia, catfish, and salmon. The problem is that many small family-run operations don't have the resources to make the investments or lack the power to recover their investments with higher prices. These small producers feel the procedures merely replicate their country standards and result in higher costs. The net impact may be a consolidation of Wal-Mart's supply base to fewer, stronger suppliers that exert control over the entire shrimp-farming supply chain.

Source: Adapted from a series of articles on Chinese operating practices: J. Spencer and N. Casey, "Toy Recall Adds to Fear of Goods Made in China," *Wall Street Journal,* August 3, 2007, pp. A1, A5; N. Zamiska and N. Casey, "Owner of Chinese Factory Kills Himself," *Wall Street Journal,* August 14, 2007, p. A2; K. Hudson and W. Watcharasakwet, "The New Wal-Mart Effect: Cleaner Thai Shrimp Farms," *Wall Street Journal,* July 24, 2007, pp. B1, B2.

Progressing from Domestic Buying to International Purchasing

An organization progresses (usually reactively) from domestic buying to international purchasing because it confronts a situation for which no suitable domestic supplier exists, or because competitors are gaining an advantage due to international purchasing. First-level firms may also find themselves driven toward international purchasing because of triggering events in the supply market. Such events could be a supply disruption, rapidly changing currency exchange rates, a declining domestic supply base, inflation within the home market, or the sudden emergence of worldwide competitors. Whatever the reason, many issues now become part of the international purchasing process that were not part of the domestic sourcing decision, or are now even more important than when sourcing was done domestically.

Information about Worldwide Sources

After identifying items to purchase internationally, a firm must gather and evaluate information on potential suppliers or identify intermediaries capable of that task. This can prove challenging if a company is inexperienced or has limited outside contacts or sources of information. The following resources can provide valuable leads when identifying potential suppliers or trade intermediaries.

International Industrial Directories

Industrial directories, which are increasingly available through the Internet, are a major source of information about suppliers by industry or region of the world. Hundreds of directories are available that identify potential international contacts. Here are some examples:

- The *World Marketing Directory* covers 50,000 major businesses in all lines having high sales volume and at least an interest in foreign trade; it is published by Dun & Bradstreet. Entries include the company's line of business and industry code.
- *Marconi's International Register* details 45,000 firms worldwide conducting business internationally; it lists products geographically under 3,500 product headings.
- *ABC Europe Production* covers 130,000 European manufacturers that export their products.
- *Business Directory of Hong Kong* details Hong Kong firms, including manufacturers; importers; exporters; banks; and construction, transportation, and service companies.

These directories, and many more, are usually available on CD-ROM or accessible through the Internet.

Trade Shows

Trade shows are often one of the best ways to gather information on many suppliers at one time. These industrial shows occur throughout the world for practically every industry. Most business libraries have a directory that lists worldwide trade shows. Internet searches will also reveal the time and place of industrial trade shows, including how to register. Examples include the International Manufacturing Technology Show; manufacturing industry professionals from the United States and 119 countries attend this show held every two years. It is estimated that over 90,000 buyers and sellers combine with over 1,200 exhibitors to meet and display the latest manufacturing technology. With a minimal amount of research, purchasers can identify trade shows related directly to their purchasing needs.

Trading Companies

Trading companies offer a full range of services to assist purchasers. These companies will issue letters of credit and pay brokers, customs charges, dock fees, insurance, and ocean carrier and inland freight bills. Clients usually receive one itemized invoice for the total services performed. One U.S.-based trading company offers more than 20 services, including

- Finding qualified sources
- Performing product quality audits
- Evaluating suppliers
- Negotiating contracts
- Managing logistics
- Inspecting shipments
- Expediting
- Performing duty classifications

The use of a full-service trading company may actually result in a lower total cost for international purchases compared with performing each activity individually. Countries such as Japan and South Korea have trading companies located in major U.S. cities. KOTRA, a Korean-based trading company, is committed to promoting mutual prosperity between Korea and its trading partners through international commerce and investment (www.kotradallas.com). Foreign trading companies offer one-stop shopping for buyers interested in the goods and services of a particular country. They will locate the sources, quote the prices, insure quality, and handle all the export and import documentation.

Third-Party Support

Experts are available to provide international sourcing assistance. Independent agents, working on commission, will act as purchasing representatives in a foreign country. They locate sources of supply, evaluate the source, and handle the required paperwork and documentation. Some agents also provide or can arrange for full-service capability.

Agents and brokers are an option when a company lacks foreign expertise or a presence in a foreign market. They help locate foreign suppliers and act as intermediaries between the buyer and seller. Direct manufacturer's representatives or sales representatives can also be a source of valuable information. Such individuals work directly for sellers as their representatives in a country. Finally, different state and federal agencies encourage and promote international trade. Services provided by these agencies are usually reasonable in cost.

Trade Consulates

Purchasers can contact foreign trade consulates located in major cities across the United States for information. Almost all consulates have trade experts who are eager to do business with American buyers. Purchasers can also contact U.S. embassies located overseas to inquire about suppliers located in a particular country. The U.S. Department of Commerce also has offices staffed by trade specialists that offer several good services at a nominal fee.

The amount and type of information required is partly a function of how a purchaser chooses to handle the foreign purchase. Purchasers that use intermediaries, such as trading companies and external agents, must search for information that identifies the best intermediaries. Purchasers that control the buying process must obtain information about suppliers from trade directories, trade shows, embassies, supplier representatives, and other sources of international information.

Supplier Selection Issues

Whether the purchaser or an external agent coordinates the international purchase, foreign suppliers must be subject to the same, or in some cases more rigorous, performance evaluation and standards as domestic suppliers. Never assume a foreign company can automatically satisfy a buyer's performance requirements or expectations. Here are some questions to ask when evaluating foreign sources:

- Does a significant total cost difference exist between the domestic and the foreign source after factoring in additional cost elements?
- Will the foreign supplier maintain any price differences over time?
- What is the effect of longer material pipelines and increased average inventory levels?
- What are the supplier's technical and quality capabilities?
- Can the supplier assist with new designs?
- What is the supplier's quality performance? What types of quality systems does it have in place?
- Is the supplier capable of consistent delivery schedules?
- How much lead time does the supplier require?
- Can we develop a longer-term relationship with this supplier?
- Are patents and proprietary technology safe with this supplier? Is the supplier trustworthy? What legal system does the supplier expect to follow?
- What are the supplier's payment terms?
- How does the supplier manage currency exchange issues?

At times buyers use trial orders to evaluate foreign sources. Purchasers may initially not be willing to rely on a foreign source for an entire purchase requirement. A buyer can use smaller or trial orders to begin to establish a supplier's performance record.

Cultural Understanding

Perhaps one of the biggest barriers to international sourcing involves the cultural differences that arise when doing business with other countries. **Culture** is the sum of the understandings that govern human interaction in a society. Culture is a multidimensional concept composed of several elements, including: (1) language, (2) religion, (3) values and attitudes, (4) customs, (5) social institutions, and (6) education. Two very important differences in culture that can affect the supply manager are values and behavior. **Values** are shared beliefs or group norms that are internalized; they affect the way people think. **Behavior** is based on values and attitudes; it affects the way people act. Understanding cultural differences will improve a purchaser's comfort and effectiveness when conducting business internationally. A major complaint about Americans is our ignorance of other cultures.

Cultural differences between countries can result in some unwelcome surprises when buying internationally. For instance, the standard procedures for negotiation and contracting are distinctly different in Asia, Europe, and the United States. Dealing with these issues requires purchasing personnel and organizations to manage different beliefs about contracting. Beliefs in developing countries about ethical issues, such as bribery, differ widely from U.S. practices. What is an illegal activity in the United States (providing bribes) is often an accepted business practice in many regions.

Language and Communication Differences

A major part of the supply manager's role is communicating requirements clearly and effectively to suppliers. Language differences can sometimes interfere with the effective communication of requirements. Not everyone understands English, and Americans will likely not understand the seller's native language.

The largest differences in communication styles across countries are message speed and level of content. Americans tend to give fast messages with the conclusions expressed first. This style is not appropriate in many countries, particularly in Europe.[10]

Dick Locke, a procurement manager who has handled buying operations in Tokyo, Europe, Mexico, and the Middle East, offers this advice about language and communication:[11]

- If a supplier is using English as a second language, the buyer should be responsible for preventing communication problems.
- To aid in communication, speak slowly, use more communication graphics, and eliminate jargon, slang, and sports and military metaphors from your language.
- Bring an interpreter to all but the most informal meetings. Allow an extra day to educate interpreters on your issues and vocabulary.
- Document, in writing, the conclusions and decisions made in a meeting before adjourning.

Logistical Issues

Buyers should not underestimate the potential effects of extended pipelines on their ability to plan and manage a worldwide supply chain. Although advanced industrial countries have a developed infrastructure, many foreign countries do not, making shipping delays a real possibility. China, for example, has 25 kilometers of paved roads, 6.5 kilometers of railways, and 17 kilometers of runways per 1,000 square kilometers of land. In comparison, the United States has 612 kilometers of paved roads, 22.7 kilometers of railways, and 189 kilometers of runways per 1,000 square kilometers.[12]

Fewer railroads, paved roads, and airports often leads to higher logistics costs and less reliable deliveries. In the United States, the ratio of logistics costs to total gross domestic product is about 10%. In developing countries, this ratio can be as high as 25% of total gross domestic product.[13] This becomes a factor when calculating the total landed cost for foreign goods. One study estimated that it takes as much as 50% more to transport goods in China than in the United States or Europe. The density of land transportation is 22% of that in the United States and 5% of that in Japan, and many roads are unpaved or in poor condition, slowing down transit times. This is further complicated by China's lack of a cross-country carrier and the small size of the average Chinese trucker's fleet (two vehicles). Additional regulations between different provinces require frequent changes of trucks when crossing province boundaries.[14]

All international shipments move by a standard set of terms. **Incoterms** are internationally recognized standard definitions that describe the responsibilities of a buyer and seller in a commercial transaction. They are used in conjunction with a sales agreement or other method of transacting the sale. The buyer and seller have an array of terms from which to choose, depending on the extent to which each party wants to be involved with the transportation and insurance. One of the complications is the modes by which an international shipment will move. Typically there will be more than one mode of transportation involved.

Modes of Transportation

EXW, CPT, CIP, DAF, DDU, and DDP are commonly used for any mode of transportation. FAS, FOB, CFR, CIF, DES, and DEQ are used for sea and inland waterway. Exhibit 10.2 on p. 358 highlights the 13 standard Incoterms.

Legal Issues

Legal systems differ from country to country. The United States uses common or case law, which often results in longer and more detailed contracts compared with countries that use code or civil law. Before IBM redesigned its purchasing process in the late 1990s, it was common for purchase contracts to be more than 40 pages in length. A redesign effort reduced this to around six pages. Many foreign countries do not like to deal with the U.S. legal system and long contracts.

Advanced industrial countries have legal systems that provide the buyer protection and fair treatment. This may not be true in developing countries. Many countries offer no effective protection against the piracy of intellectual property. It is necessary, therefore, to perform a thorough check of prospective suppliers before releasing designs or other proprietary information.

Exhibit 10.2 Incoterms 2000

Incoterms 2000 are internationally accepted commercial terms that define the respective roles of the buyer and seller in the arrangement of transportation and other responsibilities and clarify when the ownership of the merchandise takes place. They are used in conjunction with a sales agreement or other method of transacting the sale.

SERVICE	EXW EX WORKS	FCA FREE CARRIER	FAS FREE ALONGSIDE SHIP	FOB FREE ONBOARD VESSEL	CFR COST AND FREIGHT	CIF COST INSURANCE AND FREIGHT	CPT CARRIAGE PAID TO	CIP CARRIAGE INSURANCE PAID TO	DAF DELIVERED AT FRONTIER	DES DELIVERED EX SHIP	DEQ DELIVERED EX QUAY DUTY UNPAID	DDU DELIVERED DUTY UNPAID	DDP DELIV-ERED DUTY PAID
Warehouse storage	Seller	Seller	Seller	Seller	Seller	Seller	Seller	Seller	Seller	Seller	Seller	Seller	Seller
Warehouse labor	Seller	Seller	Seller	Seller	Seller	Seller	Seller	Seller	Seller	Seller	Seller	Seller	Seller
Export packing	Seller	Seller	Seller	Seller	Seller	Seller	Seller	Seller	Seller	Seller	Seller	Seller	Seller
Loading charges	Buyer	Seller	Seller	Seller	Seller	Seller	Seller	Seller	Seller	Seller	Seller	Seller	Seller
Inland freight	Buyer	Buyer/ Seller*	Seller	Seller	Seller	Seller	Seller	Seller	Seller	Seller	Seller	Seller	Seller
Terminal charges	Buyer	Buyer	Seller	Seller	Seller	Seller	Seller	Seller	Seller	Seller	Seller	Seller	Seller
Forwarder's fees	Buyer	Buyer	Buyer	Buyer	Seller	Seller	Seller	Seller	Seller	Seller	Seller	Seller	Seller
Loading on vessel	Buyer	Buyer	Buyer	Seller	Seller	Seller	Seller	Seller	Seller	Seller	Seller	Seller	Seller
Ocean/air freight	Buyer	Buyer	Buyer	Buyer	Seller	Seller	Seller	Seller	Seller	Seller	Seller	Seller	Seller
Charges on arrival at destination	Buyer	Buyer	Buyer	Buyer	Buyer	Buyer	Seller	Seller	Buyer	Buyer	Seller	Seller	Seller
Duty, taxes, and customs clearance	Buyer	Buyer	Buyer	Buyer	Buyer	Buyer	Buyer	Buyer	Buyer	Buyer	Buyer	Buyer	Seller
Delivery to destination	Buyer	Buyer	Buyer	Buyer	Buyer	Buyer	Buyer	Buyer	Buyer	Buyer	Buyer	Seller	Seller

*There are actually two FCA terms: FCA Seller's Premises, where the seller is *only* responsible for loading the goods and *not* responsible for inland freight; and FCA Named Place (International Carrier), where the seller *is* responsible for inland freight.

Source: www.i-b-.net/incoterms.html.

Sourcing Snapshot

Managing Risk: The Hidden Costs of Sourcing in China

The race by firms in the United States and other countries to source goods and services in China shows no indication of slowing down. Through experience many firms are also learning that the cost savings they initially projected may be reduced by hidden costs. Data from a study of more than 150 executives with general management (including supply chain and operations) highlights some important lessons to consider before jumping into China. Three out of four (75%) of these executives were already outsourcing at least one function in China. The most cited outsourced function was manufacturing, but respondents were outsourcing other functions such as research and development or IT support.

Some of the management issues these executives say are important to keep in mind are cultural and extend into Chinese business practices. Cultural norms are different from those in the United States, and therefore it is important to study Chinese culture and norms before entering any serious negotiations. Not doing this is a recipe for failure or much higher costs. For example, it is important to determine the nature of the relationship that will be developed. This could range from a simple agreement for standard items to a very involved partnership for a critical item. Relationships are often coupled with reciprocal obligations. For example, after one U.S. firm reached agreement on one item with a Chinese supplier, they were questioned and cajoled into agreeing that future items would be awarded to them or a supplier that they recommended.

If the firm is outsourcing operations (manufacturing) to China, the current process should be stable and operating at a competitive level. It is not a good idea to outsource a problem process, because China is a developing country and currently has a shortage of high-skilled workers as well as management expertise. Thus there will be some training required on the part of the outsourcer. Outsourcing a stable process will allow the outsourcer to train and measure the Chinese supplier. Most of the respondents in the survey indicated that the transition involves a commitment of both people and time. Most estimated it would take twice as long as originally estimated to reach a steady state of production. One key to reducing the time to steady state is to look at implementation frameworks from other firms that have had successful experiences in China.

Regarding specific outsourcing issues, don't be penny wise and pound foolish. This means visiting the site where the product is to be made. Verify the skill, quality, and turnover rate of the employees. Indications from this sample are that hidden costs can add 15–24% to the unit price when sourcing in China. These hidden costs include higher shipping costs (10–15%), warranty costs (4–7%), and travel/coordination costs (1–3%). By one estimate, 10,000 containers from China annually fall overboard. Additionally, intellectual property laws are not consistently enforced and discussions must address how intellectual property will be protected. Finally, labor rates vary widely and are increasing due to demand for Chinese goods.

In summary, any entry into China needs to be made with a clear strategy that includes a budget for travel, an understanding of the culture, calculation of the expected hidden costs, and site visits to clearly communicate expectations and process improvement plans. Extending a supply chain by 7,000 miles clearly has its challenges, and managers are now beginning to realize this and adjust savings to include these hidden costs.

Source: Adapted from a presentation by Brad Householder, "The Challenges and Hidden Costs of Outsourcing," PRTM Group, Waltham, MA, November 2005.

International contracts can be used if the country the buyer is doing business with follows the **United Nations Convention on Contracts for the International Sale of Goods (CISG)**. The CISG took effect on January 1, 1988. The purpose was to facilitate international trade by removing legal barriers. Unless the parties have specified to the contrary, the CISG applies to sales of goods contracts between parties with places of business in the "Contracting States." Contracting States are those countries that have ratified the CISG.

Countries that are part of the World Trade Organization are expected to follow certain international trade practices and protect intellectual property. Buyers and sellers doing business across boundaries should agree, preferably in a contract, about what laws will cover the business transaction.

U.S. buyers employed by domestic or foreign-based firms must also be mindful of their conduct in dealings with foreign government officials. The Foreign Corrupt Practices Act (FCPA) was passed by Congress in 1977 to prevent companies from making questionable or illegal payments to foreign government officials, politicians, and political parties. The law prohibits U.S. citizens or their agents from making payments to foreign officials to secure or retain business, and it requires accurate record keeping and adequate controls for company transactions. Since 1998, these practices apply to foreign firms and persons who make such corrupt payments while in the United States. There is no dollar threshold on the act, making it illegal to offer even a dollar as a bribe. Enforcement focuses on the intent of the bribery more than the amount.

In 2004 Lucent Technologies fired four top executives from its China operations for making bribes. The deficiencies in China were uncovered during the company's FCPA compliance audits stemming from an investigation into its practices in Saudi Arabia.[15]

Exhibit 10.3 Role of International Purchasing Offices

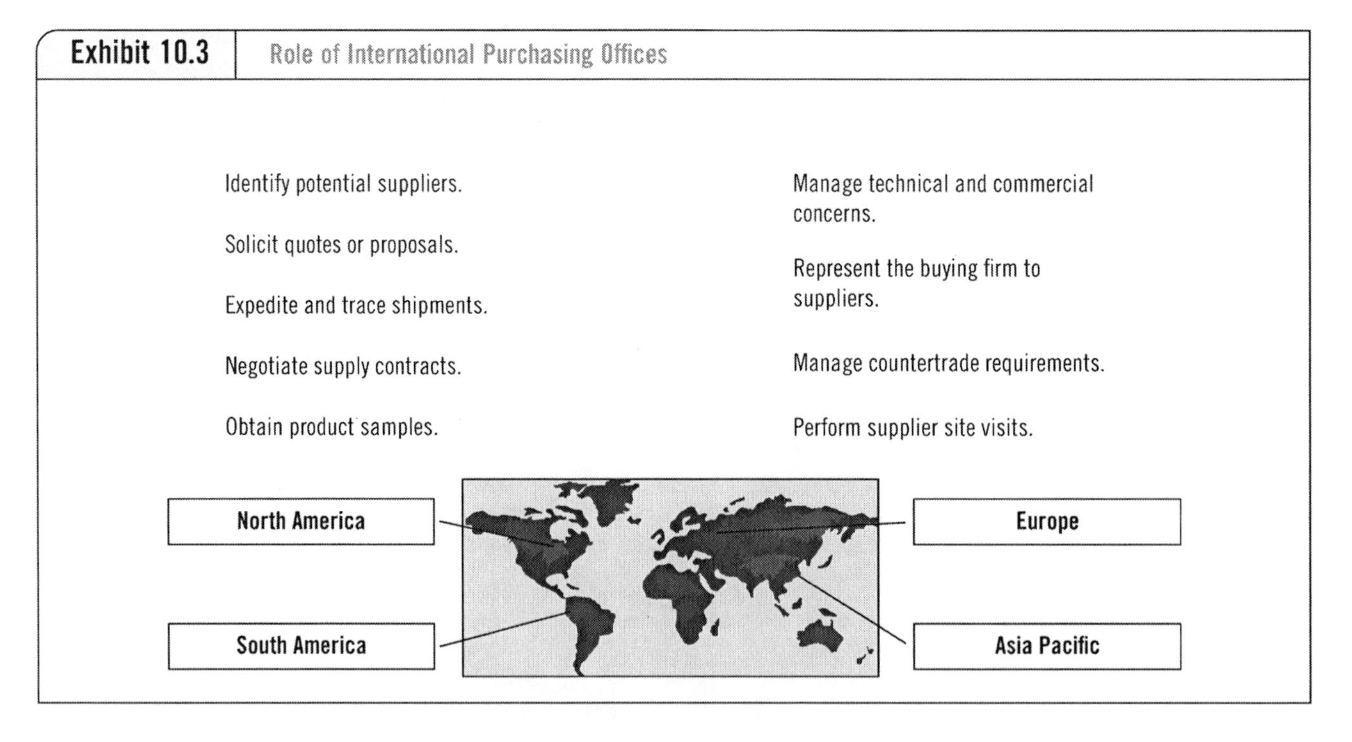

Organizational Issues

Chapter 5 provides a broad discussion of organizational issues. A logical approach when trying to meet a company's growing worldwide sourcing requirements has been the establishment of international purchasing offices (IPOs) in selected areas around the world. Foreign nationals, who usually report directly to a centralized corporate procurement office, staff the IPO. IPOs can support the sourcing needs of the entire organization, not just a single division or buying unit. Larger firms are more likely than smaller ones to have international purchasing offices. IPOs have several major functions, which Exhibit 10.3 identifies.

A 2006 study on global sourcing indicated that the growth in IPOs over the past five years corresponded to an increase in higher-level global sourcing. Firms were using their IPOs to provide operational support from the development phase through contract management of the global agreement. Specific IPO activities included facilitating import and export requirements, resolving quality and delivery performance problems, and measuring supplier performance.[16]

Another organizational issue is how to structure the overall global sourcing efforts. Recent research stated that maintaining central control and leadership over the strategic elements of a global sourcing program enhances the probability of achieving

Exhibit 10.4 Decentralized Purchasing with Centralized International Purchasing

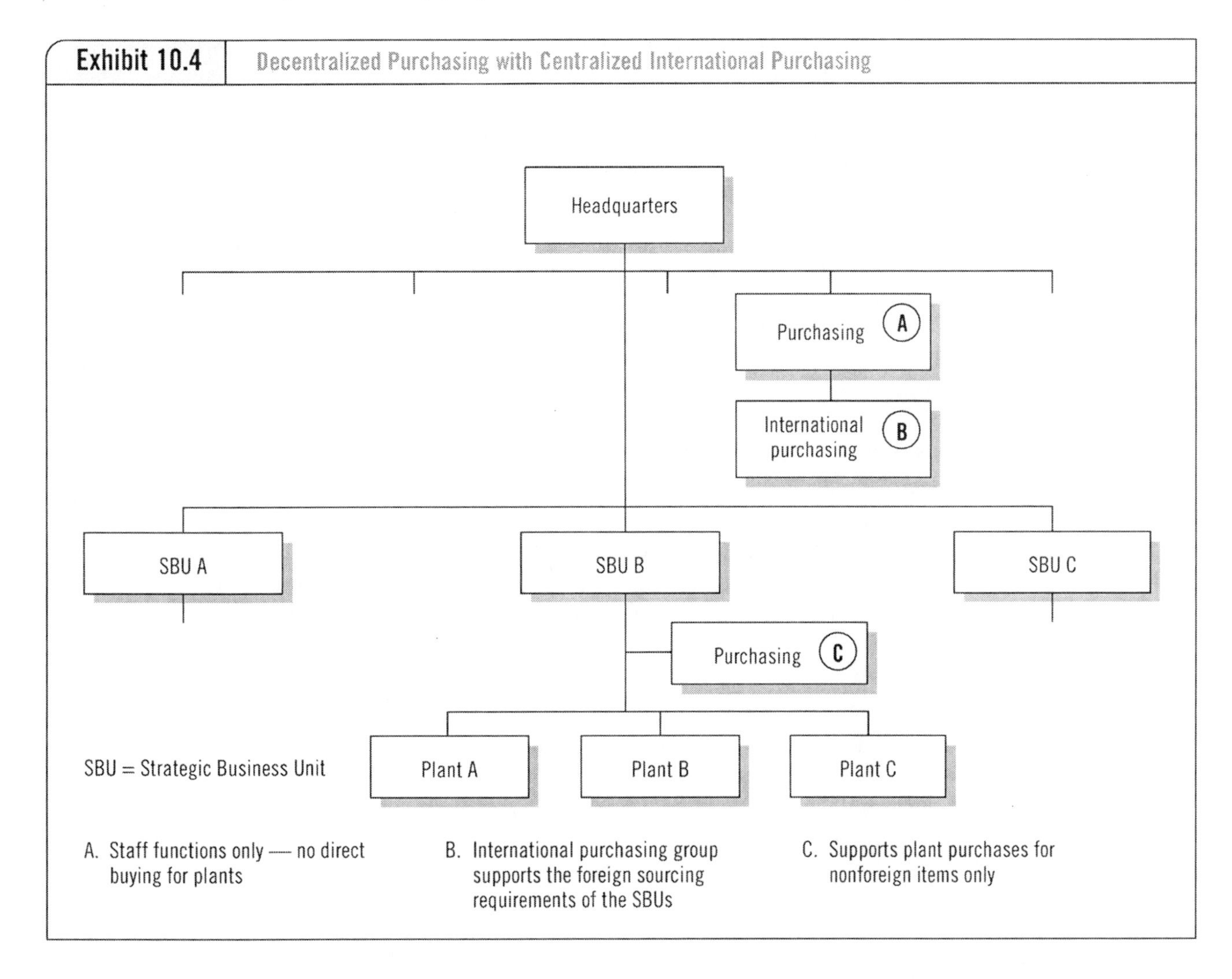

improved sourcing process outcomes.[17] This can occur even though firms may also decentralize operational activities. Exhibit 10.4 on p. 361 presents a structure that contains elements of centralized and decentralized decision making. Decentralized purchasing at the divisional or business unit level supports domestic sourcing, whereas a centralized international purchasing office supports the international requirements of the different business units.

Countertrade Requirements

A specialized form of international trade that has increased over the last 25 years is **countertrade**. This broad term refers to all international and domestic trade where buyer and seller have at least a partial exchange of goods for goods. This exchange can involve a complete trade of goods for goods or involve some partial payment to a firm in cash.

Although many companies have established a countertrade office or department, purchasing is sometimes involved in negotiating and managing countertrade agreements, including determining the market or sales value of countertrade deals or selecting appropriate products to fulfill countertrade requirements.

A country imposes countertrade demands for a number of reasons. First, some countries simply lack the hard currency to purchase imported goods. Developing nations often require Western multinationals to accept goods as at least partial payment for sales within their country. Another reason for countertrade requirements is that countertrade provides a means of selling products in markets to which a company may have otherwise lacked access. A country wishing to sell its products or services in global markets may rely upon the marketing expertise of multinational companies to market or arrange for marketing of the country's products through intermediaries.

Countertrade demands often arise when several factors are present. Items involving large dollar amounts, such as military contracts, are prime candidates for countertrade. Companies can also expect countertrade demands from a country when that country's goods have a low or nondifferentiated perception in the world marketplace. This may include items that are available from many sources, commodity-type items, or items not perceived as technologically superior or having higher quality compared with other available products. Highly valued items or those sought after by the buying country are less susceptible to countertrade demands.

Types of Countertrade

As firms have strived to meet countertrade requirements, several different forms have evolved. The five predominant types of countertrade arrangements are (1) barter, (2) counterpurchase, (3) offset, (4) buy-back, and (5) switch trading.

Barter

The oldest and most basic form of trading is **barter**, a process that involves the straight exchange of goods for goods with no exchange of currency. It requires trading parties to enter into a single contract to fulfill trading requirements. Despite its apparent simplicity, barter is one of the least-practiced forms of countertrade today.

Barter differs from other forms of countertrade in several ways. Barter involves no exchange of money between parties. Next, a single contract formalizes a barter transaction whereas other forms of countertrade require two or more contracts. Finally, barter arrangements usually relate to a specific transaction and cover a period of time shorter than that covered by other arrangements.

Counterpurchase

Counterpurchase requires a selling firm to purchase a specified amount of goods from the country that purchased its products. The amount to counterpurchase is a percentage of the amount of the original sale. This requirement usually ranges from 5 to 80% of the total value of the transaction but can actually exceed 100% under some circumstances.

This form of countertrade requires a company to fulfill its countertrade requirement by purchasing products within a country unrelated to its primary business. The countertrading company identifies a list of possible purchase items that will fulfill the countertrade requirement. The purchaser must market the unrelated goods or use a third party to assume those duties, which introduces increased complexity and cost into the transaction.

Offset

Offset agreements, which are closely related to counterpurchase, also require the seller to purchase some agreed-upon percentage of goods from a country over a specified period. However, offset agreements allow a company to fulfill its countertrade requirement with any company or industry in the country. The selling firm can purchase items related directly to its business requirements, which offers the purchaser greater flexibility. An example of an offset purchase is a U.S. aircraft manufacturer that obtains a contract to sell planes in Spain and agrees to purchase products worth 100% of the contract value in Spain.

Buy-Back

Some countertrade authorities also refer to this type of countertrade as **compensation trading. Buy-back** occurs when a firm physically builds a plant in another country or provides a service, equipment, or technology to support the plant. The firm then agrees to take a portion of the plant's output as payment. Countries lacking foreign exchange for payment but rich in natural resources can benefit from this type of countertrade arrangement. Opportunities exist for Western companies to provide the plant, equipment, and expertise to bring resources to market.

Switch Trading

This form of countertrade involves the use of a third-party trader to sell earned counterpurchase credits. **Switch trading** occurs when a selling company agrees to accept goods from the buying country as partial payment. If the selling company does not want the goods from the country, it can sell, at a discount, the credits for these goods to a third-party trader, which sells or markets the goods. The trader charges a fee for handling the transaction. The original selling company must consider the discount and third-party fee when evaluating the total cost of a countertrade arrangement with a country.

Purchasing's role in countertrade will not be as visible as marketing's role. Purchasing is usually a reactive participant that must identify supply sources that will help satisfy any countertrade requirements that a company has incurred through the sale of its product.

Costs Associated with International Purchasing

Purchasers must examine the additional costs associated with international purchasing. Whether the purchase transaction is with a domestic or foreign producer, there are certain common costs. The difference between domestic and foreign purchasing, however, is that foreign purchasing must include the additional costs associated with conducting overseas transactions. If price is a major factor, then a buyer must compare the total cost of the foreign purchase to the total cost of the domestic purchase. Exhibit 10.5 summarizes the various charges often associated with international purchasing and logistics.

Common Costs

Certain costs are common between domestic and foreign purchasing. These include the unit purchase price quoted by a supplier, tooling charges, and transportation from the supplier (common cost does not mean the costs are equal). Unit price evaluation must consider the effect of quantity discounts, minimum buys necessary

Exhibit 10.5 Elements of Total Cost for Worldwide Sourcing

Base Price

- Ascertain quantity breaks, minimum buys for shipping efficiency, and any surcharges.
- Determine price for rush shipments of smaller-than-planned quantities, which are often more.

Tooling

- Ideally, the purchaser should own the tooling and pay for it only once.
- Consider shipping tooling from a domestic source if transferable.

Packaging

- This is a hidden cost (may be expensive for long distances and multiple handlings).
- Consult a packaging supplier or internal engineer for methods to minimize cost on international shipments.

Escalation

- Determine for how long the quoted price is firm.
- Determine components of escalation (i.e., ensure that price increases are not hidden in other costs).

Transportation

- Obtain assistance from logistics personnel who have expertise in international transportation.
- Consider consolidation of shipments with other corporations from the same geographical area.
- Use multinational carriers or freight brokers to manage shipments and cost where required.
- Consult the foreign supplier as a source of information regarding freight sources.

Customs Duty

- Duties paid any time a shipment crosses international lines—can vary widely over range of goods, and often change on short notice.
- Provided by U.S. Published Tariff Schedules.
- Items may fall into more than one classification.
- May be best to discuss this with a customs agent/broker.

Insurance Premiums

- Not typically included in an ocean shipment price (need marine insurance).
- Don't pay for extra coverage that your company may already carry for international transactions.

Exhibit 10.5 Elements of Total Cost for Worldwide Sourcing (Continued)

Payment Terms
- Foreign suppliers often grant longer payment terms such as net 60.
- If dealing with intermediaries, the payment may be requested upon shipment.

Additional Fees and Commissions
- Ask supplier, customs broker, and transportation personnel if other costs may be incurred, and who is responsible for these costs.
- If your shipment is held at the port of entry due to a lack of documentation and customs officials place it in storage, a storage fee will be billed to the customer. (Who will pay for this?)

Port Terminal and Handling Fees
- U.S. port and handling charges (unloading cargo, administrative services of port personnel, and use of port).

Customs Broker Fees
- Flat charge per transaction.

Taxes
- Consider any additional taxes that may be paid.

Communication Costs
- Higher phone, travel, mailing, telex, fax, e-mail charges.

Payment and Currency Fees
- Bank transfers, bills of exchange, hedging and forward contracts.

Inventory Carrying Costs
- Higher levels of inventory will have to be held because of longer lead times.
- Costs include the interest rate forgone by investing funds, insurance, property taxes, storage and obsolescence (check with controller).

Source: Adapted from R. M. Monczka and L. C. Giunipero, *Purchasing Internationally: Concepts and Principles,* Chelsea, MI: Bookcrafters, 1990.

for shipping efficiency, the effect on price due to expedited shipments, and any supplier-specified surcharges or extras.

Transportation costs also require critical evaluation. For example, what is the effect on transportation costs if the purchaser controls a shipment directly from the supplier instead of having the supplier arrange shipment? What is the effect on transportation costs due to longer distances? International transportation often requires assistance from personnel with special expertise. A transportation group can review carrier quotations, evaluate shipping alternatives, and recommend the most efficient course of action, which may include combining international shipments with those of other purchasers to obtain favorable freight rates.

International Transaction Costs

International purchasing creates additional costs that are not part of domestic purchasing. Failure to include these costs in a total cost analysis can lead to a miscalculation of the total cost of the purchase.

For a first-time purchase, the seller may request a **letter of credit**. Letters of credit are issued by the purchaser's bank in conjunction with an affiliate bank in the seller's country. It assures the seller that the funds are in the bank. The supplier can draw against the letter of credit upon presentation of the required documents. There are two basic types of letters of credit: revocable and irrevocable. The revocable type can be changed or canceled at any time by the buyer without the seller's consent and therefore is seldom used. The irrevocable type can only be changed or canceled upon agreement of all parties.

Packaging requirements and costs are usually higher with foreign purchases because of the longer distances traveled and increased handling of shipments. Each item entering a country is also subject to a customs duty or tariff. Duty rates vary widely over seemingly small differences between items. A knowledgeable customs broker may lower duty costs as well as expedite the shipment through customs. Total cost analysis must include duty and broker fees incurred during the international transaction.

International shipments often require insurance protection. This issue is important, because unlike domestic transportation, oceangoing carrier liability is generally limited. Insurance is usually required when a third party is financing the inventory or shipment, and is provided by large firms such as Lloyd's of London.

Sourcing Snapshot

Bose Combines International Purchasing and Supply Chain Management

Companies have different experiences and approaches when developing their worldwide sourcing strategies. Bose Corporation, a manufacturer of some of the world's best-known high-fidelity speakers, is committed to just-in-time manufacturing, although it has suppliers located in North America, the Far East, and Europe. The company must blend its desire for low inventory with the need to buy from distant sources.

Controlling transportation is a central to Bose's international purchasing strategy. Bose controls its inbound and outbound transportation by taking control of shipments when the supplier turns goods over to a carrier and then relinquishing control only when finished goods are delivered to Bose's customer.

Managing a worldwide supply chain requires Bose to rely on a limited number of transportation suppliers, with whom it has developed mutually beneficial partnership agreements. Bose has a contract with PIE Nationwide, a national less-than-truckload carrier based in Jacksonville, FL, to handle North American transportation requirements. W.N. Proctor Company, a Boston-based freight forwarder and customs broker, plays a central role in Bose's critical international shipping. Bose has also established an extensive EDI system called Shipmaster, which allows the company to contact every one of PIE's 230 terminals. If Bose must expedite a shipment, Bose forwards a message directly to PIE's freight terminal.

What Shipmaster does for domestic freight, ProctorLink does for international cargo. When a shipment goes onto a plane or a ship, it goes into the Proctor system. All of the specifications—the ship, customs clearance, and so on—are included, providing the information needed to control the inventory. Proctor also provides hands-on service to Bose, such as selecting overseas agents who help move goods from the Far East to the United States.

Source: Adapted from Bose Corporation sources and public information.

Other costs include port terminal and handling fees. Depending on the exact terms of the purchase contract, a purchaser can expect charges for unloading of cargo, administrative services of port authority personnel, and general use of the port; these are U.S. port terminal and handling charges. Even if a purchaser uses a third party to manage this part of the process and receives a single invoice, these cost elements are still part of the single involved charge. Someone had to pay these charges.

A critical factor during international purchasing is keeping to a minimum the surprises that affect total cost and customer service. For example, if a shipment arrives in Long Beach, CA, without proper documentation, customs will place the shipment in warehouse storage awaiting documentation. Whether the buyer or the seller pays the storage charges should be clear in the event this issue arises.

Currency Risk

A major concern with international purchasing is managing the risk associated with international currency fluctuations. Because of this risk, companies often take steps to reduce the uncertainty associated with fluctuating currencies.

The following example illustrates the principle of currency fluctuation and risk. Suppose a U.S. company purchased a machine from Canada in June. The purchase is denominated in Canadian dollars at $100,000 paid upon delivery in November. For simplicity, assume the exchange rate in June is $1 U.S. equals $1 Canadian. By November, however, the Canadian dollar has strengthened to the point where $1 U.S. equals $0.90 Canadian (it now takes less than one Canadian dollar to purchase a U.S. dollar; the Canadian currency has appreciated vis-à-vis the U.S. dollar). Now, $100,000 U.S. only equals $90,000 Canadian. This U.S. firm needs $100,000 Canadian to pay for the machine, or $100,000 U.S./0.9 exchange rate = $111,111 U.S. If the purchaser does not protect itself from fluctuating currencies, the machine would cost $11,111 more than originally planned. On the other hand, if the U.S. dollar strengthened against the Canadian dollar during this period, the purchase would require fewer U.S. dollars in November to buy $100,000 Canadian dollars.

Companies use a variety of measures to address the risk associated with currency fluctuations. These range from very basic measures to the sophisticated management of international currencies involving the corporate finance department.

Purchase in U.S. Dollars

Buyers who prefer to pay for international purchases in U.S. dollars are attempting to eliminate currency fluctuations as a source of risk by shifting the risk to the seller. Although this appears to be an easy method of risk management, it is not always the best or most feasible approach. The foreign supplier, which is also aware of currency risks, may be unwilling to accept the risk of currency fluctuations by itself. Also, many foreign suppliers anticipate exchange rate fluctuations by incorporating a risk factor into their price. A purchaser willing to accept some of the risk may obtain a favorable price.

Sharing Currency Fluctuation Risk

Equal sharing of risk permits a selling firm to price its product without having to factor in the acceptance of risk costs. Sharing of risk requires equal division of a change in an agreed-upon price due to currency fluctuation. In the Canadian machine example, the U.S. firm realized over $11,000 in additional costs due to currency fluctuations. With equal risk sharing, the Canadian and U.S. firms would evenly divide the additional cost. This technique works best on items that have a set delivery date, such as capital equipment.

Currency Adjustment Contract Clauses

With currency adjustment clauses, both parties agree that payment occurs as long as exchange rates do not fluctuate outside an agreed-upon range or band. If exchange rates move outside the agreed-upon range, the parties can renegotiate or review the contract. This provides a mutual degree of protection because firms do not know with certainty in which direction exchange rates will fluctuate.

Purchase contracts often contain one of two types of currency adjustment clauses: delivery-triggered clauses and time-triggered clauses. Delivery-triggered clauses stipulate that the parties will review an exchange before delivery to verify that the rate is still within the agreed-upon range. If the rate falls outside the range, the buyer or seller can ask to renegotiate the contract price. Time-triggered clauses stipulate that both parties will review a contract at specified time intervals to evaluate the impact of fluctuating exchange rates. The parties review the exchange rate at scheduled intervals, and a new contract is established if the rate falls outside the agreed-upon range.

Currency Hedging

Hedging involves the simultaneous purchase and sale of currency contracts in two markets. The expected result is that a gain realized on one contract will be offset by a loss on the other. Hedging is a form of risk insurance that can protect both parties from currency fluctuations. The motivation for using hedging is risk aversion, not monetary gain. If the purpose of buying currency contracts is to realize a net gain, then the purchaser is speculating and not hedging.

Buyers and sellers trade futures exchange contracts (also referred to as "futures contracts") on commodity exchanges open to anyone needing to hedge or with speculative risk capital. In fact, the exchanges encourage speculation because speculators help create markets for buyers and sellers of futures contracts. Traders sell futures contracts in fixed currency amounts with fixed contract lengths.

Forward exchange contracts have a different focus than futures exchange contracts. Issued by major banks, these contracts are agreements by which a purchaser pays a pre-established rate for a currency in the future (as well as a fee to the bank). Trading participants include banks, brokers, and multinational companies. The use of forward exchange contracts discourages speculation. Forward exchange contracts meet the needs of an individual purchaser in terms of dollar amount and time limit.

Finance Department Expertise

Companies with extensive international experience usually have a finance or treasury department that can support international currency requirements. Finance can identify the currency a firm should use for payment based on projections of currency fluctuations. The finance department can also provide advice about hedging and currency forecasts, and whether to seek a new contract or renegotiate an existing one due to currency changes; it can also act as a clearinghouse for foreign currencies to make payment for foreign purchases.

Tracking Currency Movements

Purchasing managers should track the movement of currencies against the dollar over time to identify longer-term changes and sourcing opportunities due to changing economics. The weakening of the U.S. dollar against the euro during 2006 made exports more attractive to European countries. Purchases from Japan became more expensive to U.S. buyers in the early to mid-1990s as the Japanese yen strengthened in value from 200 yen to 100 yen per dollar. As a result, there was a financial incentive to source domestically or from countries where exchange rates were more favorable. In 2007, the yen stayed in a range between 110 and 120 yen per dollar and has not depreciated to the high 100s or the 200s of the mid-1990s.

Progressing from International Purchasing to Global Sourcing

At some point, many companies determine that moving beyond basic international purchasing might yield new and untapped benefits. Exhibit 10.6 presents international purchasing and global sourcing as a series of evolving levels or steps along a continuum. An internationalization of the sourcing process takes place as firms evolve or progress first from domestic purchasing to international purchasing, and then to the global coordination and integration of common items, processes, designs, technologies, and suppliers across worldwide locations. Level I includes those firms that only purchase domestically. Sourcing domestically could result in purchases from international suppliers that have facilities in the United States.

Referring to Exhibit 10.6, Level II represents basic international purchasing that is usually reactive and uncoordinated between buying locations or units. Moving forward, strategies and approaches developed in Level III begin to recognize that a properly executed worldwide sourcing strategy can result in major improvements.

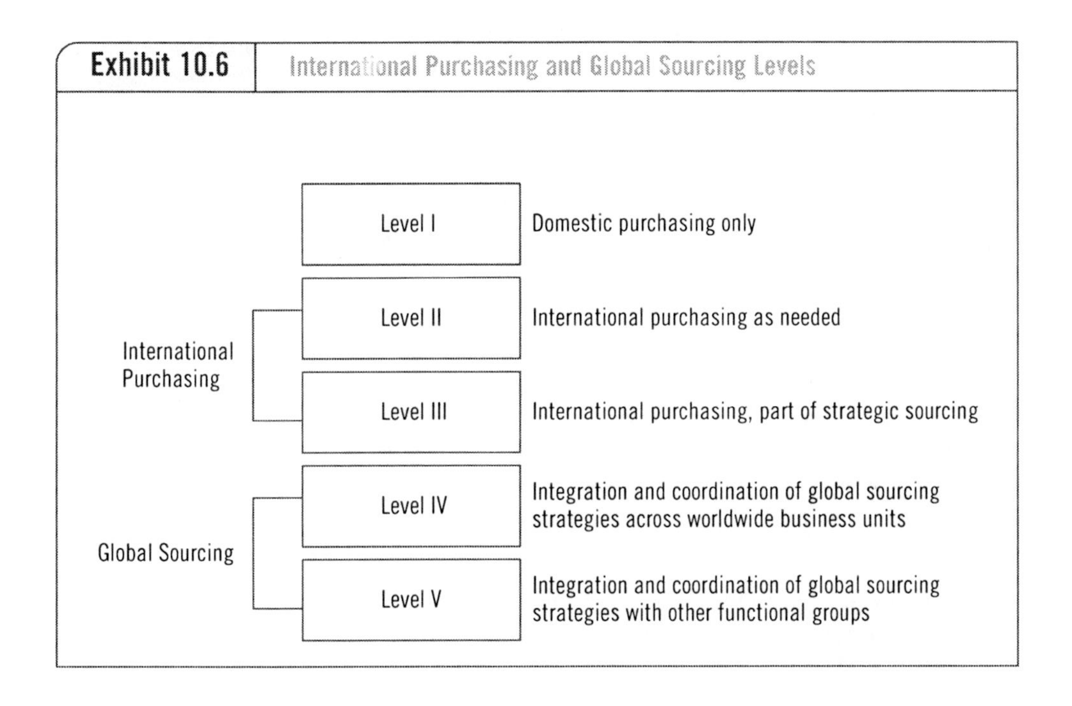

However, strategies at this level are not well coordinated across worldwide buying locations, operating centers, functional groups, or business units.

Level IV, which represents the integration and coordination of sourcing strategies across worldwide buying locations, represents a sophisticated level of strategy development. Operating at this level requires

- Worldwide information systems
- Personnel with sophisticated knowledge and skills
- Extensive coordination and communication mechanisms
- An organizational structure that promotes central coordination of global activities
- Leadership that endorses a global approach to sourcing

Although worldwide integration occurs in Level IV, which is not the case with Level III, the integration is primarily cross-locational rather than cross-functional.

Organizations that operate at Level V have achieved the cross-locational integration that firms operating at the fourth level have achieved. The primary distinction is that Level V participants integrate and coordinate common items, processes, designs, technologies, and suppliers across worldwide purchasing centers and with other functional groups, particularly engineering. This integration occurs during new-product development as well as during the sourcing of items or services to fulfill continuous demand or aftermarket requirements.

Only those firms that have worldwide design, development, production, logistics, and procurement capabilities can progress to this level. Although many firms expect to advance to Level V, the reality is that many lack the understanding or the willingness to achieve this level of sophistication.

Factors Separating Successful from Less-Successful Global Sourcing Efforts

A major research project on global sourcing, with 167 companies, identified a set of factors that drove global sourcing performance. These factors were (1) a defined process to support global sourcing, (2) centrally coordinated and centrally led decision making, (3) site-based control of operational activities, (4) real-time communication tools, (5) information sharing with suppliers, (6) availability of critical resources, (7) sourcing and contracting systems, and (8) international purchasing office support.[18] Exhibit 10.7 highlights these success factors, which are explained in more detail in the following section.

Defined Process to Support Global Sourcing

The development of a rigorous and well-defined approach or process is critical to global sourcing success. Some organizations have taken their commodity or regional strategy process and adapted it for global sourcing. When this occurs, the global process will likely weight certain factors differently (for example, more emphasis placed on risk factors and total landed cost) compared with a regional commodity development process.

A defined process helps overcome many of the differences inherent in global sourcing. Social culture and laws, personnel skills and abilities, and business culture are

Exhibit 10.7 Global Sourcing Success Factors

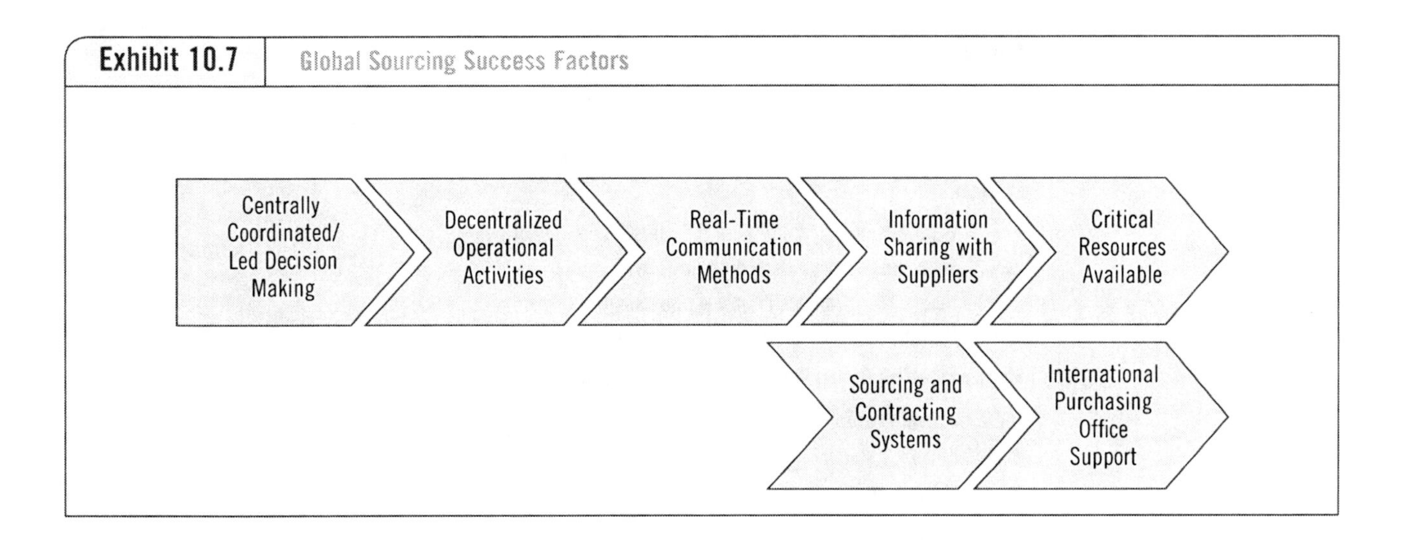

three areas where differences are the greatest across different geographic units. A global sourcing process helps align very different participants and practices around the globe. Exhibit 10.8 on p. 372 outlines the global sourcing process at a chemical company with worldwide operations.

Centrally Coordinated and Centrally Led Decision Making

Maintaining central control and leadership over activities that are strategic in nature enhances the probability of achieving a range of improved sourcing process outcomes. These benefits include

- Improved standardization or consistency of the sourcing process
- Early supplier involvement
- Supplier relationships
- Client, stakeholder, and executive satisfaction with sourcing

Site-Based and Decentralized Control of Operational Activities

Firms that also decentralize operational activities during global sourcing are likely to realize lower total cost of ownership, better inventory management, and improved performance to external customers. Operational activities at a decentralized level include

- Issuing material releases to suppliers
- Expediting orders when necessary
- Resolving performance problems
- Planning inventory levels
- Developing logistics plans

Real-Time Communication Tools

Communication complexity makes global sourcing more complex compared with domestic or regional sourcing. Global sourcing participants are often located around the world, making real-time and face-to-face communication difficult. Furthermore,

Exhibit 10.8 | A U.S. Chemical Company's Global Sourcing Process

Step 1: Identify Global Sourcing Opportunities

When identifying specific opportunities, an executive steering committee and globalization manager consider:

- What business units require the largest cost reductions?
- What does the company currently buy?
- How is the commodity currently specified?
- How much effort will it take to create a worldwide set of specifications?

Step 2: Establish Global Sourcing Development Teams

The executive steering committee forms cross-functional/cross-locational (CF/CL) teams with worldwide members to pursue global opportunities.

Step 3: Propose Global Strategy

A team charter provides project teams with responsibility for proposing a global strategy. Teams validate the original assumptions underlying the project, verify current volumes and expected savings, determine if global suppliers exist, evaluate the current set of specifications between design centers, and propose a global strategy.

Step 4: Develop Request for Proposal (RFP) Specifications

Teams are responsible for developing the request for proposal (RFP) that suppliers receive. This step consumes a large portion of the global sourcing process time.

Step 5: Release RFPs to Suppliers

On average, six suppliers receive an RFP during a global project. Project teams are responsible for following up with suppliers and answering any questions.

Step 6: Evaluate Bids or Proposals

A commercial and technical evaluation of supplier proposals occurs. Project teams will ask suppliers for their best and final offer and conduct site visits as required. Face-to-face negotiation occurs after analyzing the RFPs returned from suppliers.

Step 7: Negotiate with Suppliers

A smaller team negotiates with suppliers to finalize contract details. All negotiations are conducted at the buying company's U.S. headquarters and can last up to three days. The negotiation process lengthens if the buying company does not achieve its price and service targets.

Step 8: Award Contract(s)

Information concerning the awarded contract is communicated throughout the company via e-mail. The steering committee calculates expected savings and maintains the agreements in a corporate database.

Step 9: Implement Contract and Manage Supplier(s)

This step involves loading global agreements into the appropriate corporate systems. It also involves managing the transition to new suppliers and/or part numbers.

participants may speak several languages while adhering to different business practices, social cultures, and laws.

Many communication and coordination approaches support global sourcing efforts. Examples include regular review meetings, joint training sessions involving worldwide team members, regularly reported project updates through an intranet, and co-location of functional personnel. A common approach for coordinating work efforts is to rely on audio conferencing with a scheduled time for conference calls, usually on a weekly basis. Participants should take advantage of evolving web-based communication tools, including NetMeeting, Centra, and web-based cameras. One conclusion is clear: Successful global sourcing efforts feature well-established communication methods to help overcome the inherent complexities of the process.

It is hard to imagine a successful global sourcing effort without access to reliable and timely information. Examples of such information include a listing of existing contracts and suppliers, reports on supplier capabilities and performance, worldwide volumes by purchase type and location, and information about potential new suppliers. The ability to provide the data and information that global sourcing requires demands the development of global information technology systems and data warehouses.

Although access to a common coding system and real-time data is a major facilitator, the reality is that many firms lack essential IT capabilities. Many companies have historically grouped their procurement and engineering centers by region, whereas other companies that are the result of mergers and acquisitions usually feature different legacy systems, processes, and part numbers across locations. This forces firms to spend time and money to standardize and commonize their systems and coding schemes. Part number and commodity coding schemes have the second-lowest level of similarity from a list of 20 items when looking across all companywide locations.

Information Sharing with Suppliers

Successful global sourcing requires both access to a range of critical information and the willingness to share that information with important suppliers on a worldwide basis. Firms that share performance information with their most important worldwide suppliers realize lower purchase price and cost. Shared performance information includes details about supplier quality, delivery, cycle time, and flexibility. A second type of information sharing relates to broader outcomes. This includes assessment of the supplier's technological sophistication, future capital plans, and product variety data.

Availability of Critical Resources

Resources that affect global success include budget support for travel, access to qualified personnel, time for personnel to develop global strategies, and the availability of required information and data. The availability of time was correlated highly with team effectiveness. Teams that had the time to pursue their agenda were more effective than those that did not have the time. This is very important given the fact that most organizations use teams to coordinate their global efforts.

Sourcing and Contracting Systems

The most important way to ensure access to information is to develop technology systems that make critical information available on a worldwide basis. Firms that have systems that provide access to relevant information are more likely to report lower total costs of ownership and improved sourcing process outcomes from global sourcing. Examples of these features and the information they provide include a worldwide database of purchased goods and services; common part coding schemes;

contract management modules; and systems for measuring contract compliance, worldwide goods and services usage by location, and purchase price paid by location.

International Purchasing Office Support

As previously mentioned, IPOs support a higher level of global sourcing through greater access to product and process technology, reduced cycle times, and increased responsiveness. Additionally, the IPOs have the capabilities to provide operational support from initial negotiations through the contract management phase of the supplier selection cycle. The increasing movement to global sourcing has been enhanced by the growth of IPOs over the past five years.

Global Sourcing Benefits

Perhaps one of the most revealing and interesting differences between the international purchasing and global sourcing segments is the perception each has regarding the benefits they realize from their worldwide efforts. Exhibit 10.9 presents the top-rated benefits for each group. Although this exhibit presents only 10 benefit areas, firms that engage in global sourcing indicate they realize 16 total benefits at a statistically higher level than firms that engage in international purchasing. In fact, the average rating across all benefit areas is 30% higher for global sourcing firms compared with the overall average for international purchasing firms.

Exhibit 10.9 A. International Purchasing Benefits

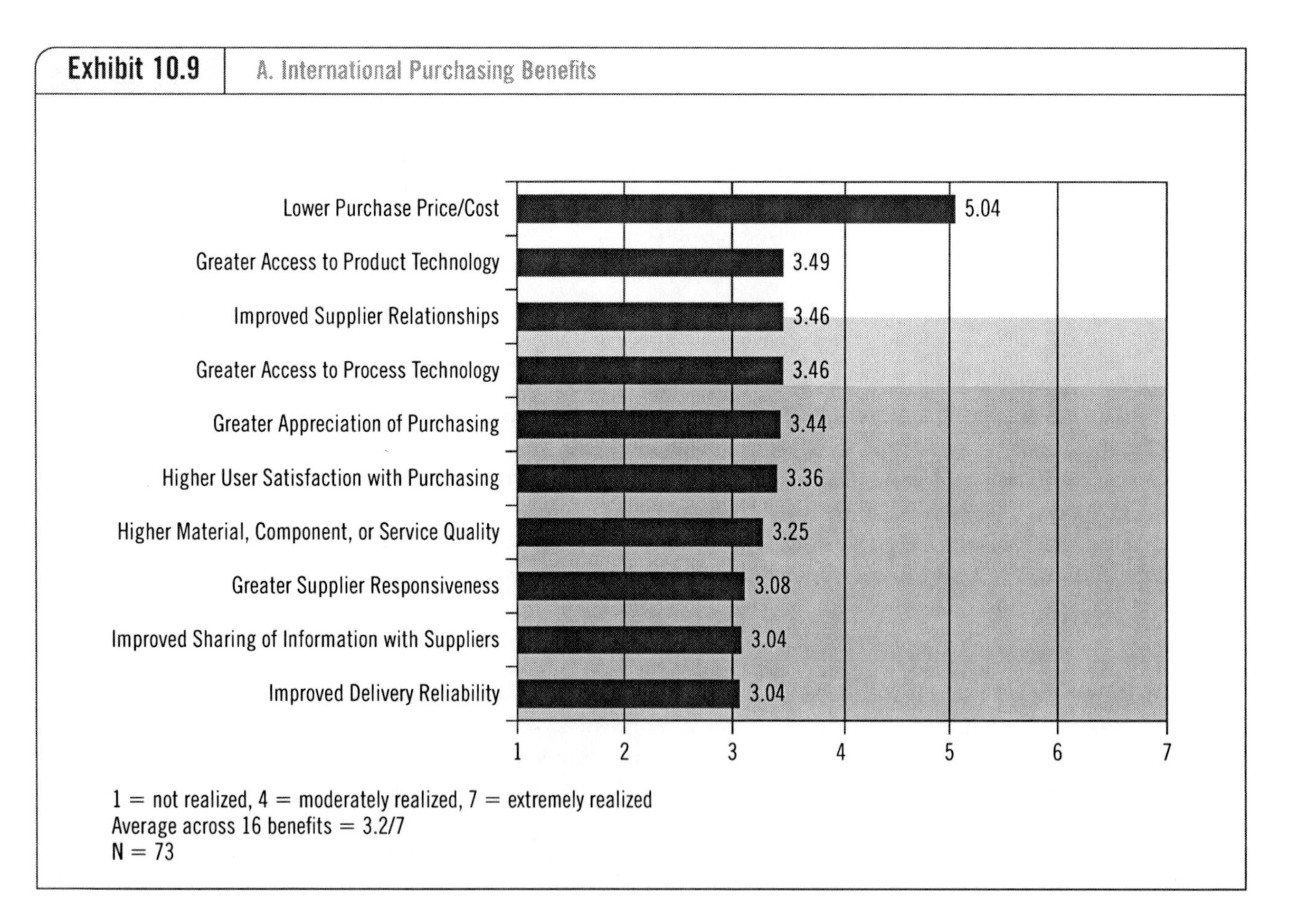

1 = not realized, 4 = moderately realized, 7 = extremely realized
Average across 16 benefits = 3.2/7
N = 73

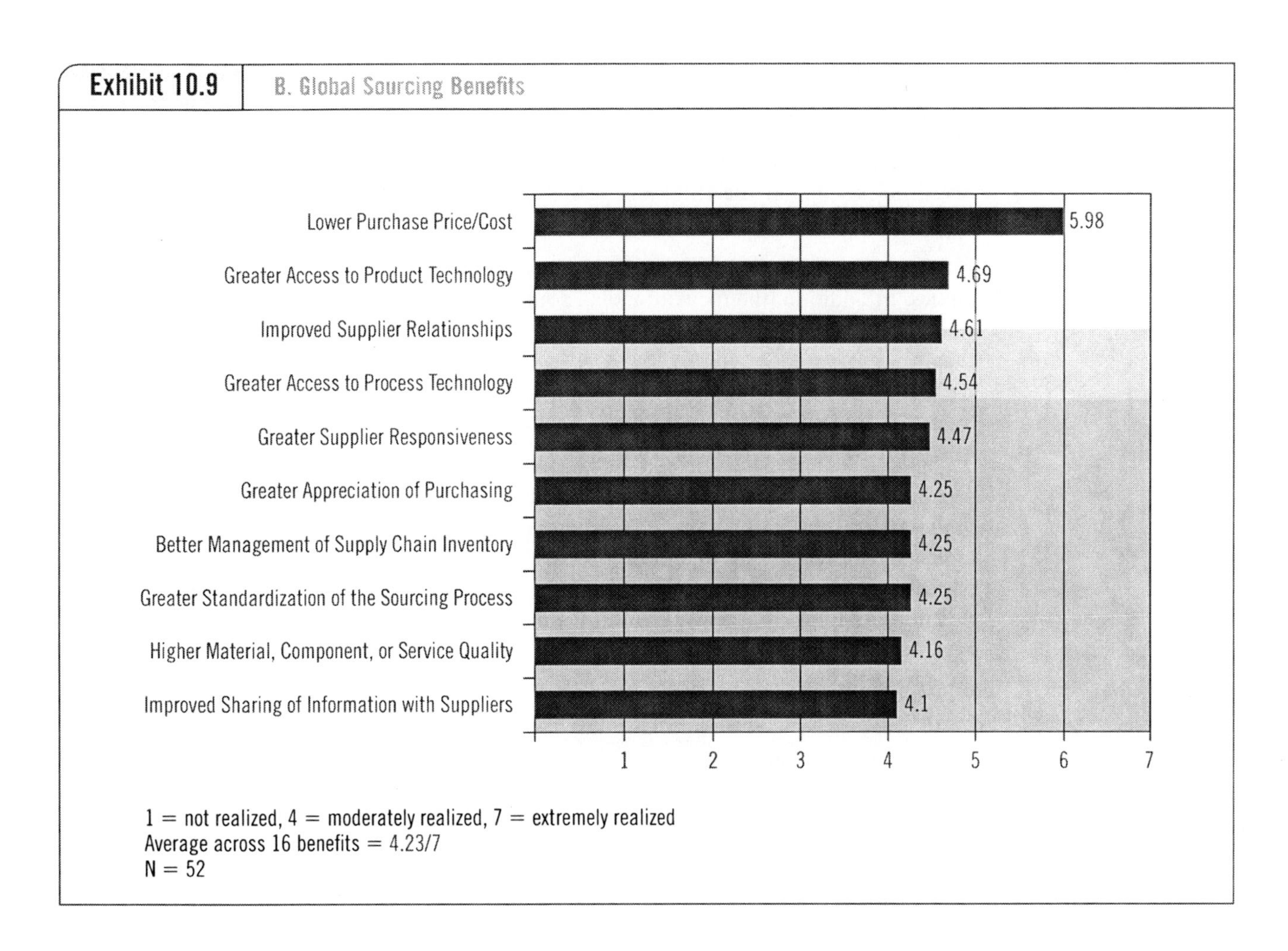

One benefit that both segments rate highly is the ability to achieve a lower purchase price or cost through worldwide sourcing. The initial benefits from international purchasing are usually price focused and are often available from basic international purchasing activities. However, firms realize many nonprice benefits only after they have taken steps to evolve toward higher sourcing levels. In particular, this includes greater access to product and process technology, an outcome that is particularly critical given the more dynamic technology changes that global sourcing firms face. Better management of supply chain inventory is also a benefit that global sourcing firms enjoy at higher levels. This is critical given the emphasis that many firms place on managing costs and inventory investment across the supply chain.

Other important benefits more readily available from global sourcing include greater supplier responsiveness, greater sourcing process consistency, improved supplier relationships, and improved sharing of information with suppliers. The benefits realized between the two groups help explain why so many firms that pursue international purchasing want to evolve toward global sourcing.

Future Global Sourcing Trends

Globalization is a continuous journey of development and improvement. Foremost in this journey is the need to develop or obtain supply management skill sets that encourage evaluating the supply network from a worldwide perspective. Other developments include the need to agree on global performance measures and to establish integrated systems between worldwide units and with suppliers. Doing this requires the continued development and refinement of integrated and coordinated global sourcing strategies across the functional organization. Greater integration between marketing, engineering, and sourcing groups should occur as firms evolve toward higher globalization levels.

We also expect a trend toward doing business with suppliers that have global capabilities. In addition, the focus of global sourcing will shift from part (i.e., component) sourcing to subsystems, systems, and services. Cost reduction pressures will also result in continued sourcing in low-cost emerging supply markets, such as China and Eastern Europe. Although very attractive from a price standpoint, these markets have hidden costs that must be identified. The ability to manage these changes will begin to separate leading companies from average firms.

Companies that produce and sell worldwide should no longer view global sourcing as an emerging approach to sourcing. The pursuit of a competitive advantage requires the development of global processes and strategies that become an integral part of a firm's supply management efforts. Understanding the critical differences between international purchasing and integrated global sourcing is essential before managers can begin to realize the benefits that this complex approach to sourcing potentially offers.

Good Practice Example — *Air Products Manages Worldwide Sourcing*

One company that has actively pursued integrated global sourcing is Air Products and Chemicals, a U.S.-based company that designs and operates industrial gas and chemical facilities worldwide. In 1999, company executives were surprised when an internal study concluded that the company would have to lower operating costs by 30% to remain competitive globally. Low-cost competitors had emerged in Asia and the Pacific, and industrial buyers were increasingly viewing the company's products as commodity items, factors that together created extensive downward pricing pressures.

Company managers concluded that one way to improve performance was global sourcing. Historically, the company operated in an engineer-to-order environment, using regional design and procurement centers. The result was highly customized design and procurement for each new project. Further, there was a lack of coordination between the company's North American and European units.

These new competitive pressures compelled the company to coordinate design and sourcing activities across its worldwide locations. Accomplishing this resulted in the development of a global engineering and procurement process. The design of each new facility now involves an extensive analysis between U.S. and European centers to identify areas of commonality, standardization, and synergy in procurement and design. Cross-functional teams, with members from the United States and Europe working jointly, develop common design specifications and contracts that satisfy each center's needs while supporting future replacement and maintenance requirements.

After five years of global sourcing experience and with more than 100 global agreements in place, Air Products is averaging 20% in cost savings compared with the regional sourcing and design practices. Furthermore, worldwide design and procurement centers have better aligned their sourcing philosophies and strategies among the centers and with the company's business strategy. Procurement managers now work with marketing to include expected savings from in-process global sourcing projects when responding to customer proposals. Integrated global sourcing is providing a new source of competitiveness to a company that operates in a mature industry.

Source: Adapted from R. M. Monczka, R. J. Trent, and K. J. Peterson, "Effective Global Sourcing and Supply for Superior Results," CAPS Research, 2006, pp. 20–21.

CONCLUSION

International purchases for raw materials, components, finished goods, and services will continue to increase. Because of this, supply management personnel at all levels must become familiar with the nuances of worldwide sourcing. Although most organizations would prefer to purchase from suppliers that are geographically close, this is not always possible. Firms operating in competitive industries must purchase from the best available sources worldwide. Developing these sources requires continual monitoring of both supply market and country trends. Currently the hot spots for sourcing are China and India. Less publicized but just as important is the low-cost-country sourcing occurring in Eastern Europe. Globalization will continue to be a major force that needs to be assessed on a company-by-company basis. Once the assessment is made, then supply management must respond with an effective global strategy.

KEY TERMS

barter, 362
behavior, 356
buy-back, 363
compensation trading, 363
counterpurchase, 363
countertrade, 362
culture, 356
forward exchange contracts, 368
global sourcing, 347
globalization, 345
hedging, 368
Incoterms, 357
international purchasing, 347
letter of credit, 365
offset, 363
switch trading, 363
United Nations Convention on Contracts for the International Sale of Goods (CISG), 360
values, 356
worldwide sourcing, 347

DISCUSSION QUESTIONS

1. Discuss whether globalization and the subsequent growth in worldwide sourcing will have a positive or negative effect over the long run in the United States. Why? What are the alternatives to worldwide sourcing?
2. China, India, and other developing countries are sourcing hot spots. Explain why and also discuss any problems you see in sourcing from these low-cost countries.
3. What are the most important reasons for pursuing worldwide sourcing today?
4. Discuss what the following statement means: Leading-edge companies must develop personnel who have global perspectives. Should personnel from organizations of all sizes have a global perspective? Why?
5. What are the advantages of establishing an international purchasing office? What services do these offices provide?
6. How does the international part-sourcing process differ from the domestic sourcing process?
7. Discuss the reasons why a firm would use a third-party external agent for worldwide sourcing.
8. Discuss some of the sources of information a buyer can use to identify potential foreign sources of supply.
9. How do international purchasing and global sourcing differ? Do you think the differences are meaningful? Why?

10. What is the difference between outsourcing and offshoring? What functions does a firm choose to offshore and why?
11. During the 1980s, many U.S. firms pursued worldwide sourcing on a reactive basis. What does this mean? What might cause a firm to shift from reactive worldwide sourcing to a proactive approach to worldwide sourcing?
12. What are the factors that separate successful from less-successful global sourcing efforts?
13. Refer to the barriers to worldwide sourcing that many firms confront. For each barrier, discuss one or more ways that a company can overcome the barrier.
14. What form of countertrade appears to offer the most purchase flexibility? Why?
15. Some purchasing managers regard countertrade as an infringement of purchasing's authority. Why might some purchasing personnel not view countertrade favorably?

ADDITIONAL READINGS

Alguire, M. S., Frear, C. R., and Metcalf, L. E. (1994), "An Examination of the Determinants of Global Sourcing," *Journal of Business and Industrial Marketing,* 9(2), 62–74.

Bozarth, C., Handfield, R., and Das, A. (1998), "Stages of Global Sourcing Evolution: An Exploratory Study," *Journal of Operations Management,* 16, 241–255.

Das, A., and Handfield, R. B. (1997), "Just-in-Time and Logistics in Global Sourcing: An Empirical Study," *International Journal of Physical Distribution and Logistics Management,* 27(3–4), 244–259.

Fraering, M., and Prasad, S. (1999), "International Sourcing and Logistics: An Integrated Model," *Logistics Information Management,* 12(6), 451.

Giunipero, L., and Monczka, R. M. (1997), "Organizational Approaches to Managing International Sourcing," *International Journal of Physical Distribution and Logistics Management,* 27(5–6), 321–336.

Kaufmann, L., and Carter, C. R. (2006), "International Supply Relationships and Non-Financial Performance: A Comparison of U.S. and German Practices," *Journal of Operations Management,* 24, 653–675.

Kotabe, M. (1994), "Global Sourcing Strategy: R&D, Manufacturing, and Marketing Interfaces," *Journal of Global Marketing,* 7(3), 157.

Locke, D. (1996), *Global Supply Management,* Boston: McGraw-Hill.

Murray, J. Y. (2001), "Strategic Alliance-Based Global Sourcing Strategy for Competitive Advantage: A Conceptual Framework and Research Propositions," *Journal of International Marketing,* 9(4), 30–58.

Petersen, K. J., Frayer, D. J., and Scannel, T. V. (2006), "An Empirical Investigation of Global Sourcing Strategy Effectiveness," *Journal of Supply Chain Management,* 36(2), 29–38.

Rexha, N., and Miyamoto, T. (2000), "International Sourcing: An Australian Perspective," *Journal of Supply Chain Management,* 36(1), 27–34.

Samli, A. C., Browning, J. M., and Busbia, C. (1998), "The Status of Global Sourcing as a Critical Tool of Strategic Planning," *Journal of Business Research,* 43(3), 177–187.

Trent, R. J., and Monczka, R. M. (2007), "Achieving Excellence in Global Sourcing," *Sloan Management Review,* Fall, 24–32.

ENDNOTES

1. Friedman, T. L. (2005), *The World Is Flat,* New York: Farrar, Straus and Giroux.
2. Friedman, pp. 24, 25.

3. Jacoby, D. (2006), "Purchasing 2015: A Global Survey by SAP and the Global Economic Intelligence Unit," Presentation.

4. Passariello, C. (2007), "Behind L'Oréal's Makeover in India: Going Upscale," *Wall Street Journal,* July 13, pp. A1, A4.

5. Glader, P. (2007), "Rio-Alcan Deal Pressures Alcoa," *Wall Street Journal,* July 13, p. A3.

6. Matthews, R. G. (2007), "Foreign Firms Build U.S. Presence," *Wall Street Journal,* August 14, p. A10.

7. The information in this section comes from a variety of sources, including data collected at the Executive Purchasing and Supply Chain Management Seminar, Michigan State University, East Lansing, 1990, 1993, 1997, 1999; "International Buying—The Facts and Foolishness" (1987), *Purchasing,* June; and "MAPI Survey on Global Sourcing as a Corporate Strategy—An Update" (1986), Machinery and Allied Products Institute, February.

8. Monczka, R. M., Trent, R. J., and Peterson, K. J. (2006), "Effective Global Sourcing and Supply for Superior Results," Tempe, AZ: CAPS Research, p. 13.

9. Jacoby.

10. Locke, D. (1996), *Global Supply Management,* Boston: McGraw-Hill, p. 46.

11. Locke, p. 51.

12. Hickey, K. (2003), "Chinese Puzzle," *Traffic World,* September 15, p. 16.

13. Hickey, p. 16.

14. Moradian, R. (2004), "The Logistics of Doing Business in China," *Inbound Logistics,* July, http://www.inboundlogistics.com/articles/3plline/3plline0704.shtml.

15. Taub, S. (2004), "Lucent Fires Four on Bribery Suspicions," *CFO.com,* April 7.

16. Monczka et al., p. 26.

17. Monczka et al., p. 24.

18. Monczka et al., pp. 24–26.

Chapter 19

PERFORMANCE MEASUREMENT AND EVALUATION

Learning Objectives

After completing this chapter, you should be able to

- Introduce a purchasing and supply measurement framework
- Review and provide insight into key purchasing and supply measurements
- Review benchmarking and its importance
- Identify key characteristics of effective measurement systems

Chapter Outline

Measuring Purchasing and Supply Performance at a Global Automotive Parts Manufacturer

OVERVIEW

This multibillion-dollar diversified manufacturer of electrical and electromechanical components and systems has worldwide operations, markets, and suppliers. Purchasing is done at the corporate, division/business, and regional levels. Global coordination is achieved through the corporate headquarters in the United States. Major operating locations are in North America, Europe, Asia/Pacific, and South America.

Purchasing is organized with companywide product and nonproduct purchasing directors reporting to the vice president of global purchasing. Global commodity directors and business unit leaders also report to the vice president or to the product/nonproduct purchasing directors. Also at corporate headquarters are purchasing staff groups, including lean operations, organization and employee development, supplier development, supplier quality, minority supplier development, strategic planning, finance, communications, e-systems, strategy and process, and risk management.

Staff number in the hundreds and are located worldwide. Annual spend is in the billions of dollars. The vice president of global purchasing reports to an executive vice president. The overall strategic intent of global purchasing is to provide the corporation with a competitive advantage through achieving extended supply chain performance excellence. Achieving this extended supply chain excellence on a worldwide basis requires vertical and horizontal integration, detailed business plans, and an integrated set of metrics to drive and measure behaviors.

The measurement system is aligned vertically and horizontally with corporate goals and other functions and business units through the strategic global purchasing plan. The plan is integrated with the critical competitive requirements through the company's executive committee. Critical drivers are cost, quality, and availability. In addition, minority purchasing spend, effective product launches, and a competitive supply base are also important.

The global purchasing plan is structured around the strategic intent of global purchasing, and key contributing elements include supplier development, cost, sourcing strategically, quality, e-systems, people, supplier relations, and accelerated change. Horizontal linkage is achieved by establishing a multiyear strategy and annual business plans. The strategy and business plans focus on the current and desired state and link together the corporate, commodity, regional, and business unit strategies and plans.

This strategy and planning process clearly provides for effective communication, project planning, and horizontal and vertical alignment with goals and resulting measurements. An extensive set of integrated financial and nonfinancial measures are in place to guide behavior and review performance. The most significant are discussed here.

COST MANAGEMENT

Two measures are most critical: (1) year-over-year price performance based on contract prices for the same or similar items, and (2) material cost improvement that can be achieved through various approaches such as design change, process improvement, packaging, and so forth.

In addition, the company's overall financial plan includes cost-reduction levels that need to be achieved by purchasing. Revenues of the firm, as they increase or decrease, influence the purchasing cost-reduction target because of the need to protect margin. The finance group makes final judgments regarding validation of purchasing cost savings.

Other important measures in use include the following:

- Quality and quality improvement based on parts per million (PPM) defective determination
- On-time delivery and availability
- Flawless on-time launch of new products
- Minority supplier spend targets
- "Rightsizing" the supply base based on an objective measurement of the appropriate number of suppliers
- Supplier relationships and development via scorecards
- People development based on number of hours of training per year
- Cost management models
- E-system applications
- Lean project

This company regularly reviews all measures above. Goals and specific targets are modified regularly, based on business needs. Examples include enhanced cost improvement and flawlessly launching new products to ensure timely introduction to the market.

Targets can be reset at any time the business requires a change. Reviews are at least monthly. There is a heavy emphasis on cost improvement. Targets are aggressive in nature, going beyond what has normally been achieved, and are in place at all purchasing levels and business units.

The purchasing performance measures are organized around the eight contributing key elements identified earlier as part of the global purchasing plan. The strategies by strategy areas and metrics are in place for the current and future states. The global purchasing business plan forces a linkage across the key elements of the corporation, including divisions, commodity teams, and regional purchasing groups.

Measured performance is regularly reported to all appropriate personnel companywide. Owners of performance across the company are established at all levels with project plans in place with appropriate metrics. For example, supplier development may include project steps and metrics for cost savings, developing supplier engineers, and implementing a supplier council.

Personal business priorities, which drive performance, are based primarily on team recognition rather than personal rewards. However, appraisals are done at the individual level and people are expected to perform at stretch levels to gain the most significant financial and nonfinancial rewards. Incentive compensation is based on overall achievement of the company's business plan and is primarily awarded at the executive level.

Significant resources are committed to the global purchasing business planning process and related measurements. Strategy and process personnel at corporate have lead roles in the planning process.

Purchasing personnel across the organization have execution responsibility, with specific personnel assigned to measurement systems input, data integrity, and enhanced systems development. Finance staff work to ensure the accuracy and validity of cost savings. Cost management personnel are developing cost models against which to evaluate purchasing and supplier performance.

Current systems provide significant support for the measurements. Cost and cost improvement are tracked and reported at all organizational levels and by division and product in considerable detail. Finance validates cost-reduction and purchasing performance to the financial plan for both direct and indirect procurement. Various other metrics are provided by SAP and internal systems models for performance monitoring.

In addition, e-systems are being enhanced and will include advanced supplier profiling and scorecards, a supplier suggestion system, and cost management.

The performance of purchasing (both direct and indirect) is critical to the financial success of the company. Top executives regularly review the performance of purchasing and the supply base, with a keen focus on cost, quality, availability, and launch. Companywide and purchasing executives drive the measurement system and critical metrics, using them to guide behavior and to reward performance.

Source: "Strategic Performance Measurement for Purchasing and Supply," CAPS Research, 2005, pp. 42–44.

Note: This case discusses an extensive purchasing and supply measurement system. It is organized around key principles of measurement.

This chapter begins with a basic overview of performance measurement and evaluation, including the reasons to measure performance and the problems associated with measurement and evaluation. Next, there is a discussion of the most common purchasing and supply chain measurement categories, with specific examples of performance measures presented. The third section discusses the development of a performance measurement and evaluation system. The fourth section discusses performance benchmarking, which is a process involving comparisons against leading firms to establish performance plans and objectives. The next section discusses the balanced scorecard. The chapter concludes with observations about performance measurement and evaluation.

Purchasing and Supply Chain Performance Measurement and Evaluation

A purchasing and supply chain performance evaluation system represents a formal, systematic approach to monitor and evaluate purchasing performance. Although this sounds easy, it is often difficult to develop measures that direct behavior or activity exactly as intended. Some firms still rely on measures that could be harmful, depending on performance objectives, rather than supporting long-term performance. For example, the ability to win significant price concessions from a supplier is still a major objective for certain price/cost performance measures. However, if a purchaser continually squeezes short-term price reductions from a supplier, will that supplier have the financial resources or the commitment to invest in longer-term performance improvements?

Modern purchasing and supply chain performance measurement and evaluation systems contain a variety of measures. Most of these measures fall into two broad categories: effectiveness measures and efficiency measures. **Effectiveness** refers to the extent to which, by choosing a certain course of action, management can meet a previously established goal or standard. **Efficiency** refers to the relationship between planned and actual sacrifices made to realize a previously agreed-upon goal.[1] Efficiency measures usually relate some input to a performance output.

Almost all measures include a standard or target against which to evaluate performance results or outcomes. It is incomplete to say, for example, that a measure will track improvement in supplier quality. We still need to compare actual improvement against a pre-established target or objective. Meeting this target, which is presumably based on world-class performance levels, will bring value to an organization. Each performance measure should include actual performance levels and a targeted performance level.

Why Measure Performance?

There are a number of reasons for measuring and evaluating purchasing and supply chain activity and performance.

Support Better Decision Making

Measurement can lead to better decisions by making performance and results visible. It is difficult to develop performance improvement plans without understanding the areas in which performance falls short. Measurement provides a track record of purchasing performance over time and directly supports decision-making activity by management.

Support Better Communication

Performance measurement can result in better communication across the supply chain, including within purchasing, between departments, with suppliers, and with executive management. For example, a purchaser must clearly communicate performance expectations to suppliers. The measures that quantify supplier performance reflect a purchaser's expectations.

Provide Performance Feedback

Measurement provides the opportunity for performance feedback, which supports the prevention or correction of problems identified during the performance measurement process. Feedback also provides insight into how well a buyer, department, team, or supplier is meeting its performance objectives over time.

Motivate and Direct Behavior

Measurement motivates and directs behavior toward desired end results. A measurement system can accomplish this in several ways. First, the selection of performance categories and objectives indicates to purchasing personnel those activities that an organization considers critical. Second, management can motivate and influence behavior by linking the attainment of performance objectives to organizational rewards, such as pay increases.

Problems with Purchasing and Supply Chain Measurement and Evaluation

Measuring and evaluating performance, including purchasing and supply chain performance, historically has had certain problems and limitations. Mark Brown, an expert on performance measurement, argued that most managers and professionals today are like a pilot trying to fly a plane with only half the instruments needed and many additional instruments that measure irrelevant data.[2] He states that practically every organization has some type of problem with its measurement system.

Too Much Data and Wrong Data

Having too much data is the most common problem an organization has with its measurement system. A second and more serious problem is that the data that managers pay attention to are often the wrong data. The metrics are selected because of history or a feeling that the measure is related to success, which may not be the case at all. In fact, measures that managers follow may sometimes be in conflict with measures used in other units or functional areas. As a general rule, employees should monitor no more than a dozen measures, with half of those being the most critical.

Measures That Are Short-Term Focused

Many small- and medium-sized organizations have a problem of relying on measures and data that are short-term focused. Typically the only data they collect are financial and operating data. In purchasing, this would mean a short-term focus on workload and supply chain activities, while ignoring the longer-range or strategic measures.

Lack of Detail

At times the data that are reported are summarized so much as to make the information meaningless. A measure that reports on a single measure of monthly supplier quality probably lacks detail. A supply manager will want to know what are the specific types of defects the supplier is experiencing, what the defects cost the buyer's company, and the supplier's quality performance over time.

An operations manager at a major automotive regional parts distribution facility receives a monthly measure of the facility's quality as measured by claims made by customers. However, he also receives reports that detail the following:

- The type of errors that are occurring (wrong part picked, damage, shortages, missed shipments, and so on)
- Which customers are making the quality claims
- Which employees are responsible for the quality errors
- The total cost of the quality claims against the facility
- The part numbers that have quality claims against them

With this information the manager can take action that will attack the root causes of the quality problems at his facility.

Drive the Wrong Performance

Unfortunately, many measures drive behavior that is not what was intended or needed. If buyers are measured on the number of purchase orders written, then they will make sure to split orders between suppliers to generate as many purchase orders as possible. Part of this is due to the fact that measuring intellectual work is difficult. However, organizations still want to look for factors that can be measured and reported. These factors may not, however, always be the right factors.

Measures of Behavior versus Accomplishments

The problem with measuring behavior is there is no guarantee the behavior will lead to desired results. A behavioral measure that tracks the amount of purchase volume covered by corporatewide contracts, for example, is becoming increasingly common. A better measure, however, is one that tracks the total savings due to the use of corporatewide contracts.

Another example of a behavioral measure is one that measures the number of meetings held by a commodity team each quarter. A better set of measures will track the performance results that occurred because of the team's actions. Although some set of behavioral measures will always be present, measures that capture accomplishments are the ones that really matter.

Purchasing and Supply Chain Performance Measurement Categories

As part of a company-focused purchasing and supply chain measurement approach, firms should follow a systematic process to maximize results and achieve vertical and horizontal alignment of purpose. Exhibit 19.1 on p. 712 illustrates the process. As indicated, company objectives drive specific company strategies such as being the low-cost producer or technology leader. These company strategies should then drive appropriate and prioritized purchasing and supply chain objectives and specific strategies.

Alignment of strategies, measures, and actions will bring together top-down direction and bottom-up targeting to produce positive contributions. In a single enterprise, this could deliver competitive advantage. Integrated purchasing and supply chain management can also produce competitive advantage for the end-to-end supply chain level, improving effectiveness and reducing overhead.

There are hundreds of purchasing and supply chain measures. Perhaps the best way to summarize the vast number of separate measures is by developing performance measurement categories as shown in Exhibit 19.1. Within each category, many separate measures relate to each general category. Most purchasing and supply chain measures fall into one of the following categories:

- Price performance
- Cost-effectiveness
- Revenue
- Quality
- Time/delivery/responsiveness
- Technology or innovation
- Physical environment and safety
- Asset and integrated supply chain management
- Administration and efficiency
- Government and social
- Internal customer satisfaction
- Supplier performance
- Strategic performance

The following sections discuss each of these categories.

Exhibit 19.1 Integrated Company/Purchasing Measurement Process

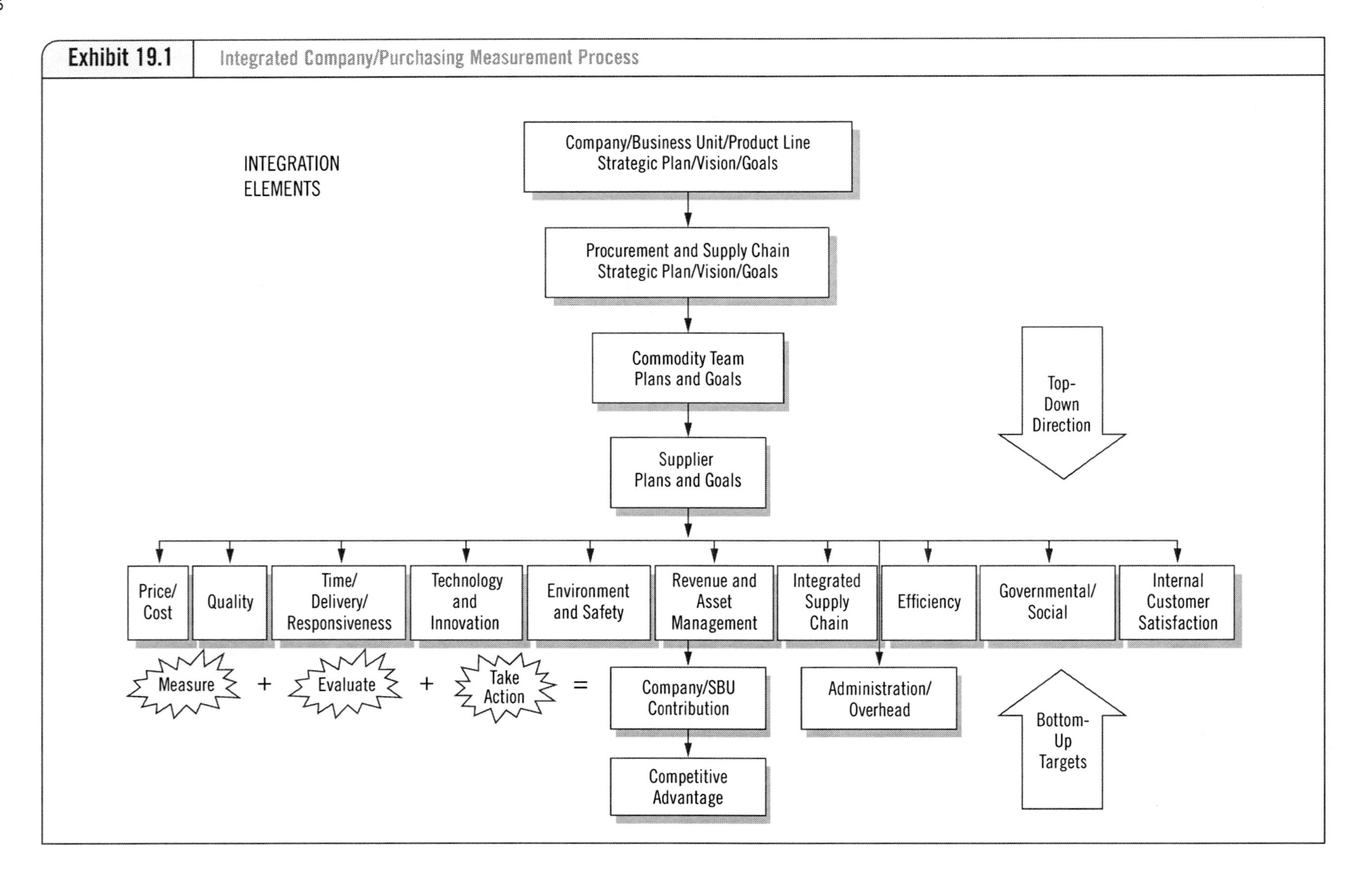

Price Performance Measures

Purchasing uses various indicators to evaluate price performance measures—in other words, how effectively it spends purchase dollars. The most common price performance measures include actual purchase price versus planned purchase price comparisons, actual purchase price(s) compared to a market index, comparisons of actual to actual purchase prices for individual and aggregated items between operating plants or divisions within an organization, and target prices achieved. Two price performance measures that are gaining importance are target prices achieved and price to market index comparisons.

Actual Price Compared to Plan

A common price performance measure is the difference between actual and planned purchase prices. Measurement of planned purchase price variance can occur at different organizational levels. One level includes actual versus planned purchases for the total material budget; this is an aggregated price performance measure. Other levels show comparisons that provide greater detail.

For example, purchasing may calculate actual versus planned price variances for each individual purchased item. Exhibit 19.2 presents various methods for calculating purchase price variance from a plan.

Actual Prices versus Market Index

Purchase price versus market index measures provide information about the relationship between actual prices and published market prices. These measures are most appropriate for market-based products where pricing is primarily a function of supply and demand. This also applies to standard and readily available products. Index

Exhibit 19.2 Purchase Price Variance from Plan

Various Formats for Measuring Purchase Price Variance

1. Purchase price variance = Actual price − Planned price
2. Purchase price variance percentage = Actual price/Planned price
3. Total purchase price variance = (Actual price − Planned price) × Purchase quantity or estimated annual volume
4. Current year dollar impact of purchase price variance = (Actual price − Planned price) × (Estimated annual volume × Percentage of requirements remaining)

Units of Measure

Dollars or percentages

Performance Reported by

Purchase item

Commodity or family group

End product

Project

Buying location or department

Buyer

Management group

Supplier

measures take into account the difference between a published index number over a designated period (such as a quarter) and the change in the actual price paid. The following illustrates this concept:

1a. Market-based index for Item X	March 31, 2007	= 125
1b. Market-based index for Item X	June 30, 2007	= 128
1c. Market index change	= (128 – 125)/125	= 2.4% increase
2a. Actual price paid for Item X	March 31, 2007	= $150
2b. Actual price paid for Item X	June 30, 2007	= $152
2c. Price paid change rate	= ($152 – $150)/$150	= 1.3% increase
3. Comparison to market	2.4% – 1.3%	= Better by 1.1%

Price Comparisons between Operations

Actual prices for similar items are also compared between plants, divisions, or business units. These comparisons provide an opportunity to identify purchase price differences within a firm. This provides visibility as to which unit is negotiating or securing the best purchase price. The comparison activity can also help identify commonly purchased items between units for purchase consolidation. A number of firms also attempt actual-to-actual price comparisons between companies to determine true price competitiveness.

Although firms are increasingly focusing on cost versus price, price performance measures are still popular, especially with firms that lack detailed cost data. Price

Sourcing Snapshot — *The Tight Squeeze at Chrysler*

Sales representatives from Detroit-area auto suppliers have been complaining about the cost-cutting pressure coming from the U.S. unit of DaimlerChrysler, which is hurting the cooperative relationships that existed between suppliers and the automotive manufacturer. During the 1990s, Chrysler extensively measured the savings generated from supplier-provided ideas. Now, facing lower sales, high rebate costs, and the cost of launching new vehicles, DaimlerChrysler announced a $600 million quarterly loss at its Chrysler unit. The red ink will likely increase the pressure at Chrysler to cut more than $2 billion as part of a $5.7 billion corporate belt-tightening. A supplier doing $300 million in business with Chrysler will now have to find an extra $3 million, and many suppliers are already struggling with razor-thin margins. Premerger Chrysler was renowned for working closely with its suppliers and received an enthusiastic response as new products were jointly developed that helped reduce Chrysler's manufacturing costs. By 1998, this strategy had helped Chrysler measure up as one of the lowest-cost producers in the world, with the highest profits per vehicle.

One supplier, complaining about the shift in performance metrics, suggested that his company may market its best technology to other automakers if the trend continues.

And that is a cost that Chrysler can ill afford.

Source: J. Green, "The Tight Squeeze at Chrysler," *Business Week,* October 9, 2000, pp. 33–34.

performance measures are also commonly used when purchasing raw materials, other commodity or standard-type items, components, systems, and contract services.

Target Prices Achieved

Target pricing is the process of determining what the external customer is willing to pay for a product or service and then assigning specific cost targets to the components, assemblies, and systems that make up the product or service. Target costing uses the following formula to determine allowable costs:

$$\text{Target Price} - \text{Profit Target} = \text{Allowable Cost}$$

Allowable cost is then allocated to various elements that make up the final product or service.

Cost-Effectiveness Measures

The measures in this category focus attention on efforts to reduce purchase costs. Cost-effectiveness measures fall into two general categories: cost changes and cost avoidance. The use of cost-effectiveness measures requires a word of caution. The method used to achieve cost reductions is critical. A cost reduction based on mutual cooperation is the same, on paper, as a cost reduction resulting from heavy-handed pressure on a supplier. Although the end result (i.e., a cost reduction) appears to be the same, the process used to achieve that result can have longer-term implications. Cooperation may reduce costs through joint improvement, whereas heavy-handed cost pressure may force a supplier to cut corners, resulting in poor quality.

Cost Changes

A cost-change measure compares the actual cost of an item or family of items over a period of time. A cost change is the increase or decrease in cost resulting from a change in purchasing strategy or practice brought about by an individual or a group.

The primary measure of concern to companies is cost reduction achieved, which is calculated by taking (New price − Prior price) × Estimated volume. For example, if the new price was $9/unit and the prior price was $10/unit with an estimated volume of 10,000 units for the next budget period, there would be a projected cost reduction of $10,000. Actual usage would determine the final cost reduction achieved.

Cost Avoidance

Cost avoidance represents the difference between a price paid and a potentially higher price (which might have occurred if purchasing had not obtained the lower price through a specific effort or action). For example, assume that purchasing paid $5.00 per unit for an item in the past, but the supplier has now quoted a price of $5.50 per unit. If the buyer negotiates a price of $5.25 per unit, then he or she has achieved a cost avoidance of $0.25 per unit, even though the price was still $0.25 higher than the prior price. Unfortunately, finance often argues that cost-avoidance savings rarely show up on a firm's profit line.

Cost-change and cost-avoidance measures differ significantly. Cost change represents an actual change from a prior-period price, whereas cost avoidance refers to the amount that would have been paid minus the amount actually paid. Purchasing departments that require tangible cost improvement should focus more on the cost-change approach. This represents actual changes that can impact a firm's overall profitability.

Cost-avoidance figures almost always require manual calculation and are sometimes subject to exaggeration. As a result, some observers have described cost-avoidance measures and figures as "soft," "funny money," and "easy to manipulate."

Revenue Measures

Revenue measures demonstrate the impact of purchasing and supply strategies and actions on revenues of the firm. For example, purchasing and supply may uncover new supplier technologies before others in the industry do and gain exclusive access, resulting in new product applications with favorable pricing and volume growth.

In addition, firms have achieved revenue growth due to royalty agreements negotiated with suppliers that have sold jointly developed technologies to other customers. Revenue from royalty generated from licensing patents and other technologies may be measured and reported.

Meeting new-product introduction dates with perfect supplier performance, enabling a first-to-market position with premium pricing, was also linked to revenue growth. Perfect-launch revenue is critical at many firms and is influenced by supplier performance.

Revenue measures for purchasing and supply are important because they link purchasing and supply strategies to the revenue elements of economic value-add. However, relatively few revenue measures are in use. Apparently, firms have not fully recognized the contribution to revenue generation that purchasing and supply can make. This is the case for direct goods and even more true on the indirect side, where the linkage of purchasing and supply strategy to revenues is less obvious or, perhaps, nonexistent.

Revenue Measure Examples

- Royalty revenues generated from supplier- or buyer-developed technology and patents initiated by purchasing or sourcing
- Supplier contribution as a reason for new business, e.g., new business development, unique technology found by purchasing, flexibility in shifting output product or service mix to meet higher profit or revenue, generating customer demand
- Return on licensing technology driven by purchasing or sourcing
- Number of patents that have led to royalties
- Number of invention disclosure forms filed
- Number of patents granted
- Value of free samples from suppliers

Quality Measures

Parts per Million

This measure expresses a maximum number (in absolute or percentage terms) of level of defects allowable for any particular product, assembly, or service. It may be expressed by using one of the following specific definitions or could be the mean time between failures for a plant or equipment item. When applied to products, components, assemblies, or systems, the traditional metric has been parts per million failing to conform to specification. As quality control has improved and the ability to manufacture to tighter tolerances has increased, this metric may also be tightened. In determining the PPM result, there is a need to measure (by factual inspection, testing, or statistically reliable sampling) the incidence of defective or nonconforming parts. The measure demands a reference point such as production, receipt, incoming inspection, or shipment. In addition, quality measures are also being developed and being used for services.

Customer Defects per Supplier

This is a measure of the number of defects from individual suppliers to indicate comparative quality performance among competing suppliers. It is also used as an absolute target for suppliers in total to attain and surpass, often as part of an assessment, certification, and reward approach. Measurement is calculated by inspecting or sampling the number of acceptable components, assemblies, or systems delivered as a proportion of the total number of those parts delivered by that supplier.

It is possible to aggregate this measure across all the different items supplied by any one supplier to arrive at an average number of defects for that supplier. However, the strategic criticality of items is not taken into account.

Field Failure Rates by Purchase Item and by Supplier

This measures the incidence of failures of components, assemblies, and systems or services when actually incorporated into the final product or service and supplied to external customers. As a measure, it indicates failures after sale, and organizations will tend to aim for a zero incidence of such failures. However, in some industries (e.g., equipment rental) this measure becomes a key measure of customer satisfaction.

The metric is calculated by developing a ratio of failures against total installed population. It is used to monitor product performance after sale, manage after-sales support costs, and provide input to supplier improvement, product design improvement, and replacement design by tracking failure rates and their root causes.

Time/Delivery/Responsiveness Measures

Time-to-Market Targets, New Products/Services

This measure is the amount of time (in weeks or months) from concept to first shipment or provision of a product or service to the external customer. The objective is continuous reduction so as to reduce the amount of time it takes to achieve break-even of investment and also to be first to market with the product or service.

On-Time Delivery/Responsiveness

These measures indicate the degree to which suppliers are able to meet customer schedule requirements. Key elements for such measures include the following:

- Due dates, scheduled or promised
- Delivery windows
- Acceptable early or late arrivals to due dates (e.g., minus two days or no days late)

The metrics are typically calculated as the percentage of shipments, services, or individual items on time or late (occasionally early). These measures can be applied in service or manufacturing businesses. Supplier and procurement performance can be measured through indices based on the above measures. These metrics can be further organized by commodity or purchase family. Percentages are calculated by company total on-time to total deliveries, and then further reported by purchase family and supplier.

Achieving New-Product Introduction Ramp-Up Schedules and Introduction Dates

These measures indicate whether procurement and supply chain management and strategic processes and suppliers are achieving necessary available volume goals at milestones and at market introduction dates for the product or service.

Cycle Time Reductions: Order Entry, Manufacturing/Operations, Distribution, and Logistics

These measures should identify total cycle time and its key components. Measures focus on reduction through elimination of delays and delivering continuous improvement to target times. Examples include supplier manufacturing cycle times, order entry, internal operations, transportation, and so forth.

Responsiveness to Schedule Changes, Mix Changes, and Design or Service Changes

These measures indicate how quickly suppliers can respond to demand or use changes, for example, the ability to adjust schedule by 50% within two weeks of scheduled delivery. Another measure could be time to achieve design changes to allowable targets. These measures recognize the need for flexibility.

Technology or Innovation Measures

First Insight/Production Outputs of New Supplier Technology

This measure would typically link to a contractual agreement whereby, for new technologies, your firm may get insight, some period of time before new technology developments are shared with other organizations. This may be an important focus in dealings with selected key technology suppliers to your firm. A specific metric can be the number of such agreements with key suppliers for critical technologies. Any target would be firm specific. A potential drawback with this measure is that no account is taken of the success or failure arising from such technology insights.

Standardization and Use of Industry Standards

These measures focus on achieving standardization of components, systems, and services and application of currently used purchased items or the use of industry-standard versus -unique items. Specific measures include reduction of different items used, percentage of new products or services made up of currently purchased items, and number of industry-unique items utilized in a new product or service. Your firm would then establish these and similar measures for product- or service-specific goals.

Physical Environment and Safety Measures

Companies are tracking the achievement of environmental and safety goals and costs associated with compliance, both voluntary compliance and where legislation enforces compliance. The objective is to drive performance improvement to achieve self-imposed or regulatory goals.

Asset and Integrated Supply Chain Management Measures

The measurement of inventory as an asset for a single enterprise may include a number of typical unit or aggregate inventory measures such as the following:

- Dollar value of inventory investment (following appropriate accounting rules)
- Inventory turnover
- Days/weeks/months of supply of inventory

The objective is to reduce inventory cost by increasing the velocity of throughput or reducing inventory carrying cost. A unique use of this measure is its application across inventory throughout various stages within a firm's supply chain and, more importantly, across firms in the aggregate supply chain (external to your firm) with specified future targets.

In addition, it is common to have additional measures that track different aspects of a firm's inventory investment. Examples include percentage of active versus inactive part numbers, total number of part numbers, working capital savings, and inventory investment by type of purchased item (for example, production items, maintenance items, and packaging materials).

It is also common to have measures that track the speed or velocity of inventory as it moves through different elements of the supply chain. This includes raw material, work-in-process, and finished-goods inventory turns. The amount of inventory maintained as safety stock is also a common measure. The accuracy of computer records that are part of the inventory location system is also closely tracked.

Transportation Cost Reduction

Transportation measures include tracking actual transportation costs against some pre-established objective, demurrage and detention costs, and premium transportation. Transportation carrier quality, delivery performance levels, and transportation lead time can also be measured.

Cost-reduction measures focus on the total transportation costs incurred per planning period to conduct business and those premium transportation costs incurred where expediting requires a nonstandard transportation method to meet internal or external requirements, for example, using air shipments when trucking is the preferred shipping mode.

Transportation costs can be measured in total dollars and as a percentage of cost of goods sold or sales revenue. Premium transportation can be measured in dollars or percentage of overall transportation costs. These costs can be measured inbound, intracompany, and outbound.

Customer Orders

These measures evaluate how well an organization is satisfying its commitment to downstream customers. Various measures include the percentage of on-time delivery, total time from customer order to customer delivery, returned orders, and warranty claims. Although we have focused primarily on purchasing and upstream supply chain activities, purchasing and materials planners are increasingly responsible for managing inventory from a total supply chain perspective. This may also include downstream activities.

E-Transactions (Number and Percentage of Suppliers/Dollars/Orders)

These measures show some degree of cross-enterprise linkage. The magnitude of use of electronic data interchange or web-based systems that link buyers and suppliers can, for example, be measured by the following:

- Absolute number of suppliers
- Percentage of suppliers
- Dollar value and percentage of orders
- Percentage of advance shipping notices
- Electronic funds transfer
- Meeting customer requirements
- Inventory throughout the supply chain
- Other

Pull Systems/Shared Schedules/Supplier Managed Inventory (SMI)

These measures establish the number (or percentage) of suppliers that are sharing schedules and operating in a pull system environment. They may also measure percentages of suppliers that are sharing schedules against those that should be. SMI measures establish the number of suppliers and magnitude of inventory being managed by suppliers for which they have financial responsibility.

Administration and Efficiency Measures

Management uses administration and efficiency measures to plan purchasing's annual administrative budget and to help control administrative expenses during a budget period. Budgeted expense items commonly include salaries, travel and living expenses, training expenses, office supplies, and other miscellaneous expenses. Salaries traditionally take the largest share of the purchasing administrative budget. The two most common methods to establish the purchasing administrative budget are the current budget plus adjustment and the use of control ratios.

Current Budget Plus Adjustment

The most common method of establishing a budget uses the current administrative budget as a starting point. Management then adjusts the budget for the next period (usually the next fiscal year) upward or downward depending on expected business conditions or other departmental requirements. Budget adjustments reflect management's view about projected purchasing workload and a firm's profitability. Decreasing workload or profits can result in a budget reduction. Conversely, increasing workload or profits may justify a budget increase.

Sourcing Snapshot

The Perfect Order at Procter and Gamble

The **perfect order** represents the ability of the supply chain to provide 100% availability in a timely, error-free manner. Procter and Gamble (P&G), a manufacturer and distributor of consumer products, defines the perfect order metric as on time to the buyer's requested delivery date, shipped complete, invoiced correctly, and not damaged in transit. In 1992, P&G began to measure its perfect orders. Initially, managers were shocked to discover that the number of perfect orders was only around 75%. Since that time, substantial improvements have been made. In 1995, 82% of orders were perfect; and by 1998, 88% were perfect. This has been achieved through continuous replenishment, having customer service representatives work closely with major customers, and improved information systems. Procter and Gamble estimates that every imperfect order costs approximately $200 as a result of redelivery, lost revenue, damage, warehouse and shipping costs, deductions, and backorders. P&G knows that continuous supply chain improvement requires measuring what is really important to the customer. And to the customer, the perfect order is important.

Source: Presentation by Ralph Drayer, Eli Broad Graduate School of Management, Michigan State University, East Lansing, December 1998.

Control Ratios

With the control ratio approach, the purchasing administrative budget is a percentage of another measure that reflects purchasing's workload. Planned dollar expenditure for direct material is often the selected workload measure.

The historical control ratio as well as negotiation between purchasing and higher management often determines the control ratio percentage used during calculation of the administrative budget. A projection of direct material purchase requirements for the next period then affects the administrative budget. Purchasing workload is assumed to be proportional to planned dollar expenditures for direct material. The purchasing administrative budget becomes the following:

$$\text{Purchasing Budget} = \text{Estimated Expenditures for Direct Materials} \times \text{Control Ratio}$$

Purchasing managers use the total budget figure to allocate resources among different departmental uses. Management must determine how many buyers are required, the size of the clerical support staff, and other budget-related issues.

Other Approaches

Current budget plus adjustment and control ratios are not the only methods used to arrive at a purchasing administrative budget or efficiency. Purchasing workload such as purchase orders processed, line items processed, and headcount may also be used to measure efficiency. Again, we must warn against emphasizing purchasing efficiency over purchasing effectiveness as a strict indicator of performance.

Governmental and Social Measures

Minority, Women, and Small Business Enterprise Objectives

In the United States there are social, state, and federal requirements that public and private organizations place a percentage of their business with minority- and women-owned business enterprises (MWBEs). These expenditures are regularly targeted at specific performance levels, tracked, and reported; they are used to drive purchasing strategy. Small-business purchases may also be included. Specific measures may include the following:

- Percentage of spend (the proportion of purchase spend from MWBE suppliers as a percentage of total annual purchase spend), calculated as follows:

$$\frac{\text{Annual Purchase (\$) from MWBE Suppliers}}{\text{Total Annual External Purchases (\$)}} = \%$$

- Number of suppliers in each MWBE category
- Growth of MWBE spend

Internal Customer Satisfaction Measures

Companies are also applying measures that indicate the degree of satisfaction with purchasing's value-add contribution. This is typically done by surveying internal customers and asking them to indicate their satisfaction with purchasing by responding to a series of check-off and open-ended questions. Supplier satisfaction surveys and measures are also used.

Supplier Performance Measures

Supplier performance measurement is an area in which many firms have made great progress. Supplier scorecards frequently contain many of the measures discussed above. Purchasers generally track supplier quality, cost, and delivery along with other performance areas. Furthermore, firms are beginning to quantify the cost associated with supplier nonperformance. The resulting cost figure represents the total cost of doing business with a supplier. Supplier total-cost measures allow direct comparisons between suppliers.

Hewlett-Packard developed a supplier performance evaluation model that evaluates supplier performance (and the teams that manage those suppliers) in the areas of T (technology contribution), Q (quality), R (supplier responsiveness), D (delivery performance), C (cost), and E (environmental performance). The FedEx supplier scorecard featured in Chapter 9 provides additional details about supplier performance measurement systems. These supplier scorecards are increasingly important in selecting, motivating, and developing suppliers.

Strategic Performance Measures

Purchasing requires measures that reflect its ability to support overall corporate and functional goals, which means a reduced emphasis on pure efficiency measures (e.g., the cost to issue a purchase order or current workload status) and greater emphasis on effectiveness measures (those that reflect purchasing's strategic contribution). Examples of the latter include tracking early supplier involvement in product design, performance gains resulting from direct supplier development efforts, and supplier-provided improvement suggestions. Within most industries, purchasing must shift from measuring itself as an administrative support function to measuring how well it provides strategic value.

Exhibit 19.3 provides examples of key strategic purchasing measures. Notice that these measures are a combination of activity- and results-oriented measures. Emphasis shifts from strict indicators of personnel performance or efficiency to how well the purchasing function supports strategic supply-base management goals and objectives. To shift from an operational to a strategic perspective, the purchasing measurement and evaluation system must also shift.

The performance indicators in Exhibit 19.3 are more strategically and externally focused than traditional performance indicators. They are also specified in terms of broader purchasing goals rather than specific activity. For example, a buyer may be responsible for a performance objective stating that 75% of the buyer's suppliers will be quality certified by the third quarter of 2007. This differs from a measure that states a buyer must process 10 requests for quotation per day on average.

Exhibit 19.3 Examples of Strategic Purchasing Measurement Indicators

- Percentage of purchasing's operating budget committed to on-site supplier visits
- Proportion of quality-certified suppliers to total suppliers
- Percentage of receipts free of inspection and material defects
- Total number of suppliers
- Proportion of suppliers participating in early product design or other joint value-added activities
- Revenue increase as a result of supplier-provided technology that differentiates end products to customers
- Percentage of operating budget allocated to supplier development and training
- Total cost supplier selection and evaluation measures
- Supplier lead-time indicators
- Purchasing's contribution to return on assets, return on investment, and economic value-added corporate measures
- Purchasing success with achieving cost reductions with Tier 2 and Tier 3 suppliers
- Percentage of purchase dollars committed to longer-term contracts
- Savings achieved from the use of companywide agreements
- Purchasing's contribution to product development cycle time reduction
- Percentage/dollar value of items purchased from single sources
- Percentage of purchase dollars committed to highest-performing suppliers
- Percentage of purchase transactions through electronic data interchange (EDI) or web-based systems
- Percentage of total receipts on a just-in-time basis
- Supplier quality levels, cost performance, and delivery performance compared with world-class performance targets
- Supplier development costs and benefits
- Continuous supplier performance improvement measures
- Reductions in working capital due to purchasing and supply chain efforts
- Contribution to return on investment and assets realized from strategic outsourcing efforts
- Savings achieved from part number reduction efforts
- Savings achieved from part standardization efforts

Developing a Performance Measurement and Evaluation System

The development of a measurement and evaluation system requires the leadership, support, and commitment of executive management, who must commit the financial resources necessary for system development. Management must also require all purchasing locations to use the same system structure, which can reduce duplication of effort and save development and training costs. This does not mean that each location must use the same performance objectives or performance criteria. It only means that the system's basic design should be similar. Executive management support also sends a message about the seriousness of tracking and improving performance.

Development of an effective measurement and evaluation system follows a general sequence of activities. These include determining which performance categories to measure, developing specific performance measures, establishing performance standards for each measure, finalizing system details, and implementing and reviewing the system and each performance measure. Exhibit 19.4 presents an overview of the development of a purchasing and supply chain performance measurement system.

Determine Which Performance Categories to Measure

A previous section discussed various performance measurement categories. The first step of the development process requires identifying which measurement categories to emphasize. Also, a firm can weight its performance measures and categories differently.

Management does not concern itself with specific performance measures during this phase of system development. The selected performance categories must relate broadly to organizational and purchasing and supply chain goals and objectives.

Selecting the performance measure categories is a critical step prior to developing specific performance measures.

Develop Specific Performance Measures

Developing specific performance measures begins once management identifies the measurement categories it will emphasize. Certain features characterize successful purchasing and supply chain performance measures.

Objectivity

Each measure should be as objective as possible. The measurement system should rely on quantitative data instead of qualitative feelings and assessments. Subjective evaluation can create disagreement between the rater and the individual or group responsible for the performance objective.

Clarity

Personnel must understand a performance measure's requirements in order to direct performance toward the desired outcome and minimize misunderstandings. All parties must be clear about what each performance measure means, agree on the

Exhibit 19.4 Developing a Purchasing and Supply Chain Performance Measurement and Evaluation System

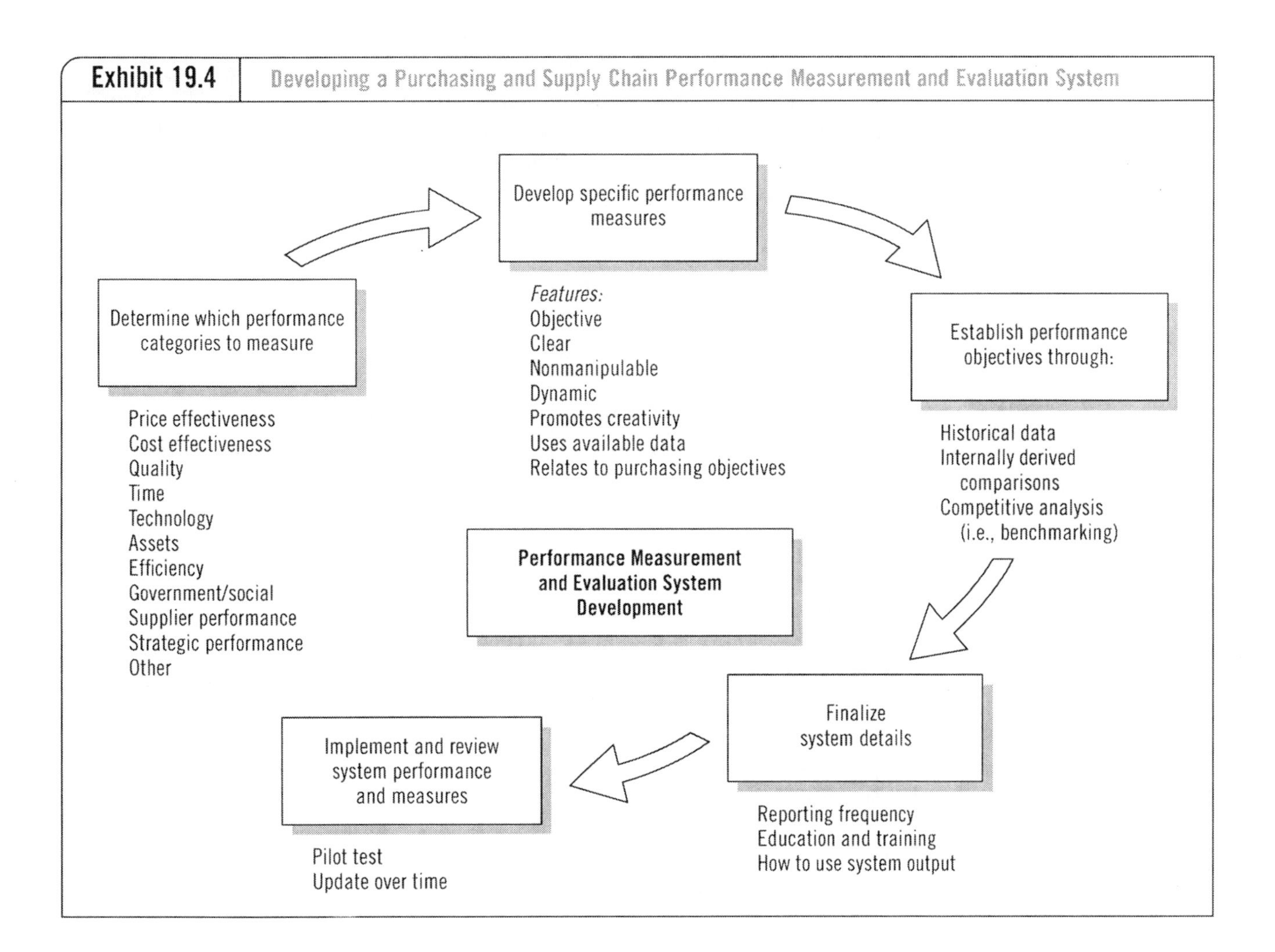

performance objectives associated with the measure, and understand what it takes to accomplish the measure. Well-understood measures are straightforward and unambiguous.

Use of Accurate and Available Data

Well-defined measures use data that are available and accurate. If a measure requires data that are difficult to generate or unreliable, the probability of using the measure on a consistent basis declines. The cost of generating and collecting the required data should not outweigh the potential benefit of using the performance measure.

Creativity

A common misconception is that a performance evaluation system should measure every possible activity. When this occurs, the measures can stifle individual creativity. The measures control behavior so tightly that the system eliminates room for personal initiative. A successful system measures only what is important while still promoting individual initiative and creativity, which may mean focusing on 5 or 6 important, clearly defined measures instead of 25 vague measures.

Directly Related to Organizational Objectives

Exhibit 19.5 illustrates how corporate goals and objectives influence purchasing goals and objectives. Other functional objectives also can influence purchasing. For example, manufacturing's goals can have a direct impact on purchasing because purchasing supports the manufacturing process. To meet its goals and objectives, purchasing executives develop strategies and action plans. Finally, management develops measures that evaluate the output or performance from the activities required to accomplish purchasing's strategies and plans. The measures serve as indicators of purchasing's progress.

Joint Participation

Joint participation means that the personnel responsible for each measure participate in developing the measure or establishing the measure's performance objective. Joint participation can go a long way toward getting the support of the personnel responsible for achieving the measure.

Dynamic over Time

A dynamic system is one that management reviews periodically, to determine whether existing measures still support purchasing's goals and objectives, if there is a need for new measures, or if performance standards or objectives require updating.

Exhibit 19.5 Linking Purchasing Measures and Corporate Objectives

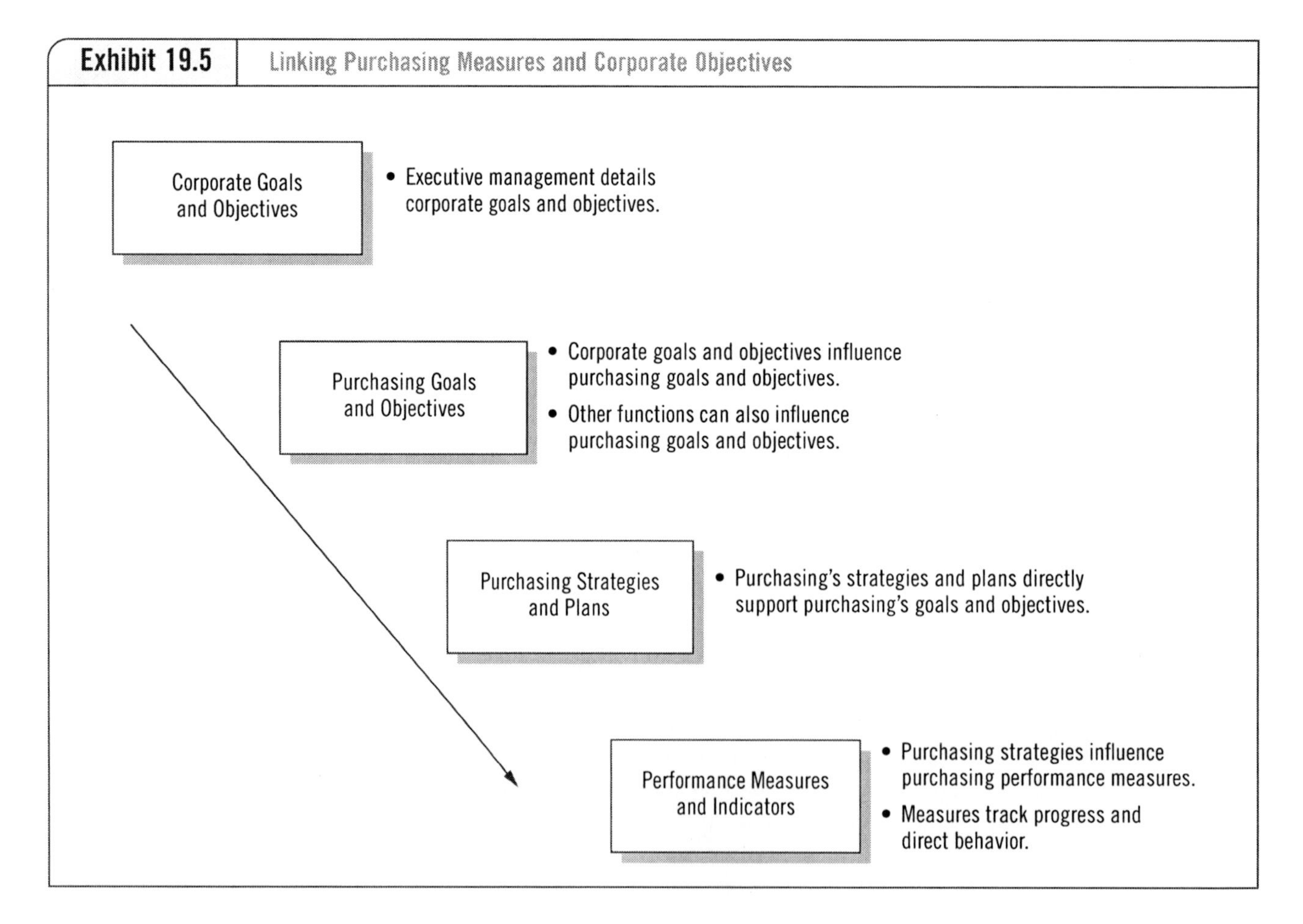

Nonmanipulable

A nonmanipulable measure is one that personnel cannot inappropriately influence the results of (i.e., the measure is cheat-proof). Ideally, the individual(s) responsible for the measure should not be responsible for supplying the data to the reporting system. This becomes an issue of accountability and integrity. The measure's output should be a true reflection of actual activity or performance results. Systems receiving their input from automated or computerized systems are generally less susceptible to data manipulation.

Establish Performance Objectives for Each Measure

Establishing an objective for each performance measure is critical. Objectives quantify the desired performance target or goal. Management must not specify objectives that are too easy. The too-easy objective can become an accepted performance standard within a department.

Performance standards or objectives must be realistic, which means the measure should be challenging yet achievable through a solid effort. An objective should not be so easy that it requires minimal effort. It should not be so difficult that it discourages personnel from even attempting to achieve the objective. The objective must also reflect the realities of a firm's competitive environment. An objective that is challenging internally yet does not reflect the competitive environment is not part of a well-defined measure.

Firms commonly use three methods when establishing performance measure objectives: (1) historical data, (2) internal comparisons, and (3) external analysis.

Historical Data

This method uses past data about an activity as the basis for establishing a formal performance objective. Historical performance is often modified with a performance improvement factor to arrive at a current objective. Purchasing and supply chain managers often use the historical approach with efficiency-related measures.

Relying on historical data can create some problems. The possibility exists that past performance was less than optimal. By establishing an objective based on suboptimal performance, even with an improvement factor, a firm risks continuing suboptimal performance. Also, historical data provide no insight about the performance capabilities of competitors or other leading firms. In addition, the firm's goals, strategies, and financial objectives will drive purchasing and supply goals. Purchasing cannot be a value contributor without contributing to firm success through goal achievement.

Internal Comparisons

A firm can perform internal comparisons between departments or business units. The best internal performance level can become the basis for a companywide performance objective. Firms with multiple business units often compare and rank performance internally across different performance categories.

This approach, which offers some advantages over the historical approach, also has disadvantages. A firm that stresses comparisons between internal units can lose sight of its external competition. Unhealthy rivalry can also develop between internal business units or departments. Furthermore, there is no guarantee that the best-performing internal unit matches the best-performing unit of a direct competitor.

External Analysis

This approach requires examination of the practices and performance objectives of competitors or other leading firms. The advantage of this approach is that it requires an external assessment at very specific levels of detail. A later section discusses benchmarking as a competitive-analysis approach for establishing performance objectives.

Finalize System Details

The next phase of implementation requires management to consider issues such as the frequency of performance reporting, the education and training of system users, and the final determination of how to use system output.

Performance-Reporting Frequency

A sound measurement and evaluation system provides regular reporting of performance results. The actual reporting frequency can differ from measure to measure. Management must determine what frequency supports the most effective use of each measure. A measure that tracks the status of inbound transportation shipments, for example, must be available on a frequent (daily or real-time) basis. A summary measure evaluating overall supplier performance may require only weekly or monthly reporting.

Education and Training

A firm must train its personnel and suppliers to use the performance measurement and evaluation system. Each participant must understand his or her accountability and responsibility under the system and how to use the system's output to improve performance. The measurement and evaluation system is a tool, and like all tools, it requires proper education and training in its use.

Using System Output

Managers use the output of a performance measurement and evaluation system in a number of ways. Some managers rely on the output to directly evaluate the performance of purchasing personnel or suppliers. Managers may use the system to track the effectiveness of individual buyers. System output may also identify better-performing suppliers that deserve future purchase contracts.

Managers must give careful thought to how best to use system output.

Implement and Review System Performance and Measures

All systems have an implementation phase, which may include pilot or trial runs to make sure the system performs as planned. The measurement and evaluation system, along with each performance measure, must be subject to periodic review. Having a system that contains obsolete or inappropriate measures can be more damaging than having no formal system at all.

Performance Benchmarking: Comparing Against the Best

An ongoing approach for establishing performance standards, processes, measurements, and objectives is benchmarking, a process that is not exclusively a purchasing or supply chain practice or approach per se. Rather, it is an approach used by corporate- and functional-level executives and managers. Benchmarking has definite applications, however, when establishing purchasing and supply chain management performance objectives and action plans. Before discussing specific benchmarking applications, we must first gain an understanding of the benchmarking process.

Benchmarking Overview

Benchmarking is the continuous measuring of products, services, processes, activities, and practices against a firm's best competitors or those companies recognized as industry or functional leaders.[3] Formally, the benchmarking process or activity requires measuring performance against that of best-in-class companies, determining how the best-in-class achieve their performance levels, and using that information as the basis for establishing a company's performance targets, strategies, and action plans.[4]

Benchmarking does not always involve comparisons against competitors. Firms often rely on comparisons with noncompetitors as a source of information, especially when benchmarking a process or functional activity common to firms across different industries (for example, supply chain management). It is usually easier to obtain benchmarking data and information from a cooperative noncompetitor.

Benchmarking is necessary for firms that are not industry leaders. Unfortunately, many U.S. firms did not recognize the need for performance benchmarking until after foreign competitors captured worldwide market share. Industry leaders should also practice performance benchmarking on a regular basis. A firm may not retain market leadership if it is unaware of the actions and capabilities of its competitors.

Types of Benchmarking

There are three basic types of performance benchmarking.[5] The first type is **strategic benchmarking**, which involves a comparison of one firm's market strategies against those of another. Strategic benchmarking usually involves comparisons against leading competitors, allowing a firm to gain an in-depth understanding of their market strategies.[6] With this knowledge, a firm can develop strategies and plans to counter or pre-empt the competition.

The second type of benchmarking is **operational benchmarking**, a process that the purchasing function follows when it performs benchmarking comparisons. Operational benchmarking focuses on different aspects of functional activity and identifies methods to achieve best-in-class performance. Selecting the function and the activities within that function to benchmark are critical to the success of operational benchmarking. Firms should benchmark functional activities that provide the greatest return over time.

The third type of benchmarking is **support-activity benchmarking**. During this process, support functions within an organization demonstrate their cost-effectiveness against external providers of the same support service or activity. Firms are increasingly using support-activity benchmarking as a way of controlling internal overhead and rising costs.

Benchmarking Benefits

There are a number of ways that a company hopes to benefit from actively pursuing performance benchmarking.[7] The benchmarking process helps identify the best business or functional practices to include in a firm's business plans, which can lead directly to performance improvement. Benchmarking can also break down a reluctance to change. Managers begin to see what it takes to maintain corporate or functional leadership by viewing the outside world. Benchmarking can also serve as a source of market intelligence. For example, competitive benchmarking may uncover a previously unrecognized technological breakthrough. Finally, valuable professional contacts between firms can result from the benchmarking process.

Benchmarking Critical Success Factors

Certain factors are critical to benchmarking success. Performance benchmarking must become an accepted process within a firm or function and not simply another fashionable program or fad. Personnel must view performance benchmarking as a permanent part of a system that establishes goals, objectives, and competitive strategies. Executive management support for the process is critical.

A firm must also be willing to commit the necessary legwork to data gathering. A firm must identify which company is the best-in-class for an activity, identify why that company is best, and quantify the benchmarked performance measure. The success of the benchmarking process depends on detailed and accurate benchmarked data and information that becomes part of a firm's action plans and performance objectives.

Managers must view benchmarking as a way to learn from outside companies and improve internal operations on a continuous basis.[8] Some individuals resist the benchmarking process because of a reluctance to recognize the value of a competitor's way of doing business—the "not invented here" syndrome. One way around this syndrome is to benchmark a noncompetitor's activities and performance wherever possible. Obviously, strategic benchmarking requires comparisons against direct competitors. For functional activities, however, a firm can study the performance and methods of noncompetitors.

Information and Data Sources

A solid source of benchmarking data includes trade journals, other business library resources, and the World Wide Web. Trade journals and other industry publications often feature firms that have distinguished themselves in some way. If this is not adequate, a firm can contact a benchmark target directly to request further information.

Industrywide conferences and professional seminars are also good sources of information, particularly at a functional level. These meetings often serve as a forum for the exchange of ideas about different topics. Leading firms often make presentations at industry trade meetings. These meetings can provide clues about which firms are the most highly regarded in a particular business area or practice.

Suppliers are another source of information. Purchasers can ask suppliers to identify the firms they believe are the best for each benchmark performance area. A firm can also rely on a professional consultant or other industry experts to identify benchmarking candidates.

An ongoing major purchasing benchmarking initiative conducted by CAPS Research (jointly sponsored by the Institute of Supply Management and W. P. Carey School of Business at Arizona State University) is another important source of information.

This effort includes specific industry-by-industry performance benchmarks and an ongoing study of leading-edge supply strategies. The CAPS Strategic Sourcing and Excellence Model provides the framework for the supply strategy and practice research. Data are collected via focus group visioning sessions, field research, and Internet-based surveys and assessments. Research findings about industry benchmarks and current and future supply chain strategies and practices are available at Knowledge Central, an online database sponsored by CAPS Research (http://www.capsresearch.org).

The Benchmarking Process

Robert Camp noted that there are five distinct steps or phases before a firm fully receives the benefits of the performance benchmarking process.[9] Exhibit 19.6 on p. 732 graphically presents these five phases.

Planning

During this initial phase of the benchmarking process, a firm addresses issues such as which products or functions to benchmark, which companies to select as benchmarking targets (competitors, noncompetitors, or both), and how to identify data and information sources. Benchmarking plans should focus on process and methods rather than simply on quantitative performance results. The process and methods cause the quantitative end results.

Analysis

Data and information collection and analysis occur during the second phase. A firm must determine how and why the benchmarked firm is better. A variety of questions should be asked:

- In what product or functional areas is the benchmarked company better?
- Why is the benchmarked company better?
- How large is the gap between the benchmarked company and our company?
- Can we include the benchmarked company's best practices directly in our operating plans?
- Can we project future performance levels and rates of change?

This phase is critical because it requires management to interpret and understand the benchmarked company's processes, methods, and activities.

Integration

Integration is the process of communicating and gaining acceptance of the benchmarking findings throughout an organization. During this phase, management begins to establish operational targets and functional goals based on the benchmarking findings.

Exhibit 19.6 Benchmarking Implementation Phases

Phase	Stage	Characteristics
Phase 1	Planning	• Determine which products, processes, or functions to benchmark • Identify benchmark target • Determine data and information requirements
Phase 2	Analysis	• Determine how and why benchmark target is better • Determine how to include benchmark company's best practices • Identify future trends and performance levels
Phase 3	Integration	• Communicate benchmark findings to key personnel • Establish operational targets and functional goals based on benchmarking findings
Phase 4	Action	• Include personnel responsible for carrying out plans during formulation of action plans • Develop a schedule for review and updating of goals and plans • Develop system to communicate benchmarking progress
Phase 5	Maturity	• Continuous use of benchmarking at all organizational levels • Continuous performance improvement resulting from the benchmarking process

Action

The action phase requires translating the benchmark findings into detailed action plans. Critical items during this phase include having personnel directly responsible for carrying out the plans involved with formulation of the plans, developing a schedule for updating plans and objectives over time, and developing a reporting system to communicate progress toward benchmarking goals.

Maturity

A firm reaches maturity when benchmarking becomes an accepted process for establishing performance plans and objectives. Another indicator of benchmarking maturity occurs when a firm realizes continuous performance improvement as a direct result of performance benchmarking.

A formal process, such as benchmarking, is essential for establishing performance targets and action plans that are externally focused. Without external comparisons, most organizations run the risk of losing sight of what defines best practices or what the competition is doing. Purchasing and supply chain managers must endorse this practice when attempting to establish plans, measures, and objectives that represent best-in-class performance.

Balanced Scorecard for Purchasing and Supply

The balanced scorecard was first presented by Robert S. Kaplan and David P. Norton in 1992. The original premise was that a total reliance on financial measures was leading organizations to make poor decisions. Kaplan and Norton argued that firms must go beyond financial measures, which are lagging indicators, and utilize measures that are leading indicators of performance.

They further suggested that the most appropriate measures that would cause organizations to do the right things would be those metrics that measure the strategy of the firm, its functional activities, and processes.

According to Kaplan and Norton, the balanced scorecard included four key linked performance measurement areas:

1. How do customers see us? (customer satisfaction perspective)
2. What must we excel at? (operational excellence perspective)
3. Can we continue to improve and create value? (innovation perspective)
4. How do we look to shareholders? (financial perspective)

In addition, Kaplan and Norton stressed that measurement itself is not the objective. Measurement and specific metrics provide clarity to general statements and a strategy focus around which to provide performance recognition and rewards.

The balanced scorecard and its related ideas have been adapted by numerous companies and applied to purchasing and supply.

Exhibit 19.7 on p. 734 is one example of a balanced scorecard for purchasing and supply. Included are measures related to the following questions:

1. How do we look to shareholders? (financial perspective)
2. How do our customers see us? (internal and external perspectives)
3. What must we excel at? (operational excellence perspective)
4. What do we need to do to improve? (innovation perspective)

Based on the company's purchasing and supply strategies, the balanced scorecard would then be connected to a specific set of appropriate performance measurements. The result will be a scorecard by department or people with specific key performance indicators.

A Summary of Purchasing Measurement and Evaluation Characteristics

A review of purchasing and supply chain performance and measurement systems supports a number of conclusions. These fall into two categories: system characteristics and human resource characteristics.

Exhibit 19.7 Case Example of Strategic Performance Measures—Semiconductor Manufacturer

Financial

- Revenue
  - Revenue from suppliers based on process improvements
  - Royalty revenue from patents
- Cost
  - Cost for direct material, indirect spend, and capital spend
  - Bill of material cost versus target
  - Savings on direct materials used by contract manufacturers
  - Administrative costs per headcount
  - Maverick spend

Operational Excellence

- Contract price enforcement
- Audit results and severity of errors
- Payment terms in contracts
- Most favored customer clauses in contracts
- Not to exceed pricing in contracts
- Keeping pricing current in ERP database
- Strategic sourcing plans in place

Customer Satisfaction

- Internal
  - Number of plant shutdowns
  - Single-source risk mitigation
  - Internal stakeholder survey
  - Factory quality incidents
  - Supplier business continuity
  - Tool performance
  - On-time delivery
  - Ramp-up readiness
  - Percentage of spend with preferred suppliers
- External
  - Customer quality incidents

Innovation

- New-product development
  - Performance versus data milestones in the new-product innovation (NPI) process
  - Current estimated cost against target in NPI process
  - Cost savings initiated by purchasing/supply in the NPI process
- People development
  - Training hours
  - Leadership development pipeline
  - Employee morale

System Characteristics

1. Measurement is not free. An evaluation system must compare the costs associated with measurement against the benefits. Furthermore, increased measurement does not necessarily mean improved performance. The amount and type of measurement should be enough to achieve the intended result but not cause negative or dysfunctional behavior.
2. Not all aspects of performance lend themselves to quantitative measurement. Negotiating skill and obtaining supplier cooperation are two examples of performance categories that are difficult to quantify.
3. Purchasing and supply chain managers are better served by a few precisely defined and thoroughly understood measures than by many poorly defined measures.
4. An effective measurement system requires a database that provides consistent and reliable data. All personnel must have access to the same data when calculating and reporting purchasing performance indicators.
5. Periodic review of the purchasing and supply chain measurement system should occur to eliminate unimportant or unnecessary performance measures, add new measures as required, and re-evaluate performance measure objectives or targets.

6. There is no best way to measure performance. Performance measures differ from firm to firm and industry to industry. No established industry purchasing performance standards have yet emerged. However, the movement toward performance benchmarking does support the development of performance indicators common to more than one firm.
7. Measurement-reporting requirements and content vary by position and level within the organization. Careful planning helps guarantee effective use of the system at each organizational level.
8. A single, overall productivity measure representing purchasing and supply chain performance is not feasible.
9. Many industries need to shift from operational measures focusing on activity to strategic measures assessing a desired end result (for example, increased participation by suppliers during new-product development).
10. The strategies and plans used to produce a performance measure's result are probably more important than the end performance result itself.
11. A balanced scorecard approach is an effective method of measurement and evaluation for purchasing and supply.

Human Resource Characteristics

1. A measurement and evaluation system is not a substitute for effective management. The system is a tool that can be used to assist in the efficient and effective operation of the purchasing and supply chain function.
2. An effective system requires communication. Responsible personnel must clearly understand the performance measure, its performance expectation, and the role of the measure during the performance evaluation process.
3. Measures must reinforce positive behavior and be positively linked to an organization's reward system and not serve as punitive tools. If management uses the measures solely as a means to identify nonperforming individuals, negative, dysfunctional, or beat-the-system behavior may result.

Good Practice Example

Using Measurement to Drive Continuous Supply Chain Improvement at Accent Industries

Accent Industries, a U.S.-based consumer goods company, manufactures products for direct shipment to retailers worldwide. This company's strategy is to excel across various operational aspects of service by being the industry leader in price, service, and convenience. Accent has developed a set of organizational objectives that it believes are critical to worldwide success. These objectives include being a low-cost producer; providing the highest quality to customers; and offering the best customer service, delivery, and responsiveness in the industry. The company has also developed a set of purchasing and supply chain performance measures that it believes directly supports its organizational directives.

When implementing its purchasing and supply chain measurement system, Accent followed a series of defined steps:

Step 1: Conduct cross-functional discussions and benchmarking to establish measures, measurement objectives, and performance targets.

Step 2: Formalize measurement objectives into written policy and procedures.

Step 3: Formally communicate measures and objectives to the supply base.

Step 4: Receive feedback from suppliers.

Step 5: Modify, if necessary, performance measures and their objectives.

Step 6: Implement final distribution of the measurement objective and process.

Step 7: Collect and maintain performance data.

Accent relies on a wide range of purchasing and supply chain measures that relate directly to the company's corporate objectives. A sample of the more critical measures include the following:

QUALITY

- Supplier defects in parts per million
- Internal manufacturing defects in parts per million
- Internal process capability
- Damage
- Number and cost of warranty claims

PRICE/COST

- Actual price to market price comparisons
- Price/cost reductions
- Tooling cost management
- Transportation cost management

CYCLE TIMES

- New-product development cycle time

DELIVERY AND SERVICE

- Supplier on-time delivery

INVENTORY/FORECASTING

- Total inventory dollar value over time
- Raw material, work-in-process, and finished-goods inventory turns
- Forecast accuracy

Supplier quality performance is determined during on-site supplier visits and statistical inferences from product receipts. The frequency of calculation varies with each supplier's current quality levels. Suppliers with known quality problems or higher levels of defects are targeted for more frequent measurement.

Accent uses its performance measurement system to establish and convey performance objectives, track progress, and promote continuous improvement.

Each supplier is provided clear, comprehensive goals and timely feedback. Factors that are critical to effective measurement include a process for establishing aggressive but attainable goals, supplier consensus that the goals are achievable, senior management support, and accurate measurement with regular feedback.

In the future the company plans to expand its use of total cost of ownership models for supplier evaluation and selection. In addition, Accent wants to pursue the open measurement and sharing of cost elements with its suppliers.

Source: Based on interviews with company managers. Company name has been changed at the request of the company.

CONCLUSION

A purchasing and supply chain performance measurement and management system should directly support corporate goals and objectives. A measurement system that directs behavior and activity away from those goals and objectives is counterproductive and can cause greater harm than good.

There is a need to create measurement systems that are responsive to change. Firms will also increasingly require measures that focus on end results rather than on specific activities. Emphasis will increasingly shift from efficiency measures to effectiveness measures. In addition, executive management must have the ability to distinguish between good and poor purchasing practices and results. A well-developed performance measurement and evaluation system can help provide this distinction. The balanced scorecard is a useful approach to purchasing and supply measurement.

KEY TERMS

benchmarking, 729

effectiveness, 708

efficiency, 708

operational benchmarking, 729

strategic benchmarking, 729

support-activity benchmarking, 729

DISCUSSION QUESTIONS

1. What is a purchasing performance measurement and evaluation system? Why would a firm want to measure purchasing performance?
2. Why would a firm want to measure supplier performance? Describe the kinds of measures that can be used to measure supplier performance.
3. What is performance benchmarking? Why is it increasingly being used when establishing purchasing performance goals and objectives?
4. What are the three types of performance benchmarking? Which type is most commonly used by the purchasing function?
5. What is the difference between effectiveness and efficiency measures? When should a firm focus on purchasing effectiveness measures? When should a firm focus on purchasing efficiency measures?
6. Discuss the reasons why measuring and evaluating purchasing performance has historically had certain problems or limitations. Do you think the purchasing function should increase or decrease its effort to measure performance? Why or why not?
7. Consider the following statement: Some firms still rely on measures that harm rather than support purchasing's long-term performance objectives. What does this mean? Provide examples of performance measures that might actually result in a negative longer-term effect on purchasing performance.
8. What is the benefit of developing performance measures that focus on cost versus purchase price?
9. Discuss the major difference between cost-reduction and cost-avoidance measures. Why have some described the reported savings in cost-avoidance measures as "soft," "funny money," and "easy to manipulate"? When can purchasing take credit for a legitimate cost reduction or cost avoidance?

10. Assume you are responsible for developing a benchmarking program. Describe how you would go about establishing the benchmarking process. Be sure to discuss the critical issues you must address.
11. Discuss what is meant by each of the following statements:
    a. Purchasing measurement is not free.
    b. There is no best way to measure purchasing performance.
    c. Many industries need to shift from operational measures focusing on buyer activity to strategic measures focusing on a desired end result.
    d. A purchasing measurement and evaluation system is not a substitute for solid management.
12. Why is it sometimes advantageous to benchmark performance against a non-competitor?
13. Effective performance measurement systems have certain characteristics. Select three characteristics and discuss why a measure should possess that characteristic.
14. Discuss the different uses a manager has for purchasing and supply chain performance data.
15. What is required to establish a balanced scorecard to measure purchasing and supply performance?

ADDITIONAL READINGS

Avery, S. (2006), "GM Strives for Consistent Metrics," *Purchasing,* October 5.

Brown, M. G. (1996), *Keeping Score: Using the Right Metrics to Drive World-Class Performance,* New York: American Management Association, pp. 15–26.

Carter, P. L., Monczka, R. M., and Mosconi, T. (2005), "Strategic Performance Measurement for Purchasing and Supply," CAPS Research.

Cooper, R., and Kaplan, R. (1988), "Measure Costs Right: Make the Right Decisions," *Harvard Business Review,* September–October, 23–28.

D'Avanzo, R., et al. (2003), "The Link between Supply Chain and Financial Performance," *Supply Chain Management Review,* November–December, 6–7.

Eccles, R. G. (1991), "The Performance Measurement Manifesto," *Harvard Business Review,* January–February, 131–137.

"Inside Purchasing: Four Pillars of Supply Strategy" (1995), *Purchasing,* 118(10), 13.

Kaplan, R. S., and Norton, D. P. (1992), "The Balanced Scorecard—Measures That Drive Performance," *Harvard Business Review,* January–February, 71–79.

Sharman, P. (1995), "How to Implement Performance Measurement in Your Organization," *CMA Magazine,* May, pp. 33–38.

Smeltzer, L. R., and Manship, J. A. (2003), "How Good Are Your Cost Reduction Measures?" *Supply Chain Management Review,* May–June, 3–7.

Timme, S., and Williams-Timme, W. (2000), "The Financial-SCM Connection," *Supply Chain Management Review,* May–June, 33–40.

Trunick, P. A. (2007), "What You Do, Start Measuring," *Logistics Today,* August 22–24.

Vitale, R., and Mavrinac, S. C. (1995), "How Effective Is Your Performance Measurement System?" *Management Accounting,* August, 43–47.

ENDNOTES

1. van Wheele, A. J. (1984), "Purchasing Performance Measurement and Evaluation," *International Journal of Purchasing and Materials Management,* Fall, 18–19.

2. Brown, M. G. (1996), *Keeping Score: Using the Right Metrics to Drive World-Class Performance,* New York: American Management Association, pp. 15–26.

3. Camp, R. C. (1989), "Benchmarking: The Search for Best Practices That Lead to Superior Performance: Part I," *Quality Progress,* January, 66.

4. Pryor, L. S. (1989), "Benchmarking: A Self-Improvement Strategy," *Journal of Business Strategy,* November–December, 28.

5. Pryor, pp. 29–30.

6. Pryor, p. 29.

7. Camp, R. C. (1989), "Benchmarking: The Search for Industry Best Practices That Lead to Superior Performance: Part III," *Quality Progress,* March, 77–80.

8. Furey, T. R. (1987), "Benchmarking: The Key to Developing Competitive Advantage," *Planning Review,* September–October, 32.

9. Camp, R. C. (1989), "Benchmarking: The Search for Best Practices That Lead to Superior Performance: Part II," *Quality Progress,* February, 71.

LOGISTICS

Taken from SUPPLY CHAIN MANGEMENT:LOGISTIC PERSPECTIVE by John J. Coyle | C. John Langley, Jr. | Brian J. Gibson | Robert A. Novack | Edward J. Bardi, 2009 and Operations Management: Goods, Service, and Value Chains by David Alan Collier | James R. Evans, 2007

Chapter Outline

CHAPTER 12

Managing Inventories

Learning Objectives

1. To understand the different types of inventory that firms use and their role in the value chain and to become familiar with a taxonomy of inventory concepts to support the development of useful quantitative models for inventory management.

2. To learn methods for prioritizing the importance of inventory items, maintaining accurate inventory information, and using technology for inventory management.

3. To understand a class of inventory management systems for monitoring and controlling independent demand using fixed order quantities for replenishing inventory levels.

4. To understand how inventory management systems for monitoring and controlling independent demand operate using fixed time intervals between order placements.

5. To learn special inventory models that consider back orders, price breaks, one-time ordering opportunities, and simulation as methods for inventory analysis.

- "Mr. Gales, we can't pick you up before 4 P.M. today in Orlando. The plane assigned to you needs a replacement part and it is out of stock. We are sending a different plane from San Diego to pick you up, but it can't get to Orlando until 4:00 P.M. You will be in Chicago by 6:30 P.M. You might be a little late to the golf tournament kickoff dinner," said Betty Kelly, the customer service representative for Scott Gales, a professional golfer. Gales had purchased a fractional ownership of a privately owned business jet, costing $3 million plus a monthly fee of $3,000. Fractional ownership, similar to vacation timesharing, allows the customer a specific number of flying hours in a certain type of airplane. Moreover, the company promises its customers that with 4 hours notice (called a service window), it can pick them up anywhere in the continental United States. As Betty hung up the telephone, she realized the cost to fly the plane from San Diego to Orlando to pick up Gales far exceeded the cost of the replacement part that was out of stock. The company would lose considerable money on this flight but cannot afford to lose Gales—and possibly many of his colleagues—as a customer.

JAY MALLIN/Bloomberg News/Landov

- Banana Republic is a unit of San Francisco's Gap, Inc., and accounts for about 13 percent of Gap's $15.9 billion in sales. As Gap shifted its product line to basics such as cropped pants, jeans, and khakis, Banana Republic had to move away from such staples and toward trends, trying to build a name in fashion circles. But fashion items, which have a much shorter product life cycle and are riskier because their demand is more variable and uncertain, bring up a host of operations management issues. In one recent holiday season, the company had bet that blue would be the top-selling color in stretch merino wool sweaters. They were wrong. Marka Hansen, company president, noted, "The No. 1 seller was moss green. We didn't have enough."[1]

- "Where is my house mortgage? You mean you lost all of the paperwork?" H. C. Morris shouted as he talked to his banker on the telephone. "Sir, we packaged and sold the original loan to a custodian loan servicing company and they cannot find your mortgage at their warehouse. The secure and fireproof warehouse holds over 25 million home mortgage folders! Home mortgages are bought and sold many times. Do you have copies of the original loan documents?" responded the banker. "Yes, but they are photocopies and probably are incomplete," noted Morris. "Mr. Morris, we will have to re-create the entire loan package and that will take at least 2 months," said the banker. "I can't wait that long—I have to close the deal for the house in 10 days. I may lose the deal," Morris shouted again. "Sir, we will work as fast as we can but with no original mortgage documents you have no choice but to wait," sighed the banker.

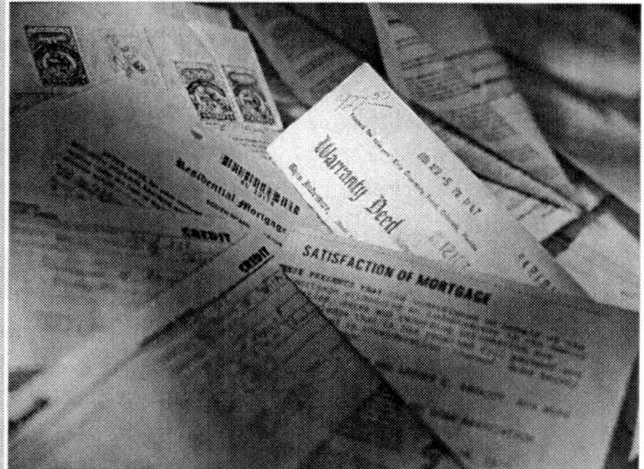

© Getty Images/PhotoDisc

Discussion Questions: Can you cite any experiences in which the lack of appropriate inventory at a retail store has caused you as the customer to be dissatisfied? Consider the off-season sale racks of clothing that you have seen at a department store. Typically, most of the items are odd sizes—for instance, S or XXL. What does this suggest about the store's inventory management decisions?

Inventory *is any asset held for future use or sale.* These assets may be physical goods used in operations and include raw materials, parts, subassemblies, supplies, tools, equipment, or maintenance and repair items. For example, a small pizza business must maintain inventories of dough, toppings, sauce, and cheese, as well as supplies such as boxes, napkins, and so on. Hospitals maintain inventories of blood and other consumables, and railroads have inventories of rail cars and maintenance parts. Retail stores such as Best Buy maintain inventories of finished goods—televisions, appliances, DVDs—for sale to customers. In some service organizations, inventories are not physical goods that customers take with them, but provide capacity available for serving customers. Some common examples are airline seats, concert seats, hotel rooms, and call center phone lines. Inventories can also be intangible; for example, many organizations maintain "inventories" of intellectual assets and best-practice knowledge bases. Thus, the concept of inventory should be interpreted broadly, although many examples in this chapter deal with physical goods.

Inventory *is any asset held for future use or sale.*

The expenses associated with financing and maintaining inventories are a substantial part of the cost of doing business (that is, cost of goods sold). Managers

Inventory management *involves planning, coordinating, and controlling the acquisition, storage, handling, movement, distribution, and possible sale of raw materials, component parts and subassemblies, supplies and tools, replacement parts, and other assets that are needed to meet customer wants and needs.*

are faced with the dual challenges of maintaining sufficient inventories to meet demand while at the same time incurring the lowest possible cost. **Inventory management** *involves planning, coordinating, and controlling the acquisition, storage, handling, movement, distribution, and possible sale of raw materials, component parts and subassemblies, supplies and tools, replacement parts, and other assets that are needed to meet customer wants and needs.* If the "right" inventory is carried and delivered at the "right" time, profits are increased through additional sales revenues, and customer service is enhanced. However, it is important to realize that having the wrong inventory or having it at the wrong time can seriously hurt a firm's performance. For example, ordering too many computers can easily lead to obsolescence and lower profits (or even losses) as new technology rapidly evolves.

Managing inventories is one of the most important functions of operations management in both manufacturing and service organizations. In the first episode, we see how the lack of the proper aircraft replacement parts can result in both unnecessary and excessive costs as well as dissatisfaction of the customer, with possible loss of future business. For this type of premium service, the airline needs to carry additional capacity in the form of extra planes to provide the service required by their high-income clients. Nearly every organization faces such problems; it is not uncommon for a restaurant to run out of certain entrees or desserts, particularly if they are "specials," and enough food was not ordered.

On the other hand, simply maintaining large stocks of inventory is costly and wasteful. The old concept of keeping warehouses and stockrooms filled to capacity with inventory has been replaced with the idea of producing finished goods as late as possible prior to shipment to the customer. Better information technology and applications of quantitative tools and techniques for inventory management have allowed dramatic reductions in inventory. For example, U.S. businesses reduced total inventory as a percentage of gross domestic product (GDP) from 8.3 to 3.8 percent from 1981 to 2000. This increases net working capital and reduces cash flow requirements to run the business, resulting in improved operational and financial efficiency. Inventory reduction is a vital part of becoming a "lean organization."

One-time, seasonal merchandise, such as that suggested in the Banana Republic episode, presents a different situation. Such firms must order far in advance of the actual selling season with little information on which to base their inventory decisions. The wrong choices can easily lead to a mismatch between customer demand and availability, resulting in either lost opportunities for sales or overstocks that might have to be sold at a loss or at least a minimal profit. Such decisions must take into account the trade-offs between ordering too much or too little, as well as other factors such as quantity discount price breaks.

The third episode illustrates the complexity of many inventory management systems and the need for modern technology. In a home mortgage warehouse, each original mortgage file folder contains up to ten legal documents per mortgage folder. A typical mortgage warehouse has to store, retrieve, copy, update, and ship 25 million individual mortgages and thus account for over 250 million documents. This includes record keeping, tracking document movement, and organizing loan portfolios. The mortgage business is slowly moving toward more modern methods for managing its inventory, such as scanning new mortgage documents and storing them in electronic form. However, converting existing paper documents into electronic form is cost-prohibitive and complicated by such legal issues revolving around original signatures versus electronic signatures.

One of the difficulties of inventory management is that every department in an organization generally views inventory objectives differently. The marketing department prefers high inventory levels to provide the best possible customer service.

Purchasing agents tend to buy in large quantities to take advantage of quantity discounts and lower freight rates. Similarly, operations managers want high inventories to prevent delays and buffer demand between workstations and processes. Financial personnel seek to minimize inventory investment, warehousing costs, and cash flow and thus would prefer small inventories. Top management needs to understand the effect that inventories have on a company's financial performance, operational efficiency, and customer satisfaction and strike the proper balance in meeting strategic objectives.

In this chapter, we examine the role of inventories in manufacturing and service organizations, along with many techniques and approaches for effectively managing them.

BASIC INVENTORY CONCEPTS

Learning Objective
To understand the different types of inventory that firms use and their role in the value chain and to become familiar with a taxonomy of inventory concepts to support the development of useful quantitative models for inventory management.

Many different types of inventories are maintained throughout the value chain—before, during, and after production—to support operations and meet customer demands (see Exhibit 12.1). **Raw materials, component parts, subassemblies, and supplies** *are inputs to manufacturing and service-delivery processes.* Examples include coal for steelmaking; automobile engines for final assembly; buns, burgers, and condiments at a quick-service restaurant; soap and shampoo at a hotel; and printer cartridges and envelopes at an office. **Work-in-process (WIP) inventory** *consists of partially finished products in various stages of completion that are awaiting further processing.* For example, a pizza restaurant might prepare a batch of pizzas with only cheese and sauce and add other toppings when orders are placed. This can improve service time during busy lunch periods. WIP inventory also acts as a buffer between workstations in flow shops or departments in job shops to enable the operating process to continue when equipment might fail at one stage or supplier shipments are late. **Finished goods inventory** *are completed products ready for distribution or sale to customers.* Finished goods might be stored in a warehouse or at the point of sale in retail stores. Finished goods inventories are necessary to satisfy customers' demands quickly without having to wait for a product to be made or ordered from the supplier.

Raw materials, component parts, subassemblies, and supplies *are inputs to manufacturing and service-delivery processes.*

Work-in-process (WIP) inventory *consists of partially finished products in various stages of completion that are awaiting further processing.*

Finished goods inventory *are completed products ready for distribution or sale to customers.*

Despite their obvious value in meeting customer demand and providing operational efficiencies, WIP and finished goods inventories have some limitations. High levels of WIP inventories, for example, can make it more difficult to change product lines, since they must be phased out when products change, thus limiting flexibility to meet changing customers' needs. In addition, large WIP inventories can hide such problems as unreliable machines, late supplier shipments, or defective parts. High levels of finished goods inventory can quickly become obsolete when technology changes or new products are introduced. The financial investment tied up in inventory that might be used more productively in the firm is clearly a concern to top management. These factors make inventory management an important activity.

Many goods move continually through the supply chain, for example, being transported by truck, train, or barge from a supplier to a factory, or from a factory to a distribution center. *Inventory that has been ordered but not yet received and is in transit is called* **pipeline inventory**. For example, if a computer manufacturer orders an average of 10,000 CD/DVD disk drives each week and it takes 4 weeks to ship from a factory in Asia to the United States, then the pipeline inventory is 40,000. Although pipeline inventory is not physically available to the user or customer, it must be accounted for to plan production and future replenishment orders.

Inventory that has been ordered but not yet received and is in transit is called **pipeline inventory**.

Exhibit 12.1 Role of Inventory in the Value Chain

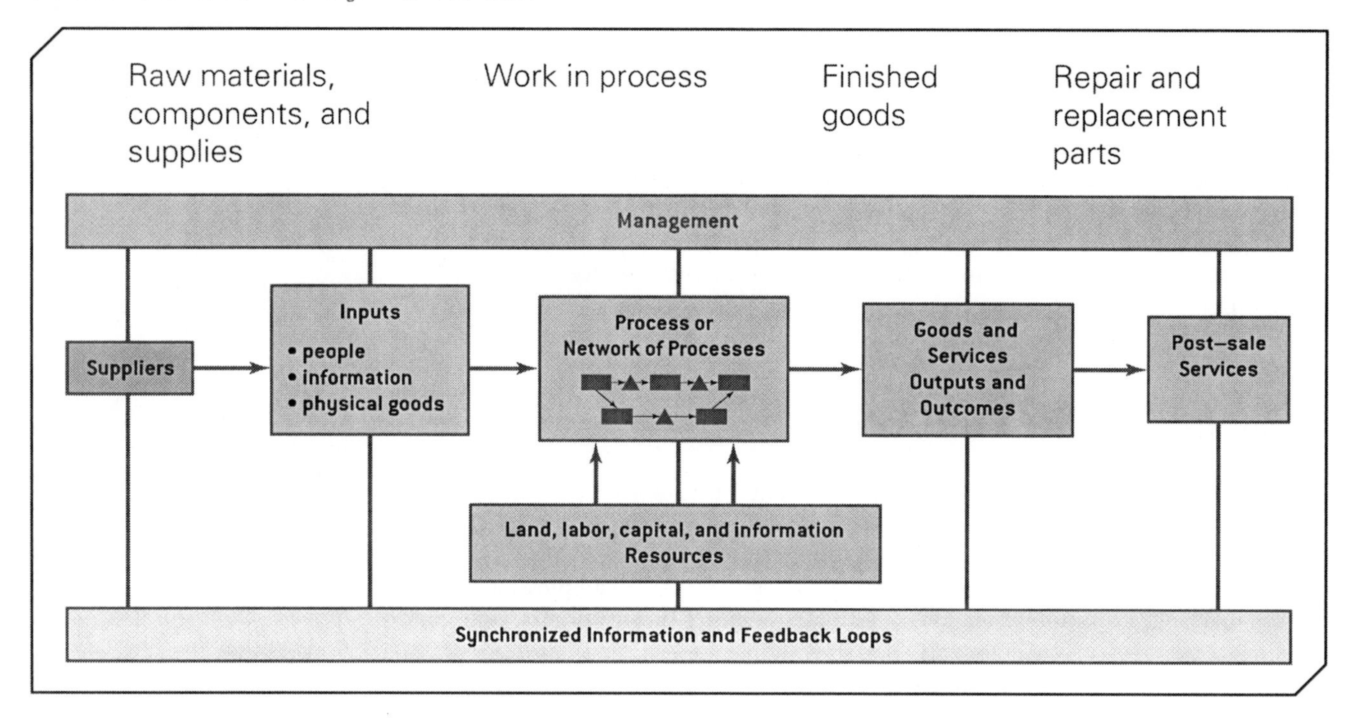

Many goods have seasonal demand cycles and the firm might not have capacity to produce enough on a regular basis, as we discussed in Chapter 10. For example, it might be impossible to produce enough lawn mowers during a short summer selling season because of limited production capacity. **Anticipation inventory** *is built up during the off-season to meet future estimated demand.* With perishable items, however, this cannot be done and firms must resort to other means to increase capacity.

Anticipation inventory *is built up during the off-season to meet future estimated demand.*

Manufacturers order raw materials or produce components on a regular basis to maintain a steady flow of inputs to support production. Similarly, wholesalers or retailers order finished goods on a regular basis to replenish their stock as customers purchase goods. For example, a retail store might have ten units of a certain type of high-definition TV in stock. It is probably not economical to order another each time one is purchased because of the high cost of shipping a single item and other administrative expenses that would be involved. Instead, the store might use some type of decision rule, such as "order seven units whenever the stock level drops to three." **Cycle inventory** *(also called* **order** *or* **lot size inventory***) is inventory that results from purchasing or producing in larger lots than are needed for immediate consumption or sale.* The term "cycle inventory" stems from the repetitive nature of the ordering or production process. As inventory is depleted and replenished, the inventory level cycles in an up-and-down pattern. Cycle inventory may take advantage of economies of scale from quantity discounts, volume shipments, or the allocation of manufacturing setup costs over many units.

Cycle inventory *(also called* **order** *or* **lot size inventory***) is inventory that results from purchasing or producing in larger lots than are needed for immediate consumption or sale.*

Customer demand is most often highly variable and uncertain. This makes it difficult for firms to plan on appropriate inventory levels. Lack of sufficient inventory can cause production lines to shut down or customers to become dissatisfied and purchase goods and services elsewhere. To reduce the risk associated with not having enough inventory, firms often maintain additional stock beyond their normal estimates. **Safety stock inventory** *is an additional amount that is kept over and above the average amount required to meet demand.*

Safety stock inventory *is an additional amount that is kept over and above the average amount required to meet demand.*

Inventory Management Decisions and Costs

Inventory managers deal with two fundamental decisions:

1. When to order items from a supplier or when to initiate production runs, if the firm makes its own items, and
2. How much to order or produce each time a supplier or production order is placed

Practical inventory management is all about making trade-offs among the costs associated with these decisions.

Inventory costs can be classified into four major categories:

1. ordering or setup costs
2. inventory-holding costs
3. shortage costs
4. unit cost of the stock-keeping units or SKUs

Ordering costs or **setup costs** *are incurred as a result of the work involved in placing purchase orders with suppliers or configuring tools, equipment, and machines within a factory to produce an item.* For purchased items, these costs stem from such activities as searching and selecting a supplier, order processing, processing receiving documents, and inspecting, unpacking and storing items that have been received. If an order (sometimes called a *shop order*) is placed within the factory, setup costs include paperwork, equipment setup and calibration, startup scrap, and the opportunity cost of producing no output while the setup is done. Order and setup costs do not depend on the number of items purchased or manufactured, but rather on the number of orders that are placed.

Ordering costs or **setup costs** *are incurred as a result of the work involved in placing purchase orders with suppliers or configuring tools, equipment, and machines within a factory to produce an item.*

Inventory-holding or **inventory-carrying costs** *are the expenses associated with carrying inventory.* Holding costs are typically defined as a percentage of the dollar value of inventory per unit of time (generally 1 year). They include costs associated with maintaining storage facilities, such as gas and electricity, taxes, insurance, and labor and equipment necessary to handle, move, and retrieve an SKU. Rent or leasing costs of warehouses, spoilage, and obsolescence might also be allocated to inventory-holding costs. However, from an accounting perspective, it is very difficult to precisely allocate such costs to an individual SKU. Essentially, holding costs reflect the opportunity cost associated with using the funds invested in inventory for alternative uses and investments. Thus, the cost of capital invested in inventory, which is the product of the value of a unit of inventory, the length of time held, and an interest rate associated with a dollar tied up in inventory, normally accounts for the largest component of inventory-holding costs. Because of the difficulty in arriving at a precise value, inventory-holding costs are often based on a combination of cost estimates derived from the accounting systems and managers' judgment. They usually range between 10 and 35 percent of the dollar value of the items.

Inventory-holding or **inventory-carrying costs** *are the expenses associated with carrying inventory.*

Note that large orders require that more inventory be carried, on average. As a result, holding costs are high but fewer orders are placed, so ordering costs are low. On the other hand, if frequent small orders are placed, ordering costs are high, but holding costs are low. These costs must be balanced to achieve a minimum-cost inventory policy.

Shortage or **stockout costs** *are costs associated with a SKU being unavailable when needed to meet demand.* These costs can reflect backorders, lost sales, or service interruptions for external customers or costs associated with interruptions to manufacturing and assembly lines for internal customers. Some examples of shortage costs are overnight shipping for emergency orders or compensation for overbooking on an airline or at a hotel. However, like holding costs, shortage costs

Shortage or **stockout costs** *are costs associated with a SKU being unavailable when needed to meet demand.*

are generally difficult to quantify precisely from an accounting perspective and often represent a judgmental "penalty cost" reflective of management policies and attitudes toward allowing shortages. Shortage costs are particularly important in stochastic demand models because uncertainty and variability often lead to shortages.

*The **unit cost** is the price paid for purchased goods or the internal cost of producing them.*

*The **unit cost** is the price paid for purchased goods or the internal cost of producing them.* In most situations, the unit cost is a "sunk cost" because the total purchase cost is not affected by the order quantity. However, the unit cost of SKUs is an important purchasing consideration when quantity discounts are offered; it may be more economical to purchase large quantities at a lower unit cost to reduce the other cost categories and thus minimize total costs. When items are produced internally, the firm must allocate costs using some accounting system to arrive at the "standard unit cost" or "cost of goods sold." Activity-based costing methods help organizations measure such costs accurately. The main challenge for operations managers is to use for all SKUs item costs that are based on consistent accounting principles and procedures.

© Getty Images/PhotoDisc

© Getty Images/PhotoDisc

*A **stock-keeping unit (SKU)** is a single item or asset stored at a particular location.*

Characteristics of Inventory Management Systems

A large variety of inventory situations are possible.[2] For instance, a self-serve gasoline station maintains an inventory of only a few grades of gasoline, whereas a large appliance store may carry several hundred different items. Demand for gasoline is relatively constant; the demand for air conditioners is highly seasonal and variable. If a gasoline station runs out of gas, a customer will go elsewhere. However, if an appliance store does not have a particular item in stock, the customer may be willing to order the item and wait for delivery or could go to another appliance store. Since the demand and inventory characteristics of the gasoline station and appliance store differ significantly, the proper control of inventories requires different approaches.

One of the first steps in analyzing an inventory problem should be to describe the essential characteristics of the environment and inventory system. This will be very useful when we develop quantitative models for making good inventory decisions. Although it is impossible to consider all characteristics here, we address the more important ones.

NUMBER OF ITEMS

Most firms maintain inventories for a large number of items, often at multiple locations. To manage and control these inventories, each item is often assigned a unique identifier, called a stock-keeping unit, or SKU. *A **stock-keeping unit (SKU)** is a single item or asset stored at a particular location.* For example, each color and size of a man's dress shirt at a department store and each type of milk (whole, 2 percent, skim) at a grocery story would be a different SKU. This helps the organization know exactly what is available at each location and facilitates ordering and accounting.

Many inventory control models determine the inventory policy for only one SKU at a time. For organizations with hundreds or thousands of distinct SKUs, applying such models might prove difficult because many variables such as demand forecasts, cost factors, and shipping times must be updated frequently. Maintaining data integrity on thousands or hundreds of thousands of SKUs can be difficult, and decisions that inventory models recommend are only as good as the quality of the input data. In such cases, SKUs are often aggregated, or partitioned, into groups with similar characteristics or dollar value. It is easier to design effective inventory systems for controlling a smaller number of groups of items.

With multiple items, there may be various constraints such as warehouse or budget limitations that affect inventory policy. Other interactions among products also must be considered. For example, certain groups of products tend to be demanded together, such as motor oil and oil filters.

NATURE OF DEMAND

Demand can be classified as independent or dependent, deterministic or stochastic, and dynamic or static. **Independent demand** *is demand for a SKU that is unrelated to the demand for other SKUs and needs to be forecast.* This type of demand is directly related to customer (market) demand. Inventories of finished goods such as toothpaste and electric fans have independent demand characteristics.

SKUs are said to have **dependent demand** *if their demand is directly related to the demand of other SKUs and can be calculated without needing to be forecast.* For example, a chandelier may consist of a frame and six lightbulb sockets. The demand for chandeliers is independent demand and would be forecast, while the demand for sockets is dependent on the demand for chandeliers. That is, for a forecast of chandeliers we can calculate the number of sockets required.

Demand is **deterministic** *when uncertainty is not included in its characterization.* In other words, we assume that demand is known in the future and not subject to random fluctuations. In many cases, demand is highly stable and this assumption is reasonable; in others, we might simply assume deterministic demand to make our models easier to solve and analyze, perhaps by using historical averages or statistical point estimates of forecasts. **Stochastic demand** *incorporates uncertainty by using probability distributions to characterize the nature of demand.* For example, suppose that the daily demand for milk is determined to be normally distributed with a mean of 100 and a standard deviation of 10. If we develop an inventory model assuming that the daily demand is fixed at 100 and ignore the variability of demand to simplify the analysis, we have a case of deterministic demand. If a model incorporates the actual probability distribution, then it is a stochastic demand model.

Demand, whether deterministic or stochastic, may also fluctuate or be stable over time. *Stable demand is usually called* **static demand**, *and demand that varies over time is referred to as* **dynamic demand**. For example, the demand for milk might range from 90 to 110 gallons per day, every day of the year. This is an example of static demand because the parameters of the probability distribution do not change over time. However, the demand for airline flights to Orlando, Florida will probably have different means and variances throughout the year, reaching peaks around Thanksgiving, Christmas, spring break, and in the summer, with lower demands at other times. This is an example of dynamic demand.

Independent demand *is demand for a SKU that is unrelated to the demand for other SKUs and needs to be forecast.*

SKUs are said to have **dependent demand** *if their demand is directly related to the demand of other SKUs and can be calculated without needing to be forecast.*

Demand is **deterministic** *when uncertainty is not included in its characterization.*

Stochastic demand *incorporates uncertainty by using probability distributions to characterize the nature of demand.*

Stable demand is usually called **static demand**, *and demand that varies over time is referred to as* **dynamic demand**.

NUMBER AND SIZE OF TIME PERIODS

In some cases, the selling season is relatively short, and any leftover items cannot be physically or economically stored until the next season. For example, Christmas trees that have been cut cannot be stored until the following year; similarly, other items, such as seasonal fashions, are sold at a loss simply because there is no storage space or it is uneconomical to keep them for the next year. In other situations, firms are concerned with planning inventory requirements over an extended number of time periods, for example, monthly over a year, in which inventory is held from one time period to the next. The type of approach used to analyze "single-period" inventory problems is different from the approach needed for the "multiple-period" inventory situation.

For multiple-period problems, we must also consider the size of the time period for planning purposes. For a manufacturer, this might be a month; for a grocery store, it might be a week. The size of the time period will affect the responsiveness of the inventory system in providing accurate and timely information to make decisions. An inventory system that updates information quarterly is clearly not as timely as one that does so daily.

LEAD TIME

*The **lead time** is the time between placement of an order and its receipt.*

*The **lead time** is the time between placement of an order and its receipt.* Lead time is affected by transportation carriers, buyer order frequency and size, and supplier's production schedules and may be deterministic or stochastic (in which case it may be described by some probability distribution). For example, rail, truck, and air transportation have different characteristics. The lead time for products shipped by air may be less variable than that for products shipped by rail. Also included in lead time is the time the supplier needs to process the order or to produce it if it is not readily available.

STOCKOUTS

*A **stockout** is the inability to satisfy the demand for an item.*

*A **back order** occurs when a customer is willing to wait for the item; a **lost sale** occurs when the customer is unwilling to wait and purchases the item elsewhere.*

*A **stockout** is the inability to satisfy the demand for an item.* When stockouts occur, the item is either back-ordered or a sale is lost. *A **back order** occurs when a customer is willing to wait for the item; a **lost sale** occurs when the customer is unwilling to wait and purchases the item elsewhere.* Back orders result in additional costs for transportation, expediting, or perhaps buying from another supplier at a higher price. A lost sale has an associated opportunity cost, which may include loss of goodwill and potential future revenue.

From a customer service viewpoint, firms never want to incur a stockout; indeed, in situations such as with blood inventories, stockouts can be tragic. In other situations, the economic consequences can be significant. For instance, the Grocery Manufacturers of America estimates that almost 40 percent of consumers would postpone a purchase or buy elsewhere when encountering a stockout, resulting in the loss of almost $200,000 in annual sales per average supermarket. More damaging is the fact that more than 3 percent of shoppers are frustrated enough to terminate the entire shopping trip and go to another store.[3] However, in many situations, back orders may be economically justified. For instance, high-value goods such as commercial jet planes or cruise ships are always made to order; no inventory is carried and a back-order state always exists. Back orders may also be planned to smooth demand on the work force because of limited capacity. When unplanned back orders occur, one of several reasons can usually be identified, including forecast inaccuracies on usage or lead time, unreliable supplier delivery, clerical errors, quality problems, insufficient safety stock, and transportation accidents. To guard against stockouts, safety stock inventory is often maintained.

PERISHABILITY

Many SKUs are perishable in that they either deteriorate or become obsolete after a certain period of time. Fruit, milk, cheese, medicines, and other consumables have a limited shelf life. Budweiser recognized the importance of freshness of beer, which remains fresh for 8 to 10 weeks, and printed a "Born On" date on every bottle. Service capacity is analogous to physical inventory in a service system. Basketball and concert tickets have no value after the game or performance, and hotel rooms cannot generate revenue if they are not rented. Other examples of perishable items are shown in Exhibit 12.2. Inventories of perishable goods must be handled differently from nonperishable goods. In many service businesses, this involves managing service capacity and is called "yield management" (see Chapter 13, "Resource Planning").

Stock-Keeping Unit (SKU)	Typical Useful Shelf Life
Milk	3 to 10 days
Newspapers	a few days
Blood	up to one year
Software	3 to 36 months due to obsolescence
Computer virus protection software	days or weeks
Human organs for transplantation	hours
Airline seat, hotel room, concert seats, sporting event seats, and so on	Time of availability until time of event

Exhibit 12.2
Examples of Perishable SKUs

INVENTORY MANAGEMENT INFRASTRUCTURE

Learning Objective
To learn methods for prioritizing the importance of inventory items, maintaining accurate inventory information, and using technology for inventory management.

Inventory management systems define the operating practices that allow for the timely ordering and delivery of the correct materials to support production or customer service objectives. The principal decisions that inventory managers must make involve how much to order and when to place orders. When purchasing from a supplier, we usually call the quantity purchased the *order quantity*. When manufacturing components within a factory, we use the term *lot size*. Later in this chapter, we will describe the logic of the two basic types of inventory management systems—a fixed quantity system (FQS), in which an order for a fixed amount is placed as necessary, and a fixed period system (FPS), in which orders are placed at fixed intervals of time. Each is useful in different inventory management situations, and various quantitative models are used to help define the best operating policies. We will also examine some special inventory management situations.

No matter what type of system or model is used, operations managers must develop a supportive infrastructure for managing inventory. Operations managers face three key issues:

1. *Setting priorities for managing SKUs*—Not all SKUs need to be managed in the same fashion. ABC analysis provides a convenient approach for prioritizing inventory items.
2. *Ensuring that inventory-related data are accurate and reliable*—Cycle counting is a popular approach for doing this.
3. *Integrating technology to support inventory management.*

ABC Inventory Analysis

One useful method for defining inventory value is ABC analysis. It is an application of the *Pareto principle*, named after an Italian economist who studied the distribution of wealth in Milan during the 1800s. He found that a "vital few" controlled a high percentage of the wealth. ABC analysis consists of categorizing inventory items or SKUs into three groups according to their total annual dollar usage:

1. "A" items account for a large dollar value but a relatively small percentage of total items.
2. "C" items account for a small dollar value but a large percentage of total items.
3. "B" items are between A and C.

Typically, A items comprise 60 to 80 percent of the total dollar usage but only 10 to 30 percent of the items, whereas C items account for 5 to 15 percent of the total dollar value and about 50 percent of the items. There is no specific rule on where to make the division between A, B, and C items; the percentages used here simply serve as a guideline. Total dollar usage or value is computed by multiplying item usage (volume) times the item's dollar value (unit cost). Therefore, an A item could have a low volume but high unit cost, or a high volume and low unit cost.

An example of using ABC analysis follows. Consider the data for 20 inventoried items of a small company shown in the spreadsheet in Exhibit 12.3. The projected annual dollar usage column is found by multiplying the annual projected usage based on forecasts (in units) by the unit cost. We can sort these data easily in Microsoft Excel, where we have listed the cumulative percentage of items, cumulative dollar usage, and cumulative percent of total dollar usage. Analysis of Exhibit 12.4 indicates that about 70 percent of the total dollar usage is accounted for by the first five items, that is, only 25 percent of the items. In addition, the lowest 50 percent of the items account for only about 5 percent of the total dollar usage. Exhibit 12.5 shows a simple histogram of the ABC analysis classification scheme for this set of data.

ABC analysis gives managers useful information to identify the best methods to control each category of inventory. Class A items represent a substantial inventory investment and typically have limited availability. In many cases, they are single-sourced and thus need close control to reduce uncertainties in supply. This involves complete, accurate record keeping, continuous monitoring of inventory

Exhibit 12.3
Usage-Cost Data for 20 Inventoried Items

	A	B	C	D
1	ABC Inventory Analysis			
2				
3		Projected		Projected
4	Item	Annual		Annual
5	Number	Usage	Unit Cost	Dollar Usage
6	1	15,000	$5.00	$75,000
7	2	6,450	$20.00	$129,000
8	3	5,000	$45.00	$225,000
9	4	200	$12.50	$2,500
10	5	20,000	$35.00	$700,000
11	6	84	$250.00	$21,000
12	7	800	$80.00	$64,000
13	8	300	$5.00	$1,500
14	9	10,000	$35.00	$350,000
15	10	2,000	$65.00	$130,000
16	11	5,000	$25.00	$125,000
17	12	3,250	$125.00	$406,250
18	13	9,000	$0.50	$4,500
19	14	2,900	$10.00	$29,000
20	15	800	$15.00	$12,000
21	16	675	$200.00	$135,000
22	17	1,470	$100.00	$147,000
23	18	8,200	$15.00	$123,000
24	19	1,250	$0.16	$200
25	20	2,500	$0.20	$500

Exhibit 12.4 ABC Analysis Calculations

	A	B	C	D	E	F	G	H
28			Projected		Projected	Cumulative	Cumulative	Cumulative
29		Number	Usage	Unit Cost	Dollar Usage	Dollar	Percent	Percent
30	Rank	Item	Annual		Annual	Usage	of Total	of Items
31	1	5	20,000	$35.00	$700,000	$700,000	26.12%	5%
32	2	12	3,250	$125.00	$406,250	$1,106,250	41.27%	10%
33	3	9	10,000	$35.00	$350,000	$1,456,250	54.33%	15%
34	4	3	5,000	$45.00	$225,000	$1,681,250	62.72%	20%
35	5	17	1,470	$100.00	$147,000	$1,828,250	68.21%	25%
36	6	16	675	$200.00	$135,000	$1,963,250	73.24%	30%
37	7	10	2,000	$65.00	$130,000	$2,093,250	78.09%	35%
38	8	2	6,450	$20.00	$129,000	$2,222,250	82.91%	40%
39	9	11	5,000	$25.00	$125,000	$2,347,250	87.57%	45%
40	10	18	8,200	$15.00	$123,000	$2,470,250	92.16%	50%
41	11	1	15,000	$5.00	$75,000	$2,545,250	94.96%	55%
42	12	7	800	$80.00	$64,000	$2,609,250	97.34%	60%
43	13	14	2,900	$10.00	$29,000	$2,638,250	98.43%	65%
44	14	6	84	$250.00	$21,000	$2,659,250	99.21%	70%
45	15	15	800	$15.00	$12,000	$2,671,250	99.66%	75%
46	16	13	9,000	$0.50	$4,500	$2,675,750	99.82%	80%
47	17	4	200	$12.50	$2,500	$2,678,250	99.92%	85%
48	18	8	300	$5.00	$1,500	$2,679,750	99.97%	90%
49	19	20	2,500	$0.20	$500	$2,680,250	99.99%	95%
50	20	19	1,250	$0.16	$200	$2,680,450	100.00%	100%

levels, frequent accuracy counts, and maximum attention to order sizes and frequency of ordering. Because of these items' large cost, small lot sizes and frequent deliveries from suppliers are common and result in very short lead times, which require close cooperation between the buyer and supplier and a high level of quality. A items require close control by operations managers.

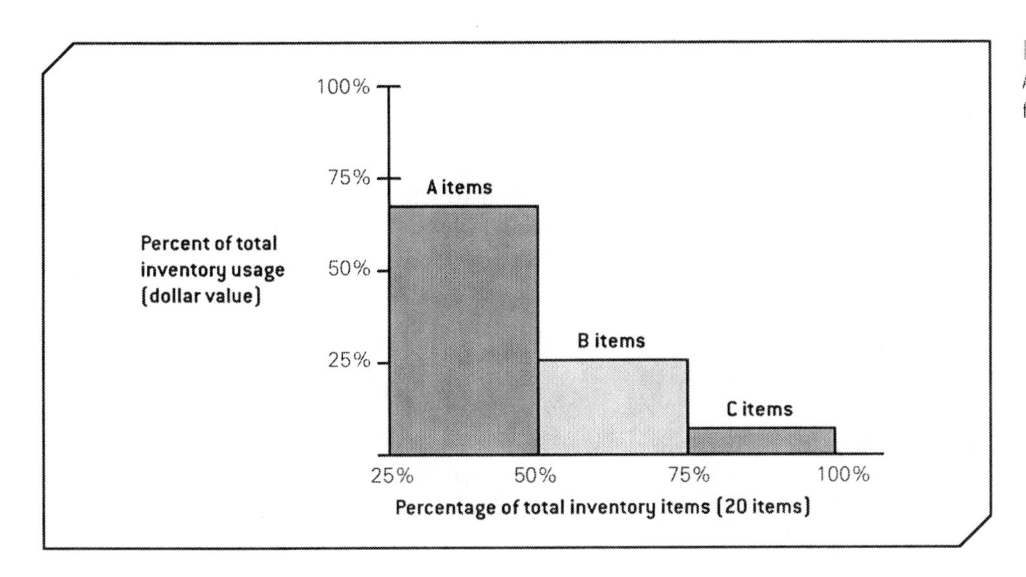

Exhibit 12.5
ABC Histogram for the Results from Exhibit 12.4

Class C items need not be as closely controlled and can be managed using automated computer systems. Large quantities of these items might be ordered to take advantage of quantity or transportation discounts, and inventory levels might simply be checked periodically without maintaining any formal records. Easy to procure from multiple suppliers, they have short lead times.

Class B items are in the middle. In many cases, these items are ordered very infrequently and consist mainly of service parts for older products still in use. Their availability may be limited, and thus long lead times can be expected. Orders are usually handled individually, which necessitates more control than is needed for C items, but they are not as critical as those for A items.

ABC analysis can be used in service organizations but may require some modifications. For example, hospitals use ABC analysis but may use more than three inventory categories. A hospital might use five categories (A, B, C, D, and E), with categories A to D defined by total dollar value. Category E, however, might be defined as a "critical SKU category" that is vital to patients' health. The SKUs might be a simple plastic clip or a tracheotomy surgical kit. Critical SKUs need very careful control to ensure their availability. Services such as a home mortgage warehouse would use ABC analysis to help control inventory and structure mortgage portfolios.

Cycle Counting

A sophisticated, computerized inventory system is worthless if it is inaccurate. Inventory systems tend to accumulate errors over time because of errors in counting and recording the amount of goods received, misidentification of the goods, theft, and so on. These errors arise from poor design of forms, untrained personnel, carelessness, or poor control. Therefore, some method of checking the actual physical inventory is necessary. One approach is to shut down the plant or warehouse periodically and count the inventory. The disadvantages of this method are that productive time is lost, and overtime premiums are usually required to accomplish the task during off-hours.

Cycle counting *is a system for repetitive physical counting of inventory throughout the year.*

An alternative to closing for inventory is cycle counting. **Cycle counting** *is a system for repetitive physical counting of inventory throughout the year.* It allows scheduling of physical counts to ensure that all parts are counted and that higher-value parts (A items) are counted more frequently than lower-value parts (B and C items). With cycle counting, inventory is counted when orders are placed and received, when the inventory record shows a zero or negative (obviously an error) balance, when the last item is removed from stock, or on a periodic basis.

There are several benefits to cycle counting. Errors can be detected on a more timely basis, and causes can be investigated and corrected. Annual physical inventory counts are eliminated, and the loss of productive time is minimized. A high level of inventory accuracy can be achieved on a continuous basis, and the firm can have a correct statement of assets throughout the year. Also, the specialized teams of cycle counters that are usually established for this become efficient in obtaining good counts, reconciling differences, and finding solutions to system errors.

The ABC classification is usually used to determine the frequency of cycle counting. Clearly, errors are more critical for A items, since their values are higher. FMC Corporation uses cycle counting this way.

Technology and Inventory Management

Modern technology has revolutionized inventory control and management and has been a major part of supply chain design activities. As described in previous chapters, Internet-based integrated operating systems connect customers and suppliers

OM SPOTLIGHT

FMC Corporation[4]

Cycle counting at FMC Corporation is based on ABC analysis, which resulted in the following breakdown.

Class	Number of Items/Percent		Value/Percent	
A	2,973	8%	$41,704,252	87%
B	4,155	12%	$4,292,290	9%
C	28,687	80%	$1,853,364	4%

The A items were subdivided into two classes: regular A items and super A items. Super A items have unit costs of $1,000 or greater. Management policy stated that super A items be counted every month, regular A items every 2 months, B items every 4 months, and C items once a year. The following schedule was established.

Class	Number of Items	Counts per Year	Work Days Between Counts	Days Available	Daily Counts
Super A	1,173	12	20	15	*
A	1,800	6	40	30	60
B	4,155	3	80	60	70
C	28,687	1	240	180	160

*See explanation.

Super A items are each counted once per month, resulting in (1,173)(12) = 14,076 counts per year. Average daily counts for the other classes of items are computed by dividing the number of items by the days available for counting (based on a 20-day work month). This all amounts to a total of 66,276 annual counts, or an average of 5,500 per month. The FMC warehouse in Bowling Green, Kentucky, where this approach is used, has achieved an inventory accuracy of 99 percent due to the cycle counting program.

on a real-time basis. Customer demand at point-of-sale terminals is communicated rapidly through the value chain to distribution facilities and factories, allowing for faster customer response and replenishment of inventory. Newer technologies such as wireless communication systems and radio frequency identification (RFID) chips are improving the efficiency and effectiveness of inventory management in supply chains.

Howmet Castings in Darien, Connecticut, for example, produces metal casting for aircraft engines and parts for wings, serving customers such as Boeing, General Electric, and Rolls-Royce. In the mid-1990s, inventories and processing times doubled as the company carried as much as $10 million of safety stock inventory to guard against late deliveries from suppliers. Today, Howmet Castings uses a software system that communicates both with original equipment manufacturers such as Boeing as well as all of its suppliers in its supply chain. The system can extract purchase order and part-type information and automatically route it to suppliers. Better communication allows the company to schedule its production and supplier orders more efficiently, thus maintaining fewer numbers of parts. Howmet estimates it gets about 80 percent of the system benefits while their suppliers realize the remaining 20 percent. The director of operations noted, ". . . excess inventory is waste. Now, I have reduced safety stock inventory to $6 million."[5] To effectively implement such a system, data formats, terminology, and databases must be standardized and maintained on master data files for access by appropriate players in the supply chain. Such systems improve contract negotiations, bulk buying, engineering design, and information sharing for daily operating decisions.

Telematic diagnostic and monitoring systems *are two-way wireless communication capabilities between equipment and its external environment.*

Telematic diagnostic and monitoring systems *are two-way wireless communication capabilities between equipment and its external environment.* Small computer chips and software are embedded in the equipment, report the equipment's location and usage, and try to recognize when something is about to go wrong. Such information is transmitted back to a company's computer and steps can be taken to perform preventive maintenance on the equipment. For example, service alerts can be sent, maintenance can be scheduled, and replacement parts can be ordered. Automobiles, jet engines, appliances, computers, and power plant equipment are just a few examples of where telematic systems are being developed.

Bar codes were one of the earliest forms of technology that dramatically improved the management and control of inventory (see, for example, OM Spotlight: Information Technology at Nissan). More recently, tiny radio frequency identification (RFID) chips embedded in packaging or products allow scanners to track SKUs as they move throughout the store.[6] RFID chips help companies locate items in stockrooms and identify where they should be placed in the store. Inventory on the shelves can easily be tracked to trigger replenishment orders. Recalled or expired products can be identified and pulled from the store before a customer can buy them, and returned items can be identified by original purchase location and date, and whether they were stolen.

Many major firms, such as Procter and Gamble and Gillette, support this technology. German retailer Metro AG will use radio frequency identification technology (RFID) to replace bar codes in its 250 stores and 10 central warehouses.[7] Metro Ag suppliers will attach RFID tags to pallets and cases, and these items will be detected by wireless readers as they move in the warehouses and stores. Metro

OM SPOTLIGHT

Information Technology at Nissan[8]

Nissan's plant in Sunderland, England produces more than 300,000 vehicles each year. When Nissan wanted to produce a third vehicle model, it was not able to add any capacity in the plant. Its current inventory system tracked inventory manually. Truck drivers were responsible for making a physical check of inventory before leaving the supplier. The system worked well and production downtime due to lack of inventory, extremely expensive for an automobile company, was never a problem. When Nissan decided to add the third line, however, the number of parts was doubled, and with the lack of capacity, Nissan knew it had to reduce its inventory. The manual system was no longer feasible; the solution was to implement a mobile data-gathering and communication system to track inventory in real time using bar code technology. This system ensures that accurate and timely parts information is available on demand and enables operations management to easily monitor job progress and cost efficiencies. When drivers check their loads at the suppliers, they scan the bar code labels of all parts. If there are any discrepancies, drivers can address the problem with the suppliers immediately. When they return to the bar code terminal at the plant, inventory information is updated immediately to a central database. All parts can be pinpointed within seconds. One benefit that this system provided to Nissan was the virtual elimination of inventory variances—the difference between what Nissan expects to get and what it actually receives—because it eliminated human error associated with the manual process.

says the system will reduce inventory by 20 percent and cut down on lost, stolen, or destroyed products. If this pilot program works, the next step is instantaneous checkout where wireless readers can read dozens of RFID tags as customers leave the store and automatically charge their credit cards or store accounts. Intel, SAP, and IBM are helping Metro AG with this initiative to work out the bugs in the wireless inventory tracking system.

One interesting application has been developed by CVS, a Rhode Island-based pharmacy chain, which is testing RFID technology to inform them when a customer has not picked up a prescription medicine. By merging RFID technology with Internet capabilities and other planning and inventory management software, managers will be able to better manage the entire value chain. Although current technology limits the range that RFID chips can transmit information, one can imagine a future scenario in which SKUs can be tracked throughout the entire value chain. Research is being conducted on home scanners that will alert customers when orange juice cartons are low and medicine is about to expire. However, this also brings up many legal and privacy issues; a watchdog organization called the Electronic Privacy Information Center advocates that retailers be required by law to disable the chips as customers leave the store.

FIXED QUANTITY SYSTEMS

Learning Objective
To understand a class of inventory management systems for monitoring and controlling independent demand using fixed order quantities for replenishing inventory levels.

In a **fixed quantity system (FQS)**, *the order quantity or lot size is fixed; that is, the same amount, Q, is ordered every time.* The order quantity might be chosen for convenience—a truck load, pallet load, or a prepackaged box of bolts. It might also be chosen based on the economics of ordering and holding inventory; we will develop some quantitative models later in this chapter. A very simple version of a FQS that is often used for small parts and in retail stores is called the *two-bin system*. Consider a supply of small parts kept in a bin with a second (full) bin in reserve. When the first bin is empty, a resupply order for another full bin is placed and the second bin is used. The second bin usually contains more than enough material to last until the new order is received. This system is easily implemented by placing a card at the bottom of the bin, which is turned in when the last item is taken. A variation of this system is often used in hardware stores or bookstores. You often see reorder forms in the form of small cards hanging on hooks for screws, bolts, and so on or inserted among the last few books on the shelf. When the card is reached, it is an indication to replenish the stock.

In a **fixed quantity system (FQS)**, *the order quantity or lot size is fixed; that is, the same amount, Q, is ordered every time.*

FQSs are used extensively in the retail industry. For example, most department stores have cash registers that are tied into a computer system. When the clerk enters the SKU number, the computer recognizes that the item is sold, recalculates the inventory position, and determines whether a purchase order should be initiated to replenish the stock. If computers are not used in such systems, some form of manual system is necessary for monitoring daily usage. This requires substantial clerical effort and commitment by the users to fill out the proper forms when items are used and is often a source of errors, so it is not recommended.

To better understand the issues associated with managing inventory using fixed quantity systems, examine the historical sales data for a product shown in Exhibit 12.6. The demand is relatively stable; approximately 10 units per day with a daily average range of 9.57 to 10.71 units. How might a manager apply a FQS system to make replenishment decisions?

Let us suppose that a fixed quantity of 70 units (about 1 week's demand) is ordered each time and that the first order arrives at the beginning of Monday on the first week. We can simulate the operation of this system on a day-to-day basis by monitoring the inventory level at the start and end of each day. We will assume

Exhibit 12.6 Historical Sales Data with Stable Demand Rate

	Week 1	Week 2	Week 3	Week 4	Week 5	Week 6	Week 7	Week 8	Week 9	Week 10
Monday	10	13	9	11	11	10	9	9	11	9
Tuesday	11	9	9	10	11	10	10	11	11	8
Wednesday	13	9	9	9	9	11	10	9	11	10
Thursday	10	10	11	10	10	11	10	8	12	10
Friday	9	10	9	10	11	9	10	9	11	10
Saturday	9	9	10	11	10	11	11	11	11	10
Sunday	9	10	11	10	8	10	9	11	8	10
Weekly Total	71	70	68	71	70	72	69	68	75	67
Daily Average	10.14	10.00	9.71	10.14	10.00	10.29	9.86	9.71	10.71	9.57
Overall Average	10.014									

that any orders are placed at the end of a day and that any receipts arrive at the beginning of a day. The first 7 days are shown in Exhibit 12.7. Because of the slight variability in the demand, we would be one unit short at the end of the week, but suppose this can be tolerated. However, if an order is not received by the next day, the firm would continue to run short, which would probably be undesirable. Therefore, the manager must plan to receive a new shipment of 70 units on the next day (Monday of Week 2).

This brings up the question of when to place the order. Unless the manager can call a supplier across town on Sunday afternoon and ensure delivery by the next morning, the manager must plan ahead and consider the lead time required to make the delivery. Suppose that the lead time is 2 days. To ensure arrival by the beginning of Day 8, the manager must order by the end of Day 5. Note that when the demand rate is essentially constant (deterministic) as it is here, managing this system is easy and its performance is highly predictable. With a stable demand of about 70 units per week, the manager can order every Friday, have delivery on Monday morning, and ensure that nearly all demand can be met.

Exhibit 12.8 shows a chart of the daily ending inventory levels over the 10-week period, obtained by extending the previous analysis (which you can easily do on a spreadsheet). You can see that when the inventory is replenished, the ending inventory on the previous day is always close to zero because of the relatively stable demand pattern.

Impact of Demand Variability

Now let us examine what happens when demand is highly variable, as shown in Exhibit 12.9. Although the average daily demand is still about 10, the variability within and between weeks is much higher than in the first example. In this example,

Exhibit 12.7
Simulation of One Order Cycle for a FQS with $Q = 70$

Day	Order Receipt	Beginning Inventory	Demand	Ending Inventory
1	70	70	10	60
2		60	11	49
3		49	13	36
4		36	10	26
5		26	9	17
6		17	9	8
7		8	9	−1

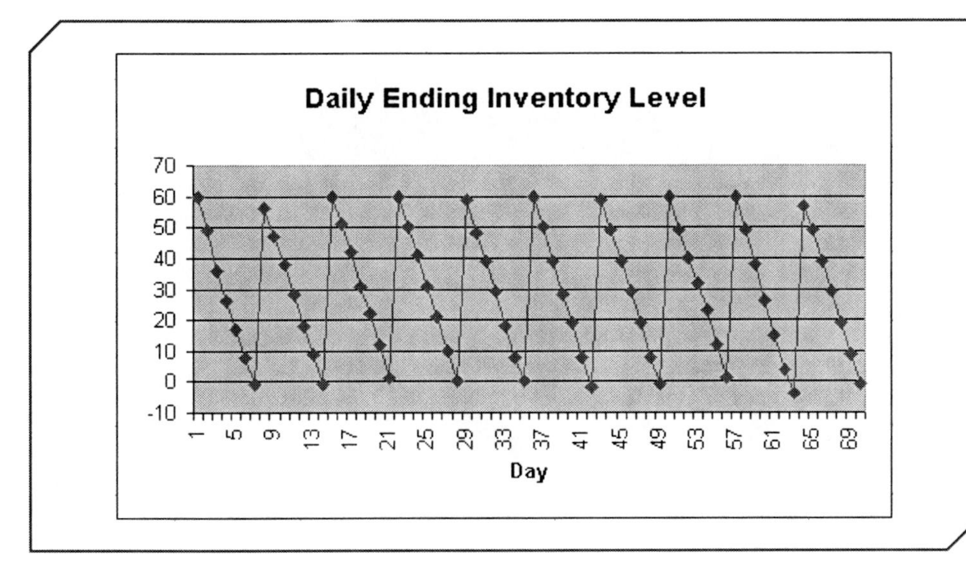

Exhibit 12.8 Simulation Chart of Ending Inventory Levels with $Q = 70$

the daily average demand ranges from 6.86 to 12.00 units. Ideally, it would be nice to plan the order so it arrives just when the inventory will reach zero, but this generally cannot be done when demand is highly variable. To see this, consider applying the same ordering policy of 70 units to arrive every Monday. Exhibit 12.10 shows the inventory pattern over the first 6 weeks, and Exhibit 12.11 shows a chart of the ending inventory over the full 10 weeks. We see that high levels of shortages occur during many weeks such as −6 on Day 6 and −11 on Day 14. This chart suggests that the inventory manager must order differently if shortages are to be avoided.

As this example shows, when demand is variable, orders cannot be placed at fixed intervals based only on average demand rates. A more appropriate way to manage a FQS is to continuously monitor the inventory level and place orders when the level reaches some "critical" value. The process of triggering an order is based on the inventory position. **Inventory position (IP)** *is defined as the on-hand quantity (OH) plus any orders placed but that have not arrived (called scheduled receipts, SR), minus any backorders (BO), or*

$$IP = OH + SR - BO \quad (12.1)$$

When the inventory position falls at or below a certain value, r, called the *reorder point*, a new order is placed.

Inventory position (IP) *is defined as the on-hand quantity (OH) plus any orders placed but that have not arrived (called scheduled receipts, SR), minus any backorders (BO).*

Exhibit 12.9 Historical Sales Data with Variable Demand

	Week 1	Week 2	Week 3	Week 4	Week 5	Week 6	Week 7	Week 8	Week 9	Week 10
Monday	10	8	8	0	8	2	11	12	11	5
Tuesday	8	5	5	10	10	6	16	2	13	12
Wednesday	20	8	17	7	11	11	13	17	19	17
Thursday	16	16	14	10	12	3	13	15	11	7
Friday	8	7	3	4	5	15	9	14	13	15
Saturday	14	8	9	13	11	12	9	6	8	10
Sunday	6	17	7	4	7	13	13	17	5	0
Weekly Total	82	69	63	48	64	62	84	83	80	66
Daily Average	11.71	9.86	9.00	6.86	9.14	8.86	12.00	11.86	11.43	9.43
Overall Average	10.01									

Exhibit 12.10 Simulation Over 6 Weeks with $Q = 70$

Day	Order Receipt	Beginning Inventory	Demand	Ending Inventory	Day	Order Receipt	Beginning Inventory	Demand	Ending Inventory
1	70	70	10	60	22	70	66	0	61
2		60	8	52	23		61	10	49
3		52	20	32	24		49	7	32
4		32	16	16	25		32	10	25
5		16	8	8	26		25	4	10
6		8	14	−6	27		10	13	0
7		−6	6	−12	28		0	4	0
8	70	58	8	50	29	70	70	8	62
9		50	5	45	30		62	10	52
10		45	8	37	31		52	11	41
11		37	16	21	32		41	12	29
12		21	7	14	33		29	5	24
13		14	8	6	34		24	11	13
14		6	17	−11	35		13	7	6
15	70	59	8	51	36	70	76	2	74
16		51	5	46	37		74	6	68
17		46	17	29	38		68	11	57
18		29	14	15	39		57	3	54
19		15	3	12	40		54	15	39
20		12	9	3	41		39	12	27
21		3	7	−4	42		27	13	14

Why not base the reordering decision on the physical inventory level, that is, just the on-hand quantity, instead of a more complex calculation? The answer is simple. When an order is placed but has not been received, the physical stock level will continue to fall below the reorder point before the order arrives. If the ordering process is automated, the computer logic will continue to place many unnecessary orders simply because it will see the stock level being less than r, even though the original order will soon arrive and replenish the stock. By including scheduled receipts, the inventory position will be larger than the reorder point, thus preventing duplicate orders. Once the order arrives and no scheduled receipts are outstanding, then the inventory position is the same as the physical inventory. Back

Exhibit 12.11
Simulation Chart of Ending Inventory Levels for Variable Demand Case with $Q = 70$

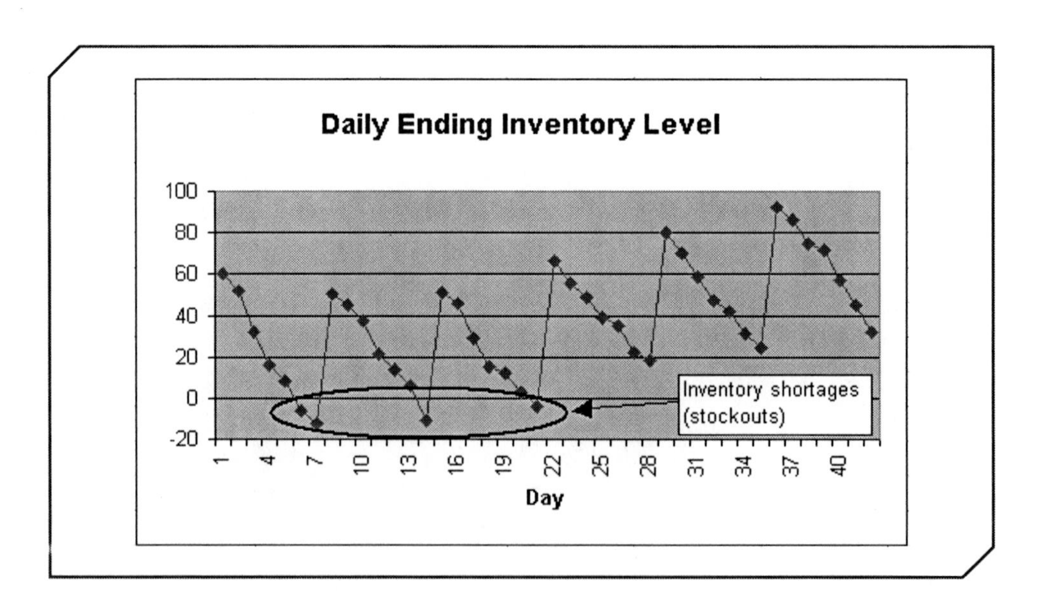

orders are included in the inventory position calculation because these items have already been sold and are reserved for customers as soon as the order arrives.

Choosing the Reorder Point

The choice of the reorder point depends on the lead time and the nature of demand. One approach to choosing the reorder point is to use the *average demand during the lead time* (μ_L). If d is the average demand per unit of time (day, week, and so on), and L is the lead time expressed in the same units of time, then the average demand during the lead time is calculated as follows:

$$r = \mu_L = d \times L \tag{12.2}$$

(From a practical perspective, it is easier to work with daily data rather than annual data, particularly if a firm does not operate 7 days per week.)

For example, in the data in Exhibit 12.9, we see that the average daily demand is about 10. Therefore, if the lead time is 2 days, the average lead time demand is $\mu_L = (10)(2) = 20$. However, if we order whenever the inventory position falls to 20 or less, we run a substantial risk of running out of stock before the next shipment arrives because of the high variability in the demand. In such cases, we need to order more and carry additional safety stock inventory; this will be addressed later in the chapter. (A more complicated situation occurs when the lead time also varies; for example, if the supplier is out of stock or a shipping delay occurs, then the customer might run out of stock. However, for simplicity, we will assume that lead times are constant.)

We can increase the level of safety stock inventory by increasing the reorder point. Suppose that instead of using the average lead time demand of 20, we increase the reorder point arbitrarily to 50 units. Exhibit 12.12 shows a portion (19 days) of a simulation of our example; that is, whenever the ending inventory is 50 or less, a fixed order for 70 units is placed to arrive after a 2-day lead time. Carefully observe how the inventory position is calculated. For instance, on Day 3, the ending inventory is 32, which is below the reorder point of 50. An order is placed, so the inventory position is

$$\text{IP} = \text{OH} + \text{SR} - \text{BO} = 32 + 70 - 0 = 102$$

Exhibit 12.12
Simulation of a Fixed Quantity System with $Q = 70$ and $r = 50$

Day	Order Receipt	Beginning Inventory	Demand	Ending Inventory	Order Placed?	Inventory Position
1	0	70	10	60		60
2	0	60	8	52		52
3	0	52	20	32	Yes	102
4	0	32	16	16		86
5	0	16	8	8		78
6	70	78	14	64		64
7	0	64	6	58		58
8	0	58	8	50	Yes	120
9	0	50	5	45		115
10	0	45	8	37		107
11	70	107	16	91		91
12	0	91	7	84		84
13	0	84	8	76		76
14	0	76	17	59		59
15	0	59	8	51		51
16	0	51	5	46	Yes	116
17	0	46	17	29		99
18	0	29	14	15		85
19	70	85	3	82		82

Notice also that the time between order placement varies. This did not happen in the first example because the daily demand was relatively constant. If we continue this simulation for the full 70-day period (instead of the 19 days in Exhibit 12.12), we obtain the results shown in Exhibit 12.13 for this ordering policy. We see that by using a larger reorder point than the average lead-time demand results in only one week where a stockout occurs. However, this occurs at the expense of carrying a higher average ending inventory.

How does the order quantity affect inventory performance? Look back at the simulation of the example in Exhibit 12.12 using a 70-unit order quantity. The average ending inventory over this first week is (60 + 52 + 32 + 16 + 8 + 64 + 58)/7 = 41.43, or about 41 units. Suppose we order 100 units instead of 70. We would only have to order every 10 days instead of every 7, but the average ending inventory over the first week increases to about 66 units. This is shown in Exhibit 12.14. We have reduced the frequency of orders at the expense of increasing the average inventory. Similarly, a smaller order quantity will increase the frequency of ordering but decrease the average inventory (construct a similar table for $Q = 30$). Holding inventory costs money, but so does ordering and shipping. Thus, inventory managers face a critical challenge in trying to balance these costs. Quantitative models, which we introduce shortly, can help in these decisions.

Summary of Fixed Quantity Systems

A summary of fixed quantity systems is given in Exhibit 12.15. Exhibits 12.16 and 12.17 contrast the performance of FQS when demand is relatively stable and highly variable. The dark lines in these exhibits track the actual inventory levels. In Exhibit 12.16, we see that the time between orders (TBO) is also constant in the deterministic case, and therefore, the ordering cycle repeats itself exactly. Here, the TBO is constant because there is no uncertainty and average demand is assumed to be constant and continuous. Recall from our previous discussion that the reorder point should be based on the inventory position (the light line), not the physical inventory level.

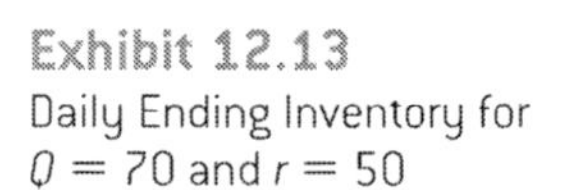
Exhibit 12.13
Daily Ending Inventory for $Q = 70$ and $r = 50$

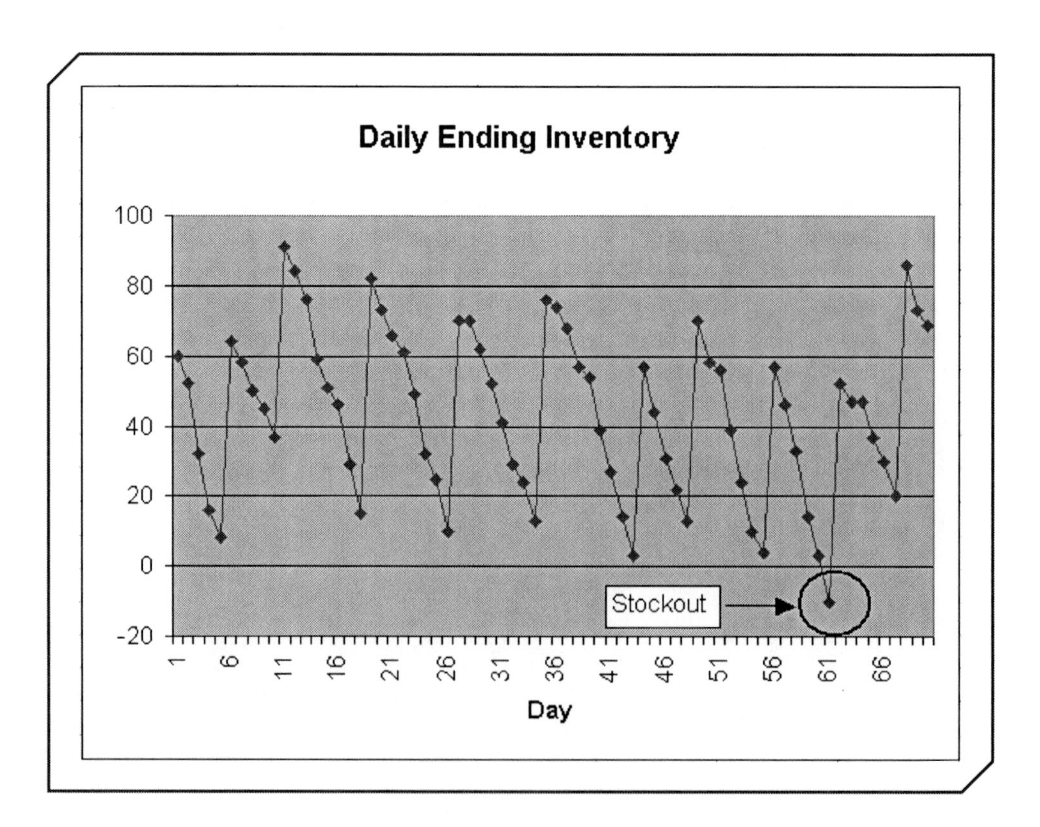

Day	Order Receipt	Beginning Inventory	Demand	Ending Inventory
1	100	100	10	90
2		90	11	79
3		79	13	66
4		66	10	56
5		56	9	47
6		47	9	38
7		38	9	29
8		29	13	16
9		16	9	7
10		7	9	−2
11	100	98	10	88
12		88	10	78
13		78	9	69
14		69	10	59

Exhibit 12.14
Simulation of a Fixed Quantity System with $Q = 100$

Managerial Decisions	Order Quantity (Q) and Reorder Point (r)
Ordering decision rule	A new order is triggered whenever the inventory position for the item drops to or past the reorder point. The size of each order is Q units.
Key characteristics	The order quantity Q is always fixed. The time between orders (TBO) is constant when the demand rate is stable. The time between orders (TBO) can vary when demand is variable.

Exhibit 12.15
Summary of Fixed Quantity System (FQS)

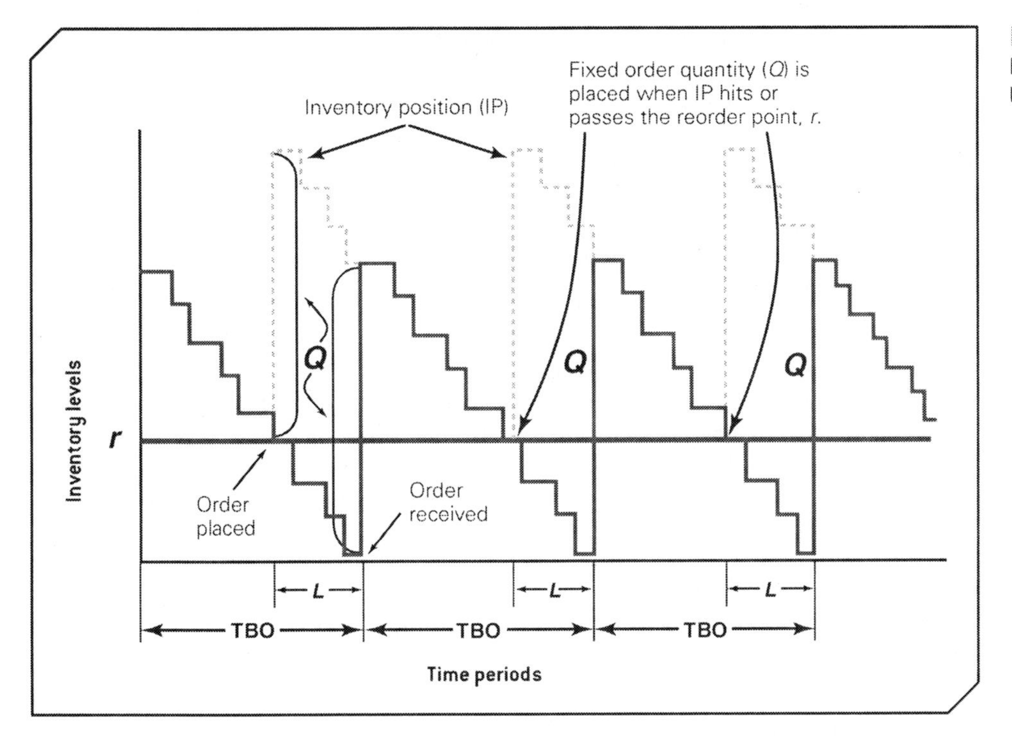

Exhibit 12.16
Fixed Quantity System (FQS) Under Stable Demand

In Exhibit 12.16 you can see that the inventory position jumps by Q when the order is placed. With the highly variable demand rate, the TBO varies while Q is constant.

Exhibit 12.17
Fixed Quantity System (FQS) with Highly Variable Demand

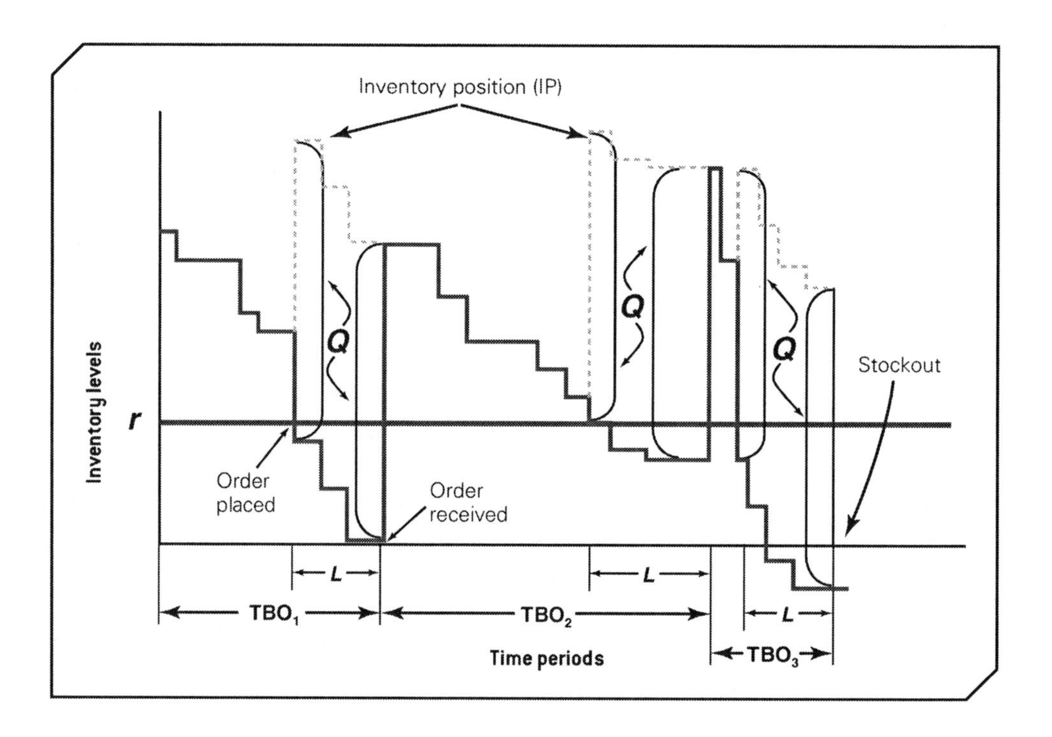

Optimal FQS Policies for Deterministic Demand: The EOQ Model

In this section, we will develop a quantitative model to find the best order quantity when demand is deterministic. Before doing so, let us gain a better understanding of the various costs that must be considered in such a model.

From this discussion of inventory costs, you may wonder how inventory models can ever be used effectively, since the important inventory costs are somewhat difficult to measure. Fortunately, inventory models are generally quite robust. That is, even if the costs used are merely good approximations, there is generally little variation in the resulting solution recommended by the inventory model. Consequently, even the simplest models have been used successfully in reducing inventory costs in many companies.

The **Economic Order Quantity** *(EOQ) model is a classic economic model developed in the early 1900s that minimizes the total cost, which is the sum of the inventory-holding cost and the ordering cost.*

The **Economic Order Quantity (EOQ)** *model is a classic economic model developed in the early 1900s that minimizes the total cost, which is the sum of the inventory-holding cost and the ordering cost.* Several key assumptions underlie the quantitative model we will develop:

- Only a single item (SKU) is considered.
- The entire order quantity (Q) arrives in the inventory at one time. No physical limits are placed on the size of the order quantity, such as shipment capacity or storage availability.
- Only two types of costs are relevant—order/setup and inventory-holding costs.
- No stockouts are allowed.
- The demand for the item is deterministic and continuous over time. This means that units are withdrawn from inventory at a constant rate proportional to time. For example, an annual demand of 365 units implies a weekly demand of 365/52 and a daily demand of 1 unit.
- Lead time is constant.

Despite these limitations—particularly the assumption of deterministic demand, which is generally not true in practice—the EOQ model provides important insights into the economics of inventory management systems and is the basis for more advanced and realistic models.

Under the assumptions of the model, the cycle inventory pattern, similar to those shown earlier in Exhibits 12.8 and 12.11, is greatly simplified. This is shown in Exhibit 12.18. Suppose that we begin with Q units in inventory. Because units are assumed to be withdrawn at a constant rate, the inventory level falls in a linear fashion until it hits zero. Because no stockouts are allowed, a new order can be planned to arrive when the inventory falls to zero; at this point, the inventory is replenished back up to Q. This cycle keep repeating. This regular pattern allows us to compute the total cost as a function of the order quantity, Q.

CYCLE INVENTORY

From the constant demand assumption, the average cycle inventory can be easily computed as the average of the maximum and minimum inventory levels:

$$\text{Average cycle inventory} = (\text{Maximum inventory} + \text{Minimum inventory})/2 = Q/2 \qquad \textbf{(12.3)}$$

If the average inventory during each cycle is $Q/2$, then the average inventory level over any number of cycles is also $Q/2$.

TOTAL COST MODEL

The inventory-holding cost can be calculated by multiplying the average inventory by the cost of holding one item in inventory for the stated period. The period of time selected for the model is up to the user; it can be a day, week, month, or year. However, because the inventory-holding costs for many industries and businesses are expressed as an annual percentage or rate, most inventory models are developed on an annual cost basis. Let

I = annual inventory-holding charge expressed as a percent of unit cost
C = unit cost of the inventory item or SKU

The cost of storing one unit in inventory for the year, denoted by C_h, is given by $C_h = I \times C$. Thus, the general equation for annual inventory-holding cost is

$$\text{Annual inventory-holding cost} = \left(\begin{array}{c}\text{Average}\\ \text{inventory}\end{array}\right)\left(\begin{array}{c}\text{Annual holding}\\ \text{cost}\\ \text{per unit}\end{array}\right) = \frac{1}{2}QC_h \qquad \textbf{(12.4)}$$

The second component of the total cost is the ordering cost. Because the inventory-holding cost is expressed on an annual basis, we need to express ordering costs as an annual cost also. Letting D denote the annual demand for the

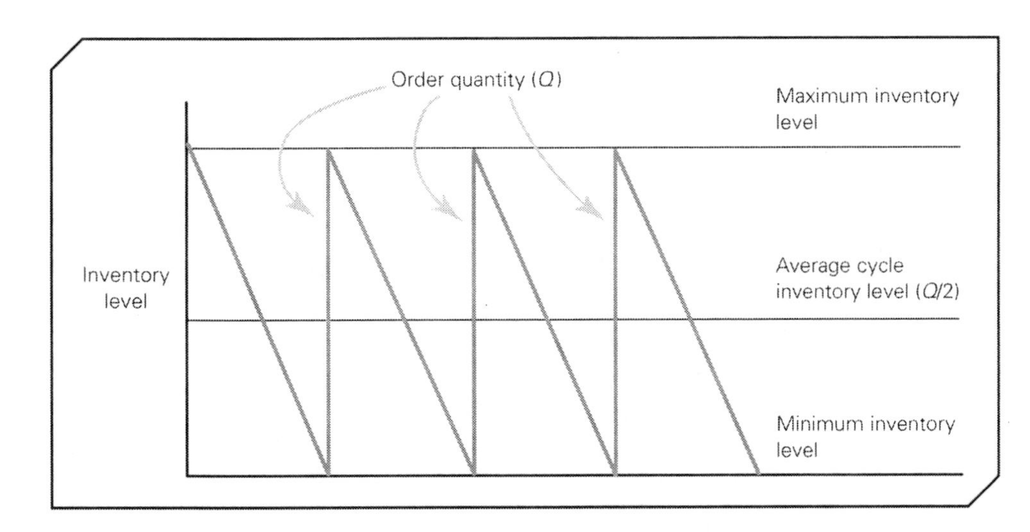

Exhibit 12.18
Cycle Inventory Pattern for the EOQ Model

product, we know that by ordering Q items each time we order, we have to place D/Q orders per year. If C_o is the cost of placing one order, the general expression for the annual ordering cost is shown in Equation (12.5).

$$\text{Annual ordering cost} = \left(\begin{array}{c}\text{Number of}\\ \text{orders}\\ \text{per year}\end{array}\right)\left(\begin{array}{c}\text{Cost}\\ \text{per}\\ \text{year}\end{array}\right) = \left(\frac{D}{Q}\right)C_o \quad \textbf{(12.5)}$$

Thus the total annual cost—inventory-holding cost given by Equation (12.6) plus order or setup cost given by Equation (10.3)—can be expressed as

$$TC = \frac{1}{2}QC_h + \frac{D}{Q}C_o \quad \textbf{(12.6)}$$

OPTIMAL ORDER QUANTITY

The next step is to find the order quantity Q that minimizes the total cost expressed in Equation (12.6). By using differential calculus, we can show that the quantity that minimizes the total cost, denoted by Q^*, is given by Equation (12.7). Q^* is referred to as the *economic order quantity*, or *EOQ*.

$$Q^* = \sqrt{\frac{2DC_o}{C_h}} \quad \textbf{(12.7)}$$

REORDER POINT

As we noted earlier for any FQS, the reorder point is simply the average demand during the lead time as given by Equation (12.2). For the EOQ model, the only difference is that the demand per unit of time is assumed to be constant and continuous. Thus, Equation (12.2) applies here, with d being a constant, rather than an average, value. In this case, operation of the FQS under the EOQ assumptions is simplified, as shown in Exhibit 12.19.

Exhibit 12.19
Relationship Between Reorder Point and Lead Time

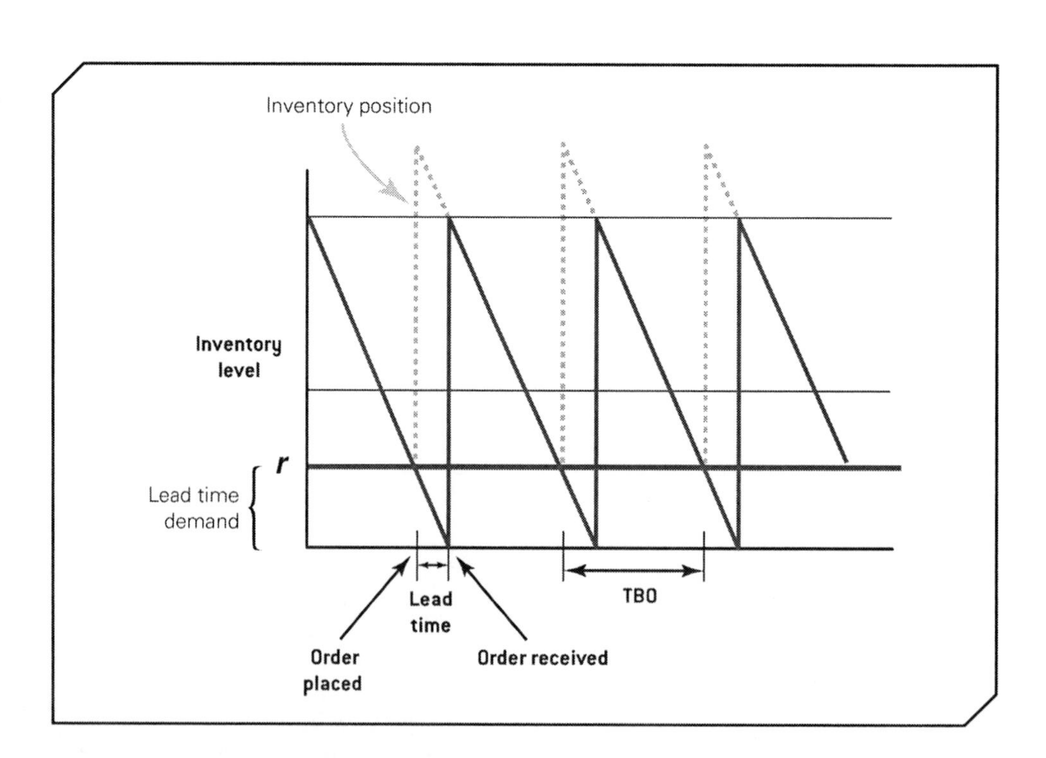

APPLYING THE EOQ MODEL

To illustrate the use of the EOQ model, let us consider the situation faced by the Merkle Pharmacies, a chain of stores in the Midwest United States. The company operates a central distribution center and ships goods purchased from manufacturers to individual stores. As its product line has grown, Merkle's managers have expressed concern about high inventory costs. As a result, Merkle's inventory manager has been asked to make a detailed cost analysis of selected items to see if a better inventory policy can be established. The inventory manager has selected one product, a popular mouthwash, for an initial study. The sales over the past 6 months have been:

Comstock Images

Month	Demand (cases)
1	2,025
2	1,950
3	2,100
4	2,050
5	1,975
6	1,900
Total cases	12,000
Average cases per month	2,000

The inventory manager has been using the average number of cases per month as the basis for the ordering policy for this product.

Although the monthly sales data do not show a perfectly constant demand rate, the variability from month to month is low; therefore, a constant rate of 2,000 cases per month appears to be acceptable. Currently, Merkle's cost is \$12.00 per case. The company estimates its cost of capital to be 12 percent. Insurance, taxes, breakage, handling, and pilferage are estimated to be approximately 6 percent of item cost. Thus the annual inventory-holding costs are estimated to be 18 percent of item cost. Since the cost of one case is \$12.00, the cost of holding one case in inventory for one year is $C_h = IC = 0.18(\$12.00) = \$2.16$ per case per year.

The next step in the inventory analysis is to determine the cost of placing an order. The cost includes the salaries of the purchasing agents and clerical support staff, transportation costs, and miscellaneous costs such as paper, postage, and telephone costs, which are estimated to be \$38.00 per order regardless of the quantity requested in the order. Note that the fixed cost of the purchasing department is not included in order cost. From this information, we have

$$\begin{aligned} D &= 24{,}000 \text{ cases per year} \\ C_o &= \$38 \text{ per order} \\ I &= 18 \text{ percent} \\ C &= \$12.00 \text{ per case} \\ C_h &= IC = \$2.16 \end{aligned}$$

Thus, the minimum-cost economic order quantity (EOQ) as given by Equation (12.7) is

$$\text{EOQ} = \sqrt{\frac{2(24{,}000)(38)}{2.16}} = 919 \text{ cases (rounded to a whole number)}$$

For the data used in this problem, the total-cost model based on Equation (12.6) is

$$\begin{aligned} TC &= \frac{1}{2}Q(\$2.16) + \frac{24{,}000}{Q}(\$38.00) \\ &= 1.08Q + \frac{912{,}000}{Q} \end{aligned}$$

For the EOQ of 919, the total cost is calculated to be

$$1.08 \times 919 + (24{,}000/919) \times (\$38.00) = \$1{,}984.90.$$

We can compare this total cost using EOQ with the current purchasing policy of $Q = 2{,}000$. The total annual cost of the current order policy is

$$TC = \$1.08(2{,}000) + \$912{,}000/2{,}000 = \$2{,}616.00$$

Thus, the EOQ analysis has resulted in a $2,616.00 − $1,984.90 = $631.10, or 24.1 percent, cost reduction. Notice also that the total ordering costs ($992) are equal to the total inventory holding costs ($992). In general, this will always be true for the EOQ model.

To find the reorder point, let us suppose that the lead time to order a case of mouthwash from the manufacturer is 3 days. Considering weekends and holidays, Merkle operates 250 days per year. So, on a daily basis, the annual demand of 24,000 cases corresponds to a demand of 24,000/250 = 96 cases. Thus we anticipate 288 cases to be sold during the 3-day lead time using Equation (12.2). Therefore, Merkle should order a new shipment from the manufacturer when the inventory level reaches 288 cases, using Equation (12.7). Also note that the company will place 24,000/919 = 26.12, or approximately 26, orders per year. With 250 working days per year, an order would be placed every 250/26 = 9.6 days. This represents the average time between orders (TBO) of 9.6 days in Exhibit 12.19.

As this example illustrates, the EOQ model can identify potential savings by improving ordering policies. Using spreadsheets or other computer technology, it would be easy to compute optimal policies for all SKUs or a major subgroup of SKUs.

SENSITIVITY ANALYSIS OF THE EOQ MODEL

Studying how model results change as inputs to the model change is called **sensitivity analysis.**

Because the inventory-holding charge and ordering cost are at best estimates, we may want to conduct an analysis on how the ordering policy might change as these estimates change. *Studying how model results change as inputs to the model change is called* **sensitivity analysis**. This is easy to do on a spreadsheet as shown in Exhibit 12.20. The spreadsheet also provides a variety of information from the EOQ model.

In the lower portion of the spreadsheet, we vary both the carrying charge and the order cost to understand how the optimal order quantity and total cost would change. As you can see, the value of Q^* appears relatively stable, even with some variations in the cost estimates. Based on these results, it appears that the best order quantity is somewhere around 850 to 1,000 cases and definitely not near the current order quantity of 2,000 cases. We also see that the total cost would not change very much even if the cost estimates are in error. Thus, there is very little risk associated with implementing the calculated order quantity of 919 cases. EOQ models in general are insensitive to small variations or errors in the cost estimates. Notice that the total cost curve in Exhibit 12.21 is relatively flat (shallow) around the minimum total cost solution.

Sensitivity analysis can also be used to evaluate the impact of other changes in model parameters, such as the annual demand (which generally is uncertain) or the unit cost of the item. We can also determine, for instance, that a 50 percent reduction in the order cost would result in a 41 percent reduction in the total cost. In an in-house manufacturing context, this would suggest that companies should try to reduce setup costs associated with making parts and components.

EOQ Models for Stochastic Demand

Stockouts occur whenever the lead time demand exceeds the reorder point in a deterministic situation. When demand is stochastic, then using the EOQ based only on the average demand will result in a high probability of a stockout. One way to

Exhibit 12.20 Spreadsheet for EOQ Model Calculations and Sensitivity Analysis (Economic Order Quantity Model.xls)

	A	B	C	D	E
1	**Economic Order Quantity Model**				
2					
3	**Model Inputs**			**Model Outputs**	
4					
5	Annual Demand, D	24,000		Optimal Order Quantity	918.94
6	Ordering Cost, Co	$38.00		Annual Holding Cost	$ 992.45
7	Unit Cost, C	$12.00		Annual Ordering Cost	$ 992.45
8	Carrying Charge, I	18%		Total Annual Cost	$ 1,984.90
9	Operating Days/Year	250		Maximum Inventory Level	918.94
10				Average Inventory Level	459.47
11				Number of Orders/Year	26.12
12				Cycle Time (Days)	9.57
13					
14					
15	**Sensitivity Analysis**				
16					
17			Optimal Order	Projected Total Cost	
18	Carrying Charge	Order Cost	Quantity	Using Optimal EOQ	Using Q = 919
19	16%	$ 36	948.68	$ 1,821.47	$ 1,822.39
20	16%	$ 40	1000.00	$ 1,920.00	$ 1,926.85
21	20%	$ 36	848.53	$ 2,036.47	$ 2,042.95
22	20%	$ 40	894.43	$ 2,146.63	$ 2,147.41

Exhibit 12.21 Chart of Holding, Ordering, and Total Costs

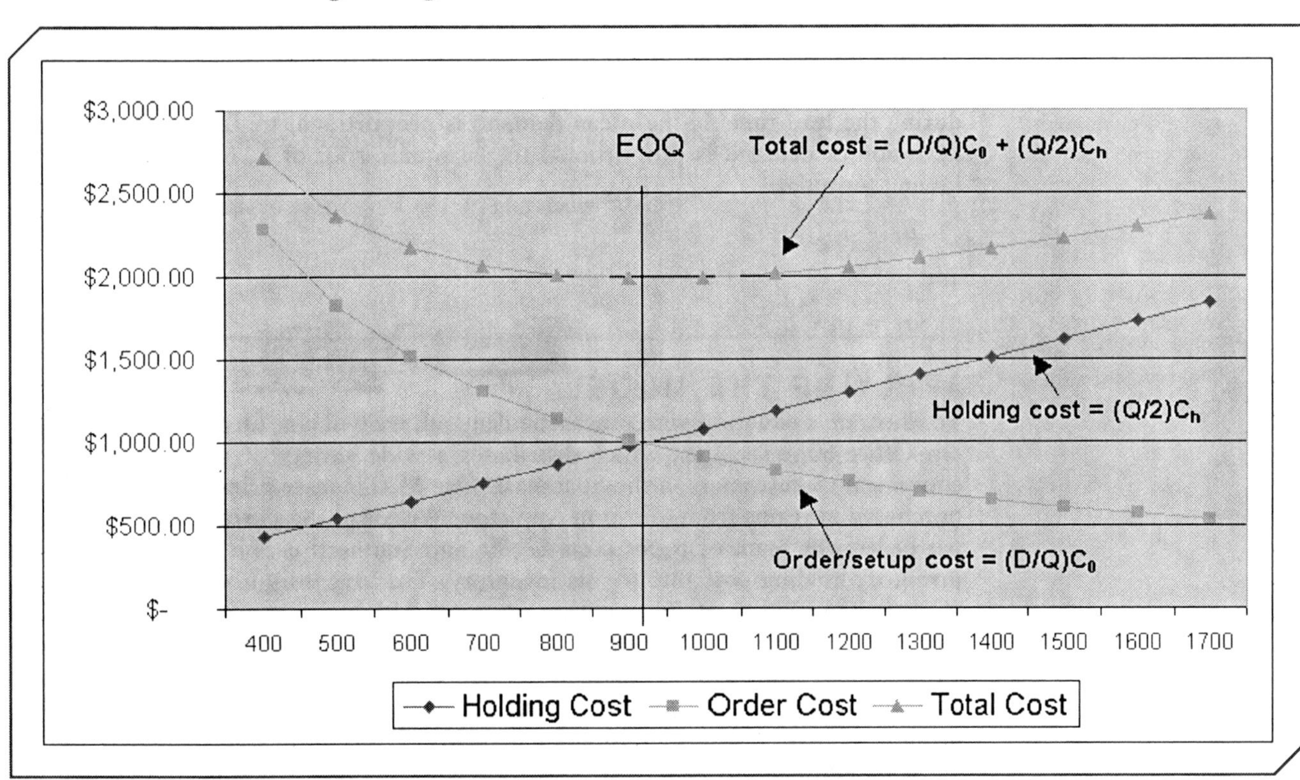

Exhibit 12.23
Reorder point allowing a 5 percent chance of a stockout

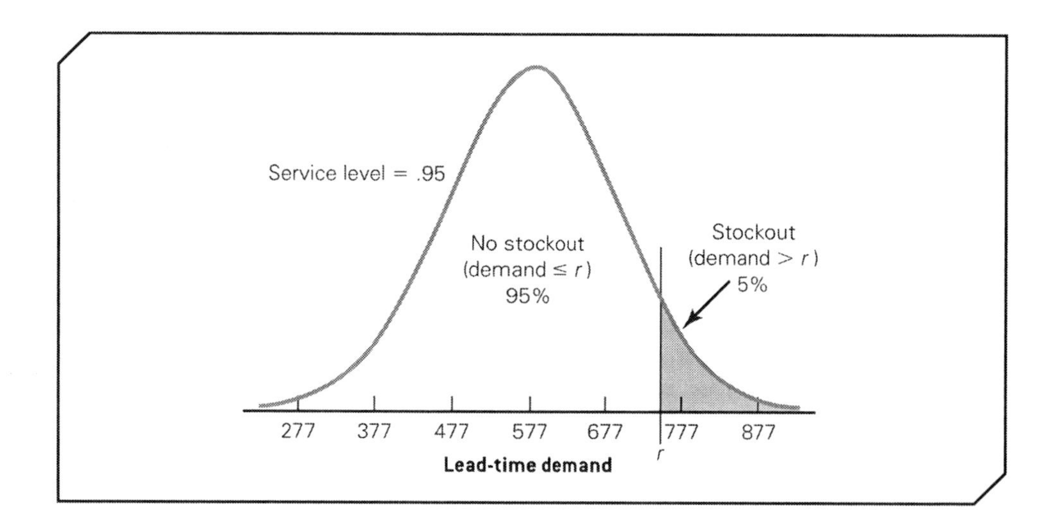

If the demand rate were constant at 15,000 reams per year as in the basic EOQ model, then the optimal policy would be $Q^* = 1{,}333$, $r = 577$, resulting in a total annual cost of approximately $1,013. If demand is stochastic with the previous assumptions, then $Q^* = 1{,}333$, $r = 742$, and total order, cycle inventory, and safety stock inventory cost is $1,138. Notice that the additional safety stock required to meet the 5 percent risk of a stockout, 165 units, incurs an additional cost of $125 per year.

Exhibit 12.24 Spreadsheet for Safety Stock Analysis (Southern Office Supplies.xls)

	A	B	C	D	E	F
1	**Southern Office Supplies**					
2						
3	**Model Inputs**			**EOQ Model Results**		
4						
5	Annual Demand	15,000		Optimal Order Quantity	1332.78	
6	Ordering Cost	$ 45.00		Annual Holding Cost	$ 506.46	
7	Unit Cost	$ 3.80		Annual Ordering Cost	$ 506.46	
8	Carrying Charge	20%		Total Annual Cost	$1,012.92	
9						
10	Lead Time Demand					
11	Mean (μL)	577				
12	Standard dev. (σL)	100				
13						
14						
15	**Safety Stock Analysis**					
16						Additional
17	Service	Probability	Normal probability	Reorder	Safety	Safety
18	Level	of Stockout	z-value	Point	Stock	Stock Cost
19	0.99	0.01	2.326	810	233	$ 176.80
20	0.95	0.05	1.645	741	164	$ 125.01
21	0.90	0.10	1.282	705	128	$ 97.40
22	0.85	0.15	1.036	681	104	$ 78.77
23	0.80	0.20	0.842	661	84	$ 63.96

Exhibit 12.24 is a spreadsheet for computing the costs associated with normal inventory levels using the EOQ model as well as additional costs incurred for various safety stock levels. (The z-values are found by using the Microsoft Excel function NORMINV.) We see that decreasing the service level permits a lower safety stock, although it increases the probability of a stockout. Thus, the manager must make a trade-off between inventory costs and customer service.

Safety Stock in Complex Supply Chains

Many organizations stock inventory at multiple locations in their supply chain. For example, large distributors and retail chains might have many warehouses located throughout a region, country, or around the world. Individual retail stores each represent an inventory stocking point. Such a strategy provides close proximity to the customer and improves customer response and service.

When demand is divided evenly among the multiple locations and they can transfer inventory to one another as necessary, then for a fixed service level it is possible to show that the average total inventory in the system varies with the square root of the number of inventory locations. That is, using an EOQ policy with safety stock to provide a particular service level, doubling the number of locations increases the average inventory by a factor of $\sqrt{2}$. For example, the EOQ for Southern Office Supplies was 1,333 reams, and to provide a 95 percent service level a safety stock of 164 reams was required. Thus, total average inventory is $Q/2$ + Safety stock, or 1,333/2 + 164 = 830.5 reams. If Southern Office Supplies expands to 4 stores, then total average inventory needed to provide the same service level will increase to $\sqrt{4} \times 830.5$, or 1,661 reams. For 16 stores, it would be $\sqrt{16} \times 830.5 = 3{,}322$ reams. Because of the assumption that inventory can be transferred among locations, each location does not need to stock the full amount calculated by the service-level analysis.

FIXED PERIOD SYSTEMS

Learning Objective
To understand how inventory management systems for monitoring and controlling independent demand operate using fixed time intervals between order placement.

An alternative to a fixed order quantity system is a **fixed period system (FPS)**—*sometimes called a periodic review system—in which the inventory position is checked only at fixed intervals of time, T, rather than on a continuous basis.* At the time of review, an order is placed for sufficient stock to bring the inventory position up to a predetermined maximum inventory level, M, sometimes called the *replenishment level*, or *"order-up-to" level*. The OM Spotlight on Hewlett-Packard describes the use of a FPS at that company.

A **Fixed Period System (FPS)** *is an alternative to a fixed order quantity system.*

In our discussion of the sales data with a stable demand rate (Exhibit 12.6), you might have observed that using a fixed order quantity also resulted in a constant time interval between orders. Suppose that we use a FPS system with a time interval between orders of $T = 7$ days, and as before, assume a 2-day lead time. To have orders arrive on Mondays, we review the ending inventory level on Thursdays (beginning with day 5). The order quantity is computed as M minus the ending inventory at the time of review (Thursday). The value of M must be large enough to safely cover the expected demand until the next review period *and* during the lead time, that is, over a length of time equal to $T + L$. Therefore, we will set $M = 90$ to cover the demand during the review period (an average of 70 units) and the 2-day lead time (about 20 units). Exhibit 12.25 shows a simulation of this ordering policy for the first 3 weeks. Note that the amount ordered at any time varies because the order quantity is calculated by subtracting the inventory level at the time of review from the replenishment level. The chart in Exhibit 12.26 shows the ending daily inventory over all 10 weeks. Note that this is very similar to Exhibit 12.19 for the FQS system. In fact, when demand is stable and deterministic, both systems are essentially the same.

OM SPOTLIGHT

Hewlett-Packard[9]

The Hewlett-Packard (HP) Company has complex supply chains for its products. The Vancouver Division manufactures one of HP's popular printers and ships them to distribution centers (DCs) in the United States, Far East, and Europe. Because the printer industry is highly competitive, HP's dealers like to carry as little inventory as possible but must supply goods to end users quickly. Consequently, HP operates under a lot of pressure to provide high levels of availability at the DCs for the dealers. DCs operate as inventory stocking points with large safety stocks to meet a target off-the-shelf fill rate, where replenishment of goods comes from manufacturing.

The basic principles that planners follow are to set a target inventory level, usually expressed in weeks of supply, for each product at each DC based on the desired fill rate. This is a function of the length and variability of the lead time to replenish the stock from the factory and the level and variability of demand. Planners review the actual inventory position each week. This weekly review period corresponds to the frequency with which products are shipped from the factory to the DCs in Europe and Asia. Studies have shown that this frequency allows the plant to maximize the use of its shipping containers. The quantity needed to bring the inventory position back to the target level becomes the production requirement at the factory, which carries no inventory. Thus, the lead time is the sum of the transportation time to ship from the factory, the manufacturing flow time at the factory, and any possible delays due to material shortages or process disruptions. HP developed a quantitative model to compute cost-effective target inventory levels to meet fill rate requirements. The model helped to improve inventory investment by over 20 percent.

Hewlett Packard

Exhibit 12.25
Simulation of FPS System with $M = 90$ Units and $T = 7$ Days

Day	Order Receipt	Beginning Inventory	Demand	Ending Inventory	Order Quantity
1		70	10	60	
2		60	11	49	
3		49	13	36	
4		36	10	26	
5		26	9	17	73
6		17	9	8	
7		8	9	−1	
8	73	72	13	59	
9		59	9	50	
10		50	9	41	
11		41	10	31	
12		31	10	21	69
13		21	9	12	
14		12	10	2	
15	69	71	9	62	
16		62	9	53	
17		53	9	44	
18		44	11	33	
19		33	9	24	66
20		24	10	14	
21		14	11	3	

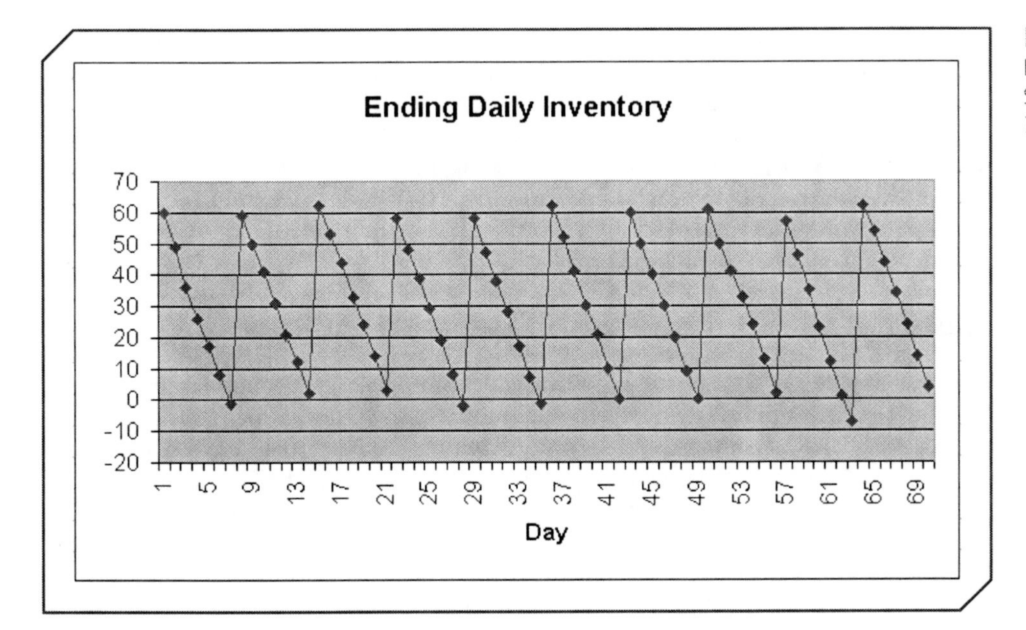

Exhibit 12.26
Ending Daily Inventory for FPS System with $M = 90$ Units and $T = 7$ Days

There are two principal decisions in a FPS:

1. the time interval between reviews, and
2. the replenishment level.

We can set the length of the review period judgmentally based on the importance of the item or the convenience of review. For example, management might select to review noncritical SKUs every month and more-critical SKUs every week. We can also incorporate economics using the EOQ model.

The EOQ model provides the best "economic time interval" for establishing an optimal policy for a FPS system under the model assumptions. This is given by

$$T = Q^*/D = EOQ/D \tag{12.11}$$

The optimal replenishment level is computed by

$$M = \mu_{T+L} = d(T + L) \tag{12.12}$$

where T is the time interval between orders or review period based on the EOQ, d = demand per time period (days, weeks, months, and so on), L is the lead time in the same time units, and μ_{T+L} is the demand during the lead time plus review period.

Periodic review systems usually involve stock clerks making the rounds and physically checking the inventory levels. Notice that if the lead time is always shorter than the time between reviews, any order placed will be received before the next review time. In this case, the inventory position at the time of review will be the same as the actual physical inventory, and therefore, the ordering decision can be made by checking the physical inventory (rather than having to compute the inventory position). This makes implementation easier. The replenishment level M for each item can be identified by a tag on the shelf, and the stock clerk needs only to compare it to the number of items remaining. The advantage of a periodic review system is that inventory need not be monitored continuously, which would be difficult to do unless the system were automated.

Periodic review systems are useful when a large number of items is ordered from the same supplier, because several orders can be placed at the same time. Shipments can be consolidated, resulting in lower freight rates. Periodic review systems can simplify administrative requirements for managing inventory. For example, inventory analysts can be assigned to review groups of SKUs at fixed intervals, for instance Group A every Monday, Group B on Tuesday, and so on. In practice, the review period also depends on the capacity of the staff to perform the work.

Periodic review systems are often used to control "C" items in an ABC classification, and "A" items are usually controlled using continuous review systems. The greater the control placed on monitoring inventory levels, the higher the cost of monitoring work and information processing, but better control may result in fewer stockouts and improved customer service.

Fixed Period Systems with Stochastic Demand

Things change when demand is highly variable. If a one-week economic time interval ordering policy is applied to the data in Exhibit 12.9, we find a high risk of a shortage, as the chart in Exhibit 12.27 shows. As with the FQS system, we see a substantial risk of a stockout, even though the average daily demand is the same over the 10-week period. Therefore, we must carry safety stock to protect against shortages.

We will assume that demand during some time interval t is described by a probability distribution having mean μ_t and standard deviation σ_t. The optimal time between review periods (T) is computed by Equation (12.11). The replenishment level M under stochastic conditions is computed using the following formula:

$$M = \mu_{T+L} + z \times \sigma_{T+L} \tag{12.13}$$

where μ_{T+L} = expected demand during the time interval $T + L$

z = the number of standard deviations necessary to achieve the acceptable service level

σ_{T+L} = standard deviation of demand during the time interval $T + L$.

Note that this calculation is similar to Equation (12.12) in that the first term, μ_{T+L}, represents the expected demand during the review period and lead time, and $z \times \sigma_{T+L}$ represents the safety stock required.

We can use the same statistical principles as in the stochastic demand model for the FQS to calculate μ_{T+L} and σ_{T+L}. If we know the mean μ_t and standard deviation σ_t for demand over a time interval t, then

$$\mu_{T+L} = \mu_t(T + L) \tag{12.14}$$

Exhibit 12.27
Daily Ending Inventory for High Variability Sales Data

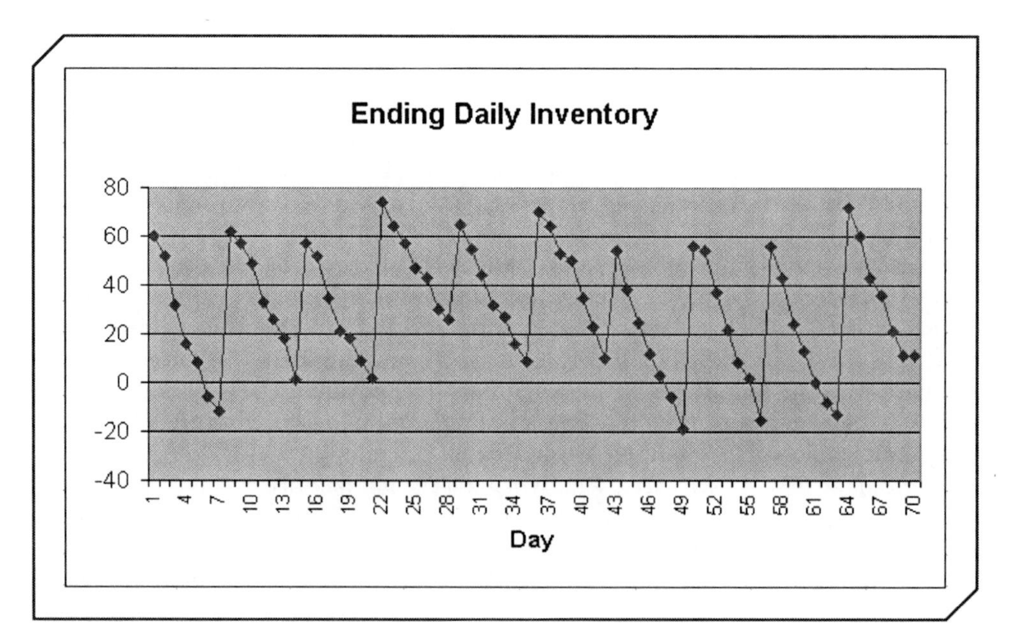

We may compute σ_{T+L} using the following formula:

$$\sigma_{T+L} = \sigma_t \sqrt{(T + L)} \quad \textbf{(12.15)}$$

APPLYING THE MODEL

We will return to the Southern Office Supplies example where we previously computed $Q^* = 1{,}333$ reams and $r = 742$ reams, assuming a 95% service level and a 2-week lead time. We use the same assumptions that weekly demand is normal with a mean of 288.46 and a standard deviation of approximately 71.

Using Equation (12.11), we compute the review period as

$$T = Q^*/D = 1{,}333/15{,}000 = .0889 \text{ years}$$

If we assume 260 working days/year, this is approximately 5 weeks. From Equations (12.14) and (12.15), we obtain

$$\mu_{T+L} = \mu_t(T + L) = 288.46(5 + 2) = 2{,}019.22 \text{ units}$$

and

$$\sigma_{T+L} = \sigma_t\sqrt{T + L} = 71\sqrt{5 + 2} = 187.85 \text{ units}$$

Using Equation (12.13) and assuming a 5 percent risk of a stockout,

$$M = \mu_{T+L} + z\sigma_{T+L} = 2{,}019.22 + 1.645(187.85) = 2{,}328.23 \text{ units}$$

Therefore, we review the inventory position every 5 weeks and place an order to replenish the inventory up to a level of 2,328 units. Exhibit 12.28 shows a simulation of the operation of this system for Southern Office Supplies. The vertical double-headed arrows show the order quantities at each review period. Note that the safety stock maintains an adequate level of inventory to reduce the risk of stockouts.

Summary of Fixed Period Systems

A summary of fixed period systems is given in Exhibit 12.29. Exhibit 12.30 shows the system operation graphically. In Exhibit 12.29, at the time of the first review, a rather large amount of inventory (IP_1) is in stock, so the order quantity (Q_1) is

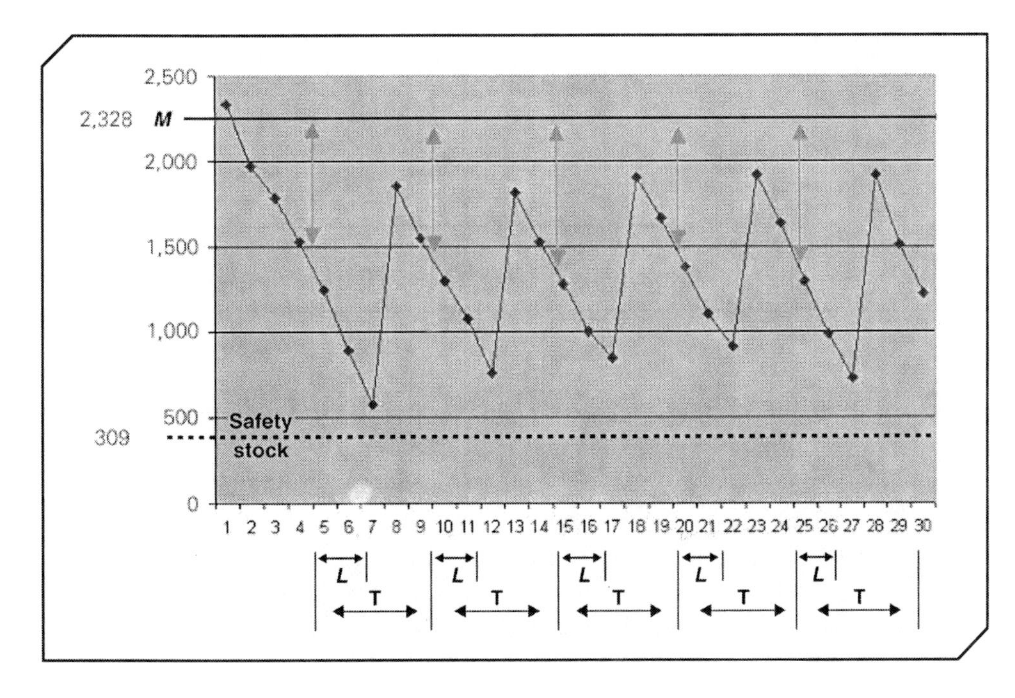

Exhibit 12.28
Simulation of Southern Office Supplies' Periodic Review Model

relatively small. Demand during the lead time was small, and when the order arrived, a large amount of inventory was still available. At the third review cycle, the stock level is much closer to zero since the demand rate has increased (steeper slope). Thus, the order quantity (Q_3) is much larger, and during the lead time, demand was high and some stockouts occurred. Note that when an order is placed at time T, it does not arrive until time $T + L$. Thus, in using a FPS, managers must cover the risk of a stockout over the time period $T + L$ and, therefore, must carry more inventory.

Exhibit 12.29
Summary of Fixed Period Inventory Systems

Managerial Decisions	Review Period (T) and Replenishment Level (M)
Ordering decision rule	Place a new order every T periods, where the order quantity at time t is $Q_t = M - IP_t$. IP_t is the inventory position at the time of review, t.
Key characteristics	The review period, T, is constant and placing an order is time triggered. The order quantity Q_t varies at each review period. M is chosen to include the demand during the review period and lead time, plus any safety stock. Stockouts can occur when demand is stochastic and can be addressed by adding safety stock to the expected demand during time $T + L$ (see Equation (12.13)).

Exhibit 12.30
Operation of a Fixed Period System (FPS)

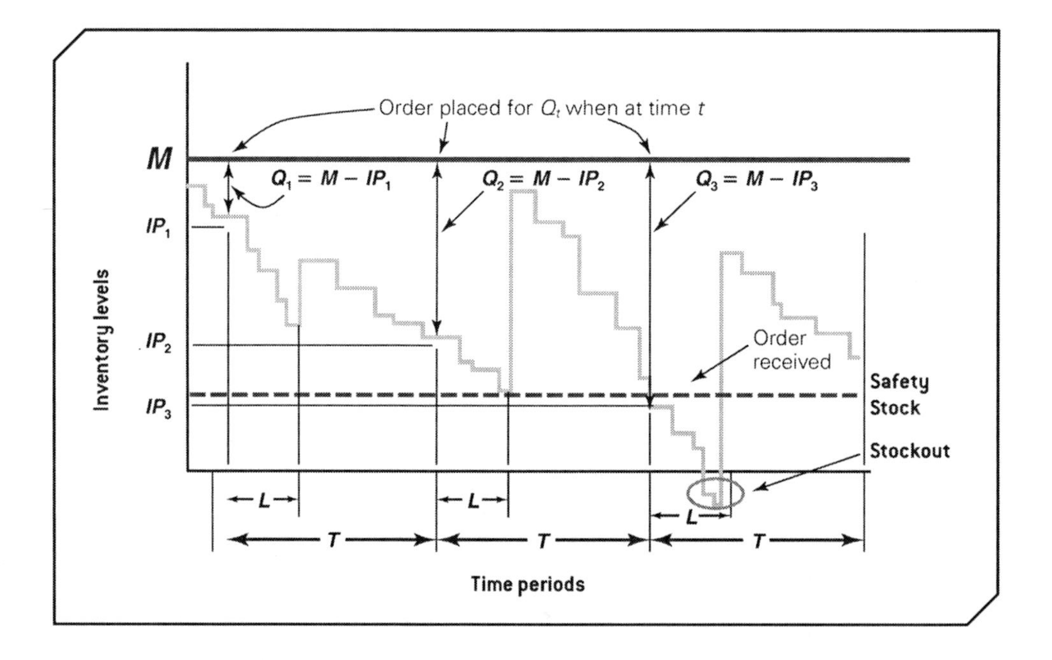

CHOOSING BETWEEN FIXED ORDER QUANTITY AND FIXED PERIOD SYSTEMS

The choice of which system—FQS or FPS—to use is not an easy decision—it is part science and part human judgment. It depends on a variety of factors, such as how many total SKUs the firm must monitor, whether computer or manual systems are used, availability of technology and human resources, the ABC profile, and the strategic focus of the organization, such as customer service or cost minimization.

FQSs maintain tighter control of inventories, because orders can be placed to ensure that stockout risks are minimized. Nevertheless, FQSs are somewhat more complex because they require continual monitoring and updating of the inventory position. This requires that accurate records of inventory positions be maintained. With today's computer systems, however, this is usually easy to do.

FPS systems are easier to manage because the inventory levels need only be checked periodically. Inventory analysts can be assigned groups of SKUs to review at fixed intervals, for instance, Group A every Monday, Group B on Tuesday, and so on. Also, in situations in which manual records must be updated, FPS systems might be more economical than FQS. FPSs are useful when a large number of items is ordered from the same supplier, because many individual orders can be placed at the same time. Thus, shipments can be consolidated into single purchase orders and trucks, resulting in lower freight rates.

An item's classification in an ABC scheme often influences the choice of inventory control system. A items require closer control and therefore benefit from more frequent reveiw periods in an FPS system or perhaps consideration of using an FQS system. C items would require less control and therefore FPS systems with longer review periods are more useful. Managers should consider the advantages and disadvantages of each type of system and the relative economics in making a decision.

SPECIAL MODELS FOR INVENTORY MANAGEMENT

Learning Objective
To learn special inventory models that consider back orders, price breaks, one-time ordering opportunities, and simulation as methods for inventory analysis.

Many other models have been developed for special inventory situations. It is impossible to describe all of them in this chapter. We will describe a few of the more common models that relate to some important types of inventory decisions.

EOQ Model with Back Orders

There are cases in which it may be desirable—from an economic point of view—to plan for and allow shortages. This situation is most common when the value per unit of the inventory is very high, and hence the inventory-holding cost is high. An example is a new-car dealer's inventory. Most customers do not find the specific car they want in stock but are willing to back-order it. Allowing back orders reduces the total cost for the customer because inventory-holding costs would typically be incorporated into the sales price, but it requires the customer to wait for the product. We present an extension to the EOQ model that allows for back orders. If we let S indicate the number of back orders that have accumulated when an order of size Q is received, the inventory system has these characteristics:

- With S back orders existing when a new shipment of size Q arrives, the S back orders will be shipped to the appropriate customers immediately, and the remaining $(Q - S)$ units will be placed in inventory.
- $Q - S$ will be the maximum inventory level.
- The inventory cycle of T days will be divided into two distinct phases: t_1 days when inventory is on hand and orders are filled as they occur and t_2 days when there is a stockout and all orders are placed on back order.

The inventory pattern for this model, where negative inventory represents the number of back orders, is shown in Exhibit 12.31.

Back-ordering costs usually involve labor and special-delivery costs directly associated with the handling of back orders. Another portion of the back-order cost can be expressed as a loss of goodwill with customers due to their having to wait for their orders. Since the goodwill cost depends on how long the customer has to wait, it is customary to adopt the convention of expressing all back-order costs in terms of how much it costs to have a unit on back order for a stated period of

Exhibit 12.31
Inventory Pattern for Back-Order Situation

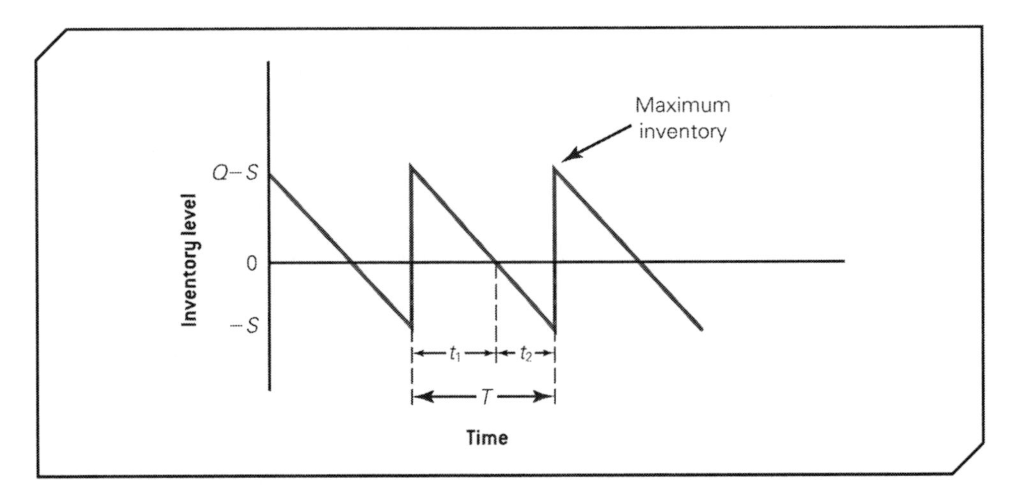

time. This method of computing cost is similar to the method we used to compute the inventory-holding cost.

Admittedly, the back-order cost rate (especially the customer goodwill cost) is difficult to determine in practice. However, noting that EOQ models are rather insensitive to the cost estimates, we should feel confident that reasonable estimates of the back-order cost will lead to a good approximation of the overall minimum-cost inventory decision. Letting C_b be the cost to maintain one item on back order for one year, the three sources of cost in this planned-shortage inventory model can be expressed as in the following equations:

$$\text{Inventory-holding cost} = \frac{(Q - S)^2}{2Q} C_h$$

$$\text{Ordering cost} = \frac{D}{Q} C_o$$

$$\text{Back-ordering cost} = \frac{S^2}{2Q} C_b$$

Thus our total-annual-cost back-order model expression (TC) becomes

$$TC = \frac{(Q - S)^2}{2Q} C_h + \frac{D}{Q} C_o + \frac{S^2}{2Q} C_b \quad \textbf{(12.16)}$$

The minimum-cost values for Q and S can be found using calculus and are

$$Q^* = \sqrt{\frac{2DC_o}{C_h}\left(\frac{C_h + C_b}{C_b}\right)} \quad \textbf{(12.17)}$$

and

$$S^* = Q^*\left(\frac{C_h}{C_h + C_b}\right) \quad \textbf{(12.18)}$$

APPLYING THE MODEL

To illustrate the use of this model, consider an electronics company that is concerned about an expensive part used in television repair. The cost of the part is $125, and the inventory-holding rate is 20 percent. The cost to place an order is estimated to be $40. The annual demand, which occurs at a constant rate throughout the year, is 800 parts. Currently, the inventory policy is based on the EOQ model, with

$$Q^* = \sqrt{\frac{2DC_o}{C_h}} = \sqrt{\frac{2(800)(40)}{0.20(125)}} = 51 \text{ parts}$$

The total annual cost of inventory-holding and ordering has been

$$TC = \frac{1}{2}QC_h + \frac{D}{Q}C_o = \frac{1}{2}(51)(0.20)(125) + \left(\frac{800}{51}\right)(40)$$

$$= \$637.50 + 627.50 = \$1{,}265.$$

Because of the relatively high inventory investment, back-ordering is being considered.

On an annual basis, an item back-order cost of \$60 was assigned. Using Equations (12.17) and (12.18), the optimal order quantity, Q^*, and the optimal number of back orders, S^*, become

$$Q^* = \sqrt{\frac{2(800)(40)}{0.20(125)}\left(\frac{0.20(125) + 60}{60}\right)} = 60 \text{ parts}$$

and

$$S^* = 60\left(\frac{0.20(125)}{0.20(125) + 60}\right) = 18 \text{ parts}$$

Both Q^* and S^* have been rounded to whole numbers to simplify the remaining calculations. We find the following total costs associated with the inventory policy by using Equation (12.16) as follows:

$$\text{Inventory-holding cost} = \frac{(Q - S)^2}{2Q}C_h$$

$$= \frac{(60 - 18)^2}{2(60)}(0.20)(\$125) = \$367.50$$

$$\text{Ordering cost} = \frac{D}{Q}C_o = \frac{800}{600}(\$40) = \$533.33$$

$$\text{Back-ordering cost} = \frac{S^2}{2Q}C_b = \frac{(18)^2}{2(60)}(\$60) = \$162.00$$

The total cost is \$1,062.83, and hence the back-ordering policy provides a \$1,265 − \$1,062.83 = \$202.17, or 16 percent, cost reduction when compared to the EOQ model. Note that the daily demand for the part is (800 parts)/(250 days) = 3.2 parts per day. Since the maximum number of back orders is 18, we see that the length of the back-order period will be 18/3.2 = 5.6 days.

Quantity Discount Model

Many suppliers offer discounts for purchasing larger quantities of goods. This often occurs because of economies of scale of shipping larger loads, from not having to break apart boxes of items, or simply as an incentive to increase total revenue. You might have noticed such incentives at stores like Amazon.com, where CDs or DVDs are often advertised in discounted bundles—for example, two CDs by the same artist for a lower price than buying them individually.

To incorporate quantity discounts in the basic EOQ model requires us to include the purchase cost of the item in the total cost equation. We did not include the purchase cost of the item in the EOQ model because it does not affect the optimal order quantity. Because the annual demand is constant, the total annual purchase cost remains the same no matter what the individual order quantities are. However, when the unit price varies by order quantity, as would be the case with price breaks for quantity discounts, we need to incorporate that into the model. For example, a company might offer several discount categories. As an example, suppose that for every item ordered up to 1,000, a base unit price applies; if the order is for 1,001 to 2,000 items, a discounted unit price (of, perhaps, 2 percent) applies; for every additional item ordered beyond 2,000, a larger discount (say, 4 percent) applies. We cannot use the EOQ formula, because different purchase costs result in different holding-cost rates, and a calculated EOQ may not even fall within the appropriate discount category.

To compute the optimal order quantity, a three-step procedure is used.

Step 1. Compute Q^* using the EOQ formula for the unit cost associated with each discount category.

Step 2. For Q^*s that are too small to qualify for the assumed discount price, adjust the order quantity upward to the nearest order quantity that will allow the product to be purchased at the assumed price. If a calculated Q^* for a given price is larger than the highest order quantity that provides the particular discount price, that discount price need not be considered further, since it cannot lead to an optimal solution.

Step 3. For each of the order quantities resulting from steps 1 and 2, compute the total annual cost using the unit price from the appropriate discount category. The total annual cost can be found by adding the purchase cost (annual demand, D, times the unit cost, C) to Equation (12.6):

$$TC = \frac{Q}{2}C_b + \frac{D}{Q}C_o + DC \qquad \textbf{(12.19)}$$

The order quantity yielding the minimum total annual cost is the optimal order quantity.

APPLYING THE PROCEDURE

We illustrate this procedure using the example illustrated for the EOQ model. Suppose that the manufacturer of mouthwash offers this quantity-discount schedule:

Discount Category	Order Size	Discount	Unit Cost
1	0 to 3,999	0	$12.00
2	4,000 to 11,999	3%	11.64
3	12,000 and over	5%	11.40

The 5 percent discount looks attractive; however, the 12,000-case order quantity is substantially more than the EOQ recommendation of 919 cases. The purchase discount might be outweighed by the larger holding costs that would have to be incurred if this quantity was ordered.

The Excel spreadsheet in Exhibit 12.32 performs the necessary calculations. In column F we place the larger of the EOQ and the minimum order size for each discount category. For example, the EOQ for discount category 2 is

$$Q_2^* = \sqrt{2DC_o/C_b} = \sqrt{\frac{2(24{,}000)(38)}{(0.18)(11.64)}} = 933$$

However, since this is below the minimum required order size, we adjust the order quantity up to 4,000. Similarly, the EOQ for discount category 3 is 943, so we set the order quantity to 12,000. The cost calculations appear in columns G through J.

As you can see, a decision to order 4,000 units at the 3 percent discount rate yields the minimum-cost solution. Note that the sum of the inventory and ordering

Exhibit 12.32 Spreadsheet for Quantity-Discount Model Calculations (Quantity Discount Model.xls)

	A	B	C	D	E	F	G	H	I	J
1	**Quantity Discount Inventory Model**									
2										
3	Annual demand		24,000							
4	Cost per unit		$ 12.00							
5	Carrying charge		18%							
6	Order cost		$ 38.00							
7										
8		Min.			Unit		Annual	Annual	Annual	Total
9	Discount	Order		Unit	Holding	Order	Holding	Ordering	Purchase	Annual
10	Category	Size	Discount	Cost	Cost	Quantity	Cost	Cost	Cost	Cost
11	1	EOQ	0%	$12.00	$ 2.16	919	$ 992	$ 992	$288,000	$289,985
12	2	4,000	3%	$11.64	$ 2.10	4000	$ 4,190	$ 228	$279,360	$283,778
13	3	12,000	5%	$11.40	$ 2.05	12000	$ 12,312	$ 76	$273,600	$285,988

costs with $Q^* = 4{,}000$ is \$4,190.40 + 228.00 = \$4,418.40. This portion of the total cost is substantially more than the \$1,984.90 cost associated with the 919-unit order size. In effect, the quantity-discount savings of 3 percent per unit is so great that we are willing to operate the inventory system with a substantially higher inventory level and substantially higher inventory-holding cost. Provided space is available to handle larger inventories, purchasing in larger quantities to obtain discounts is economically sound. Exhibit 12.33 shows a graph of the total cost that clearly shows the effect of the price breaks on the total cost and the optimal order quantity.

Exhibit 12.33 Graph of Total Cost for Quantity Discount Example

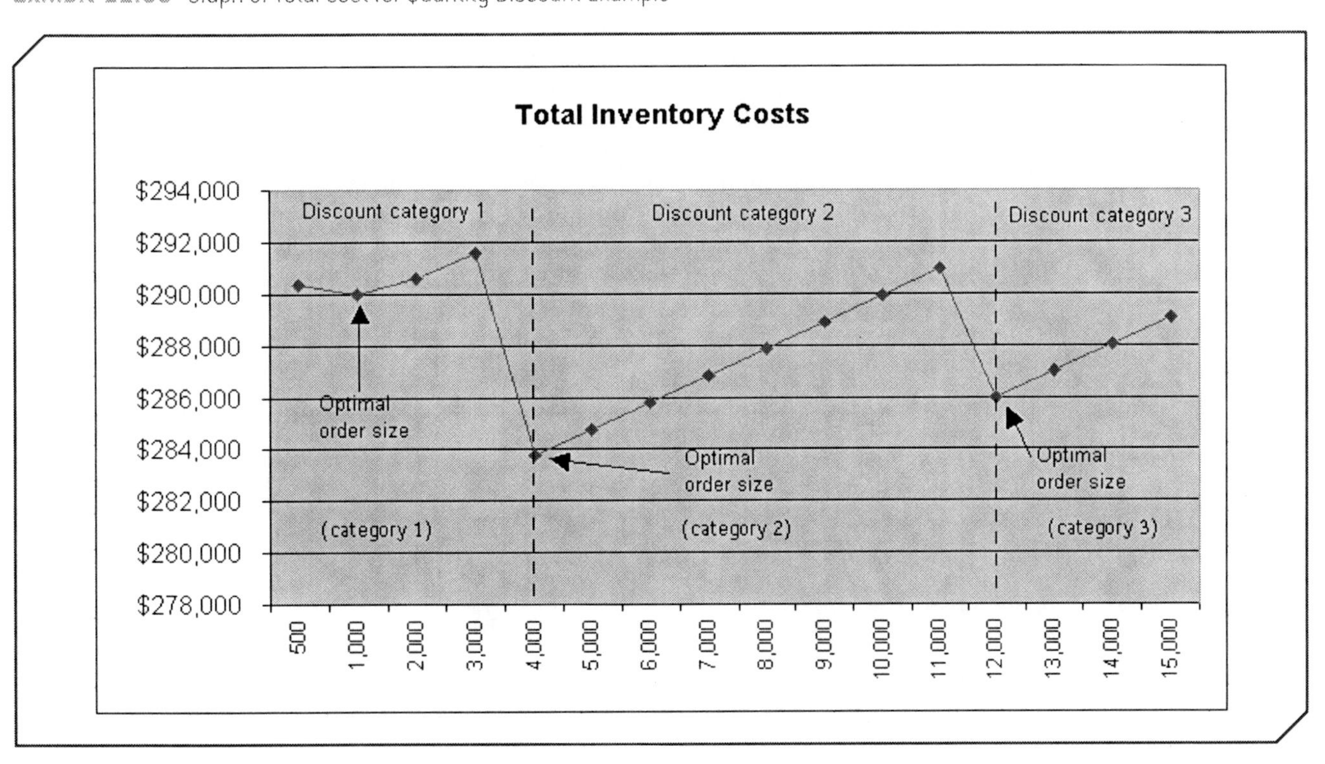

Single-Period Inventory Model

The single-period inventory model applies to inventory situations in which one order is placed for a good in anticipation of a future selling season where demand is uncertain. At the end of the period the product has either sold out or there is a surplus of unsold items to sell for a salvage value. Single-period models are used in situations involving seasonal or perishable items that cannot be carried in inventory and sold in future periods. One example is the situation faced by Banana Republic in one of the opening episodes; others would be ordering dough for a pizza restaurant, which stays fresh for only 3 days, and purchasing daily newspapers and seasonal holiday items such as Christmas trees. In such a single-period inventory situation, the only inventory decision is how much of the product to order at the start of the period. Because newspaper sales are a typical example of the single-period situation, the single-period inventory problem is sometimes referred to as the *newsvendor problem.*

The newsvendor problem can be solved using a technique called *marginal economic analysis*, which compares the cost or loss of ordering one additional item with the cost or loss of not ordering one additional item. The costs involved are defined as

c_s = the cost per item of overestimating demand (salvage cost); this cost represents the loss of ordering one additional item and finding that it cannot be sold.

c_u = the cost per item of underestimating demand (shortage cost); this cost represents the opportunity loss of not ordering one additional item and finding that it could have been sold.

The optimal order quantity is the value of Q^* that satisfies Equation (12.20):

$$P(\text{demand} \leq Q^*) = \frac{c_u}{c_u + c_s} \quad \textbf{(12.20)}$$

To illustrate this model, let us consider a buyer for a department store who is ordering fashion swimwear. The purchase must be made in the winter, and the store plans to hold an August clearance sale to sell any surplus goods by July 31. Each piece costs $40 per pair and sells for $60 per pair. At the sale price of $30 per pair, it is expected that any remaining stock can be sold during the August sale. We will assume that a uniform probability distribution ranging from 350 to 650 items, shown in Exhibit 12.34, describes the demand. The expected demand is 500.

The retailer will incur the cost of overestimating demand whenever it orders too much and has to sell the extra items available after July. Thus, the cost per item of overestimating demand is equal to the purchase cost per item minus the August sale price per item; that is, $c_s = \$40 - \$30 = \$10$. In other words, the retailer will lose $10 for each item that it orders over the quantity demanded. The cost of underestimating demand is the lost profit (opportunity loss) due to the fact that it could

Exhibit 12.34
Probability Distribution for Single Period Model

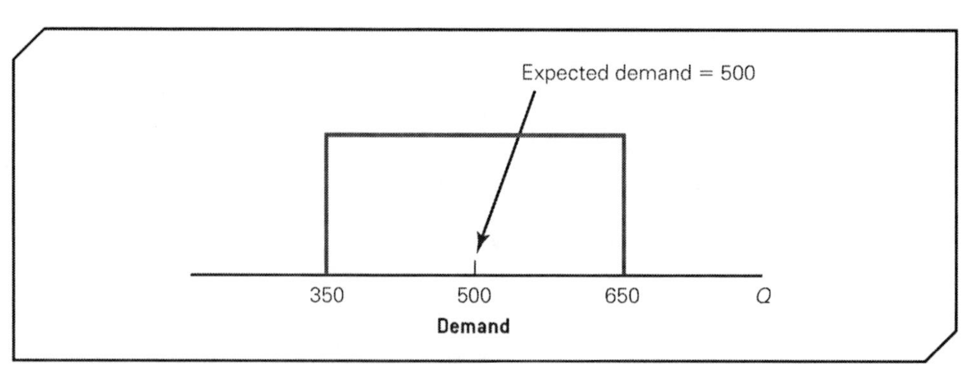

have been sold but was not available in inventory. Thus the per-item cost of underestimating demand is the difference between the regular selling price per item and the purchase cost per item; that is, c_u = \$60 − \$40 = \$20. The optimal order size must satisfy this condition:

$$P(\text{demand} \le Q^*) = \frac{c_u}{c_u + c_s} = \frac{20}{20 + 10} = \frac{20}{30} = \frac{2}{3}$$

Because the demand distribution is uniform, the value of Q^* is two-thirds of the way from 350 to 650. Thus, $Q^* = 550$ swimwear SKUs. Note that whenever $c_u < c_s$, the formula leads to the choice of an order quantity more likely to be less than demand; hence a higher risk of a stockout is present. However, when $c_u > c_s$, as in the example, the optimal order quantity leads to a higher risk of a surplus.

If the demand distribution were other than uniform, then the same process applies. To illustrate, suppose demand is normal with a mean of 500 and a standard deviation of 100. With c_u = \$20 and c_s = \$10 as previously computed, the optimal order quantity, Q^*, must still satisfy the requirement that $P(\text{demand} \le Q^*) = 2/3$. We simply use the table of areas under the normal curve (Appendix A) to find the Q^* where this condition is satisfied. This is shown in Exhibit 12.35.

In Exhibit 12.35, the area to the left of Q^* is $P(\text{demand} \le Q^*) = .667$. Therefore, the area between the mean, 500, and Q^* is .1667. This fact allows us to use Appendix A and determine that Q^* is $z = 0.43$ standard deviations above the mean. Therefore,

$$Q^* = \mu + 0.43\sigma = 500 + .43(100) = 543$$

Simulation Models for Inventory Analysis

In this chapter, we have concentrated on simple analytical inventory-decision models. But what should you do when the characteristics of an inventory system do not appear to agree with the assumptions of any inventory decision model? In this case, there are two alternatives: (1) attempt to develop and use a specially designed decision model that correctly reflects the characteristics of the system, or (2) develop and experiment with a computer simulation model that will indicate the impact of various decision alternatives on the cost of operating the system. Computer simulation is a powerful tool because it does not rely on restrictive assumptions the way that many analytical models do. Simulation has the flexibility to model unique features such as actual probability distributions that are difficult to represent in purely mathematical terms (see the OM Spotlight: Risk-Based Inventory Modeling

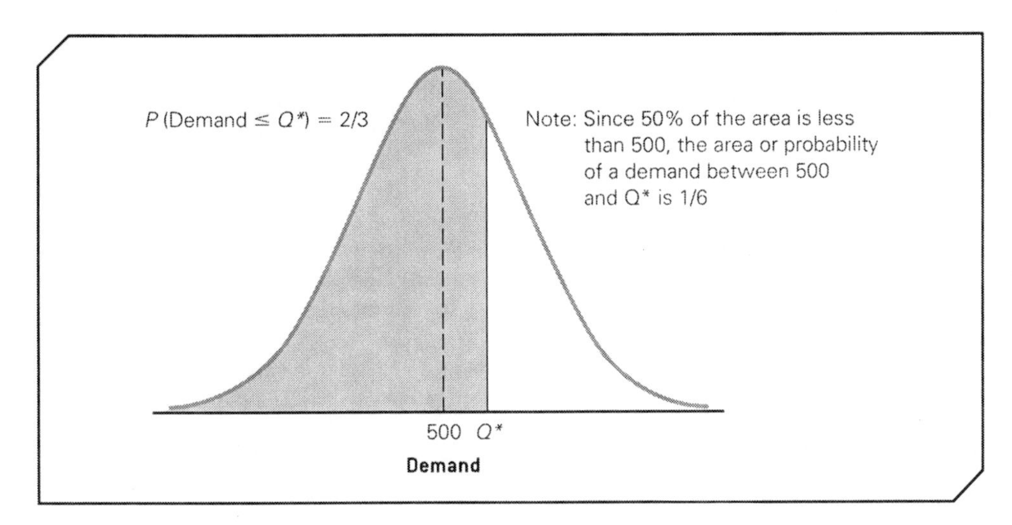

Exhibit 12.35
Optimal Order Quantity for Normally Distributed Demand Case

at Weyerhaeuser). However, building and using a simulation model can be expensive and usually requires more effort and time than analytical models. Supplementary Chapter D provides a general introduction to computer simulation in OM and includes an application to inventory analysis.

OM SPOTLIGHT

Risk-Based Inventory Simulation Modeling at Weyerhaeuser[10]

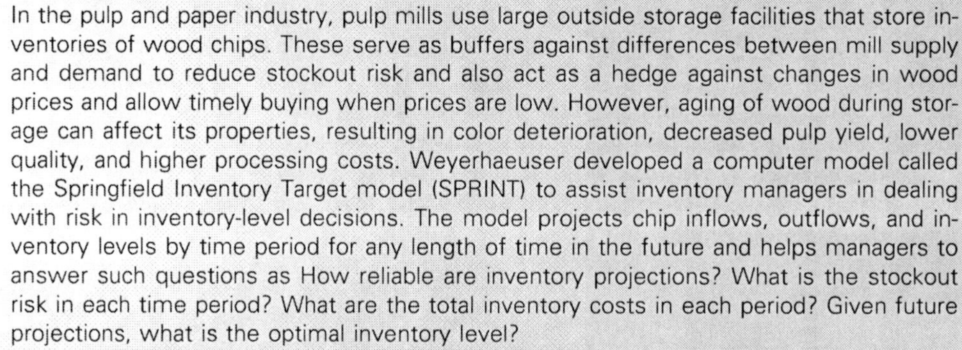

In the pulp and paper industry, pulp mills use large outside storage facilities that store inventories of wood chips. These serve as buffers against differences between mill supply and demand to reduce stockout risk and also act as a hedge against changes in wood prices and allow timely buying when prices are low. However, aging of wood during storage can affect its properties, resulting in color deterioration, decreased pulp yield, lower quality, and higher processing costs. Weyerhaeuser developed a computer model called the Springfield Inventory Target model (SPRINT) to assist inventory managers in dealing with risk in inventory-level decisions. The model projects chip inflows, outflows, and inventory levels by time period for any length of time in the future and helps managers to answer such questions as How reliable are inventory projections? What is the stockout risk in each time period? What are the total inventory costs in each period? Given future projections, what is the optimal inventory level?

The model uses probability distributions for each chip supply or usage volume and uses simulation to project expected chip deliveries, usages, and ending inventories over time, allowing the manager to assess the probability of a stockout and to translate this risk into a dollar cost. By repeatedly running the simulation model for different scenarios, the model helps managers to identify the inventory level that results in the minimum total inventory cost, balancing carrying costs with stockout costs. SPRINT has taken a lot of the guesswork out of making inventory decisions by providing objective assessments of costs and risks. Its principal benefit has been to allow managers to reduce inventories and stay within acceptable risk levels, lowering annual inventory costs by at least $2 million.

PR NewsWire
WEYERHAEUSER COMPANY

SOLVED PROBLEMS

SOLVED PROBLEM #1

Perform an ABC analysis for the items in Exhibit 12.36.

Solution:

Sorting the items in the descending order of total value we get the data in Exhibit 12.37.

The first four items account for 53 percent of dollar value and 16.6 percent of the items carried, while the last three items account for about 10 percent of the dollar value. Thus, the following classification would be reasonable. There is no correct breakdown into A, B, and C categories, so the decision is part science (ABC analysis) and part management judgment.

Inventory Classification	Item Number
A	4, 3, 5, 12
B	11, 7, 6, 10, 8
C	9, 1, 2

Item No.	Annual Item Usage	Item Value $	Item No.	Annual Item Usage	Item Value $
1	8,800	$68.12	7	112,000	$ 7.59
2	9,800	58.25	8	198,000	3.19
3	23,600	75.25	9	210,000	2.98
4	40,000	53.14	10	168,000	4.27
5	60,000	26.33	11	100,000	9.00
6	165,000	4.52	12	7,000	13.57

Exhibit 12.36
ABC Data for Solved Problem #1

Exhibit 12.37 Data for Solved Problem 1 Solution

Item No.	Annual Usage	Item Value $	Total $ Value	Cumulative No. Items	Cumulative Percent of Items	Cumulative Dollars $	Cumulative Percent of Value
4	40,000	53.14	2,125,600	40,000	3.43%	2,125,600	17.61%
3	23,600	75.25	1,775,900	63,600	5.46	3,901,500	32.32
5	60,000	26.33	1,579,800	123,600	10.61	5,481,300	45.40
12	70,000	13.57	949,900	193,600	16.62	6,431,200	53.27
11	100,000	9.00	900,000	293,600	25.20	7,331,200	60.73
7	112,000	7.59	850,080	405,600	34.81	8,181,280	67.77
6	165,000	4.52	745,800	570,600	48.97	8,927,080	73.95
10	168,000	4.27	717,360	738,600	63.39	9,644,440	79.89
8	198,000	3.19	631,620	936,600	80.38	10,276,060	85.12
9	210,000	2.98	625,800	1,146,600	98.40	10,901,860	90.31
1	8,800	68.12	599,456	1,155,400	99.16	11,501,316	95.27
2	9,800	58.25	570,850	1,165,200	100	12,072,166	100.00

SOLVED PROBLEM #2

A wholesaler of consumer electronics operates 52 weeks per year. The following information is for one of the video cassette recorders that it stocks and sells.

Demand = 4,500 units/year
Standard deviation of weekly demand = 12 units
Ordering costs = $40/order
Holding costs (C_h) = $3/unit/year
Cycle-service level = 90% (z-value = 1.28)
Lead time = 2 weeks
Number of weeks per year = 52 weeks

1. Using the fixed order quantity system to control inventory, compute the EOQ.
2. Compute the reorder point and state the order decision rule.
3. Compute the total order and inventory-holding costs.

   The firm decided to change to a fixed period system to control the item's inventory.
4. Compute the replenishment level.
5. Suppose it is time to review the inventory position, and the current inventory = 300 units (no scheduled receipts or back orders). Compute the number of units, if any, that need to be ordered using a fixed period system.
6. Compare safety stock between the fixed order quantity and fixed period models. Why the difference?

Solution:

1. $EOQ = \sqrt{\frac{2DC_o}{C_h}} = \sqrt{\frac{2(4{,}500)40}{3}}$

   $= 346.4 \rightarrow 346$ units

2. $R = dL + z\sigma_L = (4{,}500/52)2 + 1.28(12\sqrt{2})$
   $= 173.08 + 21.72 = 194.8 \rightarrow 195$ units

   Order decision rule: Place a new order for 346 units when the inventory position drops to or past the reorder point of 195 units.

3. $TC = \frac{1}{2}QC_h + \frac{D}{Q}C_o$

   $= (346/2) \times \$3 + (4{,}500/346) \times \$40$
   $= \$519 + \$519 = \$1{,}038$

4. $T = \frac{EOQ}{D}(52 \text{ weeks/year}) = \frac{346}{4{,}500}(52)$
$= 4.00$ weeks
$M = d(T + L) + z\sigma_{T+L}$
$= \frac{4{,}500}{52}(4 + 2) + 1.28(12)\sqrt{(4 + 2)}$
$= 519.23 + 37.62 = 556.85 = 557$

5. Order quantity $(Q_1) = M - IP_1 = 557 - 300 = 257$ units

6. Safety stock for the fixed order quantity model is 21.7 units versus 37.8 units for the fixed period model. This is due to the fact that the Q and R model must protect against stockouts over the lead time (L), while the T and M model must protect against stockouts over a longer time period, $T + L$. By reducing lead times and review periods, safety stock can be reduced. It cost \$48.3 more to carry the safety stock for the T and M system than the Q and R system (that is, 37.8 − 21.7 units times \$3/unit/year = \$48.3) to maintain the same service level of 90 percent.

SOLVED PROBLEM #3

Assume the quantity-discount schedule in Exhibit 12.38 is appropriate. If annual demand is 150 units, ordering cost is \$20 per order, and annual inventory-carrying cost is 25 percent, what order quantity would you recommend?

Exhibit 12.38 Data for Solved Problem 3

Order Size	Discount	Unit Cost
0 to 49	0%	\$30.00
50 to 99	5	28.50
100 or more	10	27.00

Solution:

Following the quantity discount procedure, we compute:

$Q_1 = \sqrt{2(150)(20)/[0.25(30)]} = 28.28$;
use $Q_1 = 28$

$Q_2 = \sqrt{2(150)(20)/[0.25(28.5)]} = 29.02$;
use $Q_2 = 50$ for a 5% discount

$Q_3 = \sqrt{2(150)(20)/[0.25(27)]} = 29.81$;
use $Q_3 = 100$ for a 10% discount

Category	Unit Cost	Order Quantity	Inventory Cost	Order Cost	Purchase Cost	Total Cost
1	\$30.00	28	\$105.00	\$107	\$4,500	\$4,712.00
2	28.50	50	178.13	60	4,275	4,335.00
3	27.00	100	337.50	30	4,050	4,417.50

$Q = 50$ to obtain the lowest total cost. The 5 percent discount is worthwhile.

SOLVED PROBLEM #4

Juanita Sutherland, the manager of Houston Oaks Aquarium Store, wants to set up a fixed period inventory control model to order the store's fish food. Cichlid Pellets in the 8-ounce jar is a top-selling SKU, so Juanita wants to demonstrate the advantages of formal inventory control methods to her district manager. Currently, she reviews this SKU and places an order every 2 months for 8,700 jars (that is, 52,000/6, or about 8,700) but has been experiencing stockouts of the item. This was the order policy in place at the store when she became the new store manager. She collected the following information:

Demand = 52,000 jars/year
Standard deviation of weekly demand = 110 jars
Ordering costs = \$45/order
Holding costs (C_h) = \$0.50/jar/year
Cycle-service level = 98% (z-value = 2.05)
Lead time = 2 weeks
Number of weeks per year = 52 weeks

1. Define a fixed period model based on the economics of the store.
2. At the most recent review a store employee found 1,500 jars on hand with no scheduled receipts or back orders. How many jars should now be ordered?
3. If she changed to a fixed order quantity system, define this model.
4. Compare the total order and inventory-holding cost of the fixed order quantity system with their current order policy of Q = 8,700 jars.

Solution:

1. $$EOQ = \sqrt{\frac{2DS}{H}} = \sqrt{\frac{2(52{,}000)45}{0.50}} = 3{,}060 \text{ jars}$$

$$T = \frac{EOQ}{D}(52 \text{ weeks/year}) = \frac{3{,}060}{52{,}000}(52)$$

$$= 3.06 \text{ weeks} \cong 3.0 \text{ weeks}$$

$$M = d(T + L) + z\sigma_{T+L}$$

$$= \frac{52{,}000}{52}(3 + 2) + 2.05(110)\sqrt{(3 + 2)}$$

$$= 5{,}000 + 504.2 = 5{,}504 \text{ jars}$$

Order decision rule: Place an order every 3 weeks where the order quantity equals $Q_t = 5{,}504 - IP_t$.

The current ordering policy of T = 2 months and a fixed Q = 8,700 jars is neither a fixed order quantity nor fixed period model but a combination of both (that is, both T and Q are fixed). One result of the current ordering policy is to create erratic average inventory levels with the fixed Q, so there are periods with excess inventory and then periods where stockouts occur.

2. $Q_1 = 5{,}504 - IP_1 = 5{,}504 - 1{,}500 = 4{,}004$ jars

3. First, we know from our previous calculations that the EOQ = 3,060 jars.

$$R = dL + z\sigma_L = (52{,}000/52)(2) + 2.05(110)\sqrt{2}$$
$$= 2{,}000 + 318.9 = 2{,}319 \text{ jars}$$

Order decision rule: Place a new order for 3,060 jars when the inventory position drops to or past the reorder point of 2,319 jars.

4. Current Order Policy

$$TC = \frac{1}{2}QC_h + \frac{D}{Q}C_o$$

$$= (8{,}700/2) \times 0.50 + (52{,}000/8{,}700) \times 45$$
$$= \$2{,}175 + \$270 = \$2{,}445$$

Fixed Order Quantity Policy

$$TC = \frac{1}{2}QC_h + \frac{D}{Q}C_o$$

$$= (3{,}060/2) \times 0.50 + (52{,}000/3{,}060) \times 45$$
$$= \$765 + \$765 = \$1{,}530$$

The total annual savings for this one SKU is substantial at \$915 (\$2,445 − \$1,530) and should help justify more formal inventory systems at the Houston Oaks Aquarium Store.

SOLVED PROBLEM #5

Grateful Fred sells souvenir T-shirts at rock concerts. The shirts are specially ordered with the city and date of the concert, so he cannot take them to another city after the concert. He buys the shirts for \$15 each and sells them for \$35 before and during the concert. He sells any remaining shirts outside the concert grounds for \$10 after the concert ends and can usually dispose of all of them. For a typical concert, demand is normally distributed, with a mean of 2,500 and standard deviation of 200. How many shirts should Fred order?

Solution:

$$C_o = \$15 - \$10 = \$5$$
$$C_u = \$35 - 15 = \$20$$

$$P(\text{demand} \leq Q^*) = \frac{C_u}{C_u + C_o} = \frac{20}{20 + 5} = .80$$

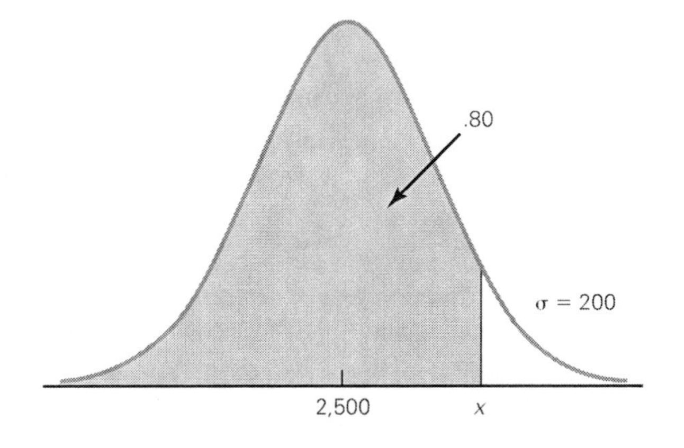

From Appendix A, z = .84. Thus,

$$Q^* = \mu + .84\sigma = 2{,}500 + .84(200)$$
$$= 2{,}668 \text{ shirts}$$

KEY TERMS AND CONCEPTS

ABC analysis
Anticipation inventory
Average total inventory at multiple stocking points
Back order
Back-order model
Chance of stockout and service levels
Cycle (order or lot size) inventory
Cycle counting
Dependent demand
Deterministic demand
Dynamic demand
Economic Order Quantity (EOQ)
Finished goods inventory
Fixed period system (FPS)
Fixed quantity system (FQS)
Independent demand
Inventory
Inventory costs
  Inventory holding (carrying) cost
  Order (setup) cost
  Shortage (stockout) costs
  Unit (item) cost
Inventory management
Inventory position (IP)
Lead time
Lost sale
Marginal economic analysis
Newsvendor problem
Number of SKUs
Operating, surplus, excess, obsolete, and new-product inventory
Perishable inventory
Pipeline inventory
Price breaks
Radio frequency identification (RFID) tags
Raw materials, component parts, subassemblies, and supplies
Reorder point
Safety stock inventory
Sensitivity analysis of EOQ
Service level
Single and two-bin system
Single-period model and decision rule
Static demand
Stochastic demand
Stock-keeping unit (SKU)
Stockout
Telematic diagnostic and monitoring systems
Time between orders (TBO)
Time period size
Total costs
  Inventory
  Order
  Safety Stock
Work-in-process (WIP) inventory

QUESTIONS FOR REVIEW AND DISCUSSION

1. Define inventory and provide some examples.
2. What is inventory management? Why is it an important function in OM?
3. How does inventory affect a firm's financial performance?
4. Explain the different types of inventories maintained in a typical value chain and state their purpose.
5. Discuss some of the issues that a small pizza restaurant might face in inventory management, forecasting, purchasing, and supplier partnerships.
6. Summarize the taxonomy for inventory management systems.
7. What is a SKU? Provide some examples in both goods and services.
8. Explain the difference between independent and dependent demand, deterministic and stochastic demand, and static and dynamic demand. Provide an example of an inventory item for each combination of these demand types (for example, independent, stochastic, and static, and so on).
9. Define *lead time*. What factors affect lead time?
10. Describe the two different types of stockouts that firms often face. What must be done to prevent them?
11. Define perishable inventory and provide some examples. How does fresh fruit differ from a concert seat even though both are perishable?
12. Explain the ABC classification for inventory. Of what value is ABC analysis?

13. What is cycle counting? How can it best be implemented?
14. Explain how modern technology such as bar coding and radio frequency identification help in inventory management.
15. What is a fixed quantity inventory system and how does it operate? What impact does demand variability have on the performance of a FQS?
16. Define inventory position. Why is inventory position used to trigger orders in a FQS rather than the actual stock level?
17. Explain how to determine the reorder point in a FQS.
18. Define and explain the different types of inventory costs that managers must consider in making replenishment decisions. How can these costs be determined in practice?
19. How does order cost differ from setup cost?
20. What is the EOQ model? What assumptions are necessary to apply it? How do these assumptions change the nature of the cycle inventory pattern graphically?
21. Explain how the total annual inventory cost is expressed in the EOQ model.
22. Discuss the sensitivity of the EOQ model's optimal solution to changes in the model parameters. Why is this important?
23. How must the EOQ model be changed to apply it in a stochastic demand situation?
24. Define service level. Why is it not necessarily desirable to attempt to attain a 100 percent service level?
25. Describe the structure and operation of a fixed period inventory system. Clearly explain how it differs from a FQS.
26. Would a pizza restaurant use a fixed order quantity or period system for fresh dough (purchased from a bakery on contract)? What would be the advantages and disadvantages of each in this situation?
27. Why does the fixed period model have to cover the time period of $T + L$ whereas the fixed order quantity model must cover only the time period L? Why is this important?
28. Explain the difference between the EOQ model and the extension to handle back orders.
29. Why are quantity discounts often given by suppliers? How do these affect the customer's inventory decisions?
30. Provide some situations where the single-period inventory model is applicable.
31. When is simulation useful in analyzing inventory systems?
32. List some products in your personal or family "inventory." How do you manage them? (For instance, do you constantly run to the store for milk? Do you throw out a lot of milk because of spoilage?) How might the ideas in this chapter change your way of managing these SKUs?
33. Interview a manager at a local business about its inventory and materials-management system, and prepare a report summarizing its approaches. Does it use any formal models? Why or why not? How does it determine inventory-related costs?

PROBLEMS AND ACTIVITIES

1. The Welsh Corporation uses 10 key components in one of its manufacturing plants. Perform an ABC analysis from the data in Exhibit 12.39. Explain your decisions and logic.
2. Develop an ABC histogram for the data in Exhibit 12.40.
3. MamaMia's Pizza purchases its pizza delivery boxes from a printing supplier. MamaMia's delivers on average 200 pizzas each month. Boxes cost 20 cents each, and each order costs $10 to process. Because of limited storage space, the manager wants to charge inventory holding at 30 percent of the cost. The lead time is 1 week, and the restaurant is open

Exhibit 12.39 ABC Data for Problem 1

SKU	Item Cost $	Annual Demand
WC219	$ 0.10	12,000
WC008	1.20	22,500
WC916	3.20	700
WC887	0.41	6,200
WC397	5.00	17,300
WC654	2.10	350
WC007	0.90	225
WC419	0.45	8,500
WC971	7.50	2,950
WC713	10.50	1,000

Exhibit 12.40
ABC Data for Problem 2

Item Number	Annual Usage	Unit Cost	Item Number	Annual Usage	Unit Cost
1	2,400	$19.51	11	500	$ 40.50
2	6,200	32.60	12	2,000	15.40
3	8,500	10.20	13	2,400	14.60
4	3,200	6.80	14	6,300	35.80
5	6,000	4.50	15	4,750	17.30
6	750	55.70	16	2,700	51.75
7	8,200	3.60	17	1,600	42.90
8	9,000	44.90	18	1,350	25.30
9	5,800	35.62	19	5,000	67.00
10	820	82.60	20	1,000	125.00

360 days per year. Determine the economic order quantity, reorder point, number of orders per year, and total annual cost. If the supplier raises the cost of each box to 25 cents, how would these results change?

4. Refer to the situation in Problem 3. Suppose the manager of MamaMia's wants to order 200 boxes each month. How much more than the optimal cost will be necessary to implement this policy?

5. A&M Industrial Products purchases a variety of parts used in small industrial tools. Inventory has not been tightly controlled, and managers think that costs can be substantially reduced. The items in Exhibit 12.41 comprise the inventory of one product line. Perform an ABC analysis of this inventory situation.

6. Given the weekly demand data in Exhibit 12.42, illustrate the operation of a continuous-review inventory system with a reorder point of 75, an order quantity of 100, and a beginning inventory of 125. Lead time is 1 week. All orders are placed at the end of the week. What is the average inventory and number of stockouts?

7. Crew Soccer Shoes Company is considering a change of its current inventory control system for soccer shoes. The information regarding the shoes is as follows:

   Demand = 100 pairs/week
   Lead time = 3 weeks
   Order cost = $35/order
   Holding cost = $2.00/pair/yr
   Cycle service level = 95%
   Standard deviation of weekly demand = 50
   Number of weeks per year = 52

   a. The company decides to use a fixed order quantity system. What would be the reorder point and the economic order quantity?
   b. In this system, at the beginning of the current week, the materials manager, Emily Eddins, checked the inventory level of shoes and found 300 pairs. There were no scheduled receipts and no back orders. Should she place an order? Explain your answer.
   c. If the company changes to a periodic review system and reviews the inventory every two weeks (P = 2), how much safety stock is required?

Exhibit 12.41
Data for Problem 5

Part Number	Annual Demand	Item Cost $	Part Number	Annual Demand	Item Cost $
A367	700	$ 0.04	P157	13	$ 3.10
A490	3,850	0.70	P232	600	0.12
B710	400	0.29	R825	15,200	0.12
C615	600	0.24	S324	20	30.15
C712	7,200	2.60	S404	400	0.12
D008	680	51.00	S692	75	12.10
G140	45	100.00	T001	20,000	0.005
G147	68,000	0.0002	X007	225	0.15
K619	2,800	5.25	Y345	8,000	0.16
L312	500	1.45	Z958	455	2.56
M582	8,000	0.002	Z960	2,000	0.001
M813	2,800	0.0012			

Exhibit 12.42 Data for Problem 6

Week	Demand	Week	Demand
1	25	7	50
2	30	8	35
3	20	9	30
4	40	10	40
5	40	11	20
6	25	12	25

8. Exhibit 12.43 gives the daily demand of a certain oil filter at an auto supply store. Illustrate the operation of a fixed order quantity inventory system by graphing the inventory level versus time if $Q = 40$, $R = 15$, and the lead time is 3 days. Assume that orders are placed at the end of the day and that they arrive at the beginning of the day. Thus, if an order is placed at the end of Day 5, it will arrive at the beginning of Day 9. Assume that 30 items are on hand at the start of Day 1.

9. For the data given in Problem 8, illustrate the operation of a fixed period inventory system with a reorder level of 40, a reorder point of 15, and a review period of 5 days.

10. Wildcat Tools is a distributor of hardware and electronics equipment. Its socket wrench inventory needs better management. The information regarding the wrenches is as follows:

    Demand = 50 wrenches per month
    Lead time = 1 month
    Order cost = $20/order
    Holding cost = $2.40/wrench/yr
    Back-order cost = $15/back order
    Cycle-service level = 90%
    Standard deviation of monthly demand = 20 wrenches
    Current on-hand inventory is 65 wrenches, with no scheduled receipts and no backorders.

    a. The company decides to use a continuous review system. What are the recommended reorder point, safety stock, and economic order quantity?
    b. Based on the information calculated in part a, should an order be placed? If yes, how much should be ordered?
    c. The company wants to investigate the fixed period system with a twice per month review (P = 2 weeks). How much safety stock is required?

11. Tune Football Helmets Company is considering changing the current inventory control system for football helmets. The information regarding the helmets is as follows:

Exhibit 12.43 Data for Problem 8

Day	Demand	Day	Demand
1	6	14	0
2	8	15	2
3	5	16	4
4	4	17	7
5	5	18	3
6	6	19	5
7	1	20	9
8	1	21	3
9	3	22	6
10	8	23	1
11	8	24	9
12	6	25	1
13	7		

Demand = 200 units/week
Lead time = 2 weeks
Order cost = $60/order
Holding cost = $1.50/unit/yr
Cycle-service level = 95%
Standard deviation of weekly demand = 60
Number of weeks per year = 52

a. The firm decides to use a fixed period system to control the inventory and to review the inventory every 2 weeks. At the beginning of the current week, D. J. Jones, the materials manager, checked the inventory level of helmets and found 450 units. There were no scheduled receipts and no back orders. How many units should be ordered?
b. If the firm changes to a fixed quantity system, what would be the reorder point and the economic order quantity?

12. The reorder point is defined as the demand during the lead time for the item. In cases of long lead times, the lead-time demand and thus the reorder point may exceed the economic order quantity, Q^*. In such cases, the inventory position will not equal the inventory on hand when an order is placed, and the reorder point may be expressed in terms of either inventory position or inventory on hand. Consider the EOQ model with $D = 5{,}000$, $C_o = \$32$, $C_h = \$2$, and 250 working days per year. Identify the reorder point in terms of inventory position and in terms of inventory on hand for each of these lead times.
    a. 5 days
    b. 15 days
    c. 25 days
    d. 45 days

13. The XYZ Company purchases a component used in the manufacture of automobile generators directly

from the supplier. XYZ's generator production, which is operated at a constant rate, will require 1,200 components per month throughout the year. Assume ordering costs are $25 per order, item cost is $2.00 per component, and annual inventory-holding costs are charged at 20 percent. The company operates 250 days per year, and the lead time is 5 days.

a. Compute the EOQ, total annual inventory-holding and -ordering costs, and the reorder point.
b. Suppose XYZ's managers like the operational efficiency of ordering in quantities of 1,200 items and ordering once each month. How much more expensive would this policy be than your EOQ recommendation? Would you recommend in favor of the 1,200-item order quantity? Explain. What would the reorder point be if the 1,200-item quantity were acceptable?

14. The maternity ward of a hospital sends one baby blanket home with each newborn baby. The following information is available for the baby blankets:

Demand = 80 blankets/week
Standard deviation in weekly demand = 7 blankets
Desired cycle-service level = 96%
Delivery lead time = 2 weeks (delivery of the blankets, not the babies!)
Annual holding cost = $2.00
Ordering cost = $8.00/order
Cost of one blanket = $6.00
The hospital is open 52 weeks each year.

a. As the new maternity ward manager, you decide to improve the current ordering methods used for items that are stocked in the maternity ward. Calculate the economic order quantity for baby blankets.
b. Baby blankets are currently ordered in quantities of 200. How much would the maternity ward save in total annual relevant costs by changing to the EOQ?
c. You decide that a fixed order quantity system will be used for ordering the blankets. Name and calculate what must be known for implementing such a system.

15. Tele-Reco is a new specialty store that sells television sets, videotape recorders, video games, and other television-related products. A new Japanese-manufactured videotape recorder costs Tele-Reco $600 per item. Tele-Reco's inventory-carrying cost is figured at an annual rate of 22 percent. Ordering costs are estimated to be $70 per order.

a. If demand for the new videotape recorder is expected to be constant at a rate of 20 items per month, what is the recommended order quantity for the videotape recorder?
b. What are the estimated annual inventory-holding and -ordering costs associated with this product?
c. How many orders will be placed per year?
d. With 250 working days per year, what is the cycle time for this product?

16. Nation-Wide Bus Lines is proud of the 6-week driver-training program it conducts for all new Nation-Wide drivers. The program costs Nation-Wide $22,000 for instructors, equipment, and so on and is independent of the number of new drivers in the class as long as the class size remains less than or equal to 35. The program must provide the company with approximately five new fully trained drivers per month. After completing the training program, new drivers are paid $1,800 per month but do not work until a full-time driver position is open. Nation-Wide views the $1,800 as a holding cost necessary to maintain a supply of newly trained drivers available for immediate service. Viewing new drivers as inventory SKUs, how large should the training classes be in order to minimize Nation-Wide's total annual training and new-driver idle-time costs? How many training classes should the company hold each year? What is the total annual cost of your recommendation?

17. Brauch's Pharmacy has an expected annual demand for a leading pain reliever of 800 boxes, which sell for $6.50 each. Each order costs $6.00, and the inventory-carrying charge is 20 cents. The expected demand during the lead time is normal, with a mean of 25 and a standard deviation of 3. Assuming 52 weeks per year, what reorder point provides a 95 percent service level? How much safety stock will be carried? If the carrying charge were 25 cents instead, what would be the total annual inventory-related cost?

18. A product with an annual demand of 1,000 SKUs has C_o = $30 and C_h = $8. The demand exhibits some variability such that the lead-time demand follows a normal distribution, with a mean of 25 and a standard deviation of 5.

a. What is the recommended order quantity?
b. What are the reorder point and safety-stock level if the firm desires at most a 2 percent probability of a stockout on any given order cycle?
c. If the manager sets the reorder point at 30, what is the probability of a stockout on any given order cycle? How many times would you expect to stock out during the year if this reorder point were used?

19. The B&S Novelty and Craft Shop in Bennington, Vermont sells a variety of quality handmade items to tourists. It will sell 300 hand-carved miniature replicas of a colonial soldier each year, but the demand pattern during the year is uncertain. The replicas sell for $20 each, and B&S uses a 15 percent annual inventory-holding cost rate. Ordering costs are $5 per order, and demand during the lead time follows a normal distribution, with a mean of 15 and a standard deviation of 6.
   a. What is the recommended order quantity?
   b. If B&S is willing to accept a stockout roughly twice a year, what reorder point would you recommend? What is the probability that B&S will have a stockout in any one order cycle?
   c. What is the safety-stock level and annual safety-stock cost for this product?

20. The manager of an inventory system believes that inventory models are important decision-making aids. Although the manager often uses an EOQ policy, he has never considered a back-order model because of his assumption that back orders are "bad" and should be avoided. However, with top level management pressure for cost reduction, you have been asked to analyze the economics of a back-ordering policy for some products. For a specific product with $D = 800$ units per year, $C_o = \$150$, $C_h = \$3$, and $C_b = \$20$, what is the economic difference in the EOQ and the back-order model? If the manager adds constraints that no more than 25 percent of the units may be back-ordered and that no customer will have to wait more than 15 days for an order, should the back-order inventory policy be adopted? Assume 250 working days per year. If the lead time for new orders is 25 days for the inventory system, find the reorder point for both the EOQ and the back-order models.

21. Marilyn's Interiors sells silk floral arrangements in addition to other home furnishings. Because space is limited and she does not want to tie up a lot of money in inventory, Marilyn uses a back-order policy for most items. A popular silk arrangement costs her $40 to assemble and Marilyn sells an average of 15 per month. Ordering costs are $30, and she values her inventory holding cost at 25 percent. Marilyn figures the back-order cost to be $40 annually. What is the optimal order quantity and planned back-order level? What if customer cancellations and other loss of goodwill increase the back-order cost to $100 annually?

22. Apply the EOQ model to the quantity-discount situation shown in the following data:

Discount Category	Order Size	Discount	Unit Cost
1	0 to 99	0 percent	$10.00
2	100 or more	3 percent	$ 9.70

Assume that $D = 500$ units per year, $C_o = \$40$, and the annual inventory-holding cost is 20 percent. What order quantity do you recommend?

23. Allen's Shoe Stores carries a basic black dress shoe for men that sells at an approximate constant rate of 500 pairs of shoes every three months. Allen's current buying policy is to order 500 pairs each time an order is placed. It costs $30 to place an order, and inventory-carrying costs have an annual rate of 20 percent. With the order quantity of 500, Allen's obtains the shoes at the lowest possible unit cost of $28 per pair. Other quantity discounts offered by the manufacturer are listed below:

Order Quantity	Price per Pair
0-99	$36
100-199	32
200-299	30
300 or more	28

What is the minimum-cost order quantity for the shoes? What are the annual savings of your inventory policy over the policy currently being used?

24. The J&B Card Shop sells calendars featuring a different Colonial picture for each month. The once-a-year order for each year's calendar arrives in September. From past experience the September-to-July demand for the calendars can be approximated by a normal distribution with $\mu = 500$ and $\sigma = 120$. The calendars cost $3.50 each, and J&B sells them for $7 each.
   a. If J&B throws out all unsold calendars at the end of July (that is, salvage value is zero), how many calendars should be ordered?
   b. If J&B reduces the calendar price to $1 at the end of July and can sell all surplus calendars at this price, how many calendars should be ordered?

25. The Gilbert Air-Conditioning Company is considering the purchase of a special shipment of portable air-conditioners manufactured in Mexico. Each unit will cost Gilbert $80 and it will be sold for $125. Gilbert does not want to carry surplus air-conditioners over until the following year. Thus all supplies will be sold to a wholesaler, who has agreed to take all surplus units for $50 per unit. Assume that the air-conditioner demand has a normal distribution with $\mu = 20$ and $\sigma = 6$.
   a. What is the recommended order quantity?
   b. What is the probability that Gilbert will sell all units it orders?

CASES

MARGATE HOSPITAL

Cost-containment activities have become particularly important to hospital operations managers, stimulated by major revisions in health care reimbursement policies and significant growth in marketing activities by private-sector health care organizations. Recognizing that poor inventory control policies reflect ineffective use of organizational assets, many hospital managers have sought to institute more systematic approaches to the control of supply inventories.

At Margate Hospital, analysts collected data on 47 disposable SKUs in a pulmonary therapy unit. These data are shown in Exhibit 12.44 (the file Margate ABC Data.xls is available on the Student CD-ROM). Four of the SKUs are designated as critical to patient care. The hospital administrator wants to develop better inventory management policies for these items. Using the data, propose a breakdown for an ABC analysis, and clearly outline how each category of items might be managed by the hospital.

Exhibit 12.44
Hospital Data for ABC Analysis

SKU	Total Annual Usage	Average Unit Cost		SKU	Total Annual Usage	Average Unit Cost	
1	212	$ 24.00		25	8	$ 58.00	
2	210	$ 5.00		26	7	$ 65.00	
3	172	$ 27.00		27	5	$ 86.00	
4	117	$ 50.00		28	5	$ 30.00	
5	100	$ 28.00		29	4	$ 84.00	
6	94	$ 31.00		30	4	$ 78.00	
7	60	$ 58.00		31	4	$ 56.00	
8	50	$ 21.00		32	4	$ 53.00	
9	48	$ 55.00		33	4	$ 49.00	
10	48	$ 15.00		34	4	$ 41.00	
11	33	$ 73.00		35	4	$ 20.00	
12	27	$210.00	Critical	36	3	$ 72.00	Critical
13	27	$ 7.00		37	3	$ 61.00	
14	19	$ 24.00		38	3	$ 8.00	
15	18	$ 45.00	Critical	39	2	$134.00	
16	15	$160.00	Critical	40	2	$ 67.00	
17	12	$ 87.00		41	2	$ 60.00	
18	12	$ 71.00		42	2	$ 52.00	
19	12	$ 50.00		43	2	$ 38.00	
20	12	$ 47.00		44	2	$ 29.00	
21	12	$ 33.00		45	1	$ 48.00	
22	10	$ 37.00		46	1	$ 34.00	
23	10	$ 34.00		47	1	$ 29.00	
24	8	$110.00					

COLORADO TECHNICAL COLLEGE[11]

At Colorado Technical College, demand patterns in the copy-center environment had been highly seasonal, following a similar pattern during each school year, and had exhibited an increasing trend from year to year. Requests for low-demand items (odd colors of paper, for example) were very erratic, while use of high-demand items (such as $8^1/_2 \times 11$, white, three-hole paper) was predictably seasonal. Unacceptably high stock levels of low-demand items were being maintained, and emergency orders on high-demand items were frequent. Data records were sparse and had been kept with little consistency, often being just monthly orders with no record of beginning or ending inventories or increased inventory with no ordering. Several of the 75 stock-keeping items (SKUs) were obtained via discount cost schedules, and one source had a $150 minimum-order requirement. Lead times generally had minor variances, with means of 1 to 10 working days.

Storage space was insufficient to accommodate a 1-week supply during peak demand and was partitioned into product families. Stockout penalties were very high, and managers placed orders at the verbal request of the workers.

The workers were well seasoned, experienced, and highly proficient in the intuitive management of the copy center. Daily work schedules were highly erratic; hence, time available to maintain an inventory control system would be very irregular. Polite political tensions existed between managers and workers, resulting from a history of poor communication, lack of resources available to assist in controlling the inventory, lack of accountability for inventory decisions, and a previous failure to implement a manual inventory control system. The workers were resistant to management control, and managers were not satisfied with the way inventory was being managed. It was evident that an inventory system was needed to achieve a balance between the workers' need for flexibility to adapt to uncertain and highly varying demand and managers' desire that the inventory be managed efficiently.

The problem solution therefore required that the workers operate an inventory control system yet be unable to manipulate the system into practical ineffectiveness. The operators would have to be given sufficient historical demand data to allow for intelligent deviation from a suggested ordering pattern and the freedom to fine-tune the ordering patterns when those patterns began to violate the constraints of limited inventory space and high stockout penalties. System integrity would have to be beyond compromise, and any deviations from a suggested order pattern would be flagged to prevent accidental, duplicate, or oversized orders.

Questions for Discussion

1. How do the behavioral and political concerns affect the design of the inventory management system?
2. Develop a thorough set of recommendations, taking into account the unique characteristics of demand and other information that would affect inventory management decisions. Present your findings in a report to the copy center manager.

KINGSTON UNIVERSITY HOSPITAL

Bonnie Ebelhar, Kingston University's director of materials management, glanced again at the papers spread across her desk. She wondered where the week had gone. On Monday, the director of university operations, Drew Paris, had asked Ebelhar to look into the purchasing and supplies systems for the hospital. Paris specifically wanted Ebelhar to evaluate the current materials management system, identify ways to reduce costs, and recommend a final plan of action. Paris explained that the university was under pressure to cut expenses, and hospital inventory did not seem to be under control. Not knowing quite what to look for, Ebelhar had spent a good part of the week collecting information—information she had organized on the papers that now covered her desk.

As Ebelhar reviewed her notes, she was struck by the variations in order sizes and order frequencies for any given hospital stock-keeping item. In some cases, items stocked out before new orders came in, whereas for other items, excessively high stock levels were being carried at (too) many hospital stocking points. She wondered whether there might be a more efficient and economical way of managing the hospital and university's inventories. Ebelhar had been exposed to inventory control techniques during her undergraduate college days.

Hospital and university supply orders were classified as either regular stock or special order. The hospital was the originator of almost all special orders. Regular stock items were characterized by their long-standing and frequent use throughout the university and hospital as well as by a low risk of obsolescence. When a hospital unit (department) needed a regular stock item, that unit generally requisitioned the item. If the item were in stock, it would be delivered by the unit's next delivery date. Last year, 19,000 requisitions had been submitted to university purchasing from the hospital units.

The process of adding an item to the regular university stock list took several months. To begin the process, one of the hospital's units had to submit a purchase request (not a purchase order) to university purchasing. After receiving such a request, university purchasing would determine whether or not to carry the item. When the university did not carry an item, individual hospital units could carry the item on a special-order basis. Special-order items were supposed to be those of an experimental nature or critical to patient health care. Hospital units requiring these special items bypassed the university purchasing system. Once a special order was placed, the hospital unit informed university purchasing so that it could eventually authorize payment on the vendor's invoice. Hospital unit coordinators or head nurses were responsible for preparing and/or authorizing special orders. In total, these special orders required a significant amount of work that took unit coordinators and head nurses away from their duties. This past year, the hospital's 31 units had issued 16,000 special orders. These were in addition to the hospital's 19,000 regular requisitions, mentioned previously.

A large number of these special orders were actually placed for supplies with widespread use throughout the hospital. In many of these cases, none of the hospital's units involved had ever requested university purchasing to include the item on the regular stock list. One unit's head nurse explained that many units were afraid of stocking out of these items if they were under university control. University purchasing didn't understand the importance and technical nature of hospital inventory. The nurse cited the months-long period university purchasing needed to place new items on the regular stock list and the long lead times sometimes involved in receiving orders requisitioned from the list.

A small but significant number of special orders were placed for or by doctors with specific brand preferences. They were unwilling to use particular items that purchasing ordered and stocked. Typically, the preferred brands were more expensive than the regular SKUs carried. These orders were most common where purchases could be broken up so that state bidding procedures did not have to be followed.

Record keeping varied by order type. University purchasing maintained ongoing records only on regular stock items. Once regular stock materials were delivered to a hospital unit, university inventory clerks input this information into the university computer. University purchasing record-keeping responsibilities ended once SKUs were delivered to a hospital unit. For special orders, the hospital was responsible for recording inventory on hand and disbursements. University purchasing kept no records on the hospital's special-order inventories or for the 215 secondary hospital stocking points.

Technically, the individual hospital units were responsible for keeping inventory records and controlling materials once they were in the unit. In practice, however, few of the hospital units had any formal methods of record keeping or inventory control. Unit coordinators or head nurses arranged the ordering of materials when supplies seemed low or when hospital doctors requested a specific item. For several years, there had not been any hospitalwide physical inventory audit in the 31 hospital units. The only recent inventory audit was by the Surgical Intensive Care Unit, which discovered large amounts of obsolete and overstocked inventory items.

Since the university was a state institution, strict bidding and purchasing procedures had to be followed for both regular stock and special orders. For example, three written bids were required for an individual order of $1,000 or more. The processing of these bids often took up to 2 months. For orders between $500 and $999, three telephone bids were necessary. In these situations, purchases could be made only from the lowest bidder. Orders under $500, or items on the state contract list, could be ordered over the phone, without any bids. State contract list items were those for which statewide needs had been combined and one contract let to cover all of them.

In emergency situations, university purchasing would authorize individual hospital departments to place both regular and special orders without following the state guidelines. Ebelhar had found evidence that some hospital units were abusing this procedure, by using emergency orders to circumvent bidding requirements on big-ticket items, when the preferred vendor was unlikely to be the lowest-priced supplier.

Vendors delivered the hospital's regular stock supplies to the university warehouse. After orders were checked in, notification was sent to the hospital storeroom, and then some or all of the regular order was transferred to the hospital storeroom. Since the hospital storeroom's capacity was limited, backup regular stock was retained at the university warehouse in some cases. Special orders were shipped directly to the hospital storeroom. Once the supplies reached the hospital storeroom, the clerks placed the items in numbered bins. In addition to receiving shipments, the hospital storeroom clerks prepared and made scheduled deliveries to the hospital units, conducted visual inventory checks of the bins, ordered replenishment stock, and filled any walk-up orders.

Each week, hospital storeroom clerks made one delivery to each of the hospital's 31 units; deliveries took place daily between 7:00 A.M. and 9:00 A.M. Once supplies were delivered to the unit, a unit assistant was responsible for stocking the unit's central supply area and resupplying any ancillary stocking locations. There were no dollar limits on the amount of supplies that a hospital unit could carry at any one time. As a result, most departments carried as many supplies as was physically possible. The stock levels of the central supply area in each of individual hospital units could vary dramatically from week to week. Stock levels in the ancillary locations, however, tended to remain constant. For example, a hospital cart would have a specific list of what items to carry and how many of each. Unit personnel would then be responsible for replenishing the cart, as needed, on a daily basis.

Ebelhar had gathered information on the costs of purchasing and storing hospital supplies. She estimated that, on average, the purchasing, payables, and receiving personnel spent 6 to 7 hours processing a single purchase order. Individual purchase orders typically included three supply items (SKUs). The average hospital storeroom's wage was $15 an hour; with employee benefits and associated overhead, the cost of one worker-hour came to $18.

Ebelhar realized that a significant amount of time was spent by hospital personnel in preparing requisitions and issuing special orders. However, she was unsure how to quantify this time. After all, anywhere from 1 to 15 hospital units might requisition a particular regular stock item before the university needed to issue another order. And, in the case of special orders, processing times could

Exhibit 12.45
Kingston University Hospital SKU Data*

		Case Size		Cost Per Case	Order Lead Time
Fetal Monitoring Kits		20 kits		$844.00	5 weeks
Strike Disinfectant		4 gallons		$ 64.20	2 weeks
Fetal Monitoring Kits+					
Beginning Balance	80	Week	1		
Receipts	125	Week	3		
Ending Balance	74	Week	16		
Strike Disinfectant++					
Beginning Balance	96	Week	1		
Receipts	200	Week	7		
Ending Balance	110	Week	16		

*These inventory balances are for the central hospital storeroom only. The receipts are reasonable estimates of their current order quantities (*Q*).
+Number of individual kits, not cases.
++In gallons, not cases.

range from a half-hour to half a day, depending on the item. Between the hospital storeroom and the university warehouse, the university allocated 26,750 square feet of storage space to hospital uses. As mentioned earlier, the university stored an average of $2.15 million in hospital supplies in this space. Records indicated that the average annual variable and semivariable cost for storage space this year would be $2.60 per square foot. Five warehouse workers and storeroom clerks were required to handle the hospital's supplies. These individuals each earned $24,000 a year; benefits and overhead rates for these employees were the same as for other personnel, about 20 percent. Other warehouse costs, including obsolescence and taxes, were expected to reach $100,000 this year.

Ebelhar wondered how to determine an inventory-carrying cost; she was not sure what to include in the computation. In her previous jobs, Ebelhar had normally included interest or other opportunity costs when determining carrying cost. In this situation, she was unsure as to what cost components to include in the inventory-carrying cost. After all, the state allocated funds for fairly specific purposes, and the university could draw down these funds whenever necessary. The state generated these funds through tax revenues and bond issues. Recently, the state had floated a bond issue at 8.9 percent.

After reviewing her notes on the hospital's materials management situation, Ebelhar decided to take a closer look at some individual regular stock items. She sorted through the papers on her desk and found two items of interest: Fetal Monitoring Kits and Strike Disinfectant. Both SKUs were considered critical to the hospital's operations. Data on these two SKUs are shown in Exhibits 12.45 to 12.48.

Ebelhar wondered whether inventory control techniques would improve inventory ordering policies and save the state and university money. As a starting point, she decided to use the information she had collected on the Fetal Monitoring Kits and the Strike Disinfectant to evaluate and compare various inventory management systems and decision rules. A few of the questions of interest to Ebelhar are as follows:

Exhibit 12.46
Kingston University Hospital Aggregate Weekly Demand as Measured by Hospital Requisitions

Week	Fetal Kits*	Strike+
1	12	31
2	14	27
3	0	1
4	1	12
5	5	11
6	9	8
7	8	4
8	7	15
9	26	15
10	11	16
11	6	10
12	10	9
13	2	8
14	8	5
15	7	10
16	5	4
Total	131	186
Mean	8.19	11.63
Standard deviation	6.12	8.02
Cycle-service level	97%	90%

*Fetal Monitoring Kit demand is quoted for individual kits, not cases.
+Strike Disinfectant demand is quoted in gallons.

1. What are good estimates of order cost and inventory-holding cost?
2. Define and graph a fixed order quantity (*Q* and *r*) inventory system for the two example SKUs.

Exhibit 12.47
Kingston University Hospital Fetal Monitoring Kits—Special One-Time Audit Results

	Hospital Unit	On-Hand Supply*
1.	Thomas Wing	12
2.	David Wing—Obstetrics	14
3.	Burn Center	6
4.	Coronary	6
5.	Davis Wing	10
6.	Delivery Room	16
7.	Pediatric Intensive Care	8
8.	Emergency Room	16
9.	Surgical Intensive Care	18
	Total Average Stock	106

3. Compute the total order and inventory-holding costs for the Q and r system, and compare to their current order Qs.
4. Define and graph a fixed period (T and M) inventory system for the two example SKUs.
5. Evaluate the relative size of carrying inventory at one hospital main storeroom site, 31 hospital departments and wards, and 215 stocking points in rooms, carts, and so on. What are the implications? How many stocking points do you recommend and why? Justify.
6. What should Ebelhar recommend to improve inventory-related performance? Explain. Justify.

Given the hospital's climate, current practices, and the materials management situation, Ebelhar wondered whether inventory management could really make a difference at this hospital.

Exhibit 12.48
Kingston University Hospital Strike Disinfectant—Special One-Time Audit Results

	Hospital Unit	On-Hand Supply*
1.	Thomas Wing	2
2.	Blood Bank	8
3.	Burn Center	4
4.	Coronary	3
5.	Cardiac Cath Laboratory	5
6.	Andrew Wing	2
7.	Delivery Room	2
8.	Dentistry	1
9.	Emergency Room	2
10.	Family Practice	1
11.	Hematology	12
12.	Internal Medicine	2
13.	Medical Intensive Care	2
14.	Medical Technology	4
15.	Chris Wing	3
16.	David Wing—Obstetrics	6
17.	Operating Room	8
18.	Oral Surgery	5
19.	Otolaryngology	4
20.	Pediatric Intensive Care	2
21.	Radiology	2
22.	Renal Division	3
23.	Respiratory Therapy	6
24.	Surgical Intensive Care	14
	Total Average Stock	103

*On-hand supply of gallons of Strike Disinfectant found last week during the special audit. This count was taken on Thursday for all hospital units and their respective secondary stocking points.

ENDNOTES

[1] Lee, Louise, "Yes, We Have a New Banana," *BusinessWeek*, May 31, 2004, pp. 70–72.

[2] A more complete technical classification and survey of inventory problems is given in Silver, E. A., "Operations Research in Inventory Management," *Operations Research* 29 (1981), pp. 628–645.

[3] Grocery Manufacturers of America, "Full-Shelf Satisfaction—Reducing Out-of-Stocks in the Grocery Channel, 2002 Report. www.gmabrtands.com/publications

[4] Cantwell, Jim, "The How and Why of Cycle Counting: The ABC Method," *Production and Inventory Management* 26, no. 2, 1985, pp. 50–54.

[5] "Hot Potato," *Chief Information Officer (CIO) Magazine*, January 15, 2003, p. 72.

[6] "Chips Soon May Replace Bar Codes," *The Sun News*, Myrtle Beach, S.C., July 9, 2003, pp. 1D and 3D.

[7] Delany, K. J., "Inventory Tool to Launch in Germany," *The Wall Street Journal*, January 12, 2004, p. B5.

[8] "Accurate Inventory Fuels Nissan Plant's Drive to Add Third Production Line," *Frontline Solutions*, August 2000, pp. 25, 30.

[9] Hau, L. Lee, Billington, Corey, and Carter, Brent, "Hewlett-Packard Gains Control of Inventory and Service Through Design for Localization," *Interfaces* 23, no. 4, July–August, 1993, pp. 1–11.

[10] Finke, Gary, "Determining Target Inventories of Wood Chips Using Risk Analysis," *Interfaces* 14, no. 5, September–October 1984, pp. 53–58.

[11] This case was inspired by Hayes, Timothy R., "An Inventory Control System for The Colorado School of Mines Quick Copy Center," *Production and Inventory Management Journal* 35, no. 4, Fourth Quarter 1994, pp. 50–53.

Chapter 10

TRANSPORTATION—MANAGING THE FLOW OF THE SUPPLY CHAIN

Learning Objectives

After reading this chapter, you should be able to do the following:

- Explain the role transportation plays in the supply chain.
- Discuss the service and cost characteristics of the primary transportation modes.
- Discuss the key activities involved in transportation planning and execution.
- Explain current transportation management strategies used to improve supply chain performance.
- Use service and cost metrics to analyze transportation performance.
- Describe how information technology supports transportation planning and execution.

Supply Chain Profile — *Forecast 2006: In Search of Better Practices*

What place does logistics have in the overall business process? The primary elements of transportation haven't changed much over the years, but the complexity certainly has. With supply chains extended over a wider geography, demand has been concentrated at ports of entry, putting pressure on port operations and domestic long-haul transportation capacity. Shippers and consignees are learning that being a good customer to carriers is one of the best ways to ensure access to freight capacity.

Bill Hutchinson, vice president of global transportation with retailer Best Buy Co., Inc., says the focus has to be on controllable costs versus those costs shippers can't influence or control. He pays special attention to ways of improving supply chain operations and efficiency. In Hutchinson's view, aligning with others in the supply chain includes closer cooperation with carriers.

With truckload carriers currently turning away some loads and choosing what they will carry and for whom, the tables have clearly turned. One motor carrier reports turning down volumes equal to 70 percent of the loads it did haul during parts of the third-quarter peak period. That's not an aberration. That same carrier says in nonpeak operations it could carry 30 percent more freight if it had drivers.

The rate of growth in freight volumes may be slowing, as indicated by some economic reports and forecasts, but there is still more freight chasing capacity than the other way around. Shippers are courting carriers, budgeting rate increases rather than fighting them, and doing all they can to become more attractive to carriers in order to lock in capacity for the coming year.

Best Buy's Hutchinson talks about timely payment of bills and a focus on reducing claims as steps shippers can take to reduce costs and retain quality carriers. More shippers will have to look at extending hours to address carrier constraints brought about by the current set of Hours of Service rules. That can even mean opening on Saturday during peak periods.

Off-peak operations aren't limited to efforts to improve carrier efficiency. The Port of Los Angeles' Pier Pass program set fees to encourage carriers to handle and move freight off the port during off-peak hours. That effort achieved its two-year volume goal within two months, shifting thousands of loads to off hours. Pier Pass reports for September indicated that one-third of daily container volumes were moving in off-peak hours. When Saturday traffic was added, 40 percent of the nearly 400,000 containers were moved in off-peak hours.

Higher accessorial charges and more stringent enforcement of detention charges have more shippers looking at ways to track dwell time. Accurate information on the time a trailer or container spends in your yard or at your dock can help mitigate some detention charges, but it can also point to areas where operations can be improved. As costs escalate, the return on systems that can help monitor and warn of potential detention charges improves.

Transportation technology also plays a role in improving business processes and helps produce better financial results. Kevin Smith, senior vice president of supply chain and logistics at drug store chain CVS Corp., found that improving throughput had a number of direct and indirect benefits. Efficient transportation planning and scheduling are critical for a company like CVS, with 103,000 truck dispatches per year. Planning inbound and outbound shipments improves distribution center dock efficiency and helps turn trailers faster. Also, the coordination of transportation with pick and pack operations contributes to lower inventories.

Manufacturing or retail, large or small, logistics professionals have a difficult challenge for the near- to mid-term. Internal efforts to improve transportation efficiency and contain costs are important. However, the external interface with carriers and other supply chain partners is also critical. Being a good customer to carriers and a good supply chain partner to suppliers and customers will be critical to retain capacity and market access.

Source: Adapted from Perry A Trunick, "Forecast 2006: In Search of Better Practices," *Logistics Today* (December 2005): 1–8. Reprinted with permission.

Introduction

Transportation involves the physical movement of people and goods between origin and destination points. As individuals, we rely heavily on transportation to get to work and back home each day, to bring us the products that we need, and to increase our access to society. From a business standpoint, the transportation system links geographically separated partners and facilities in a company's supply chain—customers, suppliers, channel members, plants, warehouses, and retail outlets. Be it by truck, train, plane, ship, pipeline, or fiber optic wire, transportation facilitates the creation of time and place utility in the supply chain.

Transportation also has major economic impact on the financial performance of businesses. In 2006, more than $800 billion was spent on freight transportation in the United States.[1] This figure represents nearly 63 percent of all expenditures for logistics activities, far exceeding the amount of money spent on warehousing, inventory management, order processing, and other fulfillment system expenses. Thus, transportation costs must be taken into account during the development of supply chain strategies and processes.

This chapter focuses on the role of transportation in logistics management and the supply chain. We focus on the key methods, strategies, and decisions required for the cost-efficient, effective flow of goods between sellers and buyers. As you will learn, proper management of these transportation issues is vital to the fulfillment of customer demand and the ultimate success of an organization.

The Role of Transportation in Supply Chain Management (SCM)

Conceptually, a supply chain is a network of organizations that are separated by distance and time. Transportation provides the critical links between these organizations, permitting goods to flow between their facilities. By bridging these buyer-seller gaps, transportation allows organizations to extend the reach of their supply chains beyond local supplier capabilities and market demand. With efficient, effective transportation capabilities, organizations can build global supply chains that leverage low-cost sourcing opportunities and allow them to compete in new markets.

Transportation service availability is critical to demand fulfillment in the supply chain. As the Supply Chain Profile points out, demand for transportation service can exceed capacity in a strong economy. To address this challenge, Best Buy works closely with carriers to ensure that enough equipment and drivers are available to move flat screen televisions, computers, and game systems to retail stores in a timely fashion. Best Buy must focus on being a good customer—unloading freight quickly, minimizing driver wait time, and paying bills as scheduled—to prevent carriers from shifting capacity to other customers. A transportation shortage would negate the organization's efforts to build and fulfill customer demand because the product inventory would not reach the stores in a timely fashion.

Transportation efficiency promotes the competitiveness of a supply chain. In terms of supply management, cost-effective transportation helps companies gain access to higher-quality, lower-priced materials and realize economies of scale in production. Likewise, low-cost transportation improves demand fulfillment opportunities. By keeping transportation expenses reasonable, the total landed cost of a product (its production costs plus transportation costs and related supply chain fulfillment costs) can be competitive in multiple markets. For example, if a Switzerland-based manufacturer sells watches for $105 plus $10 for order processing and delivery versus $120 for a similar quality domestic watch, the Swiss company can compete effectively in the local market.

Not only must transportation costs be effective, but service capabilities must also be in line with customer requirements. Inexpensive transportation is of little value to a supply chain if the product does not arrive as scheduled and damage-free to the correct location. High-quality, customer-focused transportation has a direct impact on an organization's ability to provide the "Seven R's of Logistics"—getting the right product, to the right customer, in the right quantity, in the right condition, at the right place, at the right time, and at the right cost. Additionally, transportation can create supply chain flexibility. By working with carriers that offer a range of transit times and service options, organizations can satisfy supply chain demands for expedited, next-day service as well as more economical, standard delivery requests.

In addition to the linking and customer service roles, transportation plays a key role in supply chain design, strategy development, and total cost management.

- Transportation service availability, capacity, and costs influence decisions regarding the number and location of supply chain facilities. For example, many organizations attempt to avoid locating distribution facilities in the state of Florida due to transportation costs. With little freight originating in the state, carriers compensate for the empty outbound trips by charging higher rates to move freight into Florida.
- Transportation capabilities must align with the company's strategy. In its 2004 annual report, Amazon.com described a business strategy that strives to earn repeat customer purchases by providing fast and reliable fulfillment and timely customer service.[2] To accomplish this goal, Amazon.com needs to partner with carriers that deliver customer orders consistently and quickly, provide shipment visibility, and charge reasonable shipping rates.
- Intentional tradeoffs should be made between transportation and related activities (e.g., procurement, production, and inventory management) to optimize supply chain efficiency. For example, retailers can hold lower safety stock levels if the cost of more frequent, faster deliveries does not exceed the inventory carrying cost savings. Similarly, manufacturers can employ lean production strategies if lot sizes can be minimized without creating excessive transportation costs.

Given these critical roles, it is clear that proactive management of transportation processes is fundamental to the efficient and economical operation of a company's supply chain. Company leadership must not treat transportation as a "necessary evil" or an afterthought to production and marketing. Instead, they must consider transportation issues when developing organizational plans, integrate transportation into supply chain processes, and optimize total supply chain cost rather than minimize transportation costs. Leading organizations like Best Buy, Amazon.com, and CVS have already moved in this direction. They recognize that supply chains can only achieve time and place utility through effective transportation processes that physically move goods to the place desired at the time required by their key supply chain participants—the customers.

Challenges to Carrying out This Role

While transportation can provide valuable support to an organization's supply chain, it is a mistake to assume that these roles can be accomplished with ease. There are numerous obstacles—supply chain complexity, competing goals among supply chain partners, changing customer requirements, and limited information availability—to synchronizing transportation with other supply chain activities. Further compounding the challenge is a variety of supply chain trends and external issues that must be addressed by the organization.

The growth of outsourcing, particularly offshore manufacturing, creates major transportation challenges. The increasing reliance on global supply chains that extend from China, India, and other emerging countries to Main Street, USA, requires transportation processes to connect buyers and sellers that are thousands of miles apart. While the vast distances produce higher transportation costs, the extended transit times and greater potential for supply chain disruptions necessitate higher inventory levels. Organizations must consider these higher delivery and inventory carrying costs when assessing the financial benefits of global sourcing and offshore manufacturing.

Customer demands for tailored services and defect-free delivery also impact the transportation function. The shift to smaller, more frequent deliveries limits the ability of organizations to move product in economic truckload or container load quantities. Shrinking order cycle requirements result in higher costs for faster delivery and longer fulfillment operation hours. And, the desire for real-time shipment visibility requires technological strength. Organizations must align their operations with high-quality carriers that provide a balanced mix of capacity, speed, and consistency at a reasonable cost.

Transportation capacity constraints pose another challenge to organizations needing to move freight through the supply chain. In many situations, transportation demand outstrips the capacity of our infrastructure. Port facilities must grapple with the volume of containers bearing products from the Far East, and highways in major cities suffer from congestion. Carriers also struggle to keep pace with freight growth whether it be hiring and retaining enough truck drivers or putting enough locomotives into service. The outcomes of the capacity crunch include higher freight rates, shipment delays, and limited negotiating capabilities. As noted in the Supply Chain Profile, organizations must take a more collaborative, flexible approach to working with carriers that currently hold greater power in shipper-carrier relationships.

Rising transportation rates present another major concern for organizations. After numerous years of enjoying low freight expenses fostered by excess carrier capacity, the situation has reversed. Capacity has shrunk due to greater demand for transportation services and industry consolidation from carrier mergers, acquisitions, and bankruptcies. The remaining carriers are now in a strong position to increase rates to cover the rising costs of labor, insurance, and other expenses. They have also built fuel surcharges into contracts with their customers, which add an extra charge to the customer's freight bill. During 2005, fuel surcharges ranged from 10 to 22 percent of transportation rates based on U.S. Department of Energy index price calculations for fuel. Though organizations have limited control over surcharges and rate increases, they can take steps to control transportation spending such as using lower cost modes of transportation when feasible, maximizing equipment utilization, or consolidating freight into larger shipments.

The transportation industry is also impacted by governmental requirements that affect cost structures and service capabilities. Historically, government regulation of transportation has focused on competition and pricing. For nearly 100 years, these rules limited opportunities to and incentives for carriers to develop unique service offerings and tailored pricing. Economic deregulation of most modes by 1980 and ocean shipping in 1998 gave carriers the freedom to operate with little governmental intrusion, sparking much needed competition based on services, price, and performance. An extended discussion of economic regulation can be found in Appendix 10A.

While the government has taken a market-focused approach toward carrier competition, this does not mean that it has adopted a hands-off approach to the transportation industry. Regulation is growing in areas where the transportation industry has the potential to impact the quality of life, the safety of citizens, and the growth of commerce. Most recently, legislation has been passed to improve the safety of the transportation industry, reduce its impact on the environment, and defend the country against terrorism.

- Protection of the traveling public is a primary driver of transportation safety regulation. Federal and state laws limit the size of transportation equipment, combined freight and equipment weight, and travel speed. Regulations also exist to ensure that commercial vehicle operators are properly qualified. For example, the Commercial Motor Vehicle Safety Act of 1986 requires drivers to pass a skills and knowledge test before receiving a commercial driver's license. Most recently, concerns regarding operator fatigue led to revision of the 1935 commercial vehicle driver hours of service (HOS) rules. The new HOS regulations allow 11 hours of driving time within a consecutive 14-hour period after which drivers must be off duty for 10 hours. Previously, driving time was limited to 10 hours in a 15-hour period that could be interrupted by off-duty breaks, followed by 8 hours off duty.
- A wide variety of environmental protection issues are also addressed by governmental regulation. Federal and state regulations have been in effect since the 1970s to control aircraft noise pollution. Transportation of hazardous materials—flammable and combustible substances, poisons, and radioactive materials—is highly regulated to minimize the risks to life, property, and the environment. Air pollution is another key issue. Vehicle emission regulations such as the Heavy-Duty Highway Diesel Rule, which took effect in 2007, require lower sulfur levels in fuel as well as cleaner-burning engines.
- The events of September 11, 2001, and the continued threat of terrorism have led to security-focused legislation that directly impacts the transportation industry. The Trade Act of 2002 contains requirements mandating the

advance electronic filing of all import and export cargo information for all modes of transportation. As part of this regulation, the Bureau of Customs and Border Protection (CBP) enforces the "24 Hour Rule," which requires ocean carriers to provide complete manifest information for all cargo bound for the United States to the CBP 24 hours prior to loading aboard a vessel in a foreign port. Specific attention is given to the movement of food products. The Public Health Security and Bio-terrorism Preparedness and Response Act of 2002 requires traceability of food products across supply chains, as well as detailed cargo information for imported food products.

When initiating legislation to benefit society, the government makes a significant effort to avoid unnecessary restriction of the flow of legitimate trade. Despite these efforts, it can be expensive for carriers to comply with government mandates. For example, industry experts estimate that the upcoming vehicle emissions regulation will lead to higher fuel prices and raise truck engine prices by $5,000 to $8,000, plus the new engines are expected to be less fuel efficient than current models.[3] Regulation also impacts organizations whose freight flows through the transportation system. Like many other mandates, the HOS regulations have led to rate increases and prompted organizations to revise their shipping strategies.

Ultimately, this variety of external issues makes it difficult to develop transportation processes that mesh well with supply chain requirements. Individual organizations must make a concerted effort to overcome these constraints to move freight in the most cost-efficient, customer-supportive manner possible. Fortunately, a variety of modal options exists to handle the task of moving freight in today's challenging environment.

Modes of Transportation

The primary modes of transportation available to the logistics manager are truck, rail, air, water, and pipeline. Additionally, intermodal transportation combines the use of two or more of the basic modes to move freight from its origin to destination. Each mode has different economic and technical structures, and each can provide different qualities of link service. This section provides an overview of each mode from the perspectives of service characteristics, volume and type of freight handled, cost structure, carrier types and service offerings, equipment variety, and current industry trends. Comparisons of the service capabilities, freight rates, and tradeoffs between the modes are provided in the discussion of modal selection later in the chapter.

Collectively, the U.S. transportation system moves approximately 19.5 billion tons of goods for businesses, valued at nearly $13 trillion.[4] Table 10-1 provides key data for each mode of transportation. In terms of **ton-miles** (an output measurement combining weight and distance, or tonnage multiplied by miles transported), truck and rail are similar. However, the trucking industry dominates the U.S. transportation market in terms of the value of goods moved, followed by multimodal transportation.

In terms of freight expense, organizations spent $801 billion for transportation services in 2006. Almost 80 percent of the total was spent on trucking services at $635 billion, an increase of $27 billion over the previous year. Rail follows with 6.7 percent; air, 4.7 percent; water, 4.6 percent; and pipeline, 1.2 percent.[5] The combined levels of freight value, volume, and spending suggest that truck, multimodal, and air transportation are premium-priced services for moving higher-value goods. In contrast, rail, water, and pipeline provide more economically priced services for lower-value commodities.

Table 10-1 Shipment Characteristics by Mode of Transportation (2002)

MODE OF TRANSPORTATION	VALUE OF GOODS (BILLIONS)	TONS (MILLIONS)	TON-MILES (BILLIONS)
Truck	$9,075	11,712	1,515
Rail	392	1,979	1,372
Water	673	1,668	485
Air	563	6	13
Pipeline	896	3,529	688
Multiple modes	1,121	229	233

Source: Bureau of Transportation Statistics, "Pocket Guide to Transportation" (January 2006): 23.

Motor Carriers

Motor carriage is the most widely used mode of transportation in the domestic supply chain. This mode is very much a part of an organization's supply chain with trucks, ranging from the smallest delivery van to the largest tractor-trailer combinations, moving their freight. The sophisticated U.S. highway network permits trucks to reach all points of the country. Thus, trucking companies have excellent accessibility to virtually all freight shipping and receiving locations. This accessibility, combined with the industry's excellent service capabilities, has made trucking the mode of choice for high-value, time-sensitive goods.

The trucking industry is highly competitive and made up of 573,469 private, for-hire, and other U.S. interstate motor carriers.[6] These companies range in size from single-truck, owner-operator service providers to national carriers like Yellow Roadway Corporation whose 70,000 employees generated more than $9.1 billion in revenue from its trucking operations in 2004.[7] Of the $509 billion spent on trucking in 2004, 65 percent was spent on intercity transportation service versus 35 percent for local service.

The economic structure of the motor carrier industry contributes to the vast number of carriers in the industry. First, there are not significant cost economies of scale that make it impossible for small carriers to compete. The equipment and licensing costs are not out of reach for most organizations. Second, most expenses are incurred as the result of moving freight; thus, trucking is a high-variable-cost, low-fixed-cost business. Trucking companies typically do not require extensive terminal and equipment investment and do not have to maintain the highway infrastructure. The U.S. government builds and maintains the highway, and motor carriers pay for highway use through fees such as use taxes and licensing charges. Thus, variable operating costs—wages and benefits, fuel, maintenance, and tires—have a greater impact on the economics of trucking companies.

Much of the freight moved by the trucking industry is regional in nature, moving within a 500-mile radius of the origin. Some of the primary commodities handled by this mode include consumer-packaged goods, electronics, electrical machinery, furniture, textiles, automotive parts, and other finished and semifinished goods. Shippers rely on the trucking industry to transport these goods because they are time sensitive and need superior protection while in transit.

The trucking industry is comprised of for-hire and private fleet operations. Private fleets transport freight that is owned by the organization that is operating the trucks. The National Private Truck Council estimates that there are 135,000 private fleets used primarily by manufacturers and retailers in the United States, with 35,000 of them running 10 or more vehicles.[8] These organizations operate 6 million of the 7.4 million commercial trucks running on U.S. roads. Wal-Mart operates the largest private trucking fleet in the world with 6,753 tractors and 44,500 trailers in operation.[9]

For-hire trucking companies move freight for other organizations. The three general types of for-hire carriers include the following:

- **Truckload carriers (TL)** handle single large shipments per trailer that exceed 15,000 pounds or use the full cubic capacity of a trailer. TL carriers provide direct service, picking up the load at the origin point and delivering it directly to the destination without stopping at freight-handling terminals.
- **Less-than-truckload (LTL) carriers** move multiple shipments ranging from 150 pounds up to 15,000 pounds in each trailer. National LTL carriers use a hub-and-spoke network of local and regional terminal facilities to sort and consolidate shipments moving to a particular market area. Regional LTL carriers focus their efforts on a particular area of the country.
- **Small package carriers** handle shipments up to 150 pounds and move multiple shipments on a single van or truck. They use networks similar to LTL carriers to move freight efficiently throughout the country. United Parcel Service (UPS) and FedEx Ground are the two largest small package ground carriers in the country.

The lines between these carrier types has blurred over the past few years. Carriers have responded to customer desires for transportation providers with multiple capabilities through acquisition activities. For example, FedEx acquired Viking Freight in 1998 and American Freightways in 2001, adding LTL services to their existing small package ground and express capabilities. UPS made a similar move into LTL, purchasing Overnite Transportation in 2005. Additionally, regional LTL carriers are offering some direct TL-like services, and TL carriers are providing multistop deliveries for their customers. Suffice it to say that the trend will continue with carriers serving new markets, handling different sized freight, and meeting unique customer service requirements as long as it is profitable for them to do so.

The flexibility of the trucking industry to handle the varying commodities and shipment sizes discussed above is provided by a wide range of equipment options. No longer are carriers limited to straight trucks and tractors hauling 35-foot trailers. New equipment innovations and less restrictive regulations allow carriers to use single trailers up to 53 feet long and twin 28-foot trailers. In a limited number of states, specially trained truck drivers are allowed to move longer combination vehicles (LCVs) on designated highways. Figure 10-1 highlights the variety of equipment combinations used in the trucking industry.

While motor carriers enjoy an enviable position in the transportation industry, they face daunting challenges in the future—rising costs, labor issues, and competition. Trucking companies have been able to pass along rising fuel and insurance costs during the latest economic expansion, but may not be able to do so if capacity exceeds demand. The shortage of truck drivers that has contributed to capacity shortages is

Figure 10-1 Motor Carrier Equipment Options

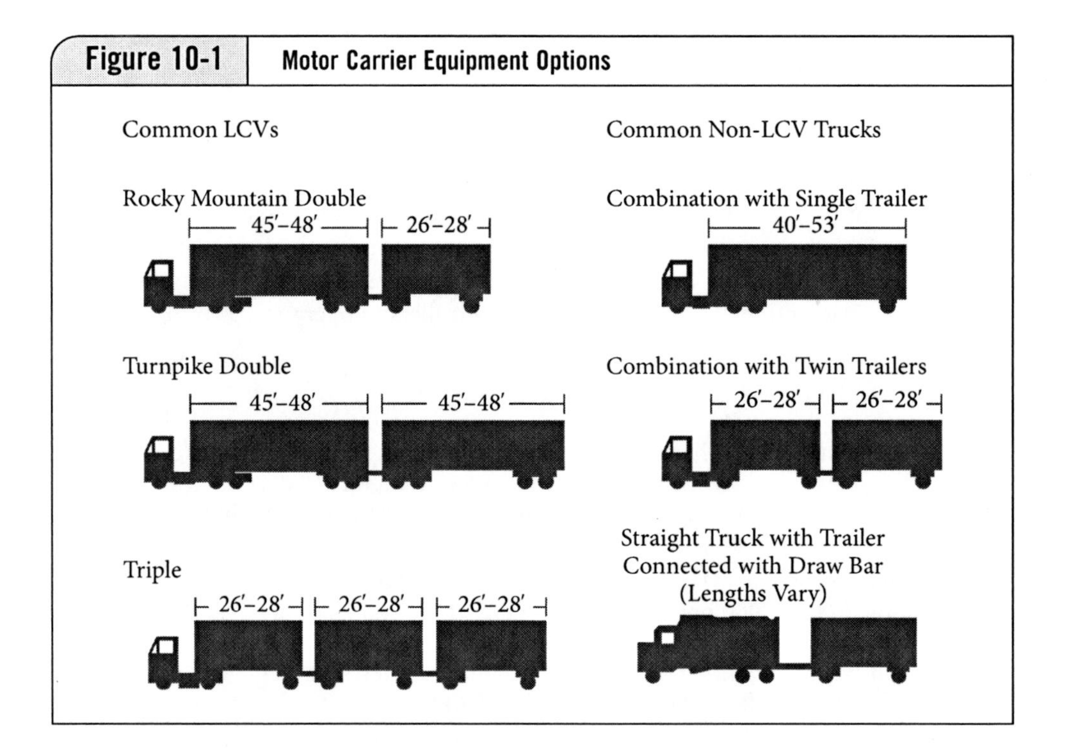

projected to get worse over time. The American Trucking Association estimates that the industry need for 20,000 additional drivers will jump to 111,000 by 2014. Finally, competition will remain fierce within the trucking industry as well as with other modes of transportation. Customers expect near perfect performance and will look for different options if service disruptions occur.

Railroads

Railroads transport a significant volume of freight in the United States, moving more than 1.8 billion tons of freight annually. The combination of volume and the average shipment length of 975 miles make rail the highest ton-mile mode of transportation. These activity levels have been achieved despite a lack of direct accessibility to all parts of the supply chain. Perceptions of rail being a slow, inflexible, and inconsistent mode are challenges that must be overcome if the industry is to compete for higher-value, more profitable freight.

Although there are 556 railroads in the United States, the industry is dominated by a very small number of large firms. The extensive merger and acquisition activity during the last decade shrunk the number of U.S. Class I railroads (linehaul railroads with revenues in excess of $290 million) to seven. These Class I carriers generated more than 92 percent of total rail industry revenues ($42.2 billion), handled 30.1 million loads, including 11 million intermodal trailers and containers.[10] Four of these companies—BNSF Railway, CSX Transportation, Norfolk Southern Railway, and Union Pacific Railroad—have evolved as the dominant carriers in the industry. None of these major rail carriers services the entire country by itself; they work together via interline agreements to provide coast-to-coast rail service.

This mode's economic structure partly accounts for the limited number of rail carriers. Railroads, which fall within that infamous group of business undertakings labeled as "natural monopolies," require a large investment in terminals, equipment, and trackage to begin operation; and the accompanying huge capacity allows railroads to be a decreasing cost industry. As output (ton-miles) increases, the average per-unit production cost decreases. Thus, having fewer railroads in operation in a given area and permitting those few firms to realize inherent large-scale output economies are economical and beneficial to society.

Railroad transportation is primarily used for the long-distance movement of low-value raw materials and manufactured products. Primary commodities handled include coal, chemicals, farm products, minerals, food, and other basic materials. These products tend to be shipped in large quantities and stockpiled by customers to gain transportation efficiencies. Railroads also handle some high-value goods, primarily automobiles and intermodal containers filled with imported finished goods. In fact, intermodal volume is rising faster on a percentage basis than traditional rail freight.

The rail industry is comprised of the following two carrier types:

- **Linehaul freight carriers** provide service between major markets and customers within those markets. These carriers move freight in container, carload, and unit train quantities. The eight Class I railroads are linehaul carriers that provide a full array of interregional or regional services.
- **Shortline carriers** provide the local and regional links between individual customers and the national rail network of the Class I railroads. They serve smaller markets, handle local delivery service, and facilitate the interline process—activities that the long-haul carriers no longer find profitable. Some shortline railroads have been consolidated via holding companies. An example is RailAmerica, Inc., an operator of 46 shortline and regional railroads with approximately 8,800 miles of tracks in the United States and Canada.

Railroads can move almost any type of freight—liquid or gas, slurry or solid, hazardous or harmless—in very large quantities. From tri-level auto racks capable of holding up to 15 vehicles to tank cars that hold nearly 20,000 gallons of corn syrup, equipment exists to move the customer's freight. Hopper cars, boxcars, intermodal well cars, gondolas, and other specialized equipment are available from railroads, railcar leasing companies, or private owners.

Rail equipment can be organized into loads and transported in one of the three following primary ways:

- Manifest trains contain a mixture of equipment and freight for multiple customers. These mixed trains travel through multiple rail yards where railcars may be added to or removed from the train, depending on their destination and the route of the train. This time-consuming assembling and disassembling of trains, called **classification**, can easily add more than 24 hours to the delivery process.
- Unit trains move an entire block of railcars carrying a single commodity (e.g., coal) from the origin to a single destination. Unit trains use one type of railcar and eliminate the need to stop for the time-consuming rail yard classification activities. These types of trains move directly from origin to destination and operate on priority schedules. Thus, they can provide service that is as fast or faster than trucks, especially on cross-country moves.
- Intermodal trains are special types of unit trains that focus on the long-distance or linehaul movement of intermodal containers and trailers. These trains move products from port and other high-volume origin points to

major market areas where the containers are offloaded and given to trucking companies for final customer delivery.

The rail industry faces a number of challenges moving forward. Capacity is a key issue as volume has surged. Railroad companies have responded by adding new crews and locomotives, but the impact on service and capacity has been limited. With the track infrastructure remaining largely unchanged, the additional freight, crews, and equipment have continued to clog the system. Interest in intermodal rail service is high (due in part to trucking industry capacity issues), but service quality is an issue among potential customers. To take advantage of this opportunity, Class I railroads must address their congestion issues and deliver goods on time.

Air Carriers

Historically, air cargo transportation has been viewed as an expensive, "use only in an emergency" mode. The advent of e-commerce, the growth of global supply chains, and initiatives to reduce inventory and order cycle time have changed this outdated perspective, and in doing so, contributed to a sustained increase in demand for air transportation. While air cargo transportation remains a small and specialized mode in terms of tonnage, the value of goods handled continues to rise and U.S. spending increased from $29 billion in 2003 to $31 billion in 2004. International air transportation is projected to grow at an annual rate of 6.3 percent over the next 20 years.[11]

While the Federal Aviation Administration activity report identifies 491 air cargo carriers, the domestic market is dominated by 14 major carriers with revenues in excess of $1 billion from freight and/or passenger operations. The majority of air cargo revenue is generated by FedEx, UPS Air, DHL, and the United States Postal Service (USPS). International air freight movement is handled by a broader range of organizations with FedEx, Korean Air Lines, Lufthansa, UPS, and Singapore Airlines recording the largest ton-kilometers activity in the industry.

The air carrier cost structure consists of high variable costs in proportion to fixed costs, somewhat akin to the motor carrier cost structure. Like motor and water carriers, air carriers do not invest heavily in facility infrastructure or byways. The government builds terminals and provides traffic control of the airways. Air carriers pay variable lease payments and landing fees for their use. Equipment costs, though quite high, are still a small part of the total cost.

Air transportation is used to ship small quantities of high-value, low-weight, semifinished, and finished goods. Primary commodities handled by this mode include computers, precision instruments, electronics, pharmaceuticals, perishable foods, periodicals, and apparel. Companies are willing to pay a high premium to transport these goods because they are very time sensitive and need superior protection while in transit.

The following two primary carrier types dominate this mode:

- **Combination carriers** move freight and passengers, often on the same trip, with cargo loaded in the belly of the aircraft. As demand has grown, some of the larger international carriers have dedicated equipment specifically to cargo movement and provide scheduled service to meet the growing needs of global commerce. Of the 12 major airlines that are combination carriers, Northwest Airlines, American Airlines, United Airlines, and Delta Air Lines handle the most freight ton-kilometers each year.
- **Air cargo carriers** focus exclusively on the movement of letters and envelopes, packages, and freight. Some carriers provide scheduled daily service through

a highly coordinated network, while others provide on-demand service for customers who need more immediate, direct transportation or the full capacity of the aircraft. Air carriers can also be separated on the basis of service capabilities.

- **Integrated carriers** provide door-to-door service, a consistent schedule of pickup and delivery windows, and standard expedited service through their hub-and-spoke networks. Because these carriers make air transportation of time-sensitive goods such a simple, well-controlled process, they dominate the U.S. domestic market for next-day and second-day movement of letters, small packages, and small shipments. Examples include FedEx, UPS, and DHL.
- **Nonintegrated carriers** provide on-demand, air-only service from airport to airport. They rely on freight forwarders or the customer to provide delivery service to and from the airport. The advantages of these carriers are the speed and flexibility of unscheduled direct service and the potential for same-day cargo movement.

Air cargo carriers employ a wide variety of aircraft to move freight domestically and around the world. Propeller planes capable of handling only a few thousand pounds are used to move letters and small packages from smaller markets to consolidation points and sort operations. Jets ranging in size up to the largest Boeing 747-400 freighter (capacity of nearly 27,500 cubic feet and 124 tons of freight) are used for long-range domestic and international service. Aircraft like the Anatov 124 can transport unique products of up to 150 tons with dimensions as large as 13 feet high by 19 feet wide. Whatever the shipment requirement may be, an aircraft with an appropriate combination of payload, range, and speed is likely available.

The air cargo industry faces numerous obstacles to profitable growth, including cost issues, competition, and security challenges. First, the rising cost of kerosene-type jet fuel directly impacts the success of the industry. It is estimated that every additional penny paid for a gallon of jet fuel costs the industry $195 million annually. Some of these costs may be recouped through fuel surcharges, but the growth of next-day trucking services is already putting pressure on the domestic air cargo industry. Air carriers may find it difficult to pass along increased costs in the face of this growing competition. Finally, the industry is under pressure from costly security mandates. Homeland security fees, cargo screening costs, training, and related security expenses are estimated to have an annual impact of more than $4 billion on the industry according to the Air Transport Association.

Water

Water transportation has played a significant role in the development of many countries and is a major facilitator of international trade. In the United States, 81 percent of water transportation spending is related to international freight movement with the other 19 percent split between coastal, inland, and Great Lakes traffic. Globally, water carriers dominate all other modes, garnering approximately 50 percent of the international freight revenue and handling 99 percent of the tonnage. Although very slow and limited by the natural infrastructure, water carriers offer tremendous capacity (e.g., one barge holds as much freight as 15 rail cars or 60 trucks), efficient fuel consumption, and low cost.

The 877 carriers in the U.S. domestic water industry generated $5 billion of revenues in 2004. More than a billion tons of freight are handled annually by the domestic fleet, which includes 416 ocean-going ships, 57 Great Lakes ships, more than 27,000 inland barges, and 5,200 towboats and tugs. The volume and fleet size have slowly declined over the past five years. In contrast, the market for international services is growing, with the U.S. market generating $22 billion in revenues for carriers. Volume also increased by 8 percent for imports and exports over the prior year, with container traffic leading the way.

The economics of ocean transportation is similar to that of airlines. To begin operation, these carriers require no investment for the right-of-way—nature provides the "highway" and government entities known as port authorities provide unloading and loading services, storage areas, and freight transfer facilities. The water carriers pay user fees for these port services only when used. Large ocean-going ships require significant capital investments, but cost is spread over a large volume of freight transported during the lengthy life span of most ships.

The domestic carriers compete vigorously with railroads for long-distance movement of low-value, high-density, bulk cargoes that mechanical devices can easily load and unload. Like the railroads, water carriers allow customers to cost effectively move large quantities of raw materials like petroleum, coal, iron ore, chemicals, forest products, and other commodities. In contrast, water carriers handle a wider variety of goods. Every conceivable type of cargo is transported via international water carrier, from low-value commodities to imported automobiles. Many imported consumer goods flow to the United States from the Far East in 20- and 40-foot ocean shipping containers.

Two primary carrier types dominate the for-hire portion of the water industry as follows:

- **Liner services** employ a wide variety of ships in their fixed route, published schedule service. Liner service carriers like Maersk, Neptune Orient Line, Mattson Navigation, P&O Nedloyd, etc., typically handle smaller, individual shipments for their customers, including containers, pallets, and other unit loads.
- **Charter services** lease ships to customers on a voyage or time basis and follow routes of the customer's choosing. The charter customer normally uses the entire capacity of the ship for large-volume freight. Charter services operate similarly to taxicab service (customer-specified route, tailored service), while liner service is much like a scheduled bus service (fixed route, standard service).

Ocean transportation of goods ranging from crude oil to electronics is facilitated by a wide range of specialized ships. The most widely used options include the following:

- **Container ships** are critical to the globalization of trade. These ships are specially designed to carry standardized containers, which are commonly rated in TEUs (20-foot equivalent units) or FEUs (40-foot equivalent units). The average ship is capable of transporting over 2,100 TEUs with future construction focusing on huge ships designed to carry in excess of 9,000 TEUs. Container ships have the flexibility to carry a wide variety of cargo, including many products that require special handling, temperature control, and so on.
- **Bulk carriers** carry cargoes with low value-to-weight ratios, such as ores, grain, coal, and scrap metal. Very large openings on these ships' holds allow easy loading and unloading. Watertight walls dividing the holds allow a ship to carry more than one commodity at a time.

- **Tankers** carry the largest amount of cargo by tonnage, usually on a charter basis. These ships range in size from World War II–era tankers of 18,000 tons to very large crude carriers (VLCCs), some of which top 500,000 tons. Tankers are constructed in much the same way as bulk carriers, but with smaller deck openings. New tankers are required to be double-hulled to protect the environment in case of a collision.
- **General cargo ships** are usually engaged to transport shipload cargoes on a charter basis and have large cargo holds and freight-handling equipment to facilitate the loading and unloading of a large variety of freight. The self-sufficiency of these ships allows them to load and discharge cargo at ports that lack up-to-date cargo-handling equipment. This feature is very important for ships transporting goods to less-developed portions of the world.
- **Roll-on, roll-off (RO–RO) vessels** are another type of ship proving its value in international trade. RO–ROs are basically large ferry ships. The carrier drives the cargo directly onto the ship using built-in ramps and drives or tows it off at its destination. Larger RO–ROs can transport 2,000 or more automobiles, as well as freight trailers, containers, farm and construction equipment, and other wheeled vehicles.

The major challenges faced by carriers in international water transportation relate to capacity, trade imbalances, and rising costs. As demand has soared for container shipping outbound from Asia, ship capacity has been pushed to the limit. Carriers are responding by ordering new equipment, but construction time for these mega-ships is lengthy. The imbalance of international trade between export-dominant Asian countries and import-dominant North America creates equipment availability problems at the origin and destination port congestion issues. Both problems result in supply chain delays that impact demand fulfillment. Finally, the industry is experiencing double-digit cost increases due to security compliance and rising fuel expenses. These costs must be passed on to customers if ocean carriers are to maintain their slim profit margins.

Pipeline

Pipelines are the "hidden giant" of the transportation modes, quietly handling a significant proportion of all intercity ton-mileage of freight. It is a unique mode of transportation as the equipment is fixed in place and the product moves through it in high volume. Pipelines effectively protect the product from contamination and also provide a warehousing function. Pipelines provide the most economical form of transportation with the lowest cost per ton of any mode.

The United States has the largest network of energy pipelines of any nation in the world. The oil pipeline network alone in the United States is more than 10 times larger than that in Europe. There are 174 operators of hazardous liquid pipelines that primarily carry crude oil and petroleum products. Some organizations focus strictly on pipeline transportation, while large oil companies like ExxonMobil, BP, and Shell also operate pipeline systems individually or via joint ventures. The natural gas pipeline industry is much less concentrated with 826 organizations involved in the transmission of product and another 1,241 involved in the final distribution of natural gas.

Pipeline costs are predominantly fixed. Pipeline operators must build their own right-of-way, which is a rather expensive proposition. Variable costs in the industry are very low as little labor is required to operate the pipelines and limited fuel is needed to run pumps. The construction of a pipeline becomes cost effective when product flows continuously, allowing the fixed costs to be spread over a high volume of goods.

The vast majority of products moved by pipeline are liquids and gases, the economically feasible products to flow via this mode. Common liquid products include crude oil and petroleum-based fuels for transportation and home heating. Widely distributed gaseous products include natural gas for home heating and propane, anhydrous ammonia, and carbon dioxide used in agricultural and industrial applications. In the past, attempts have been made to move solid product in a slurry form, but this has not proved to be competitive with water and rail transportation.

The pipeline industry is comprised of for-hire and private carriers that maintain their own infrastructures. For-hire carriers of liquid products can move different products through their system at the same time, separated by a batching plug that maintains the integrity of individual products. Private carriers include petroleum and natural gas companies that use pipelines to move product to and from their refineries, processing plants, and storage facilities. Companies, like a power plant or a chemical plant, may operate a small pipeline system to bring fuel to the plant or to move feedstocks from one plant to another.

The oil system is made up of the following three primary types of pipelines:

- **Gathering lines** are very small pipelines, usually from 2 to 8 inches in diameter. They are used together and move oil from both onshore and offshore oil wells to trunk lines. It is estimated that between 30,000 to 40,000 miles of gathering lines exist, primarily in the larger oil producing states.
- **Trunk lines**, measuring from 8 to 24 inches in diameter, bring crude oil from extraction points to refineries. There are approximately 55,000 miles of crude oil trunk lines in the United States, including the well-known Trans-Alaska Pipeline System. This 800-mile long, 48-inch diameter pipeline connects Prudhoe Bay on Alaska's North Slope to Valdez, the northernmost ice-free port in North America.
- **Refined product pipelines** carry petroleum products—gasoline, jet fuel, home heating oil, and diesel fuel—from refineries to large fuel terminals with storage tanks in almost every state in the country. These pipelines vary in size from relatively small 8- to 12-inch diameter lines up to 42-inch diameter lines. The total mileage nationwide of refined products pipelines is approximately 95,000 miles. These pipelines deliver petroleum products to large fuel terminals with storage tanks. Major industries, airports, and electrical power generation plants can be supplied directly by pipeline.[12]

Natural gas pipelines use similar networks of gathering lines, transmission lines, and main distribution lines to move product closer to the market. The major difference is the direct delivery of natural gas to homes and businesses using local distribution lines. These distribution lines, found below street level in almost every city and town, account for the vast majority of pipeline mileage in the United States—1.8 million miles.

The ongoing issues for the pipeline industry are safety and security. Compared to other modes, pipelines have enviable safety and environmental records with spills amounting to only one gallon per million barrel-miles. Continued vigilance is key from a regulatory compliance perspective, as well as prevention of catastrophic events. Any type of incident such as a major pipeline leak, fire, or explosion would be costly in terms of cleanup, fines, and negative publicity. Pipeline operators must also be cognizant of security risks that pipelines present and take actions to protect their assets and the flow of vital petroleum products through the supply chain. Contingency plans to deal with disruptive events like Hurricane Katrina or a terrorist attack on pipeline operations must also be maintained.

Intermodal Transportation

While the five primary modes give supply chain managers numerous transportation options, another group of alternatives exist. **Intermodal transportation service** refers to the use of two or more carriers of different modes in the origin-to-destination movement of freight. Shifting freight between modes may seem inefficient and time consuming, but the improved reach and combined service advantages created by intermodal transportation offset these issues. These primary benefits of intermodalism include the following:

- Greater accessibility is created by linking the individual modes. The road infrastructure allows trucks to reach locations that are inaccessible to other modes, especially air transportation, water transportation, and pipelines. For example, air transportation can only move freight between airport facilities. Trucks provide the flow between the origin and departure airport as well as the arrival airport and the customer destination. Railroads can also facilitate the use of domestic river transportation and international ocean transportation. Getting low sulfur coal from a Wyoming mine to a utility company in Japan would be best accomplished through a combination of rail and water transportation.
- Overall cost efficiency can be achieved without sacrificing service quality or accessibility. In other words, intermodal transportation allows supply chains to utilize the inherent capabilities of multiple modes to control cost and fulfill customer requirements. If a furniture manufacturer needed to move 20 loads of furniture from North Carolina to California, a combination of truck and rail transportation would improve upon truck-only service. The speed and accessibility of trucks would be used for the initial pickup and final delivery, while the cross-country transportation would be handled by the cost-efficient railroads.
- Intermodal transportation facilitates global trade. The capacity and efficiency of ocean transportation allow large-volume shipments to be transported between continents at relatively low per-unit costs. The speed of air transportation allows perishable goods to flow quickly between countries. The final domestic leg of the delivery can take place via truck. The ocean-truck combination makes product competitive across global markets by keeping the landed cost in check. The air-truck combination facilitates expedited distribution of "hot commodities" like fashion and rapid replenishment of products that are in high demand.

Although no universal statistics are kept on intermodal transportation, there is strong evidence that intermodal transportation is growing in importance and volume. The number of containers flowing from around the world through U.S. ports has increased from 10 million TEUs in 1985 to 38.5 million TEUs in 2004. Experts predict that this trend will continue with intermodal container volume reaching 80 million TEUs in 2015. Domestic flows of intermodal freight are also on the rise. The U.S. rail system moved 8.1 million containers and 2.9 million trailers in 2004. This continues the upward trend of the last two decades. To put it in perspective, Wal-Mart moved approximately 720,000 TEUs in 2005 though intermodal channels. If lined up end to end, these containers would stretch 3,750 miles.

Much of this intermodal growth can be attributed to the development of standardized containers that are compatible with multiple modes. A standard dry box container looks much like a truck trailer without the chassis; can be lifted, stacked, and moved from one piece of equipment to another; and is built to standard dimensional height and width specifications in a variety of lengths (10-, 20-, and 40-foot marine containers for international transportation and 40-, 48-, and 53-foot containers for domestic truck/rail transportation). Specialized containers are also available for handling temperature-sensitive goods (refrigerated containers), commodities (tank and dry bulk cargo containers), and other unique cargoes.

Other factors have contributed to the growth of intermodal transportation. They include better information systems to track freight as it moves through the supply chain and the development of intermodal terminals to facilitate efficient freight transfers between modes. In addition, new generations of ocean vessels, railcars, and truck trailers are being built specifically to handle intermodal freight in greater quantity and with greater ease.

Ocean carriers are continually developing larger containerships to handle international intermodal traffic. These vessels have evolved from first generation ships, capable of handling less than 1,000 TEUs (pre-1960), to fourth generation Post-Panamax ships that can hold more than 4,000 TEUs. These ships are relatively fast (speeds of up to 25 knots), serve Pacific or Atlantic routes only (as they cannot pass through the Panama Canal), and can only serve deep-water ports. Future construction will focus on even larger containerships. RO–RO ships and combination vessels can also handle intermodal freight.

The rail industry also offers a variety of equipment for moving intermodal shipments. Initial efforts focused on moving standard truck trailers on flatbed rail cars. This was called "piggy-back" service or trailer on flatcar (TOFC) service. This type of service is shrinking in favor of container on flatcar (COFC) service and double-stack container services. These methods allow rail companies to carry a wider variety of containers—everything from 10-foot ocean containers to 53-foot domestic freight containers—in nearly any combination. Double-stack service is especially efficient.

The freight services provided by intermodal transportation can be viewed in terms of product-handling characteristics as follows:

- **Containerized freight** is loaded into/onto storage equipment (a container or pallet) at the origin and delivered to the destination in/on that same piece of equipment with no additional handling. For example, if a load of DVD players needed to be shipped from the factory to the market, the players would be loaded into a 40-foot container at the factory in Taiwan, transferred to the port via truck, and then loaded on a containership bound for Los Angeles. Upon arrival, the container would be moved from the ship onto another truck and delivered to the retailer's distribution center.
- **Transload freight** involves goods that are handled and transferred between transportation equipment multiple times. Transload freight primarily consists of bulk-oriented raw materials that must be scooped, pumped, lifted, or conveyed from one container to another when transferred from one mode to another. For example, orange juice concentrate may be picked up using a rail tank car, pumped into the hold of a cargo ship for the linehaul move, and then pumped into a tank truck for final delivery.

Another way to look at the intermodal option is based on the type of service used. Figure 10-2 depicts the most prevalent forms of intermodal transportation, including truck-rail, truck-air, and truck-water, although other combinations are also used. Some carriers (e.g., CSX, Maersk Sealand, and FedEx) have multimodal capabilities, allowing them to utilize the most efficient and economical combination of intermodal transportation for their customers. In the majority of cases, the

Figure 10-2 Widely Used Intermodal Transportation Combinations

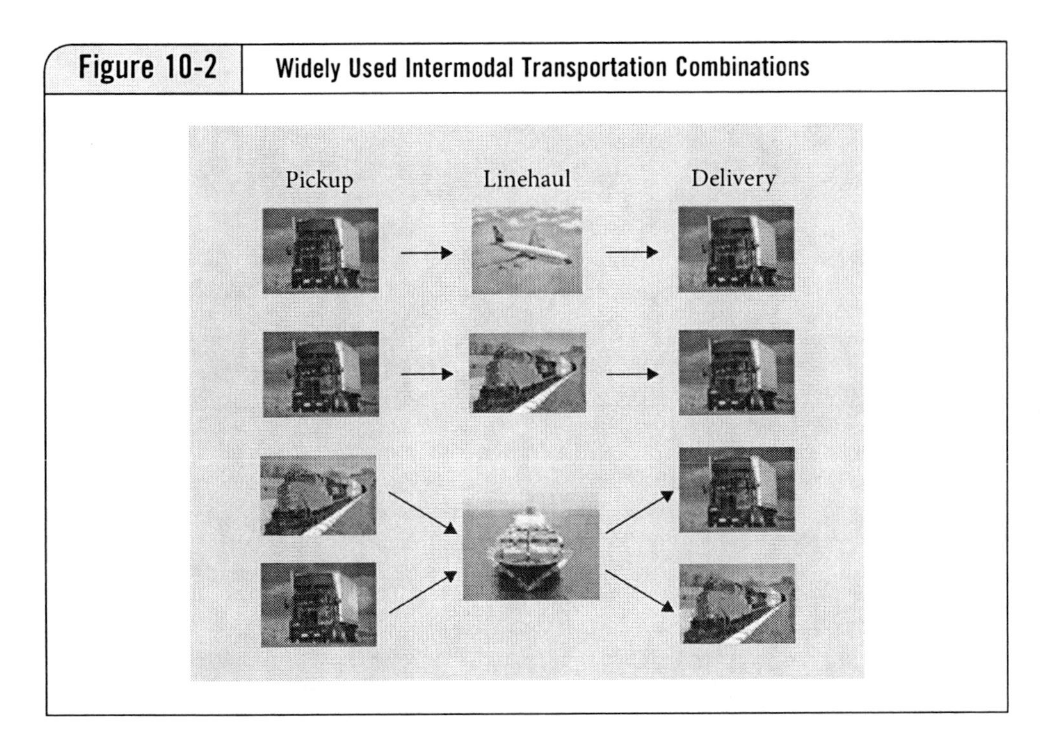

carrier makes the determination of what mode or modal combinations to use. After all, when customers drop overnight letters in the express delivery box, they are not concerned about the combination of modes used as long as the letters arrive on time!

The most pressing issue in the intermodal transportation market is congestion. While the ocean carriers are adding capacity to meet the growing demand levels, transfer points can quickly get clogged with freight. The U.S. seaport facilities along the Pacific coast have struggled to keep product flowing through their facilities in a timely fashion during peak shipping seasons. Intermodal capacity problems in the rail industry have also surfaced. Equipment shortages, transfer facility congestion, and labor issues create delivery delays and supply chain disruptions. Significant infrastructure investment, equipment purchases, and operator hiring will be needed to overcome existing challenges and prepare for the anticipated growth of intermodal transportation.

Transportation Planning and Strategy

Understanding the modal options is an important aspect of transportation management. However, before the freight begins to flow, other vital issues must also be addressed. Supply chain professionals must make a series of interrelated transportation decisions and design processes that properly align with the organization's supply chain strategies. These planning issues, highlighted in Figure 10-3, are discussed next.

Functional Control of Transportation

The initial decision for any organization is straightforward but important—determining which department(s) will be responsible for each part of the transportation process. Whenever you buy goods, sell goods, or do both, somebody has to be responsible for making key decisions and managing the process. Even in a simple purchase over the

Figure 10-3 Framework of Transportation Management Planning Activities

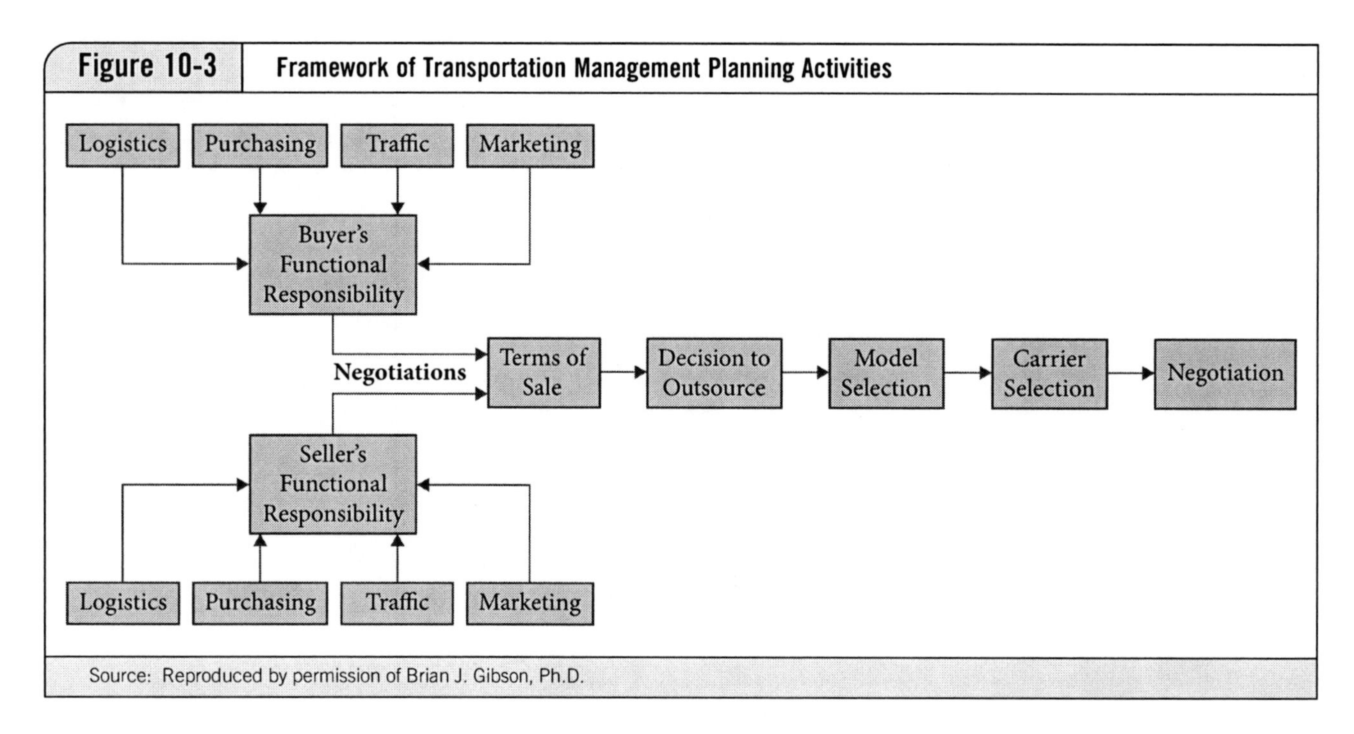

Source: Reproduced by permission of Brian J. Gibson, Ph.D.

Internet, you have to select a carrier (UPS, FedEx, USPS, etc.), service level (next-day, second-day, etc.), insurance coverage, and a related price. A failure on your part to take responsibility can result in the seller making decisions that do not fit your budget or service needs.

In most organizations, responsibility for transportation decisions falls to one or more of the following departments—logistics, procurement, and marketing. Historically, transportation was divided into two separate issues, inbound transportation of goods purchased and outbound transportation of goods sold. In this structure, the purchasing department controls inbound transportation decisions, while marketing has responsibility for outbound transportation control. Often, this decision-making structure leads to a secondary focus on transportation in lieu of procurement costs or customer demands. In the worst-case scenario, these departments arbitrarily relegate decision making to suppliers and customers. The outcome is limited opportunity to leverage transportation efficiencies and services for the benefit of all supply chain partners.

Today, savvy organizations assign transportation decision-making responsibility to a single department (e.g., logistics, distribution, operations, transportation, etc.). This department strives to coordinate inbound and outbound transportation, develop common goals, leverage purchasing power, and procure quality service in support of supply chain excellence. The results of single department control and coordination can be impressive. Many companies have been able to bolster capacity, improve freight visibility and control, enhance customer service, and reduce empty miles, all while better managing their transportation spend.

Terms of Sale

Free-on-board (FOB) terms of sale specify when the ownership and title of the goods pass from a seller to a buyer. This is a critical issue as it determines control over mode and carrier selection, transportation rate negotiation, and other key decisions.

Another important aspect of FOB terms is the determination of in-transit freight accountability. FOB terms determine where the buyer's responsibilities begin and where the seller's responsibilities end. If the terms are FOB origin, title (ownership) to the goods changes hands at the origin—usually the shipping point or seller's distribution center loading dock. From that point on, the goods belong to the buyer, and any loss or damage is the responsibility of the buyer. If the terms are FOB destination, the title transfers at the destination—typically the buyer's unloading dock. The seller has total responsibility for the goods until they are delivered to the buyer.

A related issue is the responsibility for carrier payment. In general, the seller pays the carrier for the transportation service cost under FOB destination terms, while the buyer pays the carrier under FOB origin terms. However, exceptions to these guidelines do occur. The option for Freight Prepaid or Freight Collect should be specified with the FOB terms. In cases where the seller has more clout with carriers, it is wise to have the seller negotiate transportation rates under the Freight Prepaid option. Freight Collect is typically used when the buyer has more power with carriers. Table 10-2 highlights the six different FOB payment responsibility options with their respective buyer and seller duties.

Strategically, the use of FOB origin for product purchases and FOB destination for product sales makes sense for the firm with well-organized, integrated logistics functions. The strategies work well independently, providing greater visibility of inbound freight and opportunities to consolidate outbound freight. Nissan, for example, purchases production parts using FOB origin terms to have better control over the just-in-time (JIT) delivery process. It sells the finished Pathfinders, Frontiers, and other models to Nissan dealerships on a FOB destination basis, leveraging the company's purchasing power and expert knowledge of the car delivery process.

Coordination of supply chain freight movement can also be achieved through these terms of sale. Some organizations work to integrate the flow of goods into and out of

Table 10-2 Key Responsibilities Under FOB and Freight Payment Terms

FOB TERM AND FREIGHT PAYMENT RESPONSIBILITY	WHO OWNS GOODS IN TRANSIT?	WHO HANDLES FREIGHT CLAIMS?	WHO SELECTS AND PAYS CARRIER?	WHO ULTIMATELY BEARS FREIGHT COSTS?	BEST USED WHEN _____ HAS GREATER INFLUENCE WITH CARRIER
FOB Origin, Freight Collect	Buyer	Buyer	Buyer	Buyer	Buyer
FOB Origin, Freight Prepaid	Buyer	Buyer	Seller	Seller	Seller
FOB Origin, Freight Prepaid & Charged Back	Buyer	Buyer	Seller	Buyer The seller adds freight costs to goods invoice.	Seller
FOB Destination, Freight Prepaid	Seller	Seller	Seller	Seller	Seller
FOB Destination, Freight Collect	Seller	Seller	Buyer	Buyer	Buyer
FOB Destination, Freight Collect & Allowed	Seller	Seller	Buyer	Seller The buyer deducts freight cost from goods payment.	Buyer

their facilities to leverage the combined volume with carriers for lower rates. It is also possible to retain carrier capacity or improve access to equipment by generating continuous moves. Optimization of the movement of product across the supply chain is another potential benefit of coordination. To make this strategy work, the organization must gain control over both its inbound and outbound freight.

At times, both the seller and the buyer want to use the FOB terms to be in control of the freight. Multiple factors should impact which organization ultimately manages the transportation process—power, expertise, and risk. As mentioned earlier, it is common for the organization with the greater volume with carriers to use this power to negotiate lower freight rates and greater service levels. Transportation expertise is a related issue, and the company with the greater competency should control the freight. Finally, the company with a greater amount of strategic risk or the most to lose in the case of delivery problems should control the transportation process.

Decision to Outsource Transportation

The organization with FOB freight control and procurement responsibility must analyze the transportation "make or buy" decision. Firms must choose between transporting goods using a private fleet (the "make" option) and using external service providers to move freight (the "buy" option). The decision involves multiple considerations and can be difficult. The primary options are discussed next.

Private fleets account for nearly half of all U.S. freight transportation spending and more than half the miles traveled. Companies like Wal-Mart, Briggs and Stratton, DuPont, and Frito Lay have all chosen to move freight (primarily finished goods) on company-owned and/or company-operated equipment. These companies use private fleets for a variety of economic, customer service, and marketing reasons. They have proven that a well-run private fleet can operate at costs competitive with for-hire carriers while providing greater scheduling flexibility and control over transit time. Intangible benefits such as the promotional impact and prestige of having highly visible company trucks on the road can also be gained. Many organizations have turned their trailers into 48- to 53-foot rolling billboards.

On the other hand, some organizations have decided that it is best to have external experts move the freight and/or manage the transportation process. For-hire carriers in all modes (e.g., Schneider National, Lufthansa, Canadian Pacific Railway, Hyundai Merchant Marine, etc.) have the expertise, flexibility, and capacity to move freight for a wide variety of customers. External service providers also offer a variable cost, simplified, headache-free alternative to private transportation.

By using for-hire carriers, the customers do not have to incur the large capital cost of starting a private fleet, invest the time needed to build transportation expertise, or take on the potential risks (liability for accidents, compliance with government regulations, dealing with unions, etc.) inherent in operating a private fleet. As a result, the for-hire transportation industry is huge. More than $636 billion is spent on for-hire freight transportation each year in the United States.

Another alternative to a private fleet is third-party logistics (3PL), discussed previously in Chapter 4. Third-party firms provide a wide array of transportation services. Dedicated contract carriage is one such service of 3PLs (e.g., Ryder and Exel) and truckload carriers (e.g., Werner Enterprises and J. B. Hunt). Under this arrangement, the 3PL serves as the organization's private fleet and devotes a management team, drivers, and equipment to the relationship. Another service is traffic management where the 3PL provides transportation planning and tactical decision making, handles administrative functions like freight bill auditing, and coordinates supply chain activities. Finally, some 3PLs provide international transportation assistance in the areas of documentation, carrier and route selection, Customs clearance, and other tasks that impact the timely, cost-effective flow of goods across borders.

Until recently, the make or buy decision has favored the external strategy. Many organizations eliminated their private fleets in favor of for-hire transportation services. Other organizations turned private fleets over to 3PLs that operate the fleets under a dedicated contract carriage agreement. Few organizations considered adding or expanding private fleets until very recently. With capacity shortages and price increases fresh in their minds, some organizations are rethinking their options. They have reportedly put private fleets into selective operation to improve access to much needed equipment and gain greater control over costs.

Modal Selection

A critical transportation management issue is modal selection; it affects how fast and economically product will flow across portions of the supply chain. If an organization has determined that controlling the transportation process and using external service providers (for-hire carriers or 3PLs) are in its best interest, it must then determine which mode(s) of transportation to use. Choosing among the six modal options is a function of three factors—modal capabilities, product characteristics, and modal freight pricing.

All modes provide the same basic service of moving freight from point to point in the supply chain. However, a review of Table 10-1 reveals that the modes serve different customer requirements. A vast variation in value of goods, tons, and ton-miles handled exists between the modes. The reason for the different uses is that each mode has unique attributes and capabilities that impact its ability to serve specific customer requirements. Many of these unique attributes are summarized in Table 10-3.

Numerous studies have been conducted over the years to identify the most important performance capabilities in modal selection. These studies commonly identify accessibility, transit time, reliability, and product safety as the key determinants in choosing a mode. Of course, cost is another critical consideration in modal selection. A discussion of each capability and relevant modal performance is provided next.

Accessibility Accessibility determines whether a particular mode can physically perform the transport service required. Accessibility considers the mode's ability to reach origin and destination facilities and provide service over the specified route in question. The geographic limits of a mode's infrastructure or network and the operating scope that governmental regulatory agencies authorize also affect accessibility. Accessibility problems often eliminate a mode from consideration during the selection process.

- **Accessibility advantage:** Motor carriage, because of its inherent ability to provide service to virtually any location. Given the road networks in most countries, motor carriage is more accessible to sellers and buyers than any other mode for domestic transportation.
- **Accessibility disadvantage:** Air, rail, and water. All face accessibility limitations due to infrastructure issues. Air transportation is affected by the number and location of airports. Rail transportation can directly serve only those customers that are adjacent to rail tracks. Water transportation is

Table 10-3 Comparison of Modal Capabilities

MODE	STRENGTHS	LIMITATIONS	PRIMARY ROLE	PRIMARY PRODUCT CHARACTERISTICS	EXAMPLE PRODUCTS
Truck	• Accessible • Fast and versatile • Customer service	• Limited capacity • High cost	• Move smaller shipments in local, regional, and national markets	• High value • Finished goods • Low volume	• Food • Clothing • Electronics • Furniture
Rail	• High capacity • Low cost	• Accessibility • Inconsistent service • Damage rates	• Move large shipments of domestic freight long distances	• Low value • Raw materials • High volume	• Coal/coke • Lumber/paper • Grain • Chemicals
Air	• Speed • Freight protection • Flexibility	• Accessibility • High cost • Low capacity	• Move urgent shipments of domestic freight and smaller shipments of international freight	• High value • Finished goods • Low volume • Time sensitive	• Computers • Periodicals • Pharmaceuticals • Business to consumer (B2C) deliveries
Water	• High capacity • Low cost • International capabilities	• Slow • Accessibility	• Move large domestic shipments via rivers and canals • Move large shipments of international freight via oceans	• Low value • Raw materials • Bulk commodities • Containerized finished goods	• Crude oil • Ores/minerals • Farm products • Clothing • Electronics • Toys
Pipeline	• In-transit storage • Efficiency • Low cost	• Slow • Limited network	• Move large volumes of domestic freight long distances	• Low value • Liquid commodities • Not time sensitive	• Crude oil • Petroleum • Gasoline • Natural gas

limited by the availability and depth of waterways. Still, all three modes serve virtually every major market thanks to intermodalism. These modes provide the long-distance linehaul service, while motor carriers provide pickup and delivery activities that occur away from the air, water, or rail terminals.

Transit Time Transit time is critical in supply chain management because of its impact on inventory availability, stockout costs, and customer satisfaction. Transit time is the total elapsed time that it takes to move goods from the point of origin to the destination (i.e., door to door). This includes the time required for pickup activities, terminal handling, linehaul movement, and customer delivery. Companies typically monitor average transit time for their service providers. Transit time is impacted by the speed of the mode and the ability of the mode to handle pickup and delivery responsibilities.

- **Transit time advantage:** Air transportation is very fast for the linehaul move but loses some velocity as pickup and delivery activities must be handled by truck. Motor carriage is also relatively fast because it can provide more direct movement from origin to destination far more often than any other mode.
- **Transit time disadvantage:** Rail, water, and pipeline are extremely slow with average transit speeds of 22 miles per hour, 5–9 miles per hour, and 3–4 miles per hour, respectively.

Reliability Reliability is a critical issue. Many companies feel that transit time reliability is more important than speed as it impacts their ability to plan supply chain activities. Reliability refers to the consistency of the transit time provided by a transportation mode. It is easier to forecast inventory needs, schedule production, and determine safety stock levels if it is known with some certainty when goods will arrive. Reliability is measured by the statistical variation in transit time.

Modal reliability is impacted by a variety of factors including equipment and labor availability, weather, traffic congestion, freight-handling requirements, number of terminal stops involved, and other factors. Internationally, reliability is impacted by distance, port congestion issues, security requirements, and border crossings, especially when the two countries do not have a proactive trade agreement.

- **Reliability advantage:** Motor carriers and air carriers, as they are the most reliable (variability relevant to average transit time). Numerous carriers in both modes achieve on-time delivery performance in the 98 percent or greater level.
- **Reliability disadvantage:** Water carriers and rail carriers. Historically, they have been slow and consistent, but with the capacity and congestion challenges, they have become less consistent. As a result, some customers have reduced their use of these modes when possible.

Product Safety Safety is critical to the achievement of customer service, cost control, and supply chain effectiveness. From a safety standpoint, goods must arrive at the destination in the same condition they were in when tendered for shipment at the origin. Proper precautions must be taken to protect freight from loss due to external theft, internal pilferage, and misplacement, as well as damage due to poor freight-handling techniques, poor ride quality, and accidents. Safety is often pursued through substantial protective packing.

- **Safety advantage:** Air transportation and motor carriage have the best reputations for product security. Their equipment provides excellent ride quality and protection from the elements. Faster transit times also reduce the opportunity for theft and other mishaps.
- **Safety disadvantage:** Rail and water face significant challenges to maintaining product integrity. Goods moving via rail encounter a great deal of vibration created by steel wheels on steel track, swaying, and jarring from freight cars being coupled at speeds of up to 10 miles per hour. Water transportation often exposes goods to the elements (corrosive salt water, heat, etc.), excessive movement (sway, pitch, roll, etc.), and rough handling during the loading and unloading processes.

Cost The cost of transportation is an important consideration in the modal selection decision, especially when a low-value commodity needs to be moved. Transportation costs include the rate for moving freight from origin to destination plus any accessorial and terminal fees for additional services provided. Examples of these additional costs include inside delivery to a retailer located inside a mall, packing freight in crates for international delivery, or setting up a delivery of furniture in a residential location. A number of factors are taken into consideration when freight rates are developed, including weight of the shipment, distance from origin to destination, nature and value of the product, and the speed required. A detailed discussion of freight ratemaking is provided in Appendix 10B.

- **Cost advantage:** The cost of transportation service varies greatly between and within the modes. In general, pipeline, water, and rail service are low-cost transportation methods. They move large quantities of product over extremely long distances at very reasonable rates, creating a very low cost per ton-mile for their customers. The tradeoff, of course, is slow speed, which forces a company to hold a greater level of inventory to meet demand during these longer transit times.
- **Cost disadvantage:** Motor carriage and air transportation are high-cost modes compared to the others. On average, motor carriage is about 10 times more expensive than rail, and air service is more than twice the cost of motor carriage. It is important to note that while these average costs can be used for general comparisons, each transportation situation is unique, and these higher cost modes are appropriate options.

Given the varying capabilities and cost of each transportation mode, it is obvious that modal selection is not a quick and easy process. Table 10-4 provides a comparative summary of the relevant modal capabilities. These factors must be considered in conjunction with freight costs. The total supply chain cost and service quality of moving, storing, and fulfilling demand for a product must be considered in the modal selection decision. Also, care must be taken to choose the mode with the greatest feasibility and desirability for the supply chain being served. Feasibility of a mode is determined in large part by the product being transported and the capability of the mode to effectively move the product. Desirability focuses on the mode or combination of modes with the ability to meet supply chain requirements.

Table 10-4 Performance Rating of Modes

	MODE OF TRANSPORTATION				
CRITERIA	TRUCK	AIR	RAIL	WATER	PIPELINE
Accessibility*	1	3	2	4	5
Transit time*	2	1	3	4	5
Reliability*	2	3	4	5	1
Security*	3	2	4	5	1
Cost**	4	5	3	2	1

*1 = Best to 5 = Worst

**1 = Lowest cost to 5 = Highest cost

The nature of a product—size, durability, and value—may eliminate some modes from consideration as they cannot physically, legally, and/or safely handle the goods. Product size considerations of weight, cube, density, and shape greatly impact modal selection. Lightweight small electronics and apparel are more suitable to air and motor transportation, while larger, longer products (e.g., lumber) gravitate toward rail and water transportation. Heavy goods, especially when moved in large quantity, also tend to be moved by rail and water. Low-density products such as pillows, plastic plates, and ping pong balls are poor candidates for air transportation as they absorb valuable capacity that could be used for other revenue-generating freight. They tend to be moved by truck or intermodal container. Shape is another factor that must be considered. If your product exceeds certain dimensions, air and motor carriage may not be a cost-effective option.

Durability is another key consideration in the modal selection process. Fragile products (glass, computers, etc.) must be shipped via modes with the best ride quality. Temperature-sensitive goods (food, pharmaceuticals, some hazardous chemicals, etc.) must move via modes with consistent warming or cooling capabilities. Perishable goods (magazines, newspapers, flowers, etc.) require modes with the fastest transit times. The superior speed and freight protection capabilities of air and motor carriage serve these types of low durability, high time sensitivity products well.

Product value is a critical factor in modal selection. If a company spends too much on transportation relative to the value of a product, it will not be able to sell the product at a competitive price. Generally, an inverse relationship exists between product value and the impact of transportation on its value. Transportation is a major cost in low-value products but a minor cost in high-value products. For example, transportation costs comprise 27 percent of stone, glass, and clay product costs but only 4 percent of clothing costs. Thus, water, rail, and pipeline are generally more suitable for low-value, bulk commodities, while truck and air costs can be more readily absorbed by higher-value finished goods. However, incurring higher transportation costs in proportion to product value may be warranted in some supply chains. If a company can generate a customer service advantage, hold less inventory, reduce warehouse space, or eliminate protective packaging by using a faster, more reliable mode of transportation, the additional cost can be justified.

Shipment characteristics—size, route, and required speed—cannot be ignored in modal selection. The product size issue discussed earlier can be extended to shipments in that modal capacities must be matched to the total weight and dimensions of shipments. Origin points, destination points, and specified routes affect modal accessibility and must be factored into selection decisions. Infrastructure availability, geographic distance, natural challenges like oceans and mountains, and man-made obstacles such as borders and development tend to limit modal selection to two or three realistic options. Finally, the shipment-related requirements of speed, reliability, and safety must be matched to the modal customer service capabilities discussed earlier.

The general strategy regarding modal selection focuses on determining which mode or combination of modes best suits the requirements of the freight buyer. This long-range decision requires an analysis of the best fit and balance between modal capabilities, product characteristics, supply chain requirements for speed and service, and freight transportation cost. Short of major price, infrastructure, service quality, or technological changes in the modes, the decision does not need to be revisited frequently.

Carrier Selection

Carrier selection is a specialized purchasing decision that typically will be made by a logistics, transportation, or traffic manager who has expertise and experience in the purchase of transportation services. After the modal decision has been made, attention turns to selecting the individual transportation service providers within the mode. Like the modal decision, carrier selection is based on a variety of shipment criteria and carrier capabilities: transit time average and reliability, equipment availability and capacity, geographic coverage, product protection, and freight rates.

A major difference between modal and carrier selection is the number of options. Modal selection involves six primary options, but the carrier selection may involve fewer or many more alternatives. In the case of rail transportation, many markets are only served by a single carrier. The choice is limited—either use that carrier or find another mode. At the other extreme is truckload transportation where dozens of carriers serve a particular market. Time and effort must be expended in evaluating potential carrier capability, service quality, and price.

Another difference is the frequency of the decision. Carrier selection requires more active and frequent engagement of the transportation buyer than does the more long-range modal selection decision. This engagement does not focus on choosing a new carrier for each freight move; it focuses more on the transportation buyer remaining vigilant and managing the performance of chosen carriers. It is critical to monitor each carrier's service level and freight rates on an ongoing basis. Should carrier performance deteriorate, it may be necessary to select new service providers.

The type of service provided within a mode impacts carrier selection. Most carriers have their roots in one of two types of service—direct service or indirect service—between which customers must choose. Direct service provides immediate point-to-point flows of goods. Indirect service requires interim stops and/or transfer of freight between equipment. Direct service provides the advantage of speed and safety because freight is handled less and moves without detour to the destination. Indirect service gives up speed and subjects the freight to additional handling but offers lower cost because carriers can consolidate the freight for more efficient transportation. A passenger example of these alternatives is limousine service versus bus service. You will pay more for limo service to take you directly to your destination because you have exclusive use of the vehicle. In contrast, you save money by taking a bus but may have to take a slower, less direct route.

Within a mode, most carriers have the capabilities to provide a similar level of service, but these service levels can and do vary greatly from one transportation company to another. Also, since the cost structures are essentially the same for carriers in a given mode, their rates tend to be aligned for a given movement. Given this similarity, transportation rates tend not to be the most important criterion in carrier selection. Service performance is the key determinant for this decision. Carrier selection research suggests that reliability of on-time delivery and on-time pickup, technical capabilities, carrier response to emergencies, information sharing, freight damage experience, carrier financial stability, and total transit time are among the most important criteria to transportation service buyers.[13] Of course, the relative importance of these selection criteria will be influenced by an individual organization's supply chain structure and freight requirements.

Carrier selection strategy commonly focuses on concentrating the transportation buy with a limited number of carriers. Using a small group of carriers helps the organization leverage its purchasing dollars for lower overall rates, build relationships with service providers who gain a better understanding of freight flows and requirements over time, and effectively monitor performance of the carrier base. A core carrier strategy takes this concentration focus to a greater depth with the organization narrowing its carrier base to a select few service providers that have proven to be the best carriers in terms of service quality and cost efficiency. These core carriers ultimately handle the vast majority of an organization's freight, sometimes in a dedicated fleet capacity. In many cases, the core carriers become an indispensable extension of the organization's transportation management team; they are able to manage freight flows across the supply chain with limited direction or oversight. The ability to rely on the transportation expertise of trusted core carriers also allows the organization to focus its attention on other supply chain issues.

Rate Negotiations

Following the significant economic deregulation of most transportation modes more than 25 years ago, transportation buyers focused on carrier competition to reduce transportation expenses. Buyers would pit carriers against each other for freight and ultimately award the business to the carrier offering the greatest discount from published rates. This led to destructive competition within the trucking industry, and bankruptcies were a common result. Many decentralized organizations ended up with a hodgepodge of carriers, often numbering in the hundreds, as individual facilities negotiated independent deals with carriers. Not only was it difficult to manage such a large number of carriers, but it was also impossible for organizations to leverage their freight volume with carriers for better rates.

Over time, organizations have shifted from decentralized transportation purchases based on published rate discounts to centralized freight rate negotiations with carriers. These negotiations focus on developing contracts with carriers for a tailored set of transportation services at a specific price. Key negotiation issues for the buyer include equipment availability, delivery speed and consistency, freight protection and problem resolution, billing accuracy, and the cost of service. Transportation companies focus on volume commitments, shipment frequencies, origin-destination combinations, freight characteristics, and related cost issues that impact their ability to serve the buyer profitably. When the parties successfully complete a mutually desirable negotiation, a contract for transportation services is developed and signed. It is estimated that more than 80 percent of commercial freight moves under contractual rates today.

The strategy of centralized, contract-based rate negotiation aligns well with the core carrier concept described previously. Leveraging volume with a small set of carriers whose capacity and capabilities to provide tailored services align well with the buyer's needs makes great sense and benefits both organizations. The buyer only contracts and pays for services that are needed, gains a commitment for scarce capacity, and locks into competitive rates for a specified period of time. The carrier receives a relatively stable volume of business across a set of geographic lanes which allows it to plan for greater labor and equipment utilization efficiency and reduce the cost of operations. The contracts also promote the creation of a mutually beneficial, long-term relationship in which the parties collaborate to create greater supply chain value (see the On the Line feature) beyond transportation savings.

Transportation Execution and Control

When a shipment needs to be moved across the supply chain, transportation planning efforts culminate and execution processes take center stage. Decisions must be made regarding shipment size, route, and delivery method; freight documents must be prepared; in-transit problems must be resolved; and service quality must be monitored.

Shipment Preparation

When the need for transportation service is generated by a customer request, replenishment signal, or pre-scheduled order, the delivery process is set in motion. All of the prior work to identify the correct modes and carriers, secure capacity, and control transportation spending culminates in shipment preparation and handoff to a carrier for delivery. Given the size, service requirements, and destination of a particular shipment, the transportation managers must choose the most appropriate carrier. Steps can also be taken to minimize transportation cost and protect the shipment.

To ensure maximum effectiveness in the shipment-carrier matching process, many organizations maintain a corporate transportation routing guide. These documents specify the carriers to be used by internal personnel and vendors for freight moves that are controlled by the organization. The routing guides commonly provide instructions for carton and shipment labeling, insurance and billing requirements, advanced shipping notification, and other pertinent information.

Some routing guides are simple one- or two-page documents that plainly state shipment requirements. For example, Hallmark's straightforward routing guide is easy to read and leaves no room for misinterpretation. It instructs Hallmark distribution centers to ship LTL shipments that are between 401 and 7,500 pounds or greater than 25 cartons via Yellow Freight, FOB destination, Freight Collect. Similar instructions are provided for parcel, truckload, and airfreight shipments.[14] Other companies create more detailed routing guides with specific sections for inbound, outbound, and returns freight; regional routing information; origin-destination tables and matrices; and related shipping requirements.

The strategy behind routing guides is to promote supply chain excellence through transportation. Genentech, a biotechnology company, states at the top of its routing guide: "The objective is to provide suppliers with detailed instructions that will aid in streamlining the processes of receiving, stocking and consuming materials while reducing freight and handling costs."[15] Routing guides also help organizations maintain centralized control over the number of carriers used and avoid off-contract or "maverick" buying of transportation services. Another goal is to ensure that contractual volume commitments to specific carriers are achieved, as a failure to meet these commitments can result in higher transportation rates or penalty fees.

In preparing freight for delivery, transportation managers have the ability to make last-minute, cost-saving decisions. As the individual orders and delivery requests are received, efforts should be made to consolidate freight, coordinate shipment deliveries, and take full advantage of container capacity. Multiple orders destined for a single location can be combined into a single shipment with one set of documentation. This can be especially cost-effective for small package and parcel shipments. For example, the cost of shipping 10 items that weigh five pounds apiece in 10 separate shipments to a destination is more than twice the cost of sending those same 10 items in a single 50-pound shipment. Consolidation of LTL shipments into TL deliveries or creating TL

On the Line *United Front*

Confidential contracts allow shippers and ocean carriers to develop a "more creative relationship" that extends beyond rates, according to Robert Sappio, senior vice president for trans-Pacific trade for APL Limited, a global container shipping company. The regulatory changes established in the Ocean Shipping Reform Act (OSRA) make such contracts possible.

"Either we can have an ax fight over rates and the last $50 per TEU, or we can take advantage of OSRA and be more collaborative and benefit both of us," he told the audience at the *Journal of Commerce*'s Trans-Pacific Maritime (TPM) Conference.

Sappio said APL and a few of its largest customers have formed "collaborative" relationships that address the shippers' needs while providing the carrier with predictable business. He noted that APL has been able to establish such partnerships with only a few of its shippers because the exchange of information requires a high degree of trust that can't be developed overnight. "Shippers and carriers are just starting to see the benefits of collaborative contracts," Sappio explained.

An example of this kind of relationship exists between APL and Toys "R" Us, which ships 45,000 TEUs of cargo a year to stores in 20 different countries with APL and six other container lines. Michael R. Jacobs, senior vice president of logistics for Toys "R" Us," said APL consults with Toys "R" Us across its entire supply chain and helps the retailer understand how it can be improved. In return, he said, Toys "R" Us focuses on using "APL's most profitable trade lanes and also on lanes that are the most difficult for us."

Jacobs knows these kinds of relationships aren't for everyone. "You need to trust your partner," he said. To make such a collaborative relationship work, Jacobs claims, "You need to figure out how to make your carrier more profitable. That's why there are only a few carriers you can sign multiyear contracts with."

Jacobs and Sappio believe that rates remain important, but they're only part of the equation. According to Sappio, Toys "R" Us is "no different than any other shipper looking for the best rate and last sailing out of Yantian," but the companies have learned they can help each other by understanding one another's needs.

"We try to understand their service needs to see if some of them can rate a lower level of service, so we can differentiate on services and rates," Sappio explains. But because Toys "R" Us enjoys a collaborative relationship and has a multiyear contract, APL offers it a higher level of service than a shipper that has a purely transactional relationship. Toys "R" Us works to understand APL's cost structure so that it can help the carrier provide the service it needs and the rates it can afford to pay.

This kind of radical thinking goes against the grain of the stormy relationship that has characterized shipper-carrier relations. It's what David Lim, chief executive officer of Neptune Orient Lines, the parent company of APL Ltd., focused on during his TPM Conference speech. Lim called for a "progressive transformation" of carrier services so that they can provide "end-to-end" solutions where "neither we nor our customers should be focused on the cost of shipping or warehousing or any of the other component service in the supply chain." He said that by pricing services across the supply chain instead of on each component service, the industry could "cushion and attenuate the cycles inherent in the shipping segment of global cargo supply chains."

Source: Adapted from Peter T. Leach, "United Front," *Journal of Commerce* (March 14, 2005): 1. Reproduced by permission of the *Journal of Commerce*.

stop-off deliveries of multi-destination LTL shipments can also generate cost savings. The key to reducing cost is giving the transportation manager advanced knowledge of freight volume, destinations, and service requirements, as well as the lead time to develop efficient delivery decisions.

The transportation operation is the last line of defense in protecting product integrity and value. Prior to loading the shipment, an accurate freight count should be taken to ensure that the invoice and related documents are correct, packaging should be inspected to ensure that the contents are not likely to be damaged en route, and the freight container should be examined for safety and product protection problems (e.g., obvious signs of leakage and other freight exposure issues). During the loading process, the freight must be stacked properly and stabilized to withstand vibration, swaying, and other ride quality issues. Of course, it is imperative to use carriers with an effective track record of damage- and shortage-free delivery service.

Freight Documentation[16]

Freight does not move by itself. Shipments are accompanied by related documents that spell out the details of the shipment—what it is, where it is going, who owns it, and more. The type and variety of documents required depend on the origin and destination points, characteristics of the freight, mode(s) being used, and carrier handling the freight. A simple truckload delivery of dry groceries from the Opelika, Alabama, Wal-Mart distribution center to the Wal-Mart store in Auburn, Alabama, via the company's private fleet, will require only a basic bill of lading. In contrast, a shipment of fireworks moving from Liuyang City, China, to Las Vegas, Nevada, will require extensive paperwork. Suffice it to say that the more complex the transportation requirements, the more documents are needed to facilitate the uninterrupted flow of goods through the supply chain. The most prevalent documents include the bill of lading, freight bill, and claims form.

The **bill of lading** is probably the single most important transportation document. It originates the shipment, provides all the information the carrier needs to accomplish the move, stipulates the transportation contract terms including the scope of the carrier's liability for loss and damage, acts as a receipt for the goods the shipper tenders to the carrier, and, in some cases, shows certificate of title to the goods. Figure 10-4 shows a typical bill of lading with the essential types of shipment information contained in the document.

The bill of lading is created by the shipper of the goods and is either negotiable or nonnegotiable. A straight bill of lading is nonnegotiable and the carrier must deliver the goods only to the specific receiving organization and destination in return for freight charge payment. An order bill of lading is negotiable and serves as a title to the goods listed on the document. The owner of the goods has the right to transfer title to the goods to another party and reroute the shipment to a location other than the one listed on the bill of lading.

Bills of lading also differ by type of move. An inland bill of lading is used for overland transportation and provides the required information for the domestic movement of goods by truck, rail, water, or combinations of these modes. An ocean bill of lading is a "contract of carriage" between an exporter and an ocean carrier to transport goods to a specified market overseas. A through bill of lading covers both the domestic and international transport of export goods between specified points for a specified charge. An air waybill is a bill of lading that covers both domestic and international flights transporting goods to a specified destination. It establishes the terms between a shipper and an air transportation company for the transport of goods.

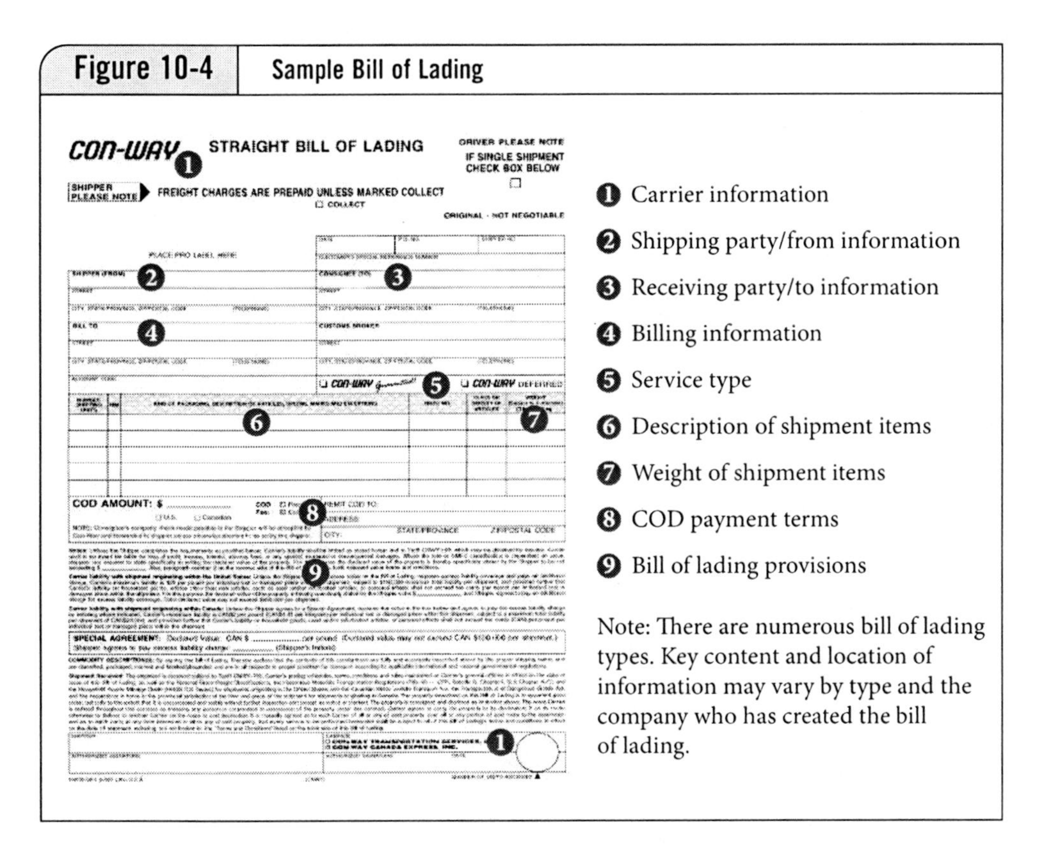

Figure 10-4 Sample Bill of Lading

The **freight bill** is the carrier's invoice for the fees the carrier charges to move a given shipment. The freight bill lists the shipment, origin and destination, consignee, items, total weight, and total charges. The freight bill differs from the bill of lading in that the freight bill sets forth the charges applicable to the shipment, while the bill of lading sets forth the terms of the shipment and is a document of title. Figure 10-5 shows a freight bill used by a LTL trucking company.

The total charges specified in the freight bill are based on the rate negotiated by the freight buyer and carrier, the size of the shipment, and supplementary fees for accessorial services. Freight bills are submitted by the carrier when the freight is picked up by

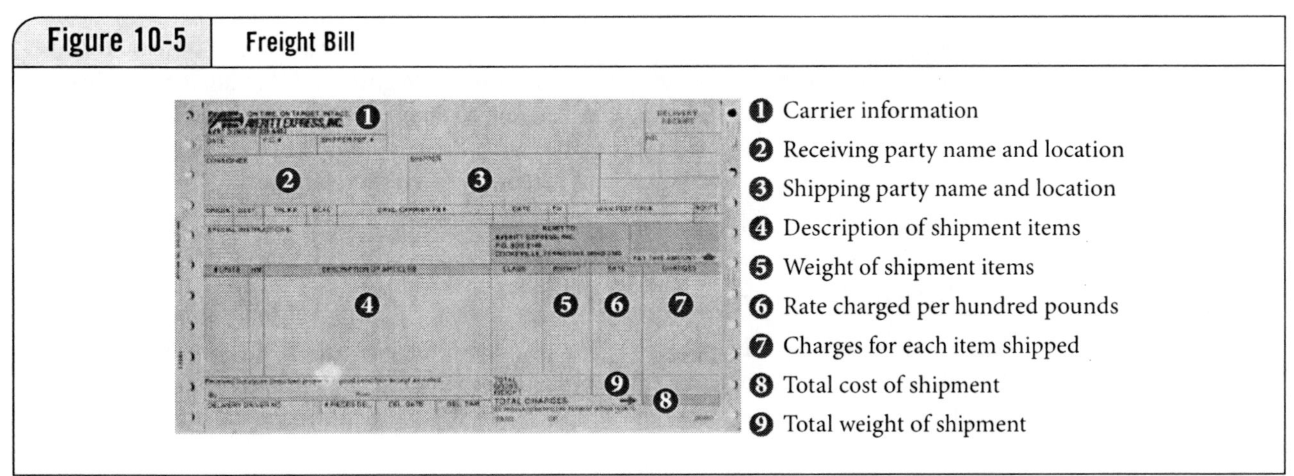

Figure 10-5 Freight Bill

the carrier (prepaid basis) or when the freight is delivered (collect basis). In most contracts, the freight buyer has a specified number of days to pay the bill after carrier submission and may receive a discount for early payment.

A **freight claims form** is a document that the transportation buyer files with the carrier to recoup monetary losses resulting from the carrier's failure to properly protect the freight. The shipper must file in writing freight claims with the carrier within a timeframe specified in the contract. Freight claims can be filed for visible damage or shortages that are detected when the product is received and inspected, concealed losses that are not discovered until packages are opened, or for financial losses due to unreasonable delays. Claims can be supported by photographs of the damage, notations of problems on the delivery receipt, and proof of the damaged goods' monetary value (e.g., the invoice, price catalog, etc.).

Freight claims are intended to compensate the transportation buyer an amount equal to the value of the goods had the carrier safely delivered them. Carrier liability is limited if the shipper elected to send the goods under a released value (i.e., valuing the freight at less than its full worth) in exchange for lower freight rates. Carriers are not liable for freight claims if the damage is attributable to some uncontrollable factor such as the following:

- Natural disaster of some other "act of God"
- Military attack or similar "act of public enemy"
- Government seizure of freight or "act of public authority"
- Failure to adequately package the freight or other negligent "act of the shipper"
- Extreme fragility, perishability, or similarly problematic "inherent nature of the goods"

A number of other documents may also be required to move freight efficiently through the supply chain. These include critical transaction documents like the commercial invoice that provides a record or evidence of a transaction between an exporter and importer, or the certificate of origin that authenticates the country of origin for the goods being shipped. Both are used for commodity control and duty valuation by the country of import. In addition to the transportation documents described earlier, valuable and sometimes necessary paperwork includes a shipper's letter of instructions, dock receipts, shipment manifests, dangerous goods declaration forms, and insurance certificates.

Documentation-based freight delays and disruptions can be minimized with attention to detail. Accurate and thorough information is a straightforward, yet critical, issue. Carriers and governmental authorities may halt the flow of goods if documents appear to be inaccurate, incomplete, or fraudulent. Availability of documents prior to the tendering of goods to carriers is also critical. Most carriers will not accept freight without the necessary paperwork. For international freight, the U.S. Customs 24-Hour Advance Vessel Manifest Rule requires carriers to submit cargo information a full day before it is loaded onto vessels with a port of call in the United States. Transportation buyers must factor this rule into their plans for delivering freight and paperwork to carriers or risk denial of loading, missed voyages, and supply chain disruptions.

Maintain In-Transit Visibility

Management of the transportation process does not end when the documents and freight are given to the carrier. It is important to control the freight and manage key events as product moves across the supply chain. Visibility of in-transit freight is a key facilitator of this control as it prevents freight from temporarily "falling off the radar screen." The goal of visibility is to provide the location and status of the shipments, regardless of the position in the supply chain, enabling transportation buyers to make decisions on the fly in the interest of better meeting customer needs. These accurate and up-to-the-minute shipment data make it possible for organizations to respond to problems as they are developing and to manage the supply chain as a single entity rather than disjointed functions.

Technology facilitates the ability to monitor product flowing across the supply chain. Time definite carriers and truckload carriers are using satellite tracking capabilities to maintain constant visibility of equipment. Equipment operators are increasingly equipped with cell phones and notebook computers with satellite uplinks, allowing frequent and timely contact. Leading integrated carriers like FedEx and UPS offer extensive tracking capabilities that are accessible to transportation buyers at no cost via the Internet. Such tools encourage carriers and their customers to proactively manage issues and exceptions as they become apparent rather than after they become major supply chain disruptions.

By itself, in-transit visibility of product adds little value to the supply chain. This information is not valuable unless it is somehow put to use. Thus, visibility tools must be linked to other capabilities and processes to have an impact on supply chain event management. These additional pieces of an event management solution include a clear supply chain strategy, ongoing collaboration with key customers and suppliers, appropriate business processes that can be used to act upon visibility information, and integrated communications systems through the supply chain.[17]

Monitor Service Quality

Upon completion of freight delivery, transportation managers must take the time to analyze the outcome of all their transportation strategy, planning, and decision-making efforts. This is accomplished through a coordinated, ongoing effort to monitor carrier performance. The focal point of this monitoring effort should be the commitments made by the carriers during contract negotiation. Service and cost issues with the greatest potential impact on the supply chain warrant the constant attention of the transportation buyer as well as the carrier.

A key requirement for service quality monitoring is information. The transportation manager must have information regarding the customer service demands and the service level that current carriers provide. Without it, the transportation manager cannot make a rational evaluation of performance. This information must be compiled from multiple sources—shipment date and cost from the freight bill, arrival date from the delivery receipt, and shipment damage information from the receiving party—to gain a full picture of delivery performance and carrier service quality. Numerous transportation metrics are used to consolidate all of the information from various sources and shipments into useful knowledge.

A popular strategy for developing an objective, holistic view of carrier service quality is to develop standardized scorecards or evaluation reports. Most scorecards use a weighted point plan to emphasize key criteria for each carrier used. The transportation manager assigns weight factors to the criteria, measures carrier performance, and multiplies the results by the weighting factor or percentage. An overall carrier score is obtained by summing the weighted scores for the criteria. The scores are shared with carriers to identify service quality issues and performance improvement opportunities.

Table 10-5 Transportation Performance Scorecard

PERFORMANCE CRITERIA	WEIGHT FACTOR	PERFORMANCE EVALUATION	POTENTIAL SCORE	CRITERIA SCORE
On-time delivery	8	>98% = 5 96.01–98% = 4 94.01–96% = 3 92.01–94% = 2 <92% = 0	40	
Loss and damage rate	5	<0.5% = 5 0.5–1% = 4 1–1.5% = 3 1.5–2% = 2 >2% = 0	25	
Billing accuracy	3	>99% = 5 97–99% = 3 95–96% = 1 <95% = 0	15	
Equipment condition	2	Safe, clean, correct type = 5 Poor condition, incorrect = 0	10	
Customer service	2	Superior = 5 Good = 4 Average = 3 Fair = 2 Unacceptable = 0	10	
		Total Score	**100**	

Source: Reproduced by permission of Brian J. Gibson, Ph.D.

Some organizations use the results to make future purchase decisions or streamline their carrier base.[18] Table 10-5 provides an example scorecard that emphasizes delivery timeliness and freight protection, two key service quality issues discussed next. In this example, a carrier providing 96.6 percent on-time deliveries would receive 32 points for the category (weight factor of 8 multiplied by the performance evaluation score of 4).

Transportation Metrics

The quality of transportation services is tangible—the key service requirements are generally observable and quantifiable. This allows organizations to monitor activities through transportation metrics or key performance indicators (KPIs). Transportation KPIs are objective measures of carrier or private fleet performance that are critical to the success of the organization. KPIs can be used to evaluate current performance versus historical results, internal goals, and carrier commitments. They can also be used to benchmark results against those achieved by competitors, world-class organizations, and other links in the supply chain.

Many aspects of transportation performance can be evaluated. Important issues include transportation spending efficiency, freight protection, delivery service quality, and customer satisfaction, among others. The challenge lies in narrowing down the vast array of metrics available to monitor transportation performance to a limited, manageable number of KPIs that reflect the transportation needs and objectives of a supply chain. Properly chosen KPIs provide numerous benefits: they signal to carriers an organization's transportation priorities, they "keep score" of carrier performance, and they maintain organizational focus on the ever-rising expectations of supply chain partners and customers.

The two primary categories of transportation KPIs include service quality and efficiency. Service quality means doing things right the first time according to customer-defined requirements and expectations. The "Seven R's" effectively identify the focus and scope of transportation service quality KPIs—"at the right time" targets transit time, "in the right condition" concentrates on freight protection, and "at the right cost" pertains to billing accuracy issues. While there are other, more qualitative aspects of service, these three issues are fundamental to the success of supply chains as described in the following discussion.

The focus on lean supply chains and just-in-time operations makes consistent, on-time delivery a critical requirement. Multiple studies suggest that on-time delivery is the most important KPI used by transportation buyers to evaluate their carriers.[19] Timely service facilitates inventory rationalization through lower safety stock levels, provides consistent replenishment to reduce out-of-stock problems, and reduces supply chain uncertainty and the resulting bullwhip effect.

- On-time delivery KPIs measure the ratio of shipments delivered in a timely fashion (i.e., the date and time promised by the carrier) to the total shipments delivered by the carrier. Most transportation buyers set 95 percent as a minimum acceptable level of performance from their motor carriers with goals of 98 percent or above.
- Delivery consistency metrics compare the average origin to destination transit time of shipments to the transit time promises made by carriers. Sizable deviations from these promises and significant variation from the transit time average suggest that carriers are not providing adequate service and corrective action should be taken.

Freight protection is another key element of transportation service quality. It's not enough to get the shipment to its destination quickly: it has to get there safely and completely. Time and money are sacrificed when freight is damaged or lost. Supply chains supporting just-in-time operations and continuous replenishment retail distribution systems are especially vulnerable to delivery disruptions, as they keep little to no safety stock on hand to replace the unavailable goods.

- Claims-free delivery is a primary freight protection KPI. The ratio of claims-free deliveries (no need for a freight claim due to loss, damage, or any other reason) to the total number of deliveries is evaluated by the transportation buyer. Perfection is the goal—most organizations will accept nothing less than 99 percent claims-free deliveries. A high level of claims indicates that carriers are not taking adequate steps to protect the freight or that the freight packaging is insufficient. Service failures must be diagnosed and corrected immediately to prevent future claims.

Since transportation rates and service requirements are tailored to a specific customer's requirements, it is imperative that carriers apply the correct shipment data, rate structures, and charges to each customer. Billing accuracy KPIs measure a carrier's ability to properly translate customer bill of lading information and instructions to the freight bills. Incorrect data entry or application of contract provisions can lead to overstatement of rates and accessorial service charges, improper deliveries, misrouted freight, and incorrect payment due dates.

- Freight bill accuracy KPIs measure the ratio of accurate freight bills to the total number of freight bills. The minimum acceptable accuracy level is 95 percent for most organizations, with a goal of 100 percent accuracy. Billing errors create administrative correction costs, and continued problems lead to the use of third-party firms to audit freight bills, a non-value-adding inspection activity that adds expense to the supply chain.

The ultimate service quality KPI is the execution of perfect deliveries, the ratio of defect-free deliveries to the total number of deliveries made. Transportation buyers should seek out high-quality carriers that are capable of consistently providing flawless service that is on-time, damage-free, accurate, responsive, and cost-effective. Defect-free transportation eliminates the need for rework, reduces administrative intervention, and tempers the use of premium service, as well as promoting customer satisfaction, inventory reduction, and reduced variation in the supply chain.

While service quality is critically important for customer satisfaction, transportation service efficiency cannot be ignored. Organizations need to balance their service requirements and the expenses related to moving freight. Transportation costs must be kept low in proportion to the value of the goods or they will not have a competitive landed cost. If cost didn't matter, many more shipments would move via air express to minimize transit time. Proper and effective use of equipment is another efficiency issue as is the productive use of transportation labor. Transportation efficiency KPIs help keep organizations focused on these goals.

Transportation is the single largest logistics expense and it is imperative that organizations get the greatest "bang for their buck" when buying transportation services. Aggregate efficiency measures focus on the total transportation spending versus goal or budget. Item-level KPIs focus on the transportation expense per unit of measure (e.g., pound, case, selling unit, etc.). It is a simple calculation of total freight cost divided by the number of units shipped. Understanding what is spent to move each unit highlights transportation's impact on the overall cost of goods. This KPI also provides a baseline from which improvement efforts can be made.

Asset utilization is a critical aspect of transportation cost control. Moving empty or partially loaded equipment is inefficient and expensive. It is estimated that 18 percent of all truck movement involves empty equipment, a multibillion-dollar cost. This is not only a carrier challenge; customers ultimately pay for these empty miles in the form of higher rates. Equipment utilization KPIs also help buyers work toward effective freight deployment. Comparison of shipment weight or cube to the available equipment capacity helps organizations identify opportunities to improve utilization. As more capacity of a container is used, the freight cost is spread across a greater number of units, and the transportation cost per unit is reduced.

Efficiency measures can also be used to evaluate and improve the performance of carriers and private fleets. Labor productivity KPIs ensure that equipment operators, freight handlers, and other personnel are performing at acceptable levels. Minimization of loading/unloading time improves carrier employee and equipment turnaround time, keeping both in productive use. These and similar KPIs directly benefit carriers by focusing on cost control. Freight buyers that contribute to efficient carrier operations reduce their exposure to equipment detention and accessorial charges, as well as put themselves in a solid position to negotiate more advantageous freight rates.

Systematic measurement of KPIs in transportation brings substantial benefits. KPIs can help organizations take a proactive, knowledge-based approach to transportation decision making. Transportation KPIs are instrumental for monitoring quality and dealing with service issues in a timely fashion before they have a major impact on the supply chain. KPIs also help organizations pinpoint inefficiencies and develop strategies for supply chain cost reduction. Finally, KPI data can be used to analyze cost-service level tradeoffs. This knowledge can be used to make better carrier selection and assignment decisions. However, a failure to identify, measure, and monitor relevant KPIs puts the organization in a reactive mode and limits the transportation manager's ability to make informed, timely decisions.

Transportation Technology

The dynamic nature of transportation, combined with the wide array of delivery requirements and options, create a complex environment for transportation buyers and managers. Multiple factors must be considered when developing strategies and making operational decisions, if appropriate and economical decisions are to be made. Fortunately, software and information technology tools have been developed to support transportation planning, execution, and performance evaluation. In this final section of the chapter, the primary technologies are presented.

Transportation Management Systems

Software tools related to the movement of goods across the supply chain are lumped together in a general category called **transportation management systems (TMS)**. TMS is defined as information technologies used to plan, optimize, and execute transportation operations.[20] This simple definition captures the essence of TMS, presenting it as a melting pot of applications used to assist managers in nearly every aspect of transportation, from basic load configuration to complex transportation network optimization.

The planning capabilities of TMS assist transportation buyers and managers with the key pre-shipment decisions discussed earlier. These individuals cannot adequately evaluate the thousands of potential lane/mode/carrier/service/price combinations in their supply chains without technological help. TMS tools allow organizations to consider a vast array of transportation options in a matter of minutes versus hours or days of manual design activity. In addition, freight planning tools can be linked to order management systems, warehouse management systems, and supply chain planning tools to gain timelier, more comprehensive information. With this knowledge, better supply chain decisions and tradeoffs can be made. Critical TMS planning applications include the following:

- **Routing and scheduling**—proper planning of delivery routes has a major impact on customer satisfaction, supply chain performance, and organizational success. Thus, this is a critical TMS capability sought by transportation decision makers. TMS software uses mathematical methods and optimization routines to evaluate possible combinations in which routes could be run and chooses the most economical one. Only those feasible routes that satisfy relevant constraints (container capacity, delivery windows, transit speed, and operator restrictions) are considered. Typical TMS output includes a detailed schedule of the routes, cost analysis, and route maps.

- **Load planning**—effective preparation of safe, efficient deliveries can be accomplished via TMS load optimization programs. These programs help transportation managers build a database of package dimensions, loading requirements (e.g., top load, keep upright, etc.), and equipment capacity. Then, the specifics of a shipment or multiple shipments traveling together, such as weight, cube, and number of cartons, are entered into the TMS. In a matter of seconds or minutes, the TMS software optimizes how product should be stacked on pallets and/or arranged in the container. The optimization results in more efficient use of cargo space, fewer loads being shipped, and less damage to the product.

TMS execution tools help transportation managers streamline some of their shipment activities. With multiple shipments needing delivery each day, manual processes are susceptible to errors, missed deadlines, and customer service failures. Various TMS capabilities automate repetitive activities to reduce labor costs and accuracy problems. For example, standardized templates can be used to ensure that complete and accurate shipment data are provided in transportation documents. Other tools post detailed shipment information to a shared network or a Web site to promote shipment visibility and provide greater freight control. Three of the key execution tools include the following:

- **Load tendering**—organizations may have a number of approved carriers that could be used for a particular shipment. However, their rates may differ slightly based on the origin-destination locations and shipment size. Rather than subjectively assigning loads to carriers, a TMS database determines which carriers are eligible to move the freight and then tenders the freight to the best carrier. The tendering decision takes into consideration routing guide requirements, carrier cost, transit time, and required service capabilities contained in the database. As a result, contract compliance is improved and freight costs are optimized.
- **Status tracking**—maintaining visibility of shipments as they move across the supply chain through delivery confirmation can be a time-consuming task. The in-transit progress of shipments can be monitored using TMS in conjunction with satellite capabilities and other visibility tools. Shipment status information, especially notifications regarding problems and shipments at risk of late delivery, can be shared with key stakeholders. The goal of this TMS tool is to provide timely information regarding potential delivery exceptions so that corrective actions can be taken.
- **Appointment scheduling**—to avoid facility congestion, equipment delays, and operator inefficiency, organizations are using TMS capabilities to automate the scheduling function. TMS tools provide the real-time visibility necessary to make appointment scheduling easier and more accurate. Many systems support Internet-based access to the scheduling system where carriers can schedule pickup and delivery times at specific dock locations. These systems help carriers avoid time-intensive phone calls, interim stops, and wait time.

TMS analytical tools provide organizations with the ability to make post-shipment evaluations of carrier performance, customer service, and network cost. The data required for analysis can be spread across the entire supply chain in a variety of documents and information systems. It is critical to collect these data in a timely fashion so that the KPIs can be measured, performance assessed and benchmarked, and corrective action taken. TMS help organizations assemble and make sense of the vast array of transportation data that are generated by freight movement. Two useful analytical applications are as follows:

- **Performance reporting and scorecarding**—managing carrier performance requires extensive data collection and calculation as discussed earlier in the section on transportation metrics. TMS tools can automate the collection of data, measurement of KPIs, and dissemination of periodic reports. These reports can provide information on overall performance, as well as the results in specific segments of the transportation operation. Customized reports like monthly carrier performance scorecards and benchmarking analyses can also be generated. These tools provide transportation managers with timely, objective information upon which future decisions can be made.
- **Freight bill auditing**—payments made to carriers must reflect the agreed-upon contractual rates and the services rendered. To ensure that they are neither being over- nor undercharged for freight services, many organizations are turning to TMS software to reconcile invoices with their contracts. These tools automate a manual process that does not always catch discrepancies in a timely, accurate manner.

This range of capabilities has led to widespread interest in TMS. It is viewed as a critical tool for managing transportation cost and service across the supply chain. The worldwide estimated market for TMS was $893.3 million in 2004, up $20 million from the previous year according to ARC Advisory Group.[21] Continued growth of TMS implementation is expected. Organizations seeking shipment visibility, collaboration with supply chain partners, and operational efficiency are purchasing the software with the expectation that TMS tools will help them address the growing challenges of limited available capacity, rising freight rates, and fuel surcharges.[22]

Emerging Technologies

Event management systems (EMS) seek to provide visibility of in-transit freight, as well as integrate processes and information flows across supply chain partners. EMS products require users to specify what kind of information they want to receive and to set acceptable time parameters for various events in the delivery process. These events include normally occurring activities, such as shipment pickup and delivery, as well as potentially problematic events. If the events don't happen within the specified timeframe, the parties are notified.[23] While event notification capabilities are maturing, the challenge is to develop a generation of EMS embedded with the intelligence to support decision making and automatically resolve some problems. Visibility, notification, and decision support are all needed to proactively manage transportation events and gain control over supply chain flows.

Radio-frequency identification (RFID) is not for inventory management only. Numerous opportunities to use RFID in transportation are also being identified. Battery-powered active RFID tags are capable of initiating communications, performing independent monitoring and control functions, and performing diagnostics. Thus, active tags are useful for transportation tracking and tracing activities such as managing equipment and locating assets in port facilities. RFID can also be combined with global positioning systems (GPS) to provide real-time status of goods in transit. Monitoring product quality and safety can also be accomplished through the sensing capabilities of the tags.[24] Internal container temperature spikes, unauthorized opening of containers, or any other unexpected activity will trigger alerts so that an appropriate response can be made. As organizations learn to harness the benefits of active RFID tags, they will

Supply Chain Technology — *Making Rock-Tenn's Transportation Manageable*

When the enterprise is as wide as the country and the number of plants and shipments are large by any measure, getting control of the shipping function is critical to a company's success. Whether it's beefing up the bottom line, remaining ahead of the competition, or just getting rid of cumbersome manual work, employing a transportation management system proves to be the right step in solving these issues and in getting even more functionality in the bargain.

Ben Cubitt, vice president of supply chain at the Norcross, Georgia, headquarters of Rock-Tenn Co., is heading the company's effort to manage transportation through implementation of a new TMS for its six divisions and 80 plants across the country. Rock-Tenn is a manufacturer of packaging products, merchandising displays, and recycled paperboard. The company's customer base includes Wal-Mart, Kraft, Procter & Gamble, Nestle, Clorox, and Del Monte.

"We have inbound, outbound, interfacility, cross border and more," Cubitt says. "We were decentralized. I call us collaborative now and we are moving toward central management. TMS is a huge part of that."

"We looked at all of the options when thinking of a TMS," recalls Cubitt. "At the end of the day we made two determinations. We thought hosted was better. But what drove it even more was we wanted to outsource the load control center. We didn't want to build that. We felt very good about a hosted system for TMS, especially with 80 sites and six divisions. With multiple systems, that made a lot of sense. We wanted someone with a strong control center, one common system, one place for rates and one place for issue reporting. Transplace gives us a common TMS over all of that."

Cubitt places a high priority on establishing good relationships with carriers and implementing routing guidelines. "Even with 80 sites, we really had very little leverage with carriers," he notes. "The number of carriers we used was just astounding. Where we used major national carriers we wouldn't see the same ones across all six divisions. We've now gone through more than a year of rationalizing the carrier base, something that continues today."

Rock-Tenn is primarily a truckload shipper with a significant amount of rail use as well. Cubitt is trying to increase rail and intermodal shipments substantially and thinks the new TMS will help in optimizing loads there. Since some of the company's LTL shipments tend to be large, there are opportunities to use the TMS to build truckload shipments from them.

Tracking and tracing of shipments were important features to Rock-Tenn's selection of the Transplace TMS. The company's major customers "want us to have strong capabilities and to be able to provide information," notes Cubitt. "We need to know where our freight is and to be able to share cost and delivery information back and forth. That is a business requirement for us." TMS allows Rock-Tenn to fulfill those needs.

Source: Roger Morton, "TMS Right Now," *Logistics Today* (May 2007): 5, 48.

enrich product visibility with greater shipment detail and bolster freight protection as it flows across the supply chain.

The challenge of technology is that it is forever changing and expanding. While the TMS capabilities and emerging tools discussed above represent the leading edge of technology for managing supply chain flows, they may soon be yesterday's news. Thus, the most important idea to take away from this section is the importance of information technology in transportation. Simply stated, technology helps us manage the vast volume of data and options in transportation in order to make better decisions regarding modal and carrier selection, routing, packaging, loading, and many other activities. These decisions lead to greater customer service, tighter cost control, and competitive advantage in the supply chain.

SUMMARY

- Without question, transportation is a very dynamic activity and a critical supply chain process. Not only is it the largest logistics cost component in most supply chains, but it also directly impacts fulfillment speed and service quality. By providing the physical links between key participants across domestic and global supply chains, transportation facilitates the creation of time and place utilities. Organizations with highly efficient and effective transportation processes can differentiate their product in the marketplace through lower landed costs and greater inventory availability.
- Managing the transportation process for maximum supply chain impact requires considerable knowledge of transportation options, planning, decision making, analytical skills, and information sharing capabilities.
- Transportation is a key supply chain process and must be included in supply chain strategy development, network design, and total cost management.
- Numerous obstacles—global expansion of supply chains, rising costs, limited capacity, and government regulation—must be overcome to synchronize transportation with other supply chain processes.
- Fulfillment of supply chain demand can be accomplished through five modal options or the intermodal use of truck, rail, air, water, and pipeline transportation.
- Multiple planning activities occur prior to carrier and mode selection: who will be responsible for managing the transportation function within the organization, what terms of sale and payment will be used, and how goods will be transported must all be determined with a strategic supply chain focus.
- Mode selection is based on the relative strengths of each modal/intermodal option in terms of accessibility, transit time, reliability, safety and security, transportation cost, and the nature of the product being transported.
- Carrier selection focuses on the type of service required (direct or indirect), geographic coverage, service levels, and carrier willingness to negotiate reasonable rates.
- Most commercial freight moves under contractual rates that are negotiated directly between freight buyers and transportation companies for specific volumes of tailored services at mutually agreed-upon prices.
- Shipment routing guides help organizations ensure internal compliance with service contracts and maintain centralized control over freight tendering decisions.
- Freight documentation provides the details of each shipment, sharing critical information that promotes uninterrupted flows of goods through the supply chain. Domestic transportation documents include the bill of lading, freight bill, and freight claims, while international freight requires additional paperwork such as a commercial invoice, shipper's letter of instructions, certificate of origin, and insurance certificates.
- Organizations must continue to manage freight after it has been tendered to carriers by maintaining in-transit visibility of shipments and monitoring carrier performance.
- Numerous metrics are available to evaluate transportation service quality in terms of carrier timeliness, freight protection, accuracy, and perfect deliveries. Service efficiency measures focus on spending proficiency, asset utilization, and labor productivity.
- Transportation management systems are widely used information technologies that support the effective planning, execution, and analysis of transportation processes. Emerging tools such as event management and RFID have the potential to improve supply chain visibility and dynamic response to potential challenges.

STUDY QUESTIONS

1. Discuss the role of transportation in the supply chain. Provide examples of how transportation can positively and negatively impact supply chain performance.
2. Describe the major challenges faced by transportation managers in the current environment.
3. What are the primary capabilities, advantages, and disadvantages of each of the basic modes?
4. Use the Business and Company Resource Center (http://academic.cengage.com/bcrc) to develop a basic overview report (primary service offerings, annual sales, current stock price, and recent news) for one domestic or international transportation company from each SIC code:
   a. SIC 4011—Railroads, Linehaul Operating
   b. SIC 4213—Trucking, Except Local
   c. SIC 4513—Air Courier Services
   d. SIC 4412—Deep Sea Foreign Transportation of Freight
5. Discuss the primary considerations and issues that must be factored into modal and carrier selection.
6. Use the Business and Company Resource Center (http://academic.cengage.com/bcrc) and company Web sites to compare the service offerings for the following carriers:
   a. J. B. Hunt (http://www.jbhunt.com) and New Penn (http://www.newpenn.com)
   b. DHL International (http://www.dhl.com) and Polar Air Cargo Worldwide, Inc. (http://www.polaraircargo.com)
   c. Maersk Line (http://www.maerskline.com) and Wallenius Wilhelmsen Logistics (http://www.2wglobal.com)
   d. Canadian National Railway Company (http://www.cn.ca) and Alaska Railroad (http://www.akrr.com)
7. Describe the purpose and value of freight documentation. Discuss the function of the following documents: bill of lading, freight bill, and freight claim.
8. How would a transportation manager monitor the quality of service provided by the carriers used? What types of metrics would be used?
9. What role does information technology play in the management of transportation planning, execution, and analysis?

NOTES

1. Rosalyn Wilson, *18th Annual State of Logistics Report* (Oak Brook, IL: Council of Supply Chain Management Professionals, 2007).
2. Amazon.com Annual Report (2004): 3–4. Retrieved February 3, 2006, Accessible via the World Wide Web at http://library.corporate-ir.net/library/97/976/97664/items/144853/2004_Annual_report.pdf.
3. Bridget McCrea, Bracing for Clean Air, *Logistics Management* (September 2004).
4. Bureau of Transportation Statistics, U.S. Department of Commerce, and U.S. Census Bureau, Transportation Commodity Flow Survey, *2002 Economic Census* (December 2004).

5. Rosalyn Wilson, *18th Annual State of Logistics Report* (Oak Brook, IL: Council of Supply Chain Management Professionals, 2007).

6. ATA Standard Trucking and Transportation Statistics (Q3, 2004).

7. The Transport Topics Top 100 For-Hire Carriers, *Transport Topics* (2005).

8. Bridget McCrea, Return of the Private Fleet, *Logistics Management* (July 2004).

9. The Transport Topics Top 100 Private Carriers, *Transport Topics* (2005).

10. Association of American Railroads, Overview of the U.S. Freight Railroads (January 2006). Retrieved March 8, 2006, from http://www.aar.org/PubCommon/Documents/AboutTheIndustry/Overview.pdf.

11. IATA, *Freight Forecast 2005-2009* (2005).

12. Underview of Pipelines, retrieved February 15, 2006, from http://www.pipeline101.com/Overview/energy-pl.html.

13. Shane R. Premeaux, Motor Carrier Selection Criteria: Perceptual Differences between Shippers and Motor Carriers, *Transportation Journal* (Winter 2002).

14. Shipment Routing Guide for Hallmarks Corporate Store Group, retrieved February 10, 2006, from http://www.hallmark.com/wcsstore/HallmarkStore/images/Content/routing_srg_stores.pdf.

15. Genentech: Contact UsSuppliersSupplier Transportation Information, retrieved February 10, 2006, from http://www.gene.com/gene/contact/transportation.jsp#ltl.

16. For an extensive discussion of freight documentation, see John J. Coyle, Edward J. Bardi, and Robert A. Novack, *Transportation*, 6th ed. (Mason, Ohio: Thomson South-Western, 2006), Chapter 11.

17. Kevin R. Fitzgerald, "More than Meets the Eye," *DC Velocity* (January 2003).

18. Brian J. Gibson and Jerry W. Wilson, "Carrier Scorecarding: Purposes, Processes, and Benefits," *Journal of Transportation Management*, Vol. 15, No. 1 (2004).

19. Carol Birkland, "Stating the Obvious," *Fleet Equipment* (February 2002) and Thomas A. Foster, "You Cant Manage What You Dont Measure," *Logistics Management* (May 1998).

20. Chad W. Autrey, Stanley E. Griffis, Thomas J. Goldsby, and L. Michelle Bobbitt, "Warehouse Management Systems: Resource Commitment, Capabilities, and Organizational Performance," *Journal of Business Logistics*, No. 2 (2005).

21. James A. Cooke, "Software Gets Friendlier," *Logistics Management* (July 2005).

22. James A. Cooke, "Upgrade Time," *Logistics Management* (May 2005).

23. Bridget McCrea, "EMS Completes the Visibility Picture," *Logistics Management* (June 2005).

24. Bob Trebilcock, "Get Active," *Modern Materials Handling* (November 2005).

CASE 10-1

Supreme Sound Explosion

Supreme Sound Explosion (SSE), located in Memphis, Tennessee, produces concert quality sound systems for rock, rap, and country musicians. Recently, the company partnered with two new suppliers to create an innovative line of speakers called Blasters. Blasters provide 100 decibels more sound versus competitors' speakers. Interest in the product is great as potential buyers want to reduce the number of sound system components that need to be taken on tour. This is no small matter when you consider that groups like the Rolling Stones and U2 regularly use dozens of tractor trailers to move equipment during their stadium tours. Tour costs can be reduced if equipment is streamlined and fewer trucks are needed to haul the equipment between tour stops. Also, more tour stops can be scheduled as loading/unloading/setup/tear down time is reduced.

One of the key suppliers makes woofers in Athens, Georgia, while the other makes tweeters in Portland, Oregon. Two tweeters are inserted into each woofer to make a Blaster. SSE assembles Blasters and uses existing suppliers for other required components. While SSE has negotiated per-unit purchasing costs with two suppliers, decisions regarding delivery of the components remain. Each supplier has proposed two different delivery options. The proposals are now in the hands of SSE's operations manager who has limited experience with transportation issues. Demand for Blasters is expected to be 400 units per month, and production is scheduled to begin in less than a month.

Product and delivery characteristics are shown in the following table:

	WOOFERS	TWEETERS
Manufactured in	Athens, GA	Portland, OR
SSE purchase price	$740 each	$2,380 per pair
Weight	48 pounds	6 pounds
Dimensions	36" (L) x 24" (W) x 24" (H)	12" (L) x 8" (W) x 6" (H)
Characteristics	Sturdy, bulky, not easily damaged, supplier maintains sizeable inventory	Compact, vibration and moisture sensitive, supplier builds to order
Delivery options	W1—delivery via LTL once per week with FOB origin, Freight Collect terms. The freight cost per delivery is $832 with an expected transit time of two days. W2—delivery via TL every other week with FOB destination, Freight Collect terms. The freight cost per delivery is $932 with an expected transit time of one day.	T1—delivery via LTL once per week with FOB destination, Freight Collect and Allowed. The freight cost per delivery is $689 with an expected transit time of five days. T2—delivery via airfreight two times per week with FOB origin, Freight Collect terms. The freight cost per delivery is $669 with an expected transit time of two days.

CASE QUESTIONS

1. What is the delivery cost per unit of woofers and tweeters for each option?
2. Why do the delivery costs of woofers and tweeters vary among the four options?
3. Which option do you recommend for the delivery of woofers and tweeters? Why?
4. What responsibilities will SSE have under your recommendation in Question 3?
5. What other supply chain issues and costs must SSE take into consideration when making these transportation decisions?

APPENDIX 10A

Federal Regulation of the Transportation Industry

Federal regulation of transportation has been with us since the Act to Regulate Commerce passed in 1887. The years immediately preceding the enactment of this law were full of turmoil, for both shippers and carriers. Inland transportation was basically by railroad, and the carriers charged high rates when possible and discriminated against small shippers. Control over the transportation industry was important to U.S. economic growth, and a stable transportation service supply that would be compatible with the needs of an expanding society was essential.

Economic Regulation[1]

The need for federal economic regulation of transportation is rooted in the significance of transportation to the overall U.S. economy. Transportation enables business to accomplish the very foundation of economic activity—the exchange of commodities from areas of oversupply to areas of undersupply. The transportation activity benefits all citizens; thus, it can be argued that the government should provide transportation, just as it provides public interest functions such as the court system and national defense.

Traditionally, however, private enterprise has provided freight transportation. Fueled by the dollars that shippers spend, transportation companies commit to various transportation services; such resource allocation is more efficient than what a political allocation could produce. Since the free enterprise marketplace has imperfections that may allow monopolies to develop, government control of transportation attempts to allocate resources in the public's interest by maintaining and enforcing the competitive market structure.

Despite arguments for economic regulation of the transportation industry, the regulatory cycle has come full circle to the point where most of the regulation adopted between 1887 and 1973 has been eliminated or reduced. Table 10A-1 highlights the major legislative efforts to regulate, and later deregulate, economic aspects of the transportation industry. Current federal economic regulation of transportation is very minimal, and marketplace forces are the major controls used to enforce a competitive market structure.

The lessening of federal economic regulatory controls over transportation began with the passage of the **Airline Deregulation Act** in 1978. This act effectively returned the airline industry to a free marketplace by eliminating most economic regulation. The **Staggers Rail Act of 1980** and the **Motor Carrier Act of 1980** soon followed. These two acts eliminated most of the economic regulation for the railroad and trucking industries. Further reduction of federal power over the industry occurred with the enactment of the **ICC Termination Act of 1995**, which eliminated the Interstate Commerce Commission, reduced or eliminated most economic regulation over motor and water carriers, and established the Surface Transportation Board to administer the remaining railroad regulations. The current status of federal regulation of the transportation modes is as follows:

Table 10A-1 Chronology of Major Transportation Regulation

DATE	ACT	NATURE OF REGULATION
Initiation Era		
1887	Act to Regulate Commerce	Regulated railroads and established Interstate Commerce Commission (ICC); rates must be reasonable; discrimination prohibited
1903	Elkins Act	Prohibited rebates and created filed rate doctrine
1906	Hepburn Act	Established maximum and joint rate controls
1910	Mann-Elkins Act	Shipper given right to route shipments
1912	Panama Canal Act	Prohibited railroads from owning water carriers
Positive Era		
1920	Transportation Act of 1920	Established rule of ratemaking; pooling and joint use of terminals allowed; began recapture clause
1933	Emergency Transportation Act	Financial assistance to railroads
Intermodal Era		
1935	Motor Carrier Act	Federal regulation of trucking similar to railroads
1938	Civil Aeronautics Act	Federal regulation of air carriers; established Civil Aeronautics Board (CAB)
1940	Transportation Act	Provided for federal regulation of water carriers; declaration of national transportation policy
1942	Freight Forwarder Act	Federal regulation of surface freight forwarders
1948	Reed-Bulwinkle Act	Antitrust immunity for joint ratemaking
1958	Transportation Act	Eliminated umbrella (protective) ratemaking; provided financial aid to railroads
1966	Department of Transportation Act	Established U.S. Department of Transportation
1970	Rail Passenger Service Act	Established Amtrak
1973	Regional Rail Reorganization Act	Established Consolidated Rail Corporation
Deregulation Era		
1976	Railroad Revitalization and Regulatory Reform Act	Rate freedom; ICC could exempt railroad operations; abandonment and merger controls began
1977	Airline Deregulation Act	Deregulated air transportation; sunset CAB
1980	Motor Carrier Act	Eased entry restrictions; permits rate negotiation
1980	Staggers Rail Act	Permits railroads to negotiate contracts; allowed rate flexibility; defined maximum rates
1993	Negotiated Rates Act	Provided for settlement options for motor carrier undercharges
1994	Trucking Industry Regulatory Reform Act	Eliminated motor carrier filing of individual tariffs; ICC empowered to deregulate categories of traffic

continued

Table 10A-1 Continued

DATE	ACT	NATURE OF REGULATION
1994	FAA Reauthorization Act	Prohibited states from regulating interstate trucking
1995	ICC Termination Act	Abolished ICC; established Surface Transportation Board (STB); eliminated most economic regulation of trucking
1998	Ocean Shipping Reform Act	Eliminated authority of shipping conferences over contracts; modified contract filing requirements

Source: John J. Coyle, Edward J. Bardi, and Robert A. Novack, *Transportation,* 6th ed. (Mason, Ohio: Cengage South-Western, 2006), Chapter 2. Reproduced by permission.

- **Motor Carriers.** All rate and tariff-filing regulations are eliminated except for household goods and noncontiguous trade (continental United States and Alaska, for example). The common carrier concept is eliminated, but the carriers are held liable for damage. All carriers may contract with shippers. Antitrust immunity is granted carriers for collective ratemaking (for example, joint publishing of a freight classification), and the carriers must provide tariffs (containing rates and rules) to shippers upon request. In essence, little federal economic control is exercised over these modes.
- **Railroads.** In theory, rail economic regulation still exists. The STB has jurisdiction over rail rates and rules, as well as routes, services, facilities, and mergers. The railroads are subject to the common carrier obligations to provide service to all shippers; to not discriminate against persons, places, or commodities; to charge reasonable rates; and to be liable for damage to the goods. The filing of rail tariffs and contracts is not required. The railroad industry remains the most highly regulated transportation mode, but complete rate deregulation exists over certain types of rail traffic—intermodal freight, for example.
- **Air Transportation.** In 1977, economic regulation of air transportation was eliminated; the marketplace determines rates and services. Safety regulation, however, remains a major thrust of federal controls over air carriers. Such safety regulations as the controls over the number of landings and takeoffs permitted at an airport indirectly determine the level of service provided by an air carrier and whether an air carrier can provide service to a particular airport (availability of landing slots).
- **Ocean Transportation.** The Shipping Act of 1984 initiated the economic deregulation of the ocean shipping industry, removing the requirement for Federal Maritime Commission (FMC) approval of rates and conference agreements (ocean conferences are a group of carriers that band together to set common prices). This act expanded antitrust immunity to conference members and allowed independent contracting by conference members but required contracts to be filed with the FMC for public dissemination. The Ocean Shipping Reform Act of 1998 greatly diminished the power of the conferences by eliminating their authority over conference members' participation in service contracts with customers. OSRA also changed tariff-filing rules in that contract rates are not made public (though basic information—port ranges, commodities, and minimum commitments—still must be published). These revisions have hastened the economic deregula-

tion of ocean shipping, with greatly expanded use of contracts and a significant reduction in the number of ocean conferences.

- **Freight Forwarders and Brokers.** Both forms of transportation are required to register with the STB, and the broker must post a $10,000 surety bond to ensure the carrier used will receive payment from the broker. However, there are no federal economic controls over the rates or services provided by these two intermediaries. A freight forwarder is considered a carrier and is held liable for freight damage, whereas the broker is not considered a carrier and is not liable for freight damage.

Safety Regulation[2]

Noneconomic regulation primarily focuses on transportation safety, promotion, and research issues. Established in 1966, the U.S. Department of Transportation (DOT) was charged with providing the United States with a national transportation policy aimed at improving the safety and efficiency of the transportation system.[3] The DOT is now partitioned into 13 administrations and bureaus, each charged with specific responsibilities.[4] The primary DOT agency for each major mode of transportation is identified in the following paragraphs.

The Federal Highway Administration (FHWA) primarily affects the motor carrier industry. The FHWA is charged with the broad responsibility of ensuring that U.S. roads and highways continue to be the safest and most technologically up to date. The agency conducts safety research, technology, and outreach projects aimed at reducing the frequency and severity of crashes, mitigating congestion, and protecting the environment. The FHWA provides financial and technical support to states for constructing, improving, and preserving the U.S. highway system.

The Federal Motor Carrier Safety Administration (FMCSA) was established as a separate entity from FHWA in the Motor Carrier Safety Improvement Act of 1999. The goals of this agency are to improve the safety of commercial motor vehicles and to reduce crashes, injuries, and fatalities involving large trucks and buses. This agency develops, maintains, and enforces federal regulations; administers the commercial driver's license program; and regulates hazardous materials transportation. Most recently the FHWA has altered the amount of time that truck drivers can work each day through the Hours of Service regulation.

The Federal Aviation Administration (FAA) primarily affects the airline industry. The major responsibilities of the FAA include regulation of air safety, promotion of air commerce, and monitoring of air space. The agency's Aviation Safety office controls the certification, production approval, and continued airworthiness of aircraft and certifies pilots, mechanics, and others in safety-related positions. The FAA also provides federal grant money to plan and develop public airports and to improve technical capabilities at airport facilities.

The Federal Railroad Administration (FRA) affects rail companies. This agency's responsibilities focus on the enforcement of railroad safety issues. The FRA Operations Practices Division examines and ensures that carrier operating rules, employee qualification guidelines, and carrier training and testing programs are in compliance with the Railroad Safety Act of 1970; railroad occupational safety and health standards; the Hours of Service Act; and accident and personal injury reporting requirements. The FRA also administers federal assistance to some carriers to ensure the continuation of freight and passenger rail service.

The Maritime Administration (MARAD) is responsible for promoting and operating the U.S. merchant marine. The agency's mission is to strengthen the U.S. maritime transportation system—including infrastructure, industry, and labor—to meet the economic and security needs of the country.[5] In times of war, the United States relies heavily on water carriage for overseas shipments of troops and materials. To keep U.S. ships properly maintained and in seaworthy condition, the federal government offers water carriers subsidies. These subsidies are administered by the MARAD. Given the importance of maritime vessels in national defense, the federal government has also granted the maritime industry an antitrust exemption. The exemption allows carriers to form shippers' conferences and to discuss specific rates. Some large customers oppose shippers' conferences because they allow carriers to monopolize certain trade routes. Some industry experts expect antitrust immunity to disappear, ending shippers' conferences and deregulating the industry much like the other transportation modes.

While the U.S. Coast Guard (USCG) is a branch of the armed forces, it also works with the DOT to promote marine safety and environmental protection. The USCG is responsible for enforcing maritime law, developing and enforcing safety regulations, assisting in rescue efforts, and protecting U.S. borders. Its mission is to protect the public, the environment, and U.S. economic interests—in the nation's ports and waterways, along the coast, on international waters, or in any maritime region as required to support national security.[6]

SUMMARY

Regulation is a dynamic component of the transportation process that is always subject to change. While we are currently in a time of limited economic regulation, governments actively develop transportation policies and regulations to address safety, security, and environmental challenges; meet societal requirements; and adapt to technological change. The intention of such regulation is positive but can have a major impact on the cost, time, and ease with which product flows across the supply chain. Thus, transportation managers must remain vigilant and factor current and pending legislation into their planning processes.

NOTES

1. For an extensive discussion of economic regulation, see John J. Coyle, Edward J. Bardi, and Robert A. Novack, *Transportation*, 6th ed. (Mason, Ohio: Cengage South-Western, 2006), Chapter 2.

2. Adapted from David J. Bloomberg, Stephen LeMay, and Joe B. Hanna, *Logistics* (Upper Saddle River, NJ: Prentice-Hall, Inc., 2002): 95–96.

3. DOT Act of 1966, Public Law 89-670, Sec. 2(b)(1).

4. For more information regarding these U.S. DOT agencies, see http://www.dot.gov/DOTagencies.htm.

5. "MARAD Mission, Goals, and Vision," retrieved March 8, 2006, from the Internet: http://www.marad.dot.gov/welcome/mission.htm.

6. "United States Coast Guard Overview," retrieved March 8, 2006, from the Internet: http://www.uscg.mil/top/about/.

APPENDIX 10B

Basis of Transportation Rates

Transportation ratemaking would be a simple process if carriers sold all transportation services on a ton-mile basis, charging customers *X* dollars to move each ton of a product each mile. However, carriers cannot operate in such a simplistic manner. Multiple factors must be considered by carriers and their customers when determining how much it costs to move a product from origin to destination. With 33,000 major shipping points in the United States alone, a countless array of commodities, varying shipment sizes, and unique service requirements, the challenge of ratemaking becomes clear.

Ratemaking has become a sophisticated activity with tremendous efforts being made to optimize the negotiated price of transportation services. Customers recognize the need for carriers to charge rates that earn a reasonable profit margin or the carrier will not be in business over the long run. This section briefly discusses primary factors that are incorporated into the transportation rate development process. To ensure that transportation rates are fair and reasonable for both parties, the following issues must be considered: (1) the cost and value of service, which affect the different rates the carrier establishes for different commodities; (2) the distance between origin and destination; (3) the weight of the shipment; (4) the characteristics of the commodity being transported; and (5) the level of service required.

Cost of Service

Basing rates on the **cost of service** considers the supply side of pricing. The cost of supplying the service establishes the floor for a rate; that is, the supply cost permits the carrier's viability by providing the rate's lower limit (see Figure 10B-1).

Figure 10B-1 Limits on Rates

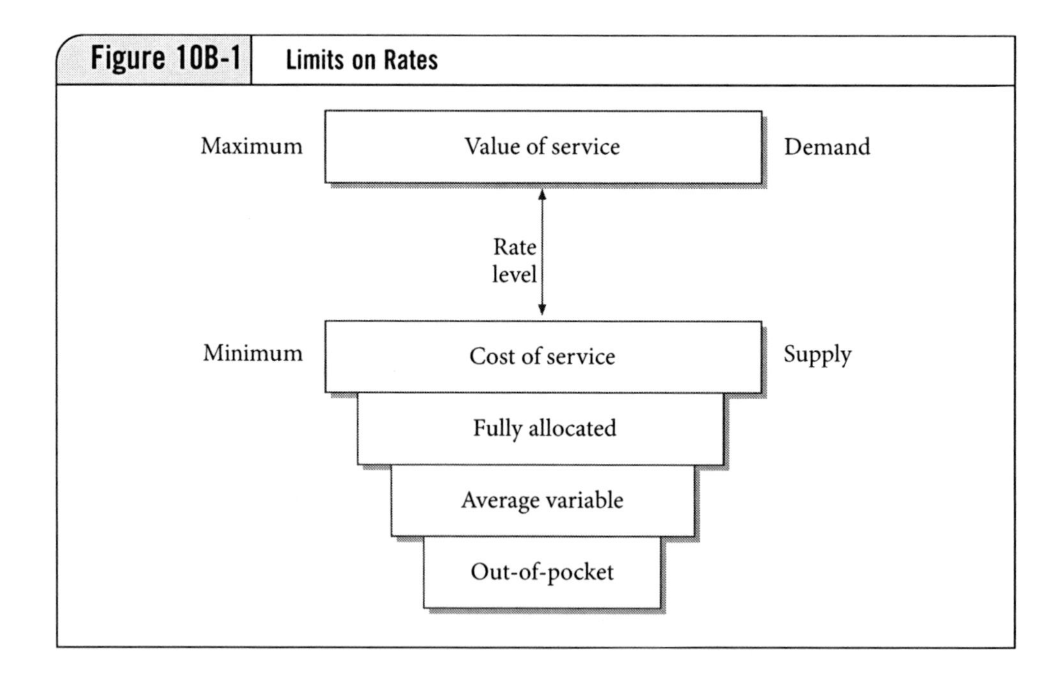

The continual problem of what cost basis to use has plagued this area. Carriers have used fully allocated (average total) costs, as well as average variable costs and out-of-pocket (marginal) costs. In essence, this problem sets up subfloors to the lower rate limit: the carrier will base the higher limit on fully allocated costs and the lower limit on out-of-pocket costs.

Common and **joint costs** also increase the problem of using service cost as a basis for rates. The carrier incurs common and joint costs when producing multiple units of output; the carrier cannot directly allocate such costs to a particular production unit. A joint cost is a particular type of common cost in which the costs a carrier incurs in producing one unit unavoidably produce another product. For example, moving a commodity from A to B unavoidably produces the movement capacity and cost from B to A—the backhaul. The procedure the carrier uses to assign these common and joint costs determines the cost basis, permitting latitude for cost variations and, consequently, for rate variations.

Value of Service

Value of service pricing considers the demand side of pricing. We may define value of service pricing as "charging what the traffic will bear." This basis considers the transported product's ability to withstand transportation costs. For example, in Figure 10B-2, the highest rate a carrier can charge to move producer A's product to point B is $0.50 per unit. If the carrier assesses a higher rate, producer A's product will not be competitive in the B market area. Thus, value of service pricing places the upper limit on the rate.

Generally, rates vary by transported product. The cost difference associated with various commodity movements may explain this, but this difference also contains the value of service pricing concept. For higher-value commodities, transportation charges are a small portion of the total selling price. From Table 10B-1, we can see that the

Figure 10B-2 Example of Value of Service Pricing

Maximum rate = $0.50

A ———————————————— B

A's production cost = $2.00

B's production cost = $2.50

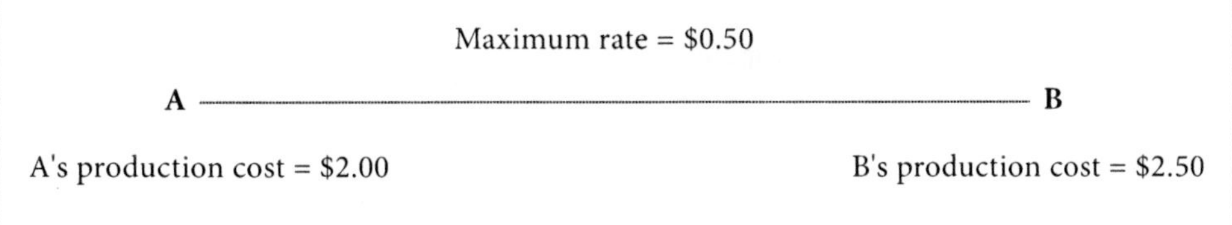

Table 10B-1 Transportation Rates and Commodity Value

	COAL	DIAMONDS
Production value per ton*	$30.00	$10,000,000.00
Transportation charge per ton*	10.00	1,000.00
Total selling price	$40.00	$10,001,000.00
Transportation cost as a percentage of selling price	25%	0.01%

*Assumed.

transportation rate for diamonds, for a given distance and weight, is 100 times greater than that for coal; but transportation charges amount to only 0.01 percent of the selling price for diamonds, as opposed to 25 percent for coal. Thus, high-value commodities can sustain higher transportation charges, and carriers price the transport services accordingly—a specific application of demand pricing.

Distance

Rates usually vary with respect to **distance**; that is, the greater the distance the commodity moves, the greater the cost to the carrier and the greater the transportation rate. However, certain rates do not relate to exact point-to-point distance. One example of these is a **blanket rate** or **zone rate**.

A blanket rate does not increase as distance increases; the rate remains the same for all points in the blanket area the carrier designates. The postage stamp rate is an extreme example of a blanket rate. No matter what distance you ship a first class letter domestically, your cost as the shipper (sender) is the same. In freight transportation, carriers develop zones that contain a particular area such as a city's commercial zone, a given state, a region, or a number of states, for example. In each case, the transportation rate is the same regardless of the particular freight pickup/delivery location within the zone. This simplifies the ratemaking process as multiple locations are assigned to the same zone rather than treating every origin and destination point as unique locations for pricing purposes. UPS, FedEx, and other small package carriers use zone rates extensively.

While transportation rates increase as distance increases, the increase is not directly proportional to distance. This relationship of rates to distance is known as the **tapering rate principle**. As Figure 10B-3 shows, the rate increases as distance increases, but not linearly. The rate structure tapers because carriers spread terminal costs (cargo handling, clerical, and billing) over a greater mileage base. These terminal costs do not vary with distance; as the shipment's movement distance increases, the terminal cost

Figure 10B-3 Example of the Tapering Rate Principle

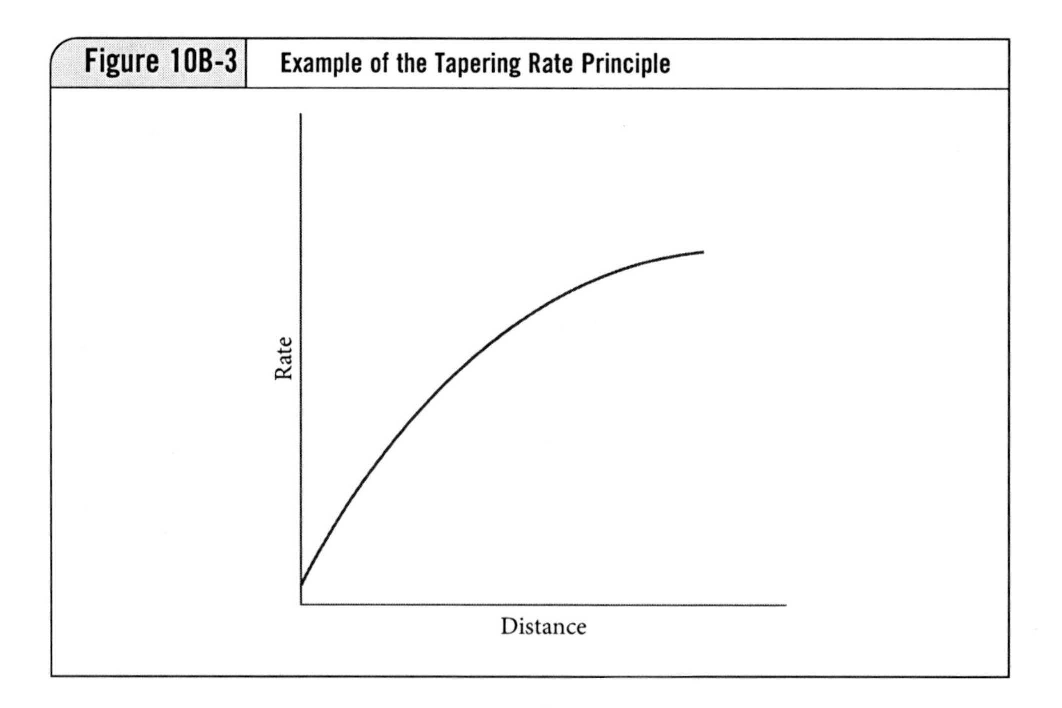

per mile decreases. The intercept point in Figure 10B-3 corresponds to the terminal costs.

Weight of Shipment

Carriers quote freight rates in cents per hundredweight (actual weight in pounds divided by 100 = hundredweight, or cwt) and determine the total transportation charge by the total weight of the shipment in cwt, and the appropriate rate per cwt. The rate per cwt relates to the shipped volume: carriers charge a lower rate for volume shipments and a higher rate for less-than-volume quantities. In essence, carriers offer a quantity discount for shipping large volumes (buying service in a large quantity). This is partly due to the fact that some of the basic shipment costs like document preparation, shipment pickup, and shipment delivery are spread over a larger amount of freight.

Railroads term these quantity discounts **carload (CL)** and **less-than-carload (LCL)**; motor carriers call them **truckload (TL)** and **less-than-truckload (LTL)**. The CL and TL rates represent the lower, volume rates; and the LCL and LTL rates denote the higher, less-than-volume rates.

One noteworthy exception to the rate-volume relationship is the **any-quantity (AQ) rate**, which bears no relationship to volume shipped. The rate per cwt remains constant regardless of the volume a firm tenders to the carrier for shipment; that is, no quantity discount is available.

Commodity Characteristics

Another ratemaking consideration is the type of product being moved. If carriers must take out-of-the-ordinary steps to protect freight, devote extra capacity to lightweight freight, or have specialized equipment to handle certain commodities, the cost of providing transportation service increases. The freight price must reflect the increased cost of the additional service to maintain carrier profitability. Hence, carriers consider commodity density, stowability, ease or difficulty of handling, and liability issues when developing freight rates.

Freight density reflects the weight *and* volume of freight. If a carrier developed rates on weight alone, bulky and lightweight products (e.g., potato chips) would move very inexpensively versus compact and heavy products (e.g., canned soups) even though the potato chips would take up far more space in the container. To adjust for density issues, carriers charge higher rates per cwt for low-density products than they do for higher-density products. For example, air carriers compare the true weight of the freight and the dimensional weight of the freight (package length × width × height/166), using the higher of the two weights in the calculation of freight rates. This prevents low-density freight from commandeering critical capacity at unreasonably low rates.

Stowability refers to how the product being shipped will affect the space utilization in the container. Certain products ship well and waste little space (e.g., a television set in a square box), while other products stow poorly and force a carrier to haul air (e.g., a fully assembled bicycle). Products resulting in wasted space are typically charged a higher price per unit.

Ease of handling is another ratemaking consideration. The more that goods must be handled, the greater the cost to the carrier. Handling requirements may include re-palletizing or re-packing goods, ordinary cross-docking of LTL shipments, the use of specially trained labor, and the need for special handling equipment. Logically, products with more specialized handling requirements are charged higher rates by carriers to offset the costs involved in providing the services.

Carriers must also assess their potential liabilities when developing rates. The more susceptible a shipment is to loss, damage, or theft, the greater the carrier's risk. Fragile or easily damaged freight results in more liability claims from shippers. Hence, carriers develop higher rates for valuable products (e.g., plasma TVs) and delicate products (e.g., Waterford crystal) to offset the financial risk of moving such products. Lower rates are afforded to sturdy products (e.g., wood flooring) that aren't likely to be stolen or damaged.

Efforts have been made to simplify these product characteristic issues. Rather than evaluating every commodity independently, classification systems have been developed to group together products with similar transportation characteristics for the purpose of ratemaking. For example, the trucking industry has long relied on the National Motor Freight Classification (NMFC) as a pricing tool that provides a comparison of commodities moving in interstate, intrastate, and foreign commerce. The NMFC groups commodities into one of 18 classes based on an evaluation of the four transportation characteristics discussed earlier. Together, these characteristics establish a commodity's "transportability."[1]

Level of Service

Another critical factor in transportation ratemaking is the service requirements of the freight buyer. The demand for faster and time-definite service is increasing in all modes of transportation. When a customer requires faster than normal service or guaranteed delivery times, carriers often need to break from their standard processes to accommodate the requirement. This could involve dispatching trailers before they are full, putting an additional operator and piece of equipment into service, deviating from normal routes, or a number of other exceptions. Any of these steps will likely reduce the efficiency of the carrier's operations and cause it to incur additional expenses. Thus, customers are charged premium rates to offset the additional costs created by their more demanding service requirements.

FedEx (and many other carriers) offers numerous service-level options and charges accordingly. The current nondiscounted rates obtained from the company's Web site for moving a single carton weighing 10 pounds from Atlanta to New York are as follows:

- $91.93 for "First Overnight" service with delivery by 8:30 a.m.
- $64.06 for "Priority Overnight" service with delivery by 10:30 a.m.
- $56.53 for "Standard Overnight" service with delivery by 3:00 p.m.
- $25.03 for "2Day" service with delivery by 4:30 p.m. on the second business day

As this example reveals, the rates vary significantly even for time differences as little as two hours. Freight buyers must objectively evaluate their need for extremely fast service because they will pay a major premium for it.

SUMMARY

This appendix provides a primer on transportation ratemaking. It addresses the key factors that should be included in all rate development initiatives—cost and value of service, shipment distance and size, commodity characteristics, and service characteristics. While no ratemaking initiative can ignore these considerations, other factors may be added to the analysis, depending on the situation. An extensive discussion of these additional factors, mode specific rate issues, and rate types (e.g., released value rates, deferred rates, and incentive rates) can be found in freight transportation textbooks.

NOTES

1. For more information on freight classification, visit http://www.nmfta.org.

Chapter 12

SUPPLY CHAIN NETWORK ANALYSIS AND DESIGN

Learning Objectives

After reading this chapter, you should be able to do the following:

- Understand the critical need in certain companies for new and improved logistics/supply chain networks.
- Identify factors that may suggest a need to redesign a logistics/supply chain network.
- Structure an effective process for logistics/supply chain network design.
- Be aware of key locational determinants, both national/regional and site-specific, and the impacts they may have on prospective locational alternatives.
- Describe the different types of modeling approaches that may be used to gain insight into logistics/supply chain network design and facility location decision making.
- Apply the simple "grid" or center-of-gravity approach to facility location.
- Discuss certain ways in which transportation alternatives and transportation costs may affect the location decision.

Supply Chain Profile — *It Takes a Village (to Distribute Goods)*

Economic Development Executive Kathy Moellenberdt accepts that pitching Topeka, Kansas, as a tourist mecca is a lost cause. "We can't talk about mountain views and oceans," she admits. But it's clear that she's ready to fight when it comes to bringing new business to the community.

Moellenberdt has set her sights on business in general, and distribution centers in particular. "Topeka is ideally situated for distribution operations," she says. "[O]ur central location lends itself to a very strong network transportation system." She's also quick to point out that Topeka offers a large, well-educated labor force and that Kansas, which has spent more than a half billion dollars to improve its highways, now boasts some of the best roads in the country.

If Topeka strikes you as an unlikely source for a marketing pitch, welcome to the new world of site selection. The big industrial regions—southern California's Inland Empire, Columbus, the Port of Houston, Indianapolis, Chicago, Memphis, the greater Atlanta area—are no longer the only ones mounting aggressive marketing campaigns. They've been joined by a horde of lesser-known but nonetheless scrappy players—Topeka, Kansas; Anchorage, Alaska; Kalamazoo, Michigan; Scranton, Pennsylvania; Little Rock, Arkansas—all hungry for new business.

To appeal to a distribution audience, these newcomers typically promote themselves as logistics hubs, or logistics villages. They emphasize the features most likely to attract a logistics professional's eye—a central geographic location; easy access to rail, highway, ocean, or air connections; lower land and building prices; tax incentives; or a bountiful labor force. Some even offer ready-to-occupy space in multi-tenant complexes specifically designed for distribution, with on-site logistics services, and, of course, easy access to multiple modes of transportation.

Ironically, it wasn't so long ago that communities actively worked to keep distribution centers (DCs) out. The prevailing opinion was that DCs made bad neighbors, the kind that attracted big trucks that would clog local roads and foul the air. A DC might bring a few jobs to the area, but not enough to outweigh the inconveniences. Apparently, the tide of public opinion has changed; nowadays, instead of pulling up the welcome mats, many regions are actively courting DCs.

Take Midlink Business Park, for example. Located in Kalamazoo, Michigan, this multi-tenant business park occupies a sprawling site that was once home to a General Motors stamping plant. In its heyday, the plant employed 4,500 workers. But in 1999, GM shuttered the facility. The property was quickly snapped up by a real estate investment firm that recognized its potential as a distribution hub. Before it opened the business park last year, the investment firm completely redeveloped and rebranded the property as a distribution complex. "Generations of families had worked here, so a lot of people had bad feelings about GM leaving," says David Smith, Midlink's president. "It became important to us to emphasize that this is not a GM facility anymore—it's a new day, with a new world business model—distribution." Today, four companies are using the site for distribution, and Midlink hopes to add more.

Another interesting example is that of Anchorage, Alaska. In the words of the head of the Anchorage Economic Development Corporation, "Geography teachers have always presented Alaska as being a little bigger than Hawaii and located in a box [on a map] off Baja,

California. But that's not the case. A lot of people don't realize you can get to London, Tokyo, and New York from Anchorage in about the same amount of time."

"In fact, Anchorage is nine hours away (by jet) from 95 percent of the industrialized world, making it an ideal gateway to international locations," says Poe. Air carriers have already discovered this. FedEx and Northwest Airlines have established sorting centers in Anchorage for processing Asia-bound cargo, and other carriers use it as a fueling and maintenance stop. Now the challenge will be to attract other types of distribution business.

To help draw that business, Anchorage is offering attractive incentive packages. And it is by no means alone. Virtually every economic development bureau—from Topeka and Kalamazoo to Alabama's Port of Huntsville and Seguin, Texas—stands ready to offer a variety of enticements if that is what it takes to seal the deal.

Overall, there is fierce competition between cities and regions to be the preferred location for new logistics and manufacturing facilities. Among the most critical factors are transportation, labor, and construction costs. Once it is apparent that these factors are likely to be acceptable, the topics of conversation then turn to economic incentives that may be offered. In any event, once the process is under way, the bidding wars are likely to intensify.

Source: Adapted from John R. Johnson, "It Takes a Village ...," *DC Velocity* (June 2006): 36–40. Copyright © 2006 Agile Business Media. Used by permission.

Introduction

As firms continue their searches for new ways to lower costs and improve service to their customers, the issue of where to locate logistics and manufacturing facilities has never been more complex or critical. In addition to enhancing the efficiency and effectiveness of a logistics/supply chain operation, the redesign of a firm's overall network can help to differentiate a firm in the marketplace. Considering the increasingly dynamic aspects of today's business world, companies are continually seeking new and improved approaches to network design and operation. Several examples illustrate this type of success:

- A leading pharmaceutical distributor with nationwide service reduced its logistics network from more than 60 to 20 distribution centers, while offering its customers a selection of service responses from which to choose (for example, same-day delivery, regular service, and so on).
- A prominent office products company shrunk its network of distribution facilities from 11 to 3, while substantially increasing the level of cross-docking activity with its customers and significantly improving logistical customer service.
- A direct-selling company with a national distribution capability reengineered its customer service operation and eliminated a major distribution point, which resulted in significant reductions to its fixed assets and operating expenses, at the same time differentiating its services to meet a recognized range of customer requirements.
- As a result of the merger of two large grocery industry manufacturers, the combined logistics network consisted of 54 distribution centers across the United States. Following careful study and analysis, with a look to the future, the company consolidated its network into 15 strategically located facilities.

This move significantly reduced the company's overall logistics costs and improved service levels to its customers.

- A major consumer products retailer developed a very large import distribution center to accommodate inbound shipments of products from its global manufacturing sites.
- A global semiconductor products manufacturer consolidated its logistics network into a single, global distribution center in Singapore and engaged a third-party supplier of express logistics services to manage its overall distribution activity. The end results included lower cost, improved service, and a new way for the firm to differentiate itself in the marketplace.
- Considering prevailing congestion at some U.S. ports located on the west coast, companies are considering changes to their shipping patterns to receive more shipments on the east coast of the United States. In turn, this has significant implications for the domestic logistics networks that support the subsequent movements of products to ultimate destinations once they have been received in the United States.

While there are also examples of the opposite situation, in which firms have justifiably expanded their logistics networks and increased the number of distribution facilities, the move to consolidate existing systems is far more prevalent. Assuming that a firm considers the impact of such a decision on total logistics cost, it is not unusual for the inventory cost savings associated with consolidating facilities to outweigh any additional transportation expense involved with moving product to the customer. Also, the use of currently available information technology, coupled with the time-sensitive capabilities of many suppliers of transportation service, can mean that such a move enhances responsiveness and the levels of service experienced by customers.

This chapter first looks at several strategic aspects of logistics/supply chain network design. While it may sometimes be that "change for the sake of change" is needed, a number of prominent factors may suggest that a redesign of the network may be necessary. Next, the process of logistics/supply chain network redesign is examined in detail. This content provides a useful framework for understanding the key steps that must be included in a comprehensive approach to network design and facility location.

Following these discussions, attention shifts to several major locational determinants. These factors may be either regionally focused or site-specific. Also included is a summary of current trends governing site selection. The chapter concludes with coverage of several modeling approaches that can be used to provide insight into the issues of logistics/supply chain network design and facility location. Several examples of transportation-specific factors are also considered.

The Need for Long-Range Planning

In the short run, a firm's logistics/supply chain network and the locations of its key facilities are givens, and the logistics manager must operate within the constraints imposed by the facility locations. Site availability, leases, contracts, and investments make changing facility locations impractical in the short run. In the long run, however, the design of the overall network must be thought of as variable. Management decisions can and should be made to change the network to meet the logistics requirements imposed by customers, suppliers, competitive changes, and the realities of the supply chain itself.

In addition, the decisions as to network design and facility location that are made today will have implications far into the future. A facility properly located under today's economic, competitive, and technological conditions may not be at an optimum location under future conditions. Today's facility location decision will have a significant effect on future costs in such areas as logistics, marketing, manufacturing, and finance. Thus, the facility location decision must seriously consider anticipated business conditions and acknowledge a critical need to be flexible and responsive to customer needs as they may change in the future. This latter concern heightens the attractiveness of the third-party logistics option for many logistics operations today.

The Strategic Importance of Logistics/Supply Chain Network Design

Why analyze the logistics/supply chain network? In essence, the answer lies in the fact that all businesses operate in a very dynamic environment in which change is the only constant. Characteristics of consumer and industrial-buyer demand, technology, competition, markets, and suppliers are constantly changing. As a result, businesses must redeploy their resources in response to and in anticipation of this ever-changing environment.

Considering the rate at which change is occurring, it is questionable whether any existing logistics/supply chain network can be truly up to date. Any network that has been in existence for a number of years is certainly a candidate for reevaluation and potential redesign. Even if the existing system is not functionally obsolete, an analysis of the existing network will probably uncover new opportunities to reduce cost and/or improve service.

This section focuses attention on several types of change that may suggest a need to reevaluate and/or redesign a firm's logistics network. While not all of these factors will affect any single firm at the same time, they represent some of the more frequently changing elements of the business environment that affect logistics and supply chain management.

Changing Customer Service Requirements

As was discussed in Chapters 1–3 and 7–8, the logistical requirements of customers are changing in numerous ways. As a result, the need to reevaluate and redesign logistics/supply chain networks is of great contemporary interest. While some customers have intensified their demands for more efficient and more effective logistics services, others are seeking relationships with suppliers who can take logistical capabilities and performance to new, unprecedented levels.

While customer service requirements may experience change, the types of customers served may also evolve over time. Consider, for example, the case of food manufacturers that have distributed their product to independent stores and regional retail chains for many years and recently added mass merchants to their list of customers. Another example is manufacturers of stationery who traditionally served a multitude of customers, from small retail to club stores, but that now focus primarily on distributors of office supply products. In these examples, change has occurred at both the customer and supply chain levels, with significant impacts on lead times, order size and frequency, and associated activities such as shipment notification, marking and tagging, and packaging.

Shifting Locations of Customer and/or Supply Markets

Considering that manufacturing and logistics facilities are positioned in the supply chain between customer and supply markets, any changes in these markets should cause a firm to reevaluate its logistics network. When the U.S. population shifted to the southeast and southwest, for example, new warehouses and distribution facilities followed the changing geo-location trends. As a result, cities such as Atlanta, Houston, Las Vegas, Reno/Sparks, and Memphis have become popular distribution center locations for companies serving these increasing population centers.

On the supply side, the service and cost requirements of the automobile industry's movement to JIT-based manufacturing have forced companies to examine the locations of logistics facilities. Many product suppliers to the automotive industry, for example, have selected nearby points for manufacturing and/or parts distribution facilities. Considering the growing, global nature of parts sourcing, automotive industry firms are also focusing on streamlining their global supply chains to achieve objectives relating to efficiency and effectiveness.

Also on the global scene, changes such as the unification initiatives of the European Union, the continued searches for lower-cost manufacturing, and the growing economic importance of China and the Asia-Pacific area in general have forced many companies to examine facility locations in terms of their suitability for competition in these rapidly developing markets. In addition to reconfiguring their overall logistics/supply chain networks, firms facing these challenges have taken steps such as establishing branch operations in these newly popular geographies and entering into joint agreements with companies that are located in and already have a significant business presence in these areas.

Sourcing of raw materials from offshore suppliers is another reason to analyze the location of existing facilities. Using Pacific Rim suppliers makes the western United States a desirable location for a distribution center, whereas an East Coast location would be more desirable for a company receiving similar materials from Europe. As world economies become more interdependent, these types of facility location decisions and priorities will become more common.

Change in Corporate Ownership

A relatively common occurrence today is for a firm to experience an ownership-related change associated with a merger, an acquisition, or a divestiture. In such instances, many companies choose to be proactive and to conduct a formal evaluation of new versus previous logistics/supply chain networks in advance of such a change. This is very helpful in terms of making sure that the newly merged or newly independent firm will have fully anticipated the logistics and supply chain impacts of the change in corporate ownership. In other instances, those having management responsibility for logistics and supply chain activities may be the last ones to find out about the impending change, and the role of network design immediately takes on a defensive posture.

Even if these logistics impacts are not part of the planning process, it is critical for firms to reassess their logistics/supply chain networks following ownership-related changes such as those identified in the preceding paragraph. Without sufficient advance planning, such changes increase the likelihood that the new operation is duplicating effort and incurring unnecessary logistics expense.

Examples of mergers/acquisitions that have had significant implications for logistics/supply chain network design include Procter & Gamble's acquisition of Gillette, the Heinz/HP Foods merger, Energizer's purchase of Schick, the acquisition of DuPont Pharmaceuticals Corporation by Bristol-Myers Squibb, the acquisition of Compaq by Hewlett-Packard Company, and the acquisition of Quaker Oats Company by Pepsi.

Cost Pressures

A major priority for many firms today is to figure out new and innovative ways to take cost out of their key business processes, including those relating to logistics. In such instances, a reevaluation of the logistics network and the functioning of the overall supply chain can frequently help to uncover new sources of such savings. Whether the answer lies in reducing cost in transportation, inventory, warehousing, or another area, a detailed examination of the current system versus alternative approaches can be exceptionally useful.

On a global basis, labor wage rates have a significant impact on the location of manufacturing and logistics operations. For example, in 2002, the average hourly compensation for the overall Chinese manufacturing sector amounted to just $0.57, which was literally about 3 percent of the U.S. hourly pay rate of $21.40 during the same year. Contrasts with other nations were equally dramatic, with hourly compensation for Chinese workers being equal to 25 percent of the pay rates of Mexico and Brazil, 10 percent of the rate of Asia's newly industrialized economies (i.e., Taiwan, Korea, Hong Kong, and Singapore), and just 3 percent of the norms of Japan and Europe. Although Chinese labor wage rates rose at rates of 13 percent in 2003 and 14 percent in 2004, recent trends such as these have not significantly reduced the gap as a percent of comparable figures from the United States.[1] In addition, companies are already searching out and locating facilities in other regions such as Africa, Latin America, and Southeast Asia. One interesting example is that of Vietnam, where Intel Corporation is building a $300 million semiconductor assembly and test facility in Ho Chi Min City.[2]

Companies considering plant modernization needs also sometimes benefit from a comprehensive cost analysis, which might accompany a reevaluation of the logistics network. A firm considering an investment of millions of dollars in an existing plant must ask, "Is this the proper location for a plant, given the current and future customer and vendor locations?"

Competitive Capabilities

Another factor relates to competitive pressures that may force a company to examine its logistics service levels and the costs generated by its network of logistics facilities. To remain competitive in the marketplace or to develop a competitive advantage, a company should frequently examine the relative locations of its facilities toward the goal of improving service and/or lowering costs. Companies often conduct this network review in light of newly developed transport alternatives.

For example, many firms locate distribution facilities near the hub operations of companies such as Federal Express, UPS, and DHL so that access to time-critical, express transportation services will be facilitated. This strategy is particularly appropriate for inventories of high-value, time-sensitive products that may need to be shipped on a moment's notice. The resulting service levels are higher, and the total cost of the comprehensive, express logistics services is lower than the total cost would be of warehousing the needed inventories at various locations throughout the company's logistics network. Essentially, the centralization of such inventories at strategically selected locations reduces the overall cost of logistics and significantly improves responsiveness in terms of delivery times. Additionally, the same result may be achieved through the use of a high-quality logistics provider, such as Forward Air Corporation, that specializes in airport-to-airport transportation of service-sensitive shipments.[3]

Corporate Organizational Change It is not unusual for logistics/supply chain network design to become a topic of discussion at the same time that a firm considers any major corporate organizational change, such as downsizing. In such instances, the strategic functioning of the firm's logistics network is viewed as something that must be protected and even enhanced through the process of organizational change.

Considering the current popularity of corporate reengineering efforts, the logistics process is frequently a prime candidate for attention. For example, many firms today have become involved in the reengineering of their order-fulfillment process, which has significant implications for the firm's logistics and supply chain activities and processes. An important component of the overall effort will include a systematic evaluation of and recommendations for change to the firm's logistics network.

Logistics/Supply Chain Network Design

A firm must consider many factors as it approaches the task of determining the optimum design of its logistics/supply chain network. These factors are identified and discussed at a later point in this chapter. At the outset, however, it is important to realize that the task of designing an appropriate logistics/supply chain network should be coordinated closely with the identification and implementation of key corporate and overall business strategies. Since the process of designing or redesigning a firm's logistics/supply chain network can be complex, it is discussed in the context of a major corporate reengineering process.

Figure 12-1 identifies the six major steps that are recommended for a comprehensive logistics/supply chain network design process. Each of these steps is discussed in detail in the following paragraphs.

Step 1: Define the Logistics/Supply Chain Network Design Process

Of initial importance is the formation of a logistics/supply chain network reengineering team to be responsible for all elements of the network design process. This team will first need to become aware of overall corporate and business strategies and the underlying business needs of the firm and the supply chains in which it is a participant.

Also in this step, it is important to establish the parameters and objectives of the network design or redesign process itself. An awareness of the expectations of senior management, for example, is essential to the effective progress of the overall reengineering process. Issues pertaining to the availability of needed resources in the areas of funding, people, and systems must be understood at an early stage in the process.

An additional topic to be addressed early on is the potential involvement of third-party suppliers of logistics services as a means of achieving the firm's logistics objectives. This consideration is critical, since it will expand the mindset of the network design team to include a consideration of logistics/supply chain network solutions that may involve externally provided as well as proprietary logistics resources.

Figure 12-1 Key Steps in the Logistics/Supply Chain Network Design Process

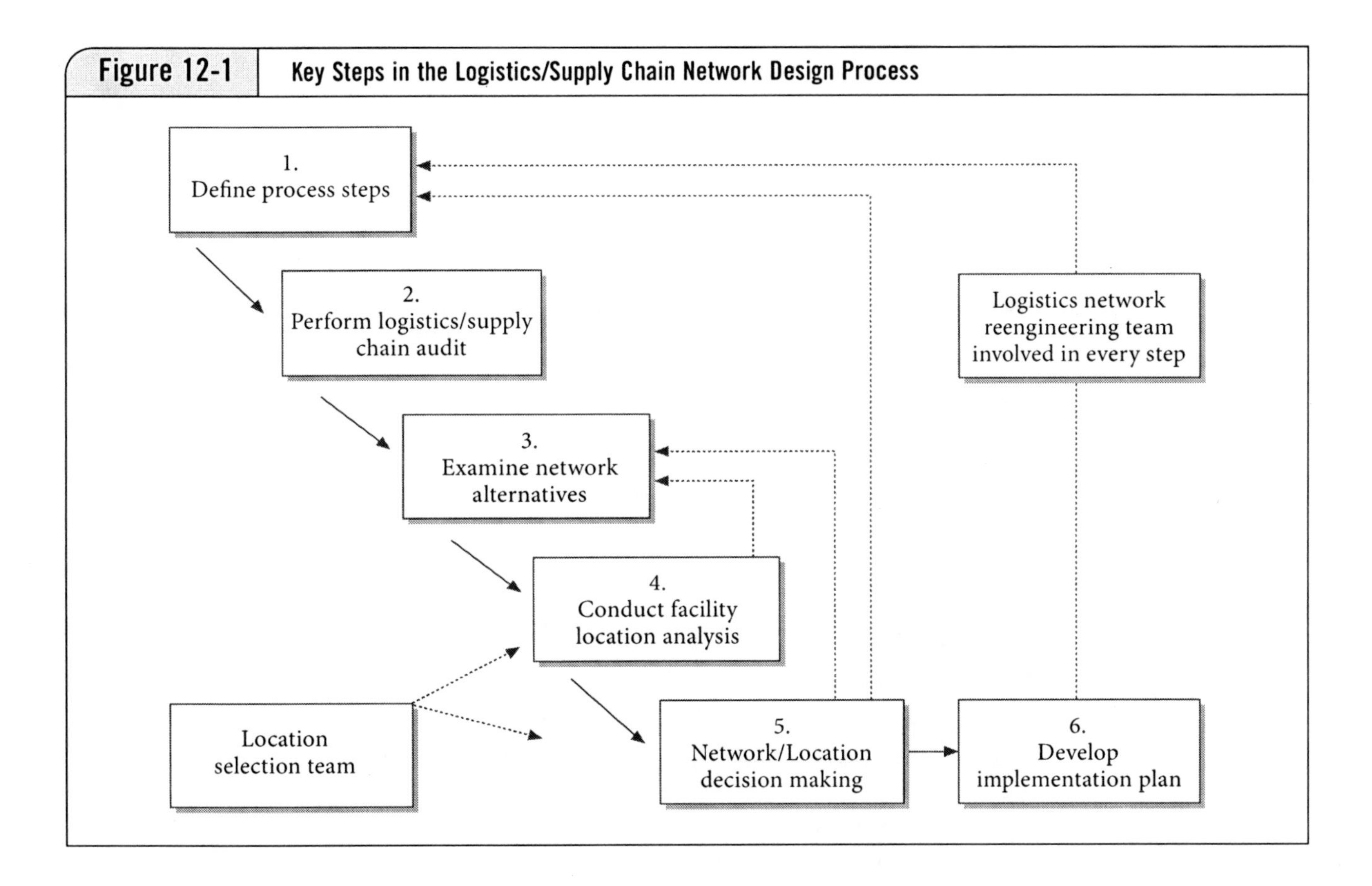

Step 2: Perform a Logistics/Supply Chain Audit

The logistics/supply chain audit provides members of the reengineering team with a comprehensive perspective on the firm's logistics process. In addition, it helps to gather essential types of information that will be useful throughout future steps in the redesign process. Figure 12-2 indicates a number of key steps that should be included in a logistics/supply chain audit. Listed here are examples of the types of information that should become available as a result of this audit:

- Customer requirements and key environmental factors
- Key logistics goals and objectives
- Profile of the current logistics/supply chain network and the firm's positioning in respective supply chain(s)
- Understanding of key logistic/supply chain activities and processes
- Benchmark, or target, values for logistics/supply chain costs and key performance measurements
- Identification of gaps between current and desired logistics/supply chain performance (qualitative and quantitative)
- Key objectives for logistics/supply chain network design, expressed in terms that will facilitate measurement

Figure 12-2 Key Steps in a Logistics/Supply Chain Audit

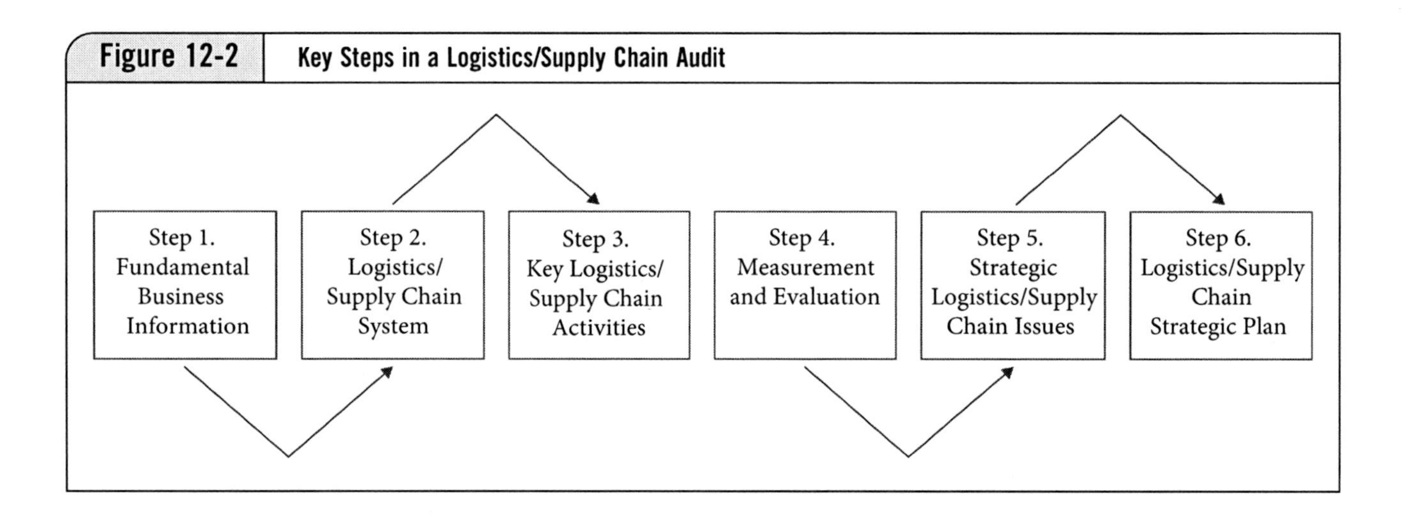

Step 3: Examine the Logistics/Supply Chain Network Alternatives

The next step is to examine the available alternatives for the logistics/supply chain network. This involves applying suitable quantitative models to the current logistics system as well as to the alternative systems and approaches under consideration. The use of these models provides considerable insight into the functioning and cost/service effectiveness of the various possible networks. Essentially, the principal modeling approach will be optimization, simulation, heuristic, or some combination of these three approaches that are explored in detail later in this chapter. Briefly, optimization approaches search for "best" solutions, simulation models replicate the functioning of the logistics/supply chain network, and heuristic techniques are able to accommodate broad problem definitions but do not provide optimum solutions.

Once an appropriate modeling procedure has been selected, it should be used to help identify a logistics/supply chain network that is consistent with the key objectives identified during the audit phase. Although, at first, reengineering teams often look to the model to suggest answers to the key questions that have been raised, they quickly realize that the modeling effort is likely to produce more insight than answers.

Once preliminary design solutions have been identified, subsequent "what-if" types of analysis should be conducted to test the sensitivity of recommended network designs to changes in key logistics variables. The results of this step should provide a valuable set of recommendations for the number and general location of logistics facilities that will help to meet the desired objectives.

Also, at this point in the network design process, it is critical to understand the geographical parameters of the logistics/supply chain under study. Although a domestic or regional perspective has been the focus of many network design projects to date, there are an increasing number of projects in which a multi-national or global perspective is necessary. State-of-the-art network design processes are currently capable of dealing with the logistics/supply chain needs of this broader geographical setting.

Step 4: Conduct a Facility Location Analysis

Once a general configuration of the desired logistics/supply chain network has been recommended, the next task is to carefully analyze the attributes of specific regions and cities that are candidates for sites of logistics facilities, distribution centers, cross-docking operations, etc. These analyses will have both quantitative and qualitative aspects. Many of the quantitative elements have already been incorporated into Step 3 of the modeling effort. The qualitative aspects, to be discussed in a later section of this chapter, include such considerations as labor climate, transportation issues, proximity to markets and customers, quality of life, taxes and industrial development incentives, supplier networks, land costs and utilities, overall supply chain and logistics infrastructure, and company preference.

The effort in this step will be facilitated by the formation of a location selection team, which will collect information on specific attributes such as those identified earlier. In addition, this team should be able to examine potential sites in terms of local factors such as topography, geology, and facility design. To supplement internally available resources, the firm may wish to engage the services of a consulting firm that specializes in assisting clients with the process of selecting a location.

The first screening by the location selection team usually eliminates areas that are uneconomical from a logistics perspective, thereby reducing the number of alternatives. For example, consider the number of potential distribution center sites in the southeastern United States. Applying the logistics/supply chain location determinant, the team may find that the optimum location is in the Tennessee/Georgia area. This definitely reduces the number of potential sites and enables the team to direct the location analysis toward a specific area.

Step 5: Make Decisions Regarding Network and Facility Location

Next, the network and specific sites for logistics facilities recommended in Steps 3 and 4 should be evaluated for consistency with the design criteria that were identified in Step 1. This step should confirm the types of change that are needed to the firm's logistics network and should do so in the context of overall supply chain positioning. Although the feasibility of involving third-party suppliers should have been incorporated into the alternatives that were evaluated in the two preceding steps, the decision to involve external suppliers will have cost and service implications as well as strategic ones.

Step 6: Develop an Implementation Plan

Once the overall direction has been established, the development of an effective implementation plan, or "blueprint for change," is critical. This plan should serve as a useful road map for moving from the current logistics/supply chain network to the desired new one. Since it was known from the beginning that this reengineering process was likely to produce recommendations for significant change, it is important that the firm commit the resources necessary to assure a smooth, timely implementation, and the continuous improvement of the network decisions that will have been made.

Major Locational Determinants

The focus of Step 4 in the logistics/supply chain network redesign process is on analyzing the attributes of specific regions and areas that are candidates for sites of logistics facilities. Table 12-1 lists a number of major locational determinants for both national/regional and site-specific locations. While these factors are listed in general order of importance, the relative weighting applied to each depends on the details of the specific location decision under consideration.

The importance of major locational determinants varies among industries and among individual companies within specific industries. For example, labor-intensive industries such as textiles, furniture, and household appliances place significant emphasis on the availability and cost of labor in both regional and local market areas. Alternatively, manufacturers of high-tech products such as computers and peripherals, semiconductors, and engineering and scientific instruments place great emphasis on assuring the availability of a highly qualified workforce with very specific technical skills and, as discussed earlier, proximity to customer markets. For industries such as drugs, beverages, and printing and publishing, in which competition or logistics costs are significant, other logistics variables are critical.

Key Factors for Consideration

This discussion focuses attention on the regional determinants shown in Table 12-1. Because the site-specific determinants cannot be generalized as readily, this level of detail should be acquired and evaluated through the efforts of the location selection team.

Labor Climate Location decision makers consider a number of factors in determining an area's labor climate. Given the typically labor-intensive nature of many logistics/supply chain operations, the cost and availability of labor are major issues of concern. Other factors to be considered include the workforce's degree of unionization, skill level, work ethic, productivity, and the enthusiasm of local public officials. The existence of right-to-work laws in certain states (which prohibit union membership as a condition of employment) and the unionization of major area employers reveal the area

Table 12-1 Major Locational Determinants

NATIONAL/REGIONAL DETERMINANTS	SITE-SPECIFIC DETERMINANTS
• Labor climate	• Transportation access
• Availability of transportation	— Truck
— Services	— Air
— Infrastructure	— Rail
• Proximity to markets and customers	— Water
• Quality of life	• Inside/outside metropolitan area
• Taxes and industrial development incentives	• Availability of workforce
• Supplier networks	• Land costs and taxes
• Land costs and utilities	• Utilities
• Company preference	

workforce's degree of unionization. Government information regarding work stoppages, productivity (value added per employee), and skill levels is available for most areas. Data regarding hourly earnings by industry and occupation are available from governmental agencies.

Another labor-related factor to be considered is the rate of unemployment in the local areas under consideration. While many other factors may seem to be quite acceptable, low levels of unemployment may require a firm to significantly increase its projected hourly wage scales to attract qualified workers. This sometimes unexpected increase may affect the overall attractiveness of a particular local area under consideration. The location study team will need to visit areas of potential interest to gather impressions and study attitudes regarding work ethic, absenteeism, potential labor-management issues, and the cooperativeness of state and local public officials.

Last, it is important to recognize that issues relating to labor climate have had a significant impact on the global evolution of "preferred" low-cost locations for manufacturing. Historically, areas such as Mexico, Puerto Rico, Philippines, China, and Southeast Asia have become very attractive locations to consider from a labor climate perspective.

Availability of Transportation Given the need by many firms for high-quality, capable transportation services, this factor is of great significance in many location decisions. Depending on the product type and industry to be served, a suitable location may require one or more of the following features: interstate highway access, availability of intermodal or local rail facilities, convenience of a major airport facility, proximity to inland or ocean port facilities, and so on. The number of serving carriers and the breadth of overall transport capabilities are factors that may need to be evaluated. Availability of capable transportation services and issues relating to transportation infrastructure may vary widely among regions of the world. In China, for example, investments in transportation infrastructure have been a key priority since they are viewed as being needed to sustain economic development.[4] For this reason, this topic deserves very deliberate and careful consideration in any network design decision.

Considering the significant service improvements that have been made in recent years by many transportation firms, most regional and local areas are strong in at least one or more areas related to transportation. For certain high-value, low-weight products, such as computers, semiconductors, and electronic equipment, the location decision may focus on identifying a single national or international geographical area from which to distribute the company's entire manufactured output. Given the time-sensitive logistics services available today from firms such as FedEx, UPS, DHL, and the postal services of many countries, this strategy is becoming more prevalent.

Proximity to Markets and Customers The nearness-to-market factor usually considers both logistics and competitive variables. Logistics variables include the availability of transportation, freight cost, and the geographical market size that can be served, for example, on a same-day or next-morning basis. The greater the number of customer firms within the market area, the greater the competitive advantage offered by the proposed location.

Although many companies place a high priority on locating logistics facilities near markets and customers, an overly complex logistics/supply chain network can be disadvantageous from a cost perspective. Also, the availability of high-quality transportation services and capable information technologies has resulted in an expansion of the geographical areas that can be served in a timely manner from key logistics facilities. In an extended sense, this has resulted in the enhanced role of global sourcing and global marketing, depending on the service needs of customers. Today's global logistics/supply chain capabilities may be enhanced to meet even greater rigorous services levels that are established and expected by customers.

Quality of Life A particular region's or area's quality of life is difficult to quantify, but it does affect the well-being of employees and the quality of work they are expected to perform. The quality-of-life factor is more important to companies that must attract and retain a mobile professional and technical workforce capable of moving to any location. Such a situation is common in the high-tech industry, especially in a company's research and development operations. The *Places Rated Almanac*[5] rates the quality of life in metropolitan areas in terms of climate, housing costs, health care and environment, crime, passenger transportation, education, recreation, the arts, and economic opportunities. Another useful source of information is *Cities Ranked and Rated.*[6]

Taxes and Industrial Development Incentives It is important to have advance knowledge of state and local taxes that apply to businesses and individuals. Prevailing business taxes, including revenue or income taxes, inventory taxes, property taxes, and so on, will have a significant impact on the cost of operating a business in the area under consideration. Personal taxes that may affect the attractiveness of a particular region or local area include taxes on income and property, as well as applicable sales taxes, excise taxes, and so forth.

Another significant factor is the availability of industrial development incentives, which are used by some states and communities to entice companies to locate in their area. Examples include tax incentives (reduced rates or tax abatements on things such as property, inventory, or sales), financing arrangements (state loans or state-guaranteed loans), reduced water and sewage rates, and rent-free buildings that are built by the community to the company's specifications. Most states have an industrial development commission that provides information about state and local inducements. In addition, early contact and discussions with representatives of the state and local-area banking institutions and financial communities will provide a wide range of useful information, as well as commitments regarding financing and other services.

In 2006, Honda Motor Company announced its plans to build a $550 million automotive assembly plant in southeastern Indiana to help meet a growing demand in North America for its vehicles. Although four other sites were in contention for this location decision, Indiana offered $141.5 million in incentives to the company, which included tax credits and abatements, training assistance, and a promise to expedite the needed highway interchange upgrades that would facilitate transportation in the vicinity of the plant site.[7] A very interesting global example of the use of tax reductions and industrial development incentives is evidenced by the Shanghai Waigaoqiao Free Trade Zone, located in the Pudong New Area, Shanghai, China.[8] This facility was established in 1990 and includes total space of 10,000 square kilometers; its customers include companies such as Intel, Hewlett-Packard, Philips, IBM, and Emerson Electric. Interestingly, companies locating in the Waigaoqiao Free Trade Zone are given five years of preferential tax treatment. Instead of paying the corporate tax ratio of 15 percent, the tax rate to be paid starts at 8 percent and increases over the five-year period to the full 15 percent.

On the Line — *Gateway Joins Dell with Major Presence in Nashville, Tennessee*

California-based Gateway, Inc., announced in May that it planned to build a new manufacturing center in La Vergne, Tennessee, which is located just east of Nashville. The 100,000-square-foot facility, which would house approximately 300 workers in the first year, would assemble Gateway's custom-ordered desktop and notebook computers, servers, and storage arrays and provide integration and software services. Gateway has built its computers overseas for years, and the plant would represent the first for the company in the United States. It would join Gateway's manufacturing facilities in Malaysia, France, Germany, and Ireland.

The $8 million deal followed other computer assembly operations announced in the Nashville area made by Dell, Quanta, and Hewlett-Packard. They must compete for workers with Dell, which has been manufacturing in Nashville since 1999 and recently announced a 1,000-person expansion of the plant. The Gateway facility shares space with an existing supplier that has a minority ownership interest in the operation. Gateway's operation is an example of how economic developers like to recruit companies to a particular area and then work on its customers, suppliers, or other partner companies to make a similar location decision.*

According to Gateway executives, "when we locate, we want to locate on the most efficient logistics supply chain location possible. Logistics is a much bigger deal than even labor costs, so the center for manufacturing really needs to be the closest in proximity to the customer base. In that standpoint, Nashville is a better center of gravity." Gateway executives say that they can serve two-thirds of their customers in less than two days from Nashville. Dell executives, on the other hand, say their own Nashville facility can reach 70 percent of its customers on the East Coast within a day. According to Tennessee state officials, Nashville's major airport and three interstate highways helped to attract both Gateway and Dell to the area. Essentially, the accessible transportation network provides both of these firms with an edge in delivery cycles and allows them to remain in close proximity to their supplier distribution centers.

Most city governments work hard to offer as many tax credits as possible to make their metropolitan areas appealing to technology companies. Gateway was eligible for Nashville's statutory jobs tax credits, at $2,000 per job created. It also received start-up training assistance. In North Carolina, Dell received incentive-based tax credits based on the number of jobs it created and the amount it invested in the state economy.

Source: Adapted from materials available in "Gateway Plant Set for Nashville," *Knoxville News-Sentinel* (May 18, 2006); "Gateway PC Assembly Operation Comes to Town," *NashvillePost.com* (May 17, 2006); and "Update: Can You Really Buy an American PC," *CIO Insight* (June 9, 2006).

** In the case of Gateway's decision to locate in Nashville, Nashville Area Chamber of Commerce's Partnership 2010, The Tennessee Valley Authority, and the Tennessee Department of Economic and Community Development all worked on promoting the benefits of a Nashville location.*

Supplier Networks In the case of a manufacturing facility, the availability and cost of raw materials and component parts, as well as the cost of transporting these materials to the proposed plant site, are of significance. For a distribution center, it is important to know how the proposed facility sites will fit with the geographic locations of key supplier facilities. In either instance, the cost and service sensitivity of the inbound movements from suppliers must be considered.

As an example, consider the case of Lear Corporation, a company that supplies seats for two Ford Motor Company truck plants. Essentially, the seats are manufactured in sequence so that they can go right off the delivery vehicle onto the Ford assembly line in the order in which they will be installed. Faced with the need to expand, and knowing that its existing plant was landlocked, Lear chose a new plant site that was 10 minutes away from one plant and 20 minutes from the other. As a result, for 20 hours per day, trucks loaded with seats leave the Lear factory every 15 minutes. According to Lear company officials, the location is about as far away from the customer as it can afford and still deliver true, just-in-time (JIT) deliveries.

Land Costs and Utilities Depending on the type of facility under consideration, issues relating to the cost of land and the availability of needed utilities are more or less critical. In the case of a manufacturing plant or distribution center, for example, a certain minimum acreage or parcel size may be needed for current use as well as future expansion. This represents a potentially significant expense. Factors such as local building codes and cost of construction are important to consider. Also, the availability and expense of utilities such as electrical power, sewage, and industrial waste disposal need to be factored into the decision-making process.

Company Preference Aside from all of the preceding types of factors, a company, or its CEO for that matter, may prefer a certain region and/or local area for the location of a logistics facility. For example, a company may prefer to locate all new facilities in rural areas within 50 miles of a major metropolitan area. Or a company may wish to locate its facilities in areas where competitors already have a presence. In other instances, a firm may wish to locate facilities in an area where it may enjoy common access with other firms to benefits such as a skilled labor supply, excellent marketing resources, or proximity to key supplier industries. This determinant is referred to as **agglomeration**, a phenomenon that sometimes explains why certain firms tend to co-locate facilities.

Current Trends Governing Site Selection

A number of trends in today's logistics environment may have a significant effect on decisions involving logistics facility location. Included among these are the following:

- Strategic positioning of inventories, such that fast-moving, profitable items may be located at "market-facing" logistics facilities. Slower-moving, less-profitable items may be located at more regional, or national, facilities. These examples are consistent with implementation of effective, inventory segmentation strategies.
- Aside from a general trend toward "disintermediation" of many wholesaler/distributor operations, companies are moving to greater use of "customer-direct" delivery from manufacturing and other upstream supply chain locations. Many times, this bypasses and diminishes the need for complete networks of distribution facilities. Increased use of "drop shipments" provides deliveries of product direct from manufacturing to the customer, thus eliminating the need for intermediate distribution capabilities.
- There is a growing use of and need for strategically located "cross-docking" facilities that serve as transfer points for consolidated shipments that need to be disaggregated or mixed into typically smaller shipments for delivery to individual customers. An example of this would be the consolidation of multiple-vendor shipments into full trailer loads being shipped to retail stores or points of use. Applied to inbound movements, this concept can significantly reduce the need for inbound consolidation facilities.

- Due diligence for location and site selection decisions is placing great emphasis on access to major airports and/or ocean ports for import and export shipments.
- Greater use of providers of third-party-logistics services, who may assume part or all of the responsibility for moving a firm's products to its customers, and/or moving its inbound parts and materials to its manufacturing process. In the global setting, many of these companies are developing specialized abilities to facilitate the movements of import and export shipments.

Modeling Approaches

This section focuses broadly on the topic of modeling approaches that can provide insight into the choice of a logistics/supply chain network design. As such, the techniques discussed here are applicable to a wide range of issues pertaining to the locations of plants, distribution centers, and customers and to the flows of product and information to support the functioning of the logistics/supply chain network. These apply to network design decisions that may be made on a domestic and/or global basis. The principal modeling approaches to be covered are optimization, simulation, and heuristic models. Detailed coverage of the grid method for facility location is included as part of the discussion of heuristic modeling approaches.

As was indicated previously, the use of appropriate modeling techniques will facilitate a comparison of the functioning and cost/service effectiveness of current versus proposed logistics/supply chain networks. Once an appropriate modeling procedure has been selected, it should be used to help identify a logistics network that is consistent with the key objectives identified earlier in the logistics/supply chain network redesign process. After preliminary solutions have been identified, subsequent what-if types of analyses should be conducted to test the sensitivity of the recommended network designs to changes in key logistics/supply chain variables.

Optimization Models

The **optimization model** is based on precise mathematical procedures that are guaranteed to find the "best," or optimum, solution, given the mathematical definition of the problem under evaluation. This means that it can be proved mathematically that the resulting solution is the best. The simple EOQ model, discussed earlier, is an example of a technique that produces an "optimum" solution.

While recognizing relevant constraints, optimization approaches essentially select an optimal course of action from a number of feasible alternatives. The optimization models in use today incorporate such techniques as mathematical programming (linear, integer, dynamic, mixed-integer linear, etc.), enumeration, sequencing, and the use of calculus.[9] Many of these have been incorporated into software packages that are commercially available.

Figure 12-3 lists the types of issues that may be addressed through the use of optimization techniques. Several advantages of this overall type of approach are as follows:

- The user is guaranteed to have the best solution possible for a given set of assumptions and data.
- Many complex model structures can be handled correctly.
- The analysis and evaluation of all alternatives that are generated result in a more efficient analysis.

Figure 12-3 Representative Strategic/Managerial Issues Relevant to Logistics/Supply Chain Network Modeling

I. **System Structure Issues**
   A. Number and Location of Raw Material Suppliers
   B. Number and Location of Plants
   C. Number and Location of Production Lines
   D. Number and Location of DCs
   E. Assignment of Plants to Suppliers
      1. DCs to Plants or Other DCs
      2. Customers to Plants or DCs

II. **Facility Ownership Issues**
   A. Owned
   B. Leased
   C. Public

III. **Facility Mission Issues**
   A. Raw Materials Suppliers
      1. Procurement Levels
      2. Costs and Capacities
   B. Plant Locations
      1. Manufacturing Levels
         a. Intermediate Products
         b. Finished Products
      2. Costs and Capacities
   C. DC Locations
      1. Throughput Levels
      2. Costs and Capacities

IV. **What-If Issues**
   A. Business Decision/Policy Issues
      1. Supply Chain Vulnerability
      2. Multi-Division Mergers
      3. Facility Capacity Changes
      4. Transportation Policy
      5. Seasonal Demand/Supply
      6. International Trade
      7. Customer Profitability
      8. Product Introductions/Deletions
      9. Alternative Networks
      10. Implementation Analysis

B. Environmental Issues
   1. Economic Climate
   2. Competitive Pressures
   3. Disaster Planning

C. Sensitivity Issues
   1. Cost versus Customer Service
   2. Cost versus Number of DCs
   3. Parametric Analysis of Inputs

Source: SAILS™: Strategic Analysis of Integrated Logistics Systems (Manassas, VA: Insight, Inc. 2006). Used with permission.

- Reliable run-to-run comparisons can be made since the "best" solution is guaranteed for each run.
- Cost or profit savings between the optimum and heuristic solution can be significant.[10]

The classic objective of a network design model has been to establish the number, location, and size of finished goods distribution centers and associated product flows so as to minimize costs and maintain or improve customer service. Now the mandate is to design the *entire supply chain*, from source of raw materials to the final customer. This emerging view encompasses procurement, multiple stages or processes of manufacturing, distribution center functions, and all related transportation flows. The supply chain function is increasingly viewed as a competitive weapon, not just a service provider; cost minimization is being supplanted by profit maximization (or enhancing shareholder equity); and national borders are dissolving. In short, answering network design questions today is virtually impossible without the help of very powerful decision support tools. There are just too many data to assimilate, and the combinations of facilities and support patterns number in the trillions. Fortunately, help is readily available for coping with this class of decision problems.[11]

One of the optimization techniques that has traditionally received significant attention is linear programming, or LP. This approach is most useful for linking facilities in a network where supply and demand limitations at plants, distribution centers, or market areas must be treated as constraints. Given an objective function that focuses attention on, for example, minimizing total cost, LP defines the optimum facility distribution pattern consistent with the problem's demand-supply constraints. Although this technique is actually quite useful, its applicability is limited due to the need for the problem formulation to be deterministic and capable of linear approximation. Also, the use of LP itself does not allow for consideration of fixed as well as variable costs of operating logistics facilities.

On a more advanced scale, the use of mixed-integer linear programming allows consideration of issues such as fixed and variable costs, capacity constraints, economies of scale, cross-product limitations, and unique sourcing requirements. One of the leading models of this type is **Strategic Analysis of Integrated Logistics Systems (SAILS™)**, developed by Insight, Inc. Figure 12-4 illustrates the supply chain complexity that may be addressed by a capable network optimization model such as SAILS™. In brief, SAILS™ is a fully integrated decision support system that can be used to build, modify,

Figure 12-4 Supply Chain Complexity

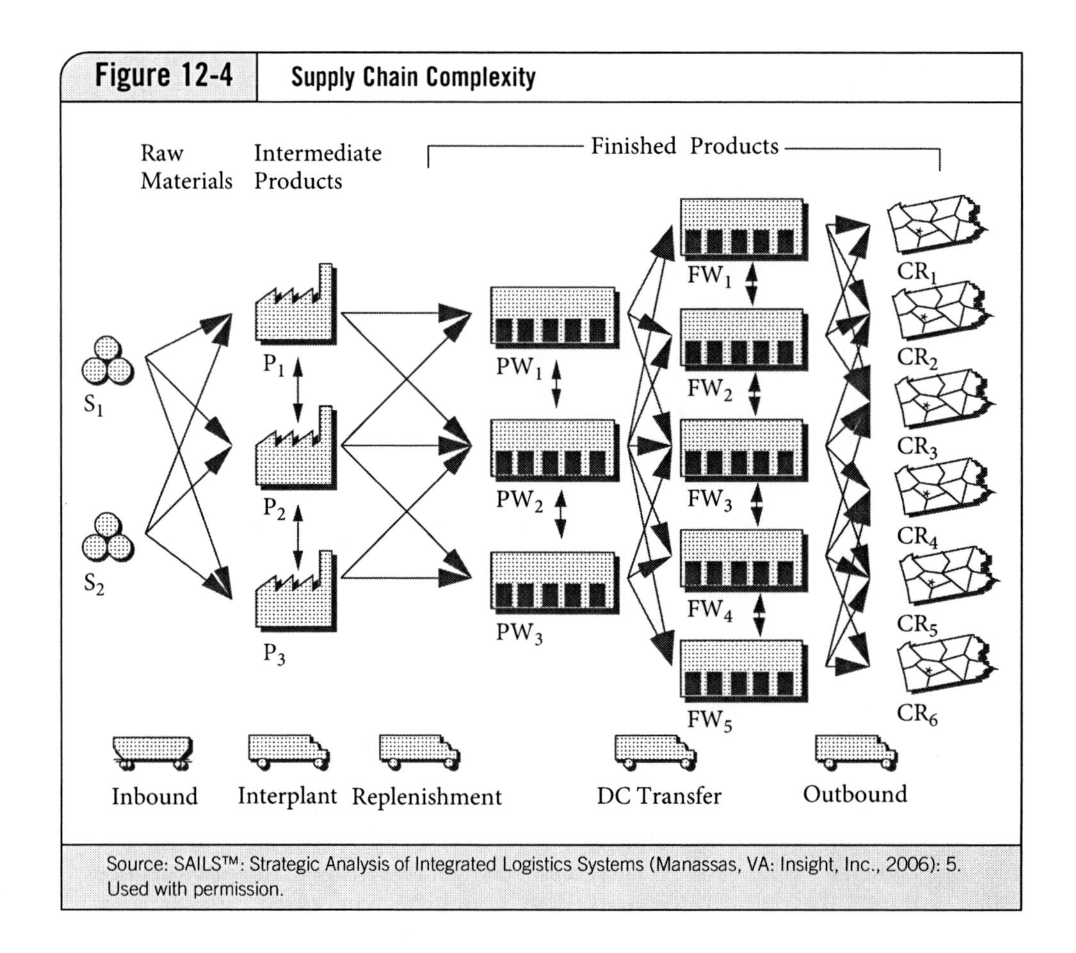

Source: SAILS™: Strategic Analysis of Integrated Logistics Systems (Manassas, VA: Insight, Inc., 2006): 5. Used with permission.

solve, and interpret sophisticated strategic supply chain design models. Although SAILS™ is an off-the-shelf software package, it may be easily customized through an extensive array of model building, input data, and processing options to meet the requirements of a particular problem formulation. Although SAILS™ was designed originally to analyze *strategic* issues that involve longer-term resource commitments, many users have successfully addressed *tactical* issues as well, such as first-level production planning, production line balancing, seasonal pre-build, etc.[12]

Once a modeling database has been created, either simple or complex, the use of SAILS™ facilitates the rapid generation and evaluation of many alternate scenarios for analysis.[13] Numerous shipment planning controls also permit the user to evaluate the network impact of various shipment planning options such as pooling, stop-offs, pickups, and direct plant shipments. SAILS™ is a highly flexible logistics modeling tool that can be used for a range of problems from the very simple to ones in which data may exist in the form of millions of shipment transactions. When a given modeling scenario has been generated, SAILS™ utilizes mixed-integer linear programming, along with an advanced technique called **network factorization**, to produce an optimum solution. Typical data inputs to SAILS™ include customer demand (either forecast or historical); aggregated product and customer identification; facility data for plants and DCs; transportation options and rates; and policy considerations such as shipment planning rules, DC inventory constraints, and customer service requirements.

Although optimization approaches typically require significant computer resources, the availability of capable systems today has greatly facilitated their ease of use. Along with improvements in model design and solver technologies, future approaches should be even more convenient for general use by those involved with the design and analysis of logistics/supply chain networks.

In addition to improved analytical techniques, the availability of insightful visual representations of logistics networks has enhanced our ability to gain insight into network alternatives. Figure 12-5 is an example of the types of "geo-mapping" alternatives that are currently available.

Simulation Models

The second approach to logistics/supply chain network design includes the development and use of **simulation models**. Simulation is defined as "the process of designing a model of a real system and conducting experiments with this model for the purpose either of understanding the behavior of the system or of evaluating various strategies within the limits imposed by a criterion or set of criteria for the operation of the system."[14] Network simulation involves developing a computer representation of the logistics/supply chain network and then observing the cost and service characteristics of the network as cost structures, constraints, and other factors are varied. It has been stated that the process of simulation is "nothing more or less than the technique of performing *sampling experiments* on the model of the system."[15]

Figure 12-5 Example Geographical-Mapping Representations

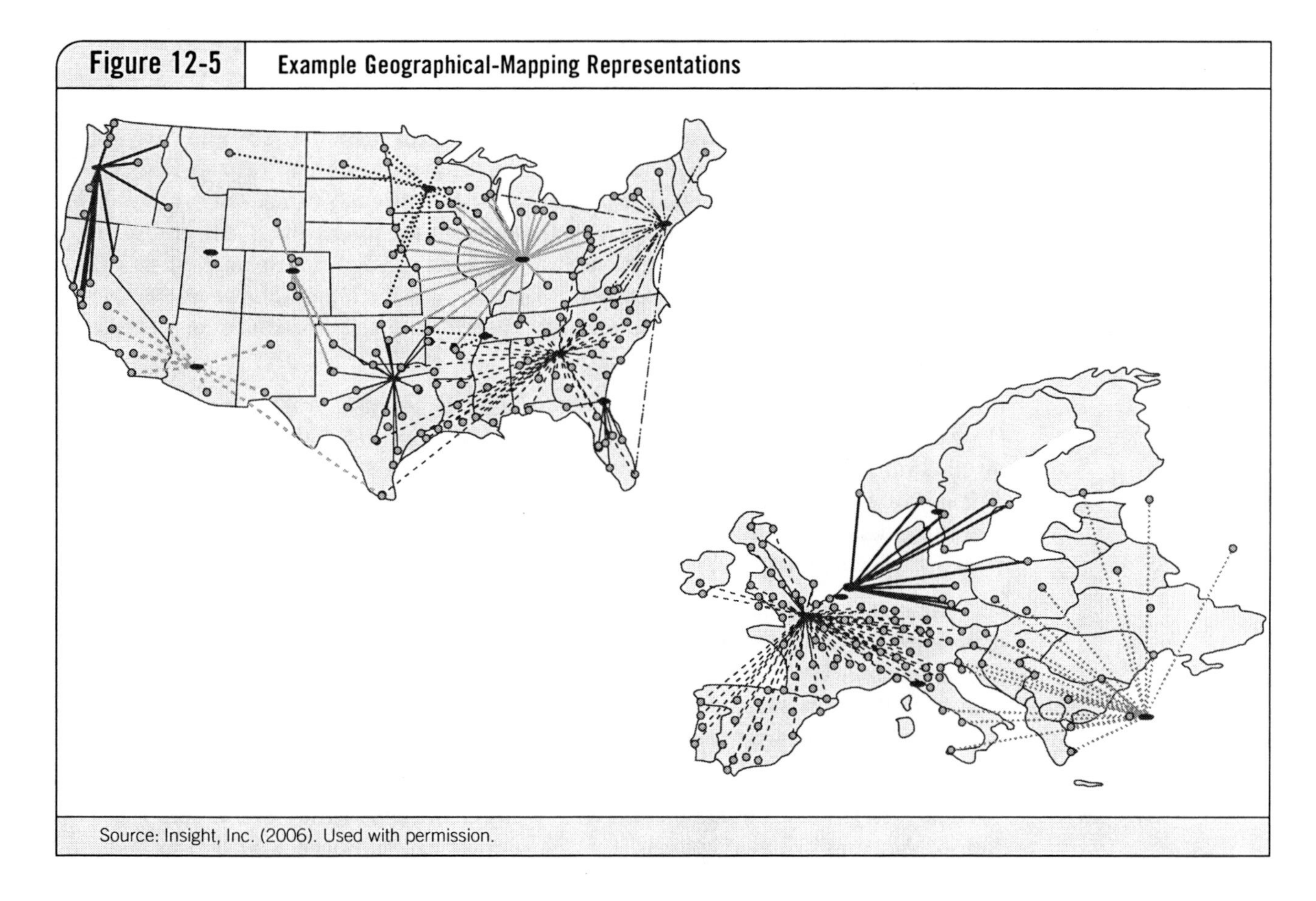

Source: Insight, Inc. (2006). Used with permission.

For location analysis, the use of simulation allows the decision maker to test the effect of alternative locations upon costs and service levels. The modeling requires extensive data collection and analysis to determine how system factors such as transportation, warehousing, inventory, materials handling, and labor costs interact. The simulation process evaluates the decision maker's selected sites to determine respective costs. Simulation does not guarantee an optimum solution but simply evaluates the alternatives that are fed into it.[16] A critical characteristic of a simulation tool is whether it is static or dynamic in nature. A dynamic tool will not only incorporate a multiperiod time perspective but also update system status for each time period based on the results of the previous time periods.

According to Ballou, simulation has value in business network planning.[17] Although it does not search directly for the best warehouse configuration, its problem description can be very rich, including cost functions that are nonlinear (inventory), stepwise (labor costs), and discontinuous (quantity discounts). Simulation continues to be used as a stand-alone approach but also is used as a supplemental methodology within other search-oriented approaches. If for no other reason, simulation is needed to replicate, or cost out, the current logistics/supply chain network of a firm so that potential improvements from location analysis can be compared to it.

Although simulation models are not designed to produce optimum solutions, they are very capable in terms of their ability to incorporate relatively comprehensive and detailed problem descriptions. Sometimes an optimization approach is used first to identify and evaluate feasible network design alternatives, and then highly customized simulation models are used to focus on the exact logistics network that will best meet the desired objectives.

Heuristic Models

Heuristic models are able to accommodate broad problem definitions, but they do not provide an optimum solution. The use of a heuristic approach can help to reduce a problem to a manageable size and search automatically through various alternatives in an attempt to find a better solution. As is indicated in the discussion of the grid technique that follows, heuristic approaches can provide a good approximation to the least-cost location in a complex decision problem. To reduce the number of location alternatives, the decision maker should incorporate into the heuristic program site characteristics considered to be optimal.

For example, the location team may consider a desirable warehouse site to be (1) within 20 miles of a major market area, (2) at least 250 miles from other company distribution centers, (3) within three miles of an interstate highway, and (4) within 40 miles of a major airport facility. The heuristic model searches for sites with these characteristics, thus reducing the number of alternative sites to those the decision maker considers practical.

Additionally, heuristic decision rules are sometimes incorporated into the decision-making process in what may appear to be "rules of thumb." Examples might include requirements to locate distribution centers at or near points of demand, to supply customers from the nearest distribution facility, to choose as the next distribution site the one that will produce the greatest cost savings, or to serve all customers within a 24-hour delivery time.[18]

As we are reminded by Ratliff and Nulty,[19] sometimes the word *heuristics* implies a "seat-of-the-pants" solution approach, involving little or no intelligence or sophistication.

They suggest that this is unfortunate, as many times, analytical heuristics can be as technically sophisticated as mathematical optimization approaches. Many heuristics are based on mathematical optimization models and algorithms, such as using practical rules to formulate a mathematical optimization model. A powerful heuristic approach is to modify a mixed-integer program by temporarily assuming the integer variables to be linear in nature, thus creating an approximate but much more solvable model. Then, the solution to this model is used as a basis for constructing a solution to the integer problem.

Supply Chain Technology — *Attracting Business by Being RFID "Friendly"*

If you want to attract DC business to your area, it's no longer enough to be business friendly. Now, you have to be RFID friendly as well.

With the RFID revolution well under way, economic development agencies are actively pitching their regions' technological capabilities in hopes of attracting RFID-enabled DC operations. In fact, two of the more aggressive promoters—North Texas and North London (yes, in England)—took the unusual step of setting up exhibits at the RFID World conference and exhibition in Dallas earlier this year.

Officials from the North Texas region have branded the Dallas/Fort Worth area as an RFID hub, and not without cause. The Dallas/Fort Worth region, where both Wal-Mart and Target carried out their initial RFID deployments, has become something of a hotbed for RFID activity. Today, the area is home to companies specializing in all facets of RFID, including chip makers, hardware companies, software developers, and consultants offering RFID implementation and integration services, according to the Metroplex Technology Business Council.

Meanwhile, the North England Inward Investment Agency (NEIIA) is promoting the ready availability of RFID expertise in North London—an area that includes Manchester, Newcastle, Liverpool, Leeds, and Sheffield. The region is home to the University of Hull's Logistics Institute, whose staff members have vast experience with RFID implementations, according to David Allison, NEIIA's chairman. "That resource alone," he says, "makes North London the ideal base for RFID-enabled companies looking to penetrate the European market."

Not to be outdone, economic development officials from the Atlanta area are also promoting their region's RFID capabilities. While other parts of the nation are experiencing a shortage of RFID expertise, these officials claim that Atlanta has no such problems. Atlanta's hometown university, Georgia Tech, produces more RFID engineers than any other school in the country.

Source: Adapted from John R. Johnson, "It Takes a Village ...," *DC Velocity* (June 2006): 36–40.

Potential Supply Chain Modeling Pitfalls to Avoid

According to Bender, a number of common pitfalls should be avoided in designing and implementing an optimum worldwide supply chain.[20] Recognizing these in advance should help to maximize the value to be achieved through use of appropriate mathematical techniques for supply chain network design.

- **Short-term horizon.** Unless modeling features are designed, implemented, and used with a long-term perspective, significant suboptimization is likely to occur.

- **Too little or too much detail.** Too little detail can make it difficult to implement results due to insufficient information; too much detail can create unnecessary complexity, making it difficult to understand the results and more difficult to implement effectively.
- **Thinking in two dimensions.** While the use of two-dimensional maps certainly helps to provide insight into supply chain problems, the geometry of the networks may ignore cost and geographical dispersions of demand. Over significant distances, and particularly for global supply chain analyses, the curvature of the earth may distort distance calculations, in which case needed adjustments must be made.
- **Using published costs.** Many "published" costs tend to represent "list" prices that need to be modified to reflect what may result after significant negotiations occur between buyers and sellers of transport services.
- **Inaccurate or incomplete costs.** Analyses based on insufficiently accurate information lead to invalid results; inaccurate cost forecasts result in suboptimal allocations of resources, typically leading to seriously flawed strategies.
- **Use of erroneous analytical techniques.** The selected techniques and approaches should be matched with the level of precision desired; the identification of modeling objectives is an important forerunner to the selection of the techniques to be utilized.
- **Lack of appropriate robustness analysis.** Since most or all model inputs have at least an element of uncertainty, it is important to understand the consequences that could result from variation in actual behavior of key model inputs; robustness analysis can help to assure the practicality and validity of the results from the selected analyses.

Example of a Heuristic Modeling Approach: The Grid Technique

Although other factors are also important, the availability and expense of transportation services are commonly included in location analyses. While transportation itself can represent a significant cost, decision makers should strive to make the final decision on the basis of the full range of relevant cost factors, as well as on the customer service implications of the network alternative being evaluated.

The grid technique is a simplistic, but well-known, heuristic approach to help companies with multiple markets and multiple supply points determine a least-cost facility location. Essentially, the grid technique attempts to determine a fixed facility (such as a plant or distribution center) location that represents the least-cost center for moving inbound materials and outbound product within a geographic grid. The technique determines the low-cost "center of gravity" for moving raw materials and finished goods.

This technique assumes that the raw materials sources and finished goods markets are fixed and that a company knows the amount of each product it consumes or sells. The technique then superimposes a grid upon the geographic area containing the raw materials sources and finished goods markets. The grid's zero point corresponds to an exact geographic location, as do the grid's other points. Thus, the company can identify each source and market by its grid coordinates.

Figure 12-6 is an example of a supply source and market environment for a company that is deciding where to locate a plant. The company, which has located supply sources and markets on the map and has superimposed a grid system over the source-market area, purchases raw materials from sources in Buffalo, Memphis, and

Figure 12-6 Grid Locations of Sources and Markets

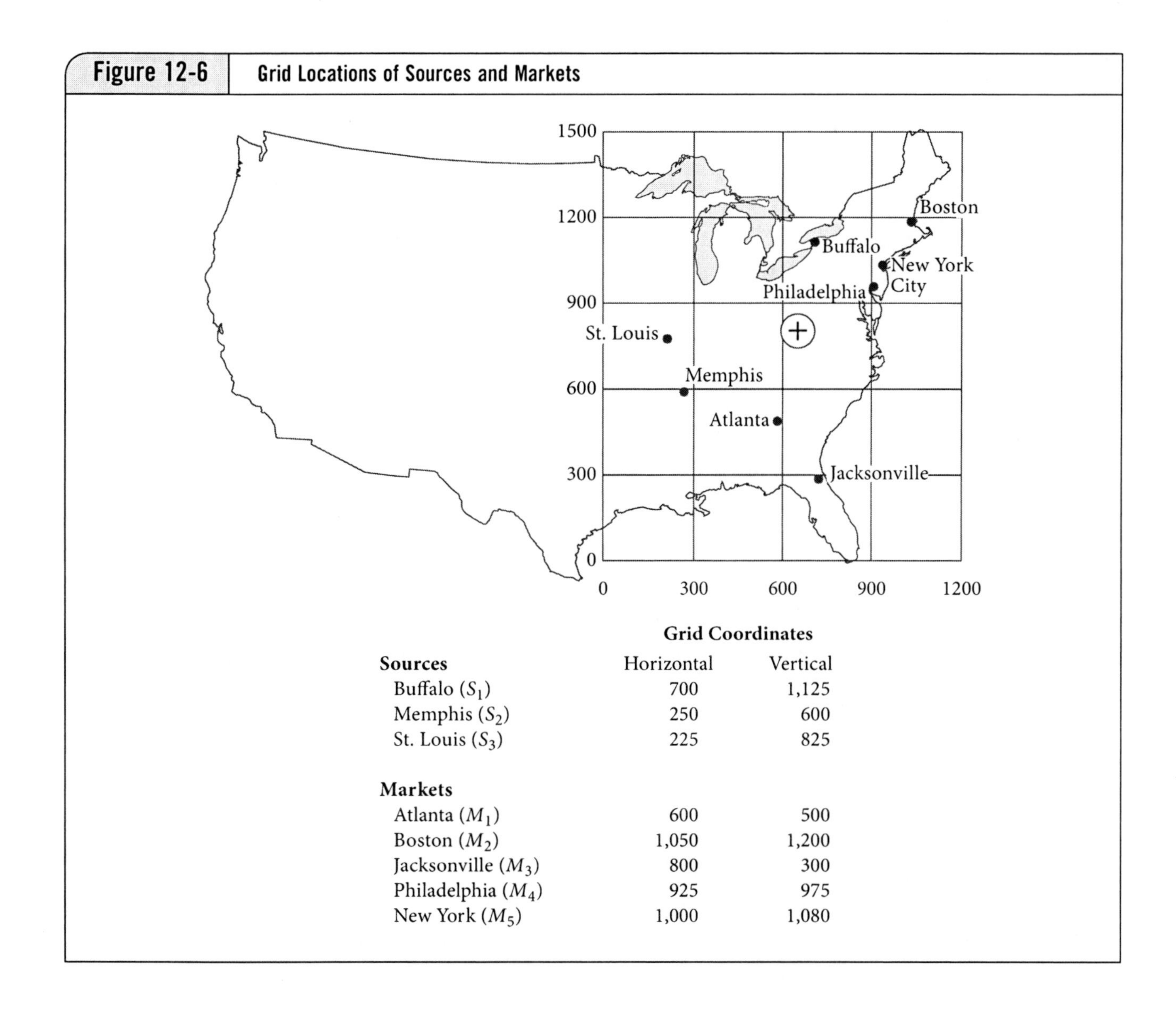

	Grid Coordinates	
Sources	Horizontal	Vertical
Buffalo (S_1)	700	1,125
Memphis (S_2)	250	600
St. Louis (S_3)	225	825
Markets		
Atlanta (M_1)	600	500
Boston (M_2)	1,050	1,200
Jacksonville (M_3)	800	300
Philadelphia (M_4)	925	975
New York (M_5)	1,000	1,080

St. Louis—S_1, S_2 and S_3, respectively. The new plant will serve five markets: Atlanta, Boston, Jacksonville, Philadelphia, and New York—M_1, M_2, M_3, M_4, and M_5, respectively.

The technique defines each source and market location in terms of its horizontal and vertical grid coordinates. For example, the Jacksonville market (M_3) has a horizontal grid coordinate of 800 and a vertical grid coordinate of 300. The Buffalo source is located at grid coordinates 700 horizontal and 1,125 vertical.

We can visualize this technique's underlying concept as a series of strings to which are attached weights corresponding to the weight of raw materials the company consumes at each source and of finished goods the company sells at each market. The strings are threaded through holes in a flat plane; the holes correspond to the source and market locations. The strings' other ends are tied together, and the weights exert their respective pulls on the knot. The strings' knotted ends will finally reach equilibrium; this equilibrium will be the center of mass, or the ton-mile center.

We can compute this concept mathematically, finding the ton-mile center, or center of mass, as follows:

$$C = \frac{\sum_{1}^{m} d_i S_i + \sum_{1}^{n} D_i M_i}{\sum_{1}^{m} S_i + \sum_{1}^{n} M_i}$$

where

C = Center of mass, or ton − mile center
d_i = Distance from 0 point on grid to the grid location of raw material i
D_i = Distance from 0 point on grid to the grid location of finished good i
S_i = Weight (volume) of raw materials purchased at source i
M_i = Weight (volume) of finished goods sold in market i

This equation will generate the least-cost location if transportation rates for raw materials and finished goods are the same. But transportation rates vary among commodities, and the ton-mile center equation does not reflect differences in the costs of moving commodities. The transportation rate pulls the location toward the location of the commodity with the higher rate. Thus, the higher rates of finished goods will draw the least-cost location toward the finished goods market and thereby reduce the distance the company moves these higher-rated goods. This will increase the distance the company transports lower-rated raw materials.

Thus, we must incorporate into our analysis the transportation rates of different products. This modification is as follows:

$$c = \frac{\sum_{1}^{m} r_i d_i s_i + \sum_{1}^{n} R_i D_i M_i}{\sum_{1}^{m} r_i s_i + \sum_{1}^{n} R_i M_i}$$

where

r_i = Raw materials rate/distance unit for raw material i
R_i = Finished goods transportation rate/distance unit for finished good i

r_i and R_i are the transportation rates per distance unit, and we assume them to be linear with respect to distance. This assumption does not correspond to the tapering principle of rates (to be discussed later in this chapter), but it does simplify the analysis.

Plant Location Example Table 12-2 presents relevant data for a plant location example, as well as the grid technique solution using a computer spreadsheet program. The grid coordinates of the raw materials sources and markets correspond to their locations on the grid in Figure 12-6. For simplicity, we will assume that this company produces only one type of finished good, so that each finished good's transportation rate is the same.

To determine the least-cost center on the grid, we must compute two grid coordinates, one for moving the commodities along the horizontal axis and one for moving them along the vertical axis. We compute the two coordinates by using the grid technique formula for each direction.

Table 12-2 provides this example's computations. The two columns at the far right contain the calculations that the grid technique equation indicates. The first calculations column contains the calculations for the horizontal numerator, or the sum of the

Table 12-2 Grid Technique Analysis of Plant Location Example

SOURCES/ MARKETS	RATE $/TON-MILE (A)	TONS (B)	GRID COORDINATES HORIZONTAL	GRID COORDINATES VERTICAL	CALCULATIONS (A) × (B) × HORIZONTAL	CALCULATIONS (A) × (B) × VERTICAL
Buffalo (S_1)	$0.90	500	700	1,125	315,000	506,250
Memphis (S_2)	$0.95	300	250	600	71,250	171,000
St. Louis (S_3)	$0.85	700	225	825	133,875	490,875
		1,500			520,125	1,168,125
Atlanta (M_1)	$1.50	225	600	500	202,500	168,750
Boston (M_2)	$1.50	150	1,050	1,200	236,250	270,000
Jacksonville (M_3)	$1.50	250	800	300	300,000	112,500
Philadelphia (M_4)	$1.50	175	925	975	242,813	255,938
New York (M_5)	$1.50	300	1,000	1,080	450,000	486,000
	TOTALS	1,100			1,431,563	1,293,188
					HORIZONTAL	VERTICAL
				Numerator: $\sum (r \times d \times S) =$	520,125	1,168,125
				$+ \sum (R \times D \times M) =$	1,431,563	1,293,188
				Sum	1,951,688	2,461,313
				Denominator: $\sum (r \times S) =$	1,330	1,330
				$+ \sum (R \times M) =$	1,650	1,650
				Sum	2,980	2,980
				Grid Center	655	826

rate times the horizontal grid coordinate times the tonnage for each raw materials source and market. The calculations at the bottom of Table 12-2 indicate the numerator and denominator of the grid technique equation.

As Table 12-2 indicates, the plant location's least-cost center in this example is 655 in the horizontal direction and 826 in the vertical direction. We measure both distances from the grid's zero point. Figure 12-6 indicates the least-cost center as point +. The least-cost location for the plant is in southeastern Ohio or northwestern West Virginia in the Wheeling-Parkersburg area.

The preceding example applied the grid technique to a plant location. Companies can use the technique to solve warehousing location problems as well. The company follows the same procedure, but the company's plants are the raw materials sources.

Advantages The grid technique's strengths are in its simplicity and its ability to provide a starting point for location analysis. Computationally, the technique is relatively easy to use. A company can generate the necessary data from sales figures, purchase records, and transportation documents (either the bill of lading or the freight bill). More exact market and source location coding is possible, as is modifying the rate-distance relationship quantification. A computer can easily handle such refinements.

The grid technique also provides a starting point for making a location decision. As we suggested earlier, transportation cost is not the only locational determinant. Using the grid technique can eliminate certain areas, permitting the decision maker to focus on an area that is logistically advantageous. For example, the grid technique may suggest Toledo, Ohio, as the least-cost location for a plant to serve the Ohio, Michigan, Indiana, and Illinois market area. This eliminates consideration of Chicago, Indianapolis, and other regional cities and permits the decision maker to concentrate the location analysis in northwestern Ohio and southeastern Michigan. This is a tremendous step forward in the location decision process.

Limitations The grid technique has limitations that the decision maker must recognize. First, it is a static approach, and the solution is optimum for only one point in time. Changes in the volumes a company purchases or sells, changes in transportation rates, or changes in raw materials sources or market locations will shift the least-cost location. Second, the technique assumes linear transportation rates, whereas actual transportation rates increase with distance but less than proportionally. Third, the technique does not consider the topographic conditions existing at the optimum location; for example, the recommended site may be in the middle of a lake. Fourth, it does not consider the proper direction of movement; most moves occur along a straight line between two points, not "vertically" and then "horizontally."

Sensitivity Analysis As mentioned in the preceding paragraph, the grid technique is a static approach; the computed location is valid only for the situation analyzed. If the transportation rates, market and source locations, and volumes change, then the least-cost location changes.

Sensitivity analysis enables the decision maker to ask what-if questions and measure the resulting impact on the least-cost location. For example, the decision maker may examine the least-cost location in light of a five-year sales projection by inserting the estimated market sales volumes into the grid technique equation and determining the least-cost location. Other what-if scenarios could include adding new markets and/or sources, eliminating markets and/or sources, and switching transportation modes, thereby changing rates.

Tables 12-3 and 12-4 perform two sensitivity analyses for the original problem in Table 12-2. The first what-if scenario considers switching from rail to truck to serve the Jacksonville market; the switch entails a 50 percent rate increase. The data in Table 12-3 show that the rate increase shifts the least-cost location toward Jacksonville; that is, the new location grid coordinates are 664 and 795, or east and south of the original location (655, 826). Therefore, a rate increase will pull the least-cost location toward the market or supply source experiencing the increase.

The second what-if sensitivity analysis considers the elimination of a Buffalo supply source and increasing by 500 tons the amount the example company purchases from Memphis. Table 12-4 shows the effect of this sourcing change. With Memphis supplying all the material the company formerly purchased from Buffalo, the new least-cost location moves toward Memphis, or south and west of the original location. Similarly, a new market or a market experiencing a sales volume increase will draw the least-cost location.

Table 12-3 Impact of Transportation Rate Change on Least-Cost Location

SOURCES/ MARKETS	RATE $/TON-MILE (A)	TONS (B)	GRID COORDINATES HORIZONTAL	VERTICAL	CALCULATIONS (A) × (B) × HORIZONTAL	(A) × (B) × VERTICAL
Buffalo (S_1)	$0.90	500	700	1,125	315,000	506,250
Memphis (S_2)	$0.95	300	250	600	71,250	171,000
St. Louis (S_3)	$0.85	700	225	825	133,875	490,875
		1,500			520,125	1,168,125
Atlanta (M_1)	$1.50	225	600	500	202,500	168,750
Boston (M_2)	$1.50	150	1,050	1,200	236,250	270,000
Jacksonville (M_3)	$2.25	250	800	300	450,000	168,750
Philadelphia (M_4)	$1.50	175	925	975	242,813	255,938
New York (M_5)	$1.50	300	1,000	1,080	450,000	486,000
	TOTALS	1,100			1,581,563	1,349,438
					HORIZONTAL	VERTICAL
				Numerator: $\sum (r \times d \times S) =$	520,125	1,168,125
				$+ \sum (R \times D \times M) =$	1,581,563	1,349,438
				Sum	2,101,688	2,517,563
				Denominator: $\sum (r \times S) =$	1,330	1,330
				$+ \sum (R \times M) =$	1,838	1,838
				Sum	3,168	3,168
				Grid Center	664	795

We can conclude from these sensitivity analyses that the rates, product volumes, and source/market locations do affect a plant's least-cost location. The least-cost location moves toward a market or source experiencing a rate or volume increase, and away from the market or source experiencing a decrease. Introducing a new market or source pulls the location toward the additional market or source.

Application to Warehouse Location in a City A special case exists for applying the grid technique to the location of a warehouse in a city. The situation's uniqueness comes from the blanket rate structure, which applies the same rate from an origin to any point within the city or commercial zone. Thus, any location within a city's commercial zone incurs the same inbound transportation cost from a company's mix of suppliers used; that is, the cost of moving supplies to a warehouse within the same city does not affect the location decision.

Since the supply volumes moving into the warehouse do not affect the location decision, the least-cost warehouse location within a city considers the cost of moving

Table 12-4 Impact of Supply Source Change on Least-Cost Location

SOURCES/ MARKETS	RATE $/TON-MILE (A)	TONS (B)	GRID COORDINATES HORIZONTAL	VERTICAL	CALCULATIONS (A) × (B) × HORIZONTAL	(A) × (B) × VERTICAL
Buffalo (S_1)	$0.90	0	700	1,125	0	0
Memphis (S_2)	$0.95	800	250	600	190,000	456,000
St. Louis (S_3)	$0.85	700	225	825	133,875	490,875
		1,500			323,875	946,875
Atlanta (M_1)	$1.50	225	600	500	202,500	168,750
Boston (M_2)	$1.50	150	1,050	1,200	236,250	270,000
Jacksonville (M_3)	$2.25	250	800	300	450,000	168,750
Philadelphia (M_4)	$1.50	175	925	975	242,813	255,938
New York (M_5)	$1.50	300	1,000	1,080	450,000	486,000
	TOTALS	1,100			1,581,563	1,349,438
					HORIZONTAL	VERTICAL
				Numerator: $\sum (r \times d \times S) =$	323,875	946,875
				$+\sum (R \times D \times M) =$	1,581,563	1,349,438
				Sum	1,905,438	2,296,313
				Denominator: $\sum (r \times S) =$	1,355	1,355
				$+\sum (R \times M) =$	1,838	1,838
				Sum	3,193	3,193
				Grid Center	597	719

finished goods from the warehouse to the customers. We modify the grid technique equation as follows:

$$C = \frac{\sum_{1}^{n} R_i D_i M_i}{\sum_{1}^{n} R_i M_i}$$

If we assume that the cost of distributing (R) the commodity throughout the city is the same, R cancels out, reducing the equation to a ton-mile center as follows:

$$C = \frac{\sum_{i}^{n} D_i M_i}{\sum_{1}^{n} M_i}$$

As before, this modified grid technique enables the decision maker to eliminate certain areas of the city and to concentrate the analysis upon sites in the general vicinity of the least-cost location's grid coordinates. To determine a specific site for the warehouse, the decision maker must consider land and facility availability, expressway systems, and highway access in this general vicinity.

Transportation Pragmatics[21]

The previous discussion showed the importance of the transportation factor in the facility location decision. We simplified the rate structure focus on the transportation factor's locational pull. In this section, we examine how dropping these transportation simplifications affects facility location, directing attention specifically toward tapering rates, blanket rates, commercial zones, foreign trade zones, and in-transit privileges.

Tapering Rates As we pointed out earlier, transportation rates increase with distance but not in direct proportion to distance. This **tapering-rate principle** results from the carrier's ability to spread certain fixed shipment costs, such as loading, billing, and handling, over a greater number of miles. As noted by Edgar M. Hoover, a tapering rate in a one-source, one-market situation pulls the location to either the source or the market but not to a point in between.

To illustrate this effect, consider the data in Table 12-5 and Figure 12-7. In this example, we assume the rates to be constant (the same) for raw materials supplied at *S* and finished products sold at *M*. The rates in Table 12-5 increase with distance but not proportionally. For example, the shipping rate from *S* is $2.00 for 50 miles and $3.00 for 100 miles, a distance increase of 100 percent but a rate increase of only 50 percent.

Table 12-5 and Figure 12-7 indicate that a location at either *S* or *M* will result in a total rate of $3.70. At any other location, the total rate is higher. Thus, the tapering rate pulls the location toward the source or the market.

Dropping rate constancy between raw materials and finished goods draws the location toward *M*, the market. In Table 12-6 and Figure 12-8, the rates for moving the finished product into the market are higher than those for moving raw materials. The location having the least total transportation cost is at *M*, where the total transportation rate is $3.70.

Blanket Rates A noted exception to the preceding rate structure is the **blanket rate**. The blanket rate does not increase with distance; it remains the same from one origin

Table 12-5 Locational Effects of Tapering Rates with Constant Rate Assumption

DISTANCE FROM *S* (MILES)	TRANSPORT RATE FROM *S*	DISTANCE TO *M* (MILES)	TRANSPORT RATE TO *M*	TOTAL TRANSPORT RATE
0	$0.00	200	$3.70	$3.70
50	2.00	150	3.50	5.50
100	3.00	100	3.00	6.00
150	3.50	50	2.00	5.50
200	3.70	0	0.00	3.70

Figure 12-7 Locational Effects of Tapering Rates with Constant Rate Assumption

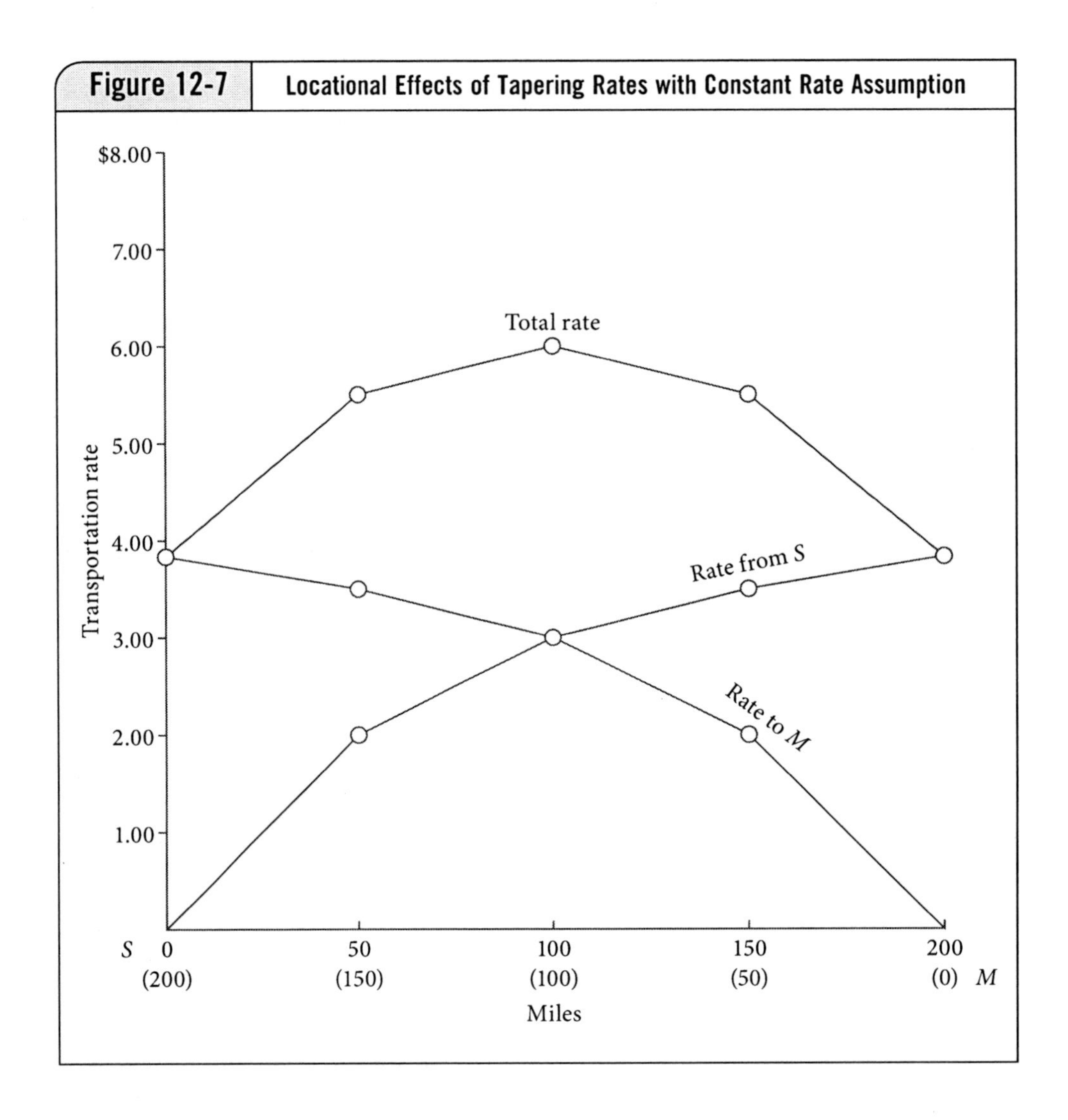

Table 12-6 Locational Effects of Tapering Rates without Constant Rate Assumption

DISTANCE FROM *S* (MILES)	TRANSPORT RATE FROM *S*	DISTANCE TO *M* (MILES)	TRANSPORT RATE TO *M*	TOTAL TRANSPORT RATE
0	$0.00	200	$5.20	$5.20
50	2.00	150	5.00	7.00
100	3.00	100	4.50	7.50
150	3.50	50	3.50	7.00
200	3.70	0	0.00	3.70

to all points in the blanket area. The carriers establish such rates to ensure a competitive price for a product in a given area, thereby ensuring demand for the product and its transportation. An example of a blanket rate would be the same rate on wine traveling from the West Coast to all points east of the Rocky Mountains, enabling the West Coast wine to compete with imported wines entering the East Coast.

Figure 12-8 Locational Effects of Tapering Rates without Constant Rate Assumption

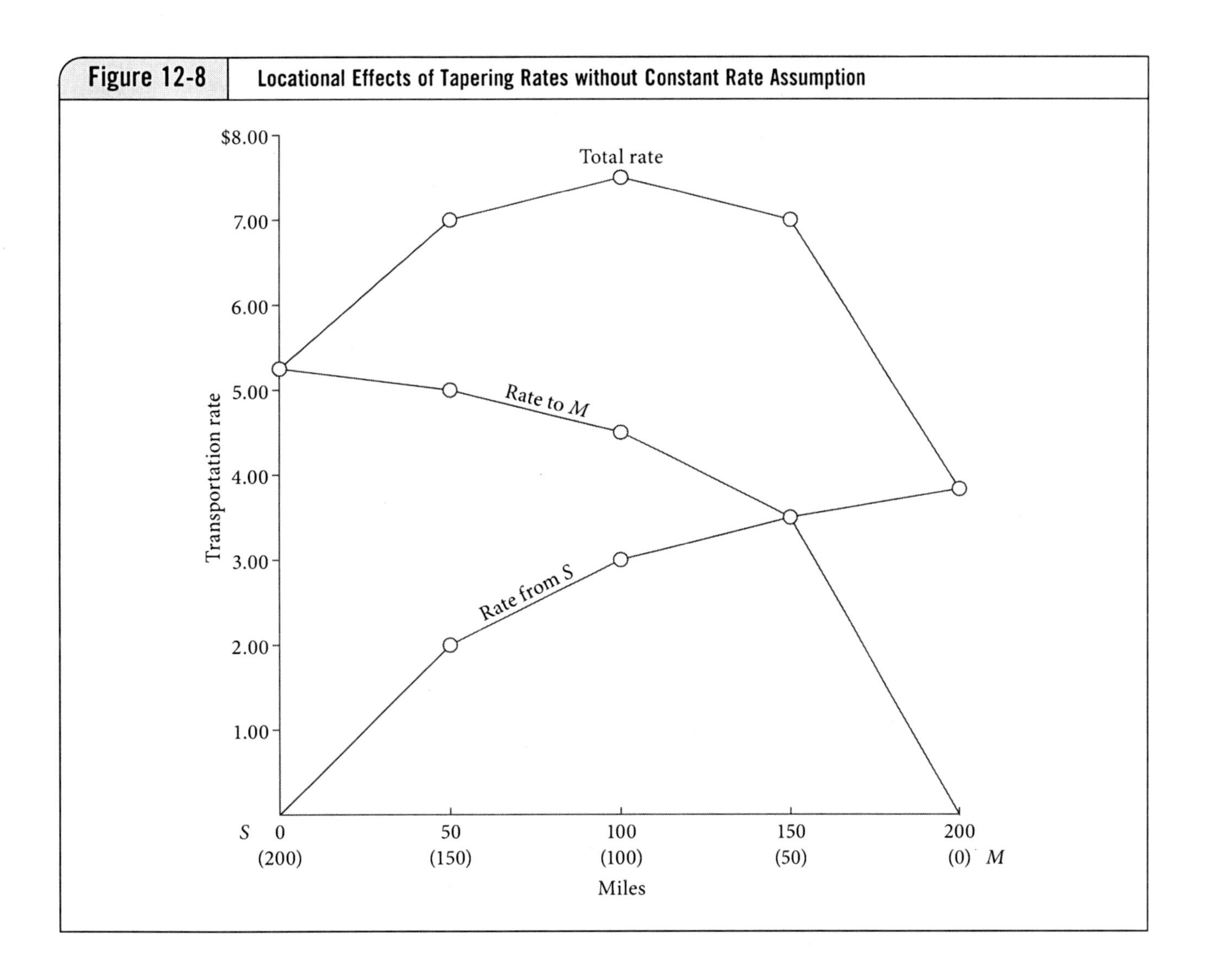

The blanket rate eliminates any transportation cost advantage or disadvantage that companies associate with a given location. In the case of the wine blanket rates, the West Coast wine producers can effectively compete in the East Coast market area with East Coast and foreign producers. The blanket rate, then, is a mutation of the basic rate-distance relationship that eliminates the transportation rate as a locational determinant; it is the exception rather than the rule in transportation rates.

Commercial Zones A specific blanket area is the **commercial zone**, the transportation definition of a particular city or town. It includes the municipality itself plus various surrounding areas. The commercial zone rates that carriers quote to a particular town or city also apply to points in the surrounding area within the commercial zone.

The commercial zone's locational impact appears near the end of the location decision process when a company selects a specific site. If the specific site is beyond the limits of a municipality's commercial zone, rates that apply to the city do not apply to the site. Also, a site outside the commercial zone reduces carrier availability, especially the availability of motor carriers that define their operating scopes in terms of point-to-point operations.

Foreign Trade Zones[22] As previously discussed, a **foreign trade zone (FTZ)** is a geographic area into which importers can enter a product and hold it without paying duties—and only paying duties or customs when is it shipped into U.S. customs territory. A variety of activities can be conducted in a FTZ, including assembling, packaging, destroying, storing, cleaning, exhibiting, re-packaging, distributing, sorting, grading, testing, labeling, repairing, combining with foreign or domestic content, or processing.[23] Advantages of FTZs include the following:

- Deferred customs duties and federal excise taxes on imports
- No duties or quota payments on re-exported materials
- Choice of duty rates paid—based either on the rate for component parts or for the finished product
- Exemption from state and local inventory taxes or foreign and domestic goods that are to be exported

The availability of FTZ benefits can impact the design of a firm's logistics network. For example, Ryder Group operates a foreign trade zone, Kelly USA, on the former Kelly Air Force Base in San Antonio, Texas. The Trade Processing Center operated by Ryder is a 40,000-square-foot facility with an on-site Mexican freight broker who serves as a liaison between Ryder's U.S. and Mexican operations. Also, the complex operates seven days a week with door-to-door services for over-the-road trucking, rail, air, and ocean transport of goods.

Another example of how a foreign trade zone can help a company is Foreign Trade Zone 50 in California.[24] This involves an electronics company that imports 40,000 electrical capacitors per year from Asia at a value of $200 per unit or 9.6 percent duty rate. The company requested permission to manipulate the merchandise (e.g., open cartons, perform quality control inspections, and repackage cartons) prior to re-exportation to Mexico. The final product then is exported to a free zone within a Mexican maquiladora for manufacturing of the finished goods. The company benefits from duty elimination within Foreign Trade Zone 50 and realizes a yearly zone savings of U.S. $768,000.

Other well-known companies that utilize foreign trade zones include Northrop Grumman, Kawasaki Motors Manufacturing Corp., BMW Manufacturing Corp., General Electric Co., JVC America, and Caterpillar, Inc.[25]

Transit Privileges Basically, the **transit privilege** permits the shipper to stop a shipment in transit and to perform some function that physically changes the product's characteristic. The lower through rate from origin to final destination (the tapering-rate principle) applies, rather than the higher combination of rates from origin to transit point and from transit point to final destination.

The transit privilege essentially makes intermediate locations, rather than just origins or destinations, optimum. The transit privilege eliminates any geographic disadvantage that companies associate with a producer's location. The intermediate point the carrier designates as a transit point enjoys the lower, long-distance through rate that applies at either the origin or the destination.

Like the blanket rate, the transit privilege is not available at all locations or for all commodities—only those sites and commodities the carrier specifies. If a commodity benefits from the availability of a transit privilege, the limited points specified by the carrier will be prime facility location alternatives.

SUMMARY

- The logistics/supply chain network design decision is of great strategic importance to logistics, the firm as a whole, and the supply chain.
- A number of factors may suggest the need to redesign the logistics/supply chain network.
- A formal, structured process for network design is preferable; the potential impacts on cost and service justify a significant effort toward following a sound process.
- Numerous factors may affect the design of a logistics network and the location of specific facilities within the context of the network.
- Principal modeling approaches to gain insight into the topic of logistics/supply chain network design include optimization, simulation, and heuristic models.
- The "grid" method represents a useful way to obtain a good, but not necessarily optimal, solution to a logistics facility location problem.
- The availability and cost of transportation affect the location decision in a number of significant and unique ways.

STUDY QUESTIONS

1. In what ways can the design of a firm's logistics/supply chain network affect its ability to create value for customers through efficiency, effectiveness, and differentiation?
2. What are the steps in the process of logistics/supply chain network design? Of these steps, which are most relevant to the task of selecting a specific site for a logistics facility?
3. Discuss the factors that cause a company to analyze the design of a logistics/supply chain network or to reconsider the location of a particular facility.
4. Why are most location decisions analyzed by a team of managers instead of a single person? What types of teams are suggested as being helpful to the task of logistics network redesign?
5. What are the major locational determinants, and how does each affect the location decision?
6. What is the difference between a regional/national location decision, and in what ways do the determinants of each differ?
7. Discuss the role of logistics variables in the decision as to where to locate a plant or distribution center.
8. What are the principal types of modeling techniques that apply to the task of logistics/supply chain network design and facility location? What are the strengths and limitations of each?
9. Describe the grid technique. What is its purpose, and how does it lead to the making of a decision? What are its strengths and limitations?

10. Using the grid technique, determine the least-cost location for the following problems:

(a)

	TONS	RATE	GRID COORDINATES(H, V)
S_1	200	0.50	2, 14
S_2	300	0.60	6, 10
M_1	100	1.00	2, 2
M_2	100	2.00	10, 14
M_3	100	1.00	14, 18
M_4	100	2.00	14, 6

	Tons	Rate	Grid Coordinates (H, V)
S_1	200	0.50	2, 14
S_2	300	0.60	6, 10
M_1	100	1.00	2, 2
M_2	100	2.00	10, 14
M_3	100	1.00	14, 18
M_4	100	2.00	14, 6

(b)

CUSTOMER	TONS	GRID COORDINATES(H, V)
A	100	1, 11
B	300	7, 11
C	200	5, 9
D	500	7, 7
E	1,000	1, 1

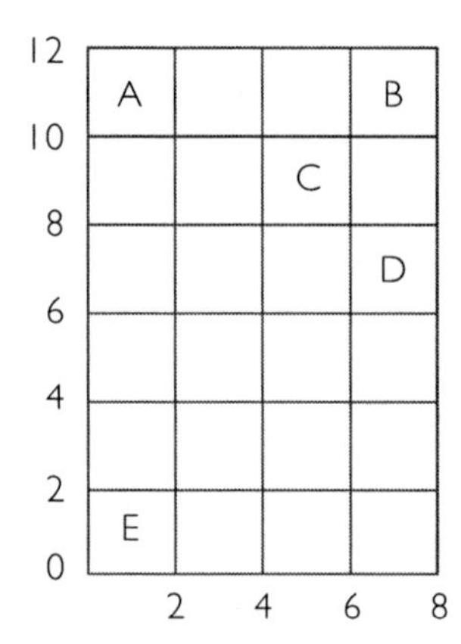

Customer	Tons	Grid Coordinates (H, V)
A	100	1, 11
B	300	7, 11
C	200	5, 9
D	500	7, 7
E	1,000	1, 1

11. Explain how tapering rates, blanket rates, commercial zones, foreign trade zones, and in-transit privileges affect the facility location decision.

NOTES

1. Morgan Stanley, 2006.
2. http://www.industryweek.com, Article ID 12125.
3. For example, see http://www.forwardair.com
4. Figures relating to the development of transportation infrastructure in China suggest that in the 50 years from 1949 to 1999, road length in China increased 16 times, highway and expressways increased by 15 times, and seaport terminals increased by 7.6 times. By the end of 1999, passenger transportation had increased by 100 times that of 1949 and cargo transportation increased 155 times. Adapted from Charles Guowen Wang, *CSCMP Global Perspectives: China* (Oak Brook, IL: Council of Supply Chain Management Professionals, 2006) and the official Web site of the China Ministry of Communications.
5. David Savageau, *Places Rated Almanac* (Foster City, CA: IDG Books Worldwide, 2000).
6. Bert Sperling and Peter Sander, *Cities Ranked and Rated: More Than 400 Metropolitan Areas Evaluated in the U.S. and Canada,* 1st ed. (Hoboken, NJ: Wiley Publishing Company, 2004).
7. *Knoxville News Sentinel* (June 29, 2006): 1.
8. *Investing in Waigaoqiao Free Trade Zone,* Shanghai Waigaoqiao Free Trade Zone United Development Co., Ltd., 2005.
9. Ronald H. Ballou, *Business Logistics Management,* 3rd ed. (Englewood Cliffs, NJ: Prentice-Hall, 1992): 297.
10. Richard F. Powers, "Optimization Models for Logistics Decisions," *Journal of Business Logistics* 10, No. 1 (1989): 106.
11. SAILS™: Strategic Analysis of Integrated Logistics Systems (Manassas, VA: Insight, Inc., 2006).
12. Ibid.
13. Ibid.
14. Robert E. Shannon, *Systems Simulation: The Art and Science* (Englewood Cliffs, NJ: Prentice-Hall, 1975): 1.
15. Frederick S. Hillier and Gerald J. Lieberman, *Introduction to Operations Research,* 3rd ed. (San Francisco, CA: Holden-Day, Inc., 1980): 643.
16. For an excellent overview of simulation modeling, see Donald J. Bowersox and David J. Closs, "Simulation in Logistics: A Review of Present Practice and a Look to the Future," *Journal of Business Logistics* 10, No. 1 (1989): 133–148.
17. Ronald H. Ballou, "Logistics Network Design: Modeling and Informational Considerations," *The International Journal of Logistics Management* 6, No. 2 (1995): 47.
18. For additional examples and a comprehensive perspective on heuristic modeling, see Ronald H. Ballou, "Heuristics: Rules of Thumb for Logistics Decision Making," *Journal of Business Logistics* 10, No. 1 (1989): 122–132.
19. Donald H. Ratliff and William G. Nulty, *Logistics Composite Modeling* (Atlanta, GA: Ratliff & Nulty, 1996): 38.
20. The content of this section has been adapted from Paul S. Bender, "How to Design an Optimum Supply Chain," *Supply Chain Management Review* (Spring 1997): 79–80.
21. Portions of this section are adapted from Edward J. Taaffe and Howard L. Gauthier Jr., *Geography of Transportation* (Englewood Cliffs, NJ: Prentice-Hall, 1973): 41–43.
22. Margaret Gordetsky, "Ryder Puts Customers in the Foreign Trade Zone," *Transport Topics* (August 28, 2000): 26.
23. Trade Information Center, http://www.ia.ita.doc.gov/ftzpage/tic.html
24. http://www.expansionmanagement.com/cmd/articledetail/articleid/15924/default.asp
25. Ibid.

CASE 12-1

Johnson & Johnson

Healthcare consumer packaged goods giant Johnson & Johnson's (J&J) European operations were comprised of 12 distribution centers in seven countries. The company's initial analysis showed there was little or no consolidation among facilities. The facilities had high operational costs (U.S. $10 million+), but transportation costs were relatively low (U.S. $6 million+). The distribution centers were geographically located to help meet the specific needs and service expectations of their European customers. Since J&J is always on the lookout for ways to streamline and improve its supply chain practices, it was very interested in ways to improve its manufacturing and distribution activities in Europe.

An initial result of applying the network optimization software was a reduction in the number of distribution centers from 12 to 2. Although this scenario was accompanied by increases in the transportation costs to customer locations, overall systems costs decreased by U.S. $7 million. Given the strategic importance of maintaining acceptably high levels of customer service, however, it was important to incorporate the requirement of retaining reasonable customer service levels (i.e., one-day service for some customers, with two-day service for others) into the formulation of the network optimization model. In addition, it also was necessary for the model to consider factors such as the expense of long-term leases, etc.

Subsequently, a network optimization model that responded to the issues discussed above was developed and utilized. The end result included a reduction in the number of distribution centers from 12 to 5, which translated into a decrease in facility costs from U.S. $10.1 million to U.S. $3.9 million. Although transportation costs increased slightly—from U.S. $6.6 million to U.S. $7.6 million, the overall network experienced a system savings of approximately U.S. $5 million. At the same time, the optimized network was able to meet customer service objectives such as those outlined above.

CASE QUESTIONS

1. What factors help to explain why J&J historically had as many as 12 distribution centers in Europe?
2. What steps in the logistics/supply chain network design process discussed in this chapter would have been most relevant to the task faced by J&J in Europe?
3. Are there other factors the network optimization study should have considered?
4. This case study focuses on the shipments from distribution centers to customer locations. What factors on the supply side, or inbound-to-DC-side, would be relevant to the analysis that was conducted?

Source: Adapted from Insight, Inc., (2006). Used with permission.

CASE 12-2

Fireside Tire Company

Fireside Tire Company, a manufacturer of radial tires for sport utility vehicles, sells its products in the automotive aftermarket and distributes them throughout the United States. Fireside has three tire production plants located in Allentown, Pennsylvania; Toledo, Ohio; and Macomb, Illinois (see map). Normally, Fireside ships tires from its plants to distribution centers, but truckload-size purchases typically are transported directly from plants to customer locations. All shipments to a region move under truckload rates applying to a minimum weight of 40,000 pounds, or 400 cwt.

Fireside management is concerned about the most economical location for a distribution center to serve its southeastern region, consisting of North Carolina, South Carolina, Georgia, Florida, Mississippi, Alabama, and southeastern Tennessee. Although an Atlanta distribution center currently serves this region, Fireside management is concerned that the Atlanta location is not the most logistically sound alternative.

To help the logistics department conduct an analysis of this region's distribution center location using the grid method, Fireside's transportation department developed the following data based on projections for 2008:

2008 SHIPMENTS TO ATLANTA				GRID COORDINATES	
FROM	CWT	RATE/CWT	MILEAGE	HORIZONTAL	VERTICAL
Toledo	15,000	$2.20	640	1,360	1,160
Macomb	5,000	2.43	735	980	1,070
Allentown	11,000	2.52	780	1,840	1,150

2008 SHIPMENTS FROM ATLANTA		GRID COORDINATES	
TO	CWT	HORIZONTAL	VERTICAL
Chattanooga	2,700	1,350	650
Atlanta	3,500	1,400	600
Tampa	4,300	1,570	220
Birmingham	2,800	1,260	580
Miami	5,300	1,740	90
Jacksonville	5,100	1,600	450
Columbia	2,200	1,600	650
Charlotte	2,900	1,590	740
Raleigh/Durham	2,200	1,700	800

The transportation department also determined that total freight expenditures from the Atlanta distribution center during 2007 were $217,000 and that the average shipment distance was 330 miles.

CASE QUESTIONS

1. Based on the available information, is Atlanta the best location for a distribution center to serve the southeastern region? If not, what would you recommend?
2. The Fireside transportation department projects a 25 percent rate increase in 2010 from all of its transportation providers. How will this affect the southeastern location?
3. Marketing anticipates that the Raleigh/Durham market will grow by 3,000 cwt in 2011, and that Fireside will serve the growth from Allentown. How will this affect Atlanta as a location?

Chapter 3

GLOBAL DIMENSIONS OF SUPPLY CHAINS

Learning Objectives

After reading this chapter, you should be able to do the following:

- Describe the scope of a global company's supply chain network and understand what questions are appropriate for the network to function on a competitive basis.
- Understand the three major phases of globalization.
- Appreciate the complexity and magnitude of the operations of some successful global companies and why global expansion is important to their growth.
- Explain how technology and service specialists can help companies, especially small- to medium-size firms, penetrate the global marketplace.
- Appreciate the importance and magnitude of the trading partner countries of the United States.
- Understand the nature of global markets and competitive strategy.
- Explain the rationale for global security measures and the balance necessary to ensure that such security measures do not impede trade.
- Discuss global transportation options and strategic intermediaries.

Supply Chain Profile — *Red Fish, Blue Fish, LLP*

Fran Fisher was contemplating a significant career and business change. Basically, he was considering changing a hobby into a new business venture. For many years, he had been involved in the media communications business. While his specialty was in radio promotions and advertising, he had experience in television not only with promotions and advertising but also as a TV "personality" as a broadcaster of college sports events. He developed a small media consulting company which was located in Greensburg, Pennsylvania, about 30 miles from Pittsburgh.

Fran had always been interested in exotic fish and had several large display tanks in his office suite and at home in his study. He purchased fish mostly through a Pittsburgh wholesaler/distributor that also sold to selected individuals. He had also bought some fish through catalog offerings, and more recently, he had made some purchases from China via the Internet.

Several of Fran's friends had been asking his advice about buying exotic fish and the necessary equipment to have a setup like he has in his office. He had even been contacted by a local dentist who was having his office remodeled. The dentist, Andy Zimmerman, had read in the trade magazine for dentists that fish tanks were becoming popular as decorations and seemed to have a soothing impact on patients, especially children. Andy even offered to pay Fran a consulting fee for his initial advice on fish purchases and wanted him to consider doing the whole setup—buying fish and equipment and installing the tanks with appropriate compensation to follow.

Fran's media consulting business was declining, and he was concerned about the future. New Internet options such as YouTube, Facebook, and others were changing the media business, especially for small companies in small market areas. He needed to change his consulting business in some way or look for new opportunities. He decided to take advantage of Andy's offer and developed a three-phase proposal—selection of types and quantity of fish, purchase and setup of tanks and related equipment, and regular cleaning and maintenance of the tanks. Fran thought that his proposal might be too high priced, but Andy accepted the whole package and seemed pleased with the price that was proposed.

SIX MONTHS LATER

Andy's office was all set up, and he seemed very pleased overall. Fran received some inquiries from other local businesses and decided to pursue this new venture at least on a part-time basis initially. His wife, Charlotte, had expressed an interest in helping with the fish business with the exception of cleaning tanks. Fran had purchased Andy's fish and all the supporting equipment from China. He was actually surprised at how easy it was to search for suppliers via the Internet and the cost savings of buying from distributors in China. His nephew, Eric Lynch, was a logistics graduate of Penn State, and he had worked in the transportation business for many years. Eric advised Fran to use Federal Express, which turned out to be a very good recommendation.

Fran's Internet surfing also exposed him to some U.S. Web sites offering exotic fish for sale. He was surprised at the differential between the prices he had paid to purchase Andy's fish in China and what the domestic Web sites were charging for comparable fish. He thought the differential would provide him enough margin to make a profit on sales in the United States and even sales in Canada and Europe if he could develop a good Web site to display fish and related equipment.

Now it was time to address some basic issues about this new business venture. Eric was interested in joining the business to provide logistics and supply chain expertise. Charlotte had become proficient with handling purchases from China and other sources. Fran felt that his media experience would enable him to develop a good Web site for his new business, which he decided should be called Red Fish, Blue Fish. He was, however, concerned about working capital and cash flow.

Andy had offered to invest in the company when Fran told him about the new business. Eric believed that they could base their business model on Dell's approach. If they took orders via the Internet and immediately contacted their Chinese suppliers they could use overnight air freight delivery, which would minimize their inventory and the need for working capital. Fran felt that they could operate the business from his current offices. He also felt that business sales, like the one he did for Andy, could be quite lucrative, and the ongoing monthly maintenance fee would help his cash flow situation. He was even considering a collaborative arrangement with a local contractor, Jim Beierlein, who would do office and business installations since some remodeling was usually required. Also, Jim could help him with some of the special packaging if he had sales in Europe or Canada.

Introduction

Globalization was identified in Chapter 1 as being one of, if not *the* leading, external factors driving change of the economic landscape for not only for-profit companies but also for not-for-profit organizations. Global trading has been with us for centuries, but the scope and magnitude of the product, information, and financial flows today are almost mind boggling. For example, the value of trade between the United States and China has grown from $285 billion in 2005 to $343 billion in 2006, which represents a 20 percent increase in one year. This is indicative of the importance of global trade flows in the world economy and, in particular, to the U.S. economy.[1]

It has been argued that globalization was initially driven by countries (1400–1800) seeking materials and goods not available in their own land, but they also had imperialistic objectives of enhancing their economic and political power. The second era of globalization (1800–2000) was driven by companies seeking goods and materials, labor, economies of scale, and markets. This era produced multinational companies with global reach and enormous economic market power.[2]

The development and growth of large multinational companies really moved the world toward globalization. These companies were the ones that initially asked the following global questions first posed in Chapter 1:

- Where in the world should we procure or purchase raw materials, semi-finished materials, components, services, etc.?
- Where in the world should we locate plants and/or supporting facilities to produce products and/or services to meet customer demand?
- Where in the world should we market and sell our products and/or services?
- Where in the world should we store and/or distribute our products or services?
- What global transportation and communication alternatives should we consider and use?
- What global partnerships or alliances should we establish for collaboration to improve our efficiency and effectiveness?

These questions should not be answered separately. They are too interrelated or synergistic and require the evaluation of alternative scenarios to answer all the questions for the optimal or best alternatives.

The scope of these questions provides an insight into the nature of being truly global. The established, successful multinational companies also created opportunities for smaller organizations to participate in the global marketplace as they "fine-tuned" their "business models" to improve efficiency and effectiveness. For example, the multinationals could purchase component parts needed for the finished products from a variety of sources in different countries. This became a common practice for auto and computer manufacturers. Companies, such as Nike, outsourced all of their manufacturing. The complexity of global trade sometimes required specialists not only in transportation but also in more specialized areas such as customs and tariffs. Such arrangements led to growing collaboration in the various supply chains.

In the second phase of globalization, companies headquartered in developed countries like the United States, Western Europe, Japan, etc., had an advantage in terms of infrastructure, educational systems, capital markets, etc. It has been suggested that the world was, figuratively speaking, tilted in favor of the developed countries. The economic advantage was such that the citizenry of the less-developed countries tended to migrate to the more developed countries, especially the United States. The well-educated and skillful immigrants added to the advantages enjoyed by the developed countries.[3]

The third era of globalization is said to have begun around the year 2000. The significant characteristic of this era is that it is being powered by individuals and smaller organizations in contrast to the countries of the first era and the large companies of the second era.[4] The critical ingredients for this new era have been the technological advances, especially in information technology and communications, which have connected the "four corners of the globe." Thus, with the enabling of more broad-based participation in the global economy without some of the massive infrastructure previously required, the world has indeed become flat. Again, the large, multinational companies have created "niche" opportunities for individuals and/or small organizations to collaborate in their supply chains.

One of the outcomes of this new global era is an "attack" on traditional, hierarchical organizational structures.[5] Businesses are being transformed into flatter, more horizontal, and more collaborative organizations that participate in more supply chains to add value and efficiency for consumers worldwide.

Chapter 1 argued that the rate of change has accelerated and is being fueled by a number of major external forces or change drivers. The synergism between globalization and technology, especially, has permanently changed the dynamics of the world's marketplace. The outcry in some quarters about outsourcing is 40 years too late and may be misguided. This new era has and will continue to spotlight supply chains as a critical part of the ability of organizations to compete economically, and it deserves special discussion.

Supply Chains in a Global Economy

In Chapter 1, a supply chain was depicted as being boundary spanning; that is, it encompasses a group of interrelated firms that should be focused on delivering the best "price/value" products and services to the ultimate customer at the end of the supply

On the Line — *Adapting to Operating in Low-Cost Regions*

Including low-cost regions in modern supply chains is now a given. But determining which regions to access for any particular purpose is still as much art as science. Ongoing discussions with key industry contacts suggest that different locations, countries, and regions have their own specific strengths (and weaknesses), and, even more importantly, regional positions shift over time.

Tracking and responding to the relative positions of low-cost regions will be an ongoing theme for global supply chain managers. Five years ago, China was *the* source for low-cost products; now, Vietnam is competing against inland China and parts of India for that same position. In terms of the importance of market proximity, whether to the United States, Europe, or emerging urban markets in India and China, it becomes even more necessary to understand how an area's character fits with a firm's global supply chain strategies.

How can buyers discover where to source materials, components, subassemblies, and finished goods? What makes a particular area attractive, and how long will it be before the next "hot" region appears on the horizon? How does a region structure itself to join the world economy in a mode that means sustainable growth and improvement for its citizens for years to come? These issues are on the agenda (or destined to be so) of supply and logistics managers all over the world.

Supply chain managers are now operating in a global business ecology. As the overseers of physical movements in the new economy, they face challenges within countries, between countries, and across regions. Researchers and managers need to cooperate so that everybody has the tools and insight needed to support continued economic success in a world where borders are still real, but transcending borders is the order of the day.

Source: Arnold Maltz, Arizona State University, *World Trade Magazine* (January 1, 2007).

chain. The supply chain also should manage three important flows, namely, materials/products, information, and financials. The best supply chains compete very successfully on a national and/or global basis.

Wal-Mart is frequently cited for its supply chain efficiency and effectiveness and rightly so. Consider, for example, that a computer manufacturer such as Hewlett-Packard will sell over 400,000 computers in one day through over 4,000 Wal-Mart stores to customers worldwide during the Christmas season. Each of the computers has component parts from a number of global providers, and the computers are usually assembled in several global locations. The synchronization of the three flows mentioned above that allows this to happen almost seamlessly is an amazing accomplishment.

Consider also that Americans spend over $35 million per hour, 24 hours per day, 365 days of the year in Wal-Mart stores, and the stores stock over 65,000 different items a year.[6] None of the above is meant to imply that the supply chains that Wal-Mart is a part of operate perfectly each and every time. In other words, Wal-Mart stores do experience shelf stockouts at times (hence the use of rain checks) or overstocks of some stock-keeping units (SKUs) occasionally.[7] However, considering the length and complexity of some of its supply chains, it minimizes such happenings using the tools, technology, and management skills discussed in this text.

The net effect of Wal-Mart's success with supply chain management has enabled it, as indicated in Chapter 1, to become the largest corporation in the world as measured by sales dollars of over $350 billion per year. Other companies have also been successful based to some extent on the efficiency and effectiveness of their supply chains, e.g., Apple, Dell, Procter & Gamble (P&G), IBM, Johnson & Johnson, General Electric, Kimberly-Clark, etc.

These companies and others have transformed themselves by changing their supply chains and their business models, which, in turn, has significantly changed the business landscape in the twenty-first century. Consider, for example, that some U.S. companies derive over 25 percent of their profit from global sales, which helps to mitigate declines or instability in domestic markets.

Adam Smith, who is credited with providing the economic rationale for capitalism in his famous book, *Wealth of Nations*, stated that division of labor or labor specialization is limited by the extent of the market or volume of demand.[8] In other words, economies and companies could improve their "wealth" by allowing specialization of tasks. The automobile assembly line is a good example of specialization wherein each individual performs a small task relative to the total product, but the output per individual is higher than if individuals each assembled a complete car. Smith's caveat, which is very relevant here, indicates that the advantage is true as long as you can sell the increased volume that is produced. We argued in 1976, in our first edition of this text, that an important role of logistics was to help extend the market area of countries or companies through improved efficiency to lower the "landed cost" in new market areas.

The logic of the rationale stated above is even more apropos for supply chains. It can be argued that supply chains help to establish the limits of what is competitively possible in the market. In other words, the cost and value at the end of the supply chain determine a firm's ability to compete in a marketplace. Good supply chains are "business power," and good supply chain managers are continually pushing the "limits" of their supply chains to be viable in both domestic and global markets.

Operating globally has become easier to accomplish for even individuals and small companies, as stated previously, because of the advances in information/communications technology and the continuing improvement of specialists such as UPS, FedEx, DHL, etc., that can provide global supply chain services at a very reasonable cost. A growing number of specialists and continuing improvements in information technology/communications are contributing to the flattening of the world. Obviously, large global companies are also contributing to this phenomenon.

It is safe to conclude that supply chains and supply chain management play an important role in the global economy and have helped to push the growth and success of companies that do "supply chaining" very well. The "train (globalization) is out of the station" and rolling down the tracks at increasing speed. Global supply chains impact all of us. We love the lower prices, the increased array of products, and the convenience (read 24/7, one-stop shopping, etc.), but we are critical of some of the outcomes when individuals lose their jobs, businesses are closed, etc. Many would argue that the advantages outweigh the disadvantages, e.g., the lower prices have saved consumers billions of dollars in purchase prices. There are tradeoffs (advantages and disadvantages), but there is no turning back. Successful organizations will continue to need effective and efficient supply chain management as they move ahead aggressively in the twenty-first century. The following chapters will address how such success can be accomplished.

In the next several sections of this chapter, we will discuss the magnitude of global operations and supply chains as well as some of the challenges and types of global supply chain services.

The Scope and Magnitude of Global Business

In Chapter 1, the concept of the world collapsing in terms of time and distance was presented. Obviously, the distance between New York City and Shanghai, China, is still the same, and these cities have not changed time zones. However, transportation, communications, and computer-related technology are making it much more convenient for business executives from different countries to meet face to face or via special information technology. The ability to connect to individuals and companies across the globe and to connect computer information systems on a 24/7 basis has provided unparalleled opportunity for collaboration horizontally and vertically in supply chains. This connectivity has allowed the type of interorganizational cooperation, visibility of flows, and real time adjustments necessary for efficient and effective supply chains.

The global data presented in this section reflect this new era. Table 3-1 presents trade data (total of imports and exports) for the top 10 U.S. trading partners. Some interesting and important relationships depicted in Table 3-1 should be noted. China is now our second largest trading partner, supplanting Mexico, which historically has been number 2. The trade volume with China was 18.2 percent of the total of the top 10 for 2006, and it increased its trade volume by 20 percent from 2005 to 2006. In 2000, China was number 4 on the top 10 list following Canada, Mexico, and Japan, and its trade volume with the United States has tripled since that time ($343 billion vs. $94 billion). This increase reflects the comments made previously about the growing importance of China. The total value of trade with these top 10 trading partners ncreased by 10.7 percent from 2005 to 2006, and since 2000 it has increased by about 53 percent in total value. Both of these percentage increases are reflective of the growing interdependence and the trade relationships with other countries. The data lend additional creditability to statements made previously about the importance of global supply chains.

India was mentioned in Chapter 1 in the context of globalization but does not appear in the top 10 countries listed in Table 3-1. India's strength has been in the area of information technology services, which tends to understate its importance for global supply chains. In 2005, 59 percent of U.S. corporate spending (off-shore) for information technology services was spent in India.[9] Interestingly, China, which is known for manufacturing various types of products, is attracting U.S. companies to establish research centers. Microsoft and Intel established research centers in Beijing in 1998, Google in 2005, and Rohm & Haas and Dupont in Shanghai in 2006.[10] The combined population of China and India, which is in excess of 2 billion people, makes them attractive as markets and as a source of imports. Consequently, it seems safe to conclude that global supply chain connections to both China and India will continue to grow. Large U.S. consumer product companies and retailers are already connected with sourcing and selling.

Even smaller companies, such as W. W. Grainger, a distributor of maintenance, repair, and operating (MRO) products, is "connecting" its supply chain to China as a source of products to buy and a market for distributing and selling its other products.

Table 3-1 Top U.S. Trading Partners

	Value of Trade ($ billions)	
Country	**2005**	**2006**
Canada	$ 499	$ 534
China	285	343
Mexico	290	332
Japan	194	208
Germany	119	130
United Kingdom	90	99
South Korea	72	78
Taiwan	56	61
France	57	61
Singapore	44	43
Total	$1,706	$1,889

Source: U.S. Bureau of the Census, Foreign Trade Statistics, 2007.

Challenges and risks are associated with doing business with or in China and India, but the opportunities are enormous. Companies will change their business models because of these opportunities. Consider the partnership between IBM and Lenovo for IBM's personal computer business or Honda Motor in India which has used different partnering strategies for different product lines.

Once risks are identified, leading companies use a variety of strategies to manage them. These risk mitigation strategies are selectively applied depending on the impact and probability of each risk. Evidence is building that those firms that apply a rigorous risk management methodology are much more likely to see the promised benefits from a global outsourcing strategy, as well as realize the payback from their overarching globalization strategy.

Global Markets and Strategy

The global business environment has changed significantly and become much more conducive to business activity between and among different countries. Companies are not just importing and exporting products but are also locating plants and other facilities in other parts of the world. Honda and Toyota used to produce cars in Japan and ship them to the United States. Now their cars are, for the most part, produced in the United States for sale in North America. U.S. companies have also located plants in other countries.

As indicated in Chapter 1, tariffs and other trade barriers have been significantly reduced among many countries, allowing a much more competitive global economy.

On the Line — *Managing the Risk Inherent in Global Outsourcing*

Many firms see globalization as much more than outsourcing. Additionally, they regard its essence as being to establish a market presence in other regions of the world and to serve as an engine for growth. Globalization in this context thus means leveraging various regions of the world for potential in several areas, which include establishing a presence in the global market for growth, resource access, and cost savings.

Of course, outsourcing is frequently a key component of the globalization strategy. But all too often the risk inherent in outsourcing decisions is not effectively assessed or managed, putting the firm's business in jeopardy.

Unfortunately, many firms have not placed their outsourcing strategy within the context of a complete global strategic plan. Invariably, pressure is exerted from the top to reduce direct, visible cost. This quickly evolves into an outsourcing strategy to take advantage of the incredible pool of low-cost labor in other regions of the world, particularly in Asia, Latin America, and Eastern Europe.

When pursuing an outsourcing strategy, it is hard for many companies to stop and consider risks because they are blinded by the huge savings potential. A couple of years ago, on a tour of seven factories in South China, the authors saw some shocking examples of where these savings are coming from (and the long-term risk therein embodied), including the following:

- Factory workers routinely working 11 hours per day, six days per week for roughly $100 per month
- An extremely intense work pace
- Competent engineers earning a maximum of $12,000 per year

In a typical financial analysis, this incredible labor cost savings is balanced with higher inventory and transportation costs. But many companies are just now realizing that risk might be the greatest potential cost.

What are the risks associated with global outsourcing? A few examples include catastrophic delays in delivery due to force majeure or even terrorism, quality and damage problems hidden by a long supply line, highly inaccurate forecasts over a long supply line, currency swings, and intellectual property issues.

Are these risks causing an outsourcing backlash? There's no clear trend. For example, one company discussed withdrawing from China, while another firm described taking everything to China. What makes the difference between success and failure? We would argue that the difference is in having a rigorous approach to analyzing and managing outsourcing risk.

Source: J. Paul Dittmann, Ph.D., University of Tennessee, *World Trade Magazine* (January 1, 2007).

This represents both a threat and an opportunity. Like deregulation of transportation, some companies have not really responded well and have lost market share or gone out of business. Other companies have taken advantage of the opportunity and expanded aggressively into global markets, e.g., General Electric, IBM, Wal-Mart, McDonald's, P&G, Kimberly-Clark, etc. Many *Fortune* 500 companies experience 50 percent or more of their sales in global markets. Such sales have helped these companies stabilize their revenues and buffet them against turbulent times in the U.S. marketplace, such as occurred in 2007.[11] Small- and medium-sized companies have also been able to be players in global markets, even a company like Red Fish, Blue Fish, LLP.

Success in the global marketplace, obviously, requires developing a cohesive set of strategies including product development, technology, marketing, manufacturing, and supply chains. Global companies tend to be more successful when their strategies help them to simultaneously achieve their business objectives at their various global locations. From a supply chain perspective, this means strategically sourcing materials and components worldwide, selecting global locations for key supply depots and distribution centers, evaluating transportation alternatives and channel intermediaries, providing customer service, understanding governmental influences on global supply chain flows, examining opportunities for collaboration with third- or fourth-party logistics companies, and other supply chain issues. We will discuss some of these topics in this chapter, and the remainder will be covered in subsequent chapters. A topic that merits special consideration is supply chain security, which will be discussed subsequently in this chapter.

From a customer service perspective, global markets and strategy have four important characteristics. First, companies want to standardize to reduce complexity, but they recognize that global markets need some customization. For example, in contrast to the U.S. market where large retail stores buy in volume quantities for delivery to their large warehouses, third-world countries have tiny retail stores that may only be 80 to 100 square feet. This means deliveries of small quantities, more frequent deliveries, different packaging, etc. P&G recently has made changes in its customer service strategy and related areas to customize for these markets. P&G recognizes that the population base is such in these countries that the total volume of sales will offset some of the lower economies of scale at the tiny stores. Customer service levels have to be adjusted for these markets in terms of delivery schedules, volumes, order fulfillment, and other areas.

Second, global competition reduces the product life cycle, as previously mentioned, since products can be copied or reengineered quickly by competitors. Technology companies are faced with this phenomenon even in the U.S. market, but other products are faced with similar experiences. Technology companies counteract with continual upgrades and new products. Apple, for example, had great success with its iPod, but it quickly followed this with the iPhone to maintain financial momentum. Shorter product life cycles present challenges for inventory management with respect to obsolete items. Customer service levels are also impacted because changes have to be made as the product matures in terms of sales volume and then declines, which reduces product profitability. Usually, companies cannot afford to provide the same level of customer service when the product volume declines.

Third, traditional organizational structures and related business models frequently change since companies get more involved in outsourcing manufacturing and some logistical activities such as transportation, warehousing, and order fulfillment. All of this impacts the supply chain and its related customer service activities. The collaboration indicated requires effective coordination among the various parties to ensure that customer service levels (on-time delivery, complete orders, reliability, etc.) are maintained. There are many challenges for supply chain managers.

Fourth, globalization introduces more volatility, as noted in Chapter 1. It is much more likely that supply chains will experience challenges with weather, terrorism, strikes, etc. The need for flexibility and responsiveness is a requisite for customer service through the supply chain. The expanded networks cover long distances and are complex.

In addition to the four areas indicated above, some of the customary strategies used in the domestic market are also challenged. Reduced order cycle time, for example, has become an important part of supply chain management since it can lead to lower inventory levels for customers, improved cash flow, and lower current assets/accounts receivable. The increased length and complexity of the supply chain make it more difficult to achieve shorter lead times.

Also, demand-driven supply or pull systems that can lower inventory levels significantly are challenged by the longer distance and complexity of multi-layered supply chains. Other strategies such as compression and "lean" supply chains are also more difficult to achieve in the global environment. None of this discussion is meant to imply that companies should not be involved in globalization. Rather it is meant to provide understanding of the challenges necessary to improve the likelihood of success. Without a doubt, globalizing has helped many U.S. companies as previously noted. Much higher sales and profits and more revenue stability are some of the advantages that have been pointed out thus far, but globalization is a two-edged sword that requires a company to be nimble and continually proactive in managing and responding to change. The topic of the next section, global supply chain security, ties in directly with this discussion of global supply chain strategy.

Supply Chain Security: A Balancing Act

Global commerce between the United States and the rest of the world came to a halt on September 11, 2001, when terrorists attacked the United States. Air transportation into and out of the United States and even some domestic flights were suspended. Ocean vessels loaded with containers and other freighter ships were prevented from unloading or loading in the major ports. Many had to anchor off the coast for days, waiting to come into the assigned port. Fresh fruits and vegetables rotted, and needed materials did not arrive on time. It was a frightening period but a time when we saw firsthand how global and interdependent with the rest of the world we had become.[12]

Before the events of September 11, 2001, ships would frequently clear U.S. ports in a matter of hours. That scenario has changed because of security measures that have been introduced. More cargo inspections, much more paperwork, and a longer time to clear U.S. borders are now a reality. Ships may be stopped and inspected and cargo inspected and checked. Some ships and items are given very close scrutiny because of their country of origin.[13]

Given the importance of global trade to the United States, a delicate balance exists between security and the efficient flow of global commerce. If security is too tight it could impede the flow of needed goods or materials, causing delays and decreased efficiency. Ports and border gateways can become congested because of security measures. Consequently, clearance time has increased from hours to days in some instances. Steps have been taken to improve the flow through border crossing.[14] This is necessary for our global economy.

Electronic filing of cargo information has helped to improve the border clearance times. The Trade Act of 2002 requires exporters to electronically submit shipping documents to U.S. Customs 24 hours after delivery to a port or 24 hours before vessel departure. For imports, the manifest must be filed by the ocean carrier or the consolidator 24 hours before the U.S.-bound cargo is loaded on the vessel in the foreign port.

Supply Chain Technology — *Zara Shows How*

Zara, the Spanish fashion leader, is an excellent example of a company that has implemented two different operations models for two different market needs. The industry's fastest growing company, Zara launches more than 11,000 new designs each year. The company has crafted a model in which product development takes three to five weeks, as opposed to the industry average of nine months; new product introductions arrive in stores every two to three weeks on average.

Because short life cycle fashions represent the bulk of Zara's sales and profits, the company deploys an onshore, rapid-response supply model based on quick feedback from stores. Each store manager tracks customer opinion using a handheld device and relays the information to the regional manager, who passes the regional data to the product-development team, which can quickly come up with a new design that meets current trends.

For this core model, the company uses mainly onshore manufacturers in Spain and Portugal, although its number of suppliers in Asia is increasing to serve growing demand in the Far East. The company books manufacturing capacity in advance, committing to make a certain number of blouses before it knows the colors and styles. The combination of instantly relaying customer insights and booking onshore capacity in advance means Zara can have new products on store shelves within weeks of the moment a store manager detects a fashion trend. Stores in Europe, the Americas, and Asia are replenished, on average, twice a week; the average product shelf life is two to three weeks.

However, for basic products like t-shirts and underwear—products that collectively make up less than 30 percent of revenues—Zara relies on low-cost offshore or near-shore manufacturers in countries such as China and Morocco. That basic-product group's larger orders, relatively predictable demand, and long shelf life make it possible to source from those lower-cost locales.

Source: Jaume Ferrer, Johan Karlberg, and Jamie Hintland, "Integration: The Key to Global Success," *Supply Chain Management Review* (March 2007): 29

Because of Canada's importance as a trading partner, an expedited procedure (FAST) has been developed to speed up clearance through the U.S.-Canadian border.[15]

The U.S. Coast Guard was authorized by the U.S. Maritime Transportation Security Act of 2002 to assess the vulnerability of U.S. ports and to deny entry to ships from countries that do not meet U.S. security standards. This act requires the development of standards for container seals and locks, cargo tracking, identification, and screening systems for ocean containers.[16] Some of these requirements have been slow in developing to meet standards.

In addition, the Customs Trade Partnership Against Terrorism (C-TPAT) was established under the direction of the U.S. Department of Homeland Security in November 2001. This voluntary initiative to secure the global supply chain was started with seven companies; by 2007, some 7,400 corporations were involved in this cooperative effort to secure the global supply chain and to facilitate legitimate cargo and conveyance. C-TPAT functions under the U.S. Customs and Border Protection (CBP) Agency, which previously was known as the U.S. Customs Service.

CBP has responsibility for the traditional role of the U.S. Customs Service, namely, preventing illegal entry of people and drugs, protecting agriculture from harmful pests and diseases, protecting the intellectual property of businesses, collecting import duties, and regulating and facilitating global trade. Partner companies in C-TPAT agree to be responsible for keeping their supply chains secure to agreed standards and to implement needed changes. One of the key features of this program is information sharing of best practices for security among members. The goal is to develop a "green lane" to speed goods across the border but also to protect the United States and the global supply chains of the participants.[17]

Ports

As indicated above, ports are a critical part of global supply chains and also a major focus for global security. Every day, thousands of containers from countries all around the world arrive at U.S. seaports. Each shipment is usually for a specific supply chain—for example, porch furniture from Thailand bound for a St. Louis retailer or shoes from China destined for a Chicago distributor.

America's ports are a vital part of its global commerce. Over $2 trillion in trade value per year passes through U.S. ports, and over $18 billion is collected in industry fees and taxes. The 50 states utilize 15 ports to handle their imports and exports; a total of about $5.5 billion worth of goods moves in and out every day. About 99 percent of the international cargo of the United States moves through its ports, or about 2.5 billion tons annually. In 1960, international trade accounted for about 9 percent of U.S. gross domestic product (GDP). Today, it is over 25 percent.[18]

U.S. ports also play a vital role for the cruise industry. In 2005, it was estimated that there were 8.6 million embarkations through U.S. ports, which was an increase of 21 percent from 2003. This flow of passenger traffic has a very positive economic impact on the U.S. economy because of the expenditures to support the cruise industry.[19]

The ports also play a vital role in national defense and security. The ports are bases of operation to deploy troops and equipment. In 2003, the Surface Deployment and Distribution Command loaded 1.6 million tons of equipment and cargo to support the war effort in Iraq. Port security is very important for military and civilian purposes, and it is a shared responsibility between the public and private sectors. C-TPAT is an excellent example of this shared responsibility.

As indicated previously in this chapter, Canada and Mexico are very important trade partners for the United States; they ranked number 1 and 3, respectively, in 2006. These two countries account for about 30 percent of the total U.S. global trade.[20] Given their importance, the next section of this chapter will discuss the **North American Free Trade Agreement (NAFTA).**

North American Free Trade Agreement

The North American Free Trade Agreement was signed by leaders of Canada, the United States, and Mexico in 1993 and was ratified by Congress in early 1994. NAFTA establishes free trade between these three countries and provides the way the agreement is to be interpreted. NAFTA states that the objectives of these three countries is based on the principles of an unimpeded flow of goods, most favored nation (MFN) status, and a commitment to enhance the cross-border movement of goods and services. MFN status provides the lowest duties or customs fees, if any, and simplifies the paperwork required to move goods between the partner countries.

Even though the U.S./Canada Free Trade Agreement has been in effect for some time, certain trade barriers still remain. For example, many U.S. companies do not recognize certain French/English requirements for packaging and ingredient labeling.

Figure 3-1 A Typical Truck Shipment Crossing into Mexico

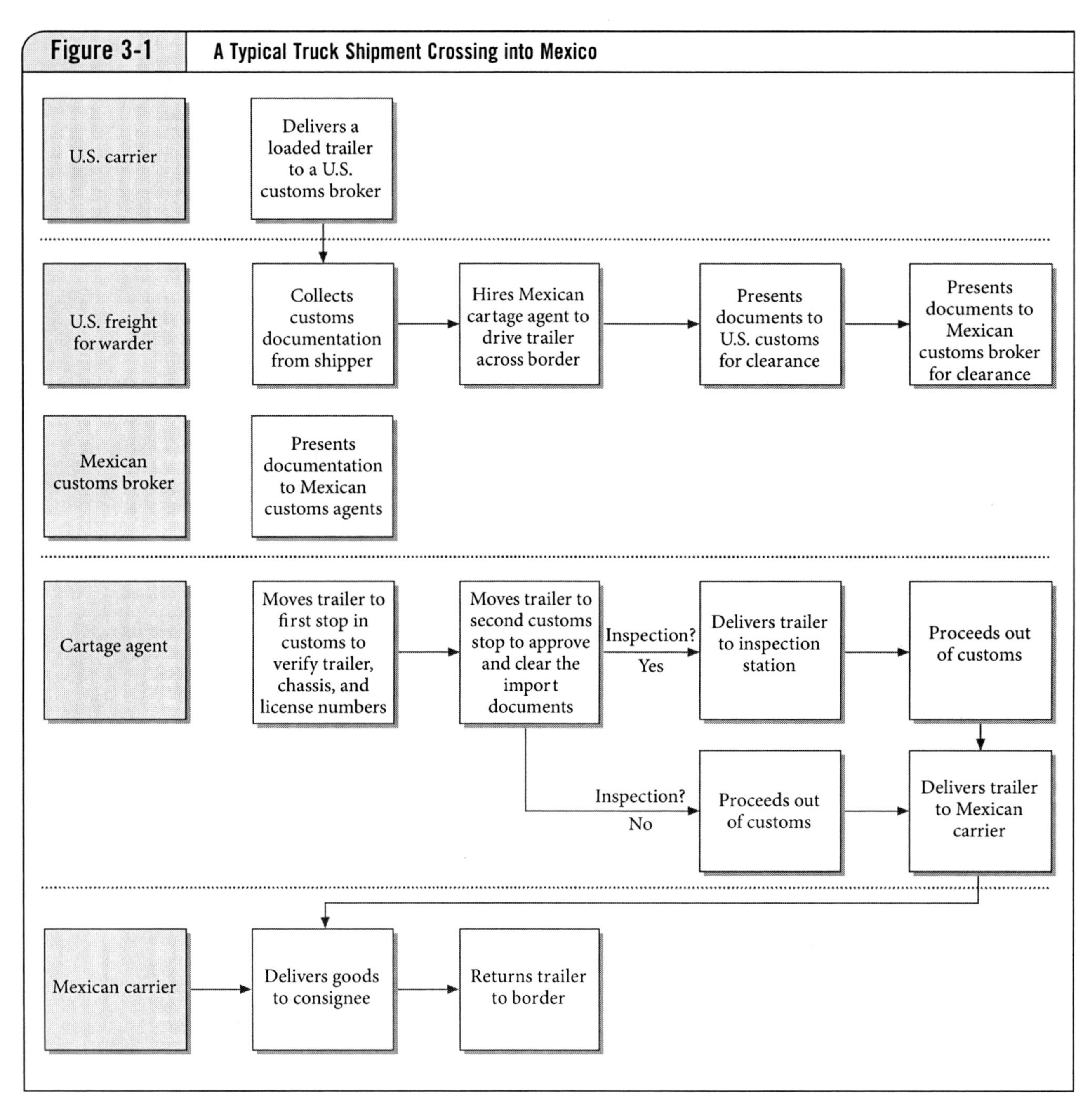

Trade with Mexico also poses some trade constraints that NAFTA did not eliminate. The supply chain barriers include a poor transportation infrastructure, restrictive foreign capital rules, and customs rules. The Mexican highway system is poor when compared to that existing in the United States and Canada. Mexico only has one railroad, which is owned and operated by the government. There are no national less-than-truckload (LTL) trucking companies, and air transportation is limited to the few airports. Foreign trucking companies are restricted from hauling intracountry shipments in all three countries; these are known as **cabotage restrictions**.

Figure 3-1 shows the procedure usually required to move a truck shipment from the United States into Mexico. The U.S. trucking company moves the shipment to the border, where a Mexican cartage carrier hauls the shipment across the border to Mexican customs and to the Mexican carrier after shipment clearance. The U.S. domestic freight forwarder submits shipment documents to the Mexican customs broker, who submits them to Mexican customs. Mexican customs inspects the documents, collects duties, inspects the goods, and clears the shipment. The Mexican cartage carrier delivers the shipment to a Mexican trucking company, which delivers it to the consignee.

The supply chain constraints will eventually be eliminated as NAFTA experience grows. Computerized customs information systems are currently operating in the United States and Canada, with Mexico a few years behind. The electronic transfer of information for NAFTA shipments into Mexico will speed the border crossing and improve logistics service.

In the long run, the goal of NAFTA is to create a better trading environment; but, in the short run, it has created some confusion due to the record keeping required to prove the origin of the product to obtain favorable tariff treatment. NAFTA's goals involve making the needed structural changes to operate a borderless logistics network in North America. Information systems, procedures, language, labels, and documentation are being redesigned. As new markets and supply sources develop, new transportation and storage facilities as well as intermediaries will need to be developed.

Maquiladora Operations

A concept that has become popular among U.S.-based firms is to use Mexican manufacturing/production facilities for subassembly or component manufacturing, or for final assembly of products such as electronic devices or television sets. While this has been occurring for some time, U.S. firms have begun to include such **Maquiladora operations** (named for the region of Mexico in which many of these plant operations are located) as formal components of their manufacturing and supply chain systems.

Essentially, in a Maquiladora operation, a U.S. manufacturer either operates or subcontracts for a manufacturing, processing, or assembly activity to be performed in Mexico. Mexican production and labor costs are lower than those in the United States, and the operations involve no local content issues. U.S. firms often send semifinished product to Mexico for final assembly, for example, and then have the finished product shipped to the United States. This concept appeals to many companies: U.S. manufacturers operate more than 2,000 Maquiladora facilities in Mexico.

One feature that adds to the feasibility of such an approach is the limited tariff duties. The importing, storing, manufacturing, and subsequent export of goods have virtually no net payment of customs duties or import charges. The duties are limited to the value-added portion of the goods, primarily labor, returning from Mexico. Effectively, this contributes to the economic efficiency of supply chain alternatives such as Maquiladora operations.

Successful Mexican Maquiladora operations have served as role models for this concept's further exploitation in Central and South American countries. Coupled with the prospect of closer trade relations between the United States and Mexico, these alternatives offer advantages to the firms utilizing them. There are some constraints in South America because of less than amicable relations with some countries.

Asian Emergence

In perhaps the most significant trend of the past 25 years, Pacific Rim countries have emerged as important players in the global business environment. While Japan has achieved a dominant position in global financial markets, other Asian countries account for significant portions of global trade growth. Hong Kong, South Korea, Singapore, and Taiwan have all assumed leadership positions in certain markets and product types, and they are among the top 10 trading partners of the United States (see Table 3-1). This trend is likely to accelerate in the future.

Many Asian countries have become preferred sources for many raw materials and components. These countries have become trusted suppliers of finished goods such as apparel, furniture, consumer electronics, and automobiles. The advantages many of these countries offer are low labor cost and high quality.

New Directions

Aside from establishing product sources in other countries, global companies are locating plants and key logistics facilities in countries that use or consume their output. For example, Japanese-based firms such as Toyota have located plants in the United States. Similarly, U.S. automobile manufacturers such as Ford and General Motors have located plants in other countries.

Some global manufacturers are using a strategy known as **focus production** in which a given plant produces one or two items of the company's total product line. The plants are typically located in different countries, requiring a global logistics system to tie the focused plant to the customer, who may be located within the producing country or a different country.

An important dimension of any supply chain is transportation links. Transportation can be depicted as the glue that holds the supply chain together. Global supply chains are very dependent upon efficient and effective transportation and the related services of channel intermediaries discussed next.

Global Transportation Options

Global transportation is usually much more complex than domestic U.S. transportation. The distances involved are greater, and the number of parties involved is typically more extensive. Because of the large expanses of water separating most regions of the world, the major modes of global transport are ocean and air. Land modes also carry freight between contiguous countries, particularly in Europe, where land routes are short.

Ocean

Transport by ship is by far the most pervasive and important global shipment method, accounting for two-thirds of all international movements. Ocean transportation's major advantages are low rates and the ability to transport a wide variety of products and shipment sizes. The primary disadvantages include long transit times (slow speed), low accessibility, and higher potential for shipment damage. The pervasive use of containers has reduced damage and increased accessibility via connections with other modes (rail and truck) for inland origins and destinations.

Ocean shipping comprises three major categories. One is **liner service**, which offers scheduled service on regular routes. Another is **charter vessels**, which firms usually hire on a contract basis and which travel no set routes. Finally, **private carriers** can be part of a firm's own supply chain. Table 3-2 contains the top 10 ocean carriers. Note the changes that occurred between 2000 and 2006 in ocean carrier rankings.

Table 3-2 Top 10 Ocean Carriers Ranked by Capacity

OCEAN CARRIER	2000	2006
A. P. Moller	1	1
Mediterrian Shipping Co. (MSC)	5	2
CMA CGM Group	12	3
Evergreen Group	2	4
Hapag-Lloyd	14	5
China Shipping (CSCL)	18	6
APL	6	7
Hanji/Senator	4	8
COSCO Container Line	7	9
NYK	8	10

Source: http://www.supplychainbrain.com.

Liner carriers offer set schedules over specific routes. They also offer set tariffs and accept certain standards of liability. Liners usually carry break-bulk shipments of less-than-shipload size. Most container and roll-on, roll-off (RO-RO) ships are liners.

Liners are operated by large steamship companies, which usually belong to **shipping conferences**. These conferences are voluntary associations of ocean carriers that operate over common trade routes and use a common tariff for setting rates on the commodities they handle. Conferences also work together to attract customers and to utilize member ships as effectively as possible.

In general, conferences provide good service with frequent and reliable schedules, published daily in the *Journal of Commerce.* Additionally, conferences help to standardize shipping on many routes by stabilizing prices and offering uniform contract rates.

Firms contract charter ships for specific voyages and/or for specified time periods. **Voyage charters** are contracts covering one voyage. The carrier agrees to carry a certain cargo from an origin port to a destination. The price the carrier quotes includes all of the expenses of the sea voyage. **Time charters** allow the use of a ship for an agreed-upon time period. The carrier usually supplies a crew as part of the contract. The charterer has exclusive use of the vessel to carry any cargo that the contract does not prohibit and assumes all expenses for the ship's operation during the charter period. **Bareboat** or **demise charter** transfers full control of the vessel to the charterer. The charterer is then responsible for the ship and all expenses necessary for the vessel's operation, including hiring the crew.

Chartering usually takes place through **ship brokers**, who track the location and status of ships that are open for hire. When a shipper needs to contract for a ship, the shipper contacts a broker, who then negotiates the price with the ship owner. The ship owner pays the broker a commission on the charter's cost.

In a logistics system, **private ocean carriers** play the same role as private carriage in general. In other words, companies utilize private ocean vessels to lower their overall costs and/or to improve their control over transportation service. The major differences between domestic and international private ocean transportation are the scale of investment, the complexity of regulations, and the greater risk international transport entails. In international operations, chartering often provides a very viable substitute for private carriage.

Air

The fast transit times that air transport provides have had an impact on global distribution. The speed of airplanes combined with a frequency of scheduled flights has reduced some global transit times from as many as 30 days to 1 or 2 days. These transit times have spurred the development of global freight services. These carriers offer door-to-door, next-day services for packages between most large American cities and a growing number of overseas points.

The world's air carriers have usually focused on passenger service, and air cargo accounts for a small percentage of international freight by weight. However, the nature of the cargo, mostly high-value, low-density items, causes the total value of airfreight cargo to be a greater proportion of the world total. Air cargoes include high-value items such as computers and electronic equipment, perishables such as cut flowers and live seafood, time-sensitive documents and spare parts, and even whole planeloads of cattle for breeding stock. Table 3-3 provides a list of major international cargo air carriers.

Most airfreight travels as **belly cargo** in the baggage holds of scheduled passenger flights. Only a few major airlines have all-freight aircraft.

In addition to short transit time, air transportation offers an advantage in packaging. This mode requires less stringent packaging than ocean transport, since air transport will not expose the shipment to rough handling at a port, to a rough ride on the

Table 3-3	Major International Cargo Air Carriers
Airborne Express	
British Airways	
BAX Global	
DHL Worldwide Express	
Emery Worldwide	
Federal Express	
Japan Airlines	
KLM Royal Dutch Airlines	
Lufthansa	
Singapore Airlines	
United Airlines	
United Parcel Service	

oceans, or to the weather. A firm using air transportation may also be able to use the same packaging for international shipping as for domestic shipping. In addition, shippers have developed special containers for air transport. These containers reduce handling costs and provide protection, but they also make intermodal shipments difficult. Their odd shapes usually require shippers to repack the shipment before transporting it by another mode. Recent container-handling innovations have made it possible to load standard 20-foot containers onto large freight aircraft.

A disadvantage of air carriage is high rates, which have precluded many shippers from transporting international shipments by air. Generally, only highly valuable, highly perishable, or urgently needed commodities can bear the higher cost of airfreight.

Motor

Companies will often use motor transport when shipping goods to an adjacent country—between the United States and Mexico or Canada, for example. It is very common in Europe, where transport distances are relatively short. Motor also plays a large part in intermodal shipments.

The advantages of international motor transport are basically the same as those for domestic shipments: speed, safety, reliability, and accessibility to the delivery site. However, motor shipment across multiple national boundaries involves a number of different import regulations. To minimize paperwork, these shipments are often made **in bond**—the carrier seals the trailer at its origin and does not open it again until it reaches its destination country.

Rail

International railroad use is also highly similar to domestic rail use, but rail's accessibility is much more limited internationally because border crossing points are scarce. Differing track gauges in various countries also prevent long-distance shipments.

Intermodal container shipments by rail are increasing. Various **maritime bridge** concepts involve railroads both for transcontinental shipments and to and from inland points. For example, a shipper using a **land bridge** substitutes land transportation for part of a container's ocean voyage, taking several days off the transit time and saving in-transit inventory costs. A prime example of a land bridge occurs on the trade route between Japan and Europe. The all-water route takes anywhere from 28 to 31 days. If the shipment travels by water from Japan to Seattle (10 days), then by rail to New York (five days), and by water from New York to Europe (seven days), the total shipping time is approximately 22 days.

Strategic Channel Intermediaries

Intermediaries play a much larger role in global supply chain operations than in the domestic United States. The scope of services that intermediaries offer is very comprehensive. Intermediaries play a strategic role in helping new and established companies venture into the global arena. Some companies require assistance in comprehending complex operations involving sources and destinations in other countries.

Foreign Freight Forwarders

For a company with little international shipping expertise, the **foreign freight forwarder** may be the answer. The foreign freight forwarder, which employs individuals who are knowledgeable in all aspects of international shipping, supplies its experts to small international shippers that find employing such individuals in their shipping departments uneconomical. Foreign freight forwarders are regulated by the Federal Maritime Commission.

Foreign freight forwarders, like their domestic counterparts, consolidate small shipments into more economical sizes. In the international arena, these larger sizes range from containers up to entire ships. Foreign freight forwarders also perform the routine actions that shipments require.

Since no two international sales are exactly alike and since shippers have varying international traffic capabilities, the forwarder usually performs the export work that the shipper cannot handle. The supply chain manager must weigh the forwarder's cost against the cost of hiring personnel to perform the same tasks.

The forwarder derives income from different sources. One source is the fees charged for preparing export documentation. Another source is the commissions the forwarder receives from carriers. These commissions are based on the amount of revenue the forwarder generates for the carrier. The third type of income comes from the price difference between the rate the forwarder charges a shipper and the lower rate per pound it pays for the consolidated shipments. The final two sources are from the provision of inland transportation and warehousing functions.

Airfreight Forwarders Airfreight forwarders perform the same functions as surface freight forwarders, but for air shipments only. They do not require a license from the federal government as foreign freight forwarders do. Airfreight forwarders primarily consolidate small shipments, which they present to the air carrier for movement to the destination.

Like the foreign freight forwarder, the airfreight forwarder generates income from fees charged for services provided and the difference between the rate charged the shipper and that paid to the air carrier. The major competitors of airfreight forwarders are the air carriers, who can go directly to the shipper and eliminate the forwarder. For small shipments, air express carriers, such as Federal Express, Emery, UPS Air, and DHL, compete directly with the forwarders.

Non-Vessel-Operating Common Carriers

The **non-vessel-operating common carrier (NVOCC)** consolidates and dispenses containers that originate at or are bound to inland points. The need for these firms arose from the inability of shippers to find outbound turnaround traffic after unloading inbound containers at inland points. Rail and truck carriers often charge the same rate to move containers, whether they are loaded or empty. NVOCCs are regulated by the Federal Maritime Commission.

To reduce these costs, the NVOCC disperses inbound containers and then seeks outbound shipments in the same containers. It will consolidate many containers for multiple-piggyback-car or whole-train movement back to the port for export. It also provides scheduled container service to foreign destinations.

Shippers and receivers of international shipments gain from the shipping expertise that NVOCCs possess and from the expanded and simplified import and export opportunities. The ocean carrier gains from the increased market area made possible by NVOCCs' solicitation services.

Export Management Companies

Often, a firm wishes to sell its products in a foreign market but lacks the resources to conduct the foreign business itself. An **export management company (EMC)** can supply the expertise such firms need to operate in foreign environments.

EMCs act as agents for domestic firms in the international arena. Their primary function is to obtain orders for their clients' products by selecting appropriate markets, distribution channels, and promotional campaigns. The EMC collects and analyzes credit data for foreign customers and advises exporters on payment terms. It also usually collects payments from foreign customers. EMCs may also supply documentation, arrange transportation, provide warehouse facilities, maintain a foreign inventory, and handle break-bulk operations.

A firm can contract with an export management company to provide its exclusive representation in a defined territory. The EMC may either purchase the goods or sell them on commission. In order to present a complete product line to importers, an EMC will usually specialize in a particular product type or in complementary products.

Using an export management company has several advantages. First, EMCs usually specialize in specific markets, so they understand in detail what an area requires. They will have up-to-date information on consumer preferences and will help the exporter to target its products most effectively. Second, EMCs will usually strive to maintain good relations with the governments of importing countries. This enables them to receive favorable customs treatment when introducing new products. EMCs also remain current on documentation requirements. This helps the goods they are importing to enter with few holdups.

Export Trading Companies

An **export trading company (ETC)** exports goods and services. The ETC locates overseas buyers and handles most of the export arrangements, including documentation, inland and overseas transportation, and the meeting of foreign government requirements. The ETC may or may not take title to the goods.

A trading company may also engage in other aspects of foreign trade, in which case it becomes a **general trading company**. One reason Japan has been successful in international trade is because of its large general trading companies, the **sogo shosha**. These firms, which consolidate all aspects of overseas trade into one entity, may include banks, steamship lines, warehouse facilities, insurance companies, sales forces, and communications networks.

A trading company allows small- to medium-size firms, which do not in and of themselves possess the resources, to engage in foreign trade. The trading company purchases their goods and sells them on the international market, taking care of all the intermediate steps. Having all the functional areas under one control makes coordination easy and speeds response time when markets fluctuate.

Customs House Brokers

Customs house brokers oversee the movement of goods through customs and ensure that the documentation accompanying a shipment is complete and accurate for entry into the country. U.S. customs house brokers are licensed by the Department of the Treasury.

Customs house brokers operate under power of attorney from the shipper to pay all import duties due on the shipment. The importer is ultimately liable for any unpaid duties. The brokers keep abreast of the latest import regulations and of the specific requirements of individual products. The next section discusses storage facilities and packaging from a global perspective.

Storage Facilities and Packaging

Storage Facilities

At several points during an international shipment, the goods being shipped may require storage. Storage may be necessary while the shipment waits for loading on an ocean vessel, after it has arrived at the destination port and is awaiting further transportation, or while customs clearance is being arranged for the merchandise. When packaged in a container, goods are protected from the weather, theft, and pilferage. A carrier or shipper can store containers outside between a journey's stages with little effect on the contents.

Noncontainerized cargo, on the other hand, requires protection if it is to arrive in good order. Ports supply several types of storage facilities to fill this need. **Transit sheds**, located next to the piers or at the airport, provide temporary storage while the goods await the next portion of the journey. Usually, the port usage fee includes a fixed number of days of free storage. After this time expires, the user pays a daily charge. **In-transit storage areas** allow the shipper to perform some required operation on the cargo before embarkation. These actions may include carrier negotiations and waiting for documentation, packing, crating, and labeling to be completed. The carrier usually provides **hold-on-dock storage** free of charge until the vessel's next departure date, allowing the shipper to consolidate goods and to save storage costs.

When goods require long-term storage, the shipper uses a warehouse. **Public warehouses** are available for extended storage periods. The services and charges offered by these facilities are similar to those of public warehouses in the domestic sphere, which are discussed in a later chapter.

Bonded warehouses, operated under customs supervision, are designated by the U.S. secretary of the treasury for the purpose of storing, repacking, sorting, or cleaning imported merchandise entered for warehousing without paying import duties while the goods are in storage. Only bonded carriers may move goods into and out of bonded warehouses. Bonded warehouses are very important in global commerce.

One purpose of bonded warehouses is to hold imported goods for reshipment out of the United States. The owner can store items in a bonded warehouse for up to three years, allowing time to decide on the goods' ultimate disposition without having to pay import duties or taxes on them. If the owner does not reexport the goods before the three years elapse, they are considered imports and are subject to all appropriate duties and taxes.

Packaging

Export shipments moving by ocean transportation require more stringent packaging than domestic shipments normally do. An export shipment undergoes more handling: it is loaded at the origin, unloaded at the dock, loaded onto a ship, unloaded from the ship at port, loaded onto a delivery vehicle, and unloaded at the destination. This handling usually occurs under unfavorable conditions—in inclement weather or with antiquated handling equipment, for example. If storage facilities are inadequate, the goods may remain exposed to the elements for a long time.

The shipper may find settling liability claims for damage to export goods very difficult. Usually, the freight handling involves many firms, and these firms are located in different countries. Stringent packaging is the key to claims prevention for export shipments.

SUMMARY

- Companies competing in global supply chains need to address some important questions for their global networks to ensure their efficiency and effectiveness.
- There have been three phases of globalization: the first was driven by countries, the second by large companies, and the third by individuals and small organizations.
- Successful global companies have transformed their supply chains on an ongoing basis to enable them to deliver low cost and high value to the ultimate customer.
- The scope and magnitude of trade flows between the United States and other countries have grown considerably in the last several decades. One interesting development has been the growth in importance of trade with China and several other Asian countries.
- Success in the global marketplace requires developing a cohesive set of strategies with respect to customer service, product development, business model, and overall supply chains.
- Supply chain security has taken on increased importance since September 11, 2001. Companies individually, jointly, and in cooperation with the various levels of government need to be actively involved. The federal government, in particular, has expanded the scope of its regulations and policies for global security.
- U.S. ports play a critical role in global supply chains since over 90 percent of global trade passes through them. Ports are also an important focus for security.
- Canada and Mexico are ranked number 1 and 3, respectively, on the list of most important trading partners with the United States. That relationship is enhanced by the North American Free Trade Agreement ratified by Congress in 1994. While the treaty had lofty goals, it still is experiencing problems with full implementation of its objectives. Nevertheless, it has fostered trade in North America.
- Global supply chains have a number of transportation and related service options available to managers. Each of the options has advantages and disadvantages that need to be analyzed.

STUDY QUESTIONS

1. Globalization has developed in three phases or eras. What are the major differences between today's third phase and the previous two phases? Do you think that there will be a fourth phase? Why or why not?

2. It has been alleged that the world has become flat. What does this description mean from a global economic perspective? What factors have contributed to this phenomenon?

3. A number of authors have observed that traditional, hierarchical organizations have changed in the current global economy. How have organizations changed? Why have they changed?

4. Wal-Mart has frequently been cited for being a successful supply chain company. Why?

5. What special role do supply chains play in the globalization of organizations? Will supply chains continue to be important in the future?

6. What is meant by the current description of the global economy that "time and distance have been collapsed or compressed"? Do you agree? Do you think that our trading relationships will be affected in the future by this phenomenon?

7. Why are customer service and its related strategy so important for companies operating global supply chains?
8. What is meant by the phrase "that supply chain security, especially on a global basis," is a balancing act?
9. Why are ports so important for global supply chains?
10. Discuss the major alternatives for global transportation.

NOTES

1. "China, India Lure Global Investors with Booming Economics and Robust Trade," *T. Rowe Price Report*, Issue 96 (Summer 2007): 1–10.
2. Thomas L. Friedman, *The World Is Flat* (New York: Farrar, Strauss and Giroux, 2005): 6–11.
3. Ibid.
4. Ibid.
5. Ibid.
6. Charles Fishman, *The Wal-Mart Effect* (New York: Penguin Press, 2006): 1–22.
7. *The Wall Street Journal* (August 9, 2007): 1.
8. Adam Smith, *Wealth of Nations*.
9. Edward Iwata, "Infosys Kicks up Growth Mode," *USA TODAY* (August 4, 2006): 1B.
10. Bob Fernandez, "U.S. Research Making Great Leap," *Philadelphia Inquirer* (November 5, 2006): E-1.
11. Timothy Aeppel, "Overseas Profits Help U.S. Firms Through the Tumult," *The Wall Street Journal* (August 9, 2007): A10.
12. J. J. Coyle, E. J. Bardi, and R. A. Novack, *Transportation*, 6th ed. (Mason, Ohio: Cengage South-Western, 2006): 232–240.
13. Ibid.
14. Ibid.
15. Ibid.
16. Ibid.
17. "Securing the Global Supply Chain," U.S. Customs and Border Protection (Washington, DC: Office of Field Operations, November 2004): 1–25.
18. "America's Ports Today," American Association of Port Authorities (Alexandria, VA: 2007): 1–8.
19. Ibid.
20. "Measurement of Commercial Motor Vehicle Travel Time and Delay at U.S. International Border Stations," U.S. Federal Highway Administration, 2002.

CASE 3-1

Red Fish, Blue Fish, LLP: A Sequel

Fran Fisher, CEO of Red Fish, Blue Fish, was meeting with Eric Lynch who now was vice president for global supply chain management for Red Fish, Blue Fish. Fran started the meeting by praising Eric for his management of their growing global enterprise. "Eric, I can hardly believe how far we have come during the last three years. Our sales have quadrupled and there is every reason to believe that we can double our current sales in more years. Our consulting sales business appears to be stabilizing, and we have to decide if we want to extend our sales area eastward into the Philadelphia, Baltimore, and DC markets. Our Internet sales have been growing geometrically not only in the United States and Canada but also in Western Europe. Interestingly, we have also had some sales in several South American countries during the last year."

"China is still our principal source for the fish that we sell, and Liu-Sheng Trading Company has become almost an extension of our company. Connie Que, COO of Liu-Sheng, and I met in Hong Kong recently to discuss our long-term needs. She assured me that they could handle our continued growth and wanted to be a 'partner' with Red Fish, Blue Fish."

Fran told Eric that he was concerned, for the long run, in depending on one source of supply, that is, Liu-Sheng Trading Company. Also, he was unsure about South American countries as a future growth market. Finally, he told Eric that the complexity of the supply chain needed to be considered.

CASE QUESTIONS

1. What are the advantages and potential disadvantages to Red Fish, Blue Fish of having China (Liu-Sheng Trading Company) as its sole source of supply? What would you recommend?
2. What supply challenge would Red Fish, Blue Fish face in expanding into South America? Do you recommend expanding aggressively into South America? Why or why not?